Jon Balserak
RTS Jackson, MS
April 16, 1992

J.C.Brown.
John Smith

THE WORKS

OF

THE REV. HUGH BINNING, M.A.,

ONE OF THE REGENTS IN THE UNIVERSITY OF GLASGOW,

AND AFTERWARDS

MINISTER OF GOVAN

COLLECTED AND EDITED

BY

THE REV. M. LEISHMAN, D.D.,

MINISTER OF THE PARISH OF GOVAN

Soli Deo Gloria Publications

"...for instruction in righteousness..."

Soli Deo Gloria Publications
213 W. Vincent Street, Ligonier, PA 15658

*

The Works of Hugh Binning
was copied from the fourth edition,
1858, Edinburgh, London, and Dublin
A. Fullarton and Co.

This Soli Deo Gloria Reprint is 1992.

*

The Works of Hugh Binning
ISBN 10877611-45-X

Introduction to The Works of Hugh Binning

by Rev. Eric Alexander

I am privileged to introduce modern readers to the Rev. Hugh Binning, a fellow-Scot who ministered in my native city of Glasgow, both in the University and in the Parish of Govan, in the seventeenth century. Binning was a remarkable scholar, illustrated by the fact that he became Professor of Philosophy in Glasgow University at the age of 19. During the three years in which he held the chair in Glasgow, he also studied theology and became minister of Govan on the River Clyde in 1650.

His ministry was brief, since he died when he was only 26, probably of tuberculosis. However, the quality of Hugh Binning's godliness and the depth of his scholarly insight were so great that he made a profound impact on his century and far beyond. Oliver Cromwell was much impressed by the skill of the case Binning argued against independency in a dispute between Presbyterian and Independents in 1651. Yet, he was most amicably disposed towards the Independents and even gave the use of his church to one of their chaplains.

Binning's ministry was marked by several features. First, he has a very distinctive style. It will be recognized by those who are acquainted with this period that the schoolmen, raising division in their exposition of a text of Scripture, and then many sub-divisions with subtle distinctions which may have escaped the hearers and readers. Binning adopted a more simple style, but clothed his thoughts in such eloquence that, in turn, some found it dificult to follow him. The elegance of his language has a power of its own, and Dr. McCrie said of him, "very few writers please me more."

Secondly, he is most thoroughly committed to the authority of Scripture. He says, "there needs be no more question about the divine authority of the Scriptures among those who have their senses exercised to discern between good and ill than among men who see and taste, concerning light and darkness, sweet and bitter." His great emphasis is that it is only when the sinner is enlightened by the Holy Spirit that he will perceive the power and authority of Scripture: "His arm must create an eye in their souls, an internal light, before it can behold that glorious brightness of God shining in the Word."

Thirdly, he preaches pastorally and to the conscience. This, together with his style, is perhaps the most notable feature of Binning's ministry. Listen to him urging the truth of I John 1:7 upon discouraged Christians:

> Now, my beloved, for you who look upon the gospel by a parcel (portion), and such a parcel as enjoins much upon you, I would earnestly beseech you to open and enlarge your hearts to receive

> the full body of the truth; to look upon that cleansing blood as well as that pure light; to consider the perpetual use of the one until you have fully attained the other. Know that the fountain is kept open and not shut; not only to admit you to come at first, but to give ready access in all after-defilements; and there is no word more comprehensive than this here, it "cleanseth from all sin." All thy exceptions, doubts, and difficulties, are about some particular sins and circumstances; thy debates run upon some exception. But here is an universal comprehensive work, that excludes all exception - no kind of sin, either for quality, or degree, or circumstance, is too great for this blood. And therefore, as you have reason to be humbled for your failings, so there is no reason to be discouraged, but rather revive your spirits and vigour again in the study of this walking in the light, knowing that one day we shall be in the light, as he is in it.

This volume consists of a series of magisterial addresses on the Common Principles of the Christian religion, a series of 40 sermons on Romans 8 entitled "The Sinner's Sanctuary", a series on I John, and miscellaneous other addresses, amongst them a delightful "Treatise on Christian Love."

Binning is both stimulation for the mind and food for the soul. It is a great benefit to the entire Christian church that this volume is being made available again, and I warmly commend it.

CONTENTS.

THE SINNER'S SANCTUARY.

FELLOWSHIP WITH GOD.

HEART-HUMILIATION.

NOTANDA.

The following Notes, by the Editor, ought to have been inserted at the foot of their respective pages.

Page 1, line 25. Nulla est tam facilis res, quin difficilis siet,
Quam invitus facias.—*Terent. Heaut.* iv. vi. 1.

"There is nothing so easy, as not to become difficult, should you do it unwillingly."

P. 1, l. 35. Nam illud verum est M. Catonis oraculum, nihil agendo, homines male agere discunt. "For that is a true oracle of M. Cato,—by doing nothing, men learn to do ill."—*Columel.* lib. xi. cap. 1.

P. 5, last line. Ει γουν αηδων ημην, εποιουν τα της αηδονος, ει κυκνος, τα του κυκνου, νυν δε λογικος ειμι, ὑμνειν με δει τον θεον. "Were I a nightingale, I would perform the office of a nightingale; or a swan, that of a swan: but since I am a rational creature, it is right that I should celebrate the praises of God."—*Epictet. Dissert.* lib. i. cap. 16.

P. 7, l. 53. Quidam vivere tunc incipiunt, cum desinendum est. Si hoc judicas mirum, adjiciam quod magis admireris: quidam ante vivere defecerunt, quam inciperent. "Some then begin to live, when they are near the close of life. If you think this wonderful, I will add what you will wonder at still more: some have ceased to live before they have begun to live."—*Senec. Epist.* xxiii.

P. 9, l. 18. Cicero represents the saying—*Amicorum omnia communia* (Friends have all things in common)—to be a Greek proverb.—*De Offic.* lib. i. cap. xvi.

P. 12, l. 50. Ubi in contrarium ducit, ipsa velocitas majoris intervalli causa fit. "When it leads to an opposite direction, velocity becomes itself the cause of a wider separation."—*Senec. De Vita Beata*, cap. i.

P. 13, l. 7. At hic, tritissima quæque via, et celeberrima, maxime decipit. "But here, every path that is most beaten, and most famous, deceives most."—*Ibid.*

P. 13, l. 16.—pergentes, non qua eundum est, sed qua itur.—"proceeding, not where we ought to go, but where others go."—*Ibid.*

P. 15, l. 30. Aut prodesse volunt, aut delectare.—*Hor. Ars Poet.* v. 333.
"They wish either to improve or delight."

P. 16, l. 6. Omne tulit punctum, qui miscuit utile dulci.—*Id.* v. 343.
"Profit and pleasure them to mix with art
Shall gain all votes."—*Francis' Translation.*

P. 37, l. 4. Pluris est oculatus testis unus, quam auriti decem.
Qui audiunt audita dicunt, qui vident plane sciunt.—*Plaut. Trucul.* ii. vi. 8.

"One eye-witness is worth more than ten witnesses who speak by hearsay. They who hear tell what they hear; they who see have a perfect knowledge of what occurs."

P. 37, l. 50. The title πολυωνυμος (distinguished by many names) was often applied by the Greeks to the principal object of their idolatrous worship. Cleanthes begins his Hymn to Jove in this way,—

κυδιστ' αθανατων πολυωνυμε,

"Most illustrious of the immortals, having many names."

The Ethiopians believed that there was one God, who was the cause of all things; but they also reverenced another God, whom they supposed to be inferior to him, and to have *no name* (ανωνυμον τινα).—*Strab. Geog.* lib. xvii. p. 822.

P. 37, l. 52. Quid est Deus? Quod vides totum, et quod non vides totum.

"What is God? Every thing which you see, and every thing which you do not see."—*Senec. Nat. Quest.* lib. i.

P. 38, l. 15. The author of the Asclepian Dialogue, uses *unus omnia* (one-all things) and *Creator omnium* (the Creator of all things,) as equivalent expressions.—*Cudworth's Intellectual System*, vol. i. p. 346.

P. 55, l. 44. God was represented by some of the ancient philosophers to be "the soul of the world, and the soul of the souls of the world."

P. 79, l. 4, and 8. Prudens futuri temporis exitum
Caliginosa nocte premit Deus;
Ridetque, si mortalis ultra
Fas trepidat.—*Hor. Carm.* lib. iii. Ode 29.

"Future events wise Providence
Hath hid in night from human sense,
To narrow bounds our search confined;
And laughs to see proud mortals try
To fathom deep eternity,
With the short line and plummet of their mind."
Creech's Translation.

P. 364, l. 37. Ουδε γαρ ὁ Ζευς
Ουθ' ὑων παντας ἁνδανει, ουτ' ανεχων.
Theognidis Sententiæ, v. 25.

PREFACE BY THE EDITOR.

The Rev. Hugh Binning entered upon his pastoral charge at a very eventful period. He was ordained in the interval between the death of Charles I. and the coronation of his son Charles II., which took place at Scone, on the first of January, 1651. In the first year of the incumbency of Binning, the fatal battle of Dunbar was fought. In different parts of Scotland, three different armies, without concert with one another, subsequently took the field, to oppose the progress of the parliamentary forces. And it was not till after the death of Binning, that General Monk succeeded in reducing the country to a state of subjection. Meanwhile, the same jealousies and animosities prevailed, which had previously divided the Scottish nation. The nobility, as well as the clergy, were opposed to one another, and adopted different views of the national interests. And what tended not a little to increase the public divisions, the Anabaptists, Quakers, and other sectarians, connected with the English army, employed themselves wherever they went, in propagating with great industry, their peculiar opinions. By keeping these things in view, the reader will be better able to understand, in the writings of Binning, numerous allusions, more or less recondite, to the particular circumstances of the times.

It was on Saturday the nineteenth of April, 1651, that Cromwell came to Glasgow, with the principal part of his army. The next day he went to hear sermon in the High church. In the forenoon, he entered the Choir, or Inner church, as it was called, and, as Principal Baillie says, "quietly heard Mr. Robert Ramsay preach a very good honest sermon, pertinent for his case."* He appeared equally unexpectedly in the afternoon, in the Nave, or Outer church, when Mr. John Carstairs delivered in his presence a lecture, and Mr. James Durham, a sermon. Both of these discourses had, like the former one, a special reference to the existing posture of public affairs. But as might have been expected, Cromwell was offended at the plain dealing of all the three clergymen, who considered it to be their duty to condemn him and his army, for their invasion of Scotland; for the contempt they manifested for the religious institutions of the country; and likewise, for their persecution of the ministers of Ireland. On the following day, therefore, he summoned them, and the other clergymen of the city, to a meeting in his own lodgings, that he might vindicate himself and his confederates from the charges which had been brought against them, and at the same time hear what his accusers had to advance in their own behalf.

At this conference, which appears to have been conducted with good temper on both sides; they who spoke most on the part of the Scottish clergy, were Mr. Patrick Gillespie, Principal of the University of Glasgow, and Mr. James Guthrie, minister of Stirling, who forfeited his life at Edinburgh soon after the Restoration. On the other side, the principal speakers were Cromwell himself, and General Lambert,† who, like many other of the parliamentary officers, was a preacher, as

* Baillie's Letters and Journals, vol. III. pp. 286—288. MSS. in Bib. Col. Glas.

† "A Letter from Head Quarters in Scotland.

"Sir, We came hither on Saturday last, April 19th. The ministers and townsmen generally staid at home, and did not quit their habitations as formerly. These ministers that are here, are those that have deserted from the proceedings beyond the water; yet they are equally dissatisfied with us. And though they preach against us in the pulpit to our forces; yet we permit them well as a soldier.* Some of Cromwell's chaplains† are also represented to have taken a share in the discussion, along with the Rev. Hugh Binning. Cromwell, it is said, was struck with the fearlessness and ability of so young a minister. "Who is that learned and bold young man?" said he. When he was told his name was Binning, he replied, "He has bound well. But," he added, putting his hand, at the same time, to his sword, "this will loose all again."

In his Memoirs of the Life of Dr. John Owen, Mr. Orme adverts to this anecdote regarding Binning, simply on the authority of a note in the Biographia Scoticana. He does not seem to have been aware that, beyond this note, there was any evidence to produce, that such a meeting as has now been described, was ever actually held. But he observes, "There is nothing improbable in the meeting, and Cromwell's pun quite accords with other anecdotes of his conversation."‡ The part which Mr. Binning is reported to have acted on this occasion, was no less characteristical of him. He was a very able disputant. But when giving utterance to his feelings, or expressing his sentiments, he was sometimes led to employ strong language.§

The following account of the object and result of the meeting at Glasgow is that which is given by Sir James Balfour:—"Oliver Cromwell, with his army, being at this tyme in Glasgow, had a conference with 8 ministers, anent the lawfulness of his engagement against this countrey and kingdome. He gave them some papers, wich they anssuered extempore, and proued to his face his periurey and breach of couenant and leauge, and his sinfull rebellion and murther, contrair to [the] expresse word of God, and leauge and couenant suorne by himselue, and most of his complices. He toke the morrow at 3 in the afternoone to his furder conference with them; and maney of his cheiffest officers did openly acknowledge, they were conuinced in reson, and neuer till now, did see the weekness of ther auen grounds. In place of keiping the appoynted meitting, (seing a fyre to begin to kindle amongest his auen,) about midnight, that same day, he commands all his armey presently to march, wnder the paine of death, backe towardes Edinburghe; and empties all his garisons be west Linlithgow, sends his horses towardes the border, and with grate haist, with his footte returns to Edinburgh and Leith; and is now bussie in repairring the breaches of Edinburgh castle."‖

We are informed, that a Report of the whole proceedings which took place on this occasion, was drawn up by Principal Gillespie, and Mr. James Guthrie.¶ But whether that Report is now in existence or not, or was ever printed, the writer has not been able to ascertain.

The invasion of Scotland, which was one of the charges brought against Cromwell, was condemned by Lord Fairfax, the commander-in-chief of the parliamentary forces. He looked upon it as an infraction of the Solemn League and Covenant, which had been very generally subscribed in England, as well as in Scotland. Feeling alarm at this, the Council of State appointed Cromwell, Lambert, Harrison, St. John, and Whitelocke to converse with him, with a view, if possible, to overcome his scruples. But after a long interview, Fairfax remained unmoved by

without disturbance, as willing to gain them by love. My Lord General sent to them to give us a friendly Christian meeting, to discourse of those things, which they rail against us for, that (if possible) all misunderstandings between us may be taken away, which accordingly they gave us on Wednesday last. There was no bitterness nor passion vented on either side, with all moderation and tenderness. My Lord General, the Major-Gen. Lambert, for the most part maintained the discourse, and on their part, Mr. James Guthrie, and Mr. Patrick Gelaspy. We know not what satisfaction they have received. Sure I am, there was no such weight in their arguments, that might in the least discourage us from what we have undertaken; the chiefest thing on which they insisted being our invasion into Scotland."—Sev. Proc. in Parl. May 1, to 8. Cromwelliana, p. 102. See also Durham's Comment. on Revel. Life of the Author, p. xi.

* Nicoll's Diary, pp. 68, 94.

† Along with Dr. John Owen, Joseph Caryl, John Oxenbridge, and Cuthbert Sydenham officiated as chaplains in the army of Cromwell in Scotland. Orme's Memoirs of Dr. Owen, p. 128 Neal's History of the Puritans, vol. iv. p. 490. Lond. 1822.

‡ Memoirs of Dr. Owen, p. 127.

§ See note, p. 512.

‖ Annals of Scotland, vol. iv. p. 298.

¶ Baillie's Letters, vol. iii. p. 290. MSS. in Bib. Col. Glas.

their arguments, and expressed his determination to resign his commission rather than proceed to Scotland with the army, which was preparing to act against that part of the kingdom. As he adhered firmly to this resolution, he was deprived of his commission, and Cromwell was appointed to succeed him. Whitelock* has furnished us with an account of what passed at the interview, which he and his friends had with Lord Fairfax. The views expressed by the different parties, therefore, as Whitelock has recorded them, will enable any one to form, it is conceived, a tolerably correct idea of the nature of the discussion which took place at Glasgow, when the same point was one of the questions at issue, and when two of the principal speakers were the very individuals who had previously argued the matter with Fairfax.

The letters which passed between Cromwell, and Colonel Dundas, the governor of Edinburgh Castle. will likewise assist us to conjecture what may have been advanced on both sides on the occasion in question, at Glasgow. Some Scottish clergymen had taken refuge there after the battle of Dunbar. It was to them principally, through Colonel Dundas, that Cromwell addressed himself. The letters were printed at the time. On examining them, it will be perceived, that the invasion of Scotland, and the other offences with which Cromwell and his party were charged at Glasgow, formed in this instance likewise, grounds of accusation on the one hand, and called forth a vindication on the other. In Hume's opinion the letters written by the parliamentary general are "the best of Cromwell's wretched compositions that remain."† But Mr. Orme says of them, "From their phraseology, I strongly suspect them to have been the production of Owen's pen."‡ One of the letters, dated September 9, 1650, addressed to "The Honourable the Governor of the Castle of Edinburgh," and signed by "O. Cromwell," contains this passage :—"The ministers in England are supported, and have liberty to preach the gospell, though not to raile ; nor under pretence thereof to overtop the civill power, or debase it as they please. No man hath been troubled in England or Ireland for preaching the gospell; nor has any minister been molested in Scotland since the coming of the army hither. The speaking truth becomes the ministers of Christ. When ministers pretend to a glorious reformation, and lay the foundation thereof in getting to themselves worldly power, and can make worldly mixtures to accomplish the same, such as their late agreement with their king, and hopes by him to carry on their designe, [they] may know, that the Sion promised and hoped for will not be built with such untempered mortar. As for the unjust invasion they mention, time was, when an army of Scotland came into England, not called by the supreame authority. We have said in our papers with what hearts and upon what accompt we came; and the Lord hath heard us, though you would not, upon as solemn an appeal as any experience can parallell. And although they seem to comfort themselves with being the sons of Jacob, from whom (they say) God hath hid his face for a time, yet it's no wonder, when the Lord hath lifted up his hand so eminently against a family, as he hath done so often against this, and men will not see his hand, if the Lord hide his face from such, putting them to shame, both for it, and their hatred at his people, as it is this day. When they purely trust to the sword of the Spirit, which is the word of God, which is powerfull to bring down strongholds, and every imagination that exalts itself, which alone is able to square and fitt the stones for the new Jerusalem; then and not before, and by that meanes, and no other, shall Jerusalem, (which is to be the praise of the whole earth,) the city of the Lord be built, the Sion of the Holy One of Israel."§

This letter was answered on the same day, and in the following terms, by the Governor of the Castle. "My Lord,—Yours I have communicate to those with me, whom it concerned, who desire me to return this answer, that their ingenuitie in prosecuting the ends of the covenant, according to their vocation and place, and adhering to their first principles, is well-known, and one of their greatest regrates

* Memorials of English Affairs from the beginning of the Reign of Charles I. to the Restoration, pp. 444—446. Lond. 1682.

† Hist. of Eng. vol. vii. p. 186. Lond. 1825.

‡ Memoirs of Dr. Owen, p. 126.

§ Thurloe's State Papers, vol. i. p. 159.

is, that they have not been met with the like; when ministers of the gospel have been imprisoned, deprived of their benefices, sequestrate, forced to flee from their dwellings, and bitterly threatned, for their faithful declarein the will of God against the godless and wicked proceedings of men, that it cannot be accounted an imaginary fear of suffering in such, as are resolved to follow the like freedom and faithfulness in discharge of their master's message; that it savours not of ingenuitie to promise liberty of preaching the gospel, and to limit the preachers thereof, that they must not speak against the sins and enormities of civill powers, since their commission carryeth them to speak the word of the Lord unto, and to reprove the sins of persons of all ranks, from the highest to the lowest; that to impose the name of railing upon such faithfull freedom, was the old practice of malignants against the ministers of the gospell, who laid open to people the wickedness of their ways, that they should not be ensnared thereby; that their consciences bear them record, and all their hearers do know, that they meddle not with civill affairs further than to hold forth the rule of the word, by which the straightnes and crookednes of men's actions are made evident. But they are sorry, that they have just cause to regrate, that men of meer civill place and employment should usurp the calling and employment of the ministry, to the scandall of the reformed kirks, and particularly in Scotland, contrary to the government and discipline therein established, to the maintenance whereof you are bound by the solemn league and covenant. Thus far they have thought fitt to vindicate their return to the offer in Colonell Whalley's letter. The other part of yours, which concerns the public as well as them, they conceive that all have been answered sufficiently in the public papers of the state and kirk. Onely, to that of the successe upon your solemn appeal, they say again, what was said to it before, that they have not so learned Christ, as to hang the equity of their cause upon events; but desire to have their hearts established in the love of the truth in all the tribulations that befall them."*

Other letters followed these, previous to the surrender of the Castle. From them, and the public papers of the time, we discover that the English army justified their invasion of Scotland, and their oppressive treatment of their opponents, in Scotland and Ireland, by representing that their part of the kingdom had been previously invaded from Scotland; that the presbyterian party was friendly to monarchy; that that party had interfered with their attempts to reform the government of England, and declared against them as sectaries; and that a second invasion of England by the Scottish nation was known to have been contemplated. On the other hand, it was affirmed that the invasion of England, by the Marquis of Hamilton, had been always disapproved of, and opposed by those who were now in power in Scotland; that in taking up arms against the people of Scotland, the English were proclaiming themselves the enemies of those who had formed a covenant with them, and helped them in the day of their distress; and that although the necessity or lawfulness of a war with England, in present circumstances, had never been determined upon, nor been even discussed either in parliament or in the assembly, there could be no doubt a design was formed to overturn both the civil and ecclesiastical institutions of the northern part of the island, and make it a mere province of England.

Richard Baxter felt the warmest sympathy at this period with the Scottish people, and with his usual intrepidity and honesty, openly arraigned the conduct of his countrymen for invading Scotland. Binning, and the ablest of his friends, could not have pled their own cause in the presence of Cromwell, and his officers, with greater power and eloquence, than he did for them, with the parliamentary soldiers and others, over whom he possessed any influence. "When the soldiers were going against the king and the Scots," says he, "I wrote letters to some of them to tell them of their sin, and desired them at last to begin to know themselves. They were the same men who had boasted so much of love to all the godly, and pleaded for tender dealing with them, and condemned those that persecuted them, or restrained their liberty, who were now ready to imbrue their swords in the blood of such as they acknowledged to be godly; and all because they dared not be as

* Thurloe's State Papers, vol. i. pp. 159, 160.

perjured, or disloyal, as they were. Some of them were startled at these letters, and thought me an uncharitable censurer, who would say that they could kill the godly, even when they were on the march to do it: for how bad soever they spoke of the cavaliers (and not without too much desert as to their morals), they confessed, that abundance of the Scots were godly men. Afterwards, however, those that I wrote to better understood me.

"At the same time, the Rump, or Commonwealth, which so much abhorred persecution, and were for liberty of conscience, made an order that all ministers should keep certain days of humiliation, to fast and pray for their success in Scotland: and that we should keep days of thanksgiving for their victories; and this upon pain of sequestration! so that we all expected to be turned out; but they did not execute it upon any, save one, in our parts. For myself, instead of praying and preaching for them, when any of the committee or soldiers were my hearers, I laboured to help them to understand what a crime it was to force men to pray for the success of those who were violating their covenant and loyalty, and going, in such a cause, to kill their brethren,—what it was to force men to give God thanks for all their bloodshed, and to make God's ministers and ordinances vile, and serviceable to such crimes, by forcing men to run to God on such errands of blood and ruin,—and what it is to be such hypocrites as to persecute, and cast out those that preach the gospel, while they pretend the advancement of the gospel, and the liberty of tender consciences, and leave neither tenderness nor honesty in the world, when the guides of the flocks, and preachers of the gospel, shall be noted to swallow down such heinous sins. My own hearers were all satisfied with my doctrine, but the committee-men looked sour, yet let me alone."*

With regard to Binning's own opinion of those whom he calls "our enemies the invaders," we find that expressed in his Case of Conscience. "They think themselves," says he, "godly and righteous, yet are not purged from their filthiness. They are given up to strong delusions to believe lies; and there is no lie greater than this, that they are a godly party, in a godly cause and way. They wipe their mouth after all their bloodshed, and say, I have done no evil. They wash their hands, as Pilate, as if they were free of the blood of those just men, whose souls cry under the altar."†

Like his friend Principal Gillespie, however, Binning appears to have kept up an amicable intercourse with some of the Independents in the army of the Commonwealth. He even gave the use of his church to the chaplain attached to Colonel Overtoun's regiment, and not only went himself to hear him preach, but exhorted his people likewise to do so. Such conduct, on his part, will be viewed differently by different people. It will be condemned by those who are servilely attached to their own particular communion, and disposed to extend the line of separation between themselves and others, even beyond the limits prescribed by their own canonical rules; but it will be approved of by all whose charity is not bounded by their own narrow pale; who, when they agree with others respecting the fundamental doctrines of religion, would grant to them, as to smaller matters, the toleration they claim for themselves; and who, withal, believe, that much of that asperity and jealousy which disturb the peace, and sully the character of the Christian world, would in all likelihood be destroyed and prevented, were they, who unhappily are separated from one another by names and forms, to become better acquainted with each other's principles, and each other's feelings. Binning was blamed by some of his brethren for his liberality. The part he had acted was brought under the consideration of one of the inferior church courts. He endeavoured to justify himself, and to show that he had done nothing inconsistent either with his Christian or his ministerial character. But not succeeding in the attempt, with true Christian forbearance, he expressed his desire to avoid giving offence to his brethren, and intimated his willingness that his conduct in similar cases should henceforward be regulated by their wishes.‡

* Orme's Life and Times of Richard Baxter, vol. i. pp. 140, 141.

† P. 520.

‡ "At Cathcart Kirk, 19th Oct., 1652.

"Mr. Robert Baylie renewed his protestation given in be him the last daye, against Mr. Hew

As a proof of the influence which, along with Cromwell, some of the independent chaplains in his army possessed over a number of the Scottish clergy, it has been asserted that it was owing to them that a change was effected in some of the forms of the presbyterian mode of worship. "It is very observable," it has been said, "that all the presbyterian ministers in Scotland made use of the Christian forms of the Lord's Prayer, Creed, and Doxology, until Oliver's army invaded Scotland, and the independent chaplains in that army thought their own dispensation was above that of Geneva. Upon this, such of the presbyterians as would recommend themselves to the Usurper, and such as had his ear, forbore those forms in the public worship, and by degrees they fell into desuetude."*

The friendship which thus subsisted between some of the English independent ministers, and some of the Scottish clergy, during the time that the parliamentary army was in Scotland, has been differently accounted for. It has been inferred that a number of the Protesters were "somewhat favourable to Independency, among the chief of whom was Mr. Patrick Gillespie."† On the other hand, it has been supposed, that some of the Independent clergy had no decided objection to presbyterianism, in the form in which that system of ecclesiastical polity existed in Scotland. Dr. Owen, in particular, has been said to have expressly declared this; nay, that he would have thought it an honour to sit as a member in one of her Assemblies.‡ There can be no doubt that the differences betwixt some of the Presbyterians and the Independents, were not originally so great as these were afterwards discovered to be, between persons distinguished by the same names. They professed to believe the same great doctrines, and conscientiously preached them; and they differed only in regard to their mode of church government. But even in regard to this, some of the earlier Independents were far from differing widely from their presbyterian brethren. The Rev. Charles Herle, who, after the death of Dr. Twisse, was made prolocutor in the Westminster Assembly, has been represented to have said, "The difference between us, and our brethren who are for independency, is nothing so great as some may conceive; at most, it does but ruffle the fringe, not any way rend the garment of Christ. It is so far from being a fundamental, that it is scarce a material difference."§ We are informed that Richard Baxter was likewise accustomed to observe, that "if all the Presbyterians had been like Mr. Marshall, and the Independents like Mr. Burroughs, their differences might easily have been compromised."‖ The only part of the country in which any ministers connected with the Church of Scotland appear to have separated from it, and joined themselves to the Independents, was the town or county of Aberdeen. A small work on Independency, bearing the title of 'A Little Stone out of the Mountain, or Church Order briefly opened,' which was written by Nicholas Lockyer, who accompanied the English army to Scotland,

Binnen moderating of the Presbyterie, in his own name, and in the name of so many as would adhere to that protestation; and that upon the additional reason, that Mr. Hew Binnen of his own accord, had gone in to hear an Englishman preach in his own kirk in the parish of Govan, who attended Colonel Overtoun's regiment; and that the said Mr. Hew, be his example and counsel, had moved the people to do the like, and did maintain the lawfulness of this his action, in the face of the presbyterie, as if the abstaining from this should have been a needless separatione upon his part, and the part of his people, though, that having found that some took offence at it, he did no more countenance that man's preaching."—(Records of Presbytery of Glasgow.) At the previous meeting, Bailiie had protested against Mr. Binning's appointment to the moderator's chair, because he maintained, another member of the presbytery had a greater number of "uncontraverted votes."—Id.

* An Apology for the Clergy of Scotland, p. 45. London, 1692.

† Orme's Mem. of Dr. Owen, p. 488.

‡ Christian Instructor, vol. xxi. p. 547. Biog. Presb. vol. i. p. 131. Lorimer's Eldership, p. 155.

§ Neal's History of the Puritans, vol. iii. p. 120.

‖ Id. p. 318. Mr. Herle, who came to Scotland with the Earl of Nottingham and the Earl of Stanford, preached in the High church of Edinburgh, on Sunday the 27th of February, 1648. Mr. Stephen Marshall, not long after, at the request of Mr. George Gillespie, one of the ministers of Edinburgh, preached in the same church, "he," says Bishop Guthry, "who being here four years ago professed to be a presbyterian, but since turned *independent*."—(Memoirs of Bishop Guthry, &c., pp. 256, 258, second edition.) Fuller, however, says of Mr. Marshall, that he died a presbyterian.—(Fuller's Worthies, book 2, p. 53, apud Neale's Hist. vol. iv. p. 134.) And Baillie represents him to have been "the best preacher in England." (Letters and Journals, vol. i. p. 440.

was printed at Leith in 1652. This was replied to, in a work from the pen of James Wood, professor of theology in St. Andrews, which was printed at Edinburgh in 1654. The title of Professor Wood's publication is, 'A Little Stone pretended to be out of the Mountain, Tried, and Found to be a Counterfeit,' &c. In that work, Wood animadverts upon a letter from "the new Independents of Aberdene," dated May 1652, and laments that "some of them had been for some years ministers" of the Established church.* It is singular enough, that in a memoir of that unhappy man, Archbishop Sharp, which was published in his own lifetime, and dedicated to himself, it is stated that Provost Jaffrey, who afterwards became a Quaker, was known to declare that Sharp "was the first man who had confirmed him in the way of Independency."†

Along with other circumstances, the disunion which prevailed throughout the church, and the causes which gave rise to it, must have had a tendency to mitigate the hostility with which the Protesting clergy regarded the army of Cromwell in general, and the effect, at the same time, of recommending them to him, and his adherents. The Protesters doubted the sincerity of Charles. Though he had subscribed their covenant, they were persuaded he had no real attachment to their church. They were of opinion, that, were he once firmly seated on the throne, their civil and religious liberties would be alike endangered. So far, therefore, could they sympathize with the parliamentary general, and the soldiers whom he commanded, in their opposition to their monarch. The Protesters drew off from the army, which after the battle of Dunbar was embodied, with the concurrence of the king, the parliament, and the commission of the church, for the defence of the monarchy, and the liberation of Scotland. This army was recruited with men of every description. Numerous commissions in it were given to known malignants. The success of an army so constituted, the Protesters thought, was to be dreaded rather than wished for. Binning and others declared they could not even pray for its success.‡ Here was another point, in regard to which they and the invading army must have felt sympathy with one another, and which must have materially altered their relative position, leading them to assume such an equivocal attitude, that it must have been difficult, even for themselves, to determine whether they were more the friends or the foes of each other.

Injustice, however, has been done to the Protesters, by representing them to have been republicans. This was by no means their character as a body, whatever may have been the opinions of individuals among them. One of the most active and able of them, was the unfortunate Mr. James Guthrie, minister of Stirling. Though he was executed after the Restoration, for his conceived disloyalty, in opposition, it is believed, to the personal wishes of the king, he never abjured his lawful prince. He wished the royal prerogative to be limited by law, as it afterwards was at the Revolution; but he did not wish it to be abolished. At great personal hazard, Guthrie maintained a public disputation on the subject of the royal authority, in the church of Stirling, with the noted Hugh Peters one of Cromwell's chaplains, and in the presence of a number of the parliamentary officers. And in the same place, and near the same period, he showed himself to be a staunch presbyterian, by engaging in a public discussion§ with Mr. J. Brown, an Anabaptist, who was chaplain to Colonel Fairfax's regiment. In his speech at his trial, he declared his loyalty in the strongest possible terms, and made the following touching, though unavailing, appeal to his judges:—"Albeit, it does become me to adore God in the holiness and wisdom of his dispensations, yet I can hardly refrain from expressing some grief of spirit, that my house and family should not only be so many months together cessed, by a number of English soldiers, and myself kept from the pulpit, for preaching and speaking against the Tender, and incorporating this nation in one commonwealth with England; and that I should thereafter, in time of Oliver Cromwell his usurping the government

* Pp. 360, 362. † Miscellanea Scotica, vol. ii. p. 32. ‡ See p. 497, *note*.

§ This was followed by a written controversy between the parties. (Wodrow MSS. vol. ix. in Bib. Ad.) The same person disputed publicly in the church of Cupar on two successive days, in 1652, with Mr. James Wood, professor of theology at St. Andrews. Lamont's Diary, p. 48.

to himself, under the name of Protector, be delated by some, and challenged by sundry of his council in this nation, for a paper published by me, wherein he was declared to be an usurper, and his government to be usurpation; that I should have been threatened to have been sent to the court, for writing a paper against Oliver Cromwell his usurping the crown of these kingdoms; that I should have been threatened with banishment for concurring in offering a large testimony, against the evil of the times, to Richard Cromwell his council, immediately after his usurping the government; I say, my lord, it grieves me, that, notwithstanding of all those things, I should now stand indicted before your lordships as intending the eradicating and subverting of the ancient civil government of this nation, and being subservient to that usurper in his designs. The God of heaven knows that I am free of this charge; and I do defy all the world, allowing me justice and fair proceeding, which I hope your lordships will, to make out the same against me."*

From the Case of Conscience, and from some expressions which Binning uttered under strong excitement, and which were repeated to Principal Baillie,† it would appear that his loyalty was somewhat shaken by the passing of the public resolutions, after the battle of Dunbar; if not before that time, by a conviction of the dissimulation of the king. He probably thought, with the framers of the western remonstrance,‡ in which he seems to have concurred, that they would not be justifiable in fighting for Charles, without some additional security being provided for the maintenance of their religious privileges, and unless some adequate restraint were imposed upon the exercise of the royal authority. His dread of arbitrary power is strongly expressed in the Case of Conscience. "The plea of necessity," says he,§ "is but a pretence to cover some design, that under its specious and plausible covering, the power of the land may be engrossed in the hands of malignants; and so by this means, all power and trust may return, as the rivers to the sea or fountain, as they judge the king, that so, in his person, there may be established an unlimited and arbitrary power."

That Binning was the author of the Case of Conscience cannot reasonably be doubted.

I. It was published, in 1693, ‖ under the name of "Mr. Hugh Binning, sometime Professor of Philosophie in the Universitie of Glasgow, and thereafter minister of God's word at Goven." Nor, so far as can be ascertained, was it denied to be his by any person, at the time of its publication. It was printed in Holland; and although, as has been objected to it, it has not attached to it the name of the printer, nor the name of the place where it was printed, neither have 'The Apologeticall Relation,' 'The True Non-Conformist,' 'The Apology for, or Vindication of, Oppressed Persecuted Ministers,' 'The History of the Indulgence,' 'Rectius Instruendum,' 'The Hind Let Loose,' and various other works by Scottish writers, which, for obvious reasons, were printed abroad, after the Restoration. In his dying Testimony, however, it is declared by Mr. Robert Smith, a graduate of Groningen, that the Rev. James Kid, who was subsequently minister of Queensferry, was sent to Holland by the Society people to superintend the printing of the Sanquhar Declaration of 1692, and "Mr. Hugh Binning's piece against association;" that Mr. Kid was imprisoned for this for a considerable time in Holland, and that after he obtained his liberty, he and Kid studied for one session together at the University of Utrecht.¶

II. It seems almost certain that the manuscript must have been obtained from the widow of the author, or from his son, both of whom were living when the pamphlet first appeared, and both of whom were intimately connected with the Society people. At a general meeting of the Society people at Edinburgh, 28th May, 1683,

* Wodrow's Hist. of the Suf. of Ch. of Scot. vol. i. p. 165, Glas. 1829. † See note, p. 512.

‡ Balfour's Annals, vol. iv. pp. 141—160. Brown's Hist. of Glas. vol. i. p. 109. Peterkin's Rec. of Kirk of Scot. p. 672.

§ P. 489. ‖ Small quarto, pp. 51.

¶ Shields' Faithful Contendings, pp. 485—488. Faithful Witness-Bearing Exemplified, *preface*, p. iv.

"It was resolved that *Mr. John Binning* should be desired to wait upon a school, for teaching some young men; and for his pains he was to have twenty-five pounds Scots per Quarter. According to this resolution, Mr. Binning did teach Latin to some of these young men for some time."* And in a letter from the Rev. James Renwick, to Sir Robert Hamilton of Preston, dated Sept. 26th, 1683, and printed from the original, he says, "Likeways, according to your direction, I challenged Mrs. Binning upon her intimacie with your sister; but she says there is noe ground for it, and I think not such as your honour apprehends. As also I challenged her upon the commendation she gave Jo. Wilsone, in her letter unto you; but she says she had not then seen his testimonie, and was sorrie when she saw it, it was so contrary both to her thoughts, and to her commendation of him."† This letter is curtailed in the printed collection of Renwick's Letters; ‡ and the passage in it, which refers to Mrs. Binning, is only partially quoted by John Howie of Lochgoin, in a note to Shields' Faithful Contendings.§

III. A copy of the original manuscript is at present in my possession, belonging to David Laing, Esq., Edinburgh, which, so far as one can judge from the orthography and hand-writing, must have been written near the time of the author. It formed part of a collection of papers chiefly of that period, of which some are docketed by Sir Archibald Johnston of Warriston. It is entitled "The Tractat, proving that there is still a Maligt. Pairty, and that wee should not associate with them, written in Januar 1651." The writer of the Life of Binning was of opinion that as "Mr. Binning died in the year 1653, and the pamphlet was not published till the year 1693," some of the Protesters would have published it, in the course of that period, "had they known that Mr. Binning was the author of it." But various circumstances may have occurred to prevent its being made public at an earlier period. And although it was not printed, it may have been read by many in manuscript. I cannot but think, though he has mistaken the Christian name of the author, that it is to Hugh Binning's Case of Conscience, that Samuel Colvill, the ungodly son of a pious mother, alludes, in that mass of ribaldry and indecency, 'The Whigs Supplication,' when describing the library of the Covenanters, he says,

"Some reads the cases of Richard Binning."‖

This mock poem of Colvill was printed for the first time in the year 1681; but according to the poet's own statement, it was circulated in MS. previous to this.¶

IV. The views of Binning are known to have accorded with the general strain of the Case of Conscience. The object of his tractate was to expose and counteract the purposes and proceedings of the Resolutioners. This was likewise Binning's object in the part he acted, on different occasions, in the presbytery of Glasgow. In the Minutes of that ecclesiastical court, he is always found opposed to the Resolutioners, and co-operating with Principal Gillespie, and the other Protesters. This will account for the tone in which Baillie speaks of him: "Behold," says he in a letter from Perth, 2d January, 1651, "the next presbytery day, when I am absent, Mr. Patrick [Gillespie] causes read again the Commission's letter, and had led it so, that by the elders' votes, the men of greatest experience and wisdom of our presbytery were the two youngest we had, Mr. Hugh Binning and Mr. Andrew Morton."** The following fact proves that the opponents, as well as the friends, of Binning in the presbytery, knew him to be decidedly averse to the public resolutions. On the 28th of May, 1651, Mr. Patrick Gillespie, Mr. John Carstairs, and Mr. Hugh Binning were chosen by the presbytery to be their representatives at the

* Faithful Contendings, p. 66.

† Memoirs of the First Years of James Nisbet, one of the Scottish Covenanters, written by himself, Append. p. 287. Edin. 1827.

‡ Pp. 54—58. § P. 486. See also Life of the Author, p. xliii. *note.*

‖ Verse 1193.

¶ Mr. Alexander Peterkin, the annotator of the Records of the Kirk of Scotland, before presenting his readers with a long extract from the 'Whigs Supplication,' (ver. 94—113.) describing an armed body of Covenanters, gravely declares, it was "taken from a MS. copy of a doggrel poem (by Cleland it is thought,) which the editor presented some years ago to the Library of the Antiquarian Society of Edinburgh." See Rec. of Kirk of Scot. p. 533.

** Baillie's Letters, vol. ii. p. 360.

ensuing General Assembly. But Mr. Robert Ramsay, and the other Resolutioners who were present, protested against their election, on the ground that they had not received notice of what was intended to be done; that Mr. Gillespie and Mr. Binning were opposed to the public resolutions in Church and State; and that the commission of the Church might yet give them some directions as to this matter. Accordingly, when the Assembly met at St. Andrews, from protesting against which, as an illegal Assembly, the Protesters derived their name, among the numerous commissions which were objected to, on that occasion, were those of Mr. Patrick Gillespie, and Mr. Hugh Binning, the Resolutioners in the presbytery having, it appears, made a different appointment of commissioners, at a meeting of their own.* So much opposed, indeed, was Binning to the public resolutions, that we find him, on the 20th of June, 1651, protesting against the insertion of a letter, from the Commission of the Church regarding them, in the presbytery Minutes. And on the 20th of August, we in like manner perceive him voting against the registration, in the Minutes of the presbytery, of various Acts of the Assembly, which had met at St. Andrews and Dundee, in July, 1651, "becaus yei were sinful in themselves, and came from an unlawful and null assemblie."†

But this is not all. Binning wrote "Some animadversions upon a paper entituled, *no separation from the armie*, &c." These, it is believed, were never printed. The manuscript copy, which I have perused, is in the hand-writing of Mr. David Anderson, the clerk, or amanuensis of Sir Archibald Johnston of Warriston, who has written on it with his own hand, "Mr. H. Binny his reply to M. D. Dickson." The title itself of the manuscript indicates the views of the author. But the similarity of its style and reasoning, and those of the Case of Conscience, is very evident. Although he was thus led, under an imperative sense of duty, to enter the lists of controversy with Mr. David Dickson, who was now Professor of Theology in the University of Edinburgh, but who at the time of the induction of the author, being a member of the presbytery, had presided at his ordination, it is pleasant to observe, that even when expressing himself most strongly, Binning treats his former colleague in the University of Glasgow, with uniform courtesy and respect. In one place he says, "If I knew not the integritie of the writter, I could hardlie spare a hard censure of him, either for dissembling what he knowes, or not reading what he condemns. But I will think neither, but rather that he is too confident of his own assertion." In another place he exclaims, "Alas! should a divine speak so? If a carnall polititian had said it, I had not thought it strange, but a godlie tender man to speake in these terms." Should it be asked how this manuscript has not formed a part of the present collection of the works of the Author, the reason is simply this. It was not conceived that the degree of interest felt at this distant period, in the controversy to which it relates, would warrant its publication, and more particularly as any one, wishing to obtain a knowledge of the principles and the policy which it advocates, may be gratified, by consulting some of the numerous pamphlets and manifestoes, which were printed at the time.

Along with the Case of Conscience, the present edition of the works of the Author includes the 'Treatise of Christian Love,' first printed at Edinburgh in 1743; and 'Several Sermons upon the most Important Subjects of Practical Religion,' which were printed for the first time at Glasgow in 1760. Neither of these is contained in the quarto edition of Binning's works that was published in 1768, at Glasgow. That was a mere reprint of the edition of 1735, which issued from the Edinburgh press. In his Address to the Reader, the publisher of the Treatise on Christian Love says, "This treatise, with a great number of excellent sermons, preached by this able minister of the gospel, many of which have never been printed, in a manuscript in folio, was found in the late Reverend Mr. Robert Woodrow, minister of Eastwood, his library." The editor of the Practical Sermons, however, informs us, in his preface, that the manuscript from which the "elegant and judicious treatise of Christian Love was first printed," *was in his hand.*‡ And he adds, "As Mr. Wodrow wrote large collections upon the lives of

* Rec. of Kirk of Scot. pp. 627, 633.

† Records of Presbytery of Glasgow

‡ P. xvii.

our most eminent Reformers, which he designed to publish if he had lived longer, so the Lives and Letters of Mr. John Knox, who was commonly styled the Re former, is now preparing for the press, to which will be added some of his essays on religious subjects, never before printed. If the publication of Mr. Knox's life be duly encouraged, some more lives of other ministers in that period will be transcribed and revised, for the benefit of the public, who desire to have them printed."* Hence we are led to conclude, that those additional works of Binning found their way to the press through the Rev. Robert Wodrow, minister of Eastwood, the son and successor of the historian. The preface to the Practical Sermons is dated "Brousterland, Sept. 12th, 1760." This is the name of a place in the parish of Kilbride, in the county of Lanark, to which it has been ascertained the son of the historian retired, for a short time, after resigning his cure in the year 1758. I observe, likewise, that a letter now before me, written in the year 1806, by the Rev. Dr. James Wodrow, minister of Stevenston, the youngest son of the historian, and addressed to the Rev. Dr. Robert Finlay, of the University of Glasgow, contains a statement, which, in the absence of more direct evidence, may be referred to, as furnishing us with some other grounds for believing that the anonymous writer of the "Brousterland" preface was the retired minister of Eastwood. The statement is, that the writer of the letter, who was much younger than his two brothers, the ministers of Tarbolton and Eastwood, had "heard" that they "had some thoughts of publishing Buchanan and Knox's Lives," written by their father.

It is to be regretted that none of Binning's writings were published by himself, or in his own lifetime. The indulgence of the reader is on this account justly claimed for them. We cannot be certain that the author's meaning has been always correctly expressed. And every one accustomed to composition must be aware, that in transcribing, or revising what has been previously written, even with some degree of care, the change of a single expression, or the insertion of an additional word, or the transposition of a solitary clause in a sentence, often makes the meaning of the writer infinitely clearer, and gives a new character altogether to his style. But we ought also to bear in mind, that the following sermons were prepared for a country audience; and that they were the ordinary weekly production of a very young clergyman, struggling with bad health, and burdened with the performance of various other arduous duties. Many, I have no doubt, will think this apology for the author unnecessary. The facts now stated, however, when taken into consideration, must increase their admiration of Binning; his copiousness, his variety, both in regard to matter and style, the beauty of his imagery, the grandeur of his conceptions, his felicitous application of the language of scripture, being all the more wonderful, when viewed in connexion with the unfavourable circumstances in which his sermons were composed.

The discourses of Binning are unquestionably a very favourable specimen of the talents and learning, as well as of the piety of the clergy of Scotland in his day. At the same time, that class of men have not had justice done to them. Adopting the tone of their persecutors, it was long the practice of court sycophants, and others, to ridicule and calumniate them. Their sermons were burlesqued, sometimes through ignorance, and sometimes through malice. Many of them were printed from the notes, or imperfect recollections of pious but illiterate persons. And if a minister was known to possess any portion of eccentricity, absurd sayings were invented for him; and when, at any time, a singular statement, or an uncouth expression, was heard to proceed from him, it was seized upon with avidity, treasured up, and repeated as an illustration of the kind of preaching that was common among the ministers of his church. It is almost inconceivable, therefore, how many, even among the intelligent classes of society, in the present day, have been led, most unwarrantably, to form their estimate of the literary qualifications of the ministers of Scotland, in the seventeenth century, from the grotesque "Pockmanty Sermon" of the Rev. James Row, minister at Monnivaird

* Pp. xxv, xxvi.

and Strowan, from Hobbes's Behemoth, from the unpolished, unauthenticated* discourses of some of the field preachers, or from that collection of profanity and obscenity entitled "Scotch Presbyterian Eloquence Display'd."†

Bishop Hall bears honourable testimony to the character and professional accomplishments of the ministers of Scotland, in the early part of the seventeenth century. In a sermon preached by him in London, on Easter Monday, 1618, he says, "For the northern part of our land, beyond the Tweed, we saw not, we heard not, of a congregation without a preaching minister; and though their maintenance generally hath been small, yet their pains have been great, and their success answerable. As for the learning and sufficiency of those preachers, whether prelates or presbyters, our ears were for some of them sufficient witnesses; and we are not worthy of our ears, if our tongues do not thankfully proclaim it to the world."

When we approach somewhat nearer the time of Binning, we can point, in the Church of Scotland, to such men as Robert Leighton, who was then the Presbyterian minister of the parish of Newbottle, and to Alexander Henderson, minister of the parish of Leuchars, in the county of Fife, men who would have done honour to any Protestant church in Europe. Nothing need be said of the piety and eloquence of Leighton, whose name has been preserved from obscurity, by his subsequent elevation to the episcopal chair, and the publication of his admirable writings. The name of Henderson may not be so familiar to some. But what

* "The sermons preached at conventicles, which are ordinarily circulated, are a very unsafe rule by which to judge of the talents of the preachers, and the quality of the discourses which they actually delivered. We have never been able to ascertain that one of these was published during the lifetime of the author, or from notes written by himself. They were printed from notes taken by the hearers, and we may easily conceive how imperfect and inaccurate these must often have been. We have now before us two sermons by Mr. Welsh, printed at different times; and upon reading them, no person could suppose that they were preached by the same individual. * * * We have no doubt that the memory of Mr. Peden has been injured in the same way. The collection of prophecies that goes under his name is not authentic; and we have before us some of his letters, which place his talents in a very different light from the idea given of them in what are called his sermons and his life." (Review of Sir Walter Scott's Tales of my Landlord, written by Dr. M'Crie. Christian Instructor, vol. xiv. pp. 127, 128.)—We are cautioned not to judge of the talents of Samuel Rutherford as a preacher "from the sermons printed after his death, and of which it is probable he never composed a single sentence." (Murray's Life of Rutherford, pp. 221—223.)—And says Patrick Walker, the simple compiler of the 'Life and Death of Mr. Daniel Cargill,' "I have seen some of Mr. Cargill's sermons in writ, but I never saw none as he spake them; and I have been much pressed to publish them, and other old sermons, which I dare not do, upon several considerations; knowing that sermons would have past then, and very edifying, which will not pass now, in this critic and censorious age, without reflections; not knowing how they were taken from their mouth, nor what hands they have come through since." Biographia Presbyteriana, vol. ii. p. 53.

† The presbyterian clergy in Scotland were much offended when this silly yet mischievous book made its appearance, as they justly looked upon it as calculated not only to blacken their reputations, but to inflict a serious injury upon religion. (See 'A Just and Modest Reproof of a pamphlet called The Scotch Presbyterian Eloquence,' pp. 36, 38. Edin. 1693.)—No one is more perseveringly held up to ridicule in it than the Rev. James Kirkton, whose character as a man of talents, and possessing a sound judgment, has been since sufficiently vindicated by the publication of his 'Secret and True History of the Church of Scotland.' Kirkton takes notice of the Scotch Presbyterian Eloquence, and informs us that its reputed authors were "Mr. Gilbert Crockat and Mr. John Munroe;" adding, "Truly one would think, a thinking man who reads this piece may wonder first, what conscience governs these men, who publish, to abuse the world, such stories, which they themselves know to be lies, as well as they whom they belie. Next, what wisdom is among them, who knew well enough there are thousands of honest people to refute their calumnies!" (p. 194.)—Provoked by an insulting reference to the book under review, an able controversial writer of that period says, "Thou hast, by the bye, mentioned the Presbyterian Eloquence. Every body knows that book to be a forgery out of the curates' shop. But to give the world a true test both of the Presbyterian and the Episcopal eloquence, let us appeal to the printed sermons on both sides. Do thou take the printed sermons of the Presbyterians, and pick out of them all the ridiculous things thou ever canst. And if I dont make a larger collection of more impious and ridiculous things, out of the printed sermons of the Episcopalians, citing book and page for them, I shall lose the cause." (Curate Calder Whipt, p. 11.)—In such a contest as is here proposed, religion must suffer, and truth be sacrificed. Lord Woodhouselee, therefore, does not hesitate to pronounce both the Presbyterian Eloquence Displayed, and the Answer to it, to be "equally infamous and disgraceful libels." Life of Lord Kames, vol. i. Append. p. 10.

says an English historian of him? "Alexander Henderson, the chief of the Scottish clergy in this reign, was learned, eloquent, and polite, and perfectly well versed in the knowledge of mankind. He was at the helm of affairs in the General Assemblies in Scotland; and was sent into England in the double capacity of a divine and plenipotentiary. He knew how to rouse the people to war, or negotiate a peace. Whenever he preached, it was to a crowded audience; and when he pleaded or argued, he was regarded with mute attention."* Mr. William Guthrie, minister of Fenwick in the county of Ayr, was another of Binning's contemporaries. His memory, like that of other Scottish ministers of that century, has suffered from his name having been attached to sermons falsely said to be his, at least in the form in which they have been printed. Let any person, however, of unsophisticated taste and true piety read 'The Christian's Great Interest,' which was the only work published by Guthrie himself, and it will not surprise him that a church, which had many such village pastors, should have fixed itself in the affections of the nation at large, and that instructed by such men, the humblest classes of the community should have had so much religious knowledge, as Bishop Burnet † somewhat reluctantly admits they possessed. The wife of Wodrow the historian was the granddaughter of William Guthrie. ‡ In his Analecta, Wodrow says, it was well ordered that Mr. Guthrie died in Angus, "for his congregation would have idolized his grave had he died among them." He also mentions that his Treatise was highly valued by Queen Mary, who caused it to be translated into the French language, and to whom it had been presented by Mr. William Carstares, chaplain to William III., and afterwards Principal of the University of Edinburgh; that Archbishop Tillotson commended it as one of the best written books in the language; and that Dr. John Owen declared, he valued it so highly, he had made it his vade mecum.§ Contrary to the general belief, the ministers of Scotland, in Binning's time, not only included among them many individuals, who were highly esteemed on account of their talents, literature, and piety; but a great number of them "were related to the chief families in the country, either by blood or marriage."‖ Binning himself, and Mr. William Guthrie minister of Fenwick, were the sons of respectable landed proprietors. Mr. Gabriel Semple, minister of Kirkpatrick of the Muir, was the son of Sir Bryce Semple of Cathcart; Mr. James Hamilton, minister of Dumfries, was the nephew of Lord Claneboy, afterwards Earl of Clanbrassil; Mr. David Fletcher, minister of Melrose, was the brother of Sir John Fletcher, King's Advocate; Mr. Patrick Scougal, minister of Saltoun, was the son of Sir John Scougal of that ilk; Mr. John Nevoy, minister of Newmills, was the brother of Sir David Nevoy of that ilk. Mr. James Hamilton, minister of Cambusnethan, was the son of Sir John Hamilton of Broomhill, and brother of the first Lord Belhaven; and to mention no others, Mr. Robert Melvil, minister at Culross, was the son of Sir James Melvil of Halhill.

One of the distinguishing peculiarities of Binning is his rejection of the endless divisions and subdivisions, which, along with their subtle distinctions, were borrowed from the schoolmen, and which disfigured and incumbered the sermons of that age. In Scotland, as well as in England, before his time, sermons were formed, as Dr. Watts expresses it, "upon the model of doctrine, reason, and use."¶ Those sermons often contained much excellent theology, which was faithfully and aptly applied to the heart and life. But the numerous parts into which they were divided, must have marred their effect, and operated as a restraint upon the eloquence of the preacher. This was plainly the opinion of Binning. "Paul speaks," says he, "of a right dividing of the word of truth, (2 Tim. ii. 15.) not that ordinary way of cutting it all in parcels, and dismembering it, by manifold divi-

* Granger's Biog. Hist. of Eng. vol. i. part ii. p. 416. London 1769.

† Burnet's Hist. of his own Times, vol. i. p. 280. Oxford 1833.

‡ Life of Professor Wodrow, p. 61.

§ Analecta, at present printing by Maitland Club, vol. i. pp. 277, 300. Biog. Presby. vol. i. pp. 236, 237.

‖ Burnet's Hist. of his Own Times, vol. i. p. 279.

¶ Watts' Works, vol. v. 350.

sions, which I judge makes it lose much of its virtue, which consists in union. Though some have pleasure in it, and think it profitable; yet I do not see that this was the apostolic way."* Binning, accordingly, had the courage and the good taste to adopt in conjunction with Leighton, a more simple and natural manner of preaching. After a building was completed, he did not think it added either to its beauty or convenience, to retain the scaffolding. For this, he was censured at the time, by Robert Baillie. But whoever will read the sermon of that learned divine, entitled 'Errors and Induration,' which was preached by him in Westminster Abbey, in the month of July, 1645, will not be astonished to find, that Baillie disapproved of a mode of preaching, which was so completely at variance with his own. "He has the new guise of preaching," said Baillie, speaking of Mr. Andrew Gray, who was the son of Sir James Gray, and one of the ministers of the High Church of Glasgow, "which Mr. Hugh Binning and Mr. Robert Leighton began, [not] containing the ordinary way of expounding and dividing a text, of raising doctrines and uses; but runs out on a discourse on some common head, in a high, romancing, and unscriptural style, tickling the ear for the present, and moving the affections in some, but leaving, as he confesses, little or nought to the memory and understanding. This we must misken, for we cannot help it."†

It has been said that Binning himself, when on his death-bed, regretted to one of his friends, that his sermons had been framed after a different model from that to which his countrymen had been accustomed; and had he lived, that "he was fully resolved to have followed that way of preaching by doctrine, reasons, and uses, qlk he declared he was then best pleased with."‡ We can easily believe this. The faithful Christian minister is not a man that is likely to be pleased with his own performances, in any circumstances, and more particularly, when he sees the hour approaching, when he expects to be called upon, to render an account of his stewardship: and should his hopes of usefulness have been disappointed, he will be more disposed, even than others, to blame the teacher. Binning, it is not improbable, thought he had done wrong, in discarding from many of his sermons formal divisions altogether, and, like many English preachers who came after him, that in passing from one extreme, he had sometimes proceeded to another. He may likewise have discovered, when catechizing some of his simple parishioners, that from want of the usual landmarks to guide them, they were not always able to follow him, when addressing them from the pulpit, or to give such a good account of his sermons, as of the discourses of some other ministers, who in preaching adhered to the rules and method of the period. §

A small volume, having for its title 'Evangelical Beauties of the late Rev. Hugh Binning,' was prepared for the press, by the Rev. John Brown of Whitburn, and published at Edinburgh, in the year 1828. Along with this interesting little work, a letter from the late Dr. M'Crie was printed, in which that judicious and popular writer says, "I am fond of Binning, he is thoroughly evangelical, is always in earnest and full of his subject, abounds in new and striking thoughts, and has many natural and unaffected beauties in his style and manner of writing. Had he paid a little more attention to order and method, and lived to correct his sermons for the press, he would, in my opinion, have carried every point of a good and great preacher. As it is, very few writers please me more. I will rejoice if the plan you propose shall be the means of producing a new edition of his works, which are far less known than they deserve to be, and have hitherto been chiefly in the

* P. 213. † Journals and Letters, vol ii. p. 385. ‡ Analecta, vol. iv. p. 171. vol. v. p. 342. MSS. in Bib. Ad.

§ "Their ministers generally brought them about them on the Sunday nights, where the sermons were talked over; and every one, women as well as men, were desired to speak their sense and their experience; and by these means they had a comprehension of matters of religion, greater than I have seen among people of that sort anywhere. The preachers went all in one track, of raising observations on points of doctrine out of their text, and proving these by reasons, and then of applying those, and shewing the use that was to be made of such a point of doctrine, both for instruction and terror, for exhortation and comfort, for trial of themselves upon it, and for furnishing them with proper directions and helps; and this was so methodical, that the people grew to follow a sermon quite through every branch of it." Burnet's History of his own Times, vol. i. p. 2?0.

hands of that class of persons least qualified for relishing some of his distinguishing excellencies." There can be little doubt, as Dr. M'Crie has here hinted, that in Binning's discourses, there is occasionally an apparent neglect of order and method, and that we could have wished, for the sake of his hearers particularly, or with a view to attract attention and assist the memory, he had more frequently stated the outlines of his plan in two or three general heads. But few surely will feel sorry that his eloquent periods are not broken down into detached fragments, or will wish that he had substituted a dry detail of disjointed particulars for his powerful and impassioned appeals to the understanding and feelings of his auditors. Few will wish that he had discussed all his texts in the way he has handled 1 Tim. i. 5.* The presbytery of Glasgow prescribed to him this text as the subject of one of his probationary discourses. That is the reason, probably, that his sermons upon it are composed upon a different plan from his others, and more in accordance with the conventional mode of the day.

Although Binning held the doctrine of predestination, in what the enemies of that scriptural doctrine consider its most repulsive form, being, like Samuel Rutherford, and David Dickson, the author of Therapeutica Sacra, and many other eminent divines of that time, a supralapsarian; he was far from exacting in others a rigid conformity to his particular opinions. It is impossible not to admire the Christian spirit that dictated the following passage in one of his sermons, "If we search the scriptures, we shall find that they do not entertain us with many and subtile discourses of God's nature, and decrees, and properties, nor do they insist upon the many perplexed questions that are made concerning Christ and his offices, about which so many volumes are spun out, to the infinite distraction of the Christian world. They do not pretend to satisfy your curiosity, but to edify your souls; and therefore they hold out God in Christ, as clothed with all his relations to mankind, in all those plain and easy properties, that concern us everlastingly,—his justice, mercy, grace, patience, love, holiness, and such like. Now, hence I gather, that the true knowledge of God consists not in the comprehension of all the conclusions that are deduced, and controversies that are discussed anent these things; but rather, in the serious and solid apprehension of God, as he hath relation to us, and consequently in order and reference to the moving of our hearts, to love, and adore, and reverence him, for he is holden out only in those garments that are fit to move and affect our hearts. A man may know all these things, and yet not know God himself; for to know him, cannot be abstracted from loving him."†

The practical character of the theology of Binning is not less remarkable. He never lost sight of the connection between truth and the conscience. All who are acquainted with his writings must be aware, that from the consideration of the more profound doctrines of Divine Revelation, he did not permit himself to be deterred by any false humility, or any mistaken idea of the incompetency of the human mind to follow in the track of the sacred writers. In the works of no author of the period, or of the theological school to which he belonged, shall we find more frequent references to the high and sacred mysteries of revealed truth. Yet are we unable to perceive, in his discourses, any symptoms of the paralyzing influence, which the discussion of such topics has not unfrequently exerted, on the compositions of other equally sound, but less skilful and comprehensive writers. His divinity was drawn immediately from the sacred scriptures; and finding it there, not only in its sublime, and often mysterious relations to the mind, and purposes of the Almighty, but also in its application to the conscience and affections of the finite creature, for whose use it was revealed,—he presented it to his hearers in all its native majesty, and at the same in all its practical simplicity.

In dealing with the consciences of sinners, in particular, this peculiarity of Bining is displayed in a manner that is singularly striking. In the sermons of those who are most opposed to the doctrines which he was at such pains to inculcate, we shall search in vain for more pungent addresses to the consciences of mankind, or more unfettered exhibitions of the gospel as a remedial scheme, in which all

* P. 600. † P. 356.

the descendants of Adam are warranted to regard themselves as having an interest. Some of his contemporaries were evidently shackled by their conceptions of the place which the doctrine of the divine decrees holds in the system of revealed truth. They hesitated to proclaim a free salvation and a willing Saviour to all mankind, simply on the ground of their common destitution as sinners; and they sought to extricate themselves from the difficulties, arising out of the doctrine of election on the one hand, and the common offers of the gospel on the other, by the chilling hypothesis, that these offers were made in reality, whatever might be their form, to convinced, or in the language of the period, "sensible" sinners only. Binning, spurning at such systematic trammels, took his stand upon the clear testimony of God in the gospel. He not only taught that Christ is the Saviour of sinners, but pressed upon every sinner the offer of the Saviour. Instead of requiring those whom he addressed, to accept of salvation, by the discovery of convictions, or feelings, or any thing else in themselves, constructive of an initial work of grace, he simply and unreservedly taught them that sinners, as such, are addressed in the gospel, and that all who are sinners have an equal warrant to accept freely, that which is thus so freely proffered. "I think," he says, "a man should seek nothing in himself, whereupon to build his coming to Christ. Though it be true, no man can come to a Saviour, till he be convinced of sin and misery, yet no man should seek convictions, as a warrant to come to Christ for salvation. He that is in earnest about this question, how shall I be saved?—I think he should not spend the time in reflecting on, and examination of himself, till he find something promising in himself; but, from discovered sin and misery, pass straightway over to the grace and mercy of Christ, without any intervening search of something in himself to warrant him to come. There should be nothing before the eye of the soul but sin and misery and absolute necessity, compared with superabounding grace and righteousness in Christ; and thus it singly devolves itself over upon Christ, and receives him as offered freely, 'without money and without price.' I know it is not possible that a soul can receive Christ, till there be some preparatory convincing work of the law, to discover sin and misery. But I hold, that to look to any such preparation, and fetch an encouragement or motive therefrom, to believe in Christ, is really to give him a price for his free waters and wine; it is to mix in together, Christ and the law, in the point of our acceptation. And for souls to go about to seek preparations for a time, resolving not at all to consider the promise of the gospel, till they have found them, and satisfaction in them, is nothing else but to go about to establish their own righteousness, being ignorant of the righteousness of Christ."*

Binning, however, it will be found, did not give his sanction to the views of those who confounded faith in Christ and the assurance of salvation. This was one of the numerous errors of the day. It was prevalent in England; and along with other heresies, it had no doubt insinuated itself, by means of the parliamentary soldiers, into some parts of Scotland. So far from the assurance of salvation being of the essence of faith, or a constant attendant upon it, there are some sincere Christians, we have reason to believe, who are all their lifetime strangers to it; while they who have attained to it, from discovering in themselves the fruits and evidences of faith, have it oftentimes clouded and suspended. This is consistent with the personal experience of many humble and pious persons, and with what we read in the Diaries of many, whose life when upon the earth was the best of all proofs that the Spirit of God dwelt in them. It is likewise confirmed by the recorded experience of the man according to God's own heart. If he was at one time elevated with hope, he was at another time depressed by fear. If, when meditating upon the divine love and mercy, he was on some occasions filled with peace and joy, he was on other occasions, when contemplating his own guilt and unworthiness, a prey to grief and perplexity. If he was heard to exclaim, 'Thou, Lord, hast made me glad through thy work; I will triumph in the works of thy hands,' he was also heard to cry out, 'Will the Lord cast off for ever? And will he be favourable no more? Is his mercy clean gone for ever? Doth his promise fail for evermore? Hath God forgotten to be gracious? Hath he in anger shut up

* P. 132. See also Sermon vi. p. 576.

his tender mercies?' A man who believes Christ to be the Son of God and the Saviour of the world, if he has searched the scriptures, has been made acquainted with the deceitfulness of the human heart, and the devices of our great adversary. It is on this account he does not always feel assured of his salvation. He is afraid that he may be deceiving himself, and be thinking more highly of himself then he ought to think. He has learned, from the parable of the sower, that some 'receive the word with joy,' and 'for a while believe;' but as they have 'no root,' they 'in time of temptation fall away.' This leads him to examine himself, and to prove himself, whether he be in the faith. This indeed is what the apostle has enjoined us all to do, thereby showing that a man may be in Christ Jesus, and yet be doubtful of his salvation; and, on the other hand, that a man may have a complete assurance of his salvation, and yet be still 'in the gall of bitterness and in the bond of iniquity.' It is from the fruits of the Spirit, therefore, that in himself as well as in others, the believer discovers the presence of the Spirit. "Both in philosophy and divinity, yea, in common sense, it is allowed to reason from the effects to the causes. Here is burning; therefore here is fire. Here is the blossoming of trees and flowers; therefore it is spring, and the sun is turning again in his course. Here is perfect day-light; therefore the sun is risen. Here is good fruit growing; therefore here is a good tree. 'Tis a consequence no less sure and infallible, here is unfeigned love to the brethren, therefore here is regeneration. Here are spiritual motions, affections, desires, acts, and operations; therefore here is spiritual life."*

These were plainly the sentiments of Binning. He distinguished, with logical precision, between faith in Christ and its consequences. In regard to the doctrine of the Antinomians, he says, "That every man is bound to persuade himself at the first, that God hath loved him, and Christ redeemed him, is the hope of the hypocrite,—like a spider's web, which, when leaned to, shall not stand. That man's expectation shall perish: he hath kindled sparks of his own,—a wild fire, and walketh not in the true light of the word, and so must lie down in sorrow."† Employing language very similar to that of Gillespie, which it would almost seem he had before him at the moment, he also says, "If the question be, as it is indeed, about the grounds of our assurance, and knowledge of our own faith, certainly it is clear as the noonday, that as the good tree is known by the fruits thereof, and the fire by the heat thereof, so the indwelling of faith in the heart is known by its purifying of the heart and working by love. It makes a man a new creature, so that he and others may see the difference. Neither is this any derogation to the free grace of Christ, or any establishing of our own righteousness, except men be so afraid to establish their own righteousness, that they will have no holiness at all, but abandon it quite, for fear of trusting in it, which is a remedy worse than the disease, because I make it not a ground of my acceptation before God, but only a naked evidence of my believing in Christ, and being accepted of God; it being known that these have a necessary connexion together in the scriptures, and it being also known that the one is more obvious and easy to be discerned than the other."‡

It will be thought that the Latin quotations, which the author has introduced into his sermons, might have been spared. These show a mind richly stored with classical learning. They are not forced or unnatural. All of them are appropriate, and many of them singularly felicitous. Still it will be conceived that they would have appeared with more propriety and better effect, in an academical disquisition, or a *concio ad clerum*, than in sermons preached in a country church. But in justice to Binning, it is proper to observe, he did nothing more than follow the example of the most celebrated preachers who had preceded him. Bishop Burnet remarks with considerable severity of the English divines, who appeared before Tillotson, Lloyd, and Stillingfleet, that their sermons were "both long and heavy, when all was pye-balled, full of many sayings of different languages."§ The sermons of the learned Joseph Mede, who died in 1638, are filled not only

* Gillespie's Miscellany questions, p. 247. Edin. 1649.

† P. 135.

‡ P. 133.

§ Hist. of his Own Times, vol. i. p. 348.

with Greek and Latin quotations, but with Hebrew, and Chaldee, and Syriac. But his biographer very ingenuously admits, that when he had occasion to quote from a work written in any of the Eastern languages, if the testimonies were long, Mede usually gave a Latin version of them, "as judging it perhaps more fit and useful to quote them in a language which might be understood by all that heard him, even by the younger students, than to make an astonishing clatter, with many words of a strange sound, and of an unknown sense to some in the auditory."* In the discourses of Jeremy Taylor, Bishop of Down, who outlived Binning, we likewise meet with innumerable quotations, both in Greek and Latin, from the classics and from the fathers. And though we might be disposed to infer the contrary, those discourses were not composed for the benefit of the learned members of a university. As the author himself has informed us, they were all preached at Golden Grove, to the family and domestics of his patron, and perhaps in addition to these, to a few of their neighbours, and as many of the peasantry on the estate as could understand English.† The common people in England were so much accustomed in those days to hear Latin spoken in the pulpit, that they were sometimes led to undervalue a preacher who did not make some use of it. When Dr. Pocock, the celebrated orientalist, was presented to the rectory of Childry, near Oxford, he considered it to be his duty to adapt his instructions to what he thought to be the capacity of his rustic parishioners. This made some of them lament to one of his friends that he was "no Latiner."‡ An unseasonable display of learning by Dr. Manton, on the other hand, when preaching in St. Paul's, on some public occasion, instead of awakening admiration, subjected him to a reproof which he felt very keenly. On returning home in the evening, a poor man following him, gently pulled him by the sleeve of his gown, and asked him if he were the gentleman who had preached that day before my Lord Mayor. He answered he was. "Sir," said he, "I came with earnest desires after the word of God, and hopes of getting some good to my soul, but I was greatly disappointed; for I could not understand a great deal of what you said,—you were quite above me." The Doctor replied, with tears in his eyes, "Friend, if I did not give you a sermon, you have given me one."§ Massillon was one of the first French preachers who abstained, in the pulpit, from the use of citations from profane authors. In the first sermon of his "Petit Careme," he has a quotation from Sallust. But he does not name the author, nor does he give the words in the original. He merely gives the meaning of them, introducing his quotation in this manner, *as one of the ancients says*, "comme dit un ancien." This, it is believed, is the only instance of the kind that is to be found in the sermons of that eloquent preacher.‖

Some may be desirous to know how it was that a practice so different from ours, and so much opposed to the good sense and the good taste of modern times, was formerly so common, or by what arguments it was attempted to be defended. Abraham Wright, one of the Fellows of St. John the Baptist's College, Oxford, undertook this task. He published a book in 1656, under this title, "Five Sermons in Five several Styles, or Waies of Preaching." These different ways of preaching were what he characterized as Bishop Andrews' way, Bishop Hall's way, Dr. Maine and Mr. Cartwright's way, the Presbyterian way, and the Independent way. All of the sermons, with the exception of the last, contain specimens of the "Babylonish dialect" of the age. But this, in the estimation of Abraham Wright, was not their least recommendation. "You are also taught from these leaves," says he,¶ "that secular learning is not so heathenish, but it may be made Christian. Plato, and Socrates, and Seneca, were not of such a reprobate sense, as to stand wholly excommunicate. The same man may be both a poet and a prophet, a philosopher and an apostle. Virgil's fancie was as high as the Magi's star, and

* Mede's Works. *General Preface.*

† Heber's Life of Bishop Taylor, p. 171.

‡ Pocock's Works, vol. i. Life of the Author, p. 22.

§ Manton's Sermons. Life of the Author, p. v.

‖ Œuvres De Massillon, tome vi. p. 4. Essai Sur L'Eloquence de la Chaire, par le Cardinal Maury, tome ii. p. 231.

¶ Address to the Christian Reader.

might lead wise men in the West as clearly to their Saviour, as that light did those Eastern sages. And so, likewise, Seneca's positions may become Saint Paul's text; Aristotle's metaphysicks convince an atheist of a God, and his demonstrations prove Shiloes advent to a Jew. That great apostle of the Gentiles had never converted those nations, without the help of their own learning. It was the Gentiles oratorie, yet not without the Holy Ghost's rhetorick, that did almost perswade Agrippa to be a Christian; and it was the Gentiles poetrie, but not without a Deitie in the verse, that taught the Athenians to know an unknown God. By which you see it is possible that Gamaliel's feet may be a step to an apostleship." This failed to convince the pious editor of the Works of the ever-memorable John Hales of Eaton, if ever he chanced to see it. The learned prebendary, for the purpose of enforcing his arguments against intemperance, chose to quote the concluding words of the Symposium of Xenophon. Lord Hailes was of opinion that this was "improper in a popular discourse," and therefore he used the liberty to leave out the quotation in his edition of the works of the author.

But this much may likewise be stated in behalf of Binning. He did not engage, like some other preachers, his contemporaries, in nice critical discussions, which could be appreciated, or understood, by none but scholars like himself; and when he brought forth a classical quotation in his sermons, if a literal translation did not accompany it, he took care at least to put all who heard him in possession of the sentiment which it contained. In this way, none of his hearers were left ignorant of what he said; while the varied and attractive form in which the important truths he inculcated were exhibited, may have recommended them to that portion of his audience whose minds were more highly cultivated, among whom it is not unlikely were some, who, on account of his fame, may have come to hear him, more or less frequently, from the contiguous city and university.

When Binning quotes the sacred scriptures, it will be perceived he does not always make use of the authorized version. In the Case of Conscience, he appears to do this; but we find from the old manuscript already referred to, that he sometimes contented himself with mentioning the chapter and verse to which he wished to direct attention, without giving the words. These, therefore, we may suppose, were added by the transcriber, when the work was about to be printed. It was not till after the death of the author that the nation generally can be said to have adopted the translation of the scriptures which was completed in the reign of King James, and which is now in common use. Before the introduction into Scotland of what is called the Geneva Bible, the translation of Tyndale and Coverdale was employed. This was superseded in a great measure by the Geneva Bible, which was an English version of the scriptures that was executed in Geneva in the year 1560, by Protestant refugees from England. In the year 1575, the General Assembly required that every parish kirk in Scotland should be provided with a copy of Bassandyne's edition of the Geneva Bible. The first edition of the present authorized version was published in 1611. But as many preferred the Geneva Bible to it, the former continued to maintain its place in Scotland for some time longer. In Boyd's "Last Battle of the Soul," printed at Edinburgh in 1629, the Geneva translation is used. It was likewise used by Dr. Balcanquhall in a sermon which was preached by him in the presence of Charles the First, in the year 1632, and published under the title of "The Honour of Christian Churches, and the Necessitie of frequenting Divine Service, and Publike Prayers in them." And we learn from Dr. Lee, that so late as the year 1639, the celebrated Alexander Henderson, in preaching before the General Assembly at Edinburgh, read a long text from the Geneva Bible, which, he tells us, appears from the proceedings of that Assembly still extant in manuscript.* About the time, however, when Binning began to preach, the version now universally adopted seems to have become much more common. Binning generally employs it. But he occasionally quotes from the Geneva translation, and sometimes from memory. It is easy to conceive that, in this transition state of the two versions, he may have been nearly equally familiar with both, and unable from his recollection at the moment to distinguish the

* Memorial for the Bible Societies in Scotland, p. 91. See also pp. 30, 90, 112.

words of the one from those of the other. We therefore find, in point of fact, that when trusting to his memory, he quotes a passage of scripture, he sometimes gives it, partly in the language of the one, and partly in the language of the other translation. One of the texts of his first sermon is Rom. xi. 36. The English reading of that text, according to the Geneva version is, 'For of him, and through him, and *for* him are all things;' but according to the authorized version, it is, 'For of him, and through him, and *to* him are all things.' Any person, however, who reads the sermon attentively, will be convinced, that when the author wrote it, he must have had before him at the time, the Geneva version, and not the other. "'All things,' says he,* 'are of him, and *for* him;' but man in a peculiar and proper way. As God, in making of man, was pleased of his goodness to stamp him with a character of his own image,—and in this he puts a difference between man and other creatures, that he should have more plain and distinct engravings of divine majesty upon him, which might show the glory of the workman,—so it appears that he is in a singular way made *for* God, as his last end. As he is set nearer God, as the beginning and cause, than other creatures; so he is placed nearer God as the end. All creatures are made *ultimo*, lastly, *for* God, yet they are all made *proxime*, nextly, *for* man."

The sacred scriptures are the Christian teacher's treasury. The knowledge of these evinced by the young and interesting author, apprizes us that he had carefully studied them, as his rule of faith and manners. But his beautiful and appropriate illustrations were not derived from the Bible alone. The stores of profane history, philosophy, and science; the apologues and mythology of the ancients, were all made tributary to him. His scholastic habits evidently gave a tinge to his discourses. When perusing some of these, we could almost imagine we are listening to the youthful Regent, while delivering, within the walls of the University of Glasgow, his dictates to a class of admiring and enthusiastic students. We are at once reminded of the "Professor of Philosophy," for instance, when we find him borrowing from Plato, and other ancient philosophers, such names as these, applied by them "to the unknown God," αυτο ον,† αυτο πνευμα,‡ and *primum intelligibile, et primum intelligens*;§ when he makes mention of "the astronomers" who "do cut and carve in their imagination cycles, orbs, and epicycles, in the heavens, because of the various and different appearances and motions of stars in them, whereas it may be, really, there is but one celestial body in which all these various lights and motions do appear;"‖ and when he tells us, that "if two superficies were exactly plain and smooth, they could join so closely together, that no air could come between them, and then they could hardly be pulled asunder."¶ All the while, however, it is evident that the knowledge of the philosopher is made subservient to the nobler purposes of the divine. The idea never occurs to us, that his secular learning is produced for display, and not to give interest to a sacred subject, or to furnish him with the means of explaining it.

The following extract will show the holy use to which the pious author consecrated his knowledge of "physiology," which, when a Regent, he was bound to teach, by the foundation-charter of the University:—"We can do nothing except we have some pattern or copy before us; but now, upon this ground which God hath laid, man may fancy many superstructures. But when he stretched out the heaven, and laid the foundation of the earth, 'who, being his counsellor, taught him?' At whom did his Spirit take counsel? Certainly, none of all these things would have entered into the heart of man to consider or contrive, Isa. xl. 12, 13. Some ruder spirits do gaze upon the huge and prodigious pieces of the creation, as whales and elephants, &c.; but a wise Solomon will go to the school of the ant to learn the wisdom of God, and choose out such a simple and mean creature for the object of his admiration. Certainly there are wonders in the smallest and most inconsiderable creatures which faith can contemplate. O the curious ingenuity and draught of the finger of God, in the composition of flies, bees, flowers, &c. Men ordinarily admire more some extraordinary things; but the truth is, the whole course of nature is one continued wonder, and that greater than any of

* P. 5. † Pp. 42, 48. ‡ P. 55. § P. 302. ‖ P. 80. ¶ P. 279.

the Lord's works without the line. The straight and regular line of the wisdom of God, who, in one constant course and tenor, hath ordained the actions of all his creatures, comprehends more wonders and mysteries, as the course of the sun, the motion of the sea, the hanging of the earth in the empty place upon nothing. These, we say, are the wonders indeed, and comprehend something in them which all the wonders of Egypt and the wilderness cannot parallel. But it is the stupid security of men, that are only awakened by some new and unusual passages of God's works beyond that straight line of nature."*

From an eloquent passage in his sermon on the text (1 John i. 5,) 'God is light,' it will likewise be seen that if Binning spoke, like a philosopher, of the properties of light, his was the language of a Christian philosopher :—" The light is, as it were, a visible appearance of the invisible God. He hath covered his invisible nature with this glorious garment, to make himself in a manner visible to man. It is true, that light is but, as it were, a shadow of that inaccessible light, *umbra Dei.* It is the dark shadow of God, who is himself infinitely more beautiful and glorious. But yet, as to us, it hath greater glory and majesty in it, than any creature besides. It is the chief of the works of God, without which the world would be without form and void. It is the very beauty of the creation, that which gives lustre and amiableness to all that is in it; without which the pleasantest paradise would become a wilderness, and this beautiful structure, and adorned palace of the world, a loathsome dungeon. Besides the admirable beauty of it, it hath a wonderful swift conveyance throughout the whole world, the upper and lower, in a moment, in the twinkling of an eye. It is carried from the one end of heaven to the other in a moment, and who can say by what way the light is parted? Job xxxviii. 24. Moreover, it carries alongst with it a beautiful influence, and a refreshing heat and warmness, which is the very life and subsistence of all the creatures below. And so, as there is nothing so beautiful, so nothing so universally and highly profitable. And to all this, add that singular property of it, that it is not capable of infection; it is of such absolute purity, that it can communicate itself to the dunghill, as well as to the garden, without receiving any mixture from it. In all the impurities it meets withal, it remains unmixed and untainted, and preserves its own nature entire. Now you may perceive, that there is nothing visible that is fitter to resemble the invisible God, than this glorious, beautiful, pure, and universally communicable creature, light. * * *

" Then add unto this, to make up the resemblance fuller, the bounty and benignity of his influence upon the world, the flowings forth of his infinite goodness, that enrich the whole earth. Look, as the sun is the greatest and most universal benefactor,—his influence and heat is the very renovation of the world. It makes all new, and green, and flourishing; it puts a youth upon the world, and so is the very spring and fountain of life to all sublunary things. How much is that true of the true light, of the substantial, of whom this sun is but a shadow! * * *

" And to complete the resemblance more, there may be something of the infallibility and incomprehensibility of the divine majesty here represented. For though nothing be clearer than the light, yet there is nothing in its own nature darker than light; that which is so manifest to the eyes, how obscure is it to the understanding! Many debates and inquiries have been about it, but yet it is not known what that is by which we know all things. Certainly such is the divine light. It is inconceivable and inexpressible, therefore is he said to dwell in light inaccessible and full of glory, 1 Tim. vi. 16. There is a twofold darkness that hinders us to see God, a darkness of ignorance in us, and a darkness of inaccessible light in him. The one is a vail upon our hearts, which blinds and darkens the souls of men, that they do not see that which is manifest of God even in his works. O that cloud of unbelief that is spread over our souls, which hinders the glorious rays of that divine light to shine into them! This darkness Satan contributes much to, who is the prince of darkness, 2 Cor. iv. 4. This makes the most part of souls like dungeons within, when the glorious light of the gospel surrounds them without. This earthliness and carnality of our hearts makes them

* P. 90.

like the earth, receive only the light in the upper and outward superfice, and not suffer it to be transmitted into our hearts to change them. But when it pleaseth him, who at the first, by a word of power, commanded light to shine out of darkness, he can scatter that cloud of ignorance, and draw away the vail of unbelief, and can by his power and art, so transform the soul, as to remove its earthly quality, and make it transparent and pure; and then the light will shine into the heart, and get free access into the soul. But though this darkness were wholly removed, there is another darkness, that ariseth not from the want of light, but from the excessive superabundance of light,—*caligo lucis nimiæ;* that is, a divine darkness, a darkness of glory, such an infinite excess and superplus of light and glory above all created capacities, that it dazzles and confounds all mortal or created understandings. We see some shadows of this, if we look up to the clear sun. We are able to see nothing for too much light. There is such an infinite disproportion here between the eye of our mind, and this divine light of glory, that if we curiously pry into it, it is rather confounding and astonishing; and therefore it fills the souls of saints with continual silent admiration and adoration."*

The comparisons, employed by Binning, have sometimes a degree of quaintness in them which is far from being displeasing, if it does not heighten their effect, as when he observes of that Great Being, whose thoughts are not as our thoughts, that he "speaks in our terms, and *like nurses with their children,* uses our own dialect."† He employs an equally vivid, though somewhat quaint comparison, when he observes, that "the best way to behold the sun, is to look at it *in a pail of water;* and the surest way to know God by, is to take him up in a state of humiliation and condescension, as the sun in the rainbow, in his words and works, which are mirrors of the divine power and goodness, and do reflect upon the hearts and eyes of all men the beams of that uncreated light."‡ We are offended, however, with the homeliness of such expressions as these, "sin's ugly face;"§ "our legs are cut off by sin;"‖ "the legs of the soul;"¶ men opposing God are "like dogs barking at the moon;"** "the pull of the Father's arm;"†† the Christian is "on speaking terms with God;"‡‡ "he drives a trade with heaven;"§§ "Christ "took up a shop, as it were, in our flesh, that he might work in us;"‖‖ Nevertheless, an obvious excuse suggests itself to us for the employment, by the author, of these, and such like familiar expressions, which are besides of singularly rare occurrence in his writings. The great object which a Christian minister, like Binning, will constantly propose to himself, when addressing his people, will be, to make himself useful to them. But he knows he cannot be useful, without being intelligible to his audience. He is thus led sometimes to lower his style, as well as to simplify his ideas, that he may reach the understandings and hearts of the youngest and the most illiterate among his hearers. This was evidently Binning's case. To the least intelligent of those whom he addressed, he sometimes spoke in their own dialect, or, to adopt his own comparison, "like nurses with their children." In so far as he did this, he followed the maxim of the great German Reformer. *Hi sunt optimi ad populum concionatores,* said Luther, *qui pueriliter, populariter, et quam simplicissime docent.* "They are the best preachers to the people, who teach them in a plain, familiar, and perfectly simple way."

A preacher, however, who is desirous to make his instructions exceedingly simple, is in danger of bringing his language too low, or of expressing himself in a manner which may not please persons of refined taste. His own good sense will teach him to avoid this if possible. But in the hurry of writing or speaking, he may not always succeed. When this happens, the fault into which he has been betrayed ought to be overlooked by those who are aware, that the business of a minister of Christ is not to interest merely, but to convince; not to afford pleasure, but to enlighten, reclaim, and admonish, 'rightly dividing the word of truth.'

It is right that the reader should know what changes have in the present edition been made upon the text of the author. To make the work as perfect as possible, it has been carefully collated with the earliest editions which could be procured of

* Pp. 301—303. † P. 74. ‡ P. 36. § P. 456. ‖ P. 165. ¶ P. 216.
** P. 76. †† P. 248. ‡‡ P. 657. §§ P. 619. ‖‖ P. 217.

his different writings. From his style being so much in advance of that of his countrymen in general, at the time he lived, it may be supposed that his language has been modernized to a considerable extent. But such is not the fact. The orthography has been altered. Greater attention than formerly has been paid to the punctuation. This was so defective in many places, as completely to obscure and pervert the meaning of the author. The references to scripture have also been corrected in numerous instances. But beyond this, nothing almost whatever has been done, with the exception of the occasional emendation of what, according to existing rules, would now be considered an ungrammatical expression, or the substitution of a modern word for one that was obsolete or provincial. The text itself, however, will show that very few changes indeed of this description have been ventured upon. It was thought better, for various reasons, that the author should be allowed to speak in his own familiar tongue, than that he should be transformed into a modern preacher. The remodelling of his style might have made it more agreeable to some readers, but it would no longer have been the style of Binning, nor characteristic of his age and country. His language, mcreover, would have lost much of its raciness in the attempt to mellow it.

An explanation of such words as have been employed by Binning, and are not now in common use, or generally understood beyond the limits of Scotland, has been given in the Notes. Many of his Latin quotations, when not translated by himself, have likewise been explained, and verified, and their authors pointed out. This, it is confessed, has been a very irksome and laborious undertaking. As the classical quotations of the author, like his quotations from scripture, have not unfrequently been made from memory, the difficulty of tracing them to their proper sources was thereby much increased. The necessary books were not always at hand to consult, and even when these were obtained, it was sometimes found to be impossible, after the most patient research, to discover the place where the saying of some ancient writer was concealed. There are few notes comparatively attached to the first part of the work, as the printing of it commenced sooner than was expected. To supply this defect, some *Notanda* have been inserted after the Life of the Author.

But in addition to some of the classical quotations of the author, various historical allusions required to be elucidated, along with certain obscure references to passing events, and the opinions and proceedings of different sects and parties. It is not pretended that every thing of this kind has had light thrown upon it. But I can say this much with confidence, that it has been my constant endeavour to discover the latent or partially disclosed meaning of the author, and to give to the candid reader the benefit of my researches, and of any knowledge, which, in consequence of my position, I possessed, of a minister of the Church of Scotland, of whom I deem it no small honour to have been a successor.

When this edition of the works of the Rev. Hugh Binning had nearly passed through the press, the Editor had unexpectedly put into his hands a manuscript volume of the sermons of the author. About fifty of these, he finds, on examination, have never been printed, most of which have been transcribed by the Rev. Robert Macward, whose handwriting is perfectly well known. The remaining part of the volume contains the forty sermons on the eighth chapter of the Epistle to the Romans, entitled 'The Sinner's Sanctuary.' These are believed to be in the handwriting of Binning himself. There can be no doubt whatever that this is the manuscript volume in folio, which is described in the preface to 'Several Sermons upon the most important Subjects of Practical Religion,' dated "Brousterland, Sept. 12th, 1760." It is there said to have been for "many years concealed in the library of John Graham, a pious and learned man, much abstracted from the world, who was a near relation of Mr. M'Ward's, with a large collection of Mr. M'Ward's own papers, which are yet among the curious and large collection of manuscripts, that were left by Mr. Wodrow, the author of the History of the Sufferings of this Church, to his sons." (Pp. xix, xx.) The writer of that preface also tells us, that he had in his possession a "quarto volume" of manuscript sermons, belonging to Binning. The Editor has not been able to ascertain what has become of this latter volume; nor can any thing be learned of the "Course of Philosophy," which the author of Binning's Life, states, he was assured was in the hands of a gentleman in Edinburgh, at the time he wrote that Life, which was about the year 1735. (See Life of the Author, p. liv.) The sermons which have not hitherto been printed, and which are contained in the manuscript volume now brought to light, may be expected to be given to the world at no distant period.

THE

LIFE OF MR. HUGH BINNING.

THERE being a great demand for the several books that are printed under Mr. Binning's name, it was judged proper to undertake a new and correct impression of them in one volume. This being done, the publishers were much concerned to have the life of such an useful and eminent minister of Christ written, in justice to his memory, and his great services in the work of the gospel, that it might go along with this impresson. We living now at so great distance from the time wherein he made a figure in the world, must be at a considerable loss in giving an exact and particular relation. However, his pious and exemplary life may in some measure be known from his writings ; and for this end, a great many bright passages might be gathered out of them, which would raise his character highly in the eyes of all good men ; for the Rev. Mr. Robert M'Ward, minister in Glasgow, observed, "That his life was his sermons put in print, by which means they who did forget what he had said in the pulpit, by seeing what he did in his conversation might remember what they had forgot; he lived as he spoke, and spoke as he lived." All due pains have been taken to procure proper materials, and good vouchers of the following narration. Some few things are learned from the prefaces prefixed to his several pieces, by worthy and able divines, who revised and published them; more accounts of him were furnished by persons of great credit, on whose veracity we can safely rely. But the most remarkable passages in his life are happily preserved, in a letter written by Mr. M'Ward,* to the Rev. Mr. James Cole-

* [Mr. Robert Macward went to England as the secretary, or amanuensis, of the famous Samuel Rutherford, when the latter was appointed one of the commissioners to the Westminster Assembly (Murray's Life of Rutherford, p. 233). When mentioning Macward's institution, as Professor of Humanity in the old college of St. Andrews, in April, 1650, Lamond says of him, that he was previously "servant to Mr. Sa. Rutherford, m. of St. Andrews" (Diary, p. 16, Edin. 1830). Sir John Chiesley was, in the same sense, and at the same period, the servant of the celebrated Alexander Henderson, another of the commissioners (Kirkton's Hist. of the Ch. of Scot., *note*, p. 71). It is justly remarked by Dr. M'Crie, when speaking of Richard Bannatyne, who was also called *the servant* of Knox, "that the word servant, or servitor, was then used with greater latitude than it is now, and, in old writings, often signifies the person whom we call by the more honourable name of clerk, secretary, or man-of-business" (Life of Knox, p. 349. *Sixth edition*). Mr. Macward succeeded Mr. Andrew Gray as one of the ministers of Glasgow, in the year 1656, chiefly through the influence of Principal Gillespie (Baillie's Letters, vol. ii. pp. 406, 407. Cleland's Annals of Glasgow, vol. i. p. 128). A sentence of banishment was unjustly passed upon him for a sermon on Amos iii. 2, which he preached in the Tron Church, Glasgow, after the Restoration. As to what he said in that sermon regarding the conduct of the parliament, Baillie declares, that "all honest men did concur with him," though he disapproves, at the same time, of Macward's "high language," and blames him, because "he obstinately stood to all," and thereby provoked his persecutors (Letters, pp. 453, 454). But it appears from Wodrow (Hist. of the Sufferings of the Ch. of Scot., vol. i. p. 213, Glasg. 1829), that when Mr. Macward understood that what had given offence was the use he had made, in his sermon, of the words "protest" and "dissent," he did not hesitate to explain he did not mean thereby a legal impugning of the acts, or authority of parliament, but "a mere ministerial testimony" against what he conceived to be sin. Macward retired to Holland.

After repeated applications from Charles the Second, the States General, on the 6th of February, 1677, ordered Mr. Macward, and other two Scottish exiles, to withdraw from the Seven Provinces of the Netherlands (Dr. M'Crie's Mem. of Veitch and Brysson, p. 367). That the States came to this determination with very great reluctance, will appear from the following passage in one of Sir William Temple's Letters: "I will only say that the business of the three Scotch ministers hath been the hardest piece of negotiation that I ever yet entered upon here, both from the particular interest of the towns and provinces of Holland, and the general esteem they have of Mackaird [Macman,* sometime minister at Sluys in Flanders. The writer of his life must in the entry confess that his part is so small, that he can scarce assume any thing to himself, but the procuring the materials from others, the copying out of those things that were of any moment, and disposing them in the best and most natural order he could think of; having studied the strictness of a severe historian, without helping out things with his invention, or setting them off by a rhetorical style of language. Nay, all that is contained in Mr. M'Ward's large letter concerning him, is told almost in his very words, with a little variation of the order wherein he had placed the same, omitting the many long digressions on several subjects which that worthy person judged fit to insist upon; taking occasion from what he had noticed concerning Mr. Binning to enlarge on the same.

John Binning of Dalvennan was married to Margaret M'Kell, a daughter of Mr. Matthew M'Kell,† minister at Bothwell, and sister to Mr. Hugh M'Kell,‡ one of

ward], being a very quiet and pious man" (Vol. iii. p. 291). It is creditable to the good feeling, though not certainly to the firmness, of the States General, that at the time they determined to require Macward and his two friends to leave the Seven Provinces, they voluntarily furnished them with a certificate, bearing that each of them had lived among them "highly esteemed for his probity, submission to the laws, and integrity of manners" (Dr. M'Crie's Mem. of Veitch and Brysson, p. 368). He was afterwards permitted to return to Rotterdam, where he had been officiating, as minister of the Scottish Church, at the time he was ordered to remove out of the country. He died there in the month of December, 1681. Dr. Steven's "History of the Scottish Church, at Rotterdam," p. 336.—Ed.]

* [In his very interesting "History of the Scottish Church, Rotterdam," Dr. Steven mentions (p. 72) that Mr. James Koelman was deprived of his charge at Sluys in Flanders, for refusing to observe the festival days, and to comply with the formularies of the Dutch church. He appears to have been a very conscientious and pious man. Among the Wodrow MSS. in the Library of the Faculty of Advocates, Edinburgh (Vol. ix. Numb. 28.), there is a copy of "A Resolution of the States of Zeeland anent the suspension of Thomas Pots, and Bernardus Van Deinse, ministers of Vlissing, because of their suffering, or causing Jacobus Coelman to preach; together with the Placiaet (or proclamation), whereby the said Coelman is for ever banished out of the province of Zeeland, Sept. 21, 1684. Extract out of the Registers of the Noble and Mighty Lords, the States of Zeeland. Sept. 21, 1684." It is set forth in this paper, that though Koelman had been suspended from his office by the States of the Land and Earldom of Zealand, in consequence of their "Resolution and penal discharge of the 21st of September, 1674, made by reason of his perverse opinions, and disobedience to his lawful high superiors," he had notwithstanding "adventured and undertaken to go about private exercises within this province, and also to preach twice publickly within the city Vlissing [Flushing] on Sabbath the 3d of this instant moneth, September, and so hath rendered himself guilty of the punishment contained in our forementioned Resolution, and penal discharge, bearing that he should be banished the province, so be he happened to hold any publick or private exercises there."

Mr. Koelman, Mr. Macward, and Mr. Brown of Wamphray, were the three clergymen who officiated at the ordination of Mr. Richard Cameron, in the Scottish Church, Rotterdam, previous to his coming to Scotland in the beginning of the year 1680 (Biographia Presbyteriana, Vol. i. p. 197). It was Richard Cameron, when, in the language of one of his friends, he was "carrying Christ's standard over the mountains of Scotland," who repeated three times that simple and pathetic prayer, before he was killed at Airs-moss, *Lord, spare the green, and take the ripe* (Id. p. 203). From a letter written from Holland, 7th December, 1685, by Mr. Robert Hamilton of Preston, it may be seen how much Mr. Koelman interested himself in the affairs of the Scottish refugees (Faithful Contendings Displayed, pp. 203—205, 214, 215). There is prefixed to a Dutch translation of Binning's Common Principles of the Christian Religion, which was executed and published by Koelman at Amsterdam in 1678, a Memoir of the author. Koelman acknowledges he had derived all his information respecting Binning from a letter which he had received from Mr. Macward, through a mutual friend. This letter, or a copy of it, with some other of Macward's MSS., was in the possession of the publisher of the duodecimo volume of the sermons of the author, printed at Glasgow, 1760 (Preface, pp. iv. xxv.). Koelman concludes his Memoir of Binning, which contains some excellent pious reflections, but almost no facts with which the English reader is not already acquainted, with a feeling allusion to his ejection from his charge at "Sluys in Vlaanderen." After this painful separation from his flock, besides writing many useful original works, he seems to have employed his leisure in translating into his native language some of the most esteemed practical writings of foreign divines, such as *Guthrie's Great Concern, Rutherford's Letters*, &c. Dr. Steven's Hist. ut supra.—Ed.]

† [Adverting to a sermon, which was preached by Mr. Matthew M'Kail, at a field meeting in the year 1669, Wodrow says, that he was "a true Nathanael, and a very plain dealer" (Hist. of the Suf. of Ch. of Scot., vol. ii. p. 127). After having been, on different occasions, brought before the Privy-council, and imprisoned, he was, on the 8th of January, 1674, upon his refusing to engage not to preach, ordered to confine himself to the parish of Carluke, and security was required from him that he would appear before the Council, at their summons (Id. vol. i. pp. 371, 372, vol. ii. p. 248. See also History of Indulgence, p. 36). He died at Edinburgh, in March 1681 (Law's Memorialls, p. 183).

Wodrow does not speak with much confidence, as to the degree of propinquity which existed be the ministers of Edinburgh; he had by her Mr. Hugh and Alexander. The father was possessed of no inconsiderable estate in the shire of Ayr, for Mr. Hugh having died before his father, John, the only son of Mr. Hugh, was served heir to his grandfather in the lands of Dalvennan. Alexander, the second son, who died about ten years ago, got the lands of Machrimore, and was married to a daughter of Alexander Crawfurd of Kerse, and is succeeded therein by his son John Binning, at present a writer in Edinburgh.

The worldly circumstances of the grandfather being so good, he was thereby enabled to give his son Hugh a liberal education, the good and desirable effects of which appeared very early upon him: the greatness of his spirit and capacity gave his parents good ground to conceive the pleasant hope of his being a promising child. When he was at the grammar-school, he made so great proficiency in the knowledge of the Latin tongue, and Roman authors, that he outstripped his condisciples, even such as were some years older than himself. When his fellow-schoolboys went to their play and diversion, he declined their society, and choosed to employ himself, either in secret duty with God, or conference with religious people. His pastime was to recreate himself in this manner. He had an aversion to sports, games, and other diversions, not from any moroseness, or melancholy of temper,

wixt Mr. Matthew M'Kail minister of Bothwell, and Mr. Hugh M'Kail, the young licentiate who was executed at Edinburgh, 22d Dec., 1666, for being concerned in the insurrection at Pentland. But Colonel Wallace, who commanded the insurgents on that unfortunate occasion, styles "Mr. Hugh M'Kell son of Mr. Matthew M'Kell minister of Bothwell." (Wallace's 'Narrative of the Rising at Pentland,' in Dr. M'Crie's Memoirs of Veitch and Brysson, p. 430.) The unhappy father was allowed to see his son, in prison, after his sentence. There is an affecting account in Naphtali (pp. 339, 345.) of this mournful interview, and of another which took place on the morning of the execution. The address of young M'Kail on the scaffold concluded with these sublime expressions—"Farewell, father and mother, friends and relations. Farewell the world, and all delights. Farewell meat and drink. Farewell sun, moon, and stars. Welcome God and Father! Welcome sweet Lord Jesus, the Mediator of the new covenant! Welcome blessed Spirit of grace, and God of all consolation! Welcome glory! Welcome eternal life! Welcome death!" (Id. p. 348. Edin. 1761.) We are told by Kirkton, that "when Mr. M'Kail died, there was such a lamentation as was never known in Scotland before: not one dry cheek upon all the street, or in all the numberless windows in the market-place." (Hist. of Ch. of Scot., p. 249.) It was discovered afterwards, that Burnet, archbishop of Glasgow, had in his possession at the time, a letter from the king, forbidding any more blood to be shed. But to the disgrace of his sacred profession, and of his feelings as a man, "Burnet let the execution go on, before he produced his letter, pretending there was no council-day between."—Burnet's Hist. of his own Times, vol. i. p. 435. Oxford, 1833.—Ed.]

‡ [All accounts agree in stating that Mr. Hugh M'Kail, minister in Edinburgh, was uncle to the preacher of the same name who was executed. The minister of Bothwell, therefore, instead of being the father, must have been the brother of the minister in Edinburgh. In the years 1636, and 1637, when Mr. Samuel Rutherford was in Aberdeen, according to his own description of himself, "a poor Joseph, and prisoner," with whom his "mother's children were angry," he wrote several letters to Mr. Hugh M'Kail, in answer to others which he received from him (Rutherford's Letters, pp. 41, 247, 272, 292. *Sixth edition.* Edin., 1738). The name of Mr. Hugh M'Kail is included in the list of ministers who, on the 19th of August, 1643, were by the General Assembly appointed Commissioners for the Visitation of the University of Glasgow (Evidence of Royal Commissioners for Visiting the Universities of Scotland, vol. ii. p. 261. London, 1837). "Mr. Hugh M'Kail, minister at Irvine," was likewise one of the ministers commissioned by the Assembly, in 1644, to visit the church in Ulster (Dr. Reid's History of the Presbyterian Church in Ireland, vol. ii. p. 57). As a further proof of the estimation in which he was held by his brethren, when it was proposed by the Assembly, in 1648, to recommend to the general session of Edinburgh six ministers, that they might choose four from these to fill their vacant churches, Mr. Hugh M'Kail was selected to be one of the number (Baillie's Letters, vol. ii. p. 303). He was a Resolutioner (Id. p. 387). He died in 1660 (Lamont's Diary, p. 121). The editor of Kirkton's History of the Church of Scotland, for the purpose of bringing ridicule upon the presbyterian clergy of that day, quotes a passage from the MS. sermons of Mr. Hugh M'Kail. We are much mistaken, however, if on reading that passage. and after making some allowance for an antiquated style, and a certain degree of quaintness, one of the characteristics of the age,—the impression produced upon the mind of any candid person, who admires strong good sense, though presented in a homely dress, is not in a very high degree favourable to the character and talents of the author (See Kirkton's History, pp. 227, 228). In the preface to Stevenson's History of the Church and State of Scotland, reference is made to a manuscript, having this title, 'A true relation of the Prelates, their practice for introducing the Service book, &c., upon the Church of Scotland; and the Subjects, their lawful proceedings in opposing the same.' This manuscript, Mr. Stevenson observes, was believed to have belonged to "one of the Mr. Mackails, once famous ministers in this church" Some information respecting it will be found in the Appendix (pp. 191, 192.) to Lord Rothes's "Relation of Proceedings concerning the Affairs of the Kirk of Scotland," printed in Edinburgh, 1830, for the Bannatyne Club.—Ed.]

being rather of an affable, cheerful, and debonair disposition; but thinking that time was too precious to be lavished away in these things. Religion and religious exercises were his choice, and the time he had to spare from his studies he spent that way. He began to have sweet familiarity with God, and to live in near communion with him, before others began seriously to lay to heart their lost and undone condition by nature, and that additional misery they expose themselves to, by walking in a wicked way and sinful course. When he arrived at the thirteenth or fourteenth year of his age, he had even then attained so much experience in the ways of God, that the most judicious and exercised Christians in the place confessed they were much edified, strengthened, and comforted by him; nay, that he provoked them to diligence in the duties of religion, being abundantly sensible that they were much outrun by a youth.

Before he was fourteen years old, he entered upon the study of philosophy in the university of Glasgow, wherein he made very considerable progress, and with as much facility outstripped his fellow-students, as he had done his condisciples in the Latin school; by which means, he came to be taken notice of in the college by the professors and students. And at the same time that he made proficiency in the liberal sciences, he advanced remarkably in religion. The abstruse depths of philosophy, which are the torture of slow engines and weak capacities, he dived into without any trouble or pain. And notwithstanding his surprising attainments and improvements, his great acumen and ready apprehension of things, whereby he was able to do more in one hour, than others in some days by hard study and close application, and though on these accounts he was much respected by the eminent ministers of the city, and learned professors of the university; yet was he ever humble, never exalted above measure, nor swelled with the tympany of pride and self-conceit, the common foible and disease of young men of any greatness of spirit.

So soon as he had finished his course of philosophy, he was made Master of Arts* with great applause; and having furnished his mind with an uncommon measure of the ancillary knowledge of letters, he began the study of divinity, with a view to serve God in the holy ministry. At which time there happened to be a vacancy in the college of Glasgow, by the resignation of Mr. James Dalrymple of Stair, who had been Mr. Binning's Master. This gentleman was so great and so good a man, that it is impossible to avoid giving an account of some of the remarkable things of his life. The first employment he had, was in the army, being a captain in William Earl of Glencairn's regiment of foot; but as he had made his studies with great application, at the earnest request of the professors of the university of Glasgow, he stood as candidate for a chair of philosophy, in a comparative trial, (in buff and scarlet, the military dress of those days,) to which he was with great applause preferred. In this station he was greatly esteemed for his uncommon abilities in philosophy, and other parts of learning. But being resolved to follow the study of the law, he soon resigned his office of professor, and entered Advocate upon the 7th of February, 1648; and quickly distinguished himself by his pleadings before the Court of Session, avoiding always to take any employment, either as advocate, or judge, in criminal matters, though often respectively pressed to accept of both; which proceeded from a delicacy in his opinion, lest, to wit, he might possibly be the instrument either of making the innocent suffer, or to acquit the guilty. In this situation he continued, till the Tender was imposed, when he, with many other eminent lawyers, withdrew from the bar. On June 26th, 1657, he was, by a commission signed by General Monk, † in name of the Protector's

* [It appears from the dedication prefixed to the "Theses Theologicæ, Metaphysicæ, Mathematicæ et Ethicæ, Preside Jacobo Darimplio, Glasg. Excudebat Georgius Andersonus, An. Dom. 1646," that "Hugo Binningus" graduated "ad diem 27 Julii, Anno Domini 1646." Under the ancient Statutes of the University, no student was entitled to receive the degree of master, till he had reached his twentieth year. But this rule was not always strictly adhered to (Report of the Royal Commission of Inquiry into the state of the Universities of Scotland, appointed in 1830, p. 220). Binning was not nineteen years of age at the date of his laureation. His distinguished contemporary, Mr. George Gillespie, took his degree in his seventeenth year.—Ed.]

† [General Monk, who, for the part he took in the restoration of Charles the Second, was made Duke of Albemarle, encouraged most during the time he was in Scotland, the *Resolutioners*, while Cromwell, on the other hand, befriended the *Protesters* (Life of General Monk, by Dr. Gumble,

council of Scotland, appointed to be one of the Judges, which was soon confirmed by a nomination directly from the Protector himself, in the month of July thereafter, which he had no inclination to accept of, being himself no favourer of the usurpation. For as he had been secretary to the commission which had been sent to the king to Breda, he had waited upon his majesty upon his landing in the North. However, being importunately pressed to accept by many eminent men, and amongst them by several ministers, who all distinguished between his serving as one of the Council under the Protector, and exercising the office of a Judge, by administrating justice to his fellow-subjects, he did accept; and his act of admission only bears his giving his oath, *de fideli administratione.* After the Restoration, he was made by the king one of the ordinary Lords of Session, by his majesty's nomination, dated at Whitehall, February 13th, 1661–2. And in the year 1671, he was created President of that Court, in the room of Sir John Gilmour of Craigmiller. In the parliament 1681, he made a great appearance for securing the Protestant religion; and by reason of the difficulties of the times, he desired leave of his majesty to retire from business, and live quietly in the country. But in this he was prevented by a commission, dated the 14th of October, 1681, which having passed the great seal, was produced the 1st of November thereafter, by which commission he was superseded as President of the Session, and in the year 1682, was obliged for his safety to retire to Holland. For though he had the king's promise that he should live undisturbed, yet he was let know that he could not be in safety; and after his retreat to Holland, several unjust but fruitless attempts were made to have him tried for treason, both before the parliament and justiciary, for no other reason than that he had always with sincerity and firmness, given his opinion to the king and his ministers, against the measures that were then followed; and which in the following reign, at length brought about the glorious Revolution: at which time, anno 1668, he attended King William in that expedition, by the success of which we were most happily delivered from tyranny and slavery. On November 1st, 1689, Sir James Dalrymple of Stair, his letter as President of the Session was produced and recorded, and he was accordingly admitted and restored to his office. In the year 1690 he was created a Viscount upon account of his great services and merit. He published, while in Holland, his Institutions of the law of Scotland, (a more full edition of which came out in 1693,) and two volumes in folio, of Decisions, from the year 1661, to 1681 inclusive. He also published a system of physics,* valued greatly at the time. And a book entitled, A Vindication of the divine attributes, was also his, in which there is discovered great force of argument and knowledge. He was looked upon before his death, as the living oracle of our law, and at present his Institutions are appealed to, as containing the true and solid principles of it.†

one of his chaplains, who was with Monk in Scotland, p. 51. London, 1671). Monk professed to be a Presbyterian ("The Mystery and Method of His Majesty's Happy Restoration, by John Price, D.D., one of the late Duke of Albemarle's chaplains." Baron Masseres' Tracts, pp. 723, 775). "In Scotland, Mr. Robert Douglas [one of the ministers of Edinburgh] was the first, so far as I can find, who ventured to propose the king's restoration to General Monk, and that very early. He travelled, it is said, *incognito* in England; and in Scotland engaged considerable numbers of noblemen and gentlemen in this project. From his own original papers, I find that when Monk returned from his first projected march into England, Mr. Douglas met him and engaged him again in the attempt."—Wodrow's Hist. of the Ch. of Scot., vol. i. p. 59.—Ed.]

* [Physiologia Nova Experimentalis. Lugd. Bat. 1686.—Ed.]

† [The appointment of Mr. James Dalrymple, as one of the Regents of the University of Glasgow, took place "iv. Id. Martii 1641" (Annales Collegii). He was then only twenty-two years of age. In the year 1635, a clause was introduced into the oath, which the Regents were required to take at their election, binding them to resign their situation in the event of their marriage. Accordingly, having married in 1643, Mr. Dalrymple vacated his charge, but was immediately afterwards re-elected. Sir Walter Scott has said of James Dalrymple, that he was "one of the most eminent lawyers that ever lived, though the labours of his powerful mind were unhappily exercised on a subject so limited as Scottish Jurisprudence, on which he has composed an admirable work." It has been properly observed, that during the whole of the seventeenth century, not only at Glasgow, but in the other universities of Scotland, "the Regents, or Teachers of Philosophy (with very few exceptions), were young men who had recently finished their academical studies, and who were destined for the church. The course of study which it was their duty to conduct, was calculated to form habits of severe application in early life, and to give them great facility both in writing and in speaking. The universities had the advantage of their services during the vigour of life, when they were unencumbered by domestic cares, and when they felt how much their reputation and interest depended on the

Mr. Binning, who had lately been his scholar, was determined after much entreaty, (of which we shall presently give an account,) to stand as a candidate for that post. The Masters of the college, according to the usual laudable custom, emitted a programme, and sent it to all the universities in the kingdom, inviting such as had a mind to dispute for a profession of philosophy, to sist themselves before them, and offer themselves to compete for that preferment, giving assurance that without partiality and respect of persons, the place should be conferred upon him who should be found *dignior et doctior*.

The Ministers of the city of Glasgow considering how much it was the interest of the Church, that well-qualified persons be put into the profession of philosophy, and that Universities by this means become most useful seminaries for the Church; and that such as had served as Regents in the college, were ordinarily brought out to the ministry, who, as the Divinity chairs became vacant, were advanced to that honour,—many instances of which I am able to condescend upon; and they knowing that Mr. Binning was eminently pious, and one of a solid judgment, as well as of a bright genius, set upon him to sist himself among the other competitors, but had great difficulty to overcome his modesty. However, they at last prevailed with him to declare, before the Masters, his willingness to undertake the dispute with others.

There were two candidates more; one of them had the advantage of great interest with Doctor Strang, principal of the college at that time; and the other a scholar of great abilities, and of the same sentiments with the Doctor, in some problematical points of divinity, which with great subtilty had been debated in the schools. Mr. Binning so managed the dispute and acquitted himself in all the parts of trial, that to the conviction of the judges he very much darkened his rivals. And as to the precise point of qualification, in respect of literature, cut off all shadow of a demur and pretence of difficulty in the decision. However, the Doctor and some of the Faculty who joined him, though they could not pretend that the candidate, they appeared for, had an equality, much less a superiority in the dispute; yet they argued, a *cœteris paribus*, that the person they inclined to prefer, being a citizen's son, having a good competency of learning, and being a person of more years, had greater experience than Mr. Binning could be supposed to have, and consequently was more fit to be a teacher of youth: Mr. Binning being but yesterday a fellow-student with those he was to teach, it was not to be expected, that the students would behave to him with that respect and regard which should be paid to a master. But to this it was replied, that Mr. Binning was such a pregnant scholar, so wise and sedate as to be above all the follies and vanities of youth, that he knew very well how to let no man despise his youth; his wit was neither vain nor light, and his fancy was obedient to his reason, and what was wanting in years was sufficiently made up by his singular endowments, and more than ordinary qualifications. A Member of the Faculty, perceiving the struggle among them to be great (and indeed the affair seemed to have been argued very plausibly on both sides), proposed a dispute between the two candidates extempore, upon any subject they should be pleased to prescribe. This being considered by the Faculty, did quickly put a period to the division among them; and those who had opposed him not being willing to engage their friend again in the lists, with such an able antagonist, yielded the question, and Mr. Binning was elected.*

exertions which they made. After serving a few years (seldom more than eight, or less than four), they generally obtained appointments in the church, and thus transferred to another field the intellectual industry and aptitude for communicating knowledge, by which they had distinguished themselves in the university. It may well be conceived that, by stimulating and exemplifying diligence, their influence on their brethren in the ministry was not less considerable than on the parishioners, who more directly enjoyed the benefit of attainments and experience more mature, than can be expected from such as have never had access to similar means of improvement." Rep. of Roy. Com. ut supra, p. 221.—Ed.]

* [About the same period, Mr. Alexander Jamieson, who was afterwards minister of Govan, obtained the appointment of Regent in the University of St. Andrews, after engaging in a public disputation. The description of what took place on that occasion, given by Mr. John Lamont of Newton, is not devoid of interest, as a picture of the times:—" 1649, Apr. 10, 11.—Ther were three younge men that did disputte for the vacant regents place in St. Leonard's Colledge, (Mr.

Mr. Binning was not full nineteen years of age, when he commenced Regent and Professor of Philosophy ;* and though he had not time to prepare a system of any part of his profession, being instantly after his election to take up his class ; yet such was the quickness and fertility of his invention, the tenaciousness of his memory, and the solidity of his judgment, that his dictates † to the scholars had a great depth

David Nauee, formerlie possessing the same, bot now deposed, as is spoken before), viz., Mr. Alex. Jamesone, ane Edenbroughe man, having for his subject, *Syllogismus ;* Mr. William Diledaffe, a Cuper man, his subiect, *Liberum Arbitrium ;* and Mr. James Weymes, a St. Androus man, he having *De Anima* for his subiect. All the tyme they had ther speeches, ther heads werre couered, bot when they came to the disputte, they were vncouered. Ther werre three of the five ministers forsaide present at the disputs, viz., Mr. Alexander Moncriefe, Mr. Walt. Greige, and Mr. Ja. Sharpe [afterwards archbishop of St. Andrews], wha had decisive voices in the electione of a Regent (thir werre the first ministers that ever had voice in the electione of a measter to ane of the colledges there ; the custome formerlie, and of olde, was, that every colledge had libertie to chose ther owne measters). For Mr. Ja. Weymes, he was the warst of the three, for in the disputs, he bracke Priscian's head verry often ; for Mr. Alex. James. and Mr. Wil. Diled. they werre judged *pares* by the whulle meitting, so that after longe debeatte, they werre forcet to cast lotts, and the lott fell upon Mr. Alex. Jamesone, wha did succeide to the forsaide vacant regent's place. Mr. Will. Diled. got a promise (bot with difficultie) of the next vacant place. Mr. Ro. Norie, professor of Humanitie in the said colledge, had no voice in the forsaide electione, because he was not present at all the meittings of the disputs."—(Lamont's Diary, p. 4. Edin. 1830.)

The last instance of a public competition for a chair in the University of Glasgow, occurred towards the close of the seventeenth century, soon after the Revolution. It is remarkable enough that in this case also, the result was ultimately determined by lot. "A programme was immediately published, and on the day appointed no less than nine candidates appeared to enter the lists in a comparative trial. All of them acquitted themselves so well during the whole course of a long trial, that the electors were at a loss whom to choose. Setting aside some of the nine who were thought less deserving, they could not find a ground of preference among the rest. It was therefore resolved, after prayer to God, to commit the choice to lot. The lot fell upon Mr. John Law, and a present of five pounds sterling was given to each of the other candidates. One of the competitors was Mr. William Jamieson, a blind man known to the learned world by his writings. He was after some years chosen to give public lectures in the college upon Ecclesiastical History, for which he had a pension from the Crown till his death."—MS. History of the University of Glasgow, written by Dr. Thomas Reid, formerly Professor of Moral Philosophy.—Ed.]

* [The day of his election was "iiij Cal. Nov. 1646" (Annal. Colleg). The *Nova Erectio*, or foundation-charter, granted to the University of Glasgow 13th July, 1577, in the minority of James VI., made provision for the appointment of three Regents, or Professors, along with the Principal. The first Regent was required to teach Rhetoric and Greek; the second Logic, Ethics, and the principles of Arithmetic and Geometry; and the third, who was also sub-principal, Physiology, Geography, *Astrology*, and Chronology (See Copy of the *Nova Erectio* in Evidence for University Commissioners for Scotland, vol. ii. p. 241. London, 1837). In the year 1581, the Archbishop of Glasgow gifted to the University the customs of the city, which enabled them to establish the office of a fourth Regent, to whom was allotted exclusively the teaching of Greek; and, sometime previous to the year 1637, a fifth Regent was chosen, who was Professor of Humanity, "humaniarum literarum" (Old Stat. Acc. of Scot., vol. xxi. Append. pp. 24, 25). This professorship, however, was not permanently established till the year 1706 (Rep. of Roy. Com. appointed in 1830, p. 241). By the foundation-charter the Regents were restricted to particular professions, or departments of academical instruction, that they might be found better qualified for the discharge of their different functions (ut adolescentes qui gradatim ascendunt, dignum suis studiis et ingeniis præceptorem reperire queant). But this practice, as will be seen from the following minute of a University Commission, was changed in the year 1642. "The Visitation after tryall, taking to consideration that everie Regent within the Colledge his beine accustomed hithertills to continue for more years togithere, in and on the same professione, so that the schollers of one and the self-same class are necessitat yearlye to change theire masters, have found it more profitable and expedient, that the present course of teaching the schollers be altered, and that everie master educate his own schollers through all the foure classes, quhilk is appointed to begin presentlie, thus, that the classes, which are taken up with the masters the zeir, they go on with them: so that Mr. David Munro having the Magistrand [or oldest] classe now, he take the Bajane classe [or the youngest students, the *Bejani*, derived from the French word *bejaune*, a novice] the next zeir" (*Sessio 2da, September* 17. Evid. for Univ. Com. ut supra, p. 260). This new mode of instruction continued to be followed till the year 1727, when the old system enjoined in the foundation-charter was revived (Rep. of Roy. Com. ut supra, p. 223). It is said that Dr. Thomas Reid, the celebrated philosopher, was an advocate of the system of ambulatory professors, which was adhered to in King's College, Aberdeen, down to the beginning of the present century (Old Stat. Acc. of Scot., vol. xxi. Append. p. 83). The first class that Binning taught was the class of the *Bejani* (Wodrow's Analecta, vol. i. p. 338. MSS. in Bib. Ad.). He and the other Regents were all styled "Professors of Philosophy." Appendix to Spottiswood's Hist. of Ch. of Scot. p. 22. London, 1777.—Ed.]

† [It was the custom of the Regents to *dictate*, to the students, their observations on such parts of the writings of Aristotle, Porphyry, and others, as were read in their classes. This was done in Latin, which was the only language allowed to be used by the students, even in their common conversation. At a meeting of commissioners from the different universities of Scotland, which was held at Edin-

of learning of that kind, and perspicuity of expression. And I am assured, that he was among the first in Scotland that began to reform Philosophy from the barbarous terms, and unintelligible distinctions of the schoolmen, and the many vain disputes and trifling subtilties, which rather perplexed the minds of the youth, than furnished them with solid and useful knowledge.*

He continued in this profession for the space of three years, and discharged his trust so well, that he gained the general applause of the university for his academical exercises. And this was the more wonderful, that having turned his thoughts towards the ministry, he carried on his theological studies at the same time, and made vast improvements therein; to which he was enabled, by his deep penetration, and a memory so retentive, that he scarcely forgot any thing he had read or heard. It was easy and ordinary for him to transcribe any sermon, after he returned to his chamber, at such a full length, as that the intelligent and judicious reader who heard it preached, should not find one sentence to be wanting.

During this period of his life, he gave a proof and evidence of the great progress he had made in the knowledge of Divinity, by a composure on that choice passage of the Holy Scripture, 2 Cor. v. 14, 'For the love of God constraineth us, because we thus judge, that if one died for all, then were all dead.'

This performance he sent to a certain gentlewoman for her private edification, who had been detained at Edinburgh for a long time with business of importance; and having perused the same, she judged it was a sermon of some eminent minister in the West of Scotland, and put it into the hands of the then Provost of Edinburgh for his opinion, who was so well satisfied with it, that supposing it to be taken from the mouth of one whom the city had formerly resolved to call, was restless till a call was brought about to him, to be one of the ministers of the city. But when the lady returned back to Glasgow, she found her mistake, by Mr. Binning's

burgh on the 24th of July, 1648, one of the resolutions agreed upon, was to this effect:—"Because the *diting* [dictating] of long notes has in time past proved a hindrance, not only to necessary studies, but also to a knowledge of the text itself, and to the examination of such things as are taught, it is therefore seriously recommended by the commissioners to the dean and faculty of arts, that the regents spend not so much time in *diting* of their notes; that no new lesson be taught till the former be examined" (Bower's History of the University of Edinburgh, vol. i. p. 244) Binning, it is said, "dictated all his notes off hand" (Wodrow's Analecta, vol. i. p. 338. MS. in Bib. Ad.). Had he lived, it was thought "he had been one of the greatest schoolmen of his time." —Id. vol. v. p. 342.—Ed.]

* [Long after the publication of the *Novum Organum* of Lord Bacon, and even after the successful application of his principles by Sir Isaac Newton and Locke, the logic and metaphysics of Aristotle continued to occupy the chief place, in the course of instruction, in the most celebrated universities of Europe. The first great reform, in the mode of teaching philosophy, introduced into the college of Glasgow, was effected through a royal visitation, which took place in 1727. "The improvements in this university," says Professor Jardine, "arising from the regulations introduced by the royal visitation, were greatly promoted by the appointment, which took place shortly afterwards, of more than one professor of singular zeal and ability. The first of these was Dr. Francis Hutcheson. This celebrated philosopher, whose mind was stored with the rarest gifts of learning, illustrated, with a copious and splendid eloquence, the amiable system of morality which is still associated with his name; producing thus the happiest effects, not only on his own students, but also on his colleagues, and infusing, at once, a more liberal spirit, and a greater degree of industry, into all the departments of teaching. Great obstacles, however, still remained. The professor of the first philosophy class, according to the practice of the times, continued to deliver his lectures in the Latin language; a method of instruction which, although it must long have proved a great impediment to the ready communication of knowledge, on the part of the teacher, and to the reception of it on the part of the pupil, was not discontinued in this college, till upon the following occasion.

"In the year 1750, Adam Smith was appointed professor of logic; and, being rather unexpectedly called to discharge the duties of his office, he found it necessary to read to his pupils, in the English language, a course of lectures on rhetoric and belles lettres, which he had formerly delivered in Edinburgh. It was only during one session, however, that he gave these lectures; for at the end of it, he was elected professor of moral philosophy: and it was on the occasion of this vacancy in the logic chair, that Edmund Burke, whose genius led him afterwards to shine in a more exalted sphere, was thought of, by some of the electors, as a proper person to fill it. He did not, however, actually come forward as a candidate; and the gentleman who was appointed to succeed Dr. Smith, without introducing any change as to the subjects formerly taught in the logic class, followed the example of his illustrious predecessor in giving his prelections in English."—Outlines of Philosophical Education, Illustrated by the Method of Teaching the Logic class, in the University of Glasgow, pp. 20, 21. Glasg. 1825.—Ed.]

asking the discourse from her. This was the first discovery he had given of his great dexterity and ability in explaining of Scripture. At the expiration of his third year as a professor of philosophy, the parish of Govan, which lies adjacent to the city of Glasgow, and is within the bounds of that presbytery, happened to be vacant. Before this time,* whoever was principal of the college of Glasgow, was also minister of Govan. For Mr. Robert Boyd of Trochrigg,† (a person of very great learning, as his commentary on the Epistle to the Ephesians, and his *Hecatombe Christiana* testify) after he had been minister at Vertuille in France, and professor of Divinity in Saumur, returned to Scotland, and was settled principal of the college, and minister of Govan. But this being attended with inconveniences,

* [The office of principal of the University of Glasgow was disjoined from the cure of the parish of Govan, in 1621; and the immediate predecessor of Binning was Mr. William Wilkie, who was deposed by the synod on the 29th of April, 1649. "Mr. William Wilkie, I thought," says Principal Baillie, "was unjustly put out of Govan, albeit his very evil carriage since, has declared more of his sins." (MS. Letters, vol. iii. p. 849, in Bib. Col. Glas.)

There are certain extracts from the letters of Mr. William Wilkie to Dr. Balcanquhal, dean of Rochester, published in Lord Hailes's Memorials and Letters (vol. ii. pp. 47, 48). The learned judge, however, has mistaken the name Wilkie for *Willie.* Not knowing, therefore, who the writer of the letter was, he says, in a note, "This *Willie* appears to have been a sort of ecclesiastical spy employed by Balcanquhal, the great confident of Charles I. in every thing relating to Scotland." (Ibid.) In his preface, Lord Hailes acknowledges that the letters he has published were "chiefly transcribed from the manuscripts, amassed with indefatigable industry by the late Mr. Robert Wodrow." But Wodrow himself states, in his Life of Dr. Strang (Wodrow MSS., vol. xiii. pp. 4, 5, in Bib. Coll. Glasg.), that he was possessed of six original letters, which had been written by Mr. William Wilkie, minister of Govan, during the sitting of the famous Glasgow Assembly in 1638, and addressed to Dr. Balcanquhal, who had come down to Scotland with the Marquis of Hamilton, the Lord Commissioner, and was then residing in Hamilton palace. He also informs us that these and some other letters were discovered "after Naseby encounter, or some other, where Dr. Balcanquhal happened to be, in a trunk found among the baggage, which fell into the hands of the parliament's army." Wilkie's letters contained an account of the proceedings of the Assembly, Wodrow says, "not very favourable to the majority there." And he then adds, it was "from these and such other informations upon the one side, Doctor Balcanquhal drew up The Large Declaration, under the King's name, in 1642." At the time of the Glasgow Assembly, Mr. William Wilkie was one of the regents of the university.

Since this was written, Wilkie's letters have been printed, without abridgment, in the Appendix to vol. i. of a new edition of Baillie's Letters, published at Edinburgh by the Bannatyne club. "The originals of all these letters are contained in folio, vol. xxv., of the Wodrow manuscripts, which is now preserved among the Archives of the Church of Scotland."—Id. p. 481.—Ed.]

† [The estate of Trochrigg, which is one of the largest in the parish of Girvan, in the county of Ayr, is now the property of John Hutchieson Fergusson, Esq. It was sold by the descendants of the ancient proprietors about the year 1782. It was to his paternal residence at Trochrigg, that Principal Boyd retired with his family in 1621, when he resigned his office as Principal of the University of Glasgow; and it was in this retreat he wrote the Latin poem, entitled, *Ad Christum Servatorem Hecatombe.* This beautiful poem has been justly described to be, carmen totius fere Christianæ Religionis, seu evangelicæ doctrinæ medullam, vel compendium verius, cultissimis dulcissimisque versibus, ex intimoque Latio petitis, stropharum Sapphicarum centuria lectori ob oculos proponens, "a song embracing almost the whole of the Christian religion, or placing before the eyes of the reader in a hundred Sapphic stanzas, the marrow, or rather a compend of evangelical doctrine, in the most polished and mellifluent verses, and in language taken from that of the Augustan age." (Poet. Scot. Musæ Sacræ p. 198, præfatio, p. vi., Edin. 1739. Life of Boyd, Wodrow MSS., vol. xv. p. 123, in Bib. Coll. Glas.)

The commentary on the Epistle to the Ephesians (Roberti Bodii A Trocheregia Scoti, In Epistolam ad Ephesios Prælectiones, fol. pp. 1236, Londini, 1652), contains the substance of the lectures, which Boyd delivered, when he was professor of theology in the University of Saumur. This is attested by his cousin, Mr. Zachary Boyd, who was one of the Regents at Saumur, and attended the delivery of them (harum prælectionum assiduus fuit auditor). Some time after the death of the learned and pious author, a copy of the *Prælectiones* was transmitted to Holland to his friend Andreas Rivetus, that he might superintend the printing of it. As Chouet, a well-known Genevese printer, happened to be in Holland at the time, Rivetus parted with the manuscripts to him, that they might be put to press immediately on his return to Switzerland. But, unfortunately, the vessel in which the manuscripts were shipped, was taken by another vessel from Dunkirk, and having thus fallen into the hands of some Jesuits, they never could be recovered. Rivetus consoled himself with the reflection that the original manuscripts, in the author's own hand-writing, were safe in Scotland in the keeping of the family. The church and the nation, however, being at this period in such a distracted state, the work was not given to the world till the year 1652, when it was published by the London Stationers' Company, (Andreæ Riveti Epistola de vita, scriptis, moribus, et felici exitu Roberti Bodii, ante Prelectiones Bodii,) though the General Assembly had passed various acts, and entered into arrangements with different printers for the purpose. See Index of Unprinted Acts for the years 1645, 1646, and 1647.—Ed.]

an alteration was made; and the presbytery having a view of supplying that vacancy with Mr. Binning, did take him upon trials, in order to his being licensed as a preacher;* and after he was licensed, he did preach at Govan, to the great satisfaction of that people. Mr. Binning was sometime after called and invited to be minister of the said parish, which call the presbytery heartily approved of, and entered him upon trials for ordination, about the 22d year of his age; and as a part of trials, they prescribed to him a common head, *De concursu et influxu divino cum actionibus creaturarum*,—the occasion of which was, that Dr. Strang, principal of the College, and a member of the presbytery, had vented some peculiar notions upon that profound subject. And having delivered a very elaborate discourse, *viva voce*, to the admiration of all who heard it, he gave in, according to custom, his thesis to be impugned by the members of the presbytery, which was the direct antithesis of Doctor Strang's opinion in his dictates to the students on that controversy. The Doctor being pitched upon to be one of his opponents, found his credit and reputation much engaged, and exerted his metaphysical and subtile talent on that occasion. But Mr. Binning maintained his ground by the weight and solidity of his defence, to the great satisfaction of all that were present; so that some were pleased to say, that young Mr. Binning appeared to be the old learned Doctor; Nay, the Doctor himself after the recounter, admiring Mr. Binning's abilities and parts, said, "Where hath this young man got all this learning and reading?"† When

* [When the Presbytery of Glasgow had met on the 22d August, 1649, "The parochineris of Govane gave in ane supplicatione, shewing that whereas yai are destitute of ane minister, and being certanelie informed of the qualifications of Mr. Hew Binnen, one of ye regents of ye colledge of Glasgow, for ye work of ye ministrie," they were unanimously desirous he should be sent to preach to them, "so soone as he shall have past his tryels." The presbytery, in consequence of this supplication, "ordaines Mr. Patrik Gillespie, moderator of the presbyterie, to wrytt to ye said Mr. Hew, to acquaint him w[t] the desyre of the parochineris of Govane, and to repar to the presbytery to undertake his tryels for ye effect forsaid." Records of the Presbytery of Glasgow.

On the 5th September, 1649, "Mr. Robert Ramsay reported Mr. Hew Binnen had exercised on the text prescribed, and had geven the brethrene full satisfaction. He is ordained to handle the contraversie, de scientia media, and to give in theses thereupon." Id.

"Sept. 19, 1649.—The qlk daye Mr. Hew Binnen gave in theses upon the contraversie prescribed unto him, de scientia media, to be sustenit by him. The presbyterie appoint him to handle this contraversie this daye eight dayes at nyne houres." Id.

"Sept. 26, 1649.—The qlk daye Mr. Hew Binnen made his Latin lesson, de scientia media, and sustenit the disputt thairupon, and was approven in both." The following ministers were present, "Mr. Patrik Gillespie, Mr. David Dicksone, Doctor Jhone Strang, Mr. Zach. Boyde, Mr. George Young, Mr. Hew Blair, Mr. Gab. Conyngham, Mr. David Benett, Mr. Matthew Mackell, Mr. Wm. Young, Mr. Arch. Dennestoune, Mr. Jhone Carstaires, Mr. James Hamilton." The presbytery "ordaines Mr. Hugh Binnen to make ye exercise this daye fyfteen dayes, and the rest of his tryels to be ye said day." Id.

On the 10th October, 1649, after Mr. Hugh had "exercised"—"compeared the laird of Pollok and the parochineris of Govane, and desyred that Mr. Hew Binnen might preach to them the next Lordis daye, qlk was granted, and he ordained to go and preach yr." Id.

On the 24th Oct., 1649, "Compeared the parochineris of Govane, and gave in ane call to have Mr. Hew Binnen to be their minister." Id.

"December 19, 1649.—The qlk day Mr. Hew Binnen handled the contraversie, de satisfactione Christi, and sustenit the disputt upon the theses given in be him, and was approven." Id.

On the 2d January, 1650, his admission to the ministerial charge of the parish of Govan is appointed to take place "next Fryday." The minister who presided on that occasion was Mr. David Dickson, who was one of the professors of Theology in the University of Glasgow. Id.—Ed.]

† [Dr. John Strang, who was the son of Mr. William Strang, minister of Irvine, was born in the year 1584. He studied at the University of St. Andrews, where he took the degree of master at sixteen. After having been a regent in St. Leonard's college for several years, he was ordained in 1614, minister of Errol, in the Presbytery of Perth. When Cameron *le grand*, as he was called, (Vide Bayle's Dict. Art. Cameron,) resigned his situation as principal of the University of Glasgow, Dr. Strang succeeded him. He died at Edinburgh, on the 20th of June, 1654, in the seventieth year of his age, and was buried near his distinguished predecessor, Principal Boyd. At his death, an old friend and very learned man, *Andreas Ramisæus octogenarius*, composed some Latin verses, as an affectionate tribute to his memory. These may be seen in a short Life of Dr. Strang, which was written by Baillie, and prefixed to Dr. Strang's work, *De Interpretatione et Perfectione Scripturæ, Rotterodami*, 1663. It is from this Life the preceding particulars respecting the learned author have been taken.

It appears to have been chiefly through the influence of Archbishop Law, who was his cousin, that Dr. Strang was made principal of the University of Glasgow. When the latter understood that *Trocheregius* wished to be reinstated in his office, a correspondence took place betwixt them, which he had finished his trials, he had the unanimous approbation of the presbytery, nay, their declaration and testimony of his fitness to be one of the ministers of the city, upon the first vacancy. And I am assured, that at the very same time the Masters of the University had it in their view to bring him back again to their society, whenever the profession of Divinity should become vacant.

He was, considering his age, a prodigy of learning, for before he had arrived at the 26th year of his life, he had such a large stock of useful knowledge, as to be philologus, philosophus, and theologus præstans,* and might well have been an ornament to the most famous and flourishing university in Europe. This was the more astonishing, if we consider his weakness and infirmity of body, not being able to read much at one time, or to undergo the fatigue of assiduous study. But this was well supplied, partly by a memory that retained every thing he heard or read, and partly by a solid penetrating judgment, whereby he digested it well, and made it his own; so that with a singular dexterity, he could bring it forth seasonably, and communicate it to the use and advantage of others, drained from the dregs he found about it, or intermixed with it; insomuch that his knowledge seemed rather to be born with him, than to have been acquired by hard and laborious study.

From his childhood he knew the Scriptures, and from a boy had been under much deep and spiritual exercise, until the time (or a little before it) of his entry upon the office of the ministry, when he came to a great calm and lasting tranquillity of mind, being mercifully relieved of all those doubtings which had for a long time greatly exercised him; and though he was of a tender and weakly constitution, yet love to Christ, and a concern for the good of precious souls committed to him, constrained him to such diligence in feeding the flock, as to spend himself in the work of the ministry. It was observed of him, that he was not much averse at any time from embracing an invitation to preach before the most experienced Christians, even the learned professors of the university, and the Reverend ministers of the city: and when one of his most intimate friends noticed herein a difference from that modesty and self-denial, which appeared in the whole of his way and conduct, he took the freedom to ask him, how he came to be so easily prevailed with to preach before persons of so great experience and judgment, whose eminent gifts and graces he highly valued and esteemed? He made this excellent reply, that when he had a clear call to mention his blessed Master's name in any place, he had no more to say, but, "Here am I, send me. What am I that I should resist his heavenly call? And when he, whose name is holy and reverend, is spoken of and to, and is there present, the presence of no other person is to be regarded or dreaded; and under that impression, I forget who is present, and who is absent."

Though he was bookish, and much intent upon the fulfilling of his ministry, he turned his thoughts to marriage, and did marry a virtuous and excellent person, Mistress Barbara Simpson,† daughter of Mr. James Simpson, a minister in Ire-

is in the highest degree honourable to the feelings and character of Dr. Strang. This correspondence is inserted by Wodrow in his *Life of Robert Boyd of Trochrig* (Wodrow MSS., vol. xv. pp. 99—104. in Bib. coll. Glasg.). Baillie represents Dr. Strang to have been an acute philosopher, and second to none in the kingdom as a disputant (nullique ad hunc usque diem, in nostra gente, hac in parte secundus. Vita Autoris, ut supra). The strongly expressed commendation of such a man was no mean compliment to Binning's talents and learning. Wodrow says, he was told by a neighbouring clergyman, Mr. Patrick Simson, minister of Renfrew, who was ordained the same year that Binning died, and who lived for some years after the commencement of the following century, "yt qn they were seeking to get old principal Strang out of the colledge, ye principal said, 'Ye are seeking to get me out of my place, qm have ye to fill my room? I know none, unless it be a young man newly come out of the school, viz., Mr. Hugh Binning'" (Analecta, vol. iv. p. 171. MSS. in Bib. Ad.).—The Presbytery Records show that the common head which was presented to Binning was not, *De concursu*, &c., but one closely allied to it, *De scientia media*.—Ed.]

* [See his epitaph, p. l.—Ed.]

† [Her name was *Mary*, or *Maria* Simpson. The inventory of the effects of "Mr. Hew Binning, at Govane, deceissit in ye moneth of Sept. 1653," is given up "be Marie Sympsone, his relict, and onlie exe^rix^ dative" (Com. Rec. Glasg.). Towards the close of her life, Mrs. Binning became connected with the Society people. She seems to have corresponded with the Rev. James Renwick, one of their ministers, who, in a letter dated July 9, 1685, speaks of her as "like to die in prison," and in another, of her having "gone to Ireland" (Renwick's Letters, pp. 104, 179). Howie of Lochgoin, the author of "Lives of the Scots Worthies," assures us that it is Mrs. Bin-

land.* Upon the day on which he was to be married, he went accompanied with his friends (amongst whom were some grave and worthy ministers) to an adjacent country congregation, upon the day of their weekly sermon. The minister of the parish † delayed sermon till they should come, hoping to put the work upon one of the ministers he expected to be there. But all of them declining it, he next tried if he could prevail with the bridegroom, and succeeded, though the invitation was not expected, and the nature of the occasion seemed to be somewhat alien from his being employed in that work. It was no difficult task to him upon a short warning to preach, having a prompt and ready gift. He was never at a loss for words and matter, and having stepped aside a little time to premeditate and implore his Master's presence and assistance (for he was ever afraid to be alone in that work) he went immediately to the pulpit, and preached upon 1 Pet. i. 15. 'But as he who hath called you is holy, so be ye holy in all manner of conversation.' At which time, he was so remarkably helped, that all acknowledged that God was with him of a truth. And the people of the parish, who had come to hear their own minister, (a truly pious and excellent man,) were so surprised and taken with him, as if God, besides his ordinary resident (so Mr. M'Ward expresses it) had sent them an extraordinary ambassador to negotiate a peace between God and them, and a prompt paranymph unto, and a skilful suitor of a spouse for Jesus Christ the blessed Bridegroom, that he might present them as a chaste virgin to this divine Husband.

However he studied in his public discourses to condescend to the capacity of the meaner sort of hearers, yet it must be owned, that his preaching gift was not so much accommodated and suited to a country congregation, as it was to the judicious and learned.‡ The subjects of sermons are so numerous and various, and the order of men's disposing of their thoughts upon these subjects so different, that a suit of clothes may be as soon made to answer every man's back, as a fixed and invariable method may be prescribed, that shall agree to every subject, and every man's taste. Mr. Binning's method was singular and peculiar to himself, much after the haranguing way.§ He was no stranger to the rules of art, and knew well how to make his method subservient to the subjects he handled. And though he tells not his discourse has so many parts, yet it wanted not method, it being *maxi-*

ning who is alluded to by Renwick in his Letters, pp. 49, 104. He likewise quotes part of a letter written to her in 1692, by Sir Robert Hamilton of Preston, who commanded the army of the Covenanters at the battle of Bothwell bridge (Shields' Faithful Contendings, pp. 486, 487). In a catalogue of the manuscripts of the Rev. Robert Wodrow, minister of Eastwood, which is in the library of the Faculty of Advocates, vol. xxiv. folio, is stated to contain "50 letters from Mrs. Binning to Mr. Ham." It is not known where this volume is now to be found.—Ed.]

* [" The Rev. James Simpson was chaplain to the Lord Sinclair's regiment. He appears to have settled in the charge of a congregation in Ulster; perhaps at Newry, which was the head-quarters of his regiment for several years.—He was still in his charge in Ireland in 1650, in which year I find the Rev. Hugh Binning, minister of Govan, was married to his daughter." Dr. Reid's History of the Presbyterian Church in Ireland, vol. i. pp. 369, 370.—Ed.]

† [What Koelman says, is this, that the adjoining parish to which he and his friends went, was the one in which, after sermon, the marriage ceremony was to be performed. Mrs. Binning, it is probable, was residing there at the time.—Ed.]

‡ [His eloquence procured for him, according to Macward, the name of "the Scots Cicero." Along with a distinct articulation, he possessed great fluency. When he preached in Glasgow, which, being the minister of a neighbouring parish, was frequently the case, he was much admired and followed (Koelman's "Het. Leven en Sterven van Mr. Hugo Binning," prefixed to his Translation of Binning's Common Principles of the Christian Religion). With regard to the estimation in which, as a preacher, he was held in his own parish, his mode of preaching being so completely different from what they had been accustomed to, it is said, "he was more valued by Govan people after his death, than when alive." Analecta, vol. i. p. 338, MSS. in Bib. Ad.—Ed.]

§ [The writer of "A Short Account of the Life and Writings of Mr. Hugh Binning," prefixed to the small volume of his sermons, published for the first time in 1760, remarks, "By the *haranguing way*, I suppose he means those sermons that are not divided or sub-divided into doctrinal observations and heads, marked by the numbers 1, 2, 3, &c. But the reader will see many of these discourses, where there are no figures, as first, second, third, or any number of heads mentioned, as regularly divided, or sub-divided, as those sermons where we will see a good number of doctrines and heads. * * * Some useful sermons have been often perplexed with a great multitude of heads, consisting of two or three sentences, without any proof or illustration, of which the hearer or reader will remember or retain less, than some sermons that contain five or six heads, or have not their distinct branches marked with different figures or places." pp. xxii, xxiii.—Ed.]

*mum artis celare artem.** His diction and language is easy and fluent, neat and fine, void of all affectation and bombast. His style is free from starch lusciousness and intricacy; every period has a kind of undesigned negligent elegance, which arrests the reader's attention, and makes what he says as apples of gold set in pictures of silver: so that, considering the time when he lived, it might be said, that he had carried the orator's prize from his cotemporaries in Scotland, and was not at that time inferior to the best pulpit orators in England, the English language having got its greatest embellishments and refinings but of late years. In his Sermons, his matter gives life to his words, and his words add a lustre to his matter. That great divine, Mr. James Durham,† an excellent judge of men, gave this verdict of him, that "there is no speaking after Mr. Binning;" and truly he had the tongue of the learned, and knew how to speak a word in season. The subject-matter of his Sermons is mostly practical, and yet rational and argumentive, fit to inform the understanding of his hearers, and move their affections: and when controversies come in his way, he shows great acuteness and judgment in discussing and determining them, and no less skill in applying them to practice. His discourses are so solid and substantial, so heavenly and sublime, that they not only feed but feast the reader, as with marrow and fatness. In the most of them, we meet with much of the sublime, expressed in a most lofty, pathetic, and moving manner. Mr. M'Ward says in his letter, "That as to the whole of Mr. Binning's writings, I know no man's pen on the heads he hath handled more adapted for edification, or which, with a pleasant violence, will sooner find or force a passage into the heart of a judicious experienced reader, and cast fire, even ere he is aware (O happy surprise!) into his affections, and set them into a flame." And in another part of the same letter, he says, "The subjects he discourses upon are handled with such a pleasant and profitable variety of thought and expression, that the hearer or reader is taken with it, as if he had never met with it before. He was such a skilful

* [It being "the perfection of art to conceal art."—Ed.]

† [Mr. James Durham, minister of the Inner High church, Glasgow, was the son and heir of John Durham of Easter Powrie, now named Wedderburn, a considerable estate in the parish of Muirhouse, and county of Forfar (Old. Stat. Acc. of Scot., vol. xiii. pp. 162, 163). In the time of the civil wars, and before he contemplated being a clergyman, he was a captain in the army. He held the office of king's chaplain, when Charles the Second was in Scotland. The description which "Old Aitkenhead, who had it from the gentlewoman," gave, of Cromwell's visit, in April 1651, to the High church of Glasgow, where Mr. Durham was preaching, is this: "The first seat that offered him was P. Porterfield's, where Miss Porterfield sat, and she, seeing him an English officer, was almost not civil. However, he got in and sat next Miss Porterfield. After sermon was over he asked the minister's name. She sullenly enough told him, and desired to know wherefore he asked. He said because he perceived him to be a very great man, and in his opinion might be chaplain to any prince in Europe, though he had never seen him nor heard of him before. She inquired about him, and found it was O. Cromwell" (Wodrow's Anal., vol. v. p. 186, MSS. in Bib. Ad.).

Mr. Durham sided neither with the Resolutionists nor Protestors. For this he was strongly blamed at the time by Principal Baillie, who took a keen part in the controversy, (Let. and Jour., vol. ii. p. 376.) though after his death, he recorded, in the following terms, his opinion of Mr. Durham's character and talents: "From the day I was employed by the presbytery to preach, and to pray, and to impose, with others, hands upon him, for the ministry at Glasgow, I did live to the very last with him in great and uninterrupted love, and in high estimation of his egregious endowments, which made him to me precious among the most excellent divines I have been acquainted with in the whole isle. O, if it were the good pleasure of the Master of the vineyard to plant many such noble vines in this land!" (Durham's Commentary upon the book of Revelation, Address to the Reader, p. vi.) The work written by Durham, entitled, "The Law Unsealed, or a Practical Exposition of the Ten Commandments," has commendatory prefaces prefixed to it, by two distinguished English puritans, Dr. John Owen, and Mr. William Jenkyn. Dr. Owen wrote likewise a preface to the "Clavis Cantici, or an Exposition of the Song of Solomon, by James Durham, minister at Glasgow," 4to. 1669. Doubts have been expressed, however, whether Wood, in his Athenæ Oxonienses, (vol. ii. p. 747. Lond. 1721.) was warranted to attribute this preface to Owen, "as the preface is anonymous" (Orme's Life of Owen, Append., p. 505). But the only copy of the work, which is in my possession, (Glas. 1723.) has attached to it the name of "John Owen, May 20, 1669."

The widow of Mr. Durham, who was the daughter of Mr. William Muir of Glanderston, a branch of the family of the Muirs of Caldwell, was, in 1679, twice committed to prison, for having in her house religious meetings, or conventicles, as they were called in those days of relentless tyranny and oppression. On one of the occasions, she was taken to Edinburgh, and imprisoned there, along with her sister, the mother of Principal Carstairs. Wodrow's Hist. of the Suff. of the Church of Scot., vol. iii. pp. 10, 54.—Ed.]

scribe, as knew how to bring out of his store things new and old; the old with such sweetness and savour as it seemed still new, and the new retained its first sweetness so as never to grow old.

He and some young ministers in the same presbytery, who had been students of divinity when he was professor of philosophy, did keep private meetings for Christian fellowship, and their mutual improvement. But finding that he was in danger of being puffed up with the high opinion they had of him, he broke up these meetings, though he still kept up a brotherly correspondence with them, for the vigorous prosecution of their ministerial work. He studied to be clothed with humility, and to hide his attainments under that veil. Though he wanted not matter and words wherewith to please and profit all his hearers, yet at every thought of his appearing in public to speak of God and Christ to men, his soul was filled with a holy tremor, which he vented by saying, "Ah! Lord, I am a child and cannot speak. Teach me what I shall say of thee, who cannot order my speech by reason of darkness." In his first Sermon, on the fourth question of our Shorter Catechism, he expresses himself in a most elegant and rapturous manner: "We are now," says he, "about this question, What God is? But who can answer it? Or if answered, who can understand it? It should astonish us in the very entry, to think we are about to speak and to hear of his majesty, 'whom eye hath not seen, nor ear heard,' nor hath it entered into the heart of any creature to consider what he is. Think ye, blind men could understand a pertinent discourse of light and colours? Would they form any suitable notion of that they had never seen, and cannot be known but by seeing? What an ignorant speech would a deaf man make of sound, when a man cannot so much as know what it is, but by hearing of it? How then can we speak of God who dwells in inaccessible light, since though we had our eyes opened, yet they are far less proportioned to that resplendent brightness, than a blind eye is to the sun's light?"

He was a great student in the books of creation and providence, and took much pleasure in meditating upon what is written in these volumes. The wonders he discovered in both, led him up to the infinitely wise and powerful Maker and Preserver of all things. Once, when he came to visit a gentleman of good learning, and his intimate acquaintance, the gentleman took him to his garden, and in their walk he discoursed with him to his great surprise of the objective declarations, which every thing makes of its Almighty Creator: and talked of the wisdom and goodness of God, particularly in clothing the earth with a green garb, rather than with a garment of any other colour; and having plucked a flower from it, he made a most savoury spiritual discourse. He so dissected and anatomized the same, as to set forth the glorious perfections of its Maker in a most taking and entertaining manner.

But the main object of his pious and devout contemplations was God in Christ reconciling the world to himself. For God who commanded the light to shine out of darkness, had shined into his heart to give him the light of the knowledge of God, in the face of Jesus Christ; so that he not only understood the mysteries of the kingdom of God himself, but it was given to him to make others know them. His preaching was in the demonstration of the Spirit, and of power. His Sermons are the very transcript of what had past betwixt God and his own soul. He spoke and wrote his experimental knowledge, and did both speak and write because he believed. He did earnestly contend for the articles of faith and truths of religion, and could never think of parting with one hoof, or the least grain of truth; being persuaded, that Christian concord must have truth for its foundation, and holiness for its attendant, without which it will decline into a defection, and degenerate into a conspiracy against religion. As to the duties of Christianity, he enforced the performance of these with all the arguments of persuasion; so that, through the blessing of God, his pulpit discourses became the power of God to the illumination of the understandings of his hearers, the renovation of their natures, the reformation of their lives, and the salvation of their souls.

The difficult part of a reprover he acted in the most prudent and gaining manner; when he did lick with his tongue the mote out of his brother's eye, he did it with all tenderness, and with the tear in his own. His words wanted neither point nor edge for drawing the blood, when the case of the offender made it an indispensable duty; and when he was necessitated to use sharpness with any, they were convinced that he honestly and sincerely intended their spiritual good. His compassion on the ignorant and them that were out of the way, made it evident how much he considered himself as encompassed with infirmities, and so within the hazard of being tempted.

He was a person of exemplary moderation and sobriety of spirit, had healing methods much at heart, and studied to promote love and peace among his brethren in the ministry. He vigorously contributed to the recovery of the humanity of Christianity, which had been much lost in the differences of the times, and the animosities which followed thereupon. These virtues and graces had such an ascendant in his soul, that when he carried coals about with him, taken from the altar to warm the souls of all, with whom he conversed, with love to God, his truths, interests and people; so he carried sanctuary water about with him to cool and extinguish what of undue passion he perceived to accompany the zeal of good and well designing persons; a temper that is rarely found in one of his age. But ripe harvest grapes were found upon this vine in the beginning of spring; and no wonder, since he lived so near the Sun of Righteousness, and lay under the plentiful showers of divine grace, and the ripening influences of the Holy Spirit.

The prevailing of the English sectarians under Oliver Cromwell, to the overthrow of the Presbyterian interest in England, and the various attempts which they made in Scotland, on the constitution and discipline of this church, was one of the greatest difficulties which the ministry had then to struggle with. Upon this he made the following most excellent reflection, in a Sermon preached on a day of public humiliation, "What if the Lord hath defaced all that his kingdom was instrumental in building up in England, that he alone may have the glory in a second temple more glorious?"* And when he observed, That the zeal of many for the Solemn League and Covenant, (by which they were sworn to endeavour the preservation of the reformed religion in Scotland, and the reformation of religion in the kingdoms of England and Ireland,) was not attended with a suitable amendment of their own lives, he takes up a bitter lamentation over them in a very remarkable paragraph: "Alas! we deceive ourselves with the noise of a covenant, and a cause of God; we cry it up as an antidote against all evils, use it as a charm, even as the Jews did their temple; and in the mean time we do not care how we walk before God, or with our neighbours. Well, thus saith the Lord, 'Trust ye not in lying words, saying, The temple of the Lord, the temple of the Lord, the temple of the Lord are these. For if ye throughly amend your ways and your doings; if ye throughly execute judgment between a man and his neighbour; if ye oppress not the stranger, the fatherless, and the widow, and shed not innocent blood in this place, neither walk after other gods to your hurt,' &c., Jer. vii. 4—6. If drunkenness reign among you, if filthiness, swearing, oppression, cruelty reign among you, your covenant is but a lie, all your professions are but lying words, and shall never keep you in your inheritances and dwellings. The Lord tells you what he requires of you, is it not to do justly, and love mercy, and walk humbly with God? Mic. vi. 8. This is that which the grace of God teaches, to deny 'ungodliness and worldly lusts,' and to 'live soberly, righteously, and godly,' towards God, your neighbour, and yourself, Tit. ii. 11, 12; and this he prefers to your public ordinances, your fasting, covenanting, preaching, and such like.†"

When the unhappy distinction betwixt the public Resolutioners and Protesters ‡

* [See page 368.—Ed.] † [See page 406.—Ed.]

‡ [The following account of the origin of the differences between the Resolutioners and Protesters, is that given by Kirkton. "After the defeat of Dumbar, the king required a new army to be levyed, wishing earnestly it might be of another mettale than that which hade been lossed. So he desired that sort of people who were called Malignants, his darlings, might be brought into places of trust, both in council and army, though they hade been secluded from both by their own consent. And this request was granted both by committee of estates and commission of the church sitting at Perth. But there was a party in both these councils, which alleadged confidently, that though the malignants were content to profess repentance for their former practices, yet they should be found to be men neither sincere in their professions, nor successful in their undertakings.

took place in this church, Mr. Binning was of the last denomination. This distinction proved to be of fatal consequences. He saw some of the evils of it in his own time, and being of a catholic and healing spirit, with a view to the cementing of differences, he wrote an excellent Treatise of Christian love,* which contains very strong and pathetic passages, most apposite to this subject, some of which we will afterwards have occasion to quote. He was no fomenter of faction, but studious of the public tranquillity. He was a man of moderate principles and temperate passions. He was far from being confident, or vehement in the managing of public affairs ; never imposing or overbearing upon others, but willingly hearkened to advice, and yielded to reason.

After he had laboured four years in the ministry, serving God with his spirit in the gospel of his Son, whom he preached, warning every man and teaching every man in great ministerial wisdom and freedom, that he might present every man perfect in Christ Jesus,—whereunto he laboured, striving according to his working, which wrought in him mightily,—he died of a consumption, when he was scarce come to the prime and vigour of life, entering on the twenty-sixth year of his age, leaving behind him a sweet savour after he was gone, and an epistle of commendation upon the hearts of his hearers. While he lived, he was highly valued and esteemed, having been a successful instrument of saving himself and them that heard him ; of turning sinners unto righteousness, and of perfecting the saints ; and died much lamented by all good people, who had the opportunity and advantage of knowing him. He was a person of singular piety, of a humble, meek, and peaceable temper, a judicious and lively preacher ; nay, so extraordinary a person, that he was justly accounted a prodigy for the pregnancy of his natural parts, and his great proficiency in human learning, and knowledge of divinity. He was too shining a light to shine long, and burned so intensely that he was soon put out. But he now shines in the kingdom of his Father, in a more conspicuous and refulgent manner, even as the brightness of the firmament, and as the stars for ever and ever.

The last Sermons he preached were those on Rom. viii. 14, 15. 'For as many as are led by the Spirit of God, they are the sons of God. For ye have not received the spirit of bondage again to fear ; but ye have received the Spirit of adoption, whereby we cry, Abba, Father.' He concluded the last of these discourses, with a reflection on these words. 'We cry, Abba, Father.' "This (says he,) is

This was the beginning of the fatal schism in the Scottish church. For though the king, to secure Scotland, was content once more to take the covenant at his coronation in Scoon (which instrument he caused burn at London) : yet the dissatisfied party continued still in their jealousies, and even of the king himself, whom they doubted most of all. This party was called Protesters and Remonstrators, as the other was called Resolutioners : which names occasioned lamentable distraction" (History of the Church of Scotland, p. 53). A more particular account of this unhappy controversy, so fatal in its results to both parties, may be seen in the introduction to Wodrow's history.

Though Baillie was a Resolutioner, he seems to have had some misgivings as to the course he adopted. "We carried unanimously at last," says he, in a letter to Mr. Spang, dated Perth, January 2, 1651, "the answer herewith sent to you. My joy for this was soon tempered, when I saw the consequence, the loathing of sundry good people to see numbers of grievous bloodshedders ready to come in, and so many malignant noblemen as were not like to lay down arms till they were put into some places of trust, and restored to their vote in parliament" (Letters and Journals, vol. ii. p. 366). In the Life of Professor Wodrow, written by his son, (pp. 29, 30. Edin. 1828,) it is said, "There were great endeavours used in the year 1659, and 1660, entirely to remove that unhappy rent 'twixt the public Resolutioners and Protesters in this church, and had not Mr. Sharp struck in by his letters from London, in order to serve his own designs, and ruin both, and made Mr. Douglas and other ministers at Edinburgh cold in this matter of the union, it had no doubt succeeded. These put Mr. Wodrow upon an inquiry into that debate, and when leaving the lessons during the vacation in the summer, he desired Mr. Baillie's directions what to read for understanding that subject. The professor said to him, Jacobe, I am too much engaged personally in that debate to give you either my judgment on the whole, or to direct you to particular authors on the one side and the other ; but taking him into his closet, he gave him the whole pamphlets that had passed on both sides in print and manuscript, laid ranked in their proper order, and said, there is the whole that I know in that affair, take them home to the country with you, and read them carefully, and look to the Lord for his guiding you to determine yourself aright upon the whole."—Ed.]

* [This treatise was afterwards printed, and is included in the present edition of the works of the author.—Ed.]

much for our comfort, that from whomsoever, and whatsoever corner in the world, prayers come up to him, they cannot want acceptance. All languages, all countries, all places are sanctified by Jesus Christ, that whosoever calls upon the name of the Lord from the ends of the earth, shall be saved. And truly it is a sweet meditation to think, that from the ends of the earth the cries of souls are heard; and that the end is as near heaven as the middle; and a wilderness as near as a paradise; that though we understand not one another, yet we have one loving and living Father, that understands all our meanings. And so the different languages and dialects of the members of this body make no confusion in heaven, but meet together in his heart and affection, and are as one perfume, one incense, sent up from the whole catholic church, which is here scattered upon the earth. O that the Lord would persuade us to cry this way to our Father in all our necessities!"* Thus having contemplated that subject concerning the adoption of children, he was taken hence to the enjoyment of the inheritance reserved in the heavens for them, and the Spirit called him by death, as the voice did John the divine, Rev. iv. 1, 'Come up hither.'

He was buried in the churchyard of Govan, where Mr. Patrick Gillespie,† then

* [See page 226.—Ed.]

† [Mr. Patrick Gillespie, who was brother to George Gillespie one of the ministers of Edinburgh, was for some time minister of Kirkcaldy. On the 4th December, 1641, "Mr. Pa. Gillespie produceit," to the magistrates and council of Glasgow, "a presentation grantit to him, be his Majestie, of the place of the Highe Kirke, instead of the bischope" (Glasgow Burgh Records). He was one of the three ministers who, in 1651, were summarily deposed by the Assembly, for their opposition to the Public Resolutions, and protesting against the lawfulness of that Assembly (Lamont's Diary, p. 33). His sentence was reversed by the Synod of Glasgow (Baillie's Letters, vol. ii. pp. 414, 415). Gillespie was evidently desirous to effect a reconciliation between the Resolutioners and Protesters, by means of mutual concessions (Id. pp. 388, 401, 411). In the year 1553, he was elected principal of the University of Glasgow, by the English sequestrators (Id. p. 371, Lamont's Diary, p. 53).

No one in Scotland had more influence with Cromwell than Principal Gillespie, who is said to have been the first minister in the Church of Scotland, who prayed publicly for him (Nicol's Diary, p. 162). In April, 1654, the Protector called him up to London, along with Mr. John Livingston of Ancrum, and Mr. John Menzies of Aberdeen, to consult with them on Scottish affairs (Life of Livingston, p. 55). He preached before the Protector in his chapel, and obtained from him, for the University of Glasgow, the confirmation of "all former foundations, mortifications, and donations made in its favour, particularly that of the bishopric of Galloway; to which he added the vacant stipends of the parishes, which had been in the patronage of the bishop of Galloway, for seven years to come; and also in perpetuity the revenues of the deanery and subdeanery of Glasgow" (Old Stat. Acc. of Scot., vol. xxi. Append. pp. 25, 26). Through his influence with the Protector, he likewise procured a grant to the town of Glasgow, "for the use of the poor who had been injured by the fire in 1653," [1652] (Brown's Hist. of Glasg., p. 120.) and "assisted and pleasured sundry in the matter of their fines" (Baillie's Letters, vol. ii. p. 390). As to what is said by the editor of Kirkton's History, that after the Restoration, "Gillespie had made great efforts for a pardon, and offered to promote episcopacy in Scotland" (p. 111), the reader is referred to a Review of that work, in the Christian Instructor (Vol. xvii. pp. 339, 340). He died not long after this at Leith (Law's Memorials, p. 11).

Gillespie's work, entitled "The Ark of the Covenant Opened," (London, printed for Tho. Parkhurst, 1677,) has a preface from the pen of Dr. John Owen, who was with Cromwell in Scotland, as one of his chaplains, and in this way, no doubt, became acquainted with Gillespie (Wood's Athenæ Oxonienses, vol. ii. p. 738. London, 1721). In his preface, Dr. Owen says, "My long Christian acquaintance with the author made me not unwilling to testify my respects unto him and his labours in the church of God, now he is at rest, for whom I had so great an esteem while he was alive." Wodrow expresses his regret, that "the other three parts" of Gillespie's work have not been printed, which, he informs us, the author "wrote and finished for the press" (Hist. of the Suff. of Ch. of Scot., vol. i. p. 204. Glasg. 1829). The Synod of Glasgow were informed, on the 8th of Oct., 1701, that "Mr. Parkhurst, at London," possessed two unpublished parts of Gillespie's Ark of the Covenant. They, therefore, appointed a committee to communicate with him on the subject, through some of the booksellers of Glasgow, "conceiving that the publishing of these pieces may be of use to the Church, from the experience they have had of the works of that worthy author already come to light, upon the same subject" (Records of Synod). On the 5th April, 1709, "Mr. Robert Wodrow reports, that Mr. Parkhurst continues still indisposed, so that nothing can be done with respect to the printing of Mr. Gillespie's book formerly mentioned. Wherefore, the Synod lets the matter fall out of their minutes." Id.

Chalmers (Caledonia, vol. iii. p. 591.) seems to have imagined that Patrick Gillespie was the "Galasp" ridiculed by Milton, in one of his sonnets. Warton says, this was "George Gillespie, one of the Scotch ministers of the Assembly of Divines" (Warton's Milton, p. 339. Lond. 1791). But Milton referred neither to the one nor the other; but to Allaster Macdonald *Macgillespic*, (*son of Archibald*) otherwise known by the name of Colkittoch, or Colkitto, who commanded the Irish principal of the university of Glasgow, at his own proper charges, (as I am credibly informed,) caused a monument* to be erected for him, on which there is to this day the following inscription in Latin :

HIC SITVS EST MR. HVGO BINNINGVS;
VIR PIETATE, FACVNDIA, DOCTRINA
CLARVS; PHILOLOGVS, PHILOSOPHVS,
THEOLOGVS PRÆSTANS; PRÆCO
DENIQVE EVANGELII FIDELIS ET
EXIMIVS, QVI E MEDIO RERVM CVRSV
SVBLATVS, ANNO ÆTATIS 26, DOM.
AVTEM 1653. MVTAVIT PATRIAM NON
SOCIETEM, EO QVOD VIVVS CVM
DEO AMBVLAVIT. ET SI QVID VLTRA
INQVIRAS, CÆTERA SILEO; CVM NEC
TV NEC MARMOR HOC
CAPIAT.

He left behind him a disconsolate widow, and an only son, called John after the grandfather, to whom the grandfather at his death had left the estate of Dalvennan;† but John having been engaged in the insurrection at Bothwell-bridge, anno 1679, it was forfeited, and he continued dispossessed of it till the year 1690, when, by the 18th act of parliament in the said year, the forfeitures and fines past since the year 1665, to the 5th day of November, 1688, were rescinded.‡ His widow

auxiliaries in Montrose's army. See the new edition of Baillie's Letters, now in course of publication, formerly quoted, vol. ii. p. 499.—Ed.]

* [This is a simple marble tablet surmounted with a heart, and the emblems of mortality. It was placed in a niche in the front wall of the old parish church; but, in 1826, when the present church was erected, which is a Gothic structure, it was removed to the vestibule. It is seen in the vignette of the title page. The inscription may be turned into English, thus: "Mr. Hugh Binning is buried here, a man distinguished for his piety, eloquence, and learning; an eminent philologist, philosopher, and theologian; in fine, a faithful and acceptable preacher of the gospel, who was removed from this world in the 26th year of his age, and in the year of our Lord 1653. He changed his country, not his company, because when on earth he walked with God. If thou wish to know any thing beyond this, I am silent as to any thing further, since neither thou nor this marble can receive it."—Ed.]

† [John Binning of Dalvennan was served heir to his grandfather on the 19th of March, 1672 (Inq. Ret. Ab. Ayr, 580). And the Retour of his heritable property, at the date of his forfeiture, specifies, as having belonged to him, the ten merk land of the ten pound land of Keires, comprehending the lands of Dalvennan, Yondertoun and Burntoun, Daluy, Milntown, The Fence, Drumore, Hillhead, Rashiefauld, Chappel, the mill of Keires, &c., in the parish of Straiton; the lands of Over Priest-Craig and Nether Priest-Craig in the parish of Colmonell; and a house, garden, and land in the parish of Maybole, in the county of Ayr.—Inq. De Possess. Quinquen. (18.)—Ed.]

‡ [The name of "Binning of Dalvennan" appears in the Act of the Scottish parliament, "Rescinding the Forefaultures and Fynes since the year 1665" (Acts of the Parl. of Scot. vol. ix. p. 165). Previous to the passing of that Act, however, a petition was presented to the parliament by Mr. Roderick M'Kenzie, who had been a Depute Advocate in the former reign, in which he stated, "That John Binning of Dalvennan having been forefault for being in armes at Bothwell-bridge, anno 1679, and the deceased Matthew Colvill, writer in Edinburgh, John Binning's greatest enemy, being very active to obtain the gift of his forefaulture, with a designe of his ruine, and the prejudice of his numerous and just creditors, the deceased Mr. James Gordon, minister at Cumber in Ireland, John Binning's father-in-law and former Curator, to whom he was oweing a considerable soume of money, came over to Scotland, at John Binning's desire, who was then in Ireland, to obtaine the said gift, to disappoint Matthew Colvill thereof, who prevailed with the petitioner to lend the money to pay the compositione and expenses of the gift." Mr. M'Kenzie also affirmed, that he had "no other security for the money soe lent, but a right to the said gift," and that the money he had advanced "to the said Mr. James Gordon for the compositione and expenses of the gift, with what he hes payed of John Binning's reall and confirmed debts, far exceeds the value of his land." In consequence of these representations, "Their Majesties High commissioner and said Estates of Parliament remitt the case of Mr. Roderick M'Kenzie, petitioner, anent the forfaulture of Dalvennan, to the consideratione of the commission nominate in the General Act recissory of ffynes and forefaulters, with power to them to hear the parties concerned thereanent, and to report to the next session of this, or any other ensuing parliament."—Id. pp. 162, 163.

John Binning was declared at this period to be "altogether insolvent." This is the reason probably, if he was not in the mean time satisfied that his claim was untenable, that his case does not appear to have been brought under the notice of parliament again, and that he did not persist in his attempts to regain possession of Dalvennan (Id. Appendix, p. 32). To confirm his title to a property, which considering the office he held, seems to have been acquired under very suspicious circumstances, M'Kenzie had contrived to get an act of parliament passed in his favour, in the year 1685. In this Act, he is lauded for "suppressing the rebellious ffanatical partie in the western and other was afterwards married to one Mr. James Gordon,* a presbyterian minister for some time in the kingdom of Ireland. She lived to a great age, and died in the year 1694, at Paisley in the shire of Renfrew, about four or five miles from Govan; which, when the people of that parish heard, the savoury memory they still had of their worthy pastor, made them to desire the friends of the defunct, to allow them to give her a decent and honourable burial, beside her deceased husband, undertaking to defray all the charges of the funeral, which was done accordingly. And to this day Mr. Binning is mentioned among them with particular veneration. He was succeeded by Mr. David Vetch,† who likewise died young.

Before I conclude this Relation, it is proper I give some account of his writings. The books published at different times under his name, which are contained in this volume, are all posthumous. Wherefore it will not be strange, if the reader shall meet with some passages in them that are less perfect and complete, since he did not intend them for the press; and that they want those finishing strokes, which such a masterly pen was able to give them. The good effects his discourses had upon the hearers, and the importunity of many judicious and experienced Christians to have them published, that they might have the same influence on such as should read them, encouraged some worthy ministers to revise and print them. And since these sermons have for a long time had the approbation both of learned divines and serious Christians, they need not any recommendation of mine.

shires of this realme, and putting the lawes to vigorous execution against them, as His Majesties Advocate Deput;" and the lands of Dalvennan are said to have been transferred to him, by "Jean Gordon, as donatrix," who was the uterine sister of John Binning, and who is described as "relect of the deceist Daniel M'Kenzie sometime ensign to the Earle of Dalhousie, in the Earle of Marr's Regiment" (Id. vol. viii. pp. 565—567). John Binning taught a school for some time (Faithful Contendings, p. 66). The General Assembly showed kindness to him, on different occasions, for his father's sake. In 1702, the Commission of the Assembly being informed by a petition from himself of his "sad circumstances," recommended him to the provincial Synods of Lothian and Tweedale, and of Glasgow and Ayr "for some charitable supply" (Rec. of Commission, Sess. 39). In 1704, he applied for relief to the General Assembly, and stated that he had obtained from the Privy Council a patent to print his father's works, of which twelve years were then unexpired, and that it was his intention to publish them in one volume. The Assembly recommended "every minister within the kingdom to take a double of the same book, or to subscribe for the same." They likewise called upon the different presbyteries in the church to collect among themselves something for the petitioner (Unprinted Acts, Sess. 11). The last application he made to the Assembly for pecuniary aid was in 1717, when he must have been far advanced in life.—Idem, 13th May.—Ed.]

* [Mr. James Gordon was minister of Comber, in the county of Down. He was ordained about the year 1646. We find his name in Wodrow's list of the non-conforming ministers in the synod of Ballimenoch in Ireland (Hist. of Suff. of Ch. of Scot. vol. i. p. 324). According to Dr. Reid, "Mr. Gordon, after having been deposed with the rest of his brethren in 1661, continued to officiate privately at Comber for many years; but about the year 1683, in his old age, he appears to have deserted his principles, and conformed to prelacy." Hist. of the Presb. Ch. in Ireland, vol. ii. pp. 129, 130.—Ed.]

† [May 14, 1654.—"Sederunt Mr. John Carstaires and the Elders.

"The qlk day the session being conveened for election and calling of a min[r] to the kirk of Govan, and having now this forenoon heard Mr. David Veetch, with whom most are satisfied, but for the satisfaction of all persons interested, who heard him never but once, both of heritors and elders, the session have delayed their election till they hear him again in the afternoon, and the session then were to meet again for that effect.

"Sederunt Mr. John Carstaires and the Elders.

"The heritors and elders having now heard the said Mr. David Veetch twise, and both being well satisfied, and clear, and unanimous, the satisfaction of the session being first enquired, and next of the heritors, which, being both of one mynd, cordially for the thing, a call was presently drawn up, and subt by moderator and clerk, also by session and heritors, according to order. After the fors[d] draught, at appointment of the presbytery and session, Mr. John preached in the s[d] church, and, after sermon, did intimat to the people their nomination of Mr. David to take charge in the ministrie of that congregation, and ordained, that if any person had any thing to object ag[t] the said Mr. David's being min[r] at the s[d] church, they would come and signifie it to the session, now presently to meet at the s[d] church for that effect, according to the practice in such cases. The session having met, and none compearand to signifie their dissent, or assent, they take their non-compearance for their signification of satisfaction; so, after three severall oyesses at the most patent door of the s[d] church, by the officer intimating the fors[d] words, none at all appeared. So the s[d] Mr David being desired to come in to session, they presented to him their unanimous and cordiall call of election to the ministrie of the kirk of Govan which he accepted." Records of Kirk-Session of Govan.—Ed.]

The first of his works that was printed,* is entitled, "The Common Principles of the Christian Religion, clearly proved, and singularly improved; or a Practical Catechism, wherein some of the most concerning foundations of our faith are solidly laid down; and that doctrine which is according to godliness, is sweetly, yet pungently pressed home, and most satisfyingly handled." Mr. M'Ward speaking of this performance, says, "That it was not designed for the press, that it contained only his notes on those subjects he preached to his flock, and which he wrote (I suppose he means † in a fair hand) for the private use and edification of a friend, from whom he had them; and when put into his hand to be revised, he says, he did not so much as alter, or add one word, to make the sense more plain, full, or emphatical." This book is an excellent exposition of the Westminster Catechism, so far as it goes, viz. to the twenty-first question, 'Who is the Redeemer of God's elect?' Mr. Patrick Gillespie writes a preface to the reader, wherein he expresses his high opinion of it in the following encomium: "In this book Mr. Binning explains many of the fundamental articles of the Christian faith, and had he lived to have perfected and finished this work, he had been upon this single account famous in the church of Christ." The Assembly's Catechism has had many expositions by pious and learned ministers, some of them by way of sermon, and others by way of question and answer. But this, so far as it goes, is not inferior to any. A learned layman, Sir Matthew Hales, chief-justice of the king's bench, the divine of the state in King Charles II.'s reign, judged the Assembly's Catechism to be an excellent composure, and thought it not below him, or unworthy of his pains to consider it. For in the second part of his 'Contemplations moral and divine,' we have his most instructive meditations upon the first three questions. These had been the employment of his *horæ sacræ*; and it is a pity he did not go on to the other questions. The shortness of Mr. Binning's life has deprived us of a complete course of useful catechetical discourses. This book was so greatly esteemed in this country, that before the year 1718, there had been no less than five impressions cast off the press;‡ and all these being sold off, a sixth was made in the said year. As they were much valued at home, so they were highly prized abroad: and as an evidence of this, I find that Mr. James Coleman, minister at Sluys in Flanders, translated them into the Dutch language.§

In the year 1670, another posthumous work was printed; it is entitled, "The Sinner's Sanctuary; being forty Sermons upon the Eighth chapter of the Epistle to the Romans, from the first verse down to the sixteenth." The Publishers in their preface acquaint us, that they were encouraged to print it, because the former treatise was universally received by the intelligent and judicious in the principles of the Christian faith. In this book, as in all his other writings, the readers will perceive a pure stream of piety and learning running through the whole, and a very peculiar turn of thought, that exceeds the common rate of writers on this choice part of the Holy Scriptures. Dr. Horton, Dr. Manton, and others, have printed a great number of useful practical discourses; but so far as he goes, he is not exceeded by any of them.

A third treatise was printed at Edinburgh, in the year 1671. The title of it is, "Fellowship with God, being twenty-eight Sermons on the First Epistle of John, Chap. 1st, and Chap. 2d, Verses 1, 2, 3." In this book, we have the true ground and foundation of attaining the spiritual way of entertaining fellowship with the Father and the Son, and the blessed condition of such as attain to it, most succinctly and distinctly explained. This book was revised and published by one A. S. who, in his preface to the reader, styles himself, his servant in the gospel of our dearest Lord and Saviour. I need give no other commendation of it, than that summary eulogium which that minister has left us. "In a word, (says he,) here are

* [12mo., Glasgow, 1659.—Ed.]

† [Macward's words are, *a prima manu*. Het Leven en Sterven van Mr. Hugo Binning.—Ed.]

‡ [A copy of "The Common Principles of Christian Religion" is now before me, which was 'Printed by R. S., Printer to the Town of Glasgow, 1666," and which bears to be "The 5 Impression."—Ed.]

§ [All the works of Binning, which were published in the lifetime of Koelman, were translated by him into the Dutch language. No fewer than four editions of these have been printed at Amsterdam.—Ed.]

to be found, convictions for atheists, piercing rebukes to the profane, clear instructions to the ignorant, milk to the babes in Christ, strong meat for the strong, strength to the weak, quickening and reviving for such as faint in the way, restoratives for such as are in a decay, reclamations and loud oyesses after backsliders to recall them, breasts of consolation for Zion's mourners. And to add no more, here are most excellent counsels and directions to serious seekers of fellowship with God, to guide them in their way, and help them forward to the attainment of that fulness of joy which is to be had in fellowship with the Father and the Son."

The last treatise that has been printed is, "Heart Humiliation, or Miscellany Sermons, preached upon some choice texts at several solemn occasions." These likewise were revised and published by the above A. S. in the year [1676]. Mr. Binning considering the great confusions and lamentable divisions that prevailed in the church in his day, and the abounding immorality and profaneness of the age, was deeply weighed therewith. His righteous soul was so vexed and grieved on these accounts, that he vented his mind in a most pathetic and moving manner, when the days of public humiliation and fasting were observed. With respect to the many fasts then appointed, and the few good effects they had, he says in his sermon on Isa. lxiv. 7.—'There is none that calleth upon thy name, that stirreth up himself to take hold of thee,'—"The fasting days of Scotland will be numbered in the roll of the greatest provocations, because there is no real and spiritual conviction of sin among us; custom now hath taken away the solemnity, and there remaineth nothing but the very name."* And in this same sermon, he says, "Doth any of you pray more in private than ye used? Or what edge is upon your prayers? Alas! the Lord will get good leave to go from us; it feareth me we would give Christ a testimonial to go over seas. Hold him, hold him! Nay the multitude would be gladly quit of him,—they cannot abide his yoke, his work is a burden, his word is a torment, his discipline is bands and cords; and what heart can ye have to keep Christ? What violence can ye offer to him to hold him still? All your entreaties may be fair compliments, but they would never rend his garment."† There are still several manuscripts of Mr. Binning's carefully preserved, which are in nothing inferior to any of his printed works. There is a valuable Treatise upon Christian Love, consisting of several sheets writ in a very small character,—it is divided into chapters; and several sermons upon very edifying subjects, useful and profitable for our times,—which are designed to be printed in a separate volume; which every body may easily discover from the style and genius of the author to be his genuine writings; his manner of thinking and writing being a talent so peculiar to himself, that it scarcely can be imitated by any other person.

Had it pleased the Almighty to have spared so valuable a life for some time longer, he would have vindicated divinity from the many fruitless questions, unintelligible terms, empty notions, and perplexed subtilties, wherewith it had been corrupted for a long time by the schoolmen. As he was excellently fitted for this, so it was much upon his heart to have reduced divinity to that native simplicity, which had been lost in most parts of the world. A good specimen of his ability this way he hath given us in his catechism; and so, though he lived but a short time, he yet lived long enough to raise the greatest expectation that hath been known of any of his standing.

Mr. M'Ward assures us, That if Dr. Strang's dictates *De Voluntate Dei circa peccata*‡ had been published before Mr. Binning's death, Mr. Binning had an ex-

* [See page 457.—Ed.] † [See page 465.—Ed.]

‡ [A contemporary of Binning, Mr. P. Simson, minister of Renfrew, informed Wodrow, "That Dr. Strang was in hazard to have been staged for his Dictates, qch wer smoothed in his printed book, *De Voluntate Dei,* and would have been removed from his place if he had not demitted" (Life of Dr. Strang. Wodrow MSS. vol. xiii. p. 9. in Bib. Coll. Glas.). Complaints regarding Dr. Strang having been presented to the General Assembly, a committee was appointed, on the 18th of June, 1646, to examine his written dictates, a copy of which was produced by Dr. Strang; and to find out whether the doctrines which he taught were in accordance with the doctrines of their own and other reformed churches, and whether there were any expressions used by him which gave countenance to the views of the enemies of the truth. This committee was composed of some of the most able men in the church, including several professors from the four universities.

amen of them ready for the press. But this treasure, to the great loss of the learned world, cannot now be found. As for his philosophical writings which he taught in the University, I am assured that his course of philosophy is in the hands of a learned gentleman in this city, who gives them an high commendation.

There is a book published under his name in 4to, consisting of fifty-one pages, with this title, 'An Useful Case of Conscience, learnedly and accurately discussed and resolved, concerning associations and confederacies with idolaters, infidels, heretics, malignants, or any other known enemies of truth and godliness.' But it is very much questioned by the most intelligent, if that book was really Mr. Binning's. The publisher does indeed put Mr. Binning's name to the title-page, but conceals his own: and he brings no manner of voucher, showing that Mr. Binning was the author, but sends it abroad into the world in a clandestine manner. Neither the name of the printer, nor of the place where it was printed, is mentioned in the title-page.* It was printed in the year 1693, when the first General Assembly

The list contains, along with others, the names of Alexander Henderson, John Sharpe, the author of *Cursus Theologicus*, Robert Douglas, George Gillespie, Robert Blair, Samuel Rutherford, James Wood, William Strahan, David Dickson, Robert Baillie, John Neave, Edward Calderwood, and Robert Leighton, afterwards Archbishop of Glasgow. On the 27th of August, 1647, the committee gave in a Report to the General Assembly, to the effect that Dr. Strang had employed some expressions in his dictates which were calculated to give offence, but that, on conferring with him, they were satisfied in regard to his orthodoxy; and that, to put an end to all doubts as to his meaning, the Doctor had gratified them, by proposing of his own accord the addition of certain words to what was previously somewhat ambiguous (Vita Autoris, Strangii De Interpret. Script.).

So far as can be collected from the imperfect account we have of the circumstances of the case, Dr. Strang discovered, it was imagined, a bias to Arminianism, whereas he seems to have been merely more of a sublapsarian than a supralapsarian. The "peculiar notions" he entertained were "vented," we have been told, "upon that profound subject," *De concursu et influxu divino cum actionibus creaturarum*, or the concurrence and influence of God in the actions of his creatures. In the two chapters of his published work, which treat expressly upon this point, we can perceive nothing that is at variance with our own Confession. But this does not warrant us to infer that the dictates, as originally delivered, and before they were amended and enlarged by the author himself, may not have contained some very objectionable language at least, especially when we look to the Report of the committee of the Assembly regarding them. Indeed, all that Baillie himself says, who was one of that committee, is, that Dr. Strang was pursued "without any ground at all *considerable*," and that "he got him *reasonably* fair off." Letters and Journals, vol. ii. p. 338.

The publication of Dr. Strang's work, "De Voluntate et Actionibus Dei circa Peccatum" (Amstelodami Apud Ludovicum et Danielem Elzevirios, 1657, 4to. pp. 886), was intrusted to Mr. William Spang, minister of the English church at Middleburgh, in Zealand. The manuscripts were sent to him by his cousin, Mr. Robert Baillie, at that time Professor of Theology in the University of Glasgow, who, after the death of his first wife, had married a daughter of Dr. Strang. "Dr. Strang, your good friend," says Baillie, in a letter to Mr. Spang, dated July 20, 1654, "having to do in Edinburgh with the lawyers, concerning the unjust trouble he was put to for his stipends, did die, so sweetly and graciously, as was satisfactory to all, and much applauded over all the city, his very persecutors giving him an ample testimony. His treatise, *Dei circa peccatum*, he has enlarged, and made ready for the press. Be careful to get it well printed, according to the constant friendship that was always betwixt you and him" (Letters, vol. ii. pp. 382, 383). At the request of Mr. Spang, Alexander Morus furnished a preface, and *Ad Lectorem Commonitio*, for Dr. Strang's work.—ED.]

* ["This is somewhat strange," observes Howie of Lochgoin, "that a nameless author should quarrel that book, because the publisher hath omitted to tell his name, and hath only inserted the author's name. He might have known that it was not long a secret that Mr. James Kid (who was afterwards settled minister in Queensferry) was the publisher, and upon that account suffered both long imprisonment at Utrecht, and the seizure of all that they could get of the books. And as for vouchers, Mrs. Binning, the relict of the worthy author, being then alive, had connexion and much correspondence with Mr. Hamilton, Mr. Renwick, and many of the persecuted Society people, and was of the same sentiments with them, as appears by several letters yet extant in their own handwrit,—and Mr. Renwick speaks of her in some of his letters, as in the 49 and 104 pages of the printed volume of his letters: but especially it appears, by a paragraph which is omitted in the printed copy, page 58, (which shall be here transcribed from the original, written with his own hand,) wherein he says, 'Likewise, according to your direction, I challenged Mrs. Binning—upon the commendation she gave to John Wilson in her letter to you. But she says, that she had not then seen his testimony, and was sorry when she saw it, that it was so contrary both to her thoughts and commendation of him.' And likewise a postscript to the 20th Letter, relative to the same matter is also omitted. And about the same time that Mr. Binning's book was printed, while Sir Robert Hamilton was prisoner, upon account of the declaration [Sanquhar Declaration] in 1692, he wrote a letter to Mrs. Binning, wherein he complains of her unwonted silence, in his honourable bonds for such a noble Master. Yet trusting her sympathy is not diminished, he adds,

of this church after the Revolution, which consisted of both Public Resolutioners and Protesters, had agreed to bury for ever all their differences about the Public Resolutions, concerning the question of employing malignants in the army, that was raised against the kingdom of England. It seems that he dreaded the frowns and censure of those worthy and faithful ministers of Jesus Christ, who had been a long time in the fire of persecution. But if we further consider, that our late glorious deliverer, King William, was in the year 1693 engaged in a defensive war with the Emperor of Germany and the King of Spain, against Louis XIV., the bloody tyrant of France and terror of Europe, who aimed at the universal monarchy thereof, and to overturn the happy revolution, the blessed benefits of which we have enjoyed ever since, it is evident, that the publisher was afraid of the resentment of the civil powers; especially when the spreading of that pamphlet might have an unhappy tendency to alienate the affections of his subjects, when he was carrying on that just and necessary war, for the preservation of our civil and religious liberties, to which we had been but lately restored. Nay, it is said, that when this pamphlet was spreading in the army in Flanders, it was like to have a bad influence on the soldiers, which made King William take an effectual method to suppress it. Further, Mr. Binning died in the year 1653, and this pamphlet was not published till the year 1693; so that, for the space of forty years it was never heard of nor made public by any of the Protesters themselves in that period, which would not have been neglected, had they known that Mr. Binning was the author of it. And lastly, Mr. Binning was of a pacific temper, and his sentiments with respect to public differences were healing, which are evident from the accounts already given of his printed books. And to show that he was a promoter of brotherly love, and of the peace of the church, I shall set down a few passages taken from his Treatise of Christian Love, which are as bright and strong for recommending the same, as any that I have met with in the writings of any of our divines, so that I can't allow myself to think he could be the author thereof. In chapter 2d of that Treatise, he says, "There is a greater moment and weight of Christianity in charity, than in the most part of those things for which Christians bite and devour one another. It is the fundamental law of the gospel, to which all positive precepts and ordinances should stoop. Unity in judgment is very needful for the well-being of Christians. But Christ's last words persuade this, that unity in affection is more essential and fundamental. This is the badge he left to his disciples. If we cast away this upon every different apprehension of mind, we disown our Master, and disclaim his token and badge."* He goes on in the same strain in the following paragraph: "The apostle Paul puts a high note of commendation upon charity, when he styles it the bond of perfection. 'Above all things (says he) put on charity, which is the bond of perfectness,' Col. iii. 14. I am sure it hath not so high a place in the minds and practice of Christians now, as it hath in the roll of the parts and members of the new man here set down. Here it is above all. With us it is below all, even below every apprehension of doubtful truths. An agreement in the conception of any poor petty controversial matter of the times, is made the badge

'O, my worthy friend, I cannot express Christ's love and kindness since the time of my bonds. He hath broke up new treasures of felt love and sweetness, and hath been pleased to give me visitations of love and access to himself, to comfort and confirm poor feckless me many ways, that this is his way that is now persecuted, and that it is his precious truths, interests, and concerns, that I am now suffering for, whatever enemies with their associated ministers and professors may allege,' &c.

"By which it is evident that they had much correspondence with Mrs. Binning. And there is yet a fair and correct manuscript copy of the foresaid book extant, which was in Sir Robert's custody, and it is more than probable that it was procured from Mrs. Binning, especially as she survived its publication without quarrelling it.

"It is unnecessary to notice what further is thrown out by the foresaid anonymous writer, against the book and the publisher, as Mr. Wodrow, in the preface to Mr. Binning's octavo volume of sermons, printed 1760, hath modestly animadverted thereupon, and says there is no reason to doubt if it was Mr. Binning's. He also ingenuously confesseth, that there is in it the best collection of scriptures he knows, concerning the sin and danger of joining with wicked and ungodly men, &c., and that it was wrote in a smooth good style, agreeable enough to Mr. Binning's sentiments in some of his sermons." Faithful Contendings Displayed, pp. 486, 487, note. See likewise Faithful Witness-bearing Exemplified, preface, p. iv.—Ed.]

* [See page 527.—Ed.]

of Christianity, and set in an eminent place above all."* And in the same chapter he adds, "This is the sum of all, to worship God in faith and purity, and to love one another. And, whatsoever debates and questions tend to the breach of this bond, and have no eminent and remarkable advantage in them, suppose they be conceived to be about matters of conscience, yet the entertaining and prosecuting of them to the prejudice of this, is a manifest violence offered to the law of God, which is the rule of conscience. It is a perverting of scripture and conscience to a wrong end. I say then, that charity and Christian love should be the moderatrix of all our actions towards men. From thence they should proceed, and according to this rule be formed. I am persuaded if this rule were followed, the present differences in judgment of godly men, about such matters as minister mere questions, would soon be buried in the gulf of Christian affection."† I shall mention only another in the same chapter. "Is not charity more excellent than the knowledge and acknowledgment of some present questionable matters about government, treaties, and such like, and far more than every punctilio of them? But the apostle goes higher. Suppose a man could spend all his substance upon the maintenance of such an opinion, and give his life for the defence of it, though in itself it be commendable, yet if he want charity and love to his brethren, if he overstretch that point of conscience to the breach of Christian affection and duties flowing from it, it profits him nothing. Then certainly charity must rule our external actions, and have the predominant hand in the use of all gifts, and in the venting of all opinions."‡ And now, having given a just character of this eminent minister of the gospel, a true account of his life, and some slight remarks upon his writings, I shall no longer detain the reader from the perusal of those treatises that are contained in this volume; from which you will know more of Mr. Binning, than from all I and others have said in his just praise. I shall now conclude, by acquainting the purchasers and readers of this volume, that I am allowed by the publishers to assure them, that the rest of his practical manuscripts are revising for the press; and that with all expedition they shall be printed; from which I am hopeful they shall receive as great satisfaction, as from any of his pieces already published.

* [See page 527.—Ed.] † [See page 528.—Ed.] ‡ [Ibid.—Ed.]

THE COMMON PRINCIPLES OF THE CHRISTIAN RELIGION, CLEARLY PROVED, AND SINGULARLY IMPROVED; OR, A PRACTICAL CATECHISM.

Original Preface.

TO THE READER.

Christian Reader,—The holy and learned author of this little book, having outrun his years, hastened to a maturity before the ordinary season, insomuch that ripe summer-fruit was found with him by the first of the spring: for before he had lived twenty-five years complete, he had got to be *Philologus, Philosophus, Theologus eximius;* whereof he gave suitable proofs, by his labours, having first professed in philosophy three years, with high approbation, in the university of Glasgow, and thence was translated to the ministry of the gospel in a congregation adjacent, where he laboured in the work of the gospel near four years, leaving an epistle of commendation upon the hearts of his hearers. But as few burning and shining lights have been of long continuance here, so he ('after he had served his own generation by the will of God,' and many had rejoiced in his light for a season) was quickly transported to the land of promise, in the 26th year of his age. He lived deservedly esteemed and beloved, and died much lamented by all discerning Christians who knew him. And, indeed, the loss which the churches of Christ, in these parts, sustained in his death, was the greater upon a double account: first, that he was a person fitted with dexterity to vindicate school-divinity and practical theology from the superfluity of vain and fruitless perplexing questions wherewith latter times have corrupted both; and had it upon his spirit, in all his way, to reduce* that native gospel simplicity, which, in most parts of the world where literature is in esteem, and where the gospel is preached, is almost exiled from the school and from the pulpit,—a specimen whereof the judicious reader may find in this little treatise. Besides, he was a person of eminent moderation and sobriety of spirit, (a rare grace in this generation,) whose heart was much drawn forth in the study of healing-ways and condescensions of love among brethren; one who longed for the recovering of the *humanity of Christianity,* which hath been well near lost in the bitter divisions of these times, and the animosities which have followed thereupon.

That which gave the rise to the publishing of this part of his manuscripts, was partly the longing of many who knew him after some fruit of his labours for the use of the church; and partly the exceeding great usefulness of the treatise, wherein, I am bold to say, that some fundamentals of the Christian religion, and great mysteries of faith, are handled with the greatest gospel-simplicity and most dexterous plainness; and are brought down to the meanest capacity and vulgar understanding, with abundant evidence of a great height and reach of useful knowledge in the author; who, had he lived to have perfected the explication of the grounds of religion in this manner—as he intended, in his opening the catechism unto his particular congregation—he had been, upon this single account, famous in the churches of Christ. But now, by this imperfect *opus posthumum,* thou art left to judge *ex ungue leonem.*

The author's method was his peculiar gift, who, being no stranger to the rules of art, knew well how to make his method subserve the matter which he handled; for, though he tell not always that his discourse hath so many parts, thou mayest not think it wants method, it being *maximam artis celare artem.* That the same Spirit which enabled him to conceive, and communicate to others, these sweet mysteries of salvation, may help thee with profit to read and peruse them, is the desire of him who is,

Thine in the service of the Gospel,

PATRICK GILLESPIE.

[The word *reduce* is here used in its literal etymological sense, as signifying *to bring back,* or to *restore.*—Ed.]

THE COMMON PRINCIPLES OF THE CHRISTIAN RELIGION.

Lecture I.

GOD'S GLORY THE CHIEF END OF MAN'S BEING.

ROM. xi. 36. "*Of him, and through him, and to him, are all things; to whom be glory for ever.*" And 1 COR. x. 31. "*Whatsoever ye do, do all to the glory of God.*"

ALL that men have to know, may be comprised under these two heads,—What their end is; and What is the right way to attain to that end. And all that we have to do, is by any means to seek to compass that end. These are the two cardinal points of a man's knowledge and exercise: *Quo et qua eundum est,*—Whither to go, and what way to go. If there be a mistake in any of these fundamentals, all is wrong. All arts and sciences have their principles and grounds that must be presupposed to all solid knowledge and right practice; so hath the true religion some fundamental principles which must be laid to heart and imprinted into the soul, or there can be no superstructure of true and saving knowledge, and no practice in Christianity that can lead to a blessed end. But as the principles are not many, but a few common and easy grounds, from which all the conclusions of art are reduced, so the principles of true religion are few and plain; they need neither burden your memory, nor confound your understanding. That which may save you 'is nigh thee,' says the apostle, (Rom. x. 8.) 'even in thy mouth.' It is neither too far above us, nor too far below us. But, alas! your not considering of those common and few and easy grounds, makes them both burdensome to the memory, and dark to the understanding. As there is nothing so easy but it becomes difficult if you do it against your will,—*Nihil est tam facile, quin difficile fiat, si invitus feceris,*—so there is nothing so plain, so common, but it becomes dark and hard if you do not indeed consider it and lay it to heart.

That which is, in the first place, to be considered is, Our end. As in all other arts, and every petty business, it hath the first place of consideration, so especially in the Christian religion. It is the first cause of all human actions, and the first principle of all deliberate motions. Except you would walk at random, not knowing whither you go, or what you do, you must once establish this and fix it in your intention—What is the great end and purpose wherefore I am created, and sent into the world? If this be not either questioned, or not rightly constituted, you cannot but spend your time, *Vel nihil agendo, vel aliud agendo, vel male agendo;* you must either do nothing, or nothing to purpose, or, that which is worse, that which will undo you. It is certainly the wrong establishing of this one thing that makes the most part of our motions either altogether irregular, or unprofitable, or destructive and hurtful. Therefore, as this point hath the first place in your catechism, so it ought to be first of all laid to heart, and pondered as the one necessary thing. 'One thing is needful,' says Christ, Luke x. 42; and if any thing be in a superlative degree needful, this is it. O that you would choose to consider it, as the necessity and weight of it require!

We have read two scriptures, which speak to the ultimate and chief end of man, which is the glorifying of God by all our actions and words and thoughts. In which we have these things of importance: 1. That God's glory is the end of our being. 2. That God's glory should be the end of our doing. And, 3. The ground of both these; because both being and doing are from him, therefore they ought to be both for him. He is the first cause of both, and therefore he ought to be the last end of both. 'Of him, and through him, are all things;' and therefore all things are also for him, and therefore all things should be done to him.

God is independent altogether, and self-sufficient. This is his royal prerogative, wherein he infinitely transcends all created perfection. He is of himself, and for himself; from no other, and for no other, 'but of him, and for him, are all things.' He is the fountain-head; you ought to follow the streams up to it, and then to rest, for you can go no farther. But the creature, even the most perfect work, besides God, it hath these two ingredients of limitation and imperfection in its bosom: it is from another, and for another. It hath its rise out of the fountain of God's immense power and goodness, and it must run towards that again, till it empty all its faculties and excellencies into that same sea of goodness. Dependence is the proper notion of a created being,—dependence upon that infinite independent Being, as the first immediate cause, and the last immediate end. You see then that this principle is engraven in the very nature of man. It is as certain and evident that man is made for God's glory, and for no other end, as that he is from God's power, and from no other cause. Except men do violate their own conscience, and put out their own eyes—as the Gentiles did, Rom. i. 19, &c.—'that which may be known' of man's chief end, 'is manifest in them,' so that all men are 'without excuse.' As God's being is independent, so that he cannot be expressed by any name more suitable than such as he takes to himself, 'I am that I am,'—importing a boundless, ineffable, absolute, and transcendent being, beside which, no creature deserves so much as to have the name of being, or to be made mention of in one day with his name, because his glorious light makes the poor derived shadow of light in other creatures to disappear, and to evanish out of the world of beings,—so it is the glorious perfection of his nature, that he doth 'all things for himself,' Prov. xvi. 4, for his own name; and his glory is as dear to him as himself. 'I am the Lord, that is my name, and [therefore] my glory will I not give to another,' Isa. xlii. 8; and xlviii. 11. This is no ambition. Indeed, for a man to seek his own glory, or search into it, 'is not glory,' (Prov. xxv. 27,) but rather a man's shame. Self-seeking in creatures is a monstrous and incongruous thing; it is as absurd, and unbeseeming a creature, to seek its own glory, as to attribute to itself its own being. Shall the thing formed say to the potter, Thou hast not made me? That were ridiculous. And shall the thing formed say, 'Tis made for itself? That were as ridiculous. Self-denial is the ornament and beauty of a creature, and therefore humility is an ornament and clothing, 1 Pet. v. 5; and honour upholds the humble spirit, Prov. xxix. 23. But God's self-seeking, and seeking of his own glory, is his eminent excellency. It is indeed his glory, because he is, and there is none else; there is nothing, besides him, but that which hath issued forth from his incomprehensible fulness. And therefore it is all the reason of the world, that as he is the beginning, so he should be the end of all things, Rev. i. 8. And there is the more reason of it, that his majesty's seeking of his own glory is not prejudicial to the creature's good, but the very communication of his fulness goes along with it: so that in glorifying himself, he is most beneficial to his own creatures. Poor creatures, indigent at home, are yet proud of nothing, and endeavour, in seeking of themselves, to engross all perfections into their own bosoms! Ambition and vainglory robs and spoils others' excellencies to clothe itself withal; and then boasts itself in these borrowed feathers! But our blessed Lord is then doing most for our advantage when he does all for his own glory. He needs not go abroad to seek perfection, but to manifest what he is in himself; he communicates of himself to us. O blessed self-seeking that gave us a being and well-being; that makes no advantage by it, but gives advantage! He hath the honour of all, but we have the profit of all.

'All things are of him, and for him;' but man in a peculiar and proper way. As God, in making of man, was pleased of his goodness to stamp him with a character of his own image—and in this he puts a difference between man and other creatures, that he should have more plain and distinct engravings of divine majesty upon him, which might show the glory of the workman—so it appears that he is in a singular way made for God, as his last end. As he is set nearer God, as the beginning and cause, than other creatures; so he is placed nearer God as the end. All creatures are made *ultimò*, lastly, for God, yet they are all made *proximè*, nextly, for man. Therefore David falls out a wondering, 'Lord, what is man, that thou art mindful of him,' 'and hast made him to have dominion over the works of thy hands, and put all things under his feet!' Psal. viii. 4, 6. The creature comes out in a direct line from God, as the beams from the body of the sun; and it is directed towards the use and service of mankind, from whom all the excellency and perfection that is in it should reflect towards God again. Man is both *proximè et ultimò* for God. We are to return immediately to the fountain of our being; and thus our happiness and well-being is perpetuated. There is nothing intervening between God and us that our use and service and honour should be directed towards: but all the songs and perfections of the creature, that are among the rest of the creatures, meet all in man as their centre, for this purpose that he may return with them all to the glorious fountain from whence they issued. Thus we stand next God, and in the middle between God and other creatures. This, I say, was the condition of our creation. We had our being immediately from God, as the beginning of all; and we were to have our happiness and well-being by returning immediately to God as the end of all. But sin coming in between God and us, hath displaced us, so that we cannot now stand next God, without the intervention of a Mediator; and we cannot stand between God and creatures, to offer up their praises to him; but 'there is one Mediator between God and man,' that offers up both man's praises and the creature's songs which meet in man.

Now, seeing God hath made all things for himself, and especially man for his own glory, that he may show forth in him the glory and excellence of his power, goodness, holiness, justice, and mercy; it is not only most reasonable that man should do all things that he doth to the glory of God, but it is even the beauty and perfection of a man,—the greatest accession that can be to his being,—to glorify God by that being. We are not our own, therefore we ought not to live to ourselves, but to God whose we are.

But you may ask, What is it to glorify God? Doth our goodness extend to him? Or is it an advantage to the Almighty that we are righteous? No indeed! And herein is the vast difference between God's glorifying of us and sanctifying of us, and our glorifying and sanctifying of him. God 'calls things that are not,' and makes them to be: but we can do no more but call things that are, and that far below what they are. God's glorifying is creative,—ours only declarative. He makes us such,—we do no more but declare him to be such. This then is the proper work that man is created for, to be a witness of God's glory, and to give testimony to the appearances and out-breakings of it in the ways of power and justice and mercy and truth. Other creatures are called to glorify God, but it is rather a proclamation to dull and senseless men, and a provocation of them to their duty. As Christ said to the Pharisees, 'If these children hold their peace, the stones would cry out,' so may the Lord turn himself from stupid and senseless man, to the stones and woods and seas and sun and moon, and exhort them to man's duty, the more to provoke and stir up our dulness, and to make us consider that it is a greater wonder that man, whom God hath made so glorious, can so little express God's glory, than if stupid and senseless creatures should break out in singing and praising of his majesty. The creatures are the books wherein the lines of the song of God's praises are written; and man is made a creature capable to read them, and to tune that song. They are appointed to bring in brick to our hand; and God has fashioned us for this employment, to make such a building of it. We are the mouth of the creation; but ere God want praises when our mouth is dumb, and our ears deaf, God will open the mouths of asses, 'of babes and sucklings,' and in them perfect praises, Psal. viii. 1, 2. Epictetus said well, *Si Luscinia essem, canerem ut Luscinia: cum autem homo sim, quid agam? Laudabo Deum, nec unquam cessabo*—If I were a lark, I would sing as a lark; but seeing I am a man, what should I do, but praise God with outceasing? It is as proper to us to praise God, as for a bird to chaunt. All beasts have their own sounds and voices peculiar to their own nature; this is the natural sound of a man. Now as you would think it monstrous to hear a melodious bird croaking as a raven; so it is no less monstrous and degenerate to hear the most part of the discourses of men savouring nothing of God. If we had known that innocent estate of man, O how would we think he had fallen from heaven! We would imagine that we were thrust down from heaven, where we heard the melodious songs of angels, into hell, to hear the howlings of damned spirits. This then is that we are bound unto, by the bond of our creation; this is our proper office and station God once set us into, when he assigned every creature its own use and exercise. This was our portion, (and O the noblest of all, because nearest the King's own person!) to acknowledge in our hearts inwardly, and to express in our words and actions outwardly, what a One he is, according as he hath revealed himself in his word and works. It is great honour to a creature to have the meanest employment in the court of this great King; but, O, what is it to be set over all the King's house, and over all his kingdom! But, then, what is that, in respect of this,—to be next to the King,—to wait on his own person, so to speak? Therefore the godly man is described as a waiting-maid, or servant, Psal. cxxiii. 2.

Well then, without more discourse upon it, without multiplying of it into particular branches, to glorify God is in our souls to conceive of him, and meditate on his name, till they receive the impression and stamp of all the letters of his glorious name; and then to express this in our words and actions, in commending of him, and obeying of him. Our souls should be as wax to express the seal of his glorious attributes of justice, power, goodness, holiness, and mercy: and as the water that receives the beams of the sun reflects them back again, so should our spirits receive the sweet warming beams of his love and glorious excellency, and then reflect them towards his Majesty, with the desires and affections of our souls. All our thoughts of him, all our affections towards him, should have the stamp of singularity, such as may declare there is none like him, none besides him; our love, our meditation, our acknowledgment should have this character on their front,—'There is none besides thee: thou art, and none else.' And then a soul should, by the cords of affection to him and admiration of him, be bound to serve him. Creation puts on the obligation to glorify him in our body and spirits which are his; but affection only puts that to exercise. All other bonds leave our natures at liberty, but this constrains, 2 Cor. v. 14; it binds on all bonds, it ties on us all divine obligations. Then a soul will glorify God, when love so unites it to God, and makes it one spirit with him, that his glory becomes its honour, and becomes the principle of all our inward affections and outward actions. It is not always possible to have and express particular thoughts of God and his glory, in every action and meditation; but, for the most part it ought to be so: And if souls were accustomed to meditation on God, it would become their very nature,—*altera natura*,—pleasant and delightsome. However, if there be not always an express intention of God's glory, yet there ought to be kept always such a disposition and temper of spirit as it may be construed to proceed from the intention of God's glory; and then it remains in the seed and fruit, if not in itself.

Now when we are speaking of the great end and purpose of our creation, we call to mind our lamentable and tragical fall from that blessed station we were constitute into. 'All men have sinned and come short of the glory of God,' Rom. iii. 23. His being in the world was for that glory, and he is come short of that glory. O strange shortcoming! Short of all that he was ordained for! What is he now meet for? For what purpose is that chief of the works of God now! The salt, if it lose its saltness, is meet for nothing, for wherewithal shall it be seasoned? Mark ix. 50. Even so, when man is rendered unfit for his proper end, he is meet for nothing, but to be cast out and trode upon; he is like a withered branch that must be cast into the fire, John xv. 6. Some things, if they fail in one use, they are good for another; but the best things are not so,—*Corruptio optimi, pessima*. As the Lord speaks to the house of Israel, 'Shall wood be taken of the vine tree to do any work?'

Even so the inhabitants of Jerusalem, Ezek. xv. 2—6. If it yield not wine, it is good for nothing. So, if man do not glorify God,—if he fall from that,—he is meet for nothing, but to be cast into the fire of hell, and burnt for ever; he is for no use in the creation, but to be fuel to the fire of the Lord's indignation.

But behold! the goodness of the Lord and his kndness and love hath 'appeaied toward man. Not by works of righteousness which we have done, but according to his mercy he saved us,' 'through Jesus Christ,' Tit. iii. 4, 5, 6. Our Lord Jesus, by whom all things were created, and for whom, would not let this excellent workmanship perish so, therefore he goes about the work of redemption,—a second creation more laborious and also more glorious than the first, that so he might glorify his Father and our Father. Thus the breach is made up; thus the unsavoury salt is seasoned; thus the withered branch is quickened again for that same fruit of praises and glorifying of God. This is the end of his second creation, as it was of the first: 'We are his workmanship created to good works in Christ Jesus,' Eph. ii. 10. 'This is the work of God, to believe on him whom he hath sent;' 'to set to our seal,' and to give our testimony to all his attributes, John vi. 29, and iii. 33. We are 'bought with a price,' and therefore we ought to glorify him with our souls and bodies. He made us with a word, and that bound us; but now he has made us again, and paid a price for us, and so we are twice bound not to be our own but his, 'and so to glorify him in our bodies and spirits,' 1 Cor. vi. ult. I beseech you, gather your spirits, call them home about the business. We once came short of our end,—God's glory and our happiness; but know, that it is attainable again. We lost both; but both are found in Christ. Awake then and stir up your spirits, else it shall be double condemnation—when we have the offer of being restored to our former blessed condition—to love our present misery better. Once establish this point within your souls, and therefore ask, Why came I hither? To what purpose am I come into the world? If you do not ask it, what will you answer, when he asks you at your appearance before his tribunal? I beseech you, what will many of you say in that day when the Master returns and takes an account of your dispensation? You are sent into the world only for this business,—to serve the Lord. Now what will many of you answer? If you speak the truth (as then you must do it,—you cannot lie then!) you must say, "Lord, I spent my time in serving my own lusts; I was taken up with other businesses, and had no leisure; I was occupied in my calling," &c. Even as if an ambassador of a king should return him this account of his negociation: "I was busy at cards and dice; I spent my money, and did wear my clothes." Though you think your ploughing and borrowing and trafficking and reaping very necessary, yet certainly these are but as trifles and toys to the main business. O what a dreadful account will souls make! They come here for no purpose but to serve their bodies and senses, to be slaves to all the creatures which were once put under man's feet: Now man is under the feet of all, and he has put himself so. If you were of these creatures, then you might be for them. You seek them as if you were created for them, and not they for you; and you seek yourselves, as if you were of yourselves, and had not your descent of God. Know, my beloved, that you were not made for that purpose, nor yet redeemed either to serve yourselves, or other creatures, but that other creatures might serve you, and ye serve God, Luke i. 74, 75. And this is really the best way to serve ourselves, and to save ourselves,—to serve God. Self-seeking is self-destroying; self-denying is self-saving, soul-saving. 'He that seeketh to save his life shall lose it, and he that loseth his life shall find it, and he that denies himself and follows me, is my disciple.' Will ye once sit down in good earnest about this business? 'Tis lamentable to be yet to begin to learn to live, when ye must die! Ye will be out of the world almost, ere ye bethink yourself, Why came I into the world? *Quidam tunc vivere incipiunt, cum desinendum est; imo quidam ante vivere desierunt quam inciperent;* this is of all most lamentable,—many souls end their life, before they begin to live. For what is our life, but a living death, while we do not live to God, and while we live not in relation to the great end of our life and being,—the glory of God? It were better, says Christ, that such 'had never been born.' You who are created again in Jesus Christ, it most of all concerns you to ask, Why am I made? And why am I redeemed? And to what purpose? It is certainly that ye may glorify your heavenly Father, Mat. v. 16; Ps. lvi. 13.

And you shall glorify him if you bring forth much fruit, and continue in his love, John xv. 8, 9. And this you are chosen and ordained unto, ver. 16; and therefore abide in him, that ye may bring forth fruit, ver. 4. And if you abide in him by believing, you do indeed honour him; and he that honoureth the Son honoureth the Father, John v. 23. Here is a compendious way to glorify God. Receive salvation of him freely, righteousness and eternal life; this sets to a seal to God's truth and grace and mercy: and whoso counts the Son worthy to be a Saviour to them, and sets to their seal of approbation to him whom God the Father hath sent and sealed, he also honours the Father; and then he that honoureth the Father, hath it not for nothing, 'for them that honour me I will honour,' 1 Sam. ii. 30, says the Lord; and 'he that serves me, him will my Father honour,' John xii. 26. As the believing soul cares for no other, and respects no other but God, so he respects no other but such a soul. 'I will dwell in the humble, and look unto the contrite;' there are mutual respects and honours. God is the delight of such a soul, and such a soul is God's delight. That soul sets God in a high place, in a throne in its heart; and God sets that soul in a heavenly place with Christ, Eph. ii. 6; yea he comes down to sit with us, and dwells in us, off his throne of majesty, Isa. lxvi. 1, 2; and lvii. 15.

Lecture II.

UNION AND COMMUNION WITH GOD THE END AND DESIGN OF THE GOSPEL.

PSALM lxxiii. 24—28. "*Thou wilt guide me with thy counsel, &c. Whom have I in heaven but thee? &c. It is good for me to draw near to God.*"—1 JOHN i. 3. "*That which we have seen and heard declare we unto you, that ye also may have fellowship with us: and truly our fellowship is with the Father, and with his Son Jesus Christ.*"—JOHN xvii. 21—23. "*That they all may be one, as thou, Father, art in me, and I in thee, that they also may be one in us,*" &c.

IT is a matter of great consolation that God's glory and our happiness are linked together; so that whoever set his glory before them singly to aim at, they take the most compendious and certain way to true blessedness. His glory is the ultimate end of man, and should be our great and last scope. But our happiness—which consists in the enjoyment of God—is subordinate to this, yet inseparable from it. The end of our creation is communion and fellowship with God, therefore man was made with an immortal soul capable of it; and this is the greatest dignity and eminency of man above the creatures. He hath not only impressed from God's finger, in his first moulding, some characters resembling God, in righteousness and holiness; but is created with a capacity of receiving more of God by communion with him. Other creatures have already all they will have,—all they can have,—of conformity to him; but man is made liker than all, and is fitted and fashioned to aspire to more likeness and conformity, so that his soul may shine more and more to the perfect day.

There was an union made already in his first moulding; and communion was to grow as a fragrant and sweet fruit out of this blessed root. Union and similitude are the ground of fellowship and communion. That union wa sgracious,—that communion would have been glorious; for grace is the seed of glory. There was a twofold union between Adam and God,—an union of state, and an union of nature; he was like God, and he was God's friend. All the creatures had some likeness to God, some engravings of his power and goodness and wisdom: but man is said to be made according to God's image, 'Let us make man like unto us.' Other creatures had *similitudinem vestigii*, but man had *similitudinem faciei*. Holiness and righteousness are God's face,—the very excellency and glory of all his attributes; and the Lord stamps the image of these upon man. Other attributes are but like his back parts; and he leaves the resemblance of his footsteps upon other creatures. What can be so beautiful as the image of God upon the soul? Creatures, the nearer they are to God, the more pure and excellent. We see in the fabric of the world, bodies the higher they are, the more pure and cleanly, the more beautiful. Now then, what was man that was 'made a little lower than the angels?'—in the Hebrew, 'a little lower than God,' *tantum non deus.* Seeing man is set next to God, his glory and beauty certainly surpasses the glory of the sun and of the heavens. Things contiguous and next other are like other. The water is liker air than the earth, therefore it is next the air. The air is liker heaven than water, therefore is it next to it. *Omne contiguum spirituali, est spirituale.* Angels and men next to God, are spirits, as he is a spirit. Now similitude is the ground of friendship. *Pares paribus congregantur; similitudo necessitudinis vinculum.* It is that which conciliates affections among men: So it is here by proportion. God sees all is very good, and that man is the best of his works; and he loves him, and makes him his friend, for his own image which he beholds in him.

At length from these two roots this pleasant and fragrant fruit of communion with and enjoyment of God grows up. This is the entertainment of friends, to delight in one another, and to enjoy one another. *Amicorum omnia communia.* Love makes all common. It opens the treasure of God's fulness, and makes a vent of divine bounty towards man; and it opens the heart of man, and makes it large as the sand of the sea to receive of God. Our receiving of his fulness is all the entertainment we can give him. O what blessedness is this, for a soul to live in him! And it lives in him when it loves him. *Anima est ubi amat, non ubi animat.* And to taste of his sweetness and be satisfied with him, this makes perfect oneness: and perfect oneness with God, who is 'the fountain of life, and in whose favour is life,' is perfect blessedness.

But we must stand a little here and consider our misery, that have fallen from such an excellency. How are we come down from heaven wonderfully? Sin has interposed between God and man; and this dissolves the union, and hinders the communion. An enemy has come between two friends, and puts them at odds; and oh! an eternal odds. Sin hath sown this discord, and alienated our hearts from God. Man's glory consisted in the irradiation of the soul from God's shining countenance; this made him light, God's face shined on him. But sin interposing has eclipsed that light and brought on an eternal night of darkness over the soul. And thus we are spoiled of the image of God, as when the earth comes between the sun and the moon. Now then, there can no beams of divine favour and love break through directly towards us, because of the cloud of our sins, that separates between God and us, and because of 'the partition-wall,' and 'the hand-writing of ordinances that was against us,'—God's holy law, and severe justice, Eph. ii. 14; Col. ii. 14.

Then, what shall we do? How shall we see his face in joy? Certainly it had been altogether impossible, if our Lord Jesus Christ had not come, who is 'the light and life of men.' The Father shines on him, and the beams of his love reflect upon us, from the Son. The love of God, and his favourable countenance, that cannot meet with us in a direct and immediate beam, they fall on us in this blessed compass, by the intervention of a mediator. We are rebels standing at a distance from God; Christ comes between, a mediator and a peace-maker, to reconcile us to God. 'God is in Christ reconciling the world. God first makes an union of natures with Christ; and so he comes near to us, down to us, who could not come up to him; and then he sends out the word of reconciliation,—the gospel, the tenor whereof is this, 'That which we have seen and heard declare we unto you, that ye also may have fellowship with us; and truly our fellowship is with the Father, and with his Son,' 1 John i. 3. It is a voice of peace and invitation to the fellowship of God. Behold, then, the happiness of man is the very end and purpose of the gospel. Christ is the repairer of the breaches; the second Adam aspired to quicken what Adam killed. He hath 'slain the enmity,' and cancelled the hand-writing that was against us, and so made peace by the blood of his cross; and then, having removed all that out of the way, he comes and calls us unto the fellowship which we were ordained unto from our creation. We who are rebels, are called to be friends; 'I call you not servants, but friends.' It is a wonder that the creature should be called a friend of God; but, O great wonder, that the rebel should be called a friend! And yet that is not all. We are called to a nearer union,—to be the sons of God; this is our privilege, John i. 12. This is a great part of our fellowship with the Father and his Son; we are the Father's children, and the Son's brethren; 'and if children, then heirs, heirs of God;' and if brethren, then co-heirs with Christ, Rom. viii. 17.

Thus the union is begun again in Christ; but as long as sin dwells in our mortal bodies, it is not perfect, there is always some separation and some enmity in our hearts; and so there is neither full seeing of God, for 'we know but in part,' and we see 'darkly,' nor full enjoying of God, for we are 'saved by hope,' and we 'live by faith, and not by sight.' But this is begun which is the seed of eternal communion; we are here partakers of the divine nature. Now then it must aspire unto a more perfect union with God whose image it is. And therefore the soul of a believer is here still in motion towards God as his element. There is here an union in affection, but not completed in fruition,—*affectu non effectu.* The soul pants after God,—'Whom have I in heaven or earth but thee? My flesh and my heart faileth,' &c. A believing soul looks upon God as its only portion,—accounts nothing misery but to be separated from him, and nothing blessedness but to be one with him. This is the loadstone of their affections and desires; the centre which they move towards, and in which they will rest. It is true, indeed, that oftentimes our heart and our flesh faileth us, and we become ignorant and brutish. Our affections cleave to the earth, and temptations with their violence turn our souls towards another end than God. As there is nothing more easily moved and turned wrong than the needle that is touched with the adamant, yet it settles not in such a posture, it recovers itself and rests never till it look towards the north, and then it is fixed,—even so, temptations and the corruptions and infirmities of our hearts disturb our spirits easily, and wind them about from the Lord, towards any other thing; but yet we are continuing with him, and he keeps us with his right hand; and therefore though we may be moved, yet we shall not be greatly commoved; we may fall, but we shall rise again. He is 'the strength of our heart,' and therefore he will turn our heart about again, and fix it upon its own portion. Our union here consists more in his holding of us by his power, than our taking hold of him by faith. Power and good-will encamp about both faith and the soul: 'We are kept by his power through faith,' 1 Pet. i. 5. And thus he will guide the soul, and still be drawing it nearer to him, from itself, and from sin, and from the world, till he 'receive us into glory,' and until we be one as with the Father and the Son,—'He in us and we in him, that we may be made perfect in one,' as it is in the words read.

This is strange. A greater unity and fuller enjoyment, a more perfect fellowship, than ever Adam in his innocency would have been capable of! What soul can conceive it? what tongue express it? None can: for it is that which 'eye hath not seen, nor ear heard, neither hath it entered into man's heart to conceive.' We must suspend the knowledge of it till we have experience of it. Let us now believe it, and then we shall find it. There is a mutual inhabitation which is wonderful. Persons that dwell one *with* another have much society and fellowship; but to dwell one *in* another is a strange thing,—'I in them, and they in me;' and therefore God is often said to dwell in us, and we to dwell in him. But that which makes it of all most wonderful and incomprehensible is that glorious unity and communion between the Father and the Son, which it is made an emblem of: 'As thou, Father, art in me, and I in thee, that they also may be one in us.' Can you conceive that unity of the Trinity? Can you imagine that reciprocal inhabitation,—that mutual communion between the Father and the Son? No: it hath not entered into the heart to conceive it! Only thus much we know, that it is most perfect, it is most glorious; and so much we may apprehend of this unity of the saints with God. O! love is an uniting and transforming thing. 'God is love, and he that dwelleth in love dwelleth in God, and God in him.' He dwelleth in us by love; this makes him work in us, and shine upon us. Love hath drawn him down from his seat of majesty, to visit poor cottages of sinners, Isa. lxvi. 1, 2; and xlvi. 3, 4. And it is that love of God reflecting upon our souls that carries the soul upward to him, to live in him, and walk with him. O how doth it constrain a soul to 'live to him,' and draw it from itself! 2 Cor. v. 15. Then the more unity with God, the more separation from ourselves and the world; the nearer God the farther from ourselves; and the farther from ourselves the more happy; and the more unity with God, the more unity among ourselves, among the brethren of our family. Because here we are not fully one with our Father, therefore there are many differences between us and our brethren; because we are not one perfectly in him, therefore we are not one, as he and the Father are one. But when he shall be in us, and we in him, as the Father is in the Son, and the Son in the Father, then shall we be one among ourselves, then shall we meet in the unity of the faith, into a perfect man, 'into the measure of the stature of the fulness of Christ,' Eph. iv. 13. Christ is the uniting principle: While the saints are not wholly one, *uni tertio*, they cannot be perfectly one *inter se*, among themselves. Consider this, I beseech you. Christ's union with the Father is the foundation of our union to God, and our union among ourselves. This is comfortable; the ground of it is laid already. Now it is not simply the unity of the Father and the Son in essence that is here meant; for what shadow and resemblance can be in the world of such an incomprehensible mystery? But it is certainly the union and communion of God with Christ Jesus as mediator, as the head of 'the church which is his body.' Therefore seeing the Father is so wonderfully well-pleased and one with Christ, his well-beloved Son and messenger of the covenant, and chief party contracting in our name, he is, by virtue of this, one with us, who are his seed and members. And therefore, the members should grow up in 'the head Christ, from whom the whole body maketh increase,' 'according to the effectual working [of the Spirit] in it,' Eph. v. 15, 16. Now, if the union between the Father and Christ our head cannot be dissolved, and cannot be barren and unfruitful, then certainly the Spirit of the Father, which is given to Christ beyond measure, must effectually work in every member, till it bring them to 'the unity of the faith,' and, 'to the measure of the perfect man, which is the fulness of Christ.' So then every believing soul is one with the Father as Christ is one, because he is the head and they the members; and the day is coming that all the members shall be perfectly united to the head Christ, and grow up to the perfect man, which is 'the stature of Christ's fulness.' 'And then shall we all be made perfect in one:' we shall be one as he is one; because he and we are one perfect man, head and members.

Now, to what purpose is all this spoken? I fear, it doth not stir up in our souls a desire after such a blessed life. Whose heart would not be moved at the sound of such words? 'Our fellowship is with the Father and with his Son.' 'We are made perfect, he in us, and we in him.' Certainly, that soul is void of the life of God that doth not find some sparkle of holy ambition kindled within, after such a glorious and blessed condition! But these things savour not, and taste not to the most part; 'the natural man knoweth them not, for they are spiritually discerned.' How lamentable is it, that Christ is come to restore us to our lost blessedness, and yet no man almost considers it or lays it to heart! O how miserable,—twice miserable—is that soul that doth not draw near to God in Christ, when God hath come so near to us in Christ; that goes a-whoring after the lust of the eyes and flesh, and after the imaginations of their own heart, and will not be guided by Christ, the way and life, to glory! 'Thou shalt destroy them, O Lord,' Psal. lxxiii. 27. All men are afar off from God, from the womb: behold, we may have access to God in Christ. Wo to them that are yet afar off, and will not draw near: 'they shall all perish!' I exhort you to consider what you are doing; the most part of you are going away from God; you were born far off, and you will yet go farther; know what you will meet with in that way,—destruction!

You have never yet asked in earnest, For what purpose you came into the world? What wonder ye wander and walk at random, seeing ye have not proposed to yourselves any certain scope and aim! It is great folly; you would not be so foolish in any petty business; but O how foolish men are in the main business! 'The light of the body is the eye;' if that be not light, 'the whole body is full of darkness.' If your intention be once right established, all your course will be orderly; but if you be dark and blind in this point, and have not considered it, you cannot walk in the light, your whole way is darkness. The right consideration of the great end would shine unto you, and direct your way. But while you have not proposed this end unto yourselves—the enjoyment of God—you must spend your time, either in doing nothing to that purpose, or doing contrary to it. All your other lawful business, your callings and occupations, are but in the by; they are not the end, nor the way, but you make them your only business; they are altogether impertinent to this end. And the rest of your walking, in lusts and ignorance, is not only impertinent, but inconsistent with it and contrary to it. If you think that you have this before your eyes, to enjoy God,—I pray you look upon the way you choose. Is your drunkenness, your swearing, your uncleanness, your contentions and railings, and such works of the flesh,—are these the way to enjoy God? Shall not these separate between God and you? Is your eating and drinking, sleeping as beasts, and labouring in your callings,—are these all the means you use to enjoy God? Be not deceived; you who draw not near God by prayer often in secret, and by faith in his Son Christ, as lost miserable sinners, to be saved and reconciled by him, you have no fellowship with him, and you shall not enjoy him afterward! You whose hearts are given to your covetousness, who have many lovers and idols besides him, you cannot say, Whom have I besides Thee in earth? No; you have many other things besides God. You can have nothing of God, except ye make him all to you,—unless you have him alone. 'My undefiled is One,' Cant. vi. 9. He must be alone, for 'his glory he will not give to another.' If you divide your affections, and pretend to give him part, and your lusts another part, you may be doing so, but he will not divide his glory so, he will give no part of it to any other thing. But as for those souls that come to him and see their misery without him, O know how good it is! It is not only good, but best, yea only good; it is *bonum*, and it is *optimum;* yea, it is *unicum.* 'There is none good, save one, even God;' and there is nothing good for us but this one, to be near God, and so near, that we may be one,—one spirit with the Lord,—'for he that is joined to the Lord is one spirit.' Rejoice in your portion, and long for the possession of it. Let all your meditations and affections and conversation proclaim this, 'Whom have I in heaven but thee? and there is none in the earth whom I desire besides thee.' And certainly he shall guide you to the end, and receive you into glory. Then you shall rest from your labours, because you shall dwell in him, and enjoy that which you longed and laboured for. Let the consideration of that end unite the hearts of Christians here. O what an absurd thing is it, that those who shall lodge together at night, and be made 'perfect in one,' should not only go contrary ways, but have contrary minds and affections!

Lecture III.

THE AUTHORITY AND UTILITY OF THE SCRIPTURES.

2 Tim. iii. 16. "*All scripture is given by inspiration of God, and is profitable for doctrine, for reproof, for correction, for instruction in righteousness.*"

We told you that there was nothing more necessary to know than what our end is, and what the way is that leads to that end. We see the most part of men walking at random,—running an uncertain race,—because they do not propose unto themselves a certain scope to aim at, and whither to direct their whole course. According to men's particular inclinations and humours so do the purposes and designs of men vary; and often do the purposes of one man change, according to the circumstances of time and his condition in the world. We see all men almost running cross one to another. One drives at the satisfaction of his lust by pleasure; another fancies a great felicity in honour; a third in getting riches; and thus men divide themselves; whereas, if it were true happiness that all were seeking, they would all go one way towards one end. If men be not in the right way, the faster they seem to move toward the mark, the farther they go from it. Wandering from the right way, (suppose men intend well) will put them farther from that which they intend. *Si via in contrarium ducat, ipsa velocitas majoris intervalli causa est.* Therefore it concerns us all most deeply to be acquainted with the true path of blessedness; for if we once mistake, the more we do, the swifter we move, the more distant we are from it indeed. And there is the more need, because there are so many by-paths that lead to destruction. What say I? By-paths! No; highways, beaten paths, that the multitude of men walk in, and never challenge, nor will endure to be challenged as if they were in an error! In other journeys, men keep the plain highway, and are afraid of any secret by-way, lest it lead them wrong: *At hic, via quæque tritissima maxime decipit.* Here the high-pathed way leads wrong, and O, far wrong!—to hell. This is the meaning of Christ's sermon, "Enter in at the strait gate, but walk not in the broad way where many walk, for it leads to destruction." Therefore I would have this persuasion once begotten in your souls, that the course of this world,—the way of the most part of men,—is dangerous, is damnable. O consider whither the way will lead you, before you go farther! Do not think it a folly to stand still now, and examine it, when you have gone on so long in their company. Stand, I say, and consider! Be not ignorant as beasts, that know no other things than to follow the drove; *quæ pergunt, non quo eundum est, sed quo itur;* they follow not whither they ought to go, but whither most go. You are men, and have reasonable souls within you; therefore I beseech you, be not composed and fashioned according to custom and example, that is, brutish, but according to some inward knowledge and reason. Retire once from the multitude, and ask in earnest at God, What is the way? Him that fears him he will teach the way that he should choose. The way to his blessed end is very strait, very difficult; you must have a guide in it,—you must have a lamp and a light in it,—else you cannot but go wrong.

The principles of reason within us are too dark and dim; they will never lead us through the pits and snares in the way. These indeed shined so brightly in Adam that he needed no light without him, no voice about him; but sin hath extinguished it much; and there remains nothing but some little spunk or sparkle, under the ashes of much corruption, that is but insufficient in itself, and is often more blinded and darkened by lusts. So that if it were never so much refined—as it was in many heathens—yet it is but the blind leading the blind, and both must fall into the ditch. Our end is high and divine,—to glorify God and to enjoy him; therefore our reason *caligat ad suprema;* it can no more steadfastly behold that glorious end, and move towards it, than our weak eyes can behold the sun. Our eyes can look downward upon the earth, but not upward to the heavens: so we have some remnant of reason in us, that hath some petty and poor ability for matters of little moment, as the things of this life; but if we once look upward to the glory of God, or eternal happiness, our eyes are dazzled, our reason confounded, we cannot steadfastly behold it, Eph. iv. 18; 2 Cor. iii. 13, 14.

Therefore the Lord hath been pleased to give us the scriptures, which may be 'a lamp unto our feet,' and a guide unto our way; whereunto we shall do well 'to take heed, as unto [a candle or] a light that shineth in a dark place, until the day dawn, 2 Peter i. 19. These are 'able to make us wise unto salvation.' Let us hear what Paul speaks to Timothy, 2 Tim. iii. 16, 'All scripture is given by inspiration of God,' &c.: where you have two points of high concernment,—the authority of the scriptures, and their utility. Their authority, for they are given by divine inspiration; their utility, for they are 'profitable for doctrine,' &c., and can make us perfect, and well 'furnished to every good work.'

The authority of it is in a peculiar way divine. 'Of him and through him are all things.' All writings of men, according to the truth of the scriptures, have some divinity in them, inasmuch as they have of truth, which is a divine thing. Yet the holy scriptures are by way of excellency attributed to God, for they are immediately inspired of God. Therefore Peter saith that 'the scriptures came not in old time by the will of man, but holy men spake as they were moved by the Holy Ghost,' 2 Peter i. 21. God by his Spirit, as it were, acted the part of the soul in the prophets and apostles; and they did no more but utter what the Spirit conceived. The Holy Ghost inspired the matter and the words, and they were but tongues and pens to speak and write it unto the people; there needed no debate, no search in their own minds for the truth, no inquisition for light; but light shined upon their souls so brightly, so convincingly, that it put it beyond all question that it was the mind and voice of God. You need not ask How they did know that their dreams or visions were indeed from the Lord; and that they did not frame any imagination in their own hearts, and taught it for his word, as many did? I say, you need no more ask that, than ask, How shall a man see light, or know the sunshine? Light makes itself manifest, and all other things. It is seen by its own brightness. Even so the holy men of God needed not any mark or sign to know the Spirit's voice; his revelation needed not the light of any other thing, it was light itself; it would certainly overpower the soul and mind, and leave no place of doubting. God, who cannot be deceived, and can deceive no man, hath delivered us this doctrine. O! with what reverence shall we receive it, as if we heard the Lord from heaven speak! If you ask, How you shall be persuaded that the scriptures are the word of God,—his very mind opened to men and made legible. Truly there are some things cannot be well proved, not because they are doubtful, but because they are clear of themselves, and beyond all doubt and exception. Principles of arts must not be proved, but supposed, till you find by trial and experience afterward that they were indeed really true. There are, no question, such characters of divinity and majesty imprinted in the very scriptures themselves, that whosoever hath the eyes of his understanding opened, though he run he may read them, and find God in them. What majesty is in the very simplicity and plainness of the scriptures! They do not labour to please men's ears, and adorn the matter with the curious garments of words and phrases; but represent the very matter itself to the soul, as that which in itself is worthy of all acceptation, and needs no human eloquence to commend it. Painting doth spoil native beauty. External ornaments would disfigure some things that are of themselves proportioned and lovely; therefore the Lord chooses a plain and simple style which is 'foolishness' to the world; but in these swaddling-clothes of the scriptures, and this poor cottage, the child Jesus, the Lord of heaven and earth, is contained. There is a jewel of the mysterious wisdom of God, and man's eternal blessedness, in this mineral. What glorious and astonishing humility is here! What humble and homely glory and majesty also! He is most high, and yet none so lowly. What excellent consent and harmony of many writers in such distant times! Wonder at it. All speak one thing to one purpose,—to bring men to God, to abase all glory, and exalt him alone. Must it not be one spirit that hath quickened all these, and breathes in them all this one heavenly song, of 'glory to God on high, and good-will towards men?' Other writers will reason these things with you to convince you and persuade you; and many think them more profound and deep for that reason, and do despise the baseness of the scriptures; but to them whose eyes are opened, the majesty and authority of God commanding and asserting and testifying to them, is more convincing, from its own bare assertion, than all human reason.

Although there be much light in the scriptures to guide men's way to God's glory and their own happiness, yet it will all be to small purpose if 'the eyes of our understanding' be darkened and blinded. If you shall surround a man with day-light, except he open his eyes, he cannot see. The scriptures are a clear sun of life and righteousness; but the blind soul encompassed with that light is nothing the wiser, but thinks the lamp of the word shines not, because it sees not; it hath its own dungeon within it. Therefore the Spirit of God must open the eyes of the blind, and enlighten the eyes of the understanding, that the soul may see wonderful things in God's law, Psal. cxix. 5, 18. The light may shine in the darkness, but 'the darkness comprehendeth it not,' John i. 5. I wonder not that the most part of men can see no beauty, no majesty, no excellency in the holy scriptures to allure them, because they are natural, and have not the Spirit of God, and so cannot know these things 'for they are spiritually discerned,' 1 Cor. ii. 14: Therefore as the inspiration of God did conceive this writing at first, and preached this doctrine unto the world, so there can no soul understand it, or profit by it, but by the inspiration of the Almighty. 'Verily there is a spirit in man, and the inspiration of the Almighty giveth him understanding,' saith Job. When the Spirit comes into the soul to engrave the characters of that law and truth into the heart which were once engraven on tables of stone, and not written with pen and ink; then the Spirit of Christ Jesus writes over and transcribes the doctrine of the gospel on 'the fleshly tables of the heart,'—draws the lineaments of that faith and love preached in the word upon the soul; then the soul is 'the epistle of Christ,' 'written not with [pen and] ink, but with the Spirit of the living

God,' 2 Cor. iii. 3. And then the soul is manifestly declared to be such, when that which is impressed on the heart is expressed in the outward man in walking, that it may be 'read of all men.' Now, the soul having thus received the image of the scriptures on it, understands the Spirit's voice in them, and sees the truth and divinity of them. The eye must receive some species and likeness of the object before it see it; it must be made like to the object ere it can behold it,—*Intelligens in actu fit ipsum intelligibile:* so the soul must have some inspiration of the Holy Ghost, before it can believe with the heart the inspired scriptures.

Now, for the utility and profit of the scriptures, who can speak of it according to its worth? Some things may be over-commended,—nay, all things but this one,—God speaking in his word to mankind. Many titles are given to human writings; some are called accurate, some subtile, some ingenious, and some profound and deep, some plain, some learned; but call them what they please, the scripture may vindicate to itself these two titles as its own prerogative,—holy and profitable. The best speaker in the world in many words cannot want sin; the best writer hath some dross and refuse; but here, all is holy, all is profitable. Many books are to no purpose but to feed and inflame men's lusts; many serve for nothing but to spend and drive over the time, without thought; most part are good for nothing but to burden and over-weary the world, to put them in a fancy of knowledge which they have not; many serve for this only, to nourish men's curiosity and vain imaginations, and contentions about words and notions; but here is a book profitable,—all profitable. If you do not yet profit by it, you can have no pleasure in it; it is only ordained for soul's profiting, not for pleasing your fancy, not for matter of curious speculation, not for contention and strife about the interpretation of it. Many books have nothing in them, but specious titles to commend them; they do nothing less than what they promise; they have a large and fair entry, which leads only into a poor cottage; but the scriptures have no hyperbolic and superlative styles to allure men; they hold out a plain and common gate and entry which will undoubtedly lead to a pleasant palace; others *et prodesse volunt et delectare,* but these certainly *et prodesse volunt et possunt,* —they both can profit you and will profit you. I wish that souls would read the scriptures as profitable scriptures, with the intention to profit. If you do not read with such a purpose, you read not the scriptures of God, they become as another book unto you. But what are they profitable for? For doctrine, and a divine doctrine; a doctrine of life and happiness. It is the great promise of the new covenant, 'You shall be all taught of God.' The scriptures can make a man learned and wise, learned to salvation; it is foolishness to the world, 'but the world through wisdom know not God.' Alas! what then do they know? Is there any besides God? And is there any knowledge besides the knowledge of God? You have a poor petty wisdom among you to gather riches and manage your business. Others have a poor imaginary wisdom that they call learning; and generally people think, to pray to God is but a paper-skill, a little book-craft; they think the knowledge of God is nothing else but to learn to read the Bible. Alas! mistake not; it is another thing to know God. The doctrine of Jesus Christ written on the heart is a deep profound learning; and the poor, simple, rudest people, may by the Spirit's teaching become wiser than their ancients, than their ministers. O, it is an excellent point of learning, to know how to be saved! What is it, I pray you, to know the course of the heavens,—to number the orbs, and the stars in them,—to measure their circumference,—to reckon their motions,—and yet not to know him that sits on the circle of them, and not know how to inhabit and dwell there? If you would seek unto God, and seek eyes opened to behold the mystery of the word, you would become wiser than your pastors; you would learn from the Spirit to pray better; you would find the way to heaven better than they can teach you, or walk in it.

Then, it is 'profitable for reproof and correction.' It contains no doctrine very pleasant to men's natural humours; but it is indeed most pleasant to a right and ordered taste. You know, the distemper of the eye, or the perverting of the taste, will misrepresent pleasant things, and sweet things to the senses, and make them appear ill-savoured and bitter. But, I say, to a discerning spirit there is nothing so sweet, so comely. 'I have seen an end of all perfection,' but none of thy law. 'Thy word is sweeter to me than the honey, or the honey-comb.' If a soul be prepossessed with the love of the world, and the lusts of the world, it cannot savour and taste of them; that vicious quality in the mind will make the pleasant gospel unpleasant. 'I piped unto you, and ye have not danced.' But however, the scriptures are then most profitable when they are least pleasant to our corruptions; and, therefore, it is an absolute and entire piece. *Et prodesse volunt et delectare. Omne tulit punctum, qui miscuit utile dulci.* There are sharp reproofs, and sad corrections of his holy law, which must make way for the pleasant and sweet gospel. There is a reproof of life,—a wounding before healing,—that whoso refuse them, despise their own soul, but 'the ear that heareth them abideth among the wise,' Prov. xv. 31, 32. Woe unto that soul that correction or reproof or threatening is grievous unto; 'he shall die,' Prov. xv. 10; 'he is brutish,' Prov. xii. 1. There is a generation of men that can endure to hear nothing but gospel-promises; that cry out against all reproving of sins, and preaching of God's wrath against unbelieving sinners, as legal, and meddling with other men's matters, especially if they reprove the sins of rulers, their public state enormities; as if the whole word of God were not profitable; as if reproofs were not as wholesome as consolations; as if threatenings did not contribute to make men flee from the wrath to come into a city of refuge. Let such persons read their own character out of wise Solomon, 'Correction is grievous to them that forsake the way.' 'Rebuke a wise man, and he will love thee; give instruction to a wise man, and he will be yet wiser,' Prov. ix. 8, 9. If we were pleasers of men, then were we not the servants of Jesus Christ; let us strive to profit men, but not to please them. Peace, peace, which men's own hearts fancy, would please them; but it were better for them to be awakened out of that dream, by reproof, by correction; and he that will do so, shall 'find more favour of him afterwards, than he that flattereth with the tongue,' Prov. xxviii. 23.

Well then, let this be established in your hearts as the foundation of all true religion, that the scriptures are the word of the eternal God, and that they contain a perfect and exact rule both of glorifying God and of the way to enjoy him. They can make you perfect to every good work. I shall say no more on this; but beseech you, as you love your own souls, be acquainting yourselves with them. You will hear, in these days, of men pretending to more divine and spiritual discoveries and revelations than the scriptures contain: but, my brethren, these can make you 'wise to salvation,' these can make you 'perfect to every good work.' Then, what needs more? All that is besides salvation, and beyond perfection, count it superfluous and vain, if not worse, if not diabolical. Let others be wise to their own destruction,—let them establish their own imaginations for the word of God, and rule of their faith,—but hold you fast what you have received, and 'contend earnestly' for it. Add nothing, and diminish nothing; let this lamp shine 'till the day dawn,'—till the morning of the resurrection; and walk ye in the light of it, and do not kindle any other sparkles, else ye shall lie down in the grave in sorrow, and rise in sorrow. Take the word of God as the only rule, and the perfect rule,—a rule for all your actions, civil, natural, and religious; for all must be done to his glory, and his word teacheth how to attain to that end. Let not your imaginations, let not others' example, let not the preaching of men, let not the conclusions and acts of Assemblies be your rule, but in as far as you find them agreeing with the perfect rule of God's holy word. All other rules are *regulæ regulatæ;* they are but like publications and intimations of the rule itself. Ordinances of assemblies are but like the herald-promulgation of the king's statute and law; if it vary in any thing from his intention, it is not valid and binding. I beseech you, take the scriptures for the rule of your walking, or else you will wander; the scripture is *regula regulans,* a ruling rule. If you be not acquainted with it, you must follow the opinions or examples of other men; and what if they lead you unto destruction?

Lecture IV.

THE SCRIPTURES REVEAL ETERNAL LIFE THROUGH JESUS CHRIST.

JOHN v. 39. "*Search the scriptures, for in them ye think ye have eternal life, and they are they which testify of me.*" EPH. ii. 20. "*And are built upon the foundation of the apostles and prophets.*"

As in darkness there is need of a lantern without and the light of the eyes within,—for neither can we see in darkness without some lamp, though we have never so good eyes, nor yet see without eyes, though in never so clear a sunshine,—so there is absolute need for the guiding of our feet in the dangerous and dark paths to eternal life (that are full of pits and snares,) of the lamp, or word written or preached, without us, and the illumination of the Holy Ghost within us. These are conjoined, Isa. lix. 21, 'This is my covenant:' 'The Spirit that is upon thee, and my words which I have put in thy mouth, will not depart out of thy mouth, nor out of the mouth of thy seed,' &c. There are words without, and there must needs be a spirit within, which makes us to behold the truth and grace contained in these words. There is a law written without, with pen and ink, and there is a law written within, upon the heart, with the Spirit of the living God. The law without is the pattern and exact copy; the law within, is the transcript or the image of God upon the heart, framed and fashioned according to the similitude of it, 2 Cor. iii. 3; Heb. viii. 10. So then, there needs be no more question about the divine authority of the scriptures, among those who have their senses exercised to discern between good and ill, than among men who see and taste, concerning light and darkness, sweet and bitter. The persuasion of a Christian is fetched deeper than the reasons of men. Their faith is 'the evidence of things not seen.' It is an eye, a supernatural eye, whereby a soul beholds that majesty and excellency of God shining in the word, which, though it shine about the rest of the world, yet 'tis not seen, because they cannot know it nor discern it. Wonder not that the multitude of men cannot believe the report that is made; that there are few who find any such excellency and sweetness in the gospel as is reported, because saith Isaiah, liii. 1, the arm of 'the Lord is not revealed to them.' The hand of God must first write on their heart, ere they understand the writings of the scriptures; his arm must create an eye in their souls, an internal light, before it can behold that glorious brightness of God shining in the word. The word is God's testimony of himself, of his grace and mercy, and good-will to mankind. Now no man can receive this testimony, unless it be sealed and confirmed by the Holy Ghost into the heart: saith Peter, 'We are his witnesses of these things, and so is also the Holy Ghost whom God hath given to them that obey him,' Acts v. 32. The word witnesses to the ear, and the Spirit testifieth to our spirits, the truth and worth of that; and therefore the Spirit is a seal and a witness. The word is the Lord's voice to his own children; bastards cannot know it, 'but my sheep know my voice,' John x. 4, 16. You know no difference between the bleating of one sheep from another, but the poor lambs know their mother's voice; there is a secret instinct of nature that is more powerful than many marks and signs: even so those who are begotten of God know his voice,—they discern that in it which all the world that hear it cannot discern,—there is a sympathy between their souls and that living word. That word is the immortal seed they are begotten of; and there is a natural instinct to love that, and to meditate in it; such an inclination to it, as in new-born babes to the breasts; so the children of God 'do desire the sincere milk of the word, that they may grow thereby,' as they were born of it, 1 Pet. ii. 2. In those scriptures which we read in your audience, you have something of their excellency, and our duty. There is a rich jewel in them, a precious pearl in that field, even Jesus Christ, and in him eternal life; and therefore we ought to search the scriptures for this jewel, to dig in the field for this pearl, the doctrine of the prophets and apostles, as a sure foundation whereupon souls may build their eternal felicity, and the hope of it. Jesus Christ is the very chief stone in that foundation, whereupon the weight of all the saints and all their hope hangs. And therefore we ought to lean the weight of our souls only to this truth of God, and build our faith only upon it, and square our practice only by it.

We shall speak something of the first, that it may be a spur to the second. The Jews had some respective opinion of the word of God; they knew that in them was eternal life; they thought it a doctrine of life and happiness, and so cried up Moses' writings, but they would not believe Christ's words. They erred, not understanding the scriptures, and so set the writings of Moses' law at variance with the preaching of Christ's gospel. What a pitiful mistake was this! They thought they had eternal life in the scriptures, and yet they did not receive nor acknowledge him whom to know was eternal life. Therefore our Lord Jesus sends them back again to the scriptures:—"Go and search them; you think, and you think well, that in them ye may find the way to eternal life; but while you seek it in them you mistake it: these scriptures testify of me, the end of the law, but you cannot behold the end of that ministry, because of the blindness of your hearts, (Rom. x. 3; 2 Cor. iii. 13, 14.) Therefore search again, unfold the ceremonies; I am wrapt in them, and life eternal with me. Dig up the law till you find the bottom of God's purpose in it,—till you find the end of the ministration,—and you shall find me, 'the way, the truth, and life;' and so you shall have that eternal life which now you do but think you have, and are beguiled. While you seek it out of me, in vain you think you have it, for it is not in the scriptures, but because they testify of me, the life and the light of men." May not this now commend the word to us? eternal life is in it. Other writings and discourses may tickle the ears with some pleasing eloquence, but that is vanishing; it is but like a musician's voice. Some may represent some petty and momentary advantage, but how soon shall an end be put to all that? So that within a little time the advantage of all the books of the world shall be gone. The statutes and laws of kings and parliaments can reach no further than some temporal reward or punishment; their highest pain is the killing of this body; their highest reward is some evanishing and fading honour, or perishing riches: but 'he showeth his word and judgments unto us, and hath not dealt so with any nation,' Psal. cxlvii. 19, 20. And no nation under the whole heaven hath such laws and ordinances; eternal life and eternal death is wrapt up in them. These are rewards and punishments suitable to the majesty and magnificence of the eternal Lawgiver. Consider, I beseech you, what is folded up here,—the scriptures show the path of life; life is of all things the most excellent, and comes nearest the blessed being of God. When we say *life*, we understand a blessed life, that only deserves the name. Now this we have lost in Adam. Death is passed upon all men, but that death is not the worst: 'tis but a consequence of a soul-death. The immortal soul—whose life consisteth in communion with God, and peace with him—is separated from him by sin, and so killed, when it is cut off from the fountain of life; what a life can it have more, than a beam that is cut off by the intervention of a dark body from the sun. Now then, what a blessed doctrine must it be that brings to light, life and immortality? especially when we have so miserably lost it, and involved our souls into an eternal death. Life is precious in itself, but much more precious to one condemned to die,—to be caught out of the paws of the lion,—to be brought back from the gibbet. O how will that commend the favour of a little more time in the world! But then if we knew what an eternal misery we are involved into, and stand under a sentence binding us over to such an inconceivable and insupportable punishment as is the curse and wrath of God; O how precious an esteem would souls have of the scriptures, how would they be sweet unto their soul, because they show unto us a way of escaping that pit of misery, and a way of attaining eternal blessedness as satisfying and glorious as the misery would have been vexing and tormenting! O that ye would once lay these in the balance together,—this present life and life eternal! Know ye not that your souls are created for eternity; that they will eternally survive all these present things? Now how do ye imagine they shall live after this life? Your thoughts and projects and designs are confined within the poor narrow bounds of your time. When you die, in that day your thoughts shall perish. All your imaginations and purposes and providences shall have an end then ; they reach no farther than that time. And if you should wholly perish too, it were not so much matter. But for all your purposes and projects to come to an end, when you are but beginning to live, and enter eternity, that is lamentable indeed ! Therefore I say, consider what ye are doing, weigh these in a balance,—eternal life and the persent life ; if there were no more difference but the continuance of the one, and the shortness of the other,—that the world's standing is but as one day, one moment to eternity,—that ought to preponderate in your souls. Do we not here flee away as a shadow upon the mountains ? Are we not as a vapour that ascends, and for a little time appears a solid body, and then presently vanisheth ? Do we not come all into the stage of the world, as for an hour, to act our part and be gone ; now then, what is this to endless eternity ? When you have continued as long as since the world began, you are no nearer the end of it. Ought not that estate then to be most in your eyes, how to lay up a foundation for the time to come ? But then, compare the misery and the vexation of this life with the glory and felicity of this eternal life. What are our days ? But few and full of trouble. Or, if you will, take the most blessed estate you have seen and heard of in this world, of kings and rich men, and help all the defects of it by your imaginations ; suppose unto yourselves the height and pitch of glory and abundance and power that is attainable on earth ; and when your fancy hath busked up such a felicity, compare it with an eternal life : O how will that vanish out of your imaginations ! If so be you know any thing of the life to come, you will even think that an odious comparison,—you will think all that earthly felicity but light as vanity, 'every man at his best estate is altogether vanity.' Eternal life will weigh down eternally, 2 Cor. iv. 17, 18. O but it hath an exceeding weight in itself,—one moment of it, one hour's possession and taste of it ! but then what shall the endless endurance of it add to its weight ? Now there are many that presume they have a right to eternal life, as the Jews did. You think, saith he, that you have it ; you think well, that you think 'tis only to be found in the scriptures ; but you vainly think that you have found it in them : and there is this reason for it, because 'you will not come to me that you might have life,' John v. 40. If you did understand the true meaning of the scriptures, and did not rest on the outward letter and ordinances, you would receive the testimony that the scriptures give of me. But now you hear not me, the Father's substantial Word, therefore 'ye have not his word abiding in you,' ver. 38. There was nothing more general among that people, than a vain carnal confidence and presumption of being God's people, and having interest in the promise of life eternal, as it is this day in the visible church. There is a multitude that are Christians only in the letter, and not in the spirit, that would never admit any question concerning this great matter of having eternal life ; and so by not questioning it, they come to think they have it, and by degrees their conjectures and thoughts about this ariseth to the stability of some feigned and strong persuasion of it. In the Old Testament the Lord strikes at the root of their persuasions, by discovering unto them how vain a thing it was, and how abominable it was before him, to have an external profession of being his people, and to glory in external ordinances and privileges, and yet to neglect altogether the purging of their hearts and consciences from lust and idol-sins, and to make no conscience of walking righteously towards men. Their profession was contradicted by their practice, 'Will ye steal, murder, and commit adultery, and yet come and stand in my house ?' Jer. vii. 9, 10. Doth not that say as much as if I had given you liberty to do all these abominations ? Even so it is this day ; the most part have no more of Christianity but a name. They have some outward privileges of baptism and hearing the word ; and, it may be, have a form of knowledge, and a form of worship ; but in the meantime they are not baptized in heart,—they are in all their conversation even conformed to the heathen world,—they hate personal reformation, and think it too precise and needless. Now, I say, such are many of you, and yet you would not take well to have it questioned whether ye shall be partakers of eternal life. You think you are wronged when that is called in question. Oh that it were beyond all question indeed ! But know assuredly that you are but Christians in the letter,—in the flesh and not in the spirit. Many of you have not so much as 'a form of knowledge'—have not so much as the letter of religion. You have heard some names in the preaching often repeated,—as Christ, and God, and faith, and heaven, and hell,—and you know no more of these but the name. You consider not and meditate not on them; and though you know the truth of the word, yet the word abideth not nor dwelleth in you. You have it in your mouth, you have it in your mind or understanding, but it is not received in love, it doth not dwell in the heart. 'Let the word of Christ dwell in you richly,' Col. iii. 16. You have it imprisoned in your minds, and shut up in a corner where it is useless, and can do no more but witness against you, and scarce that. As the Gentiles incarcerated and detained the truth of God, written by nature within them, in unrighteousness, (Rom. i. 18,) so do many of you detain the knowledge of his word in unrighteousness. It hath no place in the heart, gets no liberty and freedom to walk through the affections, and so to order the conversation of men; and therefore the most part of men do but fancy to themselves an interest and right to eternal life. You think it, and do but think it; it is but a strong imagination, that hath no strength from the grounds of it, no stability from any evidence or promise, but merely from itself; or it is but a light and vain conjecture that hath no strength in it because there is no question or doubts admitted which may try the strength of it. But then I suppose that a man could attain some answerable walking, that he had not only a form of knowledge, but some reality of practice, some inward heat of affection and zeal for God and godliness, yet there is one thing that he wants, and if it be wanting will spoil all; and it is this, which Christ reproves in the Jews, 'you will not come to me to have life;' the scriptures testify of me, but you receive not their testimony. Suppose a man had as much equity and justice towards men, piety towards God, and sobriety towards himself, as can be found amongst the best of men; let him be a diligent reader of the scriptures, let him love them, and meditate on them day and night; yet if he do not come out of himself, and leave all his own righteousness as dung behind him, that he may be found in Jesus Christ, he hath no life, he cannot have any right to life eternal. You may think this is a strange assertion, that if a man had the righteousness and holiness of an angel, yet he could not be saved without denying all that, and fleeing to Christ as an ungodly man; and you may think it as strange a supposal, that any person that reads the scriptures, and walks righteously, and hath a zeal towards God, yet are such as will not come to Christ and will not hear him whom the Lord hath sent.

But the first is the very substance of the gospel. 'There is none other name whereby men may be saved,' but by Jesus Christ,' Acts iv. 12. Life eternal is all within him. All the treasures of grace and wisdom and knowledge are seated in him, Col. i. 19; ii. 3. All the light of life and salvation is embodied in this sun of righteousness, since the eclipse of man's felicity in the garden. Adam was a living soul, but he lost his own life, and killed his posterity. Christ Jesus, the second common man in the world, is a quickening spirit. He hath not only life in himself, but he gives it more abundantly; and therefore you have it so often repeated in John, who was the disciple most acquainted with Christ, 'in him was life; and the life was the light of men,' John i. 4. And he is 'the bread of life,' that gives life to the world, John vi. 33, 35. He is 'the resurrection and the life,' xi. 25; and 'the way, the truth, and the life,' xiv. 6. The scriptures do not contain eternal life, but in as far as they lead to him who is life, and whom to know and embrace is eternal life: and therefore, saith he, 'these are they which testify of me.' Man lived immediately in God when he was in innocency; he had life in himself from God; but then he began to live in himself without dependence on God the fountain of life, and this himself being interposed between God and life, it evanished even as a beam by the intervening of any gross body between it and the sun. Now man's light and life being thus eclipsed and cut off, the Lord is pleased to let all fulness dwell in his Son Jesus Christ, and the fulness of the Godhead dwelt in him bodily, Col. ii. 9; that since there was no access immediately to God for life (a flaming fire, and sword of divine justice compassing and guarding the tree of life, lest man should touch it) there might be access to God in a mediator like unto us, that we might come to him, and might have life from God by the intervention of Jesus Christ.

Look then what is in the Holy Scriptures, and you shall find it but a letter of death and ministration of condemnation while it is separated from him. Christ is the very life and spirit of the scriptures, by whose virtue they quicken our souls. If you consider the perfect rule of righteousness in the law, you cannot find life there, because you cannot be conformed unto it; the holiest man offends in every thing, and that holy law being violated in any thing will send thee to hell with a curse. 'Cursed is he that abideth not in all things.' If you look upon the promise of life, 'do this and live;' what comfort can you find in it, except you could find doing in yourselves? And can any man living find such exact obedience as the law requires? There is a mistake among many. They conceive that the Lord cannot but be well-pleased with them if they do what they can. But be not deceived,—the law of God requires perfect doing; it will not compound with thee, and come down in its terms; not one jot of the rigour of it will be remitted. If you cannot do all that is commanded, all you do will not satisfy that promise; therefore thou must be turned over from the promise of life to the curse, and there thou shalt find thy name written. Therefore it is absolutely necessary that Jesus Christ be made under the law, and give obedience in all things, even to the death of the cross, and so be made a curse for us, and sin for us, even he 'who knew no sin.' And thus in him you find the law fulfilled, justice satisfied, and God pleased. In him you find the promise of life indeed established in a better and surer way than was first propounded. You find life by his death, you find life in his doing for you. And again, consider the ceremonial law,—what were all those sacrifices and ceremonies? Did God delight in them? Could he savour their incense and sweet smells, and eat the fat of lambs and be pacified? No, he detests and abhors such abominations! Because that people did stay in the letter, and went no further than the ceremony, he declares that it was as great abomination to him as the offering up of a dog. While they were separated from Jesus Christ, in whom his soul rested and was pacified, they were not expiations, but provocations; they were not propitiations for sin, but abominations in themselves. But take these as the shadow of such a living substance; take them as remembrances of him who was to come, and behold Jesus Christ lying in these swaddling clothes of ceremonies, until the fulness of time should come, that he might be manifested in the flesh, and so you shall find eternal life in those dead beasts, in those dumb ceremonies. If you consider this Lamb of God slain in all these sacrifices, from the beginning of the world, then you present a sweet-smelling savour to God,—then you offer the true propitiation for the sins of the world,—then he will delight more in that sacrifice than all other personal obedience.

But what if I should say, that the gospel itself is a killing letter, and ministration of death, being severed from Christ? I should say nothing amiss, but what Paul speaketh, that his gospel was 'a savour of death' to many. Take the most powerful preaching, the most sweet discourse, the most plain writings of the free grace and salvation in the gospel,—take all the preaching of Jesus Christ himself and his apostles,—and you shall not find life in them, unless ye be led by that Spirit of Christ unto himself, who is 'the resurrection and the life.' It will no more save you than the covenant of works, unless that word abide and dwell in your hearts, to make you believe in him, and embrace him with your souls, whom God hath sent. Suppose you heard all, and heard it gladly, and learned it, and could discourse well upon it, and teach others, yet if you be not driven out of yourselves, out of your own righteousness, as well as sins, and pursued to this city of refuge, Jesus Christ, you have not eternal life. Your knowledge of the truth of the gospel, and your obedience to God's law, will certainly kill you, and as certainly as your ignorance and disobedience, unless you have embraced in your soul that good thing Jesus Christ, contained in these truths, who is the diamond of that golden ring of the scriptures; and unless your soul embrace these promises as soul-saving, as containing the chief good, and 'worthy of all acceptation,' as well as your mind receive these as true and faithful sayings, 1 Tim. i. 15.

Thus ye see Jesus Christ is either the subject of all in the scriptures, or the end of it all. He is the very proper subject of the gospel. Paul knew nothing but Christ crucified in his preaching; and he is the very end and scope 'of the law for righteousness,' Rom. x. 3. All the preaching of a covenant of works, all the curses and threatenings of the Bible, all the rigid exactions of obedience, all come to this one great design; not that we set about such a walking to please God, or do something to pacify him, but that we being concluded under sin and wrath on the one hand, and an impossibility to save ourselves on the other hand, Gal. iii. 22., Rom. v. 20, 21., may be pursued unto Jesus Christ for righteousness and life, who is both able to save us, and ready to welcome us. Therefore the Gospel opens the door of salvation in Christ, the law is behind us with fire and sword, and destruction pursuing us; and all for this end, that sinners may come to him and have life. Thus the law is made the pedagogue of the soul to lead to Christ; Christ is behind us, cursing, condemning, threatening us, and he is before with stretched-out arms ready to receive us, bless us, and save us, inviting, promising, exhorting to have life. Christ is on Mount Sinai, delivering the law with thunders, Acts vii. 38; and he is on the Mount Zion, in the calm voice; he is both upon the mountain of cursings and blessings, and on both doing the part of a mediator, Gal. iii. 19, 20. It is love that is in his heart which made him first cover his countenance with frowns and threats; and it is love that again displays itself in his smiling countenance. Thus souls are enclosed with love pursuing and love receiving; and thus the law, which seems most contrary to the Gospel, testifies of Christ. It gives him this testimony, that except salvation be in him, it is nowhere else. The law says, "It is not in me, seek it not in obedience; I can do nothing but destroy you, if you abide under my jurisdiction." The ceremonies and sacrifices say, "If you can behold the end of this ministry,—if a veil be not upon your hearts, as it was upon Moses' face, (2 Cor. iii. 13.) you may see where it is; it is not in your obedience, but in the death and suffering of the Son of God whom we represent." Then the Gospel takes all these coverings and veils away and gives a plain and open testimony of him: "There is no name under heaven to be saved by, but Christ's." The Old Testament spake by figures and signs, as dumb men do, but the New speaks in plain words, and with open face. Now I say, for all this that there is no salvation but in him, yet many souls,—not only those who live in their gross sins and have no form of godliness, but even the better sort of people that have some 'knowledge' and civility and a kind of 'zeal for God,'—yet they do not 'come to him that they may have life,' they do not 'submit to the righteousness of God,' Rom. x. 2, 3. Here is the march that divides the ways of heaven and hell,—coming to Jesus Christ, and forsaking ourselves. The confidence of these souls is chiefly or only in that little knowledge, or zeal, or profession they have; they do not as really abhor themselves for their own righteousness as for their unrighteousness. They make that the covering of their nakedness and filthiness which is in itself as menstruous and unclean as any thing. It is now the very propension and natural inclination of our hearts, to stand upright in ourselves. Faith bows a soul's back to take on Christ's righteousness; but presumption lifts up a soul upon its own bottom. 'How can ye believe that seek honour one of another?' The engagements of the soul to its own credit or estimation,—the engagements of self-love and self-honour,—do lift up a soul that it cannot submit to God's righteousness, to righteousness in another. And therefore many do dream and think that they have eternal life, who shall awake in the end, and find that it was but a dream, a night-fancy.

Now from all this I would enforce this duty upon your consciences, to 'search the Scriptures' if you think to have eternal life; search them if ye would 'know Christ, whom to know is life eternal;' then again search them, for 'these are they that testify of him.' Searching imports diligence,—much diligence,—it is a serious work; it is not a common seeking of an easy and common thing, but a search and scrutiny for some hidden thing, for some special thing. It is not bare reading of the Scriptures that will answer this duty, except it be diligent and daily reading; and it is not that alone, except the spirit within meditate on them, and by meditation accomplish a diligent search. There is some hidden secret that you must search for that is enclosed within the covering of words and sentences. There is a mystery of wisdom that you must apply your hearts to search out, Eccl. vii. 25. Jesus Christ is the treasure that is hid in this field. O a precious treasure of eternal life! Now then, souls, search into the fields of the Scriptures for him 'as for hid treasure,' Prov. ii.

4. It is not only truth you must seek and buy, and not sell it, but it is life you would search; here is an object that may not only take up your understandings, but satisfy your hearts. Think not you have found all when you have found truth there, and learned it; no, except you have found life there, you have found nothing, you have missed the treasure. If you would profit by the Scriptures, you must bring both your understanding and your affections to them, and depart not till they both return full. If you bring your understanding to seek the truth, you may find truth, but not truly; you may find it, but you are not found of it. You may lead truth captive, and enclose it in a prison of your mind, and encompass it about with a guard of corrupt affections, that it shall have no issue, no outgoing to the rest of your souls and ways, and no influence on them. You may 'know the truth,' but you are not 'known of it,' nor brought into captivity to the obedience of it. The treasure that is hid in the Scriptures is Jesus Christ, whose entire and perfect name is, 'Way, Truth, and Life.' He is a living truth and true life; therefore Christ is the adequate object of the soul, commensurable to all its faculties. He has truth in him to satisfy the mind; and has life and goodness in him to satiate the heart; therefore if thou wouldest find Jesus Christ, bring thy whole soul to seek him, as Paul expresseth it. He is true and faithful, and 'worthy of all acceptation,' then bring thy judgment to find the light of truth, and thy affections to embrace the life of goodness that is in him. Now, as much as ye find of him, so much have ye profited in the Scriptures. If you find commands there which you cannot obey, search again, and you may find strength under that command. Dig a little deeper, and you shall find Jesus the end of an impossible command. And when you have found him, you have found life and strength to obey, and you have found a propitiation and sacrifice for transgressing and not obeying. If you find curses in it, search again, and you shall find Jesus Christ under that, 'made a curse for us;' you shall find him 'the end of the law for righteousness to every one that believes.' When you know all the letter of the Scripture, yet you must search into the spirit of it, that it may be imprinted into your spirits. All you know does you no good but as it is received in love; unless your souls become a 'living epistle,' and the word without be written on the heart, you have found nothing. As for you that cannot read the Scriptures, if it be possible, take that pains to learn to read them. O if you knew what they contain, and whom they bear witness of, you would have little quietness till you could read at least his love-epistles to sinners! And if you cannot learn, be not discouraged; but if your desires within be fervent, your endeavours to hear it read by others will be more earnest. But it is not so much the reading of much of it that profiteth, as the pondering of these things in your hearts, and digesting them by frequent meditation, till they become the food of the soul. This was David's way; and by this he grew to the stature of a tall and well-bodied Christian.

Lecture V.

OF THE SCRIPTURES.

EPH. ii. 20. "*And are built upon the foundation of the apostles and prophets, Jesus Christ himself being the chief corner-stone.*"

BELIEVERS are 'the temple of the living God,' in which he dwells and walks, 2 Cor. vi. 16. Every one of them is a little sanctuary and temple to his Majesty; 'sanctify the Lord of hosts in your hearts.' Though he be 'the high and lofty One that inhabits eternity,' yet he is pleased to come down to this poor cottage of a creature's heart, and dwell in it. Is not this as great a humbling and condescending for the Father to come down off his throne of glory, to the poor base footstool of the creature's soul, as for the Son to come down in the state of a servant, and become in the form of sinful flesh? But then he is a temple and sanctuary to them. 'And he shall be for a sanctuary,' (Isa. viii. 14.) a place of refuge, a secret hiding-place. Now, as every one is a little separated retired temple, so they all conjoined make up one temple, one visible body, in which he dwells. Therefore Peter calls them 'living stones, built up a spiritual house' to God, 1 Pet. ii. 5. All these little temples make up one house and temple fitly joined together, in which God shows manifest signs of his presence and working. Unto this the apostle in this place alludes. The communion and union of Christians with God is of such a nature, that all the relations and points of conjunction in the creatures are taken to resemble it, and hold it out to us. We are citizens, saith he, and domestics, household-men, and so dwell in his house; and then we are 'his house' besides. Now ye know there are two principal things in a house,—the foundation and the corner-stone; the one supports the building, the other unites it and holds it together. These two parts of this spiritual building are here pointed at. The foundation of every particular stone, and of the whole building, is the doctrine of the prophets and apostles, as holding out Jesus Christ to souls, 'the rock' on which our house shall be builded: not the apostles, or prophets, far less pastors and teachers since,—for they are but at best, 'workers together with God,' and employed in the building of the house; nor yet their doctrine, but as it holds out that 'sure foundation' that God has laid in Zion, (Isa. xxviii. 16.) which is Jesus Christ; for 'other foundation can no man lay.' And then, 'the corner-stone' is that same Jesus Christ, who reaches from the bottom even to the top of the building, and immediately touches every stone, and both quickens it in itself, and unites them together.

Well then, here is a sure foundation to build our eternal happiness upon; the word of God, that endures for ever, holds it out to us. All men are building upon something. Every man is about some establishment of his hopes,—lays some foundation of his confidence which he may stand upon. They are one of the two that Christ speaks of, Luke vi. 48, 49: one builds on the rock, another on the sand. Now as the foundation is, so is the house. A changeable foundation makes a falling house; a sure foundation makes an unchangeable house; a house without a foundation will prove quickly no house. Now whatsoever men build their hope and confidence upon,—besides the word of God, his sure promise and sure covenant, and Jesus Christ in them,—they build upon no foundation, or upon a sandy foundation. 'All flesh is grass, and the flower and perfection of it is as the flower of the field.' Here is the name and character of all created perfections,—of the most excellent endowments of mind,—of all the specious actions of man: it is all but vanishing and vanity! 'Every man at his best estate is such, yea, altogether such.' You who have no more to build upon but your prosperity and wealth, O that is but sand and dung! Would any man build a house upon a dunghill? You who have no other hope but in your own good prayers and meanings,—your own reformations and repentances,—your professions and practices,—know this, that your hope is like a spider's house, like the web that she has laboriously exercised herself about all the week over, and then when you lean upon that house it shall fall through, and not sustain your weight. Whatsoever it be, besides this 'living stone,' Jesus Christ, who is the very substance of the word and promises, it shall undoubtedly prove thy shame and confusion. But behold the opposition the prophet makes between the word and these other things: 'The word of our God shall stand for ever,' Isa. xl. 6—8. And therefore Peter makes it an 'incorruptible seed' of which believers are begotten, 1 Peter i. 23. It is the unchangeable truth and immutable faithfulness of God that makes his word so sure; 'it is builded up to the heavens.' Therefore the Psalmist often commends the word of the Lord as 'a tried word,'—as 'purified seven times.' It hath endured the trial and proof of all men,—of all temptations,—of all generations. It hath often been put in the furnace of questions and doubtings,—it hath often been tried in the fire of afflictions,—but it came forth like pure gold, without dross. This is faith's foundation, 'God hath spoken in his holiness;' and therefore, though 'all men be liars,' yet God will be found true; he deceives none, and is deceived of none. The Lord hath taken a latitude to himself in his working; he loves to show his sovereignty in much of that; and therefore he changes it in men and upon men as he pleaseth. Yet he hath condescended to limit and bound himself by his word, and in this to show his faithfulness. And therefore, though heaven and earth should pass away,—though he should annihilate this world, and create new ones,—yet 'not one jot of his word shall fail.' The earth is established sure, though it hath no foundation, for the word of his command supports it: and yet a believer's confidence is upon a surer ground. 'Though the earth should be removed, yet it cannot pass or fail,' saith our Lord. And therefore the Psalmist useth to boast in God, that though the earth were moved, and the floods lifted up their voice, yet he would not fear, because his foundation was unshaken for all that; the word is not moved, when the world is moved, and therefore he was not moved. The world's stability depends upon a word of command; but our salvation depends on a word of promise. Now ye know, promises put an obligation upon the person, which commands do not. A man may change his commands as he pleases to his children or servants, but he may not change his promises. Therefore the promises of God put an obligation upon him who is truth itself, not to fail in performance; or rather he is to himself, by his unchangeable will and good pleasure, by his faithfulness and truth, an obliging and binding law. When no creature could set bounds to him, he encloses himself within the bounds of promises to us, and gives all flesh liberty to challenge him if he be not faithful.

Now all 'the promises of God are yea and amen in Jesus Christ;' that is, established and confirmed in him. Christ is the surety of them; and so the certainty and stability of them depend upon him, at least to our sense; for God in all his dealing condescends to our weakness, that we may have strong consolation. A promise might suffice to ground our faith, but he addeth an oath to his promise, and he takes Christ surety for the performance; and therefore Christ may be called the truth indeed, —the substantial word of God,—for he is the very substance of the written and preached word. And then he is the certainty and assurance of it; the Scriptures testify of him, and lead us to this 'rock higher than we,' to build upon; and against this 'the gates of hell cannot prevail.' If the word lead not a soul into Christ himself, that soul hath no foundation. Though thou hear the word,—though thou know the word,—yea, suppose thou couldest teach others, and instruct the ignorant, —yet all that will be no foundation, as good as none, except thou do it. And what is it to do the word, but believe in him whom the word testifies of? This is the work of God, to resign thy soul to his mercies and merits, and have no confidence in the flesh; to scrape out all the rubbish of works and performances and parts out of the foundation, and singly to roll thy soul's weight upon God's promises and Christ's purchase; to look with Paul, on all things besides, in thee, and about thee, as dung and dross that thou can lean no weight upon; and to remove that dunghill from the foundation of thy hope, that Jesus Christ may be the only foundation of thy soul, as God hath laid him in the church for 'a sure foundation that whoso believeth in him may not be ashamed.' Whatever besides a soul be established on, though it appear very solid, and the soul be settled and fixed upon it, yet a day will come that will unsettle that soul and raze that foundation. Either it shall be now done in thy conscience, or it must be done at length, when that great tempest of God's indignation shall blow from heaven 'against all unrighteousness of men,' in the day of accounts. Then shall thy house fall, and the fall of it shall be great! But a soul established upon the sure promises, and upon Christ, in whom they 'are yea and amen,' shall abide that storm, and in that day have confidence before God, —have wherewith to answer in Jesus Christ, all the challenges of divine justice, and the accusations of conscience. 'He that trusts in him shall be as mount Sion, which cannot be moved.' You see all things else change, and therefore men's hopes and joys perish. Even here the temptations and revolutions of the times undermine their confidence and joy; and the blasts of the northern wind of affliction blow away their hopes.

Now as Christ is 'the foundation,' so he is 'the corner-stone' of the building. It is Christ who hath removed that 'partition-wall' between Jews and Gentiles, even the ceremonies of the one, and the atheism of the other. 'He is our peace, who hath made both one.' The two sides of the house of God are united by this corner-stone, Jesus Christ. Thus we, who were the temples of Satan, are made the temples of God. Thus poor stranger Gentiles, who had no interest in the covenant of promises, come to share with Abraham, Isaac, and Jacob, and to be founded upon the doctrine of the prophets who taught the Jewish church. Christ is the bond of Christians; this is 'the head' into which all the members should grow up into a body. Distance of place, difference of nations, distinction of languages, all these cannot separate the members of Jesus Christ; they are more one—though consisting of divers nations, tongues, and customs, and dispositions—than the people of one nation, or children of one family; for one Lord, one spirit, unites all. Alas, that all are not united in affection and judgment! Why do the sides of this house contend, and wrestle one against another, when there is such a corner-stone joining them together? Are there not many Christians who cannot endure to look upon one another, who are yet both placed in one building of the temple of God? Alas, this is sad and shameful! But that which I would especially have observed in this, is, that Jesus Christ is such a foundation that reacheth throughout the whole building, and immediately toucheth every stone of the building. It is such a foundation as riseth from the bottom to the top; and therefore Jesus Christ is both 'the author and finisher of our faith,' 'the beginning and the end.' The first stone and the last stone of our building must rise upon him, and by him; the least degree of grace and the greatest perfection of it, both are in him; and therefore Christians should be most dependent creatures,—dependent in their first being, and in after well-being,—in their being, and growing, wholly dependent upon Christ; that out 'of his fulness' they may receive grace, and then more 'grace for grace,' that al may appear to be grace indeed.

Now, I beseech you, my beloved in the Lord, to know whereupon ye are builded, or ought to be builded. There are two great errors in the time, take heed of them; one is the doctrine of some, and another is the practice of the most part. Some do prefer their own fancies and night-dreams, and the imaginations of their own heart, to the word of God; and upon pretence of revelation of new light,* do cast a mist upon that word of God which is a light that hath shined from the beginning. 'Be not deceived:' but 'try the spirits whether they be of God,' or not. There are many pretend to much of the Spirit, and therefore cry out against the word, as letter, as flesh. But, my brethren, believe not every doctrine that calls itself a spirit. That spirit is not of God that hears not God's voice: as Christ reasoneth against the Jews. Seek ye more of the Spirit of Christ which he promiseth, who is a Spirit that teacheth all things; and bringeth to remembrance these blessed sayings; and leads us in all truth. It shall be both safest and sweetest to you to meditate on that word of the prophets and apostles; and the entrance into it shall give you light,—an old light which was from the beginning, and therefore a true light—for all truth is eternal—and yet a new light to your sense and feeling. It is both an old command, and a new command; an old word, and a new word; if thou search it by the Spirit's inspiration, that old word shall be made new, that letter made spirit and life. Such are the words that Christ speaks. But yet there are many who do not reject the Scriptures in judgment, who, notwithstanding, do not build on them in practice. Alas, it may be said of the most part of professed Christians among us, that they are not built upon the foundation of the apostles and prophets, but upon the sayings of fallible and weak men! What ground have many of you for your faith; but because the minister saith so, you believe so? The most part live in an implicit faith, and practise that in themselves which they condemn in the papists. You do not labour to 'search the scriptures,' that upon that foundation you may build your faith in the questioned truths of this age; that so you may be able to answer those that ask a reason of the faith that is in you. Alas! simple souls, you believe every thing, and yet really believe nothing; because you believe not the word, as the word of the living God, but take it from men upon their authority! Therefore when a temptation cometh, from any gainsayings of the truth,—you cannot stand against it, because your faith hath no foundation but the sayings of men, or acts of assemblies. And therefore, as men whom you trust with holding out light unto you, hold out darkness instead of light, you embrace that darkness also.

* [The allusion here appears to be to the doctrines of the Quakers who, in Binning's time, were increasing in the west of Scotland, and accustomed to rail, with impunity, at ministers in the face of their congregations. See Baillie's Letters, vol. II. pp. 393, 413, 419.—Ed.]

But, I beseech you, be builded upon the foundation of the apostles and prophets; not upon *them*, but upon that whereon they were builded, the infallible truths of God. You have the Scriptures, search them; since you have reasonable souls, search them. Other men's faith will not save; you cannot see to walk to heaven by other men's light, more than you can see by their eyes. You have eyes of your own, souls of your own, subordinate to none but the God of spirits, and the Lord of consciences, Jesus Christ; and therefore examine all that is spoken to you from the word, according to the word; and receive no more upon trust from men, but as you find it upon trial to be the truth of God.

Lecture VI.

WHAT THE SCRIPTURES PRINCIPALLY TEACH: THE RUIN AND RECOVERY OF MAN: FAITH AND LOVE TOWARDS CHRIST.

2 Tim. i. 13. "*Hold fast the form of sound words, which thou hast heard of me, in faith and love which is in Christ Jesus.*"

Here is the sum of religion. Here you have a compend of the doctrine of the Scriptures. All divine truths may be reduced to these two heads,—faith and love; what we ought to believe, and what we ought to do. This is all the Scriptures teach, and this is all we have to learn. What have we to know, but what God hath revealed of himself to us? And what have we to do, but what he commands us? In a word, what have we to learn in this world, but to believe in Christ, and love him, and so live to him? This is the duty of man, and this is the dignity of man, and the way to eternal life. Therefore the Scriptures, that are given to be 'a lamp to our feet, and a guide to our paths,' contain a perfect and exact rule,—*credendorum et faciendorum*,—of faith and manners,—of doctrine and practice. We have in the scriptures many truths revealed to us of God, and of the works of his hands,—many precious truths; but that which most of all concerns us, is to know God and ourselves. This is the special excellency of the reasonable creature, that it is made capable to know its Creator, and to reflect upon its own being. Now, we have to know ourselves, what we are now, and what man once was; and accordingly to know of God, what he once revealed of himself, and what he doth now reveal. I say, the Scriptures hold out to our consideration a twofold estate of mankind, and according to these, a twofold revelation of the mystery of God. We look on man now, and we find him another thing than he was once; but we do not find God one thing at one time, and another thing at another time; for there is no 'shadow of change' in him; and 'he is the same yesterday, and to-day, and for ever.' Therefore we ask not, what he was, and what he is now; but how he manifests himself differently, according to the different estates of man. As we find in the Scriptures, man once righteous and blessed, Eccles. vii. 29; and God making him such according to his own image, 'in righteousness and true holiness,' Col. iii. 10; Eph. iv. 24; we find him in communion and friendship with God, set next to the divine majesty, and above the works of his hand, and all things 'under his feet.' How holy was he! and how happy! And happy he could not choose but be, since he was holy; being conformed and like unto God in his will and affection,—choosing that same delight, that same pleasure with God, in his understanding,—knowing God and his will, and likewise, his own happiness. In such a conformity he could not but have much communion with him, that had such conformity to him—union being the foundation of communion—and great peace and solid tranquillity in him.

Now, in this state of mankind God expresses his goodness and wisdom and power, his holiness and righteousness. These are the attributes that shine most brightly. In the very morning of the creation, God revealed himself to man as a holy and just

God, whose eyes cou d behold no iniquity; and therefore he made him upright, and made a covenant of life and peace with him, to give him immortal and eternal life,—to continue him in his happy estate, if so be he continued in well-doing; Rom. x. 5, 'do this and live.' In which covenant, indeed, there were some outbreakings of the glorious grace and free condescendency of God; for it was no less free grace and undeserved favour to promise life to his obedience, than now to promise life to our faith. So that if the Lord had continued that covenant with us, we ought to have called it grace, and would have been saved by grace as well as now; though it be true, that there is some more occasion given to man's nature to boast and glory in that way, yet not at all 'before God,' Rom. iv. 2.

But we have scarcely found man in such an estate, till we have found him sinful and miserable and fallen from his excellency. That sun shined in the dawning of the creation, but before ye can well know what it is, it is eclipsed and darkened with sin and misery: as if the Lord had only set up such a creature in the firmament of glory, to let him know how blessed he could make him, and wherein his blessedness consists, and then presently to throw him down from his excellency. When you find him mounting up to the heavens, and spreading himself thus in holiness and happiness, like a bay-tree; behold again, and you find him not; though you seek him, you shall not find him, his place doth not know him. He is like one that comes out with a great majesty upon a stage, and personates some monarch, or emperor, in the world; and then ere you can well gather your thoughts, to know what he is, he is turned off the stage, and appears in some base and despicable appearance. So quickly is man stript of all those glorious ornaments of holiness, and puts on the vile rags of sin and wretchedness, and is cast from the throne of eminency above the creatures, and from fellowship with God, to be a slave and servant to the dust of his feet, and to have communion with the devil and his angels. And now, ye have man holden out in Scripture as the only wretched piece of the creation, as the very plague of the world; the whole creation groaning under him, (Rom. viii.) and in pain to be delivered of such a burden, of such an execration and curse and astonishment. You find the testimony of the word condemns him altogether, concludes him under sin, and then under a curse, and makes all flesh guilty in God's sight. The word speaks otherwise of us than we think of ourselves: 'Their imagination is only evil continually,' Gen. vi. 5. O then, what must our affections be, that are certainly more corrupt! What then must our way be! All flesh hath corrupted their way, and done abominable works, and 'none doeth good,' Psal. xiv. 1, 2, 3. But many flee in unto their good hearts as their last refuge, when they are beaten from these outworks of their actions and ways. But the Scripture shall storm that also: 'The heart is deceitful above all things: who can know it?' it is 'desperately wicked,' Jer. xvii. 9. In a word, man is become the most lamentable spectacle in the world; a compend of all wickedness and misery enclosed within the walls of inability and impossibility to help himself, shut up within a prison of despair, a stinking, loathsome, and irksome dungeon. It is like the miry pit that Jeremiah was cast into, that there was no out-coming, and no pleasant abode in it.

Now, man's state being thus,—nay, having made himself thus, and 'sought out' to himself such sad 'inventions,' Eccl. vii. 29;—and having 'destroyed' himself, Hos. xiii. 9; What think ye? Should any pity him? If he had fallen into such a pit of misery ignorantly and unwittingly, he had been an object of compassion; but having cast himself headlong into it, who should have pity on him? Or, who should 'go aside to ask' how he did, or bemoan him? Jer. xv. 5. But behold the Lord pities man as a father doth his children, Psal. ciii. 'His compassions fail not;' he comes by such a loathsome and contemptible object, and casts his skirts over it, and saith, 'Live!' (Ezek. xvi.) and maketh it a time of love. I say, no flesh could have expected any more of God than to make man happy and holy, and to promise him life in well-doing; but to repair that happiness after it was wilfully lost, and to give life to evil-doers and sinners,—O how far was it from Adam's expectation when he fled from God! Here then is the wonder, that when men and angels were in expectation of the revelation of his wrath from heaven against their wickedness, and the execution of the curse man was concluded under, that even then God is pursuing man, and pursues him with love, and opens up to him his very heart and bowels of love in Jesus Christ! Behold then the second revelation and manifestation of God, in a way of grace, pure grace,—of mercy and pity towards lost sinners. 'The kindness and love of God our Saviour toward man [hath] appeared, not by works of righteousness which we have done, but according to his abundant mercy showed in Christ Jesus,' Tit. iii. 4—6. So then, we have this purpose of God's love unfolded to us in the Scriptures; and this is the substance of them—both Old and New Testament—or the end of them; 'Christ is the end of the law' (Rom. x. 4.) to all sinners concluded under sin and a curse. By it, our Lord Jesus, the good Ebedmelech, comes and casts down a cord to us, and draws us up out of the pit of sin and misery. He comes to this prison, and opens the doors to let captives free. So then we have God holden out to us as a redeemer, as a repairer of our breaches,—'God in Christ reconciling the world,'—'O Israel, thou hast destroyed thyself, but in me is thine help,' Hos. xiii. 9. He finds to himself 'a ransom' to satisfy his justice, Job xxxiii. 24. He finds a propitiation to take away sin,—a sacrifice to pacify and appease his wrath. He finds one of our brethren, but yet his own Son in whom he is well-pleased; and then holds out all this to sinners, that they may be satisfied in their own consciences, as he is in his own mind. God hath satisfied himself in Christ; you have not that to do. He is not now to be reconciled to us, for he was never really at odds; though he covered his countenance with frowns and threats, since the Fall, and hath appeared in fire and thunders and whirlwinds which are terrible, yet his heart had always love in it to such persons; and therefore he is come near in Christ, and about reconciling us to himself. Here is the business then, to have our souls reconciled to him, to take away the enmity within us; and as he is satisfied with his Son, so to satisfy ourselves with him, and be as well-pleased in his redemption and purchase as the Father is, and then you believe indeed in him. Now if this were accomplished, what have we more to do but to love him and to live to him? When you have found in the Scripture, and believed with the heart, what man once was, and what he now is; what God once appeared, and what he now manifests himself in the gospel; ye have no more to do but to search in the same Scriptures what ye henceforth ought to be. Ye who find your estate recovered in Christ, ask, 'What manner of persons ought we to be?' And the Scripture shall also give you that 'form of sound words,' which may not only teach you to believe in him, but to love him and obey his commands. The law that before condemned you is now by Christ put in your hands to guide you and conduct you in the way, and teacheth you how to live henceforth to his glory. 'The grace of God that bringeth salvation hath appeared unto all men, teaching us, that denying ungodliness, and worldly lusts, we should live soberly, righteously, and godly in this present world,' Tit. ii. 12. Here is the sum of the rule of your practice and conversation; piety towards God, equity towards men, and sobriety towards ourselves; self-denial, and world-denial, and lust-denial; to give up with the world and our own lusts,—henceforth to have no more to do with them,—to resign them, not for a time, not in part, but wholly and for ever in affection, and by parts in practice and endeavour; and then to resign and give up ourselves to him, to live to him, and to live in him.

Thus we have given you a sum of the doctrine of the Scriptures, of that which is to be believed, and that which is to be done as our duty. Now we shall speak a word of these two cardinal graces which are the compend of all graces,—as the objects of them are the abridgment of the Scriptures,—faith and love. These 'sound words' can profit us nothing, unless we hold them fast with faith and love.

Faith is like the fountain-gate. Streams come out of it that cleanse the conscience from the guilt of sin, and purify the heart from the filth of sin; because it is that which cometh to the 'fountain opened up in the house of David,' and draweth water out of these 'wells of salvation.' If you consider the fall and ruin of mankind, you will find infidelity and unbelief the fountain of it as well as the seal of it. Unbelief of the law of God,—of his promises and threatenings. This was first called in question; and when once called in question, it is half-denied. Hath God said so, that you shall die?—It is not far off:—'Ye shall not surely die.' Here then was the very beginning of man's ruin. He did not retain in his knowledge, and believe with his heart, the truth and faithfulness and holiness of God; which unbelief was conjoined and intermingled with much pride—'ye shall be as gods.' He began to live out of God, in himself; not remembering that his life was a stream of that divine fountain, that being cut off from it, would dry up. Now therefore, our Lord Jesus Christ,—an expert Saviour, and very learned and complete for this work, —he brings man out of this pit of misery by that same way he fell into it. He fell down by unbelief, and he brings him up out of it by faith. This is the cord that is cast down to the poor soul in the dungeon; or rather his faith is the dead-grip of the cord of divine promises which is sent unto the captive-prisoner; and by virtue thereof he is drawn out into the light of salvation. Unbelief of the law of God did first destroy man; now the belief of the gospel saves him. The not believing of the Lord's threatenings was the beginning of his ruin; and believing of his precious promises is salvation. I say no more, as our destruction began at the unbelief of the law, so our salvation must begin at the belief of it. The law and divine justice went out of his sight, and so he sinned; now the law entering into the conscience, discovers a man's sins, and makes sin abound; and that is the beginning of our remedy, to know our disease. But as long as this is hid from a man's eyes, he is shut up in unbelief; he is sealed and confirmed in his miserable estate, and so kept from Jesus Christ the remedy. Thus unbelief first and last destroys. Faith might have preserved Adam, and faith again may restore thee who hast fallen in Adam.

There is a great mistake of faith among us: some taking it for a strong and blind confidence that admits of no questions or doubts in the soul, and so vainly persuading themselves that they have it; and some again conceiving it to be such an assurance of salvation as instantly comforts the soul and looseth all objections, and so foolishly vexing their own souls, and disquieting themselves in vain, for the want of that which, if they understood what it is, they would find they have. I say, many souls conceive that to be the best faith that never doubted, and hath always lodged in them and kept them in peace since they were born. But, seeing all men were once 'aliens from the commonwealth of Israel, and strangers to the covenant of promise, and without God in the world,' and so without Christ also, it is certain that those souls who have always blessed themselves in their own hearts, and cried 'Peace, peace,' and were never afraid of the wrath to come, have embraced an imagination and dream of their own heart for true faith. It is not big and stout words that will prove it. Men may defy the devil and all his works, and speak very confidently, and yet, God knows, they are captives by him at his pleasure, and not far from that misery which they think they have escaped. Satan works in them with such a crafty conveyance that they cannot perceive it. And how should they perceive it? For we are 'by nature dead in sins,' and so cannot feel or know that we are such. It is a token of life to feel pain, a certain token, for dead things are senseless. You know how jugglers may deceive your very senses, and make them believe they see that which is not, and feel that which they feel not. Oh! how much more easy is it for Satan—such an ingenious and experimented spirit—assisted with the help of our deceitful hearts, to cast such a mist over the eyes of hearts, and make them believe any thing! How easily may he hide our misery from us, and make us believe it is well with us! And thus multitudes of souls perish in the very opinion of salvation. That very thing which they call faith,—that strong ungrounded persuasion,—is no other thing than the unbelief of the heart; unbelief, I mean, of the holy law, of divine justice, and the wrath to come; for if these once entered into the soul's consideration, they would certainly cast down that stronghold of vain confidence that Satan keeps all the house in peace by. Now this secure and presumptuous despising of all threatenings and all convictions, is varnished over to the poor soul with the colour and appearance of faith in the gospel. They think, to believe in Christ is nothing else but never to be afraid of hell; whereas it is nothing else but a soul fleeing into Christ for fear of hell, and fleeing from the wrath to come to the city of refuge.

Now again, there are some other souls quite contrary minded, that run upon another extremity. They once question whether they have faith; and always question it. You shall find them always out of one doubt into another, and still returning upon these debates, Whether am I in Christ, or not? And often peremptorily concluding that they are not in him, and that they believe not in him. I must confess, that a soul must once question the matter, or they shall never be certain. Nay, a soul must once conclude that it is void of God, and without Christ; but having discovered that, I see no more use and fruit of your frequent debates and janglings about interest. I would say then unto such souls, that if you now question it, it is indeed the very time to put it out of question. And how? Not by framing or seeking answers to your objections;—not by searching into thyself to find some thing to prove it,—not by mere disputing about it, for when shall these have an end? But simply and plainly by setting about that which is questioned. Are you in doubt if you be believers? How shall it be resolved then but by believing indeed? It is now the very time that thou art called to make application of thy soul to Christ, if thou thinkest thou cannot make application of Christ to thy soul. If thou cannot know if he be thine, then how shalt thou know it but by choosing him for thine and embracing him in thy soul? Now I say, if that time which is spent about such unprofitable debates, were spent in solid and serious endeavours about the thing in debate, it would quickly be out of debate. If you were more in the obedience to those commands, than in the dispute whether you have obeyed or not, you would sooner come to satisfaction in it. This I say the rather, because the weightier and principal parts of the gospel are those direct acts of faith and love to Jesus Christ; both these are the outgoings of the soul to him. Now again, examination of our faith and assurance are but secondary and consequent reflections upon ourselves, and are the soul returning in again to itself, to find what is within. Therefore, I say, a Christian is principally called to the first, and always called. It is the chief duty of man, which, for no evidence, no doubting, no questioning, should be left undone. If ye be in any hesitation whether you are believers or not; I am sure the chiefest thing, and most concerning, is, rather to believe than to know it. It is a Christian's being to believe; it is indeed his comfort and well-being to know it; but if you do not know it, then by all means so much the more set about it presently. Let the soul consider Christ and the precious promises, and lay its weight upon him. this you ought to do, and not to leave the other undone.

Secondly, I say to such souls, that it is the mistake of the very nature of faith that leads them to such perplexities, and causeth such inevidence. It is not so much the inevidence of marks and fruits that makes them doubt, as the misapprehension of the thing itself; for as long as they mistake it in its own nature, no sign, no mark, can satisfy in it. You take faith to be a persuasion of God's love that calms and quiets the mind. Now, such a persuasion needs no signs to know it by; it is manifest by its own presence, as light by its own brightness. It were a foolish question to ask any, how they knew that they were persuaded of another's affection? The very persuasion maketh itself more certain to the soul than any token. So then, while you question whether you have faith or not, and in the mean time take faith to be nothing else but such a persuasion, it is in vain to bring any marks or signs to convince you that you have faith; for if such a persuasion and assurance were in you, it would be more powerful to assure your hearts of itself than any thing else; and while you are doubting of it, it is more manifest that you have it not, than any signs or marks can be able to make it appear that you have it. If any would labour to convince a blind man that he saw the light, and gave him signs and tokens of the light's shining, the blind man could not believe him; for it is more certain to himself that he sees not, that any evidence can make the contrary probable. You are still wishing and seeking such a faith as puts all out of question. Now, when ministers bring any marks to prove you have true faith, it cannot satisfy or settle you, because your very questioning proves that ye have not that which ye question. If you had such a persuasion, you would not question it. So then, as long as you are in that mistake concerning the true nature of faith, all the signs of the word cannot settle you. But I say, if once you understood the true nature of faith, it would be more clear in itself unto you, than readily marks and signs could make it; especially in the time of temptation. If you would know, then, what it is indeed, consider what the word of God holds out concerning himself, or us; and the solid belief of that in the heart hath something of the nature of saving faith in it. The Lord gives a testimony concerning man, that he is 'born in sin,' that he is 'dead in sin,' and all his 'imaginations are only evil continually.' Now, I say, to receive this truth into the soul, upon God's testimony, is a point of faith. The Lord in his word 'concludes all under sin' and wrath; so, then, for a soul to conclude itself also under sin and wrath is a point of faith. Faith is the soul's testimony to God's truth; the word is God's testimony. Now then, if a soul receive this testimony within, whether it be law or gospel, it is an act of faith. If a soul condemn itself, and judge itself, that is a setting to our seal that God is true, who speaks in his law, and so it is a believing in God. I say more: to believe with the heart that we cannot believe, is a great point of sound belief, because it is a sealing of that word of God,—'The heart is desperately wicked,' and 'of ourselves we can do nothing.' Now, I am persuaded, if such souls knew this, they would put an end to their many contentions and wranglings about this point, and would rather bless God that hath opened their eyes to see themselves, than contend with him for that they have no faith. It is light only that discovers darkness, and faith only that discerns unbelief. It is life and health only that feel pain and sickness; for if all were alike, nothing could be found,* as in dead bodies. Now, I say to such souls as believe in God the Lawgiver, believe also in Christ the Redeemer. And what is that? It is not to know that I have an interest in him. No, that must come after; it is the Spirit's sealing after believing which puts itself out of question when it comes. And so if you had it, you needed not many signs to know it by; at least you would not doubt of it, more than he that sees the light can question it. But, I say, to believe in Christ is simply this: I,—whatsoever I be,—ungodly, wretched, polluted, desperate, am willing to have Jesus Christ for my Saviour; I have no other help, or hope, if it be not in him. It is, I say, to lean the weight of thy soul on this foundation-stone laid in Zion; to embrace the promises of the gospel, albeit general, as 'worthy of all acceptation,' and wait upon the performance of them. It is no other thing but to make Christ welcome; to say, "'Even so, Lord Jesus;' I am content in my soul that thou be my Saviour, to be found in thee, 'not having my own righteousness.' I am well-pleased to cast away my own as dung, and find myself no other than an ungodly man." Now it is certain that many souls that are still questioning whether they have faith, yet do find this in their souls; but because they know not that it is faith which they find, they go about to seek that which is not faith, and where it is not to be found; and so disquiet themselves in vain, and hinder fruitfulness.

Now, the faith of a Christian is no fancy; it is not a light vain imagination of the brain, but it dwells in the heart,—'with the heart man believes,' and it dwells with love. Faith and love, we need not be curious to distinguish them. It is certain that love is in it, and from it; it is in the very bosom of it, because faith is a soul-embracing of Christ; it is a choosing of him for its portion; and then upon the review of this goodly portion, and from consideration of what he is, and hath done for us, the soul loves him still more, and is impatient of so much distance from him. We find them conjoined in Scripture, but they are one in the heart. O that we studied to have these jointly engraven on the heart! As they are joined in the word, so our heart should be a 'living epistle.' Faith and love are two words but one thing under different notions. They are the outgoings of the soul to Christ for life,—the breathings of the soul after him, for more of him, when it hath once tasted how good he is. Faith is not a speculation, or a wandering thought of truth; it is the truth, not captivated into the mind, but dwelling in the heart, and getting possession of the whole man. You know, a man and his will are one; not so a man and his mind; for he may conceive the truth of many things he loves not, but whatever a man loves, that and he in a manner become one with another. Love is unitive; it is the most excellent union of distant things. The will commands the whole man, and hath the office of applying of all the faculties to their proper works. *Illa imperat, aliæ exsequuntur.* Therefore when once divine truth gets entry into the heart of a man, and becomes one with his will and affection, it will quickly command the whole man to practise and execute; and then he that received 'the truth in love' is found a walker in the truth. Many persons captivate truth in their understandings, as the Gentiles did; they hold or detain it in unrighteousness; but be-

* [That is, *felt*.—Ed.]

cause it hath no liberty to descend into the heart, and possess that garrison, it cannot command the man. But oh! it is better to be truth's captive than to captivate truth, saith the apostle, 'Ye have obeyed from the heart that form of doctrine which was delivered you,' Rom. vi. 17. O a blessed captivity! to be delivered over to truth,—that is indeed freedom, for truth makes free, John viii. 32. And it makes free where it is in freedom. Give it freedom to command thee, and it shall indeed deliver thee from all strange lords; and thou shalt obey it from the heart when it is indeed in the heart. When the truths of God,—whether promises, or threatenings, or commands,—are impressed into the heart, you shall find the expressions of them in the conversation. Faith is not an empty assent to the truth, but a receiving of it 'in love;' and when the truth is received in love, then it begins to work by love. 'Faith worketh by love,' saith Paul, Gal. v. 6. That now is the proper nature of its operation which expresses its own nature. Obedience proceeding from love to God flows from faith in God, and that shows the true and living nature of that faith. If the soul within receive the seal and impression of the truth of God, it will render the image of that same truth in all its actions.

Love is put for all obedience. It is made the very sum and compend of the law, the fulfilling of it; for the truth is the most effectual and constraining principle of obedience, and withal the most sweet and pleasant. The love of Christ constrains us to live to him, and not henceforth to ourselves, 2 Cor. v. 14, 15. As I said, a man and his will is one; if you engage it, you bind all; if you gain it, it will bring all with it. As it is the most ready way to gain any party, to engage their head whom they follow and upon whom they depend, let a man's love be once gained to Christ, and the whole train of the soul's faculties, of the outward senses and operations, will follow upon it. It was an excellent and pertinent question that Christ asked Peter, when he was going away, (if Peter had considered Christ's purpose in it, he would not have been so hasty and displeased,) "Peter, 'lovest thou me?' then 'feed my sheep.'" If a man love Christ, he will certainly study to please him, and though he should do never so much in obedience, it is no pleasure except it be done out of love. O this, and more of this in the heart, would make ministers feed well, and teach well, and would make people obey well! 'If ye love me, keep my commandments.' Love devotes and consecrates all that is in a man to the pleasure of him whom he loves; therefore it fashions and conforms one—even against nature—to another's humour and affection. It constrains not to live to ourselves, but to him,—its joy and delight is in him, and therefore all is given up and resigned to him. Now as it is certain, that if you love much you will do much, so it is certain that little is accepted for much that proceeds from love; and therefore, our poor maimed and halting obedience is called 'the fulfilling of the law.' He is well-pleased with it, because love is ill-pleased with it. Love thinks nothing too much,—all too little; and therefore his love thinks any thing from us much, since love would give more. He accepts that which is given; the lover's mite cast into the treasury, is more than ten times so much outward obedience from another man. He meets love with love. If the soul's desire be towards the love of his name; if love offer, though a farthing, his love receiving it counts it a crown. Love offering a present of duty, finds many imperfections in it, and covers any good that is in it, seems not to regard it, and then beholds it as a recompense. His love, receiving the present from us, covers a multitude of infirmities that are in it. And thus, what in the desire and endeavour of love on our part, and what in the acceptation of what is done on his part, 'love is the fulfilling of the law.' It is an usual proverb, All things are as they are taken: 'Love is the fulfilling of the law,' because our loving Father takes it so; he takes as much delight in the poor children's willingness, as in the more aged's strength; the offer and endeavour of the one pleaseth him, as well as the performance of the other.

The love of God is the fulfilling of the law, for it is a living law; it is the law written on the heart; it is the law of a spirit of life within. *Quis legem det amantibus? Major lex amor sibi ipsi est.* You almost need not prescribe any rules, or set over the head of love the authority and pain of a command, for it is a greater law to itself. It hath within its own bosom as deep an engagement and obligation to any thing that may please God as you can put upon it; for it is in itself the very engagement and bond of the soul to him. This is it, indeed, which will do him service; and that is the service which he likes. It is that only serves him constantly and pleasantly; and constantly it cannot serve him which doth it not pleasantly, for it is delight only that makes it constant. Violent motions may be swift, but not durable; they last not long. Fear and terror is a kind of external impulse that may drive a soul swiftly to some duty; but because that is not one with a soul, it cannot endure long; it is not good company to the soul. But love, making a duty pleasant, becomes one with the soul; it incorporates with it, and becomes like its nature to it, that though it should not move so swiftly, yet it moves more constantly. And what is love but the very motion of the soul to God? And so till it have attained that, to be in him, it can find no place of rest. Now this is only the service that he is pleased with, which comes from love, because he sees his own image in it; for love in us is nothing else but the impression and stamp that God's love to us makes on the heart. It is the very reflection of that sweet warm beam. So then, when his love reflects back unto himself, carrying our heart and duty with it, he knoweth his own superscription, he loves his own image in such a duty: 'if a man love me, he will keep my words: and my Father will love him, and we will come unto him, and make our abode with him,' John xiv. 23. Here now is an evidence that he likes it, for he must needs like that place he chooses to dwell in. He who hath such a glorious mansion and palace above must needs love that soul dearly, that he will prefer it to his high and holy place.

Now I know it will be the secret question and complaint of some souls, how shall I get love to God? I cannot love him, my heart is so desperately wicked; I cannot say as Peter, 'Lord, thou knowest that I love thee.' I shall not insist upon the discovery of your love unto him by marks and signs; only I say, if thou indeed from thy heart desirest to love him, and art grieved that there is not this love in thy soul to him which becomes so love-worthy a Saviour, then thou indeed lovest him, for he that loveth the love of God, loveth God himself. And wherefore art thou sad for the want of that love, but because thou lovest him in some measure, and withal findest him beyond all that thou canst think and love? But I say, that which most concerns thee is to love still more, and that thou wouldest be still more earnest to love him than to know that thou lovest him.

Now I know no more effectual way to increase love to Jesus Christ, than to believe his love. Christ Jesus is 'the author and finisher' both of faith and love; and 'we love him, because he first loved us.' Therefore the right discovery of Jesus Christ, what he is, and what he hath done for sinners, is that which will of all things most prevail to engage the soul unto him. But as long as ye suspend your faith upon the being or increase of your love and obedience—as the manner of too many is—you take even such a course as he that will not plant the tree till he see the fruits of it; which is contrary to common sense and reason.

Since this, then, is the sum of true religion, to believe in Christ, and to love him, and so live to him,—we shall wind up all that is spoken into that exhortation of the apostle's, 'Hold fast the form of sound words which thou hast heard.' You have this doctrine of faith and love delivered unto you which may be able to save your souls. Then, I beseech you, hold them fast, salvation is in them. They are 'sound words' and wholesome words; words of life, spirit and life, (as Christ speaks,) as well as words of truth. But how will you hold them fast that have them not at all,—that know them not though you hear them? You who are ignorant of the gospel, and hear nothing but a sound of words, instead of sound and wholesome words, how can you hold them fast? Can a man hold the wind in the hollow of his hand, or keep a sound within it? You know no more but a sound and a wind that passeth by your ear, without observing either truth or life in it. But then again, you who understand these sound words, and have 'a form of knowledge,' and of the letter of the law, what will that avail you? You cannot hold it fast, except you have it within you; and it is within you indeed when it is in your heart,—when the form of it is engraven upon the very soul in lo e. Now, though you understand the sound of these words, and the sound of truth in them, yet you receive not the living image of them which is faith and love. Can you paint a sound? Can you form it, or engrave it on any thing? Nay, but these sound words are more substantial and solid. They must be engraven on the heart, else you will never hold them. They may be easily plucked out of the mouth and hand by temptation, unless they be enclosed and laid up in the secret of the heart, as Mary laid them. The truth must hold thee fast, or thou canst not hold it fast; it must captivate thee, and bind thee with the golden chains of affection, which only is true freedom, or certainly thou wilt let it go. Nay, you must not only have the truth received by love into your heart, but, as the apostle speaks, you must also 'hold fast the form of sound words.' Scripture words are sound words; the Scripture-method of teaching is sound and wholesome. There may be unsound words used in expressing true matter; and if a man shall give liberty to his own luxuriant imagination to expatiate in notions and expressions, either to catch the ear of the vulgar, or to appear some new discoverer of light and gospel-mysteries, he may as readily fall into error and darkness, as into truth and light. Some men do busk up old truths, Scripture truths, into some new dress of language and notions, and then give them out for new discoveries, new lights; but in so doing, they often hazard the losing of the truth itself. We should beware and take heed of strange words that have the least appearance of evil, such as *Christed* and *Godded*.* Let us think it enough to be wise according to the Scriptures, and suspect all that as vain, empty, unsound, that tends not to the increase of faith in Christ and love and obedience unto him; as ordinarily the dialect of those called Antinomians is. Giving, and not granting, that they had no unsound mind, yet I am sure they use unsound words to express sound matter. The clothes should be shaped to the person. Truth is plain and simple; let words of truth also be full of simplicity. I say no more, but leave that upon you, that you hold fast even the very words of the Scriptures, and be not bewitched by the vain pretensions of spirit,—all spirit,—pure and spiritual service,—and such like, to the casting off of the word of truth, as *letter*, as *flesh*. And such is the high attainment of some in these days; an high attainment indeed, and a mighty progress in the way to destruction,—the very last discovery of that Antichrist and man of sin. Oh, make much of the Scripture, for you shall neither read nor hear the like of it in the world! Other books may have sound matter, but there is still something, in manner or words, unsound. No man can speak to you truth in such plainness and simplicity, in such soundness also. But here is both sound matter, and sound words; the truth holden out truly; health and salvation holden out in as wholesome a matter as is possible. Matter and manner are both divine.

Lecture VII.

OF THE NAME OF GOD.

Exod. iii. 13, 14. "*And Moses said unto God, Behold, when I come unto the children of Israel, and shall say unto them, The God of your fathers hath sent me unto you; and they shall say to me, What is his name? what shall I say unto them? And God said unto Moses, I AM THAT I AM: and he said, Thus shalt thou say unto the children of Israel, I AM hath sent me unto you.*"

We are now about this question, What God is. But who can answer it? Or, if answered, who can understand it? It should astonish us in the very entry to think that we are about to speak and to hear of his majesty, whom 'eye hath not seen, nor ear heard,' nor hath it entered into the heart of any creature to consider what he is. Think ye that blind men could have a pertinent discourse of light and colours? Would they form any suitable notion of that they had never seen, and which cannot

* [These terms were made use of, as descriptive of themselves, by the sect called the Familists. See Discovery of Familism p. 7. *apud* Baillie's Anabaptism, pp. 102, 127. Lond. 1647.—Ed.]

be known but by seeing? What an ignorant speech would a deaf man make of sound which a man cannot so much as know what it is but by hearing of it? How then can we speak of God who dwells in such inaccessible light, that, though we had our eyes opened, yet they are far less proportioned to that resplendent brightness, than a blind eye is to the sun's light?

It uses to be a question, If there be a God? Or, how it may be known that there is a God? It were almost blasphemy to move such a question, if there were not so much Atheism in the hearts of men, which makes us either to doubt, or not firmly to believe and seriously to consider it. But what may convince souls of the Divine Majesty? Truly, I think, if it be not evident by its own brightness, all the reason that can be brought is but like a candle's-light to see the sun by! Yet, because of our weakness, the Lord shines upon us in the creatures, as in a glass; and this is become the best way to take up the glorious brightness of his majesty, by reflection in his word and works. God himself dwells in 'light inaccessible, that no man can approach unto;' if any look straight to that Sun of Righteousness, he shall be astonished and amazed, and see no more than in the very darkness. But the best way to behold the sun is to look at it in a pail of water; and the surest way to know God by, is to take him up in a state of humiliation and condescension, as the sun in the rainbow, in his word and works, which are mirrors of the divine power and goodness, and do reflect upon the hearts and eyes of all men the beams of that uncreated light. If this be not the 'speech,' that 'day uttereth unto day, and night unto night,' " One self-Being gave me a being;" and if thou hear not that language that is 'gone out into all the earth,' and be not, as it were, noised and possessed with all the sounds of every thing about thee, above thee, beneath thee, yea, and within thee, all singing a melodious song to that excellent name which is above all names, and conspiring to give testimony to the fountain of their being: if this, I say, be not so sensible unto thee as if a tongue and a voice were given to every creature to express it, then, indeed, we need not reason the business with thee who hast lost thy senses. Do but, I say, retire inwardly, and ask in sobriety and sadness, what thy conscience thinks of it; and undoubtedly it shall confess a divine majesty; or at least tremble at the apprehension of what it either will not confess or slenderly believes. The very evidence of truth shall extort an acknowledgment from it. If any man denied the divine majesty, I would seek no other argument to persuade him than what was used to convince an old philosopher who denied the fire: they put his hand in it till he felt it. So, I say, return within to thy own conscience, and thou shalt find the scorching heat of that Divine Majesty burning it up, whom thou wouldst not confess. There is an inward feeling and sense of God that is imprinted in every soul by nature that leaves no man without such a testimony of God, that makes him 'without excuse;' there is no man so impious, so atheistical, but whether he will or not, he shall feel at some times that which he loves not to know or consider of; so that what rest secure consciences have from the fear and terror of God, it is like the sleep of a drunken man, who, even when he sleeps, does not rest quietly.

Now, although this inward stamp of a Deity be engraven on the minds of all, and every creature without have some marks of his glory stamped on them, so that all things a man can behold above him, or about him, or beneath him, the most mean and inconsiderable creatures, are pearls and transparent stones that cast abroad the rays of that glorious brightness which shines on them; as if a man were enclosed into a city built all of precious stones, that in the sunshine all and every parcel of it, the streets, the houses, the roofs, the windows, all of it, reflected into his eyes those sunbeams in such a manner as if all had been one mirror:—though, I say, this be so, yet such is the blockishness and stupidity of men that they do not, for all this, consider of the glorious Creator; so that all these lamps seem to be lighted in vain to show forth his glory; which, though they do every way display their beams upon us, that we can turn our eye nowhere but such a ray shall penetrate it, yet we either do not consider it, or the consideration of it takes not such deep root as to lead home to God. Therefore the Scripture calls all natural men atheists: They have 'said in their heart, there is no God,' Psal. xiv. 1. All men almost confess a God with their mouth, and think they believe in him; but alas! behold their actions and hearts, what testimony they give; for a man's walking and conversation is like an eye-witness, that one of them deserves more credit than ten ear-witnesses of professions,—*Plus valet oculatus testis unus, quam auriti decem.* Now, I may ask of you, what would ye do, how would ye walk, if ye believed there were no God? Would ye be more dissolute and profane, and more void of religion? Would not human laws bind you as much in that case as they now do? For that is almost all the restraint that is upon many,—the fear of temporal punishment, or shame among men. Set your walking beside a heathen's conversation, and save that you say, ye believe in the true God, and he denies him, there is no difference. Your transgressions speak louder than your professions, 'that there is no fear of God before your eyes,' Psal. xxxvi. 1. Your practice belies your profession; you 'profess that you know God; but in works you deny him,' saith Paul, Tit. i. 16. *Ore quod dicitis, opere negatis.*

In the words read in your audience, you have a strange question, and a strange answer; a question of Moses, and an answer of God. The occasion of it was the Lord's giving to Moses a strange and uncouth message. He was giving him commission to go and speak to a king to dismiss and let go six hundred thousand of his subjects; and to speak to a numerous nation to depart from their own dwellings, and come out whither the Lord should lead them. Might not Moses then say within himself, "'Who am I,' to speak such a thing to a king? Who am I, to lead out such a mighty people? Who will believe that thou hast sent me? Will not all men call me a deceiver, an enthusiastical fellow, that take upon me such a thing?" Well then, saith Moses to the Lord,—"Lord, when I shall say, that the God of their fathers sent me unto them, they will not believe me; they have now forgotten thy majesty, and think that thou art but even like the vanities of the nations; they cannot know their own portion from other nations' vain idols; which they have given the same name unto, and call gods as well as thou art called. Now therefore," says he, "when they ask me what thy proper name is by which thou art distinguished from all idols, and all the works of thine own hands, and of men's hands, what shall I say unto them? Here is the question." But why askest thou my name? saith the Lord to Jacob, Gen. xxxii. 29. Importing, that it is high presumption and bold curiosity to search such a wonder. Ask not my name, saith the angel to Manoah, for 'it is secret' or wonderful, Judges xiii. 18. It is a mystery, a hidden mystery, not for want of light, but for too much light. It is a secret; it is wonderful; out of the reach of all created capacity. Thou shalt call his name 'Wonderful,' Isa. ix. 6. What name can express that incomprehensible Majesty? The mind is more comprehensive than words, but the mind and soul is too narrow to conceive him. O then! how short a garment must all words, the most significant and comprehensive and superlative words be? Solomon's soul and heart was enlarged as the sand of the sea, but O it is not large enough for the Creator of it! 'What is his name, and what is his Son's name, if thou canst tell?' Prov. xxx. 4. The Lord himself expresses it to our capacity, because we are not capable of what he can express, much less of what he is. If he should speak to us of himself as he is, O, it should be 'dark sayings,' hid from the understandings of all living! We could reach no more of it, but that it is a wonder, a secret. Here is the highest attainment of our knowledge, to know there is some mystery in it, but not what that mystery is. Christ hath a name above all names, how then can we know that name? It was well said by some of old, *Deus est* πολυωνυμος, and yet ανωνυμος, *multorum nominum, et tamen nullius nominis;* he hath all names, and yet he hath no name; *quia est omnia, et tamen nihil omnium,* because he is all in all, and yet none of all; *Deus est quod vides, et quod non vides.* You may call him by all the works of his hands, for these are beams of his uncreated light, and streams of his inexhaustible sea of goodness, so that whatever perfection is in them, all that is eminently, yea, infinitely in him. Therefore saith Christ, 'There is one good, even God:' and he calls himself 'the light of life;' and therefore you have so many names of God in Scripture. There is no quality, no property, or virtue, that hath the least shadow of goodness, but he is that essentially, really, eternally, and principally; so that the creature deserves not such names but as they participate of his fulness. He is 'the true light,' the true life; the sun is not that true light, though it give light to the moon and to men, for it borrows its light and shining from him. All creatures are and shine but by reflection; therefore these names do agree to them but by a metaphor, so to speak; the propriety and truth of them is in him. As it is but a borrowed kind of speech to call a picture or image a man—only because of the representation and likeness to him it communicates in one name with him—even so, in some manner, the creatures are but some shadows, pictures, or resemblances, and equivocal shapes of God; and whatever name they have, of good, wise, strong, beautiful, true, or such like, it is borrowed speech from God whose image they have. And yet poor vain man would be wise,—thought wise really, intrinsically in himself, and properly,—calls himself so; which is as great an abuse of language as if the picture should call itself a true and living man. But then, as you may call him all things, because he is eminently and gloriously all that is in all, the fountain and end of all; yet we must again deny that he is any of these things. *Unus omnia, et nihil omnium.* We can find no name to him; or what can you call him, when you have said, 'He is light?' You can form no other notion of him but from the resemblance of this created light. But alas! that he is not; he as infinitely transcends that, and is distant from it, as if he had never made it according to his likeness. His name is above all these names; but what it is himself knows, and knows only.

If ye ask what he is, we may glance at some notions and expressions to hold him out. In relation to the creatures, we may call him Creator, Redeemer, Light, Life, Omnipotent, Good, Merciful, Just, and such like: but if you ask, what is his proper name in relation to himself, *ipse novit*, himself knows that, we must be silent, and silence in such a subject is the rarest eloquence. But let us hear what the Lord himself speaks, in answer to this question. If any can tell, sure he himself knows his own name best. "'I am (saith he) what I am.' *Sum qui sum.* 'Go tell them that I AM hath sent thee.'" A strange answer, but an answer only pertinent for such a question. What should Moses make of this? What is he the wiser of his asking? Indeed he might be the wiser; it might teach him more by silence than all human eloquence could instruct him by speaking. His question was curious, and behold an answer short and dark, to confound vain and presumptuous mortality,—'I am what I am;' an answer that does not satisfy curiosity, for it leaves room for the first question, and What art thou? But abundant to silence faith and sobriety, that it shall ask no more, but sit down and wonder.

There are three things I conceive imported in this name: God's unsearchableness, God's unchangeableness, and God's absoluteness. His ineffability, his eternity, and his sovereignty and independent subsistence, upon whom all other things depend. I say,

I. His unsearchableness. You know it is our manner of speech when we would cover any thing from any, and not answer any thing distinctly to them, we say, "It is what it is; I have said what I have said; I will not make you wiser of it." Here then is the fittest notion you can take up God into, to find him unsearchable beyond all understanding, beyond all speaking. The more ye speak or think, to find him always beyond what ye speak or think; whatever you discover of him, to conceive that infiniteness is beyond that; *ad finem cujus pertransire non potest*, the end of which you cannot reach; that he is an unmeasurable depth, a boundless ocean of perfection; that you can neither sound the bottom of it, nor find the breadth of it! Can a child wade the sea, or take it up in the hollow of its hand? Whenever any thing of God is seen, he is seen a wonder; 'Wonderful' is the name he is known by. All our knowledge reacheth no farther than admiration. 'Who is like unto thee?' Exod. xv. 11. Psalm. lxxxix. 6, 7; and admiration speaks ignorance. The greatest attainment of knowledge reacheth but to such a question as this, Who is like to thee? to know only that he is not like any other thing that we know, but not to know what he is. And the different degrees of knowledge are but in more admiration or less at his unconceivableness, and in more or less affection expressed in such pathetic interrogations, O who is like the Lord? How excellent is his name? Here is the greatest degree of saints' knowledge here-away, to ask with admiration and affection such a question that no answer can be given to, or none that we can conceive or understand so as to satisfy wondering, but such as still more increaseth it. There is no other subject but you may exceed it in apprehensions and in expressions. O how often are men's songs and thoughts and discourses above the matter! But here is a subject that there is no excess into; nay, there is no access unto it, let be excess in it. Imagination that can transcend the created heavens and earth, and fancy to itself millions of new worlds, every one exceeding another, and all of them exceeding this in perfection, yet it can do nothing here. That which at one instant can pass from the one end of heaven to the other, walk about the circumference of the heavens, and travel over the breadth of the sea, yet it can do nothing here. 'Canst thou by searching find out God?' Job xi. 7. Imagination cannot travel in these bounds, for his centre is everywhere, and his circumference nowhere, as an old philosopher speaks of God: *Deus est, cujus centrum est ubique, circumferentia nusquam.* How shall it then find him out? There is nothing sure here, but to lose ourselves in a mystery, and to follow his majesty till we be swallowed up with an—*O altitudo!* O the depth and height and length and breadth of God! O the depth of his wisdom! O the height of his power! O the breadth of his love! And O the length of his eternity! It is not reason and disputation, saith Bernard, will comprehend these, but holiness; and that by stretching out the arms of fear and love, reverence and affection. What more dreadful than power that cannot be resisted, and wisdom that none can be hid from? and what more lovely than the love wherewith he hath so loved us, and his unchangeableness which admits of no suspicion? O fear him who hath a hand that doth all, and an eye that beholds all things; and love him who hath so loved us, and cannot change! God hath been the subject of the discourses and debates of men in all ages; but oh! *Quam longe est in rebus qui est tam communis in vocibus?* How little a portion have men understood of him? How hath he been hid from the eyes of all living? Every age must give this testimony of him,—we have heard of his fame, but he is hid from the eyes of all living. I think, that philosopher that took it to his advisement, said more in silence than all men have done in speaking. Simonides being asked by Hiero, a king, what God was, asked a day to deliberate in and think upon it. When the king sought an account of his meditation about it, he desired yet two days more; and so as oft as the king asked him, he still doubled the number of the days in which he might advise upon it. The king wondering at this, asked what he meant by those delays: saith he, *Quanto magis considero, tanto magis obscurior mihi videtur,*—"the more I think on him, he is the more dark and unknown to me." This was more real knowledge than the many subtile disputations of those men who, by their poor shell of finite capacity and reason, presume to empty the ocean of God's infiniteness, by finding out answers to all the objections of carnal reason against all those mysteries and riddles of the Deity. I profess, I know nothing can satisfy reason in this business, but to lead it captive to the obedience of faith, and to silence it with the faith of a mystery which we know not. Paul's answer is one for all, and better than all the syllogisms of such men, 'Who art thou, O man! who disputest?' Dispute thou: I will believe. *Ut intelligatur, tacendum est.* Silence only can get some account of God; quiet and humble ignorance in the admiration of such a majesty is the profoundest knowledge. *Non est mirum si ignoretur, majoris esset admirationis si sciatur.* It is no wonder that God is not known; all the wonder were to know and comprehend such a wonder, such a mystery. It is a wonder indeed, that he is not more known, but when I say so, I mean that he is not more wondered at because he is passing knowledge. If our eyes of flesh cannot see any thing almost when they look straight and steadfastly upon the sun, O what can the eye of the soul behold, when it is fixed upon the consideration of that shining and glorious majesty! Will not that very light be as darkness to it, that it shall be as it were darkness and dazzled with a thick mist of light in *superlucente caligine,*—confounded with that resplendent darkness? It is said that the Lord 'covers himself with light as with a garment,' Psal civ. 2; and yet 'clouds and darkness are round about him,' Psal. xcvii. 2; and he makes darkness his [covering] secret place, Psal. xviii. 11. His inaccessible light is this glorious darkness, that strikes the eyes of men blind; as in the darkness, the sun's light is the night-owl's night and darkness. When a soul can find no better way to know him by, than by these names and notions by which we deny our own knowledge, when it hath conceived all of him it can, then, as being overcome with that dazzling brightness of his glory, to think him inconceivable and to express him in such terms as withal expresses our ignorance. There is no name agrees more to God, than that which saith, we cannot name him, we cannot know him, such as invisible, incomprehensible, infinite, &c. This, Socrates, an heathen, professed to be all his knowledge, that he knew he did know nothing, and therefore he preached an unknown God to the Athenians, to whom, after, they erected an altar with that inscription, 'To the unknown God.' I confess, indeed, the most part of our discourses, of our performances, have such a writing on them, 'to the unknown God!' because we think we know him, and so we know nothing. But oh! that Christians had so much knowledge of God, so much true wisdom, as solidly, and willingly to confess in our souls our own ignorance of him, and then I would desire no other knowledge, and growing in the grace of God, but to grow more and more in the believing ignorance of such a mystery, in the knowledge of an unknown, unconceivable and unsearchable God; that in all the degrees of knowledge we might still conceive we had found less, and that there is more to be found than before we apprehended. This is the most perfect knowledge of God, that doth not drive away darkness, but increases it in the soul's apprehension. Any increase in it doth not declare what God is, or satisfy one's admiration in it, but rather shows him to be more invisible and unsearchable. So that the darkness of a soul's ignorance is more manifested by this light, and not more covered; and one's own knowledge is rather darkened, and disappears in the glorious appearance of this light. For in all new discoveries, there is no other thing appears but this, that that which the soul is seeking is supereminently unknown, and still further from knowledge than ever it conceived it to be. Therefore, whatever you conceive or see of God, if you think ye know what ye conceive and see, it is not God ye see, but something of God's less than God; for it is said, 'eye hath not seen, nor ear heard, nor hath it entered into the heart of man to conceive, what he hath laid up for them that love him.' Now certainly, that is himself he hath laid up for them; therefore, whatever thou conceivest of him, and thinkest now thou knowest of him, that is not he; for it hath not entered into man's heart to conceive him. Therefore, this must be thy soul's exercise and progress in it, to remove all things, all conceptions from him, as not beseeming his majesty, and to go still forward in such a dark negative discovery, till thou know not where to seek him, nor find him. *Si quis Deum videat et intelligat quod vidit, Deum non vidit*, if any see God, and understand what they see, God they do not see; for, 'God hath no man seen,' 1 John iv. 12; 'and no man knows the Father but the Son, and none knows the Son but the Father.' It is his own property to know himself as it is to be himself. Silent and seeing ignorance is our safest and highest knowledge.

Lecture VIII.

THE ETERNITY AND UNCHANGEABLENESS OF GOD.

Exod. iii. 14. "*I AM THAT I AM.*"—Psal. xc. 2. "*Before the mountains were brought forth, or ever thou hadst formed the earth and the world, even from everlasting to everlasting thou art God.*"—Job xi. 7—9. "*Canst thou by searching find out God? canst thou find out the Almighty unto perfection? It is as high as heaven; what canst thou do? deeper than hell; what canst thou know? The measure thereof is longer than the earth, and broader than the sea.*"

This is the chief point of saving knowledge, to know God; and this is the first point or degree of the true knowledge of God, to discern how ignorant we are of him, and to find him beyond all knowledge. The Lord gives a definition of himself, but such an one as is no more clear than himself to our capacities; a short one indeed, and you may think it says not much—'I am.' What is it that may not say so, 'I am that I am?' The least and most inconsiderable creature hath its own being.

Man's wisdom would have learned him to call himself by some high styles, as the manner and custom of kings and princes is, and such as the flattery of men attributes unto them. You would think the superlatives of wise, good, strong, excellent, glorious, and such like, were more beseeming his majesty; and yet there is more majesty in this simple style than in all others; but a 'natural man' cannot behold it, for it is 'spiritually discerned.' 'Let the potsherd,' saith he, 'strive with the potsherds of the earth,' [Isa. xlv. 9,] but let them not strive with their Maker. So I say, let creatures compare with creatures; let them take superlative styles, in regard of others. Let some of them be called good, and some better, in the comparison among themselves; but God must not enter in the comparison. Paul thinks it an odious comparison, to compare present crosses to eternal glory: 'I think them not worthy to be compared, saith Paul, Rom. viii. 18. But how much more odious is it, to compare God with creatures? Call him highest, call him most powerful, call him most excellent, almighty, most glorious in respect of creatures, you do but abase his majesty, to bring it down to any terms of comparison with them which is beyond all the bounds of understanding. All these do but express him to be in some degree eminently seated above the creatures, as some creatures are above all others! so you do no more but make him the head of all as some one creature is the head of one line or kind under it; but what is that to his majesty? He speaks otherwise of himself, Isa. xl. 17. 'All nations before him are as nothing, and they are counted to him less than nothing.' Then, certainly, you have not taken up the true notion of God when you have conceived him the most eminent of all beings, as long as any being appears as a being in his sight before whom all beings conjoined are as nothing. While you conceive God to be the best, you still attribute something to the creature; for all comparatives include the positive in both extremes: so then, you take up only some different degrees between them who differ so infinitely, so incomprehensibly. The distance betwixt heaven and earth is but a poor similitude to express the distance between God and creatures. What is the distance betwixt a being and nothing? Can you measure it? Can you imagine it? Suppose you take the most high, and the most low, and measure the distance betwixt them, you do but consider the difference betwixt two beings, but you do not express how far nothing is distant from any of them. Now, if any thing could be imagined less than nothing, could you at all guess at the vast distance between it and a being? so it is here. Thus saith the Lord, 'all nations,' their glory, perfection, and number, all of them, and all their excellencies united,—do not amount to the value of an unit in regard of my Majesty; all of them like ciphers, join never so many of them together, they can never make up a number, they are nothing in this regard, and less than nothing. So then, we ought thus to conceive of God, and thus to attribute a being and life to him, as in his sight and in the consideration of it all created beings might evanish out of our sight; even as the glorious light of the sun, though it do not annihilate the stars, and make them nothing, yet it annihilates their appearance to our senses, and makes them disappear as if they were not. Although there be a great difference and inequality of the stars in the night,—some lighter, some darker, some of the first magnitude, and some of the second and third, &c. some of greater glory, and some of less,—but in the day-time all are alike, all are darkened by the sun's glory, even so it is here,—though we may compare one creature with another, and find different degrees of perfection and excellency, while we are only comparing them among themselves; but let once the glorious brightness of God shine upon the soul, and in that light all these lights shall be obscured, all their differences unobserved. An angel and a man, a man and a worm, differ much in glory and perfection of being: but oh! in his presence there is no such reckoning. Upon this account all things are alike, God infinitely distant from all, and so not more or less. Infiniteness is not capable of such terms of comparison. This is the reason why Christ says, 'There is none good but one, even God.' Why, because in respect of his goodness, nothing deserves that name. Lesser light, in the view of the greater, is a darkness, as less good in comparison of a greater appears evil; how much more then shall created light and created goodness lose that name and notion, in the presence of that 'uncreated Light, and self-sufficient Goodness.' And therefore it is, that the Lord calls himself after this manner, 'I am,' as if nothing else were. "I will not say," saith he, "that I am the highest, the best and most glorious that is—that supposeth other things to have some being, and some glory that is worthy the accounting of—but I am, and there is none else; I am alone; I lift up my hand to heaven, and swear I live for ever." There is nothing else can say, I am, I live, and there is nothing else; for there is nothing hath it of itself. Can any boast of that which they have borrowed, and is not their own? As if the bird that had stolen from other birds its fair feathers should come forth and contend with them about beauty; would not they presently every one pluck out their own, and leave her naked, to be an object of mockery to all! Even so, since our breath and being is in our nostrils, and that depends upon his Majesty's breathing upon us, if he should but keep in his breath, as it were, we should vanish into nothing; he looketh upon man and he is not, Job vii. 8. That is a strange look, that looks man not only out of countenance, but out of life and being. He looks him into his first nothing; and then can he say, "I live, I am?" No, he must always say of himself in respect of God, as Paul of himself in respect of Christ, 'I live, yet not I, but Christ in me.' I am, yet not I, but God in me. I live, I am, yet not I, but in God, in whom I live and have my being. So that there is no other thing, besides God, can say, 'I am;' because all things are but borrowed drops of this self-sufficient fountain, and sparkles of this primitive light. Let any thing intervene between the stream and the fountain, and it is cut off and dried up; let any thing be interposed between the sun and the beam, and it evanishes. Therefore, this fountain-being, this original light, this self-being, αυτο ον, as Plato called him, deserves only the name of being; other things that we call after that name are nearer nothing than God, and so, in regard of his majesty, may more fitly be called nothing than something. You see then how profound a mystery of God's absolute self-sufficient perfection, is infolded in these three letters, I AM, or in these four, JEHOVAH. If you ask what is God? There is nothing occurs better than this, 'I am,' or, he that is. If I should say he is the almighty, the only wise, the most perfect, the most glorious, it is all contained in that word, 'I am that I am,' *Nempe hoc est ei esse, hæc omnia esse;* for that is to be, indeed, to be all those perfections simply, absolutely, and, as it were, solely. If I say all that, and should reckon out all the scripture-epithets, I add nothing; if I say no more, I diminish nothing.

As this holds out God's absolute perfection, so we told you that it imports his eternity and unchangeableness. You know Pilate's speech, 'What I have written I have written;' wherein he meant that he would not change it; it should stand so. So this properly belongs to God's eternity, 'Before the mountains were brought forth, or ever thou hadst formed the earth and the world, even from everlasting to everlasting, thou art God,' Psal. xc. 2. Now this is properly to be; and this only deserves the name of being, which never was nothing, and never shall be nothing; which may always say, 'I am.' You know it is so with nothing else but God. The heavens and earth, with the things therein, could not say, six thousand years ago, 'I am.' Adam could once have said, 'I am,' but now he cannot say it; for that self-being and fountain-being hath said to him, return to dust. And so it is with all the generations past; where are they now? They were, but they are not. And we then were not, and now are; for we are come in their place, but within a little time, Who of us can say, 'I am?' No, 'we flee away; and are like a dream, as when one awaketh!' We 'are like a tale that is told,' that makes a present noise, and it is past. Within few years this generation will pass, and none will make mention of us; our place will not know us, no more than we do now remember those who have been before. Christ said of John, 'he was a burning and shining light;' 'he was,' saith he, but now he is not. But Christ may always say, 'I am the light and life of men.' Man is; but look a little backward, and he was not; you shall find his original. And step a little forward and he shall not be, you shall find his end. But God is 'Alpha and Omega, the beginning and the end.' But oh! who can retire so far backward as to apprehend a beginning; or go such a start forward as to conceive an end in such a being as is the beginning and end of all things, but without all beginning and end? Whose understanding would it not confound? There is no way here but to flee to Paul's sanctuary, 'O the height and breadth, and length and depth!' We cannot imagine a being, but we must first conceive it nothing, and in some instant receiving its being; and, therefore, 'Canst thou by searching find out God?' Therefore what his being is hath not entered into the heart of man to consider. If any man would live out the space but of two generations, he would be a world's wonder; but if any had their days prolonged as the patriarchs before the flood, they would be called ancient indeed, but then the heavens and earth are far more ancient. We may go backward the space of near six thousand years in our own minds, and yet be as far from his beginning as we were. When we are come to the beginning of all things, a man's imagination may yet extend itself further, and suppose to itself as many thousands of years before the beginning of time, as all the angels and men of all nations and generations from the beginning, if they had been employed in no other thing but this, could have summed up; and then suppose a product to be made of all the several sums of years, it would be vast and unspeakable; but yet your imagination could reach further, and multiply that great sum into itself as often as there are units in it. Now when you have done all this, you are never a whit nearer the days of 'the Ancient of days.' Suppose then this should be the only exercise of men and angels throughout all eternity; all this marvellous arithmetic would not amount unto the least shadow of the continuance of him who is 'from everlasting.' All that huge product of all the multiplications of men and angels, hath no proportion unto that never-beginning and never-ending duration. The greatest sum that is imaginable hath a certain proportion to the least number, that it containeth it so oft and no oftener; so that the least number being multiplied will amount unto the greatest that you can conceive. But O! where shall a soul find itself here? It is enclosed between infiniteness before and infiniteness behind,—between two everlastings; which way soever it turns, there is no outgoing; which way soever it looks, it must lose itself in an infiniteness round about it. It can find no beginning and no end, when it hath wearied itself in searching, which, if it find not, it knows not what it is, and cannot tell what it is. Now what are we then? O what are we, who so magnify ourselves! 'We are but of yesterday, and know nothing,' Job viii. 9. Suppose that we had endured the space of a thousand years, yet saith Moses, Psal. xc. 4, 'A thousand years are but as yesterday in thy sight.' Time hath no succession to thee. Thou beholdest at once what is not at once, but in several times; all that may thus happen hath not the proportion of one day to thy days. We change in our days, and are not that to-day we were yesterday; but 'he is the same yesterday, and to-day, and for ever,' Heb. xiii. 8. Every day we are dying, some part of our life is taken away; we leave still one day more behind us, and what is behind us is gone and cannot be recovered. Though we vainly please ourselves in the number of our years, and the extent of our life, and the vicissitudes of time, yet the truth is, we are but still losing so much of our being and time as passeth. First, we lose our childhood, then we lose our manhood; and then we leave our old age behind us also, and there is no more before us. Even the very present day we divide it with death. But when he moves all things, he remains immoveable. Though days and years be in a continual flux and motion about him, and they carry us down with their force, yet he abides the same for ever. Even the earth that is established so sure, and the heavens that are supposed to be incorruptible, yet they 'wax old as doth a garment;' but he is the same, and 'his years have no end,' Psal. cii. 26, 27. *Sine principio principium; absque fine finis; cui præteritum non abit, haud adit futurum; ante omnia post omnia totus unus ipse*,—He is the beginning without any beginning; the end without an end: there is nothing bypast to him, and nothing to come. *Sed uno mentis cernit in ictu, quæ sunt, quæ erunt, quæ fuerantque*,—he is one that is all, before all, after all, and in all. He beholds out of the exalted and supereminent tower of eternity, all the successions and changes of the creatures; and there is no succession, no mutation in his knowledge, as in ours. 'Known to him are all his works from the beginning.' He can declare the end before the beginning; for he knows the end of all things, before he gives them beginning. Therefore he is never driven to any consultation upon any emergence, or incident, as the wisest of men are, who could not foresee all accidents and events; but 'he is in one mind,' saith Job; and that one mind and one purpose is one for all, one concerning all. He had it from everlasting, and who can turn him? For he will accomplish what his soul desires.

Now, 'canst thou by searching find out God?' Canst thou, a poor mortal creature, either ascend up unto the height of heaven, or descend down into the depths of hell? Canst thou travel abroad, and compass all the sea and dry land, by its longitude and latitude? Would any mortal creature undertake such a voyage, to compass the universe? Nay, not only so, but to search into every corner of it, above and below, on the right hand and on the left? No certainly, unless we suppose a man whose head reaches unto the height of heaven, and whose feet is down in the depths of hell, and whose arms, stretched out, can fathom the length of the earth, and breadth of the sea; unless, I say, we suppose such a creature, then it is in vain to imagine, that either the height of the one, or the depth of the other,—the length of the one, and the breadth of the other, can be found out and measured. Now, if mortal creatures cannot attain the measure of that which is finite, O then, what can a creature do! What can a creature know of him that is infinite, and the maker of all these things? You cannot compass the sea and land, how then can a soul comprehend him, 'who hath measured the waters in the hollow of his hand, and comprehended the dust of the earth in a measure, and weighed the mountains in scales, and the hills in a balance?' Isa. xl. 12. Thou canst not measure the circumference of the heaven, how then canst thou find out him, 'who metes out heaven with the span,' 'and stretcheth them out as a curtain?' Isa. xl. 12, 22. You cannot number the nations, or perceive the magnitude of the earth, and the huge extent of the heavens, what then canst thou know of him, 'who sitteth upon the circle of the earth, and the inhabitants thereof are as grasshoppers before him?' and he spreadeth out the heavens 'as a tent to dwell in!' Isa. xl. 22. He made all the pins and stakes of this tabernacle, and he fastened them below but upon nothing, and stretches this curtain about them and above them; and it was not so much difficulty to him, as to you to draw the curtain about your bed; for 'he spake, and it was done, he commanded, and it stood fast.' Canst thou by searching find him out? And yet thou must search him; not so much out of curiosity to know what he is, for he dwelleth in 'the light which no man can approach unto,' which no man hath seen, and no man can see, 1 Tim. vi. 16; not so much to find him, as to be found of him, or to find what we cannot know when we have found. *Hic est qui nunquam quæri frustra potest, cum tamen inveniri non potest.* You may seek him, but though you never find him, yet ye shall not seek him in vain, for ye shall find blessedness in him. Though you find him, yet can you search him out unto perfection? Then what you have found were not God. How is it possible for such narrow hearts to frame an apprehension, or receive an impression of such an immense greatness, and eternal goodness? Will not a soul lose its power of thinking and speaking, because there is so much to be thought and spoken; and it so transcends all that it can think or speak? Silence then must be the best rhetoric; and the sweetest eloquence, when eloquence itself must become dumb and silent. It is the abundance and excess of that inaccessible light, that hath no proportion to our understandings, that strikes us as blind as, in the darkness, the want of light. All that we can say of God is, that whatsoever we can think or conceive, he is not that, because he hath not entered into the heart of man to conceive, and that he is not like any of those things which we know, unto which if he be not like, we cannot frame any similitude or likeness of him in our knowledge. What then shall we do? Seek him and search him indeed: but, if we cannot know him, to reverence and fear and adore what we know. So much of him may be known as may teach us our duty and show unto us our blessedness. Let then all our inquiries of him have a special relation to this end, that we may out of love and fear of such a glorious and good God, worship and serve him, and compose ourselves according to his will and wholly to his pleasure. Whatever thou knowest of God, or searchest of him, it is but a vain speculation, and a work of curiosity, if it do not lead to this end,—to frame and fashion thy soul to an union and communion with him in love; if it do not discover thyself unto thyself, that in that light of God's glorious majesty thou mayest distinctly behold thy own vileness and wretched misery, thy darkness and deadness and utter impotency. The angels that Isaiah saw attending God in the temple, had wings covering their faces, and wings covering their feet. Those excellent spirits who must cover their feet from us, because we cannot behold their glory, as Moses behoved to be veiled, yet they cannot behold his glory, but must cover their face from the radiant and shining brightness of his majesty. Yet they have other two wings to fly with. And being thus composed in reverence and fear to God, they are ready to execute his commands willingly and swiftly, Isa. vi. 1—3, &c. But what is the use Isaiah makes of all this glorious sight? 'Woe is me! I am a man of unclean lips,' &c. Oh! all is unclean, —people, and pastor! He had known, doubtless, something of it before, but now he sees it of new, as if he had never seen it. The glory of God shining on him doth not puff him up in arrogancy and conceit of the knowledge of such profound mysteries, but he is more abased in himself by it It shines into his heart and whole man, and lets him see all unclean within and without. And so it was with Job, Job xliii. 5, 6. 'I have heard of thee by the hearing of the ear;' but as long as it was hearsay, I thought myself something,—I often reflected upon myself and actions, with a kind of self-complacency and delight; but now, saith he, since I have seen thee by the seeing of the eye, 'I abhor myself and repent in dust and ashes;' I cannot look upon myself with patience,—without abhorrency and detestation. Self-love made me loathe other men's sins more than mine own, and self-love did cover mine own sins from me; it presented me to myself in a feigned likeness; but now I see myself in my true shape, and all coverings stripped off. Thy light hath pierced into my soul, and behold, I cannot endure to look upon myself. Here now is the true knowledge of God's majesty, which discovers within thee a mystery of iniquity: and here is the knowledge of God indeed, which abases all things besides God, not only in opinion but in affection, that attracts and unites thy soul to God, and draws it from thyself and all created things. This is a right discovery of divine purity and glory, that spots even the cleanness of angels, and stains the pride of all glory; much more will it represent filthiness, as filthiness without a covering. It is knowledge and science, 'falsely so called,' that puffeth up; for true knowledge emptieth a soul of itself, and humbleth a soul in itself, that it may be full of God. He that thinks he knows any thing, knows nothing as he ought to know.

This then is the first property or mark of the saving knowledge of God. It removes all grounds of vain confidence that a soul cannot trust unto itself. And then the very proper intent of it is, that a soul may trust in God, and depend on him in all things. For this purpose the Lord hath called himself by so many names in scripture, answerable to our several necessities and difficulties, that he might make known to us how all-sufficient he is, that so we may turn our eyes and hearts towards him. This was the intent of this name, I AM, that Moses might have a support of his faith; for if he had looked to outward appearance, was it not almost a ridiculous thing, and like a vain fancy, for a poor inconsiderable man to go to a king with such a message, that he would dismiss so many subjects? And was it not an attempt of some madman to go about to lead so many thousands from a wicked tyrannical king, into another nation? Well, saith the Lord, 'I am;' I, who give all things a being, will give a being to my promise. I will make Pharaoh hearken, and the people obey. Well then, what is it that this name of God will not answer? It is a creating name,—a name that can bring all things out of nothing by a word. If he be such as he is, then he can make of us what he pleases. If our souls had this name constantly engraven on our hearts, O what power would divine promises and threatenings have with us! 'I, even I, am he that comforteth thee,' saith he, Isaiah xli. 12. If we believed that it were he indeed, the Lord Jehovah, how would we be comforted! How would we praise him by his name JAH! How would we stoop unto him, and submit unto his blessed will! If we believed this, would we not be as dependent on him as if we had no being in ourselves? Would we not make him our habitation and dwelling-place; and conclude our own stability, and the stability of his church from his unvariable eternity? as the Psalmist, Psal. xcix. 1. Psal. cii. ult. How can we think of such a Fountain-Being, but we must withal acknowledge ourselves to be shadows of his goodness, and that we owe to him what we are, and so consecrate and dedicate ourselves to his glory! How can we consider such a Self-Being, Independent, and Creating Goodness, but we must have some desire to cleave to him, and some confidence to trust in him! Now, this is to know him.

When we think on his unchangeableness, let us consider our own vanity, whose glory and perfection is like a summer flower, or like a vapour ascending for a little time, whose 'best estate is altogether vanity.' Our purposes are soon broken off, and made of none effect; our resolutions change. This is a character of mortality, we are not always alike. *Non sibi constare, nec ubique et semper sibi parem eundemque esse.* To be now one thing, and then another thing, is a property of sinful and wretched man. Therefore let us 'cease from man whose breath is in his nostrils,' and 'trust not in princes' who shall die, far less in ourselves who are less than the least of men: but let us put our trust in God, 'who changeth not,' and we shall not be consumed,—our waters shall not fail,—we shall never be ashamed of any hope we have in him. There is nothing else you trust in, but undoubtedly it shall prove your shame and confusion. Whatever you hear or know of God, know that it is vain and empty, unless it descend down into the heart to fashion it to his fear and love, and extend unto the outward man to conform it to obedience; you are but 'vain in your imaginations, and your foolish hearts are darkened,' while 'when you know God, you glorify him not as God.' If that be not the fruit and end of knowledge, that knowledge shall be worse to thee than ignorance, for it both brings on judicial hardening here, and will be thy solemn accuser and witness against thee hereafter, Rom. i. 21—24 The knowledge of Jesus Christ, truly so called, is neither barren nor unfruitful, for out of its root and sap spring humility, self-abasing confidence in God, patience in tribulations, meekness in provocations, temperance and sobriety in lawful things, &c. 2 Pet. i. 5—8.

Lecture IX.

WHAT GOD IS TO US.

Exod. xxxiv. 6, 7. "*The Lord, the Lord God, merciful and gracious, long-suffering, and abundant in goodness and truth, keeping mercy for thousands.*"

There is nothing can separate between God and a people but iniquity; and yet he is very loath to separate even for that. He makes many shows of departing, that so we may hold him fast; and indeed he is not difficult to be holden. He threatens often to remove his presence from a person or nation; and he threatens, that he may not indeed remove, but that they may entreat him to stay; and he is not hard to be entreated. Who is a God like unto him, slow to anger, and of great mercy? He is long of being provoked, and not long provoked; for it is like the anger of a parent's love. Love takes on anger as the last remedy; and if it prevail, it is as glad to put it off as it was unwilling to take it on. You may see a lively picture of this in God's dealing with Moses and this people in the preceding chapter. He had long endured this rebellious and obstinate people,—had often threatened to cut them off,—and yet, as it were, loath to do it, and repenting of it, he suffers himself to be entreated for them; but all in vain to them,—they corrupted their way still more: and in the 32d chapter fall into gross idolatry, the great trespass that he had given them so solemn warning of often, whereupon great wrath is conceived. And the Lord (chap. xxxiii. 2.) threatens to depart from them,—Go your way, saith he, to Canaan, but I will not go with you; take your venture of any judgments, and the people of the land's cruelty. Here is a sad farewell to Israel; and who would think he could be detained after all that? Who would think that he could be entreated? And yet he is not entreated, he is not requested, before he gives some ground of it, and before he first condescends; go, saith he, and put off thy ornaments from thee, that I may know what to do unto thee. Will he then accept a repenting people, and is there yet hope of mercy? Should he that is going away show us the way to keep him still? And he that flees from us, will he strengthen us to pursue and follow after him? This is not after the manner of men, it is true, whose compassions fail when their passion ariseth, but this is the manner and method of grace, or of him who waits to be gracious. He flees so as he would have a follower. Yea, while he seems to go away, he draws the soul that he might run after him. Hence is that word, Psal. lxiii. 8. 'My soul followeth hard after thee; thy right hand upholdeth me.' Well, the people mourn, and put off their ornaments in sign of humiliation and abasement, but all this doth not pacify and quench the flame that was kindled. Moses takes the tabernacle out of the camp, the place of judgment where God spake with the people; and the cloud, the sign of God's presence, removes. In a word, the sign of God's loving and kind presence departs from them, to signify that they were divorced from God, and, in a manner, the Lord by Moses excommunicates all the people and rulers both, and draws away these holy things from the contagion of a profane people. But yet all is not gone. He goes far off, but not out of sight, that you may always follow him; and if you follow, he will stand still. He is never without the reach of crying, though we do not perceive him. Now, in this sad case you may have a trial who is godly. Every one that seeks the Lord will separate from the unholy congregation, and follow the tabernacle; and this affects the whole people much, that they all worship in the tent doors.

Now, in the meantime, God admits Moses to speak with him. Though he will not speak to the people, yet he will speak with their mediator, a typical mediator, to show us that God is well-pleased in Christ; and so all Christ's intercessions and requests for us will get a-hearing. When they are come once in talking, the business is taken up, for He is not soon angry, and never implacably angry,—'slow to anger,' and keeps it not long. Moses falling familiar with God, not only obtains his request for the people, but becomes more bold in a request for his own satisfaction and confirmation. He could not endure to lead that people unless God went with him; and having the promise of his going with them, he cannot endure distance with him, but aspires to the nearest communion that may be. Oh! that it were so with us. His great request is, that the Lord will show him his glory. Had he not seen much of this already; and more than any man ever saw, when he spake in the mount with God, &c.? Nay, but he would see more; for there is always more to be seen, and there is in a godly soul always more desire to see it. The more is seen, the more is loved and desired. Tasting of it only begets a kindly appetite after it; and the more tasted, still the fresher and more recent: but yet it is above both desire and fruition,—'Thou canst not see my face,' &c. All our knowledge of God,'—all our attainments of experience of him,—do but reach to some dark and confused apprehension of what he is. The clearest and nearest sight of God in this world, is, as if a man were not known but by his back, which is a great point of estrangement. It is said, in heaven we shall see him 'face to face,' and fully as he is, because then the soul is made capable of it.

Two things in us here put us in an incapacity of nearness with God,—infirmity and iniquity. Infirmity in us cannot behold his glory. It is of so weak eyes, that the brightness of the sun would strike it blind. And iniquity in us, he cannot behold it, because he is of pure eyes, that can look on no unclean thing. It is the only thing in the creation that God's holiness hath an antipathy at; and therefore he is still about the destroying of the body of sin in us, about the purging from all filthiness of flesh and spirit; and till the soul be thus purged of all sin, by the operation of the Holy Ghost, it cannot be a temple for an immediate vision of him, and an immediate exhibition of God to us. Sin is the wall of partition, and the thick cloud that eclipses his glory from us. It is the opposite hemisphere of darkness, contrary to light; according to the access or recess of God's presence, it is more or less dark. The more sin reigns in thee, the less of God is in thee; and the more sin be subdued, the readier and nearer is God's presence. But let us comfort ourselves that one day we shall put off both infirmity and iniquity; mortality shall put on immortality, and corruption be clothed with incorruption. We shall leave the rags of mortal weakness in the grave, and our menstruous clothes of sin behind us; and then shall the weak eyes of flesh be made like eagles' eyes, to behold the sun; and then shall the soul be clothed with holiness, as with a garment, which God shall delight to look upon, because he sees his own image in that glass.

We come to the Lord's satisfying of Moses' desire, and proclaiming his name before him. It is himself only can tell you what he is. It is not ministers' preaching, or other discourse, can proclaim that name to you. We may indeed speak over those words unto you, but it is the Lord that must write that name upon your heart. He only can discover his glory to your spirit. There is a spirit of life which cannot be enclosed in letters and syllables, or transmitted through your ears into your hearts, but he himself must create it inwardly, and stir up the inward sense and feeling of that name, of those attributes. Faith, indeed, 'cometh by hearing,' and our knowledge in this life is 'through a glass darkly,' through ordinances and senses; but there must be an inward teaching and speaking to your souls to make that effectual: 'the anointing teacheth you of all things,' 1 John ii. 27. Alas! it is the separation of that from the word that makes it so unprofitable. If the Spirit of God were inwardly writing what the word is teaching, then should your souls be 'living epistles,' that ye might read God's name on them. O! be much in imploring of and depending on him that teacheth to profit, who only can declare unto your souls what he is!

These names express his essence or being, and his properties; what he is in himself, and what he is to us. In himself he is Jehovah, or a Self-Being, αυτ ον, as we heard in the 3d chapter, 'I am that I am,' and El, a strong God, or Almighty God; which two hold out unto us the absolute incomprehensible perfection of God, eminently and infinitely enclosing within himself all the perfections of the creature; the unchangeable and immutable being of God, who was, and is, and is to come, without succession, without variation, or shadow of turning; and then the almighty power of God, by which without difficulty, by the inclination and beck of his will and pleasure, he can make, or unmake all,—create or annihilate,—to whom nothing is impossible. Which three, if they were pondered by us till our souls received the stamp of them, they would certainly be powerful to abstract and draw our hearts from the vain, changeable, and empty shadow of the creature, and gather our scattered affections that are parted among them, because of their insufficiency, that all might unite in one, and join with this self-sufficient and eternal God. I say, if a soul did indeed believe and consider how all-sufficient he is, how insufficient all things else are, would it not cleave to him, and draw near to him? Psal. lxxiii. ult. It is the very torment and vexation of the soul to be thus racked, distracted, and divided about many things; and therefore many, because there is none of them can supply all our wants. Our wants are infinite, our desires insatiable, and the good that is in any thing is limited and bounded; it can serve, one but for one use, and another for another use; and when all are together, they can but supply some wants, but they leave much of the soul empty. But often these outward things cross one another, and cannot consist together; and hence ariseth much strife and debate in a soul. His need requireth both, and both will not agree. But O that you could see this one universal good, one for all, and above all, your souls would choose him certainly—your souls would trust in him! Ye would say, 'Asshur shall not save us, we will not ride on horses.' Creatures shall not satisfy us, we will seek our happiness in thee and nowhere else; since we have tasted this new wine, away with the old, the new is better. I beseech you, make God your friend, for he is a great one; whether he be a friend or an enemy, he hath two properties that make him either most comfortable, or most terrible, according as he is at peace or war with souls,—eternity, and omnipotency. You were all once enemies to him. O consider what a party you have, an almighty party, and an unchangeable party! and if you will make peace with him, and that in Christ, then know he is the best friend in the world, because he is unchangeable and almighty. If he be thy friend, he will do all for thee he can do and thou hast need of. Many friends willing to do, have not ability, but he hath power to do what he wills and pleases. Many friends are changeable,—their affections dry up and of themselves die; and therefore even princes' friendship is but a vain confidence, for they shall die, and then their thoughts of favour perish with them; but he abides the same for all generations. There is no end of his duration, and no end of his affection; he can still say, 'I am that I am.' What I was, I am; and I will be what I am. Men cannot say so, they are like the brooks that the companies of Teman looked after, and thought to have found them in summer as they left them in winter; but behold they were dried up, and the companies ashamed. God cannot make thee ashamed of thy hope, because he is faithful and able. Ability and fidelity is a sure anchor to hold by in all storms and tempests.

Such is God in himself. Now, there are two manner of ways he vents himself towards the creatures,—in a comfortable way, or in a terrible way. This glorious perfection and almighty power hath an issue upon sinners, and it runs in a twofold channel, of mercy or justice; of mercy towards miserable sinners that find themselves lost, and flee unto him and take hold of his strength; and justice towards all those that flatter themselves in their own eyes, and continue in their sins, and put the evil day far off. There is no mercy for such as fear not justice, and there is no justice for such as flee from it unto mercy. The Lord exhibits himself in a twofold appearance, according to the condition of sinners. He sits on a throne and tribunal of grace and mercy, to make access to the vilest sinner who is afraid of his wrath and would fain be at peace with him; and he sits on a throne of justice and wrath, to seclude and debar presumptuous sinners from holiness. There were two mountains under the law,—one of cursings, and another of blessings. These are the mountains God sets his throne upon, and from these he speaks and sentences mankind. From the mountain of cursings, he hath pronounced a curse and condemnatory sentence upon all flesh, 'for all have sinned.' Therefore, he concludes all under sin, that all flesh might stop their mouth, and the whole world become guilty before God. Now, the Lord having thus condemned all mankind because of disobedience, he sits again upon the mountain of blessings, and pronounces a sentence of absolution, of as many as have taken with the sentence of condemnation, and appealed to his grace and mercy; and those which do not so, the sentence of condemnation stands above their heads unrepealed. He erects his tribunal of justice in the world for this end, that all flesh might once be convicted before him; and therefore he cites, as it were, and summons all men to sist themselves and compear before his tribunal, to be judged. He lays out an accusation in the word against them. He takes their consciences witness of the truth of all that is charged on them. and then pronounces that sentence in their conscience, 'Cursed is he that abideth not in all things,' which the conscience subsumes, and concludes itself accursed, and subscribes to the equity of the sentence. And thus man is guilty before God, and his mouth stopped. He hath no excuses, no pretences, he can see no way to escape from justice, and God is justified, by this means, in his speaking and judging, Psal. li. 4. The soul ratifies and confirms the truth and justice of all his threatenings and judgments, Rom. iii. 4. Now, for such souls as join with God in judging and condemning themselves, the Lord hath erected a throne of grace and tribunal of mercy in the word, whereupon he hath set his Son Jesus Christ, Psal. ii. 6; lxxxix. 14; xlv. 6; Heb. i. 8. And O! this throne is a comfortable throne. Mercy and truth go before the face of the king to welcome and entertain miserable sinners, and to make access to them. And from this throne Jesus Christ holds out the sceptre of the gospel, to invite sinners, self-condemned sinners, to come to him alone, who hath gotten all final judgment committed to him, that he may give eternal life 'to whom he will,' John v. 21, 22. O! that is a sweet and ample commission given to our friend and brother, Jesus Christ,—power to repeal sentences passed against us,—power and authority to absolve them whom justice hath condemned, and to bless whom the law hath cursed, and to open their mouth to praise whose mouth sin and guiltiness hath stopped,—power to give the answer of a good conscience to thy evil self-tormenting conscience! In a word, he hath power to give life, to make alive and heal those who are killed or wounded by the commandment. Now, I say, seeing God hath of purpose established this throne of mercy in the word, thou mayest well, after receiving and acknowledging of the justice of the curse of the law, appeal to divine mercy and grace sitting on another throne of the gospel. Thou mayest—if thy conscience urge thee to despair, and to conclude there is no hope—thou mayest, I say, appeal from thy conscience, from Satan, from justice, unto Jesus Christ, who is holding out the sceptre to thee. The minister calls thee, rise and come; stand no longer before that bar, for it is a subordinate judicatory; there is a way to redress thee by a higher court of grace. Thou mayest say to justice, to Satan, to thy own conscience,—"It is true, I confess, that I deserve that sentence; I am guilty, and can say nothing against it, while I stand alone. But though I cannot satisfy, and have not; yet there is one, Jesus Christ, who gave his life a ransom for many, and whom God hath given as a propitiation for sins. He hath satisfied and paid the debt in my name; go and apprehend the cautioner, since he hath undertaken it, nay, he hath done it, and is absolved. Thou hadst him in thy hands, O Justice! Thou hadst him prisoner under the power of death. Since thou hast let him go, then he is acquitted from all the charge of my sins; and therefore, since I know that he is now a king, and hath a throne to judge the world and plead the cause of the poor sheep, I will appeal to him, refer the cause to his decision, I will make my supplication to him, and certainly he will hear, and interpose himself between wrath and me. He will rescind this sentence of condemnation, since he himself was condemned for us and is justified, —'It is Christ that died, yea rather that is risen again,' who shall condemn me? He is near that justifies me, Rom. viii. 33, 34. Now if thou do indeed flee unto him for refuge, that city is open for thee, and nothing to prejudge thy entry. But no curse, no condemnation can enter in it, Rom. viii. 1. He will justify and absolve thee from all things whereof the law could not justify thee, but condemn thee. There is forgiveness with him, that he may be feared. David may teach thee this manner of application, (Psal. cxxx. and cxlii. 2,) of appealing from the deserved curse, to free undeserved blessing and mercy in Christ.

Let us consider this name of the Lord, and it shall answer all our suspicions of him,—all our objections against coming to him and believing in him. It is certain, ignorance is the mother of unbelief, together with the natural perverseness of our hearts. If we knew his name, we would trust in him; if his names were pondered and considered, we would believe in him. Satan knows this, and therefore his great sleight and cunning is to hold our minds fixed on the consideration of our misery and desperate estate. He keeps the awakened conscience still upon that comfortless sight, and he labours to represent God by halves, and that it is a false representation of God. He represents him as clothed with justice and vengeance,—as a consuming fire, in which light a soul can see nothing but desperation written; and he labours to hold out the thoughts of his mercy and grace, or diverts a soul from the consideration of his promises; whence it comes, that they are not established, that though salvation be near, yet it is far from them in their sense and apprehension. Therefore I say, you should labour to get an entire sight of God, and you shall see him best in his word. There he reveals himself, and there you find, if you consider, that which may make you fear him indeed, but never flee from him,—that which may abase you, but withal embolden you to come to him though trembling. Whatever thought possess thee of thine own misery, of thy own guiltiness, labour to counterpoise that with the thought of his mercy and free promises. Whatever be suggested of his holiness and justice, hear himself speak out his own name, and thou shall hear as much of mercy and grace as may make these not terrible unto thee, though high and honourable. The Lord hath so framed the expression and proclamation of his name in this place, that first a word of majesty and power is premised,—'the Lord, the Lord God,'—that it may compose our hearts in fear and reverence of such a glorious one, and make a preparatory impression of the majesty of our God, which indeed is the foundation of all true faith. It begins to adore and admire a deity, a majesty hid from the world. The thoughts of his power and glory possess the soul first, and make it begin to tremble to think that it hath such a high and holy one to deal with.

But, in the next place, you have the most sweet, alluring, comforting styles that can be imagined, to meet with the trembling and languishing condition of a soul that would be ready to faint before such a majesty. Here Mercy takes it by the hand, and gives a cordial of grace, pardon, forgiveness, &c. to it, which revives the soul of the humble, and intermingles some rejoicing with former trembling. Majesty and greatness go before to abase and humble the soul in its own eyes; and mercy and goodness second them, to lift up those who are low and exalt the humble. And in the description of this, the Lord spends more words, according to the necessity of a soul, to signify to us how great and strong consolation may be grounded on his name,—how accessible he is, though he dwell in inaccessible light,—how lovely he is, though he be the high and the lofty one,—how good he is, though he be great,—how merciful he is, though he be majestic. In a word, that those that flee to him may have all invitation, all encouragement to come, and nothing to discourage, to prejudge their welcome; that whoever will, may come, and nothing may hinder on his part. And then, after all this, he subjoins a word of his justice, in avenging sin, to show us that he leaves that as the last; that he essays all gaining ways of mercy with us; and that he is not very much delighted with the death of sinners, that so whosoever perishes may blame themselves for hating their own salvation and forsaking their own mercy.

Now whoever thou art that apprehendest a dreadful and terrible God, and thyself a miserable and wretched sinner, thou canst find no comfort in God's highness and power, but it looks terrible upon thee, because thou doubtest of his good-will to save and pardon thee. Thou sayest with the blind man, If thou wilt, thou canst do it; thou art a strong God, but what comfort can I have in thy strength, since I know not thy good-will? I say, the Lord answers thee in this name, I am 'merciful,' saith the Lord. If thou be miserable, I am merciful as well as strong; if thou have sin and misery, I have compassion and pity. My mercy may be a copy and pattern to all men to learn it of me, even towards their own brethren, Luke vi. 36. Therefore he is called 'the father of mercies,' 2 Cor. i. 3. *Misericors est cui alterius miseria cordi est.* Mercy hath its very name from misery, for it is no other thing than to lay another's misery to heart; not to despise it, not to add to it, but to help it. It is a strong inclination to succour the misery of sinners, therefore thou needest no other thing to commend thee to him. Art thou miserable, and knowest it indeed? Then he is merciful; and know that also, these two suit well.

Nay, but saith the convinced soul, I know not if he will be merciful to me, for what am I? There is nothing in me to be regarded. I have nothing to conciliate favour, and all that may procure hatred. But, saith the Lord, I am 'gracious,' and dispense mercy freely, without respect to condition or qualification. Say not, if I had such a measure of humiliation as such a one,—if I loved him so much,—if I had so much godly sorrow and repentance,—then, I think he would be merciful to me. Say not so, for behold he is gracious. He hath mercy on whom he will have mercy; and there is no other cause, no motive to procure it; it comes from within his own breast. It is not thy repentance will make him love thee, nor thy hardness of heart will make him hate thee or obstruct the vent of his grace towards thee. No! if it be grace, it is no more of works,—not works in that way that thou imaginest. It is not of repentance, not of faith in that sense thou conceivest; but it is freely, without the hire, without the price of repentance or faith, because all those are but the free gifts of grace. Thou wouldst have these graces to procure his favour, and to make them the ground of thy believing in his promises but grace is without money. It immediately contracts with discovered misery, so that if thou do discover in thyself misery and sin, though thou find nothing else, yet do not cast away confidence, but so much the more address thyself to mercy and grace, which do not seek repentance in thee, but bring repentance and faith with them unto thee. Yet there is something in the awakened conscience. I have gone on long in sin; I have been a presumptuous sinner; can he endure me longer? Well, hear what the Lord saith, I am 'long-suffering' and patient. And if he had not been so, we had been damned ere now. Patience hath a long term, and we cannot outrun it, outweary it. Why do we not wonder that he presently and instantly executed his wrath on angels, and gave them not one hour's space for repentance, but cast them down headlong into destruction, as in a moment; and yet his majesty hath so long delayed the execution of our sentence, and calls us unto repentance and forgiveness, that we may escape the condemnation of angels? His patience is not slackness and negligence, as men count it, 2 Pet. iii. 9. He sits not in heaven as an idol, and idle spectator of what men are doing; but he observes all wrongs, and is sensible of them also. And if we were mindful and sensible of them also, he would forget them. He is long-suffering. This is extended and stretched-out patience beyond all expectation, beyond all deserving, yea contrary to it. Therefore, as long as he forbears, if thou apprehend thy misery and sin, and continuance in it; do not conclude that it is desperate. 'Why should a living man complain?' As long as patience lengthens thy life, if thou desire to come to him, believe he will accept thee.

But, saith the doubting soul, I am exceeding perverse and wicked; there is nothing in me but wickedness. It so abounds in me that there is none like me. But, saith the Lord, I am 'abundant in goodness.' Thy wickedness, though it be great, it is but a created wickedness; but my goodness is the goodness of God. I am as abundant in grace and goodness as thou art in sin,—nay, infinitely more. Thy sin is but the transgression of a finite creature; but my mercy is the compassion of an infinite God,—it can swallow it up. Suppose thy sin cry up to heaven, yet mercy reaches above heaven, and is built up for ever. Here is an invitation to all sinners to come and taste,—O come and taste, and see how good the Lord is! Goodness is communicative; it diffuses itself, like the sun's light. There is 'riches of his goodness,' Rom. ii. 4. Poor soul, thou canst not spend it though thou have many wants!

But I am full of doubtings, fears, and jealousies; I cannot believe in his promises; I often question them. How, then, will he perform them? I say, saith the Lord, I am abundant in truth. He will certainly perform. Shall our unbelief, or doubting, 'make the faith of God without effect?' &c. Rom. iii. 3. God forbid! His faithfulness reaches unto the clouds; he will keep covenant with thee, whose soul hath chosen him, though thou often question and doubt of him. Indeed, thou shouldst not give indulgence to thy doubtings and jealousies, but look on them as high provocations. For what can be more grievous to fervent love than to meet with jealousy? Jealousy would quench any creature's love; but though it grieve and provoke him, yet he will not change, he will not diminish his. Only do not think your disputings and quarrelling innocent and harmless things. No certainly, they grieve the Spirit,—stir up the beloved to go away, as it were, before he please,—and make thee walk without comfort, and without fruit. Yet he will bear with, and not quench 'the smoking flax' of a believer's desires, though they do not arise to the flame of assurance.

But the wounded spirit hath one or two burdens more. I have abused much mercy, how can mercy pity me? I have turned grace into wantonness, so that when I look to mercy and grace to comfort me, they do rather challenge me. The sins of none are like mine,—none of such a heinous and presumptuous nature. But let us hear what God the Lord speaks: I keep 'mercy for thousands, forgiving iniquity, and transgression, and sin.' Thou hast wasted much mercy, but more is behind; all the treasure is not spent. Though there were many thousand worlds besides, I could pardon them all, if they would flee unto my mercy. Thou shalt not be straitened in me. Mercy will pardon thy abuse of mercy; it will forgive all faults thou dost against itself. Thou that sinnest against the Son of man, the Redeemer of the world, and remedy of sin,—yet there is pardon for thee, whatever the quality, condition, or circumstance of thy sin be. Whoever, convinced of it, and loadened with it, desirest rest to thy soul, thou mayest find it in Christ, whose former kindness thou hast answered with contempt. Many sins, many great sins, and these presumptuous sins, cannot exclude, nay, no sin can exclude a willing soul. Unbelief keeps thee unwilling, and so excludes thee.

Now, as the spider sucks poison out of the sweetest flower, so the most part of souls suck nothing but delusion and presumption and hardening out of the gospel. Many souls reason for more liberty to sin, from mercy. But behold, how the Lord backs it with a dreadful word, 'who will by no means clear the guilty.' As many as do not condemn themselves before the tribunal of justice, there is no rescinding of the condemnatory sentence, but it stands above their heads, 'he that believeth not is condemned already.' Justice hath condemned all by a sentence. He that doth not, in the sense of this, flee unto Jesus Christ from sin and wrath, is already condemned. His sentence is standing. There needs no new one. Since he flees not to mercy for absolution, the sentence of condemnation stands unrepealed. You guilty souls who clear yourselves, God will not clear you. And, alas! how many of you do clear yourselves! Do you not extenuate and mince your sins? How hard is it to extort any confession of guilt out of you, but in the general! If we condescend to particulars, many of you will plead innocency almost in every thing, though you have, like children, learned to speak these words that ye are sinners. I beseech you consider it; it is no light matter, for 'God will by no means clear the guilty;' by no means, by no entreaties, no flatteries. What! will he not pardon sin? Yes indeed: his name tells you he will pardon all kind of sins, and absolve all manner of guilty persons: but yet such as do condemn themselves, such as are guilty in their own conscience, and their mouths stopped before God,—you who do not enter into the serious examination of your ways, and do not arraign yourselves before God's tribunal daily, till you find yourselves loathsome and desperate, and no refuge for you,—you who do flatter yourselves always in the hope of heaven, and put the fear of hell always from you,—I say, God will by no means, no prayers, no entreaties, clear or pardon you, because you come not to Jesus Christ, in whom is preached forgiveness and remission of sins. You who take liberty to sin, because God is gracious, and delay repentance till the end, because God is long-suffering,—know God God will not clear you; he is holy and just as he is merciful. If his mercy make thee not fear and tremble before him, and do not separate thee from thy sins,—if remission of sins be not the strongest persuasion to thy soul of the removing of sin,—certainly thou dost in vain presume upon his mercy.

Now, consider what influence all this glorious proclamation had on Moses. It stirs up in him reverence and affection,—reverence to such a glorious Majesty, and great desire to have him amongst them, and to be more one with him. If thy soul rightly discover God, it cannot but abase thee. He 'made haste' to bow down and worship. O, God's majesty is a surprising and astonishing thing! It would bow thy soul in the dust if it were presented to thee. Labour to keep the right and entire representation of God in thy sight,—his whole name, strong, merciful, and just,—great, good, and holy. I say, keep both in thy view, for half-representations are dangerous, either to beget presumption and security when thou lookest on mercy alone; or despair when thou lookest on justice and power alone. Let thy soul consider all jointly, that it may receive a mixed impression of all. And this is the holy composition and temper of a believer,—Rejoice with trembling, love with fear; let all thy discoveries of him aim at more union and communion with him who is such a self-sufficient, all-sufficient, and eternal Being.

Lecture V.

WHAT GOD IS.

JOHN iv. 24. "*God is a Spirit, and they that worship him must worship him in spirit and in truth.*"

WE have here something of the nature of God pointed out to us, and something of our duty towards him. 'God is a Spirit,' that is his nature; and 'man must worship him,' that is his duty; and that 'in spirit and in truth,' that is the right manner of the duty. If these three were well pondered till they did sink into the bottom of our spirits, they would make us indeed Christians, not in the letter, but in the spirit. That is presupposed to all Christian worship and walking, to know what God is; it is indeed the *primo cognitum* of Christianity, the first principle of true religion, the very root out of which springs and grows up walking suitably with, and worshipping answerably of, a known God. I fear much of our religion is like the Athenians'; they built an altar to the unknown God, and like the Samaritans', who worshipped they knew not what. Such a worship, I know not what it is, when the God worshipped is not known, The two parents of true religion are the knowledge of God and of ourselves. This, indeed, is the beginning of the fear of God, which the wise preacher calls 'the beginning of' true 'wisdom.' And these two, as they beget true religion, so they cannot truly be one without the other. It is not many notions and speculations about the divine nature,—it is not high and strained conceptions of God,—that comprise the true knowledge of him. Many think they know something when they can speak of those mysteries in some singular way, and in some terms removed from common understandings, while neither themselves nor others know what they mean. And thus they are presumptuous, self-conceited, knowing nothing as they ought to know. There is a knowledge that puffs up, and there is a knowledge that casts down; a knowledge in many that doth but swell them, not grow them; it is but a rumour full of wind, a vain and empty, frothy knowledge, that is neither good for edifying others, nor saving a man's self; a knowledge that a man knows and reflects upon, so as to ascend upon the height of it, and measure himself by the degrees of it. This is not the true knowledge of God, which knows not itself, looks not back upon itself, but straight towards God, his holiness and glory, and our baseness and misery; and therefore it constrains the soul to be ashamed of itself in such a glorious presence, and to make haste to worship, as Moses, Job, and Isaiah did.

This definition of God,—if we did truly understand it, we could not but worship him in another manner. 'God is a Spirit.' Many ignorant people form in their own mind some likeness and image of God, who is invisible. Ye know how ye fancy to yourselves some bodily shape. When you conceive of him, you think he is some reverend and majestic person sitting on a throne in heaven. But, I beseech you, correct your mistakes of him. There is outward idolatry and there is inward; there is idolatry in action, when men paint or engrave some similitude of God; and there is idolatry in imagination, when the fancy and apprehension run upon some image or likeness of God. The first is among Papists, but I fear the latter is too common among us; and it is indeed all one, to form such a similitude in our mind, and to engrave or paint it without. So that the God whom many of us worship, is not the living and true God, but a painted or graven idol. When God appeared most visible to the world, as at the giving out of the law, yet no man did see any likeness at all. He did not come under the perception of the most subtle sense; he could not be perceived but by the retired understanding, going aside from all things visible. And therefore you do but fancy an idol to yourselves, instead of God, when you apprehend him under the likeness of any visible or sensible thing; and so whatever love, or fear, or reverence you have, it is all but misspent superstition, the love and fear of an idol.

I. Know then, 'that God is a Spirit;' and therefore he is like none of all those things you see, or hear, or smell, or taste, or touch. The heavens are glorious indeed, the light is full of glory; but he is not like that. If all your senses should make an inquiry, and search for him throughout the world, you should not find him. Though he be near hand every one of us, yet our eyes and ears, and all our senses, might travel the length of the earth and breadth of the sea, and should not find him, even as you might search all the corners of heaven, ere you could hear or see an angel. If you would saw a man asunder and resolve him into atoms of dust, yet you could not perceive a soul within him. Why? Because these are spirits, and so without the reach of your senses.

II. If God be a Spirit, then he is invisible, and dwells in light inaccessible, 'which no man hath seen or can see.' Then our poor narrow minds, that are drowned, as it were, and immersed in bodies of clay, and in this state of mortality, receive all knowledge by the senses, cannot frame any notion of his spiritual and abstracted nature. We cannot conceive what our own soul is, but by some sensible operation flowing from it; and the height that our knowledge of that noble part of ourselves amounts to, is but this dark and confused conception, that the soul is some inward principle of life and sense and reason. How then is it possible for us to conceive aright of the divine nature, as it is in itself, but only in a dark and general way? We guess at his majesty, by the glorious emanations of his power, and wisdom, and the rays thereof, which he displays abroad in all the work of his hands; and from all these concurring testimonies, and evidences of his majesty, we gather this confused notion of him, that he is the fountain-self-independent Being, the original of these things, and more absolute in the world than the soul is in the body; the true *Anima mundi;* the very life and the light of men, and the soul that quickens, moves, and forms all this visible world; that makes all things visible, and himself is invisible. Therefore it is that the Lord speaks to us in Scripture of himself, according to our capacities,—of his face, his right hand, and arm, his throne, his sceptre, his back parts, his anger, his fury, his repentance, his grief, and sorrow,—none of which are properly in his spiritual, immortal, and unchangeable nature. But because our dulness and slowness is such in apprehending things spiritual, it being almost without the sphere and comprehension of the soul while in the body, which is almost addicted unto the senses in the body; therefore the Lord accommodates himself unto our terms and notions; *balbutit nobiscum*,—he, like a kind father, stammers with his stammering children, speaks to them in their own dialect; but withal, would have us conceive he is not really such an one, but infinitely removed in his own being from all these imperfections. So when you hear of these terms in scripture, O beware of conceiving God to be such a one as yourselves! But, in these expressions not beseeming his Majesty, because below him, learn your own ignorance of his glorious Majesty, your dulness and incapacity to be such as the holy One must come down as it were in some bodily appearance, ere you can understand any thing of him.

III. If God be a Spirit, then he is most perfect and most powerful. All imperfection, all infirmity, and weakness in the creature, is founded in the gross and material part of it. You see the more matter and bodily substance is in any thing, it is the more lumpish, heavy, and void of all action. It is the more spiritual, pure, and refined part of the creation that hath most activity in it, and is the principle of all motions and actions. You see a little fly hath more action in it than a great mountain, because there are spirits in it which move it. The bottom of the world contains the dregs of the creation, as it were,—a mass and lump of heavy earth; but the higher and more distant bodies be from that, the more pure and subtile they are; and the more pure and subtile they be, the more action, virtue, and efficacy they have. The earth stands like a dead lump, but the sea moves; and the air being thinner and purer than both, moves more easily and swiftly. But go up higher, and still the motion is swifter, and the virtue and influence is the more powerful. What is a dead body when the soul and spirit is out of it? It hath no more virtue and efficacy than so much clay, although by the presence of the spirit of it, it was active, agile, swift, strong and nimble. So much then as any thing hath of spirit in it, so much the more perfect and powerful it is. Then I beseech you consider what a One the God of the spirits of all flesh must be,—the very Fountain-spirit,—the Self-being spirit,—αυτο πνευμα. When the soul of a man, or the spirit of a horse, hath so much virtue, to stir up a lump of earth, and to quicken it to so many diverse operations, even though that soul and spirit did not, nay, could not make that piece of earth they dwell in, then, what must his power and virtue be that made all those things? Who gave power and virtue even to the spirits of all flesh? 'Their horses,' saith God, are 'flesh and not spirit,' (Isa. xxxi. 3;) because, in comparison of his majesty, the very spirits in them are but like a dead lump of flesh. If he should draw in his breath, as it were, they would have no more virtue to save the Israelites, than so many lumps of flesh or clay. For he is the Spirit of all spirits, that quickens, actuates, and moves them to their several operations and influences. *Anima mundi, et Anima animarum mundi.* An angel hath more power than all men united in one body. Satan is called the prince of the air, and the god of this world, for he hath more efficacy and virtue to commove the air, and raise tempests, than all the swarms of multiplied mankind, though gathered into one army. If the Lord did not restrain and limit his power, he were able to destroy whole nations at once. An angel killed many thousands of Sennacherib's army in one night; what would many angels do then, if the Lord pleased to apply them to that work? O what is man that he should magnify himself, or glory in strength, or skill? Beasts are stronger than men, but man's weaker strength being strengthened with more skill, proves stronger than they. But in respect of angels he hath neither strength nor wisdom.

IV. If God be a Spirit, then he is not circumscribed by any place; and if an infinite Spirit, then he is everywhere, no place can include him, and no body can exclude him. He is within all things, yet not included nor bounded within them; and he is without all things, yet not excluded from them. *Intra omnia, non tamen inclusus in illis; extra omnia, nec tamen exclusus ab illis.* You know every body hath its own bounds and limits circumscribed to it, and shoots out all other bodily things out of the same space, so that before the least body want some space, it will put all the universe in motion, and make every thing about it to change its place, and possess another. But a spirit can pass through all of them, and never disturb them; a legion may be in one man, and have room enough. If there were a wall of brass, or tower, having no opening, neither above nor beneath, no body could enter, but by breaking through, and making a breach into it; but an angel or spirit could storm it without a breach, and pierce through it without any division of it. How much more doth the Maker of all spirits fill all in all! The thickness of the earth doth not keep him out, nor the largeness of the heavens contain him. How then do we circumscribe and limit him within the bounds of a public house, or the heavens? O! how narrow thoughts have we of his immense greatness, who, without division or multiplication of himself, fills all the corners of the world,—whose indivisible unity is equivalent to an infinite extension and divisibility! How often, I pray you, do you reflect upon this? God is near to every one of us. Who of us thinks of a divine Majesty nearer us than our very souls and consciences, 'in whom we live, and move, and have our being?' How is it we move, and think not with wonder of that first Mover in whom we move? How is it we live and persevere in being, and do not always consider this fountain-Being in whom we live and have our being? O, the atheism of many souls professing God! We do speak, walk, eat, and drink, and go about all our businesses, as if we were self-being, and independent of any; never thinking of that all-present quickening Spirit, that acts us, moves us, speaks in us, makes us to walk and eat and drink; as the barbarous people, who see, hear, speak and reason, and never once reflect upon the principle of all these, to discern a soul within. This is brutish, and in this, man who was made of a straight countenance to look upward to God, and to know himself and his Maker, till he might be differenced from all creatures below, is degenerated, and become like the beasts that perish. Who of us believes this all-present God? We imagine that he is shut up in heaven, and takes no such notice of affairs below; but certainly, he is not so far from us; though he show more of his glory above, yet he is as present and observant below.

V. If he be a Spirit, then as he is incomprehensible and immense in being, so also there is no comprehension of his knowledge. The nearer any creature comes to the nature of a spirit, the more knowing and understanding it is. Life is the most excellent being, and understanding is the most excellent life. *Materia est iners et mortua.* The nearer any thing is to the earthly matter, as it hath less action, so less life and feeling. Man is nearer an angel than beasts, and therefore he hath a knowing understanding spirit in him. There is a spirit in man, and the more or less this spirit of man is abstracted from sensual and material things, it lives the more excellent and pure life, and is, as it were, more or less delivered from the chains of the body. These souls that have never risen above, and retired from sensible things, O, how narrow are they,—how captivated within the prison of the flesh! But when the Lord Jesus comes to set free, he delivers a soul from this bondage, he makes these chains fall off, and leads the soul apart to converse with God himself, and to meditate on things not seen,—sin, wrath, hell, and heaven. And the farther it goes from itself, and the more abstracted it is from the consideration of present things, the more it lives a life like angels. And therefore, when the soul is separated from the body, it is then perfectly free, and hath the largest extent of knowledge. A man's soul must be almost like Paul's 'whether out of the body, or in the body, I know not,'—if he would understand aright spiritual things. Now then, this infinite Spirit is an all-knowing Spirit, all-seeing Spirit, as well as all-present; 'there is no searching of his understanding,' Isa. xl. 28. Psalm cxlvii. 5. 'Who hath directed the Spirit of the Lord, or, being his counsellor, hath taught him?' Isa. xl. 13. Rom. xi. 34. He calls the generations from the beginning, and known to him are all his works from the beginning. O that you would always set this God before you, or rather set yourselves always in his presence, in whose sight you are always! How would it compose our hearts to reverence and fear in all our actions, if we did indeed believe that the Judge of all the world is an eye-witness to our most retired and secret thoughts and doings! If any man were as privy to thy thoughts, as thy own spirit and conscience, thou wouldst blush and be ashamed before him. If every one of us could open a window into one another's spirits, I think this assembly should dismiss as quickly as that of Christ's, when he bade them that were without sin cast a stone at the woman. We could not look one upon another. O then, why are we so little apprehensive of the all-searching eye of God, who can even declare to us our thought before it be? How much atheism is rooted in the heart of the most holy! We do not always meditate, with David, Psal. cxxxix, on that all-searching and all-knowing Spirit, who knows our down-sitting and uprising, and understands our thoughts afar off, and who is acquainted with all our ways. O how would we ponder our path, and examine our words, and consider our thoughts beforehand, if we set ourselves in the view of such a Spirit, that is within us and without us, before us and behind us! He may spare sinners as long as he pleases, for there is no escaping from him. You cannot go out of his dominions; nay, you cannot run out of his presence, Psal. cxxxix. 7—10. He can reach you when he pleases, therefore he may delay as long as he pleases.

Lecture IX.

THE KNOWLEDGE THAT GOD IS, COMBINED WITH THE KNOWLEDGE THAT HE IS TO BE WORSHIPPED.

JOHN iv. 24. "*God is a Spirit: and they that worship him must worship him in spirit and in truth.*"

THERE are two common notions engraven on the hearts of all men by nature,—that God is, and that he must be worshipped; and these two live and die together; they are clear, or blotted together. According as the apprehension of God is clear, and distinct, and more deeply engraven on the soul, so is this notion of man's duty of worshipping God clear and imprinted on the soul; and whenever the actions of men do prove that the conception of the worship of God is obliterate or worn out,—whenever their transgressions do witness that a man hath not a lively notion of this duty of God's worship,—that doth also prove that the very notion of a godhead is worn out, and cancelled in the soul. For how could souls conceive of God as he is indeed, but they must needs, with Moses, (Exod. xxxiv. 8.) make haste to pray and worship? It is the principle of the very law of nature which shall make the whole world inexcusable, 'because that when they knew God, they glorified him not as God.' A father must have honour, and a master must have fear; and God, who is the common parent and absolute master of all, must have worship, in which reverence and fear, mixed with rejoicing and affection, predominate. It is supposed, and put beyond all question that he must be: 'he that worships him, must worship him in spirit and in truth.' It is not simply said, God is a Spirit and must be worshipped; no, for none can doubt of it. If God be, then certainly worship is due to him, for who is so worshipful? And because it is so beyond all question, therefore woe to the irreligious world that never puts it in practice! O, what excuse can you have, who have not so much as a form of godliness! Do you not know, that it is beyond all controversy that God must be worshipped? Why then do you deny that in your practice, which all men must confess in their conscience? Is not he God, the Lord, a living and self-being Spirit? Then must he not have worshippers? Beasts are not created for it; it is you, O sons of men! whom he made for his own praise; and it is not more suitable to your nature than it is honourable and glorious. This is the great dignity and excellency you are privileged with, beyond the brute beasts,—to have spirits within you capable of knowing and acknowledging the God of your spirits. Why then do you both rob and spoil God of his glory, and cast away your own excellency? Why do you love to trample on your ornaments and wallow in the puddle; like beasts void of religion, but so much worse than beasts, that you ought to be better, and were created for a more noble design? O base-spirited wretches, who hang down your souls to this earth, and follow the dictates of your own sense and lust, and have not so much as an external form of worshipping God! How far are you com-short of the noble design of your creation, and the high end of your immortal souls! If you will not worship God, know, he will have worshippers. Certainly he will not want it; because he hath designed so many souls to stand before him, and worship him, and that number will not fail. He might indeed have wanted worshippers: for what advantage is it to him? But in this he declares his love and respect to man, that he will not want honour and service from him. It is rather to put honour upon him, and to make him blessed and happy, than for any gain that can amount to himself by it. For this is indeed the true honour and happiness of man, not to be worshipped and served of other fellow-creatures, but to worship and serve the Creator. This is the highest advancement of a soul, to lie low before him, and to obey him, and have our service accepted of his Majesty. I beseech you, strive about this noble service! Since he must have worshippers, O say within your souls, "I must be one! If he had but one, I could not be content if I were not that one." Since the Father is seeking worshippers, (ver. 23,) O let him find thee! Offer thyself to him, saying, Lord, here am I. Should he seek you, who can have no advantage from you? Should he go about so earnest a search for true worshippers, who can have no profit by them? And why do ye not seek him, since to you all the gain and profit redounds? Shall he seek you to make you happy? And why do ye not seek him and happiness in him? It is your own service, I may truly say, and not his so much; for in serving him thou dost rather serve thyself; for all the benefit redounds to thyself, though thou must not intend such an end, to serve him for thyself, but for his name's sake; else thou shalt neither honour him, nor advantage thyself. I pray you let him not seek in vain, for in these afflictions he is seeking worshippers; and if he find you, you are found and saved indeed. Do not then forsake your own mercy, to run from him who follows you with salvation.

As none can be ignorant that God is, and must be worshipped, so it is unknown to the world in what manner he must be worshipped. The most part of men have some form in worshipping God, and please themselves in it so well that they think God is well pleased with it; but few there are who know indeed what it is to worship him in a manner acceptable to his Majesty. Now you know it is all one not to worship him at all, as not to worship him in that way he likes to be worshipped. Therefore, the most part of men are but self-worshippers, because they please none but themselves in it. It is not the worship his soul hath chosen, but their own invention; for you must take this as an undeniable ground, that God must be worshipped according to his own will and pleasure, and not according to your humour or invention. Therefore, his soul abhors will-worship, devised by men out of ignorant zeal or superstition, though there might seem much devotion in it, and much affection to God. As in the Israelites sacrificing their children, what more seeming self-denial,—and yet what more real self-idolatry? God owns not such a service, for it is not service and obedience to his will and pleasure, but to men's own will and humour. Therefore, a man must not look for a reward but from himself. Now, it is not only will-worship, when the matter and substance of the worship is not commanded of God, but also when a commanded worship is not discharged in the appointed manner. Therefore, O how few true worshippers will the Father find! True worship must have truth for the substance, and spirit for the manner of it; else it is not such a worship as the Father seeks and will be pleased with. Divine worship must have truth in it,—that is plain,—but what was that truth? It must be conformed to the rule and pattern of worship, which is God's will and pleasure revealed in the word of truth. True worship is the very practice of the word or truth. It carries the image and superscription and command upon it, which is a necessary ingredient in it, and constituent of it. Therefore, if thy service have the image of thy own will stamped on it, it is not divine worship but will-worship. Thus all human ceremonies and ordinances enjoined for the service of God, carry the inscription not of God, but of man, who is the author and original of them, and so are but adulterated and false coin that will not pass current with God. I fear there be many rites and vain customs among ignorant people, in which they place some religion, which have no ground in the word of God, but are only 'old wives' fables' and traditions. How many things of that nature are used upon a religious account, in which God hath placed no religion! Many have a superstitious conceit of the public place of worship, as if there were more holiness in it than in any other house; and so they think their prayers in the church are more acceptable than in their chamber. But Christ refutes that superstitious opinion of places, and so consequently of days, meats, and all such external things. The Jews had a great opinion of their temple, the Samaritans of their mountain,—as if these places had sanctified their services. But saith our Lord, (ver. 21,) 'The hour cometh when ye shall neither in this mountain nor yet at Jerusalem, worship the Father,' but it is any where acceptable, if so be ye worship in spirit and truth. Many of you account it religion to pray and mutter words of your own in the time of public prayer; but who hath required this at your hands? If ye would pray yourselves, go apart; shut the door behind thee, saith Christ. Private prayer should be in private and secret; but where public prayer is, your hearts should close with the petitions, and offer them up jointly to God. It is certainly a great sleight of that deceitful destroyer, the devil, to possess your minds with an opinion of religion in such vain babblings, that he may withdraw both your ears and your hearts from the public worship of God; for when every one is busied with his own prayers, you cannot at all join in the public service of God which is offered up in your name. The like I may say of stupid forms of prayer, and tying yourselves to a platform, written in a book, or to some certain words gotten by the heart? Who hath commanded this? Sure, not the Lord, who hath promised his Spirit to teach them to pray, and help their infirmities, who know not how, nor what to pray. It is a device of your own, invented by Satan to quench the spirit of supplication, which should be the very natural breathing of a Christian. But there are some so grossly ignorant of what prayer is, that they make use of the ten commandments, and creed, as a prayer. So void are they of the knowledge and Spirit of God, that they cannot discern betwixt God's commands to themselves and their own requests to God; betwixt his speaking to men, and their speaking to him; between their professing of him before men, and praying and confessing to him. All this is but forged, imaginary worship,—worship falsely so called, which the Father seeks not, and receives not.

But what if I should say, that the most part of your worship, even that which is commanded of God, as prayer, hearing, reading, &c. hath no truth in it, I should say nothing amiss. For though you do those things that are commanded, yet not as commanded, without any respect to divine appointment; and only because you have received them as traditions from your fathers, and because you are taught so by the precepts of men, and are accustomed so to do: therefore the stamp of God's will and pleasure is not engraven on them, but of your own will, or of the will of men. Let me pose* your consciences, many of you, what difference is there between your praying and your plowing; between your hearing, and your harrowing; between your reading in the Scriptures, and your reaping in the harvest; between your religious service and your common ordinary actions; I say, what difference is there in the rise of these? You do many civil things out of custom, or because of the precepts of men; and is there any other principle at the bottom of your religious performances? Do you at all consider these are divine appointments,—these have a stamp of his authority on them? And from the conscience of such an immediate command of God, and the desire to please him and obey him, do you go about these? I fear many cannot say it. O, I am sure all cannot, though it may be all will say it. Therefore your religious worship can come in no other account than will-worship, or man-worship. It hath not the stamp of truth on it,—an express conformity to the truth of God as his truth.

But we must press this out a little more. Truth is opposed to a ceremony and shadow. The ceremonies of old were shadows, or the external body of religion, in which the soul and spirit of godliness should have been enclosed; but the Lord did always urge more earnestly the substance and truth than the ceremony,—the weightier matters of the law, piety, equity, and sobriety, than these lighter external ceremonies. He sets a higher account upon mercy than sacrifice, and upon obedience than

* [That is, propound a nice question.—ED.]

ceremonies. But this people turned it just contrary. They summed up all their religion in some ceremonial performance, and separated those things God had so nearly conjoined. They would be devout men in offering sacrifices, in their washings, in their rites, and yet made no conscience of heart and soul piety towards God, and upright just dealing with men. Therefore the Lord so often quarrels with them, and rejects all their service as being a device and invention of their own, which never entered into his heart: Isa. i. 10—15; Jer. vii. throughout; Isa. lxvi. 3, 4; Isa. xxviii. Now, if you will examine it impartially, it is even just so with us. There are some external things in religion, which, in comparison with the weightier things of faith and obedience, are but ceremonial. In these you place the most part if not all your religion, and think yourselves good Christians, if you be baptized, and hear the word, and partake of the Lord's table, and such like; though in the meantime you be not given to secret prayer, and reading, and do not inwardly judge and examine yourselves that ye may flee unto a Mediator,—though your conversation be unjust and scandalous among men. I say unto such souls, as the Lord unto the Jews, 'Who hath required this at your hands?' Who commanded you to hear the word, to be baptized, to wait on public ordinances? Away with all this; it is abomination to his majesty! Though it please you never so well, the more it displeases him. If you say, Why commands he us to hear? &c. I say, the Lord never commanded these external ordinances for the sum of true religion; that was not the great thing which was in his heart, that he had most pleasure unto, but the weightier matters of the law, piety, equity, and sobriety, a holy and godly conversation adorning the gospel: 'What doth the Lord require of thee, but to do justly, and to love mercy, and to walk humbly with thy God?' So then, thou dost not worship him in truth, but in a shadow. The truth is holiness and righteousness. That external profession is but a ceremony. While you separate these external ordinances from these weighty duties of piety and justice, they are but as a dead body without a soul. If the Lord required truth of old, much more now, when he hath abolished the multitude of ceremonies, that the great things of his law may be more seen and loved.

If you would then be true worshippers, look to the whole mind of God, and especially the chief pleasure of God's mind, that which he most delights in ; and by any means do not separate what God hath conjoined. Do not divide righteousness towards men from a profession of holiness to God, else it is but a falsehood, a counterfeit coin. Do not please yourselves so much in external church-privileges, without a holy and godly conversation adorning the gospel; but let the chief study, endeavour, and delight of your souls be about that which God most delights in. Let the substantials of religion have the first place in the soul. Pray more in secret; that will be the life of your souls. You ought, indeed, to attend public ordinances; but, above all, take heed to your conversation and walking at home, and in secret. Prayer in your family is a more substantial worship than to sit and hear prayer in public; and prayer in secret is more substantial than that. The more retired and immediate a duty be, the more weighty it is; the more it crosses thy corruptions, and evidences the stamp of God on thy affections, the more divine it is; and therefore to serve God in these is to serve him in truth. Practice hath more of truth in it than a profession. 'When your fathers executed judgment, was not this to know me?' Duties that have more opposition from our nature, against them, and less fuel or oil to feed the flame of our self-love and corruption, have more truth in them; and if you should worship God in all other duties, and not especially in these, you do not worship him in truth.

Next, let us consider the manner of divine worship; and this is as needful to true worship as true matter; that it be commanded, and done as it is commanded,—that completes true worship. Now, I know no better way or manner to worship God in, than so to worship him, as our worship may carry the stamp of his image upon it, as it may be a glass wherein we may behold God's nature and properties. For such as himself is, such he would be acknowledged to be. I would think it were true worship indeed, which had engrvaen on it the name of the true and living God, if it did speak out so much of itself: 'That God is, and that he is a rewarder of them that seek him diligently.' Most part of our service speaks an unknown God, and carries such an inscription upon it, 'To the unknown God.'

There is so little either reverence, or love, or fear, or knowledge in it, as if we did not worship the true God, but an idol. It is said, that 'the fool says in his heart, there is no God,' because his thoughts and affections and actions are so little composed to the fear and likeness of that God, as if he did indeed plainly deny him. I fear, it may be said thus of our worship: It says, There is no God. It is of such a nature that none could conclude from it that it had any relation to the true God. Our prayers deny God, because there is nothing of God appears in them. But this is true worship, when it renders back to God his own image and name• *Unde repercussus redditur ipse sibi.* As it is a pure fountain, in which a man may see his shadow distinctly, but a troubled fountain or mire in which he cannot behold himself; so it is pure worship, which receives and reflects the pure image of God, but impure and unclean worship, which cannot receive it and return it. I pray you, Christians, consider this, for it is such worshippers the Father seeks. And why seeks he such, but because in them he finds himself? So to speak, his own image and superscription is upon them; his mercy is engraven on their faith and confidence; his majesty and power is stamped on their humility and reverence; his goodness is to be read in the soul's rejoicing, his greatness and justice in the soul's trembling. Thus there ought to be some engravings on the soul answering the characters of his glorious name. O how little of this is among them that desire to know something of God! How little true worship, even among them whom the Father hath sought out to make true worshippers! But alas, how are all of us unacquainted with this kind of worship! We stay upon the first principles and practices of religion, and go not on to build upon the foundation. Sometimes your worship hath a stamp of God's holiness and justice, in fear and terror at such a majesty, which makes you tremble before him; but where is the stamp of his mercy and grace which should be written in your faith and rejoicing? Tremble and fear indeed, but 'rejoice with trembling,' because there is mercy with him. Sometimes there is rejoicing and quietness in the soul, but that quickly degenerates into carnal confidence, and makes the soul turn grace into wantonness, and esteem of itself above what is right, because it is not counterpoised with the sense and apprehension of his holiness and justice. But O to have these jointly written upon the heart, in worship, fear, reverence, confidence, humility, and faith! That is a rare thing: it is a divine composition and temper of spirit that makes a divine soul. For the most part, our worship savours and smells nothing of God, neither his power, nor his mercy and grace, nor his holiness and justice, nor his majesty and glory: a secure, faint, formal way, void of reverence, of humility, of fervency, and of faith. I beseech you let us consider, as before the Lord, how much pains and time we lose, and please none but ourselves, and profit none at all. Stir up yourselves as in his sight; for it is the keeping of our souls continually as in his sight which will stamp our service with his likeness. The fixed and constant meditation on God and his glorious properties, this will beget the resemblance between our worship and the God whom we worship; and it will imprint his image upon it; and then it should please him, and then it should profit thee, and then it should edify others.

But more particularly: the worship must have the stamp of God's spiritual nature, and be conformed to it in some measure, else it cannot please him. There must be a conformity between God and souls. This is the great end of the gospel, to repair that image of God which was once upon man, and make him like God again. Now, it is this way that Jesus Christ repairs this image, and brings about the conformity with God, by the soul's worshipping of God suitable to his nature, which, as it grows more and more suitable to God's nature, it is the more and more like God, and happy in that likeness. Now, 'God is a Spirit,' therefore, saith Christ, you 'must worship him in spirit and in truth.' The worship then of saints must be of a spiritual nature, that it may be like the immortal divine Spirit. It is such worshippers the Father seeks. He seeks souls to make them like himself; and this likeness and conformity to God is the very foundation of the soul's happiness, and eternal refreshment. This is a point of great consequence, and I fear not laid to heart. The worship must be like the worshipped. It is a spirit must worship the eternal Spirit. It is not a body that can be the principal and chief agent in the business. What communion can God have with your bodies while your souls are removed far from him, more than with beasts? All society and fellowship must be between those that are like one another. A man can have no comfortable company with beast, or with stones, or with trees. It is men that can converse with men; and a spirit must worship the self-being Spirit. Do not mistake this, as if under the days of the gospel we were not called to an external and bodily worship,—to any service to which our outward man is instrumental. That is one of the deep delusions of this age, into which some men, 'reprobate concerning the faith,' have fallen, that there should be no external ordinances, but that Christians are now called to a worship all spirit, pure spirit, &c. This is one of the spirits, and spiritual doctrines (that call themselves so) which ye must not receive; for it is neither the Spirit of God nor of Christ that teacheth this. Not the Spirit of God the Creator, because he hath made the whole man, body and soul, and so must be worshipped of the whole man. He hath created man in such a capacity as he may offer up external actions, in a reasonable manner, with the inward affections. As the Lord hath created him, so should he serve him—every member, every part in its own capacity, —the soul to precede, and the body to follow,—the soul to be the chief worshipper, and the body its servant employed in the worship. True worship hath a body and a soul as well as a true man; and as the soul separated is not a complete man, so neither is the soul separated a complete worshipper without the body. The external ordinances of God is the body, the inward soul-affection is the spirit, which being joined together make complete worship. Neither is it the Spirit of Christ which teacheth this, because our Lord Jesus hath taught us to offer up our bodies and spirits both as a reasonable service, Rom. xii. 1, 2. The sacrifice of the bodily performance offered up by the spiritual affection and renewed mind is a living sacrifice, holy, acceptable, and reasonable. That Spirit which dwelt in Christ above measure, did not think it too base to vent itself in the way of external ordinances. He was, indeed, above all, above the law, yet did willingly come under them, to teach us, who have so much need and want, to come under them. He prayed much, he preached, he did sing and read, to teach us how to worship, and how much need we have of prayer and preaching. This was not the spirit Christ promised to his disciples and apostles, which spirit did breathe most lively in the use of external ordinances, all their days; and this is not the spirit which was at that hour in which Christ spoke, 'the hour is come and now is,' ver. 23, in which the true worship of God shall not be in the external Jewish ceremonies and rites, void of all life and inward sense of piety; but the true worship of God shall be made up of a soul and body,—of spirit and truth,—of the external appointed ordinances according to the word of truth, and the spirit of truth,—and of the spirit and inward soul-affection and sincerity, which shall quicken and actuate that external performance. There were no such worshippers then as had no use of ordinances. Christ was not such, his disciples were not such; therefore it is a new gospel, which, if an angel should bring from heaven, ye ought not to receive it.

As it is certain, then, that both soul and body must be employed in this business, so it is sure that the soul and spirit must be the first mover and chiefest agent in it, because it is a spiritual business, and hath relation to the Fountain-spirit, which hath the most perfect opposition to all false appearances and external shows. That part of man that cometh nearest God, must draw nearest in worshipping God; and if that be removed far away, there is no real communion with God. Man judges according to the outward appearance, and can reach no farther than the outward man; but God is an all-searching Spirit, who trieth the heart and reins, and therefore he will pass another judgment upon your worship than men can do, because he observes all the secret wanderings and escapes of the heart out of his sight. He misses the soul when you present attentive ears or eloquent tongues. There is no dallying with his Majesty; painting will not deceive him, his very nature is contrary to hypocrisy and dissimulation; and what is it but dissimulation, when you present yourselves to religious exercises as his people, but within are nothing like it, nothing awaking, nothing present? O consider, my beloved, what a one you have to do with! It is not men, but the Father of spirits, who will not be pleased with what pleases men, of your own flesh, but must have a spirit to serve him! Alas! what are we doing with such empty names and shows of religion? Busied with the outside of worship only, as if we had none to do with but men who have eyes of flesh. All that we do in this kind is lost labour, and will never be reckoned up in the account of true worship. I am sure you know and may reflect upon yourselves, that you make religion but a matter of outward fashion and external custom: you have never almost taken it to heart in earnest. You may frequent the ordinances,—you may have a form of godliness consisting in some outward performances and privileges,— and O, how void and destitute of all spirit, and life, and power! Not to speak of the removal of affection and the employing of the marrow of your soul upon base lusts and creatures, or the scattering of your desires abroad amongst them, for that is too palpable; even your very thoughts and minds are removed from this business; you have nothing present but an ear, or eye; and your minds are about other business; your desires, your fears, your joys, and delights, your affections, never did run in the channel of religious exercises; all your passion is vented in other things. But here you are blockish and stupid, without any sensible apprehension of God, his mercy, or justice, or wrath, or of your own misery and want. You sorrow in other things, but none here, none for sin! You joy for other things, but none here, you cannot rejoice at the gospel! Prayer is a burden, not a delight. If your spirits were chiefly employed in religious duties, religion would be almost your element, your pleasure and recreation; but now it is wearisome to the flesh, because the spirit taketh not the chief weight upon it. O! 'be not deceived, God is not mocked.' You do but mock yourselves with external shows, while you are satisfied with them. I beseech you, look inwardly, and be not satisfied with the outward appearance, but ask at thy soul, where it is, and how it is. Retire within, and bring up thy spirit to this work. I am sure you may observe that any thing goes more smoothly and sweetly with you than the worship of God, because your mind is more upon any thing else. I fear the most part of us who endeavour, in some measure, to seek God, have too much dross of outward formality, and much scum of filthy hypocrisy and guile. O! pray that the present furnace may purge away this scum. It is the great ground of God's present controversy with Scotland; but, alas! the bellows are like to burn, and we not to be purged. Our scum goes not out from us. We satisfy ourselves with some outward exercises of religion. Custom undoes us all; and it was never more undoing than when indignation and wrath are pursuing it. O! that you would ponder what you lose by it,—both the sweetness and advantage of godliness, beside the dishonour of God. You take a formal, negligent, and secure way, as the most easy way, and the most pleasing to your flesh; and I am persuaded you find it the most difficult way, because you want all the pleasant and sweet refreshment and soul-delights you might have in God, by a serious and diligent minding of religion. The pleasure and sweetness of God tasted and found, will make diligence and pains more easy than slothfulness can be to the slothful. This oils the wheels, and makes them run swiftly; formality makes them drive heavily. Thus you live always in a complaining humour,—sighing, and going backward,— because you have some stirring principle of conscience within which bears witness against you; and your formal sluggish disposition on the other hand refuses to awake and work. You are perplexed and tormented between these two. When thy spirit and affections go one way, and thy body another; when thy conscience drives on the spirit, and thy affections draw back, it must needs be an unpleasant business.

Lecture VII.

THE UNITY OF THE DIVINE ESSENCE, AND THE TRINITY OF PERSONS.

Deut. vi. 4. "*Hear, O Israel, the Lord our God is one Lord.*"—1 John v. 7. "*There are three that bear record in heaven, the Father, the Word, and the Holy Ghost, and these three are one.*"

'Great is the mystery of godliness,' 1 Tim. iii. 16. Religion and true godliness is a bundle of excellent mysteries,—of things hid from the world, yea, from the wise men of the world, (1 Cor. ii. 6.) and not only so, but secrets in their own nature, the distinct knowledge whereof is not given to saints in this estate of distance and absence from the Lord. There is almost nothing in divinity, but it is a mystery in itself, how common soever it be in the apprehensions of men. For it is men's overly,* and common and slender apprehensions of them, which make them look so commonly upon them. There is a depth in them, but you will not know it, till you search it, and sound it; and the more you sound, you shall find it the more profound. But there are some mysteries small and some great. There is a difference amongst them; all are not of one stature, of one measure. The mystery of Christ's incarnation and death and resurrection, is one of the great mysteries of religion, 'God manifest in the flesh.' Yet I conceive there is a greater mystery than it, and of all mysteries in nature or divinity I know none equal to this,—the Holy Trinity. And it must needs be greatest of all, and without controversy greatest, because it is the beginning and end of all,—*fons et finis omnium.* All mysteries have their rise here, and all of them return hither. This is furthest removed from the understandings of men,—what God himself is; for himself is infinitely above any manifestation of himself. God is greater than God manifested in the flesh, though in that respect he be too great for us to conceive. There is a natural desire in all men to know; and, if any thing be secret and wonderful, the desire is the more inflamed after the knowledge of it. The very difficulty or impossibility of attaining it, instead of restraining the curiosity of man's spirit, doth rather incense it. *Nitimur in vetitum* † is the fruit, the sad fruit we plucked and eat from the tree of the knowledge of good and evil. If the Lord reveal any thing plainly in his word to men, that is despised and set at nought, because it is plain: whereas the most plain truths, which are beyond all controversy, are the most necessary, and most profitable for our eternal salvation. But if there be any secret mystery in the Scriptures, which the Lord hath only pointed out more obscurely to us, reserving the distinct and clear understanding of it to himself, (Deut. xxix. 29,)—that is the apple which our accursed natures will long for, and catch after, though there be never so much choice of excellent saving fruit in the paradise of the Scriptures besides. If the ark be covered to keep men from looking into it, that doth rather provoke the curious spirit of man to pry into it, 1 Sam. vi. 19. If the Lord show his wonderful glory in the mount, and charge his people not to come near, lest the glorious presence of God kill them, he must put rails about it, to keep them back, or else they will be meddling. Such is the unbridled license of our minds, and the perverse dispositions of our natures, that where God familiarly invites us to come,—what he earnestly presseth us to search and know,—that we despise as trivial and common; and what he compasseth about with a divine darkness of inaccessible light, and hath removed far from the apprehensions of all living, that we will needs search into, and wander into those forbidden compasses, with daring boldness. I conceive this holy and profound mystery is one of those 'secret things' which

* [That is, careless.—Ed.]

† [The heathen poet whose words these are, ("We move towards what is forbidden,") describes well the perversity and the imbecility of our nature. Vid. Ovid. Amor. lib. iii. eleg. 4. ver. 17. Met. lib. vii. ver. 20.—Ed.]

it belongs to God to know; for who knoweth the Father but the Son, or the Son but the Father, or who knoweth the mind of God but the Spirit? Yet the foolish minds of men will not be satisfied with the believing ignorance of such a mystery, but will needs inquire into those depths, that they may find satisfaction for their reason. But, as it happeneth with men who will boldly stare upon the sun, their eyes are dazzled and darkened with its brightness; or those that enter into a labyrinth, which they can find no way to come out, but the further they go into it, the more perplexed it is, and the more intricate; even so it befalls many unsober and presumptuous spirits, who, not being satisfied with the simple truth of God, clearly asserting that this is, endeavour to examine it according to reason, and to solve all the objections of carnal wit and reason, (which is often 'enmity against God,') not by the silence of the Scriptures, but by answers framed according to the several capacities of men. I say, all this is but daring to behold the infinite glory of God with eyes of flesh, which makes them darkened in mind, and vanishing in their expressions, while they seek to behold this inaccessible light, while they enter into an endless labyrinth of difficulties out of which the thread of reason and disputation can never extricate them or lead them forth. But the Lord hath showed us 'a more excellent way,' though it may be despicable to men. Man did fall from blessedness by his curious and wretched aim at some higher happiness and more wisdom: the Lord hath chosen another way to raise him up again, by faith rather than knowledge; by believing rather than disputing. Therefore the great command of the gospel is this, to receive with a ready and willing mind whatsoever the Lord saith to us, whatsoever it may appear to sense and reason; to dispute no more, to search no more into the secret of divine mysteries, as if by searching we could find them out 'unto perfection;' but to believe what is spoken, 'till the day break, and the shadows flee away,' and the darkness of ignorance be wholly dispelled by the rising of the Sun of righteousness. We are called then to receive this truth,—That God is one, truly one, and yet there are three in this one, the Father, Son, and Holy Ghost. This, I say, you must believe, because the wisdom of God saith it, though you know not how it is, or how it can be. Though it seem a contradiction in reason, a trinity in unity, yet you must lead your reason captive to the obedience of faith, and silence it with this one answer, The Lord hath said it. If thou go on to dispute, and to inquire, 'How can these things be?' thou art escaped from under the power of faith, and art fled into the tents of human wisdom, where thou mayest learn atheism, but no religion; for the world by wisdom knew not God,' 1 Cor. i. 21. And certainly, whoever he be that will not quiet his conscience, upon the bare word of truth in this particular, but will call in the help of reason and disputation, how to understand and maintain it, I think he shall be further from the true knowledge of God and satisfaction of mind than before. There is no way here, but to flee into Paul's sanctuary, 'Who art thou, O man, that disputest?' Whenever thou thinkest within thyself? How may this be, how can one be three, and three one? then withal let this of Paul sound in thine ears, 'Who art thou, O man, who disputest?' Think that *thou* art man, think that *he* is God! Believing ignorance is much better than rash and presumptuous knowledge. Ask not a reason of these things, but rather adore and tremble at the mystery and majesty of them. Christianity is 'foolishness' to the world upon this account, because it is an implicit faith so to speak, given to God. But there is no fear of being deceived,—though he lead the blind by a way thou knowest not, yet he cannot lead thee wrong. This holy simplicity in believing every word of God, and trusting without more trying by disputation, is the very character of Christianity, and it will be found only true wisdom. For if any will become wise, he must be a fool in men's account. That he may be wise, he must quit his reason to learn true religion, which indeed is a more excellent and divine reason; neither is it contrary to it, though it be high above it.

In this place of Moses, you have the unity of God asserted, 'The Lord thy God is one Lord;' and it is indeed engraven on the very hearts of men by nature, that God is one. For all may know that the common notion and apprehension of God is, that he is a most perfect Being,—the original of all things,—most wise, most powerful, and infinite in all perfections. Now common reason may tell any man that there can be but one thing most perfect and excellent; there can be but one infinite,—

one almighty,—one beginning and end of all,—one first mover, one first cause, 'of whom are all things,' and who is of none.

Again, in this place of John, ye have a testimony of the blessed trinity of persons, Father, Son, and Holy Ghost, in that holy unity of essence. The great point which John hath in hand is this fundamental of our salvation, that Jesus Christ is the Son of God, and Saviour of the world, in whom all our confidence should be placed, and upon whom we should lean the weight of our souls. And this he proves by a two-fold testimony,—one out of heaven, another in the earth. There are three bearing witness to this truth in heaven, 'the Father, the Word, (that is, Jesus Christ, the eternal Son of God, whom this apostle calls the Word of God, or Wisdom of God, John i. 1.) and the Holy Ghost.' The Father witnessed to this truth in an audible voice out of heaven, when Christ was baptized, (Mat. iii. 17.) 'This is my beloved Son, in whom I am well-pleased.' Here is the Father's testimony of the Son when he was baptized, which was given very solemnly in a great congregation of people, and divinely, with great glory and majesty from heaven; as if the heavens had opened upon him, and the inaccessible light of God had shined down on him. This was confirmed in the transfiguration, (Mat. xvii. 5.) where the Lord gave a glorious evidence—to the astonishment of the three disciples—how he did account of him,—how all saints and angels must serve him; 'him hath God the Father sealed,' saith John. Indeed, the stamp of divinity, of the divine image, in such an excellent manner upon the man Christ, was a seal set on by God the Father, signifying and confirming his approbation of his well-beloved Son, and of the work he was going about. Then the Son himself did give ample testimony of this. This was the subject of his preaching to the world, 'I am the light and the life of men; he that believeth on me shall be saved.' And therefore he may be called the Word of God, (John i. 1.) and the Wisdom of God, (Prov. viii.) because he hath revealed unto us the blessed mystery of wisdom concerning our salvation. He is the very expression and character of the Father's person and glory, (Heb. i. 3.) in his own person; and he hath revealed and expressed his Father's mind, and his own office, so fully to the world, that there should be no more doubt of it. Out of the mouth of these two witnesses this word might be established; but, for superabundance, behold a third, the Holy Ghost witnessing at his baptism,—in his resurrection, —after his ascension. The Holy Ghost signifieth his presence and consent to that work, in the similitude of a dove; the Holy Ghost testifieth it in the power that raised him from the dead; the Holy Ghost put it beyond all question when he descended upon the apostles according to Christ's promise. For the other three witnesses on earth, we shall not stay upon it; only know, that the work of the regeneration of souls by the power of the Word and Spirit signified by water, the justification of guilty souls signified by the blood of Jesus Christ, and the testimony of the Spirit in our consciences, bearing witness to our spirits, is an assured testimony of this, that Jesus Christ, in whom we believe, is 'the Only-Begotten of the Father, full of grace and truth.' The changing, pacifying, and comforting of souls in such a wonderful manner, cries aloud that he in whom the soul believes is the true and living God, whom to know is eternal life. But mark, I pray you, the accuracy of the apostle in the change of speech. 'These three' witnesses on earth, saith he, 'agree in one,' in giving one common testimony to the Son of God and the Saviour of sinners. But as for the heavenly witnesses,—the Father, the Word, and the Holy Ghost,—however they be three after an inconceivable manner, and that they do also agree in one common testimony to the Mediator of men, yet moreover they are One. They not only agree in one, but are one God,—one simple, undivided, self-being, infinite Spirit, —holden out to us in three persons, the Father, Son, and Holy Ghost, to whom be praise and glory.

Lecture VIII.

OF THE UNITY OF THE GODHEAD AND THE TRINITY OF PERSONS.

DEUT. vi. 4. "*Hear, O Israel: The Lord our God is one Lord.*"—1 JOHN v. 7. "*There are three that bear record in heaven, the Father, the Word, and the Holy Ghost: and these three are one.*"

'ALL Scripture is given by inspiration of God, and is profitable for doctrine, for reproof, for correction, for instruction in righteousness,' 2 Tim. iii. 16. There is no refuse in it; no simple and plain history, but it tends to some edification; no profound or deep mystery, but it is profitable for salvation. Whatsoever secrets there be in the mysteries of God, which are reserved from us, though it be given us but to 'know in part,' and 'darkly' through a vail, yet as much is given to us to know as may make the man of God perfect in every good work. As much is given us to know as may build us up to eternal salvation. If there were no more use of these deep mysteries of the holy Trinity, &c. but to silence all flesh, and restrain the unlimited spirits of men, and keep them within the bounds of sobriety and faith, it were enough. That great secret would teach as much by its silence and darkness, as the plainer truths do by speaking out clearly. O that this great mystery did compose our hearts to some reverend and awful apprehension of that God we have to do with; and did imprint in our soul a more feeling sense of our darkness and ignorance. This were more advantage then all the gain of light, or increase of knowledge that can come from the search of curiosity. If men would labour to walk in that light they have attained, rather than curiously inquire after what they cannot know by inquiry, they should sooner attain more true light. If men would set about the practice of what they know, without doubt they would more readily come to a resolution and clearness in doubtful things. Religion is now turned into questions and school-debates. Men begin to believe nothing, but dispute everything, under a pretence of searching for light and resolution. But for the most part, while men look after light, they darken themselves; and this is the righteous judgment of the Lord upon the world that doth not receive the truth in love, or walk in the light of what they have already attained; therefore he gives men up to wander in their search into the dark dungeons of human wisdom and fancy, and to lose what they have already. If those things which are 'without controversy' (as the apostle speaks, 1 Tim. iii. 16.) were indeed made conscience of, and embraced in love, and practised, it were beyond all controversy that the most part of present controversies would cease. But it falls out with many, as with the dog, that, catching at a shadow in the water, lost the substance in his teeth; so they, pursuing after new discoveries in controverted things, and not taking a heart-hold and inward grip of the substantial truths of the gospel, which are beyond all controversy, do even lose what they have. Thus, even that whch they have not is taken from them, because though they have it in judgment, yet they have it not surely and solidly in affection, that it may be holden. So, to this present point if we could learn to adore and admire this holy, holy, holy One,—if we could in silence and faith sit down and wonder at this mystery,—it would be more profitable to us, and make way for a clearer manifestation of God, than if we should search and inquire into all the volumes that are written upon it, thinking by this means to satisfy our reason. I think there is more profoundness in the sobriety of faith than in the depths of human wisdom and learning. When the mystery is such an infinite depth, O but men's eloquence and wisdom must be shallow, far too shallow either to find it out, or unfold it!

But there is yet both more instruction and consolation to be pressed out of this mystery; and, therefore, if you cannot reach it in itself, O consider what it concerns us, how we may be edified by it, for this is true religion! Look upon that place of Moses,—what is the great instruction he draws from this unity of God's essence? ver. 5. 'Thou shalt love the Lord thy God with all thy heart.' Since God is one, then have no God but one, and that the true and living God; and this is the very first command of God, which flows as it were immediately from his absolute oneness and perfection of being. There is no man but he must have some God, that is, something whereupon he placeth his affection most. Every man hath some one thing he loves and respects beyond all other things, some lord and master that commands him. Therefore, saith Christ, 'no man can serve two masters.' Before a man will want a god to love and serve, he will make them, and then worship them. Yea, he will make himself, his belly, his back, his honour, and pleasure, a god; and sacrifice all his affections and desires and endeavours to these. The natural subordination of man to God, the relation he hath as a creature to a Creator, is the first and fundamental relation beyond all respects to himself or other fellow-creatures. This is the proto-natural* obligation upon the creature; therefore it should have returned in a direct line to his majesty all its affections and endeavours. But man's fall from God hath made a wretched thraw† and crook in the soul, that it cannot look any more after him, but bows downwards towards creatures below it, or bends inwardly towards itself; and so since the fall man hath turned his heart from the true God, and set it upon vanity,—upon lying vanities,—upon base dead idols which can neither help him nor hurt him. Your hearts are gone a-whoring from God, O that ye would believe it! None of you will deny but ye have broken all the commands. Yet such is the brutish ignorance and stupidity of the most part, that you will not confess that when it comes to particulars; and especially, if you should be challenged for loving other things more than God, or having other gods besides the true God, you will instantly deny it, and that with an asseveration and aversation,—"God forbid that I have another God!" Alas! this shows, that what you confess in the general is not believed in the heart, but only is like the prating of children, whom you may learn to say any thing. I beseech you consider, that what you give your time, pains, thoughts, and affections to, that is your God. You must give God all your heart, and so retain nothing of your own will if God be your God. But do ye not know that your care and grief and desire and love vents another way, towards base things? You know, that you have a will of your own which goeth quite contrary to his holy will in all things: therefore Satan hath bewitched you, and your hearts deceive you, when they persuade you that you have had no other God but the true God. Christianity raises the soul again, and advances it by degrees to this love of God, from which it had fallen. The soul returns to its first husband, from whom it went a-whoring, and now the stamp of God is so upon it, that it is changed into his image and glory. Having tasted how good this one self-sufficient good is, it gladly and easily divorces from all other lovers. It renounces former lusts of ignorance, and now begins to live in another. Love transplants the soul into God, and in him it lives, and with him it walks. It is true, this is done gradually, there is much of the heart yet unbroken to this sweet and easy yoke of love, much of the corrupt nature untamed, unreclaimed; yet so much is gained by the first conversion of the soul to God, that all is given up to him in affection and desire. He hath the chief place in the soul. The disposition of the spirit hath some stamp and impression of his oneness and singularity. My beloved is one. Though a Christian is not wholly rid of strange lords, yet the tie of subjection to them is broken. They may often intrude by violence upon him, but he is in a hostile posture of affection and endeavour against them. I beseech you, since the Lord is one, and there is none beside him, O let this be engraven on your hearts, that your inward affections and outward actions may express that one Lord to be your God, and none other beside him! It is a great shame and reproach to Christians, that they do not carry the stamp of the first principle of religion upon their walking. The condition and conversation of many declare how little account they make of the true God. Why do ye enslave your souls to your lusts, and the service of the flesh, if ye believe in this one God? Why do ye all things to please yourselves, if this one Lord be your one God? As for you, the Israel of God, who are called by Jesus Christ to partake with the commonwealth of Israel in the covenant of promises, hear, I beseech you, this, and

* [That is, the most natural.—Ed.]

† [That is, a twist or undue bend.—Ed.]

let your souls incline to it, and receive it: Your God is one Lord; have, then, no other lords over your souls and consciences; not yourselves, not others.

But in the next place, Let us consider to what purpose John leads such three witnesses, that we may draw some consolation from it. The thing testified and witnessed unto is the ground-work of all a Christian's hope and consolation, that Jesus Christ is the eternal Son of God, and Saviour of the world,—one, able to save to the uttermost all that put their trust in him; so that every soul that finds itself lost, and not able to subsist, nor abide the judgment of God, may repose their confidence in him, and lay the weight of their eternal welfare upon his death and sufferings, with assurance to find rest and peace in him to their souls. He is such an one as faith may triumph in him over the world, and all things beside. A believer may triumph in his victory, and in the faith of his victory, over hell and death and the grave; may overcome personally, 'For this is the victory that overcometh the world, even our faith,' ver. 4. And how could a soul conquer by faith, if he in whom it believes were not 'declared to be the Son of God with power?' There is nothing so mean and weakly as faith in itself. It is a poor despicable thing of itself, and that it sees, and that it acknowledges. Yea, faith is a very act of its self-denial. It is a renouncing of all help without and within itself, save only that which is laid on Christ Jesus. Therefore it were the most unsuitable mean of prevailing, and the most insufficient weapon for gaining the victory, if the object of it were not the strong God, the Lord Almighty, from whom it derives and borrows all its power, and virtue, either to pacify the conscience, or to expiate sin, or to overcome the world. O consider, Christians, where the foundation of your hope is situated! It is in the divine power of our Saviour. If he who declared so much love and good-will to sinners, by becoming so low, and suffering so much, have also all power in heaven and earth; if he be not only man near us, to make for us boldness of access, but God near God to prevail effectually with God, then certainly he is 'a sure foundation' laid in Zion, 'elect and precious.' He is an immoveable Rock of Ages; whosoever trusts their soul to him shall not be ashamed. I am sure that many of you consider not this, that Jesus Christ, who was in due time born of the virgin Mary, and died for sinners, is the eternal Son of God, equal to his Father in all glory and power. O how would this make the gospel a great mystery to souls, and the redemption of souls a precious and wonderful work, if it were considered! Would not souls stand at this anchor immoveable in temptation, if their faith were pitched on this sure foundation, and their hope cast upon this solid ground! O know your Redeemer is strong and mighty, and none can pluck you out of his hand, and himself will cast none out that comes! If the multitude of you believed this, you would not make so little account of the gospel that comes to you, and make so little of your sins which behoved to be taken away by the blood of God, and could be expiated by no other propitiation; you would not think it so easy to satisfy God with some words of custom, and some public services of form, as you do; you would not for all the world deal with God alone without this Mediator. And being convinced of sin, if you believe this solidly, that he in whom forgiveness of sin and salvation is preached is the same Lord God whom you hear in the Old Testament, who gave out the law, and inspired the prophets,—the Only Begotten of the Father, in a way infinitely removed from all created capacities,—you could not but find the Father well-satisfied in him, and find a sufficient ransom in his death and doings to pacify God, and to settle your consciences.

But as the thing testified is a matter of great consolation, so the witnesses testifying to this fundamental of our religion may be a ground of great encouragement to discouraged souls. It is ordinary, that the apprehensions of Christians take up Jesus Christ as very lovely, and more loving than any of the persons of the Godhead, either the Father or the Holy Ghost. There are some thoughts of estrangedness and distance of the Father, as if the Son did really reconcile and gain him to love us, who before hated us; and upon this mistake, the soul is filled with continual jealousies and suspicions of the love of God. But observe, I beseech you, the Father, the Son, and the Holy Ghost, all of them first agreeing in one testimony. The Father declares from heaven that he is abundantly well-pleased with his Son, not only because he is his Son, but even in the undertaking and performing of that work of redemption of sinners. It is therefore his most serious invitation and peremptory command to all to hear him, and believe in him, Mat. iii. 17; 1 John iii. 23. Nay, if we speak more properly, our salvation is not the business of Christ alone, as we imagine it, but the whole Godhead is interested in it deeply, and so deeply, that you cannot say who loves it most or likes it most. The Father is the very fountain of it, his love is the spring of all—'God so loved the world, that he gave his only-begotten Son.' Christ hath not purchased that eternal love to us, but is rather the gift, the free gift of eternal love. And therefore, as we have the Son delighting among the sons of men, Prov. viii. 31; and delighting to be employed and to do his will, Psal. xl. 8; so we have the Father delighting to send his Son, and taking pleasure in instructing him and furnishing him for it, Isa. xlii. 1. And therefore Christ often professed that he was not about his own work, but the Father's work who sent him; and that it was not his own will, but his Father's, he was fulfilling. Therefore we should not look upon the head-spring of our salvation in the Son, but rather ascend up to the Father, whose love and wisdom did frame all this. And thus we may be confident to come to the Father in the Son, knowing that it was the love of the Father that sent the Son, though indeed we must come to him only in the Son, in the name of Christ, and faith of acceptation through a Mediator; not because the Mediator purchaseth his good-will, but because his love and good-will only vents in his beloved Son Christ; and therefore he will not be known or worshipped but in him, in whom he is near sinners, and reconciling the world to himself. And then the Holy Ghost concurs in this testimony; and as the Son had the work of purchasing rights and interests to grace and glory, so the great work of applying all these privileges to saints, and making them actually partakers of the blessings of Christ's death, is committed in a special way to the Holy Ghost, 'I will send the Comforter,' &c. So then Father, Son, and Holy Ghost, all agree in one, that Jesus Christ is a sure refuge for sinners,—a plank for ship-broken men,—a firm and sure foundation to build everlasting hopes upon. There is no party dissenting in all the gospel. The business of the salvation of lost souls is concluded in this holy council of the Trinity with one voice. As at first, all of them agreed to make man,—'let us make man:' so again, they agree to make him again, to restore him to life in the second Adam. Whoever thou be that wouldst flee to God for mercy, do it in confidence. The Father, the Son, and the Holy Ghost, are ready to welcome thee,—all of one mind to shut out none, to cast out none. But to speak properly, it is but one love, one will, one counsel, and purpose in the Father, Son, and Spirit, for 'these Three are One;' and not only agree in One, they are One; and what one loves or purposes, all love and purpose. I would conclude this matter with a word of direction how to worship God, which I cannot express in fitter terms than these of Nazianzen: "I cannot think upon one, but by and by I am compassed about with the brightness of three; and I cannot distinguish three, but I am suddenly driven back unto one." There is great ignorance and mistake of this even among the best Christians. The grosser sort, when they hear of one God only, think Christ but some eminent man, and so direct their prayers to God only, excluding the Son and Holy Ghost; or when they hear of three persons,—the Father, Son, and Holy Ghost,—they straightway divide their worship, and imagine a trinity of gods. And I fear, those of us who know most, use not to worship God as he hath revealed himself,—Father, Son, and Holy Ghost, and yet one God. Our minds are reduced to such a simple unity as we think upon one of them alone; or else distracted and divided into such a plurality, that we worship in a manner three gods instead of one. It is a great mystery to keep the right middle way. Learn, I beseech you, so to conceive of God, and so to acknowledge him, and pray to him, as you may do it in the name of Jesus Christ, that all the persons may have equal honour, and all of them one honour; that while you consider one God, you may adore that sacred and blessed Trinity, and while you worship that Holy Trinity, you may straightway be reduced to an unity. To this wonderful and holy One, Father, Son, and Holy Ghost, be all praise and glory.

Lecture XIV.

OF THE DECREES OF GOD.

Eph. i. 11. "*Who worketh all things after the counsel of his own will.*"—Job xxiii. 13. "*He is in one mind, and who can turn him? and what his soul desireth, even that he doeth.*"

Having spoken something before of God, in his nature and being and properties, we come, in the next place, to consider his glorious majesty, as he stands in some nearer relation to his creatures, the work of his hands. For we must conceive the first rise of all things in the world to be in this self-being; the first conception of them to be in the womb of God's everlasting purpose and decree; which, in due time, according to his appointment, brings forth the child of the creature to the light of actual existence and being. It is certain that his majesty might have endured for ever, and possessed himself without any of these things. If he had never resolved to create any thing without himself, he had been blessed then, as now, because of his full and absolute self-sufficient perfection. His purposing to make a world, and his doing of it, adds nothing to his inward blessedness and contentment. This glorious and holy One encloses within his own being all imaginable perfections, in an infinite and transcendent manner; that if you remove all created ones, you diminish nothing; if you add them all, you increase nothing. Therefore it was in the superabundance of his perfection, that he resolved to show his glory thus in the world. It is the creature's indigence and limited condition which maketh it needful to go without its own compass, for the happiness of its own being. Man cannot be happy in loving himself. He is not satisfied with his own intrinsic perfections, but he must diffuse himself by his affections and desires and endeavours, and, as it were, walks abroad upon these legs, to fetch in some supply from the creature or Creator. The creature is constrained out of some necessity thus to go out of itself, which speaks much indigence and want within itself. But it is not so with his majesty. His own glorious Being contents him; his happiness is to know that, and delight in it, because it comprehends in itself all that is at all possible, in the most excellent and perfect manner that is conceivable,—nay, infinitely beyond what can be conceived by any but himself. So he needs not go without himself to seek love or delight, for it is all within him, and it cannot be without his own Being, unless it flow from within him. Therefore ye may find in Scripture what complacency God hath in himself, and the Father in the Son, and the Son in the Father. We find, Prov. viii., how the wisdom of God, our Lord Jesus, was the Father's delight from all eternity, and the Father again his delight; for he rejoiced always before him, ver. 30. And this was an all-sufficient possession that one had of another, ver. 22. The love between the Father and the Son is holden out as the first pattern of all loves and delights, John xvii. 23, 24. This then flows from the infinite excess of perfection and exundation of self-being, that his majesty is pleased to come without himself, to manifest his own glory in the works of his hands, to decree and appoint other things beside himself, and to execute that decree. We may consider in these words some particulars for our edification:

I. That the Lord hath from eternity purposed within himself and decreed to manifest his own glory in the making and ruling of the world; that there is a counsel and purpose of his will which reaches all things, which have been, are now, or are to be after this. This is clear, for he works all things "according to the counsel of his own will."

II. That his mind and purpose is one mind, one counsel. I mean not only one for ever, that is, perpetual and unchangeable, as the words speak,—but also one for all, that is, with one simple act or resolution of his holy will he hath determined all these several things, all their times, their conditions, their circumstances.

III. That whatsoever he hath from all eternity purposed, he in time practiseth it, and comes to execution and working; so that there is an exact correspondence betwixt his will and his work, his mind and his hand. He works according to the counsel of his will, and whatsoever his soul desireth that he doeth.

IV. That his purpose and performance is infallible,—irresistible by any created power. Himself will not change it, for 'he is in one mind;' and none else can hinder it, for 'who can turn him?' He desireth and he doeth it, as in the original. There is nothing intervenes between the desire and the doing, that can hinder the meeting of these two.

The first is the constant doctrine of the Holy Scriptures, of which ye should consider four things: 1st, That his purpose and decree is most wise. Therefore Paul cries out upon such a subject, 'O the depth of the riches both of the wisdom and knowledge of God!' Rom. xi. 33. His will is always one with wisdom; therefore you have the purpose of his will mentioned thus, 'the counsel of his will;' for his will, as it were, takes counsel and advice of wisdom, and discerns according to the depth and riches of his knowledge and understanding. We see among men these are separated often, and there is nothing in the world so disorderly, so unruly and uncomely, as when will is divided from wisdom. When men follow their own will and lusts as a law, against their conscience, that is monstrous. The understanding and reason are the eyes of the will; if these be put out, or if a man leave them behind him, he cannot but fall into a pit. But the purposes of God's will are depths of wisdom, nay, his very will is a sufficient rule and law; so that it may be well used of him, *Stat pro ratione voluntas*,* Rom ix. 11—18. If we consider the glorious fabric of the world,—the order established in it,—the sweet harmony it keepeth in all its motions and successions,—O it must be a wise mind and counsel that contrived it! Man now having the idea of this world in his mind, might fancy and imagine many other worlds bearing some proportion and resemblance to this. But if he had never seen nor known this world, he could never have imagined the thousandth part of this world; he could in nowise have formed an image in his mind of all those different kinds of creatures. Creatures must have some example and copy to look to; but what was his pattern? 'Who hath been his counsellor' to teach him? Rom. xi. 34. Who gave him the first rudiments or principles of that art? Surely none. He had no pattern given him,—not the least idea of any of these things furnished him,—but it is absolutely and solely his own wise contrivance. —2d, This purpose of God is most free and absolute; there is no cause, no reason, why he hath thus disposed all things, and not otherwise, as he might have done, but his own good will and pleasure. If it be so in a matter of deepest concernment, (Rom ix. 18.) it must be so also in all other things. We may find, indeed, many inferior causes,—many peculiar reasons for such and such a way of administration,—many ends and uses for which they serve,—for there is nothing that his majesty hath appointed but it is for some use and reason,—yet we must rise above all these, and ascend into the tower of his most high will and pleasure, which is founded on a depth of wisdom; and from thence we shall behold all the order, administration, and use of the creatures to depend. And herein is a great difference between his majesty's purpose and ours. You know there is still something presented under the notion of good and convenient, that moves our will, and inclines us for its own goodness to seek after it, and so to fall upon the means to compass it. Therefore, the end which we propose to ourselves hath its influence upon our purposes, and pleasures them; so that from it the motion seems to proceed first, and not so much from within; but there is no created thing can thus determine his majesty. Himself, his own glory, is the great end which he loves for itself, and for which he loves other things. But among other things, though there be many of them ordained one for another's use, yet his will and pleasure is the original of that order. He doth not find it, but makes it. You see all the creatures below are appointed for man, as their immediate and next end, for his use and service. But was it man's goodness and perfection which did move and incline his majesty to this appointment? No, indeed! but of his own good will he makes such things serve man, that all of them together may be for his own glory.—3d, The Lord's decree is the first rise of

* [That is, "His will stands for reason." Juv. Sat. vi. ver. 222.—Ed.]

all things that are, or have been, or are to come. This is the first original of them all, to which they must be reduced as their spring and fountain. All of you may understand that there are many things possible, which yet actually will never be. The Lord's power and omnipotency is of a further extent than his decree and purpose. His power is natural and essential to his being; his decree is of choice, and voluntary. The Father could have sent a legion of angels to have delivered his Son; the Son could have asked them, but neither of them would do it, Matt. xxvi. 53. The Lord could have raised up children to Abraham out of stones, but he would not, Matt. iii. 9. His power then comprehends within its reach all possible things which do not in their own nature and proper conception imply a contradiction; so that infinite worlds of creatures more perfect than this,—numbers of angels and men above these,—and creatures in glory surpassing them again,—are within the compass of the boundless power and omnipotency of God. But yet for all this it might have fallen out that nothing should actually and really have been, unless his majesty had of his own free will decreed what is, or hath been, or is to be. His will determines his power, and, as it were, puts it in the nearest capacity to act and exercise itself. Here, then, we must look for the first beginning of all things that are. They are conceived in the womb of the Lord's everlasting purpose, as he speaks, Zeph. ii. 2. The decree is, as it were, with child of beings, Isa. xliv. 7. It is God's royal prerogative to appoint things to come, and none can share with him in it. From whence is it, I pray you, that of so many worlds which his power could have framed, this one is brought to light? Is it not because this one was formed, as it were, in the belly of his eternal counsel and will? From whence is it that so many men are, and no more—that our Lord Jesus was slain, when the power of God might have kept him alive,—that those men, Judas, &c. were the doers of it, when others might have done it? From whence are all those actions, good or evil, under the sun, which he might have prevented, but from his good will and pleasure, from his determinate counsel? Acts iv. 28. Can you find the original of these in the creature, why it is thus, and why not otherwise? Can you conceive why, of all the infinite numbers of possible beings these are, and no other? And, what hath translated that number of creatures, which is, from the state of pure possibility to futurition or actual being, but the decisive vote of God's everlasting purpose and counsel? Therefore we should always conceive, that the creatures, and all their actions, which have, or will have any being in the world, have first had a being in the womb of God's eternal counsel, and that his will and pleasure hath passed upon all things that are and are not. His counsel has concluded of things that have been, or will be, that thus they shall be; and his counsel determined of all other things which are also possible, that they shall never come forth into the light of the world, but remain in the dark bowels of omnipotency, that so we may give him the glory of all things that are not, and that are at all.—Then, 4th. We should consider the extent of his decree and counsel; it is passed upon all things; it is universal, reaching every being or action of the universe. This is the strain of the whole Scripture. He did not, as some dream, once create the creatures in a good state, and put them in capacity henceforth to preserve them selves, or exercise their own virtue and power, without dependence on him, as an artificer makes an horologe, and orders it in all things, that it may do its business without him. He is not only a general original of action and motion, as if he would command a river to flow by his appointed channels; as if he did only work, and rule the world by attorneys and ambassadors. That is the weakness and infirmity of earthly kings, that they must substitute deputies for themselves. But this King appoints all immediately, and disposes upon all the particular actions of his creatures, good or evil; and so he is universal absolute Lord of the creature, of its being and doing. It were a long work to rehearse what the Scripture speaks of this kind; but O! that ye would read them oftener, and ponder them better, how there is nothing in this world,—which may seem to fall out by chance to you, that you know not how it is to come to pass, and can see no cause nor reason of it,—but it falls out by the holy will of our blessed Father. Be it of greater or less moment,—or be it a hair of thy head fallen, or thy head cut off,—the most casual and contingent thing,—though it surprised the whole world of men and angels, that they should wonder from whence it did proceed,—it is no surprisal to him, for he not only knew it, but appointed it. The most certain and necessary thing, according to the course of nature, it hath no certainty but from his appointment, who hath established such a course in the creatures, and which he can suspend when he pleaseth. Be it the sin of men and devils, which seems most opposite to his holiness, yet even that cannot appear in the world of beings, if it were not, in a holy, righteous, and permissive way, first conceived in the womb of his eternal counsel, and if it were not determined by him, for holy and just ends, Acts iv. 28.

The second thing propounded is, that his mind and counsel is one; one and the same, 'yesterday, to-day, and for ever.' Therefore the apostle speaks of God, that there is no shadow of change or turning in him, James i. 17. He is not a man that he should lie, neither the son of man that he should repent: hath he said, and shall he not do it?' Numb. xxiii. 19. And shall he decree, and not execute it? Shall he purpose, and not perform it? 'I am the Lord, I change not;' that is his name, Mal. iii. 6. 'The counsel of the Lord standeth for ever, the thoughts of his heart to all generations,' Psal. xxxiii. 11. Men change their mind oftener than their garments. Poor vain man, even in his best estate, is changeableness, and vicissitude itself, altogether vanity! And this ariseth, partly from the imperfection of his understanding, and his ignorance, because he does not understand what may fall out. There are many things secret and hidden, which if he discovered, he would not be of that judgment; and many things may fall out which may give ground of another resolution: and partly from the weakness and perverseness of his will, that cannot be constant in any good thing, and is not so closely united to it, as that no fear or terror can separate from it. But there is no such imperfection in him, neither ignorance nor weakness. 'All things are naked' before him; all their natures, their circumstances, all events, all emergencies, known to him are they, and 'all his works from the beginning,' as perfectly as in the end. And therefore he may come to a fixed resolution from all eternity; and being resolved, he can see no reason of change, because there can nothing appear after, which he did not perfectly discover from the beginning. Therefore, whenever ye read in the Scripture of the Lord's repenting—as Gen. vi. 7. Jer. xviii. 8.—ye should remember that the Lord speaks in our terms, and, like nurses with their children, uses our own dialect, to point out to us our great ignorance of his majesty, that cannot conceive more honourably of him, nor more distinctly of ourselves. When he changeth all things about him, he is not changed, for all these changes were at once in his mind; but when he changeth his outward dispensations, he is said to repent of what he is doing, because we use not to change our manner of dealing, without some conceived grief, or repentance and change of mind. When a man goes to build a house, he hath no mind but that it should continue so. He hath not the least thought of taking it down again; but afterwards it becomes ruinous, and his estate enlarges, and then he takes a new resolution, to cast it down to the ground and build a better. Thus it is with man; according as he varies his work, he changes his mind. But it is not so with God. All these changes of his works,—all the successions of times, the variation of dealings, the alteration of dispensations in all ages,—were at once in his mind, and all before him; so that he never goes to build a house but he hath in his own mind already determined all the changes it shall be subject to. When he sets up a throne in a nation, it is in his mind within such a period to cast it down again; when he lifts up men in success and prosperity, he doth not again change his mind when he throws them down, for that was in his mind also; so that there is no surprisal of him by any unexpected emergence. Poor man hath many consultations ere he come to a conclusion; but it is not thus with his counsel. Of all those strange and new things which fall out in our days, he hath one thought of them all from eternity. 'He is in one mind,' and none of all these things have put him off his eternal mind or put him to a new advisement about his great projects. Not only doth he not change his mind, but his mind and thought is one of all, and concerning all. Our poor, narrow, and limited minds, must part their thoughts among many businesses, —one thought for this, another for that, and one after another. But with him there is neither succession of counsels and purposes, nor yet plurality; but, as with one opening of his eye, he beholds all things as they are, so with one inclination, or nod of his will, he hath given a law, and appointed all things.* If we can at one instant, and one look, see both light and colours, and both the glass and the shadow in it, and with one motion of our wills move towards the end and the means; O, how much more may he, with one simple undivided act of his good will and pleasure, pass a determination on all things, in their times, and orders, and in his own infinite and glorious Being perceive them all with one look! How much consolation might redound from this to believing souls! Hath the Lord appointed you to suffer persecution and tribulation here? Hath he carved out such a lot unto you in this life? Then withal consider, that his majesty hath eternal glory wrapt up in the same counsel from which thy afflictions proceed. Hath he made thy soul to melt before him? Hath he convinced thee, and made thee to flee unto the city for refuge, and expect salvation from no other but himself? Then know, that life eternal is in the bosom of that same purpose which gave thee to believe this; though the one be born before the other, yet the decree shall certainly bring forth the other. And for such souls as upon this vain presumption of the infallibility of God's purposes, think it needless to give diligence in religion, know, that it is one mind and purpose that hath linked the end and the means together as a chain; and therefore, if thou expectest to be saved, according to election, thou must, according to the same counsel, make thy calling home from sin to God sure.

Thirdly, What thing soever he hath purposed, he in due time applies to the performance of it, and then the counsel of his will becomes the works of his hands, and there is an admirable harmony and exact agreement between these two. All things come out of the womb of his eternal decree, by the word of his power, even just fashioned and framed, as their lineaments and draughts were proportioned in the decree, nothing failing, nothing wanting, nothing exceeding. There is nothing in the idea of his mind but it is expressed in the work of his hands. There are no raw half-wishes in God. Men have such imperfect desires,—I would have, or do, such a thing if it were not, &c. He wavers not thus in suspense; but what he wills and desires, he wills and desires indeed. He intends, doubtless, it shall be, and what he intends he will execute and bring to pass; therefore his will in due time applies almighty power to fulfil the desire of it; and almighty power being put to work by his will, it cannot but work all things 'according to the counsel of his will;' and whatsoever his soul desireth, that he cannot but do, even as he desires, seeing he can do it. If he will do it, and can do it, what hinders him to work and do? Know then that his commands and precepts to you signifying what is your duty, they do not so much signify what he desires, or intends to work, or have done, as his approbation of such a thing in itself to be your duty; and therefore though he have revealed his will concerning our duty, though no obedience follow, yet is not his intention frustrated or disappointed; for his commands to you say not what is his intention about it, but what is that which he approves as good, and a duty obliging men. But whatsoever thing he purposes and intends should be, certainly he will do it, and make it to be done. If it be a work of his own power alone, himself will do it alone. If he require the concurrence of creatures to it,—as in all the works of providence,—then he will effectually apply the creatures to his work, and not wait in suspense on their determination. If he have appointed such an end to be attained by such means,—if he have a work to do by such instruments,—then, without all doubt, he will apply the instruments when his time comes, and will not wait on their concurrence. You see now strange things done, you wonder at them: how we are brought down from our excellency,—how our land is laid desolate by strangers,—how many instruments of the Lord's work are laid aside, how he lifts up a rod of indignation against us, and is like to overturn even the foundations of our land,†—all these were

* [Mr. Binning was a Supralapsarian. In this and the two following Lectures, he treats of the "high mystery of predestination," the consideration of which, though it should be "handled with special prudence and care," (West. Conf. of Faith, ch. 3.) is nevertheless "full of sweet pleasant and unspeakable comfort to godly persons." Art. of Ch. of Eng. Art. xvii. His views of this mysterious doctrine are stated with singular clearness, and the objections to it, which he notices and answers, are brought forward with the utmost ingenuousness and candour, and expressed, it must be admitted, as strongly as a caviller could desire.—Ed.]

† [The reader will remember that at this time the country was convulsed from one end of it to the other.—Ed.]

were not in our mind before, but they were in his mind from eternity, and therefore he is now working it. Believe then that there is not a circumstance of all this business, not one point or jot of it, but is even as it was framed and carved out of old. His present works are according to an ancient pattern, which he carries in his mind. All the measures and degrees of your affliction,—all the ounces and grain-weights of your cup, were all weighed in the scales of his eternal counsel; the instruments, the time, the manner, all that is in it. If he change instruments, that was in his mind; if he change dispensations, that was in his mind also; and seeing ye know by the scriptures that a blessed end is appointed for the godly, that all things work for their good, that all is subservient to the church's welfare; seeing, I say, you know his purpose is such as the scripture speaks, then believe his performance shall be exact accordingly, nothing deficient; no joint, no sinew in all his work of providence, no line in all his book and volume of the creature, but it was written in that ancient book of his eternal counsel, and first fashioned in that, Psal. cxxxix. 16.

Then, lastly, His will is irresistible, his counsel shall stand; who can turn him from his purpose, and who can hinder him from performance? Therefore he attains his end in the highest and most superlative degree of certainty and infallibility. Himself will not change his own purpose; for why should he do it? If he change to the better, then it reflects on his wisdom; if he change to the worse, it reflects both on his wisdom and goodness. Certainly he can see no cause why he should change it. But as himself cannot change, so none can hinder his performance; for what power, think you, shall it be, that may attempt that? Is it the power of men, of strong men, of high men, of any men? No sure! for their breath is in their nostrils, they have no power but as he breathes in them. If he keep in his breath, as it were, they perish. All nations are as nothing before him, and what power hath nothing? Is it devils may do it? No; for they cannot, though they would; he chains them, he limits them. Is it good angels? They are powerful indeed, but they neither can nor will resist his will. Let it be the whole university of the creation,—suppose all their scattered force and virtue conjoined in one,—yet it is all but finite, it amounts to no more, if you would eternally add unto it; but all victory and resistance of this kind must be by a superior power, or at least by an equal. Therefore we may conclude that there is no impediment or let, that can be put in his way, nothing can obstruct his purpose; if all the world should conspire as one man to obstruct the performance of any of his promises and purposes, they do but rage in vain. Like dogs barking at the moon, they shall be so far from attaining their purpose, that his majesty shall disabuse them, so to speak, to his own purpose. He shall apply them quite contrary to their own mind, to work out the counsel of his mind. Here is the absolute King, only worth the name of a King and Lord, whom all things in heaven and earth obey at the first nod and beckoning to them! Hills, seas, mountains, rivers, sun and moon, and clouds, men and beasts, angels and devils,—all of them are acted, moved, and inclined according to his pleasure; all of them are about his work indeed, as the result of all in the end shall make it appear, and are servants at his command, going where he bids go, and coming where he bids come, led by an invisible hand, though in the meantime they know it not, but think they are about their own business, and applaud themselves for a time in it. *Ducunt volentem fata, nolentem trahunt.** Godly men who know his will and love it, are led by it willingly, for they yield themselves up to his disposal; but wicked men, who have contrary wills of their own, can gain no more by resisting, but to be drawn along with it.

Now to what purpose is all this spoken of God's decrees and purposes, which he hath called a secret belonging to himself? If his works and judgments be a great depth, and unsearchable, sure his decrees are far more unsearchable; for it is the secret and hidden purpose of God, which is the very depth of his way and judgment. But to what purpose is it all? I say, not to inquire curiously into the particulars of them, but to profit by them. The Scripture holds out to us the unchangeableness, freedom, extent, holiness, and wisdom of them, for our advantage; and if this ad-

* [That is, "Fate leads the willing, and drags the unwilling."—Ed.]

vantage be not reaped, we know them in vain. Not to burden your memory with many particulars, we should labour to draw forth both instruction and consolation out of them. Instruction, I say, in two things especially,—to submit with reverence and respect to his majesty in all his works and ways, and to trust in him who knows all his works, and will not change his mind.

There is nothing wherein I know Christians more deficient than in this point of submission, which I take to be one of the chiefest and sweetest, though hardest duties of a Christian. It is hardly to be found among men,—a thorough compliance of the soul to what his soul desires, a real subjection of our spirits to his good-will and pleasure. There is nothing so much blessed in scripture as waiting on him, as yielding to him to be disposed upon,—'Blessed are all they that wait on him.' Pride is the greatest opposite, and he opposes himself most to that, for it is in its own nature most derogatory to the highness and majesty of God, which is his very glory. Therefore submission is most acceptable to him, when the soul yields itself and its will to him. He condescends far more to it; he cannot be an enemy to such a soul. Submission to his majesty's pleasure, is the very bowing down of the soul willingly to any thing he does or commands,—whatever yoke he puts on, of duty or suffering, to take it on willingly, without answering again, which is the great sin condemned in servants; to put the mouth in the dust, and to keep silence, because he doth it —'I was dumb, I opened not my mouth, because thou didst it.' *There* is submission indeed,—silence of mind and mouth,—a restraint put upon the spirit to think nothing grudgingly of him for any thing he doth. It is certainly the greatest fault of Christians, and ground of many more, that ye do not look to God, but to creatures in any thing that befalls you; therefore there are so frequent risings of spirits against his yoke, frequent spurnings against it, as Ephraim, unaccustomed with the yoke. So do ye; and this it is only makes it heavy and troublesome. If there were no more reason for it but your own gain, it is the only way to peace and quietness. *Durum : sed levius fit patientia, quicquid corrigere est nefas.** Your impatience cannot help you, but hurt you, it is the very yoke of your yoke; but quiet and silent stooping makes it easy in itself, and brings in more help beside, even divine help. Learn this, I beseech you, to get your own wills abandoned, and your spirits subdued to God, both in the point of duty and dispensation. If duties commanded cross thy spirit—as certainly the reality and exercise of godliness must be unpleasant to any nature—know what thou art called to, to quiet thy own will to him, to give up thyself to his pleasure singly, without so much respect to thy own pleasure or gain. Learn to obey him simply because he commands, though no profit redound to thee; and by this means thou shalt in due time have more sweet peace and real gain, though thou intendedst it not. And in case any dispensation cross thy mind, let not thy mind rise up against it. Do not fall out with Providence, but commit thy way wholly to him, and let him do what he pleases in that. Be thou minding thy duty. Be not anxious in that, but be diligent in this, and thou shalt be the only gainer by it; besides, the honour redounds to him.

Then I would exhort you, from this ground, to trust in him. Seeing he alone is the absolute Sovereign Lord of all things,—seeing he has passed a determination upon all things, and accordingly they must be,—and seeing none can turn him from his way,—O then, Christians, learn to commit yourselves to him in all things, both for this life and the life to come! Why are ye so vain and foolish as to depend and hang upon poor, vain, depending creatures? Why do ye not forsake yourselves? Why do ye not forsake all other things as empty shadows? Are not all created powers, habits, gifts, graces, strength, riches, &c. like the idols in comparison of him, who can neither do good, neither can they do ill? Cursed is he 'that trusteth in man,' Jer. xvii. 5. There needs no other curse than the very disappointment you shall meet withal. Consider, I beseech you, that our God can do all things, whatever he pleases, in heaven and earth, and that none can obstruct his pleasure. Blessed is that soul for whom the counsel of his will is engaged. And

* [This was the only consolation which one learned Roman could administer to another on the death of a friend. "This is hard :" said he, "but what cannot be remedied is more easily borne, with patience." Hor. Carm. lib. I. carm. xxiv.—Ed.

it is engaged for all that trust in him. He can accomplish his good pleasure in thy behalf, either without or against means; all impediments and thorns set in his way, he can burn them up. You who are heirs of the promises, O know your privilege! What his soul desireth, he doth even that; and what he hath seriously promised to you, he desires. If you ask, who are heirs of the promises? I would answer, simply those and those only, who do own them and challenge them, and cling to them for their life and salvation; those who seek the inheritance only by the promise, and whose soul desires them and embraces them. O if you would observe how unlike ye are to God! Ye change often, ye turn often out of the way; but that were not so ill if ye did not imagine him to be like yourselves, and it is unbelief which makes him like to yourselves,—when your frame and tender disposition changes,—when presence and access to God is removed. That is wrong, it speaks out a mortal creature indeed; but if it be so, O do no more wrong! Do not, by your suspicions and jealousies, and questionings of him, imagine that he is like unto you, and changed also. That is a double wrong and dishonour to his majesty. Hath he not said, 'I am the Lord, and change not.' 'He is in one mind, who can turn him?' How comes it then, that ye doubt of his love as oft as ye change? When ye are in a good temper, ye think he loves you: when it is not so, ye cannot believe but he is angry, and hates you. Is not this to speak quite contrary to the word; that he is a God that changes,—that he is not in one mind, but now in one, and then in another, as oft as the inconstant wind of a soul's self-pleasing humour turns about? Here is your rest and confidence, if you will be established, not within yourselves,—not upon marks and signs within you, which ebb and flow as the sea, and change as the moon,—but, upon his unchangeable nature and faithful promises. This we desire to hold out to you all, as one ground for all. You would every one have some particular ground in your own disposition and condition, and think it general doctrine only which layeth it not home so; but believe it, I know no ground of real soul-establishment, but general truths and principles common to you all; and our business is not to lay any other foundation,—or more foundations, according to your different conditions,—but to lay this one foundation, Christ and God unchangeable; and to exhort every one of you to make that general foundation your own in particular, by leaning to it, and building upon it, and clinging to it. All other are sandy and ruinous.

Let us now, in this sad time, press consolation from this. The Lord's hand is in all this. It is immediate in every dispensation, and it is only carnal mindedness that cannot see him stretching out his hand to every man, with his own portion of affliction. Know this one thing, that God is in one mind; for all these many ways and judgments, he is in one mind,—to gather the saints, to build up the Church, the body of Christ. This is his end,—all other businesses are in the by,* and subservient to this. Therefore he will change it as he pleases, but his great purpose of good to his people all the world cannot hinder. Let us then establish our souls in this consideration; all is clear above, albeit cloudy below; all is calm in heaven, albeit tempestuous here upon earth. There is no confusion, no disorder in his mind. Though we think the world out of course, and that all things reel about with confusion, he hath one mind in it, and who can turn him? And that mind is good to them that trust in him; and therefore, who can turn away our good? Let men consult and imagine what they please,—let them pass votes and decrees what to do with his people,—yet it is all to no purpose, for there is a counsel above, an older counsel, which must stand and take place in all generations. If men's conclusions be not according to the counsel of his will, they are but imaginary dreams, like the fancies of a distracted person, who imagining himself a king, sits down on the throne, and gives out decrees and ordinances. May not he who sits in heaven laugh at the foolishness and madness of men who act in all things as if they had no dependence on him, and go about their business as if it were not contrived already? It is a ridiculous thing for men to order their business, and settle their own conclusions, without once minding One above them, who hath not only a negative, but an affirmative vote in all things. It is true that God, in his deep wisdom, hath kept up

* [Or, *by the by*.—ED.]

his particular purposes secret, that men may walk according to an appointed rule, and use all means for compassing their intended ends; and therefore it is well said, *Prudens futuri temporis exitum caliginosâ nocte premit Deus.* But yet withal we should mind that of James, 'if the Lord will,' and go about all things even the most probable, with submission to his will and pleasure. And therefore, when men go without their bounds, either in fear of danger, or joy conceived in successes,—*ridetque, si mortalis ultra fas trepidet,* &c.—Excess of fear, excess of hope, excess of joy in these outward things, is, as it were, ridiculous to him, who hath all these things appointed with him. To him be praise and glory.

Lecture IV.

OF PREDESTINATION.

EPH. i. 11. "*In whom also we have obtained an inheritance, being predestinated according to the purpose of him who worketh all things after the counsel of his own will.*"—ROM. ix. 22, 23. "*What if God, willing to show his wrath, and to make his power known, endured with much long-suffering the vessels of wrath fitted to destruction; and that he might make known the riches of his glory on the vessels of mercy which he had afore prepared unto glory.*"

IN the creation of the world, it pleased the Lord, after all things were framed and disposed, to make one creature to rule over all; and to him he gave the most excellent nature, and privileges beyond the rest; so that it may appear that he had made all things for man, and man immediately for his own glory. As man was the chief of the works of his hands, so we may, according to the Scriptures, conceive that he was chiefly minded in the counsels of his heart. And that, as in the execution of his purpose in creating the world, man had the pre-eminence assigned unto him, and all seemed subordinate unto him; so, in the Lord's purposes concerning the world, his purpose about man has the pre-eminence. He, indeed, has resolved to declare the glory of his name in this world; therefore the heavens and the firmament are made preachers of that glory, Psal. xix. 1, 2, &c. But in a special manner, his majesty's glorious name is manifested in man, and about man. He hath set man, as it were, in the centre or midst of the creation, that all the creatures might direct or bring in their praises unto him, to be offered up in his and their name, to the Lord their Maker, by him, as the common mouth of the world; and the Lord hath chosen this creature above all the creatures, for the more solemn and glorious declaration of himself in his special properties. Therefore, we should gather our thoughts in this business, to hear from the Lord what his thoughts are towards us; for, certainly, the right understanding of his everlasting counsel touching the eternal state of man, is of singular virtue to conform us to the praise of his name, and establish us in faith and confidence. Predestination is a mystery, indeed, into which we should not curiously and boldly inquire beyond what is revealed; for then a soul must needs lose itself in that depth of wisdom, and perish in the search of unsearchableness. And thus the word speaks in Scripture of this subject, intimating to us, that it is rather to be admired than conceived; and that there ought to be some ignorance of these secrets, which, conjoined with faith and reverence, is more learned than any curious knowledge. But withal, we must open our eyes upon so much light as God reveals of these secrets, knowing that the light of the word is a saving, refreshing light, not confounding, as is his inaccessible light of secret glory. As far as it pleaseth his majesty to open his mouth, let us not close our ears, but open them also to his instruction, knowing, that as he will withhold no necessary thing for our salvation, so he will reveal nothing but what is profitable. This is the best bond of sobriety and humble wisdom, to learn what he teacheth us; but when he makes an end of teaching, to desire no more learning. It is humility to seek no more, and it is true wisdom to be content with no less.

There is much weakness in our conceiving of divine things. We shape and form them in our minds according to a mould of our own experience or invention, and cannot conceive of them as they are in themselves. If we should speak properly, there are not counsels and purposes in God, but one entire counsel and resolution concerning all things which are in time, by which he hath disposed all in their several times, seasons, conditions, and orders. But because we have many thoughts, about many things, so we cannot well conceive of God but in likeness to ourselves; and therefore, the Scripture, condescending to our weakness, speaks so. 'How many are thy precious thoughts towards me,' saith David; and yet, indeed, there is but one thought of him, and us, and all, which one thought is of so much virtue, that it is equivalent to an infinite number of thoughts concerning infinite objects. The Lord hath from everlasting conceived one purpose of manifesting his own glory in such several ways; and this is the head-spring of all that befalls creatures, men, and angels. But because, in the execution of this purpose, there is a certain order, and succession, and variety, therefore men do ordinarily fancy such or such a frame and order in the Lord's mind and purpose. And as the astronomers do cut and carve in their imagination cycles, orbs, and epicycles in the heavens, because of the various and different appearances and motions of stars in them, whereas it may be, really, there is but one celestial body in which all these various lights and motions do appear, so do men fancy unto themselves an order in the Lord's decree, according to the phenomena or appearances of his works in the world; whereas, it is one purpose and decree, which in its infinite compass comprehends all these varieties and orders together. This much we may indeed lawfully conceive of his decree, that there is an exact correspondence and suitableness between his majesty's purpose and execution, and that he is a wise Lord, 'wonderful in counsel, and excellent in working,' having some great plot and design before his eyes, which he intends to effect, and which is, as it were, the great light and sun of this firmament, unto which, by that same wonderful counsel, all other things are subordinate; and so in the working it shall appear exactly as his counsel did delineate and contrive it.

There is no man so empty or shallow, but he hath some great design and purpose which he chiefly aims at; shall we not then conceive, that the Lord, who instructs every man to this discretion, and teaches him, (Isa. xxviii. 26,) is himself wise in his counsel, and hath some grand project before him in all this fabric of the world, and the upholding of it since it was made? Certainly he hath. And if you ask what it is, the wise man will teach you in general—'He made all things for himself, yea, even the wicked for the day of evil,' Prov. xvi. 4. Here, then, is his great design and purpose,—to glorify himself,—to manifest his own name to men and angels. Now, his name comprehends wisdom, goodness, power, mercy, and justice. The first three he declares in all the works of his hands. All are well done and wisely done. The excellency of the work shows the wonderful counsellor and the wise contriver. The goodness of any creature in its kind, declares the inexhausted spring of a self-being from whom it proceeds; and the bringing all these out of nothing, and upholding them, is a glorious declaration of his power. But yet, in all the works of his hands, there is nothing found to manifest his glorious mercy and justice, upon which are the flower and garland of his attributes, and unto which wisdom and power seem to be subservient. Therefore his majesty, in that one entire purpose of his own glory, resolves to manifest his wrath and his mercy upon men and angels, subjects capable of it; which two attributes are as the poles about which all the wheels of election and reprobation turn as you see in that place, Rom. ix. 22, 23. Let this then be established as the end of all his works, as it is designed in his counsel, and nothing else. It is not the creature, nor any thing in the creature, which is first in his mind, but himself, and therefore of him, and for him, are all things. Here they have their rise, and thither they return, even to the ocean of God's eternal glory, from whence all did spring.

The right establishing of this will help us to conceive aright of his counsel of predestination. It is a common cavil of carnal reason, how can the Lord reject so many persons, and fore-ordain them to destruction? It seems most contrary to his goodness and wisdom, to have such an end of eternal predestination before him, in the creating of so many, to make men for nothing, but to damn them. Here carnal reason, which is enmity to God, triumphs; but consider, I say, that this is not the Lord's end and chief design, to destroy men. Even as it is not his majesty's first look, or furthest reach, to give unto others eternal life; so it is not his prime intent to sink them into eternal death, as if that were his pleasure and delight. No, indeed! Neither is the creature's happiness nor its misery that which first moves him, or is most desired of him, but himself only, and he cannot move out of himself to any business, but he must return it unto himself. Therefore the wise preacher expresses it well, 'He made all for himself, even the wicked for the day of evil.' It was not his great end of creating wicked men to damn them, or creating righteous men to save them, but both are for a further and higher end,—for himself and his own glory.

All seem to agree about this, that the great end of all the Lord's counsels and decrees is his own glory, to be manifested on men and angels; and that this must be first in his mind; not that there is first or last with him, but to speak after the manner of men. If he had many thoughts, as we have, this would be his first thought; and in this one purpose this end is chiefly aimed at, and all other things are by the Lord's counsel subordinate to this, as means to compass that. But as concerning the order of these means, and consequently of his majesty's purpose about them, men, by examining his majesty according to the creature's rules, or according to sense, bring him down far below his own infinite greatness. Some conceive that that was first, as it were, in his mind which is first done. Looking upon the execution of his purpose in the works of his power, they imagine, that as he first created man righteous, so this was his first thought concerning man, to create man for the glory of his goodness and power, without any particular determination as yet of his end. And I conceive, this is the thought of the multitude of people. They think God was disappointed in his work, when they hear he created such a glorious creature that is now become so miserable. They cannot believe that his majesty had all this sin and misery determined with him when he purposed to create him, but look upon the emergent of man's fall into sin and misery as a surprisal of his majesty;—as if he had meant another thing in creating him, and so was, upon this occasion of man's sin, driven to a new consultation about the helping of the business, and making the best out of it that might be. Thus 'through wisdom' the world knows not God. They think God altogether like themselves, and so liken him to the builder of a house, who set nothing before him in doing so, but to build it after that manner for his own ends; but then being surprised with the fall and ruin of it, takes a new advisement, and builds it up again upon another and a surer foundation. But because they cannot say, that God takes any new advisements in time, but must confess that all his counsels are everlasting concerning all the works of his hands, therefore they bring in foreknowledge to smooth their irreligious conceit of God; as if the Lord, upon his purpose of creating man, had foreseen what should befall him, and so purposed to permit it to be so, that out of it he might erect some glorious fabric of mercy and justice upon the ruins of man. And that little or nothing may be left to the absolute sovereign will of God, to which the Scripture ascribes all things, they must again imagine, that upon his purpose of sending Christ to save sinners, he is yet undetermined about the particular end of particular men, but watches on the tower of foreknowledge to espy what they will do, whether men will believe on his Son or not, whether they will persevere in faith or not; and according to his observation of their doings, so he applies his own will to carve out their reward or portion of life or death. These are even the thoughts which are inbred in your breasts by nature. That which the learned call Arminianism is nothing else but the carnal reason of men's hearts, which is enmity to God. It is that very disputation which Paul in this chapter exclaims against, 'Who art thou, O man, that disputest?'

But certainly, all this contrivance is nothing beseeming the wisdom or sovereignty of God, but reflects upon both; upon his wisdom, that he should have thoughts of creating the most noble of his creatures, and yet be in suspense about the end of the creature, and have that in uncertainty what way his glory shall indeed be manifested by it. Is it not the first and chief thought of every wise man, what he intends and aims at in his work, and according to the measure and reach of his wisdom, so he reaches further in his end and purpose? Shall we then conceive the only wise God so far to have mistaken himself, as to do that which no wise man would do? He who is of such an infinite reach of wisdom and understanding, to fall upon the thoughts of making such an excellent creature, and yet to lie in suspense within himself about the eternal estate of it, and to be in a waiting posture what way his glory should be manifested by it; whether in a way of simple goodness only, or in a way of justice, or in a way of mercy, till he should foresee, off the tower of foreknowledge, how that creature should behave itself. Our text speaks not thus; for in the place, (Eph. i.) we have the Lord, in his eternal purpose, carving out to such and such particular persons 'an inheritance,' and 'adoption of children,' for that great end 'of the glory of his grace,' ver. 11, and 5, 6. And predestination falls out, not according to our carriage, but according to the purpose of him who 'works all things' that he works, 'after the counsel of his own will,' without consulting our will. And if you inquire what are these 'all things,' certainly we must take it simply for all things that are at all, or have any real being: his power, his hand must be in it, and that according to his own counsel, without respect had to the creature's will, according to his own good pleasure, ver. 5, 11. He had no sooner a thought of working and making man, but this purpose was in it, to make such men to the praise of his glorious grace, and to fore-ordain them to an inheritance, and others to make or fit them for destruction, as the text, Rom. ix. 22, bears. Herein the great and unsearchable wisdom of God appears to be a great depth, that when he hath a thought of making such a vessel, he hath this purpose in the bosom of it, what use it shall be for, whether for honour or dishonour; and accordingly, in his counsel, he prepares it either to glory or destruction, and in time makes it fit for its use, either by sin or grace. Here is the depth that cannot be sounded by mortal men. 'O the depth of the riches both of his wisdom and knowledge! How unsearchable are his judgments, and his ways past finding out!' The whole tenor of the Scriptures shows that his majesty was not surprised and taken at unawares by Adam's fall, but that it fell out according to the determinate counsel of his will. If he knew it, and suffered it to be, certainly he permitted it, because he willed it should be so; and why may he not determine that in his holy counsel which his wisdom can disabuse to the most glorious end that can be? Why may not he decree such a fall, who out of man's ruins can erect such a glorious throne for his grace and justice to triumph into? It is more for the glory of his infinite wisdom, to bring good, and such a good out of evil, than only to permit that good should be.

Then such doctrine is repugnant to the Lord's absolute power and sovereignty, which is Paul's sanctuary, whither he flies unto as a sure refuge, from the stroke or blast of carnal reason. 'Hath not the potter power over the clay, of the same lump to make one vessel to honour, and another to dishonour?' ver. 21. Hath not the Lord more absolute dominion over us, than the potter hath over the clay, for the potter made not the clay, but the Lord hath made us of nothing? so that simply and absolutely we are his, and not our own, and so he hath an absolute right to make any use of us he pleases, without consulting our wills and deservings. Can any man quarrel him for preparing him to destruction, seeing he owes nothing to any man, but may do with his own what he pleases? What if God, willing to make known his power, and justice, and wrath, have fitted and prepared some vessels for destruction, with which in time he bears much, and forbears long, using much patience towards them, ver. 22. Can any man challenge him for it? And what if God, willing to make known the riches of his grace, have prepared some vessels to glory, shall any man's eye be evil because he is good? ver. 23. Shall man be left to be his own disposer, and the shaper of his own fortune? Sure it was not so with Esau and Jacob: they were alike in the womb. If there was any prerogative, Esau the eldest had it,—they had done neither good nor evil. What difference was then between them to cast the balance of his will? Can you imagine any? Indeed carnal reason will say that God foreknew what they would do, and so he chose or rejected them. But, why doth not the apostle answer thus unto that objection of unrighteousness in God? ver. 14. It had been ready and plain. But rather he opposes the will and calling of God, to all works past or to come. He gives no answer but this, 'he will have mercy because he will have mercy;' that is the supreme rule of righteousness, and hitherto must we flee, as the surest anchor of our hope and stability. Our salvation depends not on our willing or running, on our resolving or doing, but upon this primitive good pleasure and will of God, on which hangs our willing and running and obtaining. It is certainly an unorderly order, to flee unto that in men, for the cause of God's eternal counsels, which only flows from his eternal counsel, Eph. i. 4. Hath he chosen us because he did foreknow that we would be holy, and without blame, as men think? Or hath he not rather chosen us to be holy and without blame? He cannot behold any good or evil in the creatures, till his will pass a sentence upon it; for from whence should it come?

Seeing then this order and contrivance of God's purpose is but feigned, it seems to some that the very contrary method were more suitable even to the rules of wisdom. You know what is first in men's intention is last in execution. The end is first in their mind, then the means to compass that end. But in practice again, men fall first upon the means, and by them come at length to attain their end; therefore those who would have that first, as it were, in God's mind, which he doth first, do even cross common rules of reason in human affairs. It would seem then, say some, that this method might do well; that what is last in his execution, was first in his purpose, and by him intended as the end of what he doth first, and so some do rank his decrees; that he had first a thought of glorifying man, and to attain this end he purposed to give him grace, and for this purpose to suffer him to fall, and for all to create him. But we must not look thus upon it either. It were a foolish and ridiculous counsel, unbeseeming the poor wisdom of man, to purpose the glorifying of man whom he had not yet determined to create. Therefore we should always have it in our mind that the great end and project of all is the glory of his mercy and justice upon men; and this we may conceive is first in order, neither men's life nor death, but God's glory to be manifested upon men. Now, to attain this glorious end, with one inclination or determination of his will, not to be distinguished or severed, he condescends upon all that is done in time, as one complete and entire mean of glorifying himself, so that one of them is not before another in his mind, but altogether. For attaining this, he purposes to create man. He ordains the fall of all men into a state of sin and misery; and some of those, upon whom he had resolved to show his mercy, he gives them to Christ to be redeemed, and restored by grace; others, he fore-ordains them to destruction; and all this at once, without any such order as we imagine. Now though he intend all this at once and together, yet it doth not hence follow that all these must be executed together. As when a man intends to build a house for his own accommodation, there are many things in the house upon which he hath not several purposes; but yet they must be severally, and in some order done. First the foundation laid; then the walls raised; then the roof put on; yet he did not intend the foundation to be for the walls, or the walls for the roof, but altogether for himself. Even so the Lord purposes to glorify his mercy and justice upon a certain number of persons, and for this end to give them a being, to govern their falling into misery, to raise some out of it by a Mediator, and to leave some into it to destruction; and all this as one entire mean to illustrate his glorious mercy and justice. But these things themselves must be done not all at once, but one before another, either as their own nature requires, or as he pleases. The very nature of the thing requires that man be created before he sin; that he sin and fall before a Mediator suffer for his sin; that he have a being before he have a glorious being; and that he have a sinful and miserable being, before he have this glorious and gracious being which may manifest the grace and mercy of God. But it is the pleasure of the Lord that determines in what time and order Christ shall suffer, either before or after the conversion of sinners, or whether sinners shall be presently instated in glory, and perfectly delivered from all sin at their first conversion, or only in part during this life.

Seeing then this was his majesty's purpose, to make so many vessels of honour, upon whom he might glorify the riches of his grace and mercy; and so many 'vessels of wrath,' upon whom he might show the power of his anger; you may think what needed all this business of man's redemption. Might not God have either preserved so many as he had appointed to glory from falling into sin and misery; or at least have freely pardoned their sin without any satisfaction; and out of the exceeding riches of his mercy and power, have as well not imputed sin to them at all, as imputed their sins to Christ, who was not guilty? What needed his giving so many to the Son, and the Son's receiving them? What needed these mysteries of incarnation, of redemption, seeing he might have done all this simply without so much pains and expense? Why did he choose this way? Indeed, that is the wonder; and if there were no more end for it, but to confound mortality that dare ask him what he doth, it is enough. Should he be called down to the bar of human reason, to give an account of his matters? 'Who hath known the mind of the Lord, or, being his counsellor, hath taught him,' that is in the depths of his unsearchable understanding, that he chose to go this round, and to compass his end by such a strange circuit of means, when he might have done it simply and directly without so much pains? Yet it is not so hidden, but he hath revealed as much as may satisfy or silence all flesh. For we must consider, that his great project is not simply to manifest the glory of his goodness, but of his gracious and merciful goodness, the most tender and excellent of all; and therefore man must be miserable, sinful, and vile, that the riches of his grace may appear in choosing and saving such persons. But that it may appear also how excellent he could make man, and how vain all created perfections are, being left to themselves, therefore he first made man righteous, and being fallen into sin and misery, he might straightway have restored him without more ado. But his purpose was to give an exact demonstration of mercy, tempered and mixed with justice; and therefore he finds out the satisfaction in his eternal counsel, 'I have found a ransom.' And so he chooses Jesus Christ to be the head of these chosen souls, in whom they might be again restored unto eternal life. And these souls, he, in his everlasting purpose, gives over to the Son to be redeemed, and these the Son receives. And thus the glory of mercy and justice shines most brightly, yea, more brightly, than if he had at first pardoned. O how doth his love and mercy appear, that he will transfer our sins upon his holy Son, and accept that redemption for us; and his justice, that a redemption and price he must have, even from his Son, when once he comes in the stead of sinners! And in this point do the songs of eternity concentre.

Lecture XVI.

OF PREDESTINATION.

ROM. ix. 22.—"*What if God, willing to show his wrath, and to make his power known, endured with much long-suffering the vessels of wrath fitted to destruction.*" EPH. i. 11.—"*In whom also we have obtained an inheritance, being predestinated according to the purpose of him who worketh all things after the counsel of his own will.*"

We are now upon a high subject; high indeed for an eminent apostle, much more above our reach. The very consideration of God's infinite wisdom might alone suffice to restrain our limited thoughts, and serve to sober our minds with the challenge of our own ignorance and darkness; yet the vain and wicked mind of man will needs quarrel with God, and enter the lists of disputation with him, about his righteousness and wisdom in the counsel of election and reprobation: 'But, O man, who art thou that repliest against God,' or disputest? ver. 20. This is a thing not to be disputed, but believed; and if ye will believe no more than ye can comprehend by sense or reason, then ye give his majesty no more credit than to weak mortal man. Whatever secret thoughts do rise up in thy heart when thou hearest of God's foreordaining men to eternal life, without previous foresight or consideration of their doings, and preparing men to eternal wrath, for the praise of his justice, without previous consideration of their deservings, and passing a definitive sentence upon the end of all men, before they do either good or evil; whenever any secret surmises rise in thy heart against this, learn to answer thus; enter not the lists of disputation with corrupt reason, but put in this bridle of the fear of God's greatness, and the consciousness of thy own baseness, and labour to restrain thy undaunted and wild mind by it. Ponder that well, who thou art who disputest; who God is, against whom thou disputest—and if thou have spoken once, thou wilt speak no more—what thou art, who is as clay formed out of nothing; what he is, who is the former; and hath not the potter power over the clay? Consider but how great wickedness it is so much as to question him, or ask an account of his matters. After you have found his will to be the cause of all things, then to inquire farther into a cause of his will, which is alone the self-rule of righteousness, is to seek something above his will, and to reduce his majesty into the order of creatures. It is most abominable usurpation and sacrilege, for it both robs him of his royal prerogative, and instates the base footstool into his throne; but know, that certainly God will overcome when he is judged, Psal. l. 6. If thou judge him, he will condemn thee; if thou oppugn his absolute and holy decrees, he will hold thee fast bound by them to thy condemnation; he needs no other defence but to call out thy own conscience against thee, and bind thee over to destruction. Therefore, as one saith well, "Let the rashness of men be restrained from seeking that which is not, lest peradventure they find that which is." Seek not a reason of his purposes, lest peradventure thou find thy own death and damnation infolded in them.

Paul mentions two objections of carnal and fleshly wisdom against this doctrine of election and reprobation, which indeed contain the sum of all that is vented and invented even to this day, to defile the spotless truth of God. All the whisperings of men tend to one of these two,—either to justify themselves, or to accuse God of unrighteousness; and shall any do it and be guiltless? I confess, some oppose this doctrine, not so much out of an intention of accusing God, as out of a preposterous and ignorant zeal for God; even as Job's friends did speak much for God. Nay, but it was not well spoken, they did but speak wickedly for him. Some speak much to the defence of his righteousness and holiness, and, under pretence of that plea, make it inconsistent with these to fore-ordain to life or death without the foresight of their carriage; but shall they speak wickedly for God, or will he accept their person? He who looks into the secrets of the heart, knows the rise and bottom of such defences and apologies for his holiness to be partly self-love, partly narrow and limited thoughts of him, drawing him down to the determinations of his own greatest enemy, carnal reason. Since men will ascribe to him no righteousness, but such an one of their own shaping, and conformed to their own model, do they not indeed rob him of his holiness and righteousness?

I find two or three objections which may be reduced to this head. First, it seems unrighteousness with God, to predestinate men to eternal death, without their own evil deserving, or any forethought of it,—that before any man had a being, God should have been in his counsel fitting so many to destruction. Is it not a strange mocking of the creatures, to punish them for that sin and corruption, unto which by his eternal counsel they were fore-ordained? This is even that which Paul objects to himself, 'Is there unrighteousness with God?' Is it not unrighteousness to hate Esau before he deserves it? Is he not unrighteous, to adjudge him to death before he do evil? ver. 14. Let Paul answer for us, 'God forbid!' Why, there needs no more answer, but all thoughts or words which may in the least reflect upon his holiness are abomination. Though we could not tell how it is righteous and holy with him to do it, yet this we must hold, that it is. It is his own property to comprehend the reason of his counsels; it is our duty to believe what he reveals of them, without farther inquiry. He tells us, that thus it is clearly in this chapter; this far then we must believe. He tells us not how it is; then farther we should not desire to learn. God, in keeping silence of that, may put us to silence, and make us conceive that there is a depth to be admired, not sounded. Yet he goeth a little farther, and indeed as high as can be, to God's will—'He hath mercy on whom he will, and whom he will he hardeneth.' Now, farther he cannot go, for there is nothing above this. We may descend from this, but we cannot ascend, or rise above it. But is this any answer to the argument? A sophister could press it further, and take advantage from that very ground—What! is not this to establish a mere tyranny in the Lord; that he doeth all things of mere will and pleasure, distributes rewards and punishments without previous consideration of men's carriage? But here we must stand, and go no farther than the scriptures walk with us. Whatever reasons or causes may be assigned, yet certainly we must at length come up hither. All things are, because he so willed; and why willed we should not ask a reason, because his will is supreme reason, and the very self-rule of all righteousness. Therefore if we once know his will, we should presently conclude that it is most righteous and holy. If that evasion of the foreknowledge of men's sins and impenitency had been found solid, certainly Paul would have answered so, and not have had his refuge to the absolute will and pleasure of God, which seem to perplex it more. But he knew well that there could nothing of that kind, whether good or evil, either actually be without his will, or be to come without the determination of the same will, and so could not be foreseen without the counsel of his will upon it; and therefore it had been but a poor shift to have refuge to that starting-hole of foreknowledge, out of which he must presently flee to the will and pleasure of God, and so he betakes him straightway to that he must hold at, and opposes that will to man's doings. 'It is not of him that willeth, nor of him that runneth, but of God that showeth mercy.' If he had meant only that Jacob and Esau had actually done neither good or evil, he needed not return to the sanctuary of God's will, for still it might be said, it is of him that runs and wills and not of God's will as the first original; because their good and evil foreseen did move him to such love and hatred. It is all alike of works of men, whether these works be present or to come: therefore I would advise every one of you, whatever ye conceive of his judgment or mercy, if he have showed mercy to you, O then rest not in thyself, but arise and ascend till thou come to the height of his eternal free purpose! And if thou conceive thy sin, and misery, and judgment, thou mayest go up also to his holy counsels, for the glory of his name, and silence thyself with them. But it shall be most expedient for thee in the thought of thy miseries, to return always within, and search the corruption of thy nature, which may alone make thee hateful enough to God. If thou search thy own conscience, it will stop thy mouth, and make thee guilty before God. Let not the thought of his eternal counsels diminish the conviction of thy guilt, or the hatred of thyself for sin and corruption; but dwell more constantly upon this, because thou art called and commanded so to do. One thing remains fixed,—though he hath fore-ordained man to death, yet none shall be damned till his conscience be forced to say, that he is worthy of it a thousand times.

There is another whispering and suggestion of the wicked hearts of men against the predestination of God, which insinuates that God is an accepter of persons, and so accuses him of partial and unrighteous dealing, because he deals not equally with all men. Do ye not say this within yourselves—If he find all guilty, why does he not punish all? Why does he spare some? And if ye look upon all men in his first and primitive thought of them, as neither doing good nor evil, why does he not have mercy on all? But is thine eye evil because he is good? May he not do with his own as he pleases? Because he is merciful to some souls, shall men be displeased, and do well to be angry? Or, because he, of his own free grace, extends it, shall he be bound by a rule to do so with all? Is not he both just and merciful, and is it not meet that both be showed forth? If he punish thee, thou canst not complain, for thou deservest it; if he show mercy, why should any quarrel, for it is free and undeserved grace. By saving some, he shows his grace; by destroying others, he shows what all deserve. God is so far from being an accepter of persons according to their qualifications and conditions, that he finds nothing in any creature to cast the balance of his choice. If he did choose men for their works' sake, or outward privileges, and refuse others for the want of these, then it might be charged on him; but he rather goes over all these, nay, he finds none of these. In his first view of men he beholds them all alike, and nothing to determine his mind to one more than another, so that his choice proceedeth wholly from within his own breast —'I will have mercy on whom I will.'

But then, thirdly, Our hearts object against the righteousness of God; that this fatal chain of predestination overturns all exhortations and persuasions to godliness, all care and diligence in well-doing. For thus do many profane souls conceive—If he be in one mind, who can turn him? Then, what need I pray, since he has already determined what shall be, and what shall become of me? His purpose will take effect whether I pray or pray not; my prayer will not make him change his mind; and if it be in his mind he will do it; if he hath appointed to save us, saved we shall be, live as we list; if he hath appointed us to death, die we must, live as we can. Therefore men, in this desperate estate, throw themselves headlong into all manner of iniquity, and that with quietness and peace. Thus do many souls perish upon the stumbling-stone laid in Zion, and wrest the truths and counsels of God to their own destruction, even quite contrary to their true intent and meaning. Paul, (Eph. i. 4.) speaks another language—'He hath chosen us in him,—that we should be holy and without blame.' His eternal counsel of life is so far from loosing the reins to men's lusts, that it is the only certain foundation of holiness; it is the very spring and fountain from whence our sanctification flows by an infallible course. This chain of God's counsels concerning us, hath also linked together the end and the means,—glory and grace,—happiness and holiness,—that there is no destroying of them. Without holiness it is impossible to see God; so that those who expect the one without any desire of, and endeavour after the other, they are upon a vain attempt to loose the links of this eternal chain. It is the only eternal choosing love of God, which separated so many souls from the common misery of men. It is that only which in time doth appear, and rise as it were from under ground, in the streams or fruits of sanctification. And if the ordinance of life stand, so shall the ordinance of fruits, John xv. 16. Eph. ii. 10. If he hath appointed thee to life, it is certain he has also ordained thee to fruits, and chosen thee to be holy; so that whatever soul casts by the study of this, there is too gross a brand of perdition upon its forehead. It is true, all is already determined with him, and he is incapable of any change, or 'shadow of turning.' Nothing then wants, but he is in one mind about it, and thy prayer cannot turn him. Yet a godly soul will pray with more confidence, because it knows that as he hath determined upon all its wants and receipts, so he hath appointed this to be the very way of obtaining what it wants. This is the way of familiarity and grace. He takes with his own to make them call; and he performs his purpose in answer to their cry. But suppose there were nothing to be expected by prayer, yet I say, that is not the thing thou shouldst look to, but what is required of thee, as thy duty, to do that simply out of regard to his majesty, though thou shouldst never profit by it. This is true obedience, to serve him for his own pleasure, though we had no expectation of advantage by it. Certainly he doth not require thy supplications for this end, to move him, and incline his affections toward thee, but rather as a testimony of thy homage and subjection to him; therefore, though they cannot make him of another mind than he is, or hasten performance before his purposed time—so that in reality they have no influence upon him—yet in praying, and praying diligently, thou declarest thy obligation to him, and respect to his majesty, which is all thou hast to look to, committing the event solely to his good pleasure.

The second objection Paul mentions, tends to justify men. 'Why then doth he yet find fault? For who hath resisted his will?' Since by his will he hath chained us with an inevitable necessity to sin, what can we do? Men cannot wrestle with him; why then doth he condemn and accuse them? 'But who art thou, O man, who disputest against God?' As if Paul had said, thou art a man, and so I am, why then lookest thou for an answer from me? Let us rather both consider whom we speak of, whom thou accusest, and whom I defend. It is God; what art thou then to charge him, or what am I so to clear him? Believing ignorance is better than presumptuous knowledge, especially in those forbidden secrets in which it is more concerning to be ignorant with faith and admiration, than to know with presumption. Dispute *thou*, O man, *I* will wonder; reply *thou*, *I* will believe! Doth it become thee, the clay, to speak so to thy Former, 'Why hast thou made me thus?' Let the consideration of the absolute right and dominion of God over us,—more than any creature hath over another, yea, or over themselves,—let that restrain us, and keep us within bounds. He may do with us what he pleaseth, for his own honour and praise; but it is his will that we should leave all the blame to ourselves, and rather behold the evident cause of our destruction in our sin, which is nearer us, than to search into a secret and incomprehensible cause in God's counsel.

Lecture XVII.

OF CREATION.

HEB. xi. 3. "*Through faith we understand that the worlds were framed by the word of God; so that things which are seen were not made of things which do appear.*"—GEN. i. 1. "*In the beginning God created the heaven and the earth.*"

WE are come down from the Lord's purposes and decrees to the execution of them, which is partly in the works of creation, and partly in the works of providence. The Lord having resolved upon it to manifest his own glory, did, in that due and predeterminate time, apply his own power to this business. Having in great wisdom conceived a frame of the world in his mind from all eternity, he at length brings it forth, and makes it visible. We shall not insist upon the particular story of it, as it is set down in general, but only point at some things for our instruction.

First, Ye see who is the Maker of all things, of whom all things visible and invisible are,—it is God. And by this he useth to distinguish himself from idols, and the vanities of the nations, that he is that self-being who gave all things a being, who made the heavens and the earth. This is even the most glorious manifestation of an invisible and eternal Being. These things that are made, show him forth. If a man were travelling into a far country, and wandered into a wilderness where he could see no inhabitants, but only houses, villages, and cities built, he would straightway conceive there hath been some workmen at this; this hath not been done casually, but by the art of some reasonable creatures. How much more may we conceive when we look on the fabric of this world,—how the heavens are stretched out for a tent to cover them that dwell on the earth, and the earth settled and established as a firm foundation for men and living creatures to abide on,—how all are done in wisdom and discretion,—we cannot but straightway imagine that there must be some curious and wise contriver, and mighty creator of these things. It is here said, 'Through faith we understand that the worlds were framed.' Indeed faith only, in the word of God, gives true and distinct understanding of it. Innumerable have been the wanderings and mistakes of the wise of the world about this matter, wanting this lamp and light of the word of God, which alone gives a true and perfect account of this thing. Many strange dotages and fancies have they fallen into; yet certain it is that there is so much of the glory of God engraven without on the creature, and so much reason imprinted on the souls of men within, that, if it were not for that judicial plague of the Lord's darkening their understandings, who do not glorify him in as far as they know him, no man could seriously and soberly consider on the visible world, but he would be constrained to conceive an invisible God. Would not every one think within himself,—all these things, so excellent as they are, cannot be out of chance, neither could they make themselves, so that of necessity they must owe what they are to something beside themselves? And of this it is certain, that it cannot have its original from any other thing, else there should be no end; therefore it must be some Supreme Being, that is from no other, and of which are all things.

But next, consider when these things were made,—'In the beginning.' And what beginning is that? Certainly the beginning of the creation, and of time, to exclude eternity. Whatever may be said of that subtilty, that God might have created the world from all eternity, for it appears, even in created things, that there is no necessity of the precedent existence of the cause, since in the same instant that many things are brought into being, in the same do they bring forth their effects, as the sun in the first instant of its creation did illuminate; yet certainly we believe, from the word of the Lord, that the world is actually but of a few thousand years standing. Six are not yet run out since the first creating word was spoken, and since the Spirit of the Lord moved upon the waters. And this we know also, that if it had pleased his majesty, he might have created the world many thousand years before that; so that it might have been at this day of ten hundred times ten thousand years standing, and he might have given it as many years as there are numbers of men and angels, beasts, yea, and pickles* of sand upon the sea coast. But it was his good pleasure that that very point of time in which it was created should be the beginning of time; and from that he gives us a history of the world, upon which the church of God may rest, and so seek no other god but the God that made these heavens and earth.

This will not satisfy the ungodly curiosity and vanity of men's spirits, who will reproach the Maker for not applying sooner to his work, and sitting idle such an immeasurable space of eternity. Men wonder what he could be doing all that time, if we may call it *time* which hath no beginning, and how he was employed. I beseech you, restrain such thoughts in you with the fear of his glorious and incomprehensible majesty who gives no account of his matters! It is enough that this is his good pleasure to begin then; and he conceals his reasons, to prove the sobriety of our faith, that all men may learn an absolute and simple stooping to his majesty's pleasure. Remember that which a godly man answered some wanton curious wit, who in scorn demanded the same of him—"He was preparing hell for curious and proud fools," said he. Let us then keep our hearts as with a bridle, and repress their boundless wanderings within bounds, lest we, by looking upward, before the beginning of the world, to see what God was doing, fall headlong into the eternal pit of destruction, and into the hands of the living God. God hath shown himself marvellously these six thousand years in the upholding this world. If we did consider these continued and repeated testimonies of his glory, we should be overwhelmed with what we find, though we search no farther. And suppose we would please ourselves to imagine that it had been created many years before, yet that doth not silence and stop the insolence of men's minds; for it always might be inquired, what the Lord was doing before that time. For eternity is as immensurable before those multiplied thousands of years as before naked six. Let our imagination sit down to subtract from eternity as many thousands as it can multiply by all the varieties and numbers in the world, yet there is nothing abated from eternity.† It is as infinite in extent before that, as before the present six thousand; and yet we may conceive that the Lord hath purposed in the beginning of the world to declare more manifestly to our understanding his eternity, his self-sufficiency, and liberty;—his eternity, that when we hear of how short standing the creature is, we may go upward to God himself; and his everlasting being, before the foundations of it were laid, may shine forth more brightly to our admiration, when we can stretch our conceptions so immensurably as far beyond the beginning of the world: and yet God is still beyond the utmost reach of our imagination,—for who can find out the beginning of that which hath not a beginning to be found out,—and our most extended apprehensions fall infinitely short of the days of the Ancient of days. O how glorious, then, must his being be, and how boundless! His self-sufficiency and perfection doth herein appear, that from such an inconceivable space he was as perfect and blessed in himself as now. The creatures add nothing to his perfection or satisfaction. He was as well-pleased with his own all-comprehending being, and with the very thought and purpose of making this world, as now he is when it is made. The idea of it in his mind gave him as great contentment as the work itself when it is done! O, to conceive this aright,—it would fill a soul with astonishing and ravishing thoughts

* [That is, grains or particles.—Ed.]

† [What a sublime answer was that which one of the deaf and dumb pupils of M. Sicard gave to the question, "What is eternity?" It is "a day," said Massieu, "without yesterday or to-morrow,"—un jour sans hier ni demain. The thoughts of our author on this boundless theme are hardly less sublime.—Ed.]

of his blessedness! Poor men weary if they be not one way or other employed without; so indigent are all creatures at home, that they would weary if they went not abroad without themselves. But to think how absolutely God is well-pleased with himself, and how all imaginable perfections can add nothing to his eternal self-complacency and delight in his own being, it would certainly ravish a soul to delight in God also. And as his self-sufficiency doth herein appear, so his liberty and freedom is likewise manifested in it. If the world had been eternal, who would have thought that it was free for his majesty to make it or not, but that it had flowed from his glorious being with as natural and necessary a resultance as light from the body of the sun? But now it appears to all men, that for his pleasure they are made, and we are created; that it was simply the free and absolute motion of his will that gave a being to all things, which he could withhold at his pleasure or so long as he pleased.

Thirdly, We have it to consider in what condition he made all these things, 'very good;' and that to declare his goodness and wisdom. The creature may well be called a large volume, extended and spread out before the eyes of all men, to be seen and read of all. It is certain, if these things,—all of them in their orders and harmonies, or any of them in their beings and qualities,—were considered in relation to God's majesty, they would teach and instruct both the fool and the wise man in the knowledge of God. How many impressions hath he made in the creatures, which reflect upon any seeing eye the very image of God! To consider of what a vast and huge frame the heavens and the earth are, and yet but one throne to his majesty, the footstool whereof is this earth, wherein vain men erect many palaces; to consider what a multitude of creatures, what variety of fowls in the heaven, and what multiplicity of beasts upon the earth, what hosts, as Moses speaks (Gen. ii. 1,) and yet that none of them all are useless, but all of them have some special ends and purposes they serve for, so that there is no discord nor disorder, nor superfluity nor want in all this monarchy of the world: all of them conspire together in such a discord, or disagreeing harmony, to one great purpose,—to declare the wisdom of him who 'made every thing beautiful in its time,' and every thing most fit and apposite for the use it was created for; so that the whole earth is full of his goodness. He makes every creature good one to another, to supply one another's necessities; and then, notwithstanding of so many different natures and dispositions between elements, and things composed of them, yet all these contrarieties have such a commixion, and are so moderated by supreme art, that they make up jointly one excellent and sweet harmony or beautiful proportion in the world. O how wise must he be who alone contrived it all! We can do nothing except we have some pattern or copy before us; but now, upon this ground which God hath laid, man may fancy many superstructures. But when he stretched out the heaven, and laid the foundation of the earth, 'who, being his counsellor, taught him?' At whom did his Spirit take counsel? Certainly, none of all these things would have entered into the heart of man to consider or contrive, Isa. xl. 12, 13. Some ruder spirits do gaze upon the huge and prodigious pieces of the creation, as whales and elephants, &c.; but a wise Solomon will go to the school of the ant to learn the wisdom of God, and choose out such a simple and mean creature for the object of his admiration. Certainly, there are wonders in the smallest and most inconsiderable creatures which faith can contemplate. O the curious ingenuity and draught of the finger of God, in the composition of flies, bees, flowers, &c. Men ordinarily admire more some extraordinary things; but the truth is, the whole course of nature is one continued wonder, and that greater than any of the Lord's works without the line. The straight and regular line of the wisdom of God, who, in one constant course and tenor, hath ordained the actions of all his creatures, comprehends more wonders and mysteries, as the course of the sun, the motion of the sea, the hanging of the earth in the empty place upon nothing. These, we say, are the wonders indeed, and comprehend something in them which all the wonders of Egypt and the wilderness cannot parallel. But it is the stupid security of men, that are only awakened by some new and unusual passages of God's works beyond that straight line of nature.

Then, fourthly, Look upon the power of God in making all of nothing, which is expressed here in Heb. xi. There is no artificer but he must have matter, or his art will fail him, and he can do nothing. The mason must have timber and stones laid to his hand, or he cannot build a house; the goldsmith must have gold or silver ere he can make a cup or a ring. Take the most curious and quick inventor of them all,—they must have some matter to work upon, or their knowledge is no better than ignorance. All that they can do is, to give some shape or form, or to fashion that in some new model which had a being before. So that, whatever men have done in the world, their works are all made up of those things which appear, and art and skill to form and fashion that excellently which before was in another mould and fashion. But he needs not sit idle for want of materials, because he can make his materials; and therefore, in the beginning he made heaven and earth, not as they now are, but he made first the matter and substance of this universe, but it was as yet a rude and confused chaos or mass, all in one lump, without difference. But then his majesty shows his wisdom and art, his excellent invention, in the following days of the creation, in ordering and beautifying and forming the world as it is, and that his power might be the more known; for how easy is it for him to do all this? There needs no more for it but a word,—let it be, and it is. 'He spake, and it was done; he commanded, and it stood fast.' Not a word pronounced, and audibly composed of letters and syllables—mistake it not so—but a word inwardly formed, as it were, in his infinite Spirit. Even the inclination and beck of his will suffices for his great work. Ye see what labour and pains we have in our business,—how we toil and sweat about it,—what wrestlings and strivings in all things we do; but behold what a great work is done without pain and travail? It is a laborious thing to travel through a parcel of this earth, which is yet but as the point of the universe; it is troublesome to lift or carry a little piece of stone or clay; it is a toil even to look upward and number the stars of heaven. But it was no toil, no difficult thing to his majesty, to stretch out these heavens in such an infinite compass; for as large as the circumference of them is, yet it is as easy to him to compass them, as it is to us to span a finger-length or two. It is no difficulty to him to take up hills and mountains, as 'the dust of the balance,' in his hand, and weigh them in scales. Hath he not chained the vast and huge mass of the weighty earth and sea, in the midst of the empty place, without a supporter, without foundations or pillars? He hangeth it on nothing. What is it, I pray you, that supports the clouds? Who is it that binds up their waters in such a way that the clouds are not rent under them, even though there be more abundance of water in them than is in all the rivers and waters round about us? Job xxvi. 7, 8. Who is it that restrains and sets bounds to the sea, that the waters thereof, though they roar, yet do not overflow the land, but this almighty Jehovah, whose decree and commandment is the very compass, the bulwark over which they cannot flow? And all this he doth with more facility than men can speak. If there were a creature that could do all things by speaking, that were a strange power. But yet that creature might be wearied of speaking much. But he speaks, and it is done. His word is a creating word of power, which makes things that are not to be, and there is no wearying of him besides, for he is almighty and cannot faint. But why then did he take six days for his work? Might he not with one word of his power have commanded this world to issue out of his omnipotent virtue thus perfect as it is? What needed all this compass? Why took he six days, who in a moment could have done it all with as much facility? Indeed herein the Lord would have us to adore his wisdom as well as his power. He proceeds from more imperfect things to more perfect;—from a confused chaos to a beautiful world,—from motion to rest,—to teach man to walk through this wilderness and valley of tears, this shapeless world, into a more beautiful habitation; through the tossings of time, into an eternal sabbath of rest, whither their works shall follow them, and they shall rest from their labours. He would teach us to take a steadfast look of his work, and that we should be busied all the days of our pilgrimage and sojourning in the consideration of the glorious characters of God upon the works of his hands. We see that it is but passing looks and glances of God's glory we take in the creatures; but the Lord would have us to make it our work and business all the week through, as it was his to make them. He would in this teach us his loving care of men, who would not create man till he had made for him so glorious a house, replenished with all good things. It had been a darksome and irksome life to have lived in the first chaos without light; but he hath stretched over him the heavens as his tent, and set lights in them to distinguish times and seasons, and ordained the waters their proper bounds and peculiar channels, and then maketh the earth to bring forth all manner of fruit; and when all is thus disposed, then he creates man. To this God, the Maker of heaven and earth, be glory and praise.

Lecture XVIII.

OF CREATION.

HEB. xi. 3. "*Through faith we understand that the worlds were framed by the word of God; so that things which are seen were not made of things which do appear.*"—HEB. i. 14. "*Are they not all ministering spirits, sent forth to minister for them who shall be heirs of salvation?*"

THERE is nothing more generally known than this, that God at the beginning made the heaven and the earth, and all the host of them, the upper or the celestial, the lower or sublunary world. But yet there is nothing so little believed or laid to heart. 'Through faith we understand that the worlds were framed.' It is one of the first articles of the creed, indeed,—'Father, almighty Maker of heaven and earth.' But I fear that creed is not written in the tables of flesh, that is, the heart. There is a two-fold mistake among men about the point of believing. Some, and the commoner sort, do think it is no other than simply to know such a thing, and not to question it; to hear it, and not to contradict it, or object against it; therefore they do flatter themselves in their own eyes, and do account themselves to have faith in God, because they can say over all the articles of their belief. They think the word is true, and they never doubted of it. But, I beseech you, consider how greatly you mistake a main matter of weighty concernment. If you will search it, as before the Lord, you will find you have no other belief of these things than children use to have, whom you teach to think or say any thing. There is no other ground of your not questioning these truths of the gospel, but because you never consider them, and so they pass for current. Do not deceive yourselves: 'with the heart man believes.' It is a heart-business, a soul-matter, no light and useless opinion, or empty expression, which you have learned from a child. You say, you believe in God, the Maker of heaven and earth; and so say children, who doubt no more of it than you, and yet in sadness they do not retire within their own hearts, to think what an One he is. They do not remember him in the works of his hands. There is no more remembrance of that true God than if no such thing were known. So it is among you,—you would think we wronged you if we said, ye believed not that God made the world; and yet certainly, all men have not this faith, whereby they understand truly in their heart, the power and wisdom and goodness of God appearing in it; that is the gift of God, only given to them that shall be saved. If I should say, that you believe not the most common principles of religion, you will think it hard; and yet there is no doubt of it, that the most common truths are least believed. And the reason is plain, because men have learned them by tongue, and there is none that question them; and therefore, very few ever, in sadness and in earnest, consider of them. You say that God made heaven and earth, but how often do ye think on that God? And how often do you think on him with admiration? Do ye at all wonder at the glory of God when ye gaze on his works? Is not this volume always obversant before your eyes—every thing showing and declaring this glorious Maker. Yet who is it that taketh more notice of him than if he were not at all? Such is the general stupidity of men, that they never ponder and digest these things in their heart, till their soul receive the stamp of the glory and greatness of the invisible God, which shines most brightly in those things that are visible; and be in some measure transformed in their minds, and conformed to those glorious appearances of him, which are engraven in great characters in all that do at all appear. There is another mistake peculiar to some, especially the Lord's people, that they think faith is limited to some few particular and more unknown and hidden truths and mysteries of the gospel. Ye think that it is only true believing, to embrace some special gospel-truths, which the multitude of people know nothing of, as the tenor of the covenants of grace and works, &c. And for other common principles of God's making and ruling the world, you think that a common thing to believe them. But, saith the apostle, 'through faith we understand that the worlds were framed.' It is that same faith spoken of in the end of the 10th chapter, by which the 'just shall live.' So then, here is a point of saving faith, to believe with the heart in God, the Creator and Father Almighty; to take a view of God's almighty power, and sufficient goodness and infinite wisdom, shining in the fabric of the world, and that with delight and admiration at such a glorious fountain-being; to rise up to his majesty by the degrees of his creatures. This is the climbing and aspiring nature of faith. You see how much those saints in the Old Testament were in this; and certainly they had more excellent and beseeming thoughts of God than we. It should make Christians ashamed, that both heathens, who had no other book opened to them but that of nature, did read it more diligently than we; and that the saints of old, who had not such a plain testimony of God as we now have, did yet learn more out of the book of the creature than we do both out of it and the scriptures. We look on all things with such a careless eye; and do not observe what may be found of God in them. I think, verily, there are many Christians, and ministers of the gospel, who do not ascend into those high and ravishing thoughts of God, in his being and working, as would become even mere naturalists. How little can they speak of his majesty, or think as it becomes his transcendent glory! There is little in sermons or discourses that holds out any singular admiring thoughts of a Deity; but in all these we are as common and careless as if he were an idol.

It is not in vain that it is expressed thus: 'through faith we know that the worlds were framed.' For certainly the firm believing and pondering of this one truth would be of great moment and use to a Christian in all his journey. You may observe in what stead it is to the saints in scripture: this raises up a soul to high thoughts, and suitable conceptions of his glorious name; and so conforms the worship of his majesty unto his excellency. It puts the stamp of divinity upon it, and spiritualizes the thoughts and affections, so as to put a true difference between the true God, and the gods that made not the heavens and the earth. Alas! the worship of many Christians speaks out no diviner or higher object than a creature; it is so cold, so formal and empty, so vain and wandering. There is no more respect testified unto him, than we would give unto some eminent person. You find in the scripture how the strain of the saints' affections and devotion rises, when they take up God in his absolute supremacy above the creatures, and look on him as the alone fountain of all that is worth the name of perfection in them. A soul in that consideration cannot choose but assign unto him the most eminent seat in the heart, and gather those affections which are scattered after the creatures, into one channel, to pour them out on him who is all in all, and hath all that which is lovely in the creatures in an eminent degree. Therefore know what you are formed for,—to show forth his praise, to gather and take up from the creatures all the fruits of his praise, and offer them up to his majesty. This was the end of man, and this is the end of a Christian. You are made for this, and you were redeemed for this, to read upon the volumes of his works and word, and from thence extract songs of praise to his majesty.

As this would be of great moment to the right worshipping of God, and to the exercise of true holiness, so it is most effectual to the establishing of a soul in the confidence of the promises of God. When a soul by faith understands the world was made by God, then it relies with confidence upon that same word of God, as a word of power, and hopes against hope. There are many things in the Christian's way betwixt him and glory, which look as insuperable. Thou art often emptied into nothing, and stripped naked of all encouragements, and there is nothing remaining but the word of God's promises to thee and to the church, which seems contrary to sense and reason. Now, I say, if thou do indeed believe that the world was made by God, then out of all question thou mayest silence all thy fears with this one thought—God created this whole frame out of nothing, he commanded the light to shine out of darkness, then certainly he can give a being to his own promises. Is not his word of promise as sure and effectual as his word of command? This is the grand encouragement of the church, both offered by God, from Isa. chap. xl., and made use of by his saints, as David, Hezekiah, &c. What is it would disquiet a soul if it were reposed on this rock of creating power and faithfulness? This would always sound in its ears,—'Faint not, weary not, Jacob, I am God, and none else. The portion of Jacob is not like others.' Be it inward or outward difficulties,—suppose hell and earth combined together,—let all the enemies of a soul, or of the church assemble,—here is one for all. The God that made the heaven and the earth can speak, and it is done; command, and it stands fast! He creates peace, and who then can make trouble, when he gives quietness to a nation, or to a person? Almighty power works in saints, and for saints. Let us trust in him!

Lecture XV.

OF THE CREATION OF MAN.

GEN. i. 26, 27. "*And God said, Let us make man in our image, after our likeness; and let them have dominion over the fish of the sea, and over the fowl of the air, and over the cattle, and over all the earth, and over every creeping thing that creepeth upon the earth. So God created man in his own image, in the image of God created he him, male and female created he them.*"—With EPH. iv. 24. "*And that ye put on the new man, which after God is created in righteousness and true holiness.*" —And Heb. iii. 10. "*Wherefore I was grieved with that generation, and said, They do alway err in their heart; and they have not known my ways.*"

WHILE we descend from the meditation of the glory of God shining in the heavens, in sun, moon, and stars, unto the consideration of the Lord's framing of man after this manner, we may fall into admiration with the Psalmist, (Psal. viii.) 'Lord, what is man that thou art mindful of him? and the son of man, that thou visitest him?' It might indeed drown us in wonder, and astonish us, to think what special notice he hath taken of such a creature from the very beginning, and put more respect upon him than upon all the more excellent works of his hands. You find here the creation of man expressed in other terms than were used before. He said, 'Let there be light,' and it was; let there be dry land, &c. But it is not such a simple word as that, but 'let us make man in our image;' as if God had called a consultation about it. What! was there any more difficulty in this than in the rest of his works? Needed he any advisement about his frame and constitution? No certainly, for there was as great work of power, as curious pieces of art and wisdom, which were instantly done upon his word. He is not a man that he should advise or consult. As there is no difficulty nor impediment in the way of his power,—he doth all that he pleases, *ad nutum*, at his very word or nod, so easy are impossibilities to him,—so there is nothing hard to his wisdom, no knot but it can loose, nothing so curious or exquisite but he can as curiously contrive it, as the most common and gross pieces of the creation; and therefore, 'he is wonderful in counsel, and excellent in working.' But ye have here expressed, as it were, a counsel of the holy and blessed Trinity about man's creation; to signify to us what peculiar respect he puts upon that creature, and what special notice he takes of us, that of his own free purpose and good pleasure he was to single and choose out man from among all other creatures, for the more eminent demonstration of his glorious attributes of grace, mercy, and justice upon him; and likewise to point out the excellency that God did stamp upon man in his creation beyond the rest of the creatures, as the apostle shows the excellency of Christ above angels, 'To which of the angels said he at any time, Thou art my son?' Heb. i. 5. So we may say, of which of the creatures said he at any time, "Come, let us make them in our image after our likeness?" O how should this make us listen to hear, earnest to know what man once was, how magnified of God, and set above the works of his hands? There is a great desire in men to search into their original, and to trace backward the dark footsteps of antiquity, especially if they be put in expectation of attaining any honourable or memorable extraction? How will men love to hear of the worth of their ancestors? But what a stupidity doth possess the most part, in relation to the high fountain and head of all, that they do not aim so high as Adam, to know the very estate of human nature? Hence it is that the most part of people lie still astonished, or rather stupid and senseless, after this great fall of man, because they never look upward to the place and dignity from whence man did fall. It is certain, you will never rightly understand yourselves or what you are, till ye know first what man was made. You cannot imagine what your present misery is, till you once know what that felicity was in which man was made,—'let us make man in our image.' Some have called man μικροκοσμος, 'a little world,' a compend of the world; because he hath heaven and earth as it were married together in him—two most remote and distant natures, the dust of the earth, and the immortal spirit, which is called the breath of God, sweetly linked and conjoined together, with a disposition and inclination one to another. The Lord was in this piece of workmanship as it were to give a narrow and short compend of all his works, and so did associate in one piece with marvellous wisdom, being, living, moving, sense and reason, which are scattered abroad in the other creatures, so that a man carries these wonders about with him, which he admires without him. At his bare and simple word, this huge frame of the world started out of nothing; but in this, he acts the part of a cunning artificer,—'Let us make man.' He makes rather than creates; first raises the walls of flesh, builds the house of the body with all its organs, all its rooms; and then he puts in a noble and divine guest to dwell in it. He breathes in it the breath of life. He incloses as it were an angel within it, and marries these together in the most admirable union and communion that can be imagined, so that they make up one man.

But that which the Lord looks most into in this work, and would have us most to consider, is that image of himself that he did imprint on man,—'Let us make man in our own image.' There was no creature but it had some engravings of God upon it, some curious draughts and lineaments of his power, wisdom, and goodness upon it, and therefore the heavens are said to show forth his glory, &c. But whatever they have, it is but the lower part of that image, some dark shadows and resemblances of him; but that which is the last of his works, he makes it according to his own image, *tanquam ab ultima manu.* He therein gives out himself to be read and seen of all men as in a glass. Other creatures are made as it were according to the similitude of his footstep,—*ad similitudinem vestigii,*—but man *ad similitudinem faciei,*—according to the likeness of his face,—'in our image, after our likeness.' It is true there is only Jesus Christ his Son, who is 'the brightness of his glory, and the express substantial image of his person,' who resembles him perfectly and thoroughly in all properties, so that he is *alter idem,* another self both in nature, properties, and operations,—so like him that he is one with him, so that it is rather an *oneness,* than a likeness. But man he created according to his own image, and gave him to have some likeness to himself,—likeness I say, not *sameness* or *oneness.* That is high indeed, to be like God. The notion and expression of it imports some strange thing. How could man be like God, who is infinite, incomprehensible, whose glory is not communicable to another? It is true indeed, in those incommunicable properties he hath not only no equal, but none to liken him. In these he is to be adored, and admired as infinitely transcending all created perfections and conceptions. But yet in others he has been pleased to hold forth himself to be imitated and followed. And that this might be done, he first stamps them upon man in his first moulding of him. And if ye would know what these are particularly, the apostle expresses them, 'in knowledge,' (Col. iii. 10.) 'in righteousness and true holiness,' Eph. iv. 24. This is the 'image of him who created him,' which the Creator stamped on man, that he might seek him, and set him apart for himself to keep communion with him, and to bless him. There is a spirit given to man, with a capacity to know and to will; and here is a draught and lineament of God's face which is not engraven on any sensitive creature. It is one of the most noble and excellent operations of life, in which a man is most above beasts, to reflect upon himself, and to know himself and his Creator. There are natural instincts given to other things, natural propensions to those things that are convenient to their own nature; but none of them have so much as a capacity to know what they are, or what they have. They cannot frame a notion of him who gave them a being, but are only proportionate to the discerning of some sensible things, and can reach no further. He hath limited the eye within colours and light; he hath set a bound to the ear that it cannot act without sounds; and so to every sense he hath assigned its own proper stanse, in which it moves. But he teaches man knowledge, and he enlarges the sphere of his understanding beyond visible or sensible things, to things invisible,—to spirits. And this capacity he has put in the soul,—to know all things, and itself among the rest. The eye discerns light, but sees not itself; but he gives a spirit to man to know himself and his God. And then there is a willing power in the soul, by which it diffuses itself towards any thing that is conceived as good; the understanding directing, and the will commanding according to its direction, and then the whole faculties and senses obeying such commands, which makes up an excellent draught of the image of God. There was a sweet proportion and harmony in Adam; all was in due place and subordination. The motions of immortal man did begin within. The lamp of reason did shine and give light to it; and till that went before, there was no stirring, no choosing, no refusing; and when reason—which was one sparkle of the divine nature, or a ray of God's light reflected into the soul of man,—when once that did appear to the discerning of good and evil, this power was in the soul, to apply the whole man accordingly, to choose the good and refuse the evil. It had not been a lively resemblance of God to have a power of knowing and willing simply, unless these had been beautified and adorned with supernatural and divine graces of spiritual light and holiness and righteousness. These make up the lively colour, and complete the image of God upon the soul.

There was a divine light which did shine in upon the understanding, ever till sin interposed and eclipsed it; and from the light of God's countenance did the sweet heat and warmness of holiness and uprightness in the affections proceed; so that there was nothing but purity and cleanness in the soul, no darkness of ignorance, no muddiness of carnal affections, but the soul pure and transparent, to receive the refreshing and enlightening rays of God's glorious countenance. And this was the very face and beauty of the soul. It is that only that is the beauty and excellency of the creature,—conformity to God. And this was throughout, in understanding and affections; the understanding conformed to his understanding, discerning between good and evil. And conformed it behoved to be, for it was but a ray of that sun, a stream of that fountain of wisdom, and a light derived from that primitive light of God's understanding. And then the will did sympathize as much with his will, approving and choosing what he approved, and refusing that which he hated. *Idem velle atque nolle, ea demum firma amicitia est.** That was the conjunction, and it was more strict than any tie among men. There were not two wills; they were, as it were, one. The love of God reflecting into the soul, did, as it were, carry the soul back again unto him; and that was the conforming principle which fashioned the whole man without and within, to his likeness and to his obedience. Thus man was formed for communion with God; this likeness behoved to be, or they could not join as friends.

But now this calls us to a sad meditation, to think from whence we have fallen, and so how great our fall is. To fall from such a blessed estate, that must be great misery! Satan hath spoiled us of our rich treasure, that glorious image of holiness, and hath drawn upon our souls the very visage of hell, the lineaments of his hellish countenance. But the most part of men lie stupid, insensible of any thing, as beasts that are felled with their fall, that can neither find pain nor rise. If we could but

* [That is, "to have the same desires and aversions, that, in a word, is strong friendship."—*Sallust. in Catil.* c. xx.—Ed.]

return and consider what are all those sad and woful consequences of sin in the world,—what a strange distemper it hath put in the creation,—what miseries that one fall hath brought on all mankind,—I am sure by these bruises we might conjecture what a strange fall it hath been. Sin did interpose between God and us, and this darkened our souls and killed them. The light of knowledge was put out, and the life of holiness extinguished, and now there remains nothing of all that stately building, but some ruins of common principles of reason and honesty engraven on all men's consciences, which may show unto us what the building hath been. We have fallen from holiness, and so from happiness. Our souls are deformed and defiled. You see what an ill-favoured thing it is, to see a child wanting any members. O if sin were visible, how ugly would the shape of the soul be to us, since it lost the very proportion and visage of it, that is, God's image! Let us consider this doctrine, that we may know from whence we have fallen, and into what a gulf of sin and misery we have fallen, that the news of Jesus Christ, a Mediator and Redeemer of fallen man, may be sweet unto us. Thus it pleased the Lord to let his image be marred and quite spoiled in us, for he had this design to repair it and renew it better than of old, and for this end he hath created Christ according to his image. He hath stamped that image of holiness upon his flesh to be a pattern,—and not only so, but a pledge also,—of restoring such souls as flee unto him for refuge, unto that primitive glory and excellency. Know then, that he hath made his Son like unto us, that we might again be made like unto him. He said, let one of us be made man, in the counsel of redemption, that so it might again be said, let man be made like unto us, in our image. It is a second creation must do it; and O that you would look upon your hearts to inquire if it be framed in you! Certainly you must again be created into that image if you belong to Christ. To him be praise and glory.

Lecture XX.

GOD'S WORKS OF PROVIDENCE.

ROM. xi. 36. "*For of him, and through him, and to him are all things; to whom be glory for ever, Amen.*"—Psal. ciii. 19. "*The Lord hath prepared his throne in the heavens: and his kingdom ruleth over all.*"—Matt. x. 29. "*Are not two sparrows sold for a farthing? And one of them shall not fall on the ground without your Father.*"

THERE is nothing more commonly confessed in words, than that the providence of God reaches to all the creatures and their actions; but I believe there is no point of religion so superficially and slightly considered by the most part of men. The most part ponder none of these divine truths. There is nothing above their senses which is the subject of their meditations. And for the children of God, I fear many do give such truths of God too common and coarse entertainment in their minds, through a conceit of the commonness of them. I know not what we are taken up with in this age,—with some particular truths more remote from the knowledge of others in former times, or some particular cases concerning ourselves? You will find the most part of Christians stretch not their thoughts beyond their own conditions or interests, or some particular questions about faith and repentance, &c. And in the mean time the most weighty points of religion, which have been the subject of the meditation and admiration of saints in all ages, are wholly laid aside through a misapprehension of their commonness, as if a man would despise the sun and the air, and prefer some rare piece of stone or timber to them. Certainly, as in the disposal of the world, the Lord hath in great wisdom and goodness made the most needful and useful things most common—those without which man cannot live are always obvious to us, so that if any thing be more rare, it is not necessary—so in this universe of religion, he in mercy and wisdom hath so framed all, that those points of truth and belief which are most near the substance of salvation and necessary to it, and most fit to exercise us in true godliness,—these are everywhere to be found, partly engraven on men's hearts, partly set down most clearly and often in scripture, that a believing soul can look nowhere but it must breathe in that air of the gospel, and look upon that common Sun of righteousness, God the Creator, and the healing Sun, Christ the Redeemer, shining everywhere in scripture. The general providence of God and the special administration of Christ the Saviour, these are common, and these are essential to our happiness. Therefore the meditation of Christians should run most upon them, and not always about some particular questions or debates of the time. It is a strange thing how people should be more affected with a discourse on the affairs of the time, or on some inward thoughts of their own hearts, than if one should speak of God's universal kingdom over all men and nations. That is accounted a general and ordinary discourse; even as if men would set at nought the sun's light, because it shines to all, and every day; or would despise the water, because it may be found everywhere. Let the sun be removed for some few days, and O what would the world account of it beyond all your curious devices or rare enjoyments! This is it which would increase to more true godliness, if rightly believed, than many other things ye are busied withal. It is our general view of them makes them but general. I spoke once upon this word, Rom. xi. 36. but only in reference to the end of man, which is God's glory; but the words do extend further, and we must now consider what further they hold forth. The apostle hath been speaking of the Lord's unsearchable ways and judgments towards men in the dispensation of grace and salvation, how free and how absolute he is in that. And this he strengthens by the supreme wisdom of God, who did direct him. Why dost thou, O man, take upon thee to direct him now? For, where was there any counsellor when he alone contrived all the frame of this world, and then, by sovereign highness and supremacy over the creatures, disposed of them? For he is a debtor to none, therefore none can quarrel him for giving or not giving: for who was it that gave him first, for which he should give a recompense? Was there any could prevent him with a gift? Nay, none could, saith he, 'for of him, and through him, and to him are all things:' and therefore he must prevent men. For from whence should that gift of the creature, which could oblige him, have its rise? It must be of God, if it be a creature, and therefore he is in no man's common; he must give it ere we have it to give him again.

The words are most comprehensive. They comprehend all things, and that is very large. There is nothing without this compass, and they comprehend all the dependence of things. Things depend upon that which made them, that which preserves them, and that for which they are made. All things depend on him as their producing cause that gives them a being; 'for of him are all things.' They also depend on him as their conserving cause, who continues their being by that selfsame influence wherewith he gave it; 'for through him are all things.' And then they depend on him as their final cause, for whose glory they are, and are continued; for, 'to him are all things.' Thus you have the beginning, the continuance, and the end of the whole creation. This word may lead us through all; from God, as the beginning, the alpha and original of their being; through God, as the only supporter, confirmer, and upholder of their being; and unto God, as the very end for which they have their being. Now, to travel within this compass,—to walk continually within this circle, and to go along this blessed round,—to begin at God, and to go along all our way with him, till we arrive and end at God,—and thus to do continually in the journey of meditation, when it surveys any of his works,—this were, indeed, the very proper work, and the special happiness man was created for; and, I may say, a great part of that which a Christian is created for. Again, there would be nothing more powerful to the conforming of a soul to God, and to his obedience and fear than this, to have that persuasion firmly rooted in the heart—that of God 'are all things;' that whatever it be, good or evil, that befalls us or others,—whatever we observe in the world, that is the subject of the thoughts and discourses of men, and turns men's eyes after them,—that all that is of God; that is, it is in the world; it started out of nothing at his command; it is, because his power gave it a being; and in this consideration to overlook, and in a manner forget, all second causes; to have such affecting and uptaking thoughts of the first principle of all these motions, as to regard the lower wheels, that are next us, no more than the hand or the sword that a man strikes us with: as if these second causes had no influence of their own, but were merely acted and moved by this supreme power, as if God did nothing by them, but only at their presence. We should so labour to look on those things he doth by creatures, as if he did them alone without the creatures; as if he were this day creating a world. Certainly, the solid faith of God's providence will draw off the covering of the creature, and espy the secret almighty power which acts in every thing to bring forth his good pleasure concerning them. And then to consider, with that same seriousness of meditation, that the same everlasting arm which made them, is under them to support them; that the most noble and excellent creatures are but streams, rays, images, and shadows of God's majesty, which, as they have their being by derivation, so they have their continuance by that same continued influence; so that if he would interpose between himself and them, or withdraw his countenance, or stop his influence, the most sufficient of them all should evanish, as the sun-beams dry up the streams of a fountain, and disappear as the image of the glass, Psal. civ. 29, 30. O that place were a pertinent object of a Christian's meditation; how much of God is to be pressed out of it by a serious pondering of it! 'Thou hidest thy face, they are troubled: thou takest away their breath, they die, and return to their dust. Thou sendest forth thy Spirit, they are created.' It is even with the very being and faculties of the creature as with the image in the glass, which, when the face removes, it is seen no more. The Lord, as it were, breathes into them a being; and when he takes in his breath they perish; and when he sends it out again they are renewed. We do not wonder at the standing of the world, but think, if we had been witnesses of the making of it, we would have been filled with admiration. But certainly it is only our stupidity that doth not behold that same wonder continued, for what is the upholding of this by his power, but a very continued and repeated creation,—which influence were able to bring a world out of nothing? If this had not been before the virtue and power he employs now in making them subsist, that same alone, without any addition of power, would have in the beginning made all this to be of nothing; so that the continuance of the world is nothing else but an uninterrupted and constant flux and emanation of these things from God, as of light from the body of the sun. And then to meditate how all these things are for him and his glory, though we know no use nor end of them, yet that his majesty hath appointed them to show forth, one way or other, the glory of his name in them; and those things which to our first and foolish apprehensions seem most contrary to him, and, as it were, to spread a cloud of darkness over his glorious name—the sins and perverse doings of men and angels; the many disorders and confusions in the world, which seem to reflect some way upon him; that yet he hath holy and glorious ends in them all, yea, that himself is the end of all; I say, to meditate on these things till our soul received the stamp of reverence, and fear, and faith in God,—this would certainly be the most becoming exercise of a Christian, to bring all things down from God, that we might return and ascend with all things again unto God.

This is the most suitable employment of a man, as reasonable, much more as a Christian; that very duty he was created for. 'This people have I formed for myself; they shall show forth my praise,' Isa. xliii. 21. And this is the showing forth of his praise, to follow forth the footsteps of God in the word and in the world; and to ponder these paths of divine power and goodness and wisdom, and to acknowledge him with our heart in all these. He made many creatures on which his glory and praise is showed forth, and he made this creature man to show forth that praise and that glory which is showed forth in other creatures. O but this is a divine office! It is strange how our hearts are carried forth towards base things, and busied in many vain, impertinent, and base employments, and scarce ever mind this great one we were created for.

Certainly, this is the employment we were made for; to deduce all things from God till we can again reduce all to him with glory; to bring all down from his everlasting counsels, until we send all up to his eternal glory, together with the sacrifice of our hearts; to behold all things to be of him, that is, of his eternal counsel and decree,

—to have their rise in the bosom of that; and then, through him, to proceed out of the bosom of his decree and purpose, by his power, *quasi obstetricante potentia*, and then to return with all the praise and glory to his ever-glorious name, 'for whom are all things.' There is none but they will allow God some government in the world. Some would have him as a king, commanding and doing all by deputies and substitutes. Some would have his influence general, like the sun's upon sublunary things; but how shallow are all men's thoughts in regard of that which is? God has prepared, indeed, his throne in the heavens. That is true, that his glory doth manifest itself in some strange and majestic manner above; but the whole tenor of Scripture shows that he is not shut up in heaven, but that he immediately cares for, governs, and disposes all things in the world; for his kingdom is over all. It is the weakness of kings, not their glory, that they have need of deputies; it is his glory, not baseness, to look to the meanest of his creatures. It is a poor resemblance and empty shadow that kings have of him; he rules in the kingdoms of men, and to him belongs the dominion and the glory. He deserves the name of a king, whose beck heaven and earth obey. Can a king command that the sea flow not? Can a parliament act and ordain that the sun rise not? Or will these obey them? Yet at his decree and command the sun is dark, the sea stands still, the mountains tremble; 'at thy rebuke the sea fled.' Alas! what do we mean that we look upon creatures, and act ourselves as if we were independent in our being and moving? How many things fall out, and you call them casual, and attribute them to fortune? How many things do the world gaze upon, think upon, and discourse upon, and yet not one thought, one word of God all the time? What more contingent than the falling of a sparrow on the ground? And yet even that is not unexpected to him, but it flows from his will and counsel. What less taken notice of or known than the hairs of your head? Yet these are particularly numbered by him, and so that no power in the world can add to them or diminish from them, without his counsel. O what would the belief of this do to raise our hearts to suitable thoughts of God above the creatures; to increase the fear, faith, and love of God; and to abate from our fear of men, and our vain and unprofitable cares and perplexities? How would you look upon the affairs of men,—the counsels, contrivances, endeavours, and successes of men,—when they are turning things upside down, and plotting the ruin of his people, and establishing themselves alone in the earth? What would you think of all these revolutions at this time? Many souls are astonished at them, and stand gazing at what is done and to be done. And this is the very language of your spirits and ways; The Lord hath forsaken the earth; the Lord seeth not. This is the language of our parliaments and people. They do imagine that they are doing their own business, and making all sure for themselves. But, O what would a soul think that could escape above them all, and arise up to the first wheel of present motions! A soul that did stand upon the exalted tower of the word of God, and looked off it by the prospect of faith, would presently discover the circle in which all these wanderings and changes are confined, and see men, states, armies, nations, and all of them doing nothing but turning about in a round, as a horse in a mill, from God's eternal purpose, by his almighty power, to his unspeakable glory. You might behold all these extravagant motions of the creatures, inclosed within those limits, that they must begin here, and end here, though themselves are so beastly that they neither know of whom nor for whom their counsels and actions are. Certainly, Satan cannot break without this compass, to serve his own humour. Principalities and powers cannot do it. If they will not glorify him, he shall glorify himself by them and upon them.

Lecture XXI.

OF THE FIRST COVENANT MADE WITH MAN.

GEN. ii. 17. "*But of the tree of the knowledge of good and evil, thou shalt not eat of it; for in the day that thou eatest thereof, thou shalt surely die.*"—GEN. i. 26. "*And God said, Let us make man in our image, after our likeness: And let them have dominion over the fish of the sea, and over the fowl of the air, and over the cattle, and over all the earth, and over every creeping thing that creepeth upon the earth.*"

THE state wherein man was created at first, you heard was exceeding good,—all things very good, and he best of all, the choicest external and visible piece of God's workmanship, made according to the most excellent pattern,—'after our image.' Though it be a double misery to be once happy, yet seeing the knowledge of our misery is, by the grace of God, made the entry to a new happiness, it is most necessary to take a view of what man once was, that we may be more sensible of what he now is. You may take up this image and likeness in three branches.

First, there was a sweet conformity of the soul in its understanding, will, and affections unto God's holiness and light,—a beautiful light in the mind, derived from that fountain-light, by which Adam did exactly know both divine and natural things. What a great difference doth yet appear between a learned man and an ignorant rude person, though it be but in relation to natural things! The one is but like a beast in comparison of the other. O how much more was there between Adam's knowledge and that of the most learned! The highest advancement of art and industry in this life reaches no further than to a learned ignorance of the mysteries in the works of God, and yet there is a wonderful satisfaction to the mind in it. But how much sweet complacency hath Adam had, whose heart was so enlarged as to know both things higher and lower, their natures, properties, and virtues, and several operations! No doubt could trouble him, no difficulty vex him, no controversy or question perplex him; but above all, the knowledge of that glorious and eternal Being, that gave him a being, and infused such a spirit into him,—the beholding of such infinite treasures of wisdom, and goodness, and power in him, what an amiable and refreshful sight would it be, when there was no cloud of sin and ignorance to interpose and eclipse the full enjoyment of that uncreated light! When the aspect of the sun makes the moon so glorious and beautiful, what may you conceive of Adam's soul framed with a capacity to receive light immediately from God's countenance! How fair and beautiful would that soul be, until the dark cloud of sin did interpose itself! Then consider, what a beautiful rectitude and uprightness, what a comely order and subordination would ensue upon this light, and make his will and affections wonderfully good. 'God made man upright,' Eccles. vii. 29. There was no thraw * or crack in all,—all the powers of the soul bending upright towards that Fountain of all goodness. Now the soul is crooked and bends downward towards those base earthly things that are the abasement of the soul; then it looked upright towards God,—had no appetite, no delight but in him and his fulness, and had the moon or changeable world under its feet. There was a beauty of holiness and righteousness which were the colours that did perfect and adorn those lineaments of the image of God which knowledge did draw in the soul. 'He was a burning and a shining light,' may be truly said of Adam, who had as much life as light, as much delight in God as knowledge of him. This was the right constitution and disposition of man,—his head lifted up in holiness and love towards God; his arms stretched out in righteousness and equity towards man; and all the affections of the man under their command, they could not trouble this sea with any tempest, because they were under a powerful commander, who kept them under such awe and obedience as the centurion

* [That is, twist.—ED.]

his servants,—saying to one, Go, and he goeth, and to another, Come, and he cometh, sending out love one way, holy hatred another way. These were as wings to the bird to flee upon, as wheels to the chariot to run upon; though now it be turned just contrary, that the chariot draws the coachman, because the motion is downward. There could be no motion in an upright man's soul till the holy and righteous will gave out a sentence upon it. That was the *primum mobile*, which was turned about itself by such an *intelligentia* as the understanding. And so it was in Christ,—affection could not move him, but he did move his own affections, he troubled himself. In us the servant rides on horses, and the prince walks on foot; even as in a distempered society, the laws and ordinances proceed by an unnatural way, from the violence of unruly subjects usurping over their masters. Holy and righteous man could both raise up his affections, and compose them again, they were under such nurture and discipline. He could have said, Hitherto, and no further; in which there was some resemblance of God ruling the raging and unruly sea. But now, if once they get entry into our city, they are more powerful than the governor, and will not take laws from him, but give him rather. When we have given way to our passions, they do next what they please, not what we permit.

Next his excellency consisted in such an immunity and freedom from all fear of misery and danger, from all touch of sorrow or pain, and did enjoy such a holy complacency and delight in his own estate, as made him completely happy. In this he was like God. This is his blessedness, that he is absolutely well-pleased in himself, that he is without the reach of fear and danger, that none can impair it, none can match it. 'I am God and none else;' that is sufficiency of delight to know himself, and his own sufficiency. Indeed, man was made changeable, mutably good, that in this he might know God was above him, and so might have ground of watchfulness and dependence upon him for continuance of his happiness who made him happy. But being made so upright, no disquieting fear nor perplexing care could trouble him. Then, lastly, if you add unto this, holy satisfaction with his own state and freedom, the dominion and sovereignty he had over the creatures, as a consequent flowing from that image, you may imagine what a happy creature he was. Whatsoever contentment or satisfaction the creatures could afford, all of them willingly and pleasantly would concur to bestow it upon man, without his care or toil, as if they had accounted it their happiness to serve him. What more excellent than this order? Man counting it his happiness and delight to serve God, and creatures esteeming it their happiness to serve man, all things running towards him with all their goodness, as to a common centre; and he returning all to God, from whence they did immediately flow. Thus, besides the fulness and riches of God's goodness immediately conferred upon man, he was enriched with all the store and goodness that the earth was full of.

God having made man thus, and furnished him after this manner, he gave him a law, and then he made a covenant with him. There was a law first imprinted into Adam, and then a law prescribed unto him. There was a law written in his heart, the remainder of which Paul saith makes the Gentiles 'inexcusable;' but it was perfectly drawn in him. All the principles and notions of good and evil were exactly drawn in it. He had a natural discerning of them, and a natural inclination to all good, and aversion from all evil, as there is a kind of law imposed by God upon other creatures, which they constantly keep, and do not swerve from, even his decree and commandment, to the obedience of which they are composed and framed. The sea hath a law and command to flow and ebb, and it is that command that breaks its proud waves on the sand, when they threaten to overflow mountains. The beasts obey a law, written in their natures, of eating and drinking, of satisfying their senses, and every one hath its several instinct and propension to several operations; so God gave a more noble instinct unto man, suitable to his reasonable soul,—an instinct and impulse to please God, in such duties of holiness and righteousness, a sympathy with such ways of integrity and godliness, and an innate antipathy against such ways as were displeasing to him or dishonourable to the creature. There is a kind of comeliness and sweet harmony and proportion between such works, as the love of God and man, the use of all for his glory, of whom all things are, and man's reasonable being. Such a thing doth suit and become it. Again, other things, as the hatred of God and men, neglect and forgetfulness of him, drunkenness and abusing lusts of that kind, do disagree, and are indecent to it. O how happy was Adam, when holiness and righteousness were not written on tables of stone, but on his heart, and when there was no need of external persuasion, but there was an inward impulse, inclining him strongly, and laying a kind of sweet necessity upon him to that which was both his duty to God and men and his own dignity and privilege! This was, no question, the very beauty of his soul,—to be not only under a law proper and peculiar to himself, but to be inwardly framed and moulded to it,—to be a living law unto himself.

But besides this inward imprinted law of holiness and righteousness, which did without more rules direct and determine him to that which is in itself good, it pleased the Lord to prescribe and impose a positive law unto him, to command him abstinence from a thing neither good nor evil, but indifferent, and such a thing as of itself he might have done as well as made use of any other creature. There was no difference between the fruit which was discharged him, and the fruit of the rest of the garden; there was nothing in it did require abstinence, and nothing in him either. Yet for most wise and holy ends, the Lord enjoins him to abstain from that fruit, and puts an act of restraint upon him, to abridge his liberty in that which might prove his obedience, and not hinder his happiness, or diminish it; because he furnished him abundantly beside. You may perceive two reasons of it. One is, that the sovereign power and dominion of God over all men, may be more eminently held forth, and that visibly in such a symbol and sign. He who put man in such a well-furnished house, and placed him in a plentiful and fruitful garden, reserves one tree, 'thou shalt not eat thereof,' to let Adam see and know, that he is the sovereign owner of all things, and that his dominion over the creatures, and their service unto him, was not so much for any natural prerogative of man above them, as out of divine bounty and indulgence, because he had chosen a creature to himself to beautify and make happy. This was a standing visible testimony, to bring man continually to remembrance of his sovereignty, that being thus far exalted above other creatures, he might know himself to be under his Creator, and that he was infinitely above him; that he might remember his own homage and subjection to God, whenever he looked upon his dominion over the creatures. And truly in other natural duties which an inward principle and instinct drives unto, the suitableness and conveniency or beauty of the thing doth often preponderate, and might make man to observe them without so much regard of the will and pleasure of the Most High. But in this the Lord would have no other reason of obedience to appear but his own absolute will and pleasure, to teach all men to consider in their actings rather the will of the commander than the goodness or use of the thing commanded. And then, for this reason, it was enjoined to make a more exact trial, and to take a more ample proof of Adam's obedience. Oftentimes we do things commanded of God, but upon what ground or motive? Because our own interest lies in them,—because there is an inward weight and *pondus* of affection pressing us to them. The Lord commands the mutual duties between parents and children, between man and wife, between friends, duties of self-preservation and defence, and such like; and many are very exact and diligent in performing these, but from what principle? It is easy to discern. Not because they are commanded of God,—not so much as a thought of that for the most part,—but because of an inward and natural inclination of affection towards ourselves and our relations, which is like an instinct and an impulse driving us to those duties. And truly we may say, it is the goodness and bounty of the Lord that hath conjoined in most parts of commanded duties our own interest and advantage, our own inclination and propension with his authority, or else the toil and pain of them would overbalance the weight of his authority. Now then, in such duties as are already imprinted on man's heart, and consonant to his own reason, there cannot be a clear proof of obedience to God's will. The pure and naked nature of obedience doth not so clearly shine forth in the observation of these. It is no great trial of the creature's subjection of its will to his supreme will, when there are so many reasons besides his will, which may incline man's will unto it. But here, in a matter in itself pleasant to the senses, unto which he had a natural inclination, the Lord interposes himself by a command of restraint, to take full probation whether man would submit to his good pleasure merely for itself, or whether he would obey merely because God commands. And indeed in such like duties as have no commendation but from the will and authority of the lawgiver, it will appear whether man's obedience be pure and simple obedience, and whether men love obedience for itself alone, or for other reasons. Therefore the Lord saith, Obedience is better than sacrifice, and disobedience is rebellion. Suppose, in such things as can neither hurt us nor help us, God put a restraint upon us,—though obedience may be of less worth than in other more substantial things, yet disobedience in such easy matters is most heinous, because it proclaims open rebellion against God. If it be light and easy, it is more easily obeyed, and the more sin and wickedness in disobeying; and therefore is Adam's sin called 'disobedience' in a signal manner, (Rom. v. 19,) because, by refusing such a small point of homage and subjection, he did cast off God's power and authority over him, and would not acknowledge him for his superior. This should teach us, who believe the repairing of that image by Jesus Christ, to study such a respect and reverence to God's holy will as to do all things without more asking why it is so. If we once know what it is, there is no more question to be asked. Of creatures we must inquire a *quare* after a *quid*,—a why, after we know what their will is. But Christians should have their wills so subdued unto God's, that though no profit nor advantage were to redound by obedience, though it were in things repugnant and cross to our inclination and humour, yet we should serve and obey him as a testimony of our homage and subjection to him. And till we learn this, and be more abstracted from our own interests in the ways of obedience, even from the interests of peace, and comfort, and liberty, we do not obey him because he commands, but for our own sakes. It is the practice of Antinomians, and contrary to true godliness, to look upon the law of God as the creature's bondage, as most of us do in our walking. A Christian, in whom the image of God is renewed according to righteousness and holiness, should esteem subjection and conformity to a law, and to the will of God, his only true liberty, yea, the very beauty of the soul; and never is a soul advanced in conformity to God, till this be its delight, not a burden or task.

Lecture XXII.

OF THE FIRST COVENANT.

GAL. iii. 12. "*The law is not of faith; but the man that doeth them shall live in them.*" —GEN. ii. 17. "*But of the tree of the knowledge of good and evil, thou shalt not eat of it; for in the day that thou eatest thereof, thou shalt surely die.*

THE Lord made all things for himself, to show forth the glory of his name; and man in a more eminent and special manner, for more eminent manifestations of himself; therefore all his dealings towards men, whether righteous or sinful, do declare the glory of God. Particularly, in reference to the present purpose, he resolved to manifest two shining properties,—his sovereignty and goodness. His sovereignty is showed, in giving out a law and command to the creature; and his goodness is manifested in making a covenant with his creature; as here you see the terms of a covenant, a duty required, and a promise made, and, in case of failing, a threatening conformed to the promise. He might have required obedience simply, as the Lord and sovereign owner of the being and operations of the creatures; and that was enough of obligation to bind all flesh, that the Creator is lawgiver, that he who gives a being doth set bounds and limits to the exercise and use of that being. But it pleased the Lord, in his infinite goodness and love, to add a promise and threatening to that law and command, and so turns it to the nature of a voluntary covenant and agreement, whereby he doth mitigate and sweeten his authority and power, and condescends so low to man as to take on himself a greater obligation than he puts upon man, 'Do this, and thou shalt live.' He might then, out of his absoluteness and power, have required at the creature's hand any terms he pleased, even the hardest which could be imagined, and yet no injustice in him. He might have put laws on men to restrain all their natural liberty, and in every thing, to proclaim nothing but his own supremacy. But O what goodness and condescension is even in the very matter of the law; and then in the manner of prescribing it with a promise! In the matter, so just and equitable to convince all men's consciences, yea, even engraven on their hearts, that he lays not many burdens on, but what men's consciences must lay on themselves; that there is nothing in it all, when summed up, harder than this,—love God most of all, and thy neighbour as thyself, which all men must proclaim to be due, though it had not been required; and but one precept added by his mere will, which yet was so easy a thing, as it was a wonder the Lord of all put no other conditions on the creatures. And then for the manner; that it is propounded covenant-wise, with a promise, not to expect the creature's consent—for it did not depend on his acceptation, he being bound to accept any terms his Lord propounded—but because the matter and all was so equitable, and the conditions so ample, that if it had been propounded to any rational man, he would have consented with an admiration at God's goodness. Indeed, if we speak strictly, there cannot be a proper covenant between God and man,—there is such an infinite distance between such unequal parties, our obedience and performance being absolutely in his power. We cannot promise it as our own, and it being but our duty, we cannot crave or expect a reward in justice, neither can he owe any thing to the creature. Yet it pleased his majesty to propound it in these terms, and to stoop so low unto men's capacities, and, as it were, come off the throne of his sovereignty, both to require such duties of men, and to promise unto them such a free reward. And the reasons of this may be plain upon God's part and upon ours. In such dealing, he consulted his own glory, and man's good. His own glory, I say, is manifested in it, and chiefly the glory of his goodness and love, that the Most High comes down so low as to article with his own footstool, that he changes his absolute right into a moderate and temperate government, and tempers his lordly and truly monarchical power by such a commixture of gentleness and goodness, in requiring nothing but what man behoved to call reasonable and due, and in promising so much as no creature could challenge any title to it. When the law was promulgated, 'Do this,' eat not of this tree, Adam's conscience behoved to say, "Amen, Lord; all is due, all the reason in the world for it." But when the promise is added, and the trumpet sounds longer, "Thou shalt live!" O more than reason, more than is due, must his conscience say! It was reason, that the most high Lord should use his footstool as his footstool, and set his servant in the place of a servant, and so keep distance from him. But how strange is it that he humbles himself to make friendship with man, to assume him in a kind of familiarity and equality? And this Christ is not forgetful of. When he restores men, he puts them in all their former dignities; 'I call you not servants but friends.' Next, his wisdom doth appear in this, that when he had made a reasonable creature, he takes a way of dealing, suitable to his nature, to bring forth willing and free obedience by the persuasion of such a reward, and the terror of such a punishment. He most wisely did enclose the will of man, as it were, on both sides, with hedges of punishment and reward, which might have been a sufficient defence or guard against all the irruptions of contrary persuasions, that man might continue in obedience, and that when he went to the right hand or left, he might be kept in, by the hope of such an ample promise, and the fear of such a dreadful threatening. But then the righteousness of God doth appear in this; for there is nothing doth more illustrate the justice of the judge, than when the malefactor hath before consented to such a punishment in case of transgression, when the law is confirmed by the consent and approbation of man. Now he has man subscribing already to his judgment, and so all the world must stop their mouth and become guilty in case of transgression of such a righteous command after such warning.

But, in the next place, it is no less for man's good. What an honour and dignity was put upon man, when he was taken into friendship with God! To be in covenant of friendship with a king, O what a dignity is it accounted! And some do account it a great privilege to be in company, and converse with some eminent and great person. But may not men say with the Psalmist, Lord, 'what is man that thou art mindful of him, or the son of man that thou visitest him?' Psal. viii. Again, what way more fit and suitable to stir up and constrain Adam unto a willing and constant obedience, when he had the encouragement of such a gracious reward, and the determent of such a fearful punishment? Between these two banks might the silver streams of obedience have run for ever without breaking over. He was bound to all, though nothing had been promised. But then to have such a hope, what spirits might it add to him? The Lord had been free, upon man's obedience, either to continue him his happy estate, or to denude him of it, or to annihilate him. There was no obligation lying on him. But now, what confirmation might man have by looking upon the certain recompense of reward—when God brings himself freely under an obligation of a promise, and so ascertains it to his soul, which he could never have dreamed of, and gives him liberty to challenge him upon his faithfulness to perform it!

And then, lastly, There was no way so fit to commend God, and sweeten him unto his soul as this. Adam knew that his goodness could not extend to God; that his righteousness could not help him, nor his wickedness hurt him, and so could expect nothing from his exact obedience. But now, when God's goodness doth so overflow upon the creature, and the Lord takes pleasure to communicate himself to make others happy, though he had need of none, O how must it engage the heart of man to a delightful remembrance, and converse with that God! As his authority should imprint reverence, so his goodness thus manifested should engrave confidence. And thus the life of man was not only a life of obedience, but a life of pleasure and delight; not only a holy, but a happy life, yea, happy in holiness.

Now, as it was Paul's great business in preaching, to ride marches between the covenant of grace, and the covenant of works,—to take men off that old broken ship to this sure plank of grace that is offered by Jesus Christ to drowning souls,—so it would be our great work to show unto you the nature of this covenant, and the terms thereof, that you may henceforth find and know that salvation to be now impossible by the law which so many seek in it. We have no errand to speak of the first Adam, but the better to lead you to the second. Our life was once in the first, but he lost himself and us both; but the second, by losing himself, saves both. We have nothing to do to speak of the first covenant, but that we may lead you, or pursue you rather to the second, established on better terms and better promises.

The terms of this covenant are,—Do this and live. Perfect obedience without one jot of failing or falling,—an entire and universal accomplishment of the whole will of God,—that is the duty required of man. There is no latitude left in the bargain to admit endeavours instead of performance, or desire instead of duty. There is no place for repentance here. If a man fail in one point, he falls from the whole promise; by the tenor of this bargain, there is no hope of recovery. If you would have the duty in a word, it is a love of God with all our heart and soul, and our neighbour as ourselves; and that testified and verified in all duties and offices of obedience to God, and love to men, without the least mixture of sin and infirmity. Now, the promise on God's part is indeed larger than that duty, not only because undeserved, but even in the matter of it, it is so abundant,—life, eternal life, continuance in a happy estate. There is a threatening added, 'In the day thou eatest thou shalt surely die;' that is, thou shalt become a mortal and miserable creature, subject to misery here and hereafter; which is more pressingly set down in that word, 'Cursed is he that abideth not in all things written in the law to do them.' It is very peremptory; that men dream not of escaping wrath when they break but in one, suppose they did abide in all the rest. Cursed is every man from the highest to the lowest; the Lord Almighty is engaged against him. His countenance, his power is against him, to destroy him and make him miserable. Whoever doth fail but in one jot of the commands, he shall not only fall from that blessed condition freely promised, but lose all that he already possessed, fall from that image of God, dominion over the creatures, and incur, instead of that possessed and expected happiness, misery here on soul and body, in pains, sicknesses, troubles, griefs, &c., and eternal misery on both, without measure, hereafter,—'eternal destruction from the presence of the Lord, and the glory of his power.'

Now, 'the law is not of faith,' saith the apostle. This opens up the nature of the bargain; and the opposition between the present covenant and that which is made with lost sinners with a Mediator. This covenant is called, of works, 'Do this, and live;' to him that worketh is the promise made, though freely too. It is grace, that once a reward should be promised to obedience; but having once resolved to give it, herein justice appears in an equal and uniform distribution of the reward, according to works; so that where there is an equality of works there shall be an equality of reward, and no difference put between persons equal; which is the very freedom of the covenant of grace, that it passes over all such considerations, and deals equally in mercy with unequal sinners, and unequally, it may be, with them that are equal in nature.

You may ask, was not Adam to believe in God and did not the law require faith? I answer, Christ distinguishes a twofold faith: 'You believe in God, believe also in me.' No question he was called to believe in God the creator of the world, and that in a threefold consideration.

First, to depend on God the self-being and fountain-good. His own goodness was but a flux and emanation from that Sun of Righteousness, and so was to be perpetuated by constant abiding in his sight. The interposition of man's self between him and God did soon bring on this eternal night of darkness. Nature might have taught him to live in him in whom he had life and being and motion, and to forget and look over his own perfections as evanishing shadows. But this quickly extinguished his life, when he began to live in himself.

Next, he was obliged to believe God's word, both threatening and promise, and to have these constantly in his view. And certainly, if he had kept in his serious consideration, the inestimable blessing of life promised, and the fearful curse of death threatened,—if he had not been induced first to doubt, and then to deny the truth and reality of these,—he had not attempted such a desperate rebellion against the Lord.

Then, thirdly, he was to believe and persuade himself of the Lord's fatherly love, and that the Lord was well-pleased with his obedience; and this faith would certainly beget much peace and quietness in his mind, and also constrain him to love him, and live to him who loved him, and gave him life and happiness out of love. Yet this holds true that the apostle saith, 'the law is not of faith,' to wit, in a Mediator and Redeemer. It was a bond of immediate friendship; there needed none to mediate between God and man; there needed no reconciler where there was no odds nor distance. But the gospel is of faith in a Mediator; it is the soul plighting its hope upon Jesus Christ in its desperate necessity, and so supposes man sinful and miserable in himself, and in his own sense too, and so putting over his weight and burden upon one whom God hath made mighty to save. The law is not of faith, but of perfect works,—a watch-word brought in of purpose to bring men off their hankering after a broken and desperate covenant. It admits no repentance, it speaks of no pardon, it declares no cautioner or redeemer. There is nothing to be expected, according to the tenor of that covenant, but wrath from heaven; either personal obedience in all, or personal punishment for ever. That is the very terms of it, and it knows no other thing. Either bring complete righteousness and holiness to the promise of life, or expect nothing but death.

This may be a sad meditation to us, to stand and look back to our former estate, and compare it with that into which we are fallen. That image we spoke of, is defaced and blotted out, which was the glory of the creation; and now there is nothing so monstrous, so deformed in the world as man. The corruption of the best things is always worst; the ruins of the most noble creature are most ruinous; the spot of the soul most abominable. We are nothing but a mass of darkness, ignorance, error, inordinate lust; nothing but confusion, disorder, and distempers in the soul, and in the conversation of men; and, in sum, that blessed bond of friendship with God broken, discord and enmity entered upon our side and separated us from God, and so we can expect nothing from that first covenant but the curse and wrath threatened. 'By one man's disobedience' sin entered upon all, 'and death by sin;'

because in that agreement Adam was a common person representing us, and thus are all men once subject to God's judgment, and come short of the glory of God, fallen from life into a state of death, and, for any thing that could be expected, irrecoverably. But it hath pleased the Lord, in his infinite mercy, to make a better covenant in Christ his Son, that, what was impossible to the law, by reason of our weakness and wickedness, his Son, sent in the flesh, condemned for sin, might accomplish, Rom. viii. 3. There is some comfort yet after this; that covenant was not the last, and that sentence was not irrevocable. He makes a new transaction, lays the iniquity of his elect upon Christ, and puts the curse upon his shoulders which was due to them. Justice cannot admit the abrogation of the law, but mercy pleads for a temperament of it. And thus the Lord dispenses with personal satisfaction, which in rigour he might have craved; and finds out a ransom, admits another satisfaction in their name. And in the name of that Cautioner and Redeemer is salvation preached upon better terms: Believe and thou shalt be saved, Rom. x. 9. Thou lost and undone sinner, whoever thou art, that findest thyself guilty before God, and that thou canst not stand in judgment by the former covenant,—thou who hast no personal righteousness, and trustest in none,—come here, embrace the righteousness of thy Cautioner,—receive him, and rest on him, and thou shalt be saved.

Lecture XXII.

OF THE STATE WHEREIN MAN WAS CREATED, AND HOW THE IMAGE OF GOD IS DEFACED.

ECCL. vii. 29.—"*Lo, this only have I found, that God hath made man upright; but they have sought out many inventions.*"

THE one half of true religion consists in the knowledge of ourselves, the other half in the knowledge of God; and whatever besides this men study to know and apply their hearts unto, it is vain and impertinent, and like meddling in other men's matters, neglecting our own, if we do not give our minds to the search of these. All of us must needs grant this in the general, that it is an idle and unprofitable wandering abroad, to be carried forth to the knowledge and use of other things, and in the mean time to be strangers to ourselves, with whom we should be most acquainted. If any man was diligent and earnest in the inquiry and use of the things in the world, Solomon was. He applied his heart to seek out wisdom, and what satisfaction was in the knowledge of all things natural; and in this he attained a great degree beyond all other men. Yet he pronounces of it all after experience and trial, that 'this also is vanity and vexation of spirit,'—not only empty and unprofitable, and not conducing to that true blessedness he sought after,—but hurtful and destructive, nothing but grief and sorrow in it. After he had proved all, with a resolution to be wise, yet it was far from him; 'I said, I will be wise, but it was far from me,' ver. 23. And therefore, after long wandering abroad, he returns at length home to himself, to know the estate of mankind. 'Lo, this only have I found, that God hath made man upright; but they have sought out many inventions.' When I have searched all other things, and found many things by search, yet, says he, what doth it all concern me, when I am ignorant of myself? There is one thing concerns me more than all,—to know the original of man, what he once was made, and to know how far he is departed from his original. This only I have found profitable to men: and as the entry and preparation to that blessedness I inquire for,—to have the true discovery of our misery.

There are two things, then, concerning man, that you have to search and to know; and that not in a trifling or curious manner, as if you had no other end in it but to know it as men do in other things, but in a serious and earnest way, as in a matter of so much concernment to our eternal well-being. In things that relate particularly to ourselves, we labour to know them for some advantage besides the knowing of them, even though they be but small and lower things; how much more should we propose this unto ourselves in the search and examination of our own estate, not merely to know such a thing, but so to know it that we may be stirred up and provoked in the sense of it to look after the remedy that God holds forth. There are two things that you have to know,—what man once was made, and how he is now unmade; how happy once, and how miserable now. And answerable to these two, are branches of the text: 'God made man upright;' that he was once; 'and they have sought out many inventions;' not being contented with that blessedness they were created into, by catching at a higher estate of wisdom, have fallen down into a gulf of misery; as the man that gazed on the stars above him, and did not take notice of the pit under his feet till he fell into it; and thus man is now. So you have a short account of the two estates of men; of the estate of grace and righteousness without sin, and the estate of sin and misery without grace. You have the true story of man from the creation unto his present condition; but all the matter is to have the lively sense of this upon our hearts. I had rather that we went home bewailing our loss, and lamenting our misery, and longing for the recovery of that blessedness, than that we went out with the exact memory of all that is spoken, and could repeat it again.

'God made man upright.' At his first moulding, the Lord showed excellent art and wisdom, and goodness too. Man did come forth from under his hand in the first edition very glorious, to show what he could do; upright, that is, all right and very exactly conformed to the noble and high pattern,—endued with divine wisdom, such as might direct him to true happiness,—and furnished with a divine willingness to follow that direction. The command was not above his head as a rod, but within his heart as a natural instinct. All that was within him was comely and beautiful; for that glorious light that shined upon him, having life and love with it, produced a sweet harmony in the soul. He knew his duty, and loved it, and was able to perform it. O how much is in this one word 'upright!' Not only sincerity and integrity in the soul, but perfection of all the degrees and parts; no part of holiness wanting, and no measure of those parts; no mixture of darkness or ignorance,—no mixture of indisposition or unwillingness. Godliness was sweet and not laborious. The love of God, possessing the heart, did conform all within and without to the will of God; and O how beautiful was that conformity! And that love of God, the fountain-being, did send forth, as a stream, love and good-will to all things, as they did partake of God's image; and so holiness towards God did beget righteousness towards men, and made men to partake of one another's happiness.

This is a survey of him in his integrity as God made him, but there follows a sad 'but,'—a sad and woful exception,—'but they have sought many inventions.' We cannot look upon that glorious estate whereunto man was made, but straightway we must turn our eyes upon that misery into which he hath plunged himself, and be the more affected with it, that it was once otherwise. It is misery in a high degree to have been once happy. This most of all aggravates our misery, and may increase the sense of it, that such man once was, and such we might have been, if we had not destroyed ourselves. Who can look upon these ruins, and refrain mourning? It is said, that those who saw the glory of the first temple, wept when they beheld the second, because it was not answerable to it in magnificence and glory; so, I say, it might occasion much sadness and grief, even to the children of God, in whom that image is in part repaired, and that by a second creation, to think how much more happy and blessed man once was, who had grace and holiness without sin. But certainly, it should and must be at first, before this image be restored, the bitter lamentation of a soul, to look upon itself wholly ruinous and defaced, in the view of that glorious stately fabric which once was made. How lamentable a sight is it to behold the first temple demolished, or the first creation defaced, and the second not yet begun in many souls, the foundation-stone not yet laid! It was a sad and doleful invention which Satan inspired at first into man's heart, to go about to find out another happiness,—to seek how to be wise as God, an invention that did proceed from hell,—how to know evil experimentally and practically by doing it! That invention hath invented and found out all the sin and misery under which the world groans. It is a poor invention to devise misery and torment to the creature. This was the height of folly and madness, for a happy creature to invent how to make itself miserable and all others. Indeed, he intended another thing—to be more happy; but pride and ambition got a deserved fall; the result of all is sin and misery.

And now from the first devilish invention, the heart of man is possessed with a multitude of vain imaginations. Man is now become vain in his imaginations, and his foolish heart is darkened. That divine wisdom he was endued withal is eclipsed, for it was a ray of God's countenance; and now he is left wholly in the dark without a guide, without a director or leader. He is turned out of the path of holiness, and so of happiness. A night of gross darkness and blindness is come on, and the way is full of pits and snares, and the end of it is at best eternal misery. And there is no lamp, no light to shine in it, to show him either the misery that he is posting unto, or the happiness that he is fleeing from. There is nothing within him sufficient to direct his way to blessedness, and nothing willing or able to follow such a direction. And thus man is left to the invention and counsel of his own desperately wicked and deceitful heart; and that is above all plagues, to be given up to a reprobate mind. He is now left to such a tutor and guider, and it is full of inventions indeed. But they are all in vain, that is, all of them insufficient for this great purpose. All of them cannot make one hair that is black, white, much less redeem the soul. But besides, they are destructive. They pretend to deliver, but they destroy. A desperate wicked heart imagineth evil continually, evil against God, and evil to our own souls. And a deceitful heart smooths over the evil, and presents it under another notion; and so, under pretence of a friend, it is the greatest enemy a man hath,—a bosom-enemy. All men's inventions, thoughts, cogitations, projects, and endeavours, what do they tend to, but to the satisfaction of their lusts,—either the lusts of the mind, as ambition, pride, avarice, passion, revenge, and such like,—or the lust of the body, as pleasure to the ears and eyes, and to the flesh? Man was made with an upright soul, with a dominion over that brutish part, more like angels; but now, all his invention runs upon that base and beastly part, how to adorn it, how to beautify it, how to satisfy it; and for this his soul must be a drudge and slave. And if men rise up to any thoughts of a higher life, yet what is it for, but to magnify and exalt the flesh—to seek an excellency within, which is lost, and so to satisfy the pride and self-love of the heart. If any man comes this length, as to apprehend some misery, yet how vain are his inventions about the remedy of it. Not knowing how desperate the disease is, men seek help in themselves, and think, by industry and care and art, to raise them up in some measure, and please God by some expiations or sacrifices of their own works. Now, this tends to no other purpose but to satisfy the lusts of man's pride; and so it increases that which was man's first malady, and keeps them from the true physician. In a word, all man's inventions are to hasten misery on him, or to blindfold himself till it come on; all his invention cannot reach a delivery from this misery. Let us therefore consider this which Solomon hath found out; and if we carefully consider it, and accurately ponder it in relation to our own souls, then have we also found it with him. Consider, I say, what man once was, and what you are now, and bewail your misery and the fountain of it—our departure from the fountain of life and blessedness. Know what you are, not only weak but wicked, whose art and power lies only in wickedness; skilful and able only to make yourselves miserable. And let this consideration make you cast away all your confidence in yourselves, and carry you forth to a Redeemer who hath found a ransom—who hath found out an excellent invention to cure all our distempers and desperate diseases. The counsel of the Holy Trinity that met about—if I may so speak—our creation in holiness and righteousness after his own image, that same hath consulted about the rest of it, and hath found out this course, that one of them shall be made after man's image, and for this purpose, that he may restore again God's image unto us. O bless this deep invention and happy contrivance of heaven, that could never have bred in any breast, but in the depths of eternal wisdom; and let us abandon and forsake our own vain imaginations, and foolish inventions! Let us become fools in our own eyes, that we may become wise.

Man by seeking to be wise, became a fool; that was an unhappy invention. Now it is turned contrary; let all men take with their folly and desperate wickedness. Let not the vain thoughts and dreams of our own well-being and sufficiency lodge within us, and we shall be made wise. Come to the Father's wisdom,—unto Jesus Christ, who is that blessed invention of heaven for our remedy. How long shall vain thoughts lodge within you? O when will you be washed from them? How long shall not your thoughts transcend this temporal and bodily life? How long do you imagine to live in sin, and die in the Lord,—to continue in sin and escape wrath? Why do you delude your souls with a dream of having interest in the love of God, and purchasing his favour by your works? These are some of those many inventions man hath sought out.

Lecture XXIV.

OF SIN BY IMPUTATION AND PROPAGATION.

Rom. v. 12.—"*Wherefore, as by one man sin entered into the world, and death by sin; and so death passed upon all men, for that all have sinned.*"

This is a sad subject to speak upon; yet it is not more sad than useful. Though it be unpleasant to hold out a glass to men, to see their own vile faces into, yet is it profitable, yea, and so necessary, that till once a soul apprehend its broken and desolate condition in the first Adam, it can never heartily embrace and come to the second Adam. You have here the woful and dreadful effects and consequents of the first transgression upon all mankind. The effect is twofold,—sin and misery, or sin and death. The subject is universal in both,—'all men,' the whole world. Behold what a flood of calamity hath entered at a small cranny—by one man's transgression! May it not be said of sin in general, what the wise man speaks of strife,—'the beginning of' sin 'is as when one letteth out water?' Therefore it had been good leaving it off before it had been meddled with; it entered at a small hole, but it hath overflowed a whole world since.

That which first occurs, is, that all mankind, proceeding from Adam by ordinary birth, are involved in sin by Adam's transgression. But that may seem a hard saying, that sin and death should flow unto the whole posterity who had no accession to Adam's transgression. It would seem, that every man should die for his own iniquity, and that it should reach no further in justice. But consider, I pray you, the relation that Adam stood into, and in which he is here holden out as a figure of Christ. Adam, the first man, was a common person, representing all mankind, in whose happiness or misery all should share. God contracts with him on these terms, that his posterity's estate should depend on his behaviour. Now, if all mankind would have reaped the benefit and advantage of Adam's perseverance,—if such an undeserved reward of eternal life would have redounded by the free promise unto them all,—what iniquity is it that they also be sharers in his misery? Our stock and treasure was ventured in this vessel; and if we were to partake of its gain, why not of its loss? You see among men, children have one common lot with their parents. If the father be forfeited, the heirs suffer in it, and are cast out of the inheritance. It might appear a surer way to have the fortunes of all—so to speak—depend upon one, and their happiness assured unto them upon the standing of one, than to have every one left to himself, and his own well-being depending upon his own standing, as it is more likely one, and that the first one, shall not sin, than many; and especially when that one knew that the weight of all his posterity hung upon him, it might have made him very circumspect, knowing of how great moment his carriage was. But certainly we must look a little higher than such reasons; there was a glorious purpose of God's predominant in this, else there was no natural necessity of imputing Adam's sin to the children not yet born, or propagating it to the children. He that brought a holy One and undefiled out of a virgin who was defiled, could have brought all others clean out of unclean parents. But there is a higher counsel about it. The Lord would have all men subject to his judgment,—all men once guilty, once in an equal state of misery, to illustrate that special grace showed in Christ the more, and demonstrate his power and wrath upon others. That which concerns us most is to believe this, that sin hath overspread all; and to have the lively impressions of this were of more moment to true religion than many discourses upon it. I had rather you went home not cursing Adam, or murmuring against the Most High, but bemoaning yourselves for your wretched estate, than be able to give reasons for the general imputation and propagation of sin. You all see it is, and therefore you should rather mourn for it than ask why it is.

There is 'sin entered into the world' by imputation, and also by propagation. Adam's first sin and heinous transgression is charged upon all his posterity, and imputed unto them, even unto them who have not sinned according to 'the similitude of Adam's transgression,' that is, actually as he did. Infants, whom you call innocents,—and indeed so they are in respect of you, who are come to age,—yet they are guilty before God of that sin that ruined all. Now, that ye may know what you are, and what little reason you have to be pleased with yourselves, and absolve yourselves as ye do, I shall unbowel that iniquity unto you. First, There was in it an open banner displayed against God. When the sovereign Lord had enjoined his creature such a testimony of his homage and loyalty, and that so easy to be performed, and such as not a whit could abate from his happiness, what open rebellion was it to refuse it! It was a casting-off the sovereign dominion of God, than which nothing can be more heinous, as if the clay should refuse to serve the potter's pleasure; and therefore it is eminently and signally styled disobedience, as having nothing in it but the pure naked nature of disobedience; no difficulty to excuse it, for it was most easy; no pleasure to plead for it, for there were as good fruit beside, and a world of them; no necessity to extenuate it; so that you can see nothing in it but the ugly face of disobedience and rebellion, (ver. 19,) whereby man draweth himself from his allegiance due to his Maker, and shaketh off the yoke in reproach of the Most High. Next, you may behold the vile and abominable face of ingratitude and unthankfulness in it; and truly heathens have so abhorred unthankfulness towards men, that they could not digest the reproach of it,—*Ingratum si dixeris, omnia dixeris*, if you call me unthankful, you may call me any thing, or all things.* It is a compend of all vices. It is even iniquity grown to maturity and ripeness. But that such a fruit should grow out of such a holy and good soil, so well-dressed and manured by the Lord was a wonder! Lord, what was man that thou didst so magnify him, and make him a little lower than the angels,—that thou didst put all things sublunary under his feet, and exalt him above them! For that creature chosen and selected from among all, to be his minion, to stand in his presence, adorned and beautified with such gifts and graces, magnified with such glorious privileges, made according to the most excellent pattern, his own image, to forget all, and forget so soon; and when he had such a spacious garden to make use of, as is supposed to make up the third part of the earth, to eat of no fruit but that which was forbidden,—there is no such monstrous ingratitude can be imagined as here was acted! But then consider the two fountains from which this flowed, unbelief and pride, and you shall find it the heaviest sin in the world,—unbelief of his word and threatening. First, he was brought to question it, and to doubt of it, and then to deny it. A word so solemnly and particularly told him by the truth itself, that ever a question of it could arise in his mind or get entry, what else was it than to impute iniquity to the holy One, and that iniquity, falsehood and lying, which his nature most abhors? What was it but to blaspheme the most high and faithful God, by hearkening to the suggestions of his enemy, and to credit them more than the threatenings of God,—to give the very flat contradiction to God,—we shall not die; and to assent so heartily to Satan's slanders and reproaches of God? And this unbelief opened a door to ambition and

* [Lycurgus, the Spartan lawgiver, made no law against ingratitude, it is said, because he conceived that no one could be so irrational as to be unthankful for kindness done to him.—ED.]

pride, the most sacrilegious ingredient of all, which is most opposite to God, and unto which he most opposed himself from the beginning: "Ye shall be as gods." Was he not happy enough already, and according to God's image? Nay, but this evil principle would arise up to the throne of God, and sit down in his stead. Pride hath atheism in it; to deny the true God, and yet would be a god itself! For the footstool to lift up itself thus, what an indignity was it! And indeed this wretched aim at so high an estate hath thrown us down as low as hell. You see then how injurious this transgression was to God. There was disobedience and rebellion in it, which denies his dominion and supremacy; there was unthankfulness in it, denying his goodness and bounty; there was unbelief in it, contradicting his truth and faithfulness; and finally, pride, opposing itself to all that is in God, reaching up to his very crown of Majesty to take it off. You see then what you are guilty of, in being guilty of Adam's transgression. Many of you flatter yourselves in your own eyes that you have not done much evil, and you will justify yourselves in your comparisons with others; but I beseech you, consider this, though you had never done personally good or evil here, that which drowned the world in misery is your sin, and charged upon you. You are guilty of that which ruined all mankind, and makes the creation 'subject to vanity' and corruption. O if ye believe this, you would find more need of the second Adam than you do! O how precious would his righteousness and obedience be to you, if you had rightly apprehended your interest in the first man's disobedience!

But besides this imputation, there is much more propagated unto all, and that is a total corruption and depravation of nature in soul and body, whereby man is utterly indisposed, disabled, and made opposite unto all that is truly and spiritually good, and wholly inclined to all evil, and that continually, which is commonly called original sin,—a total averseness from God and from all goodness, an antipathy against the ways of holiness,—and a propension and strong impulse towards evil, even as a stone moves downwards. This poison and contagion of sin entering into the world hath infected all, and gone through all the members. Neither is it any wonder that it is so, when this leprosy hath defiled the walls and roof of the house,—I mean, hath made the creation 'subject to vanity' and corruption; it is no wonder that it spread abroad in his issue, and makes all unclean like himself. And truly this is it which most abases man's nature, and, being seen, would most humble men. Yea, till this be discerned, no man can be indeed humbled. He will never apprehend himself so bad as he is, but still imagine some excellency in himself, till he see himself in this glass. You talk of good natures, and good dispositions, but in our flesh, saith the apostle, 'dwelleth no good thing.' The seeds of all wickedness are in every one of us; and it is the goodness of God for preserving of human society, that they are restrained and kept down in any from the grossest outbreakings. They know not themselves, who know any good of themselves; and they know not themselves, who either are in admiration at, or in bitterness or contempt against, other sinners, whose sins are manifest to all. This were the only way to profit by looking on their evils, if we could straightway retire within and behold the root of that in ourselves, the fountain of it within us, and so grow in loathing, not of those persons, but of human nature, and in suitable thoughts of ourselves and others, and might wonder at the goodness and undeserved bounty of the Lord, that passes an act of restraint upon our corruption, and dams it up. O that we could learn to loathe ourselves in other men's evils! Thus we might reap good out of the evil, and prevent more in ourselves. But the looking upon gross provocations as singularities, makes them more general, because every man does not charge himself with the corruption that is in all these, but prefers himself to another. Therefore are reins loosed to corruption, and a sluice opened that it may come out,—that he who would not see his own image in another's face, may behold it in the glass of his own abominations. There is no point less believed than this though generally confessed, that man is dead in sins and trespasses, and impotent to help himself. You will hardly take with wickedness when you confess weakness; as if nature were only sick, but not dead,—hurt, but not killed. Therefore it is that so many do abide in themselves, and trusting to their own good purposes and resolutions and endeavours, do think to pacify God and help themselves out of their misery. But O look again, and look in upon yourselves in the glass of the word, and there is no doubt but you will straightway be filled with confusion of face, and be altogether spoiled of good confidence and hope, as you call it! You will find yourself plunged in a pit of misery, and all strength gone, and none on the right hand, or the left to help you; and then, and not till then, will the second Adam's hand, stretched out for help, be seasonable.

That which next follows is that which is the companion of sin inseparably,— Death hath passed upon all,' and that by sin. Adam's one disobedience opened a port for all sin to enter upon mankind, and sin cannot enter without this companion, death. Sin goes before, and death follows on the back of it; and these suit one another, as the work and the wages, as the tree and the fruit. They have a fitness one to another. Sowing to corruption reaps an answerable harvest, to wit, corruption. Sowing to the wind, and reaping the whirlwind, how suitable are they! That men may know how evil and bitter a thing sin is, he makes this the fruit of it in his first law and sanction given out to men,—he joins them inseparably,—sin and death, sin and wrath, sin and a curse. By death is not only meant bodily death, which is the separation of the soul from the body, but first the spiritual death of the soul, consisting in a separation of the soul from God's blessed, enlightening, enlivening, and comforting countenance. Man's true life, wherein he differs from beasts, consists in the right aspect of God upon his soul,—in his walking with God, and keeping communion with him. All things besides this are but common and base, and this was cut off. His comfort, his joy and peace in God extinct, God became terrible to his conscience; and therefore man did flee and was afraid, when he heard his voice in the garden. Sin being interposed between God and the soul, cut off all the influence of heaven. Hence arises darkness of mind, hardness of heart, delusions, vile affections, horrors of conscience. Look what difference is between a living creature and a dead carcase, so much is between Adam's soul, upright, living in God, and Adam's soul separated from God by sin. Then upon the outward man the curse redounds. The body becomes mortal which had been incorruptible. It is now like a besieged city. Now some outer forts are gained by diseases, now by pains and torments; the outward walls of the body are at length overcome; and when life hath fled into a castle within the city, the heart, that is, last of all, besieged so straitly, and stormed so violently, that it must render unto death upon any terms. The body of man is even a seminary of a world of diseases and grievances, that if men could look upon it aright, they might see the sentence of death every day performed. Then how many evils in estate, in friends and relations, in employments, which being considered by heathens, hath made them praise the dead more than the living, but him not yet born most of all, because the present life is nothing else but a valley of misery and tears, a sea of troubles, where one wave continually prevents another, and comes on like Job's messengers; before one speaks out his woful tidings, another comes with such like, or worse. But that which is the sum and accomplishment of God's curse and man's misery is that death to come,—eternal death,—not death simply, but an 'everlasting destruction from the presence of the Lord and the glory of his power;'—an infinite loss, because the loss of such a glorious life in the enjoyment of God's presence; and an infinite hurt and torment beside, and both eternal.

Now this is what we would lay before you. You are under such a heavy sentence from the womb, a sentence of the Almighty, adjudging you for Adam's guilt and your own, to all the misery in this world and in the next,—to all the treasures of wrath that are heaped up against the day of wrath. And strange it is, how we can live in peace, and not be troubled in mind, who have so great and formidable a party! Be persuaded, O be persuaded, that there shall not one jot of this be removed,—it must be fulfilled in you or your cautioner! And why then is a Saviour offered, a city of refuge opened, and secure sinners will not flee into it? But as for as many as have the inward dreadful apprehension of this wrath to come, and know not what to do, know that to you is Jesus Christ preached, the second Adam, a quickening spirit, and in, that consideration, better than the first,—not only a living soul himself, but a spirit to quicken you who are dead in sins,—one who hath undertaken for you, and will hold you fast. Adam, who should have kept us, lost himself;

Christ in a manner lost himself to save us. And as by Adam's disobedience all this sin and misery hath abounded on man, know, that the second Adam's obedience and righteousness are of greater virtue and efficacy to save, and instead of sin to restore righteousness, and instead of death to give life. Therefore you may come to him, and you shall be more surely kept than before.

Lecture XXV.

OF THE WAY OF MAN'S DELIVERY.

1 Tim. i. 15.—"*This is a faithful saying, and worthy of all acceptation, that Christ Jesus came into the world to save sinners.*"

Of all doctrines that ever were published to men, this contained here is the choicest, as you see the very preface prefixed to it imports. And truly, as it is the most excellent in itself, it could not but be sweet unto us, if we had received into the heart the belief of our own wretchedness and misery. I do not know a more sovereign cordial for a fainting soul, than this faithful saying, 'That Christ Jesus came into the world to save sinners.' And therefore we are most willing to dwell on this subject, and to inculcate it often upon you, that without him you are undone and lost, and in him you may be saved. I profess, all other subjects, howsoever they might be more pleasing to some hearers, are unpleasant and unsavoury to me. This is that we should once learn, and ever be learning—to know him that came to save us, and come to him.

We laboured to show unto you the state of sin and misery that Adam's first transgression hath subjected all mankind unto, which if it were really and truly apprehended, I do not think but it would make this saying welcome to your souls. Man being plunged into such a deep pit of misery, sin and death having overflowed the whole world, and this being seen and acknowledged by a sinner, certainly the next question in order of nature is this, hath God left all to perish in this estate? Is there any remedy provided for sin and misery? And this will be indeed the query of a self-condemned sinner. Now there is a plank after this broken ship; there is an answer sweet and satisfactory to this question; 'Christ Jesus came into the world to save sinners.'

We shall not expatiate into many notions about this, or multiply many branches of this. The matter is plain and simple, and we desire to hold out plainly and simply, that this is the remedy of sin and misery. When none could be found on the right hand or left hand, here a Saviour from heaven comes down from above, whence no good could be expected, because a good God was provoked. 'Can there any good thing come out of Nazareth?'—that was a proverb concerning him. But I think in some sense it might be said, Can any good come down from heaven, from his holy habitation to this accursed earth? Could any thing be expected from heaven but wrath and vengeance? And if no good could be expected that way, what way could it come? Sure if not from heaven, then from no airth.* Yet from heaven our help is come, from whence it could not be looked for,—even from him who was offended, and whose justice was engaged against man. That he might both satisfy justice and save man,—that he might not wrong himself nor destroy man utterly,—he sends his only begotten Son, equal with himself in majesty and glory, into the world, in the state of a servant, to accomplish man's salvation, and perform to him satisfaction. Therefore Christ came into the world to save sinners.

There were two grand impediments in the way of man's salvation, which made it impossible to man; one is God's justice, another is man's sin. These two behoved to be satisfied or removed, ere there can be access to save a sinner. The sentence of divine justice is pronounced against all mankind, 'death passed upon all,'—a sentence of death and condemnation. Now, when the righteousness and faithfulness of God is engaged unto this, how strong a party do you think that must be? What

* [That is, quarter.—Ed.]

power can break that prison of a divine curse, and take out a sinner from under Justice's hand? Certainly there is no coming out till the uttermost farthing be paid that was owing,—till complete satisfaction be given for all wrongs. Now, truly, the redemption of the soul had ceased for ever—it is so precious that no creature can give any thing in exchange for it—except Jesus Christ had come into the world, one that might be able to tread that wine-press of wrath alone, and give his life a ransom, in value far above the soul, and pay the debt of sin that we were owing to God. And, indeed, he was furnished for this purpose, a person suited and fitted for such a work;—a man, to undertake it in our name, and God, to perform it in his own strength;—a man, that he might be made under the law, and be humbled even to the death of the cross, that so he might obey the commandment, and suffer the punishment due to us; and all this was elevated beyond the worth of created actions or sufferings, by that divine nature. This perfumed all his humanity, and all done by it, or in it. This put the stamp of divinity upon all, and imposed an infinite value upon the coin of finite obedience and sufferings. And so in his own person, by coming into the world, and acting and suffering in the place of sinners, he hath taken the first great impediment out of the way; taken down the high wall of divine justice which had enclosed round about the sinner, and satisfied all its demands, by paying the price; so that there is nothing upon God's part to accuse or condemn, to hinder or obstruct salvation.

But then there is an inner wall, or dark dungeon of sin, into which the sinner is shut up, and reserved in chains of his own lusts, until the time of everlasting darkness; and when heaven is opened by Christ's death, yet this keeps a sinner from entering in. Therefore Jesus Christ, who came himself into the world to satisfy justice and remove its plea, that there might be no obstruction from that airth, he sends out his powerful Spirit with the word, to deliver poor captive sinners, to break down the wall of ignorance and blindness, to cast down the high tower of wickedness and enmity against God, to take captive and chain our lusts that kept us in bondage. And, as he made heaven accessible by his own personal obedience and sufferings, so he makes sinners ready and free to enter into that salvation by his Spirit's working in their persons. In the one, he had God, as it were, his party, and him he hath satisfied so far, that there was a voice came from heaven to testify it, 'This is my beloved Son, in whom I am well-pleased;' and therefore, in testimony of it, God raised him from the dead. In the other, he hath Satan and man's wicked nature as his party, and these he must conquer and subdue. These he must overcome, ere we can be saved. A strange business indeed, and a great work, to bring two such opposite and distant parties together,—a holy and just God, and a sinful and rebellious creature; and to take them both as parties, that he might reconcile both.

Now what do you think of this, my beloved, that such a glorious person is come down from heaven, for such a work as the salvation of sinners? I put no doubt, it would be most acceptable unto you, if you knew your misery, and knowing your misery, you could not but accept it, if you believed that it were true and faithful. I find one of these two the great obstruction in the way of souls receiving advantage by such glad tidings. Either the absolute necessity and excellency of the gospel is not considered, or the truth and reality of it is not believed. Men either do not behold the beauty of goodness in it, or do not see the light of truth in it. Either there is nothing discovered to engage their affections, or nothing seen to persuade their understandings. Therefore the apostle sounds a trumpet, as it were, in the entry, before the publication of these glad news, and commends this unto all men as a true and faithful saying, and as worthy of all acceptation. There is here the highest truth and certainty to satisfy the mind: It 'is a faithful saying.' And there is here also the chiefest good to satiate the heart: It is 'worthy of all acceptation.' Now, if you do really apprehend your lost and miserable estate, you cannot but behold that ravishing goodness in it; and behold that you cannot, till you see the other first. Whence is it, I pray you, that so many souls are never stirred with the proposition of such things in the gospel,—that the riches and beauty of salvation in Jesus Christ doth not once move them? Is it not because there is no lively apprehension of their misery without him?*

* [The discourse ends so abruptly here, as plainly to show that it is an unfinished production, and was not designed by the learned and pious author for publication.—ED.]

THE

SINNER'S SANCTUARY;

OR

A DISCOVERY MADE OF THOSE GLORIOUS PRIVILEGES OFFERED UNTO THE PENITENT AND FAITHFUL UNDER THE GOSPEL:

UNFOLDING THEIR FREEDOM FROM DEATH, CONDEMNATION, AND THE LAW, IN

FORTY SERMONS

ON THE

EIGHTH CHAPTER OF THE EPISTLE TO THE ROMANS.

The Preface.

Courteous Reader,—It floweth more from that observance—not to say honour—which is due to the laws of custom, than from any other motive, that the stationers hold it expedient to salute thee at thy entry into this book, by any commendatory epistle; having sufficient experience, that books are oft inquired after, and rated according to the respect men generally have of the author, rather than from the matter contained therein, especially if the book be divine or serious; upon which ground this treatise might have come abroad merely upon the virtue of the title-page,—Mr. Hugh Binning being so well known, and his other treatise so universally, as deserving, received by the intelligent and studious in the great mysteries of the Trinity, and other dark principles of the Christian faith.

Yet if worthiness of matter—as the curious carved stones of the temple were to the disciples—be amiable to thine eyes, and nervous sentences, solid observations, with a kind of insinuating, yet harmless behaviour, be taking with thy spirit, here they are also; and acquainting thyself with them, either as the sinner or the saint, which thine own conscience shall best inform thee of, there shall be virtue found to proceed from them, either for thy soul's refining from the dross of this corrupt age, or to a diligent heed-taking to preserve thyself pure from the pollutions which are in the world through lust, to be more and more pure against the day and coming of Christ our Saviour.

Though many elaborate pieces are already extant, and treatises of many worthies of the church be already abroad upon this golden chapter, yet he who hath seen the manyest, and knows the sublimity and darkness, withal the excellency of the subjects therein treated, shall know this work, or lamp, to have its weight and light; and though small, yet as a candle, shall increase, and add to those lights already burning upon the table of his memory or museol.* There is but one Spirit, one faith, one baptism; yet about and in these, there are diversities of gifts; and though all men naturally have but one face, yet the variety to be seen in each one, procureth both wonder and delight, there being in every one something new, something which makes it differ from all other. There is here to be found something enlarged, enlightened, and applied, which in other volumes may not be heeded, or but slenderly touched; or if it were otherwise, here it is in some other way, method, or expression: besides which, there is no new thing under the sun. And have we not, nay, choose we not, to have variety of gems, agates, rubies, and diamonds shining about us, some squared, some angled, each having their own excellency, because so formed? If this instance take not, it is because the children of this generation are wiser than the children of light.

That the work is imperfect, is for a lamentation, save for this, that while the author was contemplating upon the Spirit of adoption, and being with God, the Spirit called upon him by death, as the voice did upon the divine, saying, 'Come up hither, and I will show thee,' Rev. iv. 1. So that what David said of the waters of Bethlehem, may be said of this lame orphan, 'Is not this the blood of this good man?' The great and wise Master-builder of the church, giving this young man order to lay the foundation, and raise the building but thus high, appointing, it may be, some others to perfect and lay on the roof; yea, possibly it is squared and framed already for thy use in other treatises, and thyself to perfect the edifice of thy salvation, by joining this and that together in thy practice; Mr. Hugh Binning, showing thee in his lot, how to be rid of, or delivered from the law's condemnation, ver. 1. and some other in his quarter to demonstrate because of that, 'neither height nor depth shall be able to separate' thee 'from the love of God,' ver. 39. of this chapter.

Had this work come directly from the author's own hands, he had spoken in his own style his own mind; but that being denied, receive this posthume infant, as David did Mephibosheth; first, for its father's sake, next for its own. Though it be lame in the feet, yet it is of goodly countenance, and speaketh so well, that its language hath got an *imprimatur;* and where it is silent rest satisfied with that old refreshing cordial in such cases, *cætera desiderantur.*

* [Perhaps the word ought to be *museum*, used in the sense of a place for study.—Ed.]

THE SINNER'S SANCTUARY.

Sermon I.

Rom. viii. 1.—" *There is therefore now no condemnation to them which are in Christ Jesus, who walk not after the flesh, but after the Spirit.*"

There are three things which concur to make man miserable,—sin, condemnation, and affliction. Every one may observe that 'man is born unto trouble as the sparks fly upward;' that his days here are few and evil. He possesses 'months of vanity, and wearisome nights are appointed' for him, Job v. 6, 7; vii. 3. He 'is of few days and full of trouble,' Job xiv. 1. Heathens have had many meditations of the misery of man's life; and in this have outstripped the most part of Christians. We recount amongst our miseries, only some afflictions and troubles, as poverty, sickness, reproach, banishment, and such like. They again have numbered even these natural necessities of men amongst his miseries,—to be continually turned about, in such a circle of eating, drinking, and sleeping. What burden should it be to an immortal spirit to roll about perpetually that wheel! We make more of the body than of the soul. They have accounted this body a burden to the soul. They placed posterity, honour, pleasure, and such things, which men pour out their souls upon, amongst the greatest miseries of men, as vanity in themselves, and vexation, both in the enjoying and losing of them; but, alas! they knew not the fountain of all this misery,—sin; and the accomplishment of this misery,—condemnation. They thought trouble came out of the ground and dust, either by a natural necessity, or by chance; but the word of God discovereth unto us the ground of it, and the end of it. The ground and beginning of it was man's defection from God, and walking according to the flesh; and from this head have all the calamities and streams of miseries in the world issued. It hath not only redounded to men, but even to the whole creation, and subjected it to vanity, ver. 20 of this chapter. Not only shalt thou, O man, (saith the Lord to Adam,) eat thy meat in sorrow, but thy curse is upon the ground also, and thou who wast immortal, shalt return to that dust which thou magnifiedst above thy soul, Gen. iii. 17. But the end of it is suitable to the beginning. The beginning had all the evil of sin in it, and the end hath all the evil of punishment in it. These streams of this life's misery, they run into an infinite, boundless, and bottomless ocean of eternal wrath. If thou live according to the flesh, thou shalt die: it is not only death here, but eternal death after this. The miseries then of this present life are not a proportionable punishment of sin, they are but an earnest given of that great sum which is to be paid in the day of accounts; and that is condemnation, 'everlasting destruction from the presence of the Lord, and the glory of his power.' Now, as the law discovers the perfect misery of mankind, so the gospel hath brought to light a perfect remedy of all this misery. Jesus Christ was manifested to take away sin, and therefore his name is Jesus, 'for he shall save his people from their sins.' This is the Lamb of God that takes away the sins of the world. Judgment was by one unto condemnation of all, but now there is 'no condemnation to them which are in Christ Jesus;' so these two evils are removed, which indeed have all evil in them. He takes away the curse of the law, being made under it; and then he takes away the sin against the law by his Holy Spirit. He hath a twofold virtue, for he came by blood and water, (1 John v. 6, 7;)—by blood, to cleanse away the guilt of sin; and by water, to purify us from sin itself. But in the meantime, there are many afflictions and miseries upon us, common to men: why are not these removed by Christ? I say, the evil of them is taken away, though themselves remain. Death is not taken away, but the sting of death is removed. Death, afflictions, and all, are overcome by Jesus Christ, and so made his servants to do us good. The evil of them is God's wrath and sin, and these are removed by Jesus Christ. Now they would be taken away indeed, if it were not good they remained, for 'all things work together for good to them that love God,' ver. 28. So then we have a most complete deliverance in extent, but not in degree. Sin remains in us, but not in dominion and power. Wrath sometimes kindles because of sin, but it cannot increase to everlasting burnings. Afflictions and miseries may change their name, and be called instructions and trials, —good, and not evil: but Christ hath reserved the full and perfect delivery till another day, which is therefore called 'the day of' complete 'redemption,' and then all sin, all wrath, all misery shall have an end, and 'be swallowed up of life' and immortality, ver. 23.

This is the sum of the gospel; and this is the substance of this chapter. There is a threefold consolation answerable to our threefold evils: there is 'no condemnation to them which are in Christ.' Here is a blessed message to condemned lost sinners, who have that sentence within their breasts, ver. 1. This was the end of Christ's coming and dying, that he might deliver us from sin as well as death, and the righteousness of the law might be fulfilled in us; and therefore he hath given the Holy Spirit, and dwells in us by the Spirit, to quicken us who are 'dead in trespasses and sins.' O what consolation will this be to souls, that look upon the body of death within them, as the greatest misery, and do groan with Paul, 'O wretched man that I am!' &c., Rom. vii. 24. This is held forth to ver. 17. But because there are many grounds of heaviness and sadness in this world, therefore the gospel opposes unto all these, both our expectation which we have of that blessed hope to come, whereof we are so sure, that nothing can frustrate us of it, and also the help we get in the meantime of the Spirit to bear our infirmities, and to bring all things about for good to us, ver. 28. And from all this the believer in Jesus Christ hath ground of triumph and boasting before the perfect victory,—even as Paul doth in the name of believers, from ver. 31 to the end. Upon these considerations, he that cried out not long ago, 'O miserable man, who shall deliver me?' doth now cry out, 'who shall condemn me?' The distressed wrestler becomes a victorious triumpher; the beaten soldier becomes more than a conqueror. O that your hearts could be persuaded to hearken to this joyful sound—to embrace Jesus Christ for grace and salvation! How quickly would a song of triumph in him swallow up all your present complaints and lamentations!

All the complaints amongst men may be reduced to one of these three. I hear the most part bemoaning themselves thus: Alas for the miseries of this life, this evil world! Alas for poverty, for contempt, for sickness! Oh! miserable man that I am, who will take this disease away? Who will show me any good thing, (Psal. iv. 6,) any temporal good? But if ye knew and considered your latter end, ye would cry out more; ye would refuse to be comforted, though these miseries were removed. But I hear some bemoaning themselves more sadly,—they have heard the law, and the sentence of condemnation is within them. The law hath entered and killed them. Oh! 'what shall I do to be saved?' Who will deliver me from the wrath to come? What are all present afflictions and miseries in respect of eternity? Yet there is one moan and lamentation beyond all these, when the soul finds the sentence of absolution in Jesus Christ, and gets its eyes opened to see that body of death and sin within, that perfect man of sin diffused throughout all the members. Then it bemoans itself with Paul—'O wretched man,—who shall deliver me from this body of death?' Rom. vii. 24. I am delivered from the condemnation of the law, but what comfort is it, as long as sin is so powerful in me? Nay, this makes me often suspect my delivery from wrath and the curse, seeing sin itself is not taken away

Now, if you could be persuaded to hearken to Jesus Christ, and embrace this gospel, O what abundant consolation should ye have! What a perfect answer to all your complaints! They would be swallowed up in such a triumph as Paul's are here. This would discover unto you a perfect remedy of sin and misery, that ye should complain no more; or at least, no more as those without hope. You shall never have a remedy of your temporal miseries, unless ye begin at eternal, to prevent them. 'Seek first the kingdom of God,' and all other things 'shall be added unto you.' Seek first to flee from the wrath to come, and ye shall escape it; and besides the evil of time, afflictions shall be removed. First remove the greatest complaints of sin and condemnation, and how easy is it to answer all the lamentations of this life, and make you rejoice in the midst of them!

You have in this verse three things of great importance to consider,—the great and precious privilege, the true nature, and the special property of a Christian. The privilege is one of the greatest in the world, because it is of eternal consequence, and soul concernment; the nature is most divine,—he is one that is in Jesus Christ, and implanted in him by faith; his distinguishing property is noble, suitable to his nature and privileges,—he walks not as the world, according to his base flesh, but according to the Spirit. All these three are of one latitude,—none of them reaches further than another. That rich privilege and sweet property concentres and meets together in one man, even in the man who is in Jesus Christ. Whoever enters into Jesus Christ, and abideth in him, he meets with these two, justification and sanctification; these are nowhere else, and they are there together.

If ye knew the nature and properties of a Christian, ye would fall in love with these for themselves; but if these for your own sakes will not allure you, consider this incomparable privilege that he hath beyond all others, that ye may fall in love with the nature of a Christian. Let this love of yourselves and your own well-being pursue you into Jesus Christ, that ye may walk even as he walked; and I assure you, if ye were once in Christ Jesus, ye would love the very nature and walking of a Christian, no more for the absolution and salvation that accompanies it, but for its own sweetness and excellency beyond all other. Ye would, as the people of Samaria, no more believe for the report of your own necessity and misery, but ye would believe in Jesus Christ, and walk according to the Spirit, for their own testimony they have in your consciences. You would no more be allured only with the privileges of it to embrace Christianity, but you would think Christianity the greatest privilege, a reward unto itself. *Pietas ipsa sibi merces est*,—godliness is great gain in itself, though it had not such sweet consequents or companions. That you may know this privilege, consider the estate all men are into by nature. Paul expresses it in short, Rom. v. "By the offence of one, judgment came upon all unto condemnation;' and the reason of this is, by one man sin came upon all, and so death by sin, for 'death passed upon all, because all have sinned,' ver. 18, 12. Lo, then, all men are under a sentence of condemnation once! This sentence is the curse of the law.—'Cursed is every one that abideth not in all things commanded to do them.' If you knew what this curse were, ye would indeed think it a privilege to be delivered from it. Sin is of an infinite deserving, because against an infinite God; it is an offence of an infinite majesty, and therefore the curse upon the sinner involves eternal punishment. O what weight is in that word, (2 Thess. i. 9,) Ye 'shall be punished with everlasting destruction from the presence of the Lord and the glory of his power!' If it were duly apprehended, it would weigh down a man's soul, and make it heavy unto death. This condemnation includes both *damnum et pœnam, pœnam damni et pœnam sensus;* and both are infinite in themselves, and eternal in their continuance. What an unpleasant and bitter life would one lead, that were born to a kingdom, and yet to be banished it and lose it? But what an incomparable loss is it, to fall from an heavenly kingdom, which heart cannot conceive, and that for ever? In God's favour is life, and in his presence are rivers of pleasures for evermore. When your petty penny-losses do so much afflict your spirits, what would the due apprehension of so great a loss do? Would it not be death unto you, and worse than death, to be separated from this life; to be eternally banished from the presence of his glory? If there should be no more punishment but this only; if the wicked were to endure for ever on earth, and the godly, whom they despised and mocked, were translated to heaven, what torment would it be to your souls to think upon that blessedness which they enjoy above, and how foolishly ye have been put by it for a thing of no value? What would a rich man's advantages and gains be to him, when he considereth what an infinite loser he is? How he hath sold a kingdom for a dunghill? Now if there were any hope, that after some years his banishment from heaven might end, this might refresh him, but there is not one drop of such consolation. He is banished, and eternally banished, from that glorious life in the presence of God, which those do enjoy whom he despised. If a man were shut up all his life-time in a pit, never to see the light once more, would not this be torment enough to him? But when withal there is such pain joined with this loss; when all this time he is tormented within with a gnawing worm, and without with fire; those senses that did so greedily hunt after satisfaction to themselves, are now as sensible in the feeling of pain and torment. And when this shall not make an end, but be eternal, O whose heart can consider it! It is the comfort and ease of bodily torments here, that they will end in death. Destruction destroys itself, in destroying the body; but here is an immortal soul to feed upon, and at length the body shall be immortal. That destruction cannot quite destroy it, but shall be an everlasting destruction and living death.

This is the sentence that is once passed against us all in the word of God, and not one jot of this word shall fall to the ground: heaven and earth may fail sooner. Ye would think it were an irrepealable decree, if all the nations in the earth, and angels above, convened to adjudge a man to death, did pass sentence upon him. Nay, but this word that is daily spoken to you, which passeth this sentence upon you all, is more certain: and this sentence of death must be executed, unless ye be under that blessed exception made here and elsewhere in the gospel. I beseech you, consider what it is to have such a judge condemning you. Would not any of you be afraid, if ye were under the sentence of a king? If that judgment were above your head, who of you would sit in peace and quietness? Who would not flee from the wrath of a king, that is like the roaring of a lion? But there is a sentence of the KING of kings and nations above your heads. 'Who would not fear thee,' to whom it doth appertain, 'O King of nations?' It is not a great man that can destroy the body, that is against thee; it is not he who hath power to kill thee, and he hath also a great desire so to do. This were indeed much; but it is the great and eternal JEHOVAH, who lifts up his hand to heaven, and swears he lives for ever,—he is against thee. He who hath all power over body and soul is against thee, and so is obliged to improve his omnipotency against thee; he can kill both soul and body, and cast them into hell, and by virtue of this curse he will not spare thee, but pour out all the curses in this book. Thou wouldst be at no peace if thou wert declared rebel by the king and parliament; but alas! that is a small thing. They can but reach thy body, nay, neither can they always do that; thou mayest flee from them, but whither canst thou flee from him? Thou canst not go out of his dominions; for the earth is his, and the sea, and all that therein is. Darkness cannot hide thee from him. He may spare long, because he can certainly overtake when he pleases; men may not, because they have no assurance of finding. I beseech you, then, consider this. It is of soul consequence; and what hath a man gained, if he gain the world, and lose his soul? If the gainer be lost, what is gained? And it is of eternal consequence; and what are many thousand years to this? You can look beyond all these, and might comfort yourselves in hope; but you cannot see to the end of this. There is still more before than is past; nay, there is nothing past,—it is still as beginning.

O that ye would consider this curse of God that stands registrate upon us all? What effects had it on Christ, when he did bear it? It made his soul heavy to death:—it was a cup that he could scarcely drink. He that supported the frame of this world was almost near succumbing under the weight of this wrath. It made him sweat blood in the garden. He that could do all things, and speak all things, was put to this, 'What shall I say?' When this condemnation was so terrible to him, who was that Mighty One upon whom all help was laid, what shall it be to you? No man's sorrow was ever like his, nor pain ever like his, if all the scattered torments were united in one; but because he was God he overcame, and came out from under it. But what do you think shall be the estate of those who shall endure that same torment?—and not for three days, or three years, or some thousands of years, but beyond imagination,—to all eternity?

I beseech you consider this condemnation which ye are adjudged unto, and do not lie under it. Do ye think ye can endure what Christ endured? Do ye think ye can bear wrath according to God's power and justice? And yet the judgment is come upon all men to this condemnation. But alas! who fears him according to his wrath? Who knows the power of his anger? Ye sleep secure, as if all matters were past and over your head. We declare unto you in the Lord's name, that this condemnation is yet above you, because you have not judged yourselves. It is preached unto you that ye may flee from it; but since ye will not condemn yourselves, this righteous Judge must condemn you.

Now, since it is so, that such a condemnatory sentence is passed on all men, what a privilege must it be, to be delivered from it,—to have that sentence repealed by some new act of God's mercy and favour? David proclaims him a blessed man whose sins are forgiven and covered; and indeed he is blessed who escapes that pit of eternal misery, though there were no more. Though there were no title to an inheritance and kingdom above, to be delivered from that wrath to come upon the children of disobedience, this is more happiness than the enjoyment of all earthly delights. 'What shall a man give in exchange for his soul?' 'Skin for skin, yea, all that a man hath will he give for his life.' These riches and advantages and pleasures that men spend their labour for, all these they part with in such a hazard. The covetous man, he will cast his coffers overboard ere he will lose his life; the voluptuous man, he will suffer pain and torment in cutting off a member, ere he die. But if men knew their souls, and what an immortality and eternity expects them, they would not only give skin for skin, and all that they have, for their soul, but their life also. Ye would choose to die a thousand deaths to escape this eternal death. But 'what shall a man give in exchange for his soul?' Matt. xvi. 26; though he would give, yet what hath he to give? There are two things endear any privilege to us, and heighten the rate of it,—the necessity of it, and the preciousness of it; and these two are eminent here. Is it not necessary to be, to live, and have a being? All men think so, when they will give all they have to redeem themselves. All other things are accidental to them, they are nearest to themselves; therefore all must go, ere themselves go. But I say this is more necessary,—to be well eternally, than to be simply; to escape this condemnation, than to have a being. And this shall be verified in the last day, when men shall cry for hills and mountains to fall on them, and save them from the wrath of the Lamb, Rev. vi. 16. Men will choose rather not to be, than to fall in that wrath. O how acceptable would a man's first nothing be to him in that great day of wrath! Who shall be able to stand in it?—when kings and princes, bond and free, great and small, shall desire mountains to grind them into powder, rather than to hear that sentence of condemnation, and yet shall not obtain it. O blessed are all they that trust in him, 'when his wrath is kindled but a little,' Ps. ii. 12. Ye toil and vex yourselves, and spend your time about that body and life; but for as precious as they are to you now, ye would exchange them one day for immunity and freedom from this wrath and curse. How will that man think his 'lines are fallen in pleasant places,—how will he despise the glory of earthly kingdoms, though all united in one,—who considers in his heart how all kings, all tongues and nations, must stand before the judgment-seat of God, and the books of his law be opened, to judge them by, as also the books of their consciences, to verify his accusation, and precipitate their own sentence, and then, in the open view of all the sons of Adam, and the angels, all secrets be brought out,—their accusation read as large as their life-time, and as many curses be pronounced against every one, as there be breaches of the law of God, whereof they are found guilty; and then all these will seek into corners, and cry for mountains, but there is no covering from his presence. What do ye think the man will think within himself, who will stand before God, and be absolved in judgment by Jesus Christ, notwithstanding his provocations above many of them? What will a king then think of his crown and dominions, when he reflects on them? What will the poor persecuted Christian then think of all the glory and perfection of this world, when he looks back upon it? O know, poor foolish men, what madness is in venturing your souls for trifles! Ye run the hazard of all greatest things for a poor moment's satisfaction. Ye will repent it too late, and become wise to judge yourselves fools, when there is no place to mend it.

But this privilege is no more necessary than it is precious. Your souls are now kept captive under that sentence of everlasting imprisonment. Ye are all prisoners, and know not of it. What will ye give in ransom for your souls? Your sins and iniquities have sold you to the righteous Judge of all the earth, as malefactors, and he hath passed a sentence of your perpetual imprisonment under Satan's custody in hell. Now what will you give to redeem your souls from that pit? How few know the worth of their souls! And so they offer unto God some of their riches for them. Doth not many of you think ye have satisfied for sins, if ye pay a civil penalty to the judge? Many think their own tears and sorrow for sin may be a price to justice, at least if it be joined with amendment in time coming. And so men conceive their sins are pardoned, and their souls redeemed. But alas! the redemption of the soul is precious, yea, it ceaseth for ever; all your substance will be utterly contemned, though ye offered it. How few of you would give so much for your souls! And yet though ye give it, it will not do it,—ye must pay the uttermost farthing, or nothing. Your sorrow and reformations will not complete the sum, no, nor begin it. 'Though thou wash thee with nitre, and take much soap, yet thine iniquity is marked before me,'—yet there is still condemnation for thee. Though all the world should convene about this matter, to find a ransom for man; suppose all the treasures of monarchs, the mines and bowels of the earth, the coffers of rich men were searched; nay, let the earth, the sea, the heavens, and sun and moon be prized at the highest;—join all the merits of angels above and men below, all their good actions and sufferings, yet the sum that amounts of all that addition, would not pay the least farthing of this debt. The earth would say, it is not in me; the heaven behoved to answer so; angels and men might say, we have heard of it, but it is hid from all living. Where then is this redemption from the curse? Where shall a ransom be found? Indeed God hath found it; it is with him. He hath given his Son a ransom for many, and his blood is more precious than souls,—let be* gold and silver. Is not this then a great privilege, that if all the kingdoms of the world were sold at the dearest, yet they could not buy it? What a jewel is this! What a pearl! Whoever of you have escaped this wrath, consider what is your advantage. O consider your dignity ye are advanced unto, that you may engage your hearts to him, to become his, and his wholly! for 'ye are bought with a price,' and are no more your own; he gave himself for you, and was made a curse to redeem you from the curse. O how should you walk as privileged men, as redeemed ones!

I beseech you all to call home your thoughts, to consider and ponder on this sentence that is passed against us. There is now hope of delivery from it, if ye will take it home unto you; but if ye will still continue in the ways of sin, without returning, know this, that ye are but multiplying those curses, platting many cords of your iniquities, to bind you in everlasting chains. Ye are but digging a pit for your souls, ye that sweat in your sins, and travel in them, and will not embrace this ransom offered. The key and lock of that pit is eternal despair. O consider how quickly your pleasures and gains will end, and spare some of your thoughts from present things, to give them to eternity, that thread spun out for ever and ever;—the very length of the days of the Ancient of days, who hath no beginning of days nor end of time! Remember now of it, lest ye become as long miserable as God is blessed, and that is for ever.

All men would desire to have privileges beyond others, but there is one that carries it away from all the world, and that is the believer in Jesus Christ, who is said to be in Christ, implanted in him by faith, as a lively member of that body whereof Christ is the head. Christ Jesus is the head of that body, the church; and this head communicates life unto all the members, for 'he filleth all in all.' There is a mighty working power in the head, which diffuseth itself throughout the members, Eph. i. 19, 22, 23. There are many expressions of union between Christ and believers. There is no near conjunction among men, but this spiritual union of Christ with believers is represented to us under it. The foundation and the building have a near dependence, the corner-stone and the wall—these knit together; and Christ Jesus is the foundation and 'the chief corner-stone, in whom all the building fitly

* [That is, not to speak of.—Ed.]

framed together, groweth unto an holy temple,' Eph. ii. 20, 21. The head and members are near united, so is Christ and believers; they 'grow up into him,' Eph. iv. 15. Parents and children are almost one, so is Christ Jesus the everlasting Father, and he shows to the Father the children which he hath given him. We are his brethren, and he is not ashamed to call us so; but which is more, we are one flesh with him. There is a marriage between Christ and the church, and this is the great meditation of the song of Solomon. He is the vine tree, and we are branches planted in him. Nay, this union is so strict, that it is mutual, 'I in them,' and they 'in me.' Christ dwelleth in us by faith, by making us to believe in him, and love him; we dwell in Christ by that same faith and love, by believing in him, and loving him. Christ Jesus is our house where we get all our furniture; he is our store-house and treasure, our place of strength and pleasure, a city of refuge, a strong tower and a pleasant river to refresh us. We again are his habitation where he dwelleth by his Spirit; we are his workhouse, where he works all his curious pieces of the new creature, forming it unto the day of his espousals, the great day of redemption.

This gives us to understand what we once were. We may stand here and look back upon our former condition, and find matter both of delight and sorrow. We were once without Christ in the world, and if without Christ, then without 'hope and without God in the world,' Eph. ii. 12. I wish this were engraven on the hearts of men, that they are born out of Christ Jesus; wild olives, growing up in the stock of degenerated Adam. He was once planted a noble vine; but how quickly turned he into a degenerate plant, and instead of grapes, brought forth wild grapes, and sour! We all grow upon an 'olive tree which is wild by nature,' Rom. xi. 24. It grows out of the garden of God, in the barren wilderness, and is meet for nothing but to bring forth fruit unto death, to be cut down and cast into the fire. It is a tree which the Lord hath cursed,—'never more fruit grow upon thee henceforth:' this was the fatal sentence pronounced on Adam. O that you would know your condition by nature! how all your good inclinations, dispositions, and education, cannot make your stock good, and your fruit good! 'Israel is an empty vine,'—this is our name. Nay, but many think they bring forth fruit. Have not heathens spread forth their branches, and brought forth many pleasant fruits of temporal patience, sobriety, magnanimity, prudence, and such like? Do not some civil men many acts of civility profitable to men? Doth not many a man pray and read the scriptures from his youth up? Yes, indeed, these are fruits, but for all that, he is an empty vine, for he brings forth fruit to himself; and so, as in the original, he is a vine emptying the fruit which it gives, Hos. x. 1. All these fruits are but to himself, and from himself; he knows not to direct these to God's glory, but to his own praise or advantage, to make them his ornament; and he knows not his own emptiness, to seek all his furniture and sap from another. What were all these fair blossoms and fruits of heathens? Indeed they were more and better than any now upon the multitude of professed Christians: and yet these were but *splendida peccata*, shining sins. What is all your praying and fasting, but to yourselves, as the Lord charges the people, Zech. vii. 'Did ye at all fast unto me?' No, ye do it to yourselves. Here is the wildness and degenerateness of your natures. Either you bring forth very bitter fruits, such as intemperance, avarice, contention, swearing, &c., or else fruits that have nothing but a fair skin, like apples of Sodom that are beautiful on the tree, but being handled, turn to ashes; so there is nothing of them from God, or to God. I think every man almost entertains this secret persuasion in his breast, —that his nature may be weak, yet it is not wicked; it may be helped with education, and care, and diligence, and dressed till it please God, and profit others. Who is persuaded in heart that he is an enemy to God, and cannot be subject to God's law? Who believes that his 'heart is desperately wicked?' Oh! it is indeed 'deceitful above all things,' and in this most deceitful, that it persuades you ye have a good heart to God. Will not profane men, whose hands are defiled, maintain the uprightness of their hearts? *Nemo nascitur bonus sed fit.* I beseech you once, consider that ye are born out of Christ Jesus. Ye conceive that ye are born and educated Christians; ye have that name indeed from infancy, and are baptized. But I ask about the thing; baptism of water doth not implant you into Jesus Christ. Nay, it declares this much unto you, that by nature ye are far off from Jesus, and wholly defiled,—all your imaginations only evil. Now, I beseech you, how came the change? Or is there a change? Are not the most part of men the old men,—no new creatures? He that is in Christ is a new creature, 2 Cor. v. 17. Ye have now Adam's nature, which ye had first. Ye have borne the image of the earthly, and are ye not such yet, who are still earthly? Think ye that ye can inherit the kingdom of God thus? Can ye pass over from a state of condemnation to a state of life and no condemnation, without a change? No, believe it, ye cannot inherit incorruption with flesh and blood, which ye were born with. Ye must be implanted in the second Adam, and bear his image, ere ye can say that ye are partakers of his blessings, 1 Cor. xv. 47—49, &c. Now I may pose your consciences,—how many of you are changed? Are not the most part of you even such as ye were from your childhood? Be not deceived; ye are yet strangers from the promises of God, and without this hope in the world.

Sermon III.

VERSE 1.—"*There is therefore now no condemnation to them which are in Christ Jesus,*" *&c.*

ALL the promises are yea and amen in Christ Jesus; they meet all in him, and from him are derived unto us. When man was in integrity, he was with God, and in God, and that immediately, without the intervention of a Mediator. But our falling from God hath made us without God, and the distance is so great, as Abraham speaks to the rich man, that neither can those above go down to him, nor he come up to them. There is a gulf of separation between God and us, that there can be no meeting. And so we who are without God, are without hope in the world, Eph. ii. 12; no hope of any more access to God as before. The tree of life is compassed about with a flaming fire and a sword. God is become a consuming fire unto us, that none can come near these everlasting burnings, much less dwell with them. Since there can be no meeting so, God hath found out the way how sinners may come to him, and not be consumed. He will meet with us in Jesus Christ, that living temple, and this is the trysting-place.* There was a necessity of this Mediator, to make up the difference, and make a bridge over that gulf of separation, for us to come to God; and this is his human nature, the new and living way, the vail of his flesh. God is in Christ, therefore, reconciling the world to himself. All the light of consolation and salvation that is from God, is all embodied in this Sun of righteousness. All the streams of grace and mercy run in the channel of his well-beloved Son. It follows then, that God is not to be found out of Jesus Christ; and whosoever is without Christ, is without God in the world. 'God was in Christ reconciling the world,' and 'there is therefore no condemnation to them that are in Christ;' but God out of Christ is condemning the world, and therefore condemnation is to all that are not in Christ. When all the sons of Adam were declared rebels, because of his and their own rebellion, the Lord hath appointed a city of refuge, that whosoever is pursued by the avenger of blood, may enter into it, and get protection and safety. Without is nothing but the sword of the avenger, justice reigning in all the world beside; within this city, justice may not enter to take out any into condemnation. And therefore those souls that flee for refuge, to lay hold upon the hope set before them in Jesus Christ, justice may pursue them to the ports of this city, condemnation may follow them hard, till they enter in; but these may not enter into the ports of the city. What a miserable estate then are these souls in, that lie in their own natures, in the open fields without this city! How many foolish men apprehend no

* [This simple vernacular expression, which is used by other Scottish theological writers of the period, as employed here, is particularly expressive. It signifies a place where either foes or friends have agreed to meet. Is that place the temple of the Lord? There surely will peace and harmony prevail. Is our 'Daysman' there? He will make intercession for us, and reconcile us to God. —ED.]

danger, but sport about the ports of the city of refuge, and will not enter in! O the avenger of blood shall be upon thee ere thou know; and if it find thee out of the city, woe unto thee! All thy prayers and entreaties will not prevail. Justice is blind and deaf,—cannot deal partially, cr respect persons, cannot hear thy supplications. It is strange, that men are taken up with other petty inconsiderable things, and yet neglect to know what this is, to be in Jesus Christ, upon which their salvation depends.

Faith in Jesus Christ is the soul's flight into the city of refuge. Now none flieth but when they apprehend danger, or are pursued. This danger that a soul apprehends, is perishing and condemnation for ever. The pursuer is the law of God, and his justice; these have a sword in their hand, the curse of God, and the sentence of condemnation. God erects a tribunal in his word, wherein he judgeth men. Whosoever he hath a purpose of good-will unto, he makes the law to enter into their consciences, that the offence might abound. He sends out some messenger of affliction, or conviction, to bring them before the judgment-seat, and hear their accusation read unto them. There the soul stands trembling, and the conscience witnesseth and approveth all that the word challengeth of; so that the sinner's mouth is stopped, and can have no excuse to this accusation. Then the judge pronounces the sentence upon the guilty person, 'Cursed is every one that abideth not in all things,' &c. The soul cries, Guilty, O Lord, guilty, I deserve the curse indeed: Oh! 'what shall I do to be saved?' Then the soul looks about on the right hand, and on the left hand, to seek some refuge, but there is none. Whither shall he go from him? He looks within himself, and beholds nothing within; but the accusing witnessing conscience becomes a tormentor. The fire is kindled within, which feeds upon the fuel of innumerable sins. Now the soul is almost overwhelmed, and spies if there be any place to flee to from itself, and from that wrath, and behold the Lord discovers a city of refuge near hand, where no condemnation is, even Christ Jesus, who hath sustained the curse, that he might redeem us from it. The vision of peace is here, and thither the soul flies out of itself, and from justice, into that discovered righteousness of Christ, and so the more that the offence abounded, now the more hath grace superabounded; so that there is now no more condemnation to him.

I beseech you consider this, and let it be written on the table of your hearts. There are two tribunals that God sits upon,—one out of Christ Jesus, another in Christ Jesus. There is a throne of justice, where no sentence passes but pure unmixed justice, without any temperament of mercy; and this all men must once compear before. You know what a covenant of works God once made with us,—if thou do these things thou shalt live; if not, thou shalt die the death. According to this we must once be judged, that justice suffer no prejudice. Therefore God speaks out of his law, upon this throne, the language of mount Sinai; he reads our charge unto us, and because all the world is guilty, therefore the sentence of death is once passed upon all. Now, whoever of you come before this tribunal to be judged, know that it is a subordinate court; there is a higher court of mercy and judgment, both justice and mercy mixed together. Though mercy be the predominant, justice and judgment are the habitation of it, but mercy and truth go before the Judge's face, and come nearest sinners to give them access. And this you may appeal unto from that tribunal of justice. 'But there is forgiveness with thee,' &c., Ps. cxxx. 4, 5. And whoever comes here, Christ Jesus sits on this throne to absolve him from that sentence. If you ask what equity is in it, is not this a prejudice to justice, and an abomination to the Lord, to justify the wicked and ungodly sinner? I say, it is no iniquity, because Jesus Christ hath paid the price for us, and was made a curse for our sins, that we might be the righteousness of God in him; and therefore it is just with God to forgive sins; to relax that sinner from the condemnation of the law, that flees into Jesus Christ. You may answer justice—I will not take this for God's last word, I hear that all final judgment is committed to the Son, that he may give life to whom he will; he calls me, and to him will I go, for he hath the words of eternal life; he will justify, and who shall condemn?

Now, if any man will not now arraign himself before the tribunal of God's justice; if he will not search his guiltiness till his mouth be stopped, and hear his sentence of condemnation read, and take with it,—that man cannot come to Jesus Christ, to be absolved, for he justifieth none but self-condemned and lost sinners. So your day is but yet coming, when you must answer to justice. The tribunal of mercy shall be removed, and Christ shall sit upon a throne of pure justice, to judge those who judged not themselves. Alas for your loss, the most part of you! I pity you. You live in great peace and quietness without the ports of the city of refuge. We declare unto you in the Lord's name, you are under the curse of God: will you yet sit secure, and put the evil day far from you? Oh! rather trouble your peace for a season, with the consideration of your sins! Enter into judgment with yourselves till you see nothing but perishing in yourselves;—and there is no hazard, because salvation is brought near in the gospel. If you would not trouble yourselves so much as to judge yourselves, then you shall be judged when there is no Mediator to plead for you, none to appeal unto.

But whosoever takes the sentence of condemnation unto them, and subscribes to the righteousness of the Lord's curse upon them, we do invite all such in the Lord's name, to come in hither, even to Jesus Christ. There is no condemnation to them that are in him. If you stand scrupulous, making many questions in such a matter of so great necessity, you wrong your own soul and dishonour him. Know this, that God is in Christ reconciling the world to himself. Therefore thou condemned sinner mayest come to God in Christ. If you ask any warrant, we think there should be no such questioning, when you are in so great necessity. If a man were starving without a city, and it were told him there is plenty within, were he not a fool that would make any more business, but labour to enter in? This is enough to cross all your objections; you are in extreme necessity, and like to perish within yourself; 'he is able to save to the uttermost all that come to him.' What would you more? Let there be then a closure between absolute necessity and sufficient ability to save. Will you yet stand disputing without the city, when the avenger of blood is above your head? If you will yet press for some more ground and warrant of believing,—then I will tell you all that I know is in the word for a ground of faith. You have great misery and necessity within you,—that you grant, and it is your complaint. Christ hath mercy and sufficiency of grace in him; he is able to save to the uttermost,—that you cannot deny. But I do add this third, he is also willing to save thee, whoever will be saved by him; nay, he is more willing than thou art. If you question this, I desire you but to consider the whole tenor of the gospel. How many invitations! How many persuasions! How many promises to those who come! Yea, how many commands, and that peremptory, to believe on him! Yea, how many threatenings against you, if you will not come to him to have life! Hath he given himself for the sins of the world, and will he not be willing that sinners partake of that he was at so much pains to purchase? Think you that Christ will be content his death should be in vain? And it should be in vain, if he did not welcome the worst sinners; yea, it should be in vain if he did not draw them to him, and make them willing. But besides this, he hath promised so absolutely, and freely, and fully, as there should be no exception imaginable against it; 'him that cometh to me, I will in no wise cast out,' John vi. 37. Why do you imagine any case where Christ hath made none? Why do you sin against your own souls? Oh, if I were in Christ, say you, I would be well! and oh, that he would welcome such a sinner! Christ answers thee in express terms: 'whosoever will, let him take and drink freely.' Thou declarest thy willingness in so speaking; and he declares his willingness in so promising. Nay, thy looking afar off on him, is a fruit of his willingness; 'ye have not chosen me, but I have chosen you,' and loved you first. If ye will not yet believe this, look upon his command; this is his command, that ye believe on the Son, 1 John iii. 23. What warrant have ye to do any duty he commands? And why do ye more question this? Is not this his command? And is it not more peremptory, because a new command, and his last command? And when withal he boasts* us into his Son, that we may have life, oh, who should have the face to question any more his willingness! Other grounds than these I know none; and I think if any come to Christ, or pretend to come, on other grounds, he comes not right. If the most holy man come not in among ungodly sinners; if he do not walk upon the

* [That is, orders us into his Son.—Ed.]

grounds of his own extreme necessity, and Christ's sufficiency, he cannot come to Jesus Christ. There is a conceit among people, which, if it were not so common as it is, I would not mention it, it is so ridiculous;—how can I come to Christ so unclean and so guilty, nothing but condemnation in me? If I were such and such, I would come to him. Alas! there can nothing be imagined more absurd, or contrary even to sense and reason. If thou wert such and such, as thou fanciest a desire to be, thou wouldst not come to Christ; thou neededst him not. That which thou pretendest as a reason why thou shouldst not come, is the great reason pressed in the gospel why thou shouldst come. What madness is this? I am so unclean, I will not come to the fountain to wash;—wherefore was the fountain opened, but for sin and uncleanness? And the more uncleanness, the more need; and the more need, the more reason to come. Necessity is a great errand, and our errand is a sufficient warrant. I am pursued by the law, I have condemnation within me, and nothing but condemnation. Well then, come to Christ Jesus, the city of refuge, where no condemnation is. Wherefore was this city appointed, but for this end? I beseech you every one who useth those debates, and taketh a kind of delight in them, know what they mean, how they wrong your own souls; how they dishonour Christ, and so God the Father; nay, how foolish and ridiculous they are,—that if it were not your perplexity indeed, they deserved no answer, but a rebuke or silence. I have seen people take delight in moving objections against the truth, yea, and study earnestly how to object against any answers given from the truth. Alas! thou meddlest to thine own hurt; thou art upon a way which shall never yield thee any comfort, but keep thy soul from establishment, as a wave tossed up and down! If ye believe not, but dispute, ye shall not be established.

But I would speak a word to those that have believed, that have fled for refuge to Christ. Oh! it concerns you most of all men to study to know this condemnation that ye are delivered from, that ye may be thankful, and may keep close within this city. I say, there is no man within the world should have more thoughts, more deep and earnest meditations on the curse and wrath of God, than those who are delivered from them through Christ; and my reason is, that ye may know how great a salvation ye have received, how great a condemnation ye have escaped, and may henceforth walk as those who are bought with a price. Your creation makes you not your own, but his, because he gave that being. But your redemption should make you twice more his, and not your own, because, when that being was worse than if it had not been at all, he made it over again. So ye are twice his: first, he made you with a word, but now he hath bought you with a price, and that a dear price,—his blood. Again, the keeping this curse always in your view and sight and application of it unto your sins, will make much employment for Christ. O how will ye often flee into that city! I think they are the greatest enemies of Jesus Christ, and his grace, who would have a believer have no more use of the law. I know not who can use the law if he do it not. I know not who can apply it unto Christ, the end of it, but he. Certainly he hath not only use of the commands as a rule of obedience, but the curse also, not to make him fear again unto bondage; no, no, but to make him see always the more necessity of Jesus Christ, that he may take up house in him, and dwell in him.

Sermon XII.

VERSE 1.—"*Who walk not after the flesh, but after the Spirit.*"

IT is difficult to determine which of these is the greatest privilege of a Christian,—that he is delivered from condemnation, or that he is made to walk according to the Spirit, and made a new creature; whether we owe more to Christ for our justification, or sanctification: for he is made both to us: but it is more necessary to conjoin them together, than to compare them with each other. The one is not more necessary—to be delivered from wrath, than the other, to walk according to the

Spirit. I think it were an argument of a soul escaped from condemnation, to have the great stream and current of its affections and endeavours towards sanctification, not that they may be accepted of God, but because they are accepted of God. It is not said, there is nothing condemnable in those that are in Christ, but there is no condemnation to them. There is, indeed, a body of death, and law of sin within them, a nature defiled with original pollution, and many streams flowing from it, which the sprinkling of the blood of Christ in justification doth not take away. If any man say there is no sin in him, he is a liar, and the truth is not in him. But here is the grace and mercy of God in Jesus Christ; that removes the curse where the sin is,—that takes away the condemnation where all worthy of condemnation is. And thus the soul's justification is parallel to Christ's condemnation. There was in him nothing condemnable, no sin, no guile in his mouth; yet there was condemnation to him, because he was in stead and place of sinners. Our iniquities were laid on him, not in him; he who knew no sin was made a curse for us, that we might be made the righteousness of God in him. So then, the soul that fleeth into Jesus Christ's righteousness, though it have in it all that deserveth condemnation, yet there is no condemnation to it, because his righteousness is laid upon it, and Christ hath taken away the curse. The innocent Son of God was condemned, therefore are guilty sinners absolved. The curse was applied unto him who had no sin, but only was made sin, or sin laid on him, and therefore the sentence of absolution from the curse is applied unto them who have no righteousness, but are made the righteousness of God by free and gracious imputation. This I speak, because of many unsavoury and unsound expressions in this loose generation, that there is no sin in the justified, that justification removes it close, as if it had never been at all. I say, as the condemnation of Jesus Christ did not blot out his innocency and holiness within him, but only justice considered him on that account as a transgressor, who yet was the holy and spotless Lamb of God in himself; so likewise the justification of a sinner before God, doth not remove or blot out the very corruption and defilement of our natures, but only scrapes out our names out of the roll of his debtors, as having satisfied in our cautioner, and considers us as righteous on that account before God. And this likewise I speak for your use, that ye may loathe and abhor yourselves, as much in yourselves, who are made clean by the blood of Jesus Christ, as if ye were not washen. Nay, so much the more ye ought to remember your own sins, which he doth not remember as debt any more; and to be ashamed and confounded because they are pardoned. It is ordinary for souls to look on themselves with an eye of more complacency in themselves, when they apprehend that God looks favourably on them. I do not think that any soul can duly consider the gracious aspect of God in Jesus Christ to them, but they will the more loathe themselves. But I find it ordinary, that slight and inconsiderate thoughts of pardon beget jolly conceits in men's hearts of themselves. And this is even the sin of God's children; something is abated of our self-abhorring, when we have peace and favour spoken unto us. But I beseech all who believe there is no condemnation for them, to consider there are all things worthy of it in them, yea, nothing but what deserves it; and therefore let that aspect of God beget self-loathing and self-detestation in you. The more you apprehend he is pleased with you, be ye the more displeased with yourselves, because it is not yourselves he is pleased with, but his own well-beloved Son. The day of redemption is coming, when there shall be no condemnation, and nothing condemnable either. In heaven you shall be so, but while ye are here, this is the most important duty ye are called to,—to loathe yourselves, because of all your abominations, and because he is pacified towards you, Ezek. xvi. at the close; and chap. xxxvi. 31; and xx. 43, 44. There is a new and strange mortification now pleaded for by many,* whose highest advancement consisteth in not feeling, or knowing, or confess-

* [The following baneful and impious doctrines, which were, in England, in those days, openly proclaimed from the pulpit, and disseminated through the press, were, it seems, not altogether unknown in the northern part of the island:

1. That the moral law is of no use at all to a believer, no rule for him to walk or examine his life by, and that Christians are free from the mandatory power of it.

2. That it is as possible for Christ himself to sin, as for a child of God to sin.

3. That a child of God need not, nay ought not, to ask pardon for sin, and that it is no less than blasphemy for him to do this.

ing sin, but in being dead to the sense and conviction of the same. Alas ! whither are these reforming times gone ? Is not this the spirit of Antichrist ? I confess it is a mortification of godliness, a crucifying of repentance and holiness, a crucifying of the new man ; but it is a quickening of the old man in the lusts thereof, a living to sin. This is a part of that new (but falsely so called) gospel that is preached by some ; which, if an angel would bring from heaven, we ought not to believe it. 'Other foundation can no man lay than that which is laid' already, upon which the prophets and apostles are builded,—even Christ Jesus. Lord, give the Spirit to understand these mysteries already revealed ; but save us from these new discoveries and lights. That which we have received is able to make us perfect to salvation.

Every one pretends a claim and right to this privilege of Christians, to be pardoned and absolved from condemnation, who doth not put it out of question, though in the mean time their iniquities testify against them ; and their transgressions say in the heart of a godly man, that 'there is no fear of God before their eyes.' Therefore the apostle describes the man that is in Jesus Christ, to be such an one, that walks 'not after the flesh, but after the Spirit,'—not only to guard against the presumptuous fancy of those that live in their sins, that pretend to hope for heaven, but to stir up every justified soul to a new manner of conversation, since they are in Jesus Christ. We would speak a word of two things from this : First, That the Scripture gives marks and characters of justified and reconciled persons, that they may be known by, both to themselves and others. Next, That the Christian having escaped condemnation, hath a new manner of walking, and is a new creature in Christ.

It might seem a strange thing, that this first were questioned in this generation, (if any the most clear and important truth could pass without scanning) the very tenor of the Scripture holds out so much of it. I wonder that any man that reads this chapter, or the epistles of James and John, should have any more doubt of it. 'Hereby we do know that we know him, if we keep his commandments.' Is not this a conclusion of our state and condition, from the conformity of our walking to the will of God ? What divine truth can we be sure of, if this be uncertain ? When the beloved disciple, who knew how to preach Christ, asserts it in express terms, 1 John v. 13, 'These things have I written unto you that believe, that ye may know that ye have eternal life, and that ye may believe on the name of the Son of God.' This very thing was the great scope and purpose of that evangelic and divine epistle.

I find that Antinomians * confound this question, that they may have the more advantage in their darkness. The question is not concerning the grounds of a man's believing in Christ, but concerning our assurance, or knowledge of our believing. There is a great mistake in Christians' practice, in confounding these two. It makes Christians very unreasonable in their doubtings and exercises ; therefore let us have this before our eyes,—faith, in its first and pure acting, is rather an adherence and cleaving of a lost soul to Christ, than an evidence of its interest in him, or of his everlasting love. You know all, that it is one thing to know a thing, or love a thing, and another thing to reflect upon it, and know that I know and love it. John did write to believers, that they might know they did believe, and believe yet more. These things then are both separable, and the one is posterior to the other,—'after that ye believed ye were sealed.' The persuasion of God's love and our interest in Christ, is the Spirit's seal set upon the soul. There is a mutual sealing here. The soul, by believing and trusting in Jesus Christ, 'sets to its seal that God is true,' as John speaks, John iii. 33. When God speaks in his law, the soul receives that testimony

4. That God doth not chastise any of his children for sin.

5. That if a man, by the Spirit, know himself to be in a state of grace, though he should commit the greatest crimes, God sees no sin in him.

Three leading Antinomian teachers were brought before a committee of the House of Commons, for promulgating, in different ways, these and similar opinions, which were justly regarded as subversive of all morality.—*Gataker's 'God's Eye on his Israel,'*—preface, Lond. 1645.—Ed.]

* [" Antinomians, contending for faith of assurance, and leading men to be persuaded that God loveth every one, whom he commandeth to believe, with an everlasting love, and that 'no man ought to call in question more whether he believe or no, than he ought to question the gospel and Christ,' do with Libertines acknowledge a faith of assurance, but deny all faith of dependence on God through Christ, as if we were not justified by such a faith."—'A Survey of the spiritual Antichrist, opening the secrets of Familisme and Antinomianisme,' by Samuel Rutherford, Professor of Divinity in the University of St. Andrew's, part II. p. 235. London, 1648.—Ed.]

of his justice and holiness, subscribes to the equity and righteousness of the sentence, by condemning itself. And when Christ speaks in the gospel, the soul seals that doctrine of free salvation, by approving and consenting with all its heart to the offer, subscribes to the way of salvation in Christ, and the truth of his promises. And thus is the truth of God and Christ sealed by the soul's believing. Then the Spirit of Jesus Christ afterward, when he pleaseth, irradiates and shines upon the soul, and discovers those things that are freely given, and witnesseth to the conscience of the believer, that he is a son of God. Thus the Spirit seals the believer, and gives his testimony to his truth.*

Now if we speak of the ground of the first, viz. of believing in Christ to salvation, I know none, but that which is common to sinners, and holden out in the gospel generally to all,—our sin and misery, and absolute necessity, and Christ's invitation of all to come, and receive his full and perfect salvation. I think a man should seek nothing in himself, whereupon to build his coming to Christ. Though it be true, no man can come to a Saviour, till he be convinced of sin and misery, yet no man should seek convictions as a warrant to come to Christ for salvation. He that is in earnest about this question, how shall I be saved ?—I think he should not spend the time in reflecting on, and examination of himself, till he find something promising in himself; but from discovered sin and misery, pass straightway over to the grace and mercy of Christ, without any intervening search of something in himself to warrant him to come. There should be nothing before the eye of the soul but sin and misery and absolute necessity, compared with superabounding grace and righteousness in Christ; and thus it singly devolves itself over upon Christ, and receives him as offered freely, 'without money and without price.' I know it is not possible that a soul can receive Christ till there be some preparatory convincing work of the law, to discover sin and misery. But I hold, that to look to any such preparation, and fetch an encouragement or motive therefrom, to believe in Christ, is really to give him a price for his free waters and wine ;—it is to mix in together Christ and the law, in the point of our acceptation. And for souls to go about to seek preparations,—for a time resolving not at all to consider the promise of the gospel, till they have found them, and satisfaction in them, is nothing else but to go about to establish their own righteousness, being ignorant of the righteousness of Christ. And therefore many do corrupt the simplicity of the gospel by rigid exactions of preparations, and measures of them, and by making them conditions or restrictions of gospel commands and promises: as in this, 'Come ye that are wearied.' And from thence they seem to exclude persons not so qualified, from having a warrant to believe. Alas ! it is a great mistake of these and such words. Certainly these are not set down on purpose to exclude any who will come,—for, 'whosoever will, let him take the water of life freely;' but rather to encourage such wearied and broken souls as conceive themselves to be the only persons excluded, and to declare unto us in some measure, the nature of true faith, that a soul must be beaten out of itself, ere it can come to Christ. Therefore, I

* [These observations discover an accurate knowledge of the philosophy of the human mind, as well as of the doctrines of Scripture. It is certainly one thing to believe in the Lord Jesus Christ, and another thing to feel assured of one's salvation, or to be persuaded that we are possessed of that true faith which is the gift of God, and by which the just shall live. To identify, as is sometimes done, faith in Christ and the assurance of salvation, is calculated, on the one hand, to encourage presumption; and, on the other hand, to give rise to despair, Prov. xxx. 12; Ezek. xiii. 22, 23. What an earlier writer even than Binning says upon this subject, is not unworthy of notice: "St. Paul, wishing well to the church of Rome, prayeth for them after this sort: 'The God of hope fill you with all joy in believing.' Hence an error groweth, when men in heaviness of spirit suppose they lack faith, because they find not the sugared joy and delight which indeed doth accompany faith, but so as a separable accident, as a thing that may be removed from it; yea, there is a cause why it should be removed. The light would never be so acceptable, were it not for that usual intercourse of darkness. Too much honey doth turn into gall, and too much joy, even spiritual, would make us wantons. Happier a great deal is that man's case, whose soul by inward desolation is humbled, than he whose heart is, through abundance of spiritual delight, lifted up and exalted above measure. Better it is sometimes to go down into the pit with him who, beholding darkness, and bewailing the loss of inward joy and consolation, crieth from the bottom of the lowest hell, 'My God, my God, why hast thou forsaken me?' than continually to walk arm in arm with angels, to sit as it were in Abraham's bosom, and to have no thought, no cogitation; but 'I thank my God it is not with me as it is with other men.' No; God will have them that shall walk in light to feel now and then what it is to sit in the shadow of death. A grieved spirit, therefore, is no argument of a faithless mind."—*Hooker's Works*, vol. iii. pp. 527, 528. Oxford. 1807.—Ed.]

conclude, that not only is it a ridiculous and foolish conceit of many Christians that use to object against believing,—if I were as such and such a person, if I did love God, if I had these fruits of the Spirit, if I walked according to the Spirit, then I might believe. Alas! how directly opposite is this to the terms of the gospel! I say, if thou place satisfaction in these, and from that ground come to Jesus Christ, then thou dost not come really,—thou dost indeed establish thine own righteousness. Doth any saint, though ever so holy, consider himself under such notions of grace, when he comes to be justified? No indeed; but as an ungodly man rather, he must deny all that, though he had it. And besides, it is most unreasonable and incongruous, to seek the fruits before the tree be planted; and to refuse to plant the tree, till you can behold the fruits of it. But also, it is contrary to the free and comfortable doctrine of the gospel, for a soul to seek the discovery of any thing in itself but sin, before it apply to Jesus Christ. I say, there must be some sense of sin, otherwise it hath not rightly discovered sin; but a soul should not be at the pains to discover that sense of sin, and find it out, so as to make it a motive of believing in Christ. He ought to go straight forward, and not return as he goes. He must indeed examine himself,—not to find himself a sensible humble sinner, that so he may have ground of believing; but that he may find himself a lost perishing sinner, void of all grace and goodness, that he may find the more necessity of Jesus Christ. And thus I think the many contentions about preparations or conditions preparatory to believing, may be reconciled.

Now if the question be, as it is indeed, about the grounds of our assurance, and knowledge of our own faith, certainly it is clear as the noonday, that as the good tree is known by the fruits thereof, and the fire by the heat thereof, so the indwelling of faith in the heart is known by its purifying of the heart and working by love. It makes a man a new creature, so that he and others may see the difference. Neither is this any derogation to the free grace of Christ, or any establishing of our own righteousness, except men be so afraid to establish their own righteousness, that they will have no holiness at all, but abandon it quite, for fear of trusting in it, which is a remedy worse than the disease, because I make it not a ground of my acceptation before God, but only a naked evidence of my believing in Christ, and being accepted of God: it being known that these have a necessary connection together in the Scriptures, and it being also known that the one is more obvious and easy to be discerned than the other. Sure I am, the Lamb's book of life is a great mystery, and unless this be granted, I see not but every man's regeneration and change shall be as dark and hidden, as the hidden and secret decrees of God's election; for the Spirit may immediately reveal both the one and the other. Is it any derogation to the grace of Christ, to know what is freely given us? Doth it not rather commend his grace, when a soul looks upon itself, beautified with his comeliness, and adorned with his graces, and loathes itself in itself, and ascribes all the honour and praise to him? Is it not more injury to the fountain and fulness of grace in Christ, not to see the streams of it at all nor to consider them, than to behold the streams of grace that flow out of this fountain, as coming out of it? I think Christians may be ready to idolize their graces, and make them mediators, when they are known; but is this a good remedy of that evil, to abandon all sight and knowledge of the things freely given us of God? Shall we not speak of the freeness of grace, because men's corruptions turn grace into carnal liberty and wantonness? If these graces be in us, sure I am, it is no virtue to be ignorant of them, but rather a weakness and darkness. It must then be the light and grace of God to know them, and from thence to conclude * that assurance of faith, which is not a forced, ungrounded persuasion, and strong fancy, without any discovered reason of it. Sure I am, the apostle's counsel is, to make our election sure, by making our calling sure. How shall any venture to look into those secrets of the Lamb's book of life, and read their name there? Undoubtedly they belong not to us,—they are a light inaccessible, that will but confound and darken us more. Therefore, whoever would know their election, according to the Scriptures, must read the transcript and copy of the book of life, which is written in the hearts and souls of the elect.

* [That is, collect or obtain.—Ed.]

The thoughts of God are written in his works upon the spirits of men. His election hath a seal upon it,—' The Lord knoweth them that are his;' and who can break up this seal? 'Who hath known the mind of the Lord?' None can, until the Lord write over his thoughts in some characters of his Spirit, and of the new creature, in some lineaments and draughts of his own image, that it may be known they are the epistle of Christ, not written with ink and paper, but with the Spirit of the living God, not on tables of stone, but in fleshly tables of the heart, 2 Cor. iii. 3. Christ writes his everlasting thoughts of love and good-will to us in this epistle; and that we may not think this doth extol the creature, and abase Christ, it is added, ver. 5,—' Not that we are sufficient of ourselves,—but our sufficiency is of God.' The seeing of grace in ourselves doth not prejudge the grace of God, unless we see it independent of the fountain, and behold not the true rise of it, that we may have no matter to glory of. It is not a safe way of beholding the sun, to look straight on it. It is too dazzling to our weak eyes,—you shall not well take it up so. But the best way is to look on it in water; then we shall more steadfastly behold it. God's everlasting love, and the redemption of Jesus Christ, is too glorious an object to behold with the eyes of flesh. Such objects certainly must astonish and strike the spirits of men with their transcendent brightness. Therefore we must look on the beams of this sun, as they are reflected in our hearts; and so behold the conformity of our souls, wrought by his Spirit, unto his will; and then we shall know the thoughts of his soul to us. If men shall at the first flight climb so high, as to be persuaded of God's eternal love, and Christ's purchase for them in particular, they can do no more, but scorch their wings, and melt the wax of them, till they fall down from that heaven of their ungrounded persuasion, into a pit of desperation. The Scripture way is to go downward once, that ye may go up. First go down in yourselves, and make your calling sure, and then you may rise up to God, and make your election sure. You must come by this circle; there is no passing by a direct line, and straight through, unless by the immediate revelation of the Spirit, which is not ordinary and constant, and so not to be pretended unto.

I confess, that sometimes the Spirit may intimate to the soul God's thoughts towards it, and its own state and condition, by an immediate overpowering testimony, that puts to silence all doubts and objections, that needs no other work or mark to evidence the sincerity and reality of it. That light of the Spirit shall be seen in its own light, and needs not that any witness of it. The Spirit of God sometimes may speak to a soul,—' Son, be of good comfort, thy sins are forgiven thee.' This may break into the soul as a beam darted from heaven, without reference to any work of the Spirit upon the heart, or word of Scripture, as a mids * or mean to apply it. But this is more extraordinary. The ordinary testimony of the Spirit is certainly conjoined with the testimony of our own consciences, Rom. viii. 16. And our consciences bear witness of the work of the Spirit in us, which the Spirit discovers to be according to the word. The Spirit makes known to us things that are freely given; but, by 'comparing spiritual things with spiritual,' 1 Cor. ii. 10, 13. The fruit and special work of the Holy Ghost in us, is the *medium*, and the Spirit's light irradiates and shines upon it, and makes the heart to see them clearly. For, though we be the children of light, yet our light hath so much darkness, as there must be a supervenient and accessory light of the Spirit, to discover that light unto us. Now what is all this to us? I fear that there be many ungrounded persuasions among us,—that many build on a sandy foundation, even a strong opinion that it is well with them, without any examination of their souls and conversations according to the word; and this certainly, when the tempest blows, cannot stand. Some teach, that no man should question whether he believe or not, but presently believe. I think none can believe too suddenly; it is always in season, *nunquam sera est fides nec pœnitentia*,—it is never late in respect of the promise; and it is never too early in respect of a man's case. But I cannot think any man can believe, till the Spirit have convinced him of his unbelief; and therefore I would think the most part of men nearer faith in Jesus Christ, if they knew they wanted faith. Nay, it is a part of faith, and believing God in his word, and setting to our seal that God is true, for

* [That is, a medium between extremes.—Ed.]

a man to take with his unbelief, and his natural inability, yea, averseness to it. I would think that those who could not believe in Christ, because they sought honour one of another, and went about to kill him, they had done well to have taken with that challenge of Christ's; and if men ought to take with their sin, they ought to search and try their sin, that they may find it out, to take with it. I wonder, since Antinomians make unbelief the only sin in the world, that they cannot endure the discovery and confession of it. It seems they do not think it so heinous a sin. I confess, no man should of purpose abstain from believing in Christ, till he find out whether he hath believed or not; but whatever hath been, he is bound presently to act faith in Jesus Christ; to flee unto him as a lost sinner, to a saving Mediator. But that every man is bound to persuade himself at the first, that God hath loved him, and Christ redeemed him, is the hope of the hypocrite,—like a spider's web, which, when leaned to, shall not stand. That man's expectation shall perish; he hath kindled sparks of his own,—a wild-fire, and walketh not in the true light of the word, and so must lie down in sorrow. Many of you deceive yourselves, and none can persuade you that ye do deceive yourselves, such is the strength of that delusion and dream. It is the great part of the heart's deceitfulness, to flatter itself in its own eyes; to make a man conceive well of himself and his heart. I beseech you, do not venture your soul's salvation on such groundless opinions; never to question the matter, is to leave it always uncertain. If you would judge yourselves according to the Scriptures, many of you have the marks and characters of those who are kept without the city, and are to have their part in the lake of fire. Is there no condemnation for you, who have never condemned yourselves? Certainly the more you are averse to condemn yourselves, this sticks the closer to you. You are not all in Christ; 'they are not all Israel which are of Israel.' Many (nay the most part) are but said Christians; have no real union with Christ, or principle of life from him. The love you carry to yourselves, makes you easily believe well of yourselves; know, that self-love can blind the eyes, and make you apprehend that God loves you also. Nay, every one readily fancies that to be, which he desires to be. I beseech you, consider if you have any ground for your hopes and confidences, but such as those that will not bear out always. It would be no disadvantage to you, to have your hope shaken, that instead of a vain presumption, you may have the anchor of hope, which shall be fixed within the vail. I think one thing keeps men far from the kingdom of God,—because they know not that they believe not in him. We had gained much ground on you by the word, if we could persuade you that ye believe not, and have not believed from the womb. We might then say to you, as Christ to his disciples, 'Ye believe in God, believe also in me.' Ye have given credit to God the judge and lawgiver, pronouncing a curse on you, and a sentence that ye have hearts desperately wicked,—now, believe also in me, the Redeemer. Ye have believed God in the law, in as far as ye have judged yourselves under sin and wrath; now, believe me in the gospel, that brings a ransom from wrath, and a remedy for sin. It is this very unbelief, that is the original of the world's perishing,—unbelief of the law. Ye do not consider ye are under the condemnation of it. Ye do not believe that ye have not yet fled to Jesus Christ to escape it; and these two keep souls in a deep sleep, till judgment awake them.

But unto every one of you, I would give this direction: Let not examination of what you are, hinder you from that which is your chief duty, and his chief commandment,—to believe in him. I know many Christians are puzzled in the matter of their interest, and always wavering, because they are more taken up with that which is but a matter of comfort and joy, than that which is his greatest honour and glory. I say, to consider the precious promises; to believe the excellency and virtue of Jesus Christ, and love him in your souls, and delight in him, is the weightiest matter of the gospel. To go out of yourselves daily into his fulness, to endeavour new discoveries of your own naughtiness and his grace, this is the new and great commandment of the gospel. The obedience of it is the most essential part of a Christian walk. Now, again, to know that ye do believe, and to discern your interest in Christ, this is but a matter of comfort and of second concernment. Therefore, I say, whenever ye cannot be clear in this, ye should be always exercised in the first. For it is that we are first called to; and if souls were more exercised that way, in the consideration and belief of the very general truths and promises of the gospel, I doubt not, but the light of these would clear up their particular interest in due time. 'These ought ye to have done, and not to leave the other undone.' It is still safest to waive such a question of interest, when it is plunging,* because it puts you off your special duty, and this is Satan's intent in it. It were better if ye do question, presently to believe and abide in him, till it were put out of question.

Sermon IV.

VERSE 1.—"*Who walk not after the flesh, but after the Spirit.*"

CHRIST is made to us of God both righteousness and sanctification; and therefore, those who are in Christ do not only escape condemnation, but they walk according to the Spirit, and not according to the flesh. These two are the sum of the gospel. There is not a greater argument to holy walking than this,—there is no condemnation for you, neither is there a greater evidence of a soul having escaped condemnation, than walking according to the Spirit. We have spoken something in general of the evidence that may be had of a man's state, from his walking, and the Spirit's working in him; we would now speak of the conjunction of these two, and the influence that that privilege hath on this duty, and something of the nature of this description, 'who walk not after the flesh, but after the Spirit.'

In the creation of man, man was composed of soul and body. There was a right order, and subordination of these, suitable to their nature. In his soul he reached angels above,—in his body he was like the beasts below; and this part, his flesh, was a servant to the soul, that was acted and affected according to the desires and motives of the soul Now sin entering, as it hath defaced all the beauty of the creation, as it hath misplaced man, and driven him out from that due line of subordination to God his Maker, for he would have been equal to God, so it hath perverted this beautiful order in men, and turned it just contrary,—hath made the servant to ride on horses, and the prince to walk on foot. This is the just punishment of our first sin. Adam's soul was placed by creation under the sole command of its Creator, above all the creatures, and his own senses; but in one sin, he proudly exalted himself above God, and lamentably subjected himself below his senses, by hearkening to their persuasion. He saw it was good, and tasted it, and it was sweet, and so he ate of it. What a strange way was this! To be like God, he made himself unlike himself, liker the miserable beasts. Now, I say, this is the deserved punishment of man. His soul, that was a free prince, is made a bond-slave to the lusts of his flesh; flesh hath gotten the throne, and keeps it, and lords it over the whole man. Now therefore it is, that the whole man unregenerate, is called flesh, as if he had no immortal spirit, John iii. 6, 'that which is born of the flesh is flesh;' and this chap. ver. 8, has a description of natural men, 'they that are in the flesh;' because flesh is the predominant part that hath captivated a man's reason and will. Nay, not only the grosser corruptions in a man, that have their use and seat in his flesh and body, are under that name;—but take the whole nature of man, that which is most excellent in him, his soul and spirit, his light and understanding, the most refined principles of his conversation,—all these are now but flesh. Nay, not only such natural gifts and illuminations, but even the light of the gospel, and law of God, that someway enters his soul, changeth the nature and name,—it is all but darkness and flesh in him, because the flesh hath a dominion over all that. The clouds and vapours that arise from the flesh, bemist† and obscure all these; the corruptions of the soul are most strengthened in this sort, and most vented here. Sin is become connatural to the flesh, and so a man, by the flesh, is ensnared and subjected to sin. Christ comprehends all our prerogatives and endowments under this, John i. 13, 'born not of blood,

* [Perhaps the word should be plungy, that is *rainy*. *Chauc.*—ED.]
† [That is, cover with mist.—ED.]

nor of the will of the flesh;' and Matt. xvi. 17, 'flesh and blood hath not revealed it unto thee.' Even all the outwards of religion, and all the common privileges of Christians may be called so. What hath Abraham found according to the flesh? Rom. iv. 1. Phil. iii. 3;—which imports so much, that all those outward privileges, many illuminations, and reformations, may so far consist with the corruption of man's nature, may unite so with that, as to have one name with it. It is not all able to conquer our flesh, but our flesh rather subdues all that, and makes it serve itself, till a stronger than it come, even the Spirit, to subdue it and cast it out of the house. Thus the image of God in man is defaced; nay, the very image and nature of man, as man, spoiled. The first creation,—sin hath marred and disordered it. Now, when this second creation, or regeneration comes, the creature is made new, and formed again by the powerful Spirit of Jesus Christ. This change is made, flesh is put out of the throne, as an usurper; the spirit and soul of a man is put in a throne above it, but placed according to its due order, under a holy and spiritual law of God. And thus Jesus Christ is the repairer of the breaches, and restorer of the ancient paths and old wastes, to dwell in. Now the soul hath a new rule established to act according to, and new principles to act from. He whose course of walking was after the corrupt dictates and commands of his fleshly affections, and was of no higher strain than his own sparks of nature, and acquired light would lead him to, now he hath a new rule established,—the Spirit speaking in the word to him, and pointing out the way to him. And there is a new principle, that Spirit leading him in all truth, and quickening him to walk in it. Now this is the soul's perfect liberty, to be from under the dominion of sin and lusts; and thus the Son makes free indeed by the free Spirit. The Son was made a servant, that we might be made free, no more servants of sin in the lusts thereof: and the Spirit of the Lord, where he comes, there is liberty; there the spirit and reasonable soul of a man is elevated into its first native dignity; there the base flesh is dethroned, and made to serve the spirit and soul in a man. Christ is indeed the greatest friend of men, as they are men. Sin made us beasts, Christ makes us men. Unbelievers are unreasonable men, αλογοι, brutish, yea, in a manner, beasts;—this is an ordinary compellation in scripture. Faith makes a man reasonable,—it gives the saving and sanctified use of reason. It is a shame for any man to be a slave to his lusts and passions. It is the character of a beast upon him. He that is led by senses and affections, is degenerated from human nature; and yet such are all out of Christ. Sin reigns in them, and flesh reigns, and the principles of light and reason within are captivated, incarcerated within a corner of their minds. We see the generally received truths among men, that God is, that he is holy, and just, and good; that heaven and hell is,—these are altogether ineffectual, and have no influence on men's conversations, no more than if they were not known, even because the truth is detained in unrighteousness. The corruptions of men's flesh are so rank, that they overgrow all this seed of truth, and choke it, as the thorns did the seed, Matt. xiii. 7. Now, for you, who are called of Jesus Christ, O know what ye are called unto! It is a liberty indeed, a privilege indeed. Ye are no more debtors to the flesh;—Christ hath loosed that obligation of servitude to it. O let it be a shame unto you, who are Christians, to walk so any more, to be entangled any more in that yoke of bondage! 'He that ruleth his spirit' is greater than the mighty, 'than he that taketh a city.' Thus we are called to be more than conquerors. Others, when they conquer the world, are slaves to their own lusts; but let it be far from you to be so. Ye ought to conquer yourselves, which is more than to conquer the world. It is not only unbeseeming a Christian, to be led with passions and lusts, but it is below a man, if men were not now through sin below beasts. I beseech you, aspire unto, and hold fast, the liberty Christ hath obtained for you. Be not fashioned any more according to former lusts. Know, ye are men,—that ye have reasonable and immortal spirits in you. Why will ye then walk as beasts? 'Understand, ye brutish! and ye fools, when will ye be wise!' But I say more; know, ye are Christians, and this is more than to be a man,—it is to be a divine man, one partaker of the divine nature, and who is to walk accordingly. Christians are called to a new manner of walking, and this walking is a fruit that comes out of the root of faith, whereby they are implanted in Christ. You see these agree well together. Those who are in

Christ, 'walk not after the flesh,' &c. Walking after the flesh, is the common walk of the world, who are without God and without Christ; but Christ gives no latitude to such a walk. This is a new nature to be in Christ, and therefore it must have new operations,—to walk after the Spirit. While we look upon the conversations of the most part of men, they may be a commentary to expound this part of the words, what it is to walk after the flesh. 'The works of the flesh,' saith the apostle, Gal. v. 19, 'are manifest;'—and indeed they are manifest, because written in great letters on the outside of many in the visible church, that who runs may read them. Do but read that catalogue in Paul, and then come and see them in congregations. It is not so doubtful and subtile a matter, to know that many are yet without the verge of Christ Jesus, without the city of refuge. You may see their mark on their brow. Is not drunkenness, which is so frequent, a palpable evidence of this,—your envyings, revilings, wrath, strife, seditions, fornications, and such like? O do not deceive yourselves! There is no room in Jesus Christ for such impurities and impieties. There is no toleration of sin within this city and kingdom. Sinners are indeed pardoned, yea received and accepted; drunkards, unclean persons, &c., are not excluded from entering here,—but they must renounce these lusts, if they would stay here. Christ will not keep both,—he must either cast out the sin, or the sinner with it, if he will not part with it. I beseech you, know what ye walk after; the flesh is your leader, and whither will it lead you?—O! it is sad to think on it,—to perdition; ver. 13, 'If ye live after the flesh, ye shall die' Ye think flesh your great friend, ye do all ye can to satisfy and please it; and, O how pleasant is the satisfaction of your flesh to you! Ye think it liberty to follow it, and count it bonds and cords to be restrained. But, oh! know and consider, that flesh will lead you by the kingdom; that guide of your way, to which you committed yourself, will lead you by heaven, Gal. v. 21. It is a blind guide, corruption and humour, and will have no eyes; no discerning of that pit of eternal misery. They choose the way that is best pathed and trodden,—that is easiest, and that most walk into; and this certainly will lead you straight into this pit of darkness. Be called off this way, from following your blind lusts, and rather suffer them to be crucified. Be avenged on them for your two eyes that they have put out, and their treacherous dealing to you, in leading you the high way to destruction. Come in to Jesus Christ, and ye shall get a new guide of the way,—the Spirit that shall lead you into all truth, unto the blessed and eternal life. Christ is the way ye must walk in, and the life that we must go into at the end of our way, and the truth according to which we must walk. Now he hath given his Spirit, the Comforter, to be our leader in this way, according to this rule and pattern unto that life. In a word, the Spirit shall lead you the straight way unto Christ. You shall begin in him, and end in him. He shall lead you from grace to glory. The Spirit that came down from heaven, shall lead you back to heaven. All your walk is within the compass of Christ,—out of him is no way to heaven.

But we must not take this so grossly, as if no other thing were a walking after the flesh, but the gross abominations among men, though even these will scrape a great number from being in Christ Jesus; but it must be further enlarged, to the motions and affections of the unrenewed spirit, and the common principles according to which men walk. And therefore the apostle, Col. iii. Gal. v., nameth many things among the works of the flesh, and members of the old man, which I doubt whether many will account so of,—some natural passions that we account nothing of, because common, as anger, wrath, covetousness. What man is there amongst us, in whom some of these mentioned stir not? Many of your hearts and eyes are given to covetousness; your souls bow downward as your bodies do, and many times before your bodies. Is not the heart of men upon this world, and cannot rise above to a treasure in heaven? And therefore your callings, otherwise lawful, and all your pains and endeavours in them, hath this seal of the flesh stamped on them, and pass no otherwise with God. We see how rank the corruptions of men are, anger domineering in them, and leading them often captive. And this is ounted a light matter, but it is not so in scripture. How often is it branded with folly by the wise man! And this folly is even the natural fleshly corruption that men are born with; and in how many doth it rise up to the elevation of malice and hatred of others? And then it carries the image of the devil, rather than of human infirmity. And if we suppose a man not much given to any of these, yet what a spirit of pride and self-love is in every man, even those that carry the lowest sail, and the meanest port among men,—those that are affable and courteous, and those that seem most condescending to inferiors and equals. Yet, alas! this evil is more deeply engraven on the spirit. If a man could but watch over his heart, and observe all the secret reflections of it, all the comparisons it makes, all the desires of applause and favour among men, all the surmises and stirrings of spirit upon any affront, O how would they discover diabolic pride! This sin is the more natural and inbred, for that it is our mother-sin that brought us down from our excellency. This weed grows upon a glass window, and upon a dunghill. It lodges in palaces and cottages. Nay, it will spring and grow out of a pretended humility, and low carriage. In a word, the ambitious designs of men, the large appetite of earthly things, the overweening conceit of ourselves, and love to ourselves, the stirring of our affections, without observing a rule upon unlawful objects, or in an unlawful manner,—all these are common to men, and men walk after them. Every man hath some predominant or idol, that takes him most up. Some are finer and subtiler than others, some have their pleasures and gains without, others their own gifts and parts within; but both are alike odious before God, and both gross flesh and corruption before him.

There are two errors among men concerning this spiritual walking,—the one is the doctrine of some in these days, the other is the practical error of many of us. Many pretending to some near and high discoveries, as to Christ and the Spirit, have fallen upon the most refined and spiritualized flesh instead of the Spirit indeed. They separate the Spirit from the word, and reckon the word and law of God, which was a lamp to David's feet, among the fleshly rudiments of the world. But if they speak not 'according to the law and to the testimony,' saith Isaiah, 'it is because there is no light in them.' Thus their new light is but an old darkness, that could not endure even the darker light of the prophets. If they speak not according to the word, it is because there is no spirit in them. Is it not the Spirit the Comforter, which Christ promised to send to the apostles, and all that should believe in his name through their word? For that Spirit was a Spirit of truth, that should lead into all truth. And lest men should father their own fancies and imaginations on the Spirit of God, Christ adds, 'he shall bring all things to your remembrance,'—those things that Christ hath spoken, and we have here written. The holy apostle to the Colossians, chap. iii. when he reproves the works of the flesh, and declares they had put them off, commends unto them, in opposition to these, 'let the word of Christ dwell in you richly in all wisdom; teaching one another in psalms and spiritual songs, with grace in your hearts to the Lord,' ver. 16,—the Spirit here, not casting out the word, but bringing it in plentifully, and sweetly agreeing with it. The Spirit that Christ sent, did not put men above ordinances, but above corruptions, and the body of death in them. It is a poor and easy victory to subdue grace and ordinances,—every slave of the devil doth that. I fear, as men and angels fell from their own dignity, by aspiring higher, so those that will not be content with the estate of Christ and his apostles, but soar up in a higher strain of spirit, and trample on that ministration as fleshly and carnal,—I fear they fall from Jesus Christ, and come into greater condemnation. It is true indeed, 2 Cor. iii. 6, 'the letter killeth,' that is, the covenant of works preacheth now nothing but condemnation to men, but the Spirit of the gospel giveth life; nay, even the gospel separated from the Spirit of life in Jesus, is but a savour of death to souls. Shall we therefore separate the Spirit from the gospel and word, because the word alone cannot quicken us? David knew how to reconcile this,—'Quicken thou me according to thy word,' Psal. cxix. 25.—'Thy Spirit is good, lead me into the land of uprightness, quicken me, O Lord,' Psal. cxliii. 10, 11. The word was his rule, and the Spirit applied his soul to the rule. The word holds out the present pattern we should be conformed unto. Now if there be no more, a man may look all his days on it, and yet not be changed; but the Spirit within, transforms and changes a man's soul to more and more conformity to that pattern, by beholding it. If a man shall shut his eyes on the pattern, he cannot know what he is, and ought to be. If he look only on the Spirit's work within, and make that his rule, he takes an imperfect rule, and an incomplete copy. And yet this is the highest attainment of these aspirers to new light. They have forsaken the word as their rule, and instead of it, have another law within them, as much as is already written on their hearts, which is in substance this, as they suppose,—I am bound to do no more than I have already power to do; I am not to endeavour more holiness than I have already. These men are indeed perfect here in their own apprehension, and do not know in part, and believe in part, and obey in part, because they are advanced the length of their own law and rule, their rule being of no perfection. Paul was not so, but forgetting what he had attained, he followed on to what was before him, and was still reaching forward. Let not us, my brethren, believe every spirit, and every doctrine that comes out under that name,—Christ hath forewarned us. Pray for more of that Spirit, which may quicken the word to us, and quicken us to obey the word. There must be a mutual enlivening. The word must be made the ministration of life by the Spirit of Jesus, which can use it as a sword to divide the soul and spirit; and we must be quickened to the obedience of the truth in the word. The word is the seed incorruptible; but it cannot beget us, or be a principle of new life within us, except a living spirit come along to our hearts. Know that the word is your pattern and rule; the Spirit your leader and helper, whose virtue and power must conform you to that rule, 1 Pet. i. 22. Peter joins these two,—the purification and cleansing the soul, which Christ attributes to the word, 'Ye are clean through the word which I have spoken,' John xv. 3. Peter attributes it to the Spirit working according to the pattern of truth. It is true the Spirit of God needs no pattern to look to; nay, but we must have it, and eye it, else we know not the Spirit of truth from a lie and delusion. We cannot try the spirits but by this rule; and it is by making us steadfastly look on this glorious pattern in the word, and the example of Christ Jesus' life, that we are conformed unto Christ, as by the Spirit of the Lord, 2 Cor. iii. 13. Certainly that must be fleshly walking, which is rather conformed unto the imaginations of a man's own heart, than the blessed will of God revealed in his word. Can such walking please God, when a man will not so much as hearken to what is God's will and pleasure? As other heresies, so especially this, is a work of the flesh.

Now there is another principle amongst many of us. We account it spiritual walking, to be separated from the gross pollutions of the world, to have a carriage blameless before men. This is the notion that the multitude fancy of it. Be not deceived,—you may pass the censure of all men, and be unreprovable among them, and yet be but walkers after the flesh. It is not what you are before the world can prove you spiritual men, though it may prove many of you carnal. Your outside may demonstrate of many of you that ye walk after the flesh; and if ye will not believe it, I ask you if ye think drunkenness a walking in the Spirit? Do ye think ye are following the Spirit of God in uncleanness? Is it not that Holy Spirit that purgeth from all filthiness? Look but what your walk is, ye that are not so much as conformed to the letter of the word in any thing; who care not to read the scriptures and meditate on them. Is this walking after the Spirit of truth? If drunkenness, railing, contention, wrath, envy, covetousness, and such like, be the Spirit's way, then I confess many of you walk after the Spirit; but if these be the manifest works of the flesh, and manifestly your way and work, then why dream ye that ye are Christians?

But I suppose, that ye could be charged with none of these outward things; that you had a form of religion and godliness, yet I say, all that is visible before men cannot prove you to be spiritual walkers. Remember it is a Spirit ye must walk after; now, what shall be the chief agent here? Sure, not the body,—what fellowship can your body have with him that is a Spirit? The body, indeed, may worship that eternal Spirit, being acted by the spirit; but I say, that alone can never prove you to be Christians. We must then lay aside a number of professors, who have no other ground of confidence but such things as may be seen of men; and if they would enter their hearts, how many vain thoughts lodge there! How little of God is there! God is not almost in all our thoughts; we give a morning and evening salutation, but there is no more of God all the day throughout. And is this walking after the Spirit, which imports a constancy? And what part can be spared most, but the spirit of a man? The body is distracted with other necessary things, but we might always spare our souls to God. Now, thus should a man obey that command,—'pray always.' It is impossible that he should do nothing else but pray in an express formal way; but the soul's walking with God, between times of prayer, should compensate that. And thus prayer is continued, though not in itself, yet in meditation on God, which hath in it the seed of all worship, and is virtually prayer and thanksgiving, and all duties.

Let us then consider, if our bodies be not more exercised in religion than our souls, yea, if they be not the chief agents. How many impertinencies, and roveries, and wanderings, are throughout the day? The most part of our conversation, if it be not profane, yet it is vain, that is, unprofitable in the world. It neither advantageth us spiritually, nor glorifies God. It is almost to no purpose; and this is enough to make it all flesh. And for our thoughts, how do they go unlimited and unrestrained?—like a wild ass, traversing her ways, and gadding about, fixed on nothing,—at least not on God; nay, fixed on any thing but God. If it be spiritual service, should it not carry the seal of our spirit and affection on it? We are as so many shadows walking, as pictures and statues of Christians, without the soul and life, which consists in the temper and disposition of the spirit and soul towards God.

Sermon V.

VERSE 1.—"*Who walk not after the flesh, but after the Spirit.*"

IT is no wonder that we cannot speak any thing to purpose of this subject, and that you do not hear with fruit, because it is indeed a mystery to our judgments, and a great stranger to our practice. There is so little of the Spirit, both in teachers and those that come to be taught, that we can but speak of it as an unknown thing, and cannot make you to conceive it, in the living notion of it as it is. Only we may say in general,—it is certainly a divine thing, and another thing than our common or religious walk is. It is little experienced, so we can know the less of it; but this much we should know,—it is another thing than we have attained. It is above us, and yet such a thing as we are called to aspire unto. How should it stir up in our spirits a holy fire of ambition to be at such a thing, when we hear it is a thing attainable: nay, when Christ calls us unto himself, that we may thus walk with him! I would have Christians men of great and big projects and resolutions; of high and unlimited desires, not satisfied with their attainments, but still aspiring unto more of God, more conformity to his will, more walking after the Spirit, more separation from the course of the world. And this is indeed to be of a divine spirit. The divine nature is here, as it were, in a state of violence, out of its own element. Now, it is known by this, if it be still moving upwards, taking no rest in this place, and these measures and degrees, but upon a continual motion towards the proper centre of it,—God, his holiness, and Spirit.

We desire to speak a word of these three. First, The nature of the spiritual walking. Next, Its connection and union with that blessed state of non-condemnation. And then of the order of this, how it flows from a man's being implanted in Christ Jesus;—which three are considerable * in the words.

This spiritual walking is according to a spiritual rule, from spiritual principles, for spiritual ends. These three being established aright, the walk is even the motion of a Christian within the compass of these. It is according to the word, as the holy rule; it is from the faith and love of Jesus Christ, as the predominant principles. Nay, from the Spirit of Jesus, living in the heart by faith, and dwelling in it by love, as the first wheel of this motion, the *primum mobile*. And as it begins in the spirit, so it ends there, in the glory of Jesus Christ, and our heavenly Father. Con-

* [That is, deserving of consideration.—ED.]

sider this then,—'t is not a lawless walking and irregular walk, it is according to the rule, and the rule is perfect, and it is a motion to perfection, not a rest in what is now attained to. The course of this world is the way and rule of the children of disobedience, Eph. ii. 2. There is a spirit indeed that works in them, and a rule it works by. The spirit is that evil spirit, contrary to the Holy Spirit of God; and you may know what spirit it is that works, by the way it leads men unto—a broad way, pathed and trodden in by many travellers. It is the king's high street, the common way that most part walk into, according as their neighbours do, as the most do. But that king is the prince of this world, Satan, who blinds the eyes of many, that they may not see that pit of misery before them, which their way leads them to. A Christian must have a kind of singularity, not in opinion, but in practice rather, to be more holy, and walk more abstracted from the dregs of the world's pollution. This were a divine singularity. Indeed men may suspect themselves, that separate from the godly in opinion. They have reason to be more jealous of themselves, when they offend against the generation of the just. But if this were the intention and design of men, to be very unlike the multitude of men, nay, to be very unlike the multitude of professors, in the affection and practice of holiness, humility, and spiritual walking, I think this were an allowed way, though a singular way. Men may aspire to as great a difference as may be, from the conversations and practice of others, if there be a tending to more conformity to the word, the rule of all practice. 'The law is spiritual' and 'holy,' saith Paul, 'but I am carnal.' This, therefore, were spiritual walking,—to set that excellent spiritual rule before our eyes, that we who are carnal may be transformed and changed into more likeness to that holy and spiritual law. If a man had not an imperfect rule of his own fancy and imagination before his eyes, he could not be satisfied with his attainments, but, with Paul, would forget them,—in a manner, not know them, but reach forward still to what is before. Because so much length would be before us, as would swallow up all our progress,—this would keep the motion on foot and make it constant. A man should never say, 'Master, let us make tabernacles, it is good to be here.' No, indeed, the dwelling-place and resting would be seen to be above. As long as a man had so much of his journey to accomplish, he would not sit down in his advancement; he would not compare with others, and exalt himself above others. Why? Because there is still a far greater distance between him and his rule, than between the slowest walker and him. This made Paul more sensible of a body of death, (Rom. vii.) than readily lower Christians are. Reflections on our attainments and comparisons with others, which are so often the work of our spirit, are a retrograde motion; it makes no way but spends the time,—is a returning as we go; whereas we ought to go straight forward. I beseech you, Christians, consider what you are doing, if you would prove yourselves so indeed. I know not how you can evidence it better, than by honouring and esteeming his word and commandments,—exceeding large and precious; no end of their perfection. The word is much undervalued in the opinions of many, but it is as little cared for in the practice of most. There is certainly little of God there, where this is not magnified and honoured. There must be darkness in that way, where this candle, which was a lamp to David's feet, shines not. Some promise to us liberty, but they themselves are the servants of corruption; it is no liberty to be above all law and rule. It was innocent Adam's liberty to be conformed to a holy and just command; nay, this was his beauty. This Spirit indeed gives liberty where he is, but this liberty is from our sins and corruptions, not to them. It looses the chains of a man's own corrupt lusts off him, to walk at freedom in the way of his commandments. The Spirit enlargeth the prisoner's heart, and then he runs, but not at random, but the way of his commands, Psalm cxix. 32. It was our bondage to be as wild asses, traversing our ways,—to be gadding abroad, to change our way. Now, here is the Spirit's liberty to bring us into the way, and that way is one. Let us then learn this one principle,—the word must be the rule of your walking, both common and religious. Alas! it is not spiritual walking, to confine religion to some solemn duties. Remember, it is a walk, a continued thing, without interruption; therefore your whole conversation ought to be as so many steps progressive to heaven. Your motion should not be to begin only when you come to pray, or read, or hear, as many men do. They are in a quite different way and element when they step out of their civil callings into religious ordinances. But Christians, your motion should be continued in your eating and drinking, and sleeping, and acting in your callings, that when you come to pray or read, you may be but stepping forward in the way, out of one darker, obscurer path, into a more beaten way. Remember, this word can make us perfect to salvation. It is a principle in the hearts of folks, which is vented now by many, that the word doth not reach their particular carriages and conversations in civil matters. These are apprehended to be without the sphere and compass of the word ; while it is commonly cast up to ministers—meddle with the word and spiritual things, and not with our matters.* Truly I think, if we separate these from the word, we may quickly separate all religion from such actions ; and if such actings and businesses be without the court of the word, they are also without the court of conscience ; conscience, religion, and the word being commensurable. Therefore I beseech every one of you, take the word for the ruling of your callings and conversations among men. Extend it to all your actions, that in all these you may act as Christians as well as men. It is certainly the licentiousness of the spirits of men, that cannot endure the application of the word unto their particular actions and conversations.

Now this spiritual walk proceeds from spiritual principles. It is certain, the Spirit of Jesus Christ is he "in whom we live, and move, and have our being" spiritually. Without him we can do nothing. And therefore Christians ought to walk with such a subordination to, and dependence on him, as if they were mere instruments, and patients under his hand. Though I think, in regard of endeavoured activity, they should bestir themselves, and give all diligence, as if they acted independently of the Spirit ; yet in regard of denial of himself, and dependence on the Spirit, each one ought to act as if he did not act at all, but the Spirit only acted in him. This is the divinity of Paul,—'I laboured more abundantly than they all, yet not I, but grace in me. I live, yet not I, but Christ in me.' O how difficult a thing is it to reconcile these two in the practice of Christians, which yet cannot really be, except they be together! It is certainly one of the great mysteries of Christianity, to draw our strength and activity from another, to look upon ourselves and our actings, as these that can do nothing,—as empty vines ; and that notwithstanding of all infused and acquired principles. Whatever we ought to do in judging and discerning of our condition, yet sure I am, Christians, in the exercise and practice of godliness, should look upon themselves void of any principle in themselves either to do or think. 'Not that we are sufficient of ourselves.' The proficient and growing Christian should look no more on his own inclinations and habits than if he had none. He should consider himself an ungodly man, that no fruit can grow upon, one that cannot pray, as he is in himself. But, alas! we come to duties in the confidence of qualifications for duties, act more confidently in them because accustomed to them, and so make grace and religion a kind of art and discipline, that use and experience make expert unto. Learn now this one thing, which would be instead of many rules and doctrines to us,—to shut out of your eyes the consideration of what you are by gifts, or grace, or experience. Do not consider that, but rather fix your eyes on the grace of Jesus Christ, and upon the power and virtue of the Holy Spirit, which is given by promise ; that when the way is all the easier to you, both by delight and custom, yet you may find it to your natural principles as insuperable as at the beginning; and may still cry out, 'Draw me, and I will run after thee; lead me, and I will walk with thee.' Do not measure the call into duties by the strength thou findest in thyself, but look unto him who strengtheneth us with all might. Now, the Spirit worketh in us by subordinate spiritual principles, as believing in Christ, and loving of him, as our Lord and Saviour ; and these two acts drive on a soul sweetly in the way of obedience. Fear, where not mixed in its actings with faith and love, is a spirit of bondage; but the Christian ought to walk according to the Spirit of adoption, which cries 'Abba, Father.' Yet how many Christians are rather in a servile and slavish manner driven on by terrors and chastisements to their duty

* [In the year 1651, Warriston and some others sent a letter to Cromwell, through General Lambert, in which they charge the English army in Scotland "with divers errors, countenancing of deposed ministers to preach, *silencing of ministers that preach of state proceedings*, and suffering officers to preach," &c.—*Whitelock's Memorials*, p. 497.—Ed.]

than by love! There is a piece of liberty in Christian walking, when there is not a restraint upon the spirit, by this slavish fear. This, I say, is not beseeming those that are in Christ Jesus. You ought to have the Spirit of your Father for your leader and guide. O how sweet, and how certain and necessary also, would this walking be! The love of Christ would be an inward principle of motion, and would make our spiritual actings as easy and pleasant as natural motions are. Fear is but a violent principle, that is like the impulse of a stone thrown upward; as long as that external impression remains, it moves, but still slower and slower, and at length evanisheth. But if you believed in him, and your hearts were engaged to love him, O how would it be a pleasant and native thing to walk in his way, as a stone goeth downward! Consider your principles, that act you to matters and duties of religion. Many men there be, in whom there appears no difference of their work to beholders; but O how wide a difference doth God discern in them! Engines and artifice may make dead and lifeless things move and walk as orderly as things that have life. But the principle of this motion makes a huge difference;—the one is moved from without, the other from itself. The most part of us act as irrational and brute beasts in religion: nay, we walk as inanimate and senseless creatures. It is some one or other consideration without us moves us,—custom, censure, education, and such like. Ah! these are the principles of our religion. How many would have no religion, no form of it, if they were not among such company! And therefore we see many change it according to companies, as the fish doth its skin, according to the colour of that which is nearest it. How many would do many things they dare not for punishment and censure, and for that same dare not leave other things undone! In a word, the most part of us are such as would walk in no path of godliness, if it were not the custom of the time and fear of men that constrained us. But, my brethren, let it not be so among you, you who are in Christ Jesus. Let this be predominant in your hearts to constrain you not to live to yourselves, but unto God, even this,—that you believe Christ hath died for sinners, that they might live from sin. And from this let your hearts be inflamed with his love, that it may carry you on in a sweet and blessed necessity to walk in all well-pleasing. Let the consideration of his love lay on a constraint, but a constraint of willingness, to live to him who hath thus loved you. But as the principle is spiritual, so must the end be; and I think these two complete the mystery of the practice of Christianity,—to act from another principle unto another end; even as these two make up the mystery of iniquity in our hearts,—to act from ourselves unto ourselves. Every man naturally makes a god of himself, is his own Alpha and Omega, the beginning of his actions, and the end of them, which is proper to God. As the fall hath cut off the subordination of the soul to God in its actions, that it cannot now derive all from that blessed Fountain of all-being and well-being, so is this channel of reference of all our actions to God stopped, that they do not tend unto him, as they are not derived from him; and thus they return unto a man's self again. There is one point of self, and making it our aim and design, which possibly many do not take heed unto. It is ordinary for us to act and walk in Christian duties, for our salvation,—for obtaining of life eternal, as our chief and only end, which is but an inferior end; because we ought not to walk mainly for life, but to life. We should not walk after the command only for heaven, but in the way of it unto heaven. Our spiritual walking can never purchase us a right unto the least of his mercies. When we have done all, this should be our soul's language,—We are unprofitable servants, our righteousness extends not to thee. What gain is it to the Almighty that thou art righteous? Yet for the most part, we make our walking as a hire for the reward. The covenant of works,—doing for life, is some way naturally imprinted in our hearts, and we cannot do, but we would live in doing; we cannot walk unto all well-pleasing, but we would also walk unto pacifying of God. Self-righteousness is men's great idol, which, when all other baser and grosser idols are down, they do still seek to establish. But, Christians, observe this evil in yourselves, and suffer this mystery of godliness to be wrought in you,—the abasing of yourselves, the denial of yourselves. I would have you, in respect of diligence and earnestness, doing, walking, and running, as if ye were to be saved by it only. But again, you must deny all that, and no more consider it, or lean upon it, than if ye ought to do nothing, or did nothing. But your ends should be more divine and high, as your nature is,—to glorify God in your mortal bodies, since ye are his, and bought with a price. O how ought ye not to be your own! The great purpose of your obedience should be, a declaration of your sense of his love, and of your obligation to him. Ye ought to walk in his way, because ye are escaped condemnation, and saved by him, and not that ye may be saved only. It is the glory of our heavenly Father, and the honour of the Redeemer, for Christians to walk, even as he walked, and follow his footsteps. It commends the grace of Jesus Christ exceedingly. Therefore this cannot but be the choice and delight of a believing soul,—to walk unto all well-pleasing, to have the glory of him as their great design to aim at; who for our salvation laid aside his glory, and embraced shame and reproach. We use to walk in obedience to God, that we may pacify God for our disobedience. But let a Christian abhor such a thought. Christ's blood must pacify, but the walking of his child pleaseth him in his well-beloved Son. When he is once pacified for sin, when he once accepts your persons, your performances are his delight. Now this should be the great scope of a soul, that all its powers should be fixed on,—to please him, and live to him.

Now these three being established, we must conceive that the chief agent and party in this walking must be spiritual; therefore men's bodies are not capable of this walk after the Spirit principally. Outward ordinances are but the shell wherein the kernel must be enclosed. All our walking that is visible to men, is but like a painted or engraven image and statue, that hath no breath nor life in it, unless the Spirit actuate and quicken the same. I say not only the Spirit of God, but the spirit and soul in man; for the Spirit's immediate and divine operations are upon such a suitable subject as the immortal soul. Verily, there is a spirit in man, and the inspiration of the Almighty gives him understanding. We must not abolish the outward form, because it hath some divinity in it, even the stamp of God's authority; and therefore, those who are swelled above ordinances, I fear they be monstrous Christians. A man is composed of a spirit and a body, acted and quickened by that Spirit. Without either of these he is not a complete man. So I say, he is not a Christian that doth not worship God in the spirit and in truth both; and it is not religion that excludes either the inward soul-communion with God, or the outward ordinance and appointment of God. But, alas! this may be our complaint,—we come and worship God, and draw nigh with our bodies, but our hearts are far removed. Here is the death of many's worship,—the soul is separated from the body of it. These are but pictures and images of Christians. We have mouths and faces of saints; but O how little of divine affection or of soul-desires, breathes in us! We are deniers of the power of godliness, by resting in a form, and this is the great sin of this generation. The essentials, the vital spirits of Christianity are exhausted, and some dry bones, like an anatomy of a Christian, remain behind. I beseech you, gather your spirits to this spiritual walking: they only can follow the Spirit. Your bodies are earthly and lumpish, and the way is all upward to the holy hill. Look inwardly and measure yourselves so. Outward appearance is no just measure. Retire within your souls, and engage them in this exercise, and enter them to this motion, and your spirits will sweetly and surely act your bodies and externals, in all matters of godliness.

Sermon VI.

VERSE 1.—"*Who walk not after the flesh, but after the Spirit.*"

IT is one of the greatest mysteries in a Christian's practice, to join these two together, which the gospel hath conjoined,—justification and sanctification, and to place them in their due order. There is much miscarrying in both these, if they are either separated or misplaced. But the truth is, they cannot really be, except they be jointly. Yet, often it falls out, that in men's apprehensions and endeavours, they are disjoined. This, then, were the argument of a living, and believing Christian,

—to join the study of holiness, with the exercise of faith in Christ, for remission of sin and righteousness; and not only to join it, but also to derive it from that principle. There is both an union between these and an order established in Scripture. The most part of those that profess the gospel are of two sorts; they do either divide holiness from imputed righteousness, or Christ's righteousness from holiness. I do not say, that any man truly seeks to be covered with the righteousness of Jesus Christ, and to have his sins freely pardoned, but he will also study to walk before God in all well-pleasing. But the truth is, many do pretend and profess to seek salvation and forgiveness in Christ's blood, and have the mercy of God, and merits of Christ always in their mouth, who yet declare by their conversation that they do not so much as desire or propose to seek after holiness. I do not speak of those who are Antinomians in profession, but of a great multitude in the visible church, who are really more Antinomians, to wit, in practice, than most part of our professed Antinomians. You hear all of free grace, and free redemption in Jesus Christ, of tender and enduring mercies in God, and this you take for the whole gospel; and presently, upon the notion of mercy and grace, you conclude unto yourselves, not only immunity and freedom from all the threatenings of the word, and from hell, but likewise ye proclaim secretly in your own hearts, a liberty to sin so much the more securely. The door of mercy cast open in the gospel, and the free access to Christ manifested therein, through the corruption that is within us, proves the very occasion of many's giving indulgence to their lusts—of delaying reformation, and turning to God. You all profess, that you seek to be justified and saved by Jesus Christ; yea, you persuade yourselves to have escaped condemnation by Christ. Now then, conjoin that profession and persuasion with your walk, and O how contrary you may find them to one another! 'Your faith is vain,' for 'ye are yet in your sins,' 1 Cor. xv. 17. The grace of God appearing to some men, effectually teacheth them to deny ungodliness, and worldly lusts, and to live righteously, soberly, and godly, Tit. ii. 11, 12. But if we may conjecture your teaching by your walking, it seems the notion of grace and the gospel that is formed in your minds, hath taught you another doctrine,—to avow ungodliness and follow worldly lusts. Is there so much as a shadow of this spiritual walking in many? I confess, it is natural for every man to seek his own righteousness, and it is the arm of God that must bow men to submit to Christ's imputed righteousness. Yet, the most part of men seem to be so far from seeking any righteousness, that they are rather seeking the fulfilling of their own carnal lusts, working wickedness with greediness, not caring how little they have to put confidence into. And yet, certain it is, that how much soever a man attains to of a form of religion or civil honesty, he is ready to put his trust in it, and to lean the weight of his soul upon it. But seeing this is natural to you all, to seek heaven by doing and working, I wonder that ye do no more. How do you satisfy your consciences in the expectation of heaven, who take so little pains in religion, and are so loose and profane in your conversation? I wonder, seeing ye have it naturally engraven in your hearts to establish your own righteousness, that ye labour not to have more of it to fill your eye withal.

But again, on the other hand, there are some men, who have a form of religion, and labour to be of a blameless conversation among men, that possibly persuade themselves they are seeking holiness, and walking spiritually. But, alas! you may find it but a painted and seeming religion, that is an abomination in the sight of God; because it is to them, all the ground of their acceptation before God. If ever this question was moved in some of you, 'What shall I do to be saved?' you have condescended on such a walk, such a profession for the answer of it. It is natural to all, even those who have least appearance of godliness, to seek heaven by doing God's will. Those that have no more to speak of than their baptism, or receiving the Lord's Supper, or attending well the solemn assemblies, will ground their hope of salvation on these things. How much more will the civil and honest men, commonly so called, who pray and read, and profess godliness,—how much more, I say, will they establish that which they attain to, as the ground of their confidence before God! Now, this is a general unknown ill that destroys the world, and yet few are convinced of it, how hard it is to be driven out of ourselves, and to seek life in another. O know, that it is in a manner the crucifying of a man's self thus to deny himself,—to have a sort of righteousness, and not to trust in it. Who is he that cannot endure to look upon himself for moral vileness? Alas, men flatter themselves in their own eyes, and look with a more favourable eye on their own actions, than they ought! Who is he that abhors himself even for abominable works? But who shall be found to abhor himself for his most religious and best actions? Who casts these out of his sight as unclean and menstruous things? Therefore, I say, though thy righteousness were equal to, or exceeded any Pharisee's righteousness, thou canst not enter into heaven. The poor publican, that was a vile and profane sinner, yet had a righteousness exceeding the Pharisee's. Though he had none of his own, yet he had a righteousness without blemish, of Christ's purchasing, having by faith fled to the mercy of God, in and through a Mediator. It is not more doing, more praying, more exact walking, that can make you more righteous in God's account, in order to absolution from law-condemnation, than the profanest and most wretched sinner. But the baser and viler thou be in thine own eyes, the more thou hidest thy best doings from thine eyes, and lookest on thy uncleanness, and betakest thyself to Christ, his unspotted and perfect righteousness, the more honourable and precious thou art in his eyes. Therefore, God is said to dwell in the heart of the humble and contrite one, not for the worth of his humility and repentance; no, no, but for the pleasure he hath in the Well-beloved's righteousness. That is the beautiful garment, only in the eye of a humbled soul, that seeth nothing in itself desirable.

Therefore, I wish that this conjunction which is made in the gospel, were also engraven in your hearts, and on your practices, that is, that you would seek after holiness, without which no man shall see God. Seek to perfect it in the fear of God, but not as though ye were to be thereby justified. Seek it with that diligence and earnest study, as if ye were to be saved by it, and yet seek it, so as to be denied to your diligence, or as if ye sought it not at all. How sweet a conjunction were this in the Christian's practice, to walk and run so after the prize, as if his walking did obtain it, and yet to look upon his walking, as if it were not at all. Your diligence and seriousness in godliness should be upon the growing hand, as if doing did save you; yet you ought to deny all that, and look to the righteousness of another, as if nothing were done at all by you. How doth Paul, (Phil. iii. 8,) unite these in his practice, 'I count all loss and dung to be found in Christ, not having mine own righteousness, and yet I press forward, and follow after perfection, as having attained nothing yet.' One of these two is the original of many stumblings and wanderings in our Christian way. Either there is not a necessity and constraint laid upon the souls of many to walk in all well-pleasing, and to perfect holiness in the fear of God,—we look on it as a thing indifferent, that is to be determined according to the measure of our receivings from God, or we look on it as a thing not urging all, but belonging to ministers, or more eminent professors; and hence there ariseth much carnal liberty, in walking without the line of Christian liberty, because there is an indifference in the spirit that gives that latitude in walking; or else there is not that following of holiness in such a way, as can consist with the establishing of Christ's righteousness,—no denial of ourselves in our actions. We act as if we were sufficient of ourselves, and walk as if we were thereby justified, and commend ourselves to God in our own consciences, whenever we can have the testimony of our consciences for well-doing. And by this means the Lord is provoked. Because we do not honour the Son, the Father counts himself despised, and the Spirit is grieved and tempted to depart, and leave us to our own imaginations, till our idol which we established fall down, and our understanding return to us.

As it would be of great moment to the peace of Christians, and increase of holiness, to have that union of justification and sanctification stamped on their hearts, so especially to have the due and evangelic method and order of these impressed on their consciences, would conduce exceedingly both to their quickening and comforting. As there is nothing, that either so deadens or darkens, and saddens the spirits of the godly, as darkness in this particular, the ignorance and mistake of the method and order of that well-ordered covenant must certainly be very prejudicial to the life and consolation tendered by the gospel. This spiritual walking flows from the believer's state of non condemnation in Christ. He is once in Jesus Christ, and then he walks after the Spirit of Christ. You may make engines to cause a dead statue walk, but it cannot walk of itself till it have a principle of life in it. Walking is one of the operations of life, that flows from some inward principle, and so this spiritual walk and motion of a Christian in his course, is the proper operation of the new nature that he is a partaker of in Christ Jesus. As, then, you know it is impossible that there can be true and unfeigned walking, where there is no life, no principle within, to put the creature to motion, though a man may by art and some external impulse so act a piece of timber or stone, as it may resemble to you a walking like to living creatures, so it is not possible that any of the sons of Adam, who are by nature dead in sins, can walk spiritually, before they be united to Jesus Christ, by believing in him for righteousness and salvation. There may be such a walking of carnal unregenerate men, as may deceive all the senses and judgments of beholders. Men may be acting from base external principles in matters of religion, so that a beholder shall perceive no difference between them and others in whom Christ lives and walks; but before God it is nothing else but an artificial walk, a painted and dead business, because the Spirit that raised up Christ is not stirring in them. They are not living members of that Head that quickens all, have not been driven out of their own righteousness to Christ, the city of refuge. Their principles are no higher than walking to obtain salvation, and acceptation of God in a legal way, walking to pacify him, walking to please men and their own consciences, walking for gain or credit, or advantage in the way, walking according to custom or education in the way. These are not living principles. But when once a soul hath embraced Christ Jesus within it, he becomes in a manner a soul to actuate and quicken that soul. He animates it, and moves it in God's ways, according to the covenant of grace,—'I will put my Spirit within you, and cause you to walk in my statutes.' There is first quickening, and then walking. You who were dead in sins, hath he quickened together with Christ, Eph. ii. 1, 5; and then it follows in due order,—'I will cause you to walk in my statutes,' Ezek. xxxvi. 27. Christ comes into the heart to dwell, and then he walks in it, 2 Cor. vi. 16. And what is that,—Christ to walk in believers? It is nothing else but Christ by his Spirit making them to walk in his way. There is so little in us to principle a spiritual action, even when renewed and quickened, that we should look on ourselves not so much as workers with him, but as being acted by him. We should look on soul and body as pieces of organized clay that cannot move, but as they are moved by him as the soul and life of them; so that, according to the Scripture dialect, a Christian is nothing else, but Christ living and walking in such a person. This is it which Christ, when he is to go out of the world, instructs his disciples into, John xv. 1. He is the vine, and we the branches. The branch must be first united to the tree, and implanted into the tree, ere it bring forth fruit. Without the tree it withers. So must a soul be first ingraft in Jesus Christ, implanted in him by faith in his death and sufferings, before it can grow up into the similitude of his resurrection, or 'walk in newness of life,' as Paul speaks, Rom. vi. 4, 5. 'Without me ye can do nothing.' Ye must first be one with him, by believing in him, and receiving him as a complete Saviour, and then the sap and virtue of the tree flows into the dead branch, and it shoots forth, and blossoms and bears.

Now, if this doctrine of Christ and his apostles were duly pondered and believed, O what a change would it make on the lives and spirits of Christians! Since this is the order established in the gospel, and an order suitable both to his grace and our necessity, (as all that is in it speaketh forth an excellent contriver)—when we go about to establish our souls in another method, how is it possible that we should not weary and vex our souls in vain? How can we choose but torment ourselves and intricate ourselves still more? Our method and way is just contrary. We perplex our souls how to find the fruits of the Spirit of Christ, how to walk after the Spirit, without first closing entirely with Christ himself. We trouble ourselves to find the operations of a spiritual life, before we lay hold on Christ, who is the life of our souls. It is made an argument by many, to keep them from believing in Christ, because they do not find that spiritual life stirring in them. How cross is this to the declared mind of Christ in the gospel! It cannot choose but both darken the spirit more, and dry up the influences of the

Spirit of God, because it keeps thee from the fountain of all consolation. You may disquiet your souls by this means, but you shall never make advantage this way. Without him 'ye can do nothing:' and yet ye will not come to him, because ye have done nothing. It is strange how little reason is in it, if your eyes were opened. You refuse or delay to abide in the vine till you bring forth fruit, and fruit ye cannot bring forth till you be in the vine. You would walk, and you will not have the life from which you must walk. Paul lived indeed, but what a life! 'The life that I live is by the faith of the Son of God.' Faith in Christ transported him out of himself to Christ, or received Christ into the soul, and Christ in the soul was the life of his soul, Gal. ii. 20. Your walking is as if a dead man would essay to go. Will one expect figs of thorns, or grapes of thistles? I beseech you, know what wrong ye do to yourselves, and to Christ. Ye wrong yourselves, because ye stand in the way of your own mercy, ye stand aback from your life,—him that is 'the way, the truth, and the life.' You would walk in the way, but no man can walk in this way, but by this way. Christ must quicken you to walk in himself. Ye must get life in him, and not bring it. You are in a vain expectation of fruits from yourselves,—they will never see the sun; and when you have wearied yourselves in such a vain pursuit, you must at length come and begin here. Ye wrong Christ's grace and mercy. This order is suited of purpose for our desperate condition, and yet ye presume to reject it, and seek another. You prescribe to your skilful and tender Physician, that which would undo you. I beseech you, know the original of your miseries, doubts, barrenness, and darkness. Here it is,—you are still puzzling yourselves about grace and duties, how to fill your eyes with these, and ye neglect Christ as your righteousness, as one dead and risen again, and now sitting at God's right hand for us. You must first close with him, as ungodly men. Though you were godly, you must shut your eyes on any such thing, and lay living Jesus upon your dead and benumbed hearts. Answer all your challenges with his absolution, and stand before God, in his clothing. Put his garment immediately on your nakedness and vileness, and we may persuade you it shall yield you abundant consolation and life. Because he lives, ye shall live, and walk. If you were more frequent and serious in the consideration of his excellent majesty, of his beautiful and lovely qualifications, as the Mediator for sinners, and of the precious promises which are all 'yea and amen,' confirmed in him, and less in the vain and unprofitable debates of self-interest, and such like, I am persuaded ye would be more fruitful Christians. This is not as the business of a holiday, to be done at your first coming to Christ, and no more. No, it must run alongst all your life. The aged experienced Christian must come along as an ungodly sinner, to a blessed and living Saviour, and have no other ground of glory or confidence before God, but Christ Jesus crucified.

Sermon VIII.

VERSE 2.—"*For the law of the Spirit of life in Christ Jesus hath made me free from the law of sin and death.*"

YOU know there are two principal things in the preceding verse,—the privilege of a Christian, and the property or character of a Christian. He is one that never enters into condemnation; He that believeth shall not perish, John iii. 15. And then he is one that walks not after the flesh, though he be in the flesh, but in a more elevate way above men, after the guiding and leading of the Holy Spirit of God. Now it may be objected in many consciences,—how can these things be? Have not all sinned, and come short of the glory of God, and so the whole world is become guilty before God? Is not every man lying under a sentence of death? 'Cursed is he that abides not in all things,' &c. How then can he escape condemnation? Again, you speak of walking after the Spirit, as proper to the Christian; but whose walk is not carnal? Who is he that doth not often step aside out of the way, and follow the conduct and counsel of flesh and blood? Is not sin dwelling here in our mortal bodies? Who can say, my heart or way is clean? Therefore both that privilege and this property of a Christian, seem to be but big words, no real thing. And indeed I confess the multitude of men hath no other opinion of them but as fancied imaginary things; few believe the report of the gospel concerning the salvation of elect ones, and few understand what this spiritual walking is. Many conceive it is not a thing that belongs to men, who are led about with passions and affections, but rather to angels or spirits perfected.

However, we have in these words an answer to satisfy both objections. He grants something implicitly, and it is this: It is true indeed, Christians are under a twofold law, captives and bondmen to these,—a law of sin in their members, bringing them in subjection to the lusts of the flesh. Sin hath a powerful dominion and tyranny over every man by nature. It hath a sort of right and power over him. And likewise, every one was under a law of death, the law of God cursing him, and sentencing him to condemnation because of sin. These two were joint conquerors of all mankind. But, saith he, there is a delivery from this bondage. Freedom is obtained to believers by Jesus Christ, and so 'there is no condemnation to them which are in Christ,' and so they walk not after the leading and direction of that law of sin within them, but after the guiding of our blessed Tutor,—the Spirit of God. If you ask how this comes to pass,—by what authority, or law, or power, is this releasement and freedom obtained? Here it is,—'by the law of the Spirit of life, which is in Christ.' Christ is not an invader, or unjust conqueror, he hath fair law for what he doth, even against those laws which detain unbelievers in bondage. There is a higher and later law on his side, and he hath power and strength to accomplish his design. He opposes law unto law, and life unto death, and spirit unto flesh; a law of spirit unto a law of sin and flesh; a law of life unto a law of death; —in a word, the gospel, or covenant of grace, unto the law or covenant of works. The powerful and living Spirit of grace that wrought mightily in him, is set fore-against the power of sin and Satan in us, and against us. The one gives him right and title to conquer, the other accomplisheth him for the work; and by these two are believers in Jesus Christ made freemen, who were bondmen. That, then, which we would speak from these words, is the common lot of all men by nature, viz. to be under the power of sin, and sentence of death; the special exemption of believers in Christ, and immunity from this, or delivery from it; and then the true ground and cause of this delivery from that bondage;—which three are contained in the words. It is a purpose indeed of a high natúre, and of high concernment to us all. Our life and death is wrapt up in this. You may hear many things more gladly, but if you knew it, none so profitable. Therefore let us gather our spirits to the consideration of these particulars.

As to the first, all men are under the bondage of a twofold law,—the law of sin within them, and the law of death without them. Man was created righteous; but, saith the wise man, he 'sought out many inventions.' A sad invention indeed! He found out misery and slavery to himself, who was made free and happy. His freedom and happiness was to be in subjection to his Maker, under the just and holy commands of his Lord, who had given him breath and being. It was no captivity or restraint to be compassed about with the hedges of the Lord's holy law, no more than it is a restraint on a man's liberty to have his way hedged in, where he may safely walk, that he may keep himself within it, from pits and snares on every hand. But, alas!—if we may say alas, when we have such a redemption in Jesus Christ, —Adam was not content with that happiness, but seeking after more liberty, he sold himself into the hands of strange lords,—first sin, and then death. 'Other lords besides thee, O Lord, have had dominion over us,' Isa. xxvi. 13. This is too true in this sense; Adam seeking to be as the Lord himself, lost his own lordship and dominion over all the works of God's hands, and became a servant to the basest and most abominable of all, even that which is most hateful to the Lord,—to sin and death. And this is the condition we are now born into. Consider it, I pray you,—we are born captives and slaves, the most noble, the most ingenuous, and the most free of us all. Paul speaks of it as a privilege to be born free; to be free in man's commonwealth. It is counted a dignity to be a free citizen or burgess of a town. Liberty is the great claim of people now-a-days; and indeed it is the great advantage of a people to enjoy that mother and womb privilege and right. But, alas! what is all this to be free-born in a civil society? It is but the state of a man among men. It reaches no further than the outward man, his life or estate. But here is a matter of greater moment,—know you what state your souls are in? Your souls are incomparably more worth than your bodies, as much as eternity surpasseth this inch of time, or immortality exceeds mortality. Your souls are yourselves, indeed; your bodies are but your house or tabernacle you lodge into for a season. Now then, I beseech you, ask whether you be born free or not. If your souls be slaves, you are slaves indeed; for so the evangelist changeth these. Matthew saith, in chap. xvi. 26, 'what hath a man gained, if 'he lose his own soul?' And Luke, chap. ix. 25, saith, what hath he gained, if he 'lose himself?' Therefore you are not free indeed except your souls be free. What is it, I pray you, to enjoy freedom among men? I ask you, what are you before God, whether bond or free? This is the business indeed. The Pharisees pleaded a claim to the liberty and privilege of being Abraham's sons and children, and thought they might hence conclude they were God's children. But our Lord Jesus discovers this mistake, when he tells them of a freedom and liberty that he came to proclaim to men, to purchase to them, and bestow on them. They stumbled at this doctrine. What, say they, talkest thou to us of making us free? We were never in bondage, because we be Abraham's children. This is even the language of our hearts, when we tell you, that ye are born heirs of wrath, and slaves of sin and Satan. Here is the secret whispering of hearts;—we be Abraham's seed; we were never in bondage to any. We be baptized Christians; we have a church state,—have the privileges, and liberties, not only of subjects in the state, but of members in the church; why sayest thou, we are bondmen? I would wish ye were all free indeed, but that cannot be till you know your bondage. Consider then, I beseech you, that you may be free subjects in a state, and free members in a church, and yet in bondage, under the law of sin and death. This was the mistake; that was a ground of presumption in the Jews, and occasioned their stumbling at this stone of salvation laid in Sion. You think you have church privileges, and what needs more? Be not deceived,—you are servants of sin, and therefore not free. There are two sorts or rather two ranks of persons in God's house,—sons and slaves. The son abides in the house for ever, the slave but for a time. When the time expires, he must go out, or be cast out. The church is God's house, but many are in it that will not dwell in it. Many have the outward liberties of this house, that have no interest in the special mercies and loving kindness proper to children. The time will come, that the most part of the visible church, who are baptized, and have eaten with him at his table, and had a kind of friendship to him here, shall be cast out as bondmen, and Isaac only shall be kept within, the child of the promise. The house that is here hath some inward sanctuary, and some outer porches. Many have access to these, that never enter within the secret of the Lord, and so shall not dwell in the house above. It is not so much the business, who shall enter into the holy hill, but who shall stand and dwell in it. The day of judgment will be a great day of excommunication. O how many thousands will be then cut off from the church of the living God, and delivered over to Satan, because they were really under his power, while they were church-members and Abraham's sons! Let me tell you then, that all of us were once in this state of bondage which Christ speaks of,—he that 'committeth sin is the servant of sin,' John viii. 34; 'and the servant abideth not in the house for ever.' So that I am afraid, many of us who are in the visible church, and stand in this congregation, shall not have liberty to stand in the assembly of the first-born, when all the sons are gathered in one to the new Jerusalem. Sin hath a right over us, and it hath a power over us, and therefore it is called a law of sin. There is a kind of authority that it hath over us, by virtue of God's justice, and our own voluntary consent. The Lord in his righteousness hath given over all the posterity of Adam, for his sin, which he sinned, as a common person, representing us,—he hath given us all over to the power of a body of death within us. Since man did choose to depart from his Lord, he hath justly delivered him into the hands of a strange lord to have dominion over him. The transmitting of such an original pollution, to all men, is an act of glorious justice. As he in justice gives men over to the lusts of their own hearts now, for following of these lusts contrary to his will; so was it, at first, 'by one man's disobedience many were made sinners,' and that, in God's holy righteousness, sin entered into the world, and had permission of God to subdue and conquer the world to itself, because man would not be subject to God. But as there is the justice of God in it, so there is a voluntary choice and election, which gives sin a power over us. We choose a strange lord, and he lords it over us. We say to our lusts, come ye and rule over us. We submit our reason, our conscience, and all, to the guidance and leading of our blind affections and passions. We choose our bondage for liberty. And thus sin hath a kind of law over us, by our own consent. It exerciseth a jurisdiction; and when once it is installed in power and clothed with it, it is not so easy again to put it out of that throne. There is a conspiring, so to speak, of these two, to make out the jurisdiction and authority of sin over us. God gives us over to iniquity and unrighteousness, and we yield ourselves over to it. Rom. vi. 16, 19, We yield our members servants to iniquity. A little pleasure or commodity is the bait that ensnares us to this. We give up ourselves, and join to our idols, and God ratifies it, in a manner, and passeth such a sentence,—Let them alone, he says, go ye every one and serve your idols, Hos. iv. 17. Since ye would not serve me, be doing,—go serve your lusts, look if they be better masters than I; look what wages they will give you.

Now, let us again consider what power sin hath, being thus clothed with a sort of authority. O but it is mighty, and works mightily in men! It reigns in our mortal bodies, Rom. vi. 12. Here is the throne of sin established in the lusts and affections of the body, and from hence it emits laws and statutes, and sends out commands to the soul and whole man. Man chose at first to hearken to the counsel of his senses, that said, it was pleasant and good to eat of the forbidden fruit; but that counsel is now turned into a command. Sin hath gotten a sceptre there, to rule over the spirit which was born a free prince. Sin hath conquered all our strength, or we have given up unto it all our strength. Any truth that is in the conscience; any knowledge of God, or religion, all this is incarcerated, detained in a prison of unrighteous affections. Sin hath many strongholds and bulwarks in our flesh, and by these commands the whole spirit and soul in man, and leads captive every thought to the obedience of the flesh. You know how strong it was in holy Paul, Rom. vii.; what a mighty battle and wrestling he had, and how near he was to fainting and giving over. How then must it have an absolute and sovereign full dominion over men in nature! There being no contrary principle within, by nature, to debate with it, it rules without much controlment. There may be many convictions of conscience, and sparkles of light against sin, but these are quickly extinguished and buried. Nay, all these principles of light and knowledge in the conscience, do oftentimes strengthen sin, as some things are confirmed, not weakened, by opposition. Unequal and faint opposition strengthens the adversary, as cold, compassing springs, makes them hotter. So it is here. Sin takes occasion, by the command, to work 'all manner of concupiscence,' Rom. vii. 8. Without the law, sin is in a manner dead; but when any adversary appears, when our lusts and humours are crossed, then they unite their strength against any such opposition, and bring forth more sinful sin. The knowledge and conscience that many have, serve nothing but to make their sins greater; to exasperate and imbitter their spirits and lusts against God. 'Why tormentest thou me before the time?' It is a devilish disposition that is in us all,—we cannot endure the light, because our deeds are evil.

Let us but consider these particulars, and we shall know the power and dominion of sin. 1st, Consider the extent of its dominion, both in regard of all men, and all in every man. I say, all men,—there is none of us exempted from it; the most noble, and the most base. Sin is the catholic king, the universal king, or rather Satan, who is the prince of this world, and he rules the world, by this law of sin, which is even the contradiction of the law of God. Who of you believes this, that Satan's kingdom is so spacious,—that it is even over the most part of the visible church? This is the emperor of the world. The Turk vainly arrogates this title to himself, but the devil is truly so, and we have God's own testimony for it. All kings, all nobles, all princes, all people, rich and poor, high and low, are once subjects of this prince, ruled by this black law of sin. O know your condition, whose servants ye are! Think not within yourselves, 'we have Abraham for our father,'—we are baptized Christians. No, know that all of us are once the children of Satan, and do his works, and fulfil his will. But moreover, all that is in us is subject to this law of sin,—all the faculties of the soul. The understanding is under the power of darkness, the affections under the power of corruption, the mind is blinded, and the heart is hardened, the soul alienated from God, who is its life; all the members and powers of a man yielded up as instruments of unrighteousness, every one to execute that wicked law, and fulfil the lusts of the flesh. This dominion is over all a man's actions, even those that are in best account and esteem among men. Your honest, upright dealing with men, your most religious performances to God, they are more conformed to the law of sin, than to the law of God,—Hag. ii. 14. 'This nation, and the work of their hands, and that which they offer, is unclean.' All your works, your good works, are infected with this pollution. Sin hath defiled your persons, and they defile all your actions,—the infection is mutual. These actions again defile your persons still more: To the impure all things are impure, 'even their mind and conscience is defiled,' Tit. i. 15. Do what ye can, ye who are in nature cannot please God; it is but obedience to the law of sin that is in you.

But 2d, Consider the intenseness and force of his power, how mighty it is in working against all oppositions whatsoever, unless it be overcome by almighty power. Nothing but All-might can conquer this power. The spirit that works in men by nature, is of such activity and efficacy, that it drives men on furiously, as if they were possessed to their own ruin. How much hath it of a man's consent! And so it drives him strongly and irresistibly. Much will, desire, and greediness, will make corruption run like a river, over all its banks set in the way thereof,—counsel, persuasion, law, heaven, hell, yet men's corruption must be over all these. Preaching, threatenings, convictions of conscience, are but as flaxen ropes to bind a Samson. Sin within easily breaks them. In a word, no created power is of sufficient virtue to bind the strong man; it must be one mightier than he, and that is the Spirit of Jesus Christ. Do ye not see men daily drawn after their lusts, as beasts, following their senses as violently as a horse rusheth to the battle! If there be any gain or advantage to oil the wheels of affection, O how men run headlong! There is no crying will hold them. In sum, sin is become all one with us; it is incorporate into the man, and become one with his affections, and then these command.

Sermon VIII.

VERSE 2.—"*For the law of the Spirit of life in Christ Jesus hath made me free from the law of sin and death.*"

THAT whereabout the thoughts and discourses of men now run, is freedom and liberty, or bondage and slavery. All men are afraid to lose their liberties, and be made servants to strangers. And indeed liberty, whether national or personal, even in civil respects, is a great mercy and privilege. But alas! men know not, neither do they consider, what is the ground and reason of such changes, and from what fountain it flows, that a nation for a long time free from a foreign yoke, should now be made to submit their necks unto it. Many wonder that our nation, unconquered in the days of ignorance and darkness, should now be conquered in the days of the gospel; and there want not many ungodly spirits, that will rather impute the fault unto the reformation of religion, than take it to themselves. There are many secret heart jealousies among us, that Christ is a hard master, and cannot be served. But would you know the true original of our apparent and threatened bondage? Come and see; come and consider something expressed in these words. All your thoughts are busied about civil liberty; but you do not consider that you are in bondage while you are free, and that to worse masters than you fear. We are under a law of sin and death, that hath the dominion and sway in all men's affections and conversations; and when the glorious liberty of the sons of God is offered unto us in the gospel, when the Son hath come to make us free, we love our own chains, and will not suffer them to be loosed. Therefore it is that a nation that hath despised such a gracious offer of peace and freedom in Jesus Christ, is robbed and spoiled of peace and freedom. When this law of the Spirit of life in Christ is published, and proclaimed openly unto congregations, unto judicatories, and unto persons, yet few do regard it. The generality are in bondage to a contrary law of sin, and this they serve in the lusts thereof. Yea, —which most of all aggravates and heightens the offence,—even after we have all of us professed a subjection to the law of God, and to Jesus Christ, the King and Lawgiver, we are in an extraordinary way engaged to the Lord, by many oaths and covenants, to be his people; we did consent that he should be our King, and that we should be ruled in our profession and practice by his word and will, as the fundamental laws of this his kingdom; we did solemnly renounce all strange lords, that had tyrannized over us; and did swear against them, never to yield willing obedience unto them; namely, the lusts of the world, ignorance of God, unbelief, and disobedience. Now what became of all this work, you may know. The generality of all ranks have rebelled against that Lord and Prince, and withdrawn from his allegiance, and revolted unto the same lusts and ways—these same courses against which we had, both by our profession of Christianity and solemn oaths, engaged ourselves. And so men have voluntarily and heartily subjected themselves unto the laws of sin, and desires of the flesh. Hence is the beginning of our ruin. Because we would not serve our own God and Lord in our own land, therefore are so many led away captive * to serve strangers in another land, therefore we are like to be captives in our own land. Because we refused homage to our God, and obeyed strange lords within, therefore are we given up to the lust of strangers without.

I would have you thinking, and that seriously, that there are worse masters you serve than those you most hate, and that there is a worse bondage, whereof you are insensible, than that you fear most. You fear strangers, but your greatest evil is within you. You might retire within, and behold worse masters, and more pernicious and mortal enemies to your well-being. This is the case of all men by nature, and of all men as far as in nature; sin ruling, commanding in them, and lording it over them, and they willingly following after the commandment, and so oppressed and broken in judgment. If you could but rightly look upon other men, you might see, that they who are servants of divers lusts, are not their own men, so to speak; they have not the command of themselves. Look upon a man given to drunkenness, and what a slave is he! Whither doth not his lust drive him? Let him bind himself with resolutions, with vows, yet ye cannot be holden by them. Shame before men, loss of estate, decay of health, temporal punishment, nay, eternal, all set together, cannot keep him from fulfilling the desires of that lust, when he hath opportunity. A man given to covetousness, how doth he serve that idol! How doth he forget himself to be a man!—or to have a reasonable soul within him, he is so devoted to it! And thus it is with every man by nature. There may be many petty little gods that he worships upon occasion, but every unrenewed man hath some one thing predominant in him, unto which he hath sworn obedience and devotion. The man most civilized, most abstracted from the grosser outward pollutions,—yet certainly, his heart within is but a temple full of idols, to the love and service of which he is devoted. There are some of the fundamental laws of Satan's

* [Cromwell, in his despatches, after the battle of Dunbar, states the number of his prisoners, exclusive of officers, to be near 10,000.—*Cromwelliana*, p. 90. "The same daye the minister declaired y[t] y[r] wes a petitioune come from the prisoners at Tinmouth quho wer taiken at Dunbar, and representit to the presbyterie for support, because they wer in ane sterving conditione, and all comanders. And y[t] ye presbyterie hes recomendit the samen to ye several kirks of ye presbyterie, Therfoir ordaines that ane collectione be yranent upon Soudaye come 8 deyes, and intimation to be maid of it the next sabbathe to ye effect ye people may provide some considerable thing yranent." Records of the kirk session of Govan, 1st July, 1652. "Upon the desire of the Guinea Merchants (20th Sept., 1651,) 1,500 of the Scots prisoners were granted to them, and sent on shipboard to be transported to Guinea to work in the mines there."—Whitelock's Mem. p. 485. "Letters (25th October., 1651,) that many of the Scots prisoners and others at Shrewsbury were dead of a contagious fever."—Id. p. 488.—Ed.]

kingdom, that rule in every natural man,—either the lust of the eyes, or the lust of the flesh, or the pride of life. Every man sacrificeth to one of these his credit and honour, or his pleasure, or his profit. Self, whatever way refined and subtilized in some, yet at best it is but an enemy to God; and without that sphere of self cannot a man act upon natural principles, till a higher Spirit come in, which is here spoken of.

Oh! that you would take this for bondage, to be under this woful necessity of satisfying and fulfilling the desires of your flesh and mind, Eph. ii. 2. Many account it only liberty and freedom, therefore they look upon the laws of the Spirit of life as cords and bonds, and consult to cast them off, and cut them asunder. But consider what a wretched life you have with your imperious lusts. The truth is, sin is for the most part its own punishment. I am sure you have more labour and toil in fulfilling the lusts of sin, than you might have in serving God. Men's lusts are never at quiet, they are continually putting you on service, they are still driving and dragging men headlong, hurrying them to and fro, and they cannot get rest. What is the cause of all the disquiet, disorder, confusion, trouble, and wars in the world? From whence do contentions arise? 'Come they not hence,' saith James, iv. 1, 'even of your lusts that war in your members?' It is these that trouble the world, and these are the troublers of Israel's peace. These take away inward peace, domestic peace, and national peace. These lusts, covetousness, ambition, pride, passion, self-love, and such like, do set nation against nation, men and men, people and people, by the ears. These multiply businesses beyond necessity; these multiply cares without profit, and so bring forth vexation and torment. If a man had his lusts subdued, and his affections composed unto moderation and sobriety, O what a multitude of noisome and hurtful cares should he then be freed from! What a sweet calmness should possess that spirit! Will you be persuaded of it, beloved in the Lord, that it were easier to serve the Lord than to serve your lusts,—that they cost you more labour, disquiet, perplexity, and sorrow, than the Lord's service will; that so you may weary of such masters, and groan to be from under such a law of sin.

But if that will not suffice to persuade you, then consider, in the next room, if you will needs serve a law of sin, you must needs be subject to a law of death. If you will not be persuaded to quit the service of sin, then tell me, what think you of your wages? 'The wages of sin is death,'—that you may certainly expect; and can you look and long for such wages? God hath joined these together by a perpetual ordinance. They came into the world together,—'sin entered, and death by sin;' and they have gone hand in hand together since. And think you to dissolve what God hath joined? Before you go farther, and obey sin more, think, I pray you, what it can give you,—what doth it give you for the present, but much pain, and toil, and vexation, instead of promised pleasure and satisfaction? Sin doth with all men, as the devil doth with some of his sworn vassals and servants. They have a poor wretched life with him. They are wearied and troubled, to satisfy all his unreasonable and imperious commands. He loads them with base service, and they are still kept in expectation of some great reward; but for the present, they have nothing but misery and trouble. And at length he becomes the executioner, and perpetual tormentor of them whom he made to serve him. Such a master is sin, and such wages you may expect. Consider then, what your expectation is, before you go on, or engage further,—death. We are under a law of bodily death, therefore we are mortal. Our house is like a ruinous lodge, that drops through, and one day or other it must fall. Sin hath brought in the seeds of corruption into men's nature, which dissolve it, else it had been immortal. But there is a worse death after this, a living death, in respect of which simple death would be chosen rather. Men will rather live very miserably than die. Nature hath an aversion to it,—'skin for skin, and all for life will a man give.' Death imports a destruction of being, which every thing naturally seeks to preserve. But O what a dreadful life is it, worse than death, when men will choose death rather than life! O how terrible will it be to hear that word, 'Hills and mountains, fall on us, and cover us!' Men newly risen, their bodies and souls meet again after a long separation, and this to be their mutual entertainment one to another,—the body to wish it were still in the dust, and the soul to desire it might never be in the body! Surely if we had so much grace as to believe this, and tremble at it, before we be forced to act it, there were some hope. If we could persuade ourselves once of this, that the ways of sin, all of them, how pleasant, how profitable soever, whatsoever gain they bring in, whatsoever satisfaction they give, that they are nothing else but 'the ways of death,' and go down to the chambers of hell; that they will delude and deceive us, and so in end destroy us;—if we might once believe this with our heart, there were some hope that we would break off from them, and choose the untrodden paths of godliness, which are pleasantness and peace. However, this is the condition of all men, once to be under sin, and under a sentence of death for sin. It is the unbelief of this, and a conceit of freedom, that securely and certainly destroys the world, by keeping souls from Jesus Christ, the Prince of Life.

But there is a delivery, and that is the thing expressed in the words. There is freedom from both attainable. And I think, the very hearing of such a thing, that there is a redemption from sin and misery possible, yea, and that some are actually delivered from it; this might stir up in our hearts some holy ambition, and earnest desire after such a state. How might it awaken our hearts after it! But this is the wofulness of a natural condition, that a soul under the power of sin can neither help itself nor rightly desire help from another, because the will is captive too. This makes it a very desperate and remediless business to any human expectation, because such a soul is well-pleased with its own fetters, and loves its own prison, and so can neither long for freedom, nor welcome the Son who is come to make free. But yet, there is a freedom and delivery; and if ye ask who are partakers of it, the text declares it to you,—even those who are in Jesus Christ, and walk according to the Spirit of Christ. All those, and those only, who, finding themselves 'dead in trespasses and sins,' under the power and dominion of sin, and likewise under the sentence of death and condemnation, begin to lift up their heads upon the hope of a Saviour, and to look unto their Redeemer as poor prisoners, whose eyes and looks are strong entreaties, and instead of many requests;—such as give an entire renounce unto their former ways and prevailing lusts, and give up themselves, in testimony of their sense of his unspeakable favour of redemption, to be wholly his, and not their own. There are some souls who are free from the dominion of sin, and from the danger of death, some who were once led about with divers lusts, as well as others, who walked after the course of this world, and fulfilled the desires of the flesh, and were children of wrath, as well as others; but now they are quickened in Christ Jesus, and have abandoned their former way. They have another rule, another way, other principles. Their study is now to please God, and grow in holiness. The ways they delighted in, in former times, are now loathsome. They think that a filthy puddle, which they drank greedily of; and now it is all, or their chiefest grief and burden, that so much of that old man must be carried about with them,—and so this expresseth many groans from them with Paul, "Woe is me, miserable man! who shall deliver me?" Such souls are, in a manner, so to speak, half redeemed, who being made sensible of their bondage, groan and pant for a Redeemer. The day of their complete redemption is at hand. All of you are witnesses of this, that there are some thus freed, but they are signs and wonders indeed to the world. Their kinsmen, their acquaintance, their friends and neighbours, wonder what is become of them. They think it strange they walk not, and run not into that same excess of riot with them. But whosoever thou art, that art escaped from under the slavery of sin, wonder at the world, that doth run so madly on their own destruction. Think it strange, that thou didst run so long with them, and that all will not run in these pleasant ways with thee. Think it strange that thou runnest so slowly, when so great a prize is to be obtained,—an immortal and never-fading crown. If mortifying and crucifying the lusts of the flesh, if dying to the world, and to thyself, seem very hard and unpleasant to thee, if it be as the plucking out of thine eye, and cutting off thine hand; know then, that corruption is much alive yet, and hath much power in thee. But remember, that if thou canst have but so much grace and resolution, as to kill and crucify these lusts, without foolish and hurtful pity,—if thou canst attain that victory over thyself, thou shalt never be a loser. Thou canst not repent it afterward. To die to ourselves and the world, to kill sin within—O that makes way to a life hid from the world, one hour whereof is better than many ages in sinful pleasure! Quicken thyself often with this thought, that there is a true life after such a ath, and that thou canst not pass into it, but by the valley of the death of thy lusts. Remember, that thou dost but kill thine enemies, which embrace that they may strangle thee; and then stir up yourself with this consideration,—the life of sin will be thy death. Better enter heaven without these lusts, than go to hell with them.

Sermon II.

VERSE 2.—"*For the law of the Spirit of life in Christ Jesus hath made me free from the law of sin and death.*"

THAT which makes the delivery of men from the tyranny of sin and death most difficult, and utterly impossible unto nature, is, that sinners have given up themselves unto it, as if it were true liberty, that the will and affections of men are conquered, and sin hath its imperial throne seated there. Other conquerors invade men against their will, and so they rule against their will. They retain men in subjection by fear and not by love. And so whenever any occasion offers, they are glad to cast off the yoke of unwilling obedience. But sin hath first conquered men's judgment, by blinding it,—putting out the eye of the understanding, and then invaded the affections of men, drawn them over to its side; and by these, it keeps all in a most willing obedience. Now, what hopes are there then of delivery, when the prisoner accounts his bondage liberty, and his prison a palace? What expectation of freedom, when all that is within us conspires to the upholding that tyrannous dominion of sin, against all that would cast off its usurpation, as if they were mortal enemies?

Yet there is a delivery possible, but such as would not have entered into the heart of man to imagine; and it is here expressed,—'the law of the Spirit of life,' &c. This declares how, and by what means, we may be made free. Not indeed by any power within us, not by any created power without us. Sin is stronger than all these, because its imperial seat is within, far without the reach of all created power. There may be some means used by men, to beat it out of the outworks of the outward man, to chase it out of the external members; some means to restrain it from such gross out-breakings; but there is none can lay siege to the soul within, or storm the understanding and will, where it hath its principal residence. It is inaccessible, and impregnable by any human power. No entreaties or persuasions, no terrors or threatenings, can prevail; it can neither be stormed by violence, nor undermined by skill, because it is within the spirit of the mind; until at length some other spirit stronger than our spirit come; till the Spirit of life which is in Christ, come and bind the strong man, and so make the poor soul free. You heard that we were under a law of death, and under the power of sin. Now there is another law, answering this law, and a power to overcome this power. You may indeed ask, by what law or authority can a sinner that is bound over, by God's justice, unto death and condemnation, be released? Is there any law above God's law, and the sentence of his justice? The apostle answers, that there is a law above it, a law after it, —'the law of the Spirit of life.' Jesus Christ opposes law unto law, the law of life unto the law of death; the gospel unto the law, the second covenant unto the first. Thus it is then, Jesus Christ, the eternal Son of God, full of grace and truth, did come in man's stead, when the law and sentence of death was passed upon all mankind, and there was no expectation, from the terms of the first covenant, that there should be any dispensation or mitigation of the rigour of it. He obtains this, that so many as God had chosen unto life, their sins and their punishment might be laid on him. And so he took part of our flesh, for this end, that he might be made a curse for us, and so redeem us from the curse. Thus, having satisfied justice, and fulfilled the sentence of death, by suffering death,—'Him hath God exalted to be a Prince and a Saviour,' and the head of all things. In compensation of this great and weighty work given him by his Father, all judgment is committed to him, and so he sends out and proclaims another law in Zion; another sentence, even of life and absolution, unto all, and upon all them that shall believe in his name. Thus you see the law of death abrogated by a new law of life, because our Lord and Saviour was made under the law of death, and suffered under it, and satisfied it, that all his seed might be freed from it, and might come under a life-giving law. So that it appears to be true, that was said at first, 'there is no condemnation to them that are in Christ,'—there is no law, no justice against them.

But then another difficulty as great as the former is in the way. Though such a law and sentence of life and absolution be pronounced in the gospel, in Christ's name, yet we are dead in sins and trespasses. We neither know nor feel our misery, nor can we come to a Redeemer. As there was a law of death above our head, so there is a law of sin within our hearts, which rules and commands us; and there is neither will nor ability to escape from under it. It is true, life and freedom is preached in Christ, to all that come to him for life. To all that renounce sin's dominion is remission of sin preached. But here is the greatest difficulty,—how can a dead soul stir, rise, and walk,—how can a slave to sin, and a willing captive, renounce it, when he hath neither to will nor to do? Indeed, if all had been purchased for us, if eternal life and forgiveness of sins had been brought near us, and all the business done to our consent, and that only wanting; if these had been the terms, I have purchased life, now rise and embrace it of yourselves, truly it had been an unsuccessful business. Christ had lost all that was given him, if the moment and weight of our salvation had been hung upon our acceptation. Therefore, it is well provided for this also, that there should be a power to overcome this power, a spirit of life in Christ to quicken dead sinners, and raise them up, and draw them to him. And so, the second Adam hath this prerogative beyond the first, that he is not only a living soul in himself, but a quickening Spirit to all that are given him of the Father, 1 Cor. xv. 45. So then, as Christ Jesus hath law and right on his side, to free us from death, so he hath virtue and power in him to accomplish our delivery from sin. As he hath fair law to loose the chains of condemnation, and to repeal the sentence passed against us, without prejudice to God's justice, he having fully satisfied the same in our name, so he hath sufficient power given him to loose the fetters of sin from off us. When he hath paid the price, and satisfied the Father, so that justice can crave nothing, yet he hath one adversary to deal with. Satan hath sinners bound with the cords of their own lusts, in a prison of darkness and unbelief. Jesus Christ therefore comes out to conquer this enemy, and to redeem his elect ones from that unjust usurpation of sin,—to bring them out of the prison by the strong hand. And therefore, he is one mighty and able to save to the uttermost; he hath might to do it, as well as right to it.

Consider, then, my beloved, these two things, which are the breasts of our consolation, and the foundation of our hope. We are once lost and utterly undone, both in regard of God's justice, and our own utter inability to help ourselves, which is strengthened by our unwillingness, and thus made a more desperate business. Now, God hath provided a suitable remedy; he hath 'laid help on one that is mighty,' indeed, who hath almighty power; and by his power he first conflicted with the punishment of our sins, and with his Father's wrath, and hath overcome, discharged, and satisfied that, and so hath purchased a right unto us, to give salvation to whom he will. He conquered, and by his power obtained this supreme authority of life and death.

Now, having this authority established in his person, the next work is to apply this purchase,—actually to confer this life. And therefore he hath almighty power to raise up dead sinners; to create us again to good works; to redeem us from the tyranny of sin and Satan, whose slaves we are. He hath a Spirit of life, which he communicates to his seed; he breathes it into those souls that he died for, and dispossesseth that powerful corruption that dwells in us. Hence it comes to pass, that they walk after the Spirit, though they be in the flesh; because the powerful Spirit of Christ hath entered, and taken possession of their spirits, Isa. lix. 20, 21.

Let us not be discouraged in our apprehensions of Christ. When we look on our ruinous and desperate estate, let us not conclude, it is past hope, and past his help too. We do proclaim, in the name of Jesus Christ, that there is no sinner, howsoever justly under a sentence of death and damnation, but they may in him find a relaxation from that sentence, and that without the impairing of God's justice. And this is a marvellous ground of comfort, that may establish our souls, (1 John i. 9;) even this, that law and justice is upon Christ's side, and nothing to accuse or plead against a sinner that employs him for his advocate. But know this also, that you are not delivered from death that you may live under sin; nay, you are redeemed from death, that you may be freed from the law of sin. But that must be done by his almighty Spirit, and cannot be otherwise done.

I know not whether of these is matter of greatest comfort,—that there is in Christ a redemption from the wrath of God and from hell; and that there is a redemption too, from sin, and corruption which dwells within us. But sure I am, both of them will be most sweet and comfortable to a believer; and without both, Christ were not a complete Redeemer, nor we completely redeemed. Neither would a believing soul, in which there is any measure of this new law and divine life, be satisfied without both these. Many are miserably deluded in their apprehensions of the gospel. They take it up thus, as if it were nothing but a proclamation of freedom from misery, from death and damnation; and so the most part catch at nothing else in it, and from thence take liberty to walk after their former lusts and courses. This is the woful practical use that the generality of hearers make of the free intimation of pardon, and forgiveness of sin, and delivery from wrath. They admit some general notion of that, and stop there, and examine not what further is in the gospel; and so you will see the slaves of sin professing a kind of hope of freedom from death,—the servants and vassals of corruption, who walk after the course of this world, and fulfil the lusts and desires of their mind and flesh, yet fancying a freedom and immunity from condemnation,—men living in sin, yet thinking of escaping wrath,—which dreams could not be entertained in men, if they did drink in all the truth, and open both their ears to the gospel; if our spirits were not narrow and limited, and so excluded the one half of the gospel, that is, our redemption from sin. There is too much of this, even among the children of God,—a strange narrowness of spirit, which admits not whole and entire truth. It falls out often, that when we think of delivery from death and wrath, we forget in the mean time the end and purpose of that, which is, that we may be freed from sin, and serve the living God without fear. And if at any time we consider, and busy our thoughts about freedom from the law of sin, and victory over corruption, such is the scantiness of room and capacity in our spirits, that we lose the remembrance of delivery from death and condemnation in Christ Jesus. Thus we are tossed between two extremes,—the quicksands of presumption and wantonness, and the rocks of unbelief and despair or discouragement, both of which do kill the Christian's life, and make all to fade and wither. But this were the way, and only way, to preserve the soul in good ease,—even to keep these two continually in our sight, that we are redeemed from death and misery in Christ, and that not to serve ourselves, or to continue in our sins, but that we may be redeemed from that sin that dwells in us, and that both these are purchased by Jesus Christ, and done by his power,—the one in his own person, the other by his Spirit within us. I would have you correcting your misapprehensions of the gospel. Do not so much look on victory and freedom from sin as a duty and task, though we be infinitely bound to it; but rather as a privilege and dignity conferred upon us by Christ. Look not upon it, I say, only as your duty, as many do; and by this means are discouraged from the sight of their own infirmity and weakness, as being too weak for such a strong party; but look upon it as the one half, and the greater half, of the benefit conferred by Christ's death,—as the greater half of the redemption which the Redeemer, by his office, is bound to accomplish. He will redeem Israel from all his iniquities; 'with him is plenteous redemption,' Psal. cxxx. 7, 8. This is the plenty, this is the sufficiency of it,—that he redeems not only from misery, but from iniquity, and that all iniquities. I would not desire a believer's soul to be in a better posture here away,* than this,—to be looking upon sin indwelling as his bondage, and redemption from it as freedom; to account himself in so far free, as the free Spirit of Christ enters and writes that free law of love and obedience in his heart, and blots out these base characters of the law of sin. It were a good temper to be groaning for the redemption of the

* [That is, in this world.—Ed.]

of the soul; and why doth a believer groan for the redemption of the body, but because he shall then be freed wholly from the law of sin, and from the presence of sin? I know not a greater argument to a gracious heart, to subdue his corruption, and strive for freedom from the law of sin, than the freedom obtained from the law of death. Nor is there any clearer argument and evidence of a soul delivered from death, than to strive for the freedom of the spirit from the law of sin. These jointly help one another. Freedom from death will raise up a Christian's heart to aspire to a freedom and liberty from sin; and again, freedom from sin will witness and evidence that such an one is delivered from death. When freedom from death is an inducement to seek after freedom from sin, and freedom from sin a declaration of freedom from death, then all is well; and indeed thus it will be in some measure with every soul that is quickened by this new law of the Spirit of life, for it is the entry of this that expels its contrary, the law of sin. And indeed the law must enter; the command and the promise must enter into the soul, and the affections of the soul be enlivened thereby, or rather the soul changed into the similitude of that mould, or else the having of it in a book, or in one's memory and understanding, will never make him the richer or freer. A Christian looks to the pattern of the law, and the word of the gospel without; but he must be changed into the image of it, by beholding it; and so he becomes a living law to himself. The Spirit writes these precepts and practices of Christ's, in which he commands imitation, upon the fleshly tables of the heart. And now the law is not a rod above his head, as above a slave; but it is turned into a law of love within his heart, and hath something like a natural instinct in it. All that men can do, either to themselves or others, will not purchase the least measure of freedom from predominant corruptions; cannot deliver you from your sins, till this free Spirit that blows where he pleases, come. It is our part to hoise up sails, and wait for the wind; to use means, and wait on him in his way and order. But all will be in vain, till this stronger one come and cast out the strong man; till this arbitrary and free wind blow from heaven, and fill the sails.

Sermon X.

VERSE 3.—"*For what the law could not do, in that it was weak through the flesh, God sending his own Son in the likeness of sinful flesh, and for sin condemned sin in the flesh.*"

THE greatest design that ever God had in the world, is certainly the sending of his own Son into the world. And it must needs be some great business, that drew so excellent and glorious a person out of heaven. The plot and contrivance of the world was a profound piece of wisdom and goodness; the making of men after God's image was done by a high and glorious counsel: 'Let us make man after our image.' There was something special in this expression, importing some peculiar excellency in the work itself, or some special depth of design about it. But what think you of this consultation,—let one of us be made man, after man's image and likeness. That must be a strange piece of wisdom and grace: 'Great is the mystery of godliness, God manifested in the flesh.' No wonder though Paul cried out, as one swallowed up with this mystery; for indeed it must be some odd matter, beyond all that is in the creation, wherein there are many mysteries, able to swallow up any understanding, but that in which they were first formed. This must be the chief of the works of God, the rarest piece of them all,—God to become man, the Creator of all to come in the likeness of a creature,—he by whom all things were created, and do yet consist, to come in the likeness of the most wretched of all. Strange, that we do not dwell more, in our thoughts and affections, on this subject. Either we do not believe it, or if we did, we could not but be ravished with admiration at it. John, the beloved disciple, who was often nearest unto Christ, dwelt most upon this, and made it the subject of his preaching; 'that which was from the beginning, which we have heard, and seen, and handled,' &c. 1 John i. 1. He speaks of that mystery, as if he were embracing Jesus Christ in his arms, and holding him out to others, saying, 'Come and see.' This divine mystery is the subject of those words read, but the mystery is somewhat unfolded and opened up to you in them, yet so as it will not diminish, but increase the wonder of a believing soul. It is ignorance that magnifies other mysteries, which vilifies thorough knowledge; but it is the true knowledge of this mystery that makes it the more wonderful, whereas ignorance only makes it common and despicable.

There are three things then, of special consideration in the words, which may declare and open unto you something of this mystery:

First, What was the ground and reason, or occasion of the Son's sending into the world; next, What the Son, being sent, did in the world; and the third, For what end and use it was,—what fruit we have by it.

The ground and reason of God sending his Son, is, because there was an impossibility in the law to save man, which impossibility was not the law's fault, but man's defect, by reason of the weakness and impotency of our flesh to fulfil the law. Now, God having chosen some to life, and man having put this obstruction and impediment in his own way, which made it impossible for the law to give him life, though it was first given out as the way of life; therefore, that God should not fail in this glorious design of saving his chosen, he chose to send his own Son, in the likeness of flesh, as the only remedy of the law's impossibility. That which Christ, being sent into the likeness of flesh, did, is the condemning of sin in the flesh, by a sacrifice offered for sin,—even the sacrifice of his own body upon the cross. He came in the likeness, not of the flesh simply, for he was really a man; but in the likeness of sinful flesh,—though without sin, yet like a sinner,—as to the outward appearance, a sinner, because subject to all those infirmities and miseries which sin did first open a door for. Sin was the inlet of afflictions, of bodily infirmities and necessities, of death itself; and when the floods of these did overflow Christ's human nature, it was a great presumption to the world, who look and judge according to the outward appearance, that sin was the sluice opened to let in such an inundation of calamity. Now, he being thus in the likeness of a sinner, though not a sinner,—he, for sin, that is, because of sin, that had entered upon man, and made life impossible to him by the law; by occasion of that great enemy of God which had conquered mankind, he condemned sin in his flesh, he overthrew it in its plea and power against us. He condemned that which condemned us, overcame it in judgment, and made us free. By sustaining the curse of it in his flesh, he cut off all its plea against us. This is the great work and business, which was worthy of so noble a messenger, his own Son, sent to conquer his greatest enemy that he hates most. And then, in the third place, you see what benefit or fruit redounds to us by it: what was the end and purpose of it;—verse 4, 'that the righteousness of the law might be fulfilled in us:' that seeing it was impossible for us to fulfil the righteousness of the law, and that so it became impossible to the law to fulfil our reward of life, it might be fulfilled by him in our name; and so the righteousness of the law being fulfilled in us by Christ, the reward also of eternal life might be fulfilled by the law to us,—he having removed the impediment of our weakness, it might be not only possible, but certain to us.

You would consider then, the reason of Christ's coming. God made at first a covenant with man, promising him life upon perfect obedience to his law; and threatening death and damnation upon the transgression thereof. You see then, what was the way of life to Adam in the state of innocency. He was made able to satisfy the law with obedience, and the law was abundantly able to satisfy him, by giving life unto him. God's image upon man's soul instructed him sufficiently for the one, and the Lord's promise made to him, was as sufficient to accomplish the other; so that there was no impossibility then in the law, by reason of the strength which God gave man. But it continued not long so. Sin entering upon man, utterly disabled him; and because the strength of that covenant consisted in that mutual and joint concurrence of God's promise and man's obedience—this being broken, (the one party falling off,) that life and salvation becomes impossible to the promise alone to perform. It is sin that is the weakness and impotency of man. This is the disease which hath consumed his strength, and concluded man under a twofold impossibility; an impossibility to satisfy the curse, and an impossibility to obey the command. There are three things in the covenant of works,—a command of obedience, and a threatening of wrath and condemnation upon disobedience, and a promise of life upon obedience. Sin hath disabled us every way. In relation to the curse and threatening, man cannot satisfy it—no price, no ransom being found sufficient for the soul, for the redemption of it is precious, and ceaseth for ever. That curse hath infinite wrath in it, which must needs swallow up finite man. And then in relation to the command, there is such a diminution of all the powers of the soul, such a corruption and defilement, by reason of the first sin, that that wherein man's strength lay, which was God's image, is cut off and spoiled; so that henceforth it is become impossible to yield any acceptable obedience to the commandment. And hence it is, from our impossibility to obey in time to come, that there is a holy and faultless impossibility upon the promise, to give life unto mankind. So you see that the law cannot do it, because of our weakness. If either man, while he was made upright, had continued in obedience, or man now fallen from uprightness, could satisfy for the fault done, and walk without any blemish in time coming, then it were feasible for the law to give life to us. But the one was not done, and the other now cannot be done; and so the impossibility of life by works, is refounded upon ourselves, who would not when we could, and now neither will nor can obey. Thus we may see clearly, that all mankind must needs perish, for any thing that man can do, and according to that first transaction of God with man, unless some other way and device be found out, which indeed was far from the eyes of all living,—without the reach of their invention or imagination. I believe if all the creatures, higher or lower, that have any reason, had convened to consult of this business, how to repair that breach made in the creation by man's sin, they might have vexed their brains, and racked their inventions unto all eternity, and yet never have fallen upon any probable way of making up this breach. They might have taken up a lamentation, not as the bemoaners of Babylon's ruin,—'we would have healed thee, and thou wouldst not;'—but rather thus,—we would heal thee, but we could not, and thou wouldst not. This design, which is here mentioned of repairing the breach, by destroying that which made it, sin, lay hid in the depth of God's wisdom, till it pleased himself to vent and publish it unto poor, forlorn, and desperate man, who, out of despair of recovery, had run away to hide himself. A poor shift indeed, for him to think that he could hide himself from him to whom darkness is as light, and to flee from him whose kingdom is over all, and who is present in all the corners of his universal kingdom,—in hell, in heaven, in the utmost corners of the earth. But this silly invention shows how hopeless the case was.

Though this be the case and condition of man by nature, yet strange it is, to see every man by nature attempting his own delivery; and fancying a probability, yea, a certainty of that which is so impossible, that is, an attaining of life by ourselves, according to the law and first covenant of works. Though our strength be gone, yet, like Samson, men rise up and think to walk and rouse up themselves as in former times, as if their strength were yet in them, and many never perceive that it is gone, till they be laid hold on by Satan according to the law's injunction, and bound in the chains of everlasting darkness. But then, alas! it is too late, for they cannot save themselves, and the season of a Saviour is gone. And this, no doubt, will be the accession of the bitterness and torment that damned souls shall be into,—that they dreamed of attaining life by a law that now is nothing but a ministration of death;—that they lost life by seeking their own righteousness; and made the law more able to condemn them, by their apprehending in themselves an ability to satisfy it, and by resting in a form of obedience to it. There is something natural in it. Adam and all his posterity were once to be saved this way,—so the terms run at first, 'do this and live.' No wonder that something of that impression be retained; but that which was a virtue in Adam, while he retained integrity, and fulfilled his duty, is a mighty fault, and presumptuous madness in us, who have fallen from that blessed estate. If man, doing his duty, expected a reward, according to the promise, it was commendable; but for man, now rebellious and stubborn, and come short of the glory of God, to look for a reward from God, against whom he warreth continually, and that for rebellion and enmity, it is damnable. But besides this, I think this principle of self-righteousness is much corrupted in man now, by what it was in Adam. I conceive, though Adam looked for life upon obedience, according to the promise, yet he rested not on, and trusted not in, his obedience. I believe, a holy and righteous man would be a humble man too, and would rather glory in God's grace than in his own works. The sense of a free and undeserved promise would not suffer him to reflect so much upon his own obedience, or put such a price upon it. But now, it is conjoined with unmeasurable pride, and arises only from self-love. There is no ground of men's looking to be saved by their own doings, but the inbred pride and self-love of the heart, together with the ignorance of a better righteousness. Adam hid himself among the trees, and covered his nakedness with leaves, and truly the shift of the most part is no better. How vain and empty things do men trust unto, and from them conclude an expectation of eternal life! The most part think to be safe in the midst or thick of the trees of the church. If they be in the throng of a visible church, and adorned with church privileges, as baptism, hearing the word, and such like, they do persuade themselves all will be well. Some have civility, and a blameless conversation before men, and with such acts of righteousness, or rather wants of some gross outbreakings, do many cover their nakedness. If there be yet a larger and finer garment of profession of religion, and some outward performances of service to God, and duties to men, O then, men do enforce upon their own hearts the persuasion of heaven, and think their nakedness cannot be seen through it! These are the coverings, these are the grounds of claim and title, that men have to eternal life, and in the meantime they are ignorant of that large glorious robe of righteousness, which Christ, by his obedience and sufferings, did weave for naked sinners.

But as the impossibility of the law's saving us, by reason of the weakness of the flesh, was the ground and occasion of Christ's coming into the flesh for to supply that defect, and take away that impossibility; so the sense and sight of this impossibility in us to satisfy and fulfil the law, and of the law to give life, is the very ground and reason of a soul's coming to Jesus Christ for the supplying of this want. As the Son should not have come in the likeness of sinful flesh, unless it had been otherwise impossible, by man's doing or suffering, that life should be obtained; so will not a soul come to Christ, the Son of God, through the vail of his flesh, until it discern and feel that it is otherwise impossible to satisfy the law or attain life. That was the impulsive cause (if we may say that there was any cause beside his love) why Christ came,—even man's misery, and remediless misery. And this is the strong motive and impulsive, that drives a poor sinner unto Jesus Christ,—the sense and impression of his desperate and lost estate without him. As there was first sin, and then a Saviour dying for sin, because nothing else could suffice, so there must be in the soul, first, the apprehension of sin, and that remediless sin, sin incurable by any created power or act; and then a sight of a Saviour coming to destroy sin and the works of the devil, and destroying it by dying for it. There is no employment for this Physician upon every slight apprehension of a wound or sickness, till it be found incurable, and help sought elsewhere be seen to be in vain. Indeed, upon the least apprehension of sin and misery, men ought to come to Christ. We shall not set or prescribe any measure of conviction to exclude you, if you can but come to him indeed. Upon the least measure of it, you will not be cast out, according to his own word; but as certain it is, that men will not come to this Physician, till they find no other can save them. These two things I wish were deeply and seriously thought upon,—that you cannot satisfy God's justice for the least point of guilt; and then, that you cannot do any thing in obedience to please God. There is a strange inconsideration; yea, I may say, ignorance among us. When you are challenged and convinced of sin, (as there is no conscience so benumbed, but in some measure it accuseth every man of many wrongs,) what is the course you fall on to pacify it or please God? Indeed, if you can get any shadow of repentance, if it were but a bare acknowledgment of the fault, you excuse yourselves in your own consciences, and answer the accusation by it. Either some other good works formerly done occur to you, or some resolution for amendment in time coming. And this you think shall pacify God and satisfy justice. But, alas! you are far from the righteousness of God, and you do err even in the very foundation of religion. These are but sparks of your own kindling, and for all these, you shall lie down in darkness and sorrow. These are but the vain expiations and excuses of natural consciences, which are led to some sense of a deity by the law written in their heart. But consider this once,—you must first satisfy the curse of the law which you are under, before you can be in any capacity to please him by new obedience. Now, if you should undertake to pay for your former breaches of the law, that will eternally ruin you; and therefore, you see the punishment is lengthened throughout eternity to them who have this to undergo alone. Go then, and first suffer the eternal wrath of an infinite God, and then come and offer obedience if thou can. But now, thou art in a double error, both of which are damnable; one is, thou thinkest thou art able, by consideration and resolution, to perform some acceptable obedience to God; another, that performance of obedience, and amending in time coming, will expiate former transgressions. If either of these were true, Christ needed not to have come in the likeness of sinful flesh, because it had been possible for the law to save thee. But now, the truth is, such is the utter disability and impotency of man through sin, that he can neither will, nor do the least good, truly good and pleasant to God. His nature and person being defiled, all he doth is unclean. And then, suppose it were possible that man could do any thing in obedience to his commands, yet it being unquestionable that all have sinned, satisfaction must first be made to God's threatening, 'thou shalt die,' before obedience be acceptable, and that is impossible too. This, then, I leave upon your consciences, beseeching you to lay to heart the impossibility you are encompassed with on both hands; justice requiring a ransom, and you have none, and justice requiring new obedience again, and you can give none; old debts urging you, and new duty pressing you, and ye alike disabled for both; that so finding yourselves thus environed with indigency and impossibility within, you may be constrained to flee out of yourselves unto him that is both able and willing. This is not a superficial business, as you make it. It is not a matter of fancy, or memory, or expression, as most make it. Believe me, it is a serious business, a soul-work, such an exercise of spirit as useth to be when the soul is between despair and hope. Impossibility within, driving a soul out of itself, and possibility, yea, certainty of help without, even in Christ, drawing a soul in to him. Thus is the closure made, which is the foundation of our happiness.

Sermon IX.

VERSE 3.—"*For what the law could not do, in that it was weak through the flesh, God sending his own Son in the likeness of sinful flesh, and for sin condemned sin in the flesh.*"

FOR what purpose do we meet thus together? I would we knew it,—then it might be to some better purpose. In all other things we are rational, and do nothing of moment without some end and purpose. But, alas! in this matter of greatest moment, our going about divine ordinances, we have scarce any distinct or deliberate thought of the end and rise of them. Sure I am, we must all confess this, that all other businesses in our life are almost impertinent to the great end, the salvation of our souls, in respect of these, in which God in a manner trysts with men, and comes to dwell with them. These have the nearest and most immediate connection with God's glory and our happiness; and yet so wretched and unhappy are we, that we study and endeavour a kind of wisdom and diligence in other petty things, which are to perish with the using, and have no great reach to make our condition either better or worse; and yet we have no wisdom, nor consideration, or attention to this great and momentous matter—the salvation of our souls. Is it not high time we were shaken out of our empty, vain, and unreasonable custom, in going about such solemn duties, when the wrath of God is already kindled, and his mighty arm is shaking terribly the earth, and shaking us out of all our nests of quietness and consolation, which we did build in the creature? God calls for a reasonable service; but I must say, the service of the most is an unreasonable and brutish kind of work,—little or no consideration of what we are about, little or no purpose or aim at any real soul advantage. Consider, my beloved, what you are doing, undoing yourselves with ignorance of your own estate, and unacquaintedness with a better; whence it comes, that you live contented in your misery, and have no lively stirrings after this blessed remedy. That for which we meet together is to learn these two things, and always to be learning them,—to know sensibly our own wretched misery and that blessed remedy which God hath provided. It is the sum of the Scriptures, and we desire daily to lay it out before you, if at length it may please the Lord to awake you out of your dream, and give you the light of his salvation.

You hear of a weakness of the flesh; but if you would understand it aright, it is not properly and simply a weakness. That supposeth always some life, and some strength remaining. It is not like an infirmity, that only indisposeth to wonted action in the wonted vigour; but it is such a weakness, as the apostle elsewhere, (Eph. ii. 1,) calls deadness. It is such a weakness, as may be called wickedness, yea, enmity to God, as it is here. Our souls are not diseased properly, for that supposeth there is some remnant of spiritual life, but they are dead in sins and trespasses. And so it is not infirmity but impossibility,—such a weakness as makes life and salvation impossible by us, both utter unwillingness and extreme inability. These two concur in all mankind, no strength to satisfy justice or obey the law, and no willingness either. There is a general practical mistake in this. Men conceive that their natures are weak to good, but few apprehend the wickedness and enmity that is in them to God and all goodness. All will grant some defect and inability, and it is a general complaint. But to consider that this inability is an impossibility, that this defect is a destruction of all spiritual good in us,—the saving knowledge of this is given to few, and to those only whose eyes the Spirit opens. There may be some strugglings and wrestlings of natural spirits to help themselves, and upon the apprehension of their own weakness, to raise up themselves by serious consideration, and earnest diligence, to some pitch of serving God, and to some hope of heaven. But I do suspect that it proceeds in many from the want of this thorough and deep conviction of desperate wickedness. Few really believe that testimony which God hath given of man,—he is not only weak, but wicked, and not only so, but desperately wicked. And that is not all, the heart is deceitful, too, and to complete the account, 'deceitful above all things,' Jer. xvii. 9. A strange character of man, given by him that formed the spirit of man within, and made it once upright, and so knows best how far it hath departed from the first pattern. O who of us believes this in our hearts! But that is the deceitfulness of our hearts to cover our desperate wickedness from our own discerning, and flatter ourselves with self-pleasing thoughts. If once this testimony were received, that the weakness of the flesh is a desperate wickedness, such a wretched and accursed condition as there is no hope therein, as is incurable to any created power, and makes us incurable, and certainly lost,—then, I say, the deceitfulness of the heart were in some measure cured. Believe this desperate wickedness of your natures, and then you have deceived the deceitfulness of your hearts to your own advantage; then you have known that which none can know aright, till the searcher of the heart and reins reveal it unto them.

Thus man stands environed with impossibilities. His own weakness and wickedness, and the law's impossibility by reason of that,—these do shut up all access to the tree of life, and are instead of a flaming sword to guard it. Our legs are cut off by sin, and the law cannot help us; nay, our life is put out, and the law cannot quicken us. It declares our duty, but gives no ability; it teacheth well, but it cannot make us learn. While we are in this posture, God himself steps in to succour miserable and undone man; and here is the way,—he sends his Son in the likeness of sinful flesh, and grace and truth come by him, which do remove those impediments that stopped all access to life.

This is a high subject, but it concerns the lowest and most wretched amongst us;

and that is indeed the wonder of it, that there should be such a mystery, such a depth in this work of redemption of poor sinners, so much business made, and such strange things done for repairing our ruins. In the consideration of this we may borrow that meditation of the Psalmist's, Psal. viii. 4, 'Lord, what is man, that thou shouldest thus magnify him; and make him not a little lower than the angels, but far higher?' 'For he took not on him the nature of angels,' Heb ii. 14, 16; but took part with the poor children of flesh and blood. This deserves a pause,—we shall stay a little, and view it more fully in the steps and degrees that this mystery rises and ascends up by. But, oh! for such an ascending frame of heart as this deserves. It is a wonder it doth not draw us upward beyond our own element,—it is a subject of such admiration in itself, and so much concernment to us.

Every word hath a weight in it, and a peculiar emphasis. There is a gradation that the mystery goes upon till it come to the top. Every word hath a degree or stop in it, whereby it rises high, and still higher. 'God' sent,—that is very strange; but God sent 'his own Son,'—is most strange. But go on, and it is still stranger,—in the likeness of 'flesh,' and that 'sinful flesh,' &c. In all which degrees you see God is descending and lower and lower, but the mystery ascends and goes higher and higher; the lower God coming comes down, the wonder rises up. Still the smaller and meaner that God appears in the flesh, the greater is the mystery of godliness, God manifested in the flesh.

If you would rise up to the sensible and profitable understanding of this mystery, you must first descend into the depths of your own natural wretchedness and misery, in which man was lying when it pleased God to come so low to meet him and help him. I say you must first go down that way in the consideration of it, and then you shall ascend to the use and knowledge of this mystery of godliness.

God's sending, hath some weight of wonder in it, at the very first apprehension of it. If you did but know who he is, and what we are, a wonder it had been that he had suffered himself to be sent unto by us, that any message, any correspondence should pass between heaven and earth, after so foul a breach of peace and covenant by man on earth. Strange, that heaven was not shut up from all intercourse with that accursed earth. If God had sent out an angel to destroy man, as he sent to destroy Jerusalem, (1 Chron. xxi. 15,)—if he had sent out his armies to kill those his enemies, who had renounced the yoke of his obedience, it had been justice, Matth. xxi. 41; xxii. 7. If he had sent a cruel messenger against man, who had now acted so horrid a rebellion, it had been no strange thing. As he did send an angel with a flaming sword to encompass the tree of life, he might have enlarged that angel's commission, to take vengeance on man: and this is the wonder, he did not send after this manner. But what heart could this enter into? Who could imagine such a thing as this? God to send, and to send for peace, to his rebellious footstool! Man could not have looked for acceptance before the throne, if he had presented and sent first up supplications and humble cries to heaven; and therefore finding himself miserable, you see he is at his wits end, he is desperate, and gives it over, and so flies away to hide himself, certainly expecting that the first message from heaven should be to arm all the creatures against him to destroy him. But, O what a wonderful, yet blessed surprisal! God himself comes down, and not for any such end as vengeance, though just, but to publish and hold forth a covenant of reconciliation and peace, to convince man of sin, and to comfort him with the glad tidings of a Redeemer, of one to be sent in the likeness of flesh. It is the grandeur and majesty of kings and great men to let others come to them with their petitions; and it is accounted a rare thing if they be accessible and affable: but that the Lord of lords and King of kings, who sitteth in the circle of the heavens, and before whom all the inhabitants of the earth are as poor grasshoppers, or crawling worms, about whose throne there are ten thousand times ten thousand glorious spirits ministering unto him, as Daniel saw him, (chap. vii. 9, 10,)—that such a one should not only admit such as we to come to him, and offer our suits to his Highness, but himself first to come down unto Adam, and offer peace to him, and then send his own Son! And what were we that he should make any motion about us, or make any mission to us? Rom. v. 10. While we were yet 'enemies,' that we were when he sent. O how hath his love triumphed over his justice! But needed he fear our enmity, that he should seek peace? Nowise; one look of his angry countenance would have looked us into nothing,—'Thou lookest upon me, and I am not;' one rebuke of his for iniquity, would have made our beauty consume as the moth, far more the stroke of his hand had consumed us, Psalm xxxix. 11. But that is the wonder indeed,—while we were yet 'enemies;' and weak too, neither able to help ourselves, nor hurt him in the least, and so could do nothing to allure him, nothing to terrify him, nothing to engage his love, nothing to make him fear; yet then he makes this motion, and mission to us, 'God sending,' &c.

God sending, and 'sending his own Son,' that is yet a step higher. Had he sent an angel, it had been wonderful, one of those ministering spirits about the throne being far more glorious than man. But 'God so loved the world, that he sent his Son.' Might he not have done it by others? But he had a higher project; and verily, there is more mystery in the end and manner of our redemption, than difficulty in the thing itself. No question, he might have enabled the creature, by his almighty power, to have destroyed the works of the devil, and might have delivered captive man some other way. He needed not, for any necessity lying upon him, to go such a round as the Father to give the Son, and the Son to receive,—as God to send, and the Son to be sent. Nay, he might have spared all pains, and without any messenger, immediately pardoned man's sin, and adopted him to the place of sons. Thus he had done the business, without his Son's, or any other's travail and labour in blood and suffering. But this profound mystery, in the manner of it, declares the highness and excellency of the end God proposed, and that is the manifestation of his love; 'Behold, what manner of love the Father hath bestowed on us,' 1 John iii. 1. And 'in this was manifested the love of God toward us, that God sent his only begotten Son into the world,' 1 John iv. 9. And truly for such a design and purpose, all the world could not have contrived such a suitable and excellent mean as this. Nothing besides this could have declared such love. There is no expression of love imaginable to this,—to give his Son, and only begotten Son for us. It had been enough, out of mere compassion, to have saved us, however it had been. But if he had given all, and done all besides this, he had not so manifested the infinite fulness of love. There is no gift so suitable to the greatness and magnificence of his majesty, as this,—one that thought it no robbery to be equal with himself. Any gift had been infinitely above us, because from him; but this is not only infinitely above us, but equal to himself, and fittest to declare himself.

But then, there is yet a higher rise of the mystery, or a lower descent of God; for it is all one, God descending is the wonder ascending,—he sent his Son. Man's admiration is already exhausted in that. But if there were any thing behind, this which follows would consume it,—in the flesh. If he had sent his own Son, might he not have sent him in an estate and condition suitable to his glory, as it became the Prince and Heir of all things, him by whom all were created and do subsist? Nay, but he is sent, and that in a state of humiliation and condescendency, infinitely below his own dignity. That ever he was made a creature, that the Maker of all should be sent in the form of any thing he had made, O what a disparagement! There is no such distance between the highest prince on the throne, and the basest beggar on the dunghill, as between the only begotten of the Father, who is the brightness of his glory, and the most glorious angel that ever was made. And yet, it would be a wonder to the world, if a king should send his son in the habit and state of a beggar, to call in the poor, and lame, and blind, to the fellowship of his kingdom. It had been a great mystery, then, if God had been manifested in the nature of angels, a great abasement of his majesty. But, O what must it be for God to be manifested in the flesh, in the basest, naughtiest, and most corruptible of all the creatures, even the very dregs of the creation, that have sunk down to the bottom! 'All flesh is grass;' and what more withering and fading, even the flower and perfection of it! Is. xl. 6. Dust it is, and what baser? Gen. xviii. 27. And corruption it is, and what viler? 1 Cor. xv. 44. And yet God sent his Son in the flesh. Is this a manifestation? Nay, rather, it is a hiding and obscuration of his glory. It is the putting on of a dark veil to eclipse his brightness. Yet manifested he is, as the intendment of the work he was about required,—manifested to reproach and ignominy for our sin. This is one, and a great point of Christ's humiliation,—that he took not on him the nature of angels, but the seed of Abraham, Heb. ii. 16.

But yet, to complete this mystery more, the Son descends a third step lower, that the mystery may ascend so much the higher, in the likeness of flesh? Not so, but in the likeness of sinful flesh. If he had appeared in the prime flower and perfection of flesh, in the very goodliness of it, yet it had been a disparagement. If he had come down as glorious as he once went up, and now 'sits at the right hand of the majesty on high;' if he had been always in that resplendent habit he put on in his transfiguration; that had been yet an abasement of his majesty. But, to come in the likeness of sinful flesh, though not a sinner, yet in the likeness of a sinner,—so like as that, touching his outward appearance, no eye could discern any difference, compassed about with all those infirmities and necessities, which are the followers and attendants of sin in us; 'a man of sorrows and acquainted with grief;' a man who all his lifetime had intimate acquaintance, and familiarity with grief. Grief and he were long acquaintance, and never parted till death parted them. Nay, not only was he, in his outward estate, subject to all those miseries and infirmities unto which sin subjects other men, but something beyond all, 'his visage was more marred than any man's, and his form more than the sons of men,' Isa. lii. 14; and therefore he was a hissing and astonishment to many. He had no form nor comeliness in him, and no beauty to make him desirable; and therefore his own friends were ashamed of him, and hid their faces from him; 'he was despised and rejected of men,' Isa. liii. 2, 3. Thus you see, he comes in the most despicable and disgraceful form of flesh that can be; and an abject among men, and as himself speaks in Psal. xxii. 6, 'a worm, and not a man;' a reproach of men, and despised among the people. Now this, I say, is the crowning of the great mystery of godliness, which, without all controversy, is the mystery in all the world that hath in it most greatness and goodness combined together, that is the subject of the highst admiration, and the fountain of the sweetest consolation that either reason or religion can afford. The mysteries of the Trinity are so high, that if any dare to reach to them, he doth but catch the lower fall;* it is as if a worm would attempt to touch the sun in the firmament. But this mystery is God coming down to man, to be handled and seen of men, because man could not rise up to God's highness. It is God descending to our baseness, and so coming near us to save us. It is not a confounding but a saving mystery. There is the highest truth in it, for the understanding to contemplate and admire; and there is the greatest good in it, for the will to choose and rest upon. It is contrived for wonder and delight to men and angels. These three, which the angelic song runs upon, are the jewels of it,—'glory to God, peace on earth, and good-will toward men.'

Sermon XII.

VERSE 3.—"*For what the law could not do, in that it was weak through the flesh, God sending his own Son,*" *&c.*

OF all the works of God towards man, certainly there is none hath so much wonder in it, as the sending of his Son to become man; and so it requires the exactest attention in us. Let us gather our spirits to consider of this mystery,—not to pry into the secrets of it curiously, as if we had no more to do but to satisfy our understandings; but rather that we may see what this concerns us, and what instruction or advantage we may have by it, that so it may ravish our affections. I believe there is very palpable and gross ignorance in thousandsof the very thing itself. Many who profess Jesus Christ, know not his natures, or his glorious person,—do not apprehend either his highness as God, or his lowness as man. But truly, the thing that I do most admire, is, that those who pretend to more knowledge of this mystery, yet few of them do enter upon any serious consideration about it,—for what use and

* [That is, he will get, or meet with, a fall, or fall lower, as he, who aims at being wise above what is written, is in danger of falling into error.—ED.]

purpose it is; though it be the foundation of our salvation, the chief ground of our faith, and the great spring of our consolation. Yet to improve the knowledge of it to any purpose of that kind, is a thing so rare, even among true Christians, that it is little the subject of their meditation. I think, indeed, the lively improvement of this mystery of godliness would be very effectual to make us really what we are said to be, that is, Christians. There is something to this purpose, 1 John iv. 2, 3, 15, and v. 1. The confessing and knowing that Jesus Christ is come in the flesh, and is the Son of God, before his taking on flesh, is made a character of a spiritual man that dwelleth in God. Not that a bare external confession, or internal opinion and assent to such a truth, is of so much value,—which yet is the height that many attain unto; but it is such a soul acknowledgment, such an heart approbation of this mystery, as draws alongst the admiration and affection after it, as fixeth the heart upon this object alone, for life and salvation. The devils confessed and believed, but they trembled at it, Luke iv. 34, 41. He was afraid of what he knew, but Peter confessed and loved what he knew; yea, he did cast his soul upon that Lord whom he confessed. It is such an acknowledgment of Christ, as draweth the soul, and unites it to him, by a serious and living embracement. Such a sight of Jesus Christ, hath both truth and goodness in it, in the highest measure; and so doth not only constrain the assent of the mind, but is a powerful attractive to the heart, to come to him, and live in him. I pray you consider then what moment is in this truth, that you may indeed apply your souls to the consideration of what is in Jesus Christ thus revealed, not simply to know it, but for a further improvement of it, to seek life in him, that the stamp and impression of this Saviour may be set so deeply on your souls, as that you may express this in a real confession of him in your words and works, Tit. i. 16; Matt. vii. 21. This is indeed to know and confess that Jesus Christ is come in the flesh, to fetch thence the ground of all our hope and consolation, and to draw thence the most powerful motives to walking 'even as he walked,' to improve it for confidence in him, and obedience to him.

I shall speak then a word of these two great ends and purposes,—of God's sending his own Son, in the likeness of sinful flesh, his own glory and man's good. The song of angels at his birth shows this,—'Glory to God in the highest, peace on earth, and good will toward men.' His glory is manifested in it in an eminent manner. The glory of his wisdom,—that found out a remedy. What a deep contrivance was it! How infinitely beyond all creature inventions! Truly there are riches of wisdom, depths of wisdom in it. I think it could never have entered the thought of men or angels;—all men once to be drowned under a deluge of sin and misery, and made subjects to God's righteous judgment, and then to find out a way how to deliver and save so many! All the wisdom that shines in the order and beauty of the world seems to be but a rude draught to this. Then, herein doth the glory of his mercy and grace shine most brightly, that he transfers the punishment due to man's sin upon his own Son, that when no ransom could be found by man, he finds it out, how to satisfy his own justice, and save us. Truly, this is the most shining jewel in the crown of God's glory,—so much mercy towards so miserable sinners, so much grace towards the rebellious. If he had pardoned sin, without any satisfaction, what rich grace had it been! But truly, to provide the Lamb and sacrifice himself, to find out the ransom, and to exact it of his own Son, in our name, is a testimony of mercy and grace far beyond that. But then, his justice is very conspicuous in this work. And indeed these two do illustrate one another; the justice of God, in taking and exacting the punishment of sin upon his own well-beloved Son, doth most eminently heighten the mercy and grace of God towards us; and his grace and mercy in passing by us, doth most marvellously illustrate the righteousness of God, in making his own Son a curse for us. What testimony can be given in the world, of God's displeasure at sin, of his righteousness in punishing sin, like this! There was no such testimony of love to sinners and no such demonstration of hatred at sin imaginable. That he did not punish sin in us, but transfer it over on his most beloved Son, O what love and grace! And that he did punish his own Son, when standing in the place of sinners, O what righteousness and justice! This is that glorious mystery, the conjunction of these two resplendent jewels, justice and mercy, of love and displeasure, in one chain of Christ's incarnation, into which the angels desire to look,

1 Pet. i. 12. And truly they do wonder at it, and praise from wonder. This is it, that the praises of men and angels shall roll about eternally. David, (Ps. ciii. 20,) foreseeing this day, foretold that angels should praise him; and now it is fulfilled, when all these glorious companies of holy, powerful spirits, welcome the Son of God into the world, by that heavenly harmony of praise, Luke ii. 14.

What lumpishness and earthliness is in us, that we do not rise up above, to this melody in our spirits, to join with angels in this song; we, I say, whom it most concerns! The angels wonder, and praise and wonder at this, because the glory of God shines so brightly in it, as if there were many suns in one firmament, as the light of seven days in one. These three especially,—wisdom, mercy and grace, justice and righteousness, every one of them looks like the sun in its strength, carried about in this orb of the redemption of man, to the ravishing of the hearts of all the honourable and glorious companies above, and making them cheerfully and willingly to contribute all their service to this work, to be ministering spirits to wait on the heirs of salvation!

Now, when the glory of the highest raiseth up such a melodious song above, among angels, O what should both the glory of the highest God, and the highest good of man do to us! When the greatest glory of God, and the chiefest advantage of man are linked together in this chain, what should we do but admire and adore, adore and admire, and, while we are in this earth, send up our consent to that harmony in heaven!

In relation to our good, much might be said, but we shall briefly show unto you, that it is the greatest confirmation of our faith, and the strongest motive to humility, that can be afforded. Now, if we could be composed thus unto confidence and reverence, to glorify him by believing, and to abase ourselves, to believe in him, and walk humbly with him, upon the meditation of Christ's coming in the flesh, this would make us true Christians indeed.

There is nothing, I know, more powerful to persuade us of the reality of God's invitations and promises to us than this. We are still seeking signs and tokens of God's love, something to warrant us to come to God in Christ, and to persuade us that we shall be welcome; and many Christians puddle themselves in the mire of their own darkness and discouragement, because they cannot find any thing in themselves that can give but the least probable conjecture, that he will admit and welcome them to come to him, or that such precious promises, and sweet invitations, can belong to such sinners as they conceive themselves to be. Truly, my beloved, I think, while we exercise ourselves thus, we are seeking the sun with a candle, making that which is in itself as bright as the light to be more dark. The evidence of God's reality in offering life to you in Christ, and his willingness to receive you, is not without the compass of his invitation, and yet you seek it where it is least to be found, that is, in yourselves. But indeed, his invitations in the gospel carry the evidence in their bosom,—that which is above all other signs and evidences, that he did even send his own Son in the flesh for this purpose. Is there any thing besides this, either greater or clearer? I think we are like those who, when they had seen many signs and wonders done by Christ, which did bear testimony to all the world of his divine nature, yet they would not be satisfied, but sought out another sign, tempting him, Matt. xvi. 1. And truly, he might return this answer to us, 'O wicked and adulterous generation, that seeketh after a sign, there shall no sign be given to thee, but the sign of the prophet Jonas.' The greatest testimony that can be imagined, is given already,—that the Father should send his only-begotten and well-beloved Son into the state of a servant for man. If this do not satisfy, I know not what will. I see not how any work of his Spirit in us, can make so much evidence of his reality and faithfulness in the gospel, and of his willingness to welcome sinners. All the works of the creation, all the works of grace, are nothing to this, to manifest his love to men; and therefore there is a singular note upon it, 'God so loved the world, that he gave his Son,' John iii. 16. And in this was his love manifested, that he sent his Son, 1 John iv. 9. If men and angels had set themselves to devise and find out a pledge or confirmation of the love of God, they would have fallen upon some revelation unto, or some operation upon their spirits. But, alas this is infinitely above that. His own express image, and the brightness of his glory, is come down to bear witness of his love; nay, he who is equal with himself in glory, is given as a gift to men; and is not he infinitely more than created gifts or graces, who is the very spring and fountain of them all? 'God so loved the world,' that truly he gave no such gift besides, to testify such a love. Therefore, when all that he hath done in this kind cannot satisfy thy scrupulous mind, but thou wilt still go on, to seek more confirmation of his readiness to receive thee, I think it is a tempting of the Holy One, which may draw such an answer from him, O wicked and adulterous person, there shall no sign be given thee, but that which is darker than the former, that which thou shalt understand less. Thou mayest get what thou seekest, perhaps some more satisfaction in thy own condition, but it shall plunge thee more in the issue. Thou shalt always be unsettled, and 'unconstant as water, thou shalt not excel.' I confess indeed, if we speak of the manifestation of one's particular interest in these promises, and of an evidence of the love of God to thee, in particular, then there must needs be something wrought by the Holy Spirit on thy soul, to draw down the general testimony of God's love to mankind into a particular application to thyself. But that I do not speak of now, because that is the sealing of the Spirit after believing; and because you are always unsettled in the first and main point, of flying unto the Son, and waiting on him for life, therefore have you so much inevidence and weakness in that which follows. That which I now speak of is, that if this were cordially believed, and seriously considered, that God sent his own Son in the flesh, to save sinners, you could not readily have any doubt, but that your coming to him for salvation would be welcome. You could not say, that such precious invitations could not belong to sinners, or that he could not love the like of you. Truly, I think, if the general were laid to heart, that God hath so loved mankind, that he gave such a gift unto them, there is none could make any more question of his reality, when that gift is tendered to any in particular. Nay, I think it is the inconsideration of this general evidence and manifestation of love to the world, that makes you so perplexed in particulars. Could you have so much difficulty to believe his love to you, if you indeed believe that he hath loved the world, that is, so many thousands like you? Is there so much distance, I pray you, between you and another, as between him and all? If, then, he loves so many miserable sinners, is there any impossibility in it, but he may love you? For what is in them that might conciliate his love? I tell you, why I think the right apprehension of the general truths of the gospel would be able, like the sun in its strength, to scatter all the clouds and mists of our particular interest-debates; because I find, that those very grounds, upon which you call in question your own particular interest, if you did consider them, you would find they go a further length, to conclude against all others; and either they have no strength in your case, or they will be of equal force to batter down the confidence of all the saints, and the certainty of all the promises. What is it that troubles you, but that you are sinners, and such sinners, so vile and loathsome? From whence you do conclude, not only that you have no present assurance of his love, but that he cannot love such a one as you are. Now, I say, if this hold good, in reference to you, take heed that you condemn not yourselves in that which you approve,—that is, that you do not dispute against the interest of all the saints, who were such as you are, and the truth of those fundamental positions of the gospel, 'God so loved the world,' &c. And so you do not only wrong yourselves, but all others; and not only so, but you offer the greatest indignity to him that out of love sent his Son, and to him who, out of love, came and laid down his life. O consider how you indignify * and set at nought that great manifestation of God's love, 'God manifested in the flesh;' how you despise his love-pledge to sinners, a greater than which he could not give you, because as great as himself! O that you could see the consequence of your anxious and perplexing doubts,—that they do not only an injury to your own souls, but that they are of a more bloody nature! If they held good, they would cut off the life and salvation of all believers, and, which is worse, they would, by an unavoidable consequence, conclude an antichristian point, that Christ is not come in the flesh. I beseech you, unbowel your evils, that you may abhor them.

* [That is, treat with indignity.—Ed.]

This may strengthen our faith, and minister much consolation, in another consideration too; that which is laid down, Heb. ii. 17, and iv. 15, that he was partaker of our nature, and in all things like unto his brethren, that so he might be a merciful High Priest, able to succour us, and touched with the feeling of our infirmities. What strong consolation may be sucked out of these breasts! When it was impossible that man could rise up to God, because of his infinite highness and holiness, behold, God hath come down to man, in his lowness and baseness. He hath sent down this ladder from heaven to the earth, that poor wretched sinners may ascend upon it. It is come down, as low as our infirm, weak, and frail nature, that we may have easy coming up to it, and going up upon it to heaven. Therefore his flesh is called a 'new and living way,' because a poor sinner may be assured of welcome and acceptation with one of his own kind, his brother,—(he was not ashamed to call us brethren,)—flesh of his flesh, and bone of his bone. This may make boldness of access, that we have not God to speak to, or come to, immediately, as he is clothed with glory and majesty, and as the Jews heard him on mount Sinai, and desired a mediator between him and them; but that that great prophet promised to them hath come, and we have him between us and God,—as low as we, that we may speak to him, 'riding upon an ass,' a low ass, that every one may whisper their desires in his ear,—and yet as high as God, that he may speak to God, and have power with him. Truly, this is a sweet trysting-place to meet God in, that no sinner may have any fear to come to it, to this treaty of peace and reconciliation. How may it persuade us of that great privilege, that we may 'become the sons of God,' when the Son of God is become the Son of man, John i. 11, 12. Truly, though it be hard to be believed, that such as we should become the sons of the great King; yet it is nothing so strange as this, that the eternal and only begotten Son of the great God, should become the Son of wretched man. That highness will be easily believed, if we consider this lowness. It will not be so hard to persuade a soul, that there is a way of union and reconciliation to God, of being yet at peace with him, if this be pondered,—that God hath married his own nature with ours,—in one person, to be a pledge of that union and peace. And then, how much quickening and comfort may it yield us, that he was not only a man, but a miserable man, and that not through any necessity, but only the necessity of love and compassion. He had enough of mercy to save us as God, he had enough of love and compassion as man; but he would take on misery too, in his own person, that he might be experimentally merciful to us. Certainly, the experience of misery and infirmity must superadd some tenderness to the heart of our High Priest. But though it did not help him to be more pitiful, yet it was done for us, to help us to have more confidence in him, and boldness to come unto him. What an encouragement is it for a poor man to come unto the once poor Jesus Christ, who 'had not where to lay his head!' He knows the evil of poverty, and he chose to know it, that he might have compassion on thee. With what boldness may poor afflicted and despised believers come to him! Why? Because himself had experience of all that, and he was familiarly acquainted with grief and sorrow, therefore he can sympathize best with thee. Let us speak even of the sinful infirmities thou art subject to. That there might be a suitableness in him to help thee, he came as nigh as might be,—he was willing to be tempted to sin; and so he knows the power that temptations must have over weak and frail natures; but sin he could not, for that had been evil for us. Let this, then, give us boldness to come to him.

I would desire to persuade you to humility from this, according to the lesson Christ gives us, Matt. xi. 29, 'Learn of me, for I am meek and lowly.' And the apostle makes singular use of this mystery of the abasement of the Majesty, to abate from our high esteem of ourselves, Phil. ii. 3—6. O should not the same mind be in us that was in Christ! God abased, man exalted,—how unsuitable are these, think you! God lowly in condition and disposition; and man, though base in condition, yet high in his disposition and in his own estimation! What more mysterious than God humbled? And what more monstrous than man proud? Truly, pride is the most deformed thing in a man, but in a Christian it is monstrous and prodigious. If he did humble himself out of charity and love, who was so high and glorious, how should we humble ourselves out of necessity, who are so low and base? And out of charity and love too, to be conformed and like unto him! Nature may persuade the one, but Christianity teacheth the other,—to be lowly in mind, and esteem every one better than ourselves. To be meek, patient, long-suffering, reason may persuade it, upon the consideration of our own baseness, emptiness, frailty, and nothingness. But this lesson is taught in Christ's school, not from that motive only, —the force of necessity, but from a higher motive,—the constraint of love to Jesus Christ,—'learn of me.' Suppose there were no necessity of reason in it, yet affection might be a stronger necessity to persuade conformity to him, and following his example, who became so low, and humbled himself to the death even for us.

Sermon VIII.

VERSE 3.—"*And for sin condemned sin in the flesh.*"

THE great and wonderful actions of great and excellent persons must needs have some great ends answerable to them. Wisdom will teach them not to do strange things, but for some rare purposes; for it were a folly and madness to do great things to compass some small and petty end, as unsuitable as that a mountain should travail to bring forth a mouse. Truly we must conceive, that it must needs be some honourable and high business, that brought down so high and honourable a person from heaven as the Son of God. It must be something proportioned to his majesty and his wisdom. And indeed so it is. There is a great capital enemy against God in the world, that is sin. This arch-rebel hath drawn man from his subordination to God, and sown a perpetual discord and enmity between them. This hath conquered all mankind, and among the rest, even the elect and chosen of God, those whom God had in his eternal counsel predestinated to life and salvation. Sin brings all into bondage, and exerciseth the most perfect tyranny over them that can be imagined; makes men to serve all its imperious lusts, and then all the wages is death,—it binds them over to judgment. Now this sedition and rebellion being arisen in the world, and one of the most noble creatures carried away in this revolt, from allegiance to the divine majesty, the most holy and wise counsel of heaven concludes to send the King's Son, to compesce* this rebellion, to reduce men again unto obedience, and destroy that arch-traitor, sin, which his nature most abhors. And for this end the Son of the great King, Jesus Christ, came down into the world, to deliver captive man, and to condemn conquering sin. There is no object that God hath so pure and perfect displeasure at as sin. Therefore he sent to condemn that which he hates most (and perfectly he hates it)—to condemn sin. And this is expressed as the errand of his coming, 1 John iii. 5, 8, to 'destroy the works of the devil.' All his wicked and hellish plots and contrivances against man, all that poison of enmity and sin, that out of envy and malice he spued out upon man, and instilled into his nature; all those works of that prince of darkness, in enticing man from obedience to rebellion, and tyrannizing over him since, by the imperious laws of his own lusts; in a word, all that work that was contrived in hell, to bring poor man down to that same misery with devils; all that Christ, the only begotten Son of the great King, came (for this noble business) to destroy it,—that tower which Satan was building up against heaven, and had laid the foundation of it as low as hell, this was Christ's business down among men, to destroy that Babylon, that tower of darkness and confusion, and to build up a tower of light and life, to which tower sinners might come, and be safe, and by which they might really ascend into heaven. Some do by these words 'for sin,' understand the occasion and reason of Christ's coming, that it was, because sin had conquered the world, and subjected man to condemnation; therefore, Jesus Christ came into the world to conquer sin and condemn it, that we might be free from condemnation by sin. And this was the special cause of his taking on flesh. If sin had not entered into the world, Christ had not come into it;

* [That is, check (from *compesco*, Lat.)—ED.]

and if sin had not erected a throne in man's flesh, Christ had not taken on flesh,—he had not come in the likeness of sinful flesh. So that this may administer unto us abundant consolation. If this was the very cause of his coming, that which drew him down from that delightful and blessed bosom of the Father, then he will certainly do that which he came for. He cannot fail of his purpose, he cannot miss his end : he must condemn sin, and save sinners. And truly this is wonderful love, that he took sin only for his party, and came only for sin, or against sin, and not against poor sinners. He had no commission of the Father but this, as himself declares, John iii. 17 ; for 'God sent not his Son into the world to condemn the world, but that the world through him might be saved.' As one observes well, Christ would never have hinted at such a jealousy, or suggested such a thought to men's minds, had it not been in them before. But this we are naturally inclined unto,—to think hard of God, and can hardly be persuaded of his love, when once we are persuaded of our enmity. Indeed the most part of the world fancy a persuasion of God's love, and have not many jealousies of it, because they know not their own enmity against God. But let a man see himself indeed God's enemy, and it is very hard to make him believe any other thing of God, but that he carries a hostile mind against him. And therefore Christ, to take off this, persuades and assures us, that neither the Father nor he had any design upon poor sinners, nor any ambushment against them ; but mainly, if not only, this was his purpose in sending, and Christ's in coming,—not against man, but against sin ; not to condemn sinners, but to condemn sin, and save sinners. O blessed and unparalleled love, that made such a real distinction between sin and sinners, who were so really one! Shall not we be content to have that woful and accursed union with sin dissolved ? Shall not we be willing to let sin be condemned in us, and to have our own souls saved ? I beseech you, beloved in the Lord, do not think to maintain always Christ's enemy, that great traitor against which he came from heaven. Wonder that he doth not prosecute both as enemies ; but if he will destroy the one and save the other, O let it be destroyed, not you ; and so much the more, for that it will destroy you ! Look to him, so iniquity shall not be your ruin, but he shall be the ruin of iniquity. But if you will not admit of such a division between you and your sins, take heed that you be not eternally undivided, that you have not one common lot for ever, that is, condemnation. Many would be saved, but they would be saved with sin too. Alas ! that will condemn thee. As for sin, he hath proclaimed irreconcilable enmity against it, he hath no quarter to give it, he will never come in terms of composition with it, and all because it is his mortal enemy. Therefore let sin be condemned, that thou mayest be saved. It cannot be saved with thee, but thou mayest be condemned with it.

The words, 'for sin,' may be taken in another sense as fitly, 'a sacrifice for sin,' so that the meaning is,—Jesus Christ came to condemn and overthrow sin in its plea against us by a sacrifice for sin, that is, by offering up his own body or flesh. And thus you have the way and means how Christ conquered sin, and accomplished the business he was sent for. It was by offering a sacrifice for sin, to expiate wrath, and so satisfy justice. 'The sting' and strength 'of death is sin, and the strength of sin is the law,' as the apostle speaks it, 1 Cor. xv. 55. We had two great enemies against us, two great tyrants over us,—sin and death. Death had passed upon all mankind. Not only the miseries of this life and temporal death had subjected all men, but the fear of an eternal death, of an everlasting separation from the blessed face of God, might have seized upon all, and subjected them to bondage, Heb. ii. 15. But the strength and sting of that is sin ; it is sin that arms death and hell against us. Take away sin, and you take away the sting, the strength of death,—it hath no force or power to hurt man. But death being the wages due for sin, (Rom. vi. 23.) all the certainty and efficacy in the wages flows from this work of darkness,—sin. But now 'the strength of sin is the law.' This puts a poisonable and destructive virtue in the sting of sin, for it is the sentence of God's law, and the justice and righteousness of God, that hath made so inseparable a connection between sin and death. This gives sin a destroying and killing virtue. Justice arms it with power and authority to condemn man, so that there can be no freedom, no releasement from that condemnation, no eschewing that fatal sting of death, unless the sentence of God's law, which hath pronounced 'thou shalt die,' be repealed, and the justice of God be satisfied by a ransom. And this being done, the strength of sin is quite gone, and so the sting of death removed.

Now, this had been impossible for man to do. These parties were too strong for any created power. The strength of sin to condemn may be called some way infinite, because it flows from the unchangeable law of the infinite justice of God. Now, what power could encounter that strength, except that which hath infinite strength too? Therefore, it behoved the Son of God to come for this business; to condemn sin and save the sinner. And being come, he yokes first with the very strength of sin, for he knew where its strength did lie, and so did encounter first of all with that,—even the justice of his Father, the hand-writing of ordinances that was against us; for if once he can set them aside, as either vanquished or satisfied, he hath little else to do. Now, he doth not take a violent way in this either. He doth it not with the strong hand, but deals wisely, and (to speak so with reverence) cunningly in it; he came under the law, that he might redeem them who were under the law, Gal. iv. 4. Force will not do it, the law cannot be violated, justice cannot be compelled to forego its right. Therefore our Lord Jesus chooseth, as it were, to compound with the law, to submit unto it: He was 'made under the law,' he who was above the law, being lawgiver in mount Sinai, Acts vii. 38; Gal. iii. 19. He cometh under the bond and tie of it, to fulfil it: 'I came not to destroy the law but to fulfil it,' Matt. v. 17. He would not offer violence to the law, to deliver sinners contrary to the commination of it, or without satisfaction given unto it, for that would reflect upon the wisdom and righteousness of the Father who gave the law. But he doth it better in an amicable way,—by submission and obedience to all its demands. Whatsoever it craved of the sinner, he fulfils that debt. He satisfies the bond in his own person by suffering, and fulfils all the commandments by obedience. And thus, by subjection to the law, he gets power over the law, because his subjection takes away all its claim and right over us. Therefore it is said, that he blotted out the hand-writing of ordinances, which was against us, by nailing it to his cross; and so took it out of the way, Col. ii. 14. Having fulfilled the bond, he cancelled it, and so it stands in no force either against him or us. Thus, the strength of sin, which is the law, is removed; and by this means, sin is condemned in the flesh. By the suffering of his flesh, it is fallen from all its plea against sinners; for, that upon which it did hang, viz. the sentence of the law, is taken out of the way, so that it hath no apparent ground to fasten any accusation upon a poor sinner that flies into Jesus Christ, and no ground at all to condemn him,—it is wholly disabled in that point. For, as the Philistines found where Samson's strength lay, and cut his hair, so Christ hath in his wisdom found where the strength of sin's plea against man lay, and hath cut off the hair of it, that is, the handwriting of ordinances which was against us.

This is that which hath been shadowed out from the beginning of the world by the types of sacrifices and ceremonies. All those offerings of beasts, of fowls, and such like, under the law, held forth this one sacrifice, that was offered in the fulness of time to be a propitiation for the sins of the world. And something of this was used among the Gentiles before Christ's coming, certainly by tradition from the fathers, who have looked afar off to this day, when this sweet-smelling sacrifice should be offered up to appease Heaven. And it is not without a special providence, and worthy the remarking, that since the plenary and substantial One was offered, the custom of sacrificing hath ceased throughout the world. God, as it were, proclaiming to all men, by this cessation of sacrifices, as well as silence of oracles, that the true atonement and propitiation is come already, and the true Prophet is come from heaven, to reveal God's mind unto the world. There were many ceremonies in sacrificing observed, to hold out unto us the perfection of our atonement and propitiation. They laid their hands on the beast, who brought it, to signify the imputation of our sins to Christ, that he who knew no sin was made sin for us, that we might be made the righteousness of God in him. And truly, it is worth the observation, that even those sacrifices for sin were called sin; and so the word is used promiscuously in Leviticus, to point out unto us, that Jesus Christ should make his soul sin, (Isa. liii. 10,) that is, a sacrifice for sin, and be made sin for us, that is, a sacrifice for sin. When the blood was poured out (because without shedding of blood there was no reconciliation, (Heb. ix. 22,) the priest sprinkled it seven times before the Lord, to shadow out the perfection of that expiation for our sins, in the virtue and perpetuity thereof, (Heb. ix. 26,) that he should appear to put away sin by the sacrifice of himself;—to put it away, as if it had never been, by taking it on him and bearing it. And then the high priest was to bring in of the blood into the holy place and within the vail, and sprinkle the mercy-seat, to show unto us, that the merit and efficacy of Christ's blood should enter into the highest heavens, to appease the wrath of God. Our High Priest, by his own blood, hath entered into the holy place, having obtained eternal redemption for us, Heb. ix. 12. And truly this is that sacrifice, which being offered without spot to God, pacifies all, ver. 14. Sin hath a cry, it crieth aloud for vengeance. This blood silenceth it, and composeth all to favour and mercy. It hath so sweet and fragrant a smell in God's account, that it fills heaven with the perfume of it. He is that true scape-goat, who, notwithstanding that he did bear all the sins of his people, yet he did escape alive. Albeit he behoved to make his soul a sacrifice for sin, and so die for it; yet by this means he hath condemned sin, by being condemned for sin. By this means he hath overcome death and the grave, by coming under the power of death, and so is now alive for ever, to improve his victory for our salvation. And by taking on our sins he hath fully abolished the power and plea of them, as the goat that was sent to the wilderness out of all men's sight was not to be seen again. Truly, this is the way how our sins are buried in the grave of oblivion, and removed as a cloud, and cast into the depths of the sea, and sent away as far as the east is from the west, that they may never come into judgment against us to condemn us, because Christ, by appeasing wrath and satisfying justice by the sacrifice of himself, hath overthrown them in judgment, and buried them in the grave with his own body.

You see then, my beloved, a solid ground of consolation against all our fears and sorrows,—an answer to all the accusations of our sins. Here is one for all, one above all. You would have particular answers to satisfy your particular doubts. You are always seeking some satisfaction to your consciences besides this; but believe it, all that can be said, besides this atonement and propitiation, is of no more virtue to purge your consciences, or satisfy your perplexed souls, than those repeated sacrifices of old were. Whatsoever you can pitch upon besides this, it is insufficient; and therefore you find a necessity of seeking some other grace or qualification to appease your consciences, even as they had need to multiply sacrifices. But now, since this perfect propitiation is offered up for our sins, should not all these vain expiations of your works cease? Truly, there is nothing can pacify heaven but this; and nothing can appease thy conscience on earth but this too. If you find any accusation against you, consider Christ hath, by a sacrifice for sin, condemned sin in his own flesh. The marks of the spear, of the nails, of the buffetings of his flesh,—these are the tokens and pledges, that he encountered with the wrath due to your sins, and so hath cut off all the right that sin hath over you. If thou canst unfeignedly in the Lord's sight say, that it is thy soul's desire to be delivered from sin as well as wrath, thou wouldst gladly fly from condemnation; then come to him who hath condemned sin, by suffering the condemnation of sin, that he might save those who desire to fly from it to him.

Sermon XIV.

VERSE 4.—"*That the righteousness of the law might be fulfilled in us.*"

GOD having a great design to declare unto the world both his justice and mercy towards men, he found out this mean most suitable and proportioned unto it, which is here spoken of in the third verse,—to send his own Son to bear the punishment of sin, that the righteousness of the law might be freely and graciously fulfilled in sinners. And, indeed, it was not imaginable by us, how he could declare both in the salvation of sinners. We could not have found out a way to declare his righteousness and holiness, which would not have obscured his mercy and grace; nor a way to manifest his grace and mercy, which would not have reflected upon his holiness and justice, according to the letter of the law that was given out as the rule of life. He that doth them shall live in them; and cursed is every one that doeth them not, &c. What could we expect, if this be fulfilled, as it would appear God's truth and holiness require? Then we are gone,—no place for mercy, if this be not fulfilled, that the mercy may be showed in pardoning sin. Then the truth and faithfulness of God seem to be impaired. This is the strait that all sinners would have been into, if God had not found such an enlargement as this,—how to show mercy without wronging justice; and how to save sinners without impairing his faithfulness. Truly, we may wonder, what was it that could straiten his majesty so, that he must send his own Son, so beloved of him, and bruise him, and hide his face from him; yea, and torment him, and not let the cup pass from him for any entreaties. Might he not more easily have never added such a commination to the law,—'thou shalt die;' or more easily relaxed and repealed that sentence, and passed by the sinner without any more, than exacted so heavy a punishment from one that was innocent? Was it the satisfaction of his justice that straitened him, and put a necessity of this upon him? But truly it seems it had been no more contrary to righteousness to have passed over the sinner, without satisfaction, than to require and take it of one who was not really guilty. The truth is, it was not simply the indispensable necessity of satisfying justice, that put him upon such a hard and unpleasant work, as the bruising of his own Son; for no doubt, he might have as well dispensed with all satisfaction, as with the personal satisfaction of the sinner. But here the strait lay, and here was the urgency of the case: he had a purpose to declare his justice, and therefore a satisfaction must be had, not simply to satisfy righteousness, but rather to declare his righteousness, Rom. iii. 25. Now, indeed, to make these two shine together in one work of the salvation of sinners, all the world could not have found out the like of this,—to dispense with personal satisfaction in the sinner, which the rigour of the law required, and so to admit a sweet moderation and relaxation, that the riches of his grace and mercy might be manifested, and yet withal, to exact the same punishment of another willingly coming in the sinner's place, to the end that all sinners may behold his righteousness and justice. And so this work of the redemption of sinners hath these names of God published by himself, (Exod. xxxiv. 6, 7.) to Moses, engraven deeply upon it; mercy and goodness spelled out at length in it,—for love was the rise of all, and love did run alongst in all; yet so, as there is room to speak out his holiness, and righteousness, and justice, not so much to affright sinners, as to make his mercy the more amiable and wonderful.

I know not a more pressing ground of strong consolation, nor a firmer bulwark of our confidence and salvation, than this conjunction of mercy and justice in the business. There might have been always a secret hink* of jealousy and suspicion in our minds, when God publisheth mercy and forgiveness to us freely. O how shall the law be satisfied, and the importunity of justice and faithfulness, that hath pronounced a sentence of death upon us, answered! Shall not the righteous law be a loser this way, if I be saved, and it not satisfied by obedience or suffering! How hard would it be to persuade a soul of free pardon, that sees such a severe sentence standing against it! But now there is no place for doubting. All is contrived for the encouragement and happiness of poor sinners, that we may come to him with full persuasion of his readiness and inclinableness to pardon, since Jesus Christ hath taken the law and justice of God off our head, and us off their hand; and since he hath reckoned with them, for what is due by us, and paid it without us,—then we have a clear way, and ready access to pardon, and to believe his readiness to pardon. And this is it which is holden out here,—Christ condemning sin in the flesh, or punishing sin in his own flesh, giving a visible and sensible representation of the justice and righteousness of God in punishing sin, and that in his own flesh, offering up himself as the condemned sinner, and hanging up to the view of all the world, as an evident testimony of the justice and righteousness of God against sin, and by this means cutting off the very strength of sin,—the law, by fulfilling it.

* [Or, hesitation.—Ed.]

In Christ's sufferings you may behold, as in a clear mirror, the hatred and displeasure of God against sin, the righteousness of God in punishing sin. Him hath God set forth to the world to be a propitiation, to declare the righteousness of God, Rom. iii. 24, 25. In this crucified Lord, you may behold the sensible image and the most lively demonstration of holiness and righteousness. Christ's flesh bare the marks of both,—holiness in hating sin, righteousness in punishing it, and both in his beloved and only begotten Son's person,—in his flesh; and all for this purpose, that the law might be no loser by our salvation, 'that the righteousness of the law might be fulfilled in us,' &c.

This is that which Christ says, 'I came not to destroy the law, but to fulfil it,' Matt. v. 17; and which Paul seconds, 'Is the law then made void by faith? God forbid: it is rather established,' Rom. iii. 31. The law and justice come better to their own, by our Cautioner, than by us. There is no such way conceivable, to satisfy them fully, as this, whether you look to the commandment or the curse.

The commandment never got such satisfaction in any person, as in Christ's; he hath fulfilled it by obedience. 'It becometh us,' saith he, 'to fulfil all righteousness,' (Matt. iii. 15,) both moral and ceremonial; so that there was no guile found in his mouth,—he knew no sin, he was holy and harmless. His Father's will was his soul's delight,—'I delight to do thy will,' Ps. xl. 8. It was more to him than his necessary food, his meat and drink. There was so absolute a correspondency between his will and God's will, and between his way and his will, that it was not possible that any difference should fall between them. His obedience had more good in it (so to speak) than Adam's disobedience had evil in it, Rom. v. 18, 19. Adam's disobedience was but the sin of a finite creature, but Christ's obedience was the work of an infinite person. I think there was more real worth in Christ's obedience to the commands, than in all the united service and obedience of men and angels. All the love, delight, fear, and obedience flowing from these,—take them in one bundle, as they will be extended and multiplied to all eternity; there is something in Christ's that elevates it above all, and puts a higher price upon it. The transcendent dignity of his person,—his own Son 'made under the law,' (Gal. iv. 4,)—that is more worth than if all men and angels had been made under it. It had been no humiliation, but rather the exaltation of an angel, to be obedient to God. That subordination to a law, is the highest top of the creature's advancement. But he was such a person, as his obedience was a humbling himself: 'He humbled himself, and became obedient, even to the death,' Phil. ii. 8; and though he was the Son of God, yet he stooped to learn obedience, Heb. v. 8. Now indeed the commandment comes to it better,* by this means, to have such a glorious person under it, than if it had poor naughty us under it; and that is fulfilled by him, when otherwise it would never have been done. I suppose that justice had exacted the punishment of us. As we could never have ended suffering to all eternity, so we would never have begun new obedience to the command to all eternity. Thus, except Christ had taken it off us, and us off its hand, it would never have been fulfilled, since it was first broken. Next, the curse of the law could not get fuller satisfaction than in Christ. I suppose it had fallen upon the sinner. There is not so much worth in the creature's extremest sufferings, as to compensate the infinite wrongs done to the holiness and righteousness of God. Therefore, what was wanting in the intrinsic value of the creature's suffering, behoved to be made up in the infinite extent of it, and eternal continuance of it upon the creature. Thus, there could never be a determined time assigned, in which the curse was fulfilled, and in which justice could say,—hold, I have enough. It is as if a man were owing an infinite debt, and he could get nothing to defray it but poor petty sums, which being all conjoined, cannot amount to any proportion of it. Therefore, since he cannot get one sum in value equal to it, he must be eternally paying it in smalls, according to his capacity. And so, because the utmost farthing cannot be won at, he can never be released out of prison. But our Lord Jesus hath satisfied it to the full. He was a more substantial debtor, and because of the infinite dignity of his person, there was an intrinsic value upon his sufferings, proportioned unto the infiniteness of man's sin; so that he could pay all

* [That is, more honoured.—Ed.]

the debt in a short time, which a sinner could but have done to all eternity. Now, you know, any man would rather choose such a cautioner, that can solidly satisfy him in gross, and pay all the sum at once, than such a principal, that because of his inability, cannot amount to any considerable satisfaction in many years. And even so it is with the law and justice of God. They hold themselves better contented in Christ than in us, in his being 'made a curse,' than the falling of the curse on us, Gal. iii. 13. And therefore God testifies it to poor sinners, 'Deliver them, I have found a ransom,' Job xxxiii. 24;—and that is the ransom which Christ gave, —'his life—for many,' Matt. xx. 28.

You see then, how this conclusion follows, 'that the righteousness of the law might be fulfilled in us,' he having fulfilled it, and satisfied it so fully, both by obedience to the commandment, and submission to the curse. It is all one in God's account, as if we had done it, because Christ was surety in our stead, and a common person representing us, and therefore his paying of the debt acquits us at the hand of justice, and whatsoever he did to fulfil all righteousness, that is accounted ours, because we were represented in him, and judicially one with him. And therefore, we were condemned when he was condemned; we were dead when he died,—and so the righteousness of the law, in exacting a due punishment for sin, was fulfilled for us in him; and it is all one as if it had been personally in us. And this is laid down as the foundation of that blessed embassy or message of reconciliation to sinners, as that upon which God is in Christ reconciling and beseeching us to be reconciled, (2 Cor. v. 19—21,)—Him who knew no sin, hath he made sin for us, that we might be made the righteousness of God in him. You see the blessed exchange that he hath made with us,—he hath laid our sins on sinless Christ, and laid Christ's righteousness on sinful us. Christ took our sins on him, that he might give us his righteousness; and by virtue of this transaction and communication, as it was righteous with God to condemn sin in Christ's flesh, because our sin was upon him, so it is as just with him to impute righteousness to us, because we were in him. And as the law made him a curse, and exacted the punishment of him, it is as righteous with the Lord to give us life and salvation, and to forgive sin, as John speaks, 1st Epistle i. 9, 'If we confess our sins, he is faithful and just to forgive us our sins.'

Now consider this, my beloved, for it is propounded unto you as the greatest persuasive to move you to come to Jesus Christ,—there is such a clear and plain way in him to salvation. If this do not move your hearts, I know not what will. I do not expect that your troubles in this world,—the frequent lashes of judgment, the impoverishing and exhausting of you, the plucking away of those things you loved, the disquieting your peace so often, that any of those things that have the image of wrath upon them, can drive you to him, and make you forsake your way, when such a motive as this doth not prevail with you. O what heart could stand against the power of this persuasion, if it were but rightly apprehended! Who would not willingly fly into this city of refuge, if they did but know aright the avenger of blood that pursues them, and what safety is within? You are always imagining vain satisfactions to the law of God. How great weight doth your fancy impose upon your tears, your confessions, your reformations! If you can attain any thing of this kind, that is it which you give to satisfy justice, it is that wherewith you pretend to fulfil the law. But if it could be so, wherefore should God have sent his Son to condemn sin, and purchase righteousness by him? I beseech you, once know and consider your estate, that you may open your hearts to this Redeemer, that you may be willing to be stripped naked of all your imaginary righteousness, to put on this which will satisfy the law fully. Will you die in your sins, because you will not come to him to have life? Will you rather be condemned with sin, than saved with Christ's righteousness? And truly, there is no other altar that will preserve you but this. Now, if any, apprehending their own misery, be hardly pursued in their consciences by the law of God, I beseech you come hither, and behold it satisfied and fulfilled. I beseech you in Christ's stead to be reconciled unto God,—to lay down all hostile affections, and come to him, because God is in Christ reconciling the world, and not imputing their sins, because he hath imputed them already to Christ, 'him who knew no sin,' &c., and he is in Christ, imputing his righteousness to sinners.

Sermon XV.

VERSE 4.—" *That the righteousness of the law might be fulfilled in us,*" &c.

'THINK not,' saith our Lord and Saviour Jesus Christ, 'that I am come to destroy the law,—I am come to fulfil it,' Matt. v. 17. It was a needful caveat, and a very timeous advertisement, because of the natural misapprehensions in men's minds of the gospel. When free forgiveness of sins, and life everlasting, is preached in Jesus Christ, without our works; when the mercy of God is proclaimed in its freedom and fulness, the heart of man is subject to a woful misconceit of Christ, as if by these a latitude were given, and a liberty proclaimed to men to live in sin. That which is propounded as the encouragement of poor sinners to come to God, and forsake their own wicked way, is miserably wrested upon a mistake, to be an encouragement to revolt more and more. Righteousness and life, by faith in a Saviour, without the works of the law, is holden out as the grand persuasion of the gospel, to study obedience to the law. And yet such is the perverseness of many hearts, that, either in opinion or practice, they so carry themselves, as if there were an inconsistency between Christ and the law, between free justification and sanctification,—as if Christ had come to redeem us, not from sin, but to sin. Now, to prevent this, 'think not,' saith he, 'that I am come to destroy the law.' Do not fancy to yourselves a liberty to live in sin, and an immunity from the obligation of a commandment, because I have purchased an immunity and freedom from the curse. No, 'I am come to fulfil it' rather, not only in mine own person, but in yours also. And to this purpose Paul, Rom. iii. 31, 'Do we then make void the law by faith ?' It is so natural to our rebellious hearts to desire to be free from the yoke of obedience, and therefore we fancy such a notion of faith, as may not give itself to working in love, as is active in nothing but imagination. The apostle abominates this,—'God forbid,' he detests it, as impious and sacrilegious; 'yea, we establish it.' So then, all returns to this, one of the great ends of Christ's coming in the flesh, and one main intendment of the gospel published in his name, is not merely to deliver us from wrath, and redeem us from the curse, (Gal. iii. 13; 1 Thess. i. 10,) but also, and that especially, to redeem us from all iniquity, that we might be a people zealous of good works, (Tit. ii. 14); and to take away sin, and 'destroy the works of the devil,' 1 John iii. 5, 8. We spoke something before noon, how Christ hath fulfilled the law, and established it in his own person, by obedience and suffering,—neither of which ways it could be so well contented by any other. But there is yet a third way that he fulfils and establisheth it, and that is in our persons, 'that the righteousness of the law might be fulfilled in us, who walk not after the flesh, but after the Spirit.' He hath obliged himself to fulfil it, not only for believers, but in believers. Therefore the promises run thus, I will write my law in their hearts, and cause them to walk in my statutes, Ezek. xxxvi. 27 ; Jer. xxxi. 33. Not only I delight to do thy will, but I will make them delight to do it also. And truly, in this respect, the law is more fulfilled and established by Christ, than ever it could have been, if man had been left to satisfy it alone. If we had reckoned alone with the law, we had been taken up eternally with satisfying for the breaches of it, so that there could be no access to obedience of the command, and no acceptance either. A sinner must first satisfy the curse, for the fault done, before ever he can be in a capacity to perform new obedience on the terms of acceptation of it with God. Now the first would have taken up eternity, so that there can be no place of entry to the second ; therefore, if Christ had not found out a way of free pardon of the sins that are past, and assurance of forgiveness for the time to come, the commandments of God would be wholly frustrated. 'But there is forgiveness with thee, that thou mayest be feared,' Psalm cxxx. 4. The word is also 'worshipped.' Truly, my beloved, this is the foundation of all religion,—free forgiveness. There had been no religion, no worship of God, no obedience to his commands throughout all eternity ; there should never have been any fear, any love, any delight in God, any reverence and subjection to him, if he had not forgiveness,—a treasure of mercies with him to bestow first upon sinners. And this makes access to stand and serve in his sight. The cloud of our transgressions is so thick and dark, that there never could have been any communion with God, if he had not found out the way to scatter and blot it out, for his own name's sake. Religion, then, must begin at this great and inestimable free gift of imputed righteousness,—of accounting us what we are not in ourselves, because found so in another. It begins at remission of sins. But that is not all. This hath a further end, and truly it is but introductive to a further end; that so a soul may be made partaker of the gift of holiness within, and have that image of God renewed in holiness and righteousness. I would have you once persuaded to begin at this, to receive the free gift of another's righteousness, (Rom. v. 17,) and another's obedience, to find your own nakedness and loathsomeness without this covering, and how short all other coverings of your own works are. O that we could once persuade you to renounce yourselves, to embrace this righteousness! Then it were easy to prevail with you to renounce sin, to put on holiness. I say, first, you must renounce yourselves, as undone in all you do, as loathsome in all that ever you loved, and come under the wide and broad skirt of Christ's righteousness, which he did weave upon the earth, for to hide our nakedness. You must once have the righteousness of the law fulfilled perfectly by another, before you can have access to fulfil one jot of it yourselves, or any thing you do be accepted. And, till this foundation be laid, you do but beat the air in religion, you build on the sand.

Now, if once you were brought this length, to renounce all confidence in yourselves, and to flee into Christ's righteousness, then it were easy to lead you a step further, —to renounce the love of your most beloved sins. And the more lovely that Christ's righteousness is in your eyes, the more beauty would holiness and obedience have in them also unto you. Then you would labour to walk after the guidance of the Spirit.

I would have the impression of this deep in your hearts,—that the gospel is not a doctrine of licentiousness, but a doctrine of the purest liberty, of the completest redemption. Many think it liberty to serve their lusts; and it is indeed as bonds and cords to restrain them. There is no man but would be content to be saved from the wrath to come; and therefore many snatch at such sentences of the gospel, and take them lightly, without consideration of what further is in it. But truly if this were all, it were not complete redemption, if there were not redemption from sin too, which is the most absolute tyrant in the world. I think a true Christian would account the service of sin bondage, though it were left at his own option. He that commits sin, is the servant of sin; therefore the freedom that Christ purchaseth, is freedom from sin, John viii. 36. I will say more. We are delivered from wrath, that so we may be redeemed from sin. We have the righteousness of Christ imputed to us, that so the image of Christ may be renewed within us; this is the very end of that. I am sure any that discerns aright, knows sin to have infinitely more evil in it than punishment hath; nay, punishment is only evil, as it hath relation to sin. There is a beauty of justice and righteousness in punishment, but there is nothing in sin but deformity and opposition to his holiness. It is purely evil, and most purely hated of God. And if there were no more to persuade you that sin is infinitely more evil than pain, consider how our pain and punishment was really transferred upon the blessed Son of God, and that all this did not make him a whit the worse. But he was not capable of the real infusion of our sin. That would have made Christ as miserable, wretched, and impotent, as any of us, that would have disabled him so far from helping us, that he would have had as much need of a mediator as we,—all which were highly blasphemous to imagine. Look then how much distance and difference there was between suffering, dying Christ, and wretched men living in sin. None can say but he is infinitely better, even while in pain, nor * the highest prince in pleasure, so much disproportion there is between sin and pain; so much is the one worse than the other. Do not think then that Christ died to purchase an indulgence for you to live in sin. Truly that were to take away the lesser evil, that the greater may remain; that were to deliver from one misery, that we may be more involved in that which is the greatest of all miseries. Nay, cer-

* [That is, than.—Ed.]

tainly if Christ be a Redeemer, he must redeem us from our most potent and accursed enemy,—sin; he must take away the root, the fountain of all misery,—sin; that which conceived in its womb all pains, sorrows, sicknesses, death and hell. You have the great end of redemption expressed, Luke i. 74, 75, 'That we, being delivered from all our enemies, might serve him without fear, in holiness and righteousness.' It was that for which he made man at first, and it is that for which he hath made him again, 'created unto good works,' Eph. ii. 10. It was a higher design certainly, for which the Son of God became partaker of our nature, than only to deliver us from hell. No doubt it was to make us partakers of the divine nature, (2 Pet. i. 4;) and this is the very nature of God,—holiness and goodness. As sin is the very nature and image of the devil, so the great breach of the creation was the breaking off of this image of God. That was the heaviest fall of man, from the top of divine excellency, into the bottom of devilish deformity. Now it is this that is the great plot for which Christ came into the world,—to make up that breach, to restore man to that dignity again; so that redemption from wrath is but a step to ascend upon, to that which is truly God's design, and man's dignity,—conformity with God in holiness and righteousness.

O that you could be persuaded of this,—that Christ's business in the world was not to bring a notion of an imaginary righteousness only, by mere imputation, but to bring forth a solid and real righteousness in our hearts, by the operation of his Spirit! I say, imputation, or accounting righteous, is but a mere imagination, if this lively operation do not follow. He came not only to spread his garment over our nakedness and deformity, but really and effectually to be a physician to save our souls, to cure all our inward distempers. The gospel is not only a doctrine of a righteousness without us, but of a righteousness both without, for, and within us too;—'that the righteousness of the law might be fulfilled in us,' &c. Christ without, happiness itself without, cannot make us happy, till they come in within us, and take up a dwelling in our souls. Therefore I declare unto the most part of you who pretend to expect salvation by Jesus Christ, that you are yet in your sins, and as yet you have no fellowship in this redemption. Do you think to walk after the course of the world, and the lusts of the flesh,—to wallow in those common pollutions and uncleannesses among men, swearing, lying, contention, railing, wrath, malice, envy, drunkenness, uncleanness, and such like, and yet be in Christ Jesus? Do not deceive yourselves, 'God is not mocked.' He that is in Christ is a new creature. His endeavour and study, his affection and desire, is toward a new walk after the Spirit. Are not most of you carnal, all flesh,—the flesh gives laws, and you obey them? Are not your immortal souls enslaved to base lusts, to the base love of the world? Are they not prone to prostitute themselves to the service of your fleshly and brutish part? Why do you then imagine, that you are in Christ Jesus, partakers of his righteousness? Consider it in time, that so you may be indeed, what you now are not, but pretend to be. It is the opinion that you are in Christ already that keeps you out of him.

But, on the other hand again, there is nothing here to discourage a poor soul, that thinks subjection to sin the greatest slavery, who would as gladly be redeemed from the power of it as from hell. I say to such, whose soul's desire it is to be purged from all that 'filthiness of the flesh and spirit,' and whose continued aim is to walk in obedience,—though you have many failings, and often fall and defile yourselves again, yet this comfort is holden out here unto you,—there is no condemnation to you; Jesus Christ hath condemned sin to save you, he hath fulfilled all righteousness for you; and therefore lay you the weight of your acceptation and consolation upon what he hath done himself, and not upon what is but yet a-doing in you. Do you not find, I say, that the grace of Jesus Christ, revealed in the gospel, is that which melts your hearts most? Is not the goodness of the Lord that which persuades you most? And do not these make you loathe yourselves and love holiness? Encourage yourselves therefore in him. Hold fast the righteousness that is without you by faith, and certainly you shall find that righteousness and holiness shall in due time be fulfilled within you. I know no soul so wretched, but it may lay hold on that perfect righteousness of Christ's, and go under the covering of it, and take heart from it, if so be the desire and affection of their soul be directed to a further end, to have his Spirit dwelling within them, for the renewing of their heart 'in righteousness and true holiness.' I do not say, that this is a condition which you must perform before you venture to lay hold on Christ's righteousness without you; nowise, but rather I would declare unto you the very nature of faith in Christ, that it seeks delivery from wrath in him, not simply and lastly, but that a way may be made for redemption from sin, and that there may be a participation of that divine nature, which is most in its eye.

Sermon XVI.

Verse 4, 5.—"*Who walk not after the flesh, but after the Spirit. For they that are after the flesh,*" *&c.*

If there were nothing else to engage our hearts to religion, I think this might do it, that there is so much reason in it. Truly it is the most rational thing in the world, except some revealed mysteries of faith, which are far above reason, but not contrary to it. There is nothing besides in it, but that which is the purest reason. Even that part of it which is most difficult to man, that which concerns the moderating of his lusts and affections, and the regulating his walk and carriage;—there is nothing that Christianity requires in these matters, but that which may be persuaded by most convincing reasons, to be most suitable and comely for man, as man. You may take it in the subject in hand. There is nothing sounds harsher to men, and seems harder in religion, than such a victory over the flesh, such an abstractedness from sensual and earthly things. And yet, truly, there is nothing in the world, that more adorns and beautifies a man, nothing so elevates him above beasts as this, insomuch that many natural spirits, void of this saving light, have notwithstanding been taken with somewhat of the beauty of it, and so far enamoured with the love of it, as to account all the world mad and brutish that followed these lower things, and enslaved themselves unto them. I take the two fountains of all the pollutions, disorders, and defilements among men, to be the inconsideration and ignorance of God, that eternal Spirit and Fountain-being, and the ignorance of our own souls, those immortal spirits within us, which are derived from that Fountain-spirit. This is the misery of men, that scarce do they once seriously reflect upon their own spirits, or think what immortal souls are within them, and what affinity these have to the Fountain of all spirits. Therefore do men basely throw down themselves to the satisfaction of the lusts of the flesh. Now, indeed, this is the very beginning of Christianity, to reduce men from these baser thoughts and employments, to the consideration of their immortal souls within. And, O how will a Christian blush to behold himself in that light, to see the very image of a beast upon his nature, to look on that slavery and bondage of his far better part to the worst and brutish part in him,—his flesh!

If a man did wisely consider the constitution of his nature, from its first divine original, and what a thing the soul is, which is truly and more properly himself, than his body; what excellency is in the soul beyond the body, and so, what pre-eminency it advanceth a man unto beyond a beast,—he could not but account religion the very ornament and perfection of his nature. Reason will say, that the spirit should rule and command the body, that flesh is but the minister and servant of the spirit, that there is nothing the proper and peculiar good of man, but that which adorns and rectifies the spirit; that all those external things which men's senses are carried after with so much violence, do not better a man, as man, but are common to beasts; that in these things, man's happiness as man, doth not all consist, but in some higher and more transcending good, which beasts are not capable of, and which may satisfy the immortal spirit, and not perish in the using, but live with it. All these things, the very natural frame and constitution of man doth convincingly persuade. Now then, may a soul think within itself, O how far am I departed from my original! How far degenerated from that noble and royal dignity, that God by the stamp of his image once put upon me! How is it that I am become a slave and drudge to that baser and brutish part, the flesh? I would have you retire into your own hearts, and ask such things at them. Man being in honour, and understanding not, is even like the beasts that perish. Truly we are become like beasts, because we consider not that we are men, and so advanced by creation far above beasts. The not reflecting on the immortal, spiritual nature of our souls, hath transformed us, in a manner, into the nature of beasts, perishing beasts. Christianity is the very transforming of a beast into a man, as sin was the deforming of a man into a beast. This is the proper effect of Christianity,—to restore humanity, to elevate it, and purify it from all those defilements and corruptions that were engrossed and incorporated into it, by the state of subjection to the flesh. And therefore the apostle delineates the nature of it unto us, and draws the difference wide between the natural man and a Christian.

The natures of things are dark and hidden in themselves, but they come to be known to us by their operations and acting. Their inclinations and instincts are known this way. Grace is truly a very spiritual thing, and the nature of it lies high. Yet as Christ could not be hid in the house, neither can grace be hid in the heart,—it will be known by its working. Christ can be better hid in a house than in the heart, because, when he is in a heart, he is engaged to restore that heart and soul to its native dignity and pre-eminency over the flesh, and this cannot but cause much disturbance in the man, for a season. To change governments, to cast out usurpers, and to restore the lawful and righteous owner to the possession of his right, cannot be done secretly and easily. It will shake the very foundations of a kingdom to accomplish it. So it is here,—the restitution of the soul to the possession of its right and dominion over the flesh,—the casting out of that tyrannous and base usurper, the flesh, cannot be done, except all the man know it, feel it, and in a manner be pained with it. Now, the nature of Christianity doth lay itself open to us in these two especially, in what it minds and savours, and how it causeth to walk. Life is known especially by affection and motion. A feeling, thinking, savouring power, is a living power; so a moving, walking power is a living power, and these are here. The Christian is shortly described by his nature. He is one after the Spirit, not after the flesh; and by the proper characteristical operations of that nature, first, minding or savouring 'the things of the Spirit,' which comprehends his inward thoughts, affections, intentions, and cogitations. All his inward senses are exercised about such objects. And then he is one walking 'after the Spirit;' his motions are in a course of obedience, proceeding from that inward relish or taste that he hath of the things of God. It is not without very good reason, that the name of a Christian is thus expressed,—one 'after the Spirit.' That is his character that expresses his nature unto us. Whether ye look to the original of Christianity, or the prime subject of it, or the chief end of it, it deserves to be called by this name. The original of it is very high, as high as that eternal Spirit, as high as the God of the spirits of all flesh. Things are like their original, and some way participate of the nature of their causes. 'That which is born of the Spirit, is spirit,' John iii. 6. That which is born of God, who is a Spirit, must be spirit, 1 John v. 1. How royal a descent is that! How doth it nobilitate a man's nature! Truly, all other degrees of birth among men are vain imaginary things, that have no worth at all, but in the fancies of men. They put no real excellency in men. But this is only true nobility. This alone doth extract a man *de fæce vulgi*, out of the dregs of the multitude. There is no intrinsic difference between bloods, or natures, but what this makes, this divine birth, this second birth. All other differences are but in opinion, this is in reality. It puts the image of that blessed Spirit upon a man. Truly, such a creature is not begotten in the womb of any natural cause, of any human persuasion, or enticing words of man's wisdom, of any external mercy or judgment. No instruction, no persuasion, no allurement, nor affrightment can make you Christians in the Spirit, till the Spirit blow when he pleaseth, and create you again. It must come from above,—that power that can set your hearts aright, and make them to look straight above.

Christ Jesus came down from heaven unto the earth, and took on our flesh, that so the almighty Spirit might come down to transform our spirits, and lift them up from the earth to the heaven. We cast the seed into the ground of men's hearts, (and alas! it gets entry but in few souls, it is scattered rather on the highway side, and cannot reach into the arable ground of the heart;) but it can do nothing without the influence of heaven, except the Spirit beget you again by that immortal seed of the word. Therefore we would cease our wondering, that all the means of God's word and works do not beget more true Christians. I do rather wonder that any of Adam's wretched posterity should be begotten again, and advanced to so high a dignity, to be born of the Spirit. O that Christians would mind their original, and wonder at it, and study to be like it! If you believe and consider that your descent is from that uncreated Spirit, how powerful might that be to conform you more and more to him, and to transform more and more of your flesh into spirit! There is nothing will raise up the spirits of the children of princes more, than to know their royal birth and dignity. How should the consideration of this make your spirits suitable to your state or fortunes, as we use to say? You would labour to raise them up to that height of your original, and to walk worthy of that high calling. O that we could learn that instruction from it which Paul gives, 1 Cor. i. 30, 31, 'But of him are ye in Christ;' therefore let him that glorieth, 'glory in the Lord!' Truly, a soul possessed with the meditation of this royal descent from God, could not possibly glory in those inglorious baser things, in which men glory, and could not contain or restrain gloriation and boasting in him. The glory of many is their shame, because it is their sin, of which they should be ashamed. But suppose that in which men glory be not shame in itself, as the lawful things of this present world, yet certainly it is a great shame for a Christian to glory in them, or esteem the better of himself for them. If this were minded always,—that we are of God, born of God, what power do you think temptations, or solicitations to sin, would have over us! 'He that is born of God sinneth not,—he keepeth himself, and that wicked one toucheth him not,' 1 John v. 18, 19. Truly, this consideration imprinted in the heart, would elevate us above all these baser persuasions of the flesh. This would make sin loathsome and despicable, as the greatest indignity we could do to our own natures. The strength and advantage of sin, is to make us forget what we are, whom we have relation unto,—to drink us drunk with the puddle of the world, or then with our own jealousies and suspicions, that we may forget our birth and state, and so be enticed to any thing. If you would have wherewith to beat back all the fiery darts of the devil, take the shield of this faith and persuasion; how would it silence temptations? 'Shall I, who am a ruler, flee?' saith Nehemiah. Shall I, who am born of the Spirit; shall I, who am of God in Christ, abase myself to such unworthy and base things? Shall I dishonour my Father, and disgrace myself?

Then Christianity's chief residence, its royal seat, is in the spirit of a man, and so he is one after the Spirit. Be ye 'renewed in the spirit of your mind,' Eph. iv. 23. As it is of a high descent, so it must have the highest and most honourable lodging in all the creation, that is, the spirit of a man. Without this there is no room else fit for it, and suitable to it, in this lower world. 'My son, give me thine heart,' saith Wisdom, Prov. xxiii. 26. It cares for nothing besides, if it get not the heart, the inmost cabinet of the imperial city of this isle of man; for 'out of it are the issues of life,' that flow into all the members. Do not think that grace will lodge one night in your outward man, that you can put on Christianity upon your countenance or conversation without. Except you admit it into your souls, it can have no suitable entertainment there alone. It is of a spiritual nature, and it must have a spirit to abide in. Every thing is best preserved and entertained by things suitable to its nature; such do incorporate together, and imbosom one with another; whereas things keep a greater distance with things different in nature. A flame will die out among cold stones, without oily matter. This heavenly fire that is descended into the world, can have nothing earthly to feed upon. It must die out, except it get into the immortal spirit, and then furnish, so to speak, perpetual nourishment to it, till at length all the spirit be set on flame, and changed, as it were, into that heavenly substance, to mount up above, from whence it came. Do not think, my beloved, to superinduce true religion upon your outside, and within to be as rotten sepulchres. You must either open your hearts to Christ, or else he will not abide with you. Such a noble guest will not stay in the suburbs of the city, if you take him not into the palace; and truly the palace of our hearts is too unworthy for such a worthy guest, it hath been so defiled by sin. How vile is it? But if you would let him enter, he would wash it and cleanse it for himself.

Will you know then the character of a Christian? He is one much within. He hath retired into his own spirit, to know how it goes with it; and he finds all so disordered and confused, all so unsettled, that, he gets so much business to do at home, he gets no leisure to come much abroad again. It is the misery of men, that they are wholly without, carried into external things only; and this is the very character of a beast, that it cannot reflect inwardly upon itself, but is wholly spent on things that are presented to the outward senses. There is nothing in which men are more assimilated to beasts than this, that we do not speak in ourselves, or return into our own bosoms, but are wholly occupied about the things that are without us. And thus it fares with us, as with the man that is busy in all other men's matters, and never thinks of his own. His estate must needs ruin; all his affairs must be out of course. Truly, while we are immersed and drowned in external things, our souls are perishing, our inward estate is washing away. All our own affairs, that can only and properly be called ours, are disordered and jumbled. Therefore, Christianity doth first of all recall the wandering and vain spirit of man into itself, as that exhortation is, Psal. iv. 9, to 'commune' with his 'own heart,'—to make a diligent search of his own affairs; and, O how doth he find all out of course; as a garden neglected, all overgrown,—as a house not inhabited all dropping through,—in a word, wholly ruinous, through intolerable negligence! It was the first turn of the prodigal to return to himself, 'he came to himself,' Luke xv. 17. Truly, sin is not only an aversion from God, but it is an estrangement from ourselves, from our souls, from our own happiness. It is a madness that takes away the use of reason and consideration of our ownselves. But grace is a conversion, not only to God, but to ourselves. It bringeth a man home to his heart, maketh him sober again who was beside himself. Hence that phrase, 1 Kings viii. 47. 'When they shall turn to their own hearts, and return' It is the most laborious vanity, or the vainest labour, to compass heaven and earth,—to be so busied abroad,—to know other things, and then to know and consider nothing of that which of all things most nearly concerns us,—ourselves. 'What shall it profit a man, if he gain the whole world, and lose his soul?' for that is himself. And what shall it profit to know all, and not know his soul, to be everywhere but where he ought to be. Well, a Christian is one called home from vain impertinent diversions, one that is occupied most about his soul and spirit, how to have all the disorders he finds in himself ordered, all those distempers cured, all those defilements washed. This is the business he is about in this world, to wash his heart from wickedness, (Jer. iv. 14,)—to cleanse even vain thoughts, and shut up, from that ordinary repair,* his own heart. He is about the enclosing it to be a garden to the well-beloved, to bring forth sweet fruits. He is about the renewing of it, the adorning it with the new man, against that day of our Bridegroom's appearing, and bringing him up to celebrate the marriage. Though he be in the flesh, yet he is most taken up with his spirit, how to have it restored to that primitive beauty and excellency, the image of God in it; how to be clothed with humility, and to put on the ornament of a meek and quiet spirit,—that he accounts his beauty; how to rule his own spirit,—that he accounts only true fortitude; and thinks it a greater vassalage and victory to overcome himself than his enemy, and esteems it the noblest revenge, not to be like to other men that wrong him. He is occupied about the highest gain and advantage, viz. to save his spirit and soul; and accounts all loss to this,—to bring Jesus Christ into the heart. That is the jewel he digs for, and esteems all dung in comparison of it.

If you be Christians after the Spirit, no doubt you are busied this way about your spirits. For others, they are busied about the flesh,—to make provision for its lusts; and there needs no other mark to know them by. Alas! poor souls, to this you have never yet adverted that you have spirits, immortal beings within you,

*[That is, concourse.—Ed.]

which must survive this dust, this corruptible flesh; what will ye do, when you cannot have flesh to care for,—when your spirits can have nothing to be carried forth into, but must eternally dwell within the bosom of an evil conscience, and be tormented with that worm, the bitter remembrance of the neglect of your spirits, and utter estrangement from them, while you were in the body? Then you must be confined within your own evil consciences, and be imprisoned there for ever, because, while yet there was time and season, you were always abroad, and everywhere, but within your own hearts and consciences,—and is not that a just recompense?

Then again, as Christianity descends from the Father of spirits, into the spirit of a man, to lodge there for a while, it doth at length bring up the spirit of a man, and unites it to that eternal Spirit; and so, as the original was high and divine, the end is high too. It issues out of that Fountain, and returns with the heart of man, to imbosom itself in that again. And truly, this is the great excellency of true religion above all those things you are busied about, that it elevates the spirit of a man to God; that it will never rest till it have carried it above to the Fountain-spirit. Our spirits are sparks and chips, to speak so with reverence, of that divine Being; but now they are wholly immersed and sunk into the flesh, and into the earth by sin, till grace come down and renew them, and extract them out of that dunghill, and purify them. And then they are, as in a state of violence, always striving to mount upwards, till they be embodied, or rather inspirited, so to speak, in that original Spirit, till they be wholly united to their own element, the divine nature. You know Christ's prayer, John xvii. 'That they may be one, as we are one; I in them, and thou in me, that they may be made perfect in one,' ver. 22, 23. Then spirits have attained their perfection, then will they 'rest from their labours,' when they are one with him. This is the only centre of spirits, in which they can rest immoveable. You find all the desires and affections of the saints are as so many breathings upward, pantings after union with him, and longings to be intimately present with the Lord. Therefore a Christian is one after the Spirit, groaning to be all spirit, to have the earthly house of this tabernacle dissolved, and to be clothed upon with that house from heaven. He knows with Paul, that he is not at home, though he be at home in the body, because the body is that which separates from the Lord, which partition-wall he would willingly have taken down, that his spirit might be at home, present with the Lord, 2 Cor. v. 1, &c. 'Who knoweth (saith Solomon) the spirit of a man that ascends upward, and the spirit of the beast that goeth downward to the earth?' Eccles. iii. 21. Truly, the natural motion of man's spirit should be to ascend upward to God who gave it. When this frail and broken vessel of the body is dissolved into the elements, the higher and purer nature that lodged within it should fly upwards to heaven; even as the spirit of the beasts, being but the prime and finer part of the body, not different in nature from the earth, naturally falls down to the earth with the body, and is dissolved into the elements. But I think, the consideration of that woful disorder, that sin hath brought into the world, that all things in man are so degenerated and become brutish, both his affections and his conversation, that carnal and sensual lusts have the whole dominion over men; I say, the serious and earnest view of this might make a man suspect and call in question, whether or not there be any difference between men and beasts; whether or not there may be any spirit in the one of a higher nature than in the other? Truly, it would half persuade, that there is no immortal spirit in man, else how could he be such a beast all his time, 'serving diverse lusts?' Can it be possible, might one think, that there is any spirit in men, that can ascend to heaven, when there is no motion thither to be observed among men? I beseech you, consider this,—the spirit must either ascend or descend when it goes out of the body, as now in affection and endeavour it ascends or descends while it is in the body. There is an indispensable connection between these. Whatsoever the spirit aims at, which way soever it turns and directs its flight, thither it shall be constrained to go eternally. Do you think, my beloved, while you are in the body, to bow down yourselves to the earth, to descend into the service of the flesh all your time, never once seriously to rise up in the consideration of eternity, or lift up your heads above temporal and earthly things, and yet in the close to ascend unto heaven? No, no; do not deceive yourselves; you must go forward. This life and eternity make one straight line, either of ascent or descent, of happiness or misery; and since you have bowed down always, while in the body, there is no rising up after it. Forward you must go, and that is downward to that element, into which you transformed your spirits; that is, the earth, or below the earth,—to hell. Your spirits have most affinity with these, and down they must go, as a stone to the earth. But if you would desire to have your spirits ascending up to heaven, when they are let out of this prison, the body, take heed which way they turn. Bend and strive while here in the body. If your strugglings be to be upward to God, if you have discovered that blessedness which is in him, and if this be the predominant of your spirit, that carries it upwards in desires and endeavours, and turns it off the base study of satisfying the flesh, and the base love of the world; if thy soul be mounting aloft, on these wings of holy desires of a better life than can be found in any thing below, certainly the motion of thy spirit will be in a straight line upward. When thou leavest thy dust to the earth, angels wait to carry that spirit to that bosom of Christ, where it longed and liked most to be. But devils do attend the souls of most part of men, to thrust them down below the earth, because they did still bend down to the earth.

Sermon XVII.

VERSE 5.—"*For they that are after the flesh do mind the things of the flesh,*" &c.

THOUGH sin hath taken up the principal and inmost cabinet of the heart of man,—though it hath fixed its imperial throne in the spirit of man, and makes use of all the powers and faculties in the soul to accomplish its accursed desires, and fulfil its boundless lusts; yet it is not without good reason expressed in scripture, ordinarily under the name of 'flesh,' and a 'body of death;' and men dead in sins, are said to be yet in the flesh. The reason is, partly because this was the rise of man's first ruin, or the chiefest ingredient in his first sin,—his hearkening to the suggestions of his flesh, against the clear light and knowledge of his spirit. The apple was beautiful to look on, and sweet to the taste, and this engaged man. Thus the voluntary debasement and subjection of the spirit—which was breathed in of God—unto the service of that dust which God had appointed to serve it, hath turned into a necessary slavery, so that the flesh being put in the throne, cannot be cast out. And this is the righteous judgment of God upon man, that he that would not serve so good and so high a Lord, should be made a drudge and slave to the very dregs of the creation. Partly again, because the flesh hath in it the seeds of the most part of these evil fruits, which abound in the world. The most part of our corruptions have either their rise or their increase from the flesh; the most part of the evils of men are either conceived in the flesh or brought forth by it, by the ministry and help of our degenerate spirits. And truly this is it that makes our returning to God so hard and difficult a work, because we are in the flesh, which is like stubble, disposed to conceive flame upon any sparkle of a temptation; there are so many dispositions and inclinations in the body since our fall, that are as powerful to carry us to excess and inordinateness in affection or conversation, as the natural instincts of beasts do drive them on to their own proper operations. You know, the flesh is oftentimes the greatest impediment that the spirit hath, because of its lumpishness and earthly quality. How willing would the spirit be, how nimble and active in the ways of obedience, if it were not retarded, dulled, and clogged with the heavy lump of our flesh! 'The spirit indeed is willing, but the flesh is weak,' saith Christ, Matt. xxvi. 41. Truly I think the great remissness, negligence, weakness, fainting of Christians, in their race of Christianity, arise ordinarily from this weight that is carried about with them, that it must be some extraordinary impulse of a higher Spirit to drive us on without wearying. And because of this indisposition of the flesh, we are not able to bear much of God's presence in this life, (it would certainly confound mortality, if so much were let out of it as is in heaven,) no more than a weak eye can endure to behold the sun in its brightness. And then the flesh, as it is the greatest retardment in good, it is the greatest incitement to evil; it is a bosom enemy, that betrays us to Satan, it is near us, and connatural to us. And this is the great advantage Satan hath of a Christian, he hath a friend within every Christian, that betrays him often. You know the most part of temptations from without could have no such force or strength against us, if there were not some predisposition in the flesh, some seeds of that evil within, if they were not presented to some suitableness to our senses; and they being once engaged on Satan's side, they easily draw the whole man with them, under a false colour and pretence of friendship; therefore they are said to 'war against the soul,' 1 Pet. ii. 11, and they are said 'easily' to 'beset us,' Heb. xii. 1. Truly it is no wonder that the enemy storm our city, when the outworks, yea, the very ports of the city, are possessed by traitors. No wonder Satan approach near the walls with his temptations, when our senses, our fleshly part, are so apt to receive him, and ready to entertain all objects without difference, that are suitable to affect them.

You see then how much power the flesh hath in man, so that it is no wonder that every natural man hath this denomination, one 'after the flesh,' one carnal from the predominating part, though the worst part. Every man by nature, till a higher birth come, may be called all flesh, all fashioned and composed of the flesh, and after the flesh, even his spirit and mind being fleshly and earthly, sunk into the flesh, and transformed into a brutish quality or nature. Now the great purpose of the gospel is, to bring along a deliverer unto your spirits, for the releasing and unfettering of them from the chains of fleshly lusts. This is the very work of Christianity, to give liberty to the captive souls of men, 'and the opening of the prison to them that are bound,' Isa. lxi. 1. The souls of men are chained with their own fleshly lusts, and if at any time they can break these grosser chains, as some finer spirits have escaped out of the vilest dungeon of the flesh, and cast off these heavier chains that bind the most part of men, yet wholly escape they cannot. There be higher and lower rooms of this prison; there are some more gross, some more subtile cords and bands of the flesh; and whatsoever it be that holds a man bound, or in whatsoever house he be imprisoned, it is not much matter, since really he is bound, and his liberty restrained. If a chain of gold bind as fast as a chain of iron, there is no real difference, except that mockery is added unto it, when a man is detained in a golden prison with golden chains. Though some men, I say, escape the grosser pollutions of the flesh, yet they are fettered within some narrow, scant, and but imaginary good things; they cannot go without the compass of those. Every man is confined by nature within the circle of his own narrow bosom, or if he expatiate into the field of the world, yet how narrow, how limited are all created objects, for the infinite desires of the soul, whether it tend to the enjoyment of other creatures, or to the possession of some imaginary excellency in a man's self. How straitened are they! How imprisoned in all that compass! There is no true liberty can be found there. Though some may be disengaged from baser lusts, and the common vain employments of men; yet far they cannot go; they do but engage more with themselves the love and estimation of themselves. Without that compass they cannot possibly go, whether from another principle, or to another end. And, O how little bounds is within any created breast for the immortal spirit, that is so vast and expatiating in its desires to dwell in!

But here is the perfect redemption that is in Jesus Christ. When he comes into the soul, he unfetters and releases it, not only of the grosser lusts of the flesh, but even of those subtile invisible bands of self-love, self-seeking, of all scant, narrow, and particular objects, and sets it at liberty to expatiate in that universal good, the infinite fulness of God, and grace which is in Christ Jesus: and hence a Christian is called one 'after the Spirit;' that is, whose spirit is rid and delivered from that natural bondage and slavery to the creatures, and is espoused, at least in affection and endeavour, to the all-sufficient and self-sufficient God.

We told you, that this new nature of a Christian shows itself in affection and motion, in minding and walking; both are signs of life, and the proper actions of it. As the natural man is easily known by what he minds and savours, and what way he walks, so is the spiritual man. Minding or savouring comprehends, no doubt, all the inward acts of the soul, all the imaginations, cogitations, thoughts, affections, desires and purposes of the soul. To express it shortly, there is a concurrence of these two, cogitation and affection, the understanding and the will, in this business. The natural man knoweth not the things of the Spirit; so he cannot taste or relish them, since he doth not know them, 1 Cor. ii. 14. How can they believe on him whom they have not heard? But far more, how can men love and desire that which they do not know? Though it be hard to convince some that they know not God, nor the things of the Spirit, because they have some form of knowledge, and seem to understand, and can discourse on religion; yet I wonder that the most part of men, whose ignorance is written in their foreheads, with such palpable characters, should have so much difficulty to take with this challenge. I am sure, many that persuade themselves of heaven, are yet shut up in that dungeon of natural blindness and darkness of mind, and that so gross and thick darkness, that it is not possible to make them conceive any notion of spiritual things; the common twilight of nature is almost extinguished, and little or nothing increased by their education in the visible church. How can you prize and esteem Jesus Christ, of whom you know nothing but the bare name? How can you savour heaven, when you have never admitted one serious thought of the life to come? O that you could be persuaded, that the grace of God is inconsistent with such gross ignorance, as is in the generality of you! Truly grace is a light shining in the soul, that opens the eyes to see that light that surrounds us in the gospel. But will you consider, beloved, how ready you are to receive other things of no moment, how your memories can retain them, and your understandings receive other purposes very perplexed and laborious; but for the knowledge of your sin and misery, or of that blessed remedy showed in the gospel, we cannot make you capable of a few questions about them; and if you learn the words by heart, (as you use to speak,) yet, alas! the matter and thing itself is not in the heart or mind, you have nothing but words, as appears. If we ask about the same matter in other words and terms, it is as dark and new to you, as if you had never heard it. I beseech you consider, if you do not then mind the things of the flesh most when you are not only most capable to know these things that concern this life, but most ready to entertain such thoughts. You have no difficulty to mind the world whole weeks and years, but you can never find leisure or time to mind the life to come; and yet vainly you say, you mind it always. I beseech you, how do you mind God, and the things of God, when, if you will but recollect your thoughts, and gather the sum of them, you will not find one serious advised thought of him or his matters in a whole week! I profess, I wonder how so many can enforce upon themselves a persuasion that God is always in their heart. I think it is the height of delusion! I am sure he is not in one of ten thousand thoughts, that travel, walk, lodge, and dwell in the souls of men; and yet they will needs bear upon themselves that they always mind him. I am sure most of you cannot say, that ever you shut the doors of your hearts upon other vain objects, that you might retire to secret meditation on God, or conference with him; and I am as sure, that many men have God oftener in their mouths, by oaths and blasphemies, and irreverent speaking, and taking his holy name in vain, than in their minds, prayers or praises, or any holy meditations of him. Are you not as unwilling to fix your minds upon any sad solemn thoughts of God's justice, of hell, of heaven, of sin or misery, of death, as boys, whose heads are full of play, are loath to go to their books? Doth not your practice in this speak with these wicked men, who say, (Job xxi. 14.) 'Depart from us, we desire not the knowledge of thy ways?' How constrained are all your thoughts of religion! They are entertained as those whom you would not desire to come again. But how unconstrained, how free are all other thoughts! Our minds can rove whole days about vanity, about fancies, dreams, nothings; but you neither like to admit nor retain the knowledge of God in your mind, Rom i. 28. Do you not entertain any serious weighty thoughts of religion, that by occasion may enter as fire-brands, as hot coals in your bosom? How glad are you to get any diversion to other things! How willing to shun them, or cast them out! But if it be any temporal thing, any thing relating to this flesh, your thoughts come freely off, are steady and fixed as long as you please; your minds can travel through all the ends of the earth, to bring in some fancy of gain or advantage, or to steal by precious time, and that without wearying. Now all these things considered, my beloved, are you not carnal? I speak to the most of you, are you not those who are born of the flesh, since you mind nothing seriously, resolutely, constantly and willingly, but the things of the flesh, and the things of this life? O it is no light matter to be born of the flesh; if you continue so, you are ordained for corruption, for death; 'to be carnally minded is death,' ver. 6, of this chapter.

But I am persuaded better things of some of you, that the true light of God hath shined into your hearts, and revealed more excellent things unto you than these perishing fleshly things, viz. heavenly, substantial, and eternal things in the gospel, which you account only worthy of the fixed and continued meditation of your spirits. I am sure you perceive another beauty and excellency in these things than the world doth, because the Spirit hath revealed them unto you. It is true that your minds are yet much darkened in their apprehension of spiritual things; they are not so willing to receive them, nor so ready to retain them as you desire; they are very unsettled and unsteady in the meditations of spiritual things, and there are innumerable thoughts of other things that pass through your hearts like common inns, uncontrolled at their pleasure; all this is true, but I am sure it is the grief of your souls that your hearts are not so fixed and established as the excellency of these spiritual things require. I know it will be the aim and real endeavour of any spiritual heart, to be shutting up all the entries and doors of the mind, that vain thoughts enter not; yet enter they will, there are so many porches to enter in at, and our narrow spirits cannot watch at all. Every sense will let in objects, and imagination itself will be active in framing them, and presenting them: but yet the endeavour of a Christian will be, not to let them lodge long within. (Jer. iv. 14.) If they come in unawares, he will labour to make a diversion to a better purpose; and so still it holds good, that the current and course of a Christian's thoughts and cogitations are upon the 'things of the Spirit,'—how to get his own heart washed and cleansed,—how to be more holy and conformed to Christ,—how to be at peace with God, and keep that peace unbroken,—how to walk in obedience to God, and in duty towards men,—how to forsake himself, and withal to deny himself in all these; I say, his most serious and solemn thoughts are about these things, his resolved and advised thoughts run most on this strain, though it be true that, whether he will or not, other vain and impertinent, or not so concerning thoughts, will pass more lightly, and too frequently through his heart.

The other thing in which this spiritual life doth appear, is the current of the affections, or that relish and taste of the sweetness of the things of the Spirit, flowing from the apprehension of them in the mind. When the light is discovered indeed, (and O it is a pleasant thing for the eye to behold it, as Solomon speaks,) then the Spirit hath found an object suitable to its nature, and so it relisheth and delighteth in it: therefore the word is not simple minding, or thinking, but savouring, thinking with affection upon them, tasting and feeding upon the knowledge of them; it is a minding of them with care and delight, with earnestness φρονειν, 'O taste and see how good the Lord is,' Psal. xxxiv. 8. Some things indeed cannot be known but by some sense. You cannot make a blind man apprehend what light is, till he see it. A deaf man cannot form a notion of sounds in his mind, except he once heard them; neither can a man understand the sweetness of honey, but by tasting it. Truly spiritual things are of that nature; there is some hidden virtue and excellency in them, which is not obvious to every man that hath the bare knowledge of the letter; there is a spirit and life in them, that cannot be transmitted into your ears with the sound of words, or infused into ink and paper; it is only the inspiration of the Almighty can inspire this sensible perception, and real taste of spiritual things. Some powders do not smell till they are beaten; truly till these truths be well powdered and beaten small by meditation, they cannot smell so fragrantly to the spirit. As meats do not nourish till they be chewed and digested, so spiritual things do not relish to a soul, nor can they truly feed the soul, till they be chewed and digested into the heart by serious and earnest consideration. This is that which makes these same truths to be someway not the same; these very principles of religion received and confessed by all, to be lively in one, and dead in another. It is the living consideration of living truth, the application of truth to the heart, that makes it lively in one; whereas others keep it only beside them in a corner of their minds, or in a book, in the corner of the house. The same meat is laid to you all, the most part look on it, others contemplate it, and exercise only their understandings about it; but there are some who taste it, and find sweetness in it, who digest it by meditation and solemn avocation of their hearts from the things of the world; and therefore some are fed, some are starved.

Need we to enlarge much upon this subject. Is it not too palpable that many who fill up our churches are in the flesh, because they do mind and savour only the things of the flesh, and not of the Spirit? Will you seriously search your hearts, ask what relishes most with them? Can you say, that it is the kingdom of God or the righteousness thereof? Or is it not rather those other things of food and raiment, and such like, that have no extent beyond this narrow span of time? I am persuaded the hearts of many taste no sweetness in religion, else they would fix more upon it, and pursue it more earnestly. Are not the things of another world, the great things of the gospel, counted all strange things, (Hos. viii. 12,) as things that you have not much to do with? Do you not let the officers of Jesus Christ, all the sweet invitations of the gospel, pass by as strangers, and as if ye were unconcerned in them? What taste have they more than the white of an egg? How unsavoury a discourse or thought to a carnal heart is it, to speak of subduing the lusts of the flesh, of dying to the world, of the world to come? Who find their hearts inwardly stirred upon the proposal of Jesus Christ? But if any matter of petty gain were proffered, O how would men listen with both their ears! How beautiful in the eyes of the covetous mind is any gain and advantage! The sound of money is sweeter to him than this blessed sound of peace and salvation. How sweet is pleasure to the voluptuous! What suitableness and conveniency is apprehended in these perishing things! But how little moment or weight is conceived and believed to be in things eternal? O how substantial do things visible seem to men, and how trifling do other things invisible appear! But for you whose eyes are opened, to you Christ is precious; to you the things of the Spirit are beautiful, and all your grief is, that you cannot affect them according to their worth, or love them according to their beauty. I say, some there are, who do see a substance and subsistence only in things not seen (Heb. xi. 1.); and for things that are seen and visible in this world, they do account them shadows only in comparison of things invisible. The world apprehends no realities, but in what they see; but a Christian apprehends no solid reality in that he sees, but only in that he sees not; and therefore, as in his judgment he looks upon the one as a shadow, the other as a substance, so he labours to proportion and conform his affection to a suitable entertainment of them, to give a shadow or show of affection to the things of this life, but the marrow and substance of his heart to the things invisible of another life. Thus the apostle, 1 Cor. vii. 29. 'Rejoicing, as if we rejoiced not; enjoying, as if we possessed not; using, as if we used not:' half acts for half objects. If we give our whole spirits, the strength of our souls and minds to them, we are as foolish as he that strikes with all his strength at the air, or a feather. There is no solidity or reality in these things, able to bottom much estimation or affection; only mind them and use them as in the by, as in passing through towards your country.

Sermon XVIII.

VERSES 5, 6.—"*For they that are after the flesh do mind,*" *&c.* "*For to be carnally minded is death; but to be spiritually minded is life and peace.*"

THERE are many differences among men in this world, that, as to outward appearance, are great and wide; and indeed they are so eagerly pursued, and seriously minded by men, as if they were great and momentous. You see what a strife and contention there is among men, how to be extracted out of the dregs of the multitude, and set a little higher in dignity and degree than they. How do men affect to be honourable above the base! How do they seek to be rich, and hate poverty! These differences of poor and rich, high and low, noble and ignoble, learned and unlearned, the thoughts of men are wholly taken up with; but there is one great difference, that is most in God's eye, and is both substantial and eternal, and so infinitely surpasseth all these differences that the minds of men most run out upon; and it is here, the great difference between flesh and spirit, and them that are after the flesh, and them that are after the Spirit. This is of all other most considerable, because widest and durablest. I say, it is the widest of all, for all others put no great difference between men as men; they do reach the peculiar excellency of a man, that is, the true, and proper, good of his spiritual and immortal part; they are such as befall alike to good and bad, and so cannot have either much good or much evil in them. I have seen folly set in great dignity, and princes walking on foot, Eccles. x. 6, 7. Then certainly such titles of honour and dignity, such places of eminency erected above the multitude, have little or nothing worth the spirit of a man in them, seeing a fool, a wicked man, is as capable of them, as a wise man, or a man of a princely spirit; and so of all others, they do not elevate a man, as a man, above others. A poor, unlearned, mean man may have more real excellency in him, than a rich, learned, and great person. But this draws a substantial and vast difference indeed, such as is between flesh and spirit, such as is between men and beasts. You know what pre-eminency a man hath over a beast. There is no such wide distance among the sons of men, as between the lowest and meanest man and the chiefest beast. 'There is a spirit in man,' saith Elihu, Job xxxii. 8,—an immortal, eternal substance, of a far higher nature and comprehension. You know what excellency is in the spirit beyond the flesh, such as is in heaven beyond the earth, for the one is breathed from heaven, and the other is taken out of the dust of the earth; the one is corruptible, yea, corruption itself, the other incorruptible. How swift and nimble are the motions of the spirit, from the one end of heaven to the other! How can it compass the earth in a moment! Do but look and see what a huge difference is between a beautiful living body, and the same when it is a dead carcase, rotten and corrupted. It is the spirit dwelling within that makes the odds, that makes it active, beautiful, and comely; but in the removal of the spirit, it becometh a piece of the most defiled and loathsome dust in the world.

Now, I say, such a vast and wide difference there is between a true Christian and a natural man, even taking him in with all his common endowments and excellencies; the one is a man, the other a beast; the one is after the flesh, the other is after the Spirit. It is the ordinary compellation of the Holy Ghost, 'Man being in honour, and understanding not, is like the beasts that perish,' Psal. xlix. 20, and xciv. 8, 'Understand, ye brutish among the people,' &c.; and Psal. xcii. 6, 'The brutish man understands not this;' and Eccles. iii. 18, 'that they themselves may know that they are but beasts.' Therefore you find the Lord often turning to beasts, to insensible creatures, thereby to reprove the folly and madness of men, Isa. i. 2, and Jer. viii. 7. Man hath two parts in him, by which he hath affinity to the two most distant natures; he stands in the middle between angels and beasts. In his spirit he riseth up to an angelic dignity, and in his body he falls down to a brutish condition. Now, which of these hath the pre-eminency, *that* he is. If the spirit be indeed elevated above all sensual and earthly things, to the life of angels, that is, to communion with God, then a man is one after the spirit, an angel incarnate, an angel dwelling in flesh; but if his spirit throw itself down to the service of the flesh, minding and savouring only things sensual and visible, then indeed a man puts off humanity, and hath associated himself to beasts, to be as one of them. And indeed, a man made thus like a beast, is worse than a beast, because he ought to be far better. It is no disparagement to a beast to mind only the flesh, but it is the greatest abasement of a man, that which draws him down from that higher station God hath set him into, to the lowest station, that of beasts; and truly a Nebuchadnezzar among beasts is the greatest beast of all, far more brutish than any beast. Now such is every man by nature,—'that which is born of the flesh is flesh.' Every man as he comes out of the womb, is degenerated and fallen down into this brutish estate, to mind, to savour, to relish nothing but what relates to this fleshly or temporal being. The utmost sphere and comprehension of man, is now of no larger extent than this visible world and this present life,—'he is blind and seeth not afar off,' 2 Pet. i. 9. Truly, such is every man by nature; whereas the proper native sphere of the spirit's motion and comprehension, is as large as its endurance; that is, as long as eternity, and as broad as to reach the infiniteness of God, the God of all spirits. Now, through the slavery and bondage of men's spirits to their flesh, it is contracted into as narrow bounds as this poor life in the flesh. He that ought to look beyond time as far as eternity, and hath an immortal spirit given for that end, is now half blind; the eye of the mind is so overclouded with lusts and passions, that it cannot see far off, not so far as to the morrow after death, not so far as to the entry of eternity. And truly, if you compare the context, you will find, that whosoever doth not give all diligence to add to faith, virtue; to virtue, knowledge; to knowledge, temperance; to temperance, patience; and to patience, godliness, &c., he that is not exercised and employed about this study, how to adorn his spirit with these graces, how to have a victory over himself and the world, and in respect of these, accounts all things beside indifferent,—such a man is blind, and seeth not far off, he hath not gotten a sight of eternity, he hath not taken up that everlasting endurance, else he could not spend his time upon provision for the lusts of the flesh, but he behoved to lay such a good foundation for the time to come as is here mentioned. If he saw afar off, he could not but make acquaintance with those courtiers of heaven, which will minister an entrance into that everlasting kingdom. But truly, while this is not your study, you have no purpose for heaven, you see nothing but what is just before your eye, and almost toucheth it; and so you savour and mind only what you see.

Is not this then a wide difference between the children of this world, and the children of God? Is it not very substantial? All others are circumstantial in respect of this, this only puts a real difference in that which is best in men, viz. their spirits. The excellency of nature is known by their affections and motions; so are these here, the spiritual man savours spiritual things, the carnal man carnal things; everything sympathizes with that which is like itself, and is ready to incorporate into it; things are nourished and preserved by things like themselves. You see the swine embraces the dunghill, that stink is only a savoury smell to them, because it is suitable to their nature. But a man hath a more excellent taste and smell, and he savours finer and sweeter things. Truly it cannot choose but that it must be a nature more swinish or brutish than a swine, that can relish and savour such filthy abominable works of the flesh as abound amongst some of you. 'The works of the flesh are manifest,' Gal. v. 19. And indeed they are manifest upon you, acted in the very day-time, out-facing the very light of the gospel. You may read them, and see if they be not too manifest in you. Now, what a base nature, what abominable and brutish spirits must possess men, that they apprehend a sweetness and fragrancy in these corrupt and stinking works of the old man! O how base a scent is it, to smell and savour nothing but this present world, and satisfaction to your senses! Truly your scent and smell, your relish and taste, argues your base, and degenerate, and brutish natures, that you are on the worse side of this division,—'after the flesh.' But alas! it is not possible to persuade you that there is no sweetness, no fragrancy, nothing but corruption and rottenness, such as comes out of sepulchres opened, in all these works of the flesh, till once a new spirit be put in you, and your natures changed; no more than you can by eloquence persuade a sick man, whose palate is possessed with a vitiated bitter humour, that such things as are suitable to his vitiated taste, are indeed bitter; or make a swine to believe that the dunghill is stinking and unpleasant. Truly it is as impossible to make the multitude of men to apprehend, to relish or savour any bitterness or loathsomeness in the ways and courses they follow, or any sweetness and fragrancy in the ways of godliness, till once your tastes be rectified, your spirits be transformed and renewed.

And indeed, when once the spirit is renewed, and dispossessed of that malignant humour of corruption, and fleshly affection, that did present all things, contrary to what they are, then it is like a healthful and wholesome palate, that tastes all things as they are, and finds bitter, bitter, and sweet, sweet; or like a sound eye, that beholds things just as they are, both in colour, quantity, and distance; then the soul savours the sweet smell of the fruits of the Spirit, ver. 22, 'Love, joy, peace, long-suffering, meekness, temperance,' &c. These are fragrant and sweet to the soul, and as a sweet perfume, both to the person that hath them, and to others round about him, and to God also. These cast a savour that allures a soul to seek them, and being possessed of them, they cast a sweet smell abroad to all that are round about, and even as high as heaven. A soul that hath these planted in it, and growing out of it, is as a garden enclosed to God. These fruits are both pleasant and sweet to the soul that eats them, and as the pleasantness of the apple allured man to taste it and sin, so the beauty and sweetness of these fruits of the Spirit draw the spirit of a man after them. He hath found the savour, and seen the beauty, and this allures him to taste them, and then he invites the well-beloved to come and taste also, to eat of these fruits with him. We might instance this in many things. A Christian relishes more sweetness in temperance, in beating down his body, and bringing it into subjection, in abstaining from fleshly lusts, than a carnal man tastes in the most exquisite pleasures that the world can afford. A Christian savours a sweetness in meekness and long-suffering, he hath more delight in forgiving, and forbearing, and praying for them that wrong him, than a natural man hath in the accomplishing of the most greedy desires of revenge. O what beauty hath gentleness, goodness, and patience, in his eye! What sweetness is in the love of God to his taste! How ravishing is the joy of the Holy Ghost! How contenting that peace that passeth understanding! These are things of the Spirit that he minds and savours. Know, Christians, that it is to this ye are called, to mind these things most, and to seek them most. Beware lest the deceitfulness of sin entice you, through the treacherous and deceitful lusts that are yet living in your members. If you indeed mind these things, and, out of the apprehension of the beauty and savour of the sweetness and smell of the fragrancy of them, would be content to quit all your corrupt lusts, for to be possessed of them, then you are on that blessed and happy side of this great and fundamental division of men; you have indeed the privilege * of all others who are not renewed. Whatever be your condition in the world, you are of the Spirit; and this is better than to be rich, wise, great, and honourable. God hath not given you such things as the world go mad after; but envy them not; he hath given you better things, more real and substantial things, that make you far better and more excellent.

But then, this difference, as it is the widest, so it is the durablest; as it is substantial here, so it is perpetual hereafter. When all the other differences between men shall be abolished, this alone shall remain; and therefore you have it in the next verse, 'To be carnally minded is death, but to be spiritually minded is life and peace.' This division that is begun here, shall grow wider for all eternity. There shall be a greater difference after this life, and a more sensible separation. Death and life, eternal death and eternal life, are the two sides of this difference, as it shall shortly be stated. When all other degrees and distances of men shall be blotted out and buried in eternal oblivion, there shall no vestige or mark remain, of either wisdom, or riches, or honour, or such like, but all mankind shall be, as to these outward things, levelled and equalized; this one unseen and neglected difference in the world shall appear and shine in that day when the Lord maketh up his jewels; then he will discern between the righteous and the wicked, between him that feareth God, and him that feareth him not,' Mal. iii. 18. The carnal and spiritual man have opposite affections and motions. The spirit of the one is on a journey or walk upward, 'after the Spirit,' and the spirit of the other is on a walk downward, towards the flesh; and the further they go, the further distant they are. The one shall be taken up to the company of the spirits of just men made perfect, and to the fellowship of angels, the other shall be thrown down into the fellowship and society of devils. And truly it is no wonder it fall so low, for all its motions in the body were downward, to the fulfilling of the lusts of the flesh. Thus you see the difference will grow wider and more sensible than it is yet between the godly and ungodly; in this world it doth not so evidently appear as it will do afterward. As two men, that leave one another, and have their faces on contrary airts,* at the beginning the distance and difference is not so great and so sensible; but wait a little, and the further they go, the farther they are distant, and the wider their separation is. Even so, when a Christian begins to break off his way from the common course of the world, it doth not appear to be so different from it as to convince himself and

* [Or pre-eminence above others.—Ed.]

* [That is, directions, or different points of the compass.—Ed.]

others; but if his face be towards Jerusalem above, and his heart thitherward, certainly he will be daily moving further from the world, till the distance be sensible both to himself and others; he will be more and more transformed and renewed, till at length all be changed. No wonder then, that these two cannot meet together in the end of their course, whose course was so opposite. Though wicked men will desire to 'die the death of the righteous,' yet it is no more possible they can meet in the end, than hell and heaven can reconcile together, because they walk to two contrary points.

Sermon XIX.

VERSE 6.—"*For to be carnally minded is death; but to be spiritually minded is life and peace.*"

IT is true, this time is short, and so short that scarce can similitudes or comparisons be had to shadow it out unto us. It is a dream, a moment, a vapour, a flood, a flower, and whatsoever can be more fading or perishing; and therefore it is not in itself very considerable, yet in another respect it is of all things the most precious, and worthy of the deepest attention and most serious consideration; and that is, because it is linked unto eternity; and there is an indissolvable knot between them, that no power or art can break or loose. The beginning of eternity is continually united to the end of time; and you know all the infinite extension of eternity is uniform, it admits of no change in it from better to worse, or worse to better; and therefore the beginning of our eternity, whether it be happiness or misery, is but one perpetuated and eternized moment, so to speak. Seeing then we are in the body, and sent unto the world for this end, that we may pass through into an unchangeable eternal estate; truly, of all things it is most concerning and weighty, what way we choose to this journey's end. Seeing the time is short, in which we have to walk, and it is uncertain too, we ought, as the apostle Peter speaks, to 'give all diligence;' as long as the day remains, we should drive the harder, lest that eternal night overtake us. The shortness and uncertainty of time should constrain us to take the present opportunity, and not to let it slip over as we do; seeing it is not at all in our hand, either what is past, or what is to come, the one cannot be recalled, the other is not in our power to call and bring forward, therefore the present moment that God hath given us, should be catched hold on, and redeemed, as the apostle speaks, Eph. v. 16. We should buy it at the dearest rate of pains and expenses, from all those vain, impertinent, and trifling diversions that take it up, that we may employ it as it becomes suitable to eternity that is posting on. And then, as the shortness of it makes it the more precious and considerable, in regard of the end of it,—eternity; as the scantiness of a thing increases the rate of it, so that same consideration should make all worldly things, that are confined either in their being or use, within it, to be inconsiderable, as Paul, (1 Cor. vii. 29—31,) shows. Seeing the time is short, it remaineth, that we should rejoice, as not rejoicing; weep, as not weeping; buy, as if we possessed not; use the world, as not abusing it. Seeing all its worth is to be esteemed from the end of it, eternity, never ending; then certainly whatsoever in time doth not reach that end, and hath no connection with it, we should give it but such entertainment, as a passing bird, that is pleasant to the eye, gets of a beholder, while it is in its flight. The shortness of the day should make us double our diligence, and push on the harder in our walk or race, that so we may come in time to our place of rest; and that same should make the passenger give an overly* and passing look to all things that are by the way, and which he must of necessity leave behind him. Seeing these things, then, are so important, let us draw our hearts together to consider what the Lord speaks to us in this word; for in it you have two ways and two ends, opposite and contrary ways and walks, and as contrary

* [That is careless or slight.—ED.]

ends; the ways are, walking 'after the flesh,' and walking 'after the Spirit;' the ends to which they lead, are death and life. We spoke something of the ways, and the wide difference that is between them, what excellency is in the one beyond the other; but truly it is hard to persuade to leave off your accustomed ways and walks, because your inward sense and the inclination of your hearts are wholly perverted and corrupted by nature. You know the moving faculty is subordinate in its operations unto the knowing, feeling, and apprehending faculties: the locomotive power is given for a subsidiary and help to the apprehensive and appetitive powers, because things are convenient and disconvenient, good or evil, to the nature of the living creature, without it; and it could not by mere knowledge, or desire, or hatred of things, either come into possession of them, or eschew them. Therefore God hath given them a faculty of moving themselves to the prosecution and attainment of any apprehended good, or to the eschewing and aversion of any conceived evil. Thus, when beasts savour or smell that food which is fit for them, their appetite stirs them up to motion after it to obtain it. Now, I say, if this inward sense be corrupted, then things that are destructive will be conceived good, because they are suitable to that corrupt humour or quality that possesses the senses; and thus all the motion and walk will be disordered. The truth is, my beloved, our spirits and minds are infected with a poisonable humour, fleshly passions and lusts are predominant naturally; and, as in them that are in a fever, their organs being distempered with a bitter unsavoury humour, the pleasantest things seem unsavoury, because not suitable to that predominant humour, even so it is with you by nature. That which puts all upon motion is out of course, since the first distemper of man. Your spirits and minds are fleshly and carnal; they have a strong and deep impression of all the lusts that are in the body, and are accordingly affected; and therefore you cannot fitly judge what is good or evil for you, but according to these, (Isa. v. 20,)—you must call evil good, and good evil; bitter sweet, and sweet bitter, because you are already prepossessed thus. And therefore the ways of the flesh, those paths that lead to destruction, you cannot but look on them as pleasant, because they suit and please your corrupted sense or spirit; and so this disordered savour or smell of some fragrant perfume in the ways of the flesh, puts you upon walking in these ways; and being thus possessed and engaged, you cannot but stop your ears to all contrary persuasions. You think it against your sense and reason, to tell you that these are loathsome and unsavoury, and that the other ways of wisdom and spirit are pleasantness and peace. I say, you cannot believe this, till your hearts and spirits be purged, and your taste be pure and uncorrupted. It is certainly upon this ground that our Saviour puts such characters on the way to heaven and hell, to life and death. The one is strait and narrow, and few walk in it; the other broad and easy, and many walk in it, Matt. vii. 13. Certainly, it is not the way in itself simply, that admits of such a motion, to speak properly, as the thing is; the way to life, by the guiding of the Spirit, is easiest, plainest, shortest, and broadest. It hath all the properties of a good way, none so pleasant and plain;—how sweet and pleasant sights all the way! It is an alley of delight,—the way of his commandments; it wants not accommodation in it to refresh the traveller. The most delightful company is here; the Father and the Son, who sought no other company from all eternity, but were abundantly satisfied and rejoiced in one another. This fellowship the Christian hath to solace himself with, and he is admitted to be partaker of that joy. There is nothing that doth disburden the soul so of care and anxiety, nothing doth rid a man of so many perplexities and troubles, as this way. But the way of sin in itself is most laborious, most difficult. It hath infinite by-ways that it leads a man into, and he must turn and return, and run in a circle all the day, all his time, to satisfy the infinite lusts and insatiable desires of sin. O how painful and laborious is it to fulfil the lusts of the flesh! How much service doth it impose! How serious attention! What perplexing cares and tormenting thoughts! How many sorrows and griefs are in every step of this way! Do you not perceive what drudges and slaves sin makes you,—how much labour you have to satisfy your lusts? And you are always to begin, as near that which you seek in the end of your years, as in the beginning. How thorny, how miry is the way of covetousness! Are you not always out of one thorn into another, and cut asunder, or pierced through with many sorrows? 1 Tim vi. 10; Matt. xiii.

22. Is that a pleasant and easy way, I pray you, that makes all your sorrow and your travail grief, and suffers not your heart to take rest in the night? Eccl. ii. 22, 23. What pains of body! What plotting of mind! What labour and vexation of both must a sinner have as his constant attendance in this way! The way is intricate, deep, unpassable, that leads to that satisfaction you desire to your lusts. Your desires are impotent and impatient, the means to carry you on are weak and lame, nowise accommodated or fit for such a journey; andthis puts you always, as it were, on the rack, tormented between the impatience of your lusts, and the impotency of means, and impossibility to fulfil them. Desires and disappointments, hopes and fears, divide your souls between them. Such is the way after the flesh, an endless labyrinth of woes and miseries, of pains and cares, ever while here.

But these ways receive such names from the common opinion and apprehension of men, because of our flesh, which is predominant. The way after the flesh being suitable to it, though in itself infinitely more toilsome, seems easy and plain; but the way after the Spirit seems strait, narrow, toilsome, and laborious. Though there be infinitely more room in the way to life, because it leads to that immense universal good, it expatiates towards the All-fulness of God, yet to the flesh how narrow and strait is it, because it cannot admit of these inordinate lusts, that have swelled so immeasurably towards narrow and scanty things! The true latitude of the way of the flesh is not great, for it is all enclosed within poor, lean, narrow, created objects; but because the imagination of men supplies what is wanting really, and fancies an infinite or boundless extent of goodness in these things; therefore the sinner walks easily, without straitening to his flesh,—it is not pinched in this way of fleshly lusts. But, alas! the spirit is wofully straitened, fettered, and imprisoned, though it be not sensibly bound.

What is the reason, then, that so many walk in the way to death, but because their flesh finds no straitening, no pressure in it? It is an easy way to their natures, because suitable to the corruption that is in them; therefore men walk on without consideration of what follows. It is like a descent, or going down a hill, and so easy to our flesh. On the other hand, the way of life, after the Spirit, is an ascent upward, and it is very difficult to our earthly and lumpish flesh. Our spirits, by communion with and subjection to the flesh, are made of an earthly quality, near the element of the flesh, and so they bow naturally downward; but if once they were purified and purged, and unfettered by the Spirit of God, and restored to their native purity, they would more easily and willingly move upward, as you see the flame doth: and till this be done in you, we cannot expect that you will willingly and pleasantly walk in these pleasant walks after the Spirit; your walk will never be free and unconstrained in the paths of godliness. You may, from some external motives and impulses, move upward for a season, in some particular duties of religion, as a stone cast up; but as that impression is not from an inward principle, so it will not be constant and durable, but you will fall down to your old bias in other things, and move quite contrary, when the external impression of fear or favour, of custom or education, or such like, wears out. But the true Christian hath a spirit within him, the root of the matter in him; this carries him upward in the ways of obedience, after the motions and directions of God's Spirit. At the beginning, indeed, it is strait and uneasy to his flesh, but the difficulty is overcome if once you begin well: the beginning (as you used to say) is the half of the whole. Truly, to be well entered is half progress, afterward the bulksome and burdensome lusts of the flesh are stript off, at least in a greater measure, and then the spirit moves easily and willingly; this walk becomes a recreation, that at first was a labour. Now delight and desire are as wings to mount the soul aloft. Now it is the good pleasure of the soul to walk to all well-pleasing. Indeed the way of this world is dirty and filthy; and therefore a Christian had need to watch continually, and to gird up his loins, that his thoughts and affections hang not down to the earth, else they will take up much filth, and cannot but clog and burden the spirit, and make it drive heavily and slowly, as Pharaoh did his chariots when the wheels were off. We had need to fly aloft above the ground, and not to come down too low near it, thinking withal to double out our journey, for we shall find, that because of the remnants of flesh within us, that this world hath a magnetical attractive virtue to draw us down to it, if we be within the sphere of its activity. It is not good coming near fire with flax; we should endeavour to keep our hearts at much distance, and disengage them from our lower consolations. This world is like the pestiferous lake of Sodom, that kills all that fly over it, and makes them fall down into it.* If we fly low upon the surface of it, we cannot think but that the spiritual life will be much extinguished. But to prevent this, we should take our flight straight upward after the Spirit, (for that is the proper motion of the more pure and spiritual part of this world,) and give no rest till we be out of the reach of that infection, till we be fully escaped the pollutions of the world.

But if you cannot be persuaded to come off this way, that seems so pleasant to your flesh, that way which is the very course of the world, (for these are joined, Eph. ii. 2,) then, I beseech you, stand still, and consider whither it will lead; do but stop a little, and bethink yourselves sadly and seriously whither this will take you, where it shall end. And truly that is dreadful, the end of it is death, a never-ending death. I am sure, if you were walking by the way, and one came and told you gravely and seriously that that way is full of dangerous pits, that there are many robbers in it waiting to cut your throat, you would count the admonition worthy of so much notice as to halt and consider what to do: but now, when the Lord himself, that deserves infinite more respect and credit than men, gives you warning once, and often, day after day repeats this admonition to you, sends out many ambassadors to call you off, makes this word to sound daily in your ears, 'Oh! why will you die?' 'Such ways lead down to the chambers of death and hell;' 'to be carnally-minded' in the issue 'is death,' whatsoever you may promise to yourselves. I say, when he makes a voice to accompany us in all our walkings, this is not the way that leads to life, why do you not think it worthy of so much consideration as once to stop and sist your progress till you examine what will come of it? Are we so credulous to men, and shall not we believe God, who is truth itself, who affirms it so constantly, and obtests us so earnestly? Are we so wise and prudent in lesser things, and shall we be mad, self-willed, and refractory in the greatest things that concern us eternally? Oh! unbelief is that which will condemn the world, the unbelief of this one thing, that the walking after, and minding of the flesh is mortal and deadly. Though all men confess with their tongues this to be a truth, yet it is not really believed; the deep inconsideration and slight apprehension of this truth, makes men boldly to walk, and violently to run on, to perdition. Did you indeed believe that eternal misery is before you at the end of this way; and would you be so cruel to yourselves as to walk in it for any allurement that is in it? Did you really believe that there is a precipice into utter darkness and everlasting death at the end of this alley, would the pleasure and sweetness of it be able to infatuate you and besot you so far as to lead you on into it, like an ox to the slaughter, and a fool to the correction of the stocks? It is strange, indeed, though you neither will believe that death is the end of these things, nor yet can you be persuaded that you do not believe it. There is a twofold delusion that possesses the hearts of men; one is, a dream and fancy of escaping death though they live in sin; another is, a dream and fancy that they do believe that death is the wages of sin: we might wonder how they consist together if we did not find it by so many experiences. Your way proves that you do not believe it, that death is the end of it; and then your words evidence that you do not believe that you are unbelievers of that. O! how desperate is the wickedness, and how great is the deceitfulness, of the heart! The false prophet that is in every man's bosom, deceives him that it may destroy him. As Satan is a liar and a murderer, and murders by lying, so the heart of man is a self-murderer and a self-destroyer, and that is done by lying and deceiving. There is some lie in every sin; but there is this gross, black, fundamental lie at the bottom of all sin,—a conceit of immunity and freedom from death and hell; a strong imagination of escaping danger, even though such a way be chosen and walked into as of its own nature inevitably leads to destruction. And there is something of this

* [This was long a current tradition. But Maundrell avers that he saw "several birds flying about and over" the lake of Sodom, or Dead Sea, as it is called, "without any visible harm."—Journey from Aleppo to Jerusalem, A. D. 1696, p. 137, Edin. 1812.—Ed.]

bloody murdering flattery even in the hearts of Christians; therefore, this apostle gives us an antidote against it, and labours often to purge it out, by stirring up that knowledge they have received: 'Know ye not that the unrighteous shall not inherit the kingdom of God?' 1 Cor. vi. 9. Be not deceived, God is not mocked, for what a man soweth, that shall he reap; he that soweth to the flesh shall reap corruption, &c., Gal. vi. 7, 8. O that you might listen to this word, to this watch-word given you, and stop your course, at least for a season, to think what shall be the latter end! Know you not that such shall not inherit the kingdom? Know you not that the way to heaven lies upward? Know you not that your way lies downward towards the flesh and the earth? Are you so far demented* as to think to come to heaven by walking just downward in the lusts of the flesh? Truly this is the strongest and strangest enchantment that can be, that you think to sow one thing and reap another thing; to sow darkness and reap light; to sow corruption and reap incorruption. Is that possible in nature, to sow nettle-seed and think to reap barley or wheat? Be not deceived. O that you would undeceive your poor deluded souls, and know that it is as natural for death and hell to grow out of sin and walking after the flesh, as it is for every seed to yield its own fruit and herb! Do you then think to dissolve the course and order of nature? Truly the flesh is mortal in itself; it is ordained for corruption. You see what it turns to after the life is out, that is an emblem of the state of the fleshly soul after death. As you did abase your spirits to the service of the flesh here, and all your ploughing, and labouring, and sowing was about it, the seed which you did cast in the ground was fleshly lusts, earthly things, for the satisfaction of your flesh; so you shall reap of the flesh corruption, death, and destruction, that shall make your immortal spirits mortal and corruptible, and subject them to death and corruption with the body, as far as they are capable; it shall deprive them of all that which is their proper life and refreshment, and separate them eternally from the fountain of blessedness, and banish them out of heaven unto the fellowship of devils. And O that corruption of the incorruptible spirit is worse than the corruption of the mortal flesh, *corruptio optimi pessima!*

Now, whoever of you is thus far undeceived as to believe your danger and misery, and to discern that inbred delusion of your hearts, be not discouraged utterly, there may be hope of recovery when you see your disease. I say, if you see that hell is at the end of your way, then know that he who sent that voice to call you off that way of death, he leaves you not to your own wits to guide you into the right way, but he follows with a voice behind you, saying, 'Here is the way, walk in it,' turn not out of it to the right hand or left. And this voice sounds plainly in the word, and it is nothing else but the sound of the gospel,—that blessed sound that invites and allures you to come to Jesus Christ, 'the way, truth, and life,' the true way to the true life. All other ways, all other lives have no truth in them; it is but a cloud, a fancy that men apprehend and lay hold on. But come to this way and it will truly lead thee to the true life, eternal life. If you fly unto him out of the apprehension of your danger, you have a clear way to come to God, and as plain a way to attain life and peace. Being in Christ, you have assurance of not falling into condemnation. He is such a way as will hold you in, and not suffer you to go out of it again to the way of death. And therefore he will give you a Tutor, a Guider, and Director in this way to life and peace, and that is the Holy Spirit, to lead in all truth, and to guide your feet in the way of his commandments. So that in this new and living way of Christ, you shall have both light of the word to know where to walk, and life of the Spirit to make you walk toward that eternal life; and thus grace and truth are come by Jesus Christ. Indeed, you must suffer the mortification of your flesh, you must endure the pain of the death of your lusts, the cutting off your right hand, and plucking out your right eye, which would make you offend and stumble in the way; but let the remembrance of the life to come sweeten it all. When men undergo the hazard of losing life for a little pleasure, when, for a poor petty advantage, men will endure so much pains and trouble, O what should 'eternal life,' and such a life as the best life here is but death to it! How should it mitigate and sweeten the bitterness of mortification? How should it fortify our

* [That is, destitute of reason.—Ed.]

spirits to much endurance and patience? A battle we must have, for these lusts that we disengage from the devil, and the world besides, will lay wait for us in this way: but, when for such small and inconsiderable advantages, men will endure all the disadvantages of war, of a long war, O how should the expectation of this peace, which encloses and comprehends all felicity, all well-being, animate and strengthen us to fight in into the city of life and peace eternal!

Sermon XX.

VERSE 7.—"*Because the carnal mind is enmity against God: for it is not subject to the law of God, neither indeed can be.*"

UNBELIEF is that which condemns the world. It involves in more condemnation than many other sins; not only because more universal, but especially because it shuts up men in their misery, and secludes them from the remedy that is brought to light in the gospel. By unbelief I mean, not only that careless neglect of Jesus Christ offered for salvation, but that which is the root of that,—the inconsideration and ignorance of our desperate sinfulness and irremediless misery without Christ,—which, not being laid to heart seriously, makes such slight and superficial entertainment of a Saviour and Redeemer. Man is truly miserable and unhappy, whether he know it or not; but truly it is an accession to his misery that he knows it not, that he neither apprehends what he is now by nature, nor what he must shortly be made by justice. Indeed, if there were no remedy to be found, it were a happy ignorance to be ignorant of misery; the knowledge and remembrance of it could do nothing but add unto the bitterness of it. If a man might bury it in eternal forgetfulness, it were some ease. But now, when God hath in his mercy so appointed it, that the beginning of the belief of sin and misery shall, in a manner, be the end of misery; and seeing, whether men know it or not, they must shortly be made sensible of it, when there is no remedy to be found, then, certainly, it is the height of man's misery that he knows and considers it not. If we would apply our hearts at length to hear what God the Lord speaks,—for he only can give account of man to himself,—we might have a survey of both in these words and the preceding—of our desperate wickedness, and of our intolerable misery. For the present, by nature we are enemies to God; and shortly we must be dealt with as enemies, as rebels to the most potent and glorious King,—be punished with death, an endless living death. Experience shows how hard a thing it is to persuade you that you are really under the sentence of death; you will not suffer your hearts to believe your danger, lest it interrupt your present pleasures of sin. Nay, you will flatter yourselves with the fancied hope of immunity from this curse, and account it a cruel and rigorous doctrine,—that so many creatures made by God should be eternally miserable, or a sentence of it should be passed on all flesh. Now, that which makes us hardly to believe this is the unbelief and deep inconsideration of your sinfulness; therefore, the apostle, to make way for the former, adds, 'Because the carnal mind is enmity against God.' Do not wonder then that your ways and courses, your affections and inclinations bring forth that ghostly and dreadful end of death; seeing all these are enmity to the greatest King, who alone hath the power of life and death. They have a perfect contrariety to his holy nature and righteous will. Not only is the carnal mind an enemy, but enmity itself; and therefore it is most suitable that the sovereign power of that 'King of kings,' is stretched out to the vindication of his holiness and righteousness, by taking vengeance on all ungodliness and unrighteousness of men. If rebellion in a state or monarchy against these petty mortal gods, who shall die as men, be so heinous as to deserve death, by the consent of all nations, how much more shall enmity and rebellion against the immortal eternal King, who hath absolute right and dominion over his creatures, as over the clay, have such a suitable recompense of eternal death? Now, my beloved, if you once believed this, the enmity and opposition of your whole natures to God, you could not but fearfully apprehend what might be the issue of it; you could not bless yourselves as you do, and put the evil day far off; but certainly you would be affrighted with the terror and majesty of that God you have to do with, whom, when he awakes to judgment, you can neither resist nor escape; no standing against his wrath, and no flying from it out of his dominions; and this would dispose and incline your minds in time to hearken to the treaty of peace, which is holden out in the gospel, and to lay down the weapons of your enmity, and make peace with him in his Son the Peacemaker.

Amity and unity are the very being and beauty of the world. This universe is made up of innumerable different kinds and natures, and all these climb and walk together by the bond of peace, and concord among themselves, and with that one high understanding that directs all, and supreme will of God that moves all. It is that link of union with God, that gives and preserves being and beauty in all the creatures, as the dependence of the ray upon the sun, or the stream upon the fountain, makes them what they are, which being interrupted, they cease to be what they were: 'all things continue as thou hast ordained them, for all are thy servants,' Psal. cxix. 91. You see, then, this amity and union of subordination of the creatures to God is not dissolved to this day; but woful and wretched man alone hath withdrawn from this subordination, and dissolved this sacred tie of happy friendship, which at first he was lifted up unto, and privileged with. Amity and friendship, you know, consists in an union of hearts and wills, and a communion of all good things; it makes two one, as much as two can be, by the conspiracy of their affections in one thing, and the joint concurrence of their endeavours to communicate to one another what each hath; it takes away propriety,* and it makes a community between persons. Now, how happy was that amity! how blessed that friendship between God and man! Though man's goodness could not extend to God, yet his soul united to God by love and delight, and all that God had given him, returning that to the proper owner, acknowledging his absolute dependence on him, and claiming interest and propriety in nothing, not in himself. And then, on the other hand, the love and good-will of the infinite God placed on man, and from that fountain all the streams of happiness issuing forth towards man, the fulness of God opening up itself to him, and laying out itself towards him, God so far descending, as, in a manner, to become the creature's, to expose and dispose himself, and all in him, for poor man's use and comfort.

How joyful was that amity! But the breaking of this bond of peace is as sad and grievous. There was a woful interposal between God and us, which hath separated these chief friends ever since the beginning, and that is sin, the seeds of all enmity and discord: this hath rent asunder the bond of amity, this hath made such a total aversion of the soul from God, and imprinted such an irreconcilable enmity in the heart against the holy will of God, that there is no possibility to reunite them again, and restore the old friendship, as long as the soul is not quite changed and transformed. That first creation is so marred and defaced, that there is no mending of it till a second creation come. The carnal mind is not simply an enemy, but enmity itself; an enemy may reconcile again, and accept terms of peace, but enmity cannot reconcile to amity, without the very destruction of itself. The opposition of the heart is so perfect, that as soon may enmity unite with amity, and become one with it, as a carnal natural mind can submit to God's holy will. That which was at the beginning voluntary, is become necessary, and turned into the nature of an inbred antipathy, that no art can cure. The fall was such a disjointing of the soul from God, that no skill but infinite wisdom, no strength but Almighty power, can set it right, and put it in the first posture again. It is true, there are not many who will openly and expressly denounce war against heaven; it is not so incident,† that any man should have explicit plain thoughts of hatred against God. There are some common principles engraven by God in all men's minds, which serve as his witnesses against men, that God should be loved, served, adored, and worshipped; that there is nothing so worthy of the desires of the soul. Now, this general acknowledgment deludes the most part; for they take it for granted that they do love God with their heart, because their consciences bear witness that they ought to love him, as if it were all

* [Or property.—Ed.] † [That is, not so likely to happen.—Ed.]

one to know our duty, and to do it. Who is there but he entertains himself with this good opinion of himself, that his heart is good and true to God: for, say you, whom should I love, if I love not God? I were not worthy to live if I love not him. It is true indeed that you say, but if you did know your hearts, you would find their faces turned backward, and averted from God, and could no more please yourselves in such a confession of the truth, than the devil hath reason to think himself a believer, because he is convinced that Christ is the Son of God, and confessed it too; no more than the son that promised to go to the garden to work, and went not, had ground to think himself an obedient son, (Matt. xxi. 30.) Such a confession of duty may be extorted from damned spirits; and therefore you would not draw this vail over the wretched wickedness of your natures, to the end that you may conceive well of yourselves. It is so far from extenuating or excusing, that the very conviction of the great obligation to love and obey God, is the greatest aggravation of the enmity. It is this which makes it the purest malice and perfectest hatred, that knowing the goodness of God, convinced of our bound duty to love and serve him, yet in the very light of such a shining truth, to turn our hearts away from him, and exercise all acts of hostility against him. That you may know, then, wherein the enmity of your hearts consists, I shall instance it in three branches or evidences. There is an enmity in the understanding, that it cannot stoop to believing of the truth; there is an enmity in the will, that it cannot subject to the obedience of God's holy commands; and this is extended also to a stubborn rebellion against the will of God, manifested in the dispensations of his providence: in a word, the natural and carnal mind is incapable of faith, of obedience, and of submission. There are many things revealed in the scripture, that the natural man cannot receive or know, 'for they are foolishness to him,' 1 Cor. ii. 14. Some spirits there are lifted up above others, either by nature or education, in which this rebellion doth more evidently appear; reason in them contends with religion, and they will believe no more than they can give a reason for. There is a wisdom in some men, that despiseth the simplicity, or the inevidence* of the gospel, and accounts it foolishness: the carnal mind will needs start out from implicit trusting of God, when once it is possessed with some imagination of wisdom; therefore how many are the insurrections of men's spirits against God's absolute power over the creatures, against the mysteries of the holy Trinity and incarnation, against the resurrection of our bodies? In these, and such like, the pretended wisdom of men hath taken liberty to act enmity, and to dispute against God. But truly, the rebellion and insubjection against the truth of God, is more generally practised, even by the multitude of men, though in an unfree, hidden way; how few do believe their own desperate wickedness, though God hath testified it of man? Doth not every one apprehend some good to remain in his nature, and some power to good? What an impossibility is it to persuade you, that all mankind are under the sentence of eternal condemnation, that children, who have not done good or evil, are involved in it also? Your hearts rise against such doctrines, as if they were bloody and cruel inventions. To tell you that many are called and few chosen, that the most part of them who profess the truth are walking in the way to hell, and shall undoubtedly fall into it: you may hear such things, but you bless yourselves from them, and cannot be persuaded to admit them into your minds; the hearts of men will be giving the very lie to the God of truth, when he speaks these things in his word; God forbid that all that be true! If we should expound the law unto you, and show you that the least idle word, the lightest thoughts, the smallest inward motion of the heart deserves eternal misery; that anger is murder in God's sight; that lusting is fornication; that covetousness and love of the world is idolatry; these things you cannot know or receive. There are so many high imaginations in your minds, that exalt themselves against the knowledge of God, so many thoughts that are mustered and set in battle-array against the holy truths of God, that truly no weapons of human persuasion or instruction can be able to cast down your misapprehensions and imaginations, or reasonings of your hearts, or able to scatter these armies of rebellious thoughts, and bring them in captivity, (2 Cor. x. 4, 5.) Man's darkened mind is a stronghold, that all the repeated and continued beatings of the word, the multiplying 'precept upon pre-

* [That is, the obscurity or mystery of the gospel.—Ed.]

cept, and line upon line,' cannot storm it to make any true light shine into it. It is a dungeon, a pit so shut up and enclosed, no door nor window in it; so that albeit the Sun of righteousness shine upon it, and round about it, there is no beam of that light can enter in the hearts of many thousands. The generality are drowned as yet in a deluge of ignorance, under the very light of daily preaching. It is a night of as thick darkness within men's souls, as if there were no light about us. Certainly this declares the height of enmity, the strength of the opposition. This prison of your minds is a stronghold indeed, that is proof of all preaching or instruction; and certainly they will hold out, till almighty power storm them, and beat or batter open some entry in your souls, to receive this shining light of the gospel.

Then, there is a rebellion of the will against God's holy will revealed in his law or word; it cannot be subject to the law of God. It neither is nor can; for enmity and antipathy is sunk into its nature so, that it is the most deformed monstrous thing in the world: if the disfigured face of man's soul were visible, O how ugly were it! How would you loathe it! If there were a creature that could do nothing but hate itself, and sought its own destruction, that were a hateful enough object. But self-hatred and enmity is nothing so deformed and abominable, as for the creature's will to be set in opposition to the holy will of him that made it. It needs not much demonstration this, if you had but a little more consideration. Look back upon the tenor of your ways, set them beside the will and commands of God, and what find you? Whether agreement or disagreement? Take a view of the current of your inclinations and affections, and compare that with the holy will of God, and what find you? Friendship or enmity? You cannot digest the reproach of that, to be called enemies to God; but, I pray you, consider if there be not as perfect contrariety in your desires, affections, inclinations, and actions to the will of God as if you did profess it. What would you do if you professed yourselves enemies to God? Could you possibly vent your enmity any other way than this, in withdrawing from the yoke of his obedience, in revolting from that allegiance you owe to him? You could wrong him no further than by setting your hearts and ways contrary to his heart and ways, in loving what he hates, and hating what he loves. For his own blessed being, you could not impair it. Now, consider if that be not acted as really as if you did profess it. Can you say that cursing, swearing, lying, railing, anger, strife, envy, revenge, and such like works of darkness, are the things which his soul loves? Are these suitable to his holy will? And yet these are your inveterate customs, to which your natures are so inured and habituated, that you can no more forsake them than hate yourselves. Are filthiness, drunkenness, Sabbath-breaking, covetousness, and love of the world, are these his delight? And yet these are your delight. Again, is it not his will that ye should purge yourselves from all filthiness of flesh and spirit, and perfect holiness? Is not righteousness that which he loves, and truth in the inward parts? Doth not he look to a contrite heart, and account that a savoury sacrifice? Is it not his royal statute and commandment, of which not one jot shall fail, that ye should deny yourselves, love your enemies, forgive them that offend you, sanctify his name always in your hearts, and especially on the holy Sabbath; that ye should watch unto prayer, be sober in the use of the world, be much in watching for his second coming? Now, what repugnance is in your hearts and ways to all these? Do not the conversations of men display a banner against the gospel, and proclaim as much in reality as is said in words in Psal. ii., 'Let us cast his cords behind us, and cut his bands.' These things are unsavoury unto you, you smell nothing pleasant in them, but only in the puddle of the world, in running at random, at your own liberty, after your own imaginations; that you account only liberty. O when shall your hearts be subdued, and your affections brought in captivity to the obedience of Christ! When shall you be delivered up to the truth, and so made to obey from the heart that form of doctrine and sound words, Rom. vi. 17. This is the strongest hold that Satan hath in man's heart,—his will and affections; and this keeps out longest against Jesus Christ, till he that is stronger come and bind the strong man, and cast out the enmity, and make all captive to his loving obedience, and willing subjection, 2 Cor. x. 4, 5.

Then, thirdly, the enmity of the soul of man is acted in his rebellion against the will of God manifested in his works, in his unsubjection and unsubmissive disposition towards the good pleasure of the Lord, in carving out such and such a lot in the world. It is certain, that as the will of God is the supreme rule of righteousness, so it is the sovereign cause and fountain of all things: and therefore, how infinitely is the creature bound to be subject to him as a Lawgiver, by pleasant and willing obedience to his righteous and reasonable commands; and to submit to him as the absolute Ruler, by quiet and humble condescendence, to all the dispensations of his providence! Now, you know,—if you know any thing of yourselves,—how cross and opposite these hearts of yours are to his good pleasure; how they are set just contrary. And whence flow all murmurings, grudgings, discontents, griefs, cares, and perplexities of men, but from this fountain, the rebellion of the heart against God? There is nothing in all the creation mutinous and malecontent, but the heart of man. You see frequent examples of it, in the murmurations of the people in the wilderness. It is frequently styled, a tempting of the Lord, (Exod. xvii. 2,) importing a high provocation of his holy Majesty; a special incitement, as it were, and motive to declare his absolute power and righteousness against such; and therefore these are often conjoined, Psal. lxxviii. 17, 18. 'They sinned yet more, by provoking the most High,—and they tempted God in their hearts:' and it is added, verse 19, 'Yea, they spake against God.' Wherein you may observe a gradation of aggravations of this enmity. When men have already deserved infinite punishment at his hand, and may always look within, and find an answer to all the murmurings of their hearts, as having sinned so often against him; yet then, to rise up against his good pleasure; and after we have so often sinned, to repine at any thing coming from him. And this, certainly, is a high provocation of the most high God: it puts a kind of necessity upon him, to inflict that which thou indeed deservest; and then, this inward heart-burning against God,—it breaks out often in words, against that most high and holy One, so ver. 40, 41, and ver. 56, 57. *Provoking*, which is the plain expression of murmuring, in the margin is rendered, *rebelling against him*, and so in ver. 8, when a short account is given of them, when the character or anagram of such a people is expressed, it is set down thus, 'a stubborn and rebellious generation.' Therefore Paul, considering this woful and wretched posture of the soul, set in opposition to the always blessed will of God, and the madness and folly of it, he exhorts us, 'Neither murmur ye, as some of them murmured, and were destroyed of the destroyer; for these things happened for ensamples,' &c. 1 Cor. x. 10, 11. Truly, there is nothing more deformed and vile in itself, or more disquieting and tormenting to the soul, or more dangerous in the consequences of it, than such a posture of spirit, a discontented humour against God's providence: whether it be in withholding that good thing from us which we desire, or sending that which crosseth our humour; whether sickness, or want, or reproach, or disrespect; whatsoever it be that the heart is naturally carried to pursue or eschew. What more abominable and ugly visage, than the countenance of an angry and furious person? But when this is against God, it adds infinitely to the deformity and vileness of it. 'I do well to be angry,' is the motto of a discontented soul. It erects an imaginary sovereignty against true Sovereignty: it sets up an anti-providence; it establisheth another divine power and wisdom, and brings the majesty, highness, and holiness of God down to be tread upon by the creature. And then it is its own tormentor, a sin that needs no punishment but itself: the insurrection and mutiny of the heart against God's will, sets all the powers of the soul out of course, vexes, pains, and disquiets all. There is no peace and tranquillity but in the complacency of the heart with God's heart; as Ephraim was like a bullock unaccustomed with the yoke, (Jer. xxxi. 18.) the more he fretted and spurned at his yoke, the more it galled him, and grieved him, till he was instructed, and then he was eased. This fills the soul with hideous tormenting thoughts and cares: this feeds upon its own marrow, and consumes it,—as some have made the emblem of envy,—which is a particular kind of this enmity: as if you would imagine a creature that did waste and consume all its moisture, and marrow, and feed upon the destruction of itself. Now this is but the prelude of what follows; this self-punishment is a messenger to tell what is coming, that the most high God is engaged in his power against such a person, and shall vent his displeasure to their eternal displeasure. That is the fruit of this enmity.

Sermon XXX.

VERSES 7, 8.—" *The carnal mind is enmity against God: for it is not subject to the law of God, neither indeed can be. So then they that are in the flesh cannot please God.*"

IT is not the least of man's evils, that he knows not how evil he is; therefore the Searcher of the heart of man gives the most perfect account of it, Jer. xvii. 12. 'The heart is deceitful above all things,' as well as 'desperately wicked;' two things superlative and excessive in it, bordering upon an infiniteness, such as sin is capable of, wickedness and deceitfulness! And indeed, that which makes the wicked heart desperately and hopelessly so, is the deceitfulness of it. There are many specious coverings gotten to palliate this wickedness and enmity, and so many invisible and spiritual wickednesses in the heart, that it is no wonder that they lurk and dwell without observation. Sin is either covered with some deceivable pretext of another thing, or altogether escapes the dim eyes of men, because of its subtile and spiritual nature. Both are in this business: the enmity of man's heart against God is so subtile a thing in many, and it is shrouded over with some other pretences in all, that few get the lively discovery and sense of it. It is true, it is very gross and palpable in the most part of men,—visible, I mean, upon them, though not to themselves. Any, whose eyes are opened, may behold the black visage of rebellion in the most part of the actings and courses of men, as the apostle, (Gal. v.) speaks, 'the works of the flesh are manifest.' Truly this enmity against God is too manifest in most part, the weapons of your warfare against God being so carnal and visible, your opposition to his holy will and ways being so palpable. There is an enmity acted by many in the tenor of their conversation, without God in the world, and against God; as appears in all your inveterate and godless customs of lying, swearing, cursing, drunkenness, railing, Sabbath-breaking, neglect of prayer, and such like; which carry in their fore-brow this inscription, 'against the known God,' opposite to that of the Athenians' altar. The God whom you pretend to know and worship,—his name is every day blasphemed, his word slighted, his will disobeyed, as if you had proclaimed war against him. But there is in some (and I fear a great many) not only an acted but an affected enmity too; enmity rising up to the maturity and ripeness of malignity and hatred of the image of God, in all his children. Some are not willing to go to heaven, yet they do not disturb others in their journey; they can let others be religious about them, and rawly* desire to be like them: but others there are, who will neither enter into heaven themselves, nor let others enter, as Christ speaks of the Pharisees, Matt. xxiii. 13. They hate the light of another's conversation, because their own deeds are evil, and are reproved and condemned by it. It is said, Rev. xi. 10, the witnesses tormented them that dwelt on the earth. It is strange what a torment it is to the world that the godly are in it! Piety is an eyesore to many: if they could extirpate all that bears that image, they would think it sweet as bread, Psal. xiv. This is a more open and declared enmity against the God of heaven; and yet I know it lurks under the mask of some other thing. You pretend to hate hypocrisy only; alas! what a scorn is it for profanity to hate hypocrisy? Sure it is not because it is a sin, but for the very shadow of piety it carries. You hate the thing itself so perfectly, that you cannot endure the very picture of it. Do not deceive yourselves, the true quarrel is, because they run not to the same excess of riot with you. If they will lie, cozen, defraud, swear, and blaspheme as other men, you could endure to make them companions, as you do others; and the principle of that is, the enmity that was placed in the beginning: that mortal irreconcilable feud, betwixt the two families, are two seeds of Christ and Satan.

But, as I told you, this enmity acts in a more subtile and invisible way in some, and it is painted over with some fair colours, to hide the deformity of it. Not only the grosser corruptions of men carry this stamp, but take even the most refined piece or part in man; take his mind, take the excellency of his mind, even the wisdom of it,

* [Coldly or carelessly.—ED.]

yet that hath enmity incorporated into it, and mixed with it throughout all; for the wisdom of the flesh is enmity with God, as it may be read, φρονημα, the very prudence and reason of a natural man, which carries him to a distance from, and opposition with, the common defilements in the courses of men; yet that hath in its bosom a more exquisite and refined enmity against God; and so the more spiritual and purified it be from grosser corruptions, it is the more active and powerful against God, because it is, as it were, the very spirit and quintessence of enmity. You see it, 1 Cor. i. how the wisdom of God is foolishness to the wisdom of the world; and then again, that the wisdom of the world is the greatest folly to the only wise God. Men, that have many natural advantages beyond others, are at this great disadvantage, they are more ready to despise godliness, as too base and simple a thing to adorn their natures; as Christ said of rich men, it may be said of wise men, of learned men, of civil and blameless persons, who have a smooth carriage before the world, how hard is it for such to enter into the kingdom of heaven? Hard indeed! for they must be stripped naked of that, ere they can enter through this narrow gate; I mean, the opinion and conceit, of any worth or excellency, and so diminished in their own eyes, that they may go through this needle's eye without crushing.

The stream of enmity runs under ground often, and so hides itself under some other notion, till at length it burst forth openly. I find it commonly runs in the secret channel of amity or friendship to some other thing opposite to God: So James iv. 4. The amity of the world is enmity with God; and 1 John ii. 15. He that loveth the world, the love of the Father is not in him. There are two dark and under-ground conduits, to convey this enmity against God,—amity to the world, and amity to ourselves, self-love, and creature-love. We cannot denounce war openly against heaven, but this is the next course, to join to, or associate with, any party that is contrary to God; and thus, under the covert of friendship to ourselves, and love to the world, we war against God, and destroy our own souls. I say, first, amity to the world carries enmity to God in the bosom of it: and if you believe not this, hear the apostle's sharp and pungent question, you adulterers and adulteresses, know you not that the amity of the world is enmity with God? He doth not speak only to persons guilty of that crime, but to all natural men, who are guilty of adultery or whoredom of a more spiritual nature, but as abominable and more dangerous. There is a bond and special tie betwixt all men and God their Maker, which obligeth them to consecrate and devote themselves, their affections and endeavours, to his honour, especially when the covenant of the gospel is superadded unto that, in which Jesus Christ our Lord reveals himself, as having only right to us and our affections; as willing to bestow himself upon us; and notwithstanding of all the distance between him and wretched sinners, yet filling it up with his infinite love and wonderful condescendency, demitting himself to the form of a servant, out of love, that so he might take us up to be his chaste spouse, and adorn us with his beauty. This he challengeth of us, whoever hear and profess the gospel, this is your profession—if ye understand it—that Jesus Christ shall be your well-beloved, and ye his; that ye shall separate yourself to him, and admit no stranger in his place; that the choice and marrow of your joy, love and delight, shall be bestowed on him. Now, this bond and tie of a professed relation to that glorious husband, is foully broken by the most part, by espousing their affections to this base world. Your hearts are carried off him unto strangers, that is, present perishing things: whereas the intendment of the gospel is, to present you to Christ as pure virgins, 2 Cor. xi. 2. Truly your hearts are gone a-whoring after other things, the love of the world hath withdrawn you, or kept you in chains; these present things are as snares, nets, and bands; as an harlot's hands and heart, Eccl. vii. 26. They are powerful enchantments over you, which bewitch you to a base love, from an honourable and glorious love. O that you would consider it, my beloved, what opposition there is betwixt the love of the world and the love of the Father; betwixt amity to that which hath nothing in it, but some present bait to your deceitful lusts, and amity to God, your only lawful Husband! Affection is a transforming and conforming thing, *Si terram amas terra es;** the love of God will purify thy heart, and lift it up to more similitude to him whom thou lovest; but the love of the world assimilates it unto the

* [That is, "If thou lovest the earth, thou art earth."—Ed.]

world, makes it such a base and ignoble piece, as the earth is. Do you think marriage affection can be parted? 'My well beloved is mine;' therefore the church is the turtle, the dove to Christ, of wonderful chastity: it never joins but to one; and after the death of its marrow, it sighs and mourns ever after, and sits solitarily. You must retire, my beloved, and disengage from the love of other things, or you cannot love Christ; and if you love not Christ, you cannot have peace with the Father: and if you have not that peace, you cannot have life. This is the chain of life; the first link begins at the divorcement of all former loves and beloved idols: once the soul must be loosed in desire and delight, and that link must be fastened upon the most lovely and desirable object, Christ, the Desire of the nations: and this draws along another link of peace and life with it. Do not mistake it, religion would not hinder or prejudice your lawful business in this world: O, it were the most compendious way to advance it, with more ease to your souls! But certainly it will teach you to exchange the love of these things for a better and more heart-contenting love.

Then, amity to ourselves is enmity to God; and truly this is the last stronghold that holds out longest against God, when others may be beaten down, or surrendered. Possibly a man may attain to this, to despise these lower things, as below his natural dignity and the excellency of his spirit. Some may renounce much of that friendship with worldly and temporal things, as being sordid and base; but the enmity gets into this strong and invisible tower of darkness, self-love and pride: and therefore the apostle John makes this the last and chiefest, the pride of life, 1 John ii. 16. When the lusts of the eyes and flesh are in some measure abated, this is but growing: and what decreaseth of these, seems to accresce* unto this: as if self-love and pride did feed and nourish itself upon the ashes or consumption of other vices. Yea, it draws sap from graces and virtues, and grows thereby, till at length it kill that which nourished it: and indeed the apostle James seems to proceed to this, ver. 5, 6. when he minds us that God resisteth the proud, and giveth grace to the humble. 'Doth the scripture say this in vain?' saith he. Is not self-amity as well enmity as the amity of the world? And therefore God opposes himself unto it, as the very grand enmity. Self is the great lord, the arch-rebel, the head of all opposition, that in which they do all centre; and when all the inferior soldiers are captives, or killed, this is last in the field; it lives first in opposition, and dies last, *primum vivens, et ultimum moriens.* When a man is separated from many things, yet he may be but more conjoined to himself, and so the further disjoined from God. Of all these vile rags of the old man, this is nearest the skin, and last put off: of all the members, self is the heart, first alive, and last alive. When enmity is constrained to render up the outward members of the body, to yield them to a more smooth and fair carriage to a civil behaviour; when the mind itself is forced to yield unto some light of truth and knowledge of the gospel; yet the enmity retires into the heart, and fortifies it the stronger, by self-love and self-estimation; as in winter the encompassing cold makes the heat to combine itself together in the bowels of the earth, and by this means the springs are hotter than in summer; so the surrounding light of the gospel, or education, or natural honesty, drives the heat and strength of enmity inward, where it fortifies itself more. This is that accursed antiperistasis,† that is made by the concurrence of some advantages of knowledge and civility, and such like.

The blood of enmity against God gets in about the heart, when it is chased for fear out of the outward man: therefore, the very first and fundamental principle of Christianity, is, 'Let a man deny himself, and so he shall be my disciple.' He must

* [Increase.—Ed.]

† [Antiperistasis, (ἀντιπερίστασις, from ἀντι, περι, and ἵστημι, the act of hemming round,) a term employed in ancient times by the Peripatetics. to denote the increase of one quality by the action of another of an opposite nature, as when internal heat or inflammation is increased by external cold. It would be "a holy Antiperistasis in a Christian," it is said (p. 216) were the surrounding ignorance and wickedness of the world to make "the grace of God unite itself, and work more powerfully, as fire out of a cloud; and shine more brightly, as a torch in the darkness of the night." A learned English divine, who lived in the same age with Binning, declares, that in the case of the faithful themselves, sin derives additional power. "by *antiperistasis* from the law, to deceive, captivate, sell as a slave. to make them do that which they hated and allowed not, and do not that which they would and loved."—Bishop Reynold's Works, vol. i. p. 146. Lond. 1826.—Ed.]

become a fool in his own eyes, though he be wise, that he may be wise (1 Cor. iii. 18.); he must become as ungodly, though godly, that he may be justified by faith (Rom. iv. 5.); he must forsake himself, that he may indeed find himself, or get a better self in another; he must not eat much honey, that is not good, it would swell him though it be pleasant; he must not search his own glory, or reflect much upon it, if he would be a follower and a friend of Christ. Look, how much soever you engage to yourselves esteem, or desire to be esteemed of others, to reflect with complacency on yourselves, to mind your own satisfaction and estimation in what you do, so much you disengage from Jesus Christ, for these are contrary points. This is a direct motion towards Christ. That is an inverse and backward motion towards ourselves; and so much as we move that way, we promove not, but lose our way, and are further from the true end. Ezekiel's living creatures may be an emblem of a Christian's motion, he returns not as he goes, he makes a straight line to God, whithersoever he turn him; but nature makes all crooked lines, they seem to go forth in obedience to God, but they have a secret unseen reflexion into its own bosom. And this is the greatest act of enmity, to idolize God, and deify ourselves; we make him a cypher and sacrifice to ourselves: his peculiar, incommunicable property of Alpha and Omega, that we do sacrilegiously attribute to ourselves, the beginning of our notions, and end of them too. This is the crooked line, that nature cannot possibly move out of, till a higher Spirit come and restore her that halted, and make plain her paths.

That which is added, as a reason, explains this enmity more clearly; *because it cannot be subject*, &c. Truly these two forementioned amities of the world and of ourselves, do withdraw men wholly from the orderly subjection that they owe to the law of God. Order is the beauty of every thing, of nature, of art, of the whole universe, and of the several parts, kingdoms and republics of it. This indeed is the very beauty of the world, all things subordinate to him that made them; only miserable man hath broken this order, and marred this beauty, and he cannot be subject, ουχ ὑποτασσεται, cannot come again into that orderly station and subordination he was once into. This is the only gap or breach of the creation. And it is some other engagements that draw him thus far out of course,—the base love of the world, and the inordinate love of himself. O these make his neck stiff, that it cannot bow to the yoke of obedience: these have opposite and contrary commands, and no man can serve two masters. When the commands of the great lord, self, come in opposition with the commands of God, then he cannot be subject to the law of God. For a time, in some things, he may resemble a subjection, when the will of self and the will of God commands in one point, as sometimes they do by accident; but that is neither frequent nor constant.

Not only is he not subject, but there is worse in it, he cannot be subject to the law of God. This is certainly to throw down the natural pride of man, that always apprehends some remanent ability in himself. You think still to make yourselves better, and when convinced or challenged for sins, to make amends, and reform your lives. You use to promise these things as lightly and easily as if they were wholly in your power, and as if you did only delay them for advantage; and truly it seems, this principle of self-sufficiency is engraven on men's hearts, when they procrastinate and delay repentance, and earnest minding of religion to some other fitter season, as if it were in their liberty to apply to it when they please: and when you are urged and persuaded to some reformation, you take in hand, even as that people, Jer. xlii. 6, 20, who said, 'all that the Lord hath said, we will do:' You can strike hands, and engage to serve the Lord, as easily as that people in Joshua xxiv. 18, 19. But we may say, Oh, that there were such a heart in you! But, alas, such a heart is not in you! You cannot serve the Lord, for he is holy and jealous, and ye are not only weak, but wicked. I beseech you then, believe this one testimony that God hath given of man, even the choicest thing in man, the very wisdom of a natural man, it is not subject to God's law, and it cannot be better, neither can it be subject Resolution, industry, vows, and covenants will not effect this, till the Most High break and bow the heart. And not only has this enmity against the old law of commandments an antipathy at them, as crossing our lusts, but even against the new and living law of the Spirit of life in Christ

Here is your misery, you can neither be subject to the law as commanding to obey it, or threatening for disobedience to it, nor to the gospel as promising to believe and receive it. The law commands, but your law countermands within; the law threatens and sentences you with condemnation, but you have some self-pleasing delusion and dream in your heads, and bless yourselves in your own hearts, even though ye walk in the imagination of your hearts, contrary to the law, Deut. xxix. It is strange that you do not fore-apprehend and fear hell! But it is this delusion possesses the heart, 'you shall not die:' it was the first act of enmity, not only the transgression of the command, but unbelief of the truth of the curse: and that which first encouraged man to sin, encourages you all to lie into it, and continue in it,—a fancy of escaping wrath. This noise fills the heart; Satan whispers in the ear, Go on, you shall not die. Thus it appears, that the natural mind cannot be subject to the law of God, no persuasion, no instruction, can enforce this belief of your damnable condition upon you.

But then, when the enmity is beaten out of this fort, and a soul is really convinced of its desperate and lost estate, when the heart is brought down to subjection, to take with that dreadful sentence; yet there is another tower of enmity in the heart, that can keep out against the weapons of the gospel, such as Paul mentions, Rom. x. 3. Being ignorant of the righteousness of God, they went about to establish their own, and could not submit to the righteousness of God. There is a natural pride and stiffness of heart, that we cannot endure but to have something in ourselves to rest on, and take pleasure into: and when a soul sees nothing, it rather vexes and torments itself as grieving because it hath no ornament or covering of its own, nor rejoiceth and delighteth in that righteousness of God revealed in Christ. O the difficulty to bow down so low, as to put on another's righteousness over our nakedness! And should it be called submission? Is it not rather the elevating and exalting of the soul? Yet in respect of our natural posture of spirit, it is a matter of great difficulty to make a self-condemned sinner submit to this, to be saved freely, without money or price, by another's ransom. What empty, vain, and frivolous expiations and satisfactions will souls invent, rather than trust all to this! How long will poor souls wander abroad from hill to mountain, seeking some inherent qualification, to commend them, and leave this garden and paradise of delights, which is opened up in Christ? Souls look everywhere for help, till all hands fail; and then necessity constrains them to come hither; but indeed, when necessity brings in, charity and amity keeps in, when once they know what entertainment is in Christ. As for you, who as yet have not stooped to the sentence of wrath, how will you submit to the righteousness of God? But I wonder how you imagine this to be so easy a thing to believe. You say you did always believe in Christ, and that your hearts are still on him, and that you do it night and day. Now, there needs no other argument to persuade that you do not at all believe in the gospel, who have apprehended no more difficulty in it, no more contrariety to your rebellious natures in it. Let this one word go home with you, and convince you of your unbelief, 'The natural mind is not subject to the law of God, neither indeed can be.' How, then, do you come so easily by it? Certainly it must be feigned and counterfeit.

Sermon XXII

VERSE 8.—"*So then they that are in the flesh cannot please God.*"

It is a kind of happiness to men, to please them upon whom they depend, and upon whose favour their well-being hangs. It is the servant's happiness to please his master, the courtier's to please his prince; and so generally, whosoever they be that are joined in mutual relations, and depend one upon another; that which makes all pleasant, is this, to please one another. Now, certainly, all the dependencies of creatures one upon another, are but shadows unto the absolute dependence of creatures upon the Creator, for in him we live, and move, and have our being: the dependence of the ray upon the sun, of the stream upon the fountain, is one of the greatest in nature; but all creatures have a more necessary connexion with this Fountain-being, both in their being and well-being; they are nothing but a flux and emanation of his power and pleasure, and, as the Psalmist expresseth it, He hides his face and they are troubled; he takes away their breath, and they die, and return to their dust: He sends forth his Spirit, and they are created, and he renews the face of the earth, Psal. civ. 29, 30. You may extend this to the being and well-being, the happiness and misery of creatures; our souls which animate our bodies are but his breath which he breathed into the dust, and can retract when he pleaseth; the life of our souls, the peace, and tranquillity, and satisfaction is another breathing of his Spirit, and another look of his countenance; and as he pleases to withdraw it, or interpose between his face and us, so we live or die, are blessed or miserable. Our being or well-being hath a more indispensable dependence on him, than the image in the glass hath upon the living face.

If it be so then, certainly of all things in the world it concerns us nearest how to please him, and to be at peace with him. If we be in good terms with him in whose hands our breath is, and whose are all our ways, (Dan. v. 23.) upon whose countenance our misery or felicity hangs, then certainly we are happy. If we please him, it matters not whom we displease; for he alone hath absolute, uncontrolled, and universal power over us, as our Saviour speaks, over both soul and body. We may expect that his good pleasure towards us will not be satisfied, but in communicating his fulness, and manifesting his favour to us, especially since the goodness of God is so exundant,* as to overflow even to the wicked world, and vent itself as out of superabundance, in a river of goodness throughout the whole earth. How much more will it run abundantly towards them whom he is well pleased with. And therefore the Psalmist cries out, as being already full in the very hope and expectation of it, that he would burst, if he had not the vent of admiration and praise, O how great is his goodness, and how excellent his loving-kindness laid up for them that fear him! Psal. xxxi. 19. and xxxvi. 7. But, on the other hand, how incomparable is the misery of them who cannot please God! even though they did both please themselves and all others for the present. To be at odds with him in whom alone they can subsist, and without whose favour is nothing but wretchedness and misery, O that must be the worst and most cursed estate imaginable: to be in such a state, as do what they can, they cannot please him, whom alone to please is of only concernment, what can be invented† to that? Now, if you ask who they are that are such? These words speak it plainly, in way of inference from the former doctrine, 'So then they that are in the flesh cannot please God.' Not they in whom there is flesh; for there are remnants of that in the most spiritual man in this life: we cannot attain here to angelic purity, though it should be the aim and endeavour of every Christian. But they that are in the flesh, or after the flesh, imports the predomination of that, and an universal thraldom of nature unto it, which indeed is the state of all men that are but once born, till a second birth come, by the Spirit of Jesus Christ.

The ground of this may be taken from the foregoing discourse, and it is chiefly twofold. One is, because they are not in Jesus Christ, in whom his soul is well pleased; another is, because they cannot suit and frame their carriage according to his pleasure. Since all mankind hath fallen under the displeasure of the most high God, by sinning against him, in preferring the pleasure of the flesh, and the pleasure of Satan, to the pleasure of God, there can be no atonement found to pacify him, no sacrifice to appease him, no ransom to satisfy his justice, but that one perfect offering for sin, Jesus Christ, the propitiation for the sins of the elect world. This the Father accepts in the name of sinners; and in testimony of his acceptance, he did two several times, by a voice from heaven, declare, first to a multitude, (Matth. iii. 17.) and then to the beloved disciples, (Matth. xvii. 5.) and both times with great majesty and solemnity (as did become him), that this is his well-beloved Son, in whom his soul is well-pleased. It pleased God to make the stream of his love to take another channel after man's sin, and not to run immediately towards wretched man, but he turned the current of his love another way, to his own Son, whom he chose for that end, to reconcile

* [Exuberant or abundant.—Ed.]

† [That is, conceived like that.—Ed.]

man, and bring him into favour; and his love going about, by that compass, comes in the issue towards poor sinners with the greater force. He hath appointed Christ the meeting-place with sinners, the Daysman to lay his hand on both; and therefore he is God to lay his hand on God, and man to lay his hand on man, and bring both into a peaceable and amicable conjunction. Now then, whoever are not in Jesus Christ, as is spoken, ver. 1. certainly they cannot please God do what they can; because God hath made Christ the centre in which he would have the good pleasure of sinners meeting with his good pleasure; and therefore, without faith it is impossible to please God, (Heb. xi. 6.) not so much for the excellency of the act itself, as for the well-pleasing object of it, Christ. The love of the Father is terminate in him, his justice is satisfied in him, his love is well-pleased with the excellency of his person; he finds in him an object of delight, which is nowhere else: and his justice is well-pleased with the sufficiency and worthiness of his ransom; and without this compass, there is neither satisfaction to the one, nor to the other: so then, whatsoever you are, how high soever your degree in the world, how sweet soever your disposition, let your natures be never so good, your carriage never so smooth; yet certainly there is nothing in all this that can please God, either by an object of love, or a price for justice. You are under that eternal displeasure, which will fall on and crush you to pieces. Mountains will not be so heavy, as it will appear in that great day of his wrath, Rev. vi. I say, you cannot come from under that imminent weight of eternal wrath, unless you be found in Jesus Christ,—that blessed place of immunity and refuge,—if you have not forsaken yourselves and your own natures, and denied your own righteousness as dung, to be found in him, clothed with his righteousness and satisfaction. If the delight and pleasure of your soul do not coincide and fall in at one place with the delight and good pleasure of the Father, that is, upon his well-beloved Son, certainly the pleasure and good will of God hath not as yet fallen upon you, and met with you: therefore, if you would please God, be pleased with Christ; and you cannot do him a greater pleasure than believe in him, (John v. 23.) that is, absolutely resign yourselves unto him, for salvation and sanctification.

The other ground is, —Such as are in the flesh cannot frame their spirits, affections, and ways to God's good pleasure; for their very wisdom, the very excellency that is in them, is enmity to God, and cannot be subject to his law; and therefore they cannot please him. I am sure you may easily reflect upon yourselves, and find, not with much search, but upon all these, as the prophet (Jer. ii. 34.) speaks, that it is not the study and business you have undertaken to please God, but the bent and main of your aims and endeavours is to please yourselves, or to please men. This makes many men's pains, even in religion, displeasing to God; because they do not indeed mind his pleasure, but their own or other's satisfaction. What they do, is but to conform to the custom of the time, or commandments of men, or their own humour; and all this must needs be abominable to God. Truly, that which is in great account among men, is an abomination to God, as our Saviour speaks of the very righteousness and professed piety of the Pharisees, Luke xvi. 15.; the more you please yourselves and the world, the further you are from pleasing God. The very beginning of pleasing God is when a soul falls in displeasure at itself, and abhorrence of his own loathsomeness; therefore it is said, The humble and contrite spirit I will look unto, and dwell with him, and such sacrifices do please God, Isa. lxvi. 2. Psal. li. 17. For the truth is, God never begins to be pleasant and lovely to a soul, till it begins to fall out of love with itself, and grow loathsome in its own eyes. Therefore you may conclude this of yourselves, that with many of you God is not well-pleased, although you be all baptized unto Christ, and do all eat of that same spiritual meat, and drink of that same spiritual drink; though you have all church-privileges, yet with many of you God is not well-pleased, as 1 Cor. x. 2—5. not only because those works of the flesh that are directly opposite to his own known will, such as fornication, murmuring, grudging at God's dispensation, cursing and swearing, lying, drunkenness, anger, malice, strife, variance, and such like, abound as much among you as that old people; but even those of you that may be free from gross opposition to his holy will, your nature hath the seed of all that enmity, and you act enmity in a more covered way; you are so well-pleased with yourselves, your chief study is to please men; you have not given yourselves to this study, to conform yourselves to the pleasure of God; therefore know your dreadful condition, you cannot please God, without whose favour and pleasure you cannot but be eternally displeased and tormented in yourselves. Certainly, though now you please yourselves, yet the day shall come that you shall be contrary to yourselves, and all to you, as it is spoken as a punishment of the Jews, (1 Thess. ii. 15.) and there is some earnest of in this life. Many wicked persons are set contrary to themselves, and all to them; they are like Esau, their hand against all, and all men's hands against them; yea, their own consciences continually vexing them. This is a fruit of that fundamental discord and enmity between men and God; and if you find it not now, you shall find it hereafter.

But as for you that are in Jesus Christ, who being displeased with yourselves, have fled into the well-beloved, in whom the Father is well-pleased, to escape God's displeasure; I say unto such, your persons God is well-pleased with in Christ, and this shall make way and place for acceptance to your weak and imperfect performances. This is the ground of your peace and acceptance; and you would take it so, and it shall yield you much peace, when you cannot be pleased with yourselves. But I would charge that upon you, that as you by believing are well-pleased with Christ, so you would henceforth study to 'walk worthy of your Lord unto all well-pleasing, being fruitful in every good work, and increasing in the knowledge of God,' Col. i. 10. This is that to which you are called, to such a work as may please him, to conform yourselves even to his pleasure and will. If you love him, you cannot but fashion yourselves so as he may be pleased. O how exact and observant is love of that which may ingratiate itself in the beloved's favour! It is the most studious thing to please, and most afraid of displeasing. Enoch had a large and honourable testimony, as ever was given to man, that he pleased God, Heb. xi. 5. I beseech you be ambitious of this after a holy manner; labour to know his will, and that for this end, that you may approve it, and prove it that you may do that good and acceptable will of God. Let his pleasure be your rule, your law, to which all within you may conform itself. Though you cannot attain an exact correspondence with his pleasure, but in many things you will offend; yet certainly this will be the resolved study of your hearts how to please him; and in as far as you cannot please him, you will be displeased with yourselves. But then, I would advise you, in as far as you are displeased with yourselves for not pleasing God, be as much well-pleased with Christ, the pleasing sacrifice and atonement; and this shall please God as much as your obedience could do, or your disobedience can displease him. To him be praise and glory.

Sermon XXIII.

VERSE 9.—"*But ye are not in the flesh, but in the Spirit, if so be that the Spirit of God dwell in you. Now, if any man have not the Spirit of Christ, he is none of his.*"

APPLICATION is the very life of the word, at least it is a necessary condition for the living operation of it. The application of the word to the hearts of hearers by preaching, and the application of your hearts again to the word by meditation, these two meeting together, and striking one upon another, will yield fire. Paul speaks of a right dividing of the word of truth (2 Tim. ii. 15.); not that ordinary way of cutting it all in parcels, and dismembering it, by manifold divisions, which I judge makes it lose much of its virtue, which consists in union, though some have pleasure in it, and think it profitable; yet I do not see that this was the apostolic way, that either they preached it themselves, or recommended it to others; but rather he means, the real distribution of the food of souls unto their various conditions, as it is the duty of a steward to be both faithful and wise in that, to give every one their own portion; and as it is the pastor's duty thus to distribute the word of God unto you, so it is your part to apply it home to yourselves, without which application, the former division of the word aright will not feed your souls; if every man act not the pastor to his own heart it cannot profit. Now indeed the right application of the word to souls is the difficultest part of preaching, and it is the hardest point of hearing; in which there needs both much affection and much direction, the one to be serious and earnest in it, the other to be wise and prudent in it. Without suitable affection, it will not pass into the subtsance of the soul to feed it, no more than the stomach can digest meat, that wants convenient heat; and without discretion and wisdom, to choose our own portion, it will not yield convenient food, but increase humours and superfluities, or distemper our spirits. That which I look at in these words, is the discretion and prudence of this wise steward in God's house, after he hath represented the wretched and woful estate of them that are in the flesh, how their natures cannot but act enmity against God, how their end is death and destruction, he subjoins in due season a suitable encouragement to believers, 'You are not in the flesh,' &c. Because there is no man so sensible of that corruption that dwells within, as he that is in part renewed; as pain to a healthful body is most sensible, and as the abundance of light makes a larger discovery of what is disordered and defiled in the house; therefore such, upon the hearing of the accursed estate of men in nature, of their natural rebellion against God, and God's displeasure against them, they are most ready, I say, to apply such things to themselves, to the weakening of their own hands, and saddening of their hearts; as the upright-hearted disciples were more ready to take with the challenge of betraying Christ, than the false-hearted Judas. Therefore the apostle prevents such an abuse of the doctrine, by making application of the better part unto the Romans; but for you, 'ye are not of the flesh,' &c. Indeed, self-examination is necessary, and it is like chewing of the meat before it be sent into the stomach, it is as necessary and precedent before right application. I wish that every one of you would consider well what this living word concerns you. It is the ground of all our barrenness; no man brings this home to himself, which is spoken to all: but truly the Lord speaks to all, that every man may speak to himself, and ask at his own heart, what is my concernment in it? What is my portion? As for you whom the Lord hath put upon this search of yourselves, and hath once made you to find yourselves in the black roll of perdition, under the hazard of the eternal weight of God's displeasure, and there hath showed unto your souls a way of making peace with God, and a place of refuge in Jesus Christ, which hath sometimes refreshed and eased your hearts, and only was able to purify your consciences, and calm the storms that did arise in them; if it be henceforth your study to walk to please him, and this engagement be on your hearts, to make no peace with the flesh, and corruption that dwells in you, then, I say, the Lord calls and accounts you not carnal but spiritual: though there be much carnality in you, yet he denominates from the better part, not from the greatest part, you are not after the flesh but after the Spirit. Though Isaac be a weak young child, and Ishmael the son of the bond-woman be a strong man; yet thou art in God's account esteemed according to the promise, which shall be the ground of thy stability. Isaac must abide in the house for ever, and grow stronger and stronger, and Ishmael must be cast out and grow weaker and weaker: the one is ordained for destruction, and so is called the old man, drawing near to its grave, the other for life; and so is a new man renewed day by day. Thus they are in God's promise, and you would learn thus to look upon it, not according to their present inequality in strength, but that future inequality and difference which is wrapt up in the promise of God, and the seed whereof is in you.

As there is a woful penury and scantiness of examination in the most part of men, who are wholly spent without, and take no leisure to recognise their own souls; so there is a miserable excess, and hurtful superfluity of examination and disputation among many of God's children, who are always in reflection, and almost never in action; so much on knowing what is, that they take not much leisure to do or pursue what is not. Truly, I think when the apostle commands us to examine whether we be in the faith, and prove ourselves, he did not mean to make it our perpetual exercise, or so to press it, as we should not endeavour to be in the faith, till we know whether we be in it: that were no advancing way, to refuse to go on in our journey till we know what progress we have made, as the custom is. But simply and plainly, I think, he intended to have Christianity begin at examination, as the first returning of a soul must needs be upon some inquiry and search of the way, and knowledge upon search, that our former way was wrong, and this is only right. But if this be the porch to enter at, will you sit down and dwell in it, and not go on into the palace itself? Because you must begin to search what you have learned wrong, that now you may unlearn it, will you be ever about the learning to know your condition, and by this means never attain to the knowledge of the truth? But when you have upon any inquiry found yourselves out of the way, you should not entertain that dispute long, but hearken to the plain voice of the gospel, that sounds unto you, 'This is the way, walk in it.' 'I am the way,' saith Christ, enter at me, by believing in me. Now, once having found that you are unbelievers by nature, to suspend believing till you prove whether you be in the faith, is unreasonable and impossible; for certainly having once found yourselves void of it, you must first have it, before you know that you have it; you must first apply to action, and afterward your examination shall be more easy.

But I would tell a more profitable improvement of such representations of the sinful and miserable estate of the ungodly world, than you use to make of it: and I think it is that the apostles intend, in the frequent turning the eyes of saints about to the accursed state of the world; partly consolation, and partly some provocation to suitable walking. Things that are opposite are best known by comparison one with another; each of them cast abroad a light to see the other by. Therefore it is that the apostles do frequently remind the converted Gentiles of the wretched estate the world lies into, and themselves once were into. You see it, 1 Cor. vi. 11. 'And such were some of you: but now you are washed.' And, Eph. ii. 1. 'You who were dead in sins hath he quickened.' There is not any thing will more commend unto a Christian the grace of God towards him, nor * to look abroad round about him, and take a view of the whole world lying in wickedness; and then to look backward to what himself once was, and compare it with what the free grace of God hath made him. O what a soul-ravishing contemplation is that: 1 John. v. 19. 'And we know that we are of God, and the whole world lieth in wickedness.' How doth this heighten the price of grace, and how much doth it add to a soul's inward contentment, to think what it was of itself, and what it would undoubtedly have been, if not thus wonderfully surprised! One used always to look to those below him, that he might not envy those above him. Truly it might do well here, when a Christian is grieved and disquieted, because he hath not attained to that desired measure of the image of God, and fellowship with him, to cast a look about him to the miserable and hopeless estate of so many thousands who have the image of Satan so visibly engraven on them, and have no inward stirring after this blessed image; and reflect a little backward, to the hole of the pit whence he was taken, to look upon that primitive estate that grace found him into, so loathsome, as is described Ezek. xvi. Would not such a double sight, think you, make him break out in admiration, and be powerful to silence and compose his spirit? O to think, that I was once in that black roll of those excluded from the kingdom! 'Such were some of you;' and then to consider, that my name was taken out, and washed by the blood of Christ to be enrolled in the register of heaven. What an astonishing thing is it! You see in nature, God hath appointed contrarieties and varieties to beautify the world; and certainly, many things could not be known how good and beneficial they are, but by the smart and hurt of that which is opposite to them: as ye could not imagine the good of light, but by some sensible experience of the evil of darkness. Heat, you could not know the benefit of it, but by the vexation of cold. Thus he maketh one to commend another, and both to beautify the world. It is thus in art; contrariety and variety of colours and lines make up one beauty: diversity of sounds make a sweet harmony. Now, this is the art and wisdom of God; in the dispensation of his grace he setteth the misery of some beside the happiness of others, that each of them may aggravate another; he puts light beside darkness, spirit fore-against † flesh, that so saints may have a double

* [That is, *than* to look.—ED.] † [That is, opposite.—ED.]

accession to their admiration at the goodness and grace of God, and to their delight and complacency in their own happiness: he presents the state of men out of Christ, that you may wonder how you are translated, and may be so abundantly satisfied as not to exchange your portion for the greatest monarch's.

Then, I say, this may provoke us, and persuade us to more suitable walking. Doth he make such a difference? O do not you unmake it again! Do not confound all again, by your walking after the course of the world. Conformity to the world is a confusion of what God hath separated. Has infinite grace translated you from that kingdom of darkness to light? O then walk in that light, as children of light! Are you such? Own your stations; consider your relations, and make yourselves ashamed at the very thoughts of sin. He points out the deformed and ugly face of the conversation of the world, that you may fall in love with the beauty of holiness, as the Lacedemonians were wont to let their children see their slaves drunk, that the brutish and abominable posture of such in that sin might imprint in the hearts of their children a detestation of such a vice. Certainly, the Lord calls you to mind often what you have been, and what the world about you is; not to engage you to it, but to alienate your minds from the deformity of sin, and to commend to you the duty of obedience. You would learn to make this holy use and advantage of all the wickedness the world lieth into; to behold in it, as in a glass, your own image and likeness; that when you use to hate or despise others, you may rather loathe and dislike yourselves, as having that same common nature; and wonder at the goodness of God that makes such difference where none was. This were the way to make gain of the most unprofitable thing in the world, that is, the sins of other men; for ordinarily the seeing and speaking of them doth rather dispose us and incline us to more liberty to sin. Many look on them with delight, some with contempt and hatred of those that commit them, but few know how to speak or look on sin itself with indignation, or themselves, because of the seeds of it within them, with abhorrency. I would think if we were circumspect in this, the worse the world is, we might be the better; the worse the times are, we might spend it better; the more pride we see, it might make us the more humble; the more impiety and impurity abound, it might provoke us to a further distance from, and disconformity with, the world. Thus, if we were wise, we might extract gold out of the dunghill, and suck honey out of the most poisonable weed. The surrounding ignorance and wickedness of the world might cause a holy antiperistasis * in a Christian, by making the grace of God unite itself, and work more powerfully, as fire out of a cloud, and shine more brightly, as a torch in the darkness of the night.

As for you, whose woful estate is here described, who are yet in the flesh, and enemies to God by nature, I would desire you to be stirred up at the consideration of this, that there are some who are delivered out of that prison, and that some have made peace with God, and are no more enemies but friends, and fellow-citizens of the saints. If the case were left wholly incurable and desperate, you had some ground to continue in your sins and security; but now when you hear a remedy is possible, and some have been helped by it, I wonder that you do not, upon this door of hope offered, bestir yourselves, that you may be those who are here excepted, 'but you are not in the flesh.' Since some are, why may not I be? Will you awake yourselves with this alarm! If you had any desire after this estate, certainly such a hope as this would give you feet to come to Jesus Christ; for these are the legs of the soul,—some desire of a better estate, and some probability of it conceived by hope.

* [See Note, p. 208.—Ed.]

Sermon XXIV.

VERSE 9.—"*If so be that the Spirit of God dwell in you. Now if any man have not the Spirit of Christ, he is none of his.*"

'BUT will God in very deed dwell with men on the earth?' 2 Chron. vi. 18. It was the wonder of one of the wisest of men; and indeed, considering his infinite highness above the height of heavens, his immense and incomprehensible greatness, that the heaven of heavens cannot contain him; and then the baseness, emptiness, and worthlessness of man, it may be a wonder to the wisest of angels. And what is it, think you, the angels desire to look into, but this incomprehensible mystery of the descent of the Most High to dwell among the lowest and vilest of the creatures? But as Solomon's temple, and these visible symbols of God's presence, were but shadows of things to come, the substance whereof is exhibited under the gospel; so that wonder was but a shadow or type of a greater and more real wonder, of God's dwelling on the earth now. It was the wonder, shall God dwell with man, among the rebellious sons of Adam? But behold a greater wonder since Christ came, God dwelling in man, first personally in the man Christ, in whom the fulness of the Godhead dwelt bodily, then graciously in the seed of Christ, in man by his Spirit; and this makes men spiritual, if so be the Spirit of Christ dwell in you. You heard of the first indwelling, ver. 3. 'God sending his own Son in the likeness of sinful flesh,' the inhabitation of the divine nature in our flesh, which had the likeness of sinful flesh, but without sin; for he sanctified himself for our cause. And truly, this mysterious and wonderful inhabitation is not only a pledge of the other, that God shall dwell in sinful men by his Spirit; but, in order of nature, it hath some influence upon the other, without which God could not have dwelt in us. There is so much distance and disproportion between his Majesty and us, that we could not be well united, but by this intervening, God coming down first a step into the holy nature of the man Christ, that from thence he might go into the sinful nature of other men. Our sinful and rebellious nature behoved to be first sanctified this way, by the personal indwelling of God in our flesh; and this had made an easy passage into sinful us, for his Spirit to dwell in us powerfully and graciously; therefore the Spirit of Christ is said to dwell in us. Christ's Spirit, not only because proceeding from him as from the Father; but particularly, because the inhabitation or operation of the Spirit in us, is the proper result and fruit of that glorious union of our nature with him. He took our flesh, that he might send us his Spirit. And, O what a blessed exchange was this! He came and dwelt in our nature, that so he might dwell in us: he took up a shop, as it were, in our flesh, that he might work in us, and make us again conformed to God.

We shall not cut this asunder into many parts. You see the words contain plainly the very essential definition of a spiritual man, and of a Christian. You find a spiritual man and a Christian equivalent in this verse; that is to say, they are taken for one and the self-same thing, and so they are reciprocal, of equal extent and restraint. Every Christian is one after the Spirit, and whosoever is after the Spirit is a Christian. One of Christ's, and one after the Spirit, is one thing. Now the definition of the Christian is taken from that which really and essentially constitutes him such. He is one in whom the Spirit of Christ dwells; that makes him one after the Spirit; that makes him one of Christ's, because it is the Spirit of Christ. As if you define what a man is, you could not do it better than thus: he is one endowed with a reasonable soul. So the apostle gives you the very soul and form of a Christian, which differenceth from all others. As the soul is to the body to make up a man, so the Spirit of Christ is to the soul and Spirit of a man to make up a Christian; as the absence or presence of the soul makes or unmakes a man, so the absence or presence of this Spirit makes or unmakes a Christian, for you see he makes it reciprocal. If you be Christians, the Spirit dwells in you; but if the Spirit dwell not in you, you are not Christians.

A word then to the first of these, that a Christian and a spiritual man are commensurable one to another. It is true, there are Jews who are not Jews inwardly, but only according to the letter, Rom. ii. 28, 29. And so there are Christians so called, who are but so outwardly, and in the letter, who have no more of it but the name and visible standing in the church; but we are speaking of that which is truly that which it is called, whose praise is not of men but of God. The name of a man may be extended to a picture or image, for some outward resemblance it hath of him, but it is not a proper speech; no more is it proper to extend the name of Christians unto the pictures or images of Christians, such as are destitute of this inward life. You may be properly, according to scripture phrase, members of the visible body; but you cannot have that real and blessed relation to Jesus Christ the head, which shall be the source of happiness to all the living members. I wish you would take it so, and flatter yourselves no more with church titles, as if these were sufficient evidences for your salvation. You would all be called Christians; but it fears me you know not many of you the true meaning and signification of that word, the most comfortable sense of it is hid from you. The meaning of it is, that a man is renewed by Christ in the spirit of his mind. As Christ and the Spirit are inseparable, so a Christian and a spiritual nature are not to be found severed. Certainly, the very sound of the name whereby you are called, imports another nature and conversation than is to be found in many; you cannot say, that you have a shadow of spirituality, either in your affections or actions; or that you have any real design and study that way, but only to please your flesh, and satisfy the customs of the world. Why do you then usurp the name of Christianity? This is a common sacrilege, to give that which is holy unto dogs. Others give it to you, and you take it to yourselves. But know, that though you please yourselves and others in this, yet without such a renovation of your natures, and such a sincere study to be inwardly and outwardly conformed to the profession and nature of Christianity, you have not your praise of God; and him whom God praises not, and allows not, he cannot bless for ever. I am persuaded there are some who are not only in the letter, but in the Spirit, whose greatest desire and design is, to be indeed what they profess; and such is their praise of God, and if God praise them now, they shall be made to praise him for ever hereafter: such are allowed to take the name and honourable style of Christianity unto them. You are Christ's nearly interested in him: and if you be Christ's own, he cannot be happy without you; for such was his love, that he would not be happy alone in heaven, but came down to be miserable with us. And now that he is again happy in heaven, certainly he cannot enjoy it long alone, but he must draw up his members unto the fellowship of that glory.

Now the other thing, that which gives even being to a Christian, is, the Spirit of Christ dwelling in him. Of this inhabitation, we shall not say so much as the comparison, being strained, will yield, neither expatiate into many notions about it. I wish rather we went home with some desires kindled in us, after such a noble guest as the Holy Spirit is, and that we were begun once to weary of the base and unclean guests that we lodge within us, to our own destruction. That which I said that the Spirit is to a Christian, what the soul is to a man, if well considered, might present the absolute necessity and excellency of this unto your eyes. Consider what a thing the body is without the soul, how defiled and how deformed a piece of dust it is, void of all sense and life, loathsome to look upon.

Truly the soul of man by nature is in no better case, till this Spirit enter; it hath no light in it, no life in it, it is a dark dungeon, such as is described, Eph. iv. 18. 'Having the understanding darkened, being alienated from the life of God through the ignorance that is in them, because of the blindness of their heart.' You have both in that word darkness and deadness want of that shining light of God in the mind, so that it cannot discern spiritual things, that make to our eternal peace: all the plainness and evidence of the gospel, though it did shine as a sun about you, cannot make you see or apprehend either your own misery, or the way to help it; because your dungeon is within; the most part cannot form any sensible notion of spiritual things, that are daily sounding unto them in the word. The eye of the mind is put out, and if it be darkness, how great is that darkness! Certainly the whole man is without light, and your way and walk must be in the dark; and indeed it appears, that it is dark night with many souls, because if it were not dark, they could not run out all their speed among pits and snares in the way to destruction. And from this woful defect flows the alienation of the whole soul from the life of God; that primitive light being eclipsed, the soul is separated from the influence of heaven; and as Nebuchadnezzar's soul acted only in a brutal way, when driven out among beasts; so the soul of man, being driven out from the presence of the Lord, may act in a way common to beasts, or in some rational way in things that concern this life, but it is wholly spoiled of that divine life of communion with God. It cannot taste, smell, or savour such things. O! if it were visible unto us, the state of the ruinous soul, we would raise a more bitter lamentation over it than the Jews did over Jerusalem, or the kings and merchants have reason to do over fallen Babylon. Truly, we might bemoan it thus, 'How is the faithful city become a harlot! righteousness lodged in it, but now murderers,' Isa. i. 21. Man was once the dwelling-place of princely and divine graces and virtues; the Lord himself was there, and then how comely and beautiful was the soul! But now it is like the desolate cities, in which the beasts of the desert lie, and their houses are full of doleful creatures, where owls dwell, and satyrs dance; where wild beasts cry, and dragons in the pleasant places, Isa. xiii. 21, 22. and Jer. l. 39. So mighty is the fall of the soul of man, as of Babylon, that it may be cried, 'It is fallen, and become the habitation of devils, and the hold of every foul spirit, and a cage of every unclean and hateful bird,' Rev. xviii. 2. All the beasts flock now to it, all the birds of darkness take their lodging in it, since this noble guest left it, and took away the light from it; for the sun hath not shined on it since that day. All unclean affections, all beastly lusts, all earthly desires, all vain cogitations get lodging in this house; the Bethel is become a Beth-aven, the house of God become a house of vanity, by the continual repair of vain thoughts; the house of prayer is turned into a den of thieves and robbers. That which was at first created for the pure service and worship of God, is now a receptacle of all the most rebellious and idolatrous thoughts and affections; the heart of every man is become a temple full of idols.

This is the state of it, and worse than can be told you: now, judge if there be not need of a better guest than these. O what absolute necessity is there of such a spirit as this, to repair and reform the ruinous spirit of man, to quicken and enlighten the darkened mind of man! Even that Spirit, that made it at first a glorious palace for God; that Spirit that breathed the soul into the former clay, must repair these breaches, and create all again. Now, when the Spirit of Christ enters into this vile ruinous cottage, he repairs it and reforms it, he strikes out lights in the heart, and, by a wonderful eye-salve, makes the eyes open to see: he creates a new light within, which makes him behold the light shining in the gospel; and behold all things are new, himself new, because now most loathsome and vile; the world new, because now appears nothing but vanity in the very perfection of it; and God new, because another majesty, glory, excellency, and beauty shines into the soul, than ever it apprehended. And as the Spirit enlightens, so he enlivens this tabernacle or temple; he kindles a holy fire in his affections, which must never go out; it is such as cannot be kindled, if it go out, but by the beams of the sun, as the poets fancied the vestal-fire. The Spirit within the soul is a fire to consume his corruption, to burn up his dross and vanity. Christ comes in like a refiner, with the fire of the Spirit, and purges away earthly lusts, and makes the love of the heart pure and clean, to burn upward toward heaven. This Spirit makes a Christian soul move willingly toward God, in the ways that seemed most unpleasant: it is an active principle within him that cannot rest till it rests in its place of eternal rest and delight in God. And then the Spirit reforms this house, by casting out all these wild beasts that lodged in it, the savage and unruly affections, that domineered in man; this strong man entering in, casts them out. There is much rubbish in old waste palaces, Neh. iv. 2. O how much pains it is to cleanse them! Our house is like the house of those nobles, Jer. v. 27. 'Full of deceit, as a cage is full of birds, and our hearts full of wickedness and vanity,' Jer. iv. 14. Certainly it will be much labour to get your unclean spirits cast out, that is, the grosser and more palpable lusts that reign in you; but when these are gone forth, yet there is much wickedness and uncleanness in the heart, of a more subtle nature, and by long indwelling, almost incorporated and mingled with the soul; and this will not be gotten out with gentle sweeping, as was done,

Luke xi. 25. That takes away only the uppermost filth that lies loosest; but this must be gotten out by much washing and cleansing; therefore the Spirit enters by blood and water. There are idols in the heart, to which the soul is much engaged; it unites and closes with them, (Ezek. xxxvi.) and these must be cleansed and washed out. There is much deceit in the heart, and this lies closest to it, and is engrossed into it: and indeed this will take the help of fire to separate it; for that is of the most active nature to separate things of a diverse nature; the Spirit must by these take out your dross. And all this the Spirit will not do alone, but honours you with the fellowship of this work; and therefore you must lay your account that the operation and reformation of this house for so glorious a guest, will be laborious in the mean time. But O how infinitely is that compensated! One hour's fellowship with him alone, when all strangers are cast out, will compensate all, will make all to be forgotten; the pain of mortification will be swallowed up in the pleasure of his inhabitation; 'When I shall awake I shall be satisfied with thy likeness.' When he shall take up house fully in you, it will satisfy you to the full. In the meantime, as he takes the rule and command of your house, so for the present he provides for it; the provision of the soul is incumbent on this divine guest: and O how sweet and satisfying is it? O the peace and joy of the Holy Ghost, which are the entertainment that he gives a soul, where he reigns, and hath brought in righteousness, Rom. xiv. 17. What a noble train doth the Spirit bring alongst with him to furnish this house? Many rich and costly ornaments hang over it, and adorn it, to make it like the king's wife all glorious within; such as the ornament of a meek and quiet spirit, (1 Pet. iii. 4.) which is a far more precious and rich hanging, than the most curious or precious contexture of corruptible things; the clothing of humility, simple in show, but rich in substance, (1 Pet. v. 5.) which enriches and beautifies the soul that hath it, more than all Solomon's glory could do his person; for 'better is it to be of a humble spirit with the lowly, than divide the spoil with the proud,' Prov. xvi. 19. In a word, the Spirit makes all new, puts a new man, a new fashion and image on the soul, which suits the court of heaven, the highest in the world; and is conformed to the noblest and highest pattern, the holiness and beauty of the greatest King. And being lodged within, O what sweet fruits is the Spirit daily bringing forth to feed and delight the soul withal! Gal. v. 22, 23. And he is not only a Spirit of sanctification, but of consolation too; and therefore of all the most worthy to be received into our hearts, for he is a bosom comforter, John xiv. 16. When there is no friend nor lover without, but a soul in that posture of Heman, Psal. lxxxviii. 18. and in that desolate estate of the churches, Lament. i. 2. 'Among all her lovers she hath none to comfort her,' (ver. 17.) 'spreading forth her hands, and none to comfort her,' (ver. 21.) sighing, and none to comfort her. In such a case to have a living and overrunning spring of comfort within, when all external and lower consolations, like winter brooks that dry up in summer, have dried up and disappointed thy expectation, sure this were a happy guest, that could do this. O that we could open our hearts to receive him!

Sermon XXV.

VERSE 9.—"*If so be that the Spirit of God dwell in you. Now if any man have not the Spirit of Christ, he is none of his.*"

THERE is a great marriage spoken of, Eph. v. that hath a great mystery in it, which the apostle propoundeth as the sample and archetype of all marriages, or rather as the substance, of which all conjunctions and relations among the creatures are but the shadows. It is that marriage between Christ and his church, for which, it would appear, this world was builded, to be a palace to celebrate it into; and especially the upper house, heaven, was made glorious for that great day, where it shall be solemnized. The first in order of time was made by God himself in paradise, certainly to represent a higher mystery, the marriage of the second Adam with his spouse, which is taken out of his bloody side, as the apostle imports, Eph. v. Now there is the greatest inequality and disproportion between the parties, Christ and sinners; so that it would seem a desperate matter to bring two such distant and unequal natures to such a near union, as may cast a copy to all unions and relations of the creatures. But he who at first made a kind of marriage between heaven and earth, in the composure of man, and joined together an immortal spirit in such a bond of amity with corruptible dust, hath found out the way to help this, and make it feasible. And truly, we may conceive the Lord was but making way for this greater mystery of the union of Christ with us, when he joined the breath of heaven with the dust of the earth. In this he gave some representation of another more mysterious conjunction. Now, the way that the wisdom and love of God hath found out to bring about this marriage, is this; because there was such an infinite distance between the only begotten Son of God, who is the express character of his image, and the brightness of his glory, and us sinful mortal creatures, whose foundation is in the dust, therefore it pleased the Father, out of his good-will to the match, to send his Son down among men ; and the Son, out of his love, to take on our flesh, and so fill up that distance with his low condescendence, to be partaker of flesh and blood with the children. And now, what the Lord spoke of man fallen, in a holy kind of irony or mock, 'Behold he is become as one of us,' that men may truly say of the Son of God, not fallen down from heaven, but come down willingly, 'Lo, he is become as one of us;' like us in all things, except sin, which hath made us unlike ourselves. This bond of union you have in verse 3. Christ so infinitely above sinners, and higher than the heavens, coming down so low, to be as like sinners as might be, or could be profitable for us, in the likeness of sinful flesh, &c. But yet this bond is not near enough; that conjunction seemeth but general and infirm; both because it is in some manner common to all mankind, who shall not be all advanced to this privilege. By taking on our nature, he cometh nearer to human nature, but not to some beyond others; and besides, the distance is not filled up this way, because there is a great disproportion between that nature in Christ and in us. In him it is holy and undefiled, and separated from sin; but in us it is unclean and immersed into sin; so that, albeit he be nearer us as a man, yet he is far distant and unlike us,—a holy perfect man. Now, what fellowship can be between light and darkness, as Paul speaketh of the marriage of Christians with idolaters? Much greater distance and disagreement is between Christ and us. Therefore, it seemeth, that some of us must be changed and transformed. But him it may not be. He cannot become liker us than by partaking of our flesh; for if he had become a sinner indeed, he would have become so like us that he could not help himself nor us either. This would eclipse the glory and happiness of the marriage. But in that he came as near as could be, without disabling himself, to make us happy; and so he was contented to come in the place of sinners, and take on their debt, and answer to God's justice for it; yea, and in his own person he submitted to be tempted to sin, though it had been evil for us he had been overcome by it; yet this brings him a step lower and nearer us, and maketh the union more hopeful. But since he can come no lower, and can be made no liker us in the case we are in; then certainly—if the match hold—we must become liker him, and raised up out of our miserable estate, to some suitableness to his holy nature. And, therefore, the love and wisdom of God, to fill up the distance completely, and effectuate this happy conjunction, that the creation seemeth to groan for,—for (ver. 22.) the whole creation is pained till it be accomplished,—he hath sent his blessed Spirit to dwell in us, and to transform our natures, and make them partakers of the divine nature, (2 Pet. i. 4.) as Christ was partaker of human nature; and thus the distance shall be removed. When a blessed Spirit is made flesh, and a fleshly man made spirit, then they are near the day of espousals; and this indwelling of the Spirit is the last link of the chain that fastens us to Christ, and maketh our flesh in some measure like his holy flesh. By taking on our flesh, Christ became bone of our bone, and flesh of our flesh; but the union becometh mutual when we receive the Spirit, we become bone of his bone, and flesh of his flesh, as it is expressed Eph. v. 30, in allusion to the creation of Eve, and her marriage to Adam. The ground of the marriage is that near bond of union,—'Because she was taken out of man;' and, therefore, because of his flesh and bone, she was made one flesh with him. Even so the sinner must be partaker of the Spirit of Christ, as Christ is partaker of the flesh of sinners; and these two concurring, these two knots interchanging and woven through other, we become one flesh with him. And this is a great mystery, indeed, to bring two, who were so far asunder, so near other. Yea, it is nearer than that too; for we are said not only to be one flesh with Christ, but one spirit, 1 Cor. vi. 17. 'He that is joined unto the Lord is one spirit;' because he is animated and quickened by one spirit,—that same spirit of Christ. And, indeed, spirits are more capable of union, and more fit to embosom one with another than bodies; therefore, the nearest union conceivable is the union of spirits by affections; this maketh two souls one, for it transports their spirit out of the body where it lives, and settleth it there where it loveth.

Now, my beloved, you see what way this great marriage, that heaven and earth are in a longing expectation after, shall be brought about. Christ did forsake his Father's house when he left that holy habitation, his Father's bosom,—a place of marvellous delight, (Prov. viii. 30.) and descended into the lower parts of the earth, (Eph. iv. 9.) and, he came out from the Father into the world, John xvi. 28. This was a great journey to meet with poor sinners. But, that there may be a full and entire meeting, you must leave and forsake your father's house too, and forget your own people, Psalm xlv. 10. You must give an entire renounce to all former lovers, if you would be his. All former bonds and engagements must be broken, that this may be tied the faster. And, to hold to the subject in hand, you must forsake and forget the flesh, and be possessed of his Holy Spirit. As he came down to our flesh, you must rise up to meet him in the spirit. The Spirit of Christ must indeed prevent you, and take you out of that natural posture you are born into, and bring you a great journey from yourselves, that you may be joined unto him.

This Spirit of Christ is his messenger and ambassador, sent beforehand to fit you and suit you for the day of espousals, and, therefore, he must have a dwelling and constant abode in you. This indwelling imports a special familiar operation, and the perpetuity or continuance of it. The Spirit is everywhere in his being, and he worketh everywhere too; but here he hath a special and peculiar work in commission,—to reveal the love of God in Christ; to engage the soul to love him again; to prepare all within for the great day of espousals; to purify and purge the heart from all that is displeasing to Christ; to correspond between Christ and his spouse, between heaven and earth, by making intercession for her when she cannot pray for herself, as you find here, ver. 26. and so sending up the news of the soul's panting and breathing after Christ, sending up her groans and sighs to her Beloved, giving intelligence of all her necessities to him who is above, in the place of an advocate and interceder; and then bring back from heaven light and life, direction from her Head—for the Spirit must lead into all truth—and consolation; for Christ hath appointed the Spirit to supply his absence, and to comfort the soul in the mean time till he come again. You have this mutual and reciprocal knot in 1 John iv. 13, 'Hereby we know that we dwell in him, and he in us, by the Spirit that he hath given.' It is much nearness to dwell one with another, but much greater to dwell one in another. And it is reciprocal, such a wonderful interchange in it, we in him, and he in us; for the Spirit carries the soul to heaven, and brings Christ, as it were, down to the earth. He is the messenger that carries letters between both;—our prayers to him, and his prayers for us, and love-tokens to us, the anointing that teacheth us all things, from our Husband, (1 John ii. 27,) and revealing to us the things of God, 1 (Cor. ii. 12,) giving us the first-fruits of that happy and glorious communion we must have with Christ in heaven, as you see, verse 23. of this chapter, and sealing us to the day of redemption, Eph. i. 13; and iv. 30; supplying us with divine power against our spiritual enemies, fetching along from heaven that strength whereby our Lord and Saviour overcame all, Eph. iii. 16; Gal. v. 17. This is a presence that few have, such a familiar and love-abode. But, certainly, all that are Christ's must have it in some measure. Now whosoever hath it, it is perpetual, the Spirit dwells in them. It is not a sojourning for a season, not a lodging for a night,—as some have fits and starts of seeking God, and some transient motions of conviction or joy, but return again to the puddle; these go through them as lightning, and do not warm them or change them; but this is a constant residence; where the Spirit takes up house he will dwell, 'he dwelleth with you, and shall be in you,' and abide for ever, John xiv. 16, 17. If the Son abide in the house for ever, (John viii. 35.) much more the master of the house must abide. Now, the Spirit where he dwells hath gotten the command of that house; all the power is put in his hand, and resigned to him; for where he dwells he must rule, as good reason is. He is about the greatest work that is now to do in the world, the repairing and renewing of the ruins and breaches of man's spirit, which was the first breach in the creation, and the cause of all the rest. He is about the cleansing and washing this temple; and we may be persuaded, that he who hath begun this good work, will perform it until the day of Christ, till we be presented blameless and without spot to our Husband (Phil. i. 5, 6.); and this is the grand consolation of believers, that they have this presence assured to them by promise, that the Spirit is fixed here by an irrevocable and unchangeable covenant or donation, and will not wholly depart from them, though he may withdraw and leave you comfortless for a season, Isa. lix. 21.

Therefore I would shut up all in a word of exhortation to you, that since we have the promise of so noble and happy a guest, you would apply yourselves to seek him, and then keep him; to receive him, and then retain him. It is true that he must first prevent us; for as no man can say, 'that Jesus is the Christ, but by the Spirit of God,' so no man can indeed pray for the Spirit, but by the Spirit's own intercession within him. Where God hath bestowed any thing of this Spirit, it is known by the kindly and fervent desires after more of it. Now, since we have such a large and ample promise (Ezek. xxxvi. 27. Joel ii. 28.) of the pouring out of the Spirit, and that in as absolute and free a manner as can be imagined: and this renewed by Christ, and confirmed by his prayer to the Father for the performance of it, (John xiv. 16, 17.) and then we have a sweet and affectionate promise propounded in the most moving and loving manner than can be, Luke xi. 13, where he encourageth us to pray for the Spirit, and that from this ground, that our heavenly Father, who placed that natural affection in other fathers toward their children, whereby they cannot refuse them bread when they cry for it; he, who was the author of all natural affection, must certainly transcend them infinitely in his love to his children, as the Psalmist argues, 'Shall not he that planted the ear, hear? and he that formed the eye, see?' So may a poor soul reason itself to some confidence, shall not he who is the fountain of all natural love in men and beasts have much more himself? And if my father will not give me a stone when I seek bread, certainly he will far less do it: therefore, 'if we being evil, know how to give good things to our children, how much more shall our heavenly Father give his Spirit to them that ask him?' Alas, that we should want such a gift for not asking it! My beloved, let us enlarge our desires for this Spirit, and seek more earnestly; and no doubt affection and importunity will not be sent away empty. Is it any wonder we receive not, because we ask not, or we ask so coldly, that we teach him in a manner to deny us, *qui timide rogat,* I may say, *frigide, docet negare.* Ask frequently, and ask confidently, and his heart cannot deny. O that we could lay this engagement on our own hearts to be more in prayer! Let us press ourselves to this, and we need not press him. Albeit the first grace be wholly a surprisal, yet certainly he keeps this suitable method in the enlargements of grace, that when he gives more, he enlargeth the heart more after it, he openeth the mouth wider to ask and receive, and, according to that capacity, so is his hand open to fill the heart. O, why are our hearts shut when his hand is open! Again, I would exhort you in Jesus Christ, to entertain the Spirit suitably, and this shall keep him. To this purpose are these exhortations: 'Grieve not the Holy Spirit,' Eph. iv. 30, and 'Quench not the Spirit,' 1 Thess. v. 19. There is nothing can grieve him but sin; and if you entertain that, you cannot retain him. He is a Spirit of holiness, and he is about the making you holy; then do not mar him in his work; labour to advance this, and ye do him a pleasure. If you make his holy temple an unclean cage for hateful birds, or a temple for idols, how can it but grieve him? And if you grieve the Spirit, certainly the Spirit will grieve you, will make you repent it at the heart. Please him, by hearkening to his motions, and following his direction, and he shall comfort you. His office is to be a spring of consolation to you; but if you grieve him by walking in the imagination of your hearts, and following the suggestions of the flesh,—his enemy,—no doubt that spring will turn its channel another way, and dry up for a season toward you. It is not every sin or infirmity that grieves him thus, if so be that it grieve thee; but the entertaining of any sin, and making peace with any of his enemies, that cannot but displease him: and, O what loss you have by it! You displease your greatest friend, to please your greatest enemy; you blot and bludder* that seal of the Spirit, that you shall not be able to read it, till it be cleansed and washed again. Now, 'if any man have not the Spirit of Christ, he is none of his,' he is not a Christian. Take this along with you, who aim at nothing but the external and outward show or visible standing in the church. If you have not this Spirit, and the seal of this Spirit, found on you, Christ will not know you for his in that day of his appearing.

Sermon XXVI.

VERSE 10.—"*And if Christ be in you, the body is dead because of sin; but the Spirit is life because of righteousness.*"

GOD's presence is his working. His presence in a soul by his Spirit is his working in such a soul in some special manner, not common to all men, but peculiar to them whom he hath chosen. Now his dwelling is nothing else but a continued, familiar and endless working in a soul, till he hath conformed all within to the image of his Son. The soul is the office-house, or workhouse, that the Spirit hath taken up, to frame in it the most curious piece of the whole creation, even to restore and repair that masterpiece, which came last from God's hand, *ab ultima manu*, and so was the chiefest; I mean, the image of God, in righteousness and holiness. Now, this is the bond of union between God and us: Christ is the bond of union with God, but the Spirit is the bond of union with Christ. Christ is the peace between God and us, that makes of two one, but the Spirit is the link between Christ and us, whereby he hath immediate and actual interest in us, and we in him. I find the union between Christ and a soul shadowed out in scripture, by the nearest relations among creatures, (for truly these are but shadows, and that is the body or substance,) and because an union that is mutual is nearest, it is often so expressed, as it imports an interchangeable relation, a reciprocal conjunction with Christ. The knot is cast on both sides to make it strong. Christ in us, and we in him; God dwelling in us, and we in him; and both by this one Spirit, 1 John iv. 13. 'Hereby we know that God dwelleth in us, and we in him, by his Spirit which he hath given us.' You find it often in John, who being most possessed with the love of Christ, and most sensible of his love, could best express it: 'I in them, and they in me. He that keepeth his commands dwelleth in him, and he in him;' as the names of married persons are spelled through other,† so doth he spell out this indwelling; it is not cohabitation but inhabitation: neither that alone singly, but mutual inhabitation, which amounts to a kind of penetration, the most intimate and immediate presence imaginable. Christ dwelleth in our hearts by faith; and we dwell in Christ by love, Eph. iii. 17; and 1 John iv. Death bringeth him into the heart; for it is the very application of a Saviour to a sinful soul. It is the very applying of his blood and sufferings to the wound that sin hath made in the conscience; the laying of that sacrifice propitiatory to the wounded conscience, is that which heals it, pacifies it, and calms it. A Christian, by receiving the offer of the gospel cordially and affectionately, brings in Christ offered into his house, and then salvation comes with him. Therefore believing is receiving, (John i.) the very opening of the heart to let in an offered Saviour; and then Christ, thus possessing the heart by faith, he works by love, and 'he that dwelleth in love, dwelleth in God, and God in him.' Love hath this special virtue in it, that it transports the soul in a manner out of

* [That is, disfigure.—ED.] † [That is, blended together when read or repeated.—ED.]

itself to the Beloved, Cant. iv. 9. *Anima est ubi amat, non ubi animat;** the fixing and establishing of the heart on God is a dwelling in him; for the constant and most continued residence of the most serious thoughts and affections, will be their dwelling in their all-fulness and riches of grace in Jesus Christ. As the Spirit dwelleth where he worketh, so the soul dwelleth where it delighteth; its complacency in God making a frequent issue or outgoing to him in desires and breathings after him; and by means of this same, God dwelleth in the heart, for love is the opening up of the inmost chamber of the heart to him, it brings in the Beloved into the very secrets of the soul, to lie all night betwixt his breasts as a bundle of myrrh, Cant. i. 13. And indeed all the sweet odours of holy duties, and all the performing of good works and edifying speeches, spring out only, and are sent forth, from this bundle of myrrh that lies betwixt the breasts of a Christian, in the inmost of his heart, from Christ dwelling in the affections of the soul.

Now, this being the bond of union betwixt Christ and us, it follows, necessarily, that whosoever hath not the Spirit of Christ, 'he is none of his;' and this is subjoined for prevention or removal of the misapprehensions and delusions of men in their self-judgings; because self-love blinds our eyes, and maketh our hearts deceive themselves. We are given to this self-flattery,—to pretend and claim to an interest in Jesus Christ, even though there be no more evidence for it than the external relation that we have to Christ, as members of his visible body, or partakers of a common influence of his Spirit. There are some external bonds and ties to Christ, which are like a knot that may easily be loosed if any thing get hold of the end of it; as by our relations to Christ by baptism, hearing the word, your outward covenanting to be his people; all these are loose unsure knots; it is as easy to untie them as to tie them, yea, and more easy; and yet many have no other relation to Christ than what these make. But it is only the Spirit of Christ given to us that entitles and interesteth us in him, and him in us. It is the Spirit working in your souls mightily and continually, making your hearts temples for the offering of the sacrifice of prayer and praises, casting out all idols out of these temples, that he alone may be adored and worshipped, by the affectionate service of the heart, purging them from all filthiness of flesh and spirit. It is the Spirit, I say, thus dwelling in men that maketh them living members of the true body of Christ, lively, joined to the Head,—Christ. This maketh him yours and you his; by virtue of this he may command you as his own, and you may use and employ him as your own. Now, for want of this, in most part of men, they also want this living saving interest in Christ. They have no real but an imaginary and notional propriety and right to the Lord Jesus; for Christ must first take possession of us by his Spirit before we have any true right to him, or can willingly resign ourselves to him, and give him right over us. What shall it profit us, my beloved, to be called Christians, and to esteem ourselves so, if, really, we be none of Christ's? Shall it not heighten our condemnation so much the more that we desire to pass for such and give out ourselves so, and yet have no inward acquaintance and interest in him whose name we love to bear? Are not the most part shadows and pictures of true Christians, bodies without the soul of Christianity, that is, the Spirit of Christ, whose hearts are treasures of wickedness and deceit, and storehouses of iniquity and ignorance? It may be known what treasure fills the heart by that which is the constant and common vent of it, as our Saviour speaks, Matt. xv. 19; and xii. 34, 35, 'Out of the abundance of the heart the mouth speaketh,' the feet walk, and the hand works. Consider, then, if the Spirit of God dwelleth in such unclean habitations and dark dungeons; certainly no uncleanness or darkness of the house can hinder him to come in; but it is a sure argument and evidence that he is not as yet come in, because the prince of darkness is not yet cast out of many souls, nor yet the unclean spirits that lodge within; these haunt your hearts, and are as familiar now as ever. Sure I am, many souls have never yet changed their guests, and it is as sure that the first guest that taketh up the soul is darkness and desperate wickedness, with unparalleled deceitfulness. There is an accursed trinity, instead of that blessed Trinity, the Father, the Son, and the Holy Spirit; and when this holy Trinity cometh in to dwell, that other of hell must go out. Now, my beloved, do you think this a light matter, to be disowned by Jesus

* [That is, "The soul is where it loves, not where it animates."—Ed.]

Christ? Truly, the word of Christ, which is the character of all our evidences and rights for heaven, disowns many as bastards and dead members, withered branches; and, certainly, according to this word he will judge you: 'the word that I have spoken shall judge you in the last day.' O that is a heavy word! You have the very rule and method of proceeding laid down before you now, which shall be punctually kept at that great day. Now, why do you not read your ditty * and condemnatory sentence here registered? If you do not read it now in your consciences, he will one day read it before men and angels, and pronounce this,—I know you not for mine, you are none of mine. But if you would now take it to your hearts, there might be hope that it should go no further, and come to no more public-hearing, there were hope that it should be repealed before that day, because the first entry of the Spirit of Christ is to convince men of sin, that they are unbelievers, and without God in the world; and if this were done, then it were more easy to convince you of Christ's righteousness, and persuade you to embrace it; and this would lead in another link of the chain,—the conviction of judgment, to persuade you to resign yourselves to the Spirit's rule, and renounce the kingdom of Satan; this were another trinity, a trinity upon earth, three bearing witness on the earth that you have the Spirit of God.

VERSE 10.—"*And if Christ be in you, the body is dead because of sin,*" *&c.*

ALL the preceding verses seem to be purposely set down by the apostle for the comfort of Christians against the remnants of sin and corruption within them; for in the preceding chapter, he personates the whole body of Christ militant, showing, in his own example, how much sin remains in the holiest in this life; and this he rather instances in his own person than another, that all may know that matter of continual sorrow and lamentation is furnished to the chiefest of saints; and yet, in this chapter, he propounds the consolation of Christians more generally, that all may know that these privileges and immunities belong even to the meanest and weakest of Christians,—that, as the best have reason to mourn in themselves, so the worst want not reason to rejoice in Jesus Christ. And this should always be minded that the amplest grounds of the strongest consolation are general to all that come indeed to Jesus Christ, and are not restricted unto saints of such and such a growth and stature. The common principles of the gospel are more full of this milk of consolation, if you would suck it out of them, than many particular grounds which you are laying down for yourselves. God hath so disposed and contrived the work of our salvation, that in this life he that hath gathered much, in some respect, hath nothing over,—that is to say, hath no more reason to boast than another, but will be constrained to sit down and mourn over his own evil heart, and the emptiness of it; and he that hath gathered less hath, in some sense, no want; I mean, he is not excluded and shut out from the right to these glorious privileges which may express gloriation and rejoicing from the heart, that there might be an equality in the body; he maketh the stronger Christian to partake with the weaker in his bitter things, and the weaker with the stronger in his sweet things, that none of them may conceive themselves either despised, or alone regarded; that the eunuch may not have reason to say, 'I am a dry tree,' Isa. lvi. 3.) For, behold the Lord will give, even to such, 'a place' in his house, and 'a name better than of sons and daughters.' The soul that is in sincerity aiming at this walk, and whose inward desires stir after more of this Holy Spirit, he will not refuse to such that name and esteem that they dare not take to themselves because of their seen and felt unworthiness. Now, in this verse he proceeds further to the fruits and effects of sin dwelling in us, to enlarge the consolation against that too. Now, 'If Christ be in you, the body,' &c. Seeing the word of God hath made such a connection between sin and death, and death is the wages of sin, and that which is the just recompense of enmity and rebellion against God, the poor troubled soul might be ready to conceive that if the body be adjudged to death for sin, that the rest of the wages shall be paid, and sin having so much dominion as to kill the body, that it should exerce † its full power to destroy all. Seeing we have a visible character of the curse of God

* [That is, indictment or accusation.—ED.] † [That is, exert.—ED.]

engraven on us in the mortality of our bodies, it may look with such a visage on a soul troubled for sin, as if it were but earnest of the full curse and weight of wrath, and that sin were not fully satisfied for, nor justice fully contented by, Christ's ransom. Now, he opposes to this misconception the strongest ground of consolation,—if Christ be in you, though your bodies must die for sin, because sin dwelleth in them, yet that Spirit of life that is in you hath begun eternal life in your souls; your spirits are not only immortal in being, but that eternal happy being is begun in you; the seeds of it are cast into your souls, and shall certainly grow up to perfection of holiness and happiness, and this through the righteousness of Christ which assureth that state unto you. The comfort is, it is neither total, for it is only the death of your body; nor is it perpetual, for your bodies shall be raised again to life eternal, verse 11. And not only is it only in part, and for a season, but it is for a blessed end and purpose; it is that sin may be wholly cleansed out that this tabernacle is taken down, as the leprous houses* were to be taken down under the law, and as now we use to cast down pest-lodges, the better to cleanse them of the infection. It is not to prejudge him of life, but to install him in a better life. Thus you see that it is neither total nor perpetual, but it is medicinal and profitable to the soul,—it is but the death of the body for a moment, and the life of the soul for ever.

Sermon XXVII.

VERSE 10.—"*And if Christ be in you, the body is dead because of sin,*" &c.

THIS is the high excellency of the Christian religion, that it contains the most absolute precepts for a holy life, and the greatest comforts in death; for from these two the truth and excellency of religion is to be measured, if it have the highest and perfectest rule of walking, and the chiefest comfort withal. Now, the perfection of Christianity you saw in the rule, how spiritual it is, how reasonable, how divine, how free from all corrupt mixture, how transcending all the most exquisite precepts and laws of men, deriving a holy conversation from the highest fountain, the Spirit of Christ, and conforming it to the highest pattern, the will of God. And, indeed, in the first word of this verse, there is something of the excellent nature of Christianity holden out, 'if Christ be in you,' which is the true description of a Christian,—one in whom Christ is, which imports the divine principle and the spiritual subject of Christianity. The principle is Christ in a man,—Christ by his Spirit dwelling in him. This great apostle knew this well in his own experience, and, therefore, he can speak best in this style: 'I live, yet not I, but Christ in me,' Gal. ii. 20: importing, that Christ and his Spirit is to the soul what the soul is to the body;—that there is a living influence from heaven that acts and moves the soul of a Christian as powerfully, yet as sweetly and pleasantly, as if it were the natural motion of the soul: and truly it is the natural motion of the soul. It is that primitive life which was most connatural to the soul of man, which sin did deprive us of. All the powerful constraint and violence that Christ uses in drawing the souls of men to him, and after him, is as kindly unto them, and perfects them as much, as that impulse by which the soul moves and turns the body: a sweet compulsion and blessed violence. Now this should make Christians often to reflect upon another principle of their life than themselves; that by looking on him, who is 'the resurrection and the life,' who is 'the true vine;' and abiding in him by faith, their life may be continued and increased. It is certainly much reflection on Him who is all in all, and less upon ourselves that maintains this life; and, therefore, the most part of men being wholly strangers to this, whether in their purposes or practices, or judgings of both, unacquainted with any higher look in religion than they

* [These were booths, or other temporary erections, put up for the reception of such as were infected with the plague.—ED.]

use in their natural and civil actings, it doth give ground to assure us that they are strangers,—alienated from the life of God,—without God, and without Christ in the world.

But then the spiritual subject of Christianity is here, Christ in you, not Christ without you, in ordinances, in profession, in some civil carriage, but Christ within the heart of a man,—that is a Christian. It is the receiving of Christ into the soul, and putting him on upon the inner man, and renewing it, that makes a Christian; not being externally clothed with him, or compassed about with him, in the administration of the ordinances. It fears me, most part of us who bear the name of Christianity, have no character of it within, if we were looked and searched. Many are like the sepulchres Christ speaks of,—without, painted and fair,—within, nothing but rottenness and dead bones. What have many of you more of Christ than what a blind man hath of light? It is round about him, but not within him. The light hath shined in darkness, but your darkness cannot comprehend it. You are environed with the outward appearances of Christ in his word and ordinances; and that is all; but neither within you, nor upon many of you, is there any thing either of his light or life. Not so much as any outward profession or behaviour, suitable to the revelation of Christ, about you. As if you were ashamed to be Christians, you maintain gross ignorance, and practise manifest rebellion against his known will, in the very light of the gospel. How few have so much tincture of Christ, so much as to colour the external man, or to clothe it with any blamelessness of walking, or form of religion! How few are so much as Christians in the letter! For you are not acquainted either with letter or spirit,—either with knowledge or affection or practice. But suppose that some have put on Christ on their outward man, and colour over themselves with some performances of religious duties, and smooth themselves with civility in carriage: yet, alas! how few are they who are renewed in the spirit of their mind, and have put on Christ in their inward man, who have opened the secrets of their hearts, and received him to 'lie all night between their breasts!' How few are busied about their hearts, to have any new impression and dye upon their affections,—to mould them after a new manner,—to kill the love of this world, and the lusts of it,—and cast out the rottenness and superfluity of naughtiness which abides within! But some there are who are persuaded thus to do, to give up their spirits to religion; and all their business and care is, to have Christ within, as well as without. Now, if the rest of you will not be persuaded to be of this number, consider what you prejudge yourselves of, of all the comfort of religion; and then religion is no religion, and to no purpose, if you have no benefit by it. And certainly, except Christ be in you as a King to rule you, and a Prophet to teach you,—to subdue your lusts, and dispel your darkness, when he appears, he cannot appear to your comfort and salvation. You are deprived of this great cordial against death, and death must seize upon all that is within you, soul and body, since Christ the Spirit of life is not within you. Happiness without you will not make you happy,—salvation round about you will not save you. If you would be saved, there must be a near and immediate union with happiness. Christ in the heart, and salvation cometh with him. A Christian is not only Christ without, not imputing his sins to him, clothing him with his righteousness; but Christ within too, cleansing the heart from the love of sin, 'perfecting holiness in the fear of God.' Do not think you have any share in Christ without you, except you receive Christ within you; because Christ is one within and without, and his gifts are undivided. Therefore, true faith receives whole Christ as a complete Saviour; even as he is entirely offered, so he is undividedly received: as he is without saving us, and within sanctifying us,—Christ without, delivering from wrath,—and Christ within, redeeming from all iniquity,—these cannot be parted more than his coat that had no seam. It is a heavy and weighty word of this apostle's, 2 Cor. xiii. 5, 'Examine yourselves, whether ye be in the faith: know ye not your own selves, how that Jesus Christ is in you, except ye be reprobates?' I wish you would lay it to heart, who have never yet returned to your hearts. If Christ be not formed in you, (as Gal. iv. 19,) you are as yet among the refuse, dross, and that which must be burnt with fire. You cannot but be cast away in the day when he makes up his jewels. Where Christ is, he is the hope of glory,—he is an immortal seed of glory. How can you hope for Christ, who have nothing of him within you?

Now, the other touchstone of true religion is, the great comfort it furnishes to the soul: and, of all comforts, the greatest is that which is a cordial to the heart against the greatest fears and evils. Now, certainly the matter of greatest fear is death, not so much because of itself, but chiefly because of that eternity of unchangeable misery that naturally it transmits them unto. Now, it is only the Christian religion possessing the heart that arms a man completely against the fear either of death itself, or the consequents of it. It giveth the most powerful consolation, that not only overcometh the bitterness and taketh out the sting of death, but changeth the nature of it so far as to make it the matter of triumph and gloriation.

There is something here supposed: the worst that can befall a Christian, it is the death of a part of him, and that the worst and ignoblest part only, 'the body is dead because of sin.' Then, that which is opposed by way of comfort to counterbalance it, is, the life of his better and more noble part. And, besides, we have the fountains both of that death and this life,—man's sin the cause of bodily death, Christ's righteousness the fountain of spiritual life.

Of death many have had sweet meditations, even among those that the light of the word hath not shined upon; and, indeed, they may make us ashamed who profess Christianity, and so the hope of the resurrection from the dead, that they have accounted it only true wisdom and sound philosophy to meditate often on death; and made it the very principal point of living well, to be always learning to die; and have applied their whole studies that way, neglecting present things that are in the by, have given themselves to search out some comfort against death, or from death. Yea, some have so profited in this, that they have accounted death the greatest good that can befall man, and persuaded others to think so.* Now, what may we think of ourselves, who scarce apprehend mortality, especially considering that we have the true fountain of it revealed to us, and the true nature and consequents of it.

All men must needs know that death is the most universal king in the world, that it reigns over all ages, sexes, conditions, nations, and times: though few be willing to entertain thoughts of it; yet, sooner or later, they must be constrained to give it lodging upon their eyelids, and suffer it to storm the very strongest tower, the heart, and batter it down, and break the strings of it, having no way either to fly from it or resist it. Now, the consideration of the general inundation of death over all mankind, and the certain approaching of it to every particular man's door, hath made many serious thoughts among the wise men of the world. But being destitute of this heavenly light that shineth to us, they could not attain to the original of it; but have conceived that it was a common tribute of nature, and an universal law imposed upon all mankind by nature, having the same reason that other mutations and changes among the creatures here below have; and so have thought it no more a strange thing, than to see other things dissolved in their elements. Now, indeed, seeing they could apprehend no other bitter ingredient in it, it was no wonder that the wisest of them could not fear it; but rather wait and expect it as a rest from their labours, as the end of all their miseries.

But the Lord hath revealed unto us in his word the true cause of it, and so the true nature of it. The true cause of it is sin,—'Sin entered into the world, and death passed upon all, for that all have sinned,' Rom. v. 12. Man was created for another purpose, and upon other conditions, and a law of perpetual life and eternal

* [In some of his epistles to his friends, Cicero expresses himself as if he thought death was to be followed by utter annihilation. But he speaks very differently in some of his other writings. The following passage occurs in a work (CONSOLATIO) which has been ascribed to him:—Gorgias orator, jam ætate confectus ac morti proximus, rogatus, num libenter moreretur, maxime vero, inquit, nam tamquam ex putri miseraque domo lætus egredior.—Mortem igitur in malis nullo modo esse ponendam, sed in præcipuis bonis numerandam, debitaturum puto neminem.—"Gorgias the orator, when worn out with age and near death, being asked, whether he would die willingly, said, 'Very willingly indeed, for I depart as if I were gladly leaving a filthy and wretched house.'—I therefore think that no one will hesitate to believe, that death is not by any means to be ranked among evils, but included among things which we account good in the highest degree."—Cic. Oper. tom. iv. pp. 1347, 1348. Basil. 1681.—ED.]

happiness was passed in his favour, he abiding in the favour, and obeying the will of him that gave him life and being. Now, sin interposing, and separating between man and God, loosing that blessed knot of union and communion, it was this other law that succeeded, as a suitable recompense, 'thou shalt die:' it is resolved, in the council of heaven, that the union of man shall be dissolved, his soul and body separated, in just recompense of the breaking the bond of union with God. This is it that hath opened the sluice to let in an inundation of misery upon mankind: this was the just occasion of that righteous but terrible appointment, 'It is appointed that all men once should die, and after death come to judgment,' Heb. ix. 27; that since the body had enticed the soul, and suggested unto it such unnatural and rebellious motions of withdrawing from the blessed Fountain of life, to satisfy its pleasure, the body should be under a sentence of deprivement and forfeiture of that great benefit and privilege of life it had by the soul's indwelling, and condemned to return to its first base original, 'the dust,' and to be made a feast of worms, to lodge in the grave, and be a subject of the greatest corruption and rottenness, because it became the instrument, yea, the incitement of the soul to sin against that God that had from heaven breathed a spirit into it, and exalted it above all the dust or clay in the world. Now, my beloved, do we not get many remembrances of our sins? Is not every day presenting our primitive departure from God, our first separation from the Fountain of life by sin, to our view, and in such sad and woful effects pointing out the heinousness of sin? Do you not see men's bodies every day dissolved, the tabernacle of earth taken down, and the soul constrained to remove out of it? But what influence hath it upon us, what do the multiplied funerals work upon us? It may be, sorrow for our friends, but little or no apprehension of our own mortality, and base impression of sin, that separates our souls from God. Who is made sadly to reflect upon his original, or to mind seriously that statute and appointment of heaven, 'In that day thou shalt die?' It is strange that all of us fear death, and few are afraid of sin, that carries death in its bosom,—that we are so unwilling to reap corruption in our bodies, and yet we are so earnest and laborious in sowing to the flesh. Be not deceived, for you are daily reaping what you have sown. And, O! that it were all the harvest; but death is only the putting in of the sickle of vengeance, the first cut of it: but, O! to think on what follows, would certainly restrain men, and cool them in their fervent pursuits after sin!

Sermon XXVIII.

VERSE 10.—"*And if Christ be in you, the body is dead because of sin: but the Spirit is life because of righteousness.*"

'THE sting of death is sin, and the strength of sin is the law,' saith our apostle, 1 Cor. xv. 56. These two concur to make man mortal, and these two are the bitter ingredients of death. Sin procured it, and the law appointed it, and God hath seen to the exact execution of that law in all ages; for what man liveth and shall not taste of death? Two only escaped the common lot, Enoch and Elias; for they pleased God, and God took them: and, besides, it was for a pledge, that at the last day all shall not die, but be changed. The true cause of death is sin, and the true nature of it is penal, to be a punishment of sin: take away this relation to sin, and death wants the sting. But, in its first appointment, and as it prevails generally over men, *aculeata* * *est mors*, it hath a sting that pierceth deeper, and woundeth sorer than to the desolation of the body, it goeth into the innermost parts of the soul, and woundeth that eternally. The truth is, the death of the body is not either the first death or the last death: it is rather placed in the middle between two deaths: and it is the fruit of the first, and the root of the last. There is a death immediately hath ensued upon sin, and it is the separation of the soul from God, the Fountain of

* [Animals that have a sting are called "aculeata animalia." *Plin. Nat. Hist.* lib. xx. cap. 91. —ED.]

life and blessedness: and this is the death often spoken of, 'You who were dead in sins and trespasses,' &c. Eph. ii. 1. 'Being past feeling,' and 'alienated from the life of God,' Eph. iv. 18, 19. And truly this is worse in itself than the death of the body simply, though not so sensible, because spiritual. The corruption of the best part in man, in all reason, is worse than the corruption of his worst part. But this death, which consists especially in the loss of that blessed communion with God, which made the soul happy, cannot be found till some new life enter, or else till the last death come, which adds infinite pain to infinite loss. Now the death of the body succeeds this soul's death, and that is, the separation of the soul from the body, most suitable, seeing the soul was turned from the Fountain-spirit to the body, that the body should by his command return to dust, and be made the most defiled piece of dust. Now, this were not so grievous, if it were not a step to the death to come, and a degree of it introductive to it. But that statute and appointment of heaven hath thus linked it, 'after death comes judgment:' because, the soul in the body would not be sensible of its separation from God, but was wholly taken up with the body, neglecting and miskenning* that infinite loss of God's favour and face, therefore the Lord commands it to go out of the body, that it may then be sensible of its infinite loss of God, when it is separated from the body; that it may then have leisure to reflect upon itself, and find its own surpassing misery: and then indeed,—infinite pain and infinite loss conjoined,—eternal banishment from the presence of that blessed Spirit, and eternal torment within itself. These two concurring, what posture do you think such a soul will be into? There are some earnest of this in this life. When God reveals his terror, and sets men's sins in order before their face, O! how intolerable is it, and more insupportable than many deaths. They that have been acquainted with it, have declared it. The terrors of God are like poisonable arrows sunk into Job's spirit, and drinking up all the moisture of them. Such a spirit as is wounded with one of these darts shot from heaven, who can bear it? Not the most patient and most magnanimous spirit, that can sustain all other infirmities, Prov. xviii. 14. Now, my beloved, if it be so now, while the soul is in the body, drowned in it, what will be the case of the soul separated from the body, when it shall be all one sense, to reflect and consider itself?

This is the sting of death indeed, worse than a thousand deaths to a soul that apprehends it; and the less it is apprehended, the worse it is; because it is the more certain, and must shortly be found, when there is no brazen serpent to heal that sting. Now, what comfort have you provided against this day? What way do you think to take out this sting? Truly, there is no balm for it, no physician for it, but one; and that the Christian only is acquainted with. He in whom Christ is, he hath this sovereign antidote against the poison of death, he hath the very sting of it taken out by Christ, death itself killed, and of a mortal enemy made the kindest friend. And so he may triumph with the apostle, 'O death, where is thy sting? O grave, where is thy victory? Thanks be to God in Jesus Christ, who giveth us the victory,' 1 Cor. xv. 55. The ground of his triumph, and that which a Christian hath to oppose to all the sorrows and pains and fears of death mustered against him, is threefold; one, that death is not real; a second, that it is not total, even that which is; and then, that it is not perpetual. This last is contained in the next verse, the second expressed in this verse, and the first may be understood or implied in it. That the nature of death is so far changed, that of a punishment it is become a medicine, of a punishment for sin it is turned into the last purgative of the soul from sin; and thus the sting of it is taken away, that relation it did bear to the just wrath of God. And now as to the body of a Christian under appointment to die for sin, that is, for the death of sin, the eternal death of sin. Christ having come under the power of death, hath gotten power over it, and spoiled it of its stinging virtue. He hath taken away the poisonable ingredient of the curse, that it can no more hurt them that are in him, and so it is not now vested with that piercing and wounding notion of punishment. Though it be true that sin was the first inlet of death, that it first opened the sluice to let it enter and flow

* [That is, not knowing.—Ed.]

in upon mankind, yet that appointment of death is renewed, and bears a relation to the destruction of sin, rather than the punishment of the sinner, who is forgiven in Christ. And, O! how much solid comfort is here, that the great reason of mortality that a Christian is subject unto, is, that he may be made free of that which made him at first mortal. Because sin hath taken such possession in this earthly tabernacle, and is so strong a poison, that it hath infected all the members, and by no purgation here made can be fully cleansed out, but there are many secret corners it lurks into, and upon occasion vents itself, therefore it hath pleased God, in his infinite goodness, to continue the former appointment of death, but under a new and living consideration, to take down this infected and defiled tabernacle, as the houses of leprosy were taken down under the law, that so they might be the better cleansed, and this is the last purification of the soul from sin. And therefore, as one of the ancients said well, "That we might not be eternally miserable, mercy hath made us mortal." Justice hath made the world mortal, that they might be eternally miserable; but to put an end to this misery, Christ hath continued our mortality; else he would have abolished death itself, if he had not meant to abolish sin by death. And indeed, it would appear this is the reason why the world must be consumed with fire at the last day, and new heavens and earth succeed in its room; because, as the little house, the body, so the great house, the world, was infected with this leprosy, and so subjoined to vanity and corruption because of man's sin: therefore, that there might be no remnant of man's corruption, and no memorial of sin to interrupt his eternal joy, the Lord will purify and change all,—all the members that were made instruments of unrighteousness, all the creatures that were servants to man's lusts. A new form and fashion shall be put on all, that the body being restored, may be a fit dwelling-place for the purified soul, and the world renewed, may be a fit house for righteous men. Thus you see, that death to a Christian is not real death; for it is not the death of a Christian, but the death of sin his greatest enemy; it is not a punishment, but the enlargement of the soul.

Now, the next comfort is, that which is is but partial, it is but the dissolution of the lowest part in man, his body; so far from prejudging the immortal life of his spirit, it is rather the accomplishment of that. Though the body must die, yet eternal life is begun already within the soul, for the Spirit of Christ hath brought in life, the righteousness of Christ hath purchased it, and the Spirit hath performed it, and applied it to us. Not only there is an immortal being in a Christian that must survive the dust (for that is common to all men), but there is a new life begun in him, an immortal well-being in joy and happiness, which only deserves the name of life, that cometh never to its full perfection till the bodily and earthly house be taken down. If you consider seriously what a new life a Christian is translated unto, by the operation of the Holy Ghost, and the ministration of the word, it is then most active and lively, when the soul is most retired from the body in meditation. The new life of a Christian is most perfect in this life when it carrieth him the furthest distance from his bodily senses, and is most abstracted from all sensible engagements, as you heard; for indeed it restores the spirit of a man to its native rule and dominion over the body, so that it is then most perfect when it is most gathered within itself, and disengaged from all external entanglements.

Now, certain it is, since the perfection of the soul in this life consists in such a retirement from the body, that when it is wholly separated from it then it is in the most absolute state of perfection; and its life acts most purely and perfectly when it hath no body to communicate with, and to entangle it either with its lusts or necessities. The Spirit is life; it hath a life now which is then best when furthest from the body; and therefore it cannot but be surpassing better when it is out of the body; and all this is purchased by Christ's righteousness. As man's disobedience made an end of his life, Christ's obedience hath made our life endless. He suffered death to sting him, and by this hath taken the sting from it: and now, there is a new statute and appointment of heaven published in the gospel, 'whosoever believeth in him shall not perish, but have eternal life.' Now indeed, this hath so entirely changed the nature of death, that it hath now the most lovely and desirable aspect on a Christian, that it is no longer an object of fear, but of desire, amicable, not terrible unto him. Since there is no way to save the passenger, but to let the vessel break, he will be content to have the body splitted, that himself, that is his soul, may escape; for truly a man's soul is himself, the body is but an earthly tabernacle that must be taken down, to let the inhabitant win out to come near his Lord. The body is the prison-house that he groans to have opened, that he may enjoy that liberty of the sons of God. And now to a Christian, death is not properly an object of patience, but of desire rather; 'I desire to be dissolved and be with Christ,' Phil. i. 23. He that hath but advanced little in Christianity will be content to die; but because there is too much flesh, he will desire to live. But a Christian that is riper in knowledge and grace, will rather desire to die, and only be content to live. He will exercise patience and submission about abiding here, but groanings and pantings about removing hence, because he knoweth that there is no choice between that bondage and this liberty.

Sermon XXIX.

VERSE 10.—"*And if Christ be in you, the body is dead because of sin: but the Spirit is life because of righteousness.*"

It was the first curse and threatening wherein God thought fit to comprehend all misery, 'Thou shalt die the death in that day thou eatest.' Though the sentence was not presently executed according to the letter, yet from that day forward man was made mortal; and there seemeth to be much mercy and goodness of God intervening to plead a delay of death itself, that so the promise of life in the second Adam might come to the first and his posterity, and they might be delivered from the second death, though not from the first. Always we bear about the marks of sin in our bodies to this day, and in so far the threatening taketh place, that this life that we live in the body is become nothing else but a dying life: the life that the ungodly shall live out of the body is a living death; and either of these is worse than simple death or destruction of being. The serious contemplation of the miseries of this life made wise Solomon to praise the dead more than the living, contrary to the custom of men, who rejoice at the birth of a man-child, and mourn at their death. Yea, it pressed him further, to think them which have not at all been, better than both, because they have not seen the evil under the sun. This world is such a chaos, such a mass of miseries, that if men understood it before they came into it, they would be far more loath to enter it, than they are now afraid to go out of it. And truly we want not remembrances and representations of our misery every day, in that children come weeping into the world, as it were bewailing their own misfortune, that they were brought forth to be sensible subjects of misery. And what is all our life-time, but a repetition of sighs and groans, anxiety and satiety, loathing and longing, dividing our spirits and our time between them? How many deaths must we suffer before death come? For the absence or loss of any thing much desired, is a separation no less grievous to the hearts of men, than the parting of soul and body: for affection to temporal perishing things, unites the soul so unto them, that there is no parting without pain, no dissolution of that continuity without much vexation; and yet the soul must suffer many such tortures in one day, because the things are perishing in their own nature, and uncertain. What is sleep, which devours the most part of our time, but the very image and picture of death, a visible and daily representation of the long cessation of the sensitive life in the grave? And yet, truly, it is the best and most innocent part of our time, though we accuse it often. There is both less sin and less misery in it; for it is almost the only lineament and refreshment we get in all our miseries. Job sought to assuage his grief and ease his body; but it was the extremity of his misery that he could not find it. Now, my beloved, when you find that which is called life subject to so much misery that you are constrained often to desire you had never been born, you find it a valley of tears, a house of mourning from whence all true delight and solid happiness is banished. Seeing the very officers and serjeants of death are continually surrounding us, and walk alongst with us—though unpleasant company—in our greatest contentments, and are putting marks upon your doors, as in the time of the plague upon houses infected, 'Lord have mercy upon us,'* and are continually bearing this motto to our view, and sounding this direction to our ears, *cito, procul, diu*,—to get soon out of Sodom that is appointed for destruction, to fly quickly out of ourselves to the refuge appointed of God, even one that was dead and is alive, and hath redeemed us by his blood, and to get far off from ourselves, and take up dwelling in the blessed Son of God, through whose flesh there is access to the Father,—seeing all these, I say, are so, why do not we awake ourselves upon the sound of the promise of immortality and life, brought to our ears in the gospel? Mortality hath already seized upon our bodies, but why do you not catch hold of this opportunity of releasing your souls from the chains and fetters of eternal death? Truly, my beloved, all that can be spoken of torments and miseries in this life, suppose we could imagine all the exquisite torments invented by the most cruel tyrants since the beginning, to be combined in some one kind of torture, and would then stretch our imagination beyond that, as far as that which is composed of all torments surpasseth the simplest death; yet we do not conceive nor express unto you that death to come. Believe it, when the soul is out of the body, it is a most pure activity, all sense, all knowledge. And seeing where it is dulled and dampished † in the body, it is capable of so much grief or joy, pleasure or pain, we may conclude, that being loosed from these stupifying earthly chains, that it is capable of infinite more vexation, or contentation, in a higher and purer strain.

Therefore, we may conclude with the apostle, that all men by nature are miserable in life, but infinitely more miserable in death. Only the man who is in Jesus Christ, in whose spirit Christ dwells, and hath made a temple of his body for offering up reasonable service in it, that man only is happy in life, but far happier in death; happy that he was born, but infinitely more happy that he was born mortal, born to die; for 'if the body be dead because of sin, the Spirit is life because of righteousness.' Men commonly make their accounts, and calculate their time so, as if death were the end of it. Truly, it were happiness in the generality of men that that computation were true; either that it had never begun, or that it might end here; for that which is the greatest dignity and glory of a man—his immortal soul—it is truly the greatest misery of sinful men, because it capacitates them for eternal misery. But if we make our accounts right, and take the right period, truly death is but the beginning of our time, of endless and unchangeable endurance either in happiness or misery; and this life in the body, which is only in the view of the short-sighted sons of men, is but a strait and narrow passage into the infinite ocean of eternity; but so inconsiderable it is that, according as the spirit in this passage is fashioned and formed, so it must continue for ever; for where the tree falleth, there it lieth. There may be hope that a tree will sprout again, but truly there is no hope that ever the damned soul shall see a spring of joy; and no fear that ever the blessed spirits shall find a winter of grief. Such is the evenness of eternity, that there is no shadow of change in it.

O then, how happy are they in whose souls this life is already begun, which shall

* [Dr. Mead describes the means which were formerly resorted to in this country to check the progress of the plague. "The main import of the orders issued out at these times was, as soon as it was found that any house was infected, to keep it shut up, with a large red cross, and these words, 'Lord nave mercy upon us,' painted on the door; watchmen attending day and night to prevent any one's going in or out, except such physicians, surgeons, apothecaries, nurses, searchers, &c., as were allowed by authority: and this to continue at least a month after all the family was dead or recovered.

"It is not easy to conceive a more dismal scene of misery than this; families locked up from all their acquaintance, though seized with a distemper which the most of any in the world requires comfort and assistance; abandoned it may be to the treatment of an inhuman nurse, (for such are often found at these times about the sick,) and strangers to every thing but the melancholy sight of the progress death makes among themselves; with small hopes of life left to the survivors, and those mixed with anxiety and doubt, whether it be not better to die, than to prolong a miserable being, after the loss of their best friends and nearest relations."—*Dr. Mead's Medical Works*, p. 273.—Ed.]

† [That is, stupified.—Ed.]

then come to its meridian, when the glory of the flesh falls down like withered hay into the dust! The life as well as the light of the righteous is progressive. It is shining more and more till that day come, the day of death, only worthy to be called the present day, because it brings perfection, it mounts the soul in the highest point of the orb, and there is no declining from that again. The spirit is now alive in some holy affections and motions, breathing upwards, wrestling towards that point. The soul is now in part united to the Fountain of life, by loving attendance and obedience, and it is longing to be more closely united. The inward senses are exercised about spiritual things, but the burden of this clayey mansion doth much dull and damp them, and proves a great *remora** to the spirit. The body indisposes and weakens the soul much. It is life, as in an infant, though a reasonable soul be there, yet overwhelmed with the incapacity of the organs. This body is truly a prison of restraint and confinement to the soul, and often loathsome and ugly through the filthiness of sin; but when the spirit is delivered from this necessary burden and impediment, O how lively is that life it then lives! Then the life, peace, joy, love, and delight of the soul surmounts all that is possible here, further than the highest exercise of the soul of the wisest men surpasses the brutish-like apprehensions of an infant; and indeed then the Christian comes to his full stature, and is a perfect man when he ceaseth to be a man.

How will you not be persuaded, beloved in the Lord, to long after this life, to have Christ formed in your hearts; for truly the generality have not so much as Christ fashioned in their outward habit, but are within darkness and earthiness and wickedness; and without, impiety and profanity. Will you not long for this life? For now you are dead while you live, as the apostle speaks of widows that live in pleasure. The more the soul be satisfied with earthly things, it is the deeper buried in the grave of the flesh, and the further separated from God. Alas! many of you know no other life, than that which you now live in the body; you neither apprehend what this new birth is, nor what the perfect stature of it shall be afterwards. But truly while it is thus, you are but walking shadows, breathing clay, and no more. A godly man used to calculate the years of his nativity from his second birth, his conversion to God in Christ; and truly, this is the true period of the right calculation of life, of that life which shall not see death. True life hath but one period, that is, the beginning of it; for end it hath none. I beseech you, reckon your years thus, and I fear that you reckon yourselves, many of you, yet dead in sins and trespasses. Is that life, I pray you, to eat, to drink, to sleep, to play, to walk, to work? Is there any thing in all these worthy of a reasonable soul, which must survive the body, and so cease from such things for ever? Think within yourselves, do you live any other life than this? What is your life but a tedious and wearisome repetition of such brutish actions which are only terminate on the body? O then, how miserable are you, if you have no other period to reckon from than your birth-day! If there be not a second birth-day before your burial, you may make your reckoning to be banished eternally from the life of God.

As for you, Christians, whom God hath quickened by the Spirit of his Son, be much in the exercise of this life, and that will maintain and advance it. Let your care be about your spirits, and to hearten you in this study, and to beget in you the hope of eternal life, look much and lay fast hold on that life-giving Saviour, who, by his righteous life and accursed death, hath purchased by his own blood both happiness to us and holiness. Consider what debtors you are to him who loved not his own life and spared it not, to purchase this life to us. Let our thoughts and affections be occupied about this high purchase of our Saviour's, which is freely bestowed on them that will have it, and believe in him for it. If we be not satisfied with such a low and wretched life as is in the body, he will give a higher and more enduring life, and only worthy of that name.

* [That is, obstruction. "Mr. Prin and the Erastian lawyers are now our *remora.*"—Baillie's Letters and Journal, vol. II. p. 158.—Ed.]

Sermon XXX.

VERSE 11.—"*But if the Spirit of him that raised up Jesus from the dead dwell in you, he that raised up Christ from the dead shall also quicken your mortal bodies by his Spirit that dwelleth in you.*"

IT is true the soul is incomparably better than the body; and he is only worthy the name of a man and of a Christian who prefers this more excellent part, and employs his study and time about it, and regards his body only for the noble guest that lodges within it; and therefore it is one of the prime consolations that Christianity affords, that it provides chiefly for the happy estate of this immortal piece in man, which, truly, were alone sufficient to draw our souls wholly after religion. Suppose the body should never taste of the fruits of it, but die and rise no more, and never be awaked out of its sleep, yet it were a sufficient ground of engagement to godliness, that the life and well-being of the far better part in man is secured for eternity, which is infinitely more than all things beside can truly promise us, or be able to perform. Certainly, whatsoever else you give your hearts to, and spend your time upon, it either will leave you in the midst of your days, and at your end you shall be a fool, or you must leave it in the end of your days, and find yourselves as much disappointed; or, to speak more properly, because when your time is ending your life and being is but at its beginning, you must bid an eternal adieu to all these things whereupon your hearts are set when you are but beginning truly to be. But this is only the proper and true good of the soul,—Christ in it;—most portable and easily carried about with you; yea, that which makes the soul no burden to itself, and helps it to carry all things easily;—and then most inseparable, for Christ in the soul is the spring of a never-ending life, of peace, joy, and contentation in the fountain of an infinite goodness, and it outwears time and age, as well as the immortal being of the soul. Yea, such is the strength of this consolation, that then the soul is most closely united and fully possessed of that which is its peculiar and satisfying good, when it leaves the body in the dust, and escapes out of this prison unto that glorious liberty.

But yet, there is besides this an additional comfort comprehended in the verse read;—that the sleep of the body is not perpetual, that it shall once be awakened and raised up to the fellowship of this glory; for though a man should be abundantly satisfied if he possess his own soul, yet no man hateth his own flesh. The soul hath some kind of natural inclination to a body suitable unto it, and in this it differs from an angel; and, therefore, the apostle, when he expresseth his earnest groan for the intimate presence of his soul with Christ, he subjoins this correction,—not that we desire to be unclothed, but clothed upon it, 2 Cor. v. 1—4. If it were possible, says he, we would be glad to have the society of the body in this glory, we would not desire to cast off those clothes of flesh, but rather that the garment of glory might be spread over all, if it were not needful, because they are old and ragged and would not suit well; and our earthly tabernacle is ruinous, and would not be fit for such a glorious guest to dwell into, and, therefore, it is needful to be taken down. Well, then, here is an overplus, and, as it were, a surcharge of consolation, that seeing for the present it is expedient to put off the present clothing of flesh, and take down the present earthly house,—yet that the day is coming that the same clothes, renewed, shall be put on, and the same house repaired and made suitable to heaven, shall be built up;—that this mortal body shall be quickened with that same spirit that now quickens the soul, and makes it live out of the body; and so the sweet and beloved friends, who parted with so much pain and grief, shall meet again with so much pleasure and joy; and, as they were sharers together in the miseries of this life, shall participate also in the blessedness of the next,—like Saul and Jonathan, 'lovely and pleasant in their lives,' and though for a time separated in death, yet not always divided. Now this is the highest top of happiness, to which nothing can be added. It is comprehensive of the whole man, and it is comprehensive of all that can be imagined to be the perfective good of man.

It is no wonder, then, that the apostle reckons this doctrine of the resurrection amongst the foundations of Christianity (Heb. vi. 1, 2.), for truly these two—the immortality of the soul and the resurrection of the mortal body—are the two ground-stones or pillars of true religion, which, if they be not well settled in the hearts of men, all religion is tottering and ruinous and unable to support itself. That the soul cannot taste death or see corruption, and that the body shall but taste it, and, as it were, salute it, and cannot always abide under the power of it, these are the prime foundations upon which all Christian persuasion is built. For without these be laid down in the lowest and deepest part of the heart, all exhortations to an holy and righteous life are weak and ineffectual, all consolations are empty and vain. In a word, religion is but an airy speculation, that hath no consistence but in the imaginations of men;—it is a house upon sand, that can abide no blast of temptation, no wave of misery, but must straightway fall to the ground. From whence is it, I pray you, that the persuasions of the gospel have so little power upon men,—that the plain and plentiful publication of a Saviour is of so small virtue to stir up the hearts of men to take hold on him? How comes it to pass that the precepts and prohibitions of the most high God, coming forth under his authority, lay so little restraint on men's corruptions,—that so few will be persuaded to stop their course, and come off the ways that they are accustomed to,—that men pull away the shoulder and stop the ear, and make their hearts as adamant, incapable of being affected with either the authority or love of the gospel,—that when he pipes unto us so few dance, and when he mourns so few lament? Is it not because these two foundations are not laid, and men's hearts not digged deep by earnest consideration to receive these ground-stones of Christianity,—the belief of their soul's eternal survivance after the dust, and of the revivance and resurrection of the body, after it hath slept a while in the dust? I remember heathens have had some noble and rare conceptions about virtue, and some have laboured to enamour men with the native beauty of it, and to persuade them that it was a sufficient reward to itself.* And truly it would far more become a Christian,—who knoweth the high and divine pattern of holiness to be God himself, and so must needs behold a far surpassing beauty and excellency in the image of God than in all earthly things,—I say, it would become him to accustom himself to a dutiful observance of religion, even without any respect to the reward of it. He would train his heart to do homage to God out of a loyal affection and respect to his majesty, and from the love of the very intrinsic beauty of obedience, without borrowing always from such selfish considerations of our own happiness or misery. Notwithstanding, such is the posture of man's spirit now, that he cannot at all be engaged to the love of religion, except some seen advantage conciliate it, and therefore the Lord makes use of such selfish principles in drawing men to himself, and keeping them still with him. And, truly, considering man's infirmity, this is the spirit and life of all religion—immortality and resurrection—that which gives a lustre to all and quickens all, that which makes all to sink deep, and that which makes a Christian steadfast and immoveable, 2 Cor. v. 8. It is certainly hope that is the key of the heart, that opens and shuts it to any thing. Hence the apostle Peter (1 Epistle) first blesseth God heartily for the new birth, and, in expressing of it, makes hope the very term of that generation, and so it must be a substantial thing. 'Blessed be God, who hath begotten us again to a lively hope.' Hope hath a quickening power in it. It makes all new where it comes, and is full of spirit. It is the helmet

* [The ancient heathens seem to have looked upon a future state, says Leland, (Advantage and Necessity of the Christian Revelation, vol. ii. p. 305. Glasgow, 1819,) "as too uncertain a thing to be relied upon, and therefore endeavoured to find out motives to virtue independent on the belief of the rewards prepared for good men, after this life is at an end. They represented, in an elegant and beautiful manner, the present conveniencies and advantages of virtue, and the satisfaction which attends it; but especially they insisted upon its intrinsic excellency, its dignity and beauty, and agreeableness to reason and nature, and its self-sufficiency to happiness, which many of them, especially the stoics,—the most rigid moralists among them,—carried to a very high degree. Cicero, in his Offices, and those excellent philosophers, Epictetus and Marcus Antoninus, in their works, which seem to be the best moral treatises pagan antiquity has left us, go upon this scheme. They were sensible, indeed, that, in order to recommend virtue to the esteem of mankind, and engage them to pursue it, it was necessary to show that it would be for their own highest advantage."—Ed.]

and anchor of a Christian, that which bears the dint of temptation and makes him steady in religion. No man will put his plough in this ground, or sow unto the Spirit, but in hope; for he that soweth must sow in hope, else his plough will not go deep, 1 Cor. ix. 10. This, then, is the very spirit and life of religion,—the resurrection of the dead,—without which our faith were in vain, and men would continue still in their sins. Certainly it is the deep inconsideration of this never-ending endurance of our souls, and restitution of our bodies to the same immortality, that makes the most part of men so slight and superficial in religion, else it were not possible, if that were laid to heart, but men would make religion their business, and chief business.

We have here the two genuine causes of the resurrection of the bodies of Christians,—the resurrection of Christ and the inhabitation of his Spirit. The influence that the resurrection of Christ hath on ours, is lively and fully holden out by this apostle, 1 Cor. xv, against them who deny the resurrection from the dead: 'If Christ be not raised, your faith is in vain, you are yet in your sins, and they that are asleep are perished.' Religion were nothing but a number of empty words of show, preaching were a vanity and imposture, faith were a mere fancy, if this be not laid down as the ground-stone,—Christ raised, not as a natural person, but as a common politic person, as the first-fruits of them that sleep, ver. 17—20. where he alludes to the ceremony of offering the first-fruits of their harvest, Lev. xxiii. 10. For under the law they might not eat of the fruits of the land till they were sanctified. All was counted profane till they were some way consecrated to the Lord. Now, for this end, the Lord appointed them to bring one sheaf for all, and that was the representative of all the rest of the heap, and this was waved before the Lord, and lifted up from the earth. Now, according to the apostle's argument, Rom. xi. 16. 'If the first-fruits be holy, so is the lump,' for it represents all the lump, and therefore Jesus Christ, the chief of all his brethren, was made the first-fruits from the dead, and lifted up from the grave, as the representer of all the lump of his elect; and so it must needs follow, that they shall not continue in the grave, but must in due time partake of that benefit which he has first entered in possession of, in their name, and for them. For if this first-fruits be holy, so the whole lump must be holy; and if the first-fruits be risen, so must the lump. You see then the force of the present reason, 'If the Spirit that raised Christ dwell in you, he shall also raise you,' namely, because he raised up Christ the very first-fruits of all the rest; so that Christ's resurrection is a sure pledge and token of yours, and both together are the main basis and ground-work of all our hope and salvation, the neglect and inconsideration whereof makes the most part of pretended Christians to walk according to that Epicurean principle, 'Let us eat and drink, for to-morrow we shall die.' As if there were no life to come, they withhold nothing from their carnal minds, that can satisfy or please their lusts. But for you who desire a part in this resurrection, and dare scarcely believe so great a thing, or entertain such a high hope, because of the sight of your unworthiness, as you would be awakened by this hope to 'righteousness, and to sin no more,' verse 34th of that chapter, so you may encourage yourselves to that hope by the resurrection of Christ; for it is that which hath the mighty influence to beget you to a lively hope, 1 Pet. i. 3. Look upon this as the grand intent, and special design of Christ's both dying and rising again, that he might be the first-fruits to sanctify all the lump. Nevertheless, it is not the desert of your bodies, for they are often a great impediment and retardment to the spirit, and lodge the enemy within their walls, when he is chased out of the mind by the law of the Spirit of life; but it is the great design of God, through the whole work of redemption, and the desert of Christ your head; and therefore you may entertain that hope, but take heed to walk worthy of it, and that it is, 'if we have this hope, let us purify ourselves;' let us who believe that we are risen with Christ, set our affections on things above, else we dishonour him that is risen in our name, and we dishonour that temple of the Holy Ghost, which he will one day make so glorious.

Sermon XXXI.

Verse. 11.—"*But if the Spirit of him that raised up Jesus from the dead dwell in you, he that raised up Christ from the dead, shall also quicken your mortal bodies by his Spirit that dwelleth in you.*"

As there is a twofold death,—the death of the soul, and the death of the body—so there is a double resurrection, the resurrection of the soul from the power of sin, and the resurrection of the body from the grave. As the first death is that which is spiritual, then that which is bodily, so the first resurrection is of the spirit, then the second of the body, and these two have a connexion together; therefore saith the apostle John, 'Blessed are they who have part in the first resurrection, for on such the second death hath no power, but they shall be priests to God,' &c. Rev. xx. 6. Although death must seize on their bodies, yet the sting wherein the strength of it lies, is taken away by Christ, that it hath no power to hurt him whose spirit is raised out of the grave of sin. And truly it is hard to tell which is the greatest change, or the most difficult, to raise a body out of corruption to life, or to raise a soul out of sin to grace. But both are the greatest changes that can be, and shadowed out under the similitude of the greatest in nature; for our conversion to God is a new birth, a new creation, and a resurrection in scripture style, and so both require one and the same power, the almighty power of his Spirit: 'You who were dead in sins hath he quickened,' &c. O what a notable change! It maketh them no longer the same men, but new creatures; and therefore it is the death of sin, and the resurrection of the soul. For as long as it is under the chains of darkness and power of sin, it is free among the dead, it is buried in the vilest sepulchre. Old graves, and these full of rottenness and dead men's bones, are nothing to express the lamentable case of such a soul, and yet such are all by nature. Whatsoever excellency or endowment men may have from their birth or education, yet certainly they are but apparitions rather than any real substance, and which is worse, their body is the sepulchre of their souls, and if the corruption of a soul were sensible, we would think all the putrefactions of bodily things but shadows of it. And therefore no sooner is there any inward life begotten in a soul, but this is the very first exercise of it, the abhorrency of the soul upon the sight and smell of its own loathsomeness.

Now, there is no hope of any reviving. Though all the wisdom and art of men and angels were employed in this business, there is nothing able to quicken one such soul, until it please the Lord to speak such a word as he did to Lazarus, 'Arise, come forth,' and send his Spirit to accomplish his word, and this will do it. When the Spirit cometh into the soul, he quickeneth it, and this is the first resurrection. O blessed are they who have part in this, whose souls are drawn out of the dungeon of darkness and ignorance, and brought forth to behold this glorious light that shineth in the gospel, and raised out of the grave of the lusts of ignorance, to live unto God henceforth, for such have their part in the second resurrection to life. For you see these are conjoined, 'If the Spirit dwell in you, he shall raise you,' &c. You see here two grounds and reasons of the resurrection of body,—Christ's rising and the Spirit's indwelling. Now I find these in the scripture made the two fountains of all Christianity, both of the first and second resurrection.

The resurrection of Christ is an evidence of our justification, the cause of our quickening, or vivification, and the ground and pledge of our last resurrection; and all these are grounds of strong consolation. The first you have, Rom. iv. 25. 'Christ died for our sins, and rose for our justification;' and the 34th verse of this chapter, 'Christ is dead, yea, rather has risen again; who then shall condemn?' Here is a clear evidence, that he hath paid the debt wholly, and satisfied justice fully. Since he was under the power of death, imprisoned by justice, certainly he would not have won free, if he had not paid the uttermost farthing; therefore his glorious resurrection is a sure manifestation of his present satisfaction,—it is a public acquittance and absolution of him from all our debt, and so by consequence, of all he died for. For their debt was laid upon him, and now he is discharged. And therefore the believing soul may tremblingly boast, who shall condemn me? For it is God that justifieth. Why? Because all my sins were laid on Christ, and God hath in a most solemn manner acquitted and discharged him from all, when he raised him from the dead; and therefore he cannot, and none other can sue me, or prosecute a plea against me, since my Cautioner is fully exonered of this undertaking, even by the great Creditor God himself. But then, his resurrection is a pawn or pledge of the spiritual raising of the soul from sin: as the death of Christ is made the pledge of our dying to sin, so his rising, of our living to God, Rom. vi. 4, 5. These are not mere patterns and examples of spiritual things, but assured pledges of the divine virtue and power which he, being raised again, should send abroad throughout the world. For, as there are coronation gifts, when kings are solemnly installed in office, so there are coronation mercies, triumphal gifts. When Christ rose and ascended, he bestowed them on the world, Eph. iv. And certainly these are the greatest, the virtue of his death to kill the old man, and the power of his resurrection to quicken the new. And by faith, a believer is united and ingrafted into him, as a plant into a choice stock, and by virtue and sap coming from Christ's death and resurrection, he is transformed into the similitude of both; he groweth into the likeness of his death, by dying to sin, by crucifying these inward affections and inclinations to it; and he groweth up into the similitude of his resurrection, by newness of life, or being alive to God, in holy desires and endeavours after holiness and obedience. And thus the first resurrection of the soul floweth from Christ's resurrection.

But add unto this, that Christ's rising is the pledge and pawn of the second resurrection, that is, of the body, for he is the head, and we are the members. Now, it is the most incongruous, that the head should rise and not draw up the members after him. Certainly he will not cease till he have drawn up all his members to him. If the head be above water, it is a sure pledge that the body will win out of the water; if the root be alive, certainly the branches will out in spring-time, they shall live also. There is that connexion between Christ and believers, that wonderful communication between them, that Christ did nothing, was nothing, and had nothing done to him, but what he did, and was, and suffered, personating them, and all the benefit and advantage redounds to them. He would not be considered of as a person by himself, but would rather be still taken in with the children. As for love he came down and took flesh to be like them, and did take their sin and misery off them, and so was content to be looked upon by God as in the place of sinners, as the chief sinner, so he is content and desirous that we should look on him as in the place of sinners, as dying, as rising for us, as having no excellency or privilege incommunicable to us. And this was not hid from the church of old, but presented as the grand consolation, 'Thy dead men shall live, together with my dead body they shall rise.' And, therefore, may poor souls awake and sing. Though they must dwell in the dust, yet as the dew and influence of heaven maketh herbs to spring out of the earth, so the virtue of this resurrection shall make the earth, and sea, and air, to cast out and render their dead, Isa. xxvi. 19. Upon what a sure and strong chain hangs the salvation of poor sinners? I wish Christians might salute one another with this: 'Christ is risen, and so comfort one another with these words,'—or rather, that every one would apply this cordial to his own heart, 'Christ is risen;' and you know what a golden chain this draweth after it, therefore we must rise and live.

The other cause, which is more immediate, and will actively accomplish it, is the Spirit dwelling in us: for there is a suitable method here too. As the Lord first raised the head, Christ, and will then raise the members, and he that doth the one cannot but do the other, so the Spirit first raiseth the soul from the woful fall into sin, which killed us, and so maketh it a temple, and the body too, for both are bought with a price, and, therefore, the Spirit possesseth both. But the inmost residence is in the soul, and the bodily members are made servants of righteousness, which is a great honour and dignity, in regard of that base employment they had once; and so it is most suitable that he who hath thus dwelt in both repair his own dwelling-house. For here it is ruinous, and, therefore, must be cast down. But because it was once a temple for the holy God, therefore it will be repaired and built again. For he that once honoured it with his presence will not suffer corruption always to dwell in it; for what Christ, by his humiliation and suffering, purchased, the Spirit hath this commission to perform it; and what is it but the restitution of mankind to a happier estate in the second Adam than ever the first was into? Now, since our Lord who pleased to take on our flesh, did not put it off again, but admits it to the fellowship of the same glory in heaven, in that he died, he dies no more, death hath no more dominion over him, he will never be wearied or ashamed of that human clothing of flesh. And, therefore, certainly that the children may be like the father, the followers their captain, the members not disproportioned to the head, the branches not different and heterogeneous to the stock, and that our rising in Christ may leave no footstep of our falling, no remainder of our misery, the Spirit of Christ will also quicken the mortal bodies of believers, and make them like Christ's glorious body.

This must be done with divine power,—and what more powerful than the Spirit? For it is the spirits or subtile parts in all creatures that causeth all motions, and worketh all effects. What then is that almighty Spirit not able to do? You have shadows of this in nature, yea, convincing evidences: for, what is the spring but a resurrection of the earth? Is not the world every year renewed, and riseth again out of the grave of winter, as you find elegantly expressed, Psalm cvii? And doth not the grains of seed die in the clods before they rise to the harvest, 1 Cor. xv. All the vicissitudes and alterations in nature give us a plain draught of this great change, and certainly it is one Spirit that effects all.

But though there be the same power required to raise up the bodies of the godly and ungodly; yet, O what infinite distance and difference in the nature and ends of their resurrections! There is the resurrection of life, and the resurrection of condemnation, John v. 29. O! happy they who rise to life that ever they died! But, O miserable, thrice wretched are all others that they may not be dead for ever! The immortality of the soul was infinite misery, because it is that which eternizes their misery; but when this overplus is added, the incorruptibility of the body, and so the whole man made an inconsumable subject for that fire to feed upon perpetually, what heart can conceive it without horror! And yet we hear it often without any such affection. It is a strange life that death is the only refreshment of it; and yet this may not be had, 'they shall seek death, and it shall fly from them.' Now, my beloved, I would desire this discourse might open way for the hearty and cordial entertainment of the gospel, and that you might be persuaded to awake unto righteousness, and sin no more, 1 Cor. xv. 34. Be not deceived, my brethren, 'flesh and blood cannot inherit the kingdom of God.' Certainly, if you have no other image than what you came into the world withal, you cannot have this hope, to be conformed one day to the glorious body of Christ. What will become of you in that day, who declare now by the continued vent of your hearts that this Holy Spirit dwells not in you? And, alas! how many are such? Oh! pity yourselves, your souls and bodies both. If for love to your bodies you will follow its present lusts, and care only for the things of the body, you act the greatest enmity and hostility against your own bodies. Consider, I beseech you, the eternal state of both, and your care and study will run in another channel. And for you who have any working of the Spirit in you, whether convincing you of sin and misery, and of righteousness in Christ, or sometimes comforting you by the word applied to your heart, or teaching you another way than the world walks into, I recommend unto you that of the apostle's, 1 Cor. xv. 58. 'Wherefore, my brethren, be steadfast, &c. always abounding in the work of the Lord, knowing your labour is not in vain.'

Sermon XXXII.

VERSE 12.—"*Therefore, brethren, we are debtors, not to the flesh, to live after the flesh,*" *&c.*

ALL things in Christianity have a near and strait conjunction. It is so entire and absolute a piece, that if one link be loosed all the chain falls to the ground, and if one be well fastened upon the heart it brings all alongst with it. Some speak of all truths, even in nature, that they are knit so together that any truth may be concluded out of every truth, at least by a long circuit of deduction and reasoning. But whatsoever be of that, certainly religion is a more entire thing, and all the parts of it more nearly conjoined together, that they may mutually enforce one another. Precepts and promises are thus linked together, that if any soul lay hold, indeed, upon any promise of grace, he draws alongst with it the obligation of some precept to walk suitable to such precious promises. There is no encouragement you can indeed fasten upon, but it will join you as nearly to the commandment; and no consolation in the gospel, that doth not carry within its bosom an exhortation to holy walking. Again, on the other hand, there is no precept but it should lead you straightway to a promise; no exhortation, but it is environed before and behind with a strong consolation, to make it pierce the deeper, and go down the sweeter. Therefore, you see how easily the apostle digresseth from the one to the other,—how sweetly and pertinently these are interwoven in his discourse. The first word of the chapter is a word of strong consolation, 'There is no condemnation to them that are in Christ,' and this like a flood carries all down with it,—all precepts and exhortations, and the soul of a believer with them; and, therefore, he subjoins an exhortation to holy and spiritual walking upon that very ground. And because commandments of this nature will not float (so to speak) unless they have much water of that kind, and cannot have such a swift course except the tide of such encouragements flow fast, therefore he openeth that spring again in the preceding words, and letteth the rivers of consolation flow forth, even the hope of immortality and eternal life: and this certainly will raise up a soul that was on ground, and carry him above in motion of obedience; and, therefore, he may well, in the next place, stir them up to their duty, and mind them of their obligation: 'Therefore, brethren, we are debtors not to the flesh.' To make this the more effectual, he drops it in with affection, in a sweet compellation of love and equality, *brethren*. There is nothing so powerful in persuasion as love; it will sweeten a bitter and unpleasant reproof, and make it go down more easily, though it maketh less noise than threatenings and severity and authority; yet it is more forcible, for it insinuates itself, and in a manner surpriseth the soul, and so preventeth all resistance. As when the sun made the traveller part with his cloak,* whereas the wind and rain made him hold it faster; so affection will prevail where authority and terror cannot; it will melt that which a stronger power cannot break. The story of Elijah, 1 Kings xix. may give some representation of this. The Lord was not in the strong wind, nor in the terrible earthquake, nor yet in the fire, but in the calm still voice. The Lord hath chosen this way of publishing his grace in the gospel, because the sum of it is love to sinners, and good will towards men. He holds it forth in the calm voice of love, and those who are his ambassadors should be clothed with such an affection, if they intend to prevail with men, to engage their affections. O! that we were possessed with that brotherly love one towards another for the salvation one of another; especially, that the preachers of the gospel might be thus kindly affectioned towards others, and that you would take it thus, the calling you off the ways of sin as an act of the greatest love. But then consider the equality of this obligation, for there is nothing pressed upon you but what lieth as heavily upon them that presseth

* [" The Sun and the Wind had once a dispute which of them could soonest prevail with a certain traveller to part with his cloak. The Wind began the attack, and assaulted him with much noise and fury; but the man, wrapping his cloak still closer about him, doubled his efforts to keep it, and went on his way. And now the Sun silently darted his warm insinuating rays, which, melting our traveller by degrees, at length obliged him to lay aside that cloak which all the rage of the Wind could not compel him to resign. *Learn*, hence, said the Sun, *that soft and gentle means will often accomplish what force and fury can never effect*." (Fable of the Sun and the Wind. Boreas et Sol.) This is one of forty-two fables ascribed to Æsop, which Avienus, a Latin poet who lived in the age of Theodosius, turned into elegiac verse. The employment of apologues, which is sanctioned by scripture, seems to be a natural mode of imparting instruction. These arrest the attention, disarm prejudice, give to unwelcome truths a pleasing form, and imprint deeply on the memory the lesson that is intended to be conveyed. It is mentioned by Vincent of Beauvais, who wrote in the middle of the thirteenth century, that the preachers of his age were accustomed to quote the fables of Æsop, in order to rouse the indifference and relieve the languor of their hearers. Specul. Hist. lib. iii. cap. viii. p. 31. Ven. 1591, ap. Warton's Diss. on Gesta Romanorum, p. i.—Ed.]

it. This debt binds all. O! that the ministers of the gospel could carry the impression of this on their hearts, that when they persuade others they may withal persuade themselves, and when they speak to others they may sit down among the hearers. If an apostle of so eminent dignity levelleth himself in this consideration, 'therefore, brethren, we are debtors,'—how much more ought pastors and teachers to come in the same rank and degree of debt and obligation with others. Truly this is the great obstruction of the success of the gospel, that those who bind on burdens on others do not themselves touch them with one of their fingers; and while they seem serious in persuading others, yet withal declare by their carriage that they do not believe themselves what they bear upon others; so that preaching seemeth to be an imposture, and affections in persuading of others to be borrowed, as it were, in a scene, to be laid down again out of it. But then again, there is a misconceit among people that this holy and spiritual walking is not of common obl gation, but peculiar to the preachers of the gospel. Many make their reckoning so, as if they were not called to such high aims and great endeavours. But truly, my beloved, this is a thing of common concernment. The Holy Ghost hath levelled us all in this point of duty, as he hath equally exalted all in the most substantial dignities and privileges of the gospel. This bond is upon the highest and upon the lowest. Greatness doth not exempt from it, and meanness doth not exclude from it. Though commonly great persons fancy an immunity from the strictness of a holy conversation because of their greatness, and often mean and low persons pretend a freedom from such a high obligation because of their lowness, yet certainly all are debt-bound this way, and must one day give account. You that are poor and unlearned, and have not received great things of that nature from God, do not think yourselves free, do not absolve yourselves, for there is infinite debt besides. You will have no place for that excuse, that you had not great parts, were not learned, and so forth. For as the obligation reaches you all, so there is as patent a way to the exercise of religion in the poorest cottage as in the highest palace. You may serve God as acceptably in little, as others may do in much. There is no condition so low and abject that layeth any restraint on this noble service and employment. This jewel loses not its beauty and virtue, when it lieth in a dunghill more than when it is set in gold.

But let us inquire further into this debt. 'We are debtors,' saith he; and he instanceth what is not the creditor, by which he giveth us to understand who is the true creditor: not the flesh, and, therefore, to make out the just opposition, it must be the Spirit. We are debtors, then, to the Spirit. And what is the debt we owe to him? We may know it that same way; we owe not to the flesh so much as to make us live after its guidance and direction, and fulfil its lusts. Then, by due consequence, we owe so much to the Spirit, as that we should live after the Spirit, and resign ourselves wholly to him, his guidance and direction. There is a twofold kind of debt upon the creature, one remissible and pardonable, another irremissible and unpardonable, (so to speak,) the debt of sin, and that is the guilt of it, which is nothing else than the obligation of the sinner over to eternal condemnation by virtue of the curse of God. Every sinner cometh under this debt to divine justice, the desert of eternal wrath, and the actual ordination by a divine sentence to that wrath. Now, indeed, this debt was insoluble to us, and utterly unpayable until God sent his Son to be our cautioner; and he hath paid the debt in his own person, by bearing our curse, and so made it pardonable to sinners, obtained a relaxation from that woful obligation to death. And this debt, you see, is wholly discharged to them that are in Christ, by another sentence repealing the former curse,—ver. 1. 'There is no condemnation to them that are in Christ.' But there is another debt, which I may call a debt of duty and obedience, which, as it was antecedent to sin, even binding innocent Adam, so the obligation of the debt of sin hath been so far from taking it away that it is rather increased exceedingly, and this debt is unpardonable and indispensable. The more of the debt of sin be pardoned, and the more the curse be dispensed with, the more the sinner owes of love and obedience to God. 'She loved much, because much was forgiven,'—and the more was forgiven of sin the more she owed of love, and the more debt was discharged the more she was indebted to him. And, therefore, after this general acquittance of all believers, ver. 1 he presseth this obligation the more strongly· 'Therefore, brethren, we are debtors.' It is like that debt spoken of, Rom. xiii., 'Owe no man any thing, but love one another;' which is not meant that it is unlawful to be debtors to men, but rather, what ye owe, or all things else, pay it, and ye are free. Your debt ceases and your bond is cancelled. But as for the debt of love and benevolence, you must so owe that to all men, as never to be discharged of it, never to be freed from it. When you have done all, this hath no limitation of time or action; even so it is here. Other debts when paid, men cease to be debtors, then they are free; but here the more he pays the more he is bound to pay,—he oweth, and he oweth eternally. His bond is never cancelled as long as he continues a creature subsisting in God, and abides a redeemed one in Christ. For these continuing, his obligation is eternally recent and fresh as the first day. And this doth not at all obscure the infinite grace of God, or diminish the happiness of saints, that they are not freed from this debt of love and obedience, but rather illustrates the one and increases the other, for it cannot be supposed to consist with the wisdom and holiness of God to loose his creature from that obligation of loving obedience and subjection, which is essential to it, and it is no less repugnant to the happiness of the creature to be free from righteousness unto sin.

Now, this debt of duty and obedience hath a threefold bond, which because they stand in vigour uncancelled for all eternity, therefore the obligation arising from them is eternal too. The bond of creation, the bond of redemption, and the bond of sanctification, these are distinguished according to the persons of the Trinity, who appear most eminently in them.

We owe our being to the Father, in whom 'we live and move and have our being;' for he made us, and not we ourselves, and we are all the works of his hands. Now, the debt accruing from this is infinite. If men conceive themselves so much obliged to others for a petty courtesy as to be their servants,—if they owe more to their parents, the instruments of their bringing forth into the world, O how infinitely more owe we to God, of whom we are, and have all! Doth the clay owe so much to the potter, who doth not make it, but fashion it only? And what owe we to him that made us of nothing, and fashioned us while we were yet without form! Truly, all relations, all obligations evanish when this cometh forth; because all that a man hath is less than himself, than his immortal spirit, and that he oweth alone to God. And besides, whatsoever debt there is to other fellow-creatures in any thing, God is the principal creditor in that bond. All the creatures are but the servants of this King, which at his sole appointment bring along his gifts unto us; and, therefore, we owe no more to them than to the hands of the messenger that is sent. Now, by this account nothing is our own, not ourselves, not our members, not our goods, but all are his, and to be used and bestowed, not at the will and arbitriment of creatures, but to be absolutely and solely at his disposal who hath the sole sovereign right to them: and, therefore, you may take up the heinousness of sin, how monstrous and misshapen a thing it is, that breaks this inviolable law of creation, and withdraws the creature from subjection to him, in whom alone it can subsist. O how disordered are the courses and lives of men! Men living to themselves, their own lusts, after their own will, as if they had made themselves. Men using their members as weapons of unrighteousness against God, as if their tongues, and hands, and feet were their own, or the devil's, and not God's. Call to mind this obligation, 'remember thy Creator.' That memento would be a strong engagement to another course than most take. How absurd would you think it to please yourselves in displeasing him, if you but minded the bond of creation! But when there are other two superadded, what we owe to the Son for coming down in the likeness of sinful flesh for us, and what we owe to the Holy Ghost for quickening our spirits, and afterward for the resurrection of our bodies, whose hearts would not these overcome and lead captive to his love and obedience?

Sermon XXXIII.

VERSES 12, 13.—" *Therefore, brethren, we are debtors, not to the flesh, to live after the flesh: for if ye live after the flesh, ye shall die,*" *&c.*

WAS that not enough to contain men in obedience to God,—the very essential bond of dependence upon God as the original and fountain of his being! And yet man hath cast away this cord from him, and withdrew from that allegiance he did owe to his Maker, by transgressing his holy commandments. But God, not willing that all should perish, hath confirmed and strengthened that primitive obligation by two other as strong if not more. If the Father did most eminently appear in the first, the Son is manifested in the second, and that is the work of the redemption of man, no less glorious than his first creation. He made him first, and then he sent his own Son in the likeness of sinful flesh, to make him again by his Spirit; and now a threefold cord is not easily broken. It seems this should bind invincibly, and constrain us not to be our own, but the Lord's; and now truly, they who are in Jesus Christ, are thrice indebted wholly to God. But the two last obligations are the most special and most wonderful, that God sent his Son for us, to redeem us from sin and misery, and to restore man to happiness took on a miserable and accursed habit,—that so glorious a person gave himself for so base an one,—that so excellent a Lord became a servant for the rebel,—that he whose the earth is, and the fulness thereof, did empty himself of all to supply us,—and in a word, the most wonderful exchange be made that ever the sun saw, God for men, his life a ransom for their life. All the rare inventions and fancied stories of men come infinitely short of this. The light never saw majesty so abased and love so expressed as in this matter; and all to this purpose, that we who had undone ourselves might be made up again, and the righteousness of the law fulfilled in us. At first he made us, but it cost him nothing but a word; but now, to buy that which was taken captive by sin, and at so dear a rate,—'ye are bought with a price,' and this price more precious than the sum of heaven and earth could amount to. Suppose by some rare alchemy the earth were all converted into gold, and the heavens into precious stones, yet these corruptible and material things come as far short of this ransom as a heap of dung is unproportioned to a mass of gold or heap of jewels. Now, you that are thus bought, may ye not conclude, 'therefore we are debtors,' and whereof? Of ourselves, for we, our persons, estates, and all were sold, and all are bought with this price; therefore we are not our own, but the Lord's, and, therefore, we ought to 'glorify God in our bodies and spirits which are his,' 1 Cor. vi. 20. Should we henceforth claim an interest and propriety in ourselves? Should we have a will of our own? Should we serve ourselves with our members? O how monstrous and absurd were that! Certainly, a believing heart cannot but look upon that as the greatest indignity and vilest impiety that ever the sun shined upon. Ingratitude hath a note of ignominy, even among heathens, put upon it. They esteemed the reproach of it the compend of all reproaches, *ingratum si dixeris, omnia dixeris.* And truly it hath the most abominable visage of any vice; yea, it is all sins drawn through other* in one table. Certainly a godly heart cannot but account this execrable and detestable, henceforth to have any proper and peculiar will and pleasure, and cannot but devote itself wholly to his will and pleasure, for whose pleasure all were first created, and who then redeemed us by the blood of his Son. I wish we could have this image of ingratitude always observant to our eyes and minds when we are enticed with our lusts to study our own satisfaction. But there is another bond superadded to this, which mightily aggravates the debt. He hath given us his Spirit to dwell within, as well as his Son for us. And O the marvellous and strange effects that this Spirit hath in the favours of men! He truly repairs that image of God which sin broke down. He furnisheth the soul and supplies it in all its necessities. He is a light and life to it,—a spring of everlasting life and consolation. So that to the Spirit we owe that we are made again after his image, and the precious purchase of Christ applied unto our souls. For him hath our Saviour left to execute his latter will in

* [That is, united or interwoven.—ED.]

behalf of his children. And these things are but the first-fruits of the Spirit. Any peace, or joy, or love, or obedience, are but an earnest of that which is coming. We shall be yet more beholden to him. When the walls of flesh are taken down, he will carry forth the soul into that glorious liberty of the sons of God; and not long after he shall quicken our very dust, and raise it up in glory to the fellowship of that happiness. Now, my beloved, consider what all this tends to,—mark the inference you should make from it: 'Therefore we are debtors,' debtors indeed, under infinite obligations for infinite mercies. But what is the debt we owe? Truly it might be conceived to be some rare thing, equivalent to such unconceivable benefits. But mark what it is: 'To live after the Spirit, and not after the flesh,' to conform our affections and actions, and the tenor of our way and course to the direction of the Spirit, to have our spirits led and enlightened by the Holy Spirit, and not to follow the indictment of our flesh and carnal minds. Now, truly, it is a wonder that it is no other thing than this, for this is no other thing than what we owe to ourselves, and to our own natures, so to speak; for truly there is a conformity and suitableness of some things to the very nature of man that is beautiful,—some things are decent and becomes it, other things are undecent and uncomely, unsuitable to the very reasonable being of man, so that they put a stain and blot upon it.

Now, indeed, there is nothing can be conceived more agreeable to the very constitution of man's nature than this, that the far better and more excellent part should lead and command; and the baser and earthly part should obey and follow. That the flesh should minister and serve the spirit, 'doth not even nature itself teach it?' And yet no heavier yoke is put upon us than what our own nature hath put upon us already, which indeed is wonderful! And certainly this wonderful attempering of his laws unto the very natural exigence of the spirit of man, makes the transgression of them so much the more heinous.

Now, all these three forementioned bonds do jointly bind on this law upon man. In general, they oblige strongly to subjection and obedience to the will of God; but particularly, they have a constraining influence upon this living 'after the Spirit,' and not 'after the flesh.' Our very creation speaks this forth, when God made man after his own image, when he beautified the spirit of man with that divine similitude and likeness, in that he breathed a spirit from heaven, and took a body out of the dust, and then exalted that heavenly piece to some participation of his own nature. Doth not all this cry aloud upon us, that the order of creation is now dissolved,—that the beauty of it is marred,—that all is turned upside-down,—when men's passions and senses are their only guides, and the principles of light in their conscience are choked and stifled? Doth not all this teach us plainly that we should not 'live after the flesh,'—that we owe not so much to this brutish part as to enthrone it and empower it over us,—that it were vilest anarchy, and most intolerable confusion and usurpation, to give it the power over us, as most men do,—that there can be no order or beauty in man till the spirit be unfettered from the chains of fleshly lusts, and restored to the native dignity and pre-eminency, and so keep the body in subjection? And, indeed, Paul was so, 1 Cor. ix. 27. 'I keep my body in subjection, and beat it down,' because it is an imperious slave,—an usurping slave, —and will command, if not beaten and kept under.

Again, Christ hath put a bond upon us to this very same. He hath strengthened this obligation with a new cord, in that he gave his precious life a ransom for the souls of men. This was the principal thing he paid for—the body only being an accessory and appendix to the soul—for it is said, 'The redemption of their soul is precious, and it ceaseth for ever,' Psal. xlix. 8.; and, 'What can a man give in exchange for his soul,' Mark viii. 37. For what material thing can equalize a spirit? Many things may be had more precious and fine than the body; but all of them have no proportion to a spiritual being. Now, then, in that so dear a ransom, and so infinite a price must be given for the spirit of man, it declares the infinite worth and excellency of it above the body, and above all visible things. And here is, indeed, the greatest confirmation that can be imagined. God hath valued it; he hath put the soul of man in the balance, to find something equal in weight of dignity and worth; and when all that is in heaven and earth is put in the other scale, the soul is down-weight by far. There is such distance that there is no proportion; only the life and blood of his own Son weighs it down, and is an overvalue; and thus, in our redemption, we have a visible demonstration—as it were—of the infinite obligation of this law, not to live after that contemptible part, our flesh, but to follow after the motions and directions of an enlightened spirit; not to spend our thoughts, care, and time, upon the body, and making provision for the lusts thereof—as most men do, and all by nature are now inclined to do—but to be taken up with the immortal precious jewel that is within, how to have it rubbed and cleansed from all the filth that sin and the flesh hath cast upon it; and restored to that native beauty, the image of God in righteousness and holiness. If you, in your practice and affection, turn the scales otherwise, and make the body and things of the body, suppose the whole world, down-weight in your affection and imagination, you have plainly contradicted the just measure of the sanctuary; and, in effect, you declare that 'Christ died in vain,' and gave his life out of an error and mistake of the worth of the soul. You say he needed not have given such a price for it, seeing every day you weigh it down with every trifle of momentary fleshly satisfaction.

Lastly, The Spirit binds this fast upon us; for the soul of man he hath chosen for his habitation, and there he delights to dwell, in the heart of the contrite and humble; and this he intends to beautify and garnish, and to restore it to that primitive excellency it once had. The spirit of man is nearer his nature, and more capable of being conformed unto it; and therefore his peculiar and special work is about our spirits. First, to enlighten and convince them; then, to reform and direct them and lead them; and this binds as forcibly, and constraineth a believer certainly to resign himself to the Spirit; to study how to order his walk after that direction, and to be more and more abstracted from the satisfaction of his body; else he cannot choose but grieve the Spirit, his best friend, which alone is the fountain of joy and peace to him, and being grieved, cannot but grieve himself next.

Now, my beloved, consider, if you owe so much to the flesh, whether or not it be so steadable* and profitable unto you? And if you think it can give you a sufficient reward to compense all your pains in satisfying it, go on; but, I believe, you can reckon no good office that ever it did you, and your expectation is less. What fruit have you of all, but shame and vexation of conscience? And what can you expect but death, the last fruits of it? What then do you owe unto it? Are you debtors to its pleasure and satisfaction, which hath never done you good, and will do you eternal hurt? Consider whether you are so much bound and obliged to it as to lose your souls for it; (one of them must be,) and whether or not you be not more obliged to God the Father, and his Son Jesus Christ, to 'live after the Spirit;' though for the present it should be painful to beat down your body. You are debtors indeed, but you owe nothing to the flesh but stripes and mortification.

Sermon XXXIV.

VERSE 13.—"*For if ye live after the flesh, ye shall die: but if ye through the Spirit do mortify the deeds of the body, ye shall live.*"

THOUGH the Lord, out of his absolute sovereignty, might deal with man in such a way, as nothing should appear but his supreme will and almighty power; he might simply command obedience, and without any more persuasions, either leave men to the frowardness of their own natures, or else powerfully constrain them to their duty, yet he hath chosen that way that is most suitable to his own wisdom, and most connatural to man's nature, to lay out before him the advantages and disadvantages, and to use these as motives and persuasives of his Spirit. For since he hath by his first creation implanted in man's soul such a principle as moveth itself upon the presentation of good or evil; that this might not be in vain, he administers all the dispensations of the law and gospel in a way suitable to that, by propounding such powerful motives as may incline and persuade the heart of man. It is true,

* Or, available.—ED.

there is a secret drawing withal necessary, the pull of the Father's arm and power of the Holy Ghost; yet that which is visible or sensible to the soul is the framing of all things so as to engage it upon rational terms. It is set between two contraries, *death* and *life*,—death which it naturally abhorreth, and life which it naturally loveth. An even balance is holden up before the light of the conscience, in which obedience and sin are weighed; and it is found even to the convincing of the spirit of man, that there are as many disadvantages in the one as advantages in the other.

This was the way that God used first with man in paradise. You remember the terms run so,—'What day thou eatest thou shalt die.' He hedged him in on the one side by a promise of life, on the other by a threatening of death. And these two are very rational restraints, suited to the soul of man, and in the inward principles of it, which are a kind of instinct to that which is apprehended good or gainful.

Now, this verse runs even so in the form of words: 'If ye live after the flesh ye shall die.' You see this method is not changed under the gospel; for, indeed, it is natural to the spirit of man, and he hath now much more need of all such persuasions, because there is a great change of man's inclination to the worst side. All within is so disordered and perverse that a thousand hedges of persuasive grounds cannot do that which one might have done at first. Then they were added out of superabundance, but now out of necessity,—then they were set about man to preserve him in his natural frame and inclinations, but now they are needful to change and alter them quite, which is a kind of creation; therefore saith David, 'create in me a new spirit;' and, therefore, the gospel abounds in variety of motives and inducements, in greater variety, of far more powerful inducements, than the law. Here is that great persuasion taken from the infinite gain or loss of the soul of man, which, if any thing be able to prevail, this must do, seeing it is seconded with some natural inclination in the soul of man to seek its own gain. Yet there is a difference between the nature of such like promises and threatenings in the first covenant and in the second. In the first covenant, though life was freely promised, yet it was immediately annexed to perfect obedience as a consequent reward of it. It was firstly promised unto complete righteousness of men's persons. But in the second covenant, firstly and principally, life eternal, grace and glory is promised to Jesus Christ and his seed, antecedent to any condition or qualification upon their part. And then again, all the promises that run in way of condition, as, 'He that believeth shall not perish,' &c.; 'If ye walk after the Spirit, ye shall live.' These are all the consequent fruits of that absolute gracious disposition and resignation of grace and life to them whom Christ hath chosen. And so their believing, and walking, and obeying, cometh in principally as parts of the grace promised, and as witnesses and evidences and confirmations of that life which is already begun, and will not see an end. Besides that, by virtue of these absolute promises made to the seed of Christ, and Christ's complete performance of all conditions in their name, the promises of life are made to faith principally, which hath this peculiar virtue to carry forth the soul to another's righteousness and sufficiency, and to bottom it upon another; and in the next place, to holy walking, though mixed with many infirmities, which promise, in the first covenant, was only annexed to perfect and absolute obedience.

You heard, in the preceding verse, a strong inducement taken from the bond, debt, and duty we owe to the Spirit, to walk after it, and the want of all obligation to the flesh. Now, if honesty and duty will not suffice to persuade you, as you know in other things it would do with any honest man, plain equity is a sufficient bond to him. Yet, consider what the apostle subjoins from the damage, and from the advantage which may of itself be the topics of persuasion, and serves to drive in the nail of debt and duty to the head. If you will not take with this debt you owe to the Spirit, but still conceive there is some greater obligation lying on you, to care for your bodies and satisfy them, then, I say, behold the end of it, what fruit you must one day reap of the flesh and service of sin: 'If ye live after the flesh, you shall die.' But, then, consider the fruit you shall reap of the Spirit and holy walking: 'you shall live.' It is true, the flesh may flatter you more for the present, but the end of it will be bitter as death, *amplectitur ut strangulet*, "the flesh embraces you that it may strangle you." And so if you knew all well you would not think you owed it any thing but enmity and hatred and mortification. If your duty will not move you, let the love of yourselves and your souls persuade you, for it is an irrepealable statute: 'The wages of sin is death.' Every way you choose to fulfil the lusts of your flesh, and to make provision for it, neglecting the eternal welfare of your souls, certainly it shall prove to you 'the tree of the knowledge of good and evil;' it shall be as the forbidden fruit, which instead of performing that which was promised will bring forth death,—the eternal separation of the soul from God. Adam's sin was a breviary or epitome of the multiplied and enlarged sins of mankind. You may see in this tragedy all your fortunes, (so to speak,)—you may behold in it the flattering insinuations and deceitful promises of sin and Satan, who is a liar and murderer from the beginning, and murdered man at first by lying to him. You find the hook covered over with the varnished bait of an imaginary life and happiness: satisfaction promised to the eye, to the taste, and to the mind. And upon these enticements, man bewitched and withdrawn from his God, after these vain and empty shadows, which, when he catched hold upon, he himself was caught and laid hold upon by the wrath of God,—by death and all the miseries before it or after it. Now, here is the map of the world,—for all that is in the world is but a larger volume of that same kind, 'the lust of the eyes, the lust of the flesh, and the pride of life!' Albeit they have been known and found to be the notablest and grossest deceivers; and every man, after he hath spent his days in pursuit and labour for them, is constrained to acknowledge at length, though too late, that all that is in the world is but an imposture, a delusion, a dream, and worse; yet every man hearkens after these same flatteries and lies, that hath cast down so many wounded, and made so many strong ones to fall by them. Every man trusts the world and his own flesh, as if they were of good report and of known integrity. And this is men's misery, that no man will learn wisdom upon others' expenses, upon the woful and tragical example of so many others, but go on as confidently now, after the discovery of these deceivers, as if this were the first time they had made such promises, and used such fair words to men. Have they not been these six thousand years almost deluding the world? And have we not as many testimonies of their falsehood, as there have been persons in all ages before us? After Adam hath tasted of this tree of pleasure, and found another fruit growing on it, and that is death, should the posterity be so mad as to be meddling still with the forbidden tree? And wherefore forbidden? Because destructive to ourselves.

Know then and consider, beloved in the Lord, that you shall reap no other thing of all your labours and endeavours after the flesh, all your toiling and perplexing cares, all your excessive pains in the making provision for your lusts, and caring for the body only, you shall reap no other harvest of all, but death and corruption. Death, you think that is a common lot, and you cannot eschew it however; nay, but the death here meant is of another sort, in respect of which you may call death life. It is the everlasting destruction of the soul from the presence of God and the glory of his power. It is the falling of that infinite weight of the wrath of the Lamb upon you, in respect of which, mountains and hills will be thought light, and men would rather wish to be covered with them, Rev. vi. 16. Suppose, now, you could swim in a river of delights and pleasures, (which yet is given to none; for truly, upon a just reckoning, it will be found that the anxiety, and grief, and bitterness, that is intermingled with all earthly delights, swallows up the sweetness of them,) yet it will but carry you down ere you be aware, into the sea of death and destruction, as the fish that swim and sport for a while in Jordan, are carried down into the Dead sea of Sodom, where they are presently suffocated and extinguished;* or, as a malefactor is carried through a pleasant

* [Mr. Binning had the authority of Jerome for saying this. When speaking of the Dead sea, or as it is styled in Scripture, the Salt sea, his words are: Denique si Jordanis auctus imbribus pisces illuc influens rapuerit, statim moriuntur, et pinguibus aquis supernatant. "In fine, if the Jordan, which runs into it, should when swollen with rain, carry any fish along with it, they die immediately, and float upon the surface of the bituminous waters." (Hieron. Comment. in Ezek. cap. xlvii.) He also states that no living creature of any description was to be found in the Dead sea. (Comment. in Joel cap. ii.) According to Volney, clouds of smoke are still observed to issue from this lake; and he represents the lava and pumice stones which have been thrown upon its

palace to the gallows; so men walk through the delights of their flesh, to their own endless torment and destruction.

Seeing then, my beloved, that your sins and lusts which you are inclined and accustomed to, will certainly kill you, if you entertain them; then nature itself would teach you the law of self-defence,—to kill, ere you be killed; to kill sin, ere it kill you,—to mortify the deeds and lusts of the body, which abound among you, or they will certainly mortify you, that is, make you die. Now, if self-love could teach you this, which the love of God cannot persuade you to; yet it is well, for being once led unto God, and moved to change your course, upon the fear and apprehension of the infinite danger that will ensue. Certainly if you were but a little acquainted with the sweetness of this life, and goodness of your God, you would find the power of the former argument *a debito*, from debt and duty, upon your spirit. Let this once lead you unto God, and you will not want that which will constrain you to abide, and never to depart from him.

If you mortify the deeds of the body, you shall live. As sin decays, you increase and grow; as sins die, your souls live, and it shall be a sure pledge to you of that eternal life. And though this be painful and laborious, yet consider, that it is but the cutting off of a rotten member, that would corrupt the whole body, and the want of it will never maim or mutilate the body; for you shall live perfectly when sin is perfectly expired, and out of life; and according as sin is nearer expiring, and nearer the grave, your souls are nearer that endless life. If this do not move us, what can be said next? What shall he do more to his vineyard?

Sermon XXXV.

VERSES 13, 14.—"*For if ye live after the flesh, ye shall die: but if ye through the Spirit do mortify the deeds of the body, ye shall live. For as many as are led by the Spirit of God, they are the sons of God.*"

THE life and being of many things consists in union;—separate them, and they remain not the same, or they lose their virtue. It is much more thus in Christianity, the power and life of it consists in the union of these things that God hath conjoined; so that if any man pretend to one thing of it, and neglect the other, he hath really none of them. And to hold to the subject in hand, there are three things, which, joined together in the hearts of Christians, have a great deal of force: the duty of a Christian, and his reward, and his dignity. His work and labour seems hard and unpleasant, when considered alone, but the reward sweetens it, when it is jointly believed. His duty seems too high, and his labour great, yet the consideration of the real dignity he is advanced unto, and privilege he has received, will raise up the spirit to great and high attempts, and to sustain great labours. Mortification is the work and labour; life, eternal life, is the reward. Following the Spirit is the Christian's duty, but to be the son of God, that is his dignity.

Mortification sounds very harsh at first. The hearts of men say, 'It is a hard saying, who can bear it?' And indeed I cannot deny but it is so to our corrupt nature; and therefore so holden out in Scripture. The words chosen to press it express much pain and pains, much torment and labour. It is not so easy and trivial a business to forsake sin, or subdue it, as many think, who only think it easy because they have never tried it. It is a circumcision of the foreskin of the heart;

banks, to be likewise indubitable indications of the agency of fire. The water however of what Milton describes as—

"That bituminous lake where Sodom flam'd,"

—though excessively bitter, and so heavy that the most impetuous waves can scarcely ruffle its surface, is now perfectly transparent. M. de Chateaubriand, who mentions this, also informs us that he heard a noise upon the lake about midnight, which the Bethlehemites who accompanied him told him "proceeded from legions of small fish which come and leap about on the shore."—(Travels, vol. i. p. 397. Lond. 1812.) He adds, "M. Seetzen, who is yet travelling in Arabia, observed in the Dead sea, neither the helix nor the muscle, but found a few shell snails."—Ibid. —ED.]

and you know how it disabled a whole city, (Gen. xxxiv.) and how it enraged the heart of a tender mother, Exod. iv. 26. It is the excision or cutting off a member, and these the most dear and precious, be it the right hand or right foot, which is a living death, as it were, even to kill a man while he is alive. It is a new birth, and the pains and throes of the birth are known. Regeneration certainly hath a travailing pain within it, insomuch that Paul travailed in pain till it were accomplished in these, Gal. iv. 19. Though men conceive sin in pleasure, yet they cannot be rid of that deadly burden without throes and pains; and to half this work, or to be remiss or negligent in it, is as foolish and unwise as for a child to stay long in the place of breaking forth, as the Lord complains of Ephraim, Hos. xiii. 13. 'He is an unwise son, for he should not stay long in the place of the breaking forth of children.' It is one of the greatest follies, not to labour by all means to be rid of the incumbrances of sin. Much violence offered to it, and a total resignation of ourselves to God, may be great pain, but it is short pain; then the pleasure is greater and continues: but now Christians lengthen their pain, and draw out their cross and vexation to a great extent, because they deal negligently in the business, they suffer the Canaanites to live, and these are thorns and briers in their sides continually. Then this business is called *mortification*, as the word is here, and Col. iii. 5, which imports a higher degree of pain, for the agonies of death are terrible; and to hold it out yet more, the most painful and lingering kind of death is chosen to express it, *crucifixion*, Gal. v. 24. Now, indeed, that which makes the forsaking of sin so grievous to flesh and blood, is the engagements of the soul to it, the oneness that is between it and our natures, as they are now fallen; for you know pain ariseth upon the dissolution or division of any thing that is continued or united; and these things that are so nearly conjoined, it is hard to separate them without much violence. And truly, as the kingdom of heaven suffers violence, so we must offer violence to ourselves, to our lusts and inclinations, who are almost ourselves: and if you would be truly Christians, this must be your business and employment, to cut off these things that are dearest unto you, to cast out the very idols your hearts sacrifice unto: and if there be any thing more one with you than another, to endeavour to break the bond with that, and to be at the furthest distance from it. It is easy to persuade men to forsake some sins and courses that they are not much inclined to, and find not much pleasure or profit by them. You may do that and be but dead in sins; but if you aim at true mortification indeed, you would consider what are the chief idols and predominant inclinations of your heart, and as to set yourself impartially against all known, so particularly against the most beloved sin; because it interrupts most the communion of God, and separates from your Beloved, and the dearer it be the more dangerous certainly it is.

But to encourage and hearten you to this, I would have you look back to that former victory that Christ hath gained in our name, and look about to the assistance you have for the present, the Spirit to help you. Truly, my beloved, this will be a dead business, if you be not animated and quickened by these considerations,—that Christ died to sin and lived to God, and that in this he was a public person representing you, that so you may conclude with Paul, 'I am crucified with Christ,' Gal. ii. 20. 'We are buried with him by baptism into his death,' Rom. vi. 4. Consider that mystical union with Christ crucified, and life shall spring out of his cross, out of his grave, to kill sin in you,—that the great business is done already, and victory gained in our Head, 'This is our victory, even faith.' Believe, and then you have overcome, before you overcome; and this will help you to overcome in your own persons. And then, consider and look round about to the strong helper you have, the Spirit: 'If ye through the Spirit mortify,' &c. Stronger is he that is in you than he that is in the world. Though he does not vent all his power to you, yet you may believe that there is a secret latent virtue in the seed of grace, that it cannot be whole overcome or conquered; and there is one engaged in the warfare with us who will never leave us nor forsake us, who of set purpose withdraweth his help now and then to discover our weakness to us, that we may cleave the faster to him, who never letteth sin get any power or gather any strength, but out of wisdom to make the final victory the more glorious. In a word, he leads us through weaknesses, infirmities, faintings, wrestlings, that his strength may be perfected in weakness,—that when we are weak, then we may be strongest in him, 2 Cor. xii. 9. Our duty then is, to follow this Spirit wheresoever he leadeth us. Christ, the captain of our salvation, when he went to heaven, sent the Spirit to be our guider, to lead us thither where he is; and therefore we should resign and give up ourselves to his guidance and direction. The nature of a creature is dependence, so the very essence of a Christian consists in dependence and subordination to the Spirit of God. Nature itself would teach them that want wisdom to commit themselves to those that have it, and not to carry the reins of their own life themselves.

Truly, not only the sense of our own imperfection, of our folly and ignorance in these things that belong to life, should make us willing to yield ourselves over to the Spirit of God, as blind men to their leader, as children to their nurses, as orphans to their tutors;* but also, because the Spirit is made our tutor and leader. Christ our Father hath left us to the Spirit in his latter-will; and, therefore, as we have absolute necessity, so he hath both willingness and ability, because it is his office. 'O Lord, I know,' saith Jeremiah, 'that the way of man is not in himself: it is not in man that walketh to direct his steps,' Jer. x. 23. O it were a great point of wisdom thus to know our ignorance and folly, and this is the great qualification of Christ's disciples, simple as children, as little children, as void of conceit of their own wisdom, Mark x. 15. And this alone capacitates the soul to receive the impressions of wisdom; as an empty table is fittest to write upon, so a soul emptied of itself: whereas self-conceit draweth a number of foolish senseless draughts in the mind that it cannot receive the true image of wisdom. Thus, then, when a soul finds that it hath misled itself, being misguided by the wild-fire of its lusts, and hath hardly escaped perishing and falling headlong in the pit, this disposes the soul to a willing resignation of itself to one wiser and powerfuller, the Spirit of God; and so he giveth the Spirit the string of his affections and judgment to lead him by, and he walketh willingly in that way to eternal life, since his heart was enlarged with so much knowledge and love. And now, having given up yourselves thus, you would carefully eye your Leader, and attend all his motions, that you may conform yourself to them. Whensoever the Spirit pulleth you by the heart, draweth at your conscience, to drive you to prayer, or any such duty, do not resist that pull, do not quench the Spirit, lest he let you alone, and do not call you, nor speak to you. If you fall out thus with your Leader, then you must guide yourselves, and truly you will guide it into the pit, if left to yourselves. Therefore make much of all the impulses of your conscience, of all the touches and inward motions of light and affection, to entertain these, and draw them forth in meditation and action, for these are nothing else but the Spirit your leader plucking at you to follow him; and if you sit when he riseth to walk, if you neglect such warnings, then you may grieve him, and this cannot but in the end be bitterness to you. Certainly, many Christians are guilty in this, and prejudge themselves of the present comfort and benefit of this inward anointing, that teacheth all things, and of this bosom guide that leadeth in all truth; because they are so heavy and lumpish to be led after him: they drive slowly, and take very much pressure and persuasion to any duty; whereas we should accustom ourselves to willing and ready obedience upon the least signification of his mind. Yea, and which is worse, we often resist the Holy Ghost. He draweth, and we hold beloved sins;—he pulleth, and we pull back from the most spiritual duties. There is so much perverseness and frowardness yet in our natures, that there needs the almighty draught of his arm to make it straight, as there is need of infinite grace to pardon it.

Now, my beloved, if you have in your desires and affections resigned yourselves over to the guidance of this Spirit, and this be your real and sincere endeavour to follow it, and in as far as you are carried back, or contrary, by temptation and corruption, or retarded in your motion, it is your lamentation before the Lord,—I say unto you, cheer your hearts, and lift them up in the belief of this privilege conferred upon you, you 'are the sons of God,'—for he giveth this tutor and pedagogue to none but to his own children: 'As many as are led by the Spirit of God,

* [That is, guardians.—Ed.]

are the sons of God.' Suppose you cannot exactly follow his motions, but are often driven out or turned back, yet hath not the Spirit the hold of your heart? Are you not detained by the cord of your judgment and the law of your mind? And is there not some chain fastened about your heart which maketh it outstrip the practice by desires and affections? You are the sons of God. That is truly the greatest dignity and highest privilege, in respect of which, all relations may blush and hide their faces. What are all the splendid and glistering titles among men but empty shows and evanishing sounds in respect of this? To be called the son of a gentleman, of a nobleman, of a king, how much do the sons of men pride themselves in it? But, truly, that putteth no intrinsic dignity in the persons themselves,—it is a miserable poverty to borrow praise from another; and truly he that boasts of his parentage, *aliena laudat non sua*, he praiseth that which is another's, not his own. But this dignity is truly a dignity, it puts intrinsic worth in the person, and puts a more excellent spirit in them than that which is in the world, as is said of Caleb; and, besides, it entitles to the greatest happiness imaginable.

Sermon XXXVI.

VERSES 14, 15.—"*For as many as are led by the Spirit of God, they are the sons of God. For ye have not received the spirit of bondage again to fear,*" *&c.*

CHILDREN do commonly resemble their parents, not only in the outward proportion and feature of their countenances, but also in the disposition and temper of their spirits, and generally they are inclined to imitate the customs and carriage of their parents, so that they sometimes may be accounted the very living images of such persons, and in them men are thought to outlive themselves. Now, indeed, they that are the sons of God are known by this character, that they are led by the Spirit of God. And there is the more necessity and the more reason, too, of this resemblance of God and imitation of him in his children, because that very divine birth that they have from heaven consists in the renovation of their natures and assimilation to the divine nature; and, therefore, they are possessed with an inward principle that carries them powerfully towards a conformity with their heavenly Father; and it becometh their great study and endeavour to observe all the dispositions and carriage of their heavenly Father, which are so honourable and high, and suitable to himself, that they at least may breathe and halt* after the imitation of him. Therefore our Lord exhorts us, and taketh a domestic example and familiar pattern to persuade us the more by, 'Be ye perfect, as your heavenly Father is perfect,' Matth. v. 48. And there is one perfection he especially recommends for our imitation, mercifulness and compassion towards men, opposed to the violence, fury, and implacableness, to the oppression, and revenge, and hatred that abounds among men, Luke vi. 36. And, generally, in all his ways of holiness and purity, of goodness and mercy, we ought to be followers of him as dear children, who are not only obliged by the common law of sympathy between parents and children, but, moreover, engaged by the tender affection that he carrieth to us, Eph. v. 1. Now, because God is high as heaven, and his ways and thoughts and dispositions are infinitely above us, the pattern seems to be so far out of sight that it is given over as desperate by many to attempt any conformity to it. Therefore it hath pleased the Lord to put his own Spirit within his own children, to be a bosom-pattern and example; and it is our duty to resign ourselves to his leading and direction. The Spirit brings the copy near hand us, and though we cannot attain, yet we should follow after. Though we cannot make out the lesson, yet we should be scribbling at it, and the more we exercise ourselves this way, setting the Spirit's direction before our eyes, the more perfect shall we be.

It is high time, indeed, to pretend to this, to be a son or a daughter of God. It is a higher word than if a man could deduce his genealogy from an uninterrupted line of a thousand kings and princes. There is more honour, true honour, in it, and

* [Or attempt to walk.—ED.]

profit too. It is that which enriches the poorest, and ennobles the basest, inconceivably beyond all the imaginary degrees of men. Now, my beloved, this is the great design of the gospel, to bestow this incomparable privilege upon you, 'to become the sons of God.' But it is sad to think how many souls scarce think upon it, and how many delude themselves in it. But consider, that as many as are the sons of God, are led by the Spirit of God;—they have gotten a new leader and guide, other than their own fancy or humour, which once they followed in the ignorance of their hearts. It is lamentable to conceive how the most part of us are acted,* and driven, and carried headlong, rather than gently led, by our own carnal and corrupt inclinations. Men pretending to Christianity, yet hurried away with every self-pleasing object, as if they were not masters of themselves, furiously agitated by violent lusts, miscarried continually against the very dictates of their own reason and conscience. And I fear there is too much of these even in those who have more reason to assume this honourable title of sonship. I know not how we are exceedingly addicted to self-pleasing in every thing. Whatsoever our fancy or inclination suggests to us, that we must do without more bands, if it be not directly sinful. Whatsoever we apprehend, that we must vent and speak it out, though to little or no edification. Like that of Solomon, we deny our hearts nothing they desire, except the grossness of it restrain us. Now, certainly if we knew what we are called to, who are the sons of God, we could not but disengage more with ourselves, even in lawful things, and give over the conduct of our hearts and ways to the Spirit of our Father, whom we may be persuaded of, that he will lead us in the ways of pleasantness and peace.

Now, the special and peculiar operations of the Spirit are expressed in the following words. There are some workings of the Spirit of God that are but introductory and subservient to more excellent works; and, therefore, they are transient, not appointed to continue long, for they are not his great intendment. Of this kind are those terrible representations of sin and wrath, of the justice of God, which put the soul in a fear, a trembling fear; and while such a soul is kept within the apprehension of sin and judgment, it is shut up, as it were, in bondage. Now, though it be true, that in the conversion of a sinner, there is always something of this in more or less degrees; yet, because this is not the great design of the gospel, to put men in fear, but rather to give them confidence; nor the great intendment of God in the dispensation of the law, to bring a soul in bondage under terror, but rather, by the gospel, to free them from that bondage; therefore he hath reason to express it thus: 'Ye have not received the spirit of bondage again to fear,' &c. But there are other operations of the Spirit, which are chiefly intended, and principally bestowed, as the great gift of our Father, to express his bounty and goodness towards us; and from these he is called the Spirit of adoption, and the Spirit of intercession. The Spirit of adoption, not only in regard of that witness-bearing and testification to our consciences of God's love and favour, and our interest in it, as in the next verse, but also in regard of that child-like disposition of reverence and love and respect that he begets in our hearts towards God, as our Father. And from both these flows this next work, 'crying, Abba, Father,' aiding and assisting us in presenting our necessities to our Father, making this the continued vent of the heart in all extremities, to pour out all that burthens us in our Father's bosom. And this gives marvellous ease to the heart, and releases it from the bondage of carefulness and anxiety, which it may be subject to, after the soul is delivered from the fear and bondage of wrath.

Let us speak, then, to these in order. The first working of the Spirit is, *to put a man in fear of himself*, and such a fear as mightily straitens and embondages the soul of man. And this, though in itself it be neither so pleasant nor excellent as to make it come under the notion of any gift from God, it having rather the nature of a torment and punishment, and being some sparkle† of hell already kindled in the conscience; yet, hath made it beautiful and seasonable in its use and end, because he makes it to usher in the pleasant and refreshing sight of a Saviour, and the report

* [That is, governed. "Most people in the world are *acted* by levity and humour." *South's Sermons.*—Ed.]

† [That is, spark.—Ed.]

of God's love to the world in him. It is true, all men are in bondage to sin and Satan, and shut up in the darkness of ignorance and unbelief, and bound in the fetters of their own lusts, which are as the chains that are put about malefactors before they go to prison. 'He that commits sin, is a servant of sin,' John viii. 34. And to be a servant of sin is slavery under the most cruel tyrant. All these things are, yet how few souls do apprehend it seriously, or are weary of their prison! How few groan to be delivered! Nay, the most part account it only liberty, to hate true delivery as bondage. But some there are, whose eyes the Spirit of God opens, and lets them see their bondage and slavery, and how they are concluded under the most heavy and weighty sentence that ever was pronounced,—the curse and wrath of the everliving God, that there is no way to flee from it, or escape it, for any thing they can do or know. Now, indeed, this serious discovery cannot choose but make the heart of a man to tremble, as David, 'My flesh trembleth for fear of thee; and I am afraid of thy judgments,' Psal. cxix. 120. Such a serious representation will make the stoutest and proudest heart to fall down, and faint for fear of that infinite intolerable weight of deserved wrath, and then the soul is in a sensible bondage, that before was in a real, but insensible bondage,—then it is environed about with bitter accusations, with dreadful challenges,—then the law of God arrests and confines the soul within the bounds of its own accusing conscience. And this is some previous representation of that eternal imprisonment and banishment from the presence of God. Albeit many of you are free from this fear, and enjoy a kind of liberty to serve your own lusts, and are not sensible of any thraldom of your spirits, yet certainly the Lord will sometime arrest you, and bring you to this spiritual bondage; when he shall make the iniquities of your heels encompass you about, and the curses of his law surround you. When your conscience accuseth, and God condemneth, it may be too late, and out of date.

Alas! then what will you do, who now put your conscience by,* and will not hearken to it, or be put in fear by any thing which can be represented to you? We do not desire to put you in fear, where no fear is; but where there is infinite cause of fear, and when it is possible that fear may introduce faith, and be the forerunner of these glad tidings that will compose the soul. We desire only you may know what bondage you are really into, whether it be observed or not, that you may fear, lest you be enthralled in the chains of everlasting darkness, and so may be persuaded to flee from it before it be irrecoverable. What a vain and empty sound is the gospel of liberty by a Redeemer, to the most part who do not feel their bondage? Who believes its report, or cares much for it—because it is necessity that casts a beauty and lustre upon it, or takes the scales off our eyes, and opens our closed ears?

Now for you, who either are, or have been, detained in this bondage, under the fearful apprehension of the wrath of God, and the sad remembrance of your sins, know that this is not the prime intent and grand business, to torment you, as it were, before the time. There is some other more beautiful and satisfying structure to be raised out of this foundation. I would have you improve it thus, to commend the necessity, the absolute necessity, of a Redeemer, and to make him beautiful in your eyes. Do not dwell upon that, as if it were the ultimate or last work, but know that you are called in this rational way, to come out of yourselves into this glorious liberty of the sons of God, purchased by Christ, and revealed in the gospel. Know, 'you have not received the spirit of bondage' only 'to fear,' but to drive you to faith in a Saviour. And then you ought so to walk, as not to return to that former thraldom of the fear of wrath, but believe his love.

* [That is, set conscience aside.—Ed.]

Sermon XXXVII.

VERSES 14, 15.—"*For as many as are led by the Spirit of God, they are the sons of God. For ye have not received the spirit of bondage again to fear; but ye have received the Spirit of adoption, whereby we cry, Abba, Father.*"

THE life of Christianity, take it in itself, is the most pleasant and joyful life that can be, exempted from those fears and cares, those sorrows and anxieties, that all other lives are subject unto; for this of necessity must be the force and efficacy of true religion, if it be indeed true to its name, to disburden and ease the heart, and fill it with all manner of consolation. Certainly it is the most rich subject, and most completely furnished with all variety of delights to entertain a soul, that can be imagined. Yet, I must confess, while we consult with the experience and practice of Christians, this bold assertion seems to be much weakened, and too much ground is given to confirm the contrary misapprehensions of the world, who take it to be a sullen, melancholic, and disconsolate life, attended with many fears and sorrows. It is, alas! too evident, that many Christians are kept in bondage, almost all their lifetime, through fear of eternal death. How many dismal representations of sin and wrath, are in the souls of some Christians, which keep them in much thraldom? At least, who is it that is not once and often brought in bondage after conversion, and made to apprehend fearfully their own estate, who hath such constant uninterrupted peace and joy in the Holy Ghost, or lies under such direct beams of divine favour, but it is sometimes eclipsed, and their souls filled with the darkness of horror and terror? And truly the most part taste not so much sweetness in religion as makes them incessant and unwearied in the ways of godliness. Yet, notwithstanding of all this, we must vindicate Christianity itself, and not impute these things unto it which are the infirmities and faults of the followers of it, who do not improve it unto such an use, or use it so far as in itself it is capable. Indeed, it is true that often we are brought to fear again, yet withal it is certain that our allowance is larger, and that we have received the Spirit, not to put us in bondage again to fear, but rather to seal to our hearts that love of God, which may not only expel fear but bring in joy. I wish that this were deeply considered by all of us, that there is such a life as this attainable,—that the word of God doth not deceive us in promising fair things which it cannot perform, but that there is a certain reality in the life of Christianity, in that peace and joy, tranquillity and serenity of mind that is holden out, and that some have really found it, and do find it; and that the reason why all of us do not find it in experience, is not because it is not, but because we have so little apprehension of it and diligence after it. It is strange that all men who have pursued satisfaction in the things of this life, being disappointed, and one generation witnessing this to another, and one person to another, that, notwithstanding, men are this day as fresh in the pursuit of that, as big in the expectations as ever. And yet, in this business of religion, and the happiness to be found in it, though the oracles of God in all ages have testified from heaven how certain and possible it is, though many have found it in experience and left it on record to others, there is so slender belief of the reality and certainty of it, and so slack pursuit of it, as if we did not believe it at all. Truly, my beloved, there is a great mistake in this, and it is general too. All men apprehend other things more feasible and attainable than personal holiness and happiness in it; but truly, I conceive there is nothing in the world so practicable as this,—nothing made so easy, so certain to a soul that really minds it.

Let us take it so then; the fault is not religion's, that those who profess it are subject to so much fear and care, and disquieted with so much sorrow. It is rather because Christianity doth not sink into the hearts and souls of men, but only puts a tincture on their outside, or because the faith of divine truths is so superficial, and the consideration of them so slight, that they cannot have much efficacy and influence on the heart, to quiet and compose it. Is it any wonder that some souls be subject again to the bondage of fear and terror when they do not stand in awe to sin? Much liberty to sin will certainly embondage the spirit of a Christian to fear. Suppose a believer in Jesus Christ be exempted from the hazard of condemnation, yet he is the greatest fool in the world that would, on that account, venture on satisfaction to his lusts. For though it be true that he be not in danger of eternal wrath, yet he may find so much present wrath in his conscience as may make him think it was a foolish bargain. He may lose so much of the sweetness of the peace and joy of God as all the pleasures of sin cannot compense. Therefore to the end that you whose souls are once pacified by the blood of Christ, and composed by his word of promise, may enjoy that constant rest and tranquillity as not to be enthralled again to your old fears and terrors, I would advise and recommend to you these two things:—One is, that you would be much in the study of that allowance which the promises of Christ afford. Be much in the serious apprehension of the gospel, and certainly your doubts and fears would evanish at one puff of such a rooted and established meditation. Think what you are called to, not 'to fear' again, but to love rather, and honour him as a Father. And, then, take heed to walk suitably and preserve your seal of adoption unblotted, unrusted. You would study so to walk as you may not cast dirt upon it, or open any gap in the conscience for the re-entry of these hellish-like fears and dreadful apprehensions of God. Certainly, it is impossible to preserve the spirit in freedom if a man be not watchful against sin and corruption. David prays, 're-establish me with thy free Spirit;' as if his spirit had been abased, embondaged, and enthralled by the power of that corruption. If you would have your spirits kept free from the fear of wrath, study to keep them free from the power of sin, for that is but a fruit of this; and it is most suitable that the soul that cares not to be in bondage to sinful lusts, should, by the righteousness of God, tempered with love and wisdom, be brought under the bondage he would not, that is, of fear and terror; for by this means the Lord makes him know how evil the first is, by the bitterness of the second.

It is usual on such a scripture as this, to propound many questions, and debate many practical cases; as, whether a soul after believing can be under legal bondage; and wherein these differ, the bondage of a soul after believing, and in its first conversion; and how far that bondage of fear is preparatory to faith; and many such like. But I choose rather to hold forth the simple and naked truth for your edification, than put you upon to entertain you in such needless janglings and contentions. All I desire to say to a soul in bondage, is, to exhort him to come to the Redeemer, and to consider that his case calls and cries for a delivery. Come, I say, and he shall find rest and liberty to his soul. All I would say to souls delivered from this bondage, is, to request and beseech them to live in a holy fear of sin, and jealousy over themselves, that so they may not be readily brought under the bondage of the fear of wrath again. Perfect love casts out the fear of hell, but perfect love brings in the fear of sin. Ye that love the Lord, hate ill; and if ye hate it, ye will fear it in this state of infirmity and weakness, wherein we are. And if at any time ye, through negligence and carelessness of walking, lose the comfortable evidence of the Father's love, and be reduced again to your old prison of legal terror, do not despair for that, do not think that such a thing could not befall a child of God, and from that ground do not raze former foundations; for the scripture saith not, that whosoever believes once in Christ, and receives the Spirit of adoption, cannot fear again; for we see it otherwise in David, in Heman, in Job, &c., all holy saints. But the scripture saith, Ye have not received the spirit of bondage for that end, to fear again. It is not the allowance of your Father. Your allowance is better and larger, if you knew it, and did not sit below it.

Now, the great gift, and large allowance of our Father, is expressed in the next words, 'But ye have received the Spirit of adoption,' &c.; which Spirit of adoption is a Spirit of intercession, to make us cry to God as our Father. These are two gifts, adoption, or the privilege of sons, and the Spirit of adoption revealing the love and mercy of God to the heart, and framing it to a soul-like disposition. Compare the two states together, and it is a marvellous change,—a rebel condemned, and then pardoned, and then adopted to be a son of God,—a sinner under bondage, a bond slave to sin and Satan, not only freed from that intolerable bondage, but advanced to this liberty, to be made a son of God. This will be the continued wonder of eternity, and that whereabout the song of angels and saints will be. Accursed rebels expecting nothing but present death, sinners arraigned and sentenced before his tribunal, and already tasting hell in their consciences, and in fear of eternal perishing, not only to be delivered from all that, but to be dignified with this privilege, to be the sons of God; to be taken from the gibbet to be crowned! That is the great mystery of wisdom and grace revealed in the gospel, the proclaiming whereof will be the joint labour of all the innumerable companies above for all eternity. Now, if you ask how this estate is attainable, himself tells us, John i. 12, 'As many as believed (or received) him, to them he gave the privilege to be the sons of God.' The way is made plain and easy. Christ the Son of God, the natural and eternal Son of God, became the Son of man. To facilitate this, he hath taken on the burden of man's sin, the chastisement of our peace; and so of the glorious Son of God he became like the wretched and accursed sons of men; and therefore God hath proclaimed in the gospel, not only an immunity and freedom from wrath, to all that in the sense of their own misery cordially receive him as he is offered, but the unspeakable privilege of sonship and adoption for his sake, who became our elder brother, Gal. iv. 4, 5. Men that want children, use to supply their want by adopting some beloved friend in the place of a son; and this is a kind of supply of nature for the comfort of them that want. But it is strange, that God having a Son so glorious, the very character of his person, and brightness of his glory, in whom he delighted from eternity,—strange, I say, that he should in a manner lose and give away his only begotten Son, that he might by his means adopt others, poor despicable creatures, yea, rebellious, to be his sons and daughters. Certainly, this is an act infinitely transcending nature,—such an act that hath an unsearchable mystery in it, into which angels desire to look, and never cease looking, because they never see the bottom of it. It was not out of indigency he did it, not for any need he had of us, or comfort expected from us, but absolutely for our necessity and consolation, that he might have upon whom to pour the riches of his grace.

Sermon XXXVIII.

VERSE 15.—"*But ye have received the Spirit of adoption, whereby we cry, Abba, Father.*"

'BEHOLD what manner of love the Father hath bestowed upon us, that we should be called the sons of God,' 1 John iii. 1. It is a wonderful expression of love to advance his own creatures, not only infinitely below himself, but far below other creatures, to such a dignity. Lord, what is man that thou so magnifiest him! But it surpasseth wonder, that rebellious creatures, his enemies, should have, not only their rebellions freely pardoned, but this privilege of sonship bestowed upon them, that he should take enemies, and make sons of them, and not only sons, but heirs, co-heirs with his own only begotten Son. And then, how he makes them sons, is as wonderful as the thing itself, that he should make his own Son our brother, 'bone of our bone and flesh of our flesh;' and make him spring out as a branch or rod out of the dry stem of Jesse, who himself was the root of all mankind. This is the way; God sent his Son, made of a woman, under the law, that we might receive the adoption of sons, Gal. iv. 5. The house of heaven marries with the earth, with them who have their foundation in the dust; the chief heir of that heavenly family joineth in kindred with our base and obscure family, and by this means we are made of kin to God. 'But of him are ye in Christ Jesus,' 1 Cor. i. 30. It behoved Christ, in a manner to lose his own sonship as to men, to have it so veiled and darkened by the superadded interest in us, and his nearness to us. He was so properly a Son of man, subject to all human infirmities, except sin, that without eyes of faith, men could not perceive that he was the Son of God. And by this wonderful exchange are we made the sons of God. Whoever, in the apprehension of their own enmity and distance from God, receive Christ Jesus, offered as the peace, the bond of union between the two families of heaven and earth, that were at an infinite odds and distance; whoever (I say) believes thus in him, and flies to him, desiring to lay down the weapons of their warfare, their peace is not only made by that marriage which Christ made with our nature, but they are blessed with this power and privilege, to be the sons and daughter of the Most High. And from thence you may conclude, that if God be your Father, you can want nothing that is good. But the determination of what is good for you, whether in spiritual enlargements, or in the things of this life, you must refer to his wisdom: for his love indeed is strong as death, nothing can quench it. In the point of reality and constancy, there is nothing to shadow it out among men. The love of women is earnest and vehement, but that is nothing to it, (Isa. xlix. 15;) for they may forget, but he cannot. Yet his love is not a foolish dotage, like man's that is often miscarried with fancy and lust; but it is a rational and wise affection, administered and expressed with infinite reason and wisdom; and therefore, he chooses rather to profit us than to please us in his dealings. And we who are not so fit to judge and discern our own good, should commit all to his fatherly and wise Providence. Therefore, if you be tempted to anxiety and carefulness of mind, either through the earthliness of your dispositions, or the present straits of the time, you who have resigned yourself to Jesus Christ, should call to mind that your heavenly Father careth for you. And what need you care too? Why not use your lawful callings, be diligent in them? This is not to prejudge that; but if you believe in God, then you are obliged by that profession to abate from the superfluous tormenting thoughtfulness that is good for nothing but to make you more miserable than your troubles can make you, and to make you miserable before you be miserable, to anticipate your sorrows. If you say, God is your Father, you are tied to devolve yourselves over on him, and trust in his good will and faithfulness, and to sit down quietly as children that have parents to provide for them.

Now, the other gift is great too, 'the Spirit of adoption;' and because ye are sons, therefore hath he given you 'the Spirit of his Son,' saith this apostle, Gal. iv. 6. And so it is a kind of consectary* of the great privilege and blessed estate of adoption. They who adopt children, use to give them some kind of token to express their love to them. But as the Lord is higher than all, and this privilege to be his son or child is the greatest dignity imaginable, so this gift of his Spirit suits the greatness and glory and love of our Father. It is a father's gift indeed, a gift suitable to our heavenly Father. If a father that is tender of the education of his child, and would desire nothing so much as that he might be of a virtuous and gracious disposition, and good ingine;† I think if he were to express his love in one wish, it would be this, that he might have such a Spirit in him, and this he would account better than all that he could leave him. But if it were possible to transmit a gracious, well-disposed and understanding spirit from one to another, and if men could leave it, as they do their inheritance to their children, certainly a wise and religious parent would first make over a disposition of that to his children; as Elisha sought a double measure of Elijah's spirit, so a father would wish such a measure to his children, and, if it were possible, give it. But that may not be. All that can be done is to wish well to them, and leave them a good example for imitation. But in this our heavenly Father transcends all, that he can impart his own Spirit to his adopted children, and his Spirit is in a manner the very essential principle that maketh them children of the Father. Their natures, their dispositions, are under his power. He can as well reform them, as you can change your children's garments. He can make of us what he will. Our hearts are in his hand, as the water, capable of any impression he pleaseth to put on it: and this is the impression he putteth on his children, he putteth his Spirit in their hearts, and writeth his law in their inward parts, a more divine and higher work than all human persuasion can reach. This Spirit they receive as an earnest of the inheritance, and withal, to make them fit for the inheritance of the saints in light.

Now, the working of this Spirit of adoption, I conceive to be threefold, beside that of intercession expressed in the verse. The first work of the Spirit of adoption, that wherein a father's affection seems to break first from under ground, is, the revealing to the heart the love and mercy of God to sinners. I do not say, to such a

* [That is, corollary or consequence.—Ed.]

[† Or, good spirit.—Ed.]

soul in particular, for that application is neither first, nor universal. But herein the Spirit of adoption first appears from under the cloud of fear; and this is the first opening of the prison of bondage, wherein a soul was shut, when the plain way of reconciliation to God in Christ, and delivery from the bondage of sin and wrath, is holden out; when such a word as this comes into the soul, and is received with some gladness, 'God so loved the world that he gave his Son,' &c. 'This is a true and faithful saying,' &c. 'Come, ye that labour and are weary, and I will give rest to your souls.' When a soul is made to hear the glad tidings of liberty preached to captives, of light to the blind, of joy to the heavy in spirit, of life to the dead, though he cannot come that length as to see his own particular interest, yet the very receiving affectionately and greedily such a general report as good and true, gives some ease and relaxation to the heart. To see delivery possible, is some door of hope to a desperate sinner. But to see it, and espy more than a possibility, even great probability, though he cannot reach a certainty, that will be as the breaking open of a window of light in a dark dungeon. It will be as the taking off of some of the hardest fetters, and the worst chains, which makes a man almost to think himself at liberty. Now this is the great office of the Spirit of the Father, to beget in us good thoughts of him, to incline us to charitable and favourable constructions of him, and make us ready to think well of him, to beget a good understanding in us and him, and correct our jealous misapprehensions of him. For certainly we are naturally suspicious of God, that he deals not in sad earnest with us. Whenever we see the height of our provocation, and weight of deserved indignation, we think him like ourselves, and can hardly receive without suspicion the gospel that lays open his love in Christ to the world.

Now, this is the Spirit's work, to make us entertain that honourable thought of God, that he is most inclinable to pardon sinners; and that his mercy is infinitely above man's sin; and that it is no prejudice to his holiness or justice; and to apprehend seriously a constant reality and solid truth in the promises of the gospel; and so to convince a soul of righteousness, (John xvi.) that there is a way of justifying a sinner or ungodly person, without wrong to God's righteousness; and this being well pondered in the heart, and received in love, the great business is done. After that, particular application is more easy, of which I shall not speak now, because occasion will be given in the next verse, about the Spirit's witnessing with our spirits, which is another of the Spirit's workings: only I say this, that which makes this so difficult, is a defect in the first. But the common principles of the gospel are not really, and so seriously apprehended, because many souls do not put to their seal to witness to the promises and truth of it. Therefore the Lord often denies this seal and witness to our comfort. It is certainly a preposterous way Satan puts souls upon, first, to get such a testimony from the Spirit before they labour to get such a testimony to Christ, and echo or answer in their hearts to his word. This way seems shortest; for they would leap into the greater liberty at the first hand. But certainly it is farthest about, because it is impossible for souls to leap immediately out of bondage to assurance, without some middle step. They cannot pass thus from extremes to extremes, without going through the middle state of receiving Christ, and laying his word up in the heart; and therefore it proves the way furthest about, because when souls have long wearied themselves, they must at length turn in hither.

But there is another working of the Spirit I wish you were acquainted with. As the first work is to beget a suitable apprehension of God's mind and heart towards sinners, so the next is, to beget a suitable disposition in our hearts towards God as a Father. The first apprehends his love, the next reflects it back again with the heart of a sinner to him. The Spirit first brings the report of the love and grace of God to us, and then he carries the love and respect of the heart up to God.

You know how God complains in Malachi, 'If I be a Father, where is my fear and honour?' For these are the only fitting qualifications of children, such a reverent, respective observance of our heavenly Father, such affectionate and humble carriage towards him, as becometh both his majesty and his love. As these are tempered one with another in him, his love not abasing his majesty, and his majesty not diminishing his love; so we ought to carry, as reverence and confidence, fear and love, may be contempered one with another, so as we may neither forget his infinite greatness, nor doubt of his unspeakable love. And this inward disposition engraven on the heart, will be the principle of willing and ready obedience. It will in some measure be our meat and drink to do our Father's will. For Christ gave us an example how we should carry towards him. How humble and obedient was he, though his only begotten Son !

Sermon XXXIX.

VERSE 15.—"*Whereby we cry, Abba, Father.*"

As there is a light of grace in bestowing such incomparably high dignities and excellent gifts on poor sinners, such as, to make them the sons of God who were the children of the devil, and heirs of a kingdom who were heirs of wrath; so there is a depth of wisdom in the Lord's allowance and manner of dispensing his love and grace in this life. For though the love be wonderful, that we should be called the sons of God; yet, as that apostle speaks, it doth not yet so clearly appear what we shall be, by what we are, 1 John iii. 1. Our present condition is so unlike such a state and dignity, and our enjoyments so unsuitable to our rights and privileges, that it would not appear by the mean, low, and indigent state we are now into, that we have so great and glorious a Father. How many infirmities are we compassed about with ! How many wants are we pressed withal ! Our necessities are infinite, and our enjoyments no ways proportioned to our necessities. Notwithstanding even in this, the love and wisdom of our heavenly Father shows itself, and oftentimes more gloriously in the theatre of men's weakness, infirmities, and wants, than they could appear in the absolute and total exemption of his children from necessities. Strength perfected in weakness, grace sufficient in infirmities, hath some greater glory than strength and grace alone. Therefore he hath chosen this way as most fit for the advancing his glory, and most suitable for our comfort and edification, to give us but little in hand, and environ us with a crowd of continued necessities and wants within and without, that we may learn to cry to him as our Father, and seek our supplies from him ; and withal he hath not been sparing, but liberal in promises of hearing our cries and supplying our wants ; so that this way of narrow and hard dispensation, that at first seems contrary to the love and bounty and riches of our Father, in the perfect view of it, appears to be the only way to perpetuate our communion with him, and often to renew the sense of his love and grace, that would grow slack in our hearts, if our needs did not every day stir up fresh longing, and his returns by this means are so much the more refreshing. There is a time of children's minority when they stand in need of continual supplies from their parents, or tutors, because they are not entered in possession of their inheritance ; and while they are in this state, there is nothing more beseeming them, than in all their wants to address to their father, and represent them to him ; and it is fit they should be from hand to mouth, as you say, that they may know and acknowledge their dependence on their father. Truly this is our minority, our presence in the body, which because of sin that dwells in it, and its own natural weakness and incapacity, keeps us at much distance with the Lord, that we cannot be intimately present with him. Now, in this condition, the most natural, the most comely and becoming exercise of children, is, to cry to our Father, to present all our grievances ; and thus to entertain some holy correspondence with our absent Father, by the messenger of prayer and supplication, which cannot return empty, if it be not sent away too full of self-conceit. This is the most natural breathing of a child of God in this world. It is the most proper acting of his new life, and the most suitable expiration of that Spirit of adoption that is inspired into him, since there is so much life as to know what we want, and our wants are infinite. Therefore that life cannot but beat this way, in holy desires after God, whose fulness can supply all wants. This is the pulse of a Christian, that goeth continually, and there is much advantage to the continuity and interrupted-ness of the motion, from the infiniteness and inexhaustedness of our needs in this life, and the continual assaults that are made by necessity and temptation on the heart. 'But ye have received the Spirit of adoption, whereby we cry,' &c. He puts in his own name in the latter part, though theirs was in the former part. When he speaks of a donation or privilege, he supplies to the meanest, to show that the lowest and most despised creature is not in any incapacity to receive the greatest gifts of God; and then, when he mentions the working of that Spirit in way of intercession, because it imports necessity and want, he cares not to commit some incongruity in the language, by changing the person, that he may teach us, that weakness, infirmities, and wants, are common to the best and chiefest among Christians; that the most eminent have continual need to cry, and the lowest and obscurest believers have as good ground to believe the hearing and acceptance of their cries; that the highest are not above the weakest and lowest ordinance, and that the lowest are not below the comfort of help and acceptation in him. Nay, the growth and increase of grace, is so far from exempting men from, or setting them above, this duty of constant supplication, that by the contrary, this is the just measure of their growth and altitude in grace. As the degrees of the height of the water Nilus in its overflowing, are a sure sign of the fertility or barrenness of that year, so the overflowings of the spirit of prayer in one gives a present account how the heart is,—whether barren and unfruitful in the knowledge of Jesus Christ, or fruitful and lively, and vigorous in it. It is certain that contraries do discover one another, and the more the one be increased, that is not only the more incompatible and inconsistent with the other, but gives the most perfect discerning of it. When grace is but as twilight in the soul, and as the dawning of the day only, gross darkness and uncleanness is seen; but the more it grow to the perfect day, the more sin is seen, and the more its hated wants are discovered that did not appear; and therefore it exerciseth itself the more in opposition to sin, and supplication to God. To speak the truth, our growth here is but an advancement in the knowledge and sense of our indigency,—it is but a further entry into the idolatrous temple of the heart, which makes a man see daily new abominations worse than the former. And therefore you may easily know that such repeated sights and discoveries will but press out more earnest and frequent cries from the heart. And such a growth in humility, and faith in God's fulness, will be but as oil to feed the flame of supplication. For what is prayer, indeed, but the ardency of the affection after God, flaming up to him in cries and requests?

To speak of this exercise of an holy heart, would require more of the spirit of it than we have. But truly this is to be lamented, that though there be nothing more common among Christians in the outward practice of it, yet that there is nothing more extraordinary and rare, even among many that use it, than to be acquainted with the inward nature of it. Truly, the most ordinary things in religion are the greatest mysteries, as to the true life of them. We are strangers to the soul and life of these things, which consist in the holy behaviour and deportment of our spirits before the Father of spirits.

These words give some ground to speak of some special qualifications of prayer, and the chief principle of it. The chief principle and original of prayer, is, the Spirit of adoption received into the heart. It is a business of a higher nature than can be taught by precepts, or learned by custom and education. There is a general mistake among men, that the gift of prayer is attained by learning, and that it consists in the freedom and plenty of expression. But O! how many doctors and disputers of the world are there, that can defend all the articles of faith against the opposers of them; yet so unacquainted are they with this exercise, that the poor, and unlearned, and nothings in the world, who cannot dispute for religion, send up a more savoury and acceptable sacrifice, and sweet incense to God daily, when they offer up their soul's desires in simplicity and sincerity. Certainly this is a spiritual thing, derived only from the Fountain of spirits,—this grace of pouring out our souls into him, and keeping communication with him. The variety of words and riches of expression is but the shell of it, the external shadow; and all the life consists in the frame of the heart before God. And this none can put in frame but he that formed the spirit of man within him. Some through custom of hearing and using it, attain to a habit of expressing themselves readily in it, it may be, to the satisfaction of others; but, alas! they may be strangers to the first letters and elements of the life and spirit of prayer. I would have you who want both, look up to heaven for it. Many of you cannot be induced to pray in your family, (and I fear little or none in secret, which is indeed a more serious work,) because you have not been used, or not learned, or such like. Alas! beloved, this cometh not through education, or learning. It cometh from the Spirit of adoption; and if ye say, ye cannot pray, ye have not the Spirit; and if ye have not the Spirit, ye are not the sons of God. Know what is in the inevitable sequel of your own confessions.

But I haste to the qualifications of this divine work,—fervency, reverence, and confidence; *fervency* in crying, *reverence and confidence* in crying, 'Abba, Father;' for these two suit well toward our Father. The first, I fear, we must seek elsewhere than in prayer. I find it spent on other things of less moment. Truly, all the spirit and affection of men runs in another channel,—in the way of contention and strife, in the way of passion and miscalled zeal, and because these things whereabout we do thus earnestly contend, have some interest or coherence with religion, we not only excuse but approve our vehemency. But O! much better were that employed in supplications to God: that were a divine channel. Again, the marrow of other men's spirits is exhausted in the pursuit of things in the world. The edge of their desires is turned that way, and it must needs be blunted and dulled in spiritual things, that it cannot pierce into heaven, and prevail effectually. I am sure, many of us useth this excuse, who are so cold in it, that we do not warm ourselves. And how shall we think to prevail with God? Our spirits make little noise when we cry all the loudest. We can scarce hear any whisper in our hearts, and how shall he hear us? Certainly it is not the extension of the voice pleaseth him; it is the cry of the heart that is sweet harmony in his ears. And you may easily perceive this, if you but consider that he is an infinite Spirit, that pierceth into all the corners of our hearts, and hath all the darkness of it as light before him. How can you think that such a Spirit can be pleased with lip cries? How can he endure such deceit and falsehood, (who hath so perfect a contrariety with all false appearances,) that your heart should lie so dead and flat before him, and the affection of it turned quite another way? There were no sacrifices without fire in the Old Testament, and that fire was kept in perpetually; and so no prayer now without some inward fire, conceived in the desires, and blazing up and growing into a flame in the presenting of them to God.

The incense that was to be offered on the altar of perfume, (Exod. xxx.) behoved to be beaten and prepared; and truly, prayer would do well to be made out of a beaten and bruised heart, and contrite spirit,—a spirit truly sensible of its own unworthiness and wants; and that beating and pounding of the heart will yield a good fragrant smell, as some spices do not till beaten. The incense was made of divers spices, intimating to us, that true prayer is not one grace alone, but a compound of graces. It is the joint exercise of all a Christian's graces; seasoned with all. Every one of them gives some peculiar fragrancy to it, as humility, faith, repentance, love, &c. The acting of the heart in supplication, is a kind of compend and result of all these, as one perfume made up of many simples. But above all, as the incense, our prayers must be kindled by fire on the altar. There must be some heat and fervour, some warmness, conceived by the Holy Spirit in our hearts, which may make our spices send forth a pleasant smell, as many spices do not till they get heat. Let us lay this engagement on our hearts, to be more serious in our addresses to God, the Father of spirits; above all, to present our inward soul before him, before whom it is naked and open, though we do not bring it. And certainly, frequency in prayer will much help us to fervency, and to keep it when we have it.

Sermon XL.

Verse 15.—" *Whereby we cry, Abba, Father.*"

All that know any thing of religion, must needs know and confess that there is no exercise either more suitable to him that professeth it, or more needful for him, than to give himself to the exercise of prayer. But that which is confessed by all, and as to the outward performance gone about by many, I fear is yet a mystery sealed up from us, as the true and living nature of it. There is much of it expressed here in few words, 'whereby we cry, Abba, Father.' The divine constitution and qualifications of this divine work, are here made up of a temper of fervency, reverence, and confidence. The first I spoke of before; but I fear our hearts were not well heated then, or may be cooled since. It is not the loud noise of words that is best heard in heaven, or that is constructed to be crying to God. No, this is transacted in the heart more silently to men, but it striketh up into the ears of God. His ear is sharp, and that voice of the soul's desires is shrill, and though it were out of the depths, they will meet together. It is true, the vehemency of affection will sometimes cause the extension of the voice; but yet it may cry as loud to heaven when it is kept within. I do not press such extraordinary degrees of fervour as may affect the body, but I would rather wish we accustomed ourselves to a solid calm seriousness and earnestness of spirit, which might be more constant than such raptures can be, that we might always gather our spirits to what we are about, and avocate them from impertinent wanderings, and fix them upon the present object of our worship. This is to worship him in spirit who is a Spirit.

The other thing that composes the sweet temper of prayer, is reverence. And what more suitable, whether you consider him or yourselves? 'If I be your Father, where is my honour? and if I be your Master, where is my fear?' Mal. i. 6. While we call him Father, or Lord, we proclaim this much, that we ought to know our distance from him, and his superiority to us. And if worship in prayer carry not this character, and express not this honourable and glorious Lord, whom we serve, it wants that congruity and suitableness to him that is the beauty of it. Is there any thing more uncomely, than for children to behave themselves irreverently and irrespectively towards their fathers, to whom they owe themselves? It is a monstrous thing even in nature, and to nature's light. O how much more abominable must it be, to draw near to the Father of spirits, who made us, and not we ourselves, in whose hand our breath is, and whose are all our ways; in a word, to whom we owe not only this dust, but the living spirit that animates it, that was breathed from heaven, and finally, 'in whom we live, and move, and have our being,' and well-being; to worship such an one, and yet to behave ourselves so unseemly and irreverently in his presence, our hearts not stricken with the apprehension of his glory, but lying flat and dead before him, having scarcely him in our thoughts whom we speak to. And finally, our deportments in his sight are such, as could not be admitted in the presence of any person a little above ourselves,—to be about to speak to them, and yet to turn aside continually to every one that cometh by, and entertain communication with every base creature. This, I say, in the presence of a king, or nobleman, would be accounted such an absurd incivility, as could be committed. And yet we behave ourselves just so with the Father of spirits.

O the wanderings of the hearts of men in divine worship! While we are in communication with our Father and Lord in prayer, whose heart is fixed to a constant attendance and presence, by the impression of his glorious holiness? Whose Spirit doth not continually gad abroad, and take a word of every thing that occurs, and so mars that soul correspondence? O that this word (Psal. lxxxix. 7.) were written with great letters on our hearts, 'God is greatly to be feared in the assembly of the saints, and to be had in reverence of all them that are about him.' That one word, God, speaketh all. Either we must convert him into an idol, which is nothing; or if we apprehend him to be God, we must apprehend our infinite distance from him, and his unspeakable, inaccessible glory above us. He is greatly feared and reverenced in the assemblies that are above, in the upper courts of angels. Those glorious spirits who must cover their feet from us, because we cannot see their glory; they must cover their faces from him, because they cannot behold his glory, Isa. vi. What a glorious train hath he, and yet how reverend are they? They wait round about the throne, above and about it, as courtiers upon their king, for they are all ministering spirits, and they rest not day and night to adore and admire that holy One, crying, 'Holy, holy, holy, the whole earth is full of his glory.' Now, how much more then should he be greatly feared and had in reverence in the assembly of his saints, of poor mortal men, whose foundation is in the dust, and in the clay, and besides drink in iniquity like water? There are two points ot difference and distance from us. He is nearer angels, for angels are pure spirits, but we have flesh, which is furthest removed from his nature. And then angels are holy and clean; yet theirs is but spotted to* his unspotted holiness. But we are defiled with sin, which putteth us farthest off from him, and which his holiness hath greatest antipathy at. Let us consider this, my beloved, that we may carry the impression of the glorious holiness and majesty of God on our hearts, whenever we appear before him, that so we may serve and rejoice with trembling, and pray with reverence and godly fear. If we apprehend indeed our own quality and condition, how low, how base it is, how we cannot endure the very clear aspect of our own consciences, we cannot look on ourselves steadfastly without shame and confusion of face, at the deformed spectacle we behold. Much less would we endure to have our souls opened and presented to the view of other men, even the basest of men. We would be overwhelmed with shame if they could see into our hearts? Now then, apprehend seriously what he is, how glorious in holiness; how infinite in wisdom, how the secrets of your souls are plain and open in his sight, and I am persuaded you will be composed to a reverend, humble, and trembling behaviour in his sight.

But withal I must add this, that because he is your Father, you may intermingle confidence; nay, you are commanded so to do, and this honours him as much as reverence. For confidence in God, as our Father, is the best acknowledgment of the greatness and goodness of God. It declareth how able he is to save us, and how willing, and so ratifieth all the promises of God made to us, and setteth to a seal to his faithfulness. There is nothing he accounts himself more honoured by, than a soul's full resigning itself to him, and relying on his power and good-will in all necessities, casting its care upon him, as a loving Father, who careth for us. And truly, there is much beauty and harmony in the juncture of these two, rejoicing with trembling, confidence with reverence, to ask nothing doubting, and yet sensible of our infinite distance from him, and the disproportion of our requests to his highness. A child-like disposition is composed thus, as also the temper and carriage of a courtier hath these ingredients in it. The love of his Father, and the favour of his Prince, maketh him take liberty, and assume boldness; and withal he is not unmindful of his own distance, from his Father or master. 'Let us draw near with full assurance of faith,' Heb. x. 22. There is much in the scripture, both exhorted, commanded, and commended, of that παῤῥησία, that liberty and boldness of pouring out our requests to God, as one that certainly will hear us, and grant that which is good. Unbelief spoileth all. It is a wretched and base spirited thing, that can conceive no honourable thoughts of God, but only like itself. But faith is the well-pleasing ingredient of prayer. The lower thoughts a man has of himself, it maketh him conceive the higher and more honourable of God. 'My ways are not your ways, nor my thoughts as your thoughts, but as far above as the heavens above the earth,' Isa. lv. 8. This is the rule of a believing soul's conceiving of God, and expecting from him; and when a soul is thus placed on God, by trusting and believing in him, it is fixed; 'His heart is fixed, trusting in the Lord,' Psal. cxii. 7. O how wavering and inconstant is a soul, till it fix at this anchor, upon the ground of his immutable promises! It is tossed up and down with every wind, it is double-minded; now one way, then another, now in one mind, and shortly changed; and indeed the soul is like the sea, capable of the least or greatest commotion, James i. 6—8. I know not any thing that will either fix your hearts from wandering in prayer, or establish your hearts from trouble and disquiet after it, nothing that will so exoner† and ease

[* That is, compared to.—Ed.]

[† That is, disburthen.—Ed.]

your spirits of care as this, to lay hold on God as all-sufficient, and lay that constraint on your hearts, to wait on him and his pleasure, to cast your souls on his promises, that are so full and so free, and abide there, as at your anchor-hold, in all the vicissitudes and changes of outward or inward things. In spiritual things that concern your salvation, that which is absolutely necessary, you may take the boldness to be absolute in it, and as Job, 'though he should slay me, yet will I trust in him;' and as Jacob, 'I will not let thee go till thou bless me.' But either in outward things, that have some usefulness in them, but are not always fittest for our chiefest good; or in the degrees of spiritual gifts, and measures of graces, the Lord calls us without anxiety to pour out our hearts in them unto him. But withal we would do it with submission to his pleasure, because he knows best what is best for us. In these, we are not bound to be confident to receive the particular we ask, but rather our confidence should pitch upon his good-will and favour, that he will certainly deny nothing that himself knows is good for us. And so in these we should absolutely cast ourselves without carefulness upon his loving and fatherly providence, and resign ourselves to him to be disposed of in them as he sees convenient. There is sometimes too much limitation of God, and peremptoriness used with him in such things, in which his wisdom craves a latitude both in public and private matters, even as men's affections and interests are engaged. But ordinarily it is attended and followed with shame and disappointment in the end. And there is, on the other hand, intolerable remissness and slackness in many, in pressing even the weightiest petitions of salvation, mortification, &c. which certainly ariseth from the diffidence and unbelief of the heart, and the want of that rooted persuasion, both of the incomparable necessity and worth of the things themselves, and of his willingness and engagement to bestow them.

The word is doubled here,' Abba, Father,' the Syriac and Greek word signifying one thing, expressing the tender affection and love of God towards them that come to him. 'He that cometh to God must believe that he is, and that he is a rewarder of them that seek him diligently.' So he that cometh to God must believe that he hath the bowels and compassion of a Father, and will be more easily inclined with our importunate cries, than the fathers of our flesh. He may suffer his children to cry long, but it is not because he will not hear, but because he would hear them longer, and delights to hear their cry oftener. If he delay, it is his wisdom to appreciate and endear his mercies to us, and to teach us to press our petitions and sue for an answer.

Besides, this is much for our comfort, that from whomsoever, and whatsoever corner in the world, prayers come up to him, they cannot want acceptance. All languages, all countries, all places are sanctified by Jesus Christ, that whosoever calls upon the name of the Lord, from the ends of the earth, shall be saved. And truly it is a sweet meditation to think, that from the ends of the earth, the cries of souls are heard; and that the end is as near heaven as the middle; and a wilderness as near as a paradise; that though we understand not one another, yet we have one loving and living Father that understands all our meanings. And so the different languages and dialects of the members of this body make no confusion in heaven, but meet together in his heart and affection, and are one perfume, one incense, sent up from the whole catholic church, which here is scattered on the earth. O that the Lord would persuade us to cry this way to our Father in all our necessities!

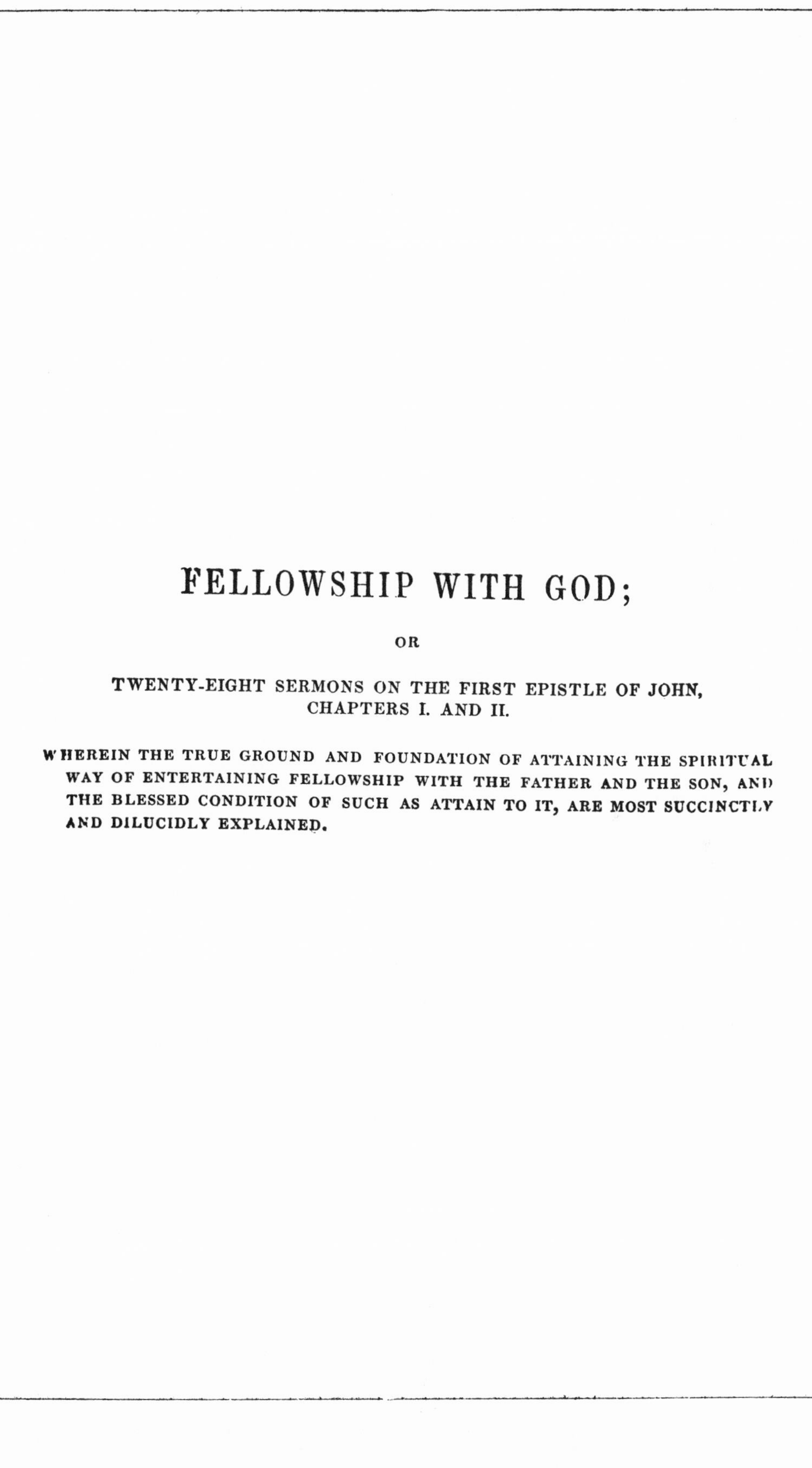

FELLOWSHIP WITH GOD;

OR

TWENTY-EIGHT SERMONS ON THE FIRST EPISTLE OF JOHN, CHAPTERS I. AND II.

WHEREIN THE TRUE GROUND AND FOUNDATION OF ATTAINING THE SPIRITUAL WAY OF ENTERTAINING FELLOWSHIP WITH THE FATHER AND THE SON, AND THE BLESSED CONDITION OF SUCH AS ATTAIN TO IT, ARE MOST SUCCINCTLY AND DILUCIDLY EXPLAINED.

TO THE

SINCERE SEEKER AFTER FELLOWSHIP WITH GOD,

AND

SERIOUSLY HEAVEN-WARD-TENDING CHRISTIAN.

Dear and Well-beloved Friend,

As thou art in thyself a rare jewel, a most precious stone, one of a thousand, yea, of ten thousand, being compared with the many thousands of common stones, I mean, external professors in the visible church, who rest on a bare name, and of whom that is verified in every nation, which our Saviour saith, Matth. xx. 16. 'Many are called, but few are chosen;' and of many of whom that is also too true in every generation, (and, oh! that it were not too manifest in this also,) which Paul observed in his time, Phil. iii. 18, 19. 'For many walk, of whom I have told you often, and now tell you, even weeping, that they are the enemies of the cross of Christ. Whose end is destruction, whose god is their belly, and whose glory is in their shame, who mind earthly things,'—and as to Christ thy Lord, most comely 'as the lily among thorns,' being his 'love among the daughters,' Cant. ii. 2. so also, thou, in a special way, art the dearly beloved and longed for, the joy and crown, of every sincere servant of Christ in the gospel, Phil. iv. 1. Thou art, if not the only, yet the chief object of their labours, their work being either to confirm and strengthen thee in thy way, that thou mayest so stand fast in the Lord, or remove impediments, make crooked things straight, and so prepare the way of the Lord before thee, or to guide thee by the light of God's word in the dark night of temptation and desertion. Now, as we are confident these sermons were preached at first by that blessed, serious labourer in the work of the ministry, Mr. Hugh Binning, with a special eye to the advancement of sincere seekers after fellowship with God, and seriously heaven-ward-tending Christians amongst his hearers, so to whom shall we direct this posthumous, and alas! unperfected work, but to thee, (O serious Christian,) who makest it thy work not only to seek after the knowledge of God in Christ, in a mere speculative way, that thou mayest know, and therein rest, as if thy work were done, but also to follow after the enjoyment of that known God, and believed on Saviour, and all the promised privileges of grace in this life, and of eternal glory in the life to come. To thee especially belong these precious soul-ravishing truths delivered in these sermons. Two things, we know, thou hast determined thy soul unto, and fixed thine eye on, as thine aim and mark in thy generation, viz. the light of knowledge and the life of practice. As to knowledge, we are confident that with the apostle Paul, 1 Cor. ii. 2. thou hast determined to know nothing but 'Christ, and him crucified;' and as to practice, with the said apostle thou prayest, that thou mayest be sincere and without offence till the day of Christ, being filled with the fruits of righteousness, which are by Jesus Christ unto the glory of God, Phil. i. 10, 11; and that thou mayest be blameless and harmless, the son of God without rebuke in the midst of a crooked and perverse nation, shining as a light in the world, Phil. ii. 15. Now in reading these sermons thou shalt perceive, that to help thee in both these, hath been the very scope and design of this serious preacher. Desirest thou to know Jesus Christ the Lord of life, either according to his eternal subsistence in the infinite understanding of the Father, as God, or as to his appearance in the flesh, as Man, or fitness as Mediator, to reconcile thee to God his Father, both in respect of willingness and ability to save? Then here thou shalt behold him delineate to the life. Wouldst thou be clearly informed anent* the only true and sure foundation of fellowship with God, the way of entertaining it, the honour or happiness of it, and sweet fruits of it, that fulness of joy that accompanies it? Here shalt thou find so clear a light as shall rejoice thy soul. Wouldst thou be fortified against the incursions and recursions of sin and Satan? Then come to this magazine, and be furnished abundantly. Desirest thou to have thy soul increased in the love of God, and to see manifest demonstrations of his love in Christ to thee? Oh! then turn in hither, and get satisfaction to thy soul's desires. If thou desirest with David, to hate sin with a perfect hatred; here, if any where, thou shalt obtain thy desire. Yet let none think that we limit the benefit and usefulness of these sermons to serious Christians only, and so by consequence exclude all others from any hope of soul-advantage in reading them. Nay, we declare, that though it be undeniable, that John did write this epistle with a special respect to the spiritual advantage of serious Christians, and that this holy preacher also had this same design, yet we dare be bold to invite all of what degree soever, to the serious perusing of them, assuring them that in so doing they shall not find their labour in vain in the Lord; for here are such pregnant demonstrations of a Deity, infinite, eternal, omnipotent, incomprehensible, governing all things by the word of his power, as may dash the boldness of the most metaphysical, notional, or profanely practical atheist, and with conviction of spirit make him cry out, as in Psal. lxxiii. 22. 'So foolish was I and ignorant, I was as a beast before thee!' Here are such clear discoveries of the vileness of sin, of its direct opposition to a holy God, and his most holy will, of its woful soul damning effects, as may convince the most profane and stout-hearted carnalist; and awake him out of his soul-destroying sleep of security and presumption. Here are so glorious evidences of God's free and inconceivable love to the world, in Christ Jesus the Son of his love, as are able to enlighten with the light of consolation, the sadliest dejected and casten down soul, under the apprehension of the curse and wrath of God due to it for sin, and raise it up to the hope of mercy in and through so clearly a revealed Saviour. In a word, here are to be found convictions for atheists, piercing rebukes to the profane, clear instructions to the ignorant, milk to babes in Christ, strong meat for the strong, strength to the weak, quickening and reviving for such as faint in the way, restoratives for such as are in a decay, reclamations and loud oyeses† after backsliders to reveal them, breasts of consolations for Zion's mourners, whether under the first convictions of the law, and pangs of the new birth, or under the challenges and compunctions of heart for recidivations and relapses after conversion, even while they are groaning under the power and burden of the body of death, Rom. vii. And to add no more; here are most excellent counsels and directions to serious seekers of fellowship with God, to guide them in their way, and help them forward to the attainment of that fulness of a joy which is to be had in fellowship with the Father and the Son. That the Lord may bless all such to whose hands these sermons shall come, with blessings suitable to their soul's condition, especially the serious Christian, for whose soul's furtherance and advancement these sermons were first penned, and now printed, is the most affectionate desire of,

Thy servant in the gospel of our dearest Lord and Saviour,

A. S.

* [That is, respecting.—Ed.]

† [Oyes, (from oyez, the old imperative of the French verb *ouir*, to hear) a word used by public criers, before making their proclamations.—Ed.]

FELLOWSHIP WITH GOD.

Sermon I.

1 John i. 1.—"*That which was from the beginning, which we have heard, which we have seen with our eyes, which we have looked upon, and our hands have handled, of the Word of life.*"

It is the great qualification of a disciple, or hearer, to be attentive and docile, to be capable of teaching, and to apply the mind seriously to it. It is much to get the ear of a man. If his ear be gotten, his mind is the more easily gained. Therefore, those who professed eloquence, and studied to persuade men to any thing, used in the entry to fall upon some thing that might stir up the attention of their hearers, or make them the more inclinable to receive instruction, or catch their favour or good-will, which is of great moment to persuasion; for it is sometimes fit to open the passages of the heart by such means, that there may be the more easy entry for instruction and persuasion. Truly there is something of this art runs here in a divine channel; as indeed all these rules of human wisdom attain their perfection, when they meet with a divine Spirit, that elevates them to a more transcendent use. Happy was that eloquence of Paul's, and something like the sweet inspiration of angels, by which they prevail with the spirits of men. 'Nevertheless, being crafty, (saith he,) I caught you with guile,' 2 Cor. xii. 16. These were *piæ fraudes*,* whereby he used to catch poor souls out of the pit, and pluck them out of the fire; and he that said, 'I will make you fishers of men,' taught them to use some holy deceit, to present some things for the allurement of souls, and so to surround and enclose them with most weighty and convincing reasons. This beloved apostle, who leaned upon Christ's bosom, and was likely to learn the very secrets of the art of fishing souls, you see how he goeth about the business. He useth an holy art in this preface. Being about to give a recapitulation of the whole gospel, and to make a short summary of the doctrine of it, for the more effectual establishment and confirmation of souls already converted, and for the powerful persuasion of others to embrace it, he useth all the skill that can be in the entry, to dispose men's hearts to receive it. Like a wise orator, he labours to make them *attentos, dociles, et benevolos*,† to stir up their attention, to conciliate their affection, and so to make them docile and easily teachable. He stirs up attention, when he shows that he is not to speak about trifling, light matters, or low things, or things that do not concern them, but concerning the greatest, most concerning, and important things to them, even the Word of life, in which all their life was wrapt up; which, though it was ancient in itself, yet withal it was a new thing to the world, and so for all respects deserved to be taken serious notice of. Then he conciliates their benevolence and good-will, by showing his own good affection towards them, and his great design in it, that it was only for their good and salvation; that he had nothing else before him, but to have them partakers with himself, in that same happiness. He had found a jewel, and he hides it not, but proclaims it, that all men may have fellowship with him, and that is, with God, and that cannot but bring in full joy to the heart. Now a soul being made thus attentive, and willing to hear, it is the best disposition that makes them most capable of being taught. If those two stays were come over,—the careless regard that is in men's hearts towards the gospel, and the suspicious thoughts

* [That is, "pious frauds."—Ed.]

† [Rhet. ad C. Heren. lib. I. cap. 4. Cic. Op.—Ed.

and prejudices against the ambassadors of it,—then what would hinder to believe it? The great miseries of men are, inconsideration and misapprehension. Either men are so noised with other things continually buzzing in their ears, and their hearts so possessed with the clamours of their lusts, and the cries of the things of this world, that they have no leisure so much as to hearken patiently to this blessed sound, or to apprehend seriously what weight and moment lies in it; and so the most part of men cannot give that earnest and deep attention that is necessarily required for this divine teaching; or else there are many mistakes and misconceptions of the gospel, which sometimes arise to that height of reasoning against God, and prejudices against them that carry this message, which usually are joined together, (and these stop the ears of men against the wisest and most powerful enchantment of preaching,) that it gains not much ground on them. O! that ye would once listen to the gospel. Hearken and incline your ears unto me, is the Lord's first great request; and if once you do but seriously apply your minds and hearts to see what is held out unto you, and to prove what good is in it, certainly these sure and everlasting mercies will mercifully and sweetly catch you with guile, and deceive you (if I may say so) to your eternal advantage. Wisdom, the Father's wisdom, begs but an equal hearing of you. Let her have but a patient hearing, and a silent impartial judgment of the heart, and she will carry it off from all that suit* you. It is lamentable that the voice of God should be out-cried by men's continual uninterrupted flood of business, that fills the heart with a continual noise, and keeps men in such a constant hurry and distemper that they can give time and patience to nothing else. And this is only the advantage the world and the lusts of it have; for if they come once under a sober and serious examination, and the other party, that is, Jesus Christ and the word of life, might have the liberty to be heard in the inward retired thoughts of the heart, it would soon be found how unequal they are, and that all their efficacy consists in our ignorance, and their strength in our weakness. Certainly Christ would carry it, to the conviction of all that is in the soul. I beseech you let us give him this attention.

He that answers a tale before he hears it, it is a folly and weakness to him. A folly certainly it is to give this gospel a repulse before ye hear it. It promiseth life and immortality, which nothing else doth. And you entertain other things upon lower promises and expectations, even after frequent experiences of their deceitfulness. What a madness then is it to hear this promise of life in Christ, so often beaten upon you, and yet never so much as to put him to the proof of it; and to put him off continually who knocks at your hearts, before you will consider attentively, who it is that thus importunes you! O, my beloved, that you would hear him to Amen. Let him speak freely to your hearts, and commune with them in the night on your beds, in your greatest retirement from other things, that you may not be disturbed by the noise of your lusts and business; and I persuade myself, you who have now least mind of this life, and joy in God, should find it, and find it in him. But to cut off all convictions and persuasions at first, and to set such a guard at your minds, to provide that nothing of that kind come in, or else that it be cast out as an enemy, this is unequal, ignorant, and unreasonable dealing, which you alone will repent of, it may be too late, when past remedy.

He propounds that which he is to speak in the fittest way, for the commendation of it to their hearts; and oh! how vast a difference betwixt this, and the ordinary subject of men's discourses. Our ears are filled continually with reports; and it is the usual way of men to delight to hear, and to report even those things that are not so delightful in themselves. And truly there are not many occurrences in the world (suppose you had a diurnal of affairs of all men every week) that can give any solid refreshment to the heart, except in the holy meditation of the vanity, vexation, and inconstancy that God hath subjected all those things unto. But it is sad that Christians, who have so noble and divine, so pleasant and profitable things to speak upon one to another, are notwithstanding as much subject to that Athenian disease, to be itching after new things continually, and to spend our time this way, to report, and to hear news. And, alas! what are those things that are tossed up and down continually, but the follies, weaknesses, impotencies and wickedness, ambition

* [That is, sue for you, or make their suit to you.—Ed.]

and avarice of men, the iniquity and impiety of the world that lies in wickedness? And is there any thing in this, either pleasant or profitable, that we should delight to entertain our own thoughts, and others' ears with them? But the subject that is here entreated of, is of another nature. Nothing in itself so excellent, nothing to us so convenient. That which was from the beginning, of the Word of life, we declare unto you. O how pleasant and sweet a voice is that which sounds from heaven, be those confused noises* are, that arise from the earth! This is a message that is come from heaven, with him that came down from it. And indeed that is the airth† from whence good news hath come. Since the first curse was pronounced upon the earth, the earth hath brought forth nothing but thorns and briars of contention, strife, sorrow, and vexation. Only from above hath this message been sent to renew the world again, and recreate it, as it were. There are four properties by which this infinitely surpasses all other things that can be told you. For itself it is most excellent; for its endurance it is most ancient; and to us it is most profitable; and both in itself, and to us, it is most certain; and by these the apostle labours to prepare their hearts to serious attention.

For the excellency of the subject that he is to declare,—it is incomparable, for it is no less than that Jewel that is hid in the mine of the scriptures, which he, as it were, digs up, and shows and offers unto them,—that Jewel (I say) which when a man hath found, he may sell all to buy it,—that Jewel, more precious than the most precious desires and delights of men, even Jesus Christ, the substantial Word of life, who is the substance of all the shadows of the Old Testament, the end of that ministry, the accomplishment of the promises, and the very life of all religion, without which there is nothing more vain and empty. It is true, the gospel is the word of life, and holds out salvation to poor sinners; but yet it is Christ that is the life of that word, not only as touching the efficacy and power of it, but as touching the efficacy of it; for the gospel is a word of life only, because it speaks of him who is the life and the light of men. It is but a report of the true life, as John said, 'I am not that light, but am sent to bear witness of that light,' John i. 8. So the gospel, though it be called 'the power of God to salvation,' (Rom. i. 16.) and 'the savour of life,' and 'the gospel of salvation,' (Eph. i. 13.) yet it is not that true life, but only a testimony and declaration of it. It hath not life and immortality in itself, but only the bringing of those to light, and to the knowledge of men, 2 Tim. i. 10. It is a discovery where these treasures are lying, for the searching and finding.

To speak of this Word of life, Jesus Christ, according to his eternal subsistence in the infinite understanding of the Father, would certainly require a divine spirit, more elevated above the ordinary sphere of men, and separate from that earthliness and impurity that makes us incapable of seeing that holy and pure Majesty. Angels were but low messengers for this. For how can they express to us what they cannot conceive themselves, and therefore wonder at the mystery of it? I confess, the best way of speaking of these things, which so infinitely surpass created capacities, were to sit down in silence, and wonder at them; and withal to taste such a sweetness, in the immense greatness and infinite mysteriousness of what we believe, as might ravish the soul more, after that which is unknown, than all the perfections of the world known and seen to the bottom can do. This doctrine of the holy Trinity hath been propagated from the beginning of the world, even among the heathens, and derived by tradition from the first fathers, or the Hebrews, to neighbour nations; and therefore they speak many divine things of that infinite, supreme Being, who is the foundation of the whole creation, and that he created all things by his most divine Word, and that his blessed Spirit is the union and bond of both, and of all things besides. It is known what mysteries the Pythagoreans§ apprehended in the number of three, what perfection they imagined to be in it; so much was let out, as might

* [That is, compared to those, &c.—Ed.] † [That is, the quarter.—Ed.]

§ [It is unquestionably a remarkable fact that Pythagoras, one of the most celebrated philosophers of antiquity, represented the Great Author of all things to be possessed of a threefold form. (Cudworthii System. Intell. cap. iv. p. 445. Jenæ 1733.) Nor is it less wonderful, as a learned writer has shown, that even the Chinese seem to have received, from the dispersed Jews, long before the birth of Christ, some knowledge of the doctrine of the Trinity. Bryant's Philo Judæus, pp. 283—290.—Ed.]

either make them without excuse, or prepare the world to receive readily the light, when it should be clearly revealed. It is commonly held forth, that this eternal Word is the birth of the infinite understanding of God, reflecting upon his own most absolute and perfect Being; which is illustrated by some poor comparison to us creatures, who form in our minds, in the understanding of any thing, an inward word or image of the object, some representation and similitude of that we understand. And this is more perfect than any external vocal expression can be. So we have a weak and finite conception of the acting of that infinite wisdom of God, by which he knows himself, that there results, as it were, upon it, the perfect substantial image, and the express character of the divine essence; and therefore is the Son of God called 'the Word' which was with God, and 'the Wisdom' of the Father, because he is, as it were, the very birth of his understanding, and not only the image of his own essence but the idea, in which he conceived, and by which he created the visible world. Then we use to conceive the Holy Ghost, as the production of his blessed will, whereby he loves, delights, and hath complacency in his own all-sufficient, all-blessed Being, which he himself alone perfectly comprehends, by his infinite understanding, and therefore called, 'the Spirit,' a word borrowed from resemblance to poor creatures, who have many impulses, and inclinations to several things, and are carried to motion and action, rather from that part which is invisible in them, the subtilest part, therefore called spirits. So the Lord applies his almighty power, and exerciseth his infinite wisdom, according to the pleasure and determination of his will, for that seems to be the immediate principle of working. Therefore there is mention made of the Spirit, in the creation of the world. He sent out his Spirit, and they were created. Psal. civ. 30. These are the weak and low attempts of men to reach the height of that unsearchable mystery. Such conjectures we have of this word of God, and his eternal generation, as if trees could take upon them to understand the nature of beasts, or as if beasts would presume to give an account of the spirit that acts in men. Certainly the distance is infinitely greater between God and us; and he must needs behold greater vanity, folly, and darkness, in our clearest apprehensions of his majesty, than we could find in the reasonings and conceptions of beasts about our nature. When our own conception in the womb is such a mystery, as made David to say, O how wonderfully am I made, and fearfully! he saw a curious art and wisdom in it that he could not understand, and he believed an infinite power he could not conceive, which surprised his soul with such unexpected matter of wonder, as made him fear and tremble at the thought of it,—I say, when the generation of a poor creature hath so much depth of wisdom in it, how canst thou think to understand that everlasting wonder of angels, the birth and conception of that eternal wisdom of God? And if thou canst not understand from whence the wind comes, and whither it goes, or how thine own spirits beat in thy veins, what is the production of them, and what their motions, how can we then conceive the procession of the holy Ghost, 'which eye hath not seen, nor ear heard, nor hath it entered into the heart of man to consider it?'

Sermon II.

1 JOHN i. 1—"*That which was from the beginning,*" *&c.*

THINGS are commended sometimes, because they are ancient, especially doctrines in religion, because truth is before error, and falsehood is but an aberration from truth; and therefore there is so much plea and contention among men, about antiquity, as if it were the sufficient rule of verity. But the abuse is, that men go not far enough backward in the steps of antiquity, that is, to the most ancient rule, and profession, and practice of truth in scripture, to Christ and his apostles, but halt in their grandfathers' tombs. But sometimes things are commended, because new. The nature of man being inclined to change and variety, and ready to surfeit and loath accustomed things, even as the stomach finds appetite for new and unusual diets, so the mind of man hath a secret longing after new doctrines and things. Now we have both these combined together in this subject, which makes it the more excellent and wonderful,—antiquity, and novelty; for antiquity, it is that which was from the beginning, and which was with the Father, and that is before all antiquity, even from eternity, not only from the beginning of time, but before all time, before all imaginable beginnings. He, of whom he speaks, Christ Jesus, the Father's Word, was with the Father from the beginning, with the Ancient of days, who infinitely and unmeasurably antedates all antiquity, to whose endurance all antiquity that is renowned among men, is but novelty, to whom the world is but as of six days standing, or but as of yesterday, if we consider that infinite, beginningless, immensurable endurance of God, before this world; what a boddom* or clew is that, that can never be untwined by the imaginations of men and angels! To all eternity they should never unwind it and come to the end of that thread of the age of the Father and the Son, who possessed one another before the hills were, and before the foundations of the mountains. This is it that maketh religion the richest and most transcendent subject in the world, that it presents us with a twofold eternity, and environs the soul before and behind with an eternity without beginning, only proper to God, and an eternity without end communicated to angels and men from God. That which was from the beginning, and before all beginning, either real or imagined, how much moment and weight is in that, to persuade a soul, and compose it, beyond all the specious and painted appearances of the world! To consider that such a Saviour is holden out unto us, to come unto, and lean upon, that is the Rock of ages, upon whose word this huge frame is bottomed, and stands firm,—one who infinitely exceeds and prevents all things visible or invisible, all their mutations and changes,—one who was possessed of the Father, as his delights, before the foundation of the world, and so most likely to reconcile him to us, and prevail with him; yea, most certainly, they must have one will, and one delight, who were undivided from all eternity; and they then rejoicing in the habitable parts of the earth, taking complacency in their own thoughts of peace and good-will they had towards us, afterwards to break forth. And if both delighted in their very projects and plots upon the business, what may we think the accomplishment of the whole design will add, if it were possible to superadd to their delight? I would have you upon this, to gather two considerations, for your edification. One, to think what an incomparably excellent Saviour we have, one with God, equal to him, yea, one with him from all eternity; and so how strong a foundation there is for faith and confidence, what a Rock to establish a tossed soul upon. Man's misery and curse being for all eternity, there is One to deliver from that, who was from all eternity. And who could purchase unto us such absolute blessedness throughout all eternity, who was not himself from all eternity? What marvellous congruity and beauty is in the ways of God? How is all fitted and framed by infinite wisdom, to the end that we may have strong consolation? Do you not see the infinite evil and heinousness of sin, in the giving of such a precious ransom for it? O how is the black visage of sin portrayed in the beauty and glory of the Mediator's person? How is it painted, even to horror, in his death? Again, what divinity and worth is put upon the immortal soul of man, that is but of yesterday, since the beginning, when he that was the delight of God, before all beginning, is weighed in the balance, as it were with it, and no other thing found sufficient for exchange and compensation, that the soul may be redeemed? And doth not this answer all the jealousies and suspicious thoughts, and fearful apprehensions, arising from the consideration of our own weakness and infirmity, when such an One is offered, as is able to save to the utmost? Then I would desire you may believe, that the Father is as well-minded to the salvation of sinners, as the Son; for they were sweet company together from all eternity, and, as it were, contrived this plot and design between them, to save and redeem mankind. Some entertain harsher thoughts of the Father, as if Christ were more accessible, and exorable. But the truth is, he hath given his Son this command, and therefore he professed, that it was not so much his will, as his Father's, he was about. Therefore correct your apprehensions; do not stand aback from the

* [That is, a bottom, or ball of thread.—Ed.]

Father, as it were, till you have prevailed with Christ. No, that is not the way. Come in your first address to the Father, in the Son, for so he wills you, not because he must be overcome by his Son's persuasion, but because he would have his love to run in that channel, through Christ to us. And indeed our Saviour was much in holding out the love of the Father, and laboured to persuade the world of it. Withal, I wish you to consider whom ye neglect and despise, who hear this gospel daily, and the Word of life holden out unto you, and yet suffer not your hearts to be moved, or stirred after him. Alas, my beloved, to forsake so great a mercy, as the eternal Word of life, as the infinite Wisdom of the Father, and to let the offer of this every day run by us, and never to find leisure and vacancy from the multitude of businesses, and throng of the thoughts and lusts of the world, never to start so far backward, as to look beyond this world, to God, and his Son Jesus Christ, never to mind seriously, either him that was before all things visible, or our own souls, that must survive and outlive all this visible frame. This, I say, is the great misery and condemnation of the world, that this eternal Light hath shined, and you love your own darkness better. But be persuaded, that one day ye will think one offer of this Word of life better than life,—better, infinitely better than the most absolute life that the attendance and concurrence of all the creatures could yield you. O then that ye would incline your ears and hearts to this that is declared unto you, to receive this Word of life, that was from the beginning; and ye may be persuaded ye shall enjoy a blessedness without end!

But here is withal a newness in this subject, which both increases admiration, and may the more engage our affection. For 'the life was manifested,' saith he, ver. 2. and he is such a Word of life, as though he was invisible, and untouchable from the beginning, yet he was lately clothed with flesh, that made him both visible and capable of being handled. Now truly these are the two poles about which the mystery, glory, and wonder of Christianity turns,—the antiquity of his real existence as God, and the lateness or novelty of his appearance in the flesh as man,—nothing so old, for he hath the infinite forestart of the oldest and most ancient creatures. Take those angels, the sons of God, who sung together in the first morning of the creation, yet their generation can soon be told, and their years numbered. It is easy to calculate all antiquity, and we should not reach six thousand years, when it is taken at the largest measure. And what are six thousand years in his sight, but as six days when they are past? And if we would run backward, as far before that point of beginning, and calculate other six thousand, yet we are never a jot nearer the age of the Son of God. Suppose a mountain of sand as big as the earth, and an angel to take from it one grain in every year, your imagination would weary itself, ere ye reckoned in what space this mountain should be diminished, or removed. It would certainly trouble the arithmetic of the wisest mathematician. Now imagine as many years, or ages of years, to have run out before the world took its beginning, as the years in which the angel would exhaust this mountain; yet we have not come a whit nearer the endurance of our Lord and Saviour, whose Being is like a circle, without beginning or end. 'Behold he is great, and we know him not, and the number of his years cannot be searched out,' Job xxxvi. 26. And who can tell his generation? The age of this Word is such a labyrinth, with innumerable turnings and windings in it, as will always lead them round that enter in it. And so they are, after the longest progress and search, but just where they were, always beginning, and never coming nearer the beginning of his duration, because it is the beginning of all things that hath a beginning, but hath none itself.

Now he that was thus blessed from everlasting, who dwelt in inaccessible light and glory, which no man hath seen, nor can see, infinitely removed from all human capacities and senses,—he, I say, begins to be manifested in the fulness of time. And to make himself visible, he takes on our flesh,—and all for this purpose, that he who was the substantial life in himself, and the eternal life, in an essential and necessary way, might become life to poor dead sinners, and communicate to them eternal life. And truly it was no wonder that all ages were in the expectation of this from the beginning of the world, since it was first promised,—that the inhabitants of heaven were in a longing expectation to see and look into this mystery, for there is something in it more wonderful than the creation of this huge frame of heaven and earth. God made himself in a manner visible, by making the visible world. His power, goodness and wisdom, are everywhere imprinted in great characters on the whole, and all the parts of it. The light, how glorious a garment is it, with which he is, as it were, clothed! The heavens, how majestic a throne! The earth, how stately a footstool! The thunder, how glorious and terrible a voice! In a word, the being, the beauty, the harmony, and proportion of this huge frame, is but a visible appearance of the invisible God. But in taking on our flesh, the Word is more wonderfully manifested, and made visible; for, in the first, the Creator made creatures to start out of nothing, at his command; but in this, the Creator is made a creature. He once gave a beginning of being to things that were not. Being before all beginning himself, he now takes a beginning, and becomes flesh, that he was not. And what is it in which he was manifested? Is it the spiritual nature of angels? But though that far excel ours, yet it is no manifestation of him to us; for he should still be as unknown as ever. Is it in the glory, perfection, and power of the visible world, as in the sun, and lights of heaven? But though that have more show of glory than the flesh of man, yet it makes not much to our comfort,—there would not be so much consolation in that manifestation. Therefore, O how wisely and wonderfully is it contrived, for the good of lost man, that the Son of God shall be made of a woman, that the Father of spirits shall be manifested in the lowest habit of our flesh; and the lower and baser that be, in which he appears, the higher the mystery is, and the richer the comfort is. Suppose the manifestation of glory should not be so great, yet the manifestation of love is so much the greater. And this is the great design, 'God so loved the world,' &c. John iii. Nay, I may say, even the glory of the only begotten Son of God was the more visibly manifested, that he appeared in so low and unequal a shape. For power to show itself in weakness, for glory to appear in baseness, for divinity to kythe* in humanity, and such glorious rays to break forth from under such a dark cloud; this was greater glory, and more majesty, than if he had only showed himself in the perfection of the creatures. Now it is easy to distinguish the vail from that it covers,—to separate infirmity from divinity. But then it had been more difficult, if his outward appearance had been so glorious, to give unto God what was God's, and to give the creatures what was the creatures'. The more near his outward shape had been to his divine nature, the less able had we been to see the glory of his divinity through it.

Now, my beloved, when both these are laid together, the ancientness of our Saviour, and withal the newness of his appearance in the flesh by which he hath come so near us, and, as it were, brought his own Majesty within our sphere, to be apprehended by us,—and for no other end but to make life and immortality to shine forth as beams from him, to the quickening of dead souls,—O how should this conjunction endear him to us! That the everlasting Father should become a child for us; that is one wonder. The next wonder is, that we who are enemies should be made the children of God by him. When the dark and obscure prophesying of this,—when the twilight of Jewish types and shadows did create so much joy in the hearts of believers, insomuch that they longed for and rejoiced to see afar off that day,—when such a dark representation of this Word of life, was the very life of the godly in the world for four thousand years,—O how much is the cause of joy increased, by the rising of the Sun of righteousness himself, and his appearing in the very darkest night of superstition and idolatry that ever was over the world! When the true Life hath risen himself, and brought to open light that life that was obscurely couched up in prophecies and ceremonies, as hid under so many clouds, O then, let us open our hearts to him, and then entertain these new and fresh tidings with new delights. Though these be now more than sixteen hundred years old, yet they are still recent to a believing heart. There is an everlasting spring in them, that sends out every day fresh consolation to souls, as refreshing as the first day this spring was opened. This is the new wine that never grows old, nay, it is rather every generation renewed, with the accession of some new manifestation of the love of God. Christ's incarnation was the first manifestation of the Son, the very morning of light and life, the day-spring visiting the world that was buried in an hellish darkness of heathen idolatry;

* [That is, to be manifested.—Ed.]

and even the church of God, in the grave of superstition, and corruption of doctrine and manners. Then did that Sun of righteousness first set up his head above the horizon. But it is but one day still. He hath been but coming by degrees to the meridian and 'shining more and more to the perfect day.' That Sun hath not set since, but made a course, and gone round about the world, in the preaching of the gospel, and brought life and light about, by succession, from one nation to another, and one generation to another. And therefore we ought to entertain it this day with acclamations and jubilation of heart, as the people that lie under the north do welcome the sun when it comes once a-year to them. 'After that the kindness and love of God our Saviour toward man appeared,' Tit. iii. 4. φιλανθρωπια, his kindly and affectionate love to mankind. That is it that shines so brightly. The beams of grace and love to men, are the rays that are scattered from this Sun of righteousness. O the hardness of men's hearts, the impenetrable obstinacy of man, that this cannot melt or pierce! How damnable and miserable a case are they into, who can neither be persuaded with the eternity of this subject, to adore it, nor moved with the late appearance of the love of God to the world, in sending of his Son,—whom neither Christ's majesty nor his humility can draw! Certainly this makes sinners under the gospel in a more deplorable condition than Sodom; because if he had not come, they had not had such sin, but now it is without excuse, &c.

Sermon III.

1 John i. 1—3.—"*That which we have heard and seen of the Word of life, declare we unto you,*" &c.

Things that are excellent in themselves, will be loved for themselves; but they become the more suitable object of affection, if they have withal some suitableness and conveniency to us. Yet neither the excellency nor conveniency of the object is sufficient to engage the heart, if there be not something in the mind too, suitable to the object; that is, the apprehension of that reality and good that is in it. For, as there is a certainty in the object, that makes it a real, not imaginary thing, so there must be a certainty in the subject, whereby the thing is apprehended to be true, good, and excellent; and then the object of affection is completed. Some things there are in nature, excellent in themselves, but they rather beget admiration than affection, because they are not suitable to our necessities. Other things of a more ordinary purchase have some conveniency to supply our wants; and though they be less worth in their own nature than precious stones and such like, yet they are more desired. But there is this lamentable disproportion betwixt our apprehensions and the things themselves, which is the ground of much disappointment, and so of vexation. The things of this world having nothing of that solid excellency, or true worth, and conveniency to our souls, nothing suitable to our immortal spirits, but being empty vain shadows, and windy husks, in stead of substantial true food; yet there are high apprehensions, and big conceits of them, which is a kind of monstrous production, or empty swelling of the mind, which because it hath no bottom of solidity, it will fail and evanish. Again, take a view of spiritual things, holden out in the gospel, and there is as incongruous and unproportioned carriage of our hearts toward them. They have a certainty and reality and subsistence in themselves; they alone are excellent, and suitable to our spirits. Notwithstanding, the mind of man is most hugely misshapen towards them by unbelief, and hath nothing in his apprehension suitable to the things themselves. They are represented as far below in the true worth, as things temporal above their just value; and therefore men are not enamoured with them, souls are not ravished after that beauty that is in them.

Now the end of these words read is, to reform this irregular, disorderly posture of our minds, to hold out to you things truly excellent, and exceedingly convenient,—things good and profitable, in the most superlative degree, in the highest rank that your imaginations can suppose; and then to persuade you, that you are not deceived with vain words, or fair promises, but that there is a certain truth, and an infallible reality in them, that you being ascertained in your souls, according to the certainty of the thing presented, you may then freely, without any reserve, give your hearts to love, embrace, and follow them. O that there might be such a meeting between your hearts and this eternal Life, that as he hath come near to us, to be suitable to us, your apprehensions might draw near to be suitable to him, and by this means, your souls might meet immediately with that Word of life, and have that constant fellowship with him that is spoken of, verse 3! So your joy should be full,—for joy is but the full peace of the desires. Fill up all the wants of the heart, and then it is full of joy. And so, when such a satisfying object is pitched on, as doth exactly correspond, and answer the inward apprehensions of the mind; then there is no more room in the heart for any other thing,—as if two superficies were exactly plain and smooth, they could join so closely together, that no air could come between them, and then they could hardly be pulled asunder.

We spoke something of the excellency of that 'Word of life' in himself, and it is but little that is said, when all is said, in respect of that which he truly is. But I fear we speak, and ye hear more of these things, than either of us lively and affectionately apprehend, or lay up in our hearts. I fear, that as we say less than is, so more than we think, I mean, seriously think upon. But we shall proceed. Such an everlasting glorious person, though he have life in himself, though he be never so excellent, as 'the Son of God,' yet what is that to us? It seems he is never a whit nearer us, or not more suitable to restore us, than the very Majesty that we offended. How far is he without our sight, and without our comprehension? He is high as heaven, who shall ascend to bring down that eternal Life to us? But stay and consider, that he is not only so glorious in himself, but so gracious to us; he is not only invisible, as God, but manifested to our senses, as man: not only hath life in himself, but is an everlasting spring of life to us; not only hath his throne in heaven with his Father, but hath come down to the world, to bring that eternal life near us, even in our mouths and hearts,—to preach it, to purchase it, to seal it, and to bestow it, and the life was manifested,—the life, and that eternal life, words of force, that have some emphasis in them. The life is much, that eternal life is more; and yet these had been little to us, if not manifested to us. Life might have remained hid in God, eternal life might have resided in Christ, the fountain, for all eternity, and nothing diminished of their happiness if these had never sprung out and vented themselves. If that life that was with the Father from the beginning had never come down from the Father, we would have missed it, not they; we alone had been miserable by it. Well then, there is a manifestation of life in Christ's low descent to death; there is a manifestation of the riches of love and grace in the poverty and emptiness of our Saviour, and thus he is suited to us and our necessities every way fitly correspondent. And now it is not only, 'as the Father hath life in himself, so the Son hath life in himself;' but there is a derivation of that life to man. That donation of life to the Son, John v. 26. was not so much for any need he had of it, as by him to bestow it on us, that it might be, 'As the living Father hath sent me, and I live by the Father: so he that eats me, even he shall live by me,' John vi. 57. As parents that retain affection to their children, albeit they have committed great injuries, for which they are driven out of their houses, yet they will, as it were, underhand bestow upon them, and exercise that same love in a covered way, by a third person, by giving to them, to impart to their children. Notwithstanding this halts too much, for our Father dissembles not his love, but proclaims it in sending his Son; nor doth Christ hide it, but declares, that he is instructed with sufficient furniture* for eternal life, that himself is the bread of life sent from heaven, that whosoever receiveth it with delight, and ponders, and meditates on it in the heart, and so digests it in their souls, they shall find a quickening, quieting, comforting, and

* [The word *furniture* had formerly a more varied and extensive signification than is now assigned to it. The old divines employed it to denote the union of the divine and human natures in the person of Christ, or the peculiar properties or qualifications with which, as the Messiah, he was furnished, to act in the character of our Mediator. "Consider that Christ's calling to the office of Mediatorship may import three things, his designation, his *furniture*, his investiture in the office." —*Gillespie's Ark of the Covenant*, p. 176. Lond. 1677.—Ed.]

strengthening virtue in him. Nay, there is a strait connection between his life and ours, 'because I live, ye shall live also;' as if he could no more want us, than his Father can want him, (John xiv. 19,) and as if he could be no more happy without us, than his Father without him. And whence is it come to pass, but from his manifestation for this very end and purpose? How should such strange logic hold? Whence such a *because*, if this had not been all his errand into the world, for which his Father dispensed to want him, as it were, and he did likewise condescend to leave his Father for a season? And now this being the business he came about, it is strange he appeared in so unsuitable and unlikely a form, in weakness, poverty, misery, ignominy, and all the infirmities of our flesh, which seemed rather contrary to his design, and to indispose him for giving life to others, whose life was a continued death in the eyes of men. And the last act of the scene seems to blow up the whole design of quickening dead sinners, when he who was designed Captain of salvation, is killed himself. For if he save not himself, how should he save others? And yet behold the infinite wisdom, power, and grace of God, working under ground, giving life to the dead by the death of life itself, saving those that are lost by one that lost himself, overcoming the world by weakness, conquering Satan by suffering, triumphing over death by crying. Like that renowned king of the Lacedemonians, who, when he heard of an oracle, that if the general were saved alive, the army could not be victorious, changed his habit, and went among the camp of his enemies, and fought valiantly till he was killed; whom when the armies of the enemies understood to be the king and general, they presently lost their hearts, and retired and fled.* So our Saviour, and captain of our salvation, hath offered himself once for all; and by being killed, hath purchased life to all that believe in his death, and that eternal life. Therefore, he is not only the Word of life in himself, and that eternal life in an essential manner, but he alone 'hath the words of eternal life,' and is the alone fountain of life to us.

Now for the certainty of this manifestation of the Word of life in our flesh, both that he was man, and that he was more than a man, even God; this, I say, we have the greatest evidence of that the world can afford, next to our own seeing and handling. To begin with the testimony set down here, of those who were ear and eye-witnesses of all, which, if they be men of credit, cannot but make a great impression of faith upon others. Consider who the apostles were, men of great simplicity, whose education was so mean, and expectations in the world so low, that they could not be supposed to conspire together to a falsehood; and especially when there was no worldly inducement leading them thereto, but rather all things persuading to the contrary. Their very adversaries could never object any thing against them, but want of learning, and simplicity, which are furthest from the suspicion of deceitfulness. Now how were it possible, think you, that so many thousands every where, should have received this new doctrine, so unsuitable to human reason, from their mouths, if they had not persuaded them that themselves were eye-witnesses of all these miracles that he did, to confirm his doctrine, and that this testimony had been above all imaginable exception? Yea, so evident was it in matter of fact, that both enemies themselves confessed, the Jews and Gentiles that persecuted that way, were constrained, through the evidence of the truth, to acknowledge, that such mighty works showed forth themselves in him, though they out of malice imputed it to ridiculous and blasphemous causes. And besides, the apostle used to provoke† to the very testimony of five hundred, who had seen Jesus rise from death, which is not the custom of liars, neither is it possible for so many, as it were, of purpose, to conspire to such an untruth, as had so many miseries and calamities following on the profession of it, 1 Cor. xv. 6.

But what say they? 'That which we have heard' of, not only from the prophets, who have witnessed of him from the beginning, and do all conspire together to give a testimony that he is the Saviour of the world, but from John, who was his messenger, immediately sent before his face, and whom all men, even Christ's enemies,

* [Codrus, respecting whom this incident is recorded, was the last king of the Athenians. His subjects, from reverence to his memory, resolved that with him should terminate their regal form of government.—*Val. Max.* lib. v. cap. 6. *Just. Hist.* lib. ii. cap. 6.—Ed.]

† [That is, appeal.—Ed.]

acknowledged to be a prophet; and therefore, his visible pointing out the Lamb of God, his declaring how near he was, and preferring of him infinitely before himself, who had so much authority himself, (and so likely to have spoken the truth, being misled with no ambition or affectation of honour,) his instituting a new ordinance, plainly pointing out the Messiah at the doors, and publishing constantly that voice, 'the kingdom of heaven is at hand:'—these we, and all the people have heard,—and heard, not with indignation, but with reverence and respect. But above all, we heard himself, the true prophet, and sweet preacher of Israel; since the first day he began to open his mouth in the ministry of the gospel, we have with attentive ears, and earnest hearts, received all from his mouth, and laid up these golden sayings in our hearts. He did not constrain them to abide with him, but there was a secret power that went from him, that chained them to him inevitably; 'Lord, whither shall we go from thee, for thou hast the words of eternal life?' O! that was an attractive virtue, a powerful conserving virtue, that went out of his mouth. We heard him, say they, and we never heard any speak like him, not so much for the pomp and majesty of his style, for he came low, sitting on an ass, and was as condescending in his manner of speech as in his other behaviour: but because 'he taught with authority.' There was a divine virtue in his preaching. Some sparkles of a divine Spirit and power in his discourses broke out from under the plainness and simplicity of it, and made our souls truly to apprehend of him what was sacrilegiously attributed in flattery to a man 'the voice of God, and not of man.' We heard him so many years speak familiarly to us, and with us, by which we were certainly persuaded he was a true man: and then we heard him in his speeches open the hidden mysteries of the kingdom of heaven, revealing the will of the Father, which no man could know, but he that was with the Father, and came down from him. We heard him unfolding all these shadows and coverings of the Old Testament, expounding Moses and the prophets, taking off the vail, and uncovering the ark and oracles: and 'how did our hearts burn within us, while he talked with us, and opened to us the scriptures?' We heard him daily in the synagogues expound the scriptures, whereof himself was the living commentary. When he read them, we saw the true exposition before our eyes.

Now, my beloved, you may be admitted to hear him too, for the sum of the living words that came from the 'Word of life' are written. His sermons are abridged in the evangelists, that you may read them, and when you read them, think within yourself, that you hear his holy mouth speak them. Set yourselves as amongst his disciples that so ye may believe, and believing, may have eternal life; for this end are they written, John xx. 30, 31.

Sermon IV.

1 John i. 1, 2—"*Which we have heard and seen,*" &c.

There is a gradation of certainty here. Hearing himself speak, is more than hearing by report; but an eye-witness is better that ten ear-witnesses, and handling adds a third assurance, for the sense of touching gives the last and greatest evidence of truth. It is true, that the sense is properly correspondent to sensible things, and of itself can only give testimony to his humanity; yet I conceive these are here alleged for both, even also to witness his glorious and divine nature, which though it did not fall under sight and handling, yet it discovered itself to be latent, under that visible covering of flesh, by sensible effects, no less than the spirit of man, which is invisible, manifests its presence in the body, by such operations sensible, as can proceed from no other principle. And therefore, this faithful witness adds, 'which we have looked upon;' which relates not only to the outward attention of the eyes, but points at the inward intention, and affection of the heart. Our senses did bring in such strange and marvellous objects to our minds, that we stood gazing, and beheld it over and over again, looked upon it with reason, concluding what it might be. We gave entertainment to our minds, to consider it wisely and deliberately, and fastened our eyes, that we might detain our hearts, in the consideration of such a glorious person. From this then ye have two things clear. One is, that the Lord Jesus Christ was a true man, and that his disciples had all possible evidence of it, which the history more abundantly shows. He conversed with them familiarly, he eat and drank with them, yea, his conversation in the world was very much condescending in outward behaviour to the customs of the world. He eat with Pharisees; when they invited him he refused not; but he was more bold with publicans and sinners, to converse with them, as being their greatest friend. He was uncivil to none; would deter none through a rigid austere conversation; and indeed, to testify the truth of his human nature, he came so low as to partake of all human infirmities without sin, and to be subject to such extraordinary afflictions and crosses, as to the eyes of the world did quite extinguish his divine glory, and bury it in misbelief. This which we speak of, as a testimony and evidence that he was man, was the very grand stumbling-block and offence of the Jews and Gentiles, which they made use of as an evidence and certain testimony that he was not God. The evidence of the one seems to give an evidence to the other. But let us consider this, for it is a sweet and pleasant subject, if our hearts were suitably framed to delight in it, that there was as much evidence to the conviction of all men's senses, of his divine majesty, as of his human infirmity,—and that there are two concurring evidences, which enlighten one another; which we shall show, partly from his own works and miracles, and partly from the more than miraculous success and progress of the gospel after him.

For the first, John testifies, that not only they saw the baseness of his outward shape, but 'the glory of the only begotten Son of God, full of grace and truth,' John i. 14. John the Baptist sent some of his disciples, because of their own unbelief, to inquire at Jesus, 'Art thou he, or look we for another?' And what answer gave he them? What reason to convince them? 'Go (saith he) and tell what ye have seen and heard, that the blind see, the lame walk, and the lepers are cleansed, the deaf hear, the dead are raised, and the poor receive the gospel.' And blessed is he whoever shall not for my outward unseemliness and baseness offend, but go by that, into the glory that shines out in such works. It is said in Luke vii. 21. that 'the same hour he cured many.' Before he spoke in answer, he answered them by his deeds. He gave a visible demonstration of that they doubted of; for they could not but see a power above created power in these works, which surpass nature and art, so many wonderful works done, so often repeated, before so many thousands, even many of his watchful and observant enemies; and all done so easily, by a word, infinite cures for number and quality wrought, which passed the skill of all physicians; devils dispossessed, life restored, water converted into excellent wine, without the maturation of the sun, or the help of the vine tree; a little bread so strangely enlarged to the satisfaction of many thousands, and more remaining than was laid down; the winds and seas obeying his very word, and composing themselves to silence at his rebuke, and infinite more of this kind. Are they not in the common apprehension of men of a degree superior to that of nature? Who could restore life but he that gave it? Whom would the devils obey, but him at whom they tremble? Who could transubstantiate water into wine, but he that created both these substances, and every year, by a long circuit of the operations of nature, turns it into wine? Who could feed seven thousand with that which a few persons would exhaust, but he that can create it of nothing, and by whose word all this visible world started out of nothing? Nay, let us suppose these things to be done only by divine assistance, by some peculiar divine influence; then certainly, if we consider the very end of this miraculous assistance of a creature, that it was to confirm the doctrine delivered by him, and make such a deep impression of the truth of it in the hearts of all, that it cannot be rooted out,—this being the very genuine end of the wisdom of God in such works, it must needs follow, that all that which Christ revealed, both of himself and the Father, of his own being with him from the beginning, of his being one with him, and being his eternal Son; all this must needs be infallibly true; for it is not supposable to agree with the wisdom and goodness of God, to manifest so much of his infinite power and glory, in so extraordinary a manner, to bear testimony to an impostor or deceiver. Therefore, though no more could be at first extorted from an enemy of Christ's doctrine, but that such mighty works did show forth themselves, which could not be done but by the divine assistance and extraordinary help of God, yet, even from that confession it may be strongly concluded, that seeing there was no other end imaginable of such extraordinary assistance, but the confirmation of his new doctrine, and that of his divine nature, being one of the chief points of it, it must needs enforce, that he was not only helped by God, as Moses, but that he was God, and did these things by his own power. By this, then, it appears, that though after so many prophecies of him, and expectations from the beginning, we see but a man, in outward appearance despisable, and without comeliness and form; yet if we could open the eyes of our souls, and fix them upon him, we behold, as through some small crannies, majesty shining in his misery, power discovering itself in his weakness, even that power that made the world, and man too. He was born indeed, yet of a virgin; he was weak and infirm himself, yet he healed all others' infirmities, even by his word. He was often an hungered, yet he could feed five thousand at one time, and seven thousand at another, upon that which would not have served his disciples, or but served them. He was wearied with travels, yet he gave rest to wearied souls. At length himself died, and that an ignominious death, notwithstanding he raised the dead by his word, and at length he raised himself by his own power. All this is included in this, 'We have seen and handled.' We saw him gloriously transfigured on the mount, where his countenance did shine as the sun, and his raiment was white as light, and two, the greatest persons in the Old Testament, came out of heaven, as it were, to yield up the administration of shadows to his substance. And we saw the heaven opening in the sight of many thousands, and heard a testimony given him from heaven, 'This is my beloved Son, hear him.' And then, when he was buried, and our hope with him, we saw him risen again, and our hope did rise with him, and then some of us handled his sides, to get full persuasion; and all of us ate and drank, and conversed with him forty days. And to make a period, at length we saw him ascending up to heaven, and a cloud receiving him as a chariot, to take him out of our sight. Thus, 'the Word was made flesh, and dwelt among us, and we have seen his glory, as of the only begotten Son of God.'

But besides that which the life and death of Jesus Christ carries engraven in it of divinity, there is one miracle, which may be said to transcend all that ever was done, and it is one continued wonder since his resurrection, even the virtue and power of that crucified Saviour to conquer the world, by such unsuitable, yea, contrary means and instruments. Heathenish religion was spread indeed universally through the world, but that was not one religion, but one name. For as many nations, as many fancied gods, and in one nation many. And true it is that Mahometanism hath spread itself far. But by what means? Only by the power of the sword, and the terror of an empire.* But here is a doctrine contrary to all the received customs and inbred opinions of men, without any such means prevailing throughout the world. Cyrus,† when he was about to conquer neighbouring nations, gave out a proclamation, "If any will follow me, if he be a foot-man, I will make him an horse-man; if he have a village, I will give him a city; if a city, I will bestow on him a country," &c. Now mark how contrary the proceeding of our Lord is: 'Go and

* ["What Mahomet did, lies within any man's reach. He was authorized by no miracle, he was countenanced by no prediction. But what was performed by Jesus Christ, is absolutely above the power and the imitation of man.

"Mahomet established himself by slaughter; Jesus Christ, by commanding us to lay down our lives: Mahomet, by forbidding his law to be read; Jesus Christ by engaging us to search and read. In a word, the two designs are in all respects so directly opposite, that Mahomet took the way, in human probability, to succeed; Jesus Christ, humanly speaking, to be disappointed. And hence, instead of so irrational a conclusion, as that because Mahomet succeeded, Jesus Christ might, in like manner, have succeeded before, we ought to infer, that since Mahomet has succeeded, Christianity must inevitably have perished, had it not been founded and supported by a power altogether divine." (Pascal's Thoughts, p. 95. Lond. 1836.) Whoever wishes to see this comparison carried farther, may consult the masterly sermons of Professor White, preached before the University of Oxford, at the Bampton Lecture. These contain a view of Christianity and Mahometanism, in their history, their evidence, and their effects. pp. 225—463. Lond. 1792.—Ed.]

† [This was Cyrus, the younger son of Darius Nothus, king of Persia, and the brother of Artaxerxes. He was slain in battle, when fighting against his own brother. Plut. in Artax.—Ed.]

preach, (saith he,) repent ye, for the kingdom of God is at hand.' Here is his proclamation, 'Repent ye.' And, 'If any man will be my disciple, let him take up his cross and follow me, and deny himself.' What disproportioned means! And yet how infinitely greater success! Cyrus could not gain the Lacedemonians to his side for all that; but Christ, though poor, despised, and contemptible while alive, and at length thought to be quite vanquished by the most shameful death, when he is lifted up upon the cross, to the view and reproach of the world, he draws all men after him. He, by a few fishermen, not commanders, nor orators, persuades the world; and within a few years, that crucified Lord is adored further and wider than any empire did ever stretch itself. All the power, majesty, and success of Alexander, could never persuade the nations, no, not his own followers, to adore him as God.* But here one nailed to the cross, crowned with thorns, rejected of all men, and within a little space, adored, worshipped, suffered for throughout the nations, yea, kings and emperors casting down their crowns at his feet, many thousands counting it their honour to die upon that account. And do not the trophies of these apostolic victories remain to this day, in every corner of the world, after so many hundred years, in so many different and so far distant nations,—that same name preached and all knees bowing to it? These things considered, how much done, and by means worse than nothing, it transcends all the miracles that ever the world wondered at. Now, my beloved, these things I mention for this end, that ye may be persuaded upon sure grounds, that he who is preached unto you, is God able to save you, and according to the evidence of these grounds, ye may believe in him, and give that cordial assent to these everlasting truths, and that welcome entertainment to him in your heart that becomes. I think certainly there is very little, even of this solid assent and persuasion of the gospel, in the hearts of the most part; because they take things or names rather implicitly, and never seriously consider what they believe, and upon what grounds. But I know not a more pleasant and profitable meditation than this, if we would enter into a serious consideration of the truth and certainty of these things we have received. O how would such evidence open the heart to an entire and full closure with them, and embracement of them!

Sermon V.

1 John i. 3.—"*That which we have seen and heard, declare we unto you, that ye also may have fellowship with us,*" &c.

There are many things that you desire to hear, and it may be are usually spoken of in public, which the generality of men's hearts are more carried after. But truly, I should wrong myself and you both, if I should take upon me to discourse in these things, which, it may be, some desire, for direction or information concerning the times; for I can neither speak of them with so much certainty of persuasion as were needful, nor can I think it an advantage, to shut out and exclude this which the apostle takes to declare, as the chief subject of his writing, which must needs be, if such things have place. Therefore I choose rather with the apostle to declare this unto you, which I can always do with a like certainty, and certainly might always

* [It has been said that the following circumstance led Alexander to lay claim to a divine origin. As he entered the temple of Jupiter Ammon in Libya, the high-priest approached him, intending to address him as his son. But not being master of the Greek language, instead of saying παιδιον, (paidion) which signifies *son*, he substituted *s* for *n*, calling him παι διος, (pai dios) which signifies *son of Jupiter*. (Plut. in Alex.) Alexander required his soldiers to address him as the son of Jupiter. This excited the indignation and contempt of Hegelochus, one of his generals. "Do we acknowledge," he said, "him to be our king, who refuses to own Philip to be his father? It is all over with us, if we can submit to these things. He who demands to be thought a God (qui postulat deus credi) despises not men only, but likewise the gods. We have lost Alexander. We have lost our king. We have encountered pride, not to be endured by the gods, to whom he equals himself, nor by men, from whom he withdraws himself."—*Quint. Curt.* lib. vi. cap. 11. See also the speech of Callisthenes in the presence of Alexander himself.—*Arrian.* lib. iv. cap. 10. —Ed.]

be done to an infinite greater advantage. There are these two peculiar excellencies in the gospel or word of life, that it is never unprofitable, nor unseasonable, but doth contain in it, at all times, the greatest advantage to the souls of men, of infinite more concernment and urgency than any other thing can be supposed to be. And then we have no doubtful disputations about it. It varies not by times and circumstances. It may be declared with the same full assurance at all times, which certainly cannot be attained in other things. I would gladly know what Paul meant, when he said, he determined to know nothing but Jesus Christ, and him crucified, (1 Cor. ii. 2.) and that he counted all dross and dung to the super-excellent knowledge of Jesus Christ, Phil. iii. 8. Sure it must amount to so much at least, that this should be the ordinary subject of the ministers of the gospel, since they are the ambassadors of Jesus Christ, not the orators of the state. Should not all other things be thought impertinent and trivial in respect of this,—the salvation of sinners? And what hath a connection with that, but Jesus Christ, and the word of life?

But though this be the most pleasant and profitable subject, yet I fear, that few of them who pretend a calling to this embassage, are thus qualified and disposed to speak and declare it, as the apostle imports, 'that which we have heard and seen,' &c. It is true, there was something extraordinary in this, because they were to be first publishers of this doctrine, and to wrestle against the rebellion of men's hearts, and the idolatry and superstition of the world;—yea, to undertake such a work, as to subdue all nations by the preaching of a crucified man to them, which seemed to reason the most desperate and impossible employment ever given or taken. Therefore, it behoved them to be the eye and ear witnesses of his doctrine, life, miracles, and all, that being themselves persuaded beyond all the degrees of certainty that reason can afford, they might be the more confident and able to convince and persuade others. But yet there is something that holds by good proportion, that he that declares this eternal life to others, should be well acquainted with it himself. He that preaches Jesus Christ, should first be conversant with him, and become his disciple and follower, before he can with any fruit become a teacher of others. Therefore the apostles, (Acts i.) chose out one that had been with them from the beginning, gone in and out with them, seen and heard all. O how incongruous is it for many of us, to take upon us to declare this unto others, which I fear, few can say they have heard and seen in a spiritual manner, and handled by experience! No question, it prevails usually most with the heart, that comes from the heart. Affection is the fire that is most suitable to set affection on flame. It is a great addition to a man's power and virtue in persuading others, to have a full persuasion settled in his own heart concerning these things. Now it is much to be lamented, that there is so little of this, and so few carry the evidence on their hearts and ways that they have been with Jesus, conversant in his company. I cannot say but the ordinances that carry their worth and dignity from God, and not from men, should be notwithstanding precious to your hearts; and that word of life, however, and by whomsoever sent, if to you it be spoken, it should be suitably received with gladness of heart. But I confess, there is much of the success disappointed, by the unsuitable carriage and disposition of instruments, which ought to be mourned under, as the greatest judgment of this nation.

Two principles hath acted this divine apostle, the exceeding love of his Master; for he loved much as he was much beloved. And this carries him on all occasions to give so hearty a testimony to him, as you see, John xxi. 24, he characteriseth himself, or circumscribes his own name thus: 'This is the disciple that testifieth these things, and wrote these things, and we know his testimony is true.' Where that divine love which is but the result and overflowing of the love Christ carries to us, fills the heart, this makes the sweetest vent, and most fragrant opening of the mouth, whether in discourse, or in prayer, or preaching, that can be. O how it perfumes all the commendation of Christ! 'Peter, lovest thou me? Feed my sheep.' These have a natural connection together,—the love of Christ in the heart, and the affectionate, hearty, serious declaration of him to others. And then, another principle hath moved him,—the love of others' salvation. 'These things I declare, that ye may have fellowship with us.' Finding in his own experience how happy he was, what a pearl he had found, how rare a jewel,—eternal life,—he cannot hide it, but proclaims it. His next wish is, now since I am thus blessed; O that all the world knew, and would come and share with me! I see that unexhausted fountain of life,—that unemptiable sea of goodness,—that infinite fulness of grace in Jesus Christ, that I, and you, and all that will, may come and be satisfied, and nothing diminished. There is that immense fulness in spiritual things, that superabundance and infinite excess over our necessities, that they may be enjoyed by many, by all, without envy or discontent, without prejudice to one another's fulness, which the scantiness and meanness of created things cannot admit. I believe, if ministers or Christians did taste of this, and had access into it to see it, and bless themselves in it,—if they might enter into this treasury, or converse into this company, they would henceforth carry themselves as those who pity the world, and compassionate mankind. A man that were acquainted with this that is in Christ, would not find his heart easily stirred up to envy, or provoked upon others' prosperity or exaltation, but rather he would be constrained to commiserate all others, that they will not know nor consider wherein their own true tranquillity and absolute satisfaction consists. He that is lifted up to this blessed society, to converse with God, were it not for the compassion and mercy he owes to miserable mankind, he might laugh at the follies and vanities of the world, as we do at children. But as the φιλανθρωπια, the affectionate, kind love our Saviour carried to human nature, made him often groan and sigh for his adversaries, and weep over Jerusalem, albeit his own joy was full, without ebb, so in some measure a Christian learns of Christ to be a lover and pitier of mankind, and then to be moved with compassion towards others, when we have fullest joy and satisfaction ourselves. O that we might be persuaded to seek after these things which may be gotten and kept without clamour and contention,—about which there needs be no strife nor envy! O! seek that happiness in fellowship with God, which, having attained, you lack nothing but that others may be as happy.

'These things I declare, that ye may have fellowship with us.' O that ministers of the gospel might say so, and might from their own experience invite others to partake with them! As Paul requests others to be followers of him, as he was of Christ, so those who succeed Paul in this embassage of reconciliation, and are sent to call to the feast, might upon good ground interpose their own experience thus: O! come and eat with us,—O! come and share with us, for it will suffice us all without division. When some get into the favour of great and eminent persons, and have the honour to be their companions, they will be very loath to invite promiscuously others to that dignity, this society would beget competition and emulation. But O! of how different a nature is this fellowship, which, whosoever is exalted to, he hath no other grief, but that his poor brethren and fellow-creatures either know not, or will not be so happy! Therefore he will always be about the declaring of this to others. But if ministers cannot use such an expression to invite you to their fellowship, yet I beseech you, beloved in the Lord, let all of us be here invited by the apostle to partake of that which will not grieve you to have fellows and companions into, but rather add to your contentment.

Moreover, this may be represented to you, that ye are invited to the very communion with the apostles. The lowest and meanest amongst you hath this high dignity in your offer, to be fellow-citizens with the saints, with the eminent pillars of the church,—the apostles.

It might be thought by the most part of Christians, who are more obscure, little known, and almost despised in the world, that they might not have so near access into the court of this great King. Some would think those who continued with him in his temptations, who waited on his own person, and were made such glorious instruments of the renovation of the world, should have some great preference to all others, and be admitted into the fellowship of the Father and the Son, beyond others; even as many would think, that Christ's mother and kinsmen in the flesh, should have had prerogatives and privileges beyond all his followers. But O! the wonderful mystery of the equal, free, and irrespective conveyance of this grace of the gospel in Christ Jesus! Neither bond nor free, neither circumcision nor uncircumcision. There is one 'common salvation,' (Jude, ver. 3,) as well as 'common faith,' Tit. i. 4, and it is common to apostles, to pastors, to people, to 'as many as shall believe in his name;' so that the poorest and meanest creature is not excluded from the highest privileges of apostles. We have that to glory into, in which Paul gloried, —that is, the cross of Christ. We have the same access, by the same Spirit, unto the Father; we have the same Advocate to plead for us, the same blood to cry for us, the same hope of the same inheritance. In a word, 'we are baptized into one body;' and for the essentials and chief substantials of privilege and comfort, the Head equally respects all the members. Yea, the apostles, though they had some peculiar gifts and privileges beyond others, yet they were forbidden to rejoice in these, but rather in those which were common to them with other saints. 'Rejoice not,' saith Christ, 'that the spirits are subject unto you, but rather rejoice because your names are written in heaven,' Luke x. 20. The height and depth of this drown all other differences.

Now, my beloved, what can be more said for our comfort? Would you be as happy as John, as blessed as Paul? Would you think yourselves well, if it were possible to be in as near relation and communion with Christ as his mother and brethren? Truly, that is not only possible, but it is holden out to you, and you are requested to embrace the offer, and come and share with them; 'He that heareth my words, and doeth them, the same is my mother, and sister, and brother.' You shall be as dear to him as his nearest relations, if you believe in him, and receive his sayings in your heart. Do not then entertain jealous and suspicious thoughts, because you are not like apostles or such holy men as are recorded in scripture. If you forsake not your own mercy, you may have fellowship with them in that which they account their chiefest happiness. There is no difference of quality or condition, no distance of other things can hinder your communion with them. There are several sizes and growths of Christians, both in light and grace. Some have extraordinary raptures and ecstacies of joy and sweetness; others attain not to that, but are rather kept in attendance and waiting on God in his ways; but all of them have one common salvation. As the highest have some fellowship with the lowest in his infirmities, so the lowest have fellowship with the highest in his privileges. Such is the infinite goodness of God, that which is absolutely necessary, and most important either to soul or body, is made more universal, both in nature and grace, as the common light of the sun to all, and the Sun of righteousness too, in an impartial way, shining on all them that come to him.

Sermon VI.

1 John i. 3.—"*And truly our fellowship is with the Father, and with his Son,*" *&c.*

It was both the great wisdom and infinite goodness of God, that he did not only frame a creature capable of society with others of his own kind, but that he fashioned him so as to be capable of so high an elevation,—to have communion and fellowship with himself. It is less wonder of angels, because they are pure incorporeal spirits, drawing towards a nearer likeness to his nature, which similitude is the ground of communion; but that he would have one of the material and visible creatures below, that for the one half is made of the dust of the earth, advanced to this inconceivable height of privilege,—to have fellowship with him,—this is a greater wonder; and for this end he breathed into man a spirit from heaven, that he might be capable of conformity and communion with him who is the Father of spirits. Now, take this in the plainest apprehension of it, and you cannot but conceive that this is both the honour and happiness of man. It is honour and dignity, I say, because the nature of that consists in the applause and estimation of those that are worthy, testified one way or another, and the highest degrees of it rise according to the degree or dignity of the persons that esteem us, or give us their fellowship and favour. Now, truly, according to this rule, the honour is incomparable, and the credit riseth infinitely above all the airy and fancied dignities of men. For the footstool to be elevated up to the throne! For the poor contemptible creature to be lifted up to the society and friendship of the most high and glorious God, the only Fountain of all the hierarchies of heaven, or degrees upon earth! So much as the distance is between God and us, so much proportionally must the dignity rise to be advanced out of this low estate to fellowship with God. The distance between creatures is not observable in regard of this; and yet poor creatures swell if either they be lifted up a little above others or advanced to familiarity with those that are above them. But what is it to pride ourselves in these things when we are altogether, higher and lower, at one view, as grasshoppers in his sight? Therefore, man being in honour, and understanding not wherein his true honour and dignity consists, he associates himself to beasts. Only the soul that is aspiring to this communion with God, is extracted out of the dregs of beastly mankind, and is elevated above mankind, and associated to blessed apostles, and holy angels, and spirits made perfect. And that were but little, though it be an honour above regal or imperial dignities, but it is infinitely heightened by this,—that their association is with God, the blessed and holy Trinity.

Now herein consists man's happiness too; for the soul being enlarged in its capacity and appetite far beyond all visible things, it is never fully satiated, or put to rest and quiet, till it be possessed with the chiefest and most universal good, that is, God. And then all the motions of desire cease. Then the soul rests from its labours. Then there is a peace and eternal rest proclaimed in the desires of the soul: 'Return unto thy rest, O my soul, for the Lord hath dealt bountifully with thee,' Psal. cxvi. 7. O what a poor short requiem do men sing to their own hearts from other enjoyments! Oftentimes men's hearts, whether dreaming or waking, speak in this manner, Soul, take thy rest; but how ill-grounded is that peace, and how false a rest, daily experience in part witnesseth, and the last day will fully declare. But O how much better and wiser were it for you to seek the favour and light of his countenance upon you, and to be united to him who is the Fountain of life, so ye might truly, without hazard of such a sad reprehension as that fool got, or grievous disappointment, say, Soul, take thy rest in God!

Man was advanced to this dignity and happiness, but he kept not his station; for the great dragon falling down from that pinnacle of honour he had in heaven, drew down with him the third part of the stars of heaven, and cast them to the earth; and thus man, who was in honour, is now associated with, and made like to, beasts or devils. He is a stranger to God from the womb; all the imaginations of his heart tend to distance from God. He is exiled and banished from God's presence, the type whereof was his being driven out of the garden. And yet he is not long out, nor far away, when the infinite love of God moves an embassage to send after him and to recall him. Many messengers are sent beforehand to prepare the way and to dispose men's hearts to peace. Many prophecies were and fore-intimations of that great embassage of love, which at length appeared. For God sent his Son, his own Son, to take away the difference, and make up the distance. And this is the thing that is declared unto us by these eye and ear witnesses, to this end, that we may know how to return to that blessed society which we had forsaken to our own eternal prejudice. Is man banished out of the paradise of God into the accursed earth? Then the Son is sent out from his own palace and the paradise above, to come into this world, and to save the world. Is there such a gulf between us and heaven? Christ hath put his own body between to fill it up. Do the cherubim watch with flaming fire to keep us from life? Then the Son hath shed his own blood in abundance to quench that fire, and so to pacify and compose all in heaven and earth. Is there such odds and enmity between the families of heaven and earth? He sent his Son, the chief heir, and married him with our nature, and in that eternal marriage of our nature with him, he hath buried in everlasting oblivion all the difference, and opened a way for a nearer and dearer friendship with God than was before. And whence was it, I pray you, that God dwelt among men, first, in a tabernacle, then in a fixed temple, even among the rebellious sons of men, and that so many were admitted and advanced again to communion with God? Abraham had the honour to be the friend of God;—O incomparable title, comprehending more than king or emperor! Was it not all from this, the anticipating virtue of that uniting and peace-making sacrifice? It was for his sake who was to come and in his flesh to lay a sure foundation for eternal peace and friendship between God and man.

Now you see the ground of our restitution to that primitive fellowship with God, my earnest desire is that ye would lay hold on this opportunity. Is such an high thing in your offer? Yea, are you earnestly invited to it, by the Father and the Son? Then sure it might at the first hearing beget some inward desire, and kindle up some holy ambition after such a happiness. Before we know further what is in it, (for the very first sound of it imports some special and incomparable privilege,) might not our hearts be inflamed, and ought not we to inquire at our own hearts, and speak thus unto them: Have I lived so long a stranger to God, the fountain of my life? Am I so far bewitched with the deceitful vanities of the world, as not to think it incomparably better to rise up above all created things, to communicate with the Father and the Son? And shall I go hence without God and without Christ, when fellowship with them is daily, freely, and plentifully holden forth? I beseech you, consider where it must begin, and what must be laid down for the foundation of this communion, even your union with Jesus Christ the Mediator between God and man. And you cannot be one with him, but by forsaking yourselves, and believing in him; and thence flows that constant abode and dwelling in him, which is the mutual entertainment of Christ and a soul, after their meeting together; 'Can two walk together except they be agreed?' We are by nature enemies to God. Now certainly reconciliation and agreement must intervene by the blood of the cross, before any friendly and familiar society be kept. Let this then be your first study, and it is first declared in the gospel. Jesus Christ is holden out as partaking with you in all your infirmities; he is represented as having fellowship with us in our sins and curses, in our afflictions and crosses, he hath fellowship in our nature, to bear our sins and infirmities. Now, since he hath partaken in these, you are invited to come and have fellowship with him in his gifts and graces, in the precious merits of his death and suffering, in his rising again and returning to glory. And this is the exchange he makes and declares in the gospel; I have taken your sins and curses, O come and take my graces, and that which is purchased by my blood. Now this is the first beginning of a soul's renewed fellowship with God, and it is the foundation of all that is to come to embrace this offer, to accept him cordially as he is represented, and to pacify and quiet our own hearts by faith in that he hath done. And this being once laid down as the ground-stone, the soul will grow up into more communion with him.

To speak aright of this communion, would require more acquaintance with it than readily will be found amongst us. But it is more easy to understand in what it is exercised and entertained, than to bring up our hearts unto it. Certainly, it must neither be taken so low and wide, as if it consisted all in these external duties, and approaches of men unto God; for there is nothing capable of communion with the Father of spirits, but a spirit. And, sure I am, the most part of us removes them, and acts little that way. It is a lamentable thing, that men pretend to please God with such vain empty shows, and bodily appearances, without any serious exercise of their souls, and attention of their minds in divine worship. Neither yet must it be taken so high, and made so narrow, as if it consisted only in these ravishments of the soul after God, which are joined with extraordinary sweetness and joy, or in such rare pieces of access and liberty. For though that be a part of it, yet is it neither universal to all God's children, nor yet constant in any. There may be some solid serious attendance on God in his ordinances, which may have more true substantial life in it, and more of the marrow of Christianity in it, though a soul should not be acquainted with these raptures, nor ever carried without the line of an equal walking with God. Therefore that which I would exhort you to, is to acquaint yourselves with Jesus Christ, and you shall find a new way opened in him, by which you may boldly come to God, and having come to God in him, you are called to walk with him, to entertain that acquaintance that is made, till all the distance and estrangedness of your hearts be worn out. And I know not any thing which is more apt, either to beget or preserve this fellowship, than the communication of your spirits often with him in prayer, and with his word in meditation. And this is not to be discharged as a custom, but the love of God within, drawing the heart willingly towards communication with him, and constraining to pour out your requests to him, and wait on him, even though ye should find that sensible sweetness that sometimes is found. It were an happy advancement in this fellowship, if converse with God, whether in prayer and solemn retirements, or in meditation, or in our ordinary walking, were become the delight of our hearts, at least that they might be carried that way towards the entertaining the thoughts of his majesty, his glory, and grace, and goodness, and wisdom shining everywhere, as from a natural instinct, even when we are not engaged with the present allurements of that sweetness that sometimes accompanies it.

Sermon VIII.

1 John i. 3, 4.—"*And truly our fellowship is with the Father, and with his Son Jesus Christ. And these things write we unto you, that your joy may be full.*"

It was sin that did first break off that fellowship that was between God and man, and cut off that blessed society in which the honour and happiness of man consisted. But that fundamental bond being loosed, it hath likewise untied all the links of society of men among themselves, and made such a general dispersion and dissipation of mankind, that they are almost like wild beasts, ranging up and down; and in this wilder than beasts, that they devour one another, which beasts do not in their own kind; and they are like fishes of the sea, without rule and government. Though there be some remnants of a sociable inclination in all men, that shows itself in their combinings in societies, and erecting governments, yet generally that which is the true bond and ligament of men, which alone can truly knit them together, is broken,—that is, love, the love of God and our neighbours. And therefore, notwithstanding of all the means used to reduce, and to contain mankind in order and harmony by government, yet there is nothing but continual rents, distractions, dissipations, divisions, and dissolutions in commonwealths amongst themselves and between nations; so that all men may be represented as lions, tigers, wolves, serpents, and such like unsociable creatures, till the gospel come to tame them and subdue them, as it is often holden out in the prophets, Isa. ii. 4; xi. 6—8; lxv. 25.

Now indeed, you have here the express end and purpose of the gospel, to make up these two great breaches in the creature, between God and men, and between men and men. It is a gospel of peace. Wherever it takes hold of men's spirits, it reduceth all to a peaceable temper, joins them to God, and one to another. For the very sum and substance of it is the love of God to mankind, and proposed for this end, to engage the love of man again; and love is the glue, the cement that alone will conjoin hearts unto this fellowship. It is a strange thing, and much to be lamented, that Christendom should be a field of blood, an aceldama, beyond other places of the world; that where the gospel is pretended to be received, that men have so far put off even humanity, as thus to bite and devour one another. Certainly it is, because where it is preached, it is not believed. Therefore, sin taketh occasion by it to become the more sinful. Always let us take heed to this, that it is the great purpose and grand design of the gospel preached to us, to restore us to a blessed society and fellowship with the Father, and withal, to a sweet fellowship among ourselves; for both you see are here.

We are called to fellowship with the Father; and what is that but to have the Father of our Lord Jesus Christ thy Father, and thou to be his son by adoption of grace? It is certainly the very marrow and extract of the whole covenant, and all the promises thereof, 'I will be your Father, and ye shall be my sons and daughters, saith the Lord Almighty,' 2 Cor. vi. 18. 'I go, 'saith Christ,' to your Father and my Father, and to your God and my God,' John xx. 17. O what a sweet complication and interchange of relations!

'I will be your God, and ye shall be my people.' Here is the epitome of all happiness and felicity. In this word all is enclosed, and without this nothing is to be found that deserves the desires of an immortal spirit. For hence it follows, that a soul is filled with the all-fulness of God (Eph. iii. 19.), for that is made over to thee who believest the gospel, and thou hast as real a right and title to it as men have to their father's inheritance. Then to have fellowship with his Son Jesus Christ is another branch of this dignity; and this is that which introduceth the other. Christ is the middle person, the Mediator between God and man, given for this end,—to recover men from their woful dispersion and separation from God, and reduce them again to that blessed society. And, therefore, our acquaintance, as it were, first begins with him, and by him we are led to the Father. No man can come to the Father but by the Son; therefore, if you have his friendship, you have done the business, for he and his Father are one.

Now this fellowship, to branch it forth more particularly, is either real or personal. Real, I mean, *κοινωνια bonorum*, a communion of all good things; a communion with him in his nature, offices, and benefits;—and this must be laid down as the foundation-stone of this fellowship. He came near us, to partake of flesh and blood with us, that we might have a way, a new and living way, consecrated,—even the vail of his flesh, to come to God by; for certainly this gives boldness to a soul to draw near to God with some expectation of success and acceptation, when it is seriously considered that our nature is so nearly conjoined already to God. By this step a soul climbs up to the majesty of God; and by means of this we become partakers of the divine nature, as God of human nature, 2 Pet. i. 4. So by the same degrees we ascend to God, that God hath descended to us. He drew near us by our nature, and we, by the intervention of that same, ascend to him, and receive his image and stamp on our souls: for the Lord did stamp his own image upon Christ's human nature to make it a pattern to us, and to represent to us, as in a visible symbol and pledge, what impression he would put upon us. Then we have fellowship with him in his offices. I need not branch them out severally. You know what he was anointed for,—to be a Priest, to offer sacrifice, and to reconcile us to God, and to make intercession for us;—to be a King, to rule us by his word and Spirit, and defend us against our enemies;—to be a Prophet, to reveal the will of God to us, and instruct us in the same. Here is a large field of fellowship. We have admittance, by faith in Jesus Christ, to the real advantage and benefit of all these. There is nothing in them but it relates to us, and redounds to us. The living virtue of that sacrifice is as fresh and recent this day, to send up a savour of rest to heaven and to pacify a troubled conscience, as the first day it was offered. That perfect sacrifice is as available to thy soul as if thou hadst offered it thyself; and this day ye have the benefit of his prayers in heaven. We partake of the strong cries and tears in the days of his flesh, and of his intercession since, more than of our own supplications. What shall I say? Ye have one to teach you all things that are needful for you, one to subdue your sins under you; and, by virtue of fellowship with Jesus Christ in these offices, there is something derived from it, and communicated to us by it, that we should be kings and priests to God our Father: kings, to rule over our own spirits and lusts in as far as grace reigns in us to eternal life, and that is truly an heroic royal spirit that overcomes himself and the world; and priests, to offer unto God continually the sacrifice of prayer and praise (1 Pet. ii. 5, 9.), which are sweet-smelling and pleasant in his sight. Yea, we should offer up our own bodies as a reasonable service, Rom. xii. 1.; and this is a holy and living sacrifice, when we dedicate and consecrate all our faculties, members, and abilities to his will and service, and do not spare to kill our lusts, which are his and our enemies.

Let us sum up all in this:—whatsoever grace or gift is in Christ Jesus, whatsoever pre-eminence he hath above angels and men, whatsoever he purchased, he purchased by his obedient life and patience in death. There is nothing of all that but the soul may be admitted to fellowship in it, by its union with him by faith. Have him, and have all that he hath. Faith makes him yours, and all that he hath is a consequential appendix to himself. The word of the gospel offers him freely to you, with all his benefits, interests, and advantages. O that our hearts may be induced to open to him!

Now being thus united to Jesus Christ, that which I would persuade next to is a personal communion; that is, a suitable entertainment of him, a conjunction of your soul to him by love, and a conspiracy of all your endeavours henceforth to please him. It is certain, that true friendship is founded on a conjunction and harmony of souls by affection, by which they cease to be two, and become in a manner one; for love makes a kind of transport of the soul into another, and then all particular and proper interests are drowned in oblivion,—no more mine and thine, but he makes an interchange, mine thine, and thine mine, my heart thine, and thy honour mine. Now, certain it is, that in this God hath given us a rare pattern, and leads the way; for he declares his love to the world in the rarest effects of it, which give the clearest demonstrations possible,—'God so loved the world that he sent his Son.' And you have the most infallible argument of the Son's love,—'Greater love hath no man than this, to lay down his life for his friends,'—but he for his enemies. Now, then, you see how the heart of God and his Son Jesus Christ is fixed from everlasting on the sons of men; so unalterably, and so fully set towards them, that it hath transported the Son out of his own glory, and brought him down in the state of a servant. But it is not yet known what particular persons are thus fixed upon, until that everlasting love break out from underground, in the engagement of thy soul's love to him; and till he have fastened this chain, and set this seal on thy heart, which makes thee impatient to want him. Thou knowest not the seal that was on his heart from eternity. But now the love of a believer being the result of his love, —this is it that is the source and spring of constant communion; and it vents itself in converse with God, and daily entertainment of him in our spirits and ways. There is a keeping of company with him in prayer and meditation, and all the ordinances. There is a communication and familiar conference of the heart with him, either in thinking on him or pouring out our requests to him. There is a mutual and daily intercourse and correspondence of that soul with God, in answering his word by obedience, in praying to him, and receiving answers from him, and then returning answer again with a letter of thanks and praise, as it were. These are the ways to increase that love of God, and kindle it up to a higher flame; and it being thus increased, it gathers in all the endeavours and abilities of the soul, and sets all on fire, as a sweet-smelling sacrifice to please him. It is henceforth the great study of the soul to remove all things that are offensive to him; for the entertaining of sin, his enemy, is most inconsistent with this true fellowship and friendship. 'If I regard iniquity in my heart, the Lord will not hear me,' Psal. lxvi. 18. This will mar that sweet correspondence in prayer and praise; for it is a breach of peace and covenant to regard and maintain his enemies. Therefore the soul that loves God will study to compose itself in all things to his good pleasure, as well as his love, that is strong as death, puts him upon a careful watching, to do all things for our profit; and so this takes in our whole carriage and walking, in religious approaches, or in common businesses, to have this as our great design,—conversing with God, and walking to all well-pleasing.

Now, if we were once enrolled in this blessed fellowship with the Father and the Son, then it follows, as a fruit and result of this, that we should have fellowship one with another. And truly the more unity with God, the more unity among ourselves: for he is the uniting, cementing principle, he is the centre of all Christians; and as lines, the farther they are from the centre, the farther distant they are from one another, so the distance and elongation of souls from God sets them at further distance amongst themselves. The nearer we come every one to Jesus Christ, the nearer we join in affection one to another; and this is imported in that of Christ's prayer, 'That they may be one in us,' John xvii. 21, 22. No unity but in that one Lord, and no perfect unity but in a perfect union with him. I would exhort to study this more,—to have fellowship one with another, as members of the same body, by sympathy, by mutual helping one another in spiritual and temporal things. Even amongst Christians that live obscurely in a city, or in a village, there is not that harmonious agreement and consent of hearts, that contention and plea of love, of gentleness and forbearance, who shall exercise most of that; but there are many jealousies, heart-burnings, grudgings, strifes, evil-speakings, &c., to the stumbling of others, and the weakening of yourselves, which certainly argue that ye are much carnal, and walk as men, and that the love of God and fellowship with him is waxed cold, and is languished and dead, &c.

Sermon VIII.

1 JOHN i. 4.—"*And these things write we unto you, that your joy may be full.*"

ALL motions tend to rest and quietness. We see it daily in the motions below, and we believe it also of the circular revolutions of the heavens above, that there is a day coming in which they shall cease, as having performed all they were appointed for. And as it is in things natural, so it is in things rational in a more eminent way. Their desires, affections, and actions, which are the motions and stretches of the soul towards that it desires and apprehends as good, tend of their own nature, and are directed by the very intention of the soul, to some rest and tranquillity, some joy and contentation of spirit. If other things that have no knowledge have their centre of rest, how much more must man, who is an understanding creature, have it by the ordination and appointment of God! But there is this wide difference in the point of capacity of happiness between man and other creatures, that they, whatsoever excellent virtues or properties they have, yet know them not themselves, and so can neither enjoy what excellency themselves have, nor have use of what is in others. For to what purpose is it to shine forth, if there be no eye to see? What advantage hath the rose in its fragrancy, if it cannot smell itself? That which is not perceived, is as if it were not. And therefore it is an evident testimony, that all these visible things were created, not for themselves, but for man's sake, who knows them, can use them, and enjoy them. Here is, then, the peculiar capacity that God hath given to man,—to discern and know what he seeks, what he hath, and possesses, that so he may be able to enjoy it, or use it, according to the nature of it. This is a great point of God's image and conformity with him, whose infinite blessedness and joy riseth from that perfect comprehension and intuitive beholding of himself, and his own incomprehensible riches. So then, man's happiness or misery must depend upon this,—both what the soul fixeth upon, and what it apprehendeth to be in it. For if that eternal and universal good, the all-fulness of God, be the centre of the soul's desires and endeavours, and there be apprehended and discovered in God that infinite excellency and variety of delights which nothing else can afford so much as a shadow of, then there cannot but result from such a conjunction of the soul's apprehension, suitable to the fulness of God, and of the excellency and goodness of God, suitable to the desires of the soul, such a rest and tranquillity, such joy and satisfaction, as cannot choose but make the soul infinitely happier than the enjoyment of any other thing could do.

This being the thing, then, which all men's desires naturally tend unto, this tranquillity and perfect satisfaction of the heart being that which carries all men's hearts after it, and that which men seek for itself, and which they seek in all other things, the great misery of man is, that he mistakes the way to it, and seeks it where it is not to be found. The generality of men are so far degenerated, both from the impression of a divine majesty, and the sense of an immortal being within themselves, that they imagine to content and ease their own hearts in these outward, inconstant, perishing things; and so their life is spent in catching at shadows, in feeding on the wind, in labouring in the fire. There is nothing so plentifully satisfies our expectations as can quit the cost, and recompense the expense of our labour, toil, grief, and travail about it. There is nothing therefore but a continual, restless agitation of the heart from one thing to another, and that in a round, circling about, from one thing that now displeases or disappoints, to things that were formerly loathed; as a sick man turns him from one side to another, or changes beds often, and at length returns, expecting to find some ease where he lay at first. And it may be judged that all circular motions are eternal, and so they can never be supposed to attain their end,—that is, rest and tranquillity. Therefore a soul thus carried in a round, by the vain imaginations of his heart, is likely never to settle and find solid rest and peace. Nay, how is it possible that they can give that tranquillity and contentation to the heart and soul of man, that are so utterly in their natures disproportioned to it, both because they are only suited to the senses, and likewise for that they are changeable? Now the soul is framed with a higher capacity, and can no more be satiated with visible things, than a man that is hungry can be satisfied with gold; and besides, it is immortal, and must have something to survive all the changes of time, and therefore is likely to rest nowhere but in that which hath eternal stability. Now, though these things cannot truly fill the heart, yet they swell the belly, like the east wind, or like the prodigal's husks, fill it with wind, which causeth many torments and distempers in the soul; and though they cannot give ease, yet they may be as thorns to prick and pierce a man through with many sorrows, as our Saviour speaks. So that there is no more wisdom or gain in this, than in gathering an armful of thorns, and enclosing and pressing hard unto them,—the more hardly and strongly we gripe them, the more grievously they pierce us; or as if a man would flee into a hedge of thorns in a tempest,—the further he thrusts into it, he is the worse pricked: and that which he is fallen into is worse than that he fleeth from. I am sure all your experiences give a harmonious testimony to this, that there is no solid, permanent, constant, and equable heart-joy and contentation in all the fancied and imaginary felicities that this world adores. There is nothing of these things, that is not lesser, and lower in actual possession, nor in the first apprehension of them afar off. Nothing in them answers either our desires or expectations; and therefore, instead of peace and tranquillity, they breed more inward torment and disquiet, because of that necessary and inevitable disappointment that attends them. Therefore the apostle passeth all these things in silence, when he is to write of purpose, to give a fulness of joy; for he knows that in them there is neither that joy, nor that fulness of joy he would wish for from them; but it is other things he writes for this end.

Now, indeed, there hath been some wiser than others, that have their apprehension far above the rest of mankind, and have laboured to frame some rules and precepts to lead man into this true rest and tranquillity. And truly, in this they have done much to discover the vanity and madness of the common practice of men, and to draw man from sensible and outward things, to things invisible and spiritual. Yet there is a defectiveness in all the rules that natural reason can reach unto. There is some crookedness withal adheres to them, which shows our departure from our original. There are many excellent discourses of morality in heathen writings, which may be very subservient to a Christian, and useful to the composing and settling of his mind, amidst all the fluctuations and uncertainties of this world. They may come well in as subsidies and guards to a Christian's heart, to preserve that peace and joy it hath from God, and keep out the ordinary tumultuous passions that disturb the most part of men. But here is the lamentable failing, that while they call a man off things without, as adventitious, they lead him but into his own spirit within, as if he could there find that rest in the very enjoyment of his poor, miserable, wretched self. But Christ Jesus calls us into our own spirits, not to dwell there. For O what a loathsome and irksome habitation is a defiled heart and a guilty conscience! But rather, that finding nothing of that joy and refreshment within, we may then freely and fully forsake ourselves, as well as the world without, and transport into God in Christ, the only habitation of joy and delight, that being filled with anguish from the world, and from ourselves, we may more willingly divorce from both, and agree to join unto Jesus Christ, and to embrace him in our hearts, who is the only Fountain of life and joy, who had no other errand and business from heaven, but to repair man's joy,—as grievous a breach as any in the creation,—a thing as much missed and sought after as any thing, yea, sought after in all things that are sought. John xv. 11. 'These things I have spoken to you, that your joy may be full.' Therefore the apostle propounds this as the end of his writing on this subject,—the word of life; these things write I 'that your joy may be full;' and the way to attain this fulness of joy, he expressed in the former verse,—by fellowship with the Father and the Son.

That which makes all other things disproportioned to the soul of man, to give it this joy, is the extreme unsuitableness between them. The soul hath an infinite capacity, and besides, an immortality of endurance, but they are condemned under impotency to supply that infinite void and inconstancy, by which they must needs perish, and leave the soul without all comfort, and with more anxiety. But in those things written here we find all things suited and proportioned to the very great exigence of the soul. There is a suitableness in them, because of their spiritual nature, whereby they may close immediately with thy spirit. Other things are material and corporeal, and what union, what fellowship can a spirit be supposed to have with them? They are extrinsic, advenient things, that never come to a nearer union with thy soul; and though they could, they would debase thy soul, and not exalt it, because of a baser inferior nature. But these things, Jesus Christ, eternal life in him, these precious promises of the gospel, these spiritual privileges of Sonship, &c., these are of a more divine nature, and by meditation and faith souls come to close with them. These are inward things more near the soul that believes, than himself is to himself; and so he may always carry them about in his heart, which may be a spring of everlasting joy. This no man can take from him. John xvi. 22. For the ground and fountain is inward, seated without the reach of all these vicissitudes and changes. Then, as they have a suitableness, so they have a fulness in them, to create fulness of joy. They are cordials to the heart, things that are in their own nature refreshing to the soul, and apt to beget heart-joy. Other things are not suitable to this, to produce any such inward soul-complacency. The things that are from without reach not so deep as the heart; they make their impressions rather on the outward senses, to tickle and please them, or the countenance, to put some pleasing shape upon it. But the wise man pronounceth all those joys that arise from external things to be superficial, only skin-deep. 'In the midst of laughter the heart is sorrowful, and the end of that mirth is heaviness,' Prov. xiv. 13. *Extrema gaudii luctus occupat.** There is no solid recreation to the soul in its retired thoughts, from all the delights of the senses; it is but like the pleasure of the itch, which no man esteems pleasure. But besides, as the things of the gospel affect the heart and soul by bringing soul-mercies and treasures, as forgiveness of sin, hope of heaven, &c., so there is a fulness in them, which may answerably fill all the corners of the heart with joy. There is an unexhaustedness in these things, an universality in Christ;—all in all, all the treasures of wisdom are in him; and may not this cause surely an high spring-tide of joy? The heart is eased upon the lowest clear apprehension of Christ and the gospel. It gives a heart-serenity and calmness to a troubled soul, that nothing else could do. Yet to make up the fulness of joy, as well as the solidity of it, to extend the measure of it, as well as to beget the true quality of it, it is requisite that not only there be a fulness in the object,—that is, full, superabundant, ample matter of rejoicing; but there must be a kind of fulness in the apprehension. It must be represented fully as it is, and the clouds of unbelief scattered; and then indeed, upon the full aspect of the gospel, and Christ in it, there is a fulness of joy that flows into the soul, as the sea is filled upon the full aspect of the moon. O that we could believe this, that there is a fulness of joy here, and nowhere else! Certainly, this alone being pondered and sunk into our hearts, would be a powerful reformer in us, and among us. How would it carry men's hearts to a disgracing and despising all the things that are held in admiration by men! How would it turn the channel of men's judgments, opinions, affections, and conversations! For certainly, whithersoever the tide of joy flows, thither the heart is carried, and this it is that all men are seeking, though they take many contrary and divers ways, as their own fancy leads them. Now, if once this were established in thy soul, that here is that truth and fulness of joy, which elsewhere is ignorantly and vainly sought, would it not divert thy desires, and turn the current of thy affections and endeavours, to fall into this ocean of gladness and delight? Elsewhere there is neither true joy nor full joy,—*nec verum nec plenum gaudium*. There is no verity in it; it is but an external garb and shadow, and there is no plenty or fulness in it. It fills not the hand of the reaper, it satisfieth not his very hunger. But here, when a soul is possessed with Christ by faith, and dwelleth in God by love, there is both reality and plenty. All the dimensions of the heart may be filled up. Some allegorize upon the triangular composition of man's heart, that no orbicular

* [These are the words of the Vulgate, signifying literally, that "grief occupies the heights of joy." A humiliating truth, akin to this, is contained in one of the maxims of Hippocrates: Ultimus sanitatis gradus est morbo proximus. "The highest state of health is as near as possible to disease."—Ed.]

thing, such as this world, can fill it exactly without vacuity, but only the blessed and holy Trinity.* Truly, we may conceive, this fulness of joy, excluding all the latent griefs of the heart, and filling up all the vacant corners, doth flow from that blessed fellowship of the Father and the Son. Now, though these two be only mentioned, yet the Holy Ghost must not be excluded, for the apostolic prayer doth attribute chiefly our fellowship with God to the Spirit; so that it is the Spirit unites our hearts, and associates them to God, and that seems to correspond between him and us. So then there is such a fellowship with the Father, Son, and Holy Ghost, that leaves no vacuity in the heart, that fills all the dimensions and corners of it with peace and joy.

But add unto this, in the third place, that these things have not only a fulness, but, withal, a durableness; not only plenty, but besides, eternity and perpetuity, to correspond to the immortality of the soul. And this, certainly, is a great congruity, and so makes up much beauty and harmony; for what more incongruous and unsuitable than for an immortal spirit to spend itself, and give up itself to that which is not, which must leave it, which is mortal, and fading in its own nature, without which it must continue infinitely longer than it can enjoy it? And what more comely than for an immortal thing to associate with eternal things, and to derive its joy from an eternal spring? For, when all things visible are done away, and things mortal abolished, then its joy none can take from it, because it takes its joy from that which must survive all these changes. Suppose any thing could for the present give a fulness of joy, and absolute content to the heart, yet, if we imagine that that thing may be separated and disjoined from the heart, and cease to be, certainly the very expectation of such an eternal separation would almost extinguish all the joy, and make it dry up of the fulness: for, may a soul think, what shall I do for ever when this well dries? Whence shall I draw water of joy? Out of what well? But now, that fear is removed, and the soul needs not lose its sweetness of the present enjoyment of God through anxious foresight of the future, because he may know that the perfect fulness that shall never ebb is but coming, and the sun is but ascending yet towards the meridian, from whence he shall never go down, but stand fixed, to be the eternal wonder and delight of angels and men.

Now, though it be true that Christians here have neither that plenty, nor that perpetuity of this joy that the object of it gives ground for; though their hearts be often filled with griefs and sorrows—partly from outward, partly from inward evils and afflictions,—yet, certainly, this ariseth but from the dark apprehension, dim belief, and slight consideration of those things that Christ spoke, and his apostles wrote unto us. We might, no question, keep our hearts in more peace and tranquillity, in all the commotions of the times or alterations in ourselves, if we did more steadfastly believe the gospel and keep more constant fellowship with God. But, however it be, there is radically a fulness of joy in every believer's heart. That seed is sown that shall one day be ripe of fulness of joy; it is always lying at the root, and reserved for them. O let us lay these things to heart, which, being laid to heart, and laid up in the heart, will fill it with this sweet fragrant perfume of peace and joy. They are written for this end; let us hear them for this end too, that our joy may be full. It is true, indeed, that this fulness of joy suits only the life to come, when the vessel is both enlarged and strengthened to contain it. Things that have strong spirits in them must have strong new bottles, such as our crazy mortal bodies are not; therefore the Lord hath reserved the just fulness, the overflowings of this joy, for the time that the soul shall be purified from all sin, and the body delivered from all corruption. Because that sin lurks in many corners of the heart now, therefore this joy cannot fill up the heart and all the vacuities of it; for it is of so

* [The first of Francis Quarles' "Emblems Divine and Moral" is the picture of a heart. A representation of the globe covers the whole of the heart, with the exception of the three angles or corners, on each of which a syllable of the word Tri-ni-tas is imprinted. Under the Emblem we find these verses:—

Reader, this book shall teach the pious heart
To soar from earth, and better views impart;
Flaming with zeal to rise to heaven above,
And make the Tri-une God the object of its love.

Frances Quarles was secretary to Archbishop Usher. He died in 1644.—Ed.]

pure and heavenly a nature that it will not compound and intermingle with sin or sinful lusts. But when nothing of that remains in th heart then it flows in apace, and leaves no corner of the heart unsatisfied and unsupplied. I would have you, who get some tastes of this joy and peace by the way, not disquieted and troubled, because it abides not to be ordinary food. If you be set down again to your ordinary spare diet of manna in the wilderness, and have not these first-fruits and grapes of Canaan sent to you, think it not strange, for the fulness which you seek you are not capable of here, but you shall be capable of it hereafter. You ought, with patience, to wait for that day when your joy shall be full. As Christ is full; full measure, heaped up and running over, will he mete out unto you then; and this shall be without the fear of any ebb or diminution of it for all eternity. Neither shall this fulness, and constant fulness, cloy the soul, or breed any satiety in it. There is fulness of joy without surfeit, without satiety; that which they have they shall always desire, and that which they desire they shall always have: everlasting desire and everlasting delight being married together in their fulness. But yet so much is attainable here as may truly be called fulness in regard of the world. The fulness of joy that all the pleasures of this earth can afford is but scarcity and want to the inward fulness of joy and contentation the poorest believers may have in God, reconciled in Christ. That which the wise man gives as the character of all earthly joy suits well: 'I said of laughter, It is mad; and of mirth, what doeth it?' Eccl. ii. 2. Truly it cannot be supposed to be more real than that which is the ground and spring of it. It must be a perfunctorious,* superficial, and empty joy that is derived and distilled from such vanities. Nay, there is a madness in it besides, for men's apprehensions to swell so excessively towards poor, narrow, and limited things. It is a monster in reason to put such a value upon nothing, and make ourselves glad upon our own dreams and fancies. There is such a manifest abuse and violation of reason in it, that it can be supposed to proceed from nothing but a distemper in men's hearts. But, besides this, there are two other characters of it given (Prov. xiv. 13.), 'Even in laughter the heart is sorrowful, and the end of that mirth is heaviness.' There is no pure earthly joy; for it hath always a mixture of grief and sadness in the inward retired closet of the heart. It is of such deadness and inefficacy that it drives not out of the heart all discontentments and anxieties; but, if the most jovial man, that seems to be transported with his delights, would but retire within and examine his own conscience, he would find those delights have but little power to affect his heart. He would find terrible and dreadful representations there, that his joys may well for a time darken them, but cannot drive them away. And then it is the very natural law and fatal necessity that grief follows those joys at the heels, yea, is perpetually attending them, to come in their place. God hath so conjoined them together, and so disposed them, that men's joy shall be mingled with grief, but their grief is pure and unmixed; and that he who draws up joy to him from the creatures, must draw grief and vexation in that same chain, inseparably annexed to it by the wise ordination of God.

But there are joys of the Holy Ghost arising from the intimation and apprehension of the gospel, from the consideration of the grace and goodness of God manifested in it, and the experience of that in the soul, which are of another stamp and nature. These, indeed, affect the heart, and give the answer of a good conscience, in the blood of Christ, which is a continual feast. These drive out the bitter a..d dreadful apprehensions of sin and wrath. These sweeten and refresh the soul in all worldly afflictions and griefs. 'The heart of man knoweth his own bitterness, and a stranger doth not intermeddle with his joy,' Prov. xiv. 10. Indeed, the torments and perplexities of a troubled soul are better felt by itself than known by others, and so are the joys of that heart that apprehends Jesus Christ and peace purchased in him. They are such as no man that is a stranger to such things in his experience can apprehend. It is a joy unspeakable. O what unspeakable content gives it to the heart! And, truly, if you did not interpose the clouds of unbelief a.d sin between you and his shining countenance, there needed not be so often an eclipse in the joys of believers. Yet the day is coming that ye shall see him fully as he is, and nothing be interposed between you and him, and then your joy shall be full, &c.

* [That is, slight.—Ed.]

Sermon II.

1 JOHN i. 5. "*This then is the message which we have heard of him, and declare unto you, that God is light,*" &c.

THE great design of the gospel is to make up the breach of man's joy, and open up the way to the fulness of it; and therefore it is the good news and glad tidings of great joy, the only best message that ever came to the world. Now it shows unto us the channel that this river of gladness and joy runs into; it discovers what is the way of the conveyance of it to the soul, and what are the banks it runs between; and that is fellowship with the Father and with the Son. In this channel that river of delight runs,—between the banks of the love of God to us, and our love to him. Herein a soul is happy, and accounts itself happy; and truly, in so much do we profit by the word, and answer the design of the gospel, by how much we estimate our happiness from this alone from the communication of God to us. Whensoever the gospel takes hold of your hearts, it will undoubtedly frame them to this,—to a measuring of all blessedness from God alone. And this will carry the heart to an undervaluing of all other things, as being too low and unworthy for this end; and so to a forsaking of every thing for the closer enjoyment of God. I fear many believers are little acquainted with this joy, because they draw not their joy singly out of the pure fountain of delight, but turn aside to other external comforts, and drown their souls in them. Now, indeed, these two cannot well consist together. If we take in any thing else to make up our happiness and comfort, so much we lose of God, and that which is truly spiritual, and therefore our hearts would be more purified from carnal delights; if we would have experience of this joy, we must hang only upon his countenance and company, else we lose the sweetness of it.

Now the apostle prosecutes this further, to discover what conformity must be between them that should keep this fellowship, and what likeness of nature and qualities is necessary for them who would be happy in God's society. 'This is the message we have heard,' saith he, 'and which we declare unto you, that God is light,' &c. Take this jointly with that which went before; 'this we declare, that ye may have fellowship with the Father and the Son.' And to the end this fellowship may hold and yield you fulness of joy, it is necessary that the nature of God be laid down as the pattern to which ye must be conformed,—'God is light,' and therefore you must be light too, if ye would have fellowship with that pure light. Now this, I say, is the full message of the gospel, that which was sent down from heaven with the Son of God, the messenger of the covenant, and which the apostles heard from him. Indeed the very manner of the proposal of these things stirs up our hearts to attention, and makes us more serious than commonly we are. That there is one, and such an one sent from heaven, with such an embassage as this is, to invite us to society with God again, one whose interest lies in this, to make us happy; and this he declares unto us, that he hath no other design but to fulfil our joy. O how powerful might this be on our hearts to conquer them, to make them willingly hearken to him! Any message that comes from heaven should be received with great reverence and respect of mortal men, because it comes from the court and palace of the great King. But when this is the substance of it, to make us happy in himself, to advance us to this incomparable dignity of society with himself, in which society there is a fulness of joy,—then how should we receive it with open hearts, and entertain it gladly! If we could take it always thus as a message from heaven, and look upon it and hear it in that notion, I think the fruit would be incomparably greater; for what is it that makes it dead and ineffectual in men's hearts, but that the apprehension of it degenerates and falls down from God to creatures; because it is not taken so as his word, carrying the stamp of his divine authority? We bring it forth, not as a message from him, but as from ourselves; and you receive it, not as from him, but from us, and thus it is adulterated and corrupted on both hands. My beloved, let us jointly mind this, that whatsoever we have to declare is a message from God to mortal men; and, therefore, let us so compose ourselves in his sight as if he were speaking to us. The conscience of a very heathen was awaked when Ehud told him he had a message from God to him. Eglon arose out of his seat, that he might hear it reverently, (Judg. iii. 20.) though it was a bloody message, as it proved in the event. Yet so much the common dictates of reason might teach you, that ye should arise and compose yourselves to reverend and awful attention to what the Lord God will speak. But when, moreover, we know that the sum of the message is to make us blessed, and raise us up to communion with him in his joy and happiness, we are not only called to reverence, as to God, but to ardent affection and desire, as to him who by all means seeks our happiness. O how happy were he that could first hear and receive this message from him, and then declare it to others! But, however, though we should fail in that, this doth not change either the authority or nature of the message itself; and therefore, if men should be so far destitute of God as not to bring it from him immediately, yet do not you forsake your own mercy too, but receive it as that which is come forth from God, receive it for itself, as carrying in its bosom a fulness of joy to you, and receive it for his sake who moved this embassage first after sinners, and his sake who carried it to sinners, that is, for the Father and the Son, to whose fellowship you are here invited. Let us then hear the message.

'This then is the message, that God is light,' &c. The ground of communion of persons is their union in nature, or likeness one to another. There is some general society between all mankind, as being conjoined in one common nature; but the contracting of that in narrower bounds of affinity and consanguinity doth enlarge the affection the more. You see it is natural for those who are joined by such relations of blood one to another, to love one another more than others out of these bonds. But true friendship draws the circle yet narrower, and contracts the love that is scattered abroad to mankind in a strange channel, to run towards one, or a few; and the foundation of this is some peculiar and particular similitude and likeness in manners, and sympathy of disposition, which makes the souls of men to melt one into another, after some converse and acquaintance together. This is the bond that knits this near society; some conformity necessarily presupposed to communion and fellowship. Now, that which holds so in the communion of man with man, must be much more needful in man's communion with God: for all the societies, combinations, and conjunctions of the creatures, are but shadows of this higher communication of the spirit of man with God the Father of spirits. And, indeed, we may find some rude draughts and resemblances of this divine society, and of the rule according to which it must be modelled, in all the friendly or near conjunctions of creatures; for every thing is best preserved and agreeth best with things of its own nature. See the disposition of the parts of the world. Things contiguous and nearest other are also likest in nature one to another. So it is among men. The several agreements and symbolizings of men's spirits in different qualities and tempers, make several sorts of men, and part them into so many companies: *Pares paribus congregantur. Simile simili gaudet.**

Now, my beloved, this same supernatural and divine society that we speak of must be constituted according to this fundamental rule, that is, it is necessary, to the end that God and man may have fellowship together, that they come nearer in likeness one to another. Now for God, you know he cannot be liker us, for he is unchangeably holy and good. That were most absurd to bring down his Majesty to partake of our wretched infirmities of sin and darkness. Indeed in this he hath come as far as his own nature and our good would permit, to communicate in our nature, and all the sinless infirmities of it. It is impossible, then, that he should make up the distance by any change of himself; but we must be changed, and some way raised up to partake of the purity of his nature, and be transformed into some likeness to him, and then is the foundation of society and fellowship laid down.

* [These are two adages. The former is quoted by Cicero as an ancient proverb in his days. (De Senect. cap. iii.) The meaning of it is, that, "equals, or persons of the same age and rank, flock together." The literal meaning of the other is, "like takes pleasure in like." It (*το ὁμοιον τῳ ὁμοιῳ φιλον*) is as old as the days of Aristotle.—Ethic. Nicom. lib. ix. cap. 3.—Ed.]

This is the apostle's meaning, in declaring to us what God is, that according to that pattern, and in that glass we may see what to conform ourselves to, and may have a particular determination of the great qualification of those who pretend to fellowship with God. 'God is light, and in him is no darkness.' Now, take the just opposition,—man is darkness, and in him is no light. Now, what communion then can light have with darkness? Either the light must become darkness, or the darkness become light. Either the light must leave its glorious purity and forsake its nature—which cannot be admitted—or else the darkness of men's souls must be wiped off, and abolished by the brightness of God's light. And then there may be a communion between the primitive light and the derivative light, between the original light and that which flows out from the original. But take darkness remaining darkness, and light remaining light, and they cannot compone* together; for the first great separation that was made in the world was between light and darkness: 'And God saw the light that it was good: and God divided the light from the darkness,' Gen. i. 4. And so it is impossible for men that live in the darkness of their minds, in ignorance, and in the darkness of sinful lusts, that they can have any fellowship with God, who is a fountain of pure light and undefiled sanctity. 'What hast thou to do to take my covenant in thy mouth,' &c.; and this God saith to the wicked. It is an incongruous and unsuitable thing, for man to pretend nearness and interest in this God, and yet be buried in darkness and hatred of the light of personal reformation, as a gold ring in a swine's nose, that rather deforms the jewel, than beautifies the beast; so are the pretensions of ignorant and wicked men, to this divine society, &c.

Sermon X.

1 John i. 5.—"*This then is the message which we have heard of him, and declare unto you, that God is light,*" &c.

Who is a fit messenger to declare this message? Can darkness comprehend the light, or apprehend it? Or can those that are blind form any lively notion of light, to the instruction and persuasion of others? Truly, no more can we conceive or speak of God, who is that pure light, than a blind man can discourse on colours, or a deaf man on sounds. 'Who is blind as the Lord's servant?' And therefore, who are more unmeet to declare this message of light? What reverence and godly fear ought this to be declared withal, when mortal man speaks of the eternal God unto mortal men? What composure of spirit should be in us? What trembling and adoration? For, at our best, we can but declare our own ignorance, and the furthest attainment in this knowledge is but a further discovery of man's darkness. We have three ways of creeping towards that glorious light of God. First, his own works are like some visible appearances of that invisible and incomprehensible God; and in these we know him, but not what he is in himself. Consider how dark and dull we are in piercing into the hidden natures of things, even below us, as beasts and plants. We behold some effects flow from them, but from what principle these do flow, that we know not. How much less can we apprehend any thing suitable of the divine Majesty, that is infinitely above us, from these wonderful and glorious works of his power and wisdom! Man is endowed with wisdom to do some excellent works of art, as planting, graffing, building, painting, weaving, and such like. But the beasts that are below us cannot apprehend from these works what the nature of man is. Now is there not a more infinite distance, a greater disproportion between us and the divine nature, so that we cannot rise up to an understanding notion of it, in itself? Nay, besides, one man will do many things which another cannot understand,—he beholds the art of it, he sees the matter, but yet he cannot pierce into the mind of the workman, and look upon that wisdom and idea of his mind. Therefore all that we can conclude from these wonderful works of God, is some silent admiration of him. If these be such, then what must he be?

* [That is, compound.—Ed.]

How infinitely distant from them, and transcendent over them? But what he is, these cannot declare, and we cannot apprehend. Then we use to climb up to the knowledge of God, by attributing to him all the perfections, excellencies, and eminences of the creatures. Whatsoever commends them, we apprehend that originally and infinitely in him; and thus we spell out that name that is most simply one, in many letters and characters, according to our mean capacity, as children when they begin to learn. So we ascribe to him wisdom, goodness, power, justice, holiness, mercy, truth, &c. All which names being taken from the creatures, and so having significations suited to our imperfections, they must needs come infinitely short of him, and so our apprehensions of them. These are scattered among the creatures, therefore they cause divers conceptions in us; but all these are united in him. He is a most simple, pure being, that eminently and virtually is all things, and properly is none of all.

Another way we have of apprehending him, by way of negation, denying all the imperfections of the creatures, and removing them at an infinite distance from him. And truly, though this be an imperfection in knowledge, yet it is the greatest knowledge we can attain to, to know rather what he is not, than what he is. He is not limited to any place, nor bounded with any measures and degrees of perfection, as creatures are; therefore we call him infinite. He is not comprehended within the limits of time, but comprehends all within himself; therefore he is eternal. He is not subject to changes and alterations; therefore called immutable. He is not compounded, as a result of divers parts; therefore he is most purely simple, and one. He is not like those things we see and hear, that fall under our senses; therefore we call him a Spirit, or a spiritual Being. Now, in all these weak endeavours of man, to detain and fix his own spirit in the contemplation of God, if he cannot reach the understanding of what God is, yet certainly he will attain this great point of wisdom,—not to be ignorant of his own ignorance. And truly, my beloved, this is the thing I would have us to learn to know, that the admiration of God in silence is the best expression of him. We would not search into these mysteries, to satisfy our curiosity, but rather compose our hearts to a continual silent wondering before him; for where our understandings are confounded, and our minds overwhelmed with the infiniteness of that glory, so that we can see nothing but our ignorance of all, this should certainly compose all to quiet admiration, for silence and wonder is the proper and natural posture of a soul that is at a stand, and can neither get forward for inaccessible light, nor will retire backward, for that it apprehends already.

'This then is the message, that God is light.' Because we cannot conceive in our poor narrow minds what God is in himself, therefore he expresseth to us often in similitudes to the creatures, and condescends to our capacity. As he stands in manifold relations to us, so he takes the most familiar names, that may hold out to our dull senses what we may expect of him. Therefore he calls himself a Father, a King, a Husband, a Rock, a Buckler, and Strong Tower, a Mountain, and whatsoever else they may represent to our hearts, that which may strengthen them in believing. But there is no creature so directly attributed to God, as light: none used to express his very nature and being, as abstracted from these relations, but this,—'God is light;' and Christ takes it to himself—'the light of the world,' and 'the life of men.' The truth is, it hath some excellency in it above all other visible creatures, that it may fitly carry some resemblance to him. The scripture calls light his garment, Psal. civ. 2. And truly it is a more glorious robe of Majesty than all the royal and imperial robes and garments of state that either angels or men could contrive. The light is, as it were, a visible appearance of the invisible God. He hath covered his invisible nature with this glorious garment, to make himself in a manner visible to man. It is true, that light is but, as it were, a shadow of that inaccessible light, *umbra Dei.* It is the dark shadow of God, who is himself infinitely more beautiful and glorious. But yet, as to us, it hath greater glory and majesty in it than any creature besides. It is the chief of the works of God, without which the world would be without form, and void. It is the very beauty of the creation, that which gives lustre and amiableness to all that is in it, without which the pleasantest paradise would become a wilderness, and this beautiful structure, and adorned palace of the world, a loathsome dungeon. Besides the admirable beauty of it, it hath a wonderful swift conveyance, throughout the whole world, the upper and lower, in a moment, in the twinkling of an eye. It is carried from the one end of heaven to the other in a moment, and who can say by what way the light is parted? Job xxxviii. 24. Moreover, it carries alongst with it a beautiful influence, and a refreshing heat and warmness, which is the very life and subsistence of all the creatures below. And so, as there is nothing so beautiful, so, nothing so universally and highly profitable. And to all this, add that singular property of it, that it is not capable of infection; it is of such absolute purity, that it can communicate itself to the dunghill, as well as to the garden, without receiving any mixture from it. In all the impurities it meets withal, it remains unmixed and untainted, and preserves its own nature entire. Now you may perceive, that there is nothing visible that is fitter to resemble the invisible God, than this glorious, beautiful, pure, and universally communicable creature, light.

Hereby you may have shadowed out unto you the nature of God, that he is an all-knowing, intelligent Being. As light is the first and principal visible thing, yea, that which gives visibility to all things, and so is in its own nature a manifestation of all things material and bodily; so God is the first object of the understanding—*primum intelligibile, et primum intelligens.* Nothing so fit an emblem of knowledge as light, and truly in that respect God is the original light, a pure intellectual light, that hath in himself the perfect idea and comprehension of all things. He hath anticipated in himself the knowledge of all, because all things were formed in his infinite understanding, and lay, as it were, first hid in the bowels of his infinite power. Therefore he is a globe or mass of light and knowledge, like the sun, from whom nothing is hid. Hell and destruction are not covered to him. There is no opacity, no darkness or thickness in the creation, that can terminate or bound this light, or hinder his understanding to pierce into it. Now as all things, by the irradiation of the light, become visible, so the participation of this glorious Sun of righteousness, and the shining of his beams into the souls of men, makes them to partake of that heavenly intellectual nature, and reflects a wonderful beauty upon them, which is not in the rest of the world.

Besides, here is represented to us the absolute purity and perfection of God's nature,—'God is light, and in him is no darkness.' Besides the purity of the light of knowledge, there is a purity of the beauty of holiness. The glorious light of God's virtue, and power, and wisdom, is communicated to all the creatures. There is an universal extent of his influence towards the good and bad, as the sun shines on both, and yet there is no spot nor stain upon his holiness or righteousness, from all his intermingling with the creatures, the worst and basest creatures. All his works are holy and righteous, even his works in unholy and unrighteous men. He draws no defilement from the basest of the creatures, nor yet from the sinfulness of it. He can be intimately present and conjoined in working, in virtue and power, in care and providence, with the dirt and mire of the streets, with the beasts of the field, and yet that is no stain upon his honour or credit, as men would suppose it to be, no more than it is a dishonour to the sun to shine on the dunghill. In a word, there is no mixture of ignorance, darkness, impurity, or iniquity in him, not the least shadow of change or turning, not the least seed of imperfection. In regard of him, the moon is not clean, and the sun is spotted. In respect of his holiness, angels may be charged with folly.

Then add unto this, to make up the resemblance fuller, the bounty and benignity of his influence upon the world, the flowings forth of his infinite goodness, that enrich the whole earth. Look as the sun is the greatest and most universal benefactor,—his influence and heat is the very renovation of the world. It makes all new, and green, and flourishing; it puts a youth upon the world, and so is the very spring and fountain of life to all sublunary things. How much is that true of the true light, of the substantial, of whom this sun is but a shadow? He is the life of the world, and the light of men. Every good gift, and every perfect donation descends from him, James i. 17. His influence is more universal to the being, to the moving, to the living of all things. And then Jesus Christ the Sun of righteousness, is carried about in the orb of the gospel, and in his beams there is a healing virtue.

These are the refreshments of poor wearied souls, that are scorched with the anger of God. There is an admirable heat and warmness of love and affection that this glorious light carries embosomed in it, and that is it that pierces into souls, and warms hearts, and quickens dead spirits, and puts a new face upon all again. This is the spring of all the life that is truly spiritual, and it hath as sweet and comfortable effects upon the souls of men, who receive the truth in love, the light in love, that is, the light with heat, as ever the sun approaching near the earth hath had upon plants and living creatures.

And to complete the resemblance more, there may be something of the infallibility and incomprehensibility of the divine Majesty here represented. For though nothing be clearer than the light, yet there is nothing in its own nature darker than light: that which is so manifest to the eyes, how obscure is it to the understanding! Many debates and inquiries have been about it, but yet it is not known what that is, by which we know all things. Certainly such is the divine light. It is inconceivable and inexpressible, therefore is he said to dwell in light inaccessible and full of glory, 1 Tim. vi. 16. There is a twofold darkness that hinders us to see God, a darkness of ignorance in us, and a darkness of inaccessible light in him. The one is a vail upon our hearts, which blinds and darkens the souls of men, that they do not see that which is manifest of God, even in his works. O that cloud of unbelief that is spread over our souls, which hinders the glorious rays of that divine light to shine into them! This darkness Satan contributes much to, who is the prince of darkness, 2 Cor. iv. 4. This makes the most part of souls like dungeons within, when the glorious light of the gospel surrounds them without. This earthliness and carnality of our hearts makes them like the earth, receive only the light in the upper and outward superfice, and not suffer it to be transmitted into our hearts to change them. But when it pleaseth him, who at the first, by a word of power, 'commanded light to shine out of darkness,' he can scatter that cloud of ignorance, and draw away the vail of unbelief, and can, by his power and art, so transform the soul, as to remove its earthly quality, and make it transparent and pure, and then the light will shine into the heart, and get free access into the soul. But though this darkness were wholly removed, there is another darkness, that ariseth not from the want of light, but from the excessive superabundance of light —*caligo lucis nimiæ*;* that is, a divine darkness, a darkness of glory, such an infinite excess and superplus of light and glory, above all created capacities, that it dazzles and confounds all mortal or created understandings. We see some shadows of this, if we look up to the clear sun. We are able to see nothing for too much light. There is such an infinite disproportion here between the eye of our mind, and this divine light of glory, that if we curiously pry into it, it is rather confounding and astonishing; and therefore it fills the souls of saints with continual silent admiration and adoration.

Sermon XX.

1 John i. 5.—"*This then is the message which we have heard of him, and declare unto you, that God is light, and in him is no darkness at all.*"

True religion consists not only in the knowledge of God, but especially in conformity to him, and communion with him. Communion and fellowship with God is the great end and design of the gospel, and it is the great result of all a Christian's pains and progress. It is not only the greatest part of religion, but the very reward of religion too, for piety hath its reward of happiness in the bosom of it, without borrowing from external things. Now, that which this sweet and fragrant fruit, which perfumes all the soul with delight, and fills it with joy, springs out of, is conformity to God. Assimilation of nature and disposition, some likeness to God imprinted on the soul again in holy affections and dispositions, a coincidency of our will with the will of God, drowning of it in the sea of his good pleasure, his law in the inward

* [That is, "the darkness of two much light."—Ed.]

parts. Now what is the root of this conformity, but the knowledge of God? This is that which hath a virtue to transform the soul into his similitude. You see then where true religion begins lowest, and by what means it grows up to the sweet fruit of that eternal joy that shall be pressed out of the grapes of fellowship with God. So then, whatsoever is declared of God unto us in his word, whatsoever is holden forth of him, is not only set forth to be the subject of our knowledge, but especially to be a pattern for imitation, and to be an inflaming motive to our affection. This is the very substance of the verse.

'This then is the message' I declare, 'that God is light;' and this I heard not from Christ only, for the satisfaction of my curiosity, nor do I declare it to you only, that you may know it, as if you had no more to do with it, but especially that ye may know what ye ought to be in conformity to that light. The end of your knowing God, is to become liker God, if so be ye would have communion with him.

Let us take this rule, then, to measure all our searchings after God, and inquirings into him. Certainly there ought to be more meditation and inquiry of heart upon this subject, because it is the spring of all life to the soul. It is that which enricheth it most, and fills it with peace, joy, and delight, and brings in a treasure into a man's heart, such as Christ speaks of—'A good man out of the good treasure of his heart,' &c. Meditation, much meditation on God, a stayedness and fixedness of spirit upon him, lays up a treasure in the heart. This is it that makes such a difference between the heart and mouth of a righteous man, and a wicked man. The heart of the wicked is little worth, for the total want of this; and therefore, their lips and tongues are void of edification, full of corruption. But where this spring floweth within, it maketh the mouth of a man like a well of life; it maketh his lips like choice silver. O the scantiness and neglect of this amongst Christians makes all to wither and decay! There is little searching after the Almighty, little employing and entertaining our spirits about him, low, slender, and single thoughts and apprehensions of him, which cannot but cause a *deliquium** and decay in all the parts of Christianity, when the very sun is eclipsed from us by our ignorance and inconsideration of him: and that so long, it must have dreadful effects upon us. Therefore, let us be exhorted to this study, to give our spirits to this employment,—to think more on God. But, as I was saying, there is need of a rule to measure us in it, and of some caution about it, that is, that we have our end rightly established, what we aim at in inquiring after, or meditating upon God. If it be only to give entertainment to the curiosity of our minds, as in the contemplation of natural things, if it be only to pry into secrets and mysteries, and to labour to comprehend that which is incomprehensible, then we lose our labour, and we are in danger to meet with a consuming fire, instead of instructing and refreshing light. I would therefore have this guarded against,—the insatiable desire and greediness of our minds after the knowledge of secret mysteries. We may set bounds here, and not overstretch or strain our understandings, to compass his infinite Being, as it is in itself. Let us rather take him up as he is revealed in the scriptures, and so meditate on him as manifested in his word and works, his grace, mercy, power, wisdom, &c. and read his name with delight in those large volumes spread before our eyes, &c.

Now the just measuring and regulating of all knowledge of God, is to direct it to a further end, to have nothing before us but this, that we may reverence, adore, fear, and love him so much the more. And this is the thing that maketh access to him most easy and sweet, when the design a soul hath, in all its searchings about him, is for this purpose, to the end it may love him, and worship him more suitably, and be more conformed to him, when he is looked upon as a pattern of our conformity, that is, the right apprehension and up-taking of him, to know that God is light, and so to know it, as in it to behold the necessity of what qualification should be in us; that is indeed to know God. My beloved, let us consider that so much we know of God, as we love him, and fear him, and are conformed unto him; for that knowledge, which is not about this work and design, is for no other purpose but to be a witness against a man, and the most heinous aggravation of his sins.

To come then to the particular in hand, 'God is light;' and that is holden out and

* [That is, a defect.—Ed.]

declared for this end, that there may be a pattern of the qualification of all that intend to enter into that society; if ye would have fellowship with God, then consider what you engage into, what manner of person he is, for the intimate knowledge of one another is presupposed to all constant friendship. You must know then what God is, if you would have communion with him, because there is no communion without some conformity, and no conformity without knowledge of him. Therefore, as he is light, so the soul must be made light in him, and enlightened by him, that would have his society. We must be transformed into that nature, and made children of light, who were children of darkness. Now, as there is a light of understanding and wisdom in God, and a light of holiness and purity, so there is in our souls, opposite to these, a darkness of ignorance and unbelief, and a darkness of sin, and impurity of affections. Now, 'what communion can light have with darkness?' Let every man ask this at his own heart, if there be no happiness without this society, and no possibility of this society, while I remain in darkness, then is it not high time to come to the light? This then is the first change that is made in a soul, the darkness of ignorance and unbelief is driven out, by the approach of that glorious light of the gospel into the heart; then is discovered unto the soul that deformity of sin, that loathsomeness in itself, that it never apprehended. Then there is a manifestation of the hidden works of darkness, of the desperate wickedness of the heart, which lay unobserved and unsuspected all the while. And now a man cannot in that view but abhor himself, for that which none else can see in him. And there is withal manifested that glorious holiness and purity in God, that inviolable righteousness, that omnipotent power, which formerly were never seriously thought upon; now these are represented to the life before a sinner. And to close up all, there is a manifestation of the grace and goodness of God in Christ, which discovers a way of salvation, and delivery from sin and wrath; and this perfumeth and refresheth all the faculties of the soul. Thus the soul is in a part conformed to that original light, when a beam is sent from it, and hath pierced into the heart, and scattered the darkness that did alienate the minds of men from God. But it is not only an illumination of the foreface, and outer side of the soul, not only a conviction of the judgment in these things; but by virtue of that divine heat that is transmitted with the light of the gospel, the soul is purified and cleansed from its grosser nature, and so is made transparent, that the light may shine into the very inwards of the heart. And this is the special point of conformity to God,—to have our souls purged from the darkness of sinful, earthly, and muddy affections,—to have them purified by the light of God, from all the works and lusts of darkness, and the shining beauty of holy affections and inclinations, to succeed and fill up the vacant room. If knowledge only reside in our brains, and send not down warm beams to quicken and inflame the heart, then it is barren and unfruitful, it is cold and unprofitable. If it hover only alone in our heads, and keep a motion there, but send down no refreshing showers to the affections, which may make us abound in good fruits, then it is like the windy clouds, clouds without rain, that pass away without any benefit to the thirsty ground. Let us then take this along with us, let the impression of this description of the divine Majesty abide in our hearts: 'God is light;' and if we often ruminate and ponder upon this, I think it will make us often to reflect upon ourselves, how we are darkness; and this will breed some carefulness and desire in the soul, how to have this darkness removed, that there may be a soul capable of divine illustration. This is it that advanceth the soul to the nearest conformity with God, the looking often upon God, till our souls be enlightened, and our hearts purified; and this again puts the soul in the nearest capacity for that blessed communion with God: 'Blessed are the pure in heart, for they shall see God,' Matt. v. 8. Truly it is not profoundness of ingine,* it is not acuteness and sharpness of wit, it is not pregnancy in understanding, or eminency in parts, that will dispose the soul to this blessed vision of God, and frame it to a capacity of fellowship with him. No, there needs no extraordinary parts for this, nothing but that the heart be purified from corruptions, those inward earthly qualities, that are like so many vicious and gross humours, filling the organ of the sight; these, pride, conceit, self-love, passion, anger, malice, envy, strife,

* [That is, genius.—Ed.]

covetousness, love of pleasures, ambition, these, I say, that possess the hearts of the most excellent natural spirits, cast a mist upon their eyes, and hinder them to see God, or enjoy that delight in him, that some poor, weak, and ignorant creatures, whose hearts the Lord had purged from sin, do find in God. Therefore if any of you have an aim at this, to have fellowship with God, know both for your direction and your encouragement, that 'God is light.' For your direction, because that must be your pattern, and if you have no study that way to be like him in holiness, you shall not see him. But take it likewise for an encouragement, for that style carries not only the necessity of what he must be, but it holds out likewise the fountain and storehouse of all our qualifications; for 'God is light.' The original, primitive light,—all must borrow of him, and that light is freely and impartially communicable to poor sinners: 'with thee is the fountain of light, and in thy light shall we see light.' Let a soul that apprehends its own darkness and distance from him thus encourage itself: My light is but a beam derived from his light, and there is no want in him. He is a sun of righteousness. If I shut not up my heart through unwillingness and unbelief, if I desire not to keep my sins, but would be purged from them, then that glorious light may shine without stop and impediment into my heart. He is not only light in his own nature, but he is a light to us, and if he please to remove that which is interposed between him and us, it shall be day-light in our hearts again. Thus a soul may strengthen itself to wait on him, and by looking thus up to him, and fixing on him, we shall be enlightened, and our faces not be ashamed.

Sermon VII.

1 JOHN i. 6.—"*If we say that we have fellowship with him, and walk in darkness, we lie,*" &c.

THERE is nothing in which men suffer themselves to be so easily deceived as in this highest concernment of religion, in which the eternal interest of their souls lies. There is no delusion either so gross or so universal in any other thing, as in this thing, in regard of which all other things are nothing. This hath overspread the world, (to speak only of that part which pretends to Christianity,) a strong, pertinacious, and blind fancy of being in Jesus Christ and having interest in salvation. I call it a blind and ignorant fancy, for truly ignorance and darkness is the strongest foundation of such conceits. Papists call it the mother of devotion. It is true, in this sense it is the mother of a man's groundless devotion towards himself, that is, of delusion. This, together with self-love, which always hoodwinks the mind, and will not suffer a serious impartial examination of a man's self; these, I say, are the bottom of this vain persuasion, that possesseth the generality of men. Now, what it wants of knowledge, it hath of wilfulness. It is a conceit altogether void of reason, but it is so wilful and pertinacious, that it is almost utterly inconvincible, and so it puts souls in the most desperate forlorn estate that can be imagined. It makes them, as the apostle speaks, (Eph. v. 6.) *υἱοὺς τῆς ἀπειθείας, children of impersuasion;*— it is rendered commonly, 'children of disobedience.' And, indeed, they are joined together. They are children of disobedience, carrying the manifest characters of wrath upon them; yet they are withal children of impersuasion, incapable of any persuasion contrary to these deluding insinuations of their own minds. Though they be manifest to all men to be sons of disobedience, living in rebellion against God, yet it is not possible to persuade them of it. They are as far from conviction of what they are, as reformation to what they should be. Notwithstanding, if men would but give an impartial and attentive ear to what the apostle says here, I suppose the very frame of his argument is so convincing, that he could not but leave some impression. If any thing will convince a child of impersuasion, the terms here propounded are fittest, 'God is light, and in him is no darkness.' Hence it follows, by unavoidable consequence, as clear as the light, that no man can have fellowship with God that walks in darkness.

Those that delude themselves in this matter are of two kinds. The generality pretend to Christianity in general, and to an interest in salvation; but if we descend into the chief parts and members of Christianity, as holiness, fellowship with God, walking after the Spirit, and such like, these they do not so much as pretend to. And withal, they think they have a dispensation from such strictness, and make it a sufficient plea that they are not such, because they never professed to be such. Others again, though fewer, can pretend even to these higher points of Christianity, as communion with God, walking after the Spirit, and indeed in this they are more consonant to their profession of Christianity. But, as the apostle saith, there may be a practical lie in it too, if we consider and compare their practice with their profession.

I would speak a word, by way of preparation, to you who are of the first sort, that is, the very multitude of professing Christians, because you do not profess so much as others, and do not give out yourselves for the students of holiness, you think yourselves exempted from the stroke of all this soul-piercing doctrine. You think readily it is not pertinent to apply this to you of walking contrary to your profession, and so committing this gross lie in not doing the truth. 'If any man say I have fellowship with God,' &c. And who will say that, say ye? Who will speak such a high word of himself as this? Therefore, since you do not presume so high, you think you have escaped the censure that follows.

But, I beseech you, consider what your professions import, and what you engage yourselves to, even by the general profession of Christianity. I know you will all say you are Christians, and hope to be saved. Now, do ye understand what is included in that? If any man say that he is a Christian, he really says that he hath fellowship with God; if any man say he is a Christian, he says he hath fellowship with Christ, and is partaker of his Spirit; for, as the apostle (Rom. viii. 9.) declares unto you, 'If any have not the Spirit of Christ, he is none of his;' that is, he is no Christian. For what is it, I pray you, to be a Christian? Is it not to be a new creature, formed again by the Spirit of Christ? 2 Cor. v. 17. Therefore, in as far as you pretend to be Christians, and yet are not professors of holiness, and think you have a dispensation from such a walking in God and after Christ, you fall under a twofold contradiction, and commit a twofold lie: first, between your profession and practice; then in your profession itself,—your practice is directly cross to the very general profession of Christianity. But besides that, there is a contradiction in the bosom of your profession. You affirm you are Christians, and yet refuse the profession of holiness. You say ye hope for heaven, and yet do not so much as pretend to godliness and walking spiritually. Nay, these you disjoin in your profession, which are really one, without which the name of Christianity is an empty, vain, and ridiculous appellation. There must be then a great darkness of misapprehension in your minds, that you take on the name of Christians, and will not know what it imports; and therefore in the mean time, you profess that which destroys and annuls your former profession. Now, certainly, this is a grosser lie, a flatter contradiction, than needs much inquiry into, to find it out. It is so palpable, that I wonder that these very common and received principles of truth do not rise up within to testify against it; for if ye do not own the profession of holiness and communion with God, what advantage have you then of Christianity? Tell me, what will it serve you for? Can it save you? Can a bare, empty, contradicted, and blasphemed title save you? And if it do not save you, it will make your condemnation the greater. Let this then first be settled in our hearts, and laid down as a principle,—that the most general profession of Christianity lays an inviolable bond and obligation upon us, to all that is imported in the particular expressions of a Christian's nature, walk, and society. Whether we take it so or not, thus it is: to be a Christian infolds all that can be said; and if it do not import these, it is not true to its own signification nor conformed to Christ's meaning. You may deprave the world as you please, and deform that holy calling so, as it may suit to your carriage, but according to this word, in this acceptation of it, you shall be judged; and if your Judge shall in that great day lay all this great charge upon you, what will it avail you now to absolve yourselves in your imaginations, even from the very obligation itself?

Let us suppose, then, that you are convicted of this, that Christianity, in the most general and common acceptation, is inclusive of fellowship and communion with God, and that you profess and pretend to both; then let us apply this just rule of the apostle's, to examine the truth and reality of such a profession. The rule is straight, and so may be a trial both of that which is straight and crooked: *Rectum sui et obliqui index.* And here the application being made, there is a discovery of the falsehood and crookedness of most men's hearts. This golden rule of examination is a rule of proportion, so to speak, or it is founded upon the harmony that should be between profession and practice, words and deeds; and upon that conformity should intercede between those that have communion one with another. Now apply these to the generality of Christians, and behold there is no harmony and consent between their speaking and walking. Their calling and profession, as Christians, imports communion with God, who is the pure unmixed light, and yet they declare otherwise, that themselves are in darkness of ignorance, and walk in the darkness of sin, and so that communion must be pretended, where there is no conformity and likeness to God intended. The result then of all is this; herein is the greatest lie, and most dangerous withal, committed,—it is the greatest lie, because it takes in all a man's conversation, which all alone makes up one great universal lie, a lie composed of infinite contrarieties, of innumerable particular lies; for every step, every word, and action, is in its own nature contrary to that holy profession, but all combined together, makes up a black constellation of lies—one powerful lie against the truth. And, besides, it is not against a particular truth, but against the whole complex of Christianity. And error is a lie against such a particular truth as it opposeth; but the tract and course of an ignorant ungodly conversation is one continued lie against the whole bulk and body of Christianity. It is a lie drawn the length of many weeks, months, and years, against the whole frame of Christian profession. For there is nothing in the calling of a Christian, that is not retracted, contradicted, and reproached by it. Oh! that ye could unbowel your own ways, and see what a cluster of lies and incongruities is in them; what reproaches and calumnies these practical lies cast upon the honour of your Christian calling; how they tend of their own nature, to the disgracing of the truth, and the blaspheming of God's name! These things ye would find, if ye would rip up your own hearts and ways; and if you found how great that lie is, you could not but fear the danger of it: for it being no less than a denying of Jesus Christ, and a real ab-renunciation of him, it puts you without the refuge of sinners, and is most likely to keep you without the blessed city, for 'there shall in no wise enter therein anything that defileth, or maketh a lie,' Rev. xxi. 27. What shall then become of them whose life all along is but one continued lie?

Sermon XIII.

1 JOHN i. 6.—"*If we say that we have fellowship with him, and walk in darkness, we lie,*" *&c.*

THAT which is the sum of religion, sincerity, and a correspondency between profession and practice, is confirmed by reason, and much strengthened by nature itself; so that religion, reason, and nature, conspire in one, to hold out the beauty and comeliness of sincerity, and to put a note and character of infamy and deformity upon all hypocrisy and deceit, especially in the matters of religion. There is nothing so contrary to religion, as a false appearance, a show of that which is not: for religion is a most entire and equable thing, like itself, harmonious in all parts of it, the same within and without, in expression and action, all correspondent together. Now, to mar this harmony, and to make it up of unequal, dissimilar parts, and to make one part give the lie to the other, the course of a man's life, in ignorance, negligence, and sin, proclaiming contrary to the profession of Christianity: this is to make religion a monstrous thing, to deny the nature of it, and in our imaginations to contrive an impossible union of inconsistent things. It is a creature made up of contradictions, which can have no subsistence in the truth, but only in the fancies of deluded souls; one professing Christianity, and so by consequence fellowship with the original light, the Sun of righteousness, and yet darkness of ignorance possessing the mind, and the heart carried away in the ways of the lusts of ignorance, and walking in that darkness. This is a monster in Christianity, one so far misshapen, that the very outward form and visage of it doth not remain. But I told you, reason confirms this. For what more suitable to the very natural frame and constitution of a reasonable being, than that the outward man should be the image and expression of the inward, and that they should answer one another, as face answers face in the water, that the tongue should be the interpreter of the mind, and the actions of a man's life the interpreter of his tongue? Here is that beautiful proportion, and that pleasing harmony, when all these, though different in their own nature, yet conjoin together, and make up one sweet concord. Now truly, if we take upon us the profession of Christianity, and yet our ordinary and habitual speeches are carnal and earthly, never salted with grace, often poisoned with blasphemies, oaths, and cursings, and often defiled with filthy speeches, and often intermingled with reproaches of others; if our conversation be conformed to the course of the world, according to those lusts that hurry away multitudes of mankind to perdition, and look to the heart within, and behold never any labour about the purifying of it from corruption, never any mortification of evil affections, and little or no knowledge of the truth, not so much as may let Christ into the soul: this, I say, is as unreasonable and absurd, as it is irreligious. It wholly perverts that beautiful order, makes an irreconcilable discord between all the parts in man, that neither mind, nor mouth, nor hands, answer one another, nor all of them, nor any of them answer that holy calling a man pretends to. Such a one pretends ordinarily the goodness of his heart towards God, but now the tongue cannot interpret the heart. It is exauctorated out of that natural office, for the ordinary current is contrary to that pretended goodness of the heart; for 'a good man, out of the good treasure of his heart, sendeth forth good things,' but all these are either evil, or never seasoned with that spiritual goodness. Then the ways and actions of a man's life which ought to interpret and expound his professions, these are rendered altogether incapable of that. They give no confirmation to them, but rather a manifest contradiction; for what are your multiplied oaths, drunkennesses, fornications, railings, contentions, lyings, sabbath-profanations, your woful neglect of prayer in secret, and in your families, your continuing in these evils that ever you walked into? What are they, I say, but a manifest violation of both religion and reason, and a clear confirmation that ye are liars, and the truth is not in you?

There is something even in nature to declare the absurdity and unnaturalness of this general discordance between men's profession and practice. Look upon all the creatures, and do they not all with one voice proclaim sincerity? Hath not every beast and every bird its own outward shape, outward gesture, and voice, and external workings, which declare the inward nature of it? And is not this a staple, known rule in nature, that every thing is known by the effects of it, a lion by his roaring, a lark by its singing, a horse by his neighing, and an ox by his lowing? &c. All these speak forth nothing but sincerity, insomuch, that if these marks and signs should be confounded, and beasts use them indifferently, all human knowledge should suddenly fall to nothing, this would put such a confusion both in the world and mankind. O how doth this condemn those who pretend to this high calling of Christianity! And yet there is no way left to discern them by, nothing appearing in them, and ordinarily proceeding from them, which may give a signification of the inward truth of their fellowship with God; but rather that which gives a demonstration of the vanity of the pretension. There were no consent in nature, if that were not, neither is there any harmonious agreement in religion, where this proportion and correspondence is not kept in a man's life. The very heathens did not account them philosophers, but those that expressed their doctrines in works, as well as words; and truly, the liveliest image of truth is in practice. They commended them that were sparing in words, and abundant in deeds, who had short speeches, but long and large discourses in their life. And what is this, but that which our Saviour everywhere, from his own example, inculcates upon us? These words are emphatic, to *do the truth,* to *walk in the light,* to *do his words,* to *believe with the heart,* and such like: all which declare, that in so far we have the truth, and have fellowship with the Light, as it is impressed in the affection, and expressed again in the conversation. For the infinite truth and the infinite life is one, and the original Light and primitive life and love is one too, and whoever truly receives the truth and light, as it is, cannot but receive him as the living truth and life-giving Light, and so be heated and warmed inwardly by his beams, which will certainly cause some stirring and working without. Forasmuch as in nature heat is always working, so is the fire of love, kindled in the heart, incessant that way. 'Faith worketh by love.' For action is the very life of life, that which both shows it and preserves it.

Now what shall we say, to carry these things home to your hearts? Where shall convincing words be had which may break the hardness of your hearts? It is strange that you are in such a deep dream of delusion, that nothing can awake you out of it. And how little is that in which you have to please yourselves? Some external privileges, the temple of the Lord, his covenant, and the seals of it, your ordinary hearing the word, and such like. But are there not many things in your hearts and ways that act the most contradictory lie to these that can be? For wherefore do we thus meet together? Do you know an end, or propose any? I scarce believe it of the most part. We come out of custom, and many as by constraint, and with little or no previous consideration of the great end of this work. And when ye go forth, what fruit appears? Your ordinary carnal and civil discourses succeed; and who is it either bows his knee to pray for the divine blessing, or entertains that holy word either in his own meditation, or speaks of it to the edification of others? Are you not, the most part of you, that ground of which Christ speaks, that lies in 'the way side,' and every thing comes and takes the seed up? Do you either listen and apply your hearts to a presentness in hearing? Or is there any more account of it, than a sound in the ear, or any footstep or impression left in the heart, more than of the flight of a bird in the air? And, alas! how many souls are choked and stifled, the truth suffocated in the very springing, by the thorns of the cares of this world, and the throng and importunity of businesses, and earthly desires? How many good motions come to no maturity by this means? How few of you use to pray in secret, and dedicate a time for retirement from the world, and enjoyment of God? Nay, you think you are not called to it, and if any be induced to it, and to public worship in their families, yet all the day over is but a flat contradiction to that. What earthly-mindedness! What unholiness of affection! What impurity of conversation! What one lust is subdued? What one sin mortified? Who increaseth more in knowledge of the truth, or in love of God? Is it not midnight with the most part of you? O the darkness of the ignorance of your minds, by which you know not that religion you profess, more than Turks who persecute it! And what are the ways in which ye walk? Are they not such ways as will not come to the light, and hate the light, because it reproves them? John iii. 19, 20; xi. 9, 10. Are they not such in which men stumble, though they seem to walk easily and plainly in them? Yet, O that everlasting stumble that is at the end of them, when you shall fall out of one darkness of sin and delusion into another extreme, eternal darkness of destruction and damnation! O that fearful dungeon and pit of darkness you post into! Therefore, if you love your own souls, be warned. I beseech you be warned to flee from that utter darkness. Be awaked out of your deceiving dreams, and deluding self flattering imaginations, and 'Christ shall give you light.' The discovery of that gross darkness you walked in, in which you did not see whither you went; I say, the clear discerning of what it is, and whither it leads, is the first opening of that light, the first visit of that morning-star, that brings salvation.

If ye will not be convinced of that infinite danger you are in, yet ye are not the further from it. He that walketh in darkness lieth, &c. His strong confidence and persuasion hath a lie, a contradiction in the bosom of it, and that will never bottom any true happiness. It is a lie acted by the hand, the foot, and all the members, a lie against the holy truth and word of God, and the very reproach of the name of Christ; a lie against yourselves, and your own professions, a foul-murdering lie, as well as a Christ-denying lie. And this lie, as a holy man saith, hath filled houses, cities, families, countries. It hath even overspread the whole nation, and filled all with darkness, horror, confusion, trouble, and anguish. Once being a holy nation by profession of a covenant with God, and our open, manifest, universal retraction of that, by an unholy, ungodly, and wicked conversation; this hath brought the sword against a hypocritical nation, and this will bring that far greater, incomparably more intolerable day of wrath upon the children of disobedience. Therefore let me exhort all of you, in the name of the Lord, as ye desire to be admitted to that eternally blessed society within the holy city, and not to be excluded among those who commit abomination, and make a lie, that ye would henceforth impose this necessity upon yourselves, or know that it is laid upon you by God, to labour to know the will and truth of God, that you may see that light that shines in the gospel; and not only to receive it in your minds, but in your hearts by love, that so you may endeavour in all sincerity the doing of that truth, the conscionable practising of what you know. And this, as it is a great point of conformity to the light, so it will make you capable of more light from God; for he delights to show his liberality, where he hath any acceptance. Be not satisfied, O be not satisfied, with knowing these truths, and discoursing upon them; but make them further your own, by impressing them deeply in your hearts, and expressing them plainly in your ways! This is 'pure religion and undefiled,' James i. 27. And 'is not this to know me, saith the Lord?' Jer. xxii. 16. Practice is real knowledge, because it is living knowledge. It is the very life and soul of Christianity, when there needs no more but the intimation of his will to carry the whole man. This is what we should all aspire unto, and not satisfy ourselves in our poor attainments below this.

Sermon XIV.

1 John i. 7.—"*But if we walk in the light, as he is in the light, we have fellowship one with another, and the blood of Jesus Christ his Son cleanseth us from all sin.*"

Art is the imitation of nature, and true religion is a divine art, that consists in the imitation of God himself, the author of nature. Therefore it is a more high and transcendent thing, of a sublimer nature than all the arts and sciences among men. Those reach but to some resemblance of the wisdom of God, expressed in his works; but this aspires to an imitation of himself in holiness, which is the glory of his name, and so to a fellowship with himself. Therefore there is nothing hath so high a pattern, or sublime an end. God himself, who is infinitely above all, is the pattern, and society with God is the end of it: and so it cannot choose, but where religion makes a solid impression on a soul. It must exceedingly raise and advance it to the most heroic and noble resolutions that it is capable of, in respect of which elevation of the soul after God, the highest projects, the greatest aspirings, and the most elevating designs of men, are nothing but low, base, and wretched, having nothing of true greatness of mind in them, but running in an earthly and sordid channel, infinitely below the poorest soul that is lifted up to God.

Since we have then so high a pattern as God, because he is infinitely removed from us in his own nature, we have him expressed to us under the name and notion of light, which makes all things manifest; not only as dwelling in inaccessible light, that is, in his own incomprehensible, ineffable essence, even before this light was created; for he is in the light, and was in the light, when there was no sun to give light, because he was in himself environed, so to speak, with the infinite light and splendour of his own understanding, and beauty of his own holiness, and so dwelling in an all-fulness and self-sufficiency of blessedness; not only is he thus in the light, but he is a light to poor sinners, the most communicative Being, that ceaseth not continually to send forth streamings of that light and life into dark and dead souls. And therefore he is not only light in himself, but a sun of righteousness, most beneficial in his influences, most impartial and free in his illumination ; and so he is often called, —'my light and my salvation,' 'our light,' 'a light to me,' Psal. xxvii. 1; Micah vii. 8; Isa. xlii. 6, 7. Now, it is this emission of light from him that first drives away that gross darkness that is over souls ; for till then, in the darkness all was hid and covered, nothing seen, neither ourselves, nor God, neither the temper of our hearts, nor the course of our ways, nor the end they lead to. But it is the breaking in of a beam of that Sun of Righteousness that maketh any such discovery; as motes are not seen till the sun shine, though the house be full of them. In darkness there is nothing but confusion and disorder ; and light only makes that disorder visible to the soul, to the affecting of the heart. Now, when once the soul hath received that light, there is a desire kindled in the heart after more of it ; as when the eye hath once perceived the sweetness and pleasantness of the light, it opens itself and exposeth itself to a fuller reception of more. And so the soul that is once thus happily prevented by the first salutation and visit of that day-spring from on high, while he is sitting in darkness, and in the shadow of death, (Luke i. 78, 79) afterwards follows after that light, and desires nothing more than to be imbosomed with it. That tender preventing mercy so draws the heart after it, that it can never be at perfect rest till the night be wholly spent, and all the shadows of it removed, and the sun clearly up above the horizon, and that is the day of that clear vision of God's face. But in the mean time, this is the great ambition and endeavour of such an one, to walk in that light, and this is the very entertainment of that fellowship with God. He is already in the light, that is, to say, he is translated from a state of darkness to light, and endued with the living and saving knowledge of God in Jesus Christ. This is his state. He is in the light, one enlightened from above, having his eyes opened to discover the mystery of the iniquity of his own heart, and to see far off, to that bottomless pit of misery which his way would lead him to; one who hath by this divine illustration discovered eternal things, and seen things not seen ; and withal, gotten some knowledge of salvation by the remission of sins. Now, such an one, being thus in the light, his duty is, and his infinite dignity besides, to walk in that light, that is, to lead all his life under that eternal light of God, which shines in the word, and to bring it all forth in his view ; to make our whole course a progressive motion towards heaven, wherein that glorious light shines most gloriously. It is almost all one with that of Paul's, to have our conversation in heaven. For, to walk in the light, is a kind of elevation of our actions, a raising them up to heaven, to that pure light ; for after that and towards that is the soul's design.

Now to express to you in what it consists, I desire not to branch it forth in many particulars, which rather distract the mind than affect the heart. Only you may know, it consists especially in the inward retirements of the soul to God, and the outward shining of that light in our conversation to others. These are the chief parts of it, borrowing from his light, and then lending and imparting it to others, by a holy conversation. Truly, we must needs conceive that the most lively and unmixed partaking of the light of God, and the sweetest society with him, is in the secret withdrawings of the soul from the world, and reposes upon God those little intervals, and, as it were, stolen hours of fellowship with God, that are taken from the multitude and throng of our business. These are the fittest opportunities of the transforming the soul into his similitude, and of purifying it as he is pure, of filling it with divine light and love; for then the heart lies, as it were, perpendicularly under his beams, and is opened before him, to give admission and entry to this transforming light; and it is the shining of God's countenance then upon the soul that draws it most towards conformity with him, and leaves an impression of light and love upon the soul.

Oh! that you were more acquainted with this, this aprication, so to speak, that is, sunning yourselves, and warming in the sun, the exposing and opening of your hearts frequently in secret, before this Sun of Righteousness. Now this, if you were acquaint with it, would make your light so to shine before men, as your heavenly Father may be glorified, Matt. v. 16,—and that is the walking in that light of God. This makes a Christian to come forth, as Moses from the Mount, with his face shining. He comes out from the retired access to God, with a lustre upon his carriage, that may beautify the gospel; and (as one saith well) with the tables of the law in both his hands, written in his practice, the light of the law shining in his life. And truly this is the Christian's diurnal motion in his lower sphere, wherein he carries about that light that is derived from the higher light. In all his converse with men, it shines from him to the glorifying of him that is the Father of lights, walking righteously and soberly, without offence, doing good to all, especially the children of light; extending offices of love and benevolence to every one; forbearing and forgiving offences, not partaking with other men's sins; and, finally, declaring in word and deed, that we have communion with the fountain of pure light, and one day expect to be translated out of this lower orb, where we are so far distant from him, and fixed in the highest of all, where we may have the immediate, full, uninterrupted, and clearest aspect of his countenance, which shall then make the description that is here given of God communicable to us, that, as he is light, and in him is no darkness, so we, being fully and perfectly shined upon by him, may be light likewise, without any mixture of darkness, as here it is not.

Now, my beloved in the Lord, this is that we are called unto, to walk thus in the light, in the light of obedience and sanctification; and that is the great thing ye would learn to aspire unto, rather than to enjoy the light of consolation. Indeed, I conceive, that which maketh many of us walk in darkness, as is spoken in Isa. l. 10, that is, without comfort, peace, and joy, and without clear discerning our interest in God, is, because we walk in another darkness, that is, of sin and distance from God. The one darkness is introductive of the other; nay, they cannot be long without one another. The dark cloud of bold sinning, and careless uncircumspect walking, that cannot but eclipse the light of consolation, and fill the soul with some horror, anguish, and confusion. Therefore, if ye would walk in the light of joy and comfort, O take heed nothing be interposed between God and your souls! You must likewise walk in the light of his law, which is as a lamp to the feet; and this light, as the ray, begets that light of comfort, as the splendour, which is the second light of the sun. I know it is a disconsolate and sad condition, to walk without the light of the knowledge of our interest in God; but I would earnestly recommend unto you two things to support you, and help you in that. One is, that you do not give over the chief point of this society with God, that is, walking in the light of his law and commandments, but that you do the more seriously address yourself to the one, that you want the other. Certainly, it ought to be no hinderance of your obedience, and patient continuing in obedience, that you know not your own interest, and that his countenance shines not so upon you. You know that sweet resolution, 'I will wait upon the Lord, who hides his face,' &c. (Isa. viii. 17; Mic. vii. 7;) and his own command, Isa. l. 10; Hos. xii. 6. Ye that walk in such darkness, nevertheless, 'stay upon God.' Truly, there could be no greater evidence of thy interest than this,—to give patient attendance upon him in the ways of obedience, till he shine forth. This would in due time 'bring forth thy righteousness as the light,' if we would not subtract and withdraw ourselves from under the light, because it is presently overclouded. Then, moreover, you would know, that all this while that your interest in Christ lies dark and under a cloud, you would then be most in the application of that blood to your souls, most in trusting and staying upon the name of God, and his absolute promises. Suppose thou do not as yet know that he is thine, yet dost thou not know that he is made thine by believing in him? And therefore, while it is inevident that it is already, thou oughtest so much the more to labour, that what is not may be. Now, if thou canst not apply him to thy soul, as thine own possession, yet thou mayest, and so much the more oughtest to apply thy soul to him, and resign and offer thyself to him, as willing to be his possession, to be his, and no more thine own. In a word, when thine own experimental feeling of the work of God's Spirit fails within thee, then so much the more insist, and dwell upon the meditation and belief of the general promises, which are the proper object of faith, and not of sense. As our own interest is the proper object of sense, and not of faith: therefore the defect in the one needs not redound upon the other. To sum up all in one word,—if thou thinkest that thou hast not yet believed in Christ, and hast no interest in him, I will not dispute with thee, to persuade thee thou art mistaken, for all this debate would be in the dark, because thou art in darkness. But one thing I would say unto thee,—labour to do that which thou wouldest do, which thou must do, if such a case were granted. Suppose it were so, that thou had no interest in him, what wouldst thou do then? I am sure thou wouldst say, I would labour by any means to have him mine. Why then thou knowest that cannot be before believing, and receiving him on his promises, and not at all but by believing. Therefore, since that this is it you must at length turn unto, suppose the case were decided, why do you not presently, rather without more wearying yourselves in the greatness of your way, turn in thither, as to a place of refuge, without further disputing in the business; and so by believing in Christ, and waiting upon him in his ways, you shall put that out of question, which debating would make an endless question. The Lord make you wise to know the things that belong to your peace.

Sermon IV.

1 John i. 7.—" *And the blood of Jesus Christ his Son cleanseth us from all sin.*"

Can two walk together except they be agreed? As darkness cannot have fellowship with light, till it be changed into some conformity to the light; even so there can neither be any fellowship in walking, nor conformity in nature, between God and us, who are enemies to him by nature, unless there be some agreement and reconciliation of the difference. Now, here is that which maketh the atonement,—' The blood of Jesus his Son cleanseth us from all sin.' This is it that takes away the difference between God and men, and makes reconciliation for us. This blood hath quenched the flame of indignation and wrath kindled in heaven against us. And this alone can quench and extinguish the flames and furies of a tormented soul, that is burned up with the apprehension of his anger. All other things thou canst apply or cast upon them will be as oil to increase them, whether it be to cool thyself in the shadows of the world's delights, such a poor shift as the rich glutton would have taken in hell. Those drops of cold water that thou canst distil out of the creature will never give any solid ease to thy conscience. Thou mayest abate the fury of it, or put it off for a season. Thou who art afraid of hell and wrath, mayest procure some short vacancy from those terrors by turning to the world; but certainly they will recur again, and break out in a greater fire like a fever that is not diminished, but increased by much drinking cold water. Or if thou go about to refresh thyself and satisfy thy challenges by thy own attainments in religion, and by reflection upon thy own heart and ways, finding something in thy esteem that may counterbalance thy evils, and so give thee some confidence of God's favour; those, I say, are but deceitful things, and will never either quench the displeasure of God for thy sins, but rather add fuel to it, because thou justifiest thyself, which is an abomination before him. Nor yet will it totally extinguish and put to silence the clamours of thy conscience, but, that some day thou shalt be spoiled of all that self-confidence and self-defence, and find thyself so much the more displeasing to God, that thou didst please thyself and undertake to pacify him. Therefore, my beloved, let me, above all things, recommend this unto you as the prime foundation of all religion, upon which all our peace with God, pardon of sin, and fellowship with God must be built,—that the blood of Jesus Christ be applied unto your consciences by believing; and that, first of all, upon the discovery of your enmity with God, and infinite distance from him, you apply your hearts unto this blood, which is the atonement—to the reconciling sacrifice, which alone hath virtue and power with God. Do not imagine that any peace can be without this. Would ye walk with God, which is a badge of agreement? Would ye have fellowship with God, which is a fruit of reconciliation? Would ye have pardon of sins, and the particular knowledge of it, which is the greatest effect of favour,—and all this, without and before application of Christ, ' who is our peace,' in whom only the Father is well-pleased? Will ye seek these, and yet dispute this point of believing, as if it were possible to attain these without the sprinkling of that blood on the heart, which indeed cleanseth it from an evil-accusing conscience? If you desire to walk in the light, as he is in the light, why weary ye yourselves in bye-ways? Why take ye such a compass of endless and fruitless agitation, and perplexity of mind, and will not rather come straightway at it, by the door of Jesus Christ? For he is the new and living way into which you must enter, if ye would walk in the light. And the wounds of his side, out of which this blood gushed, these open you a way of access to him, because he was pierced for us. That stream of blood, if ye come to it and follow it all along, it will certainly carry you to the sea of light and love, where you have fellowship with God. And, oh! how much comfort is in it, that there is such a stream running all the way of our walking with God—all the way of our fellowship! That fountain of Christ's blood runs not dry, but runs along with the believer, for the cleansing of his after pollutions, of his defilements, even in the very light itself. This, then, as it is the first foundation of peace and communion with God, so it is the perpetual assurance and confirmation of it, that which first gives boldness, and that alone which still continues boldness in it. It is the first ground, and the constant warrant and security of it, without which it would be as soon dissolved as made. If that blood did not run along all this way, to wash all his steps; if the way of light and fellowship with God were not watered and refreshed with the continual current of this blood, certainly none could walk in it without being consumed. Therefore it is, that the mercy of God, and riches of grace in Christ, hath provided this blood for us, both to cleanse the sins of ignorance before believing, and the sins of light after believing, that a poor sinner may constantly go on his way, and not be broken off from God by his infirmities and escapes in the way.

You see, then, the gospel runs in these two golden streams,—pardon of sin, and purity of walking. They run undividedly, all along in one channel; yet without confusion one with another, as it is reported of some great rivers that run together between the same banks, and yet retain distinct colours and natures all the way, till they part. But these streams that glad the city of God never part one from another. The cleansing blood and the purifying light, these are the entire and perfect sum of the gospel. Purification from sin, the guilt of sin, and the purity of walking in the light flowing from that, make up the full complexion of Christianity, which are so nearly conjoined together, that if they be divided they cease to be, and cannot any of them subsist, save in men's deluded imagination. The end of washing in the blood of Christ is, that we may come to this light, and have fellowship with it. For the darkness of hell, the utter darkness of the curse of God, which overspreads the unbelieving soul, and eclipses all the light of God's countenance from him,—that dark and thick cloud of guiltiness, that heap of unrenewed conversation; this, I say, must be removed by the cleansing of the blood of Christ, and then the soul is admitted to enjoy that light, and walk in it. And it is removed chiefly for this end, that there may be no impediment in the way of this fellowship. This blood cleanseth, that you, being cleansed, may henceforth walk in purity; and there is no purity like that of the light of God's countenance and commands. And so you are washed in the blood of Christ, that you may walk in the light of God; and take heed that you defile not your garments again. But if so be, (and certainly it will be, considering our weakness,) that you defile yourselves again, like foolish children, who, after they have washed, run to the puddle again, forgetting that they were cleansed; if either your daily infirmities trouble, or some grosser pollution defile and waste your conscience, know that this blood runs all along in the same channel of your obligation to holy walking, and is as sufficient now as ever, to cleanse you from all sin, from sins of daily incursion, and sins of a grosser nature. There is no exception in that blood, let there be none in your application to it and apprehension of it. Now, this is not to give boldness to any man to sin, or continue in sin, because of the lengthened use and continued virtue and efficacy of the blood of Christ; for if any man draw such a result from it, and improve it to the advantage of his flesh, he declares himself to have no portion in it, never to have been washed by it. For what soul can in sobriety look upon that blood shed by the Son of God, to take away the sins of the world, and find an emboldening to sin from that view? Who can wash and cleanse here, and presently think of defilement, but with indignation?

I speak these things the rather, because there is a twofold misapprehension of the gospel among Christians, and on both hands much darkness and stumbling is occasioned. We have poor narrow spirits, and do not take entire truth in its full comprehension, and so we are as unfit and unequal discerners of the gospel, and receivers of it, as he that would judge of a sentence by one word, of a book by one page, of a harmony by one note, and of the world by one parcel of it. The beauty and harmony of things consist in their entire union; and though there should appear many discrepancies and unpleasant discords in several parts, yet all united together, makes up a pleasant concert. Now this is our childish foolishness, that we look upon the gospel only by halves, and this being alone seen, begets misapprehensions and mistakes in our minds; for ordinarily we supply that which we see not with some fancy of our own. When the blood of Jesus Christ is holden out in its full virtue, in the large extent of its efficacy, to cleanse all sin, and to make peace with God, and wipe away all transgressions, as if they had never been; the generality of you never apprehending much your own desperate condition, nor conceiving an absolute necessity of a change; you think this is all that is in the gospel, and begin to flatter yourselves, and bless yourselves, though you live in the imaginations of your own hearts, and never apprehend the absolute need and inevitable sequel of walking in purity after pardon. And, alas! there is something of this sometimes overtakes the hearts of true believers, in the slight and overly consideration of the mercy of God, and blood of Christ; you do not lay the constraint upon your hearts to a holy conversation. I say, it is not because you apprehend that blood, that you take more liberty to the flesh, but rather because you too slightly and superficially consider it, and that but the one half of it, without piercing into the proper end of that cleansing, which is, that we may walk in purity.

But, on the other hand, some believing souls, having their desires enlarged after more holiness and conformity to God, and apprehending not only the necessity of it, but the beauty and comeliness of it, yet finding withal how infinitely short they come, and how oft their purposes are broken and disappointed, and themselves plunged in the mire of their own filthiness; this doth discourage them, and drives them to such a despondency and dejection of spirit, that they are like to give over the way of holiness as desperate. Now, my beloved, for you who look upon the gospel by a parcel,* and such a parcel as enjoins much upon you, I would earnestly beseech you to open and enlarge your hearts to receive the full body of the truth; to look upon that cleansing blood as well as that pure light; to consider the perpetual use of the one, until you have fully attained the other. Know that the fountain is kept open, and not shut; not only to admit you to come at first, but to give ready access in all after-defilements; and there is no word more comprehensive than this here, it 'cleanseth from all sin.' All thy exceptions, doubts, and difficulties, are about some particular sins and circumstances; thy debates run upon some exception. But here is an universal comprehensive word, that excludes all exception—no kind of sin, either for quality, or degree, or circumstance, is too great for this blood. And therefore, as you have reason to be humbled under your failings, so there is no reason to be discouraged, but rather to revive your spirits and vigour again in the study of this walking in the light, knowing that one day we shall be in the light, as he is in it. Nay, take this along with you, as your strength and encouragement to your duty, as the greatest provocation to more purity,—that there is so constant readiness of pardon in that blood.

Sermon XVI.

1 John i. 8.—"*If we say that we have no sin, we deceive ourselves, and the truth is not in us.*"

'The night is far spent, the day is at hand,' Rom. xiii. 12. This life is but as night, even to the godly. There is some light in it,—some star-light, but it is mixed with

* [That is, who look upon a part or portion of the gospel, as if that were the whole of it.—Ed.]

much darkness of ignorance and sin; and so it will be, till the sun arise, and the morning of their translation to heaven come. But though it be called night in one sense, in regard of that perfect glorious perpetual day in heaven, yet they are called the children of light, and of the day, and are said to walk in the light, and are exhorted to walk honestly as in the day, because, though there is a mixture of darkness in them, of weakness in their judgments, and impurity in their affections, yet they are *nati ad majora*, "born to greater things," and aspiring to that perfect day. There is so much light as to discern these night-monsters, their own corruptions, and Satan's temptations,—to fight continually against them. They are about this noble work, the purifying themselves from sin and darkness; so that they lie in the middle, between the light of angels and glorified spirits, that hath no darkness in it, and the midnight of the rest of the world, who are buried in darkness and wickedness, and lie entombed in it, as the word is, 1 John v. 19, 'The whole world, (κεῖται,) lieth in wickednes: but we know that we are of God:' therefore the apostle subjoins here very seasonably a caution or correction of that which was spoken about the walking in the light, and fellowship with God; which words sound out some perfection, and, to our self-flattering minds, might possibly suggest some too high opinion of ourselves. If we, even we that have fellowship with God, even I, the apostle, and you believing Christians; if we say, we have no sin, no darkness in us, we do but deceive ourselves, and deny the truth. But who will say that I have no sin? Solomon gives a challenge to all the world, Prov. xx. 9, 'Who can say, I have made my heart clean, I am pure from my sin?' And, indeed, there is no man so far a stranger to himself, but if he, in sobriety and calmness, retire into his own heart, the very evidence of the impurity of it will extort this confession from him. As it useth to be said of an atheist, he feels that Divine majesty within his secret thoughts and conscience which he denieth with his mouth; and he is often forced to tremble at the remembrance of him whom he will not confess.* So if there be any so far bewitched and enchanted into so gross and impudent a delusion, as to assert his own perfection and vacancy from sin, and freedom from obligation to any divine command (as this time is fruitful of such monsters), yet I dare be bold to say, that in the secret and quiet reflections on themselves, they find that which they will not confess. Inwardly they feel what outwardly they deny, and cannot but sometime or other be filled with horror and anguish in their consciences, by that inwardly witnessing and checking principle, when God shall give it liberty to exercise its power over them. The end of such will be, as of professed atheists. They pretend the securest contempt and most fearless disregard of God; but then, when he awakes to judgment, or declares himself in something extraordinary, they are subject to the most panic fears and terrors, because then there is a party armed within against them, which they had disarmed in security, and kept in chains. So, whensoever such men, of such high pretensions, and sublime professions, who love to speak nothing but mysteries, and presume to such glorious discoveries of new lights of spiritual mysteries; when these, I say, have flattered themselves for a season, in the monstrous exorbitant conceit of their own perfection, and immunity from sin, and, it may be, deceived some others too; when they have lived some time in this golden dream of innocency, the time will come, either when the mighty hand of God is on them here, or when they must enter eternity, that they shall awake,

* [A celebrated English preacher, who was cotemporary with Binning, makes a similar remark: "No question but those that have been so bold as to deny that there was a God, have sometimes been much afraid they have been in error, and have at last suspected there was a God, when some sudden prodigy hath presented itself to them and roused their fears. And whatsoever sentiments they might have in their blinding prosperity, they have had other kind of notions in them in their stormy afflictions, and, like Jonah's mariners, have been ready to cry to him for help, whom they disdained to own so much as in being, while they swam in their pleasures. The thoughts of a Deity cannot be extinguished, but they will revive and rush upon a man, at least under some sharp affliction. Amazing judgments will make them question their own apprehensions." (Charnock's Works, vol. I. p. 42. Lond. 1682.) An ancient historian relates, concerning Caligula the Emperor of Rome, whose licentiousness knew no bounds, and who professed the utmost contempt for the gods of his country, that, when it thundered, he was accustomed from fear of the gods he derided, to shut his eyes, cover his head, and even conceal himself under a bed.—Suet. in Calig. cap. 51. Seneca de Ira, lib. I. cap. 16.—Ed.]

and find all their iniquities in battle array, mustered by the Lord of hosts, in their conscience against themselves; and then they shall be the rarest examples of fear, terror, and unbelief, who pretended to the greatest confidence, clearness, and innocency. My beloved, let us establish this as an infallible rule, to discern the spirits by, and to know what religion is,—if it tend to glorify God, and abase man, to make him more humble, as well as holy,—if it give the true and perfect discovery of God to man, and of man to himself,—that is true religion and undefiled. But away with those sublime speculations, those winged and airy mysteries, those pretensions to high discoveries and new lights, if they do not increase that good old light of 'humble walking with thy God,' &c. If they tend to the loosing of the obligation of divine commands on thee; if they ravish man so high that he seeth not himself any more to be a poor, miserable, and darkened creature, certainly that is no fellowship with the pure light, which is not continually the discovery and further manifestation of more sin and darkness in us. For, what is a man's light in the dark night of this life, but the clearest light of that darkness that is in man? And his holiness, what is it, but the abhorring of himself for that? It is true, something further is attained than the knowing of this; but it is always so far short of that original pattern, that the best way of expressing our conformity to it, is by how much we apprehend our distance and deformity from it.

But, my beloved, this is not all that is here meant, nor mnst we take it so grossly, as if this did only check the open professors of a sinless, spotless sanctity. Nay, certainly, there is another way of saying this than by the tongue, and many other ways of self-deceiving than that gross one, many more universal and more dangerous, because less discernible. There is something of this, that even true believers may fall into, and there is something of it more common to the generality of professed Christians.

Among believers in Christ there is much difference in self-judging; extreme contrarieties, both between diverse persons, and in one and the same, at diverse times. You know that some are kept in the open view of their own sins and infirmities, and while they aim at holiness, they are wholly disabled to that worthy endeavour by their discouragements, arising from the apprehension of their own weakness and infinite short-coming. Now, to elevate and strengthen such spirits, that word was seasonably cast in, 'and the blood of Jesus Christ cleanseth from all sin:' for it properly belongs to the comfort of such fainting souls; and it is all one as if he had said, up and be doing, and the blood of Christ shall cleanse your evil doings. He goeth not about to persuade them to have better thoughts of themselves, or lower apprehensions of their sins, but only to have higher and more suitable thoughts of Christ, and the virtue of his blood; and this is the only cure,—not to abate from that low esteem of ourselves, but to add to the esteem, and grow in the lively apprehension of Christ. I would not counsel you to think yourselves better, but to think better of him, that all your confidence may arise from him.

Now there are others, (and it may be that same person at another time,—for the wind of temptation veers about, and is sometimes in one corner, sometimes in another;—our adversary useth many stratagems, and will seem to flee before us, in yielding us the victory over our unbelief, that he may in his flight return and throw some other dart upon us unawares,) when they have attained any fervency of desires, and height of design after holiness and walking with God, and this is seconded with any lively endeavours, and this confirmed and strengthened with those presences of God, and accesses into the soul, that fill it with some sweetness;—then, I say, they are ready to apprehend too highly of themselves, as if they had attained, and to look below upon others with some disdain. Then there is not that present discovery of themselves, that may intermingle humble mourning with it, but a kind of unequal measuring their attainments by their desires, which in all true Christians are exceedingly mounted above themselves. Now, indeed, this is in effect, and really to say, 'we have no sin.' Herein is a delusion, a self-deceiving fancy, that begets too much self-pleasing. Let us know where our stance is,*

* [That is, place or station.—Ed.]

infinitely below either our duty or our desire; and remind this often, that we may not be in hazard to be drunk with self-love and self-deceit in this particular. Besides, are there not many Christians, who, having been once illuminated, and had some serious exercises in their souls, both of sorrow for sin and fear of wrath, and comfort by the gospel, and being accustomed to some discharge of religious duties in private and public, sit down here, and have not mind of further progress? They think, if they keep that stance, they are well, and so have few designs or endeavours after more communion with God, or purification from sin. Now this makes them degenerate to formality. They wither and become barren, and are exposed by this to many temptations which overcome them. But, my beloved, is not this really and indeed to say, 'we have no sin?' Do not your walking and the posture of your spirits import so much, as if you had no sin to wrestle with, no more holiness to aspire unto; as if ye had no further race to run to obtain the crown? Do not deceive yourselves, by thinking it sufficient to have so much honesty and grace, as in your opinion may put you over the black line, in irregeneration, as if ye would seek no more than is precisely necessary for salvation. Truly, if ye be so minded, you give a miserable hint, that you are not yet translated from the black side of darkness. I do not say that all such are unconverted; but, if you continue thus, without stirring up yourselves to a daily conversion and renovation, ye do too much to blot out the evidence of your conversion, and at length it may prove to some a self-destroying deceit, when they shall find themselves not passed over that line that passeth between heaven and hell, which they were studying to find out, only that they might pass so far over it, as might keep their soul and hell asunder, without earnest desires of advancement towards heaven in conformity to God. Now, for the generality of professed Christians, though there be none who have that general confession of sin oftener and more readily in their mouths; yet, I suppose, it is easy to demonstrate that there is much of this self-deceit in them, which declares that the truth is not in them. You know both God and man construct* of men by their ways, not by their words; and the Lord may interpret your hearts by their dispositions, and raise a collection of atheism out of all together: 'The fool hath said in his heart,' &c. Even so say I, many pretended Christians say in their heart, 'we have no sin.' How prove ye that? I seek nothing else to prove it, than your own ordinary clearings and excusings of yourselves. Ye confess ye are sinners, and break all the commands; yet come to particulars, and I know not one of twenty that will cordially or seriously take with almost any sin. Yea, what you have granted in a general, you retract and deny it in all the particulars, which declares both that even that which you seem to know, you are altogether strangers to the real truth of it, and that you are over-blinded with a fond love of yourselves. I know not to what purposes your general acknowledgments are, but to be a mask or shadow to deceive you, to be a blind to hide you from yourselves; since the most part of you, whensoever challenged of any particular sin, or inclination to it, justify yourselves: and whenever ye are put to a particular confession of your sins, you have all rapt up in such a bundle of confusion, that you never know one sin by another. Certainly, ye deceive yourselves, and the truth is not in you.

Let me add, moreover, another instance. Do you not so live, and walk in sin so securely, so impenitently, as if you had no sin, no fear of God's wrath? Do not the most part contentedly and peaceably live in so much ignorance of the gospel, as if they had no need of Christ, and so, by consequence, as if they had no sin? For if you did believe in the heart, and indeed consider that your hearts are sinks of iniquity and impurity, would you not think it necessary to apply to the Physician? And would you not then labour to know the Physician, and the gospel, which is the report of him? Certainly, inasmuch as you take no pains for the knowledge of a Saviour, you declare that you know not your sin; for if ye know the one, ye could not but search to know the other. What is the voice of most men's walking? Doth it not proclaim this, that they think there is no sin in them? For if there be sin in you, is there not a curse upon you, and wrath before you? And if you did really see the one, would you not see the other? And did you see it, would it not

* [That is, judge.—ED.]

drive you to more serious thoughts? Would it not affright you? Would it not cause you often to retire into yourselves, and from the world? And, above all, how precious would the tidings of a Saviour be, that now are common and contemptible? Would you not every day wash in that blood? Would the current of repentance dry? But, forasmuch as you are not exercised this way, give no thoughts nor time for reconcilement with God, walk without any fear of hell, and without any earnest and serious study of changing your ways, and purifying your hearts; in a word, though ye confess sin in the general, yet your whole carriage of heart and ways declare so much, that you think it not a thing much to be feared, or that a man should busy himself about it; that a man may live in it, and be well here and hereafter. And is not this to deny the very nature of sin, and to deceive your own souls?

Sermon XVII.

1 John i. 9.—"*If we confess our sins, he is faithful and just to forgive us our sins,*" &c.

The current of sin dries not up, but runs constantly while we are in this life. It is true, it is much diminished in a believer, and it runs not in such an universal flood over the whole man as it is in the unbeliever. Yet there is a living spring of sin within the godly, which is never ceasing to drop out pollution and defilement, either upon their whole persons, or, at least, to intermingle it with their good actions. Now, there is no comfort for this, but this one, that there is another stream of the blood of Jesus Christ that never dries up, is never exhausted, never emptied, but flows as full and as free, as clear and fresh as ever it did: and this is so great, and of so great virtue, that it is able to swallow up the stream of our pollutions, and to take away the daily filth of a believer's conversation. Now indeed, though the blood of Jesus Christ be of such infinite virtue and efficacy, that it were sufficient to cleanse the sins of the whole world, it would be an over-ransom for the souls of all men, there is so much worth in it. That flood of guiltiness that hath drowned the world,—this flood of Christ's blood that gushed out of his side, is of sufficient virtue to cleanse it perfectly away. Notwithstanding of this absolute universal sufficiency, yet certain it is, that it is not actually applied unto the cleansing of all men's sins, but yet the most part of men are still drowned in the deluge of their own wickedness, and lie entombed in darkness; therefore it concerns us to know the way of the application of this blood to the cleansing of sinners; and this way is set down in this verse, 'If we confess our sins, he is just to forgive.' There was something hinted at obscurely in the preceding verse; for when he shows, that such as say they have no sin, who either, by the disposition of their hearts, or carriage of their ways, do by interpretation say that they want sin, such deceive themselves, and the truth is not in them, and so they have no benefit of that blood that cleanseth from all sin. And so it is imported here, that though the blood of Christ be fully sufficient to cleanse all sin, yet it is not so prostituted and basely spent upon sinners, as to be bestowed upon them who do not know their sins, and never enter into any serious and impartial examination of themselves. Such, though they say they are sinners, yet never descending into themselves to search their own hearts and ways, and so never coming to the particular knowledge of their sins, and feeling of them, they cannot at all make application of that blood to their own consciences, either seriously or pertinently. Though the river and fountain of Christ's blood run by them, in the daily preaching of the gospel, yet being destitute of this daily self-inspection and self-knowledge, being altogether ignorant of themselves, they can no more wash here than those who never heard of this blood. They being strangers to themselves, sets them at as great distance and estrangement from the blood of Christ, as if they were wholly strangers to the very preaching of this blood. Let us, then, have this first established in our hearts,—that there is no cleansing from sin, without the knowledge of sin; and there is no true knowledge of sin, without a serious soul examination of sin. These are knit together in their own nature. For how should our sins be pardoned, when we know nothing of them but in a confused generality that can never affect the heart? How should our sins not be opened and discovered before the holiness of God, when they are always covered unto us, and hid from our eyes? Certainly, the righteousness and wisdom of God require, that such a monstrous thing, so great an enemy of God's holiness, be not wholly passed away in silence without observation. If we do not observe, he will; for to what purpose should pardon be so lavished upon them who are not capable of knowing what favour and grace is in it? And certainly, that none can know without the feeling knowledge of the height and heinousness of sin. Now, I pray you, how should you know your sins, when you will not allow any time for the searching of yourselves? Many cannot say, that ever they did purposely and deliberately withdraw from the world, and separate their spirits for this business of self-examination; and therefore you remain perpetually strangers to yourselves, and as great strangers to the power and virtue of this blood.

Now, in this verse, he declares it plainly in what way and method sin is pardoned by this blood. By the former verse, we have so much, that it is necessary we must search and try our ways, that so we may truly know our sins, and charge them upon ourselves; and here it is superadded, that we must confess them to him: and the promise is annexed, 'he is just and faithful to forgive.' Now, this confession of sin is very fitly subjoined, both to that which he declared of that great end of that gospel,—communion with God,—and that which was immediately holden forth of the remaining virtue of Christ's blood. For might a poor soul say, How shall I come to partake of that blessed society? I am a sinner, and so an enemy to God; how shall this enmity be removed? And if the answer be made, 'The blood of Jesus Christ cleanseth from all sin,' and so maketh access for a sinner to enter into this society; yet a question remains, and how shall the virtue of that be applied to my soul? It is sufficient, I know, for all, but what way may I have the particular benefit of it? Here it is fully satisfied, 'if we confess our sins, God is just and faithful to forgive.' He lieth under some obligation to pardon us. Now, many of you may think, if this be the way, and these be the terms of pardon, then we hope all shall be pardoned; for if there be no more but to confess our sins, who will not willingly do that, and who doth not daily do it? As one said, "if it be sufficient to accuse, none will be innocent," *si accusasse sufficiat, nemo innocens erit;* so you may think, *si confiteri sufficiat, nemo reus erit,* "if it be sufficient to confess, none will be guilty." But, my beloved, let us not deceive ourselves with the present first apprehensions of words that occur in this kind. It is true, as ye take confession, there is nothing more ordinary; but, if it be taken in the true scripture meaning, and in the realest sense, I fear there is nothing among men so extraordinary. I desire you may but consider how you take this word in your dealings with men;—you take it certainly in a more real sense than you use it in religion. If any had done you some great wrong or injury, suppose your servant, or inferior, what acknowledgment would you take from him of his wrong? If he confessed his wrong only in general ambiguous terms; if he did it either lightly, or without any sense or sorrow for it; if he did withal excuse and extenuate his fault, and never ceased, notwithstanding of all his confession, to do the like wrong when occasion offered, would you not think this a mockery, and would it not rather provoke you than pacify you? Now, when you take words in so real and deep significations in your own matters, what gross delusion is it, that you take them in the slightest and emptiest meaning in those things that relate to God? And I am sure the most part of men's confessions are of that nature which I have described,—general, ignorant, senseless, without any particular view, or lively feeling, of the vileness and loathsomeness of sin, and their own hearts. Whenever it comes to particulars, there is a multitude of extenuations and pretences to hide and cover the sin; and generally men never cease the more from sinning. It puts no stop in their running, as the horse to the battle. To-day they confess it, and to-morrow they act it again with as much delight as before. Now, of this I may say, 'Offer it to thy governor, and see if he will be pleased with thee,' or let another offer such an acknowledgment of wrong to thee, and see if it will please thee; and if it will not, why deceive ye yourselves with the outward visage of things in these matters that are of greatest soul-concernment? Should they not be taken in the most inward and substantial signification that can be, lest you be deceived with false appearances, and, while you give but a shadow of confession, you receive but a shadow of forgiveness, such a thing as will not carry and bear you out before God's tribunal? Therefore we must needs take it thus, that confession of sin is the work of the whole man, and not of the mouth only. It is the heart, tongue, and all that is in a man, joining together to the acknowledgment of sin, and God's righteousness; therefore it includes in it, not only a particular knowledge of our offences, and the temper of our hearts, but a sensible feeling of the loathsomeness and heinousness of these. And this is the spring that it flows from,—a broken and contrite heart, that is bruised under the apprehensions of the weight of guiltiness, and is embittered with the sense of the gall of iniquity that possesseth the heart. Here, then, is the great moment of confession and repentance; what is the inward fountain it flows from? If the heart be brought to the distinct and clear view of itself, and to discern the iniquity and plague of it, and so to fall down under the mighty hand of God, and before his tribunal, as guilty, as not being able or willing to open his mouth in an excuse or extenuation of sin, or to plead for compassion from any consideration in himself; a soul thus placed between iniquities set in order and battle-array, on the one hand, and the holy law and righteousness of God, on the other hand; the filthiness of the one filling with shame and confusion, and the dreadfulness of the other causing fear and trembling: in this posture, I say, for a soul to come and fall at the Judge's feet, and make supplication to him in his Son Christ; thus being inwardly pressed to vent and pour out our hearts before him, in the confession of our sins, and to flee unto the city of refuge,—his mercy and grace that is declared in Jesus Christ,—this, I say, is indeed to confess our sins: for then confession is an exoneration and disburdening of the heart,—it flows from the abundance of the inward contrition of it. And as this must be the spring of it, so there is another stream that will certainly flow from the ingenuous confession of our sins, that is, a forsaking of them. These are the two streams that flow from one head and spring, the inward fountain of contrition and sorrow for sin; there is a holy indignation kindled in the heart against sin, and an engagement upon such a soul, as indeed flees to mercy, to renounce sin; and here is the complete nature of true repentance. Solomon joins them, 'He that confesseth and forsaketh shall have mercy,' Prov. xxviii. 13. And this is opposed to covering of sins—for 'he that covereth his sins shall not prosper.' And what is that to cover his sin? Confessing them in a general confused notion, without any distinct knowledge, or sense of any particular guiltiness? That is a covering of sins. Or confessing sin, and not forsaking of it? That is a covering of sin: for to act sin over again with continual fresh delight and vigour, is to retract our confessions, and to bury and cover them with the mould of new transgressions. Now, take this unto you, you 'shall not prosper!' What can be said worse? For you are but in a dream of happiness, and you shall one day be shaken out of it, and that fancied pardon shall evanish, and then your sins that you covered in this manner, shall be discovered before the Judge of the world, and you 'shall not stand in judgment.'

Sermon XVIII.

1 John i. 9.—"*If we confess our sins, he is faithful and just to forgive us our sins,*" *&c.*

The freedom of God's grace, and the greatness of his wisdom, shine forth most brightly in the dispensation of the gospel, and both of them beautify and illustrate one another. That there is, first, an expiation of sin by the blood of Jesus Christ, that a way is laid down of reconciling the world, and that by the blood of the cross, that peace is purchased, and so preached unto sinners, as a thing already procured, and now only to be applied unto the soul by faith;—herein doth the inestimable riches of the grace of God expose itself to the view of angels and men. That the great work of redemption is ended, ere it come to us; and there remains nothing, but to publish it to the world, and invite us to come and receive it, and have a part in it;—all is ready, the feast prepared, and set on the table, and there wants nothing but guests to eat of it, and these are daily called by the gospel to come to this table, which the wisdom of the Father hath prepared for us, without either our knowledge or concurrence. Besides, the very terms of proposing the gospel, speak forth absolute freedom. What can be more free and easy than this? Christ is sent to die for sinners, and to redeem them from the curse,—only receive him, come to him, and believe in him. He hath undertaken to save, only do you consent too, and give up your name to him:—ye have nothing to do to satisfy justice, or purchase salvation, only be willing that he do it for you, or rather acquiesce in that he hath done already, and rest on it. But how shall our sins be pardoned, and justice satisfied? Only confess your sins to him, and ye are forgiven, not for your confession, but for Christ; only acknowledge thine iniquity and wrongs, and he hath taken another way to repair his justice than by thy destruction and condemnation. He is so far from extending his justice against thee, that he is rather engaged upon his faithfulness and justice to forgive thee, because of his promise.

Yet, ye would not conceive so of this manner of proposal of forgiveness and salvation, as if the requiring of such a thing as repentance in thee were any derogation from the absoluteness of his grace: for it is not required, either to the point of satisfaction to God's justice, and expiation of sin, for that is done already upon the cross. Christ was not offered to save sinners, he was not sent upon the previous condition of their repentance: nay, 'while we were yet enemies, Christ died for the ungodly.' So that to the business of our redemption there was no concurrence upon our part, nor influence upon it by our carriage; for he considered us as sinners, and miserable, and so saved us. And now, to the actual application of these preventing mercies,—it is true, it is needful in the wise and reasonable dispensation of God, that sinners be brought to the knowledge and sensible acknowledgment of their sin and misery, and so be upon rational inducements of misery within, and mercy without, of self-indigency, and Christ's sufficiency, be drawn unto Jesus Christ, and so to a partaking of those purchased privileges of forgiveness of sin, peace with God, &c. I say, all this is so far from diminishing a jot of that absolute freedom of grace, that it rather jointly proclaims the riches of grace and wisdom both, that repentance should be given to an impenitent sinner, and faith freely bestowed on an unbelieving sinner; and withal, that remission and salvation, together with faith and repentance, should be brought to us by his death, while we were yet enemies;—this doth declare the most unparalleled bounty and grace that the heart of man can imagine; and withal, that remission of sins is joined to confession, and salvation to faith, herein the wisdom of God triumphs; for what way is it possible to declare that freedom of grace, to the sensible conviction of a sinner, and so to demonstrate it to all men's consciences, except by making them return within, to see their own absolute unworthiness, vileness, and incorrespondency to such mercies, and so drawing an acknowledgment of his grace from the mouths and consciences of all? How shall a soul know that rich superabundant grace, if he know not the abundance of his sins? How shall he profess the one, except he withal confess the other? Let us imagine an impenitent sinner, continuing in rebellion, pardoned and forgiven: and is there any thing more contrary to common sense and reason, to be in God's favour, and yet not accepting that favour; to be a friend, and yet an enemy; to have sins forgiven, and yet not known, not confessed? These, I say, sound some plain dissonancy and discord to our very first apprehensions. Certainly, this is the way to declare the glory of his grace, in the hiding and covering of sin, even to discover sin to the sinner; else if God should hide sin, and it be hid withal from the conscience, both thy sin and God's grace should be hid and covered, neither the one nor the other would appear. Take it thus then,—the confession of sin is not for this end, to have any casual influence upon thy remission, or to procure any more favour and liking with God; but it is simply this, the confession of sin is the most accommodate way of the profession and publication of the grace of God in the forgiving of sins. Faith and repentance are not set down as conditions pre-required on thy part, that may procure salvation or forgiveness, but they are inseparably annexed unto salvation and forgiveness, to the end that they may manifest to our sensible conviction, that grace and freedom of grace which shines in forgiveness and salvation.

'He is just and faithful,' &c. Herein is the wonder of the grace of God increased, that when we are under an obligation to infinite punishment for sin, and bound guilty before his justice, that the 'most great and potent Lord,' who can easily rid himself of all his enemies, and do all his pleasure in heaven and earth, should come under an obligation to man to forgive him his sins. A strange exchange! Man is standing bound by the cords of his own sins over the justice of God,—he is under that insoluble tie of guiltiness. God in the meantime is free, and loosed from the obligation of the first covenant, that is, his promise of giving life to man. We have loosed him from that voluntary engagement, and are bound under a curse. And yet, behold the permutation of grace,—man is loosed from sin, to which he is bound, and God is bound to forgive sin, to which he was not bound. He enters into a new and voluntary engagement by his promise, and gives right to poor creatures to sue and seek forgiveness of him, according to his faithfulness. Yet in this plea, as it becomes us to use confidence, because he gives us ground by his promises, so we should season it with humility, knowing how infinitely free and voluntary his condescension is, being always mindful, that he may in righteousness exact punishment of us for sin, rather than we seek forgiveness from him. And yet seek it we ought, because he hath engaged his faithful promise; which opportunity to neglect, and not to improve, either through fear or security, were as high contempt and disobedience to him, as those sins by which we offend him.

Certainly, the very name of God, revealed to us or known by nature's light, those general characters of his name, mercy and goodness, power and greatness, might suffice to so much, as to make us, in the apprehensions of our own guiltiness and provocations of his holiness, to look no other way than to his own merciful and gracious nature. Suppose we had nothing of a promise from him, by which he is bound; yet, as the very apprehension of the general goodness, and unlimited bounty, and original happiness that is in God, ought naturally to draw the creature towards him in all its wants, to supplicate his fulness, that can supply all necessities, without lessening his own abundance; even so, if we did only apprehend that God is the fountain of mercy, and that he is infinitely above us and our injuries, and that all our being and well-being eternally consists in his sole favour; this, I say, alone considered, might draw us to a pouring out our hearts before him, in the acknowledgment of our guiltiness, and casting ourselves upon his mercy, as the term is used in war, when there is no quarter promised, and no capitulation made. It is the last refuge of a desperate sinner, to render unto God upon mercy, to resign himself to his free disposal. Since I cannot but perish, may a soul say, without him, there is no way of escaping from his wrath, I will rather venture, and 'go in to the King, and if I perish, I perish.' There is more hope in this way to come to him, than to flee from him. Perhaps he may show an act of absolute sovereign goodness, and be as glorious in passing by an offence, as just in punishing it. Do I not see in man, in whom the divine Majesty hath imprinted some characters of conscience and honesty, that it is more generous and noble to forgive than to revenge? And do I not see generally among men, clemency and compassion are commended above severity and rigour, though just, especially towards those who are inferior, weak, unable to resist, and have yielded themselves to mercy. Now, shall I not much more apprehend that of God which I admire in a sinful man? Shall not that be most perfect in him which is but a maimed and broken piece of his image in lost man? Certainly, it is the glory of God to conceal an offence as well as to publish it, and he can show as much greatness and majesty in mercy as in justice; therefore I will wholly commit myself to him. I think a man ought to reason so, from the very natural knowledge he hath of God. But when ye have not only his name and nature published, but his word and promise so often proclaimed, himself come under some tie to receive and accept graciously all sinners that fly in under the shadow of his wings of mercy; then, O with how much persuasion and boldness should we come to him, and lay open our sins before him, who not only may pardon them, and not only is likely to do it, seeing he hath a gracious nature, but certainly will pardon them, cannot but do it, because his faithfulness requireth it! Certainly, he hath superadded his word to his name, his promise to his nature, to confirm our faith, and give us ample ground of strong consolation.

There is another more suitable notion about the justice of God, in forgiving sin. It hath some truth in the thing itself, but whether it be imported here, I dare not certainly affirm. Some take his faithfulness in relation to his word of promise, and his justice in relation to the price and ransom paid by Christ, importing as much as this,—whatever sinner comes to God in Christ, confessing his own guiltiness in sincerity, and supplicating for pardon, he cannot in justice refuse to give it out unto them, since he hath taken complete satisfaction of Christ. When a sinner seeks a discharge of all sin, by virtue of that blood, the Lord is bound by his own justice to give it out and to write a free remission to them; since he is fully paid, he cannot but discharge us, and cancel our bonds. So then a poor sinner that desires mercy, and would forsake sin, hath a twofold ground to suit* this forgiveness upon—Christ's blood, and God's own word, Christ's purchase and payment, and the Father's promise; he is just and righteous, and therefore he cannot deny the one, nor yet take two satisfactions, two payments for one debt; and he is faithful, so he cannot but stand to the other, that is, his promise, and thus is forgiveness ascertained and assured unto the confessing sinner. If any would take this in relation to confession, as if it reflected upon that which preceded; and the meaning should be, if any man confess his sin, he is just to requite confession with remission,—he cannot in righteousness deny one that deserves it so well, he is just to return some suitable recompense to such a humble confession; this sense were a perverting of the whole gospel, and would overturn the foundations of grace. For there is no connection between our confession and his remission, but that which the absolute good pleasure of his will hath made; besides, that repentance is as free grace given from the exalted Prince, as remission of sins is.

Sermon XX.

1 JOHN i. 9, 10.—"*If we confess our sins, he is faithful and just to forgive us our sins, and to cleanse us from all unrighteousness. If we say we have not sinned, we make him a liar*," &c.

AND who will not confess their sin, say you? Who doth not confess sins daily, and, therefore, who is not forgiven and pardoned? But stay, and consider the matter again. Take not this upon your first light apprehensions, which in religion are commonly empty, vain, and superficial; but search the scriptures, and your own hearts, that ye may know what confession means. It may be said of that external custom of confession that many of you have, that the Lord hath not required it,—'sacrifices and burnt-offerings thou wouldest not.' Some external submissions and confessions, which you take for compensation for sins and offences against God, —these, I say, are but abomination to the Lord; but 'a broken and a contrite heart, O God, thou wilt not despise,' Psal. li. 16, 17. And, 'Lo, I come to do thy will, I delight in it,' Psal. xl. 7, 8. When external professions and confessions are separated from the internal contrition of the heart and godly sorrow for sin; and when both internal contrition and external profession and confession are divided from conformity, or study of conformity to God's will, then they are in no better acceptance with God than those external sacrifices which God rejected, though he had required them, because they were disjoined from the true life of them and spiritual meaning, that is, faith in a mediator, and love to obedience. If confession flow not from some contrition of heart, if there be not some inward spring of this kind, the heart, opened and unfolding its very inside before God, breaking in pieces, which makes both pain or sense, and likewise gives the clearer view of the inward parts of the heart; and if it

* [That is, to sue for.—ED.]

be not joined with affection to God's will and law, earnest love to new obedience, it is but a vain, empty, and counterfeit confession, that denies itself. I suppose, a man that confesses sin which he feels not, or forsakes not, in so doing, he declares that he knows not the nature of sin; he may know that such an action is commonly called sin, and, it may be, is ashamed and censured among men, and therefore he confesseth it; but while he confesseth it without sense or feeling, he declares that he takes it not up as sin, hath not found the vileness and loathsomeness of the nature of it, nor beheld it as it is a violation of the most high Lord's laws, and a provocation of his glorious holiness. Did a soul view it thus, as it is represented in God's sight, as it dishonours that glorious Majesty, and hath manifest rebellion in it against him, and as it defiles and pollutes our spirits; he could not, I say, thus look upon it, but he would find some inward soul-abhorrence and displeasance at it, and himself too. How monstrous would it make him in his own sight? It could not but affect the heart, and humble it in secret before God; whereas your forced and strained confessions made in public, they are merely taken on then, and proceed from no inward principle. There is no shadow of any soul-humiliation in secret, but as some use to put on sackcloth when they come to make that profession, and put it off when they go out, so you put on a habit of confession in public, and put it off you when you go out of the congregation. To lie mourning before the Lord, in your secret retirements,—that you are strangers to. But I wonder how you should thus mock God, that you will not be as serious and real in confessing as in sinning. Will you sin with the whole man, and confess only with the mouth? Will ye act sin with delight, and not confess it with a true sorrow that indeed affects the heart? Now, do you honour God by confessing, when the manner of it declares, that you feel not the bitterness of sin, and conceive not the holiness and righteousness of God, whom you have to do withal? Even so, when you confess sin, which you do not forsake, you in so far declare that you know not sin, what it is you confess, and so, that you have mocked him who will not be mocked; for, what a mockery is it, to confess those faults which we have no solid effectual purpose to reform, to vomit up your sins by confession, that we may with more desire and lust lick up the vomit again, and to pretend to wash, for nothing else, but to return to the puddle, and defile again! My brethren, out of the same fountain comes not bitter water and sweet, James iii. 11. Since that which ordinarily proceeds from you is bitter, unsavoury to God and man, carnal, earthly, and sensual, your ways are a displayed banner against God's will, then lay your account, all your professions and acknowledgments are of the same nature,—they are but a little more sugared over, and their inward nature is not changed, is as unacceptable to God, as your sins are.

I would give you some characters out of the text, to discover unto you the vanity and emptiness of your ordinary confessions. The confession of sin must be particular, universal, perpetual, or constant:—particular, I say, for there are many thousands who confess that they are sinners, and yet do not at all confess their sins: for, to confess sins, is to confess their own real actual guiltiness, that which they indeed have committed, or are inclined to do. So the true and sincere confession of a repenting people is expressed, 1 Kings viii. 38, ' What prayer or supplication soever be made by any man, which shall know the plague of his own heart, and spread forth his hands, then hear thou in heaven, and forgive every man whose heart thou knowest." Now consider whether or not you be thus acquainted with your own hearts and ways, as to know your particular plague and predominant sin. Are you not rather wholly strangers to yourselves, especially the plague of your hearts? There are few that keep so much as a record or register of their actions done against God's law, or their neglect of his will; and therefore, when you are particularly posed about your sins, or the challenge of sin, you can speak nothing to that, but that you never knew one sin by another; that is, indeed, you never observed your sins, you never knew any sin, but contented yourself with the tradition you received that you were sinners. But if any man be used to reflect upon his own ways,—yet generally, the most part of men are altogether strangers to their hearts,—if they know any evil of themselves it is at most but something done or undone, some commission or omission, but nothing of the inward fountain of sin is discovered. I beseech you, then, do not deceive yourselves with this general acknowledgment that you are sinners, while in the meantime your real particular sins are hid from you, and you cannot choose but hide in a generality from God. Certainly, you are far from forgiveness, and that blessedness of which David speaks, (Psal. xxxii.) for this belongs to the man 'that hideth not his sins, in whose heart there is no guile.' And this is the plainness and sincerity of the heart, rightly to discern its own plagues, and unfold them to him. David, no doubt, would at any time have confessed that he was a sinner, but mark how heavy the wrath of God was on him for all that, because he came not to a plain, ingenuous, and humble acknowledgment of his particular sins. 'I confessed my sin, and mine iniquity I hid not.' While you confess only in general terms, you confess others' sins rather than yours; but this is it—to descend into our own hearts, and find out our just and true accusation, our real debt, to charge ourselves as narrowly as we can, that he may discharge us fully, and forgive us freely.

Next, I say, confession must be universal, that is, of all sin, without partiality or respect to any sin. I doubt if a man can truly repent of any sin, except he in a manner repent of all sin; or truly forsake one sin, except there be a divorcement of the heart from and forsaking of all sin: therefore the apostle saith, 'If we confess our sins,' not sin simply, but sins, taking in all the body and collection of them; for it is opposed to that, 'if we say we have no sin,' &c. Then there lies a necessity upon us to confess what we have; we have all sin, and so should confess all sins. Now, my meaning is not, that it is absolutely necessary that a soul come to the particular knowledge and acknowledgment of all his sins, whether of ignorance or infirmity; nay, that is not possible; for 'who can understand his errors?' saith David; 'cleanse thou me from secret sins,' Psal. xix. 12. There are many sins of ignorance, that we know not to be sins, and many escapes of infirmity, that we do not advert to, which otherwise we might know. Now, I do not impose that burden on a soul, to confess every individual sin of that kind; but this certainly must be,—there must be such a discovery of the nature of sin, and the loathsomeness of it in God's sight, and the heinous guilt of it, as may abase and humble the soul in his presence; there must be some distincter and clearer view of the dispositions and lusts of the heart, than men attain generally unto; and, withal, a discovery of the holy and spiritual meaning of God's law, which may unfold a multitude of transgressions, that are hid from the world, and make sin to abound in a man's sight and sense—for when the law enters, sin abounds; and to close up this, as there are many sins now discovered unto such a soul, which lay hid before, the light having shined in upon the darkness, and, above all, the desperate wickedness of the heart is presented; so there is no sin known and discerned, but there is an equal impartial sorrow for it, and indignation against it. As a believer hath respect to all God's commands, and loves to obey them, so the penitent soul hath an impartial hatred of all sin, even the dearest and most beloved idol, and desires unfeignedly to be rid of it. Hence your usual public confessions of sin are wiped out of the number of true and sincere confessions, because you pretend to repent of one sin, and in the meantime, neither do ye know a multitude of other sins that prevail over you, nor do you mourn for them, nor forsake them. Nay, you do not examine yourselves that way, to find out the temper of your hearts, or tenor and course of your ways. You pretend to repent for drunkenness, or such like, and yet you are ordinary cursers, swearers, liars, railers, neglecters of prayer, profaners of the Sabbath, and such like, and these you do not withal mourn for. In sum, he that mourns only for the sin that men censure, knoweth and confesseth no sin sincerely. If you would indeed return unto God from some gross evils, you must be divorced in your affections from all sin.

Then this confession should be perpetuated and continued as long as we are in this life, for that is imported by comparing this verse with those it stands between. 'If we say we have no sin,' if we say at any time, while we are in this life, if we imagine or dream of any such perfection here, 'we lie.' Now, what should we do then, since sin is always lodging in our mortal bodies, during this time of necessary abode beside an ill neighbour? What should be our exercise? Even this,—confess your sins, confess, I say, as long as you have them, draw out this the length of that. Be continually groaning to him under that body of death, and mourning under your daily infirmities and failings. That stream of corruption runs continually,—let the stream of your contrition and confession run as incessantly; and there is another stream of Christ's blood, that runs constantly too, to cleanse you. Now, herein is the discovery of the vanity and deceitfulness of many of your confessions, public and private; the current of them soon dries up, there is no perpetuity or constancy in them, no daily humbling or abasing yourselves, but all that is, is by fits and starts, upon some transient convictions, or outward censures and rebukes; and thus men quickly cover and bury their sins in oblivion and security, and forget what manner of persons they were. They are not under a daily impartial examination of their ways, take notice of nothing but some solemn and gross escapes, and these are but a short time under their view.

Now, let me apply a little to the encouragement of poor souls, who being inwardly burdened with the weight of their own guiltiness, exoner themselves by confession in his bosom. As you have two suits, and two desires to him,—one, that your sins may be forgiven, another, that they may be subdued; so he hath two solemn engagements and ties to satisfy you,—one to forgive your sins, and another to cleanse you from all unrighteousness. The soul that is truly penitent, is not only desirous of pardon of sin,—that is not the chief or only design of such a soul in application to Christ,—but it is withal to be purified from sin and all unrighteousness, and to have ungodly lusts cleansed away. And herein is the great approbation of such an one's reality,—it will not suffice or satisfy such an one, to be assured of delivery from wrath and condemnation, but he must likewise be redeemed from sin, that it hath no dominion over him. He desires to be freed from death, that he may have his conscience withal purged 'from dead works to serve the living God,' Heb. ix. 14. He would have sin blotted out of an accusing conscience, that it may be purged out of the affections of the heart, and he would have his sins washed away, for this end especially, that he may be washed from his sins, Rev. i. 5. Now, as this is the great desire and design of such a heart, in which there is no guile, to have sin purified and purged out of us, as well as pardoned, so there is a special tie and obligation upon God our Father, by promise, not only to pardon sin, but to purge from sin; not only to cover it with the garment of Christ's righteousness, and the breadth of his infinite love, but also to cleanse it by his Spirit effectually applying that blood to the purifying of the heart. Now, where God hath bound himself voluntarily, and out of love, do not ye lose him by unbelief, for that will bind you into a prison: but labour to receive these gracious promises, and to take him bound as he offers. Believe, I say, that he will both forgive you, and in due time will cleanse your heart from the love and delight of sin. Believe his promise, and engagement by promise to both, and this will set a seal to his truth and faithfulness. There is nothing in God to affright a sinner, but his justice, holiness, and righteousness; but unto thee who, in the humble confession of thy sins, fliest into Jesus Christ, that very thing which did discourage thee, may now encourage and embolden thee to come, for 'he is just and faithful to forgive sins.' His justice being now satisfied, is engaged that way to forgive, not to punish.

Sermon XX.

1 John i. 10.—"*If we say that we have not sinned, we make him a liar, and his word is not in us.*"

There is nothing in which religion more consists, than in the true and unfeigned knowledge of ourselves. The heathens supposed that sentence, γνωθι σεαυτον, 'Know thyself,' descended from heaven. It was indeed the motto of the wisest and most religious amongst them. But certain it is, that the true and sincere understanding of ourselves descends from 'the Father of lights,' and is as great a gift as man is capable of, next to the knowledge of God himself. There is nothing more necessary to man, either as a man or as a Christian, either as endowed with reason or professing religion, than that he should be thoroughly acquainted with himself, his own heart, its dispositions, inclinations, and lusts, his ways and actions; that while he travels abroad to other creatures and countries, he may not commit so shameful an absurdity, as to be a stranger at home, where he ought to be best acquainted. Yet how sad is it, that this which is so absolutely needful and universally profitable, should be lying under the manyest difficulties in the attainment of it? So that there is nothing harder, than to bring a man to a perfect understanding of himself:—what a vile, haughty, and base creature he is—how defiled and desperately wicked his nature—how abominable his actions; in a word, what a compound of darkness and wickedness he is—a heap of defiled dust, and a mass of confusion—a sink of impiety and iniquity, even the best of mankind, those of the rarest and most refined extraction, take them at their best estate. Thus they are as sepulchres painted without, and putrified within—outwardly adorned, and within all full of rottenness and corruption: 'the imagination of his heart only evil continually.' Now, I say, here is the great business and labour of religion,—to bring a man to the clear discerning of his own nature,—to represent unto him justly his own image, as it is painted in the word of God, and presented in the glass of the law; and so by such a surprising monstrous appearance, to affect his heart to self-abhorrency in dust and ashes, and to have this representation, however unpleasant, yet most profitable, continually observant to our minds, that we may not forget what manner of persons we are. Truly, I may say, if there be a perfection in this estate of imperfection, herein it consists; and if there be any attainment of a Christian, I account this the greatest,—to be truly sensible of himself, and vile in his own eyes.

It was the custom of Philip,* king of Macedonia, after he had overcome the famous republic of Greece, to have a young man to salute him first every morning with these words, *Philippe homo es*,—Philip, thou art a man; to the end that he might be daily minded of his mortality, and the unconstancy of human affairs, lest he should be puffed up with his victory; and this was done before any could have access to speak with him, as if it were to season and prepare him for the actions of the day. But O how much more ought a Christian to train up his own heart and accustom it this way, to be his continual remembrancer of himself; to suggest continually to his mind, and whisper this first into his ear in the morning, and mid-day, and evening,—*peccator es*, thou art a sinner; to hold our own image continually before us, in prayer and praises, in restraints, in liberties of spirit, in religious actions, and in all our ordinary conversation, that it might salt and season all our thoughts, words, and deeds, and keep them from that ordinary putrefaction and corruption of pride and self-conceit, which maketh all our ointment stink.

'If we say we have no sin, we make him a liar.' Why is this repeated again, but to show unto us, even to you Christians who believe in Christ, and are washed in his blood, how hard it is to know ourselves aright? If we speak of the grosser sort of persons, they scarce know any sin, nor the nature and vileness of any that they know; therefore they live in security and peace, and bless themselves in their own hearts, as if they had no sin. For such, I say, I shall only say unto them, that your self-deceiving is not so subtile, but it may soon be discerned: your lie is gross, and quickly seen through. But I would turn myself to you Christians, who are in some measure acquainted with yourselves; yet there is something against you from this word. After ye have once got some peace from the challenge of sin, and hope of pardon, you many times fall out of acquaintance with yourselves. Having attained, by the Lord's grace, to some restraint of the more visible outbreakings of sin, you have not that occasion to know yourselves by; and so you remain strangers to your hearts, and fall into better liking with yourselves, than the first sight of yourselves permitted you. Now, my beloved in the Lord, herein you are to be blamed, that you do not rather go to the fountain, and there behold the streams, than only to behold the fountain in the streams. You ought rather, upon the Lord's testimony of man, to believe what is in you, before you find it, and see it breaking out;

* [Many of the speeches and actions of Philip, who was the father of Alexander the Great, are worthy of being remembered. A collection of his most memorable sayings has been made by Erasmus, in his Apothegmata Opus. (pp. 268—279. Lutetiæ 1547.) The conduct of Philip, in many respects, however, was very unlike that of a wise and virtuous prince. Like mankind in general, though he was reminded daily of this, he too often forgot that he was mortal.—Ed.]

and keep this character continually in your sight, which will be more powerful to humble you than many outbreakings. I think we should be so well acquainted with our own natures, as to account nothing strange to them that we see abroad; but rather think all the grossness and wickedness of men suitable and correspondent to our spirits,—to that root of bitterness that is in them. The goodness of God in restraining the appearance of that in us, which is within us in reality, should rather increase the sense of our own wickedness, than diminish it in our view.

Indeed, self-love is that which blinds us, and bemists us in the sight of ourselves. We look upon ourselves through this false medium, and it represents all things more beautiful than they are; and therefore the apostle hath reason to say, 'We deceive ourselves, and we make God a liar.' O how much practical self-conceit is there in the application of truth! There are many errors contrary to the truths themselves, and many deceivers and deceived, who spread them; but I believe there are more errors committed by men in the application of truths to their own hearts, than in the contemplation of them; and more self-deceiving than deceiving of others. It is strange to think, how sound, and clear, and distinct a man's judgment will be against those evils in others, which yet he seeth not in himself; how many Christians will be able to decipher the nature of some vices, and unbowel the evils of them, and be quick-sighted to espy the least appearance of them in another, and to condemn it; and yet so partial are they in judging themselves,—self-love so purblinds them in this reflection, that they cannot discern that in themselves, which others cannot but discern! How often do men declaim against pride, and covetousness, and self-seeking, and other evils of that kind? They will pour out a flood of eloquence and zeal against them; and yet it is strange they do not advert, that they are accusing themselves, and impannelling themselves in such discourses, though others, it may be, will easily perceive a predominancy of these evils in them. 'Who art thou, O man, who judgeth another, and doest the same thing? Canst thou escape God's judgment?' Rom. ii. 1. Consider this, O Christian, that thou mayest learn to turn the edge of all thy censures and convictions against thyself, that thou mayest prevent all men's judgments of thee, in judging thyself all things that men can judge thee, that is, a chief of sinners, that hath the root of all sin in thee; and so thou mayest anticipate the divine judgment too, 'for if we judge ourselves, we shall not be judged.' Labour thou to know those evils that are incident to thy nature, before others can know them, that is, in the root and fountain, before they come to the fruit and stream; to know sins in the first conceptions of them, before they come to such productions as are visible; and this shall keep thee humble, and preserve thee from much sin, and thou shalt not deceive thyself, nor dishonour God, in making him a liar, but rather set to thy seal to this truth, and his word shall abide in thee.

There is a common rule that we have in judging ourselves, by comparing ourselves amongst ourselves, which, as Paul saith, 'is not wisdom,' 2 Cor. x. 12. When we do not measure ourselves by the perfect rule of God's holy word, but parallel ourselves with other persons, who are still defective from the rule, far further from it than any one is from another: this is the ordinary method of the judging of self-love. We compare with the worst persons; and if we be not so bad as they, we think ourselves good. If not so ignorant as some are, we presume that we know; if not so profane as many, we believe ourselves religious. 'Lord, I am not as this publican,' so say many in their hearts,—there is a curser, a swearer, a drunkard, a blind ignorant soul, that neglects prayer in private and public, and upon these ruins of others' sins, they build some better estimation of themselves. But, I pray you, what will that avail you, to be unlike them, if you be more unlike your pattern than they are unlike you? It must be, others will compare with those that are good, but it is with that which is worst in them, and not that which is best. How often do men reckon this way,—here is a good man, here is an eminent person, yet he is such and such, subject to such infirmities, and here self-love flatters itself, and, by flattering, deceives itself My beloved, let us learn to establish a more perfect rule, which may show all our imperfections. Let our rule ascend, that our hearts may descend in humility. But when our rule and pattern descends to men of like infirmities, then our pride and self-conceit ascends; and the higher we be that way in our own account, the lower we are indeed, and in God's account; and the lower we be in ourselves we lose nothing by it: for, as God is higher in our account, so we are higher in God's account, according to that standing rule, Matth. xxiii. 12, 'Whosoever shall exalt himself shall be abased, and he that shall humble himself shall be exalted.'

Sermon XXX.

1 JOHN ii. 1.—"*My little children, these things write I unto you, that ye sin not. And if any man sin, we have an advocate with the Father*," &c.

THE gospel is an entire uniform piece; all the parts of it are interwoven through other, and interchangeably knit together, so that there can be no dividing of it any more than of Christ's coat that was without seam. If you have it not altogether by the divine lot, you cannot truly have any part of it, for they are so knit together, that if you disjoin them, you destroy them; and if they cease to be together, they cease altogether to be. I speak this, because there may be pretensions to some abstracted parts of Christianity. One man pretends to faith in Jesus Christ, and persuasion of pardon of sin, and in this there may be some secret glorying arising from that confidence; another may pretend to the study of holiness and obedience, and may endeavour something that way to do known duties, and abstain from gross sins. Now, I say, if the first do not conjoin the study of the second; and if the second do not lay down the first as the foundation, both of them embrace a shadow for the thing itself, because they separate those things that God hath joined, and so can have no being but in men's fancy, when they are not conjoined. He that would pretend to a righteousness of Christ, without him, must withal study to have the righteousness of the law fulfilled within him; and he that endeavours to have holiness within must withal go out of himself, to seek a righteousness without him, whereupon to build his peace and acceptance with God; or else, neither of them hath truly any righteousness without them, to cover them, or holiness within, to cleanse them. Now, here the beloved apostle shows us this divine contexture of the gospel. The great and comprehensive end and design of the gospel is, peace in pardon of sin, and purity from sin: 'These things I write unto you, that you sin not,' &c. The gospel is comprised in commands and promises; both make one web, and link in together. The immediate end of the command is, 'that we sin not;' nay, but there is another thing always either expressly added, or tacitly understood—'but if any man sin,' that desires not to sin, 'we have an advocate with the Father.' So the promise comes in as a subsidiary help to all the precepts. It is annexed to give security to a poor soul from despair; and therefore the apostle teacheth you a blessed art of constructing all the commands and exhortations of the gospel, those of the highest pitch, by supplying the full sense with this happy and seasonable caution or caveat, 'but if any man sin,' &c. Doth that command, 'Be ye holy as I am holy, perfect as your heavenly Father,' which sounds so much unattainable perfection, and seems to hold forth an inimitable pattern; doth it, I say, discourage thee? Then, use the apostle's art, add this caution to the command, subjoin this sweet exceptive,—'but if any man,' that desires to be holy, and gives himself to this study, fail often, and fall and defile himself with unholiness, let him not despair, but know, that he hath 'an advocate with the Father.' If that of Paul's urge thee, 'present your bodies a living sacrifice,—and be not conformed to the world,' but transformed, and 'glorify God in your bodies and spirits,' which are his, (Rom. xii. 1, 2; 1 Cor. vi. 20;)—and, cleanse yourselves 'from all filthiness of the flesh and spirit,' (2 Cor. vii. 1;)—and, 'walk in the Spirit,' and 'walk as children of the light,' &c.;—if these do too rigorously exact upon thee, so as to make thee lose thy peace, and weaken thy heart and hands, learn to make out a full sentence, and fill up the full sense and meaning of the gospel, according as you see it done here. 'But if any man,'—whose inward heart-desires, and chief designs are toward these things, who would think himself happy in holiness and conformity to God, and estimates his blessedness or misery, from his union or separation from God,—'sin,' then 'we have an advocate with the Father, even Jesus Christ the righteous,' who hath all that we want, and will not suffer any accusation to fasten upon us, as long as he lives 'to make intercession for us.'

On the other hand, take a view of the promises of the gospel. Though the immediate, and next end of them is, to give peace to troubled souls, and settle us in the high point of our acceptance with God, yet certainly they have a further end, even purity from sin, as well as pardon of sin, cleansing from all sin and filthiness, as well as covering of filthness. 'These things I write unto you, that ye sin not.' What things? Consider what goes before, and what follows after, even the publication of the word of life, and eternal life in him, the declaration of our fellowship with God in Christ, the offering of the blood of Christ, able to cleanse all sin, the promise of pardon to the penitent, confession of sin,—all these things I write, 'that ye sin not;' so that this seems to be the ultimate end and chief design of the gospel, unto which all tends, unto which all work together. The promises are for peace, and peace is for purity; the promises are for faith, and faith is for purifying of the heart, and performing the precepts, so that, all at length returns to this, from whence, while we swerved, all this misery is come upon us. In the beginning it was thus, —man was created to glorify God, by obedience to his blessed will; sin interposeth and marreth the whole frame, and from this hath a flood of misery flowed in upon us. Well, the gospel comes offering a Saviour, and forgiveness in him. Thus peace is purchased, pardon granted, the soul is restored unto its primitive condition and state of subordination to God's will; and so redemption ends where creation began, or rather in a more perfect frame of the same kind. The second Adam builds what the first Adam broke down, and the Son re-creates what the Father in the beginning created, yea, with some addition. In this new edition of mankind, all seems new—'new heavens, and new earth;' and that because the creature that was made old, and defiled with sin, is made new by grace. Now, hence you may learn the second part of this lesson that the apostle teaches us; as ye ought to correct, as it were, precepts of the gospel, by subjoining promises in this manner, so ye ought to direct promises towards the performance of his precepts, as their chief end. Whensoever you read it written, 'The blood of Christ cleanseth us from all sin;'—'If we confess, he is faithful to forgive our sins;'—'God so loved the world that he gave his Son;'—'He that believeth hath everlasting life,' &c.—then make up the entire sense and meaning, after this manner, 'These things are written that we sin not.' Is there a redemption from wrath published? Is there reconciliation with God preached? And are we beseeched to come and have the benefit of them? Then say, and supply within thine own heart, 'These things are written, published, and preached, that we may not sin.' Look to the furthest end of these things, it is, 'that we sin not.' The end of things, the scope of writings, and the purpose of actions, is the very measure of them, and so that is the best interpreter of them. The scope of scripture is by all accounted the very thread that will lead a man right in and out of the labyrinths that are in it. And so it is used as the rule of the interpretation in the parts of it. Now, my beloved in the Lord, take here the scope of the whole scriptures, the mark that all the gospel shoots at, 'These things I write unto you, that ye sin not.' You hear, it is true, of pardon of sin, of delivery from wrath, of not coming into condemnation, of covering offences, of blotting them out as a cloud; all these you read and hear of; but what do they all aim at? If you consider not that attentively, you shall no more understand the plain gospel, than you can expound a parable without observing the scope of it. Do you think these have no further aim, than to give you peace, and to secure you from fears and terrors, that you may then walk as you list, and follow the guiding of your own hearts? Nay, if you take it so, you totally mistake it. If you do not read on, and find all these things written to this end, 'that ye sin not,' you err, not understanding, or misunderstanding, the scriptures.

'These things I write unto you, little children.' To enforce this the more sweetly, he useth this affectionate compellation, 'little children,' for in all things affection hath a mighty stroke, almost as much as reason. It is the most suitable way to prevail with the spirit of a man, to deal in love and tenderness with it; it insinuates more sweetly, and so can have less resistance, and therefore works more strongly. It is true, another way of terrors, threatenings, and reproofs, mingled with sharp and heavy words of challenges, may make a great deal of more noise, and yet it hath not such virtue to prevail with a rational soul. The Spirit of the Lord was not in the wind, nor in the earthquake, nor in the fire, but in the still and calm voice which came to Elijah, 1 Kings xix. 11, 12. These suit not the gentle, dove-like disposition of the Spirit; and though they be fit to rend rocks in pieces, yet they cannot truly break hearts, and make them contrite. The sun will make a man sooner part with his cloak than the wind; such is the difference between the warm beams of affection, and the boisterous violence of passions or terror. Now, O that there were such a spirit in them who preach the gospel, such a fatherly affection, that with much pity and compassion they might call sinners from the ways of death! O there is no subject, in which a man may have more room for melting affections, nothing that will admit of such bowels of compassion as this,—the multitude of souls posting to destruction, and so blindfolded that they cannot see it! Here the fountain of tears might be opened to run abundantly. The Lord personates a tender-hearted father or husband often, 'Oh, why will ye die? Ye have broken my heart with your whorish heart: O Jerusalem, how oft would I, but thou wouldst not!' When he, who is not subject to human passions, expresseth himself thus, how much more doth it become us poor creatures to have pity on our fellow-creatures? Should it not press out from us many groans, to see so many perishing, even beside salvation. I wish you would take it so, that the warning you to flee from the wrath to come, is the greatest act of favour and love that can be done to you. It becomes us to be solicitous about you, and declare unto you, that you will meet with destruction in those paths in which you walk; that these ways go down to the chambers of death. O that it might be done with so much feeling compassion of your misery, as the necessity of it requires! But, why do many of you take it so hard to be thus forewarned, and have your danger declared unto you? I guess at the reason of it. You are in a distemper as sick children distempered in a fever, who are not capable of discerning their parents' tender affection, when it crosseth their own inclinations and ways.

Sermon XXII.

1 John ii. 1.—"*My little children, these things write I unto you, that ye sin not: And if any man sin, we have an advocate with the Father,*" &c.

Christ Jesus came by water and by blood, not by water only, but by blood also, and I add, not by blood only, but by water also, chap. v. 6. In sin there is the guilt binding over to punishment, and there is the filth or spot that defileth the soul in God's sight. To take away guilt, nothing so fit as blood: for there is no punishment beyond blood; therefore saith the apostle, 'without the shedding of blood there is no remission of sin,' Heb. ix. 22; and for the stain and spot, nothing is so suitable as water, for that is generally appointed for cleansing. And some shadow of this the heathens had, who had their lustrations in water, and their expiations by blood;* but more significantly and plainly, the Jews, who had their purifications

* [There is no fact, connected with the history of former times, which can be more easily proved than this, that religious sacrifices were prevalent throughout every part of the Gentile world. Animals, which were deemed suitable for sacrifice by one nation, might be considered improper for such a purpose by another. But in the most remote countries victims of one kind or another, and not unfrequently human victims, were seen bleeding on the altars of superstition, and with the death of these, the idea of substitution, or of presenting life for life, was almost invariably connected. When sacrificing her victim, Ovid makes his votaress exclaim.—"Take heart for heart, I beseech thee, take entrails for entrails. We give to thee this life for a better one."—

Cor pro corde, precor, pro fibris sumite fibras.
Hanc animam vobis pro meliore damus.
Fast. lib. vi. v. 161.

But "as Kennicot observes from Delaney, whatever practice has obtained universally in the world, by sprinkling of water, (Num. viii. 7.) and expiations by sacrificing of slain beasts. But all these were but evanishing shadows; now the substance is come, Jesus Christ is come in water and blood; in water, to cleanse the spots of the soul, to purify it from all filthiness; and in blood, to satisfy for sin, and remove the punishment. You have both in these words of the apostle, for he labours to set out unto us the true Christ, whole and entire, 'these things I write unto you, that ye sin not.' Here is the proper end of the water—and 'if any man sin, we have Christ a propitiation for our sins.' Here is the blood—the end of the blood is to save us, the end of the water is that we sin not, since we are saved. He came in the blood of expiation, because we had sinned. He came in the water of sanctification, that we might not sin. His blood speaks peace to the soul, and the water subjoins, 'but let them not return to folly.' His blood cries, 'behold thou art made whole,' and the water echoes unto it, 'sin no more, lest a worse thing befall thee,' John v. 14. These two streams of water and blood, which are appointed for purity and pardon, run intermingled all along, and so the proper effects of them are interchangeably attributed to either of them; 'he hath washed us in his blood,' (Rev. i. 5; vii. 14.) 'and the blood of Christ cleanseth us from all sin.' Then, certainly, this blood cannot be without water, it is never separated from it. The proper effect of blood is to cover sin; but because the water runs in that channel, and is conveyed by the blood thither, therefore it doth cleanse sin, as well as cover it.

'These things I write unto you, that ye sin not.' This then is the design of the whole gospel, the great and grand design,—to destroy sin, and save the sinner. There is a treaty of peace made with the sinner, and 'Christ is the peace-maker.' A tender of life and salvation is made to him, but there is no treaty, no capitulation or composition with sin; out it must go, first out of its dominion, then out of its habitation. It must first lose its power, and then its being in a believer. Yea, this is one of the chief articles of our peace, not only required of us as our duty, that we should destroy that which cannot but destroy us; for, if any man will needs hug and embrace his sins, and cannot part with them, he must needs die in their embracements, because the council of heaven hath irrevocably passed a fatal sentence against sin, as the only thing that in all the creation hath the most perfect opposition to his blessed will, and contrariety to his holy nature,—but also, and especially, as the great stipulation and promise upon his part, 'to redeem us from all our iniquities, and purify us to himself, a people zealous of good works;' and not only to redeem us from hell, and deliver us from wrath, Tit. ii. 14. He hath undertaken this great work, to compesce* this mutiny and rebellion that was raised up in the creation by sin, else what peace could be between God and us, as long as his enemy and ours dwelt in our bosom, and we at peace with it.

Now, take a short view of these things that are written in the preceding chapter, and you shall see that the harmonious voice of all that is in the gospel, is this, 'that we sin not.' Let me say further, as 'these things are written that we sin not,' so

must have obtained from some dictate of *reason*, or some demand of *nature*, or some principle of *interest*, or else from some powerful influence or injunction of some Being of universal authority. Now the practice of animal sacrifice did not obtain from *reason*, for no reasonable notions of God could teach men that he could delight in blood, or in the fat of slain beasts. Nor will any man say, that we have any natural *instinct* to gratify, in spilling the blood of an innocent creature. Nor could there be any temptation from appetite to do this in those ages, when the whole sacrifice was consumed by fire; or when, if it was not, yet men wholly abstained from flesh; and consequently this practice did not owe its origin to any principle of *interest*. Nay, so far from any thing of this, that the destruction of innocent and useful creatures is evidently *against nature*, *against reason*, and *against interest*; and therefore must be founded in an authority, whose influence was as powerful as the practice was universal: and that could be none but the authority of God, the sovereign of the world; or of Adam, the founder of the human race. If it be said of Adam, the question still remains, what motive determined him to the practice? It could not be nature, reason, or interest, as has been already shown; it must therefore have been the authority of his Sovereign: and had Adam enjoined it to his posterity, it is not to be imagined that they would have obeyed him in so extraordinary and expensive a rite, from any other motive than the command of God. If it be urged, that superstitions prevail unaccountably in the world; it may be answered, that all superstition has its origin in true religion; all superstition is an abuse; and all abuse supposes a right and proper use. And if this be the case in superstitious practices that are of lesser moment and extent, what shall be said of a practice existing through all ages, and pervading every nation?—See Kennic. Two Diss. pp. 210, 211. and Rev. Exam. Diss. 8. p. 85—89." Magee on the Atonement, vol. II. part I. pp. 27—29.—ED.]

* [That is, restrain.—ED.]

all things are done 'that we sin not.' Take all the whole work of creation, of providence, of redemption,—all of them speak one language, 'that we sin not.' 'Day unto day uttereth speech, and night unto night showeth knowledge: there is no speech or language where their voice is not heard,' Psalm xix. 2, 3. And, as in that place, their voice proclaims the glory, majesty, and goodness of God, so they, with the same sound, proclaim and declare, that we should not sin against such a God, so great, and so good. All that we see suggests and insinuates this unto our hearts; all that we hear whispers this unto our ears, 'that we sin not, that he made us, and not we ourselves, and that we are the very work of his hands.' This speaks our absolute and essential dependence on him, and therefore proclaims with a loud voice, that sin, which would cut off this subordination, and loose from this dependence upon his holy will, is a monstrous, unnatural thing. Take all his mercies towards us, whether general or particular, the transcendent abundance of his infinite goodness in the earth, that river of his riches that runs through it, to water every man, and bring supply to his doors, that infinite variety that is in heaven and earth, and all of them of equal birth-right with man; yet by the law of our Maker, a yoke of subjection and service to man is imposed upon them, so that man is, in a manner, set in the centre of all, to the end, that all the several qualifications and perfections that are in every creature, may concentre and meet together in him, and flow towards him. Look upon all his particular acts of care and favour towards thee, consider his judgments upon the world, upon the nation, or thine own person. Put to thine ear, and hear. This is the joint harmonious melody, this is the proclamation of all, 'that we sin not,' that we sin not against so good a God, and so great a God. That were wickedness, this were madness. If he wound, it is 'that we sin not:' if he heal again, it is 'that we sin not.' Doth he kill? It is 'that we sin not!' Doth he make alive? It is for the same end. Doth he shut up and restrain our liberty, either by bondage, or sickness, or other afflictions? Why, he means 'that we sin not.' Doth he open again? He means the same thing, 'that we sin no more, lest a worse thing befall us.' Doth he make many to fall in battle, and turn the fury of that upon us? The voice of it is, that you who are left behind should 'sin no more.' Is there severity towards others, and towards you clemency? O the loud voice of that is, 'sin not!' But alas, the result of all is, that which is written, Psal. lxxviii. 32.—'Nevertheless they sinned still.' In the midst of so many concurring testimonies, in the very throng of all the sounds and voices that all the works of God utter, in the very hearing of these, nevertheless to sin still, and not to return and inquire early after God,—this is the plague and judgment of the nation.

But let us return to the words, 'these things,' &c. 'That which is written of the word of life, that which was from the beginning, and was manifested unto us,' that is written 'that we sin not:' For, saith this same apostle, chap. iii. 5, 8, 'And ye know that he was manifested to take away our sins, and in him is no sin;' yea, for this very purpose, saith he, 'that he might destroy the works of the devil.' Now, this is the great business, that drew the Son out of the Father's bosom,—to destroy the arch-enemy and capital rebel, sin, which, as to man, is a work of Satan's, because it first entered in man by the devil's suggestion and counsel. All that misery and ruin, all those works of darkness and death, that Satan had by his malice and policy wrought upon and in poor mankind, Jesus was manifested in the flesh without sin, to destroy and take away sin out of our flesh, and to abolish and destroy Satan's work, which he had builded upon the ruins of God's work, of the image of God, and to repair and renew that first blessed work of God in man, Eph. iv. 23, 24.

Now, O how cogent and persuading is this; one so high, come down so low, one dwelling in inaccessible glory, manifested in the flesh, in the infirmity and weakness of it, to this very purpose, to repair the creation, to make up the breaches of it, to destroy sin, and save the sinner! What force is in this to persuade a soul that truly believes it, 'not to sin!' For, may he think within himself, shall I save that which Christ came to destroy, shall I entertain and maintain that which he came to take away, and do what in me lies to frustrate the great end of his glorious and wonderful descent from heaven? Shall I join hands, and associate with my lusts, and war for them, 'which war against my soul,' and him that would save my soul? Nay, let us conclude, my beloved, within our own hearts,—Is the Word and Prince of life manifested from heaven, and come to mar and unmake that work of Satan, that he may rescue me from under his tyranny? Then God forbid that I should help Satan to build up that which my Saviour is casting down, and to make a prison for myself, and cords to bind me in it for everlasting. Nay, will a believing soul say, rather let me be a worker together with Christ. Though faintly, yet I resolve to wrestle with him, to pull down all the strongholds that Satan keeps in my nature, and so to congratulate and consent to him, who is the avenger and assertor of my liberty.

Then consider the greatest end and furthest design of the gospel, how it is inseparably chained and linked into this, 'that we sin not.' We are called to fellowship with the Father and the Son, and herein is his glory and our happiness. Now, this proclaims with a loud voice, 'that we sin not;' for, what more contrary to that design of union and communion with God, than to sin, which disunites and discommunicates the soul from God. The nature of sin you know, is the transgression of his law; and so it is the very just opposition of the creature's will to the will of him that made it. Now, how do ye imagine that this can consist with true friendship and fellowship, which looseth that conjunction of wills and affections, which is the bond of true friendship, and the ground of fellowship? *Idem velle atque idem nolle, hæc demum vera amicitia est.** The conspiracy of our desires and delights in one point with God's, this sweet coincidency makes out communion; and what communion then can there be with God, when that which his soul abhors is your delight, and his delight is not your desire? 'What communion hath light with darkness?' Sin is darkness. All sin, but especially sin entertained and maintained, sin that hath the full consent of the heart, and carrieth the whole man after it, that is Egyptian darkness, an universal darkness over the soul. This being interposed between God and the soul, breaks off communion, eclipses that soul totally. Therefore, my beloved, if you do believe that you are called unto this high dignity of fellowship with God, and if your souls be stirred with some holy ambition after it, consider that 'these things are written that ye sin not.' Consider what baseness is in it, for one that hath such a noble design, as fellowship with the Highest, to debase his soul so far and so low, as to serve sinful and fleshly lusts. There is a vileness and wretchedness in the service of sin, that any soul, truly and nobly principled, cannot but look upon it with indignation, because he can behold nothing but indignity in it. 'Shall I who am a ruler,' saith Nehemiah, 'shall such a man as I flee? and who is there, that being as I am, would flee? Neh. vi. 11. A Christian hath more reason. Shall such a man as I, who am born again to such a hope, and called to such a high dignity; shall I, who aim and aspire so high as fellowship with God, debase and degrade myself with the vilest servitude? Shall I defile in that puddle again, till my own clothes abhor me, who aim at so pure and so holy a society? Shall I yoke in myself with drunkards, liars, swearers, and other slaves of sin? Shall I rank myself thus, and conform myself to the world, seeing there is a noble and glorious society to incorporate with, the King of kings to converse with daily? Alas, what are these worms that sit on thrones to him? But far more, how base are these companions in iniquity, your pot companions? &c. And what a vile society is it like that of the bottomless pit, where devils are linked together in chains?

Sermon XXIII.

1 John ii. 1.—"*My little children, these things write I unto you, that ye sin not. And if any man sin, we have an advocate with the Father,*" &c.

In the gospel we have the most perfect provision against both these extremities, that souls are ready to run upon, the rock of desperate distrust, and the quicksands of presumptuous wantonness. It may be said to be a well-ordered covenant in all

* See note, page 96.

things, that hath caveated and cautioned the whole matter of our salvation, in such a way, that there is neither place for discouragement and downcasting, nor yet room for liberty in sin. There is no exemption from the obligation of God's holy law, and yet there is pardon for the breach of it, and exemption from the curse. There is no peace, no capitulation with sin, and yet there is peace concluded with the sinner, who is, by that agreement, bound to fall out with sin. There is no dispensation for sin, and from the perfection of holiness, and yet there is an advocation for the sinner, who aims and studies after it. So that, in sum, the whole gospel is comprised in this,—'he speaks peace to his saints, but let them not return to folly; thou art made whole, sin no more.' All that is in the gospel saith this, 'that thou shouldst sin no more.' But because sin is necessarily incident, therefore all that is in the gospel speaks this further,—though ye be surprised in sin, yet believe; and this is the round in which a believer is to walk,—to turn from pardon to purity, and from pollution again to pardon, for these voices and sounds are interchanged continually. If ye have sinned, believe in Christ the advocate and sacrifice, and, because ye have believed, sin not; but if ye be overtaken in sin, yet believe. And as this is daily renewed, so the soul's study and endeavour in them, should be daily renewed too. If ye have sinned, despair not; if ye be pardoned, yet presume not. After sin there is hope, it is true, because 'there is forgiveness with him;' but after forgiveness, there must be fear to offend his goodness; for there is forgiveness with him, that he may be feared, Psal. cxxx. 4. And this is the situation I would desire my soul in,—to be placed between hope of his mercy and fear of sin, the faith of his favour and the hatred of sin, which he will not favour; and how happy were a soul to be confined within these, and kept captive to its true liberty!

I spake a little before, how those fundamental truths that are set down before, do all aim at this one mark, 'that we sin not; now I proceed. That declaration what God is, verse 5, is expressly directed to this purpose and applied, verse 6—'God is light,' and therefore 'sin not,' for sin is darkness; 'he is light,' for purity and beauty of holiness, and perfection of knowledge,—that true light in which is no darkness,—that unmixed light, all homogeneous to itself,—therefore 'sin not;' for that is a work of the night, and of the darkness, that proceeds from the blindness and estrangement of your minds, and ignorance of your hearts; and it cannot but prepare and fit you for those everlasting chains of darkness. Call God what you will; name all his names, styles, and titles; spell all the characters of it, and still you may find it written at every one of them, 'sin not.' Is he light? Then sin not. Is he life? Then sin not; for sin will separate you from his light and life; sin will darken your souls and kill them. Is he love? Then sin not. 'God is love,' saith John; O then sin not against love! Hatred of any good thing is deformed; but the hatred of the beautiful image of the original love, that is monstrous. 'God is love,' and in his love is your life and light; then to sin against him is not simple disobedience, nor is it only grosser rebellion, but it hath that abominable stain of ingratitude in it. Do you read, that it is written, 'he is holy?' Then sin not, for this is most repugnant to his holiness,—'his holy eyes cannot see it.' Therefore, if thou wouldst have him look upon thee with favour, thou must not look upon sin with favour, or entertain it with delight. Is it written, that he is great and powerful?—Then sin not—that were madness. Is it written, that he is good and gracious? Then it is written, that ye sin not, for that were wickedness; it were an unspeakable folly and madness, to offend so great a God, that can so easily avenge himself; and it were abominable perverseness and wickedness, to sin against so good and gracious a God, who, though he may avenge himself, yet offers pardon and peace, and beseecheth us to accept it. Is he just? Then sin not; for 'he will not acquit the wicked nor hold them guiltless,'—them who do acquit themselves, and yet hold by their sins. And is he merciful? Then, O then, sin not, because he hath acquitted thee, because he is ready to blot out thy guilt! Wilt thou sin against mercy that must save thee? Again, is it written, that the blood of Jesus Christ cleanseth from all sin? That is written, that ye sin not. It is true, it is written, because ye have sinned already, that ye may know how it may be pardoned. But, moreover, it is written, 'that ye sin no more,' that so, more sin may be prevented, at least, deliberate continued walking in sin. So that this blood hath a twofold virtue and use, to be the greatest encouragement to a soul troubled for sin, and the chiefest argument and inducement for a soul not to sin. This medicine, or this plaster, hath two notable virtues, restorative and preservative, to restore the bones that already are broken, through falling in sin; and to preserve our feet from further falling in sin. It hath a healing virtue for those bruises that are in the soul; and, besides, it is an antidote and sovereign preservative against the poison and infection of sin and the world. What motive is like this? The Son of God shed his blood for our sins; they cost a dear price. O how precious was the ransom! More precious than gold, and silver, and precious stones, because the redemption of the soul is so precious, that it would have ceased for ever without it. Now, what soul can deliberately think of this, and receive it with any affection into the heart, but shall find the most vehement persuasion against sin? He cannot but behold the heinousness and infinite evil that is in it, which required such an infinite recompense. And can a soul on that view run to the puddle and defile again, when he sees how dearly the fountain for cleansing was purchased? Can a believing heart have such treacherous thoughts harboured within it, to crucify afresh the Lord of glory, and, as it were, to trample under feet his blood? No, certainly, he that believes in this blood cannot use it so dishonourably and basely: as it is written, that he 'sin not,' so he reads it, and believes it, that he may not sin, as well as because he hath sinned. Many speak of this blood, and think they apply it to the cleansing of their sin past; but it is rather that they may sin with more liberty, as if the end of vomiting up a surfeit of sin were to surfeit more; and the end of washing, were nothing else but to defile again. Certainly this blood is not for such souls,—not one word of comfort in the word,—not one drop of hope in the blood, to those who pretend to believe in Christ's blood, and continue in sin, as fresh and lively as ever they did, nothing abated of their desires or customs. But if we confess our sins, God will forgive, say you, and this we may do at any time, and this we do daily. Nay, but saith John, this is 'written that you sin not;' not to encourage you to sin. It is not recorded for this end, that you may live after your own imaginations and former customs, with security and peace, upon this presumption, that pardon is easily procurable, if I say, 'God have mercy upon me,' ere I die. Do not deceive yourselves, for it is written just for the contrary, 'that you sin no more, and return no more to folly.' If he had said, if we sin, though we confess, yet he is just to punish us, you would then be driven to desperation, and from that to a desperate conclusion. Since we must be punished, however, let us not punish ourselves here, in mortifying our flesh,—'let us eat and drink, for to-morrow we shall die.' Die we must, let us deserve it; for where there is no hope, there is no help for reformation.

But now, when there is such an unexpected proposal of grace; when God, who is free to punish us, becomes indebted by his promise to forgive our debts, we humbly submitting to him, and confessing our guiltiness; this surprisal of clemency and moderation should, yea, certainly will, overcome any heart that truly believes it, and conquer it to his love and obedience. The more easily he forgives sin, the more hardly will a believing heart be drawn to sin. You know any ingenuous spirit will more easily be conquered by kindness and condescendency, than severity and violence. These 'cords of love are the bands of a man,' suited to the nature of men in whom there is any sparkle of ingenuousness remaining. How often have men been engaged and overcome by clemency and goodness, who could not be conquered by force of arms! Enemies have been made friends by this means, such power is in it to knit hearts together. Augustus, when he was acquainted with the conspiracy of one of his chief minions, Cinna, whom he had made a friend of an enemy, by kindness and courtesy, takes the same way to make of a traitor a constant friend. He doth not punish him as he had done others, but calls for him, and declares unto him his vile ingratitude, that when he had given him life and liberty, he should conspire to take away his prince's life. Well, when he is confounded and astonished, and cannot open his mouth, saith Augustus, I give thee thy life again, first an open enemy, and now a traitor; yet from this day, let an inviolable friendship be bound up between us, and so it proved; for this way of dealing did totally overcome his heart, and blot out all seditious thoughts.* But, O how incomparably greater is his condescendency and clemency, whose person is so high and sacred; whose laws are so just and holy, and we so base and wretched,—to pardon such infinite guilt, rebellion, and treachery, against such an infinite majesty; and that, when a soul doth but begin to blush, and be ashamed with itself, and cannot open its mouth! I say, this rare and unparalleled goodness and mercy being considered, cannot but tame and daunt the wildest and most savage natures. Wild beast are not brought into subjection and tamed, but by gentle usage. It is not fierceness and violence can cure their fierceness, but meekness and condescendency to follow their humours, and soft dealing with them. As a rod is not bowed by great strength, but broken, even so those things of the promise of pardon for sin, of the grace and readiness of God to pardon upon the easiest terms, are written for this end, that our wild and undaunted natures may be tamed, and may bow and submit willingly to the yoke of his obedience, and may henceforth knit such a sacred bond of friendship and fellowship with God, as may never be broken.

But, say ye, who is he that sins not? Who can say, my heart is pure, and my way is clean? Who can say, I have no sin? And therefore that cannot be expected which you crave. Nay, but saith the apostle, 'These things I write unto you, that ye sin not.' Because sin is in all, therefore you excuse yourselves in your sins, and take liberty to sin. But the very contrary is the intent of the declaring unto us that we have sin; he shows that none want it, not that ye may be the more indulgent towards it, but the more watchful against it. It is not to make you secure, but rather to give you alarm. Even the best and holiest,—it is an alarm to them, to tell them that sin is *in confiniis*, in their very borders, that the enemy is even in their quarters, yea, in their bosom. Certainly, this should so much the more excite us against it, and arm us for it every moment, lest either by fraud or force, by secret undermining or open violence, it draw us away from God. This word, 'if we say we have no sin, we lie,' is a watchword given to men, a warning to enter in consideration of themselves; for the enemy being within, there is no flying from him. We carry him about with us, and being within, he is less discerned, and therefore we ought to awake, and so walk circumspectly, with eyes in our head, lest we be surprised at unawares, either in that time we know not of, or at that place we least suspect. And to others of you, who have never attained any victory over your sins, and scarce have a discerning of them, I would only say this, that the universality of sin's inhabitation, or being in all men, even the godly, will not excuse sin's domination and reign in you. It is strange, that since the holiest have need of continual watching against this bosom enemy, that ye who have both little knowledge and strength, should think ye may live securely, and not trouble yourselves. If they have need to take heed, how much more have ye, since it is but in them, but it reigns in you?

Sermon XXIV.

1 John ii. 1.—"*And if any man sin, we have an advocate with the Father,*" &c.

There is here a sad supposition, but too certain, that any man may sin; yea, that all men will sin, even those who have most communion with God, and interest in the blood of Christ. Yet they are not altogether exempted from this fatal lot of mankind. It is incident even to them to sin, and too frequently incident: but yet we have a happy and sweet provision, for indemnity from the hazard of sin,—'we

* [Lucius Cinna was the grandson of Pompey the Great. It was through the intercession of Livia, the wife of Augustus, that Cinna was pardoned. 'Do,' said she to Augustus, 'what physicians are accustomed to do, who, when the remedies they have employed do not succeed, try others which are entirely different. You have done no good by severity.—Try now the effect of clemency. Forgive Lucius Cinna. Now that he has been discovered, he cannot injure you, but he can advance your reputation.'—Seneca de Clem. lib. I. cap. 9.—Ed.]

have an advocate with the Father.' Grant the probability, yea, the necessity and certainty of that supposal, 'if any man do sin,' yet there is as much certainty of indemnity from sin, as of necessity of falling into sin. It is not more sure, that we shall carry about with us matter of sorrow and mourning; but that it is as sure, that we have always without us matter of rejoicing.

Let me then speak a word to these particulars: *First,* That sin is incident to the best, even after all persuasions, convictions, resolutions, desires, and designs to avoid sin. *Next,* That it is usual for sins after mercy, convictions, and resolution, to appear so heinous, that they may seem to overtop the mercy of God, and the merits of Christ; a soul is most apt to be troubled with guilt contracted after pardon, and a desire of purity. But withal, I would, in the *Last* place, represent to you, that there is no ground of despair or discouragement for such an one, though there be ground of humiliation and mourning. There is a provision made in the gospel against these continually incident fears; there is a security against the hazard of surprising sins; and, this comfort belongs only to such souls as unfeignedly desire not to sin, and are in some measure persuaded by the grace of God not to sin, not to those who willingly give themselves up to their own lusts. It is as common a doctrine as any, that sin hath some lodging in every man's heart and flesh, and is not totally cast out, but only bound with chains within, that it do not exercise its old dominion over a believer. But I fear, the most common truths, though they be most substantial in themselves, are yet but circumstantial in our apprehensions, and very rarely and extraordinarily have place in the deeper and more serious thoughts of our hearts. They are commonly confessed, it is true, but as seldom considered, I am sure. For who did truly ponder the inclineableness of our nature to sin, the strong propension of the heart to evil, the deceitfulness of sin itself, and the many circumstantial helps and additions it gets to its strength, but would stand in awe, and watch seriously over himself. I dare say, many sin, rather because of a misapprehended immunity from it, and a misreckoning of their own measure and strength, than because of the strength of sin itself. I know no one thing makes sin so strong as this,—that we do not apprehend our own weakness, and so give over watchfulness, which is the greatest and best part of our armour of defence, when it is done in faith, and this watch kept on the tower of the Lord's promises. The apprehension of our escaping the pollutions of the world, and of some strength to resist them: this adds no more strength to us, but diminisheth and taketh from our vigilance, and so exposeth us, as it were, naked and secure, to the cruelty of our adversary. I would wish every Christian to be thoroughly acquainted, and often conversant in two books of sophistry, I may so term them,—the deceitfulness of his own heart, and the deceivableness of sin, Jer. xvii. and Heb. iii. 13. These are the volumes he would daily turn over, to learn to discern the sophistications, self-flatteries, blindness, darkness, and self-love of his own heart; to take off the deceiving mask of pretences and appearances of good, and behold sensibly the true and real inclinations of the heart to wickedness, to passion, pride, uncleanness, malice, envy, and all those affections of the flesh:—to find out the true beating of the pulse of the heart. And indeed this just discerning and discovery of the thief in the soul, is a great part of his arraignment; for if sin lie under the view of an eye that hates it, and loves God, much of its power and virtue, which lie in darkness, is taken away. I press this the more, because I verily apprehend it to be the plague of many Christians, who have some general insight into the matter of good and evil, and espy some more gross corruption in themselves, and have some affection to good. Yet this estrangedness to our own hearts, and the vein or strain of them, the not unbowelling of our hidden affections, and not discerning of the poison of pride, self-love, love of the world, and such like lusts, which are intermingled in all that we do, and spread, as it were, universally through the whole man; this, I say, makes most of us to be subject to so many surprisals by sin. We are often routed before we draw up; and often conquered ere we consider. This makes us such unproficients in mortification, so that scarce any sin is killed, while the roots of all sin lie hid under the ground from us. Then withal, I desire you to study how deceivable a thing sin is,—how many deceitful fair pretences it is covered with. It hath the voice of Jacob, but the hands of Esau. Look, what it is that is pleasant or suitable to our natural spirits,—it insinuates itself always under the shadow of that; and if there be not much heedfulness and attention, and much experience of the wiles of that subtile one, it is a great hazard to be catched with it unadvisedly, while we clasp about another thing, which is presented as a bait and allurement. Now, is it any wonder that a poor soul be drawn to sin often, when our enemy doth not for the most part profess hostility, but friendship, and under that colour pleads admission within our ports? And, besides, we have a treacherous friend in our bosom, that betrays us into his hands; that is, our own deceitful hearts. These things I mention to put you in remembrance of what condition you are in, in this world, and what posture you should be in. Watch, I say, and when ye have done all, stand with your loins girt; and though you cannot possibly escape all sin, yet certainly it is not in vain thus to set against it, and keep a watch over it, for by this means you shall escape more sin, and sin less, as he that aims at the mark, though he do not hit it, yet shall ordinarily come nearer it, than he that shoots only at random; and as the army that is most vigilant and watchful, though they cannot prevent all losses and hazards, yet commonly are not found at such a loss, as those who are proud, confident, and secure.

Now, as it is supposed, that sin is ordinarily incident to the child of God, so it is especially to be caveated, that he despair not in his sins; for it is imported in this provision, that the believer is in great hazard upon new lapses into sin, either of daily incursion, or of a grosser nature, to be discouraged. As there is so much corruption in any man's heart, as will turn the grace of God into wantonness, and incline him, upon the proposal of free grace, to presume to take liberty to the flesh; so that same corruption, upon another occasion, works another way, upon the supposal of new sins, aggravated with preceding mercy and grace in God, and convictions and resolutions in him, to drive him into despondency and dejection of spirit, as if there were no pardon for such sins. And indeed, it is no wonder if the soul be thus set upon, if we set aside the consideration of the infinite grace of God, that far surpasseth the ill deserts of men. To speak of the very nature of the thing itself, there is no sin in its own nature more unpardonable than sin after pardon; nothing so heinous, aggravated with so many high circumstances, which mingleth it with the worst ingredients, as this sin, after so much grace revealed in the gospel, to the end that we may not sin. Sins washed so freely, in so precious a fountain, and yet to defile again; sins forgiven so readily and easily, the debt whereof, in justice, the whole creation was not able to pay, and yet to offend so gracious a Father; a soul being thoroughly convinced of the vanity, folly, and madness of sin, of the deceitfulness and baseness of its pleasures, and set in a posture against it, as the most deadly enemy; and yet, after all this, to be foiled, deceived, and insnared:—here, I say, are very piercing considerations, which cannot but set the challenge very deep into the heart of a Christian, and wound him sore. How will he be filled with shame and confusion of face, if he look upon God, every look or beam of whose countenance represents unto the soul the vilest and most abominable visage of sin! Or if he look into himself, there is nothing but self-condemning there. He finds his own conscience staring him as a thousand witnesses. Thus the soul of a believer being environed, he is ready to apprehend, that though God should have pardoned the sins of his ignorance, yet that there is more difficulty in this,—to pardon his returnings to folly; and therefore are some put to harder exercise, and greater terrors, after conversion, than in the time of it. The sins of ignorance being, as it were, removed as a cloud, and scored out in a heap; but the sins of knowledge after mercy, lying more distinctly and clearly in the view of the soul, it is more difficult to blot them out of the conscience, and sprinkle the heart from an evil conscience. These things I speak to you for this reason, that you may be afraid to sin. I suppose that there is no hazard of eternal damnation by sin. Grant that you know beforehand, that if you sin, there is yet forgiveness with him, and there is no hazard of perishing by it; yet, sure I am, it is the most foolish adventure in the world, to take liberty on that account; for though there be indemnity that way, as to thy eternal estate, yet I am persuaded, that there is more damage another way, in thy spiritual estate in this world, than all the gains of sin can countervail. There is a necessary loss of peace, and joy, and communion of the Holy Ghost. It is inevitable, in the very ordinary and natural course and connection of things, but that sin, that way indulged, will eclipse thy soul, and bring some darkness of sorrow and horror over it. To speak after the manner of man, and in the way of reason itself, the entertainment of that which God hates will deprive thee of more solid joy and sweetness in him, than all the pleasures of sin could afford. Therefore I dare not say to you, as one too unadvisedly expresseth it, "Fear not, though you do sin, of any hurt that can come by these sins: for if you sin, it shall do you no hurt at all:"* I say, this were indeed but to make you too bold with sin. I had rather represent unto you, that though ye be secured in your eternal estate, and there can come no condemnation that way, yet there is much hurt comes by sin, even in this world; and sure, I think it a very rational and Christian inducement, to prevail with a Christian not to sin, to tell him that he shall make a foolish bargain by it, for he shall lose much more than he can gain. Is there no hurt or loss incident to men, but eternal perdition? Nay, my beloved, there is a loss Christians may sustain by sinning freely, which all the combined advantages of sin cannot compensate. Is not one hour's communion with God, are not the peace of your own consciences, and the joy of the Spirit, such inestimable jewels, that it were more suitable for a man to sell the world, and buy them, than to sell them, and buy a poor momentary trifling contentment, which hath a sting in the tail of it, and leaves nothing but vexation after it? O these bruises in David's bones, these breaches in his spirit, that loss of the joy of his salvation! Let these teach you who are escaped the great hurt of sin, to fear, at least, to be hurt by it this way, more than ever you can expect to be helped by it.

But then, I desire to add this in the third place, that there is provision made against the discouragement of those souls that desire not to sin, and yet sin against their desire. If the challenge I spoke of be written in thy conscience, as it were with the point of a diamond, deeply engraven; yet my beloved, consider, that 'if any man sin, we have an advocate,' &c. There is an express caution against thy discouragement. Certainly our Saviour hath provided for it. Since the case is so incident, and the supposition so ordinary, it is not conceivable that he hath not caveated and secured thy salvation in such cases: for he knew certainly before he pardoned thee, and visited thee at first, that thou wast to be subject unto this necessary burden of sin, and that it would often-times molest and trouble you, and sometimes prevail over you. All this he knew, that when he should order your forces, and draw out against sin, with the greatest desire and resolution, that yet you might be foiled unexpectedly; and this was not unknown to him, when he showed mercy at first. Therefore, since his love is unchangeable, and his wisdom, being infinite, saith it should be so, he would never have cast his love on such persons, if these things, which were then before him, could make him change. Now, I grant there is more wonder in the pardon of following sins, than in the first pardon; and therefore you should still love more, and praise more. But what is this wonder to the wonder of his grace? It is swallowed up in that higher wonder, for his thoughts and ways are not like ours; his voice is, 'Return, thou backsliding sinner, to thy first husband, though thou hast played the harlot.' Therefore, I desire that whatsoever be presented in that kind, to aggravate your sins, let it humble you more indeed, and make you hate sin; but let it not hinder you to think as highly of his mercy and grace, and to set that in the heavens above it.

* [Language of this description was in common use with the Antinomians of the time, as may be seen in Edwards' Gangræna, (Part First, p. 22. Lond. 1646.) Gataker's Antinomianism Discovered and Confuted, (pp. 18, 19. Lond. 1652.) and other similar works written about this period.—ED.]

Sermon XXV.

1 John ii. 1.—"*And if any man sin, we have an advocate with the Father,*" &c.

It is the natural office of the conscience to accuse a man in evil doing. As every man by sin is liable to the judgment of the supreme court of heaven, so he is likewise subject to the inferior court of his own conscience; for the most high God hath a deputy within every man's breast, that not only is a witness, but a judge, to fasten an accusation, and pronounce a sentence upon him according to the law of God. And while it is so, that a man is accused in both courts, at the supreme tribunal, and the lower house of a man's own conscience; when man's accuser is within him, and God, his righteous Judge, above him, who can come in to plead such a man's cause? A person self-condemned, who shall plead for his absolution? If he cannot but accuse himself, and stop his mouth, being guilty before God of the transgression of all his law, then what place for an advocate to accuse him, or defend his cause? And who is it that can enter in the lists with God, who, because the supreme and highest Judge, must be both Judge and party? Where shall a daysman be found to lay his hands on both, and advocate the desperate-like cause of sinners? Truly, here we had been at an eternal stand, and here had the business stuck for ever, for anything that the creation could imagine, had not the infinite grace and wisdom of God opened themselves to mankind, in opening a door of hope to broken and outlaw sinners. And behold, here is the provision made for the security and salvation of lost souls,—there is one able and mighty to save,—a person found out fit for this advocation, who taketh the broken cause of sinners in hand, and pleads it out, and makes out justice to be for them, and not against them,—'If any man sin, we have an advocate,' &c.

There is one thing imported, that sin maketh a man liable to a charge and accusation, and brings him under the hazard of judgment. Indeed it is hard enough to endure an accusing conscience, and a spirit wounded with the apprehension of wrath. When our Saviour would express great affliction, he doth it thus—'A man's enemies shall be those of his own house.' If a domestic enemy be so ill, what shall a bosom enemy be; when a man's accuser is not only beside him, but within him,—not only in the house with him, but in the field too,—carried about with him whithersoever he goeth, so that he can have no retiring or withdrawing place from it! Indeed, some poor souls make a mad escape from under the challenge of their consciences; they get away from their keepers to more excess in sin, or make some vain diversion to company, and other things of the world. But the end thereof shall be more bitterness, for that will not still sleep within them, but shall awake upon them with more terror, and one day put them in such a posture, that all the comforts of the world shall be but as a drop of water to a man in a burning fever, or as oil to a flame. But, as I told you, that is not the greatest matter, to be self-accused, and self-condemned, if there were not a higher tribunal, which this process originally flows from, one greater than the conscience, who speaks to us in his word, and hath written his charge and sentence against us, and this is it which sets the soul most on edge; and it is but the very apprehension of that higher judgment, which is the gall and wormwood, the poison of those challenges in the conscience. I would desire you to look upon this, and consider that there is a sentence passed in the word of God upon all your actions, that the wrath of God is revealed in the scriptures as due to you, however you may flatter yourselves in your sins, and fancy an immunity from wrath, though you live in sin. I wish ye were once persuaded of this,—that all sinners must once appear before God's tribunal and hear the righteous sentence of the dueness of punishment pronounced; I say, all must once appear, either to hear and believe it, or to see it executed. The wisdom of God requires, that all men's guilt, which is a transgression of the law, should once come to a judicial trial and decision by the law; and either this must be done in your own consciences here, that ye may sist yourselves before him, and take with your sins, and humble yourselves in his sight, and then the matter is put over upon a Mediator: or else you must give him leave, nay he will take leave, to cite you to appear, to see the sentence executed which was pronounced, since ye would not apply it to your own hearts. O! happy is that soul that anticipates that great day of final judgment, by a previous self-judgment and self-trial. Well, then, hath the scriptures included all under sin, that all men might be guilty, and every mouth stopped before God, Rom. iii. 19. What shall we do then? Since righteousness and justice is against us, who can plead for us? It would seem that there could be no relaxing, no repealing, no dispensing with this law; at least that if there be anything of that kind, that righteousness and judgment can have no hand in it. Yet, behold what follows, 'we have an advocate,' &c. And an advocate's office is to sue out the client's right, from principles of justice. Elsewhere Christ hath the office of a Judge, here he is an advocate for the party, and both of these may have a comfortable consideration, John v. 22: 'The Father judgeth no man, but hath committed all judgment to the Son.' And yet, here we have an advocate with the Father, and that is, with the Father as judge. These do not cross one another, but make out our abundant consolation, that one entire office of our Saviour is represented under all these various notions suited to our capacity. A Judge he is: yea, his tribunal is the highest and supreme, from which there is no appeal; the ultimate decision lies here of all capital, or soul cases and causes. It is true, the Father doth not wholly divest himself of judgment and authority in the matters of life and death, for the gospel is his contrivance, as it was the Son's, but Christ is, as it were, substituted his vicegerent, in the administration of the second covenant. You read of a preparatory tribunal erected in the word by God the Creator, that is, of the law which condemns us. Now, such is the mercy and grace, and free love of God, that he hath relaxed that sentence as to the persons. He hath not taken that advantage which in justice he had against us; but upon some valuable considerations hath committed to the Son a royal power of prescribing new laws of life and death, and new terms of salvation; and Christ having, at his Father's will, satisfied the law, in what it did threaten us, he is, as it were, in compensation of such a great service, made Lord and King 'both of the dead and living,' (Rom. xiv. 9;) and 'all things in heaven and earth are given to him,' Matt. xxviii. 18; John xiii. 3. And therefore, whatever soul is aggrieved under the accusation and charge of the law, hath liberty, yea, and is called to it, of duty, to appeal unto this new erected tribunal, where Christ sits to dispense life, according to the terms of grace; and he may be sure the Father will not judge him according to the law, if the Son absolve him in the gospel.

Now, with this it consists, that he who hath all final judgment in his hand, yet is our advocate in another consideration, as we consider God the Father sitting upon the tribunal of justice, and proceeding according to the terms and tenor of his first law, or covenant of life and death. Then Christ comes in with his advocation for poor sinners, and sustains their persons, and maintains their cause, even from the principles of justice. He presents his satisfactory sacrifice, and pleads that we are not to be charged with that punishment that he hath suffered, because he hath indeed fulfilled our legal righteousness; and by this means the law's mouth is stopped, which had stopped our mouth, and the sinner is absolved, who was found guilty. Thus you see the salvation and absolution of believers is wonderfully secured, for there is a sentence for it in the court of the gospel, pronounced by the Son. But lest you think he should usurp such an absolute power, then hear, that he is an advocate to plead out the equity and justice of it, before the very tribunal of the law, that the law itself being the rule, the Father himself, who made the law, being the Judge, the poor soul that flies unto him as a refuge, may be saved, since what it craved of us it gets in him, and is as fully satisfied that way, as it could have been by us. Therefore, that same righteousness which bids condemn the sinner, commands to save the believer in Christ, though a sinner. What shall a soul then fear? Who shall condemn? It is Christ that justifieth; for he is judge of life and death, and that is much. But it is the Father that justifieth, and that is more: whatsoever tribunal you may be cited unto, you may be sure. Is it the gospel? Then the Son is judge. Is it the law? Then the Son is advocate. He will not only give life himself, but see that his Father do it, and warrant you from all back-hazards. Nay, before the matter shall misgive, as he comes down from off the throne, to stand at the bar and plead for sinners, who devolve themselves upon him, so he will not spare, if need require, to degrade himself further, if I may say so, and of an advocate become a supplicant. And truly he ceased not in the days of his flesh to pray for us, 'with strong cries and tears,' Heb. v. 7. And now he still lives to make intercession for us. He can turn from the plea of justice, to the intercession and supplication of mercy, and if strict justice will not help him, yet grace and favour he is sure will not disappoint him.

There is a divine contexture of justice and mercy in the business of man's redemption; and there is nothing so much declares infinite wisdom, as the method, order, and frame of it. Mercy might have been showed to sinners, in gracious and free pardon of their sins, and dispensing with the punishment due to their persons, yet the Lord's justice and faithfulness in that first commination might be wronged and disappointed by it, if no satisfaction should be made for such infinite offences, if the law were wholly made void both in the punishment, as also to the person. Therefore, in the infinite depths of God's wisdom, there was a way found out to declare both mercy and justice, to make both to shine gloriously in this work; and indeed that is the great wonder of men and angels, such a conjunction or constellation of divine attributes in one work. And indeed, it is only the most happy and favourable aspect in which we can behold the divine Majesty. The Psalmist, Psalm lxxxv., expects much good from this conjunction of the celestial attributes, and prognosticates salvation to be near at hand, and all good things, as the immediate effect of it. There is a meeting there, as it were, of some honourable personages, (ver. 10, 11.) such as are in heaven. The meeting is strange, if you consider the parties,—Mercy and Truth, Righteousness and Peace. If Mercy and Peace had met thus friendly, it had been less wonder; but it would seem, that Righteousness and Truth should stand off, or meet only to reason and dispute the business with Mercy. But here is the wonder,—Mercy and Truth meet in a friendly manner, and 'kiss one another.' There is a perfect agreement and harmony amongst them, about this matter of our salvation. There was a kind of parting at man's fall, but they met again at Christ's birth. Here is the uniting principle, 'Truth springing out of the earth.' Because he who is 'the truth and the life,' was to spring out of the earth, therefore 'righteousness will look down from heaven,' and countenance the business, and this will make all of them to meet with a loving salutation.

Now, as this was the contexture of the divine attributes in the business of redemption; so our Lord and Saviour taketh upon him divers names, offices, and exercises, different functions for us, because he knoweth that his Father may justly exact of man personal satisfaction, and hath him at this disadvantage, and that he might have refused to have accepted any other satisfaction from another person. Therefore he puts on the habit and form of a supplicant and intercessor for us; and so, while he was in the flesh, he ceased not to offer up 'prayers and supplications with strong cries and tears;' and he is said still 'to make intercession for us.' As he learned obedience, though a Son, so he learned to be a humble supplicant, though equal with God. Because our claim depends wholly on grace, he came off the bench, and stood at the bar, not only pleading but praying for us, entreating favour and mercy to us. And then, he personates an advocate in another consideration, and pleads upon terms of justice, that we be pardoned, because his Father once having accepted him in our stead, he gave a satisfaction in value equal to our debt, and performed all that we were personally bound to. So then you may understand how it is partly an act of justice, partly an act of mercy, in God to forgive sin to believers, though indeed mercy and grace is the predominant ingredient, because love and grace was the very first rise and spring of sending a Saviour and Redeemer, and so the original of that very purchase and price. He freely sent his Son, and freely accepted him in our stead; but once standing in our room, justice craves that no more be exacted of us, since he hath done the business himself.

A sinner stands accused in his own conscience, and before God; therefore, to the end that we get no wrong, there is a twofold advocate given us, one in the earth, in our consciences, another in the heavens with God. Christ is gone up to the highest tribunal, where the cause receives a definitive sentence, and there he manageth it above; so that though Satan should obtrude upon a poor soul a wrong sentence in its own conscience, and bring down a false and counterfeit act, as it were, extracted out of the register of heaven, whereby to deceive the poor soul, and condemn it in itself, yet there is no hazard above; he dare not appear there, before the highest court, for he hath already succumbed on earth. When Christ was here, the prince of the world was judged and cast out, and so he will never once put in an accusation into heaven, because he knoweth our faithful advocate is there, where nothing can pass without his knowledge and consent. And this is a great comfort, that all inferior sentences in thy perplexed conscience, which Satan, through violence, hath imposed upon thee, are rescinded above in the highest court, and shall not stand to thy prejudice, whoever thou be that desirest to forsake sin and come to Jesus Christ.

But how doth Christ plead? Can he plead us not guilty? Can he excuse or defend our sins? No, that is not the way. That accusation of the word and law against us is confessed, is proven, all is undeniably clear; but he pleads satisfied, though guilty,—he presents his satisfactory sacrifice, and the savour of that perfumes heaven, and pacifieth all. He shows God's bond and discharge of the receipt of the sum of our debt, and thus is he cleared, and we absolved. Therefore I desire you, whoever you are that are challenged for sin, and the transgression of the law, if ye would have a solid way of satisfaction and peace to your consciences, take with your guiltiness. Plead not "not guilty." Do not excuse or extenuate, but aggravate your guilt. Nay, in this you may help Satan, accuse yourselves, and say that you know more evil in yourselves than he doth, and open that up before God. But, in the meantime, consider how it is managed above. Plead thou also, "satisfied in Christ though guilty;" and so thou mayest say to thy accuser, If thou hast any thing to object against me, why I may not be saved, though a sinner, thou must go up to the highest tribunal to propone it, thou must come before my judge and advocate above; but forasmuch as thou dost not appear there, it is but a lie, and a murdering lie.

Now this is the way that the Spirit advocates for us in our consciences, John xiv. and xv. 26. Παρακλητος is rendered here "Advocate," there "Comforter." Both suit well, and may be conjoined in one, and given to both, for both are comfortable advocates,—Christ with the Father, and the Spirit with us. Christ is gone above for it, and he sent the Spirit in his stead. As God hath a deputy-judge in man, that is, man's conscience, so the Son, our advocate with God, hath a deputy-advocate to plead the cause in our conscience, and this he doth, partly by opening up the Scriptures to us, and making us understand the way of salvation in them, partly manifesting his own works and God's gifts in us by a superadded light of testimony, and partly by comforting us against all outward and inward sorrows. Sometimes he pleads with the soul against Satan "not guilty," for Satan is a slanderous and a false accuser, and cares not *calumniari fortiter ut aliquid hæreat*, to calumniate stoutly, and he knoweth something will stick.* He will not only object known sins and transgressions of the law, but his manner is to cast a mist upon the eye of the soul, and darken all its graces, and then he brings forth his process, that they have no grace, no faith in Christ, no love to God, no sorrow for sin. In such a case, it is the Spirit's office to plead it out to our consciences, that we are not totally guilty, as we are charged; and this is not so much a clearing of ourselves, as a vindication of the free gifts of God, which lie under his aspersion and reproach. Indeed, if there be a great stress here, and, for wise reasons, the Spirit forbear to plead out this point, but leave a poor soul to puddle it out alone, and scrape its evidences together in the dark,—I say, if thou find this too hard for thee to plead not guilty, then my advice is, that ye wave and suspend that question. Yield it not wholly, but rather leave it entire, and do as if it were not. Suppose that article and point were gained against thee, what wouldst thou do next? Certainly, thou must say, I would then seek grace and faith from him who giveth liberally. I would then labour to receive Christ in

* [How inconsistent is this maxim of Machiavel with the semblance even of Christian integrity! Pascal, however, has supplied us with ample proofs, not only from the books of the Jesuits, but from their public Theses, that they hold it to be perfectly justifiable to calumniate their enemies, or to charge them with crimes of which they know them to be innocent. He declares that this doctrine is so generally received by them, (si constante,) that should a man dare to oppose it, he would be treated by them as a fool.—Les Provinciales, tome troisieme, quinzieme lettre.—Ed.]

the promises. I say, do that now, and thou takest a short and compendious way to win thy cause, and overcome Satan. Let that be thy study, and he hath done with it.

But in any challenge about the transgression of the law, or desert of eternal wrath, the Spirit must not plead "not guilty," for thou must confess that; but in as far as he driveth at a further conclusion, to drive thee away from hope and confidence to despondency of spirit; in so far the Spirit clears up unto the conscience that this doth nowise follow from that confession of guiltiness, since there is a Saviour that hath satisfied for it, and invites all to come, and accept him for their Lord and Saviour.

Sermon XXVI.

1 John ii. 1.—"*We have an advocate with the Father, Jesus Christ the righteous.*"

There is no settlement to the spirit of a sinner that is once touched with the sense of his sins, and apprehension of the justice and wrath of God, but in some clear and distinct understanding of the grounds of consolation in the gospel, and the method of salvation revealed in it. There is no solid peace-giving answer to the challenges of the law and thy own conscience, but in the advocation of Jesus Christ, the Saviour of sinners. And therefore the apostle propones it here for the comfort of believers who are incident to be surprised through the suddenness of sin, and often deceived by the subtlety of Satan, whose soul's desires and sincere endeavours are to be kept from iniquity, and therefore they are made to groan within themselves, and sometimes sadly to conclude against themselves, upon the prevailing of sin. Here is the cordial, I say. He presents to them Jesus Christ standing before the bar of heaven, and pleading his satisfaction in the name of such souls, and so suiting forth an exemption and discharge for them from their sins. So he presents us with the most comfortable aspect, Christ standing between us and justice, the Mediator interposed between us and the Father, so there can come no harm to such poor sinners, except it come through his sides first, and no sentence can pass against them, unless he succumb in his righteous cause in heaven.

The strength of Christ's advocation for believers consists partly in his qualification for the office, partly in the ground and foundation of his cause. His qualification we have in this verse, the ground and foundation of his pleading in the next verse, in that 'he is the propitiation for our sins;' and upon this very ground his advocation is both just and effectual.

Every word holds out some fitness, and therefore every word drops out consolation to a troubled soul. 'With the Father,' speaks out the relation he and we stand in to the Judge. He hath not to do with an austere and rigid Judge, that is implacable and unsatisfiable, who will needs adhere peremptorily to the letter of the law, for then we should be all undone. If there were not some paternal affection, and fatherly clemency and moderation in the Judge; if he were not so disposed, as to make some candid interpretation upon it, and in some manner to relax the sentence, as to our personal suffering, we could never stand before him, nor needed any advocate appear for us. But here is the great comfort,—he is Christ's Father and our Father, so himself told us, (John xx. 17,) 'I go to my Father and your Father, and my God and your God.' And therefore we may be persuaded that he will not take advantage, even in that which he hath in justice, of us, and though we be apprehensive of his anger, in our failings and offences; and this makes us often to be both afraid and ashamed to come to him, measuring him after the manner of men, who are soon angry, and often implacably angry. We imagine that he cannot but repel and put back our petitions, and therefore we have not the boldness to offer them; yet he ceaseth not to be our Father and Christ's Father. And if ye would have the character of a father, look (Jer. xxxi. 18,) how he stands affected towards ashamed and confounded Ephraim, how his bowels move, and his compassions yearn towards him as his pleasant child. The truth is, in such a case, in which we are captives against our will, and stumble against our purpose, he pities us as a father doth his children, knowing that we are but dust and grass, Psal. ciii. 13—17. See the excellent and sweet application of this relation by the Psalmist—if it stir him, it stirs up rather the affection of pity, than the passion of anger. He pities his poor child, when he cries out of violence and oppression; and therefore, there are great hopes that our advocate Jesus Christ shall prevail in his suits for us, because he, with whom he deals,—the Father,—loves him, and loves us, and will not stand upon strict terms of justice, but rather attemper all with mercy and love. He will certainly hear his well-beloved Son, for in him he is well-pleased; his soul rests and takes complacency in him; and for his sake he adopts us to be his children; and therefore he will both hear him in our behalf, and our prayers too, for his name's sake.

But this is supperadded to qualify our advocate,—he is the Christ of God, anointed for this very purpose, and so hath a fair and lawful calling to this office. He takes not this honour to himself, but was called thereto of his Father, Heb. v. 4. As he did not make himself a priest, so he did not intrude upon the advocateship; 'but he that said, Thou art my Son,' called him to it. If a man had never so great ability to plead in the law, yet, except he be licentiate and graduate, he may not take upon him to plead a cause. But our Lord Jesus hath both skill and authority; he hath both the ability and the office; was not a self-intruder or usurper, but the council of heaven did licentiate him, and graduate him for the whole office of mediatorship: in which there is the greatest stay and support for a sinking soul, to know that all this frame and fabric of the gospel was contrived by God the Father, and that he is master-builder in it. Since it is so, there can nothing control it or shake it, since it is the very will of God, 'with whom we have to do,' that a mediator should stand between him and us; and since he hath such a mind to clear poor souls, that he freely chooseth and giveth them an able Advocate, it is a great token that he hath a mind to save as many as come and submit to him, and that he is ready to pardon, when he prepares so fit an Advocate for us, and hath not left us alone to plead our own cause.

But the anointing of Christ for it, implies both δυναμιν and ἐξουσιαν, *potentiam et potestatem*, the gifts for it as well as the authority, and the ability as well as the office; for God hath singularly qualified him for it,—given him the Spirit above measure, Isa. lxi. 1. He received gifts not only to distribute to men, but to exercise for men, and their advantage, Psal. lxviii. 18. And therefore the Father seems to interest himself in the cause as it were his own. He furnisheth our Advocate, as if it were to plead the cause of his own justice against us; he upholds and strengthens Christ in our cause, as really as if it were his own, Isa. xlii. 1, 6, which expresseth to us the admirable harmony and consent of heaven to the salvation of as many as make Christ their refuge, and desire not to live in sin. Though they be often foiled, yet there is no hazard of the failing of their cause above, because our Advocate hath both excellent skill, and undoubtable authority.

Yea, he is so fully qualified for this that he is called Jesus the Saviour; he is such an Advocate that he saves all he pleads for. The best advocate may lose the cause, either through the weakness of itself, or the iniquity of the judge; but he is the Advocate and the Saviour, that never succumbed in his undertaking for any soul. Be their sins never so heinous—their accusation never so just and true—their accuser never so powerful, yet they who put their cause in his hand; who flee in hither for refuge, being wearied of the bondage of sin and Satan, he hath such a prevalency with the Father, that their cause cannot miscarry. Even when justice itself seems to be the opposite party, yet he hath such marvellous success in his office, that justice shall rather meet amicably with mercy and peace, and salute them kindly, (Psal. lxxxv. 10, 11,) as being satisfied by him, that he come short in his undertaking.

But there is another personal qualification needful, or all should be in vain,—'Jesus the righteous.' If he were not righteous in himself, he had need of an advocate for himself, and might not plead for sinners; but he is righteous and holy, no guile found in his mouth; without sin, an unblameable and unspotted High Priest, else he could not mediate for others, and such an Advocate too, else he could not plead for others. Heb. vii. 26. As this perfected his sacrifice, that he offered not for his own sins, neither needed he, so this completes his advocateship, and gives it a mighty influence for his poor clients, that he needs not plead for himself. If, then, the law cannot attach our Lord and Saviour; can lay no claim to him, or charge against him, then certainly, all that he did behoved to be for others; and so he stands in a good capacity to plead for us before the Father, and to sue out a pardon to us, though guilty; for if the just was delivered for the unjust, and the righteous suffered for the unrighteous, much more is it consistent with the justice of the Father, to deliver and save the unrighteous and unjust sinner for the righteous Advocate's sake. 'If ye seek me, then let these go free,' saith he, John xviii. 8. So he in effect pleads with God his Father, O Father, if thou deal with me, the righteous One, as with an unrighteous man, then, in all reason and justice, thou must deal with my poor clients, though unrighteous, as with righteous men. If justice thought she did me no wrong to punish me, the righteous, then let it not be thought a wrong to justice to pardon, absolve, and justify the unrighteous.

Now, if he be so righteous a person, it follows necessarily, that he hath a righteous cause, for an honest man will not advocate an unjust cause. But how can the cause of believers be said to be righteous, when justice itself, and the law, indicts the accusation against them? Can they plead not guilty; or he for them? There is a twofold righteousness, in relation to a twofold rule; a righteousness of strict justice, in relation to the first covenant; and this cannot be pleaded, that our cause is exactly conformable to the covenant of works. We cannot, nor Christ in our name, plead any thing from that, which holds forth nothing but personal obedience, or else personal satisfaction. But yet our cause may be found to be righteous, in relation to the second covenant, and the rule and terms of it, in as far as God hath revealed his acceptance of a surety in our stead and hath dispensed with the rigour of the law, according to that new law of grace and righteousness contempered together. The cause of a desperate lost sinner may be sustained before the righteous Judge; and it is upon this new account that he pleads for us, because he hath satisfied in our stead; and now it is as righteous and equitable with God, to show mercy and forgiveness to believing sinners, as it is to reveal wrath and anger against impenitent sinners.

I know there will be some secret whisperings in your hearts upon the hearing of this. Oh! it is true; it is a most comfortable thing for them whose advocate he is. There is no fear of the miscarrying of their cause above; but as for me, I know not if he be an advocate for me, whether I may come into that sentence, 'We have an advocate,' &c. I confess it is true, he is not an advocate for every one, for while he was here, he prayed not for the world, but them that were given him out of the world, (John xvii.); much more will he not plead for the world, when he is above. He is rather witnessing against the unbelieving world. But yet, I believe his advocation is not restrained only to those who actually believe, as neither his supplication was, John xvii. But as he prayed for those who should hereafter believe, so he still pleads for all the elect, not only to procure remission to the penitent, but repentance to the impenitent. There is one notable effect of the advocation and intercession of Christ, which indeed is common to the world, but particularly intended for the elect, that is, the present suspension of the execution of the curse of the law, by virtue whereof there is liberty to offer the gospel, and call sinners to repentance. No question, the sparing of the world, the forbearance and long-suffering of God towards sinners, is the result and fruit of our Lord's intercession and advocation in heaven; and so, even the elect have the benefit of it before they believe; but it is so provided, that they shall never sensibly know this, nor have any special comfort from it, till they believe, and so Christ doth not plead for pardon to their sins till they repent. He pleads even before we repent, but we cannot know it; yet he pleads not that pardon be bestowed before they repent, and so the saving efficacy of his advocation is peculiar and proper in the application to believing souls.

Now, consider, I say, whether or not thou be one that finds the power of that persuasion,—'My little children, I write unto you that ye sin not,' &c. Canst thou unfeignedly say, that it is the desire and endeavour of thy soul not to sin; and that thou art persuaded to this, not only from the fear and terror of God, but especially from his mercy and goodness in the gospel? This is one part of the character of snch as Christ's advocation is actually extended to. Moreover, being surprised with sin, and overcome beside thy purpose, and against thy desire, dost thou apprehend sin as thy greatest misery, and arraign thyself before the tribunal of God; or art thou attached in thy own conscience, and the law pleaded against thee, before the bar of thy own conscience? Then, I say, according to this scripture, thou art the soul unto whom this comfort belongs; thou art called of God to decide the controversy in thy own conscience. By flying up, and appealing to that higher tribunal, where Christ is advocate, thou mayest safely give over, and trust thy cause to him.

But, on the other hand, O how deplorable and remediless is the condition of those souls who have no cause of this kind stated within their own consciences; who are not pursued by Satan and sin, but rather at peace with them, amicably agreeing with them, acting their lusts and will! You who have no bonds upon you, to restrain you from sin, neither the terror of the Lord persuadeth you, nor the love of Christ constrains you; you can be kept from no beloved sin, nor pressed to any serious and spiritual labour in God's service; and then when you sin, you have no accuser within, or such an one as you suppress, and suffer not to plead it out against you, or cite you before God's tribunal. I say unto you, (and, alas! many of you are such,) you do not, you cannot know, that you have an interest in this Advocate. You can have no benefit or saving advantage from Christ's pleading, while you remain thus in your sins. Alas! poor souls, what will ye do? Can you manage your own cause alone? Though you defraud and deceive your own consciences now; though ye offer violence to them, do ye think so to carry it above? Nay, persuade yourselves you must one day appear, and none to speak for you; God your Judge; your conscience your accuser; and Satan, your tormentor, standing by; and then woe to him that is alone, when the Advocate becomes Judge. In that day blessed are all those that have trusted in him, and used him formerly as an Advocate against sin and Satan; but woe to those for ever, who would never suffer this cause to be pleaded, while there was an Advocate!

Sermon XXVIII.

1 John ii. 2.—"*And he is the propitiation,*" &c.

Here is the strength of Christ's plea, and ground of his advocation, that 'he is the propitiation.' The advocate is the priest, and the priest is the sacrifice; and such efficacy this sacrifice hath, that the propitiatory sacrifice may be called the very propitiation and pacification for sin. Here is the marrow of the gospel, and these are the breasts of consolation which any poor sinner might draw by faith, and bring out soul refreshment. But truly, it comes not out but by drawing, and there is nothing fit for that but the heart, that alone can suck out of these breasts the milk of consolation. The well of salvation in the word is deep, and many of you have nothing to draw with; you want the bucket that should be let down, that is, the affectionate meditation and consideration of the heart; and therefore you go away empty. You come full of other cares, and desires, and delights, no empty room in your hearts for this, no soul longings and thirstings after the righteousness of God; and therefore you return as you came, empty of all solid and true refreshment. Oh, that we could draw it forth to you, and then drop it into your hearts, and make it descend into your consciences!

In these words, you may consider more distinctly, who this is, and then, for whom he is made a sacrifice, and withal, the efficacy of this sacrifice, and the sufficiency. Who this is, is pointed out as with the finger. 'He is,' that is, 'Jesus Christ, the righteous.' The apostle demonstrates him as a remarkable person, as in his evangel the Baptist doth:—'Behold the Lamb of God, which taketh away the sins of the world.' And the church, (Isa. lxiii. 1,) taketh a special notice of this person, 'Who is this that cometh from Edom?' And that which maketh him so remarkable, is his strange habit, after the treading the wine-press of wrath alone,—that he was made a bloody sacrifice to pacify God. And to show you how notable a person he is, he is signally and eminently pointed out by the Father, Isa. xlii. 1, 'Behold my servant,' &c., as if he would have the eyes of all men fixed upon him, with wonder and admiration. And for this end, he singled him out from the multitude, by a voice from heaven, which testified unto him particularly, 'This is my well-beloved Son; hear him.' Therefore the apostle had reason to say, (2 Cor. v. 14.) that he is 'one for all,' so notable an one, that he may serve for all. He stands in more value in the count of God than all mankind. All creatures are ciphers, which being never so much multiplied, come to nothing, amount not beyond nothing; but set him before them, put Christ on the head of them, and he signifies more than they all do, and gives them all some estimation in the count. And so they stand in Paul's calculation, (Phil. iii.) which he makes with very great assurance and confidence, 'Yea, doubtless, I count all dung, but the superexcellent knowledge of Christ,'—Christ is only the figure that hath signification, and gives signification to other things.

But in this business, the consideration of the persons interested, *he* and *us*, maketh us behold a great emphasis in the gospel. *He* a propitiation, and that for *our* sins, is a strange combination of wonders. If it had been some other person less distant from us, that were thus given for us, and standing in our room, then we should have better understood the exchange. Things of like worth, to be thus shuffled together, and stand in one another's place, is not so strange. But between the persons mentioned, *him* and *us*, there is such an infinite distance, that it is wonderful how the one descends to the room of the other, to become a sacrifice for us. O that we could express this to our own hearts, with all the emphasis that it hath! He the Lord, and we the servants; he the King, and we the poor beggars; he the brightness of his Father's glory, and we the shame and ignominy of the whole creation; he counting it no robbery to be equal with God, and being in the form of God, and we not equal to the worst of creatures, because of sin, and being in the form of devils! Had it been a holy and righteous man for sinners, it had been a strange enough exchange; but he is not only holy and harmless, but higher than the heavens. O what a vast descent was this, from heaven to earth, from a Lord to a servant, from an eternal Spirit to mortal flesh, from God to creatures! And to descend thus far for such persons, not only unworthy in themselves, such as could not conciliate any liking, but such as might procure loathing,—as is described, Ezek. xvi.; Rom. v. 6; 1 Pet. iii. 18,—'while we were enemies,' and might have expected a commissioner from heaven, with vengeance against us. Behold how the mysterious design of love breaks up, and opens itself to the world, in sending his own Son for us! And this is exceedingly aggravated from the absolute freedom of it, that there was nothing to pre-engage him to it, but infinite impediments in the way to dissuade him; many impediments to his affection, and many difficulties to his power, and then, no gain nor advantage to be expected from such creatures, notwithstanding of such an undertaking for them.

Now, herein is the strongest support of faith, and the greatest incentive to love, and the mightiest persuasive to obedience that can be. I say, the strongest support of faith; for, a soul apprehending the greatness and heinousness of sin, and the inviolableness of God's righteousness, with the purity of his holiness, can hardly be persuaded, that any thing can compense that infinite wrong that is done to his Majesty, though ordinarily the small and superficial apprehension of sin makes a kind of facility in this, or an empty credulity of the gospel. The reason why most men do not question and doubt of the gospel, and of their acceptance before God, is not because they are established in the faith, but rather because they do not so seriously and deeply believe, and ponder their own sins, and God's holiness; which, if many did, they would find it a greater difficulty to attain to a solid and quieting persuasion of the grounds of the gospel: they would find much ado to settle that point of the readiness of God, to pardon and accept sinners. But now, I say, all this difficulty, and these clouds of doubts will evanish at the bright appearance of this Sun of righteousness, that is, at the solid consideration of the glorious excellency of him that was given a ransom for us. Herein the soul may be satisfied, that God is satisfied, when he considers what a person hath undertaken it, even Jesus the righteous, the only Son of God, in whom his soul delighteth; whose glorious divine Majesty puts the stamp of infinite worth upon all his sufferings, and raiseth up the dignity of the sacrifice, beyond the sufferings of all creatures. For there are two things needful for the full satisfaction of a troubled soul, that apprehends the heinousness of sin, and height of wrath; nothing can calm and settle this storm, but the appearance of two things; *first*, of God's willingness and readiness to pardon sin, and save sinners; *next*, of the answerableness of a ransom to his justice, that so there may be no impediment in his way to forgive. Now, let this once be established in thy heart, that such an one, so beloved of God, and so equal to God, is the propitiation for our sins, that 'God hath sent his only begotten Son,' for this very business, unrequired and unknown of us; then, there is the clearest demonstration of these two things, that can be,—of the love of God, and of the worth of the ransom. What difficulty can be supposed in it, actually to pardon thy heinous sins, when his love hath overcome infinitely greater difficulties, to send One, his own Son, to procure pardon, John iii. Certainly, it cannot but be the very delight of his heart to forgive sins, since he 'spared not his Son' to purchase it; since he hath had such an everlasting design of love, which broke out in Christ's coming. And then, such a person he is, that the merit of his sufferings cannot but be a valuable and sufficient compensation to justice for our personal exemption, because he is one above all, of infinite highness. And therefore his lowness hath an infinite worth in it,—of infinite fulness, and therefore his emptiness is of infinite price, of infinite glory, and so his shame is equivalent to the shame and malediction of all mankind. So then, whatsoever thou apprehendest of thy own sins, or God's holiness, that seemeth to render thy pardon difficult, lay but in the balance with that, first, the free and rich expression of the infinite love of God, in sending such an one for a ransom; and sure, that speaks as much to his readiness and willingness, as if a voice spake it just now from heaven; and then, to take away all scruple, lay the infinite worth of his person, who is the propitiation, with thy sins, and it will certainly outweigh them; so that thou mayest be fully quieted, and satisfied in that point, that it is as easy for him to pardon, as for thee to confess sin and ask pardon; nay, that he is more ready to give it thee, than thou to ask it.

But, in the next place, I desire you to look upon this, as the greatest incentive of affection. O how should it inflame your hearts to consider, that such an one became a sacrifice for our sins; to think that angels hath not such a word to comfort themselves withal! Those innumerable companies of angels, who left their station, and were once in dignity above us, have not such glad tidings to report one to another in their societies, as we have. They cannot say, 'He is the propitiation for our sins.' This is the wonderful mystery, that blessed 'angels desire to look into.' They gaze upon it, and fix the eyes of their admiration upon 'God manifested in the flesh,' wondering at the choice of mortal man, before immortal spirits, that he is a ransom for them, and not for their own brethren who left their station. How should this endear him to our souls, and his will to our hearts, who hath so loved us, and given himself for us! Hath he given himself for us, and should we deny ourselves to him, especially when we consider what an infinite disparity is between the worth, and difference in the advantage of it. He gave his blessed self a sacrifice, he offered himself to death for us, not to purchase any thing to himself, but life to us. And what is it he requires but your base and unworthy self,—to offer up your lusts and sins in a sacrifice by mortification, and your hearts and affections in a thanksgiving offering, wherein your own greatest gain lies too? For this is truly to find and save yourselves, thus to quit yourselves to him.

The efficacy of this is holden out in the word, 'propitiation for our sins.' The virtue of Christ's sacrifice is to pacify justice, and make God propitious, that is, favourable and merciful to sinners. In which there are three considerable things imported. One is, that sin is the cause of enmity between God and man, and sets us at an infinite distance,—that sin is a heinous provocation of his wrath. Another is expressed, that 'Christ is the propitiation,'—in opposition to that provocation, he pacifies wrath, and then conciliates favour, by the sacrifice of himself. All the expressions of the gospel import the damnable and deplorable estate that sin puts man into; *reconciliation* imports the standing enmity and feud between God and man; *propitiation* imports the provocation of the holy and just indignation of

God against man, the fuel whereof is our sins; *justification* implies the lost and condemned estate of a sinner, under the sentence and curse of the law. All that is in the gospel reminds us of our original, of the forlorn estate in which he found us, none pitying us, nor able to help us. I would desire that this might first take impression on your hearts,—that sin sets God and man at infinite distance; and not only distance, but disaffection and enmity. It hath sown the seeds of that woful discord, and kindled that contention, which, if it be not quenched by the blood of Christ, will burn to everlasting, so that none can dwell with it, and yet sinners must dwell in it. There is a provoking quality in it, fit to alienate the holy heart of God, and to incense his indignation, which, when once it is kindled, who can stand before it? Do but consider what you conceive of wrongs done to you, how they stir your passions and provoke your patience, so that there is much ado to get you pacified; and what heinousness must then be in your offences against God, both in regard of number and kind? O that you could but impartially weigh this matter, you would find, that in the view of God, all wrongs and injuries between men evanish! 'Against thee, thee only, have I sinned.' That relation and respect of sin to God, exhausts all other respects of injuries towards men. It is true, that his Majesty is free from passion, and is not commoved and troubled as your spirits are. Yet such is the provoking nature of sin, that it cries for vengeance, and brings a sinner under the dreadful sentence of divine wrath, which he both pronounceth and can execute without any inward commotion or disturbance of spirit. But, because we conceive of him after our manner, therefore he speaks in such terms to us. But that which he would signify by it, is, that the sinner is in as dreadful and damnable a condition by sin, as if the Lord were mightily inflamed with anger and rage. The just punishment is as due and certain as if he were subject to such passions as we are; and so much the more certain, that he is not. Now, I desire you to consider, how mightily the heinousness of sin is aggravated, partly by the quality of the persons, and partly by the consideration of his benefits to us. A great man resents a light wrong heavily, because his person makes the wrong heavier. O! what do you think the Most High should do, considering his infinite distance from us, his glorious majesty and greatness, his pure holiness, his absolute power and supremacy? What vile and abominable characters of presumption and rebellion do all these imprint upon disobedience! Shall he suffer himself to be despised and neglected of men, when there is no petty creature above another, but will be jealous of his credit, and vindicate himself from contempt? And then, when ingratitude is mingled in with rebellion, it makes sin exceeding sinful; and sinful sin exceeding provoking. To proclaim open war against the holy and righteous will of him to whom we owe ourselves, and all that we are or have; to do evil, because he is good, and be unthankful, because he is kind to take all his own members, faculties, creatures, and employ them as instruments of dishonour against himself, there is here fuel for feeding everlasting indignation; there is no indignity, no vileness, no wickedness to this. All the provocations of men, how just soever, are in the sight of this groundless and vain, like a child's indignation. All are but imaginary injuries, consisting but in opinion, in regard of that which sin hath in the bosom of it against God.

But how shall any satisfaction be made for the injury of sin? What shall pacify his justly deserved anger? Here is the question indeed, that would have driven the whole world to a *nonplus*, if once the majesty and holiness of God had been seen. But the ignorance of God's greatness, and men's sinfulness, made the world to fancy some expiations of sin, and satisfactions to God, partly by sacrifices of beasts, partly by prayer, and repentance for sins.

Sermon XXVIII.

1 John ii. 3.—"*And hereby we do know that we know him, if we keep his commandments.*"

This age pretends to much knowledge beyond former ages; knowledge, I say, not only in other natural arts and sciences, but especially in religion. Whether there be any great advancement in other knowledge, and improvement of that which was, to a further extent and clearness, I cannot judge; but I believe there is not much of it in this nation, nor do we so much pretend to it. But, we talk of the enlargements of divine knowledge, and the breaking up of a clearer light in the point of religion, in respect of which we look on former times, as the times of ignorance and darkness, which God winked at. If it were so indeed, I should think the time happy, and bless the days we live in, for as many sour and sad accidents as they are mixed withal. Indeed, if the variety of books, and multiplicity of discourses upon religion; if the multitude of disputes about points of truth, and frequency of sermons, might be held for a sufficient proof of this pretension, we should not want store enough of knowledge and light. But, I fear that this is not the touchstone of the Holy Ghost, according to which we may try the truth of this assertion; that this is not the rule, by which to measure either the truth, or degrees of our knowledge; but for all that, we may be lying buried in Egyptian darkness; and while such a light seems to shine about us, our hearts may be a dungeon of darkness, of ignorance of God and unbelief, and our ways and walk full of stumblings in the darkness. I am led to entertain these sad thoughts of the present times from the words of the apostle, which give us the designation of a true Christian, to be the knowledge of God, and the character of his knowledge, to be obedience to his commands. If, according to this level, we take the estimate of the proportion of our knowledge and light, I am afraid lest there be found as much ignorance of God, and darkness, as we do foolishly fancy that we have of light. However, to find it, will be some breaking up of light in our hearts; and to discover how little we know indeed upon a solid account, will be the first morning star of that Sun of righteousness, which will shine more and more to the perfect day. Therefore we should labour to bring our light to the lamp of this word, and our knowledge to this testimony of unquestionable authority, that having recourse 'to the law and to the testimony,' we may find if there be light in us, or so much light as men think they see. If we could but open our eyes to the shining light of the scripture, I doubt not but we should be able to see that which few do see, that is, that much of the pretended light of this age is darkness and ignorance. I do not speak of errors only that come forth in the garments of new light, but especially of the vulgar knowledge of the truth of religion, which is far adulterated from the true metal and stamp of divine knowledge, by the intermixture of the gross darkness of our affections and conversation, as that other is from the naked truth; and therefore both of them are found light in the balance of the sanctuary, and counterfeit by this touchstone of obedience.

To make out this examination the better, I shall endeavour to open these three things unto you, which comprehend the words: 1st, That the knowledge of God in Jesus Christ, is the most proper designation of a Christian; 'Hereby we know that we know him,' which is as much as to say that we are true Christians;—2dly, That the proper character of true knowledge, is obedience, or conscionable practising of what we know;—and then, lastly, That the only estimate or trial of our estate before God, is made according to the appearance of his work in us, and not by immediate thrusting ourselves into the secrets of God's hidden degrees: 'Hereby we know,' &c. Here then, in a narrow circle, we have all the work and business of a Christian. His direct and principal duty is, to know God, and keep his commands, which are not two distinct duties, as they come in a religious consideration, but make up one complete work of Christianity, which consists in conformity to God. Then the reflex and secondary duty of a Christian, which makes much for his comfort, is, to know that he knows God. To know God, and keep his commands, is a thing of indispensable necessity to the being of a Christian; to know that we know him is of great concernment to the comfort and well-being of a Christian. Without the first, a man is as miserable as he can be, without the sense and feeling of misery, because he wants the spring and fountain of all happiness; without the second, a Christian is unhappy, indeed, for the present, though he may not be called miserable, because he is more happy than he knows of, and only unhappy, because he knows not his happiness.

For the first, then, knowledge is a thing so natural to the spirit of a man, that the desire of it is restless and insatiable. There is some appetite of it in all men, though in the generality of people (because of immersedness in earthly things, and the predominancy of corrupt lusts and affections, which hinder most men's souls to wait upon that more noble inquiry after knowledge, in which only a man really differs from a beast) there be little or no stirring that way; yet some finer spirits there are, that are unquiet this way, and, with Solomon, give themselves, and apply their hearts to search out wisdom. But this is the curse of man's curiosity at first, in seeking after unnecessary knowledge, when he was happy enough already, and knew as much of God and his works, as might have been a most satisfying entertainment of his spirit; I say, for that wretched aim, we are to this day deprived of that knowledge which man once had, which was the ornament of his nature and the repast of his soul. As all other things are subdued under a curse for sin, so especially this which man had is lost, in seeking that which he needed not; and the track of it is so obscured and perplexed, the footsteps of it are so indiscernible, and the way of it is like a bird in the air, or a ship in the sea, leaving us few helps to find it out, that most part of men lose themselves in seeking to find it; and therefore, in all the inquiries and searchings of men after the knowledge even of natural things that come under our view, there is at length nothing found out remarkable, but the increase of sorrow, and the discovery of ignorance, as Solomon saith, Eccles. i. 18. This is all the jewel that is brought up from the bottom of this sea, when men dive deepest into it; for the wisest of men could reach no more, though his bucket was as long as any man's, chap. vii. 23. 'I said, I will be wise, but it was far from me; that which is far off and exceeding deep, who can find it out?' Knowledge hath taken a far journey from man's nature, and hath not left any prints behind it to find it out again, but, as it were, hath flown away in an instant, and therefore we may ask, with Job, chap. xxviii. ver. 1, 12, 'Surely there is a vein for the silver, &c. But where shall wisdom be found? and where is the place of understanding?' What Utopian isles is she transported unto, that mortal men, the more they seek her, find more ignorance,—the further they pursue, they see themselves at the further distance? Thus it is in those things that are most obvious to our senses; but how much more in spiritual and invisible things is our darkness increased, because of the dulness and earthiness of our spirits that are clogged with a lump of flesh! For God himself, that should be the *primum intelligibile* of the soul, the first and principal object, whose glorious light should first strike into our hearts, Job testifies 'how little a portion is known of him.' When we cannot so much as understand 'the thunder of his power,' that makes such a sensible impression on our ears, and makes all the world to stand and hearken to it, then how much less shall we conceive the invisible Majesty of God? In natural things, we have one vail of darkness in our minds to hinder us; but in the apprehension of God, we have a twofold darkness to break through, the darkness of ignorance in us, and "the darkness of too much light" in him —*caliginem nimiæ lucis*, which makes him as inaccessible to us as the other; the over-proportion of that glorious majesty of God to our low spirits, being as the sun in its brightness to a night owl, which is dark midnight to it. Hence it is, that those holy men who know most of God, think they know least, because they see more to be known, but infinitely surpassing knowledge. Pride is the daughter of ignorance only, 'and he that thinketh he knoweth anything, knoweth nothing as he ought to know,' saith the apostle, 1 Cor. viii. 2. For he that knoweth not his own ignorance, if he know never so much, is the greatest ignorant; and it is a manifest evidence that a man hath but a superficial touch of things, and hath never broken the shell, or drawn by the vail of his own weakness and ignorance, that doth not apprehend deeply the unsearchableness of God, and his mysteries; but thinketh he hath in some measure compassed them, because he maketh a system of divinity, or setteth down so many conclusions of faith, and can debate them against adversaries, or because he hath a form and model of divinity, as of other sciences, in his mind. Nay, my beloved, holy Job attained to the deepest and fullest speculation of God, when he concluded thus, 'Because I see thee, I abhor myself;' and as Paul speaks, 'If any man love God, he is known of God, and so knows God,' 1 Cor. viii. 3. From which two testimonies I conclude, that the true knowledge of God consists not so much in a comprehension of all points of divinity, as in such a serious apprehension and conception of the divine Majesty as enkindles and inflames these two affections, love and hatred, towards their proper objects; such a knowledge as carries the torch before the affection; such a light as shines into the heart, as Paul's phrase is, 2 Cor. iv. 6, and so transmits heat and warmness into it, till it make the heart burn in the love of God, and loathing of himself. As long as a man doth but hear of God in sermons, or read of him in books, though he could determine all the questions and problems in divinity, he keeps a good conceit of himself; and that 'knowledge puffeth up,' and swells a man into a vain tumour; the venom of poison blows him up full of wind and self-confidence; and commonly they who doubt least are not the freest of error and misapprehension. And truly, whoever seriously reflects upon the difficulty of knowledge, and darkness of men's minds, and the general curse of vanity and vexation that all things are under, so that what is wanting cannot be numbered, nor that which is crooked made straight,—he cannot but look upon too great confidence and peremptoriness in all points, as upon a race at full speed in the dark night, in a way full of pits and snares. Oftentimes our confidence flows not from evidence of truth, but the ignorance of our minds, and is not so much built upon the strength of reason, as the strength of our passions, and weakness of our judgments.

But when once a man comes to see God, and know him in a lively manner, then he sees his own weakness and vileness in that light, and cries out with Isaiah, 'Wo is me, I am a man of polluted lips;' and he discerns in that light, the amiableness and loveliness of God, that ravisheth his heart after it; and then, as Jeremiah saith, he will not glory in riches, or strength, or beauty, or wisdom, but only in this, that he hath at length gotten some discovery of the only fountain of happiness. Then he will not think so much of tongues and languages, of prophesyings, of all knowledge of controversies; neither gifts of body nor of mind, nor external appendages of providence will much affect him. He would be content to trample on all these, to go over them into a fuller discovery and enjoyment of God himself.

If we search the scriptures, we shall find that they do not entertain us with many and subtile discourses of God's nature, and decrees, and properties, nor do they insist upon the many perplexed questions that are made concerning Christ and his offices, about which so many volumes are spun out, to the infinite distraction of the Christian world. They do not pretend to satisfy your curiosity, but to edify your souls; and therefore they hold out God in Christ, as clothed with all his relations to mankind, in all those plain and easy properties, that concern us everlastingly,—his justice, mercy, grace, patience, love, holiness, and such like. Now, hence I gather, that the true knowledge of God, consists not in the comprehension of all the conclusions that are deduced, and controversies that are discussed anent these things; but rather, in the serious and solid apprehension of God, as he hath relation to us, and consequently in order and reference to the moving of our hearts, to love, and adore, and reverence him, for he is holden out only in those garments that are fit to move and affect our hearts. A man may know all these things, and yet not know God himself: for to know him, cannot be abstracted from loving of him.—'They that know thy name will trust in thee,' and so love thee, and fear thee! For it is impossible but that this will be the natural result, if he be but known indeed, because there is no object more amiable, more dreadful withal, and more eligible and worthy of choice; and therefore, seeing infinite beauty and goodness, and infinite power and greatness, and infinite sufficiency and fulness, are combined together with infinite truth, the soul that apprehends him indeed, cannot but apprehend him as the most ravishing object, and the most reverend too; and, if he do not find his heart suitably affected, it is an evident demonstration that he doth not indeed apprehend him, but an idol. The infinite light, and the infinite life, are simply one, and he that truly without a dream sees the one, cannot but be warmed and moved by the other.

So then, by this account of the knowledge of God, we have a clear discovery that many are destitute of it, who pretend to it. I shall only apply it to two sorts of persons; one is, of those who have it only in their memories, another, of those who have it only in their minds or heads. Religion was once the legitimate daughter of judgment and affection, but now, for the most part, it is only adopted by men's memories, or fancies. The greatest part of the people cannot go beyond the repetition of the catechism or creed. Not that I would have you to know more: but you do not understand that, only ye repeat words, without the sensible knowledge of the meaning of them; so that if the same matter be disguised with any other form of words, you cannot know it, which showeth, that you have no familiarity with the thing itself, but only with the letters and syllables that are the garments of it. And for others that are of greater capacity, yet, alas! it comes not down to the heart, to the affecting, and moulding, and forming of it. A little light shines into the mind, but your hearts are shut up still, and no window in them. Corrupt affections keep that garrison against the power of the gospel. That light hath no heat of love, or warmness of affection with it, which showeth that it is not a ray or beam of the Sun of righteousness, which is both beautiful for light, and beneficial for influence, on the cold, and dead, frozen hearts of mankind, and by its approaching, makes a spring-time in the heart.

But all men pretend to know God. Such is the self-love of men's hearts, that it makes them blind in judging themselves: therefore the Holy Ghost, as he designs a Christian by the knowledge of God, so he characterizeth knowledge by keeping the commandments. 'Hereby we know,' &c. So that religion is not defined by a number of opinions, or by such a collection of certain articles of faith, but rather by practice and obedience to the known will of God; for, as I told you, knowledge is a relative duty, that is, instrumental to something else, and by anything I can see in scripture, is not principally intended for itself, but rather for obedience. There are some sciences altogether speculative, that rest and are complete in the mere knowledge of such objects, as some natural sciences are. But others are practical, that make a further reference of all things they cognosce upon, to some practice and operation. Now, perhaps some may think that the scripture, or divinity, is much of it merely contemplative, in regard of many mysteries infolded in it, that seem nothing to concern our practice. I confess much of that, that is raised out of the scriptures, is such, and therefore it seems a deviation and departure from the great scope and plain intent of the simplicity and easiness of the scriptures, to draw forth with much industry and subtilty, many things of mere speculation and notion, dry and sapless to the affection, and unedifying to our practice, and to obtrude these upon other men's consciences, as points of religion. I rather think, that all that is in the scriptures, either directly hath the practice of God's will for the object of it, or is finally intended for that end; either it is a thing that prescribeth our obedience, or else it tends principally to engage our affections, and secure our obedience; and so those strains of elevated discourses of God, his nature and properties, of his works, and all the mysteries infolded in them, are directed towards this end, further than mere knowing of them, to engage the heart of a believer to more love, and reverence, and adoration of God, that so he may be brought more easily and steadily to a sweet compliance, and harmonious agreement to the will of God, in all his ways. Nay, to say a little more, there are sundry physical or natural contemplations of the works of God in scripture, but all these are divinely considered, in reference to the ravishment of the heart of man, with the wisdom, and power, and goodness of God. And this shows us the notable art of religion, to extract affection and obedience to God, out of all natural contemplations; and thus true divinity engraven on the soul, is a kind of mistress science, *architectonica scientia*,* that serves itself of

* [The philosophy of Aristotle was called architectonica, (*αρχιτεκτονικη, pertaining to building*, from *αρχος a leader*, and *τικτων* an *artificer*,) as if every kind of knowledge had been rendered subservient to it.—Ed.]

all other disciplines,* of all other points of knowledge. Be they never so remote from practice, in their proper sphere, and never so dry and barren, yet a religious and holy heart can apply them to those divine uses of engaging itself further to God and his obedience: as the Lord himself teacheth us—'Who would not fear thee, O King of nations,' Jer. x.; and, 'fear ye not me who have placed the sand,' &c. Jer. v. 22. So praise is extracted, Psal. civ.; and admiration, verses 1, 33. So submission and patience under God's hand is often pressed in Job. Therefore, if we only seek to know these things that we may know them, that we may discourse on them, we disappoint the great end and scope of the whole scriptures; and we debase and degrade spiritual things, as far as religion exalts natural things in the spiritual use. We transform it into a carnal, empty, and dead letter, as religion, where it is truly, spiritualizeth earthly and carnal things into a holy use. &c.

* [That is, arts or sciences.—Ed.]

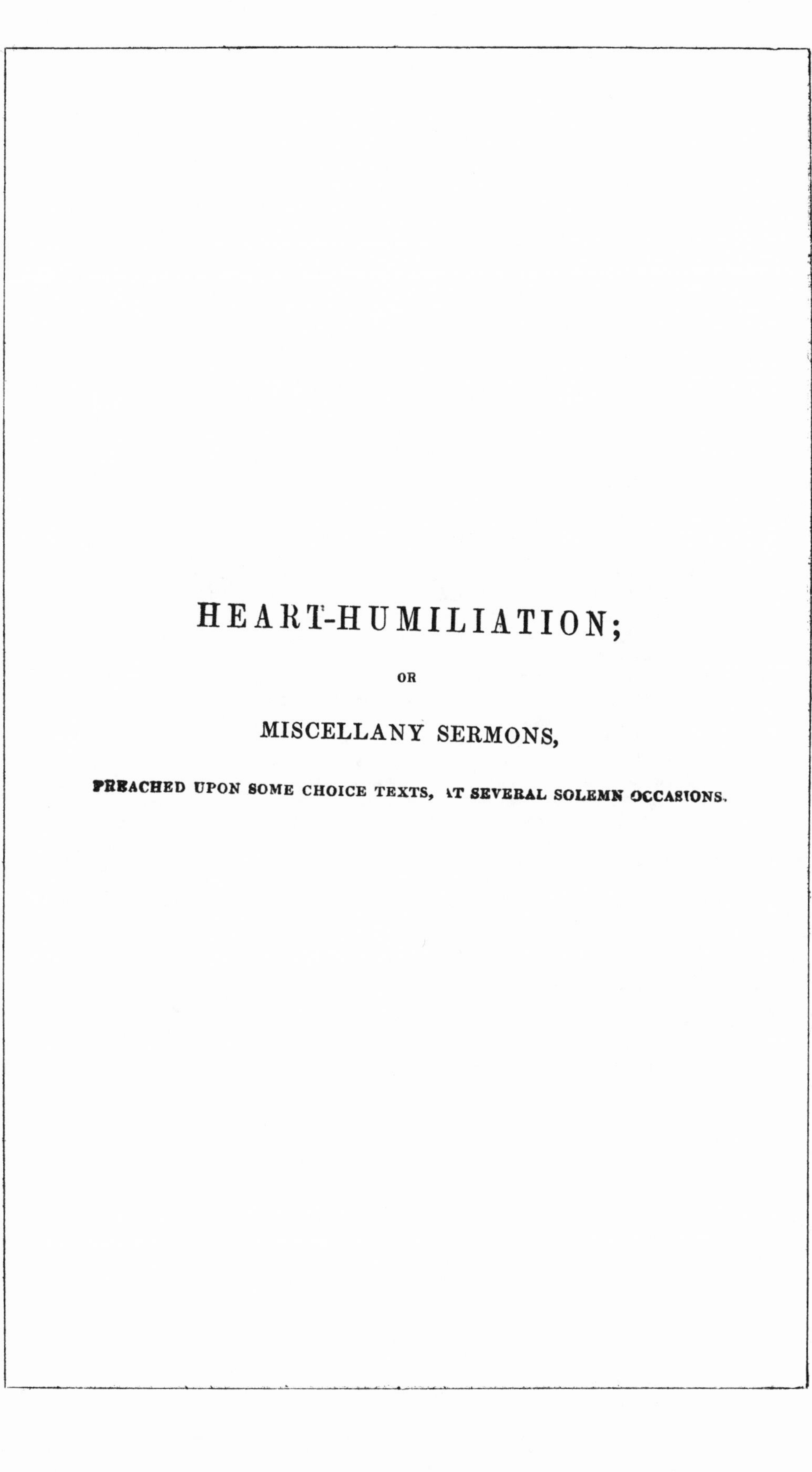

HEART-HUMILIATION;

OR

MISCELLANY SERMONS,

PREACHED UPON SOME CHOICE TEXTS, AT SEVERAL SOLEMN OCCASIONS.

To the Reader.

CHRISTIAN READER,

THIS holy preacher of the gospel had so many convictions upon his spirit of the necessity of the duties of humiliation and mourning, and of people's securing the eternal interest of their souls for the life to come, by flying into Jesus Christ for remission of sins in his blood, that he made these the very scope of his sermons in many public humiliations, as if it had been the one thing which he conceived the Lord was calling for in his days: a clear evidence whereof thou shalt find manifested in these following sermons upon choice texts, wherein the author endeavoureth, not only to lay before thee the necessity of these duties of soul-humiliation, but also showeth thee the gospel-manner of performing them, the many soul-advantages flowing from the serious exercise of them, and the many soul-destroying prejudices following upon the neglect of them; but above all, thou shalt find him so fully setting forth the sinfulness of sin, and the utter emptiness of self, as may convince the most pharisaically elated spirits, and make them cry out with Ezra, chap. ix. 6, 'O my God, I am ashamed, and blush to lift up my face to thee, my God; for our iniquities are increased over our head, and our trespass is grown up unto the heavens.' Here thou mayest read such pregnant demonstrations of the righteousness and equity of the Lord's dealing, even in his severest punishments inflicted upon the children of men, as may silence every whisperer against providence, and make them say, as Lam. iii. 22, 'It is of the Lord's mercies we are not consumed, even because his compassions fail not.' And lastly, thou shalt perceive the inconceivable fitness and fulness of Christ as a Saviour, and his never enough to be admired tenderness and condescending willingness to accept of humble, heart-broken, and heart-panting sinners after him; with such plainness of speech demonstrated, as may enable the most bruised reed to quench all the fiery darts of the devil, whereby he laboureth to affright them from making application to Jesus for salvation. Now that the Lord would make those and such-like labours of his faithful servants useful and advantageous to thy soul, Christian reader, is the prayer of thy servant in the gospel of our dearest Lord and Saviour,

A. S.

HEART-HUMILIATION.

Sermon I.

AT A PUBLIC FAST IN JULY, FIRST SABBATH, 1650.*

DEUT. xxxii. 4—7.—"*He is the Rock, his work is perfect: for all his ways are judgment,*" &c.

THERE are two things which may comprehend all religion,—the knowledge of God and of ourselves. These are the principles of religion, and are so nearly conjoined together, that the one cannot be truly without the other, much less savingly. It is no wonder that Moses craved attention; and that, to the end he may attain it from an hard-hearted deaf people, he turns to the heavens and to the earth,—as it were to make them the more inexcusable. The matter of his song is both divine and necessary. Throughout it all, he insists upon these two,—to discover what they were in themselves, and what God was to them. He parallels their way with his way, that they, finding the infinite distance, might have other thoughts of themselves and of him both. It is a song, it is true, but a sad song. The people of God's mourning should be of this nature,—mixed, not pure sorrow. It is hard to determine whether there be more matter of consolation or lamentation, when such a comparison is made to the life; when God's goodness and our evils are set before our eyes, which may most work the heart to such affections. Nay, I think it possible they may both contribute to both these. Is there any more abasing and humbling principle than love? How shall the sinner loathe himself in his glorious presence? Will not so much kindness and mercy, so often repeated, as oft as it is mentioned, wound the heart in which there is any tenderness? And, again, when a soul beholds its own ingratitude and evil requital of the Lord's kindness, how vile and how perverse it is, how must it loathe itself in dust and ashes! Yet is not all

* [The Records of the Presbytery of Glasgow show, that this Fast was appointed by the commission of the General Assembly. "The commissioun of the Generall Assemblie, upone the 25 day of Junij 1650, did emit ane seasonable warning concerning the present dangeris and dewties unto all the memberis of the kirk. 1. To draw neir to God; to murne for thair awin iniquiteis, and for all the synnes, prophanitie and bakslydinges of the land; to studie to mak peace with God in Cryst Jesus; to searche and try our wayis, and to return speedilie to the Lord; and to lift up our hartis with our handis to God in the heavines, that he may spair and save his pepill, that thai be not a prey to the enymie," &c. (Nicol's Diary of Public Transactions in Scotland, p. 17. Printed by Bannatyne Club, Edin. 1836.) On the 28th of June, a copy of this warning was presented to the Scottish parliament, who thanked the commission of the General Assembly for it, and requested them to delay the printing of it for a few days, that it might be accompanied with a Declaration from them suited to the existing crisis. (Sir James Balfour's Annals of Scotland, vol. iv. p. 63.) When the Presbytery of Glasgow met on the 31st of July, 1650, "the brethrene that wer present declaired that yei had keepit the fast, that yei had read the warning." (Presb. Rec.) See also Lamont's Diary, 7th July, 1650. The appointment of Fasts, to be observed on the Lord's day, was at a subsequent period disapproved of by the Church of Scotland. "Albeit by the treatise of fasting emitted by the Assembly 25 December, 1565, the Sundays were appointed for some fasts, as being for the greater ease of the people; and since by the last act of Assembly 1646, a fast is appointed on the Sabbath next, except one, preceding the then following General Assembly; yet seeing the work to be performed on the first day of the week is, by divine institution, already determined, we ought to set about it exactly, which we all acknowledge to be a thanksgiving and not a fast. Extraordinary duties are not to interfere with the ordinary, nor is one duty to shuffle out another. If either should be allowed, it would look somewhat like the reverse of redeeming the time, for thereby diligence is rather diminished than doubled in the service of God."—Overtures of the General Assembly, 1705.—ED.]

ground of hope removed. Such a sad sight may make mixed affections. If we be so perverse and evil, then he is infinitely good, and his mercy and goodness are above our evils; if we have dealt so with him, yet is he the Rock that changes not, he is a God of truth, and will not fail in his promise. Nay, though it be sad to be so evil, void of all goodness, yet may the soul bless him for evermore, that he hath chosen this way to glorify his name, to build up his praise upon our ruin. May not a soul thus glory in sad infirmities, because his strength is perfected in them, and made manifest? May not a soul choose emptiness in itself, that it may be beholden to his fulness? How refreshing a view might the saddest look on our misery and emptiness be, if we did behold his purpose of manifesting his glory in it! You see here a comparison instituted between two very unequal parties, God and man; there is no likeness, let be equality in it, yet there is almost an equality in unlikeness. The one is infinitely good and perfect; well, what shall we compare to him? Who is like thee, O God, among the gods?' Angels' goodness, their perfection and innocency, hath not such a name and appearance in his sight. So then, there can be no comparison made this way. Let no flesh glory in his sight in anything, but, 'let him that glorieth, glory in the Lord,' for in the sight of the glorious Lord, all things do disappear and evanish. But surely nothing, though most perfect, can once come within terms of reckoning beside him for any worth. Moses sees nothing to set beside God, that will appear in its own greatness and native colours, but the creatures' evil and sin; and if this be not infinite absolutely, or equal to his goodness, yet it comes nearest the borders of infiniteness. So then, is God most perfect? Is he infinite in goodness, in truth, in righteousness, &c.,—and so infinite, that before him nothing appears good?—' There is none good save one, that is God.' Yet we may find another infinite, and it is in evil sinful man; and these two contraries set beside other, do much illustrate each other. It is true that his grace superabounds, and his goodness is more than the creatures' sinfulness; yet, I say, you shall not find anything that cometh nearer the infiniteness and degrees of his goodness, than the sinfulness of men. How much the more glorious he appears, so much the more vile and base doth it appear.

If ye did indeed ponder and weigh these two verses in the balance of the sanctuary, would not your heart secretly ask this question within you, Do I thus requite the Lord? O foolish and unwise! Yea, would you not account yourselves mad, to forsake the fountain of living waters, and dig broken cisterns to yourselves? O of how great moment were this to humble yourselves to-day! This day ye are called to mourning and afflicting your souls. Now, I know not a more suitable exercise for a day of humiliation, or a principle that may more humble and abase your souls, than the serious and deep consideration of these two,—what God is, and hath been to us, and what we are, and have proved to him; what hath made so many formal humiliations that have provoked him to anger? Certainly we do not either seriously think on any of these, or if one of them, yet not on both. The most part of you know no more in such a day, but a name and ceremony of a little abstinence. Is this to sanctify a day to the Lord,—when ye do not so much as the people who bowed down their head for a day, and spread sackcloth under them? I wonder how ye think to pacify his wrath, and are not rather afraid of adding fuel and oil to the flame of his indignation. Ye come here and sit as in former times, and what do ye more either here or at home? There is no soul-affliction, no, not for a day. The most part of you are no more affected with your sins and his judgments, than if none of these things were. Now, I pray you, what shall the Lord say to us, when he speaks to the Jews in such terms, Isa. lviii. 5,—'Is it such a fast that I have chosen, a day for a man to afflict his soul?' And do ye so much as afflict it for a day, or at all? Is this then the fast that he will choose, to abstain from your breakfast in the morning, and at night to compensate the want of it, and no more?* Is this an acceptable day to the Lord? The Lord upbraids the Jews,

* [" The abstinence is commanded to be from Saterday at eight of the clock at night, till Sonday eftir the exercise at eftir noone, that is, after five of the clock. And then onlie bread and drink to be used, and that with great sobrietie, that the bodie craving necessarie food, the soul may be provoked earnestly to crave of God, that which it most neideth, that is mercie for our former unthankfulnes, and the assistance of his holie spirit in tyme to cum." (*The Ourdoure and Doctrine*

'Wilt thou call this a fast?' And what reason have we to ask you, is it possible ye think ye do indeed fast to the Lord? I cannot think that the most part of you dare say, that ever ye fasted or afflicted your souls.

Always here is the way, if we consider it. To spend a day acceptably to the Lord, enter into a serious consideration of his Majesty, and yourselves. Study on these two till ye find your hearts bear the stamp of them, enlarge your hearts in the thoughts of them. Both are infinite,—his goodness and power and mercy, and your sin and misery,—no end of them. Whatever ye find good in God, write up answerably to it, so much evil and sin in yourselves and the land; and what evil ye find in yourselves and the land, write up so much goodness and mercy in his account. All the names of his praise would be so many grounds of your confusion in yourselves, and would imprint so many notes of reproach and disgrace upon the creature found so contrary to him. This is even the exercise God calls us to this day,—to consider his ways to us, and our ways to him; how he hath walked, and how we have walked. Because ye lose the sight of these two, he sends affliction,—because in our prosperity and peace we forget God, and so ourselves; as ye find this people did, 'when they waxed fat they kicked against him, and forgat that he was their Rock.' We are so much taken up with our own ease and peace, that we do not observe him in his dealings; therefore doth the Lord trouble our peace, remove those things we are taken up with, make a public proclamation of affliction, and blessed be his name whose end is gracious. He means this,—it is the proclamation of all his judgments,—turn your eyes off your present ease here, consider what I am, and what yourselves are. No nation so soon buries the memory of his mercies, O how soon are they drowned in oblivion! And we forget our own provocations as suddenly. Therefore must he write our iniquities upon a rod, that we may read them in great letters; and he writes his former goodness in the change of his dispensations, when his way to us changes, that we may know what is past. This is the great design that God hath in the world,—to declare himself and his own name, that it may be wondered and admired at by men, and this cannot be but by our ruin, abasing us in the dust. He therefore uses to stain the pride of all glory, that his alone may appear without spot. This is then the great controversy of God with men and nations in all generations. They will not see him alone exalted, and will not bow before him, and see their own vileness. Why doth he overturn kingdoms and thrones? Why doth he shake nations so often? Here it is; God's controversy will never cease, till all men acknowledge him in his highness and holiness, as the sole fountain of all life, and find themselves vile, less than nothing, nay, worse than nothing, and emptiness. If ye would then have God at peace with the land and yourselves, here is the compendious way,—set him up a throne of eminency in your hearts, and put yourselves in the dust, take with your own guiltiness and naughtiness, and impossibility to help yourselves in yourselves. Hold these two still in your eyes, that he may be alone exalted.

Look how unequal a match, ver. 4, 5, 'He is the Rock,' a rock indeed! If we speak of strength, lo! he is strong; if of stability, he is the Lord, and changes not, 'the Ancient of days.' Hast not thou heard and considered this, that the Almighty faints not, and wearies not? He holds forth himself in such a name to his people, a ready, all-sufficient, perpetual, and enduring refuge to all that trust in him, and fly unto him as a rock higher than they. And this is the foundation that the church is builded on, against which the gates of hell shall not prevail. God's omnipotency is for defence, his eternity, faithfulness, and unchangeableness to make that sure. His mercy and goodness makes a hole in that rock to enter in, a ready access for poor shipwrecked and broken men, who have no other refuge. This is our rock, on which the church is builded, Jesus Christ, 1 Cor. x. 4.; Matt. xvi. 18. Were God inaccessible in himself, an impregnable rock, how would sinners overcome him, and enter in to him to be saved from wrath? Nay but Jesus Christ hath made a plain way and path, out of the waves of sin and misery, into this rock higher

of the General Fast, set down by John Knox, and John Craig, at the Appoyntment of the Assemblie in the year 1565, *Apud Dunlop's Confessions,* vol. ii. p. 686.) This Order was afterwards observed in all the fasts appointed by the General Assembly. (Id. p. 699.)—ED.]

than we; and so the poor soul that is lost in its own eyes, and sees no refuge, is forced to quit the broken ship of created confidence, for fear of perishing. Here doth it find a door in this rock to enter. And there is water to drink of, 'a fountain of living waters' comes out of it, and that is Christ.

Now, all these names of his praise rub so many marks of shame on his people. O how sad is the secret reproof and expostulation contained in this commendation of God! He hath been a rock to us, our refuge that we fled unto, and found sure; for as, in our straits, we mounted upon his power and were supported, when 'the floods lifted up their waves,' yet have we left our rock, gone out from our strength. He offers himself a rock unto us, his fulness and all-sufficiency for us, and yet we leave the fountain of living waters, and dig broken cisterns, had rather choose our own broken ships in which to toss up and down. He abides for ever the same; though we change, he changes not. How may it reprove our backslidings, that we depart from our rock! And where shall we find a refuge in the day of indignation? Is there any created mountain, but some floods of the time will cover? Therefore it is folly and madness to forsake this rock that is still above the floods; 'he is mightier than the noise of many waters.' It may reprove our unbelief,—we change our faith according to his dispensation, our faith ebbs and flows as the tide of his providence, and thus we are as sticks floating in the water, tossed up and down. But would ye be established as mount Sion? Would ye be unmoveable in the midst of great waters, that they shall not come near unto you? Then, by all means get upon this rock, that abides unmoved in the midst of the waves. Though they should beat upon it, and the wind blow, yet it is proof of all tempests. All things might be driven up and down about you with the Lord's dispensation, but ye should abide the same, and might look round about you on the troubled sea of men's minds, of lands and estates. If you come here, ye may make shipwreck, but ye shall not drown; though ye lose the creature's comfort and defence, yet ye are on your rock, which is established before the rocks and mountains. You may be sure of salvation. He that made the rocks and winds and seas, is your rock.

'His work is perfect.' As he doth not trouble himself when all is troubled about him, so he keeps him also in perfect peace, whose mind is stayed on him; so also what he doth among men, though it cannot pass without man's censure, yet it is in itself perfect, complete, without spot or defect. What is the subject of all men's questions, doubts, complaints, censures, expostulations, and such like, of which the world is full? It is some one work of God or other; there is no work of his providence, but some man finds a fault in it, and would be at the mending of it. *Neque Deus cum pluit, omnibus placet:** if he give rain, he displeases many; if he withhold it again, we are as little pleased. The reason of all this misconstruction is, we look on his work by parcels,† and take it not whole and entire. [Viewed] so, it is perfect, and cannot be made better. 'His works are perfect,' in relation to the beginning and original of them, his own everlasting purpose. Men often bring forth works by guess, by their purpose, so no wonder it answer not their desire. But 'known to him are all his works from the beginning,' and so he doth nothing in time, but what was his everlasting pleasure. Often we purpose well, and resolve perfectly, but our practice is a cripple, execution of it is maimed and imperfect. But all his works are carved out, and done just as he designed them, without the least alteration; and, if it had not been well, would he have thought on it so, and resolved it beforehand? His works are perfect, in relation to the end to which he appointed them. It may be it is not perfect in itself: a blind eye is not so perfect as a seeing eye; nay, but in relation to the glory of his name, who hath a purpose to declare his power by restoring that sight, it is as perfect. And in this sense, all the imperfection of the creatures and creation, all of them are perfect works, for they accomplish the end wherefore they were sent; and so the night declares his name, and utters a speech as well as the day, the winter as the summer, the wilderness as the fruitful field. For what is the perfection of the creature, but in as far as it accomplishes his purpose and end, as the maker of it serves himself with it? And therefore all his work is perfect, for it is all framed in wisdom to his own ends,

* [That is, "Nor does God please all, when he sends rain."—Ed.] † [That is, parts.—Ed.

in number, measure, and weight; it is so exactly agreeing to that, that you could not imagine it better. Again, his work is perfect, if we take it altogether, and do not cut it in parcels, and look on it so. Is there any workmanship beautiful, if ye look upon it in the doing? While the timber lies in one part, and the stones in another, is that a perfect building? When ye see one arm here, another there, and a leg scattered beside them, hath that image any comeliness? Certainly no; but look upon these united, and then they are perfect. Letters and syllables make no sense, till ye conjoin them in words, and words in sentences. Even so is it here; if ye look on the day alone, the light of it being perpetual would weary us, the night alone would be more so; but the interchange of them is pleasant,—day and night together make a distinct language of God's praise. So God hath set prosperity and adversity the one over against the other. One of them, it may be, seems imperfect; nay, but it is a perfect work that is made up of both. Spots in the face commend the beauty of the rest of it.

If ye would then look upon God's work aright, look on it in the sanctuary's light, and ye shall say, 'He hath done all well.' Join the end with the beginning, and behold they agree very well. Many things among us seem out of order, many things uncomplete, The reformation of England, how great obstruction was in the way of it? Is that now a perfect work? Yes, certainly; for if we knew his end and purpose, it is very well, and could not be bettered by the art of all men; 'his thoughts are far above our thoughts.' The prosperous and uninterrupted success of that party in England, is it a perfect work? Yes, certainly; for if ye could behold their end, ye would say so; 'they are set in slippery places, their foot shall slide in due time.'*

Entertain this thought in your heart, that he hath done all well. Let not your secret thoughts so much as call them in question. If once ye question, ye will quickly censure them. Hold this persuasion, that nothing can be better than what

* [The army of the Commonwealth was now on its march towards Scotland, under the command of Cromwell, who had been appointed by the English parliament captain-general of their forces. But the hopes of the people of Scotland had been revived by the arrival of Charles II. from Breda, about a fortnight before this, who, at the mouth of the river Spey, before he landed, had signed the national covenant, and also the solemn league and covenant, though the commissioners appointed to receive his subscription appear, on too good grounds, to have suspected his sincerity. (Sir Edward Walker's Hist. Disc., p. 158. Life of Rev. J. Livingston, written by himself, p. 51. Glasg. 1754.) A letter, addressed by Charles to the Committee of Estates, immediately after the battle of Dunbar, and dated Perth, 12 September, 1650, contains the following passage: "Wee cannot but acknowledge that the stroake and tryall is very harde to be borne, and would be impossible for us and you, in humane strength, but in the Lord's wee are bold and confident, whoe hath always defended this antient kingdome, and transmitted the governement of it upon us from so many worthy predecessors, whoe in the lyke difficulties have not fainted; and they had only the honor and civill liberties of the land to defend, but wee have with your religion, the gospel, and the covenant, *against which Hell shall not prevaile*, much lesse a number of sectaries stirred up by it. Wee acknowledge, that what hath befallen is just from God for our sinns, and those of our house; and the whole land, and all the families in it, have lykewise helped to pull downe the judgement, and to kindle this fierce wrath. Wee shall strive to be humbled, that the Lord may be appeased, and that he may returne to the thousands of his people, and *comfort us according to the days wee have beene afflicted, and the yeares that wee have seene evill*. You are going, you say, upon the deuties, for reliefe of the afflicted land, (you do well to do soe,) and to try the instrumentall causes and occasions of the disaster and surpryssal. Looke not too much upon second causes; the pryme and originall, and only cause, is God's just displeasure: for the causes of defeats in armys, they are harder to be found out than in any other of the actions of men, a word, a sounde, the mooving or remooving of any body or squadron, may be, and have beane, the causes of the losse of battles; and how often have pannicke feares seazed upon them, that never any ground or resone could be given for? Lay not the fault upon this or that, coming doune, or not staing upon a ground of advantage, or upon this person or the other. That is the worst way of all, for nothing devided nor in discord can stand or prosper, but leaste of all ane army; any thing of that kynde is the sodaine ruine of it. Upon any other constitution it will not worke so soone. Therefore wee intreete and charge you, as ye feare God, love his cause in your hands, have affection to your countrie, or respect to us; that you will remember, you are brethren in a covenant, and that you now stand up and joyne together as one man for religion, your countrie, your wives, children, liberties, and us, as your predecessors have done in their difficulties in their generations. Wee shall as willingly as any of them be ready to hazarde our lyfe (nay to lay it down) with you for God, the covenant, and the honor and freedom of this hitherto unconquered kyngdome, with any handful you have together, or when it shall be thought convenient." (Thurloe's State Papers, vol. i. p. 163.) The gross hypocrisy of Charles, in putting his name to a letter containing sentiments like these, and thus exciting false expectations in the minds of his credulous subjects, must be apparent to all who are acquainted with his subsequent history.—Ed.]

he doth, nothing can be added, and nothing diminished from them, he doth all in number, weight, and measure. It is so exactly correspondent to his purpose and design, as if it were weighed out, and measured out for that end.

Let this secretly reprove your hearts. The perfection of his works stains our works. O how imperfect are they! And which is worse, how impudent and bold are we to censure his, and absolve our own? If he have a hand in our work, these imperfect works are perfect in regard of him. As we have a hand in his perfect works, his perfect works are imperfect in regard of us.

Sermon XX.

DEUT. xxxii. 4, 5.—" *He is the Rock, his work is perfect; for all his ways are judgment; a God of truth, and without iniquity; just and right is he. They have corrupted themselves; their spot is not the spot of his children,*" &c.

THERE are none can behold their own vileness as it is, but in the sight of God's glorious holiness. Sin is darkness, and neither sees itself, nor any thing else, therefore must his light shine to discover this darkness. If we abide within ourselves, and men like ourselves, we cannot wisely judge ourselves; our dim sparkle will not make all the imperfections and spots appear. But, if men would come forth into the presence of his Majesty, who turns darkness into light, and before whom hell is naked,—O how base and vile would they appear in their own eyes! Is it any wonder that the multitude of you see not yourselves, when holy Isaiah and Job had this lesson to learn? Isaiah gets a discovery of his own uncleanness in the sight of God's glorious holiness, (chap. vi. 5,) which I think made all his former light darkness. He cries out 'unclean,' as if he had never known it before; and so Job, 'Since I saw thee I abhorred myself in dust and ashes.' Ye hear much of him, and it doth not abase you; but if ye saw him, ye would not abide yourselves; ye would prefer the dust you tread on to yourselves. Ye who know most, there is a mystery of iniquity in your hearts, that is not yet discerned, ye are but yet on the coast of that bottomless sea of abomination and vileness. Among all the aggravations of sin, nothing doth so demonstrate the folly, yea, the madness of it, as the perfection, goodness, and absolute unspottedness of God. It is this that takes away all pretence of excuse, and leaves the same nothing,—no place in which to hide its confusion and nakedness and shame. And therefore it is that Moses, when he would convince this people of their ways, and make them inexcusable, draws the parallel of God's ways and their ways, declares what God is, how absolutely perfect in himself, and in his works, who had given no cause of provocation to them to depart from him, and then, how odious must their departing be! When both are painted on a board before their eyes, it makes sin become exceedingly sinful. When the Lord would pierce the hearts of his people, and engrave a challenge with the point of a diamond, he useth this as his pen,—'Have I been a wilderness unto Israel? a land of darkness? Why say my people, We are lords; we will come no more to thee?' Jer. ii. 31. 'What iniquity have your fathers found in me, that they are gone far from me, and have walked after vanity?' Jer. ii. 5.

There are two things in sin that exceedingly abuse the creature,—the iniquity of it, and the folly and madness of it. It is contrary to all equity and reason to depart from him that hath made us, and given us a law, to whom we are by so many obligations tied; but what is the folly and madness of it, to depart from the fountain of living waters, and dig broken cisterns that can hold none? verse 13. This is a thing that the heavens may be astonished at; and, if the earth had sense to understand such a thing, the whole fabric of it would tremble for horror at such madness and folly of reasonable souls; and this evil hath two evils in it,—we forsake life and love death; go from him and choose vanity. It is great iniquity to depart without an offence on his part. He may appeal to all our consciences, and let them sit down and examine his way most narrowly,—'What iniquity have ye found in me?' What cause have ye to leave me! But when withal he is a living fountain, he is our glory, he is a fruitful land, a land of light, our ornament and attire, in a word, our life and our consolation, our happiness and our beauty; what word shall be found to express the extreme madness of men to depart from such an one, and change their glory into that which doth not profit? If either he were not a fountain of living waters, or if there were any fountain beside, that could yield water to satisfy the insatiable desires of men, it were more excusable; but what shadow shall be found to cover such an iniquity that is both infinite sin, and incomparable loss? It is the scripture's style given to natural men, 'fools and simple.' All sin hath folly in it, but the people of God's departing from him hath extremity of folly in it, beside iniquity, because they do embrace a dunghill instead of a throne; they make the maddest exchange that can be imagined, glory for shame, life for death,—at least, consolation and peace, for vanity and vexation and anguish of spirit.

If ye would be duly affected with the sight of your own evils, look upon them in this consideration, and, in the view of God, your large portion, ye will be forced to confess yourselves beasts in his sight, Psal. lxxiii. 22. Oh! that men would consider how good and blessed the Lord is, how he is alone, and nothing beside him in heaven and earth,—all broken cisterns, all dung and unprofitable, all vanity and vexation,—he only self-sufficient, all others insufficient; and therefore a proportioned good for our necessity and desires; and I am sure ye would be constrained to cry out with David, 'Whom have I in heaven but thee, or in the earth beside thee? It is good for me to draw near to God.' Ye would look on drawing near, and walking with him, and before him, not only as the most reasonable thing, but the best thing, most beautiful for you, most profitable for you, and all other ways would be looked on as the ways of death.

'His work is perfect.' The Lord looked, and behold all was good that was made. So it was at first. The fabric of this world was an exquisite and perfect work, a suitable demonstration of his infinite wisdom, wonderful in all the parts of it, and in the unity and harmony of the whole. But so also his work of providence is perfect. Divine wisdom hath framed and contrived all, and it cannot be better. If anything seem imperfect in itself, yet it is perfect in relation to his glorious ends he directs it unto. And so would we look on all the works among us. If anything seemed a spot and disgrace of the creation, certainly the sin of men and angels;—nay, but even that is so ordered by his holy sovereignty, that in relation to his majesty, it may be called a perfect work. If ye do but consider what a glorious high throne he hath erected to himself for justice and judgment to be the habitation of it, and mercy and truth to go before it, upon the ruins of defaced man; what a theatre of justice he hath erected upon the angels' fall, ye would call it as perfect a work as is in the world. His work is one in the world, subordinate to one great design of manifesting his own glorious justice and mercy, omnipotency and wisdom. Now what do ye see of it but parcels? Though ye comprehend all your time in one thought, yet certainly ye cannot judge it aright; for it is but one work that all the several buildings and castings down, all the several dispensations of his providence, from the beginning to the end, make up; and when we think upon these disjoined, limit our consideration within the bounds of our own time, can we rightly apprehend it? Nay, which is worse, we use to have no more within the compass of our thought, but some present thing, and how much more do we err then? What beauty, what perfection can such a small part have? But it is present to him, who beholds with a glance all these parts. Though succeeding in many generations, he sees it altogether, joins the end with the beginning, sees the first mould, the first foundation-stone, and the last completing, all flowing from himself, and returning thither, and ending in himself. He hath made an interchange in nature, which might teach us;—the night alone hath no beauty. Nay, but it beautifies the day. Your darkest hours and tempests, public and personal, are they perfect works? Yes, certainly, if ye compound them with your sunshines and calms. Several colours make pictures beautiful,—the one is as needful as the other; and if ye did consider your profit more than your honour and pleasure, ye would say so. He doth not model his works according to our fancy to please us, but our good to profit us, and he is wiser than we; and so then it is the most perfect work in itself, that possibly displeaseth us most. Therefore ye would judge of his dealing by another rule than your own satisfaction; for please you and perish you. If he spared the rod, he should hate us indeed; fond love is real hatred. Christians, if ye would judge his works by his word, and not by your sense,—by your well, and not by your will, certainly ye would say, as the men did of Christ, 'He hath done all well.' The world would discover to you a perfection, even in imperfection, a perfection in infirmities, that ye should not only rejoice in them, but glory in them. 'Most gladly therefore will I glory,' &c. saith Paul. Are infirmities a perfect work? Or is the suffering of Paul, to be buffetted and tempted, a perfect work? What comfort is in it? Yes, much. Infirmities alone are infirmities indeed; nay, but infirmities in me, and strength in Jesus; weakness in me, and strength dwelling in me,—these make up one perfect work, that could as little want the infirmities as the strength. The glory of God, and our well and consolation, require the one, as well as the other; they could not be complete without any of them. What do ye think of the times now? Are England's apostacy, and Ireland's desolation,* perfect works? That great work of reformation, that seemed to be above our shoulders, is now razed to the ground, and the very foundations removed? Is deformation a perfect work? Certainly, if we look on these things in the scripture's light, and consider them in relation to him who is the chief builder, and doth in heaven and earth what he pleaseth; that deformation is a perfect work, though not a perfect reformation. Though we could not inform you of the perfection of it, yet the general might silence us; all this shall be no miss, no mar in the end. His work, at the end of accounts, shall appear so complete, as if it had never had interruption. He is wise, and knows what he doth; if this were not for his glory and his people's good, certainly it should not be. Was not the people's wandering in the wilderness forty years a most strange work—a longer interruption of the expected and begun voyage out of Egypt? What human reason would have styled this work with perfection? Did they not often murmur against it? Yet Moses calls this a perfect work also. What if the Lord be digging the ground deeper in England, that the foundation may be the surer? What if he be on a work of judgment, filling the cup of many deluded blasphemers, that he may have another cup of wrath prepared? What if this be his great purpose, to execute vengeance upon a profane generation, that will not abide the very name and form of godliness, by those who pretend to the name of it as their honour? What if the Lord hath defaced all that this kingdom was instrumental in building up in England, that he alone may have the glory in a second temple more glorious?† Many things there may be in his mind; and 'he is in one mind, and who can turn him?' and what his soul desireth, even that he doth; and this may be enough to satisfy us, he sees and knows all his works from the beginning.

And without all controversy he hath provided it so, that the reproach of his name shall be made up with* the more shining of his glory, and the afflictions of his people shall be compensed with songs of deliverance. May ye not give him so much credit, as ye would give to a skilful man in his own trade? Ye know it is his name, 'excellent in counsel, and wonderful in working.' Then take his work, expound it according to his word, and not your apprehension. It may be his work appears not excellent; nay, but if ye knew his counsel, ye would think it so. His wonderful counsel makes all his works excellent; and therefore do not take upon you to judge his works, unless ye could wade the depth of his counsels, else ye declare yourselves to be both ignorant and presumptuous. 'There is a time to build, and a time to cast down; a time for every thing,' saith the wise man. Now, I say, he knows the time and season, he does every thing in his time. If ye come by a workman that is casting down a house that in your appearance seems good, would ye condemn him

* [The narrative of Hume presents an affecting picture of the cruelties perpetrated at the time of the Irish insurrection and massacre. (Hist. of Eng. vol. iv. pp. 361—366. Lond. 1825.) It is said that "200,000 Protestants in two months space, were murdered, and many by exquisite torments; and many more were despoiled of all their worldly fortunes." (May's Breviary, p. 33. First printed in the year 1655. Reprinted London, 1813.) For several years after this period, Ireland was laid waste by contending armies, and by the wild rage of the native inhabitants.—Ed.]

† [A reference to this passage may be seen in the Life of the Author prefixed to the Work.—Ed.]

‡ [That is, compensated.—Ed.]

presently? No, but stay till ye see what he will do next, wait till the due time, and when ye see a better piece of workmanship on that ground, ye shall absolve him. Though God often change his work, do not think he changes his counsel and purposes as men do; no, 'he is in one mind, and who can turn him?' Therefore he had that change in his mind when he made the work; when he erected such a throne, he had this in his mind to cast it down within such a space, and so his change—his throwing down—is as perfect in his mind, as his building up. Ye have large and big apprehensions of temporal kingdoms and crowns of government, and such like, as if they were great, yea, only things, but they are not so to him. All this world and its standing, all the kingdoms and their affairs are not his great work and business. He hath a great work, the bringing of many sons to glory, and the completing of Jesus Christ; building of that glorious mystical building, the holy temple made up of living stones, of which Christ is the foundation, and chief corner-stone both; and it is this that he attends to most. Other works among men, though they have more noise, they are less concerned. All these are but in the by, and subservient to his great design, and like the scaffolds of a building, that are, it may be, sometimes very needful. Nay, but when the building is completed, he shall remove all these, he hath no more use of them: kings shall be thy nurse fathers, kings shall bow to thee. He is not much concerned in government nor in governors, but for his little flock's sake; and if these were gathered, all these shall have an end, and the flock alone abide for ever.

'And all his ways are judgment.' This is to the same purpose,—his ways and his works are one. And this is the perfection of his work, that it is all right and equal; whether they be in justice or mercy, they are all righteous and holy, no iniquity in them; his ways are straight and equal, exact as if they were measured by an exact even rule; but because we make application of a crooked rule to them, we do imagine that they are crooked; as the blind man judges no light to be, because he sees it not. How may the Lord contend and plead with us, as with that people, Ezek. xviii. 25. Is it possible that any can challenge him and clear themselves, who will be justified of all when he is judged, and before whom no flesh can be justified? And yet, behold the iniquity of men's hearts. There is a secret reflection of our spirits upon his Majesty, as if his ways were not equal, whenever we repine against them, and when we do not take with our iniquity, and stop our mouths with dust. Behold, the Lord will assert his own ways, and plead with all flesh this controversy, that all his proceedings are full of equity. He walks according to a rule, though he be not tied to a rule. He walks according to the rules of wisdom, justice, and mercy, though his illimited sovereignty might be a sufficient ground of clearing of all his proceedings. But we walk not according to a rule, though we be bound to a rule, and a rule full of equity.

Here is the equity and justice of his ways, the gospel holds it forth in a twofold consideration. *First,* If any man turn from his iniquity, and flee unto my Son as the city of refuge, he shall live, he hath eternal life; iniquity shall not be his ruin, although he hath done iniquity. O 'who is a God like unto thee, that pardoneth iniquity!' Is not this complete mercy? Whatever iniquity hath been, aggravate it as ye can, though it could have ruined a world, yet it could not have ruined thee that turnest in to Jesus Christ from iniquity. What exception can all the world have against this, or his walking according to it? And *on the other hand,* whosoever continueth in sin, though he appear to himself and others never so righteous; if he entertain and love any known sin, and will not part with it for Jesus Christ, shall not he die in his iniquity? Is there any iniquity in this, that he receive the wages of his works—his reward that he eat of the fruit of his own ways, and drink of his own devices? But how many hearts censure this way as a rigid and strict severe dealing! The multitude think it cruelty to condemn any christened soul—to put so many in hell. The civil man will think it is too hard measure that he should be ranked in hell with the profane. But certainly, all mouths shall be stopped one day, and he shall be justified when he judges. Ye that will not justify him in his sayings, and set to your seal to the truth of the word, you shall be constrained to justify him, when he executes that sentence. Ye shall precipitate your own sentence, and rather wonder at his clemency in suffering you so long.

This way of the Lord is equal and right in itself, but it is not so to every one. The just man shall walk in it and not stumble; as in an even way, nothing shall offend him, Hosea xiv. last verse. Yet for as equal and straight as it is, many other transgressors shall fall therein; they stumble even in the noon-day and highway, where no offence is. It is true, often his own people stumble in it, as David, Psal. lxxiii, and xciv. David's foot was slipping, yet a secret hold was by mercy. It often requires a wise and prudent man to understand it, because his footsteps are in the deep waters; Psal. lxxxvii. 19. His way is in the depths of the sea, his paths in great waters, so that men must wait till the Lord expound his own ways, till he come out of the waters, and make them a dry plain. And this is our advantage; the word says, 'He is near thee, in thy mouth, and neither above, nor beneath in the depths, that thou needest neither descend nor ascend to know it,' Deut. xxx. 11—14. But his way is in the depths, and his footsteps are not known, so that we ought to hold us by the word till he expound his work. His word will teach us our duty, and we may commit unto him his own way; the word is a commentary to expound his ways. David lost the sight of God's footsteps and was like to wander, till he came to the sanctuary, and this shined as a candle in a dark place; he learned there to know the unknown footsteps and to follow them. By all means embrace the word, and be satisfied with it, when ye do not comprehend his work; it teaches as much in general, as may put us to quietness; all his ways are judgment, just and true in all his ways is the King of saints. If I do not comprehend how it is,—no wonder, for he makes darkness his covering, he spreads over his most curious engines and pieces of workmanship a vail of darkness for a season; and 'who can behold him when he hides himself?' says Job; and though he withdraw the covering, yet what am I? 'Who can by searching find out God?' If I shall examine his way, what rule shall I take to try it by? If I measure by my shallow capacity, or by my crooked way, shall I have any just account of it? Will my arm measure the heavens as his doth? If I examine it, or try it by himself, he is high as heaven and unsearchable. Therefore it becomes us to hearken to his word, and believe its sentence of his work, when reason cannot comprehend it.

One thing, if it were deeply engraven on our hearts, would be a principle, of settling our spirits, in all the mysteries and riddles of providence,—the knowledge and faith of his sovereignty, of his highness, and of his wisdom. Should he give account of his matters to us? He is wise and knows his works; but is he bound to make us know them? His ways are above our thoughts and ways, as heaven is above the earth, Isa. lv. And therefore, O grasshopper in the earth, that dwelleth in tabernacles of clay, do not presume to model his ways according to thy conceptions. One thing is certain,—this is enough for faith, 'all his ways are mercy and truth to those that keep his covenant and his testimonies,' Psal. xxv. 10. And there is no way or path of God so far above our reach, and unsearchable, as his mercy in pardoning sin; and this is only the satisfying answer to all your objections and scruples. In these ye do but vent your own thoughts: but says the Lord, my thoughts are above your thoughts, as heaven above earth. Ye but speak of your own ways, but my ways are far above yours, they are not measured by your iniquity; and therefore, David subjoins, Psal. xxv. ver. 11., 'Pardon my iniquity, for it is great.'

Sermon XXX.

DEUT. xxxii. 4, 5.—"*He is the rock, his work is perfect. For all his ways are judgment. A God of truth, and without iniquity, just and right is he. They have corrupted themselves, their spot is not the spot of his children. They are a perverse and crooked generation.*"

'ALL his ways are judgment,' both the ways of his commandments and the ways of his providence, both his word which he hath given as a lantern to men's paths, and his works among men. And this were the blessedness of men, to be found walking in his ways, and waiting on him in his ways, having respect to all his commandments, and respect to himself in all his works. We all know in general that he doth all well, and that all his commandments are holy and just. Nay, but our practice and affections belie our knowledge; and for the most part, we stand cross in our humours, and affections, and conversation, both to his word and providence, and this is our misery. 'Great peace have they that love thy law.' What peace then can keep that heart and mind that is daily at variance with his statutes and judgments, when the heart would wish such a command were not, when it is an eyesore to look upon it? 'Blessed are the meek.' 'It is good for a man, both quietly to wait, and hope, and keep silence.' How then must that spirit be miserable, that stands cross unto God's dispensations, and would limit the Holy One! Do not our hearts often say, 'I do well to be angry, why is it thus with me?' But, 'who hath hardened himself against him and prospered?' His counsel must stand; and you may vex yourself, and disquiet your soul in the mean time, by impatience, but you cannot by your thought add one cubit to your stature. You may make your case worse than providence hath made it, but you cannot make it better by so doing, so that at length you must bow to him or be broken. Oh then that this were engraven on our hearts with the point of a diamond! 'All his ways are judgment;' that ye might be overcome with the equity of his command and dispensation, and your heart and tongue might not move against them. It was enough of old with the saints, 'It is the Lord, let him do what seems good in his eyes.' God's sovereignty alone pondered, may stop our mouth; but, if ye withal consider, it is perfect equity that rules all, it is divine wisdom that is the square of his works; then how ought we to stoop cheerfully unto them! One thing, ye would remember, his ways and paths are judgment, and if you judge aright of him, ye must judge his way and not his single footsteps. Ye will not discern equity and judgment in one step or two; but consider his way, join adversity with prosperity, humbling with exalting; take along the thread of his providence, and one part shall help you to understand another. There is reason in all, but the reason is not visible to us in so small parts of his way and work.

'A God of truth.' Strange it is that his majesty is pleased to clothe himself with so many titles and names for us. He considers what our necessity is, and accordingly expresses his own name. I think nothing doth more hold forth the unbelief of men, and atheism of our hearts, than the many several titles that God takes in scripture. There is a necessity of a multitude of them, to make us take up God; because we staying upon a general notion of God, rather frame in our imaginations an idol than the true God. As there is nothing doth more lively represent the unbelief of our hearts, than the multitude of promises; men that consider such frequent repetitions of one thing in scripture, so many divers expressions of one God, may retire into their own hearts, and find the cause of it, even the necessity of it. But while we look so slightly on these, we must judge it superfluous and vain. Needed there any more to be said, but, 'I am your God, I am God,' if our spirits were not so far degenerated unto atheism and unbelief? Certainly that word *Jehovah* holds forth more to angels than all the inculcated names and titles of God to us, because we are dull and slow of heart. Therefore wonder at these two when ye read the scriptures, God's condescendency to us, and our atheism and unbelief of him: they are both mysteries, and exceeding broad. There is not a name of God, but it gives us a name, and that of reproach and dishonour, so that for every one, some evil may be written down. And it is to this purpose Moses draws them out in length, that in the glass of his glorious name, the people might behold their own ugly face. This name is clear, 'he is a God of truth,' not only a true God, but truth itself; to note his excellency and eminency in it. It is Christ's name, 'I am the truth,' the substantial truth, in whom all the promises are truth, 'are yea and amen.' His truth is his faithfulness in performing his promises, and doing what his mouth hath spoken: and this is established 'in the very heavens,' Psal. lxxxix. 2. His everlasting purpose is in heaven where he dwells; and if any man can ascend up to heaven, if any creature can break through the clouds, then may his truth be shaken. His word comes down among men; nay, but the foundation of it is in heaven, and there is his purpose established; and therefore, there is nothing done in time can impair or hinder it. Ye think this world very sure; the earth hangs unmoveable, though it hang upon nothing. All the tumults, confusions, and reels which have been in the world, have never moved it to the one side. Heaven goeth about in one tenour perpetually, keeping still the same distance. Nay, but his truth is more established than so. Heaven and earth depend but upon a word of command; he hath said, 'Let it be so,' and so it is. Nay, but his word is more established. Of it saith Christ, one jot or tittle of it cannot fail, though heaven and earth should fail. He may change his commands as he pleases, but he may not change his promise; this puts an obligation on him, as he is faithful and true, to perform it; and when an oath is superadded, O how immutable are these two!—when he promises in his truth, and swears in his holiness. Is there any power in heaven and earth can break that double cord? Matth. v. 18; Heb. vi. 18. There is no name of God but it is comfortable to some, and as terrible to others. What comfort is it to a godly man that trusts in his word, 'he is a God of truth!' An honest man's word is much; his oath is more. What shall his word be, who is a God of truth? Though all men should be liars, yet God is true. Ye who have ventured your souls on his word, ye have an unspeakable advantage; his truth endures for ever, and it is established in the heavens; the ground of it is without beginning, the end of it without end. Ye are more sure than the frame of heaven and earth, for all these shall wax old as a garment. We speak of a naked word of truth; indeed it is no naked word that is God's word. His works of providence, and his dispensation to you, is a naked and bare foundation, nay, a sandy foundation, and ye who lean so much to them, is it any wonder ye so often shake and waver? All other grounds beside the word are uncertain, unstable; this only endures for ever. The creature's goodness and perfection is but as the grass, and the flower of the field. Venture not much on your dispositions and frames; thou knowest not what a day may bring forth: but his truth is to all generations, and it is well tried, as gold seven times,—all generations have tried it, and found it better than pure gold. His dispensations are arbitrary,—no rule to you. He loveth to declare his sovereignty here, and to expatiate in the creature's sight beyond its conceiving; but he hath limited himself in his word, and come down to us, and laid bonds on himself. Will he then untie them for us? Give him liberty where he loves it; take him bound where he binds himself. How may God expostulate with this generation, as those of little faith? 'How long shall I be with you?' saith Christ. How long will Christians tempt the Lord in seeking signs; and will not rest upon his only word and promises? 'O adulterous generation, how long shall I be with you, and ye will not believe?' Is it not righteousness in him, either to give you no sign at all, or to give you a sign darker than the thing itself, as he did to the Pharisees? Ye will give credit to a man's word, and will ye not believe God's? An honest man will get more trust of us, than the true and living God! Shall he not be offended with this? We declare it unto you, that he is truth itself, and will not fail in his promise: let that be your castle and refuge to enter into. Mercy and truth are two sweet companions to go along with you in your pilgrimage. David prayed for them, Psal. lxi. 7. 'O prepare thy mercy and truth to preserve me.' Who will not lie safe within these everlasting arms? What power can break through them? And this he promised to himself, (Psal. lvii. 3.) God shall send them out. Mercy made so many precious promises, and truth keeps them. Mercy is the fountain and source of all our consolation, and truth and faithfulness convey it to us, and keep it for us. It is these two that go before his face, when he sits on a throne of majesty, and makes himself accessible to sinners, (Psalm lxxxix. 14.,) and so they are the pathway he walks in towards those who seek him, Psalm xxv. 10.

But this sweet and precious name, that is as ointment poured forth to those who love him, how doth it smell of death to those who walk contrary to him? 'He is a God of truth,' to execute his threatenings on those who despise his commands; and though ye flatter yourselves in your own eyes, and cry, 'Peace, peace,' even though ye walk in the imagination of your own heart; yet certainly 'he is a God of truth.' I pray you read that sad and weighty word, that will be like a millstone about many men's necks, to sink them in hell, Deut. xxix. 20, 21. ye who 'add drunkenness to thirst,' whose rule of walking is your own lust, and whatsoever pleaseth you, without respect of his commands, and yet flatter yourselves with a dream of peace; know this for a truth, 'the Lord will not spare thee, he that made thee will not have mercy on thee. His jealousy will smoke against thee; and all the curses written in this book shall lie upon thee, and thy name shall be blotted out from under heaven.' It was unbelief of God's threatening that first ruined man; it is this still that keeps so many from the remedy, and makes their misery irrecover able. The serpent brought them to this question, 'Hath God said ye shall die.' And then presently the question entertained becometh a conclusion, 'Ye shall not surely die.' Thus ye see how the liar, from the beginning, was contrary to the God of truth; and he murdered us by lying of that God of truth, and it is the same that shuts out all hope of remedy. Ye do not as yet believe and consider that curse that was pronounced against Adam, but is now also inflicted upon us: therefore, there is no solid belief can be of the promises of the gospel; and ye who think ye believe the gospel, do but indeed fancy it, except ye have considered the true curse of God on all flesh. But if any man have set to his seal that God is true in his threatening, and subscribed unto the law, then, I beseech you, add not the unbelief of the gospel unto your former disobedience. He is 'a God of truth,' in promises and threatenings. It is strange how untoward and froward we are,—a perverse generation. We do not believe his threatenings, but fancy we receive his promises, or else, believing his threatenings, we question his promises. But know this for a truth, his last word is more weighty; and the unbelief of it is most dangerous. Ye have not kept his commands, and so the curse is come upon you. Do ye believe that? If ye do, then the gospel speaks unto you; the God of truth hath one word more, 'He that believes shall be saved,' notwithstanding of all his breaking of the law. If ye do not set your seal to this also, then ye say he is not a God of truth; ye say he is a liar. And as for you who have committed your souls to him, as to a faithful keeper, and acquiesced unto his word of promise for salvation, think how unsuitable it is for you to distrust him in other lesser things. Ye have the promise of this life, whoever hath the promises of the life to come. Therefore do not make him a liar in these. He is 'a God of truth,' and will let you want no good thing. 'Say to the righteous, it shall be well with him,' whatever be. Let heaven and earth mix through other, yet ye may be as mount Sion unmoved in the midst of many floods, because of the promises.

'Without iniquity.' Who doubts of that, say ye? What needs this be added? Who charges him with iniquity or sin? Nay, but stay and consider, and you shall find great weight in this. It is true, none dare charge him openly, or speak in express terms against his holiness, yet, if we judge of our own and other's practices and dispositions, as the Lord useth to construct of them; if we resolve our murmurings, impatience, self-absolutions, and excuses to hold off convictions, into plain language; if we would translate them into a scripture style, certainly it will be found that the most part of men, if not all, use to impute iniquity to God, and accuse him rather than take with accusations laid against themselves. And therefore the Lord useth to go to law with his people. He who is the judge of the world, that cannot do unrighteousness, he who is the potter, and we all the clay; yet he so far condescends to us for convincing us, as sometimes to refer the controversy between him and his people to other creatures, as Micah vi. 2. He calls the mountains and the foundations of the earth to judge between him and his people; and sometimes he appeals unto their own consciences, and is content, though judge, to stand and be judged by those who were guilty, as ver. 3. and Jer. ii. ver. 5, and 31. All this supposes, that when the Lord would endeavour to convince them of iniquity, they did rather recriminate, and took not with their own faults. This is a truth generally acknowledged by all, 'He who is the judge of the world doth no iniquity;' but O! that ye considered it, till the meditation of it were engraven on your spirits, the seal of God's holiness, that ye might fear before him, and never call him to account for his matters. Who can say, I have purged my heart from iniquity? Among men the holiest are defiled with it, and so are all their actions. But here is one that ye may give him an implicit faith so to speak; he is 'a God of truth,' and can speak no lie; he does no iniquity, and cannot do wrong to any man. Would there be so much impatience amongst you, and fretting against his dispensations, if ye believed this solidly?

Would ye repine against his holy and just ways, were it not to charge God with iniquity? Your murmuring and grudging at his dispensations is with child of blasphemies, and he who can search the reins sees it, and constructs so of it. You say by interpretation, that if ye had the government of your own matters, or of kingdoms, ye would order them better than he doth. How difficult a thing is it to persuade men to take with their own iniquity! O how many excuses and pretences, how many extenuations are used that this conviction may not pierce deeply! But all this speaks so much blasphemy,—that iniquity is in God. Ye cannot take with your own iniquities, but ye charge his Majesty with iniquity.

'Just and right is he.' Is this any new thing? Was it not said already, that he is 'without iniquity,' and his ways judgment? But, alas! how ignorant are we of God, and slow of heart to conceive of him as he is, therefore is there 'line upon line, and precept upon precept,' and name upon name, if it be possible, that at length we may apprehend God as he is. Alas! our knowledge is but ignorance, our light darkness, while it is shut up in the corner of our mind, and shines not into the heart, and hath no influence on our practice. And the truth is, the belief of divine truths is almost no more but a not contradicting them; we do not seriously think of them as either to consent to them, or deny them. Is there any consideration amongst us now of God's justice and righteousness, though it be frequently spoken of? And what advantage shall we have if ye do not consider them? O how hard is it to persuade men's hearts of this, that God is just, and will by no means acquit the guilty! There are so many delusions drunk in in men's hearts, contrary to his truth. 'Let no man deceive you;' 'be not deceived' with vain words; 'know ye not,' saith our apostle. These are strange prefaces. Would ye not think the point of truth subtile that there needed so much prefacing unto it? and yet what is it? Even that which all men grant,—God's wrath comes on the children of disobedience; but, alas! few men consider, but deceive themselves with dreams of escaping it. Though men know it, yet they know it not, for they walk as if they knew no such thing.

Always however this is of little moment to affect our spirits now, yet in the day that God shall set your iniquities before your face, and set his justice also before your eyes, O how sad and serious a thing will it be then! If these two verses were engraven on our hearts,—God's justice and holiness, our corruption and vileness,—I think there would be other thoughts among us than there are.

Sermon XV.

DEUT. xxxii. 5.—"*They have corrupted themselves: their spot is not the spot of his children: they are a perverse and crooked generation.*"

WE doubt this people would take well with such a description of themselves as Moses gives. It might seem strange to us, that God should have chosen such a people out of all the nations of the earth, and they to be so rebellious and perverse, if our own experience did not teach us how free his choice is, and how long-suffering he is, and constant in his choice. His people are called to a conformity with himself, 'Be ye holy, for I am holy,' (Lev. chap. xix. and xx;) and to a deformity and separation from the rest of the world in their conversation, from whom God had separated them in profession and privileges, Lev. xviii. 24. But behold what unlikeness there is between God and his people. If ye were to paint out to the life a heathen people, you needed no other image or pattern to copy at but this same description of this people. It is this that makes Moses in the preface turn to the heavens and earth, and call them to hear his song; and Isaiah begins his preaching thus, 'Hear, O heavens; and give ear, O earth,' &c. A strange thing it must be, that senseless creatures are called to wonder at. It must surpass all the wonders and prodigies of nature and art. And what is that? 'I have nourished and brought up children, and they have rebelled against me,' &c. If we consider what this people seemed once to be, and thought themselves to be, we may easily know how they corrupted themselves. If ye look on them at one time, (Exod. xix. 8 ; Deut. v. 27,) ye would call them children. There was never a fairer undertaking of obedience than this, ‘All that the Lord hath spoken we will do;’ so that the Lord commends them for speaking well, verse 28, ‘They have well said all that they have spoken,’ verse 29, ‘O that there were such an heart in them!’ But compare all this people's practice with this profession, and you shall find it exceeding contrary ; they indeed corrupted themselves, though they got warning to take heed of it: ‘Take ye therefore good heed unto yourselves, lest ye corrupt yourselves,’ Deut. iv. 15, 16. But alas, it was within them that destroyed them ; there was not such a heart in them as to hear and obey ; but they undertake, being ignorant of their own deceitful hearts, which were desperately wicked. And therefore, behold what corruption ensued and followed upon such a professed resolution. They never sooner promised obedience, but they disobeyed ; they did abominable works, and did no good, and this is to corrupt their way, Psalm xiv. 1, &c. We need not instance this longer in this people ; we ourselves are a sufficient proof of it. We may make this song our own, ‘we have corrupted ourselves.’ Once we had a fair show of zeal for God, of love and desire of reformation of life, many solemn undertakings were that we should amend our ways and doings: but what is the fruit of all? Alas, we have corrupted ourselves more than they. Israel promised, but we vowed and swore to the Most High, reformation and amendment of life in our conversations and callings. Lay this rule to our practices, and are we not a perverse and crooked generation? Oh! that we were more affected with our corruptions, and were more sensible of them ; then we could not choose but mourn for our own and the land's departing from God. Did not every man vow and swear to the most high God to endeavour reformation of his life, even a personal reformation?* But

* [When the national covenant was first subscribed by King James and his household, and by persons of all ranks, in the year 1581, a number of Jesuits and popish priests had unexpectedly made their appearance in the country. Various dispensations from the Pope likewise had been intercepted “whereby the Catholics were permitted to *promise, swear, subscribe, and do what else should be required of them, so as in mind they continued firm, and did use their diligence to advance in secret the Roman faith.* These dispensations,” says Archbishop Spotswood, “being showed to the king, he caused his minister, Mr. John Craig, form a short confession of faith, wherein all the corruptions of Rome, as well in doctrine as outward rites, were particularly abjured, and a clause inserted (because of these dispensations) by which the subscribers did call God to witness that in their minds and hearts they did fully agree to the said confession, and did not feign or dissemble in any sort. This confession [or covenant] the king, for an example to others, did publicly swear and subscribe; the like was done by the whole council and court.” (Hist. of Ch. of Scotland, pp. 308, 309.) By an ordinance of council, and at the desire of the General Assembly, the national covenant, along with a Bond for the maintenance of the true religion, and the safety of the king's person and government, was again subscribed by persons of all ranks in the year 1590. This Bond had been previously entered into and signed by his majesty, and various men of rank and station in the kingdom, in anticipation of the threatened Spanish invasion, and as a counter-association to the Holy League, which had been formed by the most powerful popish princes in Europe with a view to extirpate the reformed religion. When the national covenant was renewed in 1638, and once more subscribed by all classes of the community, the Bond which accompanied it was altered to suit the circumstances of the times. It expressed a solemn determination on the part of those who subscribed it to aim at “a personal reformation,” as well as a resolution to withhold their sanction from the late innovations in religion, “till they be tried and allowed in free Assemblies, and in Parliaments,” These are the words:—“And because we cannot look for a blessing from God upon our proceedings, except with our profession and subscription we join such a life and conversation as beseemeth Christians who have renewed their covenant with God: We therefore faithfully promise for ourselves, our followers, and all others under us, both in public, and in our particular families and personal carriage, to endeavour to keep ourselves within the bounds of Christian liberty; and to be good examples to others of all godliness, soberness, and righteousness, and of every duty we owe to God and man.” (Dunlop's Confessions, vol. II., p. 136.) The following corresponding clause is contained in the Solemn League and Covenant, which was ratified by the parliaments both of England and Scotland, and subscribed generally by the people of both kingdoms in 1643, and renewed in Scotland in 1648.—“And because these kingdoms are guilty of many sins and provocations against God, and his Son Jesus Christ, as is too manifest by our present distresses and dangers, the fruits thereof; we profess and declare before God and the world, our unfeigned desire to be humbled for our own sins, and for the sins of these kingdoms; especially that we have not, as we ought, valued the inestimable benefit of the gospel, that we have not laboured for the purity and power thereof, and that we have not endeavoured to receive Christ in our hearts, nor to walk worthy of him in our lives, which are the causes of other sins and transgressions so much abounding among us: and our true and unfeigned purpose, desire, and endeavour for ourselves, and all others under our power and charge, both in public and in private, in all duties we owe to God and to man, to amend our lives, and each one to go before another in the example of a real reformation, that the Lord

alas, where is it? 'He that is filthy' is 'filthy still.' Nay, which is worse, the evil man waxeth worse and worse. There is a great noise of a public reformation of ordinances and worship; but alas, the deformation of life and practice outcries all that noise. Nay, certainly all that is done in the public, must come to no account before God, since our practices outcry it. Public reformation is abomination, where personal corruptions do not cease. This made the Jews' solemn days hateful, their hands were 'full of blood,' Isa. i. All that ye have spent on the public will never be reckoned, since ye will not consecrate your lives to God, will not give your lusts up to him. Ye are his enemies in the mean time, though you account yourselves religion's friends. I beseech you, consider your ways. Would any of us have thought to have seen such profanity, mocking of godliness, and ignorance in Scotland in so short a time? Nay, it is to be feared that the day is not far off, when ye will corrupt yourselves, and do abominable things; yea, defile yourselves as ill as the nations that know not God.

Every man useth to impute his faults to something beside himself. Ere men take with their own iniquity, they will charge God that gave no more grace: but if men knew themselves, they would deduce their corruption and destruction both from one fountain, that is, from themselves. Ignorance of ourselves maketh us oft undertake fair, and promise so well on our own head. What was the fountain of this people's corruption, and apostatizing from their professions? The Lord hints at it, Deut. v. 25, &c. 'Oh that they had such a heart.' Alas, poor people, ye know not yourselves, that speak so well. I know thee better than thou dost thyself; I will declare unto thee thy own thought; thou hast not such a heart as to do what thou sayest; there is a desperate wicked heart within thee, that will destroy thee by lying unto thee. If thou knewest this fountain of original corruption, thou wouldest despair of doing, and say, I cannot serve the Lord. Now here is the fountain of the land's corruption this day. Why is our way corrupted? Because our hearts within were not cleansed, and because they were not known. If we had dried up the fountain, the streams had ceased; but we did only dam it up, and cut off some streams for a season: we set up our resolutions and purposes as an hedge to hold it in; but the sea of the heart's iniquity, that is above all things, hath overflowed it, and defiled our way more than in former times. Ye thought upon no other thing, but that presently ye would be all changed people, and would reform without more ado,—and thus it is with you in all your public repentances. But alas! you know not yourselves; it is still within you which will yet corrupt you; and it was within us that hath undone us; we were too confident of ourselves, and it is no wonder that the Lord suffers us to prove ourselves, that we may know what is in our heart. Now, therefore, since ye have so often tried it, I beseech you follow not such a way again. Ye are called to deny yourselves, and to follow Christ: and this is a great part of it, that ye may never expect for any good within yourselves, or the helping of any evil: 'In me is thy help found.' Look to the fountain of life, Jesus Christ, and despair of your own hearts, for they are desperately wicked, so wicked, that if ye knew them, ye would despair of them, and give them over to another hand, who can create a new heart within you. Ye use to impute your backslidings to the times, to temptations, to company, and such like. This is the way that men shift the challenges of sin: the drunkard puts it on his companion, the servant on his master that led him wrong, the people put rulers in the fault, and absolve themselves, and rulers put one another in the wrong, and absolve themselves. But, alas! all of us are ignorant of ourselves: it is not times nor temptations that corrupt us, but ourselves. No man is tempted, saith James, of God, 'but every man is tempted when he is drawn away of his own lust and enticed,' James i. 14. Temptation were no temptation, if our hearts were not wicked hearts. Nay, many of us are ready to tempt temptations, to provoke the devil to temptations: we cast ourselves open to temptations. Temptations find lust within, and lust within is the mother to conceive sin, if temptation be the father. Times do not bring evils along with them, they do but discover what was hid before. All

may turn away his wrath and heavy indignation, and establish these churches and kingdoms in truth and peace."—Ed.]

the evils and corruptions you now see among us, where were they in the day of our first love, when we were as a loving and beloved child? Have all these risen up of late? No certainly, all that you have seen and found were before, though they did not appear: before they were in the root, now you see the fruit. All the apostacy and profanity that hath been vented in these days, was all shut up within the corners of men's hearts at the beginning. Time and temptation hath but uncovered the heart, and made the inside out, hath but opened a sluice to let out this sea of corruption. It is not bred since, but seen since.

Now so it is with us; we have corrupted ourselves, and so we corrupt ourselves still more. Backsliding cometh on as gray hairs, here and there, and is not perceived by beholders. *Nemo repente fit turpissimus.** No man becometh worst at first. There are many steps between that and good. Corruption comes on men's ways as in fruits, some one part beginneth to alter, and then it groweth worse, and putrifieth and corrupteth the rest of the parts. An apple rots not all at once; so it is with us. Men begin at leisure, but they run post before all be done. In some one step of our way we take liberty and think to keep the rest clean; but when that part is corrupted, 'a little leaven leaveneth the whole lump,' and all followeth: and then he that corrupted himself, is ready to corrupt others. 'Children that are corrupters,' Isa. i. 4. Every one by his example corrupts another; and by corrupting others they again corrupt themselves more. Oh! how infectious an evil is sin, of a pestilentious nature: and truly our hearts are more ready to receive such impressions, than either a world or a devil is to make them.

'Their spot is not.' Why doth the Lord take pleasure to reckon their sins, to describe so abominable a people? Is not this Jacob in whom he saw no iniquity?† Is not this Israel, whose transgressions are not known?‡ Certainly if this people would have charged themselves so, he would not have done it. He loves to forget, when we remember our sins: but he must remember them when we forget them. What is the Lord's great controversy with men? Here it is,—How can ye say or think that ye are not polluted? Or if ye take with such a general, yet, why is not the conviction of your sin and misery so deeply engraven, as to pursue you out of all hope of remedy in yourselves, (Jer. ii. 22, 23.) 'And therefore is thine iniquity marked before me,' saith the Lord. God hath determined not to wrong his justice. If men should go away unpunished and unjudged both, where were his righteousness? If there were no record of men's transgressions, were he a righteous judge? Therefore, those who do not judge themselves must leave judgment to him: for once the mouth of all flesh must be stopped, and all become guilty before God. Why pleads the Lord with man? Because man says, 'I am innocent, I have not sinned, his anger will turn away,' Jer. ii. 35. Will any speak so in terms? No indeed, but the Lord constructs so of the most part, because they do more consider the wrongs done to them, than their own wrongs done to God. All men confess the general, that they are sinners; but who searches and tries his way to find out particulars? And in as far as ye do not charge yourselves with particular guiltiness, until ye be afraid of his anger; as long as the consideration of your sins is so superficial and shallow, that ye apprehend no danger of wrath, or immunity from it, certainly God will plead with you. Justice must so far be glorified, as once to conclude you under the sentence of death; if ye do it not now, then ye leave God to be your judge and party. But if any man shall take with his guiltiness, till his mouth be stopped, and condemn himself in God's sight, I say, mercy and grace in God must not be wronged; he that judges himself shall not be judged of the Lord. What a fair offer is this to you all the Lord offers to you! If ye will in time be your own judges, I will resign my judgment to you. If you will in earnest pass the sentence, I will neither pass it nor execute it. If ye come to the Mediator, Christ Jesus, to escape from the wrath of a judge, you shall meet with a reconciled Father,

* [Nemo repente fuit turpissimus.—Juv. Sat. II. v. 83.

"For none become at once completely vile."—Gifford's Translation.

The progress of vice is a downward course. If a wicked man, at the commencement of his sinful career, were to be told the crimes he would live to perpetrate, he would be filled with horror, and be ready, like Hazael, to exclaim with unaffected indignation, 'Is thy servant a dog to do this great thing?'—2 Kings viii. 13.—Ed.] † [Num. xxiii. 21.—Ed.] ‡ [Jer. l. 20.—Ed.]

and with such love in him as shall hide a multitude of offences. O the depth, and height, and breadth of that love! Well then, it shall be a sea to cast your offences into, that shall drown them. Had not his people many spots? Is there any man can say, I have cleansed my heart from iniquity? No, not one. Yet behold, he sees no spots in his people. He doth not make them his people because spotless, but he seeth them spotless, because he makes them his people. There is no covering that can hide men's uncleanness from his piercing eye, but one, even Jesus Christ his righteousness: and 'Blessed is he whose sins are covered.' If this covering were spread over the mouth of all hell, then hell should have a covering from his eyes. If ye therefore strip yourselves naked of your own pretences and leaves, and think not yourselves secure under any created shelter; if ye hide not your iniquity, then it shall be hid indeed; here is a covering that shall hide it from his eyes. There is no spot so heinous, none so ingrained, but the blood of Jesus can wash it as perfectly out, as if it had never been, Isa. i. 16, 17. Though your spots were such as are not incident to his children, yet this blood cleanses from one and all; it is of an infinite nature. But though it be so, that the blood of Christ cleanseth from all sin, that there is a fountain opened in the house of David for sin and for uncleanness, for sin and separation, for such heinous offences as may separate people even from the congregation of the Lord's people; yet there are some sins, some spots, that ordinarily his people are not defiled with, and in this respect they may be called 'holy and undefiled in the way.' There are some marks and characters of unregenerated men, so legible and express, that we may even read from men's conversation, that they are not the children of God. Though the blood of Christ wash from all, yet the child of God ordinarily is kept from some kind of spots; so that if a man shall be spotted with them, it is no marvel he question if he be a child or not. There are two, which I think so gross and unclean spots, that I cannot conceive how a soul washen by Jesus Christ can be defiled with them. One is, a course of profanity. The common walk of the multitude is so gross and profane, so void of God and godliness, that it witnesseth to their face that they are not the sons of God. 'He that is born of God sinneth not:' he maketh not sin his way and trade to walk into, and please himself into. What are the most part of you, I pray you? Is your spot like the spot of his children? Do not ye declare your sin as Sodom, ye drunkards, who wallow in it daily, and though ye profess repentance, yet never amend? Ye who have a custom of swearing and blaspheming his holy name, do not ye carry in your forehead a spot that is not like his children? The child of God may fall in many particulars, but it is not the spot of a child to continue in them, to add drunkenness to thirst, and yet to dream of escaping wrath. I pray you, consider it, for it is of great moment. Do ye carry such a black mark,—the devil's mark? O do not think yourselves safe. May not this persuade you? Do but compare yourselves in your converse and walk with an heathen without the church. Set aside your public profession of coming to the church, and hearing the word, and church privileges, and is the difference visible between you and them? Many of you pray no more in secret or in your families than they. Ye curse and swear as they; ye are covetous and worldly as they. If ye can, do but draw a line of difference; and if ye cannot, then I ask, what are ye? Is not this the spot of bastards? Another spot is, hatred of godliness and the godly. This is indeed the most lively image of the devil: who hates his brother is of the devil. He that hates the Son, can he love the Father? he that hates him that is begotten, hates also him that begat him: and he that loves him that begat, loves him that is begotten. Now, how can he be begotten of God, who hates that nature he is said to partake of—who hates him that is begotten? I wonder that many of your consciences are not touched with this? How can ye imagine ye are children of God, when there are none of your neighbours that your heart riseth more against, that ye can less abide, than those who seek God most diligently, whose conversation is different from the world's? Do not flatter yourselves, as if it were hypocrisy ye hated. No, no; ye can agree with profanity, and how can ye hate hypocrisy? Ye can agree with a profane hypocrite—with a profane man, that feigns and dissembles repentance; but if once he were so thoroughly changed, as to hate his former way, and forsake it, then your antipathy beginneth. What a ridiculous thing is it for profanity to take upon it to censure hypocrisy! Certainly if profanity cast out with hypocrisy, it must be because it hath a form of godliness, which it so much detesteth. It is a strange hatred at godliness that a profane man hath, that he cannot abide the very shadow of it. I beseech you who love not holiness in your own persons, who hate to be reformed yourselves, do not add this height of sin to it, as to hate it in others also. If ye be not godly yourselves, do not add this declared manifest character of a child of the devil to it, to hate godliness in others. There were some hope of you, if ye held it in reverence and estimation where ye saw it. There are many other spots not incident to his children, as this, that men will not take with their sin and the curse. It is a great difficulty to convince the most part of men how miserable they are, how void of God. All the world will not put them out of a good opinion of themselves; and I think this hath been the spot of this people, they would not take with their guiltiness—a stubborn-hearted people, whole-hearted. There needs no more to declare a number of you not to be God's children, but this,—ye have lived all your time in the opinion and belief that ye were God's children, that ye believed in him; ye never saw yourselves lost and miserable. This was the spot of this people, that they esteemed themselves children, though they had many spots that testified to their face that they were no children. They waxed worse and worse; neither mercies nor judgments amended them: 'When he slew them,' it may be, 'they sought him, and flattered him with their mouth, but their hearts were not right with him, neither were they steadfast in his covenant,' Psal. lxxviii. 34. Ye would have thought them a godly people, while under the rod for a season; but all that was but extorted and pressed out by violence of affliction, as the groans of a beast under a burden. But a little time declared that it was but flattery, though they thought themselves ingenuous; and therefore they returned to their old provocations, as a sow to the puddle, or a dog to his vomit. And is not this our spot, even the spot of great and small? If any would look upon us in our engagements and vows under trouble, we appear like his people, a praying, repenting, and believing people;* but how quickly doth all this prove flattery? Do we not still return to our old ways that we have been exemplarily punished for, and which we so solemnly engaged against? The heat of the furnace dieth out, and they wax colder and harder; a little time wears away all their tenderness. Every man seeks his own things, and no man seeks the things of Jesus Christ. This was this people's sin and spot. 'Jeshurun waxed fat and kicked, and lightly esteemed the Rock of his salvation.' When their heads were lifted up to government; when they were raised out of the waters of affliction and poverty, then they forgat God, they oppressed the poor and needy, eat up his people as bread, and could not abide to have their faults told them; they said to the seers, 'See not, and to the prophets, Prophesy not unto us right things,' &c. Isa. xxx. 10. I think likewise, that oppression is not the spot of his children, whoever uses it. And covetousness presses men to it, when power is in their hand to compass it. This is a vile spot, unworthy of any ruler, let be† a Christian. It was abhorred among Pagans. O but it cries to heaven, saith the Scripture; it hath a double cry when other sins cry once! The heinousness of it crieth once, and the poor people cry again, and both these come up to the ears of the Lord of hosts; nay, it hath the cry of murder, and another beside. He that is greedy of gain, is said to take away the life of the owners thereof, Prov. i. 19. So he is a murderer before God; and the poor man's blood crieth for vengeance, and then himself seconds it, either by prayer, or crying out for misery, Job xxxv. 9. All men's prayers and professions will not outcry these two. The people's many prayers could not be heard, (Isa. i. 15,) because their hands were 'full

* [" About the time of the first renewing of the covenant, there was a sensible change to the better in men's carriage and conversation; most of all those who joined in opposing the defection, not only reforming themselves from common and gross sins, such as drunkenness, uncleanness, swearing, profaning the Lord's day, slighting of the ordinances, self-seeking, covetousness, oppression, &c. but giving themselves to the duties of religion and righteousness, such as sobriety, edifying discourse, chaste behaviour, hallowing of the Lord's day, diligent seeking of the Lord in secret and in their families, attending on the preaching of the word as often as opportunity is offered, liberality, love, charity one toward another, a public spirit and zeal for God. But all these things are now decayed in many, and they are again grown as ill if not worse than before." Causes of the Lord's Wrath against Scotland, pp. 48, 49. Printed in the year 1653.—Ed.]

† [Much less.—Ed.]

of blood,' which had a louder cry than their prayers. The poor also oppressing the poor, is like a sweeping rain that leaves nothing behind it.

It is read in the margin, "that they are not his children,—that is their blot." And indeed it is so. It is a great blot and stain in the face of any man whoever he be, that he is not born of God—that he can reckon kindred to none but Adam. But what indignity is it and disgrace, for a people professing his name, yet to have no other generation, to reckon no higher than the earth and the earthly. What is now the great blot of our visible church? Here it is, the most part are not God's children, but called so; and it is the greater blot that they are called so, and are not.* O poor saints, esteem your honour and high privilege; ye have received this, to be the sons of God! It is no blot to you that you are poor and despised in the world; but it is, and shall be an eternal blot to the great and rich, and wise in the world, that they are not the children of God. Christianity is no blot, though it be in reproach among men, but it is really the glory and excellency of a man; but the want of it, alas! how doth it abase many high and noble, impoverish many rich, and infatuate many wise! Ye think all of you are the children of God, because ye are in the church, and partake of the ordinances and sacraments; and so did this people. But Moses did not flatter these Jews, but told both princes and people in their face, that they were not children of God, because only Israel in the letter, they had not children's manners. O that it might not be said of the most part of you, that ye are not children of God, and that that is your blot and shame! It is the shame of rulers not to be the children of God. They are wise, they are active, they are noble, but one spot disgraceth all, one fly maketh their ointment to stink, they are not gracious, many of them, but sons of men at the farthest reckoning, are not begotten again to a lively hope. 'Not many wise, not many noble, not many rich.' The scantiness of gracious men is the spot of judicatories,† that there are

* [An inference unfavourable to the religious character of the countrymen of Binning, has been too hastily drawn from this and some other passages in his works. (Orme's Mem. of Dr. Owen, p. 129.) The late Dr. M'Crie observed, that this was like "the attempts of popish writers to prove the *Reformation* a *Deformation*, by culling quotations from the sermons of such Protestant preachers as inveighed most freely against prevailing vices." (Christ. Inst. vol. xx. p. 624.) In the "Representation, Propositions, and Protestations," however, "of divers Ministers, Elders, and Professors," printed in the year 1652, and probably about the time this sermon was preached, it is affirmed, that the religious aspect of the country had undergone an unhappy change, in the course of the two preceding years. "If we look back," it is said, p. 3. "to that which we have already attained of the work of Reformation, (notwithstanding our short-coming in the power and practice of godliness,) what purity was there of worship, what soundness of doctrine, unity of faithful pastors, order and authority of assemblies; what endeavours for promoving the power of godliness, for purging of the ministry, judicatories and armies, and for employing such in places of power and trust as were of constant integrity and good affection to the cause, and of blameless conversation? And again, if we consider how in place of these, within these two years, have succeeded, for unity, division; for order, confusion; for purity of worship, outward contempt; for the power of godliness, atheism and profaneness; for purging of the ministry, judicatories and armies, sinful mixtures; for zeal, lukewarmness and toleration,—it is too palpable that we are far gone on in the way of declining, having lost much of that which we had attained, and that which remains being ready to die."—Ed.]

† [The author and the other protesters disapproved not only of the proceedings of the civil and ecclesiastical judicatures, but of the composition of these courts, after the act of classes had been rescinded on the 30th of May, 1651. In consequence of the repeal of this act, they who, on account of what was in the language of the times called malignancy, had formerly been excluded from their places in the Scottish parliament, were allowed to take possession of their seats, by signing a bond, the terms of which the parliament prescribed. This the protesters considered to be wrong as a matter both of policy and principle. They likewise declared the assembly, which in July, 1651, met at St. Andrews, and afterwards adjourned to Dundee, and also that which was held in Edinburgh, in July, 1652, to be "unlawful and corrupt," adding, that "although with the renewing of the national covenant, and with the casting out of prelates, and the corruptions introduced by them, the Lord was graciously pleased to give repentance to not a few who were involved in that defection; yet, since that time, there hath always remained a corrupt party of insufficient, scandalous, and ill-affected ministers in the kirk, enemies to the power of godliness, and obstructors to the work of reformation, * * * that party perceiving that they were not able to endure trial in a time of reformation and purging, began the last year to lift up their heads, and speak a language of their own," &c. (Representation, ut supra, pp. 11, 12.) The protesters, moreover, are found complaining at this period, "how gracious and well qualified elders are removed and kept out from church judicatories, and ignorant and profane persons brought in, and more endeavoured to be brought in in their room; how gifted and gracious young men are debarred from entering into the ministry, and a door is opened to others, whereof some are loose and profane, and many are ignorant and strangers to the work of the Lord upon their own hearts."—Letter from Protesters, subscribed

many children of the world, but few children of light in them. O how beautiful and glorious would judicatories be, if all the members were children of light! What glory would there be, if all of them did shine and enlightened one another! But what beauty or comeliness, what majesty can be in rulers or judicatures, when the image of God is not in them! This is also the spot of assemblies, synods, presbyteries, that there are few godly ministers. Alas, that this complaint should be, even among those whose office it is to beget many children to God! How few of them are begotten, or have the image of their Father! And thus church assemblies have no beauty, such as the courts of Jesus Christ should have. O that we were in love with Christianity and grace; that it were our grand question, how shall I be put among the children? The Lord seems to wonder at it, and make a question of it, How can such as we be put among the children? Jer. iii. 19. But he answers it himself, 'Thou shalt call me, My Father, and shall not turn away from me.' There is no more to do, but to take with* your wanderings and wrongs done to God, embrace him in Jesus Christ, and he becomes your Father; and if ye be children, sure ye will resolve to abide in your Father's house, and turn no more to a present world, or your former lusts.

They are a 'perverse and crooked generation.' What pleasure hath the Lord in speaking thus, when he upbraids none? Certainly, in a manner it is drawn out of him. Would he object our faults, if we did not defend them by obstinacy? Perverseness and crookedness is obstinacy and incorrigibleness against mercies and judgments,—'that which is crooked cannot be made straight,' saith Solomon. Then doth the Lord take notice of sins, when men refuse to return, and so maintain their sins. It is this which heightens provocations, and makes out the controversy,—perverseness in sin. It is not ordinary common infirmities that the Lord punisheth, either in a land or person; but when infirmities are discovered by the light of the word, when the Lord useth means to reclaim men in his providence, and yet no means prevail, then are they reckoned perverse. Now, perverseness is not the spot of his children: the child of God daily bows and folds to him, receives challenges from him, takes with iniquity and yields unto God. O that this title might not be written above the head of this generation deservedly—'This is a perverse and crooked generation!'

Sermon V.

Psal. lxxiii. 28,—"*But it is good for me to draw near to God: I have put my trust in the Lord God, that I may declare all thy works.*"

After man's first transgression, he was shut out from the tree of life, and cast out of the garden, by which was signified his seclusion and sequestration from the presence of God, and communion with him: and this was in a manner the extermination of all mankind in one, when Adam was driven out of paradise. Now, this had been an eternal separation for any thing that we could do, (for we can do nothing but depart by a perpetual backsliding, and make the distance every day wider,) except it had pleased the Lord, of his infinite grace, to condescend to draw near to us in gracious promises and offers of a Redeemer. If he had not made the first journey from heaven to earth, by sending his only Son, we should have given over the hope of returning from earth to heaven. But he hath taken away the greatest part of that distance, in drawing near to our nature; yea, in assuming our flesh into the fellowship of his glorious divinity. He hath stooped so low to meet with us, and offered himself the trysting place† between God and us, a fit meeting-place, where there is a conjunction of the interests of both parties, and now, there is no more to do, but to draw near to God in Jesus Christ, since he hath made the great journey to come down to us. We have not that

in the name of many ministers, &c. met at Edinburgh, 17th of March, 1653, by Mr. Andrew Cant, p. 6. See what is said in reply to this, in 'The Assertor's Answer,' printed in the same year, p. 18.—Ed.]

* [Acknowledge.—Ed.]

† [See note, page 126.—Ed.]

infinite gulf of satisfaction to justice to pass over; we have not the height of divine Majesty, as he is infinitely above us, and offended with us, to climb up unto. Certainly we could not but fall into the lake that is below us, if we were to aim so high. But the Lord hath been pleased to descend to us, in our mean capacity in the flesh, and fill up the immeasurable gulf of justice by the infinite merits and sufferings of his Son in our flesh. And now he invites us, he requests us, to come to him in his Son and have life. We are not come to mount Sinai, that might not be touched, that burnt with fire and tempest, where there were terrible sights and intolerable noises. I say, such a God we might have had to do with, a consuming fire, instead of an instructing light,—a devouring fire, instead of a healing Sun of righteousness, considering that there is nothing in us which is not fit and prepared fuel for everlasting burnings. But we are come—and that is the eternal wonder of angels—unto mount Sion, to be citizens in the city of God, and fellow-citizens with blessed angels and glorified spirits, to peace and reconciliation with him who was our judge. And if you ask how this may be? I answer, because we have one Jesus, the Mediator of the new covenant, to come to, whose blood crieth louder for pardon of sinners than all men's transgressions can cry for punishment of sinners, Heb. xii. 18—20, &c.

Let us then consider the first step and degree of union with God,—it consists in faith in Jesus Christ. This is the first motion of the soul in drawing near to God; for, as there is no remission without blood, so no access to God without a mediator. For if you consider what is in Jesus Christ, you will find that which will engage the desire of the heart; as also that which will give boldness and confidence to act that desire. Eternal life is promised and proposed in him;—he offers rest to weary souls, and hath it to give. That which we ignorantly and vainly seek elsewhere, here it is to be found. For personal excellencies, he is the chief infinitely beyond comparison; and for suitableness to us and our necessities, all the gospel is an expression of it; so that he is presented in the most attractive drawing manner that can be imagined. And then, when the desires are inflamed, yet if there be no oil of hope to feed it, it will soon cool again. Therefore, take a view again, and you may have boldness to enter into the holiest by the blood of Jesus. There was some kind of distance kept in the Old Testament,—none but the high priest might enter into the holiest place: but the entry of our High Priest into it, that is, into heaven, hath made it patent to all that come to him and apply his blood. There is a new and living way by the holy flesh of Christ, consecrated and made, of infinite value and use, by the divinity of his person; and, therefore, having such a one of our kindred so great with God, we may draw near with a true heart and full assurance of faith, having our consciences sprinkled, &c., Heb. x. 18—20, &c. Now, since the way is made plain to you, and the entry is opened up in the gospel, do you not find your hearts stir within you to draw near to him? Do you not find a necessity of making peace by such a Mediator? O that ye knew the great distance between God and your natures, and what the hazard is, 'Lo! they that are far from thee shall perish:' then certainly you would take hold of this invitation, and be easily drawn unto Jesus Christ. But unto you who have adventured to draw near for pardon of sin in Christ, I would recommend unto you, that you would draw yet nearer to God. After that the partition-wall of wrath and condemnation is removed, yet there is much darkness in your minds, and corruption in your natures, that separates from him; I mean, intercepts and disturbs that blessed communion you are called unto. Therefore, I would exhort you, as James, 'Draw near to God, and he will draw near to you,' chap. iv. 8; and that, wherein this most consists, is in studying that purification of our natures, that cleansing of our hearts from guile, and our hands from offences, by which our souls may draw towards a resemblance of God. This access and drawing near to God in assimilation and conformity of nature, is the great design of the gospel. 'Be ye holy, for I am holy.' Now, ye are agreed, walk with him, (Amos iii. 3,) as Enoch 'walked with God,' Gen. v. 24; that is, labour in all your conversation to set him before your eyes, and to study to be well-pleased with him in all things, and to please him in all, to conform yourselves to his pleasure in every thing. And this communion in walking especially consists in that communication of the spirit with God in prayer: this is the nearest and sweetest approach when the soul is lifted up to God, and is almost out of itself in him; and this being the ordinary exercise and motion of the soul, it exceedingly advances in the first point of nearness, that is, in conformity with God. Drawing often near in communion with him in prayer, makes the soul draw towards his likeness, even as much converse of men together will make them like one another.

Now, for the commendation of this, 'It is good.' What greater evil can be imagined than separation from the greatest good? And what greater good, than accession to the greatest good? Every thing is in so far happy and well, as it is joined with, and enjoyeth, that which is convenient for it. Light is the perfection of the earth; remove it, and what a disconsolate and unpleasant thing is it! Now, truly there is nothing suitable to the immortal spirit of man but God; and, therefore, all its happiness or misery must be measured by the access or recess, nearness or distance, of that infinite goodness. Therefore, is it any wonder, that all they that go a-whoring from him perish, as every man's heart doth? For we are infinitely bound by creation, by many other bonds stronger than wedlock, to consecrate and devote ourselves wholly to God; but this is treacherously broken. Every man turns aside to vanity and lies, and is guilty of heart-whoredom from God, and spiritual idolatry, because the affection that should be preserved chaste for him is prostitute to every base object. So then, this divorcement of the soul from God cannot but follow thereupon, even an eternal eclipse of true and real life and comfort. And whoever draws back from the fountain of life and salvation, cannot but find elsewhere perdition and destruction, Heb. x. ult. My beloved, let us set thus aside all other things which are the pursuits and endeavours of the most part of men. Men's natural desires are carried towards health, food, raiment, life and liberty, peace, and such like; but the more rational sort of men seek after some shadow of wisdom and virtue. Yet the generality of men, both high and low, have extravagant illimited desires towards riches, pleasure, preferment; and all that we have spoken is enclosed within the narrow compass of men's abode here, which is but for a moment. So that, if it were possible that all these forementioned desires and delights of men could attend any man for the space of an hundred years, though he had the concurrence of the streams of the creatures to bring him in satisfaction, though all the world should bow to him and be subject to the beck of his authority without stroke of sword, though all the creatures should spend their strength and wit upon his satisfaction; yet do but consider what that shall be within some few years, when he shall be spoiled of all that attendance, denuded of all external comforts, when the fatal period must close his life, peace, health, and all; and his poor soul also, that was drowned in that gulf of pleasure, shall then find itself robbed of its precious treasure, that is, God's favour, and so remain in everlasting banishment from his presence. Do ye think, I say, that man were happy? Nay! O happy Lazarus, who is now blessed in Abraham's bosom, who enjoys an eternity of happiness for a moment's misery! But, my beloved, you know that it is not possible even to attain to that imagined happiness here. All the gain that is found is not able to quit the cost and expense of grief, vexation, care, toiling and sweating that is about them.

But if ye would be persuaded, there is that to be found easily, which you trouble yourselves seeking elsewhere; and believe me, though the general apprehension of men be,—that peace, plenty, preferment, and satisfaction in this life, to compense their pains, are more easily attainable than fellowship and communion with God; yet I am persuaded that there is nothing more practicable than the life of religion. God hath condemned the world under vanity and a curse, and that which is crooked can by no art or strength be made straight; but he hath made this attainable by his gracious promises, even a blessed life, in approaching near to himself, the fountain of all life. And this is a certain good, an universal good, and an eternal good. It will not disappoint you as other things do, of which you have no assurance for all your toilings. This is made more infallible to a soul that truly seeks it in God. It is as certain that they cannot be ashamed through frustration, as that he is faithful. And then it is an universal good, one comprehensive of all, one eminently and virtually all things created, to be joined to the infinite all-fulness of God. This advanceth the soul to a participation of all that is in him. This is health, Psalm xlii. 11; Prov. iii. 8. This is light, John viii. 12. It is life, (John xi. 25,) liberty, (John viii. 36,) food and raiment, (Isa. lxi. 10, and John iv. 14,) and what not? It is profit, pleasure, preferment, in the superlative degree, and not scattered in so many various streams, which divide and distract the heart, but all combined in one. It is the true good of both soul and body, and so the only good of man. And lastly, it is eternal, to be coetaneous with thy soul. Of all other things it may be said, 'I have seen an end of them,' they were and are not. But this will survive time, and all the changes of it, and then it will begin to be perfect, when all perfection is at an end. Now, from all this, I would exhort you in Jesus Christ to ponder those things in your hearts, and consider them in reference to your own souls, that ye may say with David, 'It is good for me to draw near to God.'

That which all men seek after, is happiness and well-being. Men pursue nothing but under the notion of good; and to complete that which may be called good, there is required some excellency in the thing itself, and then a conveniency and suitableness to us, and these jointly draw the heart of man. But the great misery is, that there is so much ignorance and misapprehension of that which is truly good, and then, when any thing of it is known, there is so little serious consideration and application of it to ourselves; and this makes the most part of men wander up and down in the pursuit of divers things, which are not that true good of the soul, and set their hearts on that which is not, until they find their hearts fall down as wanting a foundation, and then they turn about again to some other vanity. And so the wanderings and strayings of men are infinite, because the by-ways are innumerable, though the true way be but one. Yea, the turnings and toilings of one man are various and manifold, because he quickly loses the scent of happiness in every way he falls into, and therefore must turn to another. And thus men are never at any solid setting about this great business, never resolute wherein this happiness consists, nor peremptory to follow it; but they fluctuate upon uncertain apprehensions, and diverse affections, until the time and date of salvation expire; and then they must know certainly and surely the inevitable danger and irrecoverable loss they have brought themselves to, who would not take notice of the sure way, both of escaping wrath and attaining happiness while it was to be found.

Well, then, this is the great business we have here to do; yea, to make the circle the larger, it is that great business we have to do in this world, to know wherein the true well-being and eternal welfare of our souls consist, and by any means to apply unto that, as the only thing necessary, in regard of which, all other things are ceremonies, circumstances, and indifferent things. And to guide us in this examination and application, here is one man, who, having almost made shipwreck upon the rocks which men commonly dash upon, and being by the Lord led safely by, and almost arrived at the coast of true felicity, he sets out a beacon, and lights a candle to all who shall follow him, to direct them which way they shall steer their course. Examples teach more effectually than rules. It is easy for every man to speak well upon this point in general, and readily all will acknowledge that here it is, and nowhere else. But yet all this is outcried by the contrary noise of every man's practice. These general grants of truth are recalled in the conversations of men, therefore they cannot have much influence upon any man. But when we hear one speak, and see him walk so too; when we have the example of a most wise man, who wanted not these worldly expectations which other men have, so that he not only propones it to us, but after much serious advisement, after mature consideration of all that can be said of the wicked's best estate, and the godly's worst, setting down resolute conclusions for himself,—'It is good for me to draw near to God;' yea, so determinate in it, that if none of the world should be of that mind, he would not change it,—though all should walk in other ways, he would choose to be rather alone in this, than in the greatest crowd of company in any other. Now, I say, when we have such a copy cast us, a man of excellent parts in sobriety and sadness, choosing that way, which all in words confess to be the best; should not this awake us out of our dreams, and raise us up to some more attention and consideration of what we are doing? The words, you see, are the holy resolution of a holy heart, concerning that which is the chiefest good. You see the way to happiness, and you find the particular application of that to David's soul, or of his soul to it. We shall speak a word of the thing itself, then of the commendation of it, then of the application of it.

For the thing itself,—drawing near to God,—it gives us some ground to take a view of the posture in which men are found by nature, far off from God. Our condition by nature I cannot so fitly express, as in the apostle's words, (Eph. ii. 12,)—'Without Christ, aliens from the commonwealth of Israel, strangers from the covenants of promise, having no hope, and without God in the world.' A deplorable estate indeed, hopeless and helpless! No hope in it; that is the extremity of misery, the refuse of all conditions. 'Without Christ, and without God.' Oh! these are words of infinite weight: without those, without whom it is simply impossible to be happy; and without whom it is not possible but to be miserable;—without the fountain of light, life, and consolation, without which there is nothing but pure darkness, without any beam of light; nothing but death, without the least breathing of life; nothing but vexation, without the least drop of consolation. In a word, without these, and wanting these, whom, if you want, it were good to be spoiled of all being; to be nothing, if that could be, or never to have been any thing. Men will seek death, and cannot find it. O what a loss and deprivement is the loss of God, which makes death more desirable than life; and not to be at all, infinitely preferable to any being! Now, it is true, that the bringing in of multitudes within the pale of the visible church, is some degree of access and nearness to God; for then they become citizens as to external right, in the commonwealth of the church, and have the offers of the promises made to them; in respect of which visible standing, the apostle speaks of the whole church of Ephesus, 'but now ye are made near who were far off,' (ver. 13;) notwithstanding, that many of them were found afterwards to have left their first love, Rev. ii. But yet, beloved, to speak more inwardly, and as your souls stand in the sight of God, the generality of those who are near hand in outward ordinances are yet far off from God in reality,—'without God and without Christ,' as really, as touching any soul-feeling, as those who are altogether without. The bond of union and peace was broken in paradise; sin dissolved it, and broke off that nearness and friendship with God; and from that day to this day, there hath been an infinite distance and separation betwixt man and God. The steps and degrees of it are many. There is darkness and blindness in men's minds. Such ignorance naturally possesseth the multitude, that it wholly alienates them from the life of God, Eph. iv. 18. For what fellowship can light, that pure light, have with such gross darkness as is among us? This certainly is the removal of that Sun of Righteousness from our souls, or the imposition of the clouds of transgression, that makes it so dark a night in the souls of men. And then there is nothing but enmity and desperate wickedness in the heart of man, and this keeps the stronghold of the affections, Rom. viii.; Jer. xvii. There cannot be a further elongation or separation of the soul from God, than to turn so opposite, in all inclinations and dispositions, to his holy will; for the distance between God and us is not local in the point of place; for whither shall we go from him who is everywhere? And thus he is near hand every one of us; but it is also real in the deformity and repugnancy of our natures to his holy will. But add unto this, that being thus separated in affection, and disjoined, as it were, in natural dispositions, we cannot draw near to God in any ordinance,—as the word, prayer, &c. Though we may, as that people, draw near with our lips, and ask of him our duty, and seem to delight to know him, yet there is this natural incapacity and crookedness in the heart of man, that it cannot truly approach unto the Father of spirits with any soul-desire and delight. But their hearts are removed 'far from me,' Isa. xxix. 13; Matt. xv. 8. I think men might observe that their souls act not in religious business as they should, but that they remove their souls many miles distant from their bodies,—and they cannot keep any constancy in this approach of prayer to God, cannot walk with him in their conversation, or carry him along in their meditation. But there is one point of estrangement and separation superadded to all, that there is no man can come near to God without an oblation and offering of peace; that there is no approaching to him, but as to a consuming fire, except we can bring a sacrifice to appease, and a present to please Him for our infinite offences. There the difference stands,—we cannot draw near to walk together, till we be agreed. And, truly, this unto man is impossible, for we have nothing so precious as the redemption of our souls,—nothing can compense infinite wrongs, or satisfy infinite justice. Now, this seems to make our nearness again desperate, and to put men furthest off from hope.

Notwithstanding, this is the very purpose of the gospel, preached from the beginning of the world, to remove that distance, and to take impediments of meeting out of the way; for that great obstruction, the want of a sacrifice and ransom, the Lord hath supplied it, he himself hath furnished it; and it was the great design carried on from the beginning of the world. But as the sun, the nearer he is, the more the earth is enlightened: so here, first some dawning of light appears, as a messenger of hope, to tell that the Redeemer shall come,—that the true sacrifice shall be slain; then still the nearer his own appearing, the clearer are the manifestations of him, and the great design is more opened up, till at length he breaks out in glory from under a cloud, and shows himself to the world, to be that Lamb of God that should take away the sins of the world. And now, as the apostle to the Hebrews speaks, chap. vii. 19, 'The law hath made nothing perfect, but the bringing in of a better hope did, by the which we draw nigh to God.' All the sacrifices and shadows that were under the law did but point at this perfect ransom; and the way of access to God through a Mediator was not so clear; but now the matter is made as hopeful as is possible,—the partition-wall of the law's curses, —the hand-writing against us is removed on the cross,—the enmity slain,—the distance removed by the blood of the cross, being partly filled up by his descent into our nature, partly by his lower descent in our nature to suffer death. And this is the savoury oblation that we have to present to God, and may have boldness to come nigh because of it. And when once our access is made by the blood of Jesus Christ, then we are called and allowed to come still nigher, to cleave and adhere to him as our Father, to pray unto him, to walk with him. Then we should converse as friends and familiars together; then draw nigh to his light for illumination, and to him as the fountain of life for quickening, to place our delight and desire in him, —to forsake all other things, even our wills and pleasures, and to lose them, that they may be found in his; to converse much in his company, and be often in communication with him, and meditation upon him. This is the very design and substance of the gospel. It holds forth the way of making up the breach between man and God, of bringing you nigh who are yet afar off, and nearer who are near hand. O let us hearken to it!

Sermon VII.

PROV. xxvii. 1.—"*Boast not thyself of to-morrow, for thou knowest not what a day may bring forth.*"

THERE are some peculiar gifts that God hath given to man in his first creation, and endued his nature with, beyond other living creatures, which being rightly ordered and improved towards the right objects, do advance the soul of man to a wonderful height of happiness, that no other sublunary creature is capable of. But by reason of man's fall into sin, these are quite disordered and turned out of the right channel; and, therefore, as the right improvement of them would make man happy, so the wrong employment of them loadens him with more real misery than any other creature. I mean, God hath given to man two notable capacities beyond other things;—one is, to know and reflect upon himself, and to consider what conveniency is in any thing towards himself,—what goodness or advantage redounds to himself from them, and in that reflection and comparison to enjoy what he hath; another is to look forward beyond the present time, and, as it were, to anticipate and prevent the slow motions of time, by a kind of foresight and providence. In a word, he is a creature framed unto more understanding than others, and so capable of more joy in present things, and more foresight of the time to come. He is made mortal, yet with an immortal spirit of an immortal capacity, that hath its eye upon the morrow,—upon eternity. Now, herein consists either man's happiness or misery, how he reflects upon himself, and what he chooseth for the matter of his joy and gloriation, and what providence he hath for the time to come. If those be rightly ordered, all is well; but if not, then woe unto him, there is more hope of a beast than of him.

Man's nature inclines to boasting—to glorying in something, and this ariseth from some apprehended excellency or advantage, and so is originated in the understanding power of man, which is far above beasts. Beasts find the things themselves, but they do not, they cannot reflect upon their own enjoyment of them, and therefore they are not capable of such pleasure; for the more distinct knowledge of things in relation to ourselves, the more delight ensueth upon it. Many creatures have singular qualities and virtues, but they are nothing the happier; for they know them not, and have no use of them, but are wholly destinated to the use of man, who therefore is only said to enjoy them, because he only is capable of joy from them. And this, I suppose, may give us a hint at the absolute incomprehensible blessedness, self-complacency, and delight of God. It cannot but be immeasurably great, seeing the knowledge of himself and all creatures is infinite; he comprehends all his own power, and virtue, and goodness, and therefore his delight and rejoicing is answerable. There is a glorying and boasting then that is good, which man is naturally framed unto; and this is that which David expresses, Psal. xxxiv. 2, 'My soul shall make her boast in God;' and Psal. xliv. 8, 'In God we boast all the day long, and praise thy name for ever.' When the soul apprehends that all-sufficiency, and self-sufficient fulness of God; what infinite treasures of goodness, and wisdom, and power are in him, and so how suitable and convenient he is to the condition of the soul; what a sweet correspondence there is between his fulness and our emptiness—his mercy and our misery—his infiniteness and our unsuitableness; that there is in him to fill and overflow the soul: the apprehension of this cannot but in a manner perfume the soul with the delight. You find how the senses are refreshed, when they meet with their suitable object; how a pleasant smell refresheth the scent; how lively and beautiful colours are delightful to the eye. But much more here, God is the proportioned object of the immortal spirit; he corresponds to all its capacities, and fills it with unconceivable sweetness. But, my beloved, boasting and glorying in him, ariseth not only from the proportionableness and conveniency of him to our spirits; but this must be superadded,—propriety in him. Things are loved, because excellent in themselves, or because they are our own; but we boast in nothing, we glory in nothing, but because it is both excellent in itself, and ours besides. It is the apprehended interest in any thing makes the soul rise and lift up itself after this manner,—to have such a one to be ours,—such a Lord to be our God,—one so high and sublime,—one so universally full, to be made over to thee; here is the immediate rise of the soul's gloriation. And truly, as there is nothing can be so suitable a portion, so there is nothing that can be so truly made ours as God. Of all things a believer hath, there is nothing so much his own as God,—nothing so indissolubly tied unto him,—nothing so inseparably joined. See Paul's triumph upon that account, Rom. viii. Nothing can truly be said to be the soul's own, but that which is not only coetaneous with it, that survives mortality, and the changes of the body, but likewise is inseparable from it. What a poor empty sound is all that can be spoken of him, till your souls be once possessed of him! it cannot make your hearts leap within you, but it cannot but excite and stir up a believer's heart.

Now there may be a lawful kind of gloriation, rejoicing in the works of God, consequent to the first, which is a little stream from that greater river which runs out from it, and flows into it again. A soul that truly apprehends God will take delight to view the works of God, which make such an expression of him, and are a part of the magnificence of our heavenly Father. But this is all in reference to him and not to ourselves; for then it degenerates and loseth its sweetness, when once it turns the channel towards the adorning of the creature. True boasting in God hath necessarily conjoined with it an humble and low esteem of a man's self, Psal. xxxiv. 2, 'The humble shall hear thereof, and be glad.' As humility and self-emptiness made David go out of himself, to seek satisfaction in God, and having found it, he boasts and triumphs; so there were none capable of understanding his triumph, or partaking with him in his delights, but the humble souls. Now you may perceive how far this boasting here spoken of is degenerated from that, and so how far man's nature is spoiled,—'Boast not thyself,' &c. The true boasting we were created unto, hath a sufficient foundation, even such as will bear the weight of triumph; but that which men's spirits are now naturally set upon, cannot carry, cannot sound such gloriation, and therefore this boasting makes men ridiculous. If you saw a man glorying in rags, setting forth himself to be admired in them, or boasting in some vain, despicable, and base thing, you would pity him, or laugh at him as one distempered. The truth is, the natural man is mad, hath lost his judgment, and is under the greatest distraction imaginable since the fall. That fall hath troubled his brains, and they are never settled, till the new creation come to put all right again, and compose the heart of man. I say, all other distractions are but particular, in respect to particular things; but there is a general distraction over all mankind, in reference to things of most general and most eternal concernment. Now, fools and mad persons, they retain the same affections and passions that are in men, as anger, love, hatred, grief, joy, &c., but it is so much the worse, since the judgment, which is the only directive and guide of them, is troubled. Now they are set on wrong objects, they run at random, and are under no kind of rule, and so they hurry the poor man and put him in a pitiful case. Now indeed so it is with us,—since sin entered, the soul is wholly turned off God, the only true object of delight, in which only there can be solid gloriation. The mind of man is blinded, and his passions are strong, and so they are now spent upon empty vanities, and carried headlong without judgment. Oftentimes he glories in that which is his shame, and boasts in that which is his sin, and which will cause nothing but shame, the more weight be laid upon it. There is in man an oblivion and forgetfulness of God, and in this darkness of the ignorance of God, everything is apprehended or misapprehended, as present sense suggests, and as it fancies a conveniency or excellency. Thither the soul is carried, as if it were something, and then it is but the east-wind. There is nothing beside God that is a fit matter of boasting, because it lacks one of the essential ingredients—either it is not suitable to the soul, or it is not truly our own. There wants either proportion to the vast capacity and void of our desires, and so cannot fill up that really, but only in a deluding dream or imagination, and therefore will certainly make the issue rather vexation than gloriation, or there wants property and interest in them; for they are changeable and perishing in their own nature, and by divine appointment, that they cannot be conceived to be the proper good of the immortal soul. They cannot be truly our own, because they will shortly cease to be, and before they cease to be, they may in a moment cease to be ours. That tie of interest is a draw knot, whatsoever catcheth hold of the end of it looseth it.

The object of degenerate and vicious boasting is here held out: 'Boast not thyself,' or 'of thyself.' Whatsoever be the immediate matter of it, this is always the ultimate and principal object. Since man fell from God, self is the centre of all his affections and motions. This is the great idol, the Diana, that the heart worships; and all the contention, labour, clamour, and care that is among men, is about her silver shrines, so to speak, something relating to the adorning or setting forth this idol. It is true, since the heart is turned from that direct subordination to God, the affections are scattered and parted into infinite channels, and run towards innumerable objects; for the want of that original unity, which comprehends in its bosom universal plenty, must needs breed infinite variety, to supply the insatiable appetite of the soul. And this might be enough to convince you, that your souls are quite out of course, and altogether wandered from the way of happiness, because they are poured out on such a multiplicity of insufficient, unsatisfying things, every one of which is narrow, limited, and empty, and the combination and concurrence of all being a thing either impossible or improbable to be attained. But we may conceive that men's affections part themselves into three great heads of created things: one of which runs towards the goods or perfections of the mind; another towards the goods or advantages of the body; and a third towards those things that are without us, *bona fortunæ*, riches and honour, &c. Now each of these sends out many streams and rivulets as so many branches from it; but all of them, though they seem to have a direct course towards other things, yet wind about and make a circular progress to the great ocean of self-estimation, whence they issued at first.

You may find all of these, (Jer. ix. 23,) falling under a divine interdiction and curse, as being opposite to glorying in God. While men reflect within themselves, and behold some endowments and abilities in their minds beyond other men, of which wisdom is the principal, and here stands for all inward advantages or qualifications of the soul: in that secret reflection and comparison, there is a tacit gloriation, which yet is a loud blasphemy in God's ears. It is impossible almost for a man to recognosce* and review his own parts, such as ingine,† memory, understanding, sharpness of wit, readiness of expression, goodness and gentleness of nature, but that in such a review, the soul must be puffed up, apprehending some excellency beyond other men, and taking complacency in it, which are the two acts of robbery that are in gloriation and boasting. Commonly this arises from unequal comparisons. We please ourselves that we are *deterioribus meliores*, "better than the worst," and build self-estimation upon the ruins of other men's disadvantages, as if it were any point of praise in us that they are worse; like men that stand upon a height, and measure their own altitude, not from their just intrinsic quantity, but taking the advantage of the bottom, whereby we deceive our own selves. I remember a word of Solomon's, that imports how dangerous a thing it is for a man to reflect upon, or search into his own glory, Prov. xxv. 27. 'It is not good to eat much honey: so for men to search their own glory is not glory.'

To surfeit in the excess of honey or sweet things, drives to vomit, and cloys the stomach, ver. 16. Though it be sweet, there is great need, yea, the more need of caution and moderation about it; so for a man either to search into his own breast, and reflect upon his own excellencies, to find matter of gloriation, or studiously to affect it among others, and inquire into other men's account and esteem of him, it is no glory,—it is a dangerous and shameful folly. Now this is not only incident to natural spirits, upon their consideration of their own advantages, but even to the most gracious, upon the review of spiritual endowments and prerogatives. It is such a subtile and insinuating poison that it spreads universally, and infects the most precious ointments of the soul, and, as it were, poisons the very antidote and counterpoison. So forcible is this that was first dropped into man's nature by Satan's envy, that it diffuses itself even into humility, and humiliation itself, and makes a man proud because of humility. The apostle found need to caveat this, Rom. xi. 18—20, 'Boast not,' 'be not high-minded, but fear,'—'thou standest by faith;' and chap. xii. 16, 'Mind not high things;' 'be not wise in your own conceits;' and 1 Cor. viii. 2, 'If any man think that he knoweth anything, he knoweth nothing as he ought to know.' All which gives us a plain demonstration of this, that self-gloriation and complacency, in reflection upon ourselves, is both the greatest ignorance and the worst sacrilege. It is an argument of greater ignorance for a man to think he knows than not to know indeed. It is the worst and most dangerous ignorance, to have such an opinion of our knowledge, gifts, and graces; for that puffs up, swells with empty wind, and makes a vain tumour: and then it is great sacrilege, a robbing of the honour that is due to God. 'For what hast thou that thou hast not received?' That appropriating of these things to ourselves as ours, is an impropriating of them from their right owner, that is, God, 1 Cor. iv. 7. For if thou didst apprehend that thou receivest it, where then is glorying? I would desire then, that whenever you happen to reflect upon yourselves, and observe any advantage, either natural or spiritual, in yourselves, that you may think this word sounds from heaven, 'Let him that glorieth glory in the Lord. Let not the wise man glory in his wisdom;' and so not the learned man in his learning, nor the eloquent man in his speaking, nor the ingenious man in his quickness, nor the good man in his goodness. All these things, though sweet, yet will surfeit; gloriation in them is neither glory nor gain, neither honourable nor profitable.

* [Recognise.—Ed.]

† [That is, genius or ingenuity (from *ingenium*, Lat.) "But gif corporall deth be commoun to all, why will ye jeoparde to lois eternall lyfe, to eschaip that which neither ryche nor pure, neither wyse nor ignorant, proud of stomoke nor febill of corage, and finally, no earthlie creature, by no craft nor *ingyne* of man, did ever avoid." Letter of John Knox from Dieppe.—Ed.]

Then the stream of gloriation flows in the channel of bodily gifts, as might, strength of body, beauty and comeliness of parts, and other such endowments; which, besides that it is as irrational as the former, is a sacrilegious impropriation of the most free and arbitrary gifts of God to ourselves; it is withal absurd, in that it is not so truly of ourselves. These bodily ornaments and endowments do not perfect or better a man as a man; they are but the alterable qualities of the vessel or tabernacle of a man; in which other baser creatures may far excel him. How many comely and beautiful souls are lodged within obscure and ugly cottages or bodies of clay, which will be taken down! And the great advantage is, that the soul of a man, which is a man, cannot be defiled from without, that is, from the body, though never so loathsome or deformed; the vilest body cannot mar the soul's beauty. But then, on the other hand, the most beautiful body is defiled and deformed by the filthiness of sin in the soul; and O how many deformed and ugly souls dwell in beautiful and comely bodies, which truly is no other thing than a devil in an image well carved and painted. Christians, you had need to correct this within you, even a self-complacency, joined with despising of others in the consideration of those external gifts God hath given you. What an abominable thing is it to cast up in reproach, or in your hearts to despise any other for natural imperfections, such as blindness, lameness, deformity, or such like? Let that word sound always in your ears, Who made thee to differ from another? 'Boast not thyself,' &c. But there is as strong a stream runs in the third channel as in any; gloriation arising from those outward and extrinsic differences that the providence of God makes among men, such as riches, honour, gain, &c. You find such men, Psalm xlix. 6. Prov. xviii. 11, and x. 15. That which a godly man makes the name of the Lord,—that is, the ground and foundation of his confidence for present and future times,—that the most part of men make their riches, that is, their strong city, and their high wall; their hope and expectation is reposed within it. This is the tower or wall of defence against the injuries and calamities of the times, which most part of men are building; and if it go up quickly, if they can get these several stones or pieces of gain scraped together into a heap, they straightway imagine themselves safe, as under a high wall. But there is no truth in it, it is all but in their imagination; and therefore it comes often down about their ears, and offends them, instead of being a defence. Let a man creep, as it were, from off the ground where the poor lie, and get some advantage of ground above them, or be exalted to some dignity or office, and so set by the shoulders higher than the rest of the people, or yet grow in some more abundance of the things of this life; and strange it is, what a vanity or tumour of mind instantly follows! He presently thinks himself somebody, and forgetting either who is above him, to whom all are worms creeping and crawling on the footstool; or what a sandy foundation he stands upon himself, he begins to take some secret complacency in himself, and to look down upon others below him. He applauds, as it were, unto himself, and takes it in evil part to want the approbation and *plaudite* of others. Then he cannot so well endure affronts and injuries as before; he is not so meek and condescending to his equals or inferiors. While he was poor he used entreaties, but now he answers roughly, (Prov. xviii. 23,) as Solomon gives the character of him. How many vain and empty gloriations are there about the point of birth and place, and what foolish contentions about these, as if it were children struggling among themselves about their order and rank! There is no worth in these things, but what fancy and custom impose upon them: and yet poor creatures boast in these empty things. The gentlemen despise citizens, the citizens contemn the poor countrymen, and yet their bloods in a basin have no different colours, for all this hot contention about blood and birth. 'Boast not' of thyself. Nay, to speak properly, this is not thyself,—*Qui genus laudat suum, aliena jactat.** Such parents, and such a house are nothing of thy own; these are mere extrinsic things, which are neither an honour to unworthy men, nor a disgrace to one who is worthy.

You see, beloved in the Lord, what is now the natural posture or inclination of our souls in this degenerate and fallen estate. As the rivers of paradise have changed their channels and course since the fall, so hath man's affections, and so hath his

* [That is, "He who cries up his descent, boasts of that which is another's."—Ed.]

gloriation; so that it may be truly said, that our glory is our shame and not our glory. Many glory in iniquity and sin, (Psal. x. 3, and xciv. 4,) but that shall undoubtedly be their shame and confusion before men and angels. How many godless persons will glory in swearing heinous and deep oaths, and some have contended about the victory in it! You account it a point of gallantry; but this triumph is like the devils in hell upon the devouring of souls. Some boast of drinking, and being able to drink others under the table: but we should be humbled and mourn for such abominations. Certain I am, that many boast of wicked designs, and malicious projects against their neighbours, if they can accomplish them. They account their glory not to take a wrong without giving a greater, nor to suffer an evil word without twenty worse in recompense. Alas! this boasting will one day be turned into gnashing of teeth, and this gloriation into that gnawing and ever-tormenting worm of conscience. And what will ye do in the day of that visitation? And where shall be your glory? But the most part glory and boast in things that profit not, and will become their shame, because they glory in them, that is, those gifts of God, outward or inward, temporal or spiritual, wherein there is any advancement above others; unto whom I would seriously commend this sentence to be pondered duly, 'Boast not' of thyself. Whatsoever thou art, or whatsoever thou hast, boast not of thyself for it, think not much of thyself because of it. Though there be a difference in God's donation, yet let there be none in thy self-estimation. Hast thou more wisdom and pregnancy of wit, or more learning than another? Think not more of thyself for that, than thou thinkest of the ignorant and unlearned who want it. Have that same reflection upon thine own unworthiness, that thou would think reasonable another that wants these endowments should have. Is there a greater measure of grace in thee? Boast not, reckon of thyself as abstracted and denuded of that: and let it not add to thy value or account of thyself; put not in that to make it down-weight, and to make thee prefer thyself secretly to another. Whether it be some larger fortune in the world, or some higher place and station among men, or some abilities and perfections of body or mind, which may entice thee secretly to kiss thy hand, and bow down to thyself; yet remember that thou boast not; glory not in any thing but in the Lord. Let nothing of that kind conciliate more affection to thyself, or more contempt toward others. Let not any thing of that kind be the rule of thy self-judging, but rather entertain the view of the other side of thyself, that is the worst, and keep that most in thy eye, that thou may only glory in God. If thou be a gentleman, labour to be as humble in heart as thou thinkest a countryman or poor tenant should be; if thou be a scholar, be as low in thy own sight as the unlearned should be; if rich, count not thyself any whit better than the poor; yea, the higher God sets thee in place, or parts, the lower thou oughtest to set thyself. 'Boast not' of thyself, nor any thing in thyself, or belonging to thyself; for the property of all good is taken from us since the fall, and is fallen into God's hand since we forfeited it; and there is nothing now properly ours but evil,—that is our self.

Sermon VIII.

PROV. xxvii. 1.—"*Boast not thyself of to-morrow, for thou knowest not what a day may bring forth.*"

As man is naturally given to boasting and gloriation in something (for the heart cannot want some object to rest upon and take complacency in, it is framed with such a capacity of employing other things), so there is a strong inclination in man towards the time to come, he hath an immortal appetite, and an appetite of immortality; and therefore his desires usually stretch farther than the present hour; and the more knowledge he hath above other creatures, the more providence he hath and foresight of the time to come. And so he often anticipates future things by present joy and rejoicing in them, as he accelerates in a manner by his earnest desires and endeavours after them. Now, if the soul of man were in the primitive integrity, and had as clear and piercing an eye of understanding as once it had, this providence of the soul would reach to the furthest period in time, that is, to eternity, which is the only just measure of the endurance of any immortal spirit. But since the eye of man's understanding is darkness, and his soul disordered, he cannot see afar off, nor so clearly by far. He is now, as you say, sand-blind,*—can see nothing at such a distance as beyond the bounds of time, can see nothing but at hand.

'To-morrow!' This is the narrow sphere of poor man's comprehension: all he can attain unto is to be provident for the present time. I call it all present, even that which is to come of our time, because, in regard of eternity, it hath no parts, it hath no flux or succession, it is so soon cut off as a moment, as the twinkling of an eye; and so, though a man could see the end of it, it is but a short and dim sight, it is as if a man could only behold that which is almost contiguous with his eye. These, then, are the two great ruins and decays of the nature of man: he is degenerated from God to created things, and seeks his joy and rest in them, in which there is nothing but the contrary, that is, vexation. And then he is fallen from apprehension of eternity, and the poor soul is confined within the narrow bounds of time; so that now all his providence is to lay up some perishing things for some few revolutions of the sun, for some few morrows, after which, though an endless morrow ensue, yet he perceives it not, and provides not for it; and all his glorying and boasting is only upon some presumptuous confidence and ungrounded assurance of the stability of these things for the time to come, which the wise man finding much folly in, he leaves us this counsel, 'Boast not thyself of to-morrow,'—with a most pungent reason, taken partly from the instability and inconstancy of all these outward things in which men fancy an eternity of joy, and partly from the ignorance we have of the future events,—'for thou knowest not what a day may bring forth.'

This boasting is an evil so predominant among men, that I know not any more universal in its dominion, or more hurtful to us, or displeasing to God. If it could be so embowelled unto you, as that you might truly discern the many monstrous conceptions of atheism and irreligion that are in it, it were worth the while; but I shall not digress upon the general head, I had rather keep within the limits of the text. Self-boasting, you see, is that which is here condemned, and the very name is almost enough to condemn the nature of it. But there is another particular added to restrict that, 'of to-morrow.' Of all boastings the most irrational and groundless is that which arises from presumption of future things, which are so uncertain both in themselves and to us.

It is worth the observation, that whatever be the immediate and particular matter and occasion of men's gloriation, yet self is the great and ultimate object of it; it is self that men glory in, whatsoever created thing be the reason or occasion of it. 'Boast not thyself of to-morrow.' Here we might stand and take a look of the crookedness and perverseness of man's spirit since his departure from God. Self-love and pride were the first poison that the malice of Satan dropped into man's nature; and this is so strong and pestilent, that it has spread through the whole of mankind, and the whole in every man. Every one is infected, and all in every one. What are all the disordered affections in men, but so many streams from this fountain? And from these do men's affections flow next: so that there is nothing left uncorrupted, and free of this abominable and vile ingredient; all flowing from self and returning to it again, which is both sacrilegious and unnatural. There is heinous sacrilege in it,—the spoiling of the glorious divine Majesty of his indubitable prerogative and incommunicable right of all the glory and honour of his creature. There is no usurpation like this, for the worm that crawls on the footstool to creep up to the throne, and, as it were, to king it there, to deify and adore itself, and gather in all the tribute of praise, and glory, and love, that is only due to the Lord God

* [That is, short-sighted, or having that weakness of sight which frequently accompanies a very fair complexion.—ED.]

Almighty; and invert and appropriate these to ourselves, which is, as if the axe should boast itself, as if it were no iron; or the staff, as if it were no timber. Hence it is, that of all evils in man's nature, God hath the most perfect antipathy and direct opposition against pride and self-love, because it is sacrilege and idolatry in the highest manner. It strikes at the sovereignty and honour of God's name, which is dear to him as himself; it sets up a vile idol in the choicest temple of God, that is, in the heart; and this is the abomination of desolation. Other evils strike against his holy will; but this peculiarly points at the very nature and being of the most high God, and so it is with child of blasphemy,—atheism is the very heart and life of it. And then it is most unnatural, and so monstrous and deformed. For, consider all the creation, though every one of them have particular inclinations towards their own proper ends, and so a happiness suitable to their own nature; yet how diverse, how contrary soever they be, there is no selfishness in them; they all concur and conspire to the good of the whole, and the mutual help of each other. If once that poison should infect the material world, which hath spoiled the spiritual; let once such a selfish disposition or inclination possess any part of the world, and presently the order, harmony, beauty, pleasure, and profit of the whole world should be interrupted, defaced, and destroyed. Let the sun be supposed to boast itself of its light and influence, and so disdain to impart it to the lower world, and all would run into confusion. Again, I desire you but to take a view of this humour in another's person, (for we are more ready to see others' evils than our own,) and how deformed is it? So vile is self-seeking and self-boasting, that all men loathe it in others, and hide it from others. It disgraces all actions, how beautiful soever; it is the very bane of human society, that which looses all the links of it, and makes them cross and thwart one another.

But, alas! how much more easy is it, to point out such an evil in a deformed visage, than to discern it in ourselves; and how many will hate it in the picture, who love and entertain it in their own persons! Such deceitfulness is intermingled with most desperate wickedness. I verily believe that it is the predominant of every man, good and bad, except in so far as it is mortified by grace. O the turnings and windings of the heart upon itself, in all the most apparently direct motions towards God and the good of men! What serpentine and crooked circumgirations and reflections are there in the soul of man, when the outward action and expression seems most regular and directed towards God's glory, and others' edification! Whoever of you have any acquaintance with your own spirits cannot but know this, and be ashamed and confounded at the very thought of it. Self-boasting, self-complacency, self-seeking, all those being of kin one to another, are insinuated into your best notions, and infect them with more atheism before God, than the strongest pious affection can instil of goodness into them. How often will men's actions and expressions be outwardly clothed with a habit of condescendency and self-denial! And many may declaim with such zeal and vehemency against this evil, and yet, *latet anguis*, the serpent is in the bosom, and his venom may be diffused into the heart, and the poison of self-seeking and self-boasting may run through the veins of humble-like carriage and passionate discourses for self-denial. O that we could above all things establish that fundamental principle of Christianity in our hearts, even as we would be his disciples, truly and sincerely, and not in outward resemblance,—to deny ourselves, to renounce ourselves and our lusts, to make a whole resignation of our love, will, glory, and all to him, in whom to be lost it is only truly to find ourselves!

But, though man have this strange self-idolizing humour, and a self-glorying disposition, yet he is so poor and beggarly a creature, that he hath not sufficient matter within himself to give complacency to his heart; therefore he must borrow from all external things; and when there is any kind of propriety in, or title to them, then he glories in himself for them, as if they were truly in himself. We are creatures by nature most indigent, yet most proud, which is unnatural. No man is satisfied within himself (except the good man, Prov. xiv. 14.), but he goes abroad to seek it at the door of every creature, and when there are some plumes or feathers borrowed from other birds, like that foolish bird in the fable, we begin to raise our crests, and boast ourselves, as if we had all these of our own, and were beholden to none: but as things that are truly our own will not be sufficient to feed this flame of gloriation, without the accession of outward things; so present things, and the present time, will not afford aliment enough, or fuel for this humour, without the addition of the morrow.

'Boast not thyself of to-morrow.' No man's present possession satisfies him, without the addition of hope and expectation for the future; and herein the poverty of man's spirit appears, and the emptiness of all things we enjoy here, that our present revenue, as it were, will not content the heart. The present possession fills not up the vacuities of the heart, without the supply of our imaginations, by taking so much in upon the head of the morrow, to speak so. As one prodigal and riotous waster, who cannot be served with his yearly income, but takes so much on upon his estate, upon the next year's income, before it come, begins to spend upon it, before it come itself, and then, when it comes, it cannot suffice itself; so the insatiable and indigent heart of man cannot subsist and feed its joy in complacency upon the whole world, if it were presently in its possession, without some accession of hopes and expectations for the time to come. Therefore the soul, as it were, anticipates and forestalls the morrow, and borrows so much present joy and boasting upon the head of it, which when it comes itself, perhaps it will not fill the hand of the reaper, let be* pay for that debt of gloriation that was taken on upon its name, or compense the expectation which was in it; see Job xi. 18, 20; viii. 13. Hope is like a man's house to him, but to many it is no better than a spider's web. We have then a clear demonstration of the madness and folly of men, who hang so much upon things without, and suffer themselves to be moulded and modelled in their affections, according to the variety of external accidents. First of all, consider the independence of all things upon us and our choice: there is nothing more unreasonable than to stir our passions upon that which falls not under our deliberation, as the most part of things to come are. What shall be to-morrow, what shall come of my estate, of my places, what event my projects and designs shall have,—this is not in my hand: these depend upon other men's wills, purposes, and actions, which are not in my power; and therefore, either to boast or glory upon that which depends upon the concurrence of so many causes unsubordinate to me, or to be vexed and disquieted upon the fore-apprehension of that which is not in my hand to prevent, is not only irreligious, as contrary to our Saviour's command, Matt. vi. 25. but unreasonable also, as that which even nature condemns. 'Take not thought for to-morrow;' and so by consequent, 'Boast not thyself of to-morrow;' and there is one argument from the vanity of such affections, 'Thou canst not make one hair black, nor add one cubit to thy stature,' &c. To what purpose, then, are either those vexations or gloriations, which cannot prevent evil, nor procure good? Why should our affections depend upon others' motions? This makes a man the greatest slave and captive, so that he hath not the dominion and power of himself. But the vanity of such affections is the more increased, if we consider that supreme eternal will, by which all these things are determined; and therefore, it is in vain for creatures to make themselves more miserable, or put themselves in a fool's paradise, which will produce more misery afterwards, and that, for those things which are bound up in that fatal chain of his eternal purpose. Then, in the next place, the folly of men appears from the inconstancy of these things. There is such an infinite variety of the accidents of providence, that it is folly for a man to presume to boast of any thing, or take complacency in it, because many things fall between the cup and the lip,† the chalice and the chin, as the proverb is. There is nothing certain, but that all things are uncertain,—that all things are subject to perpetual motion, revolution, and change,—to-day a city, to-morrow a heap. And there is nothing between a great city and a heap but one day; nothing between a man and no man but one hour. Our life is subject to infinite casualties; it may receive the fatal stroke from the meanest thing, and most unexpected; it is a bubble floating upon the water: for this world is a watery element, in continual motion with storms,

* [Much less.—Ed.]

† [This is a literal translation of a Greek proverb, which is quoted by Aulus Gellius, (Noct. Att. lib. xiii. cap. 17.) and which has been rendered into Latin thus:—*Multa cadunt inter calicem labrumque supremum.*—Ed.]

and in these, so many poor dying creatures rise up, and swim and float awhile, and are tossed up and down by the wind and wave; and the least puff of wind or drop of rain sends it back to its own element. We are a vapour appearing for a very little time—a creature of no solidity—a dream—a shadow and appearance of something; and this dream or apparition is but for a little time, and then it evanisheth, not so much into nothing, for it was little distant from nothing before, but it disappears rather. All human affairs are like the spokes of a wheel, in such a continual circumgiration, as a captive king, who was drawing Sesostris's chariot, said, when he was looking often behind him. The king of Egypt, Sesostris, demanded for what end did he look so often about him? Says he, "I am looking to the wheel, musing upon the vicissitudes and permutations of it, how the highest parts are instantly the lowest." And this word repressed the king's vain-glory.* Now, in this constant wheeling of outward things, which is the soul that enjoys true quiet and peace? Even that soul that is fixed, as it were, in the centre upon God, that hath its abode in him; though the parts without be in a continual violent motion, yet the centre of the wheel is at much peace, is not violently turned, but gently complies to the changes of the other. And then consider the madness of this,—'Thou knowest not,' &c. There are two reasons in the things themselves,—inconstancy, and independency on us; but this is as pressing as any,—our ignorance of them; they are wholly in the dark to us, as it were in the lower parts of the earth. As there is no more in our power but the present hour,—for to yesterday we are dead already, for it is past and cannot return, it is as it were buried in the grave of oblivion; and to to-morrow we are not yet born, for it is not come to the light, and we know not if ever it will come,—so there is no more in our knowledge but the present hour. The time past, though we remember it, yet it is without our practical knowledge, it admits of no reformation by it; and the time to come is not born to us, and it is all one as if we were not born to it. And indeed, in the Lord's disposing of all affairs under the sun, after this method, there is infinite wisdom and goodness both, though at the first view men would think it better that all things went on after an uniform manner, and that men knew what were to befall them. Yet, I say, God hath herein provided for his own glory and the good of men,—his own glory, while he hath reserved to himself the absolute dominion and perfect knowledge of his works, and exercises them in so great variety, that they may be seen to proceed from him; and for our good,—for what place were there for the exercise of many Christian virtues and graces, if it were not so? What place for patience, if there were no cross dispensations? What place for moderation, if there were no prosperity? If there were not such variety and vicissitude, how should the evenness and constancy of the spirit be known? Where should contentment and tranquillity of mind have place? For it is a calm in a storm properly, not a calm in a calm,—that is no virtue. If the several accidents of providence were foreseen by us, what a marvellous perturbation and disorder would it make in our duty! Who would do his duty out of conscience to God's command, to commit events to him? Now, there is the trial of obedience, to make us go by a way we know not, and resign ourselves to the all-seeing providence, whose eyes run to and fro throughout the earth. Therefore, that no grace may want matter and occasion of exercise; that no virtue may die out for want of fuel, or rust for lack of exercise, God hath thus ordered and disposed the world. There is no condition, no posture of

* [Diod. Sic. Bibl. lib. i. p. 68.

> Venit ad occasum, mundique extrema Sesostris,
> Et Pharios currus regum cervicibus egit.
>
> *Lucan.* lib. x. ver. 276.
>
> "The farthest west our great Sesostris saw,
> Whilst captive kings did his proud chariot draw."
>
> *May's Translation.*

Sesostris was so much affected and humbled, by the delicate appeal of the enslaved monarch, that he immediately commanded him, and the other unhappy kings who were harnessed to his car, to be removed from it.—Theophylact. Hist. Maurit. lib. vi. chap. ii. Joan. Tzetz. Hist. Chiliad. iii. 69.—Ed.]

affairs, in which he hath not left a fair opportunity for the exercising of some grace. Hath he shut up and precluded the acting of one or many through affliction, then surely he hath opened a wide door, and given large matter for self-denial, humility, patience, moderation; and these are as precious as any that look fairest. In a word, I think the very frame and method of the disposing of this material world speaks aloud to this purpose. You see, when you look below, there is nothing seen but the outside of the earth, the very surface of it only appears, and there your sight is terminated; but look above, and there is no termination, no bounding of the sight,—there are infinite spaces, all are transparent and clear without and within. Now, what may this present unto us? One says, it shows us that our affections should be set upon things above, and not on things below, seeing below there is nothing but an outward appearance and surface of things,—the glory and beauty of the earth is but skin deep; but heavenly things are alike throughout, all transparent; nothing to set bounds to the affections; they are infinite, and you may enlarge infinitely towards them. I add this other consideration, that God hath made all things in time dark and opaque, like the earth. Look to them, you see only the outside of them, the present hour, and what is beyond it you know no more, than you see the bowels of the earth; but eternity is both transparent and conspicuous throughout, and infinite too. Therefore God hath made us blind to the one, that we should not set our heart, nor terminate our eyes upon any thing here; but he hath opened and spread eternity before us in the scriptures, so that you may read and understand your fortune,—your everlasting estate in it. He hath shut up temporal things and sealed them, and wills us to live implicitly, and give him the trust of them without anxious foresight; but eternity he hath unveiled and opened unto us. Certain it is, that no man, till he be fully possessed of God, who is an all-sufficient good (Psal. iv.), can find any satisfaction in any present enjoyment, without the addition of some hope for the future. Great things without it will not content. For what is it all to a man if he have no assurance for the time to come? And mean things with it will content. Great things with little hope and expectation, fill with more vexation instead of joy; and the greater they be, this is the more increased. Again, mean and low things, with great hopes and large expectations, will give more satisfaction; therefore, all mankind have a look towards the morrow, and labour to supply their present defects and wants, with hope or confidence of that. I would exhort you who would indeed have solid matter of gloriation, and would not be befooled into a golden dream of vain expectations of vain things, that ye would labour to fill up the vacuities of present things with that great hope, the hope of salvation, which will be as an helmet to keep your head safe in all difficulties, 1 Pet. i. 3; Heb. vi. 18, 19; Rom. v. 5. It is true, other men's expectations of gain and credit, and such things, do in some measure abate the torment and pain of present wants and indigencies; but certain it is, that such hope is not so sovereign a cordial to the heart, as to expel all grief, but leaves much vexation within. But then also, the frequent disappointment of such projects and designs of gain, honour, and pleasure, and the extreme unanswerableness of these to the desires and hopes of the soul, even when attained, must needs breed infinitely more anxiety and vexation in the spirit, than the hope of them could give of satisfaction; yea, the more the expectation was, it cannot choose but the greater shame and confusion must be. Therefore, if you would have your souls truly established, and not hanging upon the morrow uncertainly, as the most part of men are, get a look beyond the morrow, unto that everlasting day of eternity, that hath no morrow * after it; and see what foundation you can lay up for that time to come, as Paul bids Timothy counsel the rich men in the world, who thought their riches and revenues, their offices and dignities, a foundation and well-spring of contentment to them and their children, and are ready to say with that man in the parable, 'Soul, take thy rest, thou hast enough laid up for many years!' 'Charge them,' says he, &c. 1 Tim. vi. 16—19. O a charge worthy to be engraven on the tables of our hearts, worthy to be written on the ports of all cities, and the gates of all palaces! You would all have a foundation of lasting joy, says he; but why seek you

* [See note † page 98.—Ed.]

lasting joy in fading things, and certain joy in uncertain riches, and solid contentment in empty things, and not rather in the living God, who is the unexhausted spring of all good things? Therefore, if you would truly boast of to-morrow, or sing a solid *requiem* to your own hearts, there is another treasure to be laid up in store against the time to come,—the time only worthy to be called time, that is eternity; and that is, study to do good, and be rich in good works, in works of piety, of mercy, of equity, of sobriety. This is a better foundation for the time to come; or, rather receive and embrace the promise of eternal life made to such,—that free and gracious promise of life in the gospel; and so you may supply all the wants and indigencies of your present enjoyments, with the precious hope of eternal life which cannot make ashamed. But what is the way that the most part of men take to mitigate and sweeten their present hardships? Even like that of the fool in the parable Luke xii.. They either have something laid up for many years, or else their projects and designs reach to many years. The truth is, they have more pleasure in the expectation of such things, than in the real possession; but that pleasure is but imaginary also. How many thoughts and designs are continually turning in the heart of man,—how to be rich, how to get greater gain, or more credit! Men build castles in the air, and fancy to themselves, as it were, new worlds of mere possible things; and in such an employment of the heart, there is some poor deceiving of present sorrows, but at length they recur with greater violence. Every man makes romances for himself, pretty fancies of his own fortune, as if he had the disposing of it himself. He sits down, as it were, and writes an almanack and prognostication in his own secret thoughts, and designs his own prosperity, gain, and advantage, and pleasures or joys; and when we have thus ranked our hopes and expectation, then we begin to take complacency in them, and boast ourselves in the confidence of them, as if there were not a supreme Lord who gives a law to our affairs, as immediately as to the winds and rains.

Now, that you may know the folly of this, consider the reason which is subjoined, —'For thou knowest not what a day may bring forth.' There is a concurrence of inconstancy in all things, and ignorance in us, which might be sufficient to check our folly of confident and presumptuous expectation from them, and gloriation in them; so that, whether we look about us to the things themselves, or within us to ourselves, all things proclaim the folly and madness of that which the heart of man is set upon. And this double consideration the apostle James opposes to the vain hopes and confident undertakings of men, chap. iv. 13, &c., which place is a perfect commentary upon this text: he brings in an instance of the resolutions and purposes of rich men, for the compassing of gain by merchandise, whereby you may understand all the several designs and plots of men, that are contrived and ordered, and laid down in the hearts of men, either for more gain, or more glory, or more pleasure and ease. Now, the grand evil that is here reproved, is not simply men's care and diligence in using lawful means for their accommodation in this life, or yet their wise and prudent foresight in ordering of their affairs for attaining that end, for both these are frequently recommended and commended by the wise man Prov. vi. 6, and xxiv. 27. But here is the great iniquity,—that men in all these contrivings and actings, carry themselves as if they were absolute independents, without consideration of the sovereign universal dominion of God. No man almost reflects upon that glorious Being, which alone hath the negative and definitive sentence in all the motions and affairs of the sons of men, or considers, that it is not in man that walks to direct his paths; that when all our thoughts and designs are marshalled and ordered, and the completest preparation made for reaching our intended ends, that yet the way of man is not in himself, that all these things are under a higher and more absolute dominion of the most high God. Whose heart doth that often sound unto,—'A man's heart deviseth his way, but the Lord directeth his steps;' and so is not bound by any rule to conform his executions to our intentions? For he works all according to the counsel of his own will, and not ours; and therefore, no wonder that the product of our actions does not answer our intentions and devices, because the supreme rule and measure of them is above our power, and without our knowledge. And therefore, though there were never so many devices in the heart of man, never so wisely or lawfully contrived and ordered; though the mine be never so well prepared, and all ready for the firing of it; yet 'the counsel of the Lord, that shall stand,' Prov. xix. 21, and xvi. 9. That higher determination may blow up our best consultations or drown them, for man's goings are of the Lord; how then can a man understand his paths? Prov. xx. 24. And yet the most part of men, in all these things, lose the remembrance of this fatal and invincible subordination to God, and propose their own affairs and actions, as if themselves were to dispose of them; and when their own resolutions and projects seem probable, they begin to please themselves in them, in the forethought of what they will do, or what they may have or enjoy to-morrow afterward: there is a present secret complacency and gloriation, without any serious reminding the absolute dependence of all things upon the will of God, and their independence upon our counsels without forecasting and often ruminating upon the perpetual fluctuation and inconstancy of human affairs; but, as if we were the supreme moderators in heaven and earth, so we act and transact our own business in a deep forgetfulness of him who sits in heaven, and laughs at all our projects and practices; and therefore, the Holy Ghost would have this secret but serious thought to season all our other purposes and consultations,—'If the Lord will,' &c. Whereas though we ought to say and think this, it is scarce minded; and then we know not what shall be to-morrow, for our life itself is a vapour. Herein is a strong argument,—you lay your designs for to-morrow, for a year, for many years, and yet ye know not if ye shall be to-morrow. How many men's projects are cast beyond that time that is measured out in God's counsel! And what a ridiculous thing must that be to him, if it be not done with submissive and humble dependence on him! In a word, time is with child of innumerable things, conceived by the eternal counsel of God. Infinite and inconceivably various are those conceptions which the womb of time shall at length bring forth to light. Every day, every hour, every minute is travailing in pain, as it were, and is delivered of some one birth or another; and no creature can open its womb sooner, or shut it longer, than the appointed and prefixed season. There is no miscarrying as to him whose decrees do properly conceive them, though to us they seem often abortive. Now, join unto this, to make the allusion full, as long as they are carried in the womb of time, they are hid from all the world. The womb is a dark lodging, and no understanding nor eye can pierce into it, to tell what is in it, till it break forth; and therefore, children born are said to come to the light: for till then, they are to us in a cloud of darkness, that we cannot tell what they are. So then, every day, every hour, every moment is about to bring forth that which all the world is ignorant of, till they see it; and oh! that then they understood it. We know not whether the morrow's or next hour's birth may be a proportioned child, or a monster; whether it will answer the figure and mould that is in our mind, or be misshapen and deformed to our sense. Men's desires and designs may be said to conceive, for they form an inward image and idea within themselves, to which they labour to make the product and birth of time conformable; and when it answers our preconceived form, then we rejoice as for a man-child. But for the most part it is a monster as to our conception; it is an aberration from our rule; it is either mutilated and defective of what we desire, or superfluous or deformed, which turns our expectation into vexation, and our boasting into lamentation. But the truth is, time brings forth no monsters as to the Lord's decrees, which are the only just measures of all things. It may be said of every thing under the sun, as David speaks of himself in the womb, 'My substance was not hid from thee, when I was made in secret, and curiously formed in the lowest parts of the earth,' &c. Psal. cxxxix. 15. His eyes see all their substance, yet being unperfect, and in his everlasting book all their members are written; the portraiture of every thing is drawn there to the life, and these in continuance are fashioned, just as they were written and drawn, and so they exactly correspond to his preconception of them; whatever deformity they may have as to us, yet they are perfect works, and beautiful to him.

Sermon VIII.

ISAIAH i. 10, 11, &c.—"*Hear the word of the Lord, ye rulers of Sodom; give ear unto the law of our God, ye people of Gomorrah,*" &c.

It is strange to think what mercy is mixed with the most wrath-like strokes and threatenings. There is no prophet whose office and commission is only for judgment; nay, to speak the truth, it is mercy that premises threatenings. The entering of the law, both in the commands and curses, is to make sin abound, that grace may superabound, so that both rods and threatenings are the messengers of Jesus Christ, to bring sinners to him for salvation. Every thing should be measured and named by its end; so, call threatenings promises, call rods and judgments mercies; name all good, and good to you, if so be you understand the purpose of God in these. The shortest preaching in the Bible useth to express itself what it means, though it be never so terrible. This is a sad and lamentable beginning of a prophet's ministry; the first word is, to the heavens and to the earth:* a weighty and horrible regrate† of this people, as if none of them were to hear, as if the earth could be more easily affected than they. The creatures are taken witnesses by God of their ingratitude, and then who shall speak for them? If heaven and earth be against them, who shall speak good of them? Will their own conscience? No certainly; it will, in the day of witnessing and judging, precipitate its sentence, and spare the judge the labour of probation; 'a man's enemy shall be within his own house,' though now your consciences agree with you. Nay, why doth the Lord speak to them? Because the people consider not, because consciences have given over speaking to them, therefore the Lord directs his word to the dumb earth. Yet how gracious is he, as to direct a second word even to the people, though a sad word? It is a complaint of iniquity and backsliding, and such as cannot be uttered; yet it is mercy to challenge them, yea, to chasten them. If the Lord would threaten a man with pure and unmixed judgments, if he would frame a threatening of a rod of pure justice, I think it should be this, 'I will no more reprove thee, nor chasten thee;' and he is not far from it, when he says, 'Why shall ye be stricken any more?' &c. ver. 5. As if he would say, It is in vain now to send a rod, ye receive no correction; I sent the rod, that it might open your hearts and ears to the word, and seal your instruction;—but to what purpose is it?—Ye grow worse and worse. Well, the prophet compares here sin and judgment, and the one far surmounts the other. Ye would think a desolate country, burnt cities, desolation made by strangers, a sufficient recompense of their corruption and misorders, of their forsaking and backsliding. Ye would think now, if your present condition and the land's pressed you to utter Jeremiah's lamentation, a sadder than which is not almost imaginable, ye would think, I say, that you had received double for all your sins. And yet, alas! how are your iniquities of infinite more desert? All that were mercy, which is behind infinite and eternal punishment. That there is room left for complaint, is mercy; that there is a remnant left, is mercy.

Now, to proclaim unto this people, and convince them that their judgment was not severe, he gives them one word from God. And, indeed, it is strange, that when the rod is sent, because of the despising of the word, that after the despising of both word and rod, another word should come. Always this word is a convincing word, a directing word, and a comforting word. These use to be conjoined, and if they be not always expressed, we may lawfully understand them. We may join a consolation to a conviction, and close a threatening with a promise, if we take with a threatening. Jonah's preaching expressed no more but a threatening and denunciation of judgment; but the people understood it according to God's meaning, and made it a rule of direction, and so a ground of consolation. How inexcusable are we, who have all these expressed unto us, and often inculcated, 'line upon line, and precept upon precept,' and yet so often

* ["Hear, O heavens, and give ear, O earth," ver. 2.—Ed.]
† [Regret, or accusation.—Ed.]

divide the word of truth, or neglect it altogether. Most part fancy a belief of the promises, and neither consider threatenings nor commands. Some believing the threatenings, are not so wise for their own salvation as to consider what God says more, but take it for his last word. Shall not Nineveh rise up in judgment against this generation? They repented at one preaching, and that a short one, and in appearance very defective; and yet we have many preachings of the Son of God and his apostles in this Bible,—both law and gospel holden forth distinctly, and these spoken daily in our audience, and yet we repent not.

This is a strange preface going before this preaching, and more strange in that it is before the first preaching of a young prophet. He speaks both to rulers and people, but he gives them a name, such as certainly they would not take to themselves; but seeing he is to speak the word of the Lord, he must not flatter them, as they did themselves. Is not this the Lord's people, his portion and inheritance which he chose out of the nations? Are not these rulers the princes of Judah, and the Lord's anointed? Were they not both in covenant with God, and separated from the nations both in privileges and profession? How then are they 'rulers of Sodom' and 'people of Gomorrah' likened to the worst of the nations, and not likened to them, but spoken of, as if they were indeed all one. When ye hear the preface, ye would think that the prophet was about to direct his speech to Sodom and Gomorrah; but when you look upon the preaching, ye find he means Judah and Jerusalem; and these are the rulers and people he speaks of. Certainly, according as men walk, so shall they be named and ranked. External privileges and profession may give a name before men, and separate men from men before the world, but they give no name, make no difference before God, if all other things be not suitable to these. 'He is not a Jew,' saith Paul, 'who is one outwardly,' but he who hath that circumcision in the heart, in the spirit, and not in the letter. Outward profession and signs may have praise of men, but it is this that hath praise of God, Rom. ii. 28, 29. Circumcision and uncircumcision, baptism or unbaptism, availeth nothing, but a new creature. A baptized Christian and an unbaptized Turk are alike before God, if their hearts and ways be one, Gal. vi. 15. All Christians profess faith, and glory in baptism, but it avails nothing except it work by love, Gal. v. 6.

Now, what name shall we give you? How shall our rulers be called? How shall ye, the people, be called? If we shall speak the truth, we fear it will instruct you not, but irritate you; yet the truth we must speak, whether ye choose or whether ye refuse. You would all be called Christians, the people of God; but we may not call you so, except we would flatter you, and deceive you by flattering, and murder you by deceiving. We would gladly name you Christians in the spirit, saints chosen and precious. O that we might speak so to rulers and people! but, alas, we may not call you so, except ye were so indeed; we may not call you Christians, lest ye believe yourselves to be so. And yet, alas, ye will think yourselves such, speak what we can. Would you know your name then? I perceive you listen to hear what it is. But understand, that it is your name before God, which bears his account of you. What matter of a name among men? It is often a shadow without substance, a name without the thing. If God name you otherwise, you shall have little either honour or comfort in it; when men bless you and praise you, if the Lord reckon you among the beasts that perish, are ye honoured indeed? Well, then, hear your name before God. What account hath he of you? Ye rulers are rulers of Sodom, and ye people are people are of Gomorrah. And if ye think this a hard saying, I desire you will notice the way that the prophet Isaiah takes to prove his challenge against them, and the same may be alleged against rulers and people now. We need no proof but one of both; see ver. 23,—'Thy princes are rebellious,' because, though they hear much against their sins, yet they never amend them, they pull away their shoulder; if they hear, yet they harden their heart. Is there any of them hath set to to pray in their families, though earnestly pressed? Well, what follows? 'Every one loves gifts.' Covetousness, then, and oppression proves rulers to be rulers of Sodom. Shall their houses stand, 'shalt thou reign, because thou closest thyself in cedar?' Jer. xxii. 15. No certainly; men shall one day take up a proverb against them. 'Woe to him that increaseth that which is not his,' and 'ladeth himself with thick clay: they shall be 'for booties' to the Lord's spoilers, Hab. ii. 6. Woe to them, for they have consulted shame to their houses, and sinned against their own soul. Their design is to establish their house, and make it eminent, but they take a compendious way to shame and ruin it. Alas, it is too public, that rulers seek their own things, for themselves and their friends; and for Jesus and his interests they are not concerned. But are ye, the people, any whit better? O that it were so! But alas, when ye are involved in the same guiltiness, I fear ye partake of their plagues! What are ye then? 'People of Gomorrah.' Is not the name of God blasphemed daily because of you? Are not the abominations of the Gentiles the common disease of the multitude, and the very reproach of Christianity? Set apart your public services and professions, and is there any thing behind in your conversation, but drunkenness, lying, swearing, contention, envy, deceit, wrath, covetousness, and such like? Have not the multitude of them been as civil, and carried themselves as blamelessly, and without offence, as the throng of our visible church? What have ye more than they? It is true, ye are called Christians, and ye boast in it. Ye know his will, and can speak of points of religion, can teach and instruct others, and so have, as it were, in your minds a form and method of knowledge,—the best of you are but such. But I ask, as Paul did the Jews in such a case, 'Thou that teachest another, teachest thou not thyself? Thou that makest a boast of the law, through breaking of it, dishonourest thou God?' Rom. ii. 17—23. Why then, certainly all thy profession and baptism avail nothing, and will never extract thee from the pagans, with whom thou art one in conversation. Thy profession is so far from helping thee in such a case, that it shall be the most bitter ingredient in thy cup of judgment, for it is the greatest aggravation of thy sin, for through it God's name is blasphemed. If they had not known, they had not had sin. Pagans' sin is no sin in respect of Christians. If ye consider Christ's sermon, Matt. xi., ye will say Isaiah is a meek and moderate man in regard of him. Isaiah calls them people of Gomorrah, but Christ will have them worse, and their judgment more intolerable than theirs. And that not only the profane of them, but the civil and religious-like who believe not in him. Well, then, here is the advantage ye get of your name of Christianity, of your privilege of hearing his word daily; ye who never ponder it, to tremble at it, or to rejoice in it, who cannot be moved either to joy or grief for spiritual things; neither law nor gospel moves the most part of you. I say, here is all your gain,—ye shall receive a reward with Gentiles and pagans; yea, ye shall be in a worse case than they in the day of the Lord. The civil Christian shall be worse than the profane Turk; and ye shall not then boast that ye were Christians, but shall desire that ye had dwelt in the place where the gospel had never been preached. It is a character of the nations, that they call not on God, and of heathen families, that they pray not to him, (Jer. x. 25,) and wrath must be poured on them. What, then, are the most part of you? Ye neither bow a knee in secret nor in your families, to God. Your time is otherwise employed; ye have no leisure to pray twice or thrice a-day alone, except when ye put on your clothes ye utter some ordinary babblings. Ye cannot be driven to family worship. Shall not God rank you in judgment with those heathen families? Or shall it not be more tolerable for them than for you? And are not the most part of you every one given to covetousness, your heart and eye after it, seeking gain and advantage more than the kingdom of heaven? Doth not every one of you, as you have power in your hand, oppress one another, and wrong one another? Now, our end in speaking thus to you, is not to drive you to desperation. No, indeed; but as there was a word of the Lord sent to such by Isaiah, so we bring a word unto you. That which ruins you, is your carnal confidence. Ye are presumptuous as this people, and cry, 'The temple of the Lord,' the work of the Lord, &c. as if these would save you. Know, therefore, that all these will never cover you in the day of wrath. Know there is a necessity to make peace with God, and your righteousness must exceed the righteousness of a profession, and external privileges and duties, or else ye shall be as far from the kingdom of heaven as Sodom and Gomorrah. We speak of rulers' sins, that ye may mourn for them, lest ye be judged with them. If ye do not mourn for them in secret, know that they are your sins, ye are companions with them. Many fret, grudge, and cry out against oppression, but who weeps in secret? Who prays and deprecates God's wrath, lest it come upon them? And while it is so, the oppression of rulers becomes the sin of the oppressed themselves.

'Hear the word of the Lord.' It were a suitable preparation for any word that is spoken, to make it take impression, if it were looked on 'as the word of the Lord,' and 'law of our God.' And truly no man can hear aright unless he hear it so. Why doth not this word of the Lord return with more fruit? Why do not men tremble or rejoice at it? Certainly, because it is not received as God's word. There is a practical heresy in our hearts, which rather may be called atheism—we do not believe the Scriptures. I do not say men call it in question; but I say, ye believe them not. It is one thing to believe with the heart, another thing not to doubt of it. Ye doubt not of it, not because ye do indeed believe it, but because ye do not at all consider it. It is one thing to confess with the mouth, and another thing to believe with the heart; for ye confess the Scriptures to be God's word, not because ye believe them, but because ye have received such a tradition from your fathers; have heard it from the womb unquestioned. O that this were engraven on your heart,—that these commands, these curses, these promises are divine truths, the words and the oath of the Holy One! If every word of truth came stamped with his authority, and were received in the name of God himself, what influence would it have on the spirits and the practices of men? This would be a great reformer, would reform more in a month, than church and state hath done these many years. Why are rulers and people not converted and healed for all that is spoken? Here it is, 'Who believes our report?' Who believes that our report is thy own testimony, O Lord? When ministers threaten you in God's name,—if his authority were stamped on the threatening, if men did seriously apprehend it were God's own voice, would they not tremble? When the gospel and the joyful sound comes forth, if he apprehended that same authority upon it, which ye who are convinced believe to be in the law, would ye not be comforted? Finally, I may say, it is this point of atheism, of inconsideration and brutishness, that destroys the multitude, makes all means ineffectual to them, and retards the progress of Christians. Men do not consider, that this word is the word of the eternal, and true, and faithful God, and that not one jot of it will fail. Here is a point of reformation I would put you to; if ye mind indeed to reform, let this enter into your hearts and sink down, that the law and gospel is the word of God, and resolve to come and hear preachings so, as the voice 'of Jesus Christ, the true and faithful witness.' If ye do not take it so now, yet God will judge you so at the end. 'He that despiseth you, despiseth me; and he that hears not you, hears not me.' If ye thought ye had to do with God every Sabbath, would ye come so carelessly, and be so stupid and inconsiderate before the Judge of all the earth? But ye will find in the end, that it was God whom ye knew not.

Sermon IV.

ISAIAH i. 11.—"*To what purpose is the multitude of your sacrifices unto me? saith the Lord,*" &c.

THIS is the word he calls them to hear, and a strange word. Isaiah asks, What mean your sacrifices? God will not have them. I think the people would say in their own hearts, What means the prophet? What would the Lord be at? Do we anything but what he commanded us? Is he angry at us for obeying him? What means this word? Is he not repealing the statute and ordinance he had made in Israel? If he had reproved us for breach of commands, for omission and neglect of sacrifices, we would have taken with it; but what means this reproof for well-doing? The Lord is a hard master. If we neglect sacrifices, and offer up the worst of the flock, he is angry; if we have a care of them, and offer them punctually, and keep appointed days precisely, he is angry. What shall we do to please him? I think many of you are put to as great a non-plus, when your prayers and repentance and fasting are quarrelled; do ye not say in your hearts, we know not what to do? Ministers are angry at us if we pray not, and our praying they cry out against; they command us to repent and fast, and yet say that God will abhor both these. This is a mystery, and we shall endeavour to unfold it to you from the word. It concerns us to know how God is pleased with our public services and fastings: for the most part of people have no more religion. Ye all, I know, desire to know what true religion is. Consult the Scriptures, and search them, for there ye shall find eternal life. We frame to ourselves a wrong pattern and copy of it, and so we judge ourselves wrong. Our narrow spirits do not take in the latitude of the Scripture's religion, but taking in one part we exclude another, and think God rigid if it be not taken off our hand so. But, I pray, consider these three things, which seem to make up the good old way, the religion of the Old and New Testaments:—

First, Religion takes in all the commands,—it is universal, hath respect to all the commandments, Psal. cxix. 6. It carries the two tables in both hands, the first table in the right hand, and the second in the left. These are so entirely conjoined, that if you receive not both, you cannot receive any truly.

Secondly, It takes in all the man, his soul and spirit as well as his body; nay, it principally includes that which is principal in the man, his soul and spirit, his mind and affections. If ye divide these, ye have not a man present but a body; and what fellowship can bodies have with him who is a Spirit? If ye divide these among themselves, ye have not a spirit indeed present: if the mind be not present, surely the heart cannot; but if the mind be, and the heart away, religion is not religion, but some empty speculation. The mind cannot serve but by the heart: where the heart is, there a man is reckoned to be.

Thirdly, It takes in Jesus Christ as all, and excludes altogether a man's self. He worships God in the spirit, but he rejoices not in himself, and in his spirit, but in Jesus Christ, and hath no confidence in himself, or the flesh, Phil. iii. 3, 8. It includes the soul and spirit, and all the commands, but it denies them all, and embraces Jesus Christ by faith, as the only object of glorying in and trusting in. All a man's self becomes dross in this consideration. Now, the first of these is drawn from the last, therefore it appears first—I say, an endeavour in walking in every thing commanded, of conforming our way to the present rule and pattern, is a stream flowing from the pure heart within. A man's soul and affections must once be purified, before it sends out such streams in conversation. And from whence doth that pure heart come? Is it the fountain and original? No certainly. The heart is desperately wicked above all things, and how will it cleanse itself? But this purity proceeds from another fountain,—from faith in Jesus Christ: and it is this that lies nearest the uncreated fountain, Christ himself; it is the most immediate conduit, the mouth of the fountain, or the bucket to draw out of the deep wells of salvation. All these are conjoined in this order, 1 Tim. i. 5.—'The end of the commandment is love.' Ye know love is said elsewhere to be the fulfilling of the law; and when we say love, we mean all duties to God and man, which love ought immediately to principle. Now this love proceeds from a pure heart, cleansed and sanctified, which pure heart proceeds from faith unfeigned. So then, we must go up in our searching from external obedience all alongst, till we arrive at the inward fountain of Christ dwelling in us by faith; and then have ye found true religion indeed. Now, ye may think possibly, we have used too much circumlocution: what is all this to the present purpose? Yes, very much. Ye shall find the Lord rejecting this people's public worship and solemn ordinances upon these three grounds,—either they did not join with them the observation of weightier commands, or they did not worship him in them with their spirits; had not souls present, or they knew not the end and use for which God had appointed these sacrifices and ceremonies; they did not see to the end of all, which was Jesus Christ.

First, then, I say, the people were much in external sacrifices and ceremonies, commanded of God, but they were ignorant of the end of his commands, and of the use of them. Ye know in themselves they had no goodness, but only in relation to such an end as he pleased they should lead to; but they stayed upon the ceremony and shadow, and were not led to use it as a means for such an end; and so, though they fancied that they obeyed, and pleased God, yet really they wholly perverted his meaning and intention in the command; therefore doth the Lord plead with them in this place for their sacrificing, as if it had been murder. They used to object his commands. What, says the Lord, did I command these things? Who required them? Meaning certainly, who required them for such an end, to take away your sin? Who required them but as a shadow of the substance to come? Who required them but as signs of that Lamb and sacrifice to be offered up in the fulness of time? And forasmuch as ye pass over all these, and think to please me with the external ceremony, was that ever my intent or meaning? Certainly ye have fancied a new law of your own, I never gave such a law; therefore it is said, Psal. l. 13.—God pleads just after this manner, 'Will I eat the flesh of bulls, or drink the blood of goats?' &c.; and Micah vi. 7, 'Will the Lord be pleased with thousands of rams, or with ten thousands of rivers of oil?' He who hath no pleasure in sinful men, what pleasure can he have in beasts? Therefore, it was to signify to them (who thought God would be pleased with them for their offering) that he could not endure them; it was worse to him to offer him such a recompense, than if they had done none at all. He is only well pleased in his well-beloved Son; and when they separate a lamb or a bullock from the well-beloved, what was it to him more than 'a dog's neck' or 'swine's flesh?' It was his creature, as these are, and no more, Isa. lxvi. 3. Now that they looked never beyond the ceremonies, is evident, because they boasted in them; they used to find out these as a remedy of their sins, and a mean to pacify God's wrath, Micah vi. 6. Paul bears witness of it, 2 Cor. iii. 13—15. Moses had a vail of ceremonies over his face, and the children of Israel could not steadfastly look to the end of that mystery, Christ Jesus, but their minds were blinded, and are so to this day in the reading of the scriptures; and this vail of hardness of heart shall be done away when Christ returns to them again. Now, I say, it is just so with us. There was never a people liker other than we are like the Jews. We have many external ordinances, preaching, hearing, baptism, communion, reading, singing, praying in public, extraordinary solemnities of fasting and thanksgiving, works of discipline and government, public reproof to sinners, confessions and absolutions. What would ye think if we should change the terms of sacrifices and new moons, and speak all this to you? To what purpose is the multitude of your fasts and feasts, of your preachings and communions, of your praying in secret, and in your families, of conference and prayer with others, of running to and fro to hear preaching, to partake of the Lord's table? I am full of them, I delight not in them. When ye come here on the Sabbath, who required at your hand to tread my courts? Come no more to hear the word, run no more after communions, seek no more baptism to your children, call no more solemn assemblies, it is all iniquity. O, say ye, that is a strange preaching indeed! Must we pray no more, hear no more, sing no more? Did not God command these? Why do ye discharge them? We do not mean so, that these should not be, but they should be in another way: all these want the soul and life of them, which is Jesus Christ in them. Do ye not think yourselves religious, because ye frequent these? The multitude of the people think that these please God, and pacify his wrath: ye have no other thing in your mind but these. If ye can attain any sorrow or grief for sin, or any tears to signify it, presently you absolve yourselves for your repentance. The scandalous who appear in public, think the paying of a penalty to the judge, and bowing the knee before the congregation,* satisfies God. Ye miss nothing when ye have these. I speak to the pro-

* [Agreeably to the course of discipline in former ages, (Hooker's Eccl. Pol. vol. iii. p. 15,) they who had been convicted of any gross crime were required by the First Book of Discipline, (chap. ix.) and by subsequent enactments of the Church of Scotland, to confess their sin in the hearing of the whole congregation. The same thing was required of delinquents by the canons of the Church of England. Dr. Grey, in his Impartial Examination of Neale's History of the Puritans, (App. pp. 62—68,) has, from original documents which were in his own possession, furnished us with various forms, according to which, towards the end of the sixteenth century, offenders were appointed to make their confession, in different parts of England, in their respective parish-churches. The fines which, in cases of scandal, were exacted by the ecclesiastical courts of Scotland, were imposed and defined by acts of parliament. Power to levy these was given to justices

fessors of religion also, who pretend to more knowledge than others, when ye have gone about so many duties, ye are well satisfied if ye get liberty in them. If ye can satisfy yourselves, ye doubt not of God's satisfaction; and if ye do not satisfy yourselves in your duties, ye cannot believe his satisfaction. Ye get the ordinance, and miss nothing. Now, I say, in all this ye do not reach to the end of this ministry, Jesus Christ; ye do not steadfastly behold him, to empty yourselves in his bosom, to turn over all the unrighteousness of your holy things upon him who bears it. That which pleaseth you, is not 'he in whom the Father is well-pleased,' but the measure of your own duty. O, the establishing of our own righteousness is the ruin of the visible Church! This is the grand idol, and all sacrifice to it. Know, therefore, that the most part of your performances are abomination and iniquity, because ye have so much confidence in them, and put them not upon Christ as filthy rags, or do not cover them with his righteousness, as well as your wickedness. I know ye will say, that ye are not satisfied with them, and that is still the matter of your exercise. Well, I affirm, in the Lord's name, from that ground, that ye have confidence in them, for if your diffidence and disquietness arise from it, your confidence and peace must come from it also. Is there any almost that maintain faith, except when their own conditions please them well? And that faith I may call no faith, at least not pure and cleanly entire faith. As for the multitude of you, you must know this, that God is not pleased with your prayers, and fasting, and hearing, &c. because ye have such an esteem of them, because ye can settle yourselves against all threatenings, and never once remember of Jesus Christ, or consider the end of his coming into the world; because ye find no necessity of pardon for your prayers and righteousness, but stretch the garment of these over the uncleanness of your practices. What delight hath the Lord in them, when they are put in his Son's place? Will he not be jealous that his Son's glory be not given to another?

In the *second* place, the Lord rejects their performances, because there was nothing but a mere shadow of service, and no worshipping of God in the Spirit. Ye know what Christ saith, 'God is a Spirit, and he that worships him must do it in spirit and in truth,' John iv. 24. It is the heart and soul that God delights in, 'My son, give me thy heart,' for if thou give not thy heart, I care for nothing else. The heart is the whole man. What a man's affection is, that he is. Light is not so,—it brings not the man alongst with it. Christ Jesus hath given himself for us, and he requires that we offer ourselves to him. If we offer a body to frequent his house, our feet to tread in his courts, our ears to hear his word, what cares he for it, as long as the soul doth not offer itself up in prayer or hearing? And this was the sin of this people, Isaiah xxix. 13. They draw near with the lips, and their heart is far from the Lord. Now are we not their children, and have succeeded to this? Is there any thing almost in our public services, but what is public? Is there any thing but what is seen of men? Ye come to hear, ye sit and hear, and is there any more? The most part have their minds wandering, no thoughts present; for your thoughts are removed about your barns and corns, or some business in your head; and if any have their thoughts present, yet where are affections, which are the soul and spirit of religion, without which it is no true fire but wild fire, if it be not both burning and shining? Are ye serious in these ordinances? Or rather, are ye not more serious in any thing beside? And now, especially, when God's providence calls you to earnest thoughts, when it cries to all

of the peace, who were frequently members of the kirk session, or parochial consistory of their district. In the year 1648, the General Assembly "recommended to every congregation, to make use of the 9th act of the parliament 1645, at Perth, for having magistrates and justices in every congregation." (Rec. of Kirk of Scot. p. 511, Edn. 1839.) It was in this way, it would seem, or from elders acting both in a civil and in an ecclesiastical capacity, that the practice of exacting fines by kirk sessions arose and was continued. "You object that our church sessions did exact fines. But if you consider, that these fines, which you mention, are particularly imposed and determined by statute, and thereby appointed to be applied to pious uses; and therefore the demanding and uplifting thereof only, as well for the more summary and effectual restraint of sin, as for the end whereto they are destined, is in use to be exercised by kirk sessions, or rather by their officers and beadles in deficiency of the magistrate, this your scruple must quickly cease." 'The True Non-Conformist,' p. 55, printed abroad in the year 1671.—ED.]

men to enter into consideration of their own ways, I pray you, is there any soul-affliction in your fasts even for a day? Is there any real grief or token of it? Not a fast in Scripture without weeping! We have kept many, and have never advanced so far. Shall the Lord then be pacified? Will not his soul abhor them? How shall they appease him for your other provocations, when they are as oil to the flame, to increase his indignation? The most part of Christians are guilty here; we come to the ordinances, as it were, to discharge a custom, and perform a ceremony, that we may have it to say to our conscience that it is done, and there is no more intent and purpose. We do not seek to have soul-communion with God. We come to sermon to hear some new thing, or new truth, or new fashion of it; to learn a notional experience of cases. But alas, this is not the great purpose and use of these things. It is to have some new sense of those things we know. We know already, but we should come to get the truth more received in our love, to serve God in our spirits, and to return to him ourselves in a sacrifice acceptable. This is the greater half, if not the whole of religion,—love to Jesus Christ who loved us, and living to him, because he died for us, and living to him because we love him. Now, all our ordinances and duties should be channels to carry our love to him, and occasions of venting our affections.

Thirdly, The Lord rejected this people's services, because they were exact and punctual in them, and neglected other parts of his commandments; and this is clearly expressed here, 'I will not hear' your prayers, though there be many of them. Why? 'Your hands are full of blood.' Ye come to worship me, and pray to me, and yet there are many abominations in your conversation, which you continue in, and do not challenge in yourselves. Ye have unclean hands; and shall your prayers be accepted, which should come up with pure hands? They took his covenant in their mouth, and offered many sacrifices, but what have ye to do with these things, saith the Lord, since ye hate to be reformed, since ye hate personal reformation of your lives, and in your families? What have ye to do to profess to be my people? Psal. l. 16, 17. The Lord requires an universality, if ye would prove sincerity: if ye have respect to any of his commands, as his commands, then will ye respect all. If ye be partial, and choose one duty that is easy, and refuse another harder,—will come to the church and hear, but will not pray at home,—will fast in public, but not in private,—then, says the Lord, ye do not at all obey me, but your own humour; ye do not at all fast unto me, but unto yourselves. As much as your interest lies in a duty, so much are ye carried to it. And I take this to be the reason why many are so eager in pursuing public ordinances, following communions, and conferences with God's people, ready to pray in public rather than alone. If ye would follow them into their secret chamber, how much indifferency is there! How great infrequency, how little fervency! Well, says the Lord, did ye pray to me when ye prayed among others? No, ye prayed either to yourselves, or the company, or both. Did ye seek me in a communion? No, saith the Lord, ye sought not me, but yourselves: if ye sought me indeed with others, you would be as earnest, if not more, to seek me alone, Zech. vii. 6. And again, the Lord especially requires the weightier matters of the law to be considered. As it was among the Jews, their ceremonies were commanded, and so good; but they were not so much good in themselves as because they were means appointed for another end and use. But the moral law was binding in itself, and good in itself, without relation to another thing; and therefore Christ lays this heavy charge to the Pharisees, 'Ye tithe mint and anise, Matt. xxiii. 23. 'Woe unto you, for ye neglect the weightier matters of the law, judgment, mercy, and faith: these ye ought to have done, and not left the other undone.' Are there not many who would think it a great fault to stay away from the church on the Sabbath or week day, and yet will not stick to swear,—to drink often? 'Woe unto you, for ye strain at a gnat, and swallow a camel;' therefore are the prophets full of these expostulations. The people seemed to make conscience of ceremonies and external ordinances, but they did not order their conversation aright; they did not execute judgment, and relieve the oppressed, did not walk soberly, did not mortify sinful lusts, &c. Alas, we deceive ourselves with the noise of a covenant,* and a cause of

* [See Note, page 375.—Ed.]

God; we cry it up as an antidote against all evils, use it as a charm, even as the Jews did their temple; and, in the mean time, we do not care how we walk before God, or with our neighbours: well, thus saith the Lord, 'Trust ye not in lying words,' &c. Jer. vii. 4, 5, 6. If drunkenness reign among you, if filthiness, swearing, oppression, cruelty reign among you, your covenant is but a lie, all your professions are but lying words, and shall never keep you in your inheritances and dwellings. The Lord tells you what he requires of you. Is it not to do justly, and walk humbly with God? Mic. vi. 7. This is that which the grace of God teaches, to deny 'ungodliness and worldly lusts,' and to 'live soberly, righteously, and godly,' towards your God, your neighbour, and yourself,' Tit. ii. 11, 12; and this he prefers to your public ordinances, your fasting, covenanting, preaching, and such like.* 'Is not this to know me?' saith the Lord, Jer. xxii 15, 16. You think you know God when you can discourse well of religion, and entertain conferences of practical cases. You think it is knowledge to understand preachings and scripture; but thus saith the Lord, to do justly to all men, to walk humbly towards God, to walk soberly in yourselves, is more real knowledge of God, than all the volumes of doctors contain, or the heads of professors. Is this knowledge of God to have a long flourishing discourse containing much religion in it? Alas, no! to do justly, to oppress none, to pray more in secret, to walk humbly and soberly, this is to know the Lord. Practice is real knowledge indeed: it argues, that what a man knows, he receives in love, that the truth hath a deep impression on the heart, that the light shines into the heart to inflame it. What is knowledge before God? As much as principles, affection, and action, as much as hath influence on your conversations; if you do not, and love not what you know, is that to know the Lord? Shall not your knowledge be a testimony against your practice, and no more?

Sermon X.

ISAIAH i. 16.—"*Wash you, make you clean, put away the evil of your doings from before mine eyes; cease to do evil,*" &c.

If we would have a sum of pure and undefiled religion, here it is set down in opposition to this people's shadow of religion, that consisted in external ordinances and rites. We think that God should be as well-pleased with our service as we ourselves, therefore we choose his commands which our humour hath no particular antipathy against and refuse others. But the Lord will not be so served: as he will not share with the world, and divide the soul and service of man with creatures, so as mammon should get part, and he his part. No, if we choose the one, we must refuse the other; for so will he not suffer his word and commands to be divided: there must be some universality in respect of the gospel and the law, and a conjunction of these two, or we cannot please him.

If religion do not include the gospel, we are yet upon the old covenant of works, according to which none can be justified. If it do not include the law in the hands of a mediator, then we turn the grace of God unto wantonness. If it shut out Jesus Christ and have no use of him, how can either we or our performances stand or be accepted before his holy eyes? If it exclude the law that Christ came to establish, how can he be pleased with our religion? both of these offer an indignity to the Son of God. The sum, then, of Christian religion is believing and sanctification of the Spirit unto obedience. That is the root and fountain, this is the fruit and stream; justification of our persons, and sanctification of our lives and hearts. This is pure religion and undefiled. And therefore Isaiah says, 'Wash you, make you clean,'—cleanse in the only true fountain of Christ's blood. It is not your purifications of the law, your many washings with water and hyssop; it is not the blood of bulls and of goats can purge your consciences from dead works: they

* [This passage is quoted in the Life of the Author.—ED.]

do but purify your flesh, but cannot wash your souls worse defiled. This blood of Jesus Christ is that clean water that he must sprinkle on you, if you would be clean. If you take any other water, any other righteousness but his, and wash thyself therewith, suppose it be snow water that washeth cleanest,—thy most exact conversation; yet, he will plunge thee in the mire, till thine own clothes abhor thee, Job ix. 30, 31. Now, when you have washed your persons, (ye need not, save to wash your feet, says Christ,)—your daily conversation, reform it in the virtue of that blood, for we are not called 'to uncleanness, but unto holiness;' and therefore, 'put away the evil of your doings,' &c. God hath put away the guilt of your doings by justification, now put ye away the evil of your doings by sanctification, &c. And if ye would know what sanctification is, 'cease to do evil;' do not return to the old puddle to wallow in it. Ye that are cleansed by this blood, O think how unbeseeming it is to you to defile yourselves again with those things ye are cleansed from! but now, 'learn to do well.' Ye are given up to Christ, ye must be his disciples, and he will teach you. 'Learn of me,' saith Christ, (ye need no other law almost but his example; he is a visible and speaking law,) yet 'seek judgment.' As ye ought to look on my example, so especially ponder that word and rule of practice and behaviour that I have left behind me, and given out as the lawgiver of the redeemed. Have I redeemed you; and should not I be the redeemed and ransomed one's king? Is there any society in the world wants a law, order, and government? Neither must ye who are delivered from bondage, enfranchised and made free indeed. Now, ye should of all men most live by a law. And when ye know that rule, then apply it to your several vocations and callings. Let the magistrate act according to it, and every man according to it. Religion consists not in a general notion, but condescends to our particular practice, to reform it. You see then what we would press upon your consciences. It is true religion that we would have you persuaded unto. All men have some kind of religion, even heathens who worship idols; but the true religion respects the true and living God. Now, what is it to worship the true and living God? What is the service of him that may be called religion indeed? Should we be the prescrivers of it?* No certainly, he must carve solely in that, or else it cannot please him; therefore 'to the law and to the testimony:' if ye speak not according to this, and worship not according to this word of God, 'it is because there is no light' in you. Ye may have a religion before men pure and undefiled, but if it be not so before God and the Father, I pray you to what purpose is it? I am sure it is all lost labour; nay, it is labour with loss, instead of gain. O that ye were persuaded to look and search the scriptures. Think ye to have eternal life out of them?—and think ye to have eternal life by them, who do not labour to know the way of it set down there? Every one of you hath a different model of religion, according to your fancies and breedings, according as your lusts will suffer you. The rule that the most part walk by is the course and example of the world. Is not this darkness, and gross darkness? Others model their duties according to their ability. They will do all they can do with ease, and without troubling themselves, and they think God may be well-pleased with that. I pray you consider and hear the word of the Lord, and law of your God. Hath he set down here the rule and perfect pattern of true religion, and will ye never so much own it, as to examine yours according to it? The scriptures are the touchstone; if you would not have a counterfeit religion deceiving you in the end, when ye have trusted to it, I pray you try it by the word of God. Oh! that this principle were once sunk into your hearts,—I may not walk at random; if I please myself, and satisfy my own will, if that be not also God's will, I shall have neither gain nor comfort of it. His will is manifested in his word,—I will search and find what God hath required of me; for if I be not certain of his will, I may be doing all my days, and sweating out my life, and yet lose my pains and toil. I say, this word of the Lord that Isaiah calls to the people to hear, ver. 10, will at length judge you. Your religion will be tried in the day of accounts according to it, not according to your rules and methods

* [That is, the persons who prescribe or appoint it.—Ed.]

ye have prescribed unto yourselves. Now, if ye in the meantime shall judge yourselves, according to another rule, and absolve yourselves, and in the end God shall judge you according to this word, and condemn you, were ye not fools in neglecting this word?

The whole will of God concerning your duty may be summed up in two; John hath one of them, 1 John iii. 23, 'And this is his commandment, that we should believe on the name of his Son Jesus Christ, and love one another, as he gave us commandment;' and Paul hath another to the Thessalonians, 1 Thess. iv. 3, 'This is the will of God, even your sanctification.' And these two make up this text, so that it unites both gospel and law. The commandment of the law comes forth, and it is found that we have broken and are guilty, that we cannot answer for one of a thousand. The law entering makes sin abound. Our inability, yea, impossibility of obedience is more discovered. Well, then, the gospel proclaims the Lord Jesus Christ for the Saviour of sinners, and commands us, under pain of damnation, to believe in him,—to cast our souls on him, as one able to save, as one who hath obeyed the law for us; so that this command of believing in Christ is answerable to all the breaches of the law, and tends to make them up in Christ. When he proclaimed the law on mount Sinai, with terror, that which ye hear expressed is not his first commandment, which ye are in the first instance to obey, for all these we have broken; but it hath a gospel command in its bosom, it leads to Jesus Christ; and if ye could read the mind of God in it, ye would resolve all these commands which condemn you and curse you, into one command of believing in the Son, that ye may be saved from that condemnation. And if ye obey this command, which is his last command, and most peremptory, then are the breaches of all the rest made up, the intent of all the rest is fulfilled, though not in your obedience, yet in Christ's, which is better than ours. Believing in Christ presents God with a perfect righteousness, with an obedience even to the death of the cross. When a sinner hears the holy and spiritual sense of the law, and sees it in the light of God's holiness, O how vile must he appear to himself, and how must he abhor himself! What original pollution, what actual pollution, what a fountain within, what uncleanness in streams without, will discover itself! Now, when the most part of men get any sight of this, presently they fall a-washing and cleansing themselves, or hiding their filthiness. And what water take they? Their own tears and sorrows, their own resolutions, their own reformations. But alas, we are still more plunged in our own filthiness; that is still marked before him, because all that is as foul as that we would have washen away. What garment do men take to hide themselves ordinarily? Is it not their own righteousness? Is it not a skirt of some duty that is spread over transgressions? Do not men think their sins hid, if they can mourn and pray for a time? Their consciences are eased by reflection upon this. But alas, thine iniquity is still marked! Shall filthiness hide filthiness? Thy righteousness is as a vile garment, as a menstruous cloth, (Isa. lxiv. 6,) as well as thine unrighteousness; how then shall it cover thine nakedness? Seeing it is so then, what is the Lord's mind concerning our cleansing? Seeing stretched out hands and many prayers will not do it, what shall I do? The Lord hath showed thee what thou shalt do; and that is, that thou do nothing in relation to that end, that thou shouldst undertake to wash away the least spot by all thy repentance. Yet must thou wash and make clean, and the water is brought new unto you, even the blood of Jesus Christ that cleanseth from all sin. Wash in this blood, and ye shall be clean. And what is it to wash in this blood? It is to believe in Christ Jesus, to lay hold on the all-sufficient virtue of it, to trust our souls to it, as a sufficient ransom for all our sins; to spread the covering of Christ's righteousness over all our righteousness and unrighteousness, as having both alike need to be hid from his holy eyes. Jesus Christ 'came by water and by blood,' (1 John v. 6;) by water to sanctify, and by blood to justify; by the power and cleansing virtue of the Holy Ghost, to take away sin in the being of it; and by the virtue of his blood, to take away sin in the guilt and condemnation of it.

Now, I conceive he presses a twofold exercise upon them in this washing, and both have relation to the blood of Jesus Christ; to wit, repentance and faith If they be not all one, yet they are in this point inseparably conjoined. Repentance waters and saps the roots of believing, which otherwise would dry up; therefore, instead of outward forms and ceremonies of religion, he presseth them to inward sorrow and contrition of heart for sin, that they might present an acceptable sacrifice to God, 'a contrite heart.' This is more pleasing than many specious duties of men without, Psal. l. 7, &c. But when I press upon you repentance, do not conceive that we would have it preparatory to faith, that ye should sit down and mourn for your sins for a time, till your hearts be so far humbled, and then ye might come as prepared and fitted to Jesus Christ. This is the mistake of many Christians, which keeps them from solid settling. We find it ordinary, souls making scruples and objections against coming to Jesus Christ, because of want of such preparations, of measures of humiliation and contrition, which they prescribe to themselves, or do behold in others. And so they sit down and apply themselves to such a work, apply their consciences to the law and curse; and they find, instead of softening hardness, instead of contrition of spirit, more dulness and security; at least they cannot get satisfaction to themselves in that they seek, and thus they hang their head over their impenitent hearts, and lament, not so much that repentance is not, as that they cannot find it in themselves. Alas! there are many diseases in this one malady. If it were embowelled unto you, ye would not believe that such a way were so contradictory to the gospel. For, first, ye who are so, have this principle in your hearts, which is the foundation of it: I cannot come to Christ so unclean, I must be a little washen ere I come, the most gross uncleanness and hardness of my heart must be taken away, and so I shall be accepted. Alas, what derogation is this to the blessed Saviour! What absurdity is it! I am too unclean to come to the fountain, I must be a little purged before I come to this fountain that cleanseth from all sin. I pray you, why was the fountain opened? Was it not for sin and uncleanness? And this thou sayest by interpretation, if I were so and so humbled, then I might come, and be worthy to come; when the want of such a measure debars thee as unworthy, doth not the having of it in thy estimation make thee worthy? And so ye come with a present in your hand to Jesus Christ, with a price and reward to him who gives freely. Again, thou deniest Christ to be the only fountain of all grace, and so it is most dishonourable to him. If thou would have repentance before thou come to him, where shalt thou have it? Wilt thou find it in thy heart, which is desperately wicked? Wilt thou seek it of God, and not seek it in the mediator Jesus Christ? God out of a mediator will not hear thee. In a word, there is both extreme sin and extreme folly in this way: great sin, because it contradicts the tenor of the gospel, it dishonours the Lord Jesus, the exalted Prince, as if he were not the fountain of all grace; it is contrary both to the freedom of his grace, and to the fulness of it also. It is great folly; for thou leavest the living fountain, and goest seeking water in a wilderness; thou leavest the garden where all herbs grow, and wanderest abroad to the wild mountains; and because thou canst not find what thou seekest, thou sittest down and weepest beside it. Repentance is in Christ, and no repentance so pleasing to God as the mournings and relentings of a pardoned sinner; but thou seekest it far from him, yea, refusest him for want of that which thou mayest have by choosing him. Therefore we declare this unto you, that whatever ye be, whatever ye want, if ye think ye stand in need of Jesus Christ, embrace him. If ye be exceeding vile in your own eyes, and cannot get repentance as ye would to cleanse yourselves, here is the fountain opened, and ready to wash in. Yet this we must tell you, that no sinner can believe but he that repents,* not because repentance is required as a preparation to give a man a war-

* [" The longer I live in the world the less fond am I of that divinity that stand upon quirks and subtilties. What should drive us upon determining whether faith or repentance goes first? What valuable ends or purposes in religion can it serve to promote? What edification can it give to an audience to dispute learnedly about a point of this nature? . . . I cannot but heartily approve what Mr. Robert Blair, an eminent light of this church now in glory, said upon the question in hand. He told his people from the pulpit, that it was a very needless one. 'Tis just (said he,) as if you should ask me, when we are to walk, which foot should we lift first. If we should walk to purpose we must make use of both limbs; and so despatched the thorny question. I wish we may all imitate the wisdom of that great and good man. Is it not sufficient for us to declare that both are necessary, without determining the nice point of priority and posteriority?" (Essay on Gospel and Legal Preaching, by a Minister of the Church of Scotland, pp. 22, 23. Edin. 1723.) "Mr.

rant and right to believe,—I know no ground of faith but our necessity, and the Lord's promise and command unto us,—but because no soul can truly fly into Jesus Christ to escape sin's guilt, but he that desires to be delivered from sin itself; and therefore the most part of you fancy a faith which you have not, because there is no possibility that men will come out of themselves, till they be pressed out by discovered sin and misery within. Your woulds and wishes after Christ and salvation, that many of you have, are not the real exercises of your soul's flying unto him for salvation. If ye did indeed turn into Jesus Christ, your hearts would turn the back upon sin, and these sins ye seek remission of. Now, all the desire that many men have of Christ, is this,—I would fain have his salvation, if I might keep my sin; I would gladly be delivered from the guilt of sin, if he would let me keep still the sin. But will Christ make any such bargain?

If this blood only wash from sin, O how many lie in their sins, and wallow in their filthiness! 'There is a generation pure in their own eyes, and yet are not washed from their filthiness,' Prov. xxx. 12. O that ye believed this! If ye be not now washed, eternity shall find you unclean, and woe to the soul that enters eternity with all the pollution of its sins: can such a soul enter into the high and holy place, the clean city? No, certainly; it must be without among the dogs and swine, it must be kept in darkness for ever. It is, then, of great importance that ye be washen from your filthiness. Now, I ask you, is it so or not? Are ye made clean and washen from the guilt of your sins? Every one of you almost will say so and think so; and yet says the scripture, 'There is a generation pure in their own eyes, and yet are not washed.' Is there a generation such? Is there any such? Oh! then, think it is possible you may be mistaken in the opinion of your own cleanness. Do any conceive themselves pardoned, and yet are not so? Think it is possible you may have deceived yourselves, especially since ye have never examined it. But are there so many so, a whole generation,—the most part of men? Then, as you love your souls, try, for it is certain that the most part of you must be deceived. Is there a generation in the visible church not washen, and yet every one thinks himself clean? Then certainly the most part are in a great delusion. Will ye then once examine whether or not ye be deluded with them? It shall be your peace to know it, while it may be amended. But how comes it to pass, that so many hearing of the gospel, and lying near this fountain, are not cleansed? I think certainly, because they will not have a thorough cleansing, they get none at all. All men would love Christ's blood well to pardon sin, but who will accept of the water to sanctify them from sin? But Christ came with both. Shall this blood be spent upon numbers of you, who have no respect to it, but would still wallow in your filthiness? Would ye have God pardoning these sins ye never throughly resolved to quit? But how is it that so many men are clean in their own eyes, and yet not washed? I think indeed, the reason of it is, they make a kind of washing, which they apprehend sufficient, and yet know not the true fountain. We find men taking much soap and nitre, when convinced of sin, or charged with it, and thereupon soon absolving themselves. If ye ask their grounds, they will tell you, they repent and are sorry for it; they purpose to make amends, and they think amendment a good compensation for the past wrong. They will, it may be, vow to drink no more for a year after they have been drunk; they will confess their sin in public, and all this they do without having any thought of Jesus Christ, or the end of his coming, and can absolve themselves from such grounds, though in the mean time

Robert Blair, born in Irvine, was first a Regent in the College of Glasgow, at which time he was licensed to preach the gospel, and was from the beginning zealous for truth and piety." (Livingston's Memorable Characteristics, p. 73.) Mr. Blair died in 1666 in the 73d year of his age. (See Memoirs of the Life of Mr. Robert Blair, the first part written by himself, p. 128, Edin. 1754.) Mr. James Durham, Minister of the High Church of Glasgow, a short time before his death, intrusted to him the publication of his "Dying Man's Testament to the Church of Scotland, or a Treatise concerning Scandal," to which Mr. Blair wrote a preface. Principal Baillie gives this account of Blair, "Truly, I bear that man record that in all his English vogages, in many passages of the Assembly, private and public, he contributed as much to the pacifying of our differences as any, and much more than many." Journals and Letters, vol. i. p. 306.—Ed.]

Christ come not so much as in their mind; and therefore are they not really washed. All thy righteousness is unclean before God, and thy repentances defile thee; and yet because of some such duties, thou deceivest thyself, and art clean in thine own eyes. These have some beauty in thy eyes, and thou puttest them between thy filthiness and thy eye, and so conceivest that thou art clean. I think a reason also, why many men are clean in their own eyes, and conceive that God hath pardoned their sin, is because they have forgotten it. It is not recent in their memory, and makes no present wound in their conscience; and therefore, they apprehend God such as themselves,—they think he hath forgotten it also. But oh! how terrible shall it be, when God brings to remembrance, and sets our sins in order before us! Ye think God cares not for your sins, that he forgives them, because he is silent at them, Psal. l. 21. But the Lord shall one day set them before thee, and thou shalt know they were still marked before him.

Ye who have washen in this blood, ye may rejoice, for it shall make you clean every whit. Your iniquities that so defiled you, shall not be found. O the precious virtue of that blood that can purge away a soul's spots! All the art of men and angels could not reach this. This redemption and cleansing was precious, and would have ceased for ever; but this blood is the ransom, this blood cleanseth, and so perfectly, that it shall not appear, not only to men's eyes, but also God's piercing eye. Sinners, quit your own righteousness,—why defile ye yourselves more? When your eyes are opened, ye will find it so. Here is washing; apply yourselves to this fountain; and if ye do indeed so; if ye expect cleansing from Jesus Christ, I pray you return not to the puddle. Ye are not washen from sin, to sin more, and defile yourselves more; if ye think ye have liberty to do so, ye have no part in this blood.

Sermon IX.

ISAIAH i. 16.—"*Wash you, make you clean; put away the evil of your doings from before mine eyes; cease to do evil,*" &c.

THERE are two evils in sin,—one is the nature of it, another the fruit and sad effect of it. In itself it is filthiness, and contrary to God's holiness; an abasing of the immortal soul; a spot in the face of the Lord of the creatures, that hath far debased him under them all. Though it be so unnatural to us, yet it is now in our fallen estate become, as it were, natural, so that men agree with it, as if it were sunk and drunk into the very soul of man. The other is the guilt and desert of punishment and obligation to it. All men hate this, but they cannot hold it off. They eat the tree and fruit of death, they must eat death also: they must have the wages of sin, who have wrought for it. Now, the gospel hath found a remedy for lost man in Jesus Christ; he comes in the gospel with a twofold blessing, a twofold virtue, a pardoning virtue and a sanctifying virtue, 'water and blood,' 1 John v. 6. He comes to forgive sin, and to subdue sin; to remove the guilt of it, and then the self* of it. God's appointment had inseparably joined them; and Christ came not to dissolve the law, but to establish it. If he had taken away the punishment, and left the sin in its being, he had weakened the law and the prophets. That conjunction of sin and wrath, which is both by divine appointment, and suitable also unto their own natures, must stand, that divine justice may be entire; and therefore, he that comes to redeem us from the curse of the law, hath also this commission, to redeem from sin and all transgressions of the law, Rom. xi. 26, and Gal. iii. 13. He that turns away the wrath of God from men, turns also ungodliness from them which provoked his wrath; and so he is a complete redeemer, and a complete redeemer he had not been otherwise. If he had removed wrath only, and left us under the bondage of sin, it had not been half redemption; 'he that commits sin, is the servant of sin.' But this is perfect freedom and liberty, to be made free from sin, for it was sin that subjected us to wrath, and so was the first tyrant and the greatest. The

* [Or, sin itself.—ED.]

gospel then comes with a joyful sound unto you, but many of you mistake it, and apprehend it to be a doctrine of liberty and peace, and that unto sin; but if it were so, it were no joyful sound. If there were proclaimed a liberty to all men to do as they list, no punishment, no wrath to be feared, I would think that doctrine no glad news, it were but the perpetuating of the bondage of a reasonable soul. But this is glad news,—a delivery and freedom proclaimed in the gospel. From what? Not unto sin, but from sin; and this is to be free indeed. We owe more to Jesus Christ for this, than for redemption from wrath, because sin is a greater evil than wrath; yea, wrath were not so, if sin were not. Therefore he exhorts to wash, and wash so that they may make clean. Take Jesus Christ for justification and sanctification,—employ both the water and the blood that he hath come with. But because all men pretend a willingness to have Christ their Saviour, and their sins pardoned through his blood, who, notwithstanding, hate to be reformed, and would seek no more of Christ: therefore, he branches out that part of the exhortation in several particulars. All men have a general liking of remission of sins, but renouncing of it is to many a hard doctrine. They would be glad that God put their evils out of his sight, by passing them by, and forgetting them; but they will not be at the pains of putting away their evils from his sight; and therefore, the gospel which comprehends these two united, is not really received by many, who pretend to be followers of it. This is his command, that ye believe. Some pretend to obey this, and yet have no regard of that other part of his will, even their sanctification; and therefore their faith is dead, it is a fancy. If ye did indeed believe and receive Christ for pardon of sin, it were not possible but your souls would be engaged and constrained to endeavour to walk in all well-pleasing. But it is an evident token of one that is not washed from his sin, and believes not in Christ, if he conceive within his heart a greater latitude and liberty to walk after the flesh, and be emboldened to continue in sin, because of his grace and mercy; and yet such are the most part of you. Upon what ground do you delay repentance? Upon what presumption do ye continue in your sins, and put over the serious study of holiness, till a more fit time? Is it not from an apprehension of the grace and mercy of God, that ye think ye may return any time and be accepted, and so ye may in the meantime take as much pleasure in sin as you can, seeing ye may get leave also for God's mercy? I pray you consider, that you have never apprehended God's mercy aright, ye are yet in your sins, and certainly as yet are not washed from them.

'Put away the evil,' &c. When the Spirit convinces a soul, he convinces a man not only of evil doings but of the evil of his doings; not only of sin, but of the sinfulness of sin; and not only of those actions which are in themselves sinful, but also of the iniquity of holy things. I think no man will come to wash in Christ's blood, till this be discovered. If he see much wickedness, many evil doings, yet he will labour to wash away these by his own tears, and repentance, and well-doing. As long as he hath any good actions, as prayers, fasting, and such like, he will cover his evil doings by them; he will spread the skirts of such righteousness over his uncleanness; and when he hath hid it from his own eyes, he apprehends that he hath hid it from God's also. He will wash his bloody hands with many prayers, and thinks they may be clean enough. We see blasphemers of God's name use to join a prayer for forgiveness with their oath and curse, and they never trouble themselves more. O what mocking of God is this! Now, as long as it is thus, there is no employment for the Son of God's blood; they can do their own turn. Men will not come to Christ, because it is the best way, if they see any else beside. None will come till they see it is the only way; none can wash in Christ, except they wash all. If ye have any thing that needs not washing, his blood is not for you; his righteousness is not known, when ye establish all, or a part of your own. I fear the most part of you have no employment for Christ; ye have extreme need of him, but ye know it not, for there are many things which ye will not number among your sins,—your prayers, you hearing, reading, singing, public and private worship, giving alms, &c. How many of you were never convinced of any sin in these! Do ye not conceive God is well-pleased with you for them? Your conscience hath convinced you, it may be, of gross sins, as drunkenness, filthiness, swearing, &c. But ye are not convinced for your well-doing; ye find not a necessity of a Mediator for these. I think many of you never confessed any such thing, except in a general notion. Alas, how ignorant are men of themselves! We are unclean; how can any thing we do cleanse us? Are not we unclean; and do not our hands touch our own works? Shall not then our own uncleanness defile our good actions, more than they can cleanse us? Hag. ii. 13. The ignorance of this makes men go about to build up their old ruined righteousness, and still seek something in themselves, to make up wants in themselves. Always, when the light of God hath discovered you to yourselves, so that ye can turn your eye nowhere, but uncleanness fills it; though your conversation be blameless in the world, so as men can challenge nothing, yet ye have found within and without nothing, but matter of mourning; I say, this is an evidence that the Spirit hath shined and enlightened thy darkness. Now, when thou hast fled unto Jesus Christ for a covering to thy righteousness, as well as unrighteousness, it remains that thou now put away the evil of thy doings;—put not away thy doings, but the evil of them. We challenge your prayers, services, and public duties, even as the prophet did; we declare unto you that God is as ill pleased with them, as your drunkenness, whoring, intemperance, &c. The most part of you are no more acceptable when ye come to the church, than when ye go to the tavern,—your praying and cursing is almost all one. What shall we do then, say ye? Shall we pray no more, and hear no more? No, say I, put not away your prayers and ordinances, but put away the evil of them from before his sight. Rather multiply your doings, but destroy the evil and iniquity of your doings. And there is one evil or two above all, that makes them hateful to him: ye trust too much in them. Here is the iniquity, the idol of jealousy set up: ye make your doings your righteousness, and in that notion they are abomination. There is nothing makes your worship of God so hateful as this; ye think so much of it, and justify yourself by it; and then God knows what it is that ye so magnify, and make the ground of your claim to salvation. It is even an empty ceremony, a shadow without substance, a body without a soul. You speak and look and hear, you exercise some outward senses but no inward affection; and what should that be to him, who is a Spirit?

They did not observe the iniquity of their holy things; and therefore are they marked by him,—they are in his sight. They did not see so many faults in their prayers and services; they wondered why God did chide them so much; but God marks what we miss, he remembers when we forget. We cover ourselves with a vail of external duties, and think to hide all the rottenness of our hearts, but it will not be hid from him, before whom hell hath no covering. All hearts are open and naked before him. Your secret sins are in the light of his countenance. Men hear you pray, see you present at worship, they know no more, at least they see no more: nay, but the formality of thy worship, the wanderings of thy mind are in his sight. And, O how excellent a rule of walking were this, to do all in his sight and presence! O that ye were persuaded in your hearts of his all-seeing, all-searching eye, and all-knowing mind! Would ye not be more solicitous and anxious anent the frame of your hearts, than the liberty of your speech or external gesture? O how would men retire within themselves, to fashion their spirits before this all-searching and all-knowing Spirit! If ye do not observe the evils of your hearts and ways, they are in his sight, and this will spoil all acceptance of the good of them. If ye observe the evils of your well-doing, and bring these also to the fountain to wash them, and be about this earnest endeavour of perfecting holiness, of perfecting well-doings in the power and fear of God; then certainly he will not set your sins in the light of his countenance, the good of your way shall come before him, and the evil of it Christ shall take away.

'Cease to do evil,' &c. These are the two legs a Christian walks on; if he want any of them, he is lame and cannot go equally,—ceasing from evil, and doing good; nay, they are so united, that the one cannot subsist without the other. If a man do not cease from evil and his former lusts, he cannot do well, or perfect holiness. There are many different dispositions and conditions of men; there are generally one of two. Some have a kind of abstinence from many gross sins, and are called civil honest men,—they can abide an inquest and censure of all their neighbours, they can say no ill of them. But alas, there is as little good to be said: he drinks not, swears not, whores not, steals not. Nay, but what doth he well? Alas, the world cannot tell what he doth, for he prays not in secret, nor in his family,—he is void of some offences towards men; but there are many duties called to, towards both God and men, he is a stranger to. He oppresses not the poor; nay, but he is not charitable either to give to them; he defrauds no man, but whom helps he by his means? Again, there are others, they will boast of some things done; they pray, the keep they church well, they do many good turns, and yet for all that, they do not cease to do evil. They were drunkards, so they are; they can swear for all their prayers, are given to contention, to lying, to filthiness, &c. Now, I say, neither of these religions is pure and undefiled. Religion is a thorough and entire change; it is like a new creation, that must destroy the first subject, to get place for that which is to come. It is a putting off old garments, to put on new; the putting off an old form and engraven image, to make place for a new engraving. Men do not put a seal above a seal, but deface the old, and so put on the new; men do not put new clothes upon the old, but put the old off, and so they have place for the new. Religion must have a naked man. Godliness is a new suit, that will not go on upon so many lusts; no, no, it is more meet and more conformed unto the inwards of the soul than so. The cold must go out as the heat comes in. Many men do not change their garments, but mend them, put some new pieces unto them. They retain their old lusts, their heart idols, and they will add unto these a patch of some external obedience; but alas, is this godliness? Hypocrisy will be content of a mixture,—sin is the harlot, whose heart could endure to see the child parted. It can give God a part, to get leave to brook the most part; sin will give God liberty to take some of the outward man, if it keep the heart and soul. But God will not reckon on these terms, he will have all the man or nothing, for he is the righteous owner. True godliness cannot mix so, but false and counterfeit may do it well. Other men, again, possibly unclothe themselves of some practices, but they put on new clothing; they reform some passages for fear of censure, or shame, or such like. They are found, it may be, blameless, either because so educated, or their disposition is against particular gross sins; but they are not clothed upon with holiness and well-doing, and so they are but naked and bare in God's sight, not beautiful. They have swept their house, and some devil put out or kept out; but because the good Spirit enters not, ordinarily seven worse enter again into such men.

There is a great moment* of persuasion in this order of the exhortation, 'Wash you,' and then, 'put away the evil of your doings,' and 'cease to do evil.' Do not continue in your former customs. It is strange, how contrary our hearts are to God; we use to turn grace unto wantonness; we use to take more liberty to sin, when we conceive we are pardoned. But I do not know any more strong and constraining persuasion to forsake sin, than the consideration of the forgiving of it might yield. O what an inducement and grand argument to renouncing of evils, is the consideration of the remission of them! This is even that ye are now called unto, who have fled to Jesus to escape wrath: what should ye be taken up with, in all the world, but this,—to live to him henceforth, who died for us,—to forsake our own old way, and that from the constraining principle of love to him, 2 Cor. v. 14, 15. O that ye would enforce your own hearts with such a thought, when there are any solicitations to sin, to former lusts! Should I, that am dead to sin, live any longer therein? Rom. vi. 2. Should I, who am washed from such pollutions, return again to the pullutions of the world? Should I again defile myself, who am cleansed by so precious blood, and forget him that washed me? Should I return with the dog to the vomit, and with the sow to the puddle? God forbid. I pray you consider. If you be Christians indeed, give a proof of it. What hath Jesus Christ done for you? He hath given himself, his own precious blood, a ransom for us, will ye not give up yourselves to him? Will not ye give him your sins and lusts, which are not yourself, but enemies to yourself? Will not ye put away these ills, that he came into this world to destroy? Art thou a Christian, and are there yet so many sins, and works of the devil reigning in thee, and set up in God's sight?

* [That is, *power* of persuasion.—Ed.]

What an inconsistency is this! If thou be his follower, thou must put these away. Give them a bill of divorcement, never to turn again. Many a man parts with his sin, because it leaves him, he puts it not away; temptation goes, and occasion goes away, but the root of it abides within him. Many men have particular jars with their corruptions, but they reconcile again, as differences between married persons; They do not arise* to hate their sin in its sinful nature. But if thou hate it, then put it away. And who would not hate that which Christ so hated, that he came to destroy it? 1 John iii. 5. What a great indignity must it be to the gospel, to make that the ground of living in sin, which is pressed, in it, as the grand persuasion to forsake it? Seeing we are washed from the guilt of it, O let us not love to keep the stain and filth of it! Why are we washen? Was it not Christ's great intendment and purpose, to purify to himself a holy people? We are washen from the guilt of our sins, and is it to defile again? Is it not rather to keep ourselves henceforth clean, that we may be presented holy and unblameable in his sight,—that we may seek to be as like heaven as may be. But who ceases to do these evils, that he says are pardoned? Who puts away the evil of these doings, the guilt whereof he thinks God hath put away? Could ye find in your hearts to entertain those evils so familiarly, to pour out your souls unto them, if that peace of God were indeed spoken unto you? Would not the reflex of his love prove more constraining on your hearts? Were it possible, that if ye did indeed consider, that your lusts cost Christ a dear price to shed his blood, that your pleasures made his soul heavy to death, and that he hath laid down his life to ransom you from hell; were it possible, I say, that ye would live still in these lusts, and choose these pleasures of sin, which were so bitter to our Lord Jesus? I beseech you be not deceived, —if ye love the puddle still, that ye cannot live out of it, do not say that ye are washed. Ye may have washen yourselves with soap and nitre, but the blood of Christ hath not cleansed: for, if that blood sprinkled your conscience once, to give you an answer to all challenges, it could not but send forth streams to purify the heart, and so the whole man. The blood and water might be joined, the justifying Saviour, and the sanctifying Spirit; for both these are in this gospel-washing, 1 Cor. vi. 11; 1 John v. 6. 'This is he that came by water and blood, even Jesus Christ; not by water only, but by water and blood.' Not by water only, but by blood also, and I say, not by blood only, but by water also. The very purpose of forgiveness is not to lay a foundation for more sin, but that men may sin no more, but break off their sins. It is indeed impossible for a man to amend his ways, till he be pardoned, for his sin stands betwixt him and God. God is a consuming fire—the guilt of it hinders all meeting of the soul with God, at least all influence from him. But when an open door is made in Christ, that men may come and treat with God, notwithstanding of rebellions, and have the curse relaxed, O how may he go about his duty comfortably! Am I escaped from hell, why should I any more walk in the way to it? And now he hath the Spirit given for the asking. There are some cessations from sin, that are not real forsakings of it, and ceasings from it. You know men will abstain from eating for a season, that they may be made ripe for it at another time. Some do not cease from sin, but delay it only; they put it not away, but put it off only for another time, till a fitter occasion and opportunity. And this is so far from ceasing from it, that it is rather a deliberate choice of it, and election of conveniency for it. There may be some pure and simple ceasings from sin, mere abstinence, or rather mere absence of sin for a season, that is not ceasing from doing evil. The Christian's ceasing hath much action in it. It is such a ceasing from doing evil, that it is a putting away of evil; it hath a soul and spirit joined in that cessation. Sin requires violence to put it out where it hath haunted,—it is an intruding guest, and a usurping guest. It comes in first as a supplicant and beggar, prays for a little lodging for a night, and promises to be gone. The temptation speaks but for a little time, even the present time, for a little one,—it seeks but little at first, lest it be denied; but if once it be received into the soul, it presently becomes master, and can command its own time, and its abode. Then ye will not so easily put it out as ye could hold it out, for it is now joined with that wicked,

* [This is the word in the first Edition. It would seem to have been substituted for *arrive* —Ed.]

desperate party within you, the heart, and these united forces are too strong for you. According as a lust is one with a man's heart, or hath nearer connection with his heart and soul, it is the worse to put away: for, will ye drive a man from himself? It is the cutting off a right hand, or plucking out of a right eye. To make a man cease from such evils, requires that a stronger power be within him than is in the world. Men may cease for a time, for want of occasions or temptations to sin; when there is no active principle in them, restraining or keeping their souls from such sins as appear after, when no sooner is occasion offered, but they run as the horse to his course, or the stone falleth downward,—they receive fire as easily as dry stubble. That is not Christian ceasing, which is that which the soul argues itself into, from grounds of the gospel. Should I, who am dead to sin, live any longer therein? This is a principle of cessation, and this is true liberty,—when the soul can abstain from present temptations upon such grounds and persuasions of the gospel; then it is really above itself and above the world, then hath it that true victory. Many men cease only from sin, because sin ceases from them; they have not left it, but it hath left them. The old man thinks himself a changed man, because he wallows not in the lusts of the flesh, as in his youth. But, alas! no thanks to him for that, he hath not ceased from his lusts. But temptations to him, or power and ability in him to follow them hath ceased,—there is no change in his spirit within, for he can talk of his former sins with pleasure, he continues in other evils as bad, but more suitable to his age. In a word, he is so inwardly, that if he were in his body, and occasions offering as before, he would be just the same. Some, again, cease from some evils, from some principles, but, alas! they are no Christian principles. What restrains the multitude of civilians from gross scandals? Is it any thing but affectation of a good name and report in the world? Is it not fear of reproach or censure? Is it not because possibly they have no particular inclination to such evils? And yet there are many other evils of the heart as evil though more subtile, that they please themselves in, as pride, covetousness, malice, envy, ambition, &c. What shall all your abstinence be accounted of, when it is not love to Jesus Christ, or hatred of sin, that principles it? It is not the outward abstinence that will commend you: such it is, as the principles of it are. And these only are the true Christian principles of mortification,—love of Jesus Christ, which constrains men to live no more to themselves, but to be new creatures, 2 Cor. v. 14, 15; and hatred of sin in its nature as sin: a Christian should have a mortal hatred of it, as his mortal enemy. It is not Christianity to abstain from some fleshly lusts, if ye consider them not as your soul's enemies, 1 Peter ii. 11. 'Ye that love the Lord hate evil,' Psal. xcvii. 10. These are chained together. David's hatred was a soul-hatred, an abhorrency, Psal. cxix. 163, 'I hate and abhor lying.' It is like the natural antipathies that are among creatures: the soul hates not only the person of it, but the nature of it also. Men often hate sin, only as it is circumstantiate; but Christian hatred is a hatred of the nature, like the deadly feuds, which are enmities against the kind and name. 'I will put enmity between thy seed,' &c. It is a 'perfect hatred,' Psal. cxxxix. 22. And so it cannot endure any sin, because all is contrary to God's holiness and offensive to his Spirit. I would think it easier to forsake all evil, and cease from doing any evil, I mean, presumptuously, with a willing mind and endeavour, than indeed to forsake one; for as long as ye entertain so many lusts like it, they shall make way for it. It were easier to keep the whole commandments in an evangelical sense, than indeed to keep any one, for all of them help another, and subsist they cannot one without another, so that ye take a foolish course, who go about particular reformations. Ye scandalous sinners profess that ye will amend the particular fault ye are guilty of, and, in the mean time, you take no heed to your souls and lives; therefore it shall be either in vain, or not acceptable. How pleasant a life would Christians have, if they would indeed be persuaded to be altogether Christians! The halving of it neither pleaseth God nor delights you; it keeps you but in continual torment between God and Baal. Your own lusts usurp over you, and that of Christ in you challenges the supremacy; so ye are as men under two masters, each striving for the place, and were it not better to be under one settled government? If there be any tenderness of God in your hearts, or light in your consciences, they cannot but testify against your lusts, these strange lords. Your lusts, again, they drive you on against your conscience; thus ye are divided and tormented betwixt two,—your own conscience and affections. You have thus the pain of religion, and know not the true pleasure of it. You are marred in the pleasures of sin, conscience and the love of God is a worm to eat that gourd. It is gall and vinegar mixed in with them. Were it not more wisdom to be either one thing or another? If ye will have the pleasures of sin for a season, take them wholly, and renounce God, and see if your heart can endure that. If your heart cannot condescend to that, I pray you renounce them wholly, and ye shall find more exquisite and sure pleasures in godliness, at his right hand. O what a noble entertainment hath the soul in God; the peace and joy of the Holy Ghost is a kingdom indeed!

Sermon XII.

ISAIAH xxvi. 3.—"*Thou shalt keep him in perfect peace, whose mind is stayed on thee, because he trusteth in thee.*"

ALL men love to have privileges above others. Every one is upon the design and search after some well-being, since Adam lost that which was true happiness. We all agree upon the general notion of it, but presently men divide in the following of particulars. Here all men are united in seeking after some good; something to satisfy their souls, and satiate their desires. Nay, but they scatter presently in the prosecution of it, because, according to every man's fancy and corrupt humour, they attribute that good unto diverse things; and when they meet with disappointment, they change their opinion of that, but are made no wiser, for they turn from one to another of that same kind, in which their imagination hath supposed blessedness to be; and therefore they will return to that which they first loathed and rejected. Is there, then, no such thing in the world as blessedness? Is it not to be found among men? Are all men's insatiable desires in vain? Is a creature made up and composed of desires, to keep it in continual torment and vexation of spirit? No certainly, it is, and it is found by some. All the world strives about it, but the man only who trusts and believes in God, he it is, who carries it away from them,—who hath this privilege beyond the world. And why do so many miss it? Because they do not see or suspect that it is blessedness indeed which he enjoys; but, on the contrary, their corrupted imaginations represent godliness, and a godly man's self-indigency and dependence on God, as the greatest misery and shame. The godly man hides not his blessedness from the world; no, he proclaims it when he hath found it,—he would that all enjoyed it with him. And if there were no more to declare that it doth not consist in worldly things, this might suffice—they are not communicable to many, without the prejudice and loss of every one. But none will believe his report of his own estate.

If ye would consider, here is that which men toil for,—compass sea and land for; here it is; 'near thee in thy mouth.' It is not in heaven, that thou shouldst say, How shall I ascend to it? It is not in hell below, that thou shouldst say, Who shall descend? It is not in the ends of the earth. No. It is 'near thee, in thy mouth.' It is not beyond the sea, but it is 'near thee in thy mouth, even the word of faith,' which Christ preached, Rom. x. 6—8. And what says that word? Believe with thy heart, and thou shalt be saved; trust in God, and depend on him, and ye shall have peace, and that perfect peace; and this peace shall be kept by God himself. 'Blessed, then, is the man that trusts in the Lord,' Psal. xl. 4. Ye make a long journey in vain; ye spend your labour and money in vain; all the pains might be saved: it is not where ye seek it. Ye travel about many creatures; ye go to many doors, and inquire for happiness and peace, but ye go too far off; ye need not search so many coasts, it is nearer hand, in this word of the gospel—the joyful sound; it is this that proclaims peace. Peace is a comprehensive word, especially in scripture. It was the Jews' salutation, 'Peace be to you;' meaning happiness and all good things; it is Christ's salutation, 'Grace and peace.' Grace is holiness, peace is happiness, and these are either one, or inseparably conjoined as one. This was the angels' song, 'Glory to God, peace on earth,' Luke ii. 14. Blessedness was restored, or brought near to be restored, to miserable man, by Jesus Christ; and upon the apprehension of this, angels sing. It was this Christ came into the world with; and when he went away, he left this legacy to his children, 'My peace I leave you,' John xiv. 27. We lost happiness, and all men are on a vain pursuit of it since, but it is found, and found by one of our kin. Our Lord Jesus, our elder brother, he hath found it, or made it, and brought it near us in the gospel for the receiving; and whoso receives him by faith, and trusts in him, receives that privilege, that peace. He endured much trouble to gain our peace; he behoved to undergo misery to purchase our blessedness, and so it is his own, and whoso receives him receives it also.

The news of such a peace might be seasonable in the time of war and trouble, if we apprehended our need of it. It is not a peace from war and trouble, but a peace in war and trouble. 'My peace I leave with you,' and 'in the world ye shall have trouble,' John xiv. 27, and xvi. at the end. What a blessed message is it, that there is a peace, and a perfect peace attainable in the midst of wars, confusions, and calamities of the times, public and personal; a perfect peace, a complete peace, even complete without the accession of outward and worldly peace, that needs it not; nay, appears most perfect and entire in itself, when it is stripped naked of them all. Behold what a privilege the gospel offers unto you! ye need not be made miserable, but* if you please. This is more than all the world can afford you. There is no man can promise to himself immunity from public or personal dangers, from many griefs and disappointments; but the gospel bids you reckon up all your troubles and miseries that you can meet with in the world; and yet in such a case, if ye hearken to wisdom, there is a peace that will make you forget that trouble, 'Her ways are ways of pleasantness, and all her paths are peace,' Prov. iii. 17. I will undertake to make thee blessed, says wisdom, the Father's wisdom. When all the world hath given thee over for miserable; when thou hast spent thy substance on the physicians, and in vain, come to me, I can heal that desperate disease by a word. 'I create peace,' when natural causes have given it over; I create it of nothing; I will keep you 'in perfect peace.'

You have then here, three things of special concernment in these times; and all times, a blessedness, a perfect peace attainable, the way of it, and the fountain of it. The fountain of it, the preserver of it, is God himself; the way to attain it, is 'trusting in God, and staying on him.' This sweetness of peace is in God the tree of life. Faith puts to its hand, and plucks the fruit of the tree; hope and dependence on God is a kind of tasting of that fruit and eating of it; and then followeth this perfect peace, as the delightful relish and sweetness that the soul finds in God, upon tasting how gracious he is. God himself is the life of our souls, the fountain of living-waters, the life and light of men. Faith and trusting in God, draws out of this fountain,—out of this deep well of salvation; and staying on God, drinks of it, till the soul be refreshed with peace and tranquillity, such as passeth natural understanding. Christ Jesus is the tree of life, that grows in the garden of God; trusting in him by faith implants a soul in him,—roots a soul in him, by virtue of which union, it springs up and grows into a living branch; by staying and depending upon him, we live by him, and hence springs this blessed and sweet fruit of peace of soul and conscience, which grows upon the confidence of the soul placed in God, as the stalk by which it is united to the tree. Trusting and staying upon God is the soul's casting its anchor upon him in the midst of the waves and storms of sin, wrath, and trouble. The poor beaten sinner casts an anchor within the vail, on that sure ground of immutable promises in Jesus Christ; and then it rests and quiets itself at that anchor, enjoys peace in the midst of the storm,—there is a great calm, it is not moved, or not greatly moved, as if it were a fair day. David flieth unto God as his refuge, anchors upon the name of the Lord, Psal. lxii. 1, 2; and so

* [That is, unless you please.—ED.]

he enjoys a perfect calm and tranquillity. 'I shall not be moved;' because he is united to the rock, he is tied to the firm foundation, Jesus Christ, and no storm can dissolve this union; not because of the strength of that rope of faith, it is but a weak cord, if omnipotency did not compass it about also; and so we 'are kept by the power of God, through faith unto salvation.' The poor wearied traveller, the pilgrim, sits down under the shadow of a rock, and this peace is his rest under it. Faith lays him down, and peace is his rest and sleep. Faith in Jesus Christ is a motion towards him, as the soul's proper place and centre; and therefore it is called a coming to him,—flying to him as the city of refuge. It is the soul's flight out of itself, and misery and sin within, to apprehend mercy and grace, and happiness in Christ. Now, hope is the conjunction or union of the soul with him,—the soul then staying and resting on him, as in its proper place, and so it enjoys perfect peace and rest in its place; so that if ye remove it thence, then ye offer violence to it.

These two things are of greatest importance to you to know; what this perfect peace is, and what is the way to attain it. The one is the privilege and dignity, the other is the duty of a Christian, and these two make him up what he is.

I would think that man perfectly blessed, who is at peace with two things,—God and himself. If a man be at peace with creatures without him, and be at peace with himself, but have war within his own mind, that man's peace is no peace, let be perfect peace. A man's greatest enemy is within his own house. And within indeed, when it is in his bosom and soul: when a man's conscience is against him, it is worse than a world beside. *Conscientia mille testes*,* so I say, it is *mille hostes*. It is 'a thousand witnesses,' and 'a thousand enemies.' It were better to endure condemnation of any judge, of many judges in the world, than to sustain the conviction of a man's own conscience: when it accuseth, who shall excuse? John viii. 9; Rom. ii. 15. 'A merry spirit,' saith Solomon, 'is a continual feast,' Prov. xv. 15. And what must a heart be, which hath such a gnawing worm within it, as an accusing conscience, to eat it out? This is the worm of hell that dies not out, which makes hell hell indeed. This indeed will be a painful consumption, 'A broken spirit drieth up the bones,' it will eat up the marrow of the spirit and body, Prov. xvii. 22. What infirmity is there which a man cannot bear? Poverty, famine, war, pestilence, sickness, name what you will; but a wounded spirit who can bear? Prov. xviii. 14. And there is reason for it, for there is none to bear it: a sound and whole spirit can sustain infirmities, but when that is wounded, which should bear all the rest, what is behind to bear it? It is a burden to itself. If a man have trouble and war in this world, yet there is often escaping from it; a man may fly from his enemy, but when thy enemy is within thee, whither shalt thou fly? Thou canst not go from thyself; thou carriest about thee thy enemy, thy tormentor.

But suppose a man were at peace within himself, and cried peace, peace, to himself; yet if he be not at peace with God, shall his peace be called peace? Shall it not rather be named supine security? If a man be at variance with himself, and his soul disquieted within, there is more fear than danger if he be at peace with God. It is but a false alarm, that shall end well; but if he have peace in his own bosom, and yet no agreement with God, then destructions are certainly coming, his dream of peace will have a terrible wakening. A man may sleep soundly, and his enemies round about him, because he knoweth not of it; but he is in a worse estate than he that is in great fear, and his enemies either none, or far distant. The one hath present danger, and no fear, the other present fear, and no danger; and which of these think ye best? Sudden destruction awakes the one from sleep, Ezek. vii. 25. Their fear and destruction come both at once, when it is now in vain to fear, because it is past hope, Prov. i. 27. Therefore the Lord swears, that 'there is no peace to the wicked,' Isa. xlviii. 22. What! Do not they often cry peace to themselves, and put the evil day far off? No men are so without bands in life and death as they; they have made agreement with hell and death, and their own consciences; yet for all that, 'thus saith the Lord, there is no peace to the wicked.'

* [A proverb, which signifies that conscience does not deceive, and that its testimony is as overwhelming as that of a thousand witnesses.—*Quintil. Inst. Orator.* lib. v. chap. xi.—Ed.]

If God be against us, what is the matter who be with us; for he can make a man's friends his enemies, and he can make a man's enemies to be at peace with him: He makes peace and creates trouble, Isa. xlv. 7. Men can but destroy the body, but he can destroy both body and soul for ever. O what a potent and everlasting enemy is he! There is no escaping from his all-seeing eye and powerful hand, Psal. cxxxix. 7, 8. A man may fly from men, but whither shall he fly from His presence? To heaven?—He is there. To hell?—He is there. The darkness of the night hath been a covering under which many have escaped, and been saved in armies; but darkness is no covering to him, it is all one with light. He is near hand every one of us. The conscience is within us, but he is within the conscience; and how much God is above the creature, so great and dreadful a party is he above any enemy imaginable. Therefore I conclude, that that man only hath perfect peace, who is at peace with God, and with his own conscience. If a man be at peace with God, and not with himself, he wants but a moment's time of perfect peace; for, ere it be long, the God of it will speak peace unto him. But if he be at peace with God and himself, I know not what he wants of the perfect peace, of the 'peace, peace:' for it is a man's mind that makes peace or war, it is not outward things; but in the midst of peace he may be in trouble, and in the midst of trouble in peace, according as he hath satisfaction and contentment in his own breast: for what is all the grace of a Christian? It is godliness with contentment; it is not godliness and riches, godliness and honour, or pleasure, godliness and outward peace. No, no; contentment compenseth all these, and hath in it eminently all the gain and advantage of these. A man in honour, a rich man, having no contentment in it, is really as poor, as ignominious, as the poor and despised man. If contentment then be without these things, certainly they cannot be missed; for where contentment is not with them, it only is missed, and they not considered. Contentment is all the gain that men seek in riches, and honour, and pleasure; if a godly man have that same without them, he then hath all the gain and advantage, and wants nothing, but some trouble that ordinarily attends them. Outward peace cannot add to inward peace, and so the want of it cannot diminish.

We must begin at the original, if we would know rightly this peace that passeth knowledge. The fountain-head is peace with God; a stream of this is peace of conscience, and peace with the creatures. There is a peace of friendship, when persons were never enemies; and there is a peace of reconciliation, when parties at variance are made one. Innocent Adam had peace once with God as a friend,—angels continue so to this day; but now there is no such peace between men and God, for all are become enemies to God, and aliens from the commonwealth of Israel: that peace was broken by rebellion against God his maker, and all the posterity are born with the same enmity against God. On our part are hearts desperately wicked, whose imagination is only evil continually. On God's part is holy and spotless justice, that is of purer eyes than to behold iniquity, and therefore must destroy it or the sinner. On our part are so many rebellions,—Adam's actual transgression, and all our own sins and breaches of the holy law, as so many breaches of peace. On God's part are so many curses answerable to the breaches of the law: 'cursed is every one that abideth not in every thing,' &c. This curse is even the proclamation of men to be traitors, and an intimation of the righteous judgment which will come upon them. Adam was in a covenant of peace with God,—'Do, and thou shalt live; if not, thou shalt die.' Adam brake this covenant, so the peace is dissolved, and God is no more obliged to give life, but to execute the pain contained in the covenant; and in sign and token of this, look how Adam fled from God's presence, to hide himself when he heard his voice: it was a poor shift, for whither should he go from his presence? But, alas! seeking more wisdom, he lost that he had; seeking divine wisdom, he lost human. Now, there is no more making up this peace on such terms again; we have no capacity to treat with God any more; but blessed be his Majesty, who hath found out the way of agreement and reconciliation. O that ye were once persuaded of your enmity against God! ye are not born friends, though ye be born within the visible church. How dreadful a thing is it, to have the Most High and terrible God against you, to do to you according to your deservings! Ye all know this, we are enemies to God by nature; I pray you, is it but a name? Is it not worthy deep consideration? But who considereth this matter? If ye lose a friend, ye will be troubled, and the more behoveful your friend was, the more troubled you will be. If a great and potent nation proclaimed war against us, we cannot but be sensible of it; but alas! who considereth the great breach that is between God and all men, occasioned by the first man's transgression and rebellion! It is one of the degrees of health, to know the disease, and I may call it a degree of peace, a kind of preparation to peace, to know the enmity, and not generally to know it, but to ponder it till the heart be affected with it; to call a council of all the faculties and affections of the soul, to consider the great imminent danger of man's commonwealth. What is it, I pray you, that is the greatest obstruction of men's making peace with God, that makes the breach irreparable, and the wound incurable? It is this, certainly; no man apprehendeth it aright: we entertain good thoughts of our friendship with God, or that it is easy to be reconciled. Who seeth such a wide breach between God and man, that all the merits of angels and men could not make it up? Who seeth the price of redemption so precious, as it must cease for ever, for all that men and angels can do? Is not every man offering God satisfaction, either his tears, or sorrow, or amendment in time coming, or all of them? Do not men undertake to pacify God with external ordinances, and think it may suffice for their sins? Certainly ye are ignorant of the infinite separation between God and man, who imagine a treaty with him yourselves, or that ever ye can come unto speaking terms; and therefore is this war and enmity perpetual; therefore there is no peace, when ye cry, Peace, peace! When ye have peace within you, and say that ye have peace with God; yet certainly, the Lord thy God is against thee, and will not spare thee, Deut. xxix. 19. Many of you bless yourselves in your own hearts; when ye hear the curse and threatening of the law, ye say, God forbid that all that were true. Well, thus saith the Lord, All these curses that are written in this book shall lie upon thee, and the Lord shall separate thee unto evil, because ye take not with your enmity; there can be no treaty, a mediator can have no employment from you.

How shall the breach of peace be made up? Since the first covenant cannot be made up again, where shall the remedy be found? God is just and righteous, men are rebellious and sinful; can these meet, and the one not be consumed? Will not God be a consuming fire, and men as stubble before the Lord's presence? Therefore, there must be a Mediator between them, a peace-maker, to make of two one, to take up the difference. And this Mediator must be like both, and yet neither wholly the one nor the other. He must therefore be God and man, that he may be a fit day's-man betwixt God and man; and this is our Lord Jesus Christ. In his divinity he comes near to God, in his humanity he comes near to man: in his person he is between both, and he is fit to make peace; and therefore he is 'a Prince of peace,' Isa. ix. 6. And that he may be a Prince of peace, he must be both, 'an everlasting Father' like God, and a young child like unto man: God to prevail with God, and a man to engage for man; and therefore he is called 'our Peace,' Eph. ii. 14. Our Lord Jesus Christ enters into a covenant with the Father, wherein he undertakes to bear our curse, and the chastisement of our peace. He is content to be dealt with as the rebel, 'Upon me, upon me be the iniquity;' and so there comes an interruption, as it were, of that blessed peace he had with the Father. He is content that there should be a covering of wrath spread over the Father's love, that he should handle the Son as an enemy; and therefore it is, that sinners are admitted as friends,—his obedience takes away our rebellion. The cloud of the Lord's displeasure pours down upon him, that it might be fair weather to us; the armies of curses that were against us, encounter him, and he, by being overcome, overcometh; by being slain by justice, Satan and sin, overcometh all those, and killeth the enmity on the cross, making peace by his blood, Col. ii. 14, 15; Eph. ii. 15. And it is this sacrifice that hath pacified heaven,—the sweet smell of it hath gone above, and made peace in the high places.

Here, then, is the privilege of a believer,—to be at peace with God, to be one with him; and this indeed is life eternal, to be united unto the fountain of life, in whose favour is life, and whose loving-kindness is better than life. Is not this a blessed estate? Whatever a man hath done against God is all forgiven and forgotten, it shall never come into remembrance. Are not angels blessed who are friends with God? Such is the soul whose sins are pardoned through Christ,—its sins are as if they never had been. The soul is not only escaped that terrible wrath of God, but being at peace with God, all the goodness that is communicable to creatures, it shall partake of, 'that they may be one, as we are one, that they may be perfect in one,' John xvii. This Christ prayed for, and this was the end of his death,—to make of two one. So, then, the glory that Christ is partaker of with the Father, we must be partakers of with him, and all this by virtue of that peace with God by him. O if ye knew what enmity with God is! how would it endear and make precious peace with him! The one engageth all that is in God to be against a man; the other engageth all that is in him to be for a man. And is not he then a great one, whether he be a friend or an enemy; is he not the best friend and worst enemy, who hath most power, yea, all power, to employ for whom he will, and against whom he will? What a blessed change is it, to have God, of a consuming fire, made a sun, with healing and consolation! that the righteous, holy, and just God, before whom no flesh can stand, should accept so rebellious sinners, and dwell among them! He had not only power to destroy, but law against us also. What a perfect peace is it, then, that the Judge becometh a merciful Father, and the law of ordinances is cancelled, and that power employed to keep salvation to us, and us to salvation! Ye who have made peace and atonement through Christ's blood, rejoice in the hope of the glory of God; there wants nothing to make you completely blessed, but the clear and perfect sight and knowledge of your estate before God.

Now, when this peace, which is made up in heaven, is intimated unto the conscience, then all the tempests and clouds of it evanish; and this is the peace of believing, which is the soul's resting and quieting itself upon the believing favour of God. There may be a great calm above, good-will in God towards men, and yet great tempests in this lower region, no peace on earth. There is a peace of conscience which is a disease of conscience, a benumbedness of conscience, or a sleep of conscience, when men walk in the imagination of their own hearts, and flatter themselves in their own eyes, will not trouble themselves with the apprehension of the wrath of God. When souls will not suffer their sin, or the curse to enter in; this is that 'no peace' which the Lord speaks often of, it is but a dream; and when a man awaketh, alas! what a dreadful sight meets he with first,—'sudden destruction!' Sin enters into the conscience, and the law, the strength of sin; and so that peace endeth in an eternal disquietness. But what is the reason, that notwithstanding of God's justice and men's sins, so many are not afraid of him, so many pass the time without fear of wrath and hell? Is it not because they have taken hold of his strength, and made peace with him? No, indeed; but because they know not the power of his anger, to fear him according to his wrath. Who will spend one hour in the examination of his own ways, in searching out sins, in counting his debt, till he find it past payment? No, men entertain the thoughts of sin, and hell and wrath, as if it were coals in their bosom; they shake them out, they like and love any diversion from them. Oh! ignorance maketh much peace, I would say security, which is so much worse than fear, because it is so far from the remedy, that it knoweth not the evil and danger. It is not the rising of the Sun of righteousness, shining into the soul, that hath cleared them, but their perpetual darkness that blindeth them. I say, then, in the name of Jesus Christ, that ye never knew the peace of God, who knew not war with God; ye know not love, who have not known anger; but this is the soul's true peace and tranquillity, when it is once awakened to see its misery and danger—how many clouds overspread it; what tempests blow; what waves of displeasure go over its head! But when that peace, which is made in the high places, breaketh through the cloud with a voice, 'Son, be of good comfort, thy sins be forgiven thee!' when that voice of the Spirit is uttered, presently at its command the wind and waves obey; the soul is calmed, as the sea after a storm; it is not only untroubled, but it is peaceable upon solid grounds, because of the word which speaks peace in Christ. The peace of the most of you is such as ye were born and educated withal. Is it not a created peace, a spoken peace,—the fruit of the lips, and so no true peace? Ye had not your peace from the word, but ye brought it to the word; ye have no peace after trouble, and so it is not the Lord's peace.

The Christian may have peace, in regard of his own salvation and eternal things, and in regard of all things that befalleth in time; the first is, when the conscience is sprinkled with the blood of Jesus Christ, and getteth a good answer to all the challenges and accusations of conscience, and of the law and justice, 1 Pet. iii. 21; when the Spirit of God shines into the soul, with a new light to discover these things that are freely given, 1 Cor. ii. 12. And this is the sealing of the Spirit after believing, Eph. i. 13. When a soul hath put to its seal by believing God's word, and hath acknowledged God's truth and faithfulness in his word, the Spirit sealeth mutually the believer's faith, both by more holiness and the knowledge of it; and how great peace is this, when a soul can look upon all its iniquities when they compass about a man, and outward trouble sharpeneth and setteth on edge inward challenges, and yet the soul will not fear,—it hath answers to them all in Christ's blood, Psalm xlix. 5. This is a greater word than all the world can say. Many men's fearlessness proceedeth from ignorance of sin, their iniquities were never set in order before them; but if once they compassed them about, and wrath, like a fiery wall, compass them about also, so that there were no escaping, O it would be more terrible than all the armies of the world! Ye would account little of a kingdom, ye would exchange it for such a word as David hath upon good grounds.

Now, I say again, the soul that hath thus committed itself to him as a faithful keeper, may have peace in all estates and conditions; and this peace floweth from that other peace. There is a peace which guards the heart and mind, Phil. iv. 6, 7, opposed to carefulness and anxiety; and this Paul is exemplary for, "I have learned in every estate, therewith to be content, to want and abound," &c. ver. 11. The soul of a believer may be in an equal even tenor and disposition in all conditions; it may possess itself in patience. Impatience and anxiety make a man not his own man; he is not himself; he enjoys not himself; he is a burden to himself, and is his own tormentor; but if souls were stayed upon God, certainly they would possess themselves, dwell securely within their own breasts. We may find that the most part of men are exposed to all the floods and waves of the times. They move inwardly, as things are troubled outwardly; every thing addeth moment to their grief or joy; any dispensation casteth the balance, and either weighs them down with discouragement, or lifteth them up with vanity and lightness of mind; but the believer's privilege is to be unmoved in the midst of all the tossings and confusions of the times, Psal. cxxviii. 1, 2. Ye would be as mount Zion if ye trusted in God; no dispensation would enter into the soul to cast the balance upon you; ye might stand upon your rock Jesus Christ, and look about the estates, persons, affairs, and minds of men, as a troubled sea, fleeting, tossed up and down, and ye stand and not be moved, or not greatly moved, Psal. lxii. 2. And this is to be wise indeed. If I would describe a wise man, I would say, he "is one man," beside him no man is one with himself, but various, inconstant, changeable. He is unwise who is unlike himself, who changeth persons according to dispensations: wisdom is the stability of thy times, and faith is wisdom. It establisheth as mount Zion, so as a man cometh out still one,—in prosperity not exalted, in adversity not cast down, in every estate content; and this is the man who is blessed indeed. This were wisdom,—to will the same thing, and nill* the same thing. *Semper idem velle, atque idem nolle.*† I need not, says Seneca, add that exception, that it be right which you desire, for no one thing can universally and always please, if it be not good and right; so I say, he were both wise and happy, who had but one grief and one joy. Should not a believer's mind be calm and serene, seeing the true light hath shined; it should be as the upper world, where no blasts, no storms or clouds are to eclipse the sun, or cloud it. While our peace and tranquillity is borrowed from outward things, certainly it must change; but a believer's peace and tranquillity of mind, having its rise from above, from the unchangeable word of the Lord, it needeth not to change according to the vicissitudes of providence. He needeth not to care beforehand,

* [That is, not to will.—Ed.]

† [See Note, page 96. *Si vis eadem semper velle, vera oportet velis.*—"If you are desirous to have always similar wishes, it is necessary that you should wish for things that are proper." *Senec. Epist.* xcv.—Ed.]

because there is one who careth for him; and what needeth both to care? He needeth not be disquieted or troubled after, because it shall turn about to his good; all things shall do so, Rom. viii. 28. He needeth not be anxious about future events, because he hath all his burden cast upon another by prayer and supplication. What needeth he then take a needless burden? Prayer will do that which care pretends and cannot do, and that without trouble. He needeth not be troubled when things are present, for he cannot by his thought either add or diminish, take away or prevent. There is one good and necessary thing that his heart is upon, and that cannot be taken from him; and therefore all things else are indifferent, and of small concernment to him.

Now what wanteth such a man of perfect peace, who is reconciled to God, and at peace within himself? When peace guardeth the heart and mind within, compasseth it as a castle or garrison, to hold out all the vain alarms of external things, may not all the world be troubled about him? What though the floods lift up their voice, if they come not into the soul? If he be one and the same in peace and trouble, prosperity and adversity, do not lament him in the one more than the other. It is the mind that maketh your condition good or bad; but yet, I say, the believer hath likewise peace with all the creatures, which the world hath not, and even in this he is a privileged man. He is in league with the stones of the field, and in peace in his tabernacle, Job v. 23. All things are his, because he is Christ's, and all are Christ's, who is the possessor of heaven and earth, at least the righteous heir of both, 1 Cor iii. 21. The unbeliever hath no right to the creature; though there be a cessation for a time between them and him, yet that is no peace, for they will at length be armed against him. They are witnesses already against him, and groan to God for the corruption that man's sin hath subjected them unto. His table is, it may be, full, yet it is a snare unto him; he getteth ease and quietness outwardly: nay, but it slayeth the fool and destroyeth him. But the godly man is at peace, through Christ's blood, with all crosses and comforts; the sting and enmity of all evils is taken away by Christ. Poverty is made a friend, because Christ was poor; hunger and thirst is become a friend, because Christ was hungry and thirsty; reproach and contempt is at peace with him, because Christ was despised; afflictions and sorrows are reconciled to him, because Christ was a man of sorrows, and acquainted with griefs; in a word, death itself is become a friend, since Christ subdued it by tasting of it. I may say, the worst things to a natural man are become best friends to the believer; the grave keepeth his body and dust in hope. Death is a better friend than life, for it ministers an entry into glory: it is the door of eternal life: it taketh down the tabernacle of mortality, that we may be clothed upon with immortality. In sum, whatever it be, Christ hath stamped a new quality on it; it cometh through his hand, and so, if it be not good in itself, yet it is good in the use, and in his appointment, Rom. viii. 21. If it be not good, yet it worketh together for our good; it contributeth to our good, because it is in his skilful hand, who can bring good out of evil, peace out of trouble. O that ye were persuaded to be Christians indeed, to love his law, and trust in him. Great peace have all such. This were more to you than peace in the world; your peace should be as a river, for abundance and perpetuity; no drought could dry it up; it should run in time as a large river, and when time is done, it would embosom itself in eternity, in that ocean of eternal peace and joy which the saints are drowned in above; other men's peace is but like a brook that dries up in summer.

Sermon XIII.

Isaiah xxvi. 3.—"*Thou shalt keep him in perfect peace, whose mind is stayed on thee, because he trusteth in thee.*"

Christ hath left us his peace, as the great and comprehensive legacy, 'My peace I leave you,' John xiv. 27. And this was not peace in the world that he enjoyed; you know what his life was, a continual warfare; but a peace above the world, that passeth understanding. 'In the world you shall have trouble, but in me you shall have peace,' saith Christ,—a peace that shall make trouble no trouble. You must lay your accounts to have such a life as the forerunner had; but withal, as he hath left us his trouble, so hath he left us his peace; the trouble will have an end, but the joy can no man take from you. We have this sure promise to rest upon, in behalf of the church, peace shall be in Israel; a peace that the world knoweth not, and so cannot assault it, or take it away. O that ye would hearken to this word, that ye would trust in the Lord, and stay upon your God, then should your peace be as a river, Isa. xlviii. 18. There is nothing more desired in time of trouble than peace; but all peace is not better than war: some necessary war is better than evil-grounded peace. The kingdoms have been long in pain, labouring to bring forth a safe and well-grounded peace. But, alas! we have been in pain and brought forth wind; when we looked for peace, no good came, and for healing, behold trouble. But how shall we arrive at our desired haven? Certainly, if peace be well-grounded, it must have truth for its foundation, and righteousness for its companion; truth must spring out of the earth, and righteousness look down from heaven. This were the compendious way for public peace, if every man would make his own peace with God. There are controversies with God, between king, nobles, and people; and therefore God fomenteth the wars in the kingdoms. If you would have these ended, make peace with God in Christ, by flying in unto him, and resting on him; more trusting in God would despatch our wars; trusting in the arm of flesh continueth them. Always whatever be, peace or war, here is the business that more concerns you,—your eternal peace and safety; and, if ye were more careful of this, to save your own souls, you would help the public more. If you could be once persuaded to be Christians indeed, we needed not press many duties in reference to the public; and until you be once persuaded to save yourselves, by flying from the wrath to come, it is in vain to speak of public duties to you. We do therefore declare unto you the way of obtaining perfect peace,—peace as a river; if you will quit all self-confidences, flee from yourselves as your greatest enemies, and trust your souls unto the promise in Jesus Christ, and lean all your weight on him, we assure you, your peace shall run abundantly and perpetually. Whoever trusteth in creatures, in uncertain riches, in worldly peace, in whatsoever thing besides the only living and glorious Lord, we persuade him, that his peace shall fail as a brook. All things in this world shall deal deceitfully with you, as a brook which is blackish, by reason of ice; what time it waxeth warm, it shall evanish. You that looked and waited for water in it shall be confounded, because you hoped, and are ashamed because of your expectation, Job vi. 15, &c. The summer shall dry up your peace, and what will ye do? But if you pour out your souls on him, and trust in the fountain of living waters, you shall not be ashamed, for your peace shall be as a river. The elephant is said to trust that he can drink out a river; but he is deceived, for he may drink again,—it runs, and shall run for ever. If any thing would essay to take your peace from you, it is a vain attempt, for it runs like a river; it may be shallower and deeper, but it cannot run dry, because of the living fountain it proceedeth from. There is no other thing can be made sure; all besides this is uncertain, and this only is worthy to be made sure; nothing besides this can give you satisfaction.

Are your hearts asking within you, how shall this peace be attained? If you desire to know it, consider these words, 'Whose heart is stayed on thee, because he trusteth in thee.' It concerneth you much to know well, what this is that your eternal peace depends on.

Trusting in God, is the leaning of the soul's weight on God. The soul hath a burden above it, heavy and unsupportable, and this the truster casteth upon God; and so he is a loadened and weary man, whom Christ exhorteth to come to him, and he shall find ease for his soul, Matt. xi. 28; Prov. iii. 5. Leaning to ourselves, and trusting in God are opposed. Psal. xxii. 10, trusting is exponed * to be 'a casting upon God.' Psal. xxv. 1, it is called, 'a lifting up the soul to him.' This one thing is included in the bosom of trusting and believing, that a man hath many burdens too heavy for him, which would sink him down: the believer is such a one as Jehoshaphat, 2 Chron. xx. 12, 'O Lord, we have no might against this great company, neither know we what to do.' O Lord, I have an army of iniquities against me, a great company compasseth me about; an army of curses as numerous as mine iniquities; both are innumerable as the sand of the sea; I have no might against them, neither know I what to do: nay, the Lord is against me, his wrath is like the roaring of a lion; what can I do against him? The first beginning of trusting in God is distrusting ourselves; and until a man see his duty and burden beyond his strength, his burden greater than he can bear, you will never persuade him to come to Jesus Christ, and lean on him. We will not preach any such doctrine, as to discharge any to come to Christ, till they be wearied and loaden; for, when a man conceiveth that he wanteth that weariedness, whither shall he go to find it? Is there any fountain, but one, Jesus Christ, both of grace and preparations to it, if any such be? But this we preach unto you, that until you be wearied and loaden, you will not cast your burden on Jesus. We need not discharge you to come till you be such, for certainly you will not come. This is the desperate wickedness of our hearts, that we will never forsake ourselves till we can do no better. Until men be as David, 'I looked on the right hand, and there was none would know me; refuge failed me,' certainly they will not cry to God. Men will look round about them, before they will look up above them; they will cast the burden of their souls upon any thing, upon their own sorrow and contrition, upon their resolution to amend, upon external duties and privileges, upon civil honesty, until all these succumb under the weight of their salvation; and then, it may be, they will ask after him who bare our griefs. I would not willingly speak of preparations to faith, because it putteth men upon searching for something in themselves, upon fashioning their own hearts, and trimming them to come to Christ; whereas there is nothing can be acceptable to him but what cometh from him. But I think all that men intend, who speak of preparations, may be gained this way by holding out unto men the impossibility of coming to Christ, till they be emptied of themselves. Not that the one is a thing going before, to be done by us, but because they are all one; it is one motion of the soul to come out of itself, and into Jesus; it is one thing really to distrust ourselves, and to trust in him; and by this means, when the true nature of faith itself is holden out, men might examine themselves rather by it, whether they have it, than by the preparations of it.

But to come to our purpose, when the soul is pressed under burdens of sin and misery, of duty and insufficiency, and inability to do it, then the gospel discovereth unto the wearied soul a place of reposing and rest. The Lord hath established Christ Jesus, an 'ensign to the people;' those who seek unto him shall find his rest glorious,' Isa. xi. 10. When there is discovered in us all emptiness and inability, yea impossibility to save ourselves, or perform any duty, then are we led to Jesus Christ, as one who is come with grace and truth, in whom it hath pleased the Father all fulness should dwell; and the turning of the soul over upon him is trusting in him. You would not mistake this; trusting in the Lord in its first and most native acting, is not always persuasion of his good-will and love in particular. No, the soul meets first with a general promise, holding out his good-will in general; and the soul closeth with this, as a thing both good and true,—as faithful in itself, and worthy of all acceptation. This is it that we must first meet with,—an all-sufficient

* [That is, laid open or explained.—Ed.]

Saviour, able to save to the utmost all that come to him; and the soul's accepting of that blessed Saviour on the terms he is offered, this is believing in him, and trusting to him, as a complete Saviour.

Now when the soul hath disburdened itself upon God, and set to its seal to the truth of the promises in the gospel for salvation; if the light of the Spirit shine to discover this unto it, that it hath laid hold on his strength who is able to save to the utmost, then it becometh persuaded of his love in particular; and this is rather the sealing after believing, than believing itself.

When once men have hazarded their souls upon his word, and trusted in him, then they may trust in him for all particulars: he that hath given his Son for us, will he not with him give all things? This, therefore, is the continual recourse of a believer,—from discovered emptiness and insufficiency in himself, to travel unto the fulness and strength of Jesus Christ, that his strength may be perfected in weakness. Yea, when all things seem contrary, and his dispensation writes bitter things against us, yet ought we to trust in him, Job xiii. 15. There is a peace of wilfulness and violence in faith, that will look always towards his word, whatever be threatened to the contrary.

Now, from this faith in God, floweth a constant dependence and stayedness on him, they are stayed on him, because they trusted in him; for faith discovereth in God such grounds, that it may lean its weight upon him without wavering and changing. It considereth his power, his good will, and his faithfulness; he is able to perform, he is willing to do it, and he is faithful, because he hath promised. His greatness and power is a high rock, higher than we, that faith leadeth us unto. His love and good-will in Jesus Christ, maketh an open entry and ready access to that rock; and faithfulness engageth both to give a shelter and refuge to the poor sinner. Would a soul be any more tossed, would there be any place for wavering and doubting, if souls considered his excellent loving-kindness, and great goodness laid up and treasured with him for those that trust in him? Psalm xxxvi. 7. Who would not put their trust under the shadow of his wings, and think themselves safe? Again, if his eternal power were pondered, how he is able to effectuate whatever he pleaseth; what everlasting arms he hath that by a word supports the frame of the world; what he can do, if he stretch out his arm; and then, if these two immutable things, (Heb. vi. 18,) his promise and his oath, were looked upon;—how he hath engaged himself in his truth, and sworn in his holiness; would not a soul lie safely between these three? What strong consolation would such a threefold consideration yield? Would any wind or tempest blow within these walls mounted up to heaven?

Stayedness on God is nothing else but the fixedness of believing and trusting, Ps. cxii. 7, 8, 'his heart is fixed, trusting in God; his heart is established.' It is even the mature and ripe age of faith. Faith, while it is yet in infancy, in its tender years, neither can endure storms, nor can it confirm us in them; but when it hath sprung up and grown in that root of Jesse, when it is rooted and established in Jesus Christ, then it establisheth the soul. Faith abiding in him and taking root, groweth, confirmed as a tree that cannot easily be moved; and if you establish faith, you shall be established.

There are two particulars which I conceive the trusting soul is stayed on. First, in the meditation of God. Secondly, in expectation from him of all good things. When I say the meditation of God, I take in both contemplation and affection. The most part of men have but few thoughts of God at all; even those who trust in him do not consider sufficiently what a one he is in whom they believe. If faith were vigorous and lively, it would put men to often thinking on him, seeking to know him in his glorious names; the mind would be stayed upon this glorious object, as the most mysterious and wonderful one. How throng are men's minds with their vanities? When they awake, they are not still with God. The meditation of him is a burden to them; any other thing getteth more time and thoughts. But meditation addeth affection to contemplation; men may think long upon the heavens and their course, but their affections are not ravished with them. But thus is the soul stayed on God;—when the soul's desires are towards the remembrance of his name, then affection stayeth the mind upon what it pitcheth on;

and certainly the mind giveth but passing looks, constrained thoughts, where the heart is not. Here is David's meditation, Ps. i. 'My delight is in the law of the Lord.' The soul of a believer should be constant and fixed in the consideration of God, till he be wholly engaged to admiration and wondering. 'O Lord, how excellent is thy name,' Psal. viii. 1: 'and who is like unto thee?' You all say that you believe in God, and know his power,—you know he is good, he is merciful, just, long-suffering, faithful, &c. But what is all this knowledge but ignorance, and your light darkness, when it doth not press you to put your trust in his name? You know; nay, but you consider not what you know. This is trusting, when the mind is stayed on what it knoweth, when all the scattered thoughts and affections are called home, and united in one, to be exercised about this comprehensive object, 'the Lord our God.' It is not want of knowledge destroyeth you, but want of consideration of what you know, and this is brutishness. Men's hearts do not carry the seal and stamp of their knowledge, because thoughts of God and his word are but as passengers that go through a land, as lightning going through the mind, but warms it not; and so their practice carrieth no impression of it either. How base is it for those who have God for their God, to be so ignorant of him! Would not any man willingly travel about his own possessions? Have you such a large portion, believers, and should ye be taken up with other vanities? Should your hearts and minds be stayed on them, more than the living God? There is a great vanity and levity in men's minds; 'The Lord knoweth the thoughts of man that they are vanity.' There is an unsettledness of spirit,—we cannot pitch on that upon which we may be stayed; and so all the spirits of men are in a continual motion from one thing to another, for nothing giveth complete satisfaction, and therefore it must go and try one after another, to see if it can find in it what it found not in the former. And such is the inconstancy of the spirit, that it licketh up its vomit; and what thing it refused, it eateth it up as its meat. The time is spent in choosing and refusing, rejecting one thing and taking another, and again returning to what you have rejected. Thus are men tossed up and down, and unstable in all their ways, as a ship without ballasting. Now, faith and trusting in God is the ballast and weight of this inconstant ship: it is the anchor to stay it from being driven to and fro. If once men would pitch upon this one Lord, who hath in himself eminently all the scattered perfections of creatures, and infinitely more,—if you would consider him, and meditate on him, till your souls loved him, would you not be ravished with him? Would you not build your house beside him, and dwell in the meditation of his name? This would fix and establish you in duties—'when I awake, I am still with thee.' A little searching and experience discovereth emptiness in all beside; and therefore is it, that the soul removeth sooner from such a particular creature than it expected. But here is One that is 'past finding out.' The more I search and find, I find him the more above what I can search and find. The creatures are but painted and fair in men's apprehension, and at a distance; but the near enjoyment of them discovereth the delusion, and sendeth a man away ashamed, because he trusted. But the Lord God is, and there is no other. He is not as waters that fail, no liar,—he is an everlasting fountain,—the more you dig and draw, it runs the faster; he will never send any away ashamed that trust in him, because they shall find more than they expected.

Therefore the soul that is stayed on meditation of God, and knoweth him certainly, will be fixed in expectation from him. Our expectation from the creatures changeth, because it is often frustrated. Disappointment meets it. It is above what is in the creature, and so it must meet with disappointment; but as he is above our meditation, so is he far above our expectation; and if a man's experience answer his hope, he hath no reason to change his hope. The Lord hath often done things we looked not for, but we never looked for any thing, according to the grounds of the word, but it was done, or a better than it. He doth not always answer our limitations; but if he give gold, when we sought silver, are we not answered? Are we disappointed? There are three things that use most to disquiet and toss men's spirits,—sin and wrath, future events, and present calamities. Faith establisheth the soul on God in all these, and suffereth it not to be driven to and fro with these winds; it finds a harbour and refuge in God from all these. If he be pursued by the avenger of blood, God's wrath and justice, here is an open city of refuge that he may run to and be safe. If iniquities compass me about, yet I will not fear, but oppose unto that great company the many sufferings and obedience of Jesus Christ. My conscience challengeth and writeth bitter things against me, yet I have an answer in that blood that speaketh better things than Abel's. If sins prevail, he will purge them away. His mercy is above all my sin, and his virtue and power is above my sin. He hath promised, and will he not do it? Oft-times men's souls are perplexed and tossed about future events, careful for to-morrow. This is a great torment of spirit, it cutteth and divideth it,—putteth a man to his own providence, as if there were no God: but he that trusteth in God is established in this, 'His heart is fixed, trusting in the Lord.' He hath committed his soul to him, and why may he not his body? He hath nothing but his promise for eternal salvation, and may not that same suffice for temporal? He careth for me, saith faith, why then should we both care about one thing? He hath given his Son for me, the most precious gift, which the world cannot match, and will he not with him give all these lesser things? And thus the believer encloseth himself within the Father's love and providence, and is fixed, not fearing evil tidings; for what tidings can be evil, seeing our Father hath the sovereign disposing of all affairs, and knoweth what is best for us? Present dispensations often shake men, and drive them to and fro: their feet slip, and are not established; 'Thou didst hide thy face, and I was troubled.' But if you trusted in God, and considered what is in him to oppose to all difficulties and calamities, you would say, 'I shall not be moved, though the floods lift up their voice.' If you believed his love, would not this sweeten all his dealing? He maketh all work together for good. Sovereignty, righteousness, and mercy, are sure and firm ground to stand upon in all storms. You may cast anchor at any of those, and lie secure. 'It is the Lord, let him do what he pleaseth.' This was enough to quiet the saints in old times. Should he give account of his matters to us? Shall the clay say to the potter, why is it thus? His absolute right by creation maketh him, beyond all exception, do what he pleases; but beside this, he is pleased and condescendeth to reason with us, and give account of his matters, to testify to our conscience that he is righteous in all his ways. It was the ground of Jeremiah's settling, Lam. iii. 'It is of the Lord's mercy that we are not consumed.' It should have allayed and stayed Job. Know this, thou art punished less than thy iniquities deserve. Who will set a time to plead with him? Shall any be found righteous before him? And this might stop all men's mouths, and put them in the dust to keep silence; seeing he hath law to do infinitely more than he doth, why should not we rather proclaim his clemency, than argue him so very hard? If to both those you shall add the consideration of his mercy, that all his paths are mercy and truth unto you, even when he correcteth most severely, so that you may bless him as well for rods as for meat and clothing, and count yourself blessed when you are taught by the rod and the word, the one speaking to the other, and the other sealing its instruction,—if you believed that it were a fruit of his love, that 'he chasteneth every son whom he loveth,' because he will not let you depart from him, will not let you settle upon a present world, and forget your country above; therefore he compasseth you about with hedges of thorns to keep in your way; and therefore he maketh this world bitter and unpleasant, that you may have no continuing city,—if all this were believed, would not the soul triumph with Paul, 'What can separate me from the love of God?'—not past things, for all my sins are blotted out, and shall be remembered no more; not present things, for they work to good, and are a fruit of his love; not things to come, for that is to come which shall more declare his love than what is past; would not a soul sleep securely within the compass of this power, this love, and faithfulness of God, without fear of dashing or sinking?

Now, judge whether a perfect peace may not flow from all this. May it not be a perfect calm, when the mountains that environ go up to heaven? Not only doth the soul trust in God, but God keepeth the trusting soul in peace. He is the Creator of peace, and the preserver of it,—'I create peace,' I keep him in peace. The same power and virtue is required to the preserving of a thing, and the first being of it. Our faith and hope in God is too weak an anchor to abide all storms. Our cords would break, our hands faint and weary, but he is the everlasting God, who faileth not, and wearieth not. He holdeth an invisible gripe of us. We are kept by his power unto salvation, and we are kept by his power in peace. 'Thy right hand holdeth me,' saith David, and this helpeth me to pursue thee. What maketh believers inexpugnable, impregnable? Is it their strength? No indeed. But 'salvation will God appoint for walls and bulwarks.' Almighty power is a strong wall, though invisible;—this power worketh in us and about us.

Now, believers, pity the world about you, that knoweth not this peace. When they lie secure, and cry Peace, peace; alas! they are a city open without walls as the plain field,—there is no keeper there, nothing to hold off destruction. Entertain your own peace, do not grieve the Spirit who hath sealed it. If you return to folly after he hath spoken peace to you, I persuade you, you shall not maintain this peace. There may be peace with God, but no peace in thy conscience, as long as the whoredoms of thy heart are to the fore; thou mayest be secure, but security is worse than fear. Know this, that continuing in a course of sin, entertaining any known sin, shall trouble thy peace. If God hath spoken peace to thee, thou shalt not lodge that enemy in peace. 'Great peace have they that love thy law.' Obedience and delight in it doth not make peace, but it is the way of peace; and much meditation on the blessed word of God is the most excellent mean to preserve this peace, if it be secured with much correspondence with heaven by prayer, Phil. iv. 6, 7. If you would disburden your hearts daily at the throne of grace, peace should guard and keep your heart, and then your peace would be perfect indeed. But because your faith is here imperfect, your requests few and infervent, your follies and iniquities many; therefore is this promised perfection a stranger to the most part of Christians. Always what we want here, we must expect to have made up shortly. Heaven is a land of peace, and all things are there in full age: here all are in minority; it is but yet night; but when the day shall break up, and the shadows fly away, and the Prince of peace shall appear and be revealed, he shall bring peace and grace both with him, and both perfect. To Him be praise and glory.

Sermon XIV.

ISAIAH lix. 20.—"*And the Redeemer shall come unto Zion, and unto them that turn,*" *&c.*

DOCTRINES, as things, have their seasons and times. Every thing is beautiful in its season. So there is no word of truth, but it hath a season and time in which it is beautiful. And indeed that is a great part of wisdom, to bring forth everything in its season, to discern when and where, and to whom it is pertinent and edifying, to speak such and such truths. But there is one doctrine that is never out of season; and therefore it may be preached in season and out of season, as the apostle commandeth. Indeed to many hearts it is always out of season, and especially in times of trouble and anguish, when it should be most seasonable, when the opportunity may commend the beauty of it; but in itself, and to as many as have ever found the power of it on their hearts, it is always the most seasonable and pertinent doctrine,—I mean the very subject-matter of this text, the news of a Redeemer to captive sinners. It is in itself such glad tidings, and shines with so much beauty and splendour to troubled sinners, that it casteth abroad a lustre and beauty on the feet of the messengers that carry it, Isa. xl. It is a cordial in affliction, whether outward or inward: and it is withal the only true comfort of prosperity. It allayeth the bitterness of things that cross us, and filleth up the emptiness of things that pretend to please us; it giveth sweetness to the one, and true sweetness to the other. Reason then,—that should always be welcome to us, which we stand always in need of; that it should always be new and fresh in our affection, which is always recent and new in its operation and efficacy toward us. Other news, how great or good soever, suppose they were able to fill the hearts of all in a nation with joy, yet they grow stale, they lose their virtue within few days. What footsteps or remainder is of all the triumphs and trophies of nations, of all their solemnities for their victorious success at home and abroad? These great news, which once were the subject of the discourse of and delight of many thousands,—who report them now with delight? So those things that may cause joy and triumph to some at this time, as they cannot choose but make more hearts sad than glad; so they will quickly lose even that efficacy they have, and become tasteless as the white of an egg, to them that are most ravished with them. But, my beloved, here is glad tidings of a Redeemer come to Zion to save sinners, which have no occasion of sadness in them to any, but to those who are not so happy as to consider them, or believe them, and they are this day, after many hundred, I may say thousand, years since they were first published, as green and recent, as refreshing to wearied souls, as ever they were. Yea, such is the nature of them, and such an everlasting spring of consolation is in them, that the oftener they be told, and the more they be considered, the sweeter they are. They grow green in old age, and bring forth fruit, and are fat and flourishing; and indeed it is the never-dying virtue and everlasting sap of this word of life, that maketh the righteous so, Psal. xcii. 14. This word of a Redeemer at the first publishing, and for a long time, was but like waters issuing out from under the threshold, and then they came to the ancles, when it was published to a whole nation; but still the longer it swells the higher above knees, and loins, till it be a great inexhausted river, and thus it runs at this day through the world, and hath a healing virtue and a quickening virtue, Ezek. xlvii., and a sanctifying virtue, ver. 9—12. Now this is our errand to you, to invite you to come to these waters. If ye thirst, come to be quenched; if ye thirst not, ye have so much the more need to come, because your thirst after things that will not profit you, will destroy you, and your unsensibleness of your need of this is your greatest misery.

That the words may be more lively unto us, we may call to mind, the greatest and deepest design that hath been carried on in the world, by the Maker and Ruler of the world, is the marriage of Christ his Son with the Church. This was primarily intended, when he made the world, as a palace to celebrate it in; this was especially aimed at, when he joined Adam and Eve, in the beginning of time, together in paradise, that the second Adam should be more solemnly joined to the church, at the end of time, in the paradise of heaven; and this the apostle draws out as the sampler and arch-copy of all marriages and conjunctions in the creatures, Eph. v. Now this being the great design of God, of which all other things done in time are but the footsteps and low representations, the great question is, how this shall be brought about, because of the great distance and huge disproportion of the parties, He 'being the brightness of the Father's glory,' and we being wholly eclipsed and darkened since our fall;—He higher than the heaven of heavens, and we fallen as low as hell into a dungeon of darkness and misery, led away by sin and Satan, lying in that abominable posture represented in Ezek. xvi.; not only unsuitable to engage his love, but fit to procure even the loathing of all that pass by.

Now it being thus, the words do furnish us with the noble resolution of the Son, about the taking away of the distance, and the royal offer of the Father, to make the match hold the better, both flowing from infinite love, in the most free and absolute manner that can be imagined. The Son's resolution, which is withal the Father's promise, is to come into the world first to redeem his spouse, and so to marry her; 'and the Redeemer shall come unto Zion,' &c. The Father's offer, that he might not be wanting to help it forward, is to dispone,* by an irrevocable covenant, having the force of an absolute donation, his word and Spirit to Christ and his seed, to the church, even to the end of the world, (ver. 21). 'As for me, this is my covenant.' The Son hath done his part, and is to express his infinite love, infinite condescendency, and stooping below his majesty. Now, as for me, I will show my good-will to it in my infinite bounty and riches of grace to the church; he hath given himself for her,—I will give my Spirit; and thus it cannot but hold.

* [Dispone is a Scots law expression. It signifies to convey a right or property to another.—Ed.]

We shall speak a word then of these three; first, what estate and condition Christ findeth his church in, out of which she must be taken to be his spouse; then, what way and course is laid down by the council of heaven, to fill up the infinite distance between Christ and sinners; and, to close all, we shall show you the suitableness of these promises, and the wonderful fitness of this doctrine to the church, at this time Isaiah preached it, and at all times.

The first is supposed in the words. Redemption supposeth captivity or slavery; redemption of persons importeth captivity and slavery of these persons, and redemption of other things that belong to persons, importeth sale or alienation of our right to them. Of both, personal redemption is the greatest and most difficult; yet both we have need of, for our estate and fortune, so to speak, is lost, 'for all men have sinned and come short of the glory of God,' Rom. iii. 23. That inheritance of eternal life, we have mortgaged it, and given away our right to it. The favour of God and the blessedness of communion with him, was Adam's birthright, and by a free donation was made his proper inheritance and possession, to be transmitted to his posterity. But O! for how small a thing did he give it away,—for a little taste of an apple he sold his estate; and both he and we may lament over it, as the king that was constrained to render himself and all his army for want of water. When he tasted it, "For how small a thing," saith he, "have I lost my kingdom!" Then our persons are in a state of bondage, in captivity and slavery; captives under the wrath of God, and slaves or servants to sin. There needed no greater difference and deformity between Christ and us, than this,—our servitude and bondage to sin, which truly is the basest and most abominable vassalage in the world. The abasement of the highest prince, to the vilest servitude under the basest creatures in his dominion, is but a shadow of that loathsome and ugly posture of our souls. This servitude doth in a manner unman us, and transform us into beasts. Certainly it is that which, in the holy eyes of God, is more loathsome than any thing beside. He seeth not that deformity in poverty, nakedness, sickness, slavery. Let a man be as miserable as Job on his dunghill, it is not so much that, as the unseen and undiscerned posture and habit of their souls, that he abominateth. Now what a match is this, for the highest and holiest prince, the Son of the greatest King, and heir of all things! But if you add to this slavery, that captivity under the curse and wrath of God,—that all men are shut up, and enclosed in the prison of God's faithful and irrevocable sentence of condemnation, and given over by the righteous judgment of God, to be kept by Satan in everlasting chains of darkness,—he keepeth men now, by the invisible cords of their own sins, but these chains of darkness are reserved for both him and men,—now indeed, this superaddeth a great difficulty to the business. The other may be a difficulty to his mind and affection, because there is nothing to procure love, but all that may enforce hatred and loathing. But suppose his infinite love could come over this stay, could leap over this mountain by the freedom of it, yet there is a greater impediment in the way, that may seem difficult to his power, and it is the justice and power of God, enclosing sinners and shutting them up for eternal wrath, till a due satisfaction be had from or for them. You see then, how infinite the distance is betwixt him and us, and how great the difficulty is to bring about this intended union. Angels were sent with flaming swords to encompass the tree of life and keep it from man, but man is environed by the curse of the Almighty God. The justice, the faithfulness, and the power of God do guard or set a watch about him, that there is no access to him to save him, but by undergoing the greatest danger, and undertaking the greatest party that ever was dealt withal, and the strictest and severest too.

This being the case then, the distance being so vast, and the difficulty so great, the distance being twofold, between his nature and ours, and between our quality and his; an infinite distance between his divine nature and our flesh, and besides an extreme contrariety between the holiness of his nature, and the sinfulness of ours,—[there is here] such a repugnancy, as there is no reconciliation of them. You know what Paul speaketh of the marriage of Christians with idolaters: how much more will it hold here? What communion can be between light and darkness, between God and Belial? Is it possible these can be reduced to amity, and brought to so near an union? Yet for all this, it is possible; but love and wisdom must find out the way. Infinite love and infinite wisdom consulting together, what distance can they not swallow up? What difficulty can they not overcome?

And here you have it, the distance undertaken to be removed, both by the Father and the Son,—(for all this while we can do nothing to help it forward; while the blessed plot is going on, we are posting the faster to our own destruction). And this is the way condescended upon; *first*, To fill up that wide gap between his divine spiritual nature, and our mortal fleshly nature, it is agreed upon, that the Son shall come in our flesh, and be made partaker of flesh and blood with the children; and this is meant by this promise, 'the Redeemer shall come to Sion;' which is plainly expressed by his own mouth, John xvi. 28, 'I came forth from the Father, and am come into the world.' There being such a distance between his majesty and our baseness, love maketh him stoop down and humble himself to the very state of a servant, Phil. ii. 7, 8. And thus the humiliation of Christ filleth up the first distance; for 'love and majesty cannot long dwell together,' *nec in una sede morantur majestas et amor*;* but love will draw majesty down below itself, to meet with the object of it. This was the great journey Christ took to meet with us, and it is downward below himself; but his love hath chosen it, to be like us, though he should be unlike himself. How divinely doth the divine apostle speak of it, 'And the Word was made flesh, and he dwelt among us,' John i. 14. And therefore the children of Adam may in verity say of him, what the holy Trinity, in a holy irony spake of man, 'Lo, he is become as one of us.' It was a singular and eminent privilege conferred upon man in his first creation, that the Trinity in a manner consulted about him, 'Let us make man after our image;' but now when man hath lost that image, to have such a result of the council of the Trinity about it, 'let one of us be made man, to make up the distance between man and us, !—O! what soul can rightly conceive it without ravishment and wonder, without an ecstacy of admiration and affection!—that the Lord should become a servant!—the Heir of all things be stripped naked of all!—the brightness of the Father's glory, be thus eclipsed and darkened! —and in a word, that which comprehendeth all wonders in the creation,—who made all things,—be himself made of a woman! and God become a man, and all this out of his infinite love, to give a demonstration of love to the world; so high a person abased, to exalt so base and low as we are! There is a mystery in this, a great mystery, a mystery of wisdom, to swallow up the understanding with wonder; and a mystery of love, to ravish the hearts of men with affection,—depths of both, in the emptiness of the Son of God. The prophet doubted what was commanded, to seek a sign, whether in heaven above, or in the depth beneath; but what he would not ask, God gave in his great mercy, 'Behold a virgin shall conceive a Son, and they shall call his name Immanuel;' a sign indeed from heaven, and the height of heaven, because he is God; and a sign from the depth beneath too, because he is man; 'God with us,' and so composed to unite heaven and earth together; 'God with us,' that he might at length bring us to be with God. He became *Immanuel*, that he might make us *Immelanu*.† If that was given as tidings of great joy, and as the highest and deepest sign of love and favour, at that time to uphold the fainting church; O! how much more may it now comfort us, when it is not a virgin shall conceive, but a virgin hath conceived! May not the joy be increased, that the Redeemer is not to come, but come already, and hath made up that wide separation which was between us and him, by his low condescendency to his union with our nature! This is one step of advancement towards that happy marriage, that the whole creation seems to groan and travail for, Rom. viii. 22. But yet there is a great difficulty in the way. We are in a state of captivity; we are prisoners of justice, have sold ourselves and our happiness; and now our natural inheritance lies in the lake of fire and brimstone,—heirs of wrath, concluded under the curse of God; and indeed, this was insuperable to all flesh; neither men nor angels could ransom us from this. The redemption of the soul of man is so precious, and the redemption of the inheritance of man, that is, heaven, is so precious too, that none in heaven or

* [Non bene conveniunt, nec in una sede morantur,
Majestas et amor. OVID. MET. lib. ii. v. 846.—ED.]

† [The name Immanuel (עמנו אל) signifies, *God with us*. Immelanu (עמאל אנו) signifies, *we with God*.—ED.]

earth can be found, that can pay the price of them, so that it would have ceased for ever. And here the great design of Christ's union with sinners would have been marred and miscarried, if himself had not undertaken to overcome this too ; and indeed, as there could none be found to open the seals of the book of God's decrees concerning his church,—none worthy in heaven or earth but the Lamb, the Lion of the tribe of Judah, he prevailed to open it, and loose the seals thereof, Rev. v. 3—5. So there could none be found in heaven or earth, neither under the earth, worthy to undertake or accomplish this work, or able to open the seals of the book of God's curses, or to blot out the hand-writing of ordinances that was against us, or to open the prison of death in which man was shut up ; none, I say, hath been found worthy or prevailed, but the Lamb of God and Lion of the tribe of Judah ; and therefore the four and twenty elders that sit round about the throne, and the four beasts, with the innumerable company of angels, and spirits of just men made perfect, fell down before the Lamb, every one of them with harps, and they sung a new song, 'Worthy is the Lamb that was slain, to receive power, and riches, and wisdom, and strength, and honour, and glory, and blessing; for thou hast redeemed us to God by thy blood.' And every creature says Amen to this, and consents to this, to do him homage; to him who alone was worthy, and as willing to do it as worthy for it. I think the 16th verse of this chapter gives us a sensible representation of this. The preceding discourse from the beginning, holding out the sinful and deplorable condition of that people, and in them, as a type of the desperate wickedness of all mankind, and withal their desperate misery, for Paul, (Rom. iii.) maketh the application for us; and from this, concludeth all under sin, and so all under wrath, all guilty, that every mouth may be stopped; men waiting for light, and behold obscurity; for brightness, but walking in darkness; groping for the wall, like the blind, stumbling at noon-day as in the night, and in desolate places as dead men; all roaring like beasts, and mourning like doves, whenever the apprehension of the terror of God entereth. Now it is subjoined, verse 16, 'And he saw that there was no man,' &c.; as if he had waited and looked through all the world, if any would appear, either to speak or do for man, if any would offer themselves, and interpose themselves for his salvation. 'Therefore his own arm brought salvation, and his righteousness, it sustained him.' Therefore the Son of God steps in and offers himself, as if God had first essayed all others, and when heaven is full of wonder and silence, he breaks out in this, 'Lo, I come to do thy will,' Psal. xl. Since I have gotten a body to be like sinners, I will also come in their place, and I will give my life a ransom for them; and therefore it is subjoined, 'the Redeemer shall come to Zion ;' he shall come clothed with vengeance and indignation as a garment, against the enemies of his church, sin and Satan, in zeal and burning love to his designed spouse. He shall strengthen himself, and stir up his might and fury against all that detain her captive.

Now, indeed, he is the only fittest person for this business in heaven or earth; for he hath both right to do it, and he only hath might and power to accomplish it. He hath right to the redemption of sinners, because he is our kinsman, nearest of blood to us.

Now, you know the right of redemption belonged to the kinsman, Lev. xxv. 25. And therefore when the nearest kinsman could not redeem Naomi and Ruth's parcel of land, Boaz did it, as being next. And suitable to this, our Lord Jesus, when others as near could not, and were not able, he hath done it, and taken men and angels to witness, that he hath first redeemed us, that he might marry us, as Eph. v.; that he hath purchased us to be his wife. And indeed the very word imports this; *Goel,** a redeemer and kinsman, passing under one word: so Job, 'I know that my Redeemer,' or my kinsman, 'liveth:' and because our kinsman, therefore most interested in our redemption; for, for this end he became partaker of flesh and blood with the children, that he might destroy our greatest enemy, Satan, and redeem us, Heb. ii. 14. And besides, he hath right to redemption, as the Church's

* [The Goel (גאל), or nearest kinsman, was, by the Mosaic law, entitled not only to redeem a forfeited inheritance, but to avenge the blood of any of the family, by slaying the murderer, if he found him out of a city of refuge. He was therefore called the redeemer, or "avenger of blood," Josh. xx. 3.—Ed.]

husband, because he must mediate between her and all others; none can reach her, except he please, or prosecute a plea against her, as in the case of the wife's making a vow; if her husband consented not, it was void, (Numb. xxx.;) but if he heard of it and held his peace, it was confirmed. Now the Lord Jesus hath known this deplorable estate in which we are captives; and he hath testified his utter dislike of our binding over ourselves to death, and resigning ourselves to Satan; and therefore this bondage in which we are detained, is not confirmed and ratified, but he hath right remaining to redeem us from the hand of all our enemies. But then, he alone hath might and power to do it, for God hath laid help on him, and made him able and mighty to save us to the uttermost. It was not gold or silver, or corruptible things. Suppose the whole earth were turned into gold or precious stones; he must give person for person, and one person equivalent to all—his own life, his own blood for us; and the value of this was infinitely raised by the stamp of his divinity put upon it. The king for the servant,—one that knew no sin for sinners,—yea, God for man! This superadds infinite worth, and makes it an over-ransom, and over purchase, a ransom to buy our persons from hell, a purchase to redeem us to our inheritance, heaven, that we had lost; and these two styles it gets, λυτρον, αντιλυτρον.*

Now, you see the great difficulty is overcome and taken out of the way; Christ, being made a curse, hath purchased a redemption from the curse of the law, Gal. iii. 13. But yet, there is another point of vast distance, I may say contrariety and enmity, between us and him. He is holy and undefiled, all fair, and no spot in him; we are wholly defiled and depraved by sin; our souls are become the habitation of devils, and a cage of every unclean and hateful bird; in a word, he hath not only our enemies to overcome, but our own hearts to conquer, and our enmity to take away. This makes the widest separation from him. Now, he filled up much of the distance, with his taking our flesh, and he removed the great difficulty, by dying in our flesh: his humiliation to be a man, brought him nearer us; and his further humiliation to be a dying, crucified, and buried man, brought him yet a step nearer us. But nearer he cannot come, for lower he cannot be, except he were a sinner, which would mar the whole design, and take away all the comfort of his likeness to us. Therefore, since he hath come so low down to us, it is suitable we be raised up one step to meet him; and so the exaltation of sinners shall make up all the distance, and bring the two parties to that long since designed, and long desired meeting. Now, for this end and purpose, the Son undertakes the redemption of his church from sin and ungodliness as well as wrath; and therefore you have that which is expressed as the character of the redeemed in this verse. It is exponed as the great point or part of the redemption itself by the apostle, Rom. xi. 'The Redeemer shall come to Sion, and shall turn away ungodliness from Jacob.' And so his end was not only to be a partaker of our nature, but to make us partakers of the divine nature; and therefore the Father, out of his love to this business, promised to send his Spirit to dwell in our hearts, to make the word sound in our mouths and ears, and the Spirit to work in our hearts; and this exaltation of sinners to the participation of the Holy Spirit, together with Christ's humiliation to partake of our flesh, makes up the full distance, and bringeth Christ and his church to that holy patient impatience, and longing for the day when it shall be solemnized in heaven. The Spirit within us says, Come, and the bride says, Come. Even so come, Lord Jesus. And he waits for nothing, but the completing and adorning of all the rest, that there may be one jubilee for all and for ever. Now I wish we could understand the absolute and free tenor of God's covenant. There is much controversy speculative about the condition of the covenant, about the promises, whether absolute or conditional; and there is too much practical debate in perplexed consciences about this,

* [The word λυτρον denotes the price of redemption, or that which is given to purchase the freedom of those who are in a state of captivity. 'Even as the Son of man came not to be ministered unto, but to minister, and to give his life a ransom (λυτρον) for many.' (Matt. xx. 28; Mark x. 45.) Αντιλυτρον is but once used in the New Testament. Its signification is a counter-price, or the ransom that is paid, when the life or person of one is given for that of another. 'For there is but one God, and one mediator between God and men, the man Christ Jesus, who gave himself a ransom (αντιλυτρον) for all,' 1 Tim. ii. 5, 6. Vide Leigh's Critica Sacra.—Ed.]

how to find something in themselves to fit and fashion them for the redemption. But truly, if we would not disjoin and dismember the truth of God, but take it all entirely as one great design of love and mercy revealed to sinners, and so conjoin the promises of the covenant into one bundle, we would certainly find that it hath the voice of Jacob, though it seem to have the hand of Esau; we find an absolute, most free and unconditioned sense, when there is a conditional strain and shadow of words in some places. The truth is, the turning of souls from ungodliness is not properly a condition exacted from us, as a promise to be performed in us, and the chiefest part of Christ's redemption; and though some abuse the grace of God, and turn it into wantonness and liberty, yet certainly, this doctrine, that makes the greatest part of the glad news of the gospel to be redemption from sin, and the pouring out of the Spirit, is the greatest persuasive to a godly conversation, and the most deadly enemy to all ungodliness.

I thought to have spoken more of that third thing I proponed, * but take it in a word. This was always proponed to the church as the strongest cordial, it was given here as the greatest consolation in all their long captivity, that this Redeemer was afterwards to come, whose virtue was then living, and present to the quickening and comforting of souls. It was thought enough to uphold in a most desperate strait, 'To us a child is born,' Isa. ix. 6. I wish we could take it so. Certainly it was the character of a believer before Christ's coming, that he was one that was looking and waiting for the salvation of Israel, by this Redeemer. But now we are surrounded with consolation before and behind,—Christ already come, so that we may in joy say, Lo! this is our God, we have waited for him! others waited and longed, and we see him,—and Christ shortly to come again without sin, to our salvation. And what could be able to take our joy from us, if we had one eye always back to his first coming, and another always forward to his coming again?

Sermon IV.

ISAIAH lxiv. 6, 7.—"*But we are all as an unclean thing, and all our righteousnesses are as filthy rags,*" &c.

THIS people's condition agreeth well with ours, though the Lord's dealing be very different. The confessory part of this prayer belongeth to us now; and strange it is, that there is such odds of the Lord's dispensations, when there is no difference in our conditions; always we know not how soon the complaint may be ours also. This prayer was prayed long before the judgment and captivity came on, so that it had a prophecy in the bosom of it. Nay, it was the most kindly and affectionate way of warning the people could get, for Isaiah to pour forth such a prayer, as if he beheld with his eyes the calamity, as already come. And indeed it becometh us so to look on the word, as if it gave a present being to things as certain and sensible as if they were really. What strange stupidity must be in us, when present things, inflicted judgments, committed sins, do not so much affect us, as the foresight of them did move Isaiah! Always,† as this was registrate for the people's use, to cause them still look on judgments threatened, as performed and present, and anticipate the day of affliction by repentance; and also to be a pattern to them, how to deal with God, and plead with him from such grounds of mercy and covenant-interest: so it may be to us a warning, especially when sin is come to the maturity, and our secure backsliding condition is with child of sad judgments, when the harvest seemeth ripe to put the sickle into it.

There is in these two verses, a confession of their own sinfulness, from which grounds they justify God's proceeding with them; they take the cause upon themselves, and justify him in his judging, whether temporal or spiritual plagues were inflicted. In this verse, ‡ they take a general survey of their sinful estate, concluding themselves

* [That is, proposed.—ED.] † [That is, however.—ED.] ‡ [Verse 6.—ED.]

unclean, and all their performances and commanded duties, which they counted once their righteousness: and from this ground, they clear God's dealing with them, and put their mouths in the dust; and so from the Lord's judgment they are forced to enter into a search of the cause of so much sin; and from discovered sin, they pronounce God righteous in his judgment. Perceiving a great difference in the Lord's manner of dealing with them, and their fathers, they do not refound* it upon God, who is righteous in all his ways, but retort it upon themselves, and find a vast discrepance between themselves and their fathers, verse 5. And so it was no wonder that God's dispensation changed upon them. God was wont to meet others, to show himself gracious, even to prevent strokes, but now he was wroth with them. Nay, but there is good cause for it. They rejoice and wrought righteousness, but we have sinned. And this may be said in the general,—never one needeth to quarrel God for severe dealing. If he deal worse with one than with another, let every man look into his own bosom, and see reason sufficient; yea, more provocation in themselves than others. Always in this verse, they come to a more distinct view of their loathsome condition. Anybody may wrap up their repentance in a general notion of sin, but they declare themselves to be more touched with it, and condescend on particulars, yet such particulars as comprehend many others. And in this confession, you may look on the Spirit's work, having some characters of the Spirit in it.

I. They take a general view of their uncleanness and loathsome estate by sin; not only do they see sin, but sin in the sinfulness of it and uncleanness of it.

II. They not only conclude so of the natural estate they were born in, and the loathsomeness of their many foul scandals among them; but they go a further length, to pass as severe a sentence on their duties and ordinances as God hath done, Isa. i. and lxvi. The Spirit convinceth according to scripture's light, and not according to the dark spark of nature's light; and so that which nature would have busked † itself with as its ornament, that which they had covered themselves with as their garment, the duties they had spread, as robes of righteousness, over their sins to hide them; all this now goeth under the name of filthiness and sin. They see themselves wrapt up in as vile rags as they covered and hid: commanded duties and manifest breaches come in one category. And not only is it some of them which their own conscience could challenge in the time, but all of them and all kinds of them, moral and ceremonial, duties that were most sincere, had most affection in them, all of them are filthy rags now, which but of late were their righteousness.

III. There is an universality, not only of the actions, but of persons; not only all the peoples or multitudes' performances are abomination; but all of them, Isaiah, and one and other, the holiest of them, come in in this category and rank—'we are all unclean,' &c. Though the people, it may be, could not join holy Isaiah with themselves, yet humble Isaiah will join himself with the people, and come in, in one prayer. And no doubt, he was as sensible of sin now, as when he began to prophesy; and growing in holiness, he must grow also in sense of sinfulness. Seeing at the first sight of God's holiness and glory, he cried 'unclean,' &c. Isa. vi. 5, certainly he doth so now, from such a principle of access to God's holiness, which maketh him abhor himself in dust and ashes.

IV. They are not content with such a general, but condescend to two special things, two spiritual sins, viz. omission, or shifting of spiritual duties, which contained the substance of worship. 'None calleth on thee,' few or none, none to count upon, calleth on thee; that is, careth for immediate access and approaching unto God in prayer and meditation, &c. Albeit external and temple-duties be frequent, yet who prayeth in secret? or if any pray, that cannot come in count, the Lord knoweth them not, because they want the Spirit's stamp on them. This must be some other thing than the general conviction of sin which the world hath, who think they pray all their days; here people, who though they make many prayers, Isa. i., yet they see them no prayers, and no calling on God's name now. But,

V. To make the challenge the more, and the confession more spiritual and complete, there is discovered to them this ground of their slackness and negligence in all

* [That is, place it upon God or charge him with it.—ED.]
† [That is, adorned itself.—ED.]

spiritual duties, 'None stireth up himself to take hold on thee.' Here is the want of the exercise of faith: faith is the soul's hand and grip, John i. 12; Heb. vi. 18; 1 Tim. vi. 12; Isa. xxvii. 5. Nobody awaketh themselves out of their deadness and security, to lay hold on thee. Lord, thou art going away, and taking good-night of the land, and nobody is like to hold thee by the garment; no Jacobs here, who will not let thee go, till thou bless them; none to prevail with thy Majesty,—every one is like to give Christ a free passport and testimonial to go abroad, and are almost Gadarenes, to pray him to depart out of their coasts. There is a strange looseness and indifferency in men's spirits concerning the one thing necessary. Men lie by and dream over their days, and never put the soul's estate out of question; none will give so much pains, as to clear their interest in thee, to lay hold on thee, so as they may make peace with thee. Now, can there be a more ample and lively description of our estate, both of the land and of particular persons of it? Since this must not be limited to the nation of the Jews, though the prophet spake of the generality of them, yet, no doubt, all mankind is included in the first six verses; and any secure people may be included in the seventh verse, for Paul applieth even such like speeches (Rom. xi. 13.) that were spoken, as you would think, of David's enemies only. Yet the Spirit of God knowing the mind of the Spirit, maketh a more general use of their condition, to hold out the natural estate of all men out of Christ Jesus.

But there are in these two verses other two things beside the acknowledgment of sin:

I. The acknowledgment of God's righteousness in punishing them, for now they need not quarrel God, they find the cause of their fading in their own bosom. They now join sin and punishment together, whereas in the time of their prosperity they separated punishment from sin; and in the time of their security in adversity they separated sin from punishment: at one time making bare confession of sin, without fear of God's justice, at another time fretting and murmuring at his judgments, without the sense of their sin. But now they join both these, and the sight and sense of God's displeasure maketh sin more bitter, and to abound more, and to appear in the loathsome and provoking nature of it, so that their ackowledgment hath an edge upon it. And again, the sight and sense of sin maketh the judgment appear most righteous, and stoppeth their mouth from murmuring. In the time of their impenitency under the rod, their language was very indifferent, Ezek. xviii. 2. 'The fathers have eaten sour grapes, and the children's teeth are set on edge;' they have sinned and we suffer; they have done the wrong and we pay for it. But it is not so now, ver. 5. The fathers have done righteousness in respect of us, and thou wast good unto them; but we are all unclean, and have sinned, and so we are punished.

II. They find some cause and ground in God of their general defection; not that he is the cause of their sin, but in a righteous way he punished sin with sin. God hid his face, denied special grace and influence; and so they lie still in their security, and their sin became a spiritual plague. Or this may be so read,—*None calleth on thy name, when thou didst hide thy face from us, and when thou didst consume us because of our iniquities;* and so it serveth to aggravate their deep security, that, though the Lord was departing from them, yet none would keep him and hold him. Though he did strike, yet they prayed not; affliction did not awake them out of security, and so the last words, 'Thou hast consumed us,' &c., are differently exponed and read. Some make it thus, as it is in the translation, 'Thou hast hid thy face,' and left us in a spiritual deadness, that so there might be no impediment to bring on deserved judgment. If we had called on thee, and laid hold on thee, it might have been prevented, we might have prevailed with God, but now our defence is removed, and thou hast given us up to a spirit of slumber, and so we have no shield to hold off the stroke,—thou hast now good leave to consume us for our sins. Another sense may be—*Thou hast suffered us to consume in our iniquity, thou hast given us up to the hand of our sins.* And this is also a consequent of his hiding his face. Because thou didst hide thy face, thou lettest us perish in our sins; there needeth no more for our consumption, but only help us not out of them, for we can soon destroy ourselves.

First, Sin is in its own nature loathsome, and maketh one unclean before God. Sin's nature is filthiness, vileness, so doth Isaiah speak of himself, chap. vi. 5, when he saw God's holiness; so doth Job abhor himself, which is the affection which turneth a man's face off a loathsome object, when he saw God, Job xl. 4, and xlii. 6. Look how loathsome our natural condition is holden out by God himself, Ezek. xvi. You cannot imagine any deformity in the creature, any filthiness, but it is there. The filthiness and vileness of sin shall appear, if we consider *first*, that sin is a transgression of the holy and spiritual command, and so a vile thing; the commandment is holy and good, Rom. vii. And sin violateth and goeth flat contrary to the command, 1 John iii. 4. When so just and so equitable a law is given, God might have exacted other rigorous duties from us, but when it is so framed that the conscience must cry out, All is equity, all is righteous, and more than righteous; thou mightest command more, and reward none. It is justice to command, but it is mercy to promise life to obedience, which I owe;—what then must the offence be, against such a just command, and so holy? If holiness be the beauty of the creation, sin must be the deformity of it, the only spot in its face.

Secondly, Look upon sin in the sight of God's holiness and infinite majesty, and O how heinous will it appear! and therefore no man hath seen sin in the vileness of it, but in the light of God's countenance, as Isa. vi. 5; Job xl. and xlii. God is of purer eyes than to behold iniquity, he cannot look on it, Hab. i. 13. All other things beside sin, God looketh on them as bearing some mark of his own image, all was very good, and God saw it, Gen. i. and ii. Even the basest creatures God looketh on them, and seeth himself in them; but sin is only God's eyesore, that his holiness cannot away with it, it is most contrary unto him; and as to his sovereignty, it is a high contempt and rebellion done to God's Majesty. It putteth God off the throne, will take no law from him, will not acknowledge his law, but, as it were, spitteth in his face, and establisheth another god. There is no punishment so evil, that God will not own as his work, and declare himself to be the author of it, but only sin; his soul abhorreth it, his holy will is against it, he will have no fellowship with it: it is so contrary to him, contradicteth his will, debaseth his authority, despiseth his sovereignty, vilipendeth his truth. There is a kind of infiniteness in it; nothing can express it but itself, no name worse than itself to set it out; the apostle can get no other epithet to it, Rom. vii. 13, than 'sinful' sin; so that it cometh in most direct opposition unto God. All that is in God, is God himself, and there is no name can express him sufficiently. If you say God, you say more than can be expressed by many thousand other words. So it is here,—sin is purely sin, God is purely good and holy, without mixture, holiness itself; sin is simply evil, without mixture, unholiness itself. Whatever is in it, is sin, is uncleanness. Sin is an infinite wrong, and an infinite and boundless filthiness, because of the infinite person wronged. It is an offence of infinite Majesty, and the person wronged aggravateth the offence; if it be simply contrary to infinite holiness, it must be, in that respect, infinite unholiness and uncleanness.

Thirdly, Look upon the sad effects and consequences of sin,—how miserable, how ruinous it hath made man, and all the creation, and how vile must it be!

I. Look on man's native beauty and excellency, how beautiful a creature! But sin hath cast him down from the top of his excellency; sin made Adam of a friend an enemy, of a courtier with God an open rebel. Was not man's soul of more price than all the world, so that nothing can exchange it? Yet hath sin debased it, and prostituted it to all vile filthy pleasures; hath made the immortal spirit to dwell on the dunghill, feed on ashes, catch vanities, lying vanities, pour out itself to them, serve all the creatures—whereas it should have made them servants; yea, a slave to his own greatest enemy, to the ground he treadeth upon. O what a degenerate plant! It was a noble vine once in paradise, but sin hath made it a wild one, to bring forth sour grapes. What is there in all the world could defile a man? Matt. xv. 20. Nothing that goeth out or cometh in, but sin that proceedeth out of the heart. Man was all light, his judgment shined into his affections, and through all the man; but sin hath made all darkness, closed up the poor captive understanding, hath built up a thick wall of gross corrupted affections about it, so that light can neither get in nor out. The soul was like a clear running fountain, which yielded fresh clear streams of holy inclinations, desires, affections, actions, and emptied itself in the sea of immense Majesty from which these streams first flowed; but now it is a standing putrified puddle, that casteth a vile stink round about, and hath no issue towards God. Man was a glorious creature, fit to be lord over the work of God's own hands, and therefore had God's image in a special manner, holiness and righteousness, God's nature. A piece of divinity was stamped on man, which outshined all created perfections. The sun might blush when it looked on him, for what was material glory to the glory of holiness and beauty of God's image! But sin hath robbed poor man of this glorious image, hath defaced man, marred all his glory, put on an hellish likeness on him. Holiness only putteth the difference between angels in heaven and devils in hell; and sin only hath made the difference between Adam in paradise, and sinners on the cursed ground, Rom. iii. 23.

II. Sin hath so redounded through man unto all the creation, that it hath defiled it, and made it corruptible and subject to vanity, (Rom. viii. 20, &c.;) so that this is a spot in all the creature's face,—that man hath sinned, and used all as weapons of unrighteousness, so that now the creature groaneth to be delivered.

III. It hath brought on all the misery that is come on man, or that is to come; it hath brought on death and damnation as its wages, and the curse of the eternal God, Gal. iii. 13; Rom. vi. 23. How odious then an evil must it be, that hath so much evil in it; yea, all evil in the bosom of it! Hell is not evil in respect of sin, for sin deserveth hell; it hath ruined man, and made all the beautiful order of the creation to change.

IV. It separateth man from God, which is worst of all; and this is included in the text, 'We are all as an unclean thing,' or man is as a leprous man set apart, because of pollution, that may not come to the temple, or worship God; so hath iniquity separated between God and us, Isa. lix. 2. And O how sad a divorcement is this! it maketh men without God in the world, in whom we live, and move, and have our being; in whose favour is life, and at whose right hand are pleasures for evermore. Now poor man is made miserable, deprived of his felicity, which only consisted in enjoyment of God. Sin, as a thick partition-wall, is come in between, enmity also is come in, and divideth old friends, Eph. ii. 14—17: and now no heavenly or comfortable influence can break through; the night of darkness is begun which must prove everlasting. Except the partition-wall be removed, all must wither and decay as without the sun.

V. Look on the price paid for sin, on the cleansing that washeth it away, and you may see unspeakable deformity and vileness in it. The redemption of the soul is precious; silver and gold and precious stones will not do it,—that would be utterly contemned. 'What!' saith God, 'presumptuous sinner, wilt thou give me a farthing in payment of a sum which all the world, sold at the dearest, would not discharge?' Psal. xlix. 7, 8; 1 Pet. i. 18. It is no corruptible thing, but the blood of the Son of God. O what must the debt be, when the price is so infinite! the Son of God must die; nay, it is not sacrifice or offering:—'Lo, I come to do thy will;' it is Christ himself that is the ransom, Psal. xl. 6, 7. And it is not much soap or nitre, it is not much repentance and tears that will wash away this filthiness; no, it is of a deeper dye, it is crimson ingrained filthiness, Jer. ii. 22. and Isa. i. 16. Blood of bulls and goats cannot do it, but only the blood of the immaculate Lamb offered up by himself, (Heb. x. 4, 5;) the blood of Him, 'who by the eternal Spirit offered up himself without spot unto God,' Heb. ix. 14. What must sin be, that must have such a fountain opened for it? It must be strange uncleanness when the blood of Christ only can cleanse it, Zech. xiii. 1.

'We all,' &c. Mark, *first*, Sin hath gone over us all, and made all mankind unclean, Rom. iii. 10, 22. Every one of Adam's posterity is born unclean, 'For who can bring a clean thing out of an unclean?' Job xiv. 4. Consider, 1. How sin defaced innocent Adam, how one sin made him so vile, and spoiled him of the divine nature; and so the root was made unclean, and the branches must follow the root, and so are we all born and conceived in sin, Psalm li. 5. We carry in us original corruption, flowing from the first actual sin of Adam; and this maketh poor children, before they do good or evil, to be abominably vile in God's sight, even as the child is set out, Ezek. xvi. Every one cometh of evil parents, all come of Adam the rebel; what a loathsome sight would a child be to us so described, 'Cast out in the open field, to the loathing of its person in the day it is born;' and what must it all be before God, who is of purer eyes than to behold sin? *Secondly,* Unto all this we have added innumerable actual transgressions as so many filthy streams flowing out at the members, from the inward puddle of original corruption; and so how much more vile are we all nor infants can be, or Adam was in the day he was cast out of paradise! And thus, Rom. iii. from verse 10, are the branches set down in word, thought, and deed; so that all the inclinations and motions and actions of the man are only evil continually. Every man shall find his count past counting; one day's faults would weary you, but what will your whole life do? Known sins are innumerable, what must unknown be? Every man's heart is like the troubled sea, that casteth up mire and dirt daily, and cannot be at rest. The heart is daily flowing and ebbing in this corruption, it cometh out daily to the borders of all the members; and there are some high spring-tides, when sin aboundeth more. When in one member of the tongue a world of evil is, what can be in all the members? And what in the soul, that is more capable than all the world? Well, then, every man hath sinned in Adam, and hath sinned also in his own person, and sealed Adam's first rebellion by so many thousand actions like it. Every man hath approven the sin that first ruined man, and made himself much more loathsome nor Adam was; therefore all mankind may say, 'We all are as an unclean thing.' Now from all this, we would gladly discover unto you what your condition is by sin; if the Lord would shine, how vile would you be! Always we must declare this unto you in the Lord's name, you are all unclean, not only born in sin and iniquity, not only have you a body of death within you, that hath all the members; but all these members have one time or other acted and brought forth fruit unto death. How vile, then, must you be in God's sight! It is a strange love that you have to yourselves, that you cannot apprehend how God can hate you! But if he find sin in you, wonder rather how he can look upon you; we would then have you to know this, that there can be no fellowship between God and you in your natural estate. As men cannot inhabit a vile person's house, no more can God enter into your souls. There is an absolute necessity of washing, before you can be his house and temple. Hath that one sin of Adam made that glorious person so deformed, that he could not look on himself, but cover himself? And hath it been of so defiling a nature, that it hath redounded in all the posterity; and, as unclean things under the law defiled all they touched, so hath that sin subjected all the creatures to corruption? O then imagine what an unspeakable defilement must be on us all, who are not only guilty of Adam's sin, but of many thousands beside! If one sin have so much loathsomeness in it, what must so many out of number, united in one person, even as in us all? No unclean thing can enter into heaven above: know this for a truth, you cannot see God's face in the case you are born into. You know nothing of sin, who wonder that any should go to hell. No, if you knew anything of sin, you would wonder that ever God should look on such cast out in the open field in their blood.

Next, You must know the insufficiency of all things imaginable, to wash away sin's filthiness, except the blood of Christ. Since you are unclean, do you not ask, how shall we be washed? Indeed many have an easy answer, and pass it lightly. The multitude know no way to cleanse in, but the tears of repentance and mourning; and so, many think themselves clean, when they run and pour out a tear as Esau did for the blessing. But what saith the Lord? 'Though thou wash thee with nitre, and take thee much soap, yet thine iniquity is marked.' Can such an ingrained uncleanness, can such an infinite spot in the immortal soul, be so lightly dashed out? Many think baptism cleanseth them, but was not this people circumcised, as ye are baptized? And Peter tells us, it is not the washing of water, &c. 1 Pet. iii. 21. Sacrifice and offering will not do it. This people thought, sure they had satisfied God, when they brought a lamb, &c., but all this is abomination. Would not many of you think yourselves cleansed from sin, if you offered all your substance, and the fruit of your body for the sin of your soul? Nay, but you must see an absolute necessity of the opened fountain of Christ's blood, that cleanseth from all sin.

Then we would have you abhor yourselves in dust and ashes, and see nothing in all the creation so vile as you; look on sin in the sight of God's face, and how unholy will it appear! There are many sins, little ones, that in our practice pass for venal and uncontrolled; but look on the filthy loathsome nature of all sin, and hate the least offence, for it hath a kind of infiniteness in it, and blotteth the soul, defileth the person. How great a necessity is there of continual application to the fountain, of dwelling beside it, that you may wash daily! David's so often repeated and inculcated prayer, 'Wash me, cleanse me,' &c. Psalm li., declareth that he hath apprehended much uncleanness in sin, that it needeth so many applications of the precious blood. And you who have come to Jesus, and are clean, O how much owe you to free grace, that passed by you in your blood, and said, 'Live, it is a time of love!' How strange is it, that glorious Majesty cometh to own deformity, and cometh to clothe it with his own garments! Praise the virtue of that blood, that is more precious than the blood of bulls and goats, that can so throughly purge, as you shall have no more conscience of sin.

Unclean sinners, wash you, make you clean,—there is a fountain opened; though sin were as scarlet, it can perfectly change the colour of it. If you wash not while the fountain is open, it will quickly be sealed on you, and then it shall be said, when the angel sweareth by him that liveth for ever and ever, that time shall be no more, then shall it be said, 'let him that is unclean be unclean still.' Now, cleansing is offered in the gospel,—if you will love your loathsomeness so well, as not to dip yourselves in this fountain, then let the unclean be so still. Your repentance will never change your colour, though you should melt in sorrow; and therefore you who have found a way to be saved otherwise nor* by Jesus Christ, you shall be deceived. Your tears and mourning that you might have had, though Christ had never come into the world, is all you use to speak of, and build your hope on; and if you speak of Christ, it is in such terms as to buy him by such repentance; so that the truth is, you use but Christ's name as a shadow, you make no use of him; he needed not to have come into the world, for many of you could have done as well without him. But as many of you as cannot find cleansing, who see filth increase by washing, come to Christ Jesus, and say, 'If you wilt, thou canst make me clean,' Matt. viii. 2. Nothing beside Jesus can do it—believe his sufficiency. Nothing beside him will do—believe his willingness; for, for this cause he is an open fountain, that all may come and draw.

Sermon XVI.

ISAIAH lxiv. 6, 7.—"*All our righteousnesses are as filthy rags, and we all do fade as a leaf, and our iniquities, like the wind, have taken us away.*"

NOT only are the direct breaches of the command uncleanness, and men originally and actually unclean, but even our holy actions, our commanded duties. Take a man's civility, religion, and all his universal inherent righteousness,—all are filthy rags. And here the church confesseth nothing but what God accuseth her of, Isa. lxvi. 3, and chap. i. ver. 11, 12, 13, &c. This people was much in ceremonial and external duties; and therefore they cried, 'The temple of the Lord, the temple of Lord!' as if this would have outcried all their other sins; therefore were they proud, and lords in their own estimation, and innocent, Jer. ii. 31, 35. They thought the many good services they did to God might compense all their wrongs, Mic. vi. 6, 7. They gave a price to justice for their sins, even a confession of it, by offering a lamb, &c. and a purpose to amend. But, lo! what sense the prophet hath of all this, 'Lord, all our righteousnesses' are filthy likewise. Albeit we have paid the debt of sins with duties, yet now we see all these are sins themselves, and must have another sacrifice; so that all matter of boasting is now removed, and we are stript naked of all righteousness. We covered our filthiness before with duties, now both the one and the other is filthy. We would look upon two sorts of righteousnesses, the natural man's, and the converted man's, upon the one's civility and fair profession, and upon the other's real or true grace in discharge of duties, and we shall find good reason to conclude both the one and the other under filthiness, so that there is no ground of boasting, no inherent righteousness can make us accepted before God.

* [*Scottice* for *than*.—ED.]

First, then, Whatever men can do from natural principles, all the flower and perfection of men's actions, both civil and religious, is but abominable before God, as long as their persons are unjustified. Every performance is defiled by the uncleanness of the person; and therefore God heareth not sinners, (John viii.,) that is, unjustified sinners; though they pray much, yet God heareth them not. And this is lively expressed by Hag. ii. 12, 13, 14. As the priest's holy garments and flesh could not make bread or pottage holy, but the unclean body could make these unclean; so this nation's and people's performances and holy duties, could not make them holy, and their persons clean, but their unclean persons and actions made all their performances unclean. The solemn meeting and sacrifice, &c. could not make them accepted, but their unclean persons made their solemn meetings and religious duties vile and abominable in God's sight: and thus to the unclean all things are unclean, even their mind and conscience, Tit. i. 15. The unbelieving man, who is born unclean, and defiled with so much original corruption, and so many actual transgressions, defileth all things he toucheth. As a dead body, or a leprous garment, under the law, made all unclean it touched, and nothing could make it holy by touching of it; so all your civility, all your profession, will never contribute to the cleansing of your person; and your persons shall defile all your most clean actions. God loveth not that stock of Adam, and all that groweth on it must be hateful; he is only well-pleased in Jesus Christ, and with those who are transplanted out of rotten Adam into the true vine Jesus. It is such fruit only that can be acceptable; therefore, until you be sprinkled with clean water, and made clean according to the new covenant-way, you cannot please God. Believe this,—your sins and your duties are one, your oaths and your prayers are in the same account with God. What have you then to build upon, when all this is removed? You must once be stript naked of all coverings; and will not your nakedness then be great? The Pharisee went away unjustified, and the poor repenting sinner justified. What was the reason? There are not many of you have such a fair venture for heaven as he had,—so many prayers, fastings, alms, to ground your hope on. Nay, but all this would never justify his person, because once he was unclean, come of Adam, and had contracted more uncleanness, and all that is like the leprous garment, defiling all that cometh near it; so that whatever hath any dependence on a son of Adam, must contract filthiness. Now, I ask your consciences, have you so many specious coverings to adorn yourself with? Is not your outside spotted, and not so clean as the young civil man and the religious Pharisee? Certainly no; and yet you have no other ground to plead the acceptation of your persons upon, but only this, your prayers and tears, or some such duty performed by you. Well, all is uncleanness, since your persons were once unclean,—no soap nor nitre can wash it, no holy flesh make it holy, no good wishes nor duties can make it acceptable. Did not this people think of their duties as much as you do? and had more reason so to do; for our congregations have not so much form of godliness as they had, and yet God solemnly protested to them that all their works were defiled, even those which they took to wash themselves with. So your repentance and tears must be as filthy as the sin you would wash by it.

Secondly, The uncleanness of men's practice maketh unclean performances. Unclean hands maketh unclean prayers, Isa. i. 15. When men go on in sin, and use their members as instruments of unrighteousness against God, and guiltiness is above their head unrepented of and unpardoned, then whatever the members act for God in religious duties, it must be also abominable; for will God take prayers from such a mouth, that cursing cometh out of? Isa. iii. 10, 11, 12. Shall sweet water come out of one fountain with bitter? Or can a fig-tree bear both thistles and grapes? Certainly, profane conversation must make unclean profession; and therefore your coming to the church and ordinances, your praying in your families, or such like, must of necessity be defiled, since out of the same mouth cometh cursing, railing, lying, filthy speeches. Your tongues are so often employed in God's dishonour, to blaspheme his name, to slander your neighbours, to reproach the saints, that all your prayers must be of the same stamp, and as bitter as the other stream of your actions. When you stretch forth your hands to make many prayers, to take the bread and wine, shall not God hide his face from such hands as are unclean with many abominations, some murdering, some abusing their neighbours, some sabbath breaking, some filthiness? How oft have your hands and feet served you to evil turns? And therefore, your good turns will never come in remembrance. Nay, believe it, you cannot be heard of God, while you cover any offence. And this I may say in general, even to the saints; any known sin given way to, and entertained without controlment, without wrestling against it, hindereth the acceptation of your solemn approaches. If your heart regard iniquity, shall God hear? Psal. lxvi. 18. No, believe it, the least sin that you may judge at first venial, and then give it toleration and indulgence, shall separate between God's face and you. Your prayers are abomination, because of such an idol perked up in the heart beside God, that getteth the honour and worship due to him, and God must answer you according to it, Ezek. xix. 1, 3, 4. God will not be inquired of such as give allowance to sin, Ezek. xiv. 2—4. And, on the other hand, no sin, how great and heinous soever, can hinder God's gracious acceptation, when souls fly unto Jesus and turn their back upon sin, or giveth it no heart allowance. And to the multitude I say, all that you do or touch in a duty must be defiled, because your whole way is unclean, Hag. ii. 12—14. Think you to sin all the week through, and worship God on the Sabbath? Will you lie, swear, commit adultery, rail and curse, and come and stand before me, saith the Lord? No, certainly, you cannot be accepted. And will you hate reformation in your lives, and yet take his covenant in your mouth, and call yourselves by his name, "Christians?" And shall not God challenge you for that, as much as for your swearing, and cursing, and lying, &c.? Indeed the Lord putteth all in one roll, and you need not please yourselves in such things, Psal. l. 16; Jer. vii. 9, 10; for it is all one to you to go to tavern to drink, and come to the sermon,—to blaspheme God's name, and call on it; because the profanity of the one defileth the other, and the holiness of the other cannot make you holy.

Thirdly, The natural man's performances want the uprightness, reality, and sincerity that is required. It is but a painted tomb, full of rottenness within; it is but a shadow without substance, for he wanteth the spiritual part of worship, which God careth for, who will be worshipped 'in spirit and in truth,' John iv. 24. Now, what is it that the most part of you can speak of, but an outside of some few duties, soon numbered? You hear the preaching, and your hearts wander about your business. You hear, and are not so much affected as you would be to hear some old story or fable told you. A stage play acted before this generation would move them more than the gospel doth; so that Christ may take up this lamentation, 'We have piped to you, and you have not danced; lamented to you, and you have not mourned.' You use to tell over some words in your prayers, and are not so serious in any approach to God, as in twenty other things of the world. Whatever you plead of your heart's rightness, and have recourse to it, when your conversation cannot defend you, yet your hearts are the worst of all, and have no uprightness towards God; for you know that what duties you go about, it is not from an inward principle, but from education, or custom, or constraint. Are you upright, when you are forced, for fear of censure, to come here, or to pray at home? Is that sincerity and spiritual worship? And for the more polished and refined professors, you have this moth in your performances, and this fly to make your ointment to stink, that you do much to be seen of men. Therefore, what little fervour of spirit is in secret duties, there you may measure your altitude and your life. And O! how wearisome, how lifeless are secret approaches! You would not have many errands to God, if you thought no body looked upon you. And for spirituality, it is a mystery in all men's practice. Who directeth his duty to God's glory? If you get some flash of liberty, you have your desire; but who misseth God's presence in duties, which a world will approve? Who go mourning as without the sun, even when you have the sunshine of ordinances, and walk in the light of them?

And, *Fourthly*, Though your performances had uprightness of heart going along, and much affection in them, yet all are filthy, because of want of faith in Jesus Christ. When you make your duties a covering of your sins, and think to satisfy God's justice for the rest of your faults, by doing some point of your duty, then it cannot choose but be polluted in his sight. And this very thing was the cause of God's rejecting the Jews' righteousness, even because they did not look to the end of the mystery, Christ Jesus: did not pull by the vail of ceremonies, to see the immaculate Lamb of God slain for sin; and therefore doth the Lord so quarrel with them, as if he had never commanded them to do such things, Isa. i. 12, 13, 'Who hath required these things at your hands? Bring no more vain oblations;' all is abomination. Even as God should say to you, when you come to the church, Who required you to come? Who commanded you to come to hear the preaching? What have you to do to pray? What warrant have you to communicate? All your praying, hearing, communicating, is abomination; who commanded you to do these things? Would you not think it a foolish question? You would soon answer, that God himself commanded you, and will he not let us do his bidding? Indeed this people, no doubt, have said so in their heart, and wondered what it meant. Nay, but here is the mystery,—you go about these commanded duties not in a commanded way, and so the obedience is but rebellion. You bring offerings and incense, and think that I am pacified when you bring alms,—you judge you have given me a recompence; whereas, all that is mine, and what pleasure have I in these things? I never appointed you sacrifices for this end, but to lead you into the knowledge of my Son, which is to be slain in the fulness of time, and by one offering to perfect all. I commanded you to look on Jesus Christ slain, in the slain Lamb, and so to expect remission and salvation in him; but you never looked to more nor the ceremony, and made that your saviour and mediator; and therefore it is all abomination. When you slay a lamb, and offer incense, it is all one thing as to cut off a dog's neck, or kill a man. So may the Lord say to this generation, I command you to pray, to repent and mourn for sin, to come and hear the word; but withal you must deny all these, and count yourselves unprofitable servants; you must singly cast your soul's burden on Christ Jesus. But now, saith the Lord, who commanded your repentance? For when you sit down to pray, or come in public to confess sin before the congregation, you think you are washen. When you have said, you have sinned, and if you come to the length of tears and sorrow, O then, sure you are pardoned, though in the meantime you have no thought of Jesus Christ, and know no use of him! Therefore, saith the Lord, who commanded you to do these things? You think you have satisfied for your sin, when you pay a penalty; but who requireth this? I will reckon with you for these, as well as the sins you pray and mourn for, because you do not singly look to Christ Jesus. Now, if he had never come to the world, your ground of confidence would not fail you; for you might have prayed as much, mourned and confessed, and promised amendment; and so you pass by the Son of God, in whom only the Father is well-pleased. Think, then, upon this,—whatever you make your righteousness, there needeth no other thing to make it filthy, but to make it your righteousness. Your confidence in your good heart to God, prayer day and night, and such like, is the most loathsome thing in God's eyes. Except you come to this, to count your prayers, as God doth, among your oaths; to count your solemn duties among profane scandalous actions, as the Lord doth, Isa. i. and lxvi. 3, then certainly, you do adorn yourselves with them, and cover your nakedness of other faults with such leaves as Adam did, but you shall be more discovered. Your garment is as filthy as that it hideth, even because you make that use of it to hide your sin and cover it.

Next, The Lord's children have no ground of boasting either, from their own righteousness; the holiest saint on earth must abhor himself in dust and ashes, and holy Isaiah joineth himself in with a profane people. When he cometh to God to be justified, he cometh among the ungodly,—he bringeth no righteousness with him, he cometh in among them that work not. Now, you shall find good ground why it must be so:

I. There are ordinarily many blemishes in our holiest actions, spots upon our cleanest garments; often formality eateth up the life of duties, and representeth a body without a soul in it. You sit down to pray out of custom, morning and evening; and if there were no more to prove it, this may suffice. When pray you but at such times? You have an ordinary, and go not by it. No advantage is taken of providence, no necessity constraineth when occasion offereth; and so it is like the world's appointed hours. How great deadness and indisposition creepeth in! so that this is the ordinary complaint; yea, all prayers are filled with it,—scarcely any room for other petitions, because of the want of frame for prayer itself. The word is heard as a discourse, and on whom hath it operation to stir up affections, either of joy or of trembling? Christians, you come not to hear God speak, and so you meet with empty ordinances—God is not in them. How often do crooked and sinister ends creep in, and bias the spirit! Men ask, to spend on their lusts, and to satisfy their own ambition. Some would have more grace to be more eminent, or to have a more pleasant life; and this is but the seeking to spend on your lusts. If affection run in the channel of a duty, it is often muddy, and runneth through our corruptions: liberty in duties is principled with carnal affection and self-love. Will not often the wind of applause in company fill the sails, and make your course swifter and freer nor when you are alone? And often much love to a particular* maketh more in seeking it. And that which is a moth to eat up and consume all our duties is conceit and self-confidence in going about them, and attributing to ourselves after them. It is but very rare that any man both acted from Jesus Christ as the principle, and also putteth over his work on Christ singly as the end. Alas! too often do men draw out of Christ's fulness, and raise up their own glory upon it, and adorn themselves with the spoils of his honour; for we use to pray from a habit of it, and go to it as men acquainted with it, and when we get any satisfaction to our own minds, O how doth the soul return on itself, and goeth not forward as it goeth! It is so well pleased with itself, when it getteth liberty to approach, that it doth not put all over on Jesus, and take shame to itself. As long as there is a body of death within, holiness cannot be pure and unmixed; our duties run through a dirty channel, and cannot choose but contract filth. While sin lodgeth under one roof so near grace, grace must be in its exercise marred; and therefore the holy apostle must cry, Rom. vii. 19, 'The good that I would, I do not: but the evil which I would not, that I do,' and verse 24, 'O wretched man that I am! who shall deliver me from the body of this death?'

II. Though there were not such blemishes and spots in the face of our righteousness, yet it is here in a state of imperfection, and but in its minority, and so must be filthy in the Lord's sight. It was perfect holiness, according to the perfect rule of God's law, that Adam was to be justified by, according to the covenant of works; exact obedience, not one wanting,—or else all that can be done, came short of righteousness: one breach bringeth the curse on. All obedience, if there be a failing in a little, will not bring the blessing on: he that doth all, liveth; and he that doth not all, is cursed. And therefore, Christians, all you do cannot commend your persons to God, for if he examine you by the rule of the law, O how short will the holiest come! Paul and Isaiah dare not come into such a reckoning; neither is all obeyed, nor any in the measure and manner commanded. And therefore, you might cry down all your performances, when you could challenge them with no particular blot, with this—all is short of the command, and infinitely short. I have been aiming at holiness so long, I have stretched out my strength, and what have I attained? It may be, I have outstripped equals, and there seemeth to be some distance between me and others; nay, but the command is unspeakably more before me nor I am before others. I have reached but a span of that boundless perfection of holiness; it is but a grain weight of the eternal weight of grace, and I must forget it, and stand before God, as if I had lost mind of duties, appear in his presence as if I had attained nothing; for the length that is before my hand drowneth up all attainments.

III. Nay, but put the case were man perfect, yet should he not know his soul, but despise his life: the Lord putteth no trust in his servants, and his angels he chargeth with folly, and the heavens are not clean in his sight; how then must man be abominable, that hath his foundation in the dust, and drinketh in iniquity like water? How should God magnify him? or he be righteous that is born of a woman? Job xxv. 4, 6; xv. 14, 15; and iv. 18, 19. Job was a great length in the sight of his own vileness and God's holiness, when he saw this, 'Though I were perfect, yet I would not know it, but despise it; I would not answer him, though I were righteous,' chap. ix. 14, 15, 21. So unspeakably pure and clean is his holiness,

* [There is some obscurity in this sentence. The sentiment that is expressed, however, seems to be this:—*Much love to a particular object makes the act of seeking or praying for it to be loved more.*—Ed.]

that all created holiness hath a spot in it before his, and evanisheth, as the stars disappear when the sun riseth, which seem something in the darkness. The angels' holiness, the heaven's glory, is nothing to him, before whom the nations are as nothing; so that it is all the wonder of the world, that ever God stooped so far below himself, even to righteous Adam, as to make such a covenant with him, to account him righteous in obedience. 'What is man that thou shouldst magnify him? When I look to the heavens, and the sun, the work of thine hands, Lord, what is man?' What is innocent man in his integrity, that thou shouldst magnify him, to give him a place to stand before thee, magnify him to be a party-contractor with thy glorious Majesty? Psalm viii. 4—6. But now, when this covenant is broken, it is become impossible to a son of Adam ever to stand before God in his perfection, for, how should man be righteous that is born of a woman? Job xv. 14. Since we once sinned, how should our righteousness ever come in remembrance? Therefore hath God chosen another way to cover man's wickedness and righteousness both, with his own righteousness, his Son's divine human righteousness, which is so suited in his infinite wisdom for us. It is a man's righteousness, that it may agree with men, and be a fit garment to cover them; it is God's righteousness, that it may be beautiful in God's eyes, for he seeth his own image in it. And it is not the created inherent righteousness of saints glorified, that shall be their upper garment, that shall be their heaven and glory-suit, so to speak. They will not glory in this, but only in the Lamb's righteousness for evermore. Saint-holiness must have a covering above, for it cannot cover our nakedness; and all the songs of those that follow the Lamb make mention of his righteousness, even of his only. The Lamb is the light and sun of the city, the Lamb is the temple of it; in a word, he is all that is beautiful and glorious. Every saint hath put on the Lord Jesus, and is perfect through his comeliness. At least, if the holiness of spirits of just men made perfect be the glorious habit above; yet all the beauty and glory of it is from Christ Jesus, whose image it is, and the Spirit whose work it is. It shall be still true, all—all our righteousness, as ours, is filthy; and all holiness, as it hath a relation to us, cannot please God. It must be spotted before his pure eyes; but only it is accepted and clean, as it is Christ's and the Spirit's, as it is his own garment put upon us, and his own comeliness making us perfect. It is not so much the inherent cleanness of the saints' robes that maketh them beautiful in his eyes, as this, that they are washed in the blood of the Lamb, Rev. vii. 14.

Now, from all this we would speak a word to two sorts of you. *First,* There is one great point of religion that is the principal and foundation of all other, even free justification by faith in Jesus, without our own righteousness; and the most part stumble here in the entry. It is the greatest obstruction of souls coming to Christ Jesus, even the ignorant and blind conceit and fancy that almost every man hath of himself and his own performances; the world will not make many believe the half of the evil of themselves that is spoken in the word. If you have a general conviction of sinfulness and misery, yet you think to help it. If you sin, you use to make amends, run to your prayers and repentance to give God a recompence, and satisfy your own consciences. Speak now, is not this the way you think to be saved? I shall do what I can, pray and mourn for sin; and what I am not able to do, God must forgive; you will do all you are able or can, and God's mercy must come in to supply the want of your righteousness. But this is to put a new piece of cloth in an old garment, to make the rent worse. Many of you have no other ground of confidence in the world, nothing to answer the challenge of conscience or satisfy justice, but this, —I repent, I am sorry, I mourn, I shall amend, I resolve never to do the like again. Now, then, from this ground we would declare unto you, in the Lord's name, you are yet unclean, both in persons and actions unjustified, because you have no other covering but your own duties and performances: and let these be examined, and weighed in the balance of the sanctuary, and they will be found light. All your righteousness, saith the Lord, is filthiness; you are unclean, you cannot deny, both by birth and education,—you have often defiled yourselves with sins, you must confess. Now, I ask you, How will you cover that uncleanness and nakedness? How will you hide it from God's eyes and your own consciences? You know no way but this,—I will pray, I will repent and amend. So then you cover yourself with prayer, with sorrow and tears, and a resolution of amending. This, then, is all your covering and ornament,—something done by you, as many will make the wings of two good works stretch themselves out so far as to cover and hide a multitude of offences between them. Therefore I declare, in the Lord Jesus his name, unto you, whose conscience must go along in the acknowledgment and owning of your case, that you have covered yourselves with your own righteousness, that you have taken as filthy rags to cover your nakedness and sin with, as your sins are, and so you have made an addition to your uncleanness, you are more unclean by your prayers and repentance than before ; and so God is of more pure eyes than to look graciously on such as you are. You have gone about to establish your own righteousness, and have not known the righteousness of God, and so you have come short of it; you are yet persons in a state of enmity,—God is your judge, you are rebels. It concerns you much to heed this well, to judge of your own actions and persons as God judgeth of them; for if God shall judge one way, and you judge another way, you may be far mistaken in the end. If you have so good an opinion of yourselves and your duties, that you can plead interest in God for them, and absolve yourselves from such grounds ; and if God have not the same judgment, but rather think as evil of your prayers as of your cursing, and abhor the thing that satisfieth you, will it not be dreadful in the end? For his judgment shall stand, and you will succumb in judgment, since you crossed God's mind. Therefore we would have you solidly drink in this principle of religion;—that man is so unclean, and God so abhorreth him, that whatever he doth or can do, it cannot make him righteous; that no good action can make him acceptable, and take away the uncleanness of the evil actions; and that any sinful action taketh away all the cleanness of the good actions. Once believe this,—if I should sweat out my life in serving God, and never rise off my knees, if I should give my body to the fire for the truth, if I should melt away in tears for sin, all this is but filthy rags, and I can never be accepted of God for all that, but the matter of my condemnation groweth,—if I justify myself my own mouth proves me perverse: God needeth no more but my good deeds to condemn me for, in all justice: and therefore it is a thing impossible,—I will never put forth a hand, or open a mouth upon that account any more. I will serve God, because it is my duty, but life I will not expect by my service; when I have done all, it is wholly mercy that I am accepted, my good works shall never come in remembrance; I resolve to be found, not having my own righteousness. I will appear among the ungodly sinners, as one that hath no righteousness, that I may be justified only by faith in Jesus Christ. I say, drink in this truth, and let it settle in your hearts, and then we would hear numbers cry, 'O what shall I do to be saved?'

Now, *Secondly*, As for you who have fled unto Christ's righteousness only, and have cast away your own as dung and dross, as filthy rags; as you have done right in the point of justification, judge so likewise after it. We would exhort you to judge so of your best actions that are the fruits of the Spirit, judge so of them as you have a hand in them.

'All our righteousness.' Mark, Isaïah, a holy prophet, joineth himself in with the multitude. And the truth is, the more holiness, the more humility and self-abasing; for what is holiness, I pray you, but self-denial, the abasing of the creature, and exalting of Christ Jesus? This is the cross that the saints must all bear, 'Deny yourself, and follow me.' Grace doth not swell men above others; it is gifts, such as knowledge, that puffeth up; charity or love puffeth not up. Men are naturally high-minded, for pride was the first sin of Adam, and grace cometh to level men, to make the high mountains valleys for Christ's chariot; it maketh men stoop low to enter the door of the kingdom. Therefore, if you have attained any measure beyond others, if you would prove it real grace and holiness, do not exalt yourselves above others, be not high-minded, come down and sit among the ungodly, among the unclean, and let not grace given diminish the low estimation of yourself in yourself. There is a growing that is but a fancy, and men's conceit; when men grow above ordinances, above other Christians, and can see none or few Christians but themselves, such a growth is not real. It is but fancy, it is but swelling and wind, and must be pricked to let it out. A holy prophet came in among an unclean people; he did not say, 'Stand by, I am holier than thou.' Such a man as can find no Christian about him, even though to the judgment of all others, they seek God more than he, such a man hath not real solid grace,—his holiness is profane holiness, and proud holiness; for true holiness is humble holiness, and in honour preferreth others.

There is a great fault among those who have fled to Christ's righteousness in justification, that they use to come full from duties, as a stomach from a honeycomb. Ofttimes we make our liberty and access to God the ground of our acceptation; and according to the ebbings and flowings of our inherent righteousness, so doth the faith and confidence of justification ebb and flow. Christians, this ought not to be; in so doing, you make your own righteousness your righteousness before God; for when the unsatisfaction in the point of duty maketh you question your interest so often, is not the satisfaction of your minds in duties made the ground of your pleading interest? Give you liberty and access, you can believe anything; remove it, and you can believe nothing. Certainly this is a sandy foundation,—you ought to build nothing on performances, you should be as vile in your own eyes, and think your nakedness as open, when you come nearest God, when you have most liveliness, as when he hideth his face, and duty withereth. Will filthy rags be your ornament? No, Christians. Be more acquainted with the unspotted righteousness of the immaculate Lamb of God, and find as great necessity of covering your cleanest duties with it, as your foulest faults, and thus shall you be kept still humble and vile in your own eyes, and have continual employment for Christ Jesus. Your best estate should not puff you up, and your worst estate should not cast you down; therefore be much in the search of the filthiness of your holy actions. This were a spiritual study, a noble discovery to unbowel your duties, to divide them, and to give unto God what is God's, and take unto yourselves what is your own. The discovery of filthiness in them needeth not hinder his praise; and the discovery of grace in them needeth not mar your shame. God hath most glory when we have most shame; these two grow in just proportion,—so much is taken from God as is given to the creature.

Thirdly, We would also press you from this ground to long much to be clothed upon with immortality, to put off the filthy rags of time and earth-righteousness, and to be clothed upon with the white robes of the righteousness of the saints. As you would dwell near the fountain here, and be still washing your garments, and offering all your sacrifices in him who sanctifieth all, so would you pant and thirst for this spotless garment of glory. Glory is nothing but perfect holiness, holiness washen and made clean in the Lamb's blood. Your rags are for the prison and for sojourning; when you come to your Father's house, your raiment shall be changed. Therefore, Christians, every one of you aspire higher. Sit not down in attainments; forget what is behind, and press forward. Let perfect holiness be in your eye and purpose, sit not behind it. All our time-duties have much filthiness,—long for the pure stream that waters the city above. Grace is not in its native place, it is corrupted and mixed here: heaven is the own element of it, and there is grace without mixture. Undervalue all your performances, till you be above, where that which is in part shall be done away, where no unclean thing entereth.

Fourthly, This likewise holdeth out to you a continual necessity of washing. You must take up house beside the fountain opened in the house of David; and never look on any piece of inherent righteousness, but see a necessity of dipping it in the Lamb's blood. And therefore should you pray always in Christ's name, that the prayer which, of itself, would be cast as dung on our face, may have a sweet savour from him. Cover your holiness with Christ's righteousness, and make mention of it only.

Sermon XVII.

ISAIAH lxiv. 6.—"*And we all do fade as a leaf, and our iniquities, like the wind, have taken us away.*"

HERE they join the punishment with the deserving cause, their uncleanness and their iniquities, and so take it upon them, and subscribe to the righteousness of God's dealing.

We would say this much in general—*First*, Nobody needeth to quarrel God for his dealing. He will always be justified when he is judged. If the Lord deal more sharply with you than with others, you may judge there is a difference between your condition and theirs, as well as in the Lord's dispensation, even as this people do, ver. 5, 6. It is a strange saying, Lam. iii. 33. The Lord 'doth not afflict willingly, nor grieve the children of men.' That is, as we conceive, the Lord hath not such pleasure in trampling on men, as he might do on the dust of his feet. Though he be absolute sovereign Lord of the creature, and men be but as the dust of his feet, and he may do with his own what he pleaseth, and none ask, what dost thou? yet the Lord useth not to walk according to his own absoluteness,—he hath another ordinary rule whereby he worketh, a rule of justice and equity. Especially in the punishing of men, he useth not to afflict men for his pleasure, as tyrants use to destroy their people. The Lord exerciseth his sovereignty another way, and if he be absolute and unlimited in any thing, it is in showing mercy on men. But in judgment, there may be still some reason gotten for it in the creature beside the will of God; so that, to speak with reverence of his majesty, strokes are often drawn out of his hands. He getteth so much provocation ere he strike, and holdeth off so long,—threateneth, and giveth warning thus before strokes, as if it were against his will to lay on, as if his heart were broken with us.

Secondly, If men knew themselves and their own sinfulness, they would not challenge God with unrighteousness, but put their mouth in the dust, and keep silence. And it is from this ground, that this people do not charge God. Sin is of such infinite desert and demerit, because against infinite majesty, that God cannot go beyond it in punishment; and therefore Jeremiah, when he is wading out of the deep waters of sore temptation and sad discouragement, pitcheth and casteth anchor at this solid ground, 'It is of the Lord's mercy that we are not consumed,' Lam. iii. 22. What! do I mean thus to charge God, as if he dealt rigorously? No, no: It is his mercy that a remnant is left,—our strokes are not pure justice, our cup is mixed, mercy is the greatest part. Whatever is behind utter destruction, whatever is below the desert of sin, which is hell and damnation, all this must be reckoned up to mercy. That I am yet alive, and so may have hope, this is mercy, 'For why should a living man complain?' ver. 39. That a rod is come to awake us out of security, this is mercy, for we might have slept to death. And this wholesome counsel got Job of his friends,—to stay his murmuring and grudging at God's dispensations, Job. xi. 6. Why dost thou complain, Job? Know but thy sins, and there shall be no room for complaint. Look but unto God's secrets of wisdom, and his law, and see it is double to what you have known,—your obligation is infinitely more than you thought upon, and then how great and numberless must iniquities be? 'Know, therefore,' saith Zophar, 'God exacteth of thee less than thine iniquities deserve. God exacteth not according to law, he craveth not according to the obligation, but bids write down fifty in his bill of affliction, when an hundred are written in our bill of deserving. So then, complain not,—it is mercy that life is saved. Are you men, and living men? Wonder at this, and wonder not that you are not wealthy, are not honourable, seeing you are sinners: all that came on Jerusalem maketh not Ezra think God out of bounds, chap. ix. 13. As we are less than the least of God's mercies, and all our goodness deserveth none of them, so is the least sin greater than the greatest of all his judgments, and deserveth still more. Nay, if there were no more but original corruption common to men, and the filthiness that accompanieth men's good actions, yet is God righteous in punishing severely, and this people acknowledge it so. You use to inquire what sin hath such a man done, when so terrible judgments come on? Nay, inquire no more;—he is a sinner, and it is mercy there is not more, and it is strange mercy that it is not so with you also. You use to speak foolishly when God's hand is upon you: I hope I have my punishment here, I hope to suffer here for my sins. Poor souls, if God make you suffer for sins, it will be another matter. Though now your punishment be above your strength and patience, yet it is below your sin. As sin hath all evil in it, so must hell have all punishment in it. The torment of the gravel, racking with the stone, and such like, are but play to hell,—these are but drops of that ocean that you must drink out, and you shall go out of one hell into a worse; eternity is the measure of its continuance, and the degrees of itself are answerable to its duration. There is much impatience even among God's children under the rod; you vex and torment yourselves, and do well to be angry. Any piece of thwarting dispensation, that goes cross to your humour and inclination, imbitters your spirit against God, and maketh you go cross to his providence: how often do your hearts say, Why am I thus? What aileth the Lord at me? But, Christians, learn to study your own deservings, and stop your mouth with that, that you may not speak against heaven. If you knew sin well, you would not wonder at judgments, you would rather wonder that you are out of hell. Know what right God hath over you, and how little use he maketh of it against you. When you repine at a little, shall it not be righteousness with God to exact more, and let you know your deserving better? He that thinketh it rigour in God to exact fifty, it is justice that God crave an hundred. If the law require forty stripes, and he give but one, will you not rather commend and proclaim his clemency, than speak of his cruelty? Wonder that God hath spared us so long. Sin is come to great maturity. As pride is said to blossom and bud into a rod, so all sins are blossomed and budded into the very harvest, that the sickle may be put in. If we should have cities desolate, and our land consumed; if we should take up Jeremiah's lamentation, and our case be made parallel to theirs, we have then been punished less than our iniquities deserved.

There are some godless people so black-mouthed as to speak against heaven when God correcteth them; they follow the counsel of Job's wife, curse God and die. If God but touch them a little in that which is dearest unto them, they kick against the pricks, and run hard-heads with God. As we have known some foolish women, when their only child hath been removed, blaspheme, saying, What can God do more to me?—let him do what he can. O madness and wickedness of men! Cannot God do more when he casteth them into hell? Thou shalt acknowledge that it is more. Some have left off to seek God and turned profane, because of the Lord's correction; but you should know that all that is here is but arles.* If God had done his worst, you might think yourselves out of his common; nay, but he hath yet more to do, the full sum is to be paid. It were therefore wisdom yet to make supplication to thy judge.

But, *Thirdly*, Sins and iniquities have a great influence in the decay of nations and persons, and change of their outward condition, when it is joined with the wind of God's displeasure. The calamity of this people is set down in excellent terms, alluding to a tree in the fall of the leaf. We, saith he, were once in our land as a green tree busked round about with leaves and fruit: our church and state was in a flourishing condition; at least nothing was wanting to make outward splendour and glory. We were immovable in our own land; as David said in his prosperity, 'I shall never be moved,' so did we dream of eternity in earthly Canaan. But now, Lord, we are like a tree in the fall of the leaf: sin hath obstructed the influence of heaven, hath drawn away the sap of thy presence from among us, so that we did fade as a leaf before its fall; we were prepared so by our sins for judgment,—visible draughts and prognostics of it were to be read upon the condition and frame of all spirits and people; and then did our iniquities raise the storm of thy indignation, and that, like a whirlwind, hath blown the withering leaves off the tree, hath driven us out of our own land, and scattered us among strangers. Sin and uncleanness and the filthiness of our righteousness prepared us for the storm, made us light matter that could resist no judgment, made us matter combustible; and then iniquities, and sin rising up to iniquities, coming to such a degree, hath accomplished the judgment, put fire among us, made us as the birk in Yule even.†

* [That is, an earnest (*arrha*, Lat.).—Ed.]

† [Yule is a name that is still applied to Christmas, in the northern parts of England as well as in Scotland. "This name was originally given to the great annual feast, celebrated among the northern nations, at the time of the winter solstice, in honour of the sun. Hence Odin was denominated Julvatter, or the *Father of Yule.*" (Jamieson's Etymological Dictionary of the Scottish Language.) "He praised God that he was born in such a time, as in the time of the light of the gospel,—to such a place as to be king of such a kirk, the sincerest kirk of the world. The kirk of Geneva keep Pasch and *Yule*, what have they for them? They have no institution. As for our neighbour kirk in England, their service is an evil said mass in English, they want nothing of the mass but the liftings." (Speech of King James VI., to the General Assembly of the Church of Scot-

First, It is familiar in the Scripture that people in a prosperous condition are compared unto a green tree flourishing, Psal. xxxvii. 35. The wicked's prospering is like a green bay tree spreading himself in power, spreading out his arms, as it were, over more lands, to conquer them, over more people, to subject them. And this is often the temptation of the godly, and so doth the Lord himself witness of this people, Jer. xi. 16, 'I have called thy name a green olive tree, fair and of goodly fruit.' This was once their name, though it be now changed. Now they are called a fading withering tree without both leaves and fruit. Now their place doth not so much as know them, they are removed as in a moment, Psal. xxxvii. 36. And this comparison giveth us to understand something of the nature of human glory and pomp. The fairest and most beautiful excellency in the world, the prosperity of nations and people, is but like the glory of a tree in the spring or summer. Yea, the Scripture useth to undervalue it more than so, and the voice commandeth to cry, (Isa. xl. 6, 7, 8,) 'All flesh is grass, and the goodliness thereof as the flower of the field: the one withereth, and the other fadeth, because the Spirit of the Lord bloweth upon it.' A tree hath some stability in it, but the flower of the field is but of a month or a week's standing; nay, of one day's standing, for in the morning the grass is green, and the sun scorcheth it ere night, so that one sun's course shall see it both growing green and fading. So is the goodliness, the very perfection, the quintessence, so to speak, and the abstract of creatures' perfections. Outward accommodation in a world is as fading a thing as the flower is, as smoke is; it is so vanishing that it bides but a puff of his breath to blow it to nothing. Job hath a strange expression, 'Thou lookest upon me, and I am not,' Job vii. 8. The Lord needeth no more but stare on the most durable creature, and look it not only out of countenance, but also look it into its first nothing,—look it out of glory, out of being; and therefore you should not trust in those uncertain things, that can take wings and leave you. When you have accommodation outwardly to your mind, do not build your nest in it: these leaves of prosperity will not cover you always: there is a time when they will fall. Nations have their winter and their summer, persons have them likewise; as these must change in nature, so must they do in their lot. Heaven only is one day, one spring perpetually blossoming and bringing forth fruit. There is the tree of life that bringeth forth fruit every month, that hath both spring and harvest all the year over. Christians, sit not down under the green tree of worldly prosperity: if you do, the leaves will come down about you; the gourd you trust in may be eaten up in a night; your winter will come on so as you shall forget the former days as if they had never been. We desire you to be armed for changes: are not matters in the kingdom still going about? All things are subject to revolution and change, and every year hath its own summer and winter, so hath it pleased the Lord to set the one over against the other, that man might find nothing after him, Eccl. vii. 14. Therefore we would have you cast your accounts so as the former days of darkness may return, and the land be covered with mourning-clothes.

But would you know what is the original of the creatures' vanity, what is the moth that eats up the glory and goodliness of creatures' enjoyments? Here it is—sin and iniquities. It was sin that first subjected the creation to vanity, Rom. viii. 19, 20. This inferior world was to have been a durable house for an immortal soul, but sin made man mortal, and the world corruptible, and from this proceed all the tempests and disorders that seem to be in the creation. It is this still—it is sin that raiseth the storm of the Lord's wrath, which bloweth away the withered leaves of men's enjoyments. Sin drieth up all the sap and sweetness of the creature comforts,—it maketh the leaves of the tree wither, drives the sap away to the root, hindereth the influence of God's blessing to come through the veins of worldly prosperity. For what is the virtue and sap of creatures? It is even God's blessing; and therefore

land, at Edinburgh, August 1590. Calderwood's Hist. of the Ch. of Scot. p. 256.) What is called the birch or "birk in Yule-even," was probably the *Yule clog.* On Christmas eve, at no very remote period, the *Yule clog,* which was a large shapeless piece of wood, selected for the purpose, was dragged by a number of persons bearing in their hand large candles, and placed by them on the fire where it was to be burned, in compliance with an ancient superstitious custom. Our author may refer to this practice, or perhaps he had simply in view the old proverb, "He's as bare as the birk at Yule."—Henderson's Scottish Proverbs, p. 47. Edin. 1832.—Ed.]

the bread nourisheth not, but the word and command of God, Matt. iv. 4. That is a right unto the creatures by Jesus Christ, when possession of them is entered into by prayer and thanksgiving, for all right is sanctified by these, and it is the iniquities of men that separate between God and them, Isa. lix. 2. And when God is separated and divided from enjoyments, they must needs be empty shells and husks, no kernel in them, for God 'filleth all in all,' is all in all; and remove him, and you have nothing,—your meat and drink is no blessing, your table is a snare, your pleasures and laughter have sadness in them. At least, they are like the vanishing blaze of thorns under a pot; and therefore, when God is angry for sin, men's beauty consumeth as before the moth, Psalm xxxix. 11. When God beginneth to show himself terrible, because of sin, poor man, though of late spreading his boughs out, yet all falleth, and like ice, melteth as before the sun, which just now seemed as solid as stone. O but David was sensible of this, and could speak from much experience, Psal. xxxii. 3, 4. The anger of the Lord did eat him up, and dried his moisture. It might be read in his countenance,—all the world could not content him, all the showers of creatures dropping fatness could not keep sap in him, God's displeasure scorcheth so; nay, is within him, that no hiding-place is to be found in the world, no shadow of a rock among all the creatures in such a weary land. Moses and the people knew this well, Psal. xc. 5—9. The Lord's displeasure carried them away, as a flood coming down carrieth all headlong with it; it scorched them and made them wither as grass. When God setteth iniquities before him, and that which is the soul's secret, beginneth to imprint it in visible characters on the rod, and writeth his sin on his punishment; then no wonder that days be spent in vanity and grief, since they are passed over in his wrath, Job xiii. 25. Then doth a soul loathe its dainty meat, and then doth the ox low over his fodder. Meat is laid before him, and he cannot touch it, because of the terrors of the Almighty; and that which before he would not once touch, would not enter into terms of communing with, as the Lord's threatenings, he must now sit down and eat them up as his meat, how sorrowful soever, Job vi. 4—7.

But, *secondly*, when sin hath prepared a man for judgment, then, if iniquity be added to sin, this raiseth the storm, and kindleth the fire to consume the combustible matter. When sin hath given many blows, by preparatory corrections, at the root of a man's pleasure and credit, it will at length bring on a fatal stroke that shall drive the tree to the ground. There are some preparatory judgments, and some consummatory; some wither the leaf, and some blow it quite off; some make men like the harvest, ripe to put the sickle of judgment into it. The corruption of a land, the universality of it, and formality in worshipping of God, ripeneth a land for the harvest of judgment,—exposeth it to any storm,—leaveth it open to the Lord's wrath, so that there is nothing to hold his hand and keep off the stroke; but when the wind ariseth, and iniquities have made it tempestuous, then who may stand? It will sweep away nations and people as a flood, and make their place not to know them, so that there shall be neither leaf nor branch left. There is often a great calm with great provocations, and iniquities cry, 'Peace, peace!' But when once the cry of it is gone up to heaven, and hath engaged God's anger against a people or person, then it raiseth a whirlwind that taketh all away. Now, all this belongeth to you,—we told you the acknowledgment of sin was yours already; and a wonder it is, that the complaint is not ours also. Always this ought to be an admonition and example to us, on whom the ends of the world are fallen. Therefore we would declare this unto you, that sin and iniquities have judgment in the tail. Now you sit at peace, every one in his own dwelling, and spread forth your branches; but is there not much uncleanness among you? We would have you trouble your carnal peace and security; trouble your ease with thoughts of this. And we have ground to give this warning, because, if there were no more but the iniquity of our holy things—the formality of our service—the commonness of spirit in worship, this might be enough to raise the storm. You know not for what reasons to be afraid of judgment. Look but on original corruption; look on the defilement of your religious actions, and then find ground sufficient of fading away. Though now you sit still, and seem to be so settled, as you would never be moved; you dream of an eternity here—you cleave in your hearts to your houses and lands—you stick as fast to the world, and will not part with it, as a leaf to a tree; yet behold the wind of the Lord may arise, that shall drive you away; take your soul from these things, and then whose shall they be? If you will not fear temporal judgments, yet I pray you fear eternal—fear hell. May not the Lord shake you off this tree of time, and take you out of the land of the living, to receive your portion? There is not only an universal deadness of spirit on the land, but a profane spirit,—iniquities, abominable sins, abound. Every congregation is overgrown with scandals;* and for you, none may more justly complain. We are all unclean: sin is not in corners, but men declare their sin as Sodom; sin is come to the maturity—defection and apostacy† is the temper of all spirits; and, above all, the general contempt and slighting of this glorious gospel, is the iniquity of Scotland,‡ so that we wonder that the withered leaves yet stick to; that the storm is not yet raised, and we blown away. Now, you are like stones—your hearts as adamants, and cannot be moved with his threatenings; the voice of the Lord's word doth not once move you. You sin and are not afraid; nay, but when God's anger shall join with iniquity, and the voice of his rod and displeasure roar, this shall make the mountains to tremble, the rocks to move, and how much more shall it drive away a leaf? You seem now mountains; but when God shall plead, you shall be like the chaff driven to and fro. O how easy a matter shall it be to God to blow a man out of his dwelling-place! Sin hath prepared you for it; he needeth no more but blow by his Spirit, or look upon you, and you will not be. You who are now lofty and proud, and maintain yourselves against the word, when you come to reckon with God, and he entereth into judgment, you shall not stand—you will consume as before the moth; your hearts will fail you—'who may abide the day of his coming?' It will be so terrible, and so much the more terrible, that you never dreamed of it. If the example of this people will not move you, do but cast your eyes on Ireland,§ who all do fade as a leaf, and their iniquities have taken them away out of their own land. Shall not the seeing of the eye, nor the hearing of the ear teach you? What security do you promise to yourselves? Have not we sinned as much as they? Were not they his people as well as we? Certainly, since God waiteth longer on you, the stroke must be the greater: provoked patience must turn fury. If you would then prevent this

* [The records of the kirk session of the parish of Govan, during the incumbency of the author, after having been lost for many years, were fortunately recovered not long ago. These show the great strictness of the ecclesiastical discipline of those days. There were not fewer than twenty-two elders in the kirk session. Each of these had a ward, or district assigned to him, of which it was his duty to take a particular superintendence. It was hardly possible, therefore, that any irregularity of which a parishioner was guilty could be concealed; and consequently, what is recorded in the register is to be regarded, not as a specimen, but as the gross amount of the immorality of the parish. Some may affect to ridicule the severe notice that was taken of particular instances of misconduct. But the cognizance that was taken of such things is a proof of the high tone of moral and religious feeling that prevailed at that time among the office-bearers of the church. Individuals, we find, were brought before the kirk session, on account of family and domestic feuds, for quarrelling with their neighbours, for solitary instances of drunkenness, and of the use of profane language, for carrying water on the Lord's day, for sleeping in church, for resorting to taverns on the Sabbath, for calumny, and for neglecting the education of their children, &c. They who were convicted of such offences, were sometimes rebuked in private by an elder, and at other times by the minister in the presence of the eldership. It was only in the case of graver offences, the number of which was comparatively small, that a reproof was administered in the presence of the congregation.—Ed.]

† [In the "Causes of the Lord's Wrath against Scotland," agreed upon by the Commission of the General Assembly, 1650, "Backsliding and defection from the covenants, and our solemn vows and engagements," is specified (p. 46.) to be "one of the greatest and most comprehensive and provoking sins in the land." *Printed in the year* 1653.—Ed.]

‡ [This is the language of a man who did not use "at any time flattering words," or utter to his people "smooth things." From what he says here, however, and in some other sermons, and from corresponding evidence which might be adduced, we are forced to conclude that the well-known description which Kirkton has given of the state of religion in Scotland in those days, (Hist. of Ch. of Scot. pp. 48, 54, 64.) must be too highly coloured. The presence of a large military force and a state of civil warfare could not but be prejudicial, in various ways, to the religion and morality of a country. I am perfectly aware that the authority of Lord Clarendon, Bishop Burnet, Milton, and others, may be brought forward to prove that the parliamentary soldiers were kept under the strictest discipline, and were remarkable for their grave deportment. But I know likewise, that the characters of not a few of those soldiers are seriously affected by the offensive details of the ecclesiastical records of the parish with which Binning was connected.—Ed.]

§ [See Note, p. 368.—Ed.]

people's complaint, go about such a serious acknowledgment of your sins, 'Search your ways, and turn again to the Lord.' And let not every man sit down in a general notion of sin, but unbowel it until you see uncleanness; go up to the fountain head, original corruption; go down to all the streams, even the iniquity of holy things. Let every man be particular in the search of his own provocations personal; and every one be public in the general sins of the land, that you may confess out of knowledge and sense, 'We are all unclean,' &c.

Sermon XVIII.

ISAIAH lxiv. 7.—"*And there is none that calleth upon thy name, that stirreth up himself to take hold on thee,*" &c.

THEY go on in the confession of their sins. Many a man hath soon done with that: a general notion of sin is the highest advancement in repentance that many attain to. You may see here sin and judgment mixed in thorough other* in their complaint. They do not so fix their eyes upon their desolate estate of captivity, as to forget their provocations. Many a man would spend more affection, and be more pathetic in the expression of his misery, when it is pungent, nor he can do when he speaketh of his sins. We would observe, from the nature of this confession, something to be a pattern of your repentance. And it is this: When the Spirit convinceth, and men are serious in repentance, then the soul is more searching, more universal, more particular in acknowledgment of sins. These are characters of the Spirit's work.

First, The Spirit discovereth unto men, not only sin, but the loathsomeness of sin; its heinous nature; how offensive it is to God's holy eye. Many of you know abundance of evil deeds, and call them sins; but you have never taken up sin's ugly face, never seen it in the glass of the holy law, uncleanness itself, because you do not abhor yourselves. Poor and low thoughts of God make mean and shallow thoughts of sin. You should be as Job, vile, chap. xl. 4; and abhor yourselves in dust and ashes, chap. xlii. 6. As God's holiness grew great in your eyes, sin's uncleanness would grow proportionably, Isa. vi. 3, 5. And here your repentance halteth in the very entry.

But, *secondly,* The Spirit discovereth not only the uncleanness of men's natures, and leadeth them up to original corruption, but the Spirit also leadeth men along all the streams, not only those that break out, but those which go under ground, and have a more secret and subtile conveyance. It concludeth not only open breaches of the command under filthiness, but also all a man's own righteousness, though never so refined; it concludeth it also a defiled garment, so that the soul can look no where but see sin and uncleanness in its ornaments and duties. And thus it appeareth before God without such a covering, openeth up its soul, hideth not sin with the covering of duties, but seeth a necessity of another covering for all. Now, therefore, let the most part of you conclude, that you have never yet gotten your eyes open to see sin or confess it, because when you sit down to count your sins, there are many things that you call not sin,—you use not to reckon your praying and repentance among sins. Nay, because you have so much confidence in your repentance and confession, you have never repented. You must see a necessity of a covering of Christ's righteousness above all; faith in Jesus must cover repentance and itself both, with the glorious object of it. But, alas! how soon are many at an end of confession! some particular gross actions may come in remembrance, but no more. Sum up all your confessions; they have never yet pitched on the thousandth part of your guiltiness, no, not in kinds, let be in number.

But, *thirdly,* The spirit convinceth spiritually and particularly both; it convinceth of spiritual sins, as we last said, of the iniquity of holy things, and especially of the most substantial duties, faith and prayer, John xvi. 8, 9. There are not many of you have come this length, to see your want of prayer. No, your own words do

* [Or, together.—ED.]

witness against you, for you use to say, I pray day and night, I believe in God with all my heart. Now therefore, out of your own mouth shall you be condemned. When the Spirit convinceth you of sin; you will see no faith, no prayer at the first opening of the eyes. But I add, there is no true confession but it is particular: the Spirit useth not to bewilder men's spirits in a general notion only, and a wide field of unknown sins. And such are many of your convictions. You mourn for sin, as you say, and yet you cannot condescend on a particular that burdeneth your conscience; you grant you have many sins, but sit down to count them, and there is a short count of them. Now, do you not reflect back upon former humiliations in public, and former acknowledgments of sins in private? Do you not yet return upon your own hearts to lay home this sad challenge, I have never repented, I do not yet repent? Must not all your solemn approaches be iniquity and abomination, while your souls are not afflicted for sin, while you can see so few sins? The fasting days of Scotland will be numbered in the roll of the greatest provocations, because there is no real and spiritual conviction of sin among us; custom hath now taken away the solemnity, and there remaineth nothing but the very name. Is this the fast that the Lord chooseth? No, believe it, this shall add to your provocation, and rather hasten lingering judgment than keep it off. We would beseech you this day, pray for pardon of former abused fasts. If you had no more to mourn for, this might spend the day and our spirits both, and exhaust all our present supplications—even the wall of partition that stands between God and Scotland, which all our former solemn humiliations hath built up, a great deal higher than other sins could reach.

'There is none that calleth upon thy name.' Did not this people make many prayers (Isa. i. 15), before the captivity? And did they not cry, which noteth some fervency in it, and fast, a little before it in Jeremiah's time, (chap. xi. 11, and xiv. 12;) and in the time of it, Ezek. viii. 18; Mic. iii. 4; Zech. vii. 3? How, then, is it that the prophet, now on the watch-tower, looking round about him to take up the people's condition, and being led by the Spirit so far as to the case of the captives in Babel, can find no prayer, no calling? And was not Daniel so too? Dan. ix. 13. Lo, then, here is the construction that the Spirit of God putteth on many prayers and fastings in a land, 'There is none calleth on thy name;' there is none that prayeth faithfully and fervently, few to count upon that prayeth any. It may be there are many public prayers, but who prayeth in secret, and mourneth to God alone? There are many prayers, but the inscription is, 'To the unknown God,' to a nameless God; your praying is not a calling on his name, as a known God and revealed in the word.

This, then, we would say unto you, that there may be many prayers in your account, and none in God's. There are many prayers of men that God counteth no more of than the howling of a dog.

First, The cry of men's practices is often louder than their prayers, and goeth up to heaven, that the cry of prayer cannot be heard. When men's conversation is flat contrary to their supplications, supplication is no calling on his name, but charming rather. Sodom's abominations had a cry up to God, Gen. xviii. 21. So Abel's blood had a cry for vengeance, which Cain's prayers could not outcry. Thus the Lord would not hear many prayers, Isa. i. 15, because hands and practices were polluted. You that know no worship of God, but in such a solemn duty, your religion is summed up and confined within the limits of temple-worship, family-exercise, and prayer; certainly the rest of your conversation must speak more. God will not hear but such as worship him and do his will, John iv. 23. Your prayer is a dark parable, if your conversation expone* it not. This I speak for this end, to put many of you out of your false ground of confidence. You have nothing but your prayers to trust unto; and for your conversation, you never go about it effectually to reform it, but go on in that which you pray against. We declare unto you the truth, your prayers are abomination, Prov. xxviii. 9. The wicked may have prayers, and therefore think not to please God and flatter him with your mouths, when your conversation is rebellion. Since you hear not him in his commands, God will not hear you in your petitions, Prov. i. 24, 28. You stopped your ear at his reproof, God will stop his ear

* [That is, explain.—Ed.]

at your request. If you will go to heaven by your own righteousness, I pray you follow more after it, make the garment more to cover your nakedness: the skirt of a duty is not sufficient.

Secondly, When iniquity is regarded in the heart, and idols set up in God's place, God will not own such a worship, but sendeth a man to the idols he serveth, Psal. lxvi. 18; Ezek. xiv. 3, 4. Do you not often pray to God against a corruption, when your heart cleaveth unto it, and what your mouth saith, your heart contradicteth? Light and conscience often extort a confession of beloved sins, while the temper of the heart hath this language, Lord, grant not my request. And therefore, if there be a prayer for pardon of guilt, yet there is no thorough resolution to quit the sin; and as long as a soul is not resolved to quit the sin, there can be no ingenuous confession of it, and no prayer for removing the guilt can be heard. You cannot employ Christ in his office of mediatorship as a Priest to intercede and offer sacrifice for sin, unless you as sincerely employ him as a Sanctifier and Redeemer; and therefore prayer that separateth Christ's offices, and calleth not on whole Christ, calleth not on his name, for his name is Lord Jesus Christ. How can the Lord be inquired of by such a one who cometh to mock him, putteth up an idol in the heart, and yet prayeth against it, or some other sin, while he is not resolved to quit it? Shall God be resolute to help, when we are not earnest in seeking it? No wonder God answer you according to the idol; no wonder you be given up to serve idols, and your sin grow upon you as a plague for your hypocrisy. When you engage your heart too much to any creature, and come to pray and inquire of the Lord in your necessity, shall it not be righteousness with him, to send you to your god? 'When thou criest, let thy companies deliver thee,' Isa. lvii. 13. O man, cry unto thy bosom-idol, and let it help thee, since thou trustest to it, and spendest thy heart upon it! Deut. xxxii. 37, 38, 'Where is the God that drank the wine of your offerings, and did eat the fat of your sacrifices?' Where is the creature that you have made your heart an altar to, to send up the flames of your choicest thoughts and affections to it? Let this rise up, and help you now, saith the Lord. Therefore we exhort you, if you would have your prayers a delight, be upright in the thing you seek, and see that you entertain no known sin, give it no heart-allowance.

Thirdly, There are many prayers not heard, not known, because the mouth outcrieth the heart. It is the sacrifice of the contrite heart that God despiseth not. The prayers of this people were such, (Isa. xxix. 13,)—they drew near with the mouth, but the heart was far away. It is worship in spirit and truth that God loveth, John iv. 23. Since prayer is a communion of God with the creature, a meeting of one with God, and speaking face to face, God, who is a Spirit and immortal, must have a spirit to meet with, a soul to speak to him. Now, do you not find your hearts gadding abroad even in duty? Is it not most about your corns and lands in the time of solemn worship? Therefore God getteth no more but a carcase to keep communion with: he may have as much fellowship with the stones of the wall, and timber of the house, as he can have with your ears and mouths, while you remove your hearts to attend other things. And I would say more,—if your mind be present, yet your heart is gone; sometimes, yea often, both are gone abroad. Sometimes the mind and thought stayeth, but the affection and heart is not with it, and so the mind's residence is not constant. Your thought may come in as a wayfaring man, but tarrieth not all night, dwelleth not. Now speak to it, even Christians, may not your prayers often have a contrary interpretation to what they pretend? You pray so coldrifely* and formally, as God will interpret, you have no mind to it: we ask as we seemed indifferent whether our petition be granted or not. Should the Lord be affected with your petitions, when you yourselves are not affected much? Should his bowels of zeal sound within him, when yours are silent? It is fervent prayer availeth much, James v. 16. A heart sent out with the petition, and gone up to heaven, cannot but bring back an answer. If prayer carry not the seal of the heart and soul in it, God cannot own it, or send it back with his seal of acceptation.

Fourthly, Many prayers are not calling on God's name; and no wonder that

* [Coldly or indifferently.—Ed.]

when people pray, yet the Spirit says, 'None calleth on thy name;' for prayer is made, as to an unknown God, and God is not taken up according to his 'name,' which are his glorious attributes, whereby he manifesteth himself in his word. To call on God's name, is so to pray to God as to take him up as he hath revealed himself. And what is the Lord's name? Hear himself speak to Moses, Exod. xxxiii. 19, and xxxiv. 6, 7, 'The Lord, the Lord God, merciful and gracious, long-suffering, and abundant in goodness and truth. Keeping mercy for thousands: forgiving iniquity, and transgression, and sin, and that will by no means clear the guilty.' Now, to call on this name is for the soul, in prayer, to have a suitable stamp on it: every attribute of God taking deep impression in the heart, and so God's name to be written on the very petitions; and shortly, we may say, the spirit should have the impression of God's greatness and majesty, of his goodness and mercy, of his terribleness and justice. This is the order in which God proclaimeth his name. In the entry, the supplicant should behold the glorious sovereignty and infinite distance between God and the creature, that he may have the stamp of reverence and abasement upon his spirit, and may speak out of the dust, as it becometh the dust of the balance and footstool to do to him who sitteth on the circle of the heaven as his throne. And this I must say, there is little religion and godliness among us, because every man is ignorant of God. Even God's children do more study themselves, and their condition, than God's greatness and absoluteness. Who searches God's infiniteness in his word and works till he behold a wonder, and be drowned in a mystery? O but the saints of old did take up God at a greater distance from the creatures; they waded far into this boundless ocean of God's Majesty, till they were over head and ears, and were forced to cry out, 'Who can find out the Almighty to perfection?' All these are but parts of him, his back-parts. There is more real divinity and knowledge of God in one of Job's friends' discourses, one of David's prayers, than now in twenty sermons of gracious men, or many prayers or conferences of saints. But withal you must study his goodness and mercy, and this maketh up the most part of his name. The definition of God hath most of this, so that it may be said truly, that mercy is his delight. Mercy, as it were, swelleth over the rest: God were not accessible, unless mercy did temper it. Behold then greatness to humble, and goodness to make bold, that you may have access. As greatness should leave the stamp of reverence on your petitions, so should mercy and goodness imprint them with faith and confidence; and that the rather, because as Christ is said to be the Father's face, and the image of his person, (2 Cor. iv. 6. and Heb. i. 3,) so may he be called the Father's name, and so doth God himself call him, Exod. xxiii. 20, 21, The angel that went before them in the wilderness, whose voice they ought to obey, his 'name is in him;' and this angel is Christ Jesus, Acts vii. 37, 38. So then Christ Jesus is God's name. God, as he revealeth himself in the word, is 'God in Christ reconciling the world unto himself,' 2 Cor. v. 19. And therefore, Christians, you ought to pray always in Christ's name, and this is to call on his name. Not only encourage yourselves to come to God, because of a mediator, because he is God in Christ, but also offer up all your prayers in the name of Jesus, that his name called on them may sanctify them, otherwise your affectionate prayers cannot be acceptable to God, for he loveth nothing but what cometh through the Son. Prayer must have an evil savour, when it is not put in the golden censer that this angel hath to offer up incense with the prayers of the saints. And likewise you would know God's justice and wrath, that you may serve in fear and trembling: and when trembling is joined with the rejoicing of faith, this is acceptable service. You ought to fear to offend his holiness, while you are before him. Let God's terribleness have a deep impression on your spirit, both to make sin bitter, and to make mercy more sweet. Thus should prayer ascend with the seal of God's attributes, and then it is a calling on his name. Now, is there any calling on his name among us? Who maketh it his study to take up God in his glorious names? Therefore you call not on a known God, and cannot name him. Now, all of you take this rule to judge your prayers by. Think you not that you make many prayers? You both think it and say it, as you use to say, I pray both day and night. Nay, but count after this rule, and there will be found few prayers in Scotland, albeit you reckon up both private and public. Once scrape out of the count the prayers of the profane and scandalous, whose practice defileth their prayers; and again, blot out the prayers of men's tongues and mouths when hearts are absent; and again, set aside the formal, dwyning,* coldrife, indifferent supplications of saints, and the prayers that carry no seal of God's name and attributes on them, prayers made to an unknown God, and will you find many behind? No certainly,—any of you may take up the complaint in behalf of the land, 'There is none that calleth on thy name,' or few to count upon. You may say so of yourselves, if you judge thus,—I have almost never prayed, God hath never heard my voice; and you may say so of the land. This would be a well-spent day, if this were but our exercise, to find out the sins of our duties in former humiliations: if the Spirit did so convince you as to blot out of the roll of fasts all the former. If you come this length, as to be convinced solidly that you have never yet prayed and mourned for sin,—I have lived thus long, and been babbling all this while, I have never once spoken to God, but worshipped I know not what, fancied a God like myself, that would be as soon pleased with me as I was with myself;—if the Lord wrought thus on your hearts, to put you off your own righteousness, you should have more advantage in this, than in all your sabbaths and fasts hitherto.

Although the Lord's hand be upon them, and they 'fade as a leaf,' and are driven into another land, yet none calleth on his name. This maketh the complaint more lamentable, and no doubt is looked upon as a dreadful sign and token of God's displeasure, and of sorer strokes. Daniel, an eye-witness, confirmeth this foretold truth, chap. ix. 13, 'All this is come upon us, yet have we not made our prayers to the Lord our God.' Well may the Lord make a supposition and doubt of it, Lev. xxvi. 40, 41. After so many plagues are come on, seven added to seven, and again seven times more, and yet they will not be humbled; and when it is even at the door next to utter destruction and consumption, he addeth, 'If then their uncircumcised hearts be humbled, and they take with the punishment of sin,' &c. We need ask no reason of this, for 'bray a fool in a mortar, his folly will not depart from him,' Prov. xxvii. 22. Poor foolish man is a foolish man; folly is born with him, folly is his name, and so is he. He hath not so much wisdom as to 'hear the voice of the rod, and him that appointeth it.' Poor Ephraim is an undaunted heifer. Nature is a 'bullock unaccustomed with the yoke,' and so it is chastised more and more, Jer. xxxi. 18. Man is like an untamed beast, as the horse, or as the mule. Threatenings will not do it, 'God speaketh once, yea twice, and man perceiveth it not,' Job xxxiii. 14. God instructeth by the word, and men receive no instruction: all the warnings to flee from the wrath to come are as so many tales to make children afraid. He saith in his heart, 'I shall have peace, though I walk in the imagination of my own heart.' Since, therefore, he will not incline his ear to the word, God sendeth his rod to seal the word, and yet men are so wild that they fight with God's rods, and will not submit to him: a yoke must be put on Ephraim, a bridle in men's mouth, Psal. xxxii. 9. They will put God to more pains than speaking, and it shall cost them more pain; for he that will not be drawn with the cords of a man, love and entreaties, must be drawn with the cords of a beast, and yoked in a heavy yoke. Yet men are unruly, and the yoke groweth the heavier and sorer that they strive to shake it off. An uncircumcised heart cannot be humbled,—'How can the leopard change his spots? no more can my people return to me,' Jer. xiii. 23. It is strange that a people so afflicted will not take with the punishment of their iniquity, but will say in their heart, Wherefore come these things upon me? But here it is, how can an uncircumcised heart be humbled? God may beat on men with rods as on a dog, but he will run away from him still the more, Isa. ix. 13. Nay, it may be there will be more stirring after God, and more awaking by the first stroke of affliction, than when they are continued and multiplied. The uncouthness of rods may affect people something, but when his hand lieth on but a little, custom breedeth hardness, and more and more alienateth spirits from him.

Now we need no more to seal this truth, but our own experience. I think never people might speak more sensibly of it. It hath been the manner of the Lord's dealing with us, to use fair means to gain us, to threaten before he laid on, to give a proclamation before his stroke; and yet it hath been our manner from our youth

* [Languishing.—Ed.]

up to harden ourselves against him, and go on in our own way. Therefore hath the Lord, after long patience, laid on sad strokes, and smitten us, yet have we not turned to him. It may be, when the chastisement was fresh and green, some poured out a prayer, and in trouble visited God, (Isa. xxvi. 16,) but the body of the land hath not known him that smote them, and never ran into their hiding-place, but the temptation of the time, like a flood, hath carried them away with it. And for the Lord's children, how soon doth the custom of a rod eat out the sense of it, and prayer doth not grow proportionably to the Lord's rods. The Lord hath expected that some might stand in the gap and intercede, yet few or none called on his name. General corrections of the land hath made general apostacy from God, not a turning in to God; so that we may say, we never entered a furnace, but we have come out with more dross, contracted dross in the fire. Men's zeal and tenderness hath been burnt up, reprobate silver may God call us. We have had so much experience of the unprofitableness of former afflictions, that we know not what the Lord shall do with us. We think it may be the Lord's complaint of Scotland, 'Why should you be afflicted any more? you will revolt more and more,' Isa. i. 5. What needeth another rod? You are now all secure, it is true, because you are not stricken; nay, but what needeth a rod! For it cannot awake you,—all the fruit of it would be, not to purge away sin, but to increase it. General judgments will prove general temptations, and will alienate you more from me, and make you curse God and the covenant. And indeed, the truth is, we know not what outward dispensation can fall on that can affect this generation; we know not what the Lord can have behind that can work on us. Judgment hath had as much terror, mercies as much sweetness, and as much of God in the one and the other, as readily hath been since the beginning of the world. Only this we know, all things are possible to him which are impossible to us; and if the Spirit work to sanctify the rod, a more gentle rod shall work more effectually; his word shall do as much as his rod.

The case we are now into is just this—'None calleth on thee.' It is a terrible one, whether our condition be good or bad outwardly. Our peace hath put us asleep, and the word cannot put men to prayers. Now, the Lord hath begun to threaten, as you have been still in fear of new troubles, and a revolution of affairs again; yet I challenge your own consciences, and appeal to them,—whom hath the word prevailed with to put to prayer? Whom hath the rumour of approaching trouble put to their prayers? Whose spirit hath been affected with God's frowning on the land? And this yet more aggravateth your laziness; in the time that God doth show terrible things to his people in Ireland, giveth them a cup of wormwood, and to drink the wine of astonishment, are not you yet at ease? When your brethren and fellow-saints are scattered amongst you as strangers,* yet your hearts bleed not.

* ["Upon Sunday, the 27th of February [1642], a declaration was read out of the old town pulpit [Aberdeen] by our minister, Mr. William Strahan, showing the state of the Protestants in Ireland, and how their wives and bairns were miserably banished, and forced to flee into the west parts of Scotland for refuge, and the land not able to sustain them. It was found expedient that ilk parish within the kingdom should receive a collection of ilk man's charity, for their help and support, whereupon was collected of this poor parish fourscore pounds." (Spalding's 'History of the Troubles in Scotland,' vol. i. p. 34. Aberdeen, 1792.) "As a body, the presbyterians [in Ireland] suffered less by the ravages of the rebellion than any other class. The more influential of their ministers, and the principal part of their gentry, had previously retired to Scotland to escape the tyranny of Strafford and the severities of the bishops, and were thus providentially preserved." (Dr. Reid's 'History of the Presbyterian Church in Ireland,' vol. i. p. 339.) After the execution of Charles I., an oath, called the *Engagement*, was framed by the English parliament, requiring all persons to be "faithful to the commonwealth of England as now established, without a king or house of lords." The Irish ministers refused to take this oath. The republicans were irritated by this refusal, and by the loyalty of the ministers, who publicly preached against them. They therefore imprisoned some of the ministers, while others "fled to the woods, and some to Scotland." At length, at a council of war held at Carrickfergus in March, 1651, a formal act of banishment from the kingdom was passed against them. "Those that staid in the country, though they could not exercise their ministry orderly as formerly, and though their stipends were sequestered, yet they, changing their apparel to the habit of countrymen, travelled in their own parishes frequently, and sometimes in other places, taking what opportunities they could to preach in the fields, or in barns and glens; and were seldom in their own houses. They persuaded the people to constancy in the received doctrines, in opposition to the wild heresies which were then spreading, and reminding them of their duty to their lawful magistrates, the king and parliament, in opposition to the usurpation of the times; and in their public prayers always mentioning the lawful magistrate. This continued

Well, behold the end of it,—your case is a sad prognostic of the Lord's hiding his face and consuming us; nay, it is a sure token that his face is hid already. When Job's friends would aggravate his misery, they sum it up in this, 'thou restrainest prayer from God.' It is more wrath to be kept from much praying, nor to be scattered from your own houses. Therefore, if you would have the cloud of God's anger, that covereth the land with blackness, go over you, and pour out itself on others; if you would prevent the rod, hearken to the word, and stir up yourselves to much prayer, that you may be called his remembrancers. O how long shall prayer be banished this kingdom! The Lord's controversy must be great with us, for since the days of our first love there has been great decay of the spirit of prayer. The children of God should be so much in it, as they might be one with it. David was so much in prayer, as he in a manner defined himself by it, Psal. cix. 4, 'I give myself unto prayer.' In the original, there is no more but 'I prayer.' I was all prayer. It was my work, my element, my affection, my action. Nay, to speak the truth, it is the decay of prayer that hath made all this defection in the land. Would you know the original of many a public man's apostacy and backsliding in the cause of God, what maketh them so soon forget their solemn engagements, and grow particular, seeking their own things, untender in seeking the things of God?—would you trace back the desertion up to the fountain-head? Then come and see. Look upon such a man's walking with God in private, such a man's praying, and you shall find matters have been first wrong there. Alienation and estrangement from God himself, in immediate duties and secret approaches, hath made men's affections cool to his interest in public duties. And believe it, the reason why so few great men or none are so cordial, constant, and thorough in God's matters is this,—they pray not in secret; they come to parliament or council where public matters concerning the honour of God are to be debated, as any statesmen of Venice would come to the senate. They have no dependence on God to be guided in these matters; they are much in public duties, but little in secret with God. Believe it, any man's private walking with God shall be read upon his public carriage, whether he be minister or ruler.

There is yet another thing we would have you consider, to endear this duty unto you, and bind upon your consciences an absolute necessity of being much in it, and it is this. Prayer and calling on his name is often put for all immediate worship of God, especially the more substantial and moral part of service. This people was much in ceremonials, and they made these their righteousness; nay, but there was little secret conversing with God, walking humbly with him, loving him, believing in him. Well, then, prayer is, as it were, a compend and sum of all duties; it contains in it, faith, love, repentance, all these should breathe out in prayer. In a word, if we say to you, be much in prayer, we have said all, and it is more than all the rest, because it is a more near and immediate approach to God, having more solid religion in it. If you be lively in this, you are thriving Christians; and if you wither here, all must decay, for prayer sappeth and watereth all other duties with the influence of heaven.

'That stirreth up himself to take hold on thee.' This expresseth more of their condition under the rod, and while God was threatening to depart and leave them. None took so much notice of it, as to awake out of his dream, to take a fast hold of God. It was but like the grip a man taketh in his slumbering, that he soon quitteth in his sleep; none awaketh himself, as a bird stirreth up itself with its wings to flight; none do so spread out their sails to meet the wind. This importeth a great security and negligence, a careless stupidity. To take hold, to grip strongly and violently, importeth both faith acted on God, and communion with God; so that the sense is, nobody careth whither thou go,—there is none that stirreth up himself to take violent hold of thee. Men lying loose in their interest, and indifferent in the one thing necessary, do not strongly grip to it. Nobody keepeth

throughout the summer of 1651, at which time there was diligent search made anew for them. Some were again taken, others fled, and those who were taken were imprisoned first, for a time, in Carrickfergus, in lodgings where they quartered; and thereafter, Colonel Venables not gaining any ground upon them, they were sent to Scotland." Adair's MS. apud Dr. Reid's Hist. vol. ii. p. 246—248. See also a narrative of the sufferings of the Irish Presbyterians, for their religion and loyalty, in the 'Sample of Jet-Black Pr—tic Calumny,' p. 214.—Ed.]

thee by prayer and intercession; so that there is no diligence added to diligence, there is no stirring up of ourselves in security.

First, When the Lord seemeth to withdraw, and when he is angry, it is our duty to take hold the more on him; and not only to act faith, and call on him by prayer, but to add to ordinary diligence,—it should be extraordinary.

I. Then, I say, when the Lord is withdrawing and seemeth angry, we ought not to withdraw from him by unbelief, but to draw near, and take hold on him. And the Lord giveth a reason of this himself, Isa. xxvii. 4, 5, 'because fury is not in me.' It is but a moment's anger, it is not hatred of your persons but sins, it is not fury that hath no discretion in it, no difference between a friend and an enemy; it is but at least a father's anger, that is not for destruction but correction. The Lord is not implacable. Come to him and win him,—'Let him take hold of me, and let him make peace with me, if he will make peace.' He is a God whose compassions fail not; and so he is never so angry, but there is room left for manifestation of mercy on those that come to him. God's anger is not an humour and passion as ours is, he can take the poor child in his arms, admit it into his bosom, when outward dispensations frown. Men's anger is like the sons of Belial, briers and thorns, that none may come near to, lest they be hurt; but God angry, is accessible, because his anger is still tempered and mixed with clemency and mercy; and that mixture of mercy is so great and so predominant in all his dispensations here, that they being rightly understood, might rather invite to come, than scare from it. There is more mercy to welcome, than anger to drive away. Look upon the very end and purpose of God's hiding himself, and withdrawing,—it is this; that we may come and seek him early, Hosea v. 15. When God is angry, mercy and compassion principleth it, for anger is sent out to bring in wanderers. His anger is not humour, but resolute and deliberate, walketh upon good grounds, because David in his prosperity missed not God. When all things went according to his mind, then he let God of where he will; therefore, the Lord in mercy must hide his own heart with a frowning countenance, and cover himself with a cloud, that David may be troubled, and so take hold on God, Psalm xxx. 7, 8. Since, then, this is God's purpose, that you may come nearer to him, and since he goeth away that you may pursue; certainly he will never so run away as you may not find him out, nor will he run farther nor he strengtheneth thee to pursue him; thus, Psalm lxiii. 8, God was flying and David pursuing; nay, but the flyer giveth legs to the pursuer, he upholdeth him, as it were against himself: so did the angel strengthen Jacob to overcome himself. Now, shall it not be pleasant to God, that you lay hold on him as your own, even when he seemeth to be clothed with vengeance, seeing he changeth his outward countenance for this very end? He seemeth to go, that you may hold; because when you think he stayeth, you hold not; as the child, while the nurse is near, will look about it, and take hold of any thing; but when she withdraweth, the child cleaveth the faster to her.

But, II. We ought to stir up ourselves more now than any other time: times of God's withdrawing calleth for extraordinary and doubled approaches. So Hos. v. 15, 'They will seek me early.' And therefore the Lord's children in Scripture have made great advantage of such dispensations. The truth is, as long as we are well dealt with, security creepeth on, and religion is but in a decaying condition. Duties are done through our sleep; we are not as men awaking and knowing what we do, and whither we go. But when the Lord beginneth to trouble us, and hides his face, then it is time to awake out of sleep, before all be gone: and there ought to be, 1. More diligence in duties and approaching to God, because your case furnisheth more matter of supplication; and as matter of supplication groweth, prayer should grow. If necessity grow, and the cry be not according to necessity, it is ominous. And therefore David useth to make his cry go up according to his trouble. In a prosperous condition, though every thing might call a tender-hearted loving Christian to some nearness to God; yet ordinarily, if necessity press not, prayer languisheth and groweth formal. Sense of need putteth an edge on supplication, whereas prosperity blunteth it. The heart missing nothing, cannot go above sublunary things; but let it not have its will here, and the need of heaven will be the greater. Now I say, if you sit so many calls, both from a command, and from your own necessities, you do so much the more sin. Affliction will make even a hypocrite seek him, and pour out a prayer and visit him, Psalm lxxviii. and Isa. xxvi. And if you do not take advantage of all these pressures, you must be so much the more guilty; and therefore God, as it were, wondereth at their obstinacy, 'They return not to him that smiteth them!' All this is come upon us, yet have we not prayed. And, 2. It is sent for that end, that you may be more serious; and therefore you ought so much the more to awake, to lay hold on him. This is the way the Lord useth with his secure and wandering children, Psalm cxix. 67. For the Lord findeth us often gripping too strongly to a present world, and taking it in our arms, as if we were never to part with it. Men's souls cleave to outward accommodations; therefore the Lord useth to part us and our idol, that we may take hold of him the faster. It is union with himself that is our felicity, and it is that which God most endeavoureth. When he removeth beloved jewels, it is because they were a stumbling-block, and divorced the soul from God: when he seemeth to withdraw himself his going proclaimeth so much, oh! follow, or perish.

III. It is a very dangerous thing when he withdraweth and you follow not, when he is angry and you care not, do not fly in to make peace with him. Certainly his anger must wax hotter, and desertion will become a spiritual plague; rods must be tempered with much bitterness. What mixture of mercy can be in such a dispensation, where the fruit of it is to harden? But if the Lord's hardest dealing wrought you to more nearness and communion with himself; then certainly you have a fair advantage against the present trouble, and you have your cup mixed. You shall at length bless God for such dispensations; they may be reckoned for good to you.

Next, there ought to be more exercise of faith, and laying hold of the grounds of consolation in God in such a time. 1. For as difficulties grow, faith should fortify itself against them so much the more. The greater the storm be, it should fly the more into the chambers. Faith in the time of a calm day getteth no trial; faith bulketh much* because it hath not much to do. But except there be some fresh and new supplies it cannot hold out in a temptation. But it is a singular proof of a noble and divine faith,—that it can lay hold on him and keep him when he would go,—that can challenge kindness on a miskenning Jesus,†—that can stand on the ground of the promises when there is not a foot-breadth of a dispensation to build on. While all things go with you ye have no difficulty to maintain your faith; nay, but when the Lord seemeth to look angry, then awake and gather strength, and take hold on his strength. Look what is in your condition or his dispensation, what is good or ominous, then take hold on the other hand on him, and look what is in him to answer it, and swallow it up. Ye ought to be well acquainted with the grounds of consolation that are in God, in the worst case, and then ye might lay hold on him though he seemed a consuming fire. It is then a time that calleth most for securing your interest in him, a time when there is no external advantage to beguile you, a time when the only happiness is to be one with God. Therefore the man who, in such calamities and judgments, is not awakened to put his eternal estate out of question, he is in a dangerous case. For, do not most part drive over their days, and have no assurance of salvation, they dare not say either *pro* or *contra*. It may be, and it may not be. And this is the length that the most part come,—a negative peace; no positive confidence; no clear concluding, on sure grounds, an interest. Always ye are most called to this, when God afflicteth the land or you: if ye do not then make peace it is most dangerous. 2. The Lord loveth faith in a difficulty best,—it is the singlest and the cleanliest, it is that which most honoureth him, and glorifieth his truth and faithfulness, and sufficiency and mercy; for then it is most purely elevated above creatures, and pitcheth most on God; and therefore bringeth men to this, "No help for my soul, but thou art my portion." And this commendeth God most when he is set alone. Prosperity bringeth him down among creatures, and secure faith maketh little distinction; but awakening faith grippeth strongly and singly, putteth God alone.

Secondly, Oftentimes, when God is departing, none stirreth up himself to lay hold on him. Although there may be praying and doing of many duties, yet there

* [What is perhaps meant is, it *swelleth* much.—Ed.]

† [That is, *that can lay claim to the favour of his Saviour even when his Saviour turns away his face from him.*—Ed.]

is nothing beyond ordinary. The varieties and accessions of new grounds of supplications doth neither make greater frequency nor more fervency. This our experience may clear unto us both in duties and faith.

I. There is very little diligence in seeking of God in the way and means appointed, even when God seemeth to bid farewell to the land, and go away. Nobody cometh in as an intercessor. Men keep on their old way of praying, and never add to it, come what like. Who is it that riseth above his ordinary, as the tide of God's dispensation is? There ought to be such an impression made by the changes of God's countenance as might be read on the duties of his people. There should be such a distance between your ordinary and such times as between a sleeping man and a waking man, that whatever your attainment of access to God be, ye might stir up and go beyond it according as matters call. Will God count your public fasts a performance of this duty? Alas, we fast sleeping, and none stirreth up himself to these things! Is there any difference betwixt your solemn humiliation and another Sabbath? And is there any difference between a Sabbath and a week-day, save the external duty? Is not this palpably our case? Is there any wakening among us? No, security is both the universal disease and complaint; and it is become an incurable disease since it became a complaint. Doth any of you pray more in private than he used? Or what edge is on your prayers? Alas! the Lord will get good leave to go from us; it feareth me that we would give Christ a testimonial to go over seas. Hold him, hold him! Nay. the multitude would be gladly quit of him,—they cannot abide his yoke, his work is a burden, his word is a torment, his discipline is bands and cords; and what heart can ye then have to keep Christ? What violence can ye offer to him to hold him still? All your entreaties may be fair compliments, but they would never rend his garment.

II. There is no up-stirring to faith among us, and laying hold on Jesus Christ, albeit all his dispensations warn us that it is now high time. There are not many who are about this point, effectually to stir up their faith or to secure their interest. Think ye that conjectures will carry you through difficulties? The multitude think they believe much, but any temptation proveth their mistake. The most part of Scotland would deny God and his Son Jesus Christ if they were put to it. Always it is a time ye would not lie out from your stronghold,—faith only uniteth you to Christ, and if ye would be kept in any trial, stir up faith.

Thirdly, Prayer and faith, diligence and laying hold on God, must go together and help one another. Not calling on his name, and not laying hold on him go together, and have influence one upon another.

I. Faith hath influence on prayer. Laying hold on God in Christ will make right calling on his name, it learneth men how to call God, to call him Abba, Father. Faith useth to vent itself in prayer. I say, much consideration of God, and claiming into him, and to the grounds of confidence in him, must both make prayer acceptable, and carry the stamp and impression of God's name, or Christ's name, on it, and also make much prayer: for when a soul hath pitched on God as its only felicity, and thus made choice of him, it findeth in him all sufficiency, all things for all things. There is no necessity, but it findeth a supply in his fulness for it; and therefore it applieth a man to the fountain, to draw out of the wells of salvation. There is nothing can be so sweet and refreshing as for such a soul to pour out itself every day in him, to talk with him face to face. Faith engageth the heart to come to God with all things; whereas many difficulties would have been, and the secure or unsettled heart would have gone as many different ways to help them. Faith layeth hold on God, knoweth but one, and bringeth all here; and therefore access to God is a fruit of it, access unto the grace wherein we stand by faith. And again, how can prayer be acceptable as long as faith doth not principle it? It is but like a beast's groaning under a burden. Laying hold on God himself makes a man's duties acceptable, because he speaks and asks; believing that he shall receive, he trusteth God and doth not tempt him. Where lively faith is not entertained there cannot be much affection which is the oil of the wheels. There may be in some bitterness of spirit much vehemency; but that is not a pure flame of divine love that burneth upward to him; and it is soon extinguished, and lasteth no longer nor present sense, and then the soul groweth harder, as iron that had been in the fire.

II. When there is not much prayer and calling, faith cannot be strong and violent; for prayer is even the exercise of faith; if you wear out of that, faith rusteth. There may be much quietness with little prayer, but there cannot be much, and strong and lively faith; for where it getteth not continual employment it fags. And indeed prayer is a special point of holding God fast, and keeping him; therefore join these, if ye would thrive in any one of them. Your unbelieving complaints are not prayers and calling on his name, because they are not mixed with faith. As the apostle said of the word, so may it be said of prayer,—your prayers are not profitable, are not heard, because not mixed with faith. Ye use to doubt, that ye may be fervent; to question your interest, that ye may stir up your spirits to prayer. But alas! what a simple gross mistake is that? Poor soul, though thou get more liberty, shall it be counted access to God? Though you have more grief, and your bitterness doth indite more eloquence, shall God be moved with it? Know ye not that you should ask without wavering, and lift up pure hands without wrath and doubting? And yet both are there.

Fourthly, The duty we are called to in such a time when God is angry, is to lay hold on him. We would speak a word more of it. And, I. We ought to hold a departing Lord, by wrestling with him in supplication, not to let him depart till he bless, Hos. xii. 3, 4. The application of Jacob's victory over the angel is thus, 'Turn ye to the Lord, and wait on him,' &c. How had Jacob power over the angel? By supplication and weeping; so that prayer is a victory over God, even the Lord God of hosts. We ought, as it were, to strive against outward dispensation; when it saith, He is gone; when our condition saith, He is gone, or going, we ought to wrestle with it. No submission to such a departing, I mean, no submission that sitteth down with it, and is not careful how it be. Now this time calleth you to such an exercise. The Lord seemeth to be angry with us. There is a strong cloud over the land, and like to pour down upon us,—the Lord is drawing a sword again, and beginning now to lay on. Many threatenings would not put us to supplication. Now, what will the laying on of the rod do? If the former days be returning wherein ye saw much sorrow, is it not then high time for the Lord's remembrancers, and for the Lord's children to wrestle with God? As Esau was coming on Jacob, so hath God armed men, and such desperate men, as he hath made a rod to us before. If we be twice beaten with it, it is very just, for before we did not seek in to him who smote us.* You would know this, that the Lord is but seeking employment, and if ye would deal with him, ye may make advantage of the present and future calamities. And look to this laying hold on him; this is the chief thing ye should now heed. It is God himself that should be your principal object. Praying should be a laying hold on God, it should meet with himself. For the most part in the time of prosperity, we cannot meet with God singly, we have so much to do with creatures; we keep trysts so punctually with them, so that we cannot keep with God. We have so many things in our affections and thoughts, that God cannot get place, he cannot get us at leisure for the throng of our business; we lose God by catching at shadows. Well then, we are called in such a time of difficulty to come in to God himself, to draw by the vail of ordinances, that we may have communion with God himself. And this is right praying, when the soul getteth such immediate access to God, as it were, to handle him, and see him, and taste him, to exercise its senses on him. Ordinances have been of a long time a covering of his face, and he useth not now to unvail himself in the sanctuary, and let us see his glory. God is departed from preaching and praying, and the solemn meeting; so that we meet not with God,—we lay hold on a shadow of an outward ordinance, but not on God himself. Therefore, Christians, make advantage of this time. You may be brought to want ordinances, then lay hold on himself who is the substance and marrow of them. You may be denuded of outward comforts and accommodation here, then lay hold on himself in much prayer. If affliction would blow away the cloud on his face, or would scatter our idols from us, and make us single alone with God, as Jacob was, it were well sent.

II. Your exercise should be to take hold on God by faith. And, 1. Ye would

* [What is here said would seem to fix the date of this sermon. It appears to have been preached before the battle of Dunbar.—Ed.]

make peace with God, be much in direct acts of apprehending God himself in Jesus Christ. And this is according as ye take up yourselves with your own misery and necessity. Do but travel continually between your own misery and something answerable in God.

The first thing we would have you do, now when God frowns upon us, is to find out your own lost condition, and how great strangers you have been to him, even when ye have approached in many ordinances; and find a necessity of making peace with God and atonement. Now from this lay hold on Christ, as the hope set before you. Look upon that in him which will answer all your necessities, and be suitable to them. It is not matters of outward lot that should go nearest your heart. Let the world go where it will, that which concerneth you most in such a time, is the securing of your soul: for if you lose it, what gain you? what keep you? Your houses, and lands, and lives may be in hazard; nay, but one thing is more worth than all these, and in more hazard. Begin at spiritual things, and ask h w matters stand between God and thee.

2. Not only would ye be much in immediate application unto Jesus Christ, but ye would so take hold of him, as ye may be sure ye have him. Make peace, and know that ye have made it, and then shall ye be kept in perfect peace. You would never rest until you can on solid grounds answer the question. And this duty is called for from you at such a time, for 'the just shall live by faith,' in a troublesome time, Hab. ii. 4. And as ye ought to keep and hold fast confidence, and not cast it away in such a time, so should ye all seek after it. Do not only rest in this,—I know not but I may belong to Christ, I dare not say against it. O no, Christians, you should have positive clear grounds of assurance: 'I am his, and he is mine;' 'I know that my Redeemer liveth;' 'God is my portion.' And if ye conclude this solidly, I defy all the world to shake and trouble your peace: this is perfect peace, 'peace, peace,' double peace. How can ye choose but be shaken at every blast of temptation, when you are not thus solidly grounded, when you hold not at your anchor?

And, 3. Having thus laid hold on Christ as your own, lay hold on all in him as yours, and for your use. Whatever difficulty the present time, or your own condition afford, search but as much in God as may counterbalance it. Answer all objections, from his mercy, goodness, power, wisdom, unchangeableness, and this shall be more nor the trouble. God himself laid hold upon, and made ours, is more nor removing a temporal calamity. It is an eternal weight, to weigh down all crosses and disappointments. For what can present things be? Is there not in the favour of his countenance that which may drown them in oblivion? Are ye like to sink here? Is not God a sure anchor to hold by? And if ye do not this, your trouble is nothing in respect of the danger of your soul. Secure and loose lying out of God, not putting this matter to a full point, is worse nor all your outward fading. Therefore, we exhort you in the Lord's name, to fly into this name of the Lord, as a strong tower to run to and be safe. When the Lord seemeth now to be angry with us, run not away from him, though he should yet clothe himself with vengeance as a garment.

But, *first*, O ye poor people, who have never asked this question, whether have I any interest in Jesus? ask it now, and resolve it in time. If trouble come on, if scattering and desolation come on, and our land fade as a leaf, certainly the Lord's anger will drive you away, What will ye do in the time of his indignation? All of you, put this to the trial,—how matters stand between God and you.

And, *secondly*, If ye find all wrong, do not sink in discouragement; all may be amended, while it is seen wrong in time. Nay, God taketh away outward accommodation, to make you more serious in this. And it is the very voice of rods,—every one fly into your hold, every one make peace with me. You may take hold, and do it feckfully.*

Thirdly, You who have fled to Jesus, take more hold of him; you are called also to renew your faith, and begin again. Make peace with God, let your confidence be kept fast, and thus shall ye be immoveable, because he changeth not. God will

* [That is, strongly.—Ed.

not go from you if ye believe,—hold him by faith. Christ could not do great things in Galilee, because of their unbelief, and so he departed from them. As unbelief maketh an evil heart to depart from the God of all life and consolation, so doth it make God depart from us. But faith casteth a knot upon him (to speak with reverence), it fasteneth him by his own word and promise, and he cannot go by it. It is a violent hand laid on God. 'I will not let thee go till thou bless me.'

Fourthly, Faith and prayer, or holding of God, by believing in him, and much employing him, needeth much stirring up unto, and awaking. 'That stirreth up himself to take hold on thee.' Security is the moth of both these, and eateth out the life of faith and supplication: it maketh prayer so coldrife that it cannot prevail, and faith so weak that it cannot use violence.

I. Security apprehendeth no evil, no need. A secure condition is a dream that one is eating, and yet his soul is empty. Look how the people of Laish were quiet and secure, apprehending no evil; destruction cometh then on as an armed man. Always it is much necessity that administers fuel to a man's faith and supplication. David says, (Psal. xxx. 7,) 'I said in my prosperity, I shall not be moved.' Nay, but many say in adversity, and cry Peace, peace, where no peace is. Security pleadeth innocency, and then believeth immunity. 'I am innocent, therefore shall his anger turn away,' Jer. ii. 35. Security applieth not sin, and so refuseth the curse of sin and wages of it. And thus is a man in his own eyes a lord, and then he will come no more to God, Jer. ii. 31. It is almost impossible to awake men, by general judgments, to apprehend personal danger; and men never stir out of their nest till it be on fire. We can behold, or hear of our neighbours' spoiling, and violence done to them; but till the voice of a cry be heard in our own streets and fields, nobody will take the judgment to themselves. It is well said, that which is spoken to all, is spoken to none; so what is done to all in general, is done to none. The voice of a general rod speaketh not particularly, and maketh not men apprehensive of sad things; and thus men are not pressed unto prayer—are not put out of themselves; it is only necessity that saps the roots of it, and makes it green.

II. Security is lazy and not active, putteth not forth its hand to work, and so dieth a beggar, for only the hand of the diligent maketh rich. Laying hold on God is a duty that requireth much spirit in it: men do not grip things well in their slumbering. There is no duty that needeth so spiritual and lively principles. If a man do not put on such a piece of resolution and edge upon him, he cannot come to the wrestling of prayer and violence of faith. Although the exercise and acting of grace dependeth more upon the Spirit of God's present influence, than upon the soul of man; yet this is the way the Lord communicateth his influence, by stirring up and exciting the creature to its duty, as if it could do it alone. Grace is one thing, and the stirring up of it is another thing. For when we lie by and sleep over our time, and go not about the matter so seriously as it were life and death, it is but a weak hold we can take of God. According to the measure of a man's apprehending necessity, and according to the measure of his seriousness in these things, so will the hand of faith grip, and lay hold with more or less violence. As a man drowning will be put from sleeping, and when one is in extreme hazard all his strength will unite together in one to do that which at any ordinary time it could not do, so ought it to be here. A Christian assaulted with many temptations should unite his strength, and try the yondmost.* O but your whole spirits would run together, to the saving of yourselves, if ye were very apprehensive of necessity! The exercise of faith is a dead grip, that cannot part with what it grippeth. Therefore, 1. we must say to you, it is not so easy a thing as you believe, to lay hold on God,—there must be stirring up to it. And when the Lord speaketh of our stirring ourselves, certainly he meaneth this likewise, that he must stir us, ere we stir ourselves. 2. Above all, be afraid of a secure condition: it is the enemy of communion with God and spiritual life. Therefore, look about you, and apprehend more your necessity, and then give no rest and quietness to yourself, till you have employed and engaged him; be as men flying to lay hold on the refuge set before you. 3. It must be a time of little access to God, and little faith, when we are all secure, and nobody goeth about religion as their work and business. We

* [That is, his utmost.—Ed.

allow ourselves in it; therefore, we do exhort you, *first*, To purpose this as your end to aim at, and purpose by God's grace to take more hold of God. There is little minding of duty, and that maketh little doing of it. Once engage your hearts to a love and desire of more of this, come to a point of resolution; I must know him more, and trust more in him, be more acquaint with him. And, *secondly*, Put yourselves in the way of duty. It is God that only can stir you up, or apply your hearts to the using of violence to God: but ye would be found in the outward means much, and in these ways God will meet with you, if you wait on him in them.

'For thou hast hid thy face from us.' Here is the greatest plague, a spiritual plague. The last verse was but the beginning of sorrows, 'We all do fade,' &c. But lo, here the accomplishment of misery, God hiding his face, and consuming them in the hand of their sins.

First, The Lord's hiding of his face, and giving up a people to melt away in their sins; punishing with judicial blindness and security, is the worst judgment, it filleth the cup full. This complaint goeth on still worse; and certainly it is worse nor their fading as a leaf and exile out of their land. It is not without reason, that great troubles and afflictions are so expressed, 'Thou didst hide thy face;' as David said, 'Thou didst hide thy face, and I was troubled;' importing as much, as it is not trouble that doth trouble, but God's hiding of his face that maketh trouble trouble. It is in so far trouble, as it is a sign of his displeasure, and as the frowns of his countenance are upon it; therefore, the saints, aggravating their affliction, say, 'Thou hidest thy face.' You know the face is the place wherein either kindness or unkindness appeareth. The Lord's countenance, or face, is a refreshful sweet manifestation of himself to a soul; it is the Lord using familiarity with a spirit, and this made David more glad than corn and wine. Now, the hiding of the face, the withdrawing of his countenance, is, when the Lord in his dispensation and dealing doth withhold the manifestation of himself, either in life or consolation: when he covereth himself with clouds round about, that neither can a soul see into the backside of it—into his own warm heart, nor can the sun-beams shine through to quicken and refresh the soul. The Lord draweth over his face a vail of a crossing dispensation, or such like.

There is a desertion of the soul in the point of life and spiritual action, and there is a desertion in regard of consolation. The varieties of the Lord's desertions run upon these two. As a Christian's life is action or consolation, and the Lord's influence is either quickening or comforting, so his withdrawing is either a prejudice to the one or the other. Sometimes he goeth 'mourning all the day,' nay, but he is 'sick of love;' sometimes he is a bottle dried in the smoke, and his moisture dried up. The Christian's consolation may be subtracted, and his life abide, but he cannot have spiritual consolation, if he be not lively. This life is more substantial,—comfort is more refreshful,—life is more solid,—comfort sweet; that is true growing solid meat, this but sauce to eat it with.

The hiding here meant is certainly a spiritual punishment. The Lord denying unto this people grace to understand the voice of the rod,—he appearing as a party against them,—leaving them to their own carnal and lazy temper, and thus they lay still under God's displeasure. Now, there is nothing like this:

I. Because it is a spiritual punishment, and estates are not to be valued and laid in the balance with the soul. Albeit men are become so brutish as to abase their souls, and prostitute them to any thing, yet all a man hath is not considerable to it.

II. It is a more excellent thing that is removed by it,—'In his favour is life,'—all felicity and happiness is in God's countenance. If a man have not this, what hath he else? Losses are according as the thing is. Nay, but here is more,—'My Lord is taken from me, my God hath forgotten me.' And indeed, if man's true happiness be in communion with God, certainly, any interruption coming in must be sad, and make a man more miserable than the world knoweth. There is a greater emphasis in that word, 'Thou hast hid thy face,' than if he had said, all the world hideth their face and maketh a scorn of us.

Therefore, *first*, Know what is the worst thing of the times. Many of you think sword and pestilence, and the burdens of the time, the worst things; and if you were now to complain, the saddest complaint would be,—affliction is laid on our loins.

But know this, if your cities were desolate; if your land were made a wilderness, and we captives in another land, there is yet a worse thing than all these; and think you not this strange? Nay, I say, there is something worse already in us, that we know not of, and it is this,—'Make the hearts of this people hard.' A spirit of slumber and deadness from the Lord upon the land: there are multitudes he will never show his face unto; it is still vailed from them, and they know him not. Ye that think all were well, if ye had peace and prosperity, and know no hiding of God's countenance,—no anger but when he striketh, certainly you know not what his countenance is; by all these things men neither know love nor hatred. 2. Whatever calamity come upon you outwardly, deprecate most spiritual plagues and God's deserting. If you have God's countenance, it may make you glad in much sadness. You would be most careful lest any partition-wall came in; lest his countenance change on you, if you grieve his Spirit and break his heart. Seek to have his face to shine, and this shall be a sun with healing under his wings. O but Christ's countenance is comely, when it is seen without clouds! but often it is overclouded with much provocation.

Secondly, The Lord's hiding of his face hath influence on the temper of spirits and disposition in duties. The truth is in general, 'In him we live, and move, and have our being;' and more especially, in many things that are spiritual, we are of ourselves able to do nothing. The creature's holiness, and especially our life, is but as the rays that the Sun of righteousness sendeth forth round about him, and if any thing come between it evanisheth. As the marygold that openeth its leaves when the sun riseth, and closeth when it goeth down again, so exactly doth our spiritual constitution follow the motions of his countenance, and depend wholly on them Thou hidest thy face, and they are troubled, Psal. xxx. 7. The Lord needeth no more but discountenance us, and we are gone.

Always, I. Be more dependent creatures. We use to act as from habits within, without any subordination to the Lord's grace without us; but we find that our sufficiency is not of ourself. How often doth your spiritual condition change on you in an hour? You cannot command one thought of God, or act from any habit of grace, even then when you can bring forth other gifts in exercise. Ye find that grace findeth more difficulties, more interruptions,—therefore learn to attend the changes and motions of his countenance.

II. When you find your heart dead, and you concluded under an impossibility of taking hold of God in a lively manner, then, I pray you, look unto the Lord's suspending of his influence, and let your whole endeavours be at the throne of grace to help it. It will not be your own provoking of yourself to your duty, but you must put yourself upon God, that he may cause his face to shine.

III. Though the Lord's hiding his face be often a cause of our deadness, and his desertion maketh all to wither, yet we have often a culpable hand in it; and he hides his face being provoked so to do. One thing we may mention, grieving of the Holy Ghost whereby we are sealed, quenching the motions of the Spirit, maketh the Spirit cover his face with a vail and hide it. There is here ordinarily a reciprocal or mutual influence. Our grieving him makes him withdraw his countenance; and his withdrawing his countenance maketh us to wither and grow barren.

IV. The most sure and infallible token of the Lord's hiding his face, is security, and a spirit of deadness and laziness; when folk go about duties dreaming, and do all as it were through their sleep. Therefore we may conclude sad things on this land, that the Lord hideth his face from us. And therefore arise, and do not settle and quiet yourself in such a condition. The Lord is angry; needeth any more be said? No more needeth to kind children; but the rod must follow this to make anger sensible.

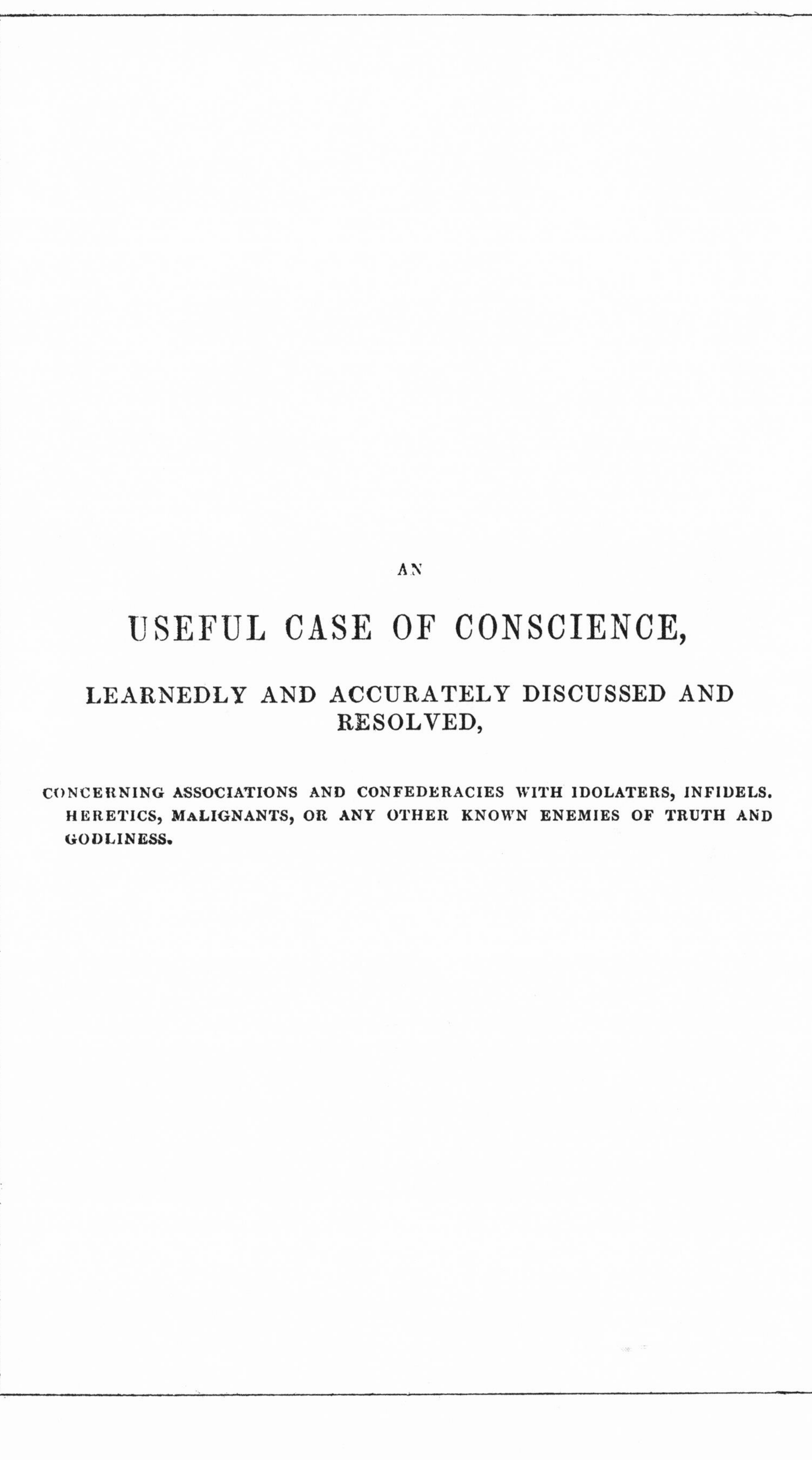

AN

USEFUL CASE OF CONSCIENCE,

LEARNEDLY AND ACCURATELY DISCUSSED AND RESOLVED,

CONCERNING ASSOCIATIONS AND CONFEDERACIES WITH IDOLATERS, INFIDELS. HERETICS, MALIGNANTS, OR ANY OTHER KNOWN ENEMIES OF TRUTH AND GODLINESS.

AN USEFUL

CASE OF CONSCIENCE, &c.

THAT THE PRESENT PUBLIC RESOLUTIONS AND PROCEEDINGS DO IMPORT A CONJUNCTION WITH THE MALIGNANT PARTY IN THE KINGDOM, AND OF THE SIN, DANGER, AND SCANDAL OF THAT WAY.

SECTION I.

THAT THERE IS A MALIGNANT PARTY STILL IN THE KINGDOM.

In the entry to this business, the importunity of not a few makes it needful to speak somewhat to a question which unto this time hath been unquestioned, as beyond all exception, that is, whether there be yet in Scotland a malignant party? Or, whether there be at this time any party who may and ought, in reason and Christian prudence, to be reputed and looked upon as malignants and disaffected to the covenanted cause of God? It seems the more needful to speak somewhat of this, 1. Because some ministers are become slack and silent in this point, as if now there were no need of watchfulness and warning against any such party. 2. Because the expressions of many of the people of the land run that way, that there are now no malignants in Scotland, and that it is but a few factious ministers that will still keep up these names, that they may more easily, with others of their own stamp, weaken and divide the kingdom, for carrying on of their own ends. 3. Because the inclinations and resolutions of the public judicatories, in reference to most of the party who carried that name, do clearly import that they do think they are no more to be looked upon as malignants, as appears from several of their papers, especially the letter written for satisfaction to the presbytery of Stirling. And therefore this must be laid down as the foundation of what follows: That there is still in the land, not only a few persons, but a party considerable for number, power, and policy, who are malignant and disaffected to the covenant and cause of God. We would join heartily in the desire of many, that these and other such like odious names of different parties and factions were taken away; but we cannot join in the reasons of this desire which are ordinarily given. We wish the name malignant were obsolete and antiquate, if so be the thing itself, which is such a root of bitterness, were extirpated out of the church. Yea, though the thing itself remained, if men would hate it for itself, and account it more odious and hateful than the name imports, we would be glad it were no more heard of, because we find this prejudice, by all such appropriated names, that people generally look upon that which goes under that name as the only sin, and as if there were not that root of bitterness, in all which it grows out of, in any; and so conceive themselves good Christians if they fall not under that hateful appellation of malignants. But seeing this bitter fruit of enmity, against godliness and the godly, comes to more ripeness and maturity in many of this generation than in others, who yet are unconverted; and seeing it hath been the custom of the church of God in all generations, to discriminate many more ungodly and known haters of godliness and his people from the common sort of natural people, and to comprehend them under these names of wicked, of malignant, of enemies, as may appear in the Old Testament, especially in the

Psalms; and that more especially in our days, that name hath been appropriated to such who have declared themselves, in their words or actions, to be haters of godliness and the power thereof, and his people, or have arisen to the height of actual opposition against these, we cannot be blamed for using such a name still, for distinction's sake. We proceed to some reasons.

I. The constant and continued proceedings of the General Assembly and their commissioners for many years past unto this day.

There is not almost any of their warnings, declarations, or remonstrances, which doth not assert this, and warn against it; and that not only before the king's home-coming and taking of the covenant, but also since that time, as is evident by the Declaration emitted by the commission in July last;* the Declaration of the Assembly itself, a little after;† by the Declaration emitted at Stirling since the defeat at Dunbar;‡ the Causes of the Fast upon that defeat;§ the Remonstrance to the king

* [It is evident from this, and similar references to recent events, that the Case of Conscience must have been written in the early part of the year 1651. The proceedings of the commission of the General Assembly, from July 1650 to July 1561, fill a large MS. volume of more than 400 pages. These proceedings have never been printed, with the exception of certain detached papers, which are found engrossed in the controversial pamphlets and journals of the times.—Peterkin's 'Records of the Kirk of Scotland,' p. 592.—Ed.]

† [" The Gen. Assembly itself at Edinburgh, in July thereafter, did, upon the 19 of that moneth, publish a Declaratione, in which they give warning concerning Malignants thus:—' We exhort all these who are in publick trust in ye comitee of Estates, or otherwise, not only to take good head of their private walking, that it be suitable to the Gospel of Jesus Christ, and of their families and followers, that they bee void of offence, but also be straight in the cause and covenant, and not to seek themselves, nor befriend any who have been enemies to the Lord's work, self-seeking, and conniving at, and complying with, and pleading for Malignants, having been publick sins that have been often complained of: and we wish to God yr were no cause to complain of these things still, notwithstanding of the solemne confession of them, and ingadging against them. God forbid that any mocke the Lord. He is a severe avenger of all such things; and there is the more reason at this time not to own Malignants, because it is ordinary with men so to be taken with the sense of the dangers qch is before them as not to look back to that which is behind them. There may be inclinations in some to employ these men, and make use of them, that we may be strengthened in this and in our neighbour land; but God hath hitherto cursed all such counsels, and blasted such resolutions: and if we shall again fall into this sin, as our guilt shal be so much the greater by reasone of many promises and ingadgments to the contrair, so we may expect ane heavier judgment from the Lord upon it. Let us keep the Lord's way, and though we be few and weake, the Lord shall be with us, and make us to prosper and prevail. They are not fit for the work of God, and for the glorious dispensations of his more than ordinary works of power and providence in these times, who cannot beleive nor act any thing beyonde what sense and reasone can make clear unto them from the beginning unto ye end of their undertakings. Former experiences and present straits call upon us that we should act and follow our deutie in such a way as may magnify the Lord, and make it known to others that we may live by Faith." '—' The Waters of Sihor, or the Lands Defectione; By Mr. James Guthrie, Minister of Stirling,' Wodrow MSS. vol. xvii. p. 41, in Bib. Ad. —Ed.]

‡ [" At Stirlinge, the 12 of Septem. 1650. A shorte declaratione and varninge to all the congregations of the Kirk of Scotland, from the commissioners of the General Assembly.

" Albeit the Lord quhosse judgments are vnsearchable, and quhosse wayes past finding out, hes brought the land werey low wnder the hand of ane prewaillinge enemey, yet must we not forbeare to declair the mynd of God, nor vthers refusse to hearken thereto. It wer superfluous to give answer to the maney calumnies and reproches that are blazed abroad; for albeit in every thing we cannot justify the conducte of the armey, yet we hold it our deutie to desyre every one not to beleive groundless reports, bot rather to eye the Lord, and looke vpe to the hand that smytts them. And therfor, in the first place, we exhort and varne all the inhabitants of the land, to searche out ther iniquities, and to be deeplie humbled before the Lord, that he may turn away his wraith from us. The Lord hath wounded us and chasteissed ws sore, wiche sayes that our iniquities are muche, and that our sins are increessed. It concerneth the King to mourne for all the grivous provocations of his father's housse, and for all his auen guiltiness; and to consider if he hes come to the covenant, and joined himselve to the Lord, upone politicke interests, for gaining a croune to himselve rather then to advance religione and righteousness; that it is iniquitie quhilk God will not forgett excepte it be speedilie repented offe. It concerns our nobles and judges to consider wither ther carriadge in publicke matters be straight and equall, or rather savoring of seeking themselves and the thinges of this worlde; and how they walke in ther families, and in ther privat conversations. There is in maney a grate deall of perversenes and incorrigiblenes in regard of forsaking some and performing some deuties, notwithstanding publecke confessions and engagements; and this cannot bot heighlie provock the Lord. And it concerneth the officers of the armey, especially thesse quho are cheiffe among them, to weight weell quhat the Lord hes against them, and to repent of ther diffidence and carnall way of acting and undervaluing of Gods people. And ministers have also neid to searche themselves concerning ther faithfullness to be sound, for wiche God is angrie: doutles even amongest thesse is muche negligence. Albeit the Lord hes suffred that armey of perfideous at Perth after his escape; together with the Remonstrance given in by them to the parliament;|| all which do clearly hold forth this truth.

and blasphemous sectaries to prevaill. Yet, God forbid that the land should complay with him, quhatever may be the plauseable and faire carriage of some of that enimey, yet doubtless there is ane levin of error and hypocrassy amongest them, wich all the lovers of treuth wold decern and avoyd. As the Lord hes trayed the stability and integritie of his people in the land heirtofore, by the prevailling of malignants, so doeth he now tray them by the prevailling of sectaries; and wee trust they will thinke it ther deutie and commendatione to prove staidfast against them als weill as the other.

3. Nather wold men be lesse cairfull and active to opposse the enimey, then they have beine in opposeing malignants heirtofor; our religione, lives, liberties and estaits, are als muche in hazard now as ever; all the ordinances of Jesus Christ in the land are in danger, and the foundatione lyke to be overturnid by thesse men quho are oblidged, by the band of the covenant, to mantiene all thesse; and it wer a grate guiltines to ly doune and complay, and crutche under the burden of the strange impositions that they will lay upon us, and as men without head, to suffer our land to be brought in bondage and ourselves to be robbed of all thesse things quhilk are most precious and deire to us. If wee should doe so, the Lord wold be angrie with us, and our posterity could not bot curss us.

4. We would not think that all danger from the malignants is now gone, seeing that ther is a grate maney suche in the land, quho still retein ther former principales, therfor we wolde, with als muche watchfullnes and tendernes now as ever, avoyde ther snars, and beware of complayance and conjunctione with them, and take head, that under a pretence of doing for the king and kingdome they gett not power and strenth unto ther handes, for advanceing and promoveing ther old malignant desseinges. Doubtles our saftie is in holding fast our former principales, and keeping a straighte faithe, without declyning to the right hand ore to the lefte.

5. It concernes all the inhabitants of the land to bewarre of murmuring and complaning against Gods dispensations, and questioning the treuthe and goodnes of our causse or quarreling with God, or blaming or casting off the covenant, becausse of aney thing that hath befallin them; that wer a grate iniquitie not to be pardoned. Lett us beare the indignatione of the Lord patientlie, becausse wee have sinned against him, untill he plead our causse and execut judgment for us; he will bring us fourthe to the light, and we shall behold his righteousnes."—Sir James Balfour's Annales, vol. iv. pp. 98—102.—Ed.]

§ [" Causes of a soleme publicke humiliatione upone the defait of the army, to be keepit throughout all the congregations of the Kirk of Scotland.

Albeit soleme publicke humiliations hes beine muche slighted, and gone about in a formall way by maney in this land, so that it is not one of the least of our provocations that we have drawn neire to God with our mouthes and keepit our heartes fare from him; for wich the Lord hath turned the wisdome of the wysse unto foollishnes, and the strenthe of the strong men unto weaknes; yet seing it is a dutie that hath oftin provin comfortable to uswards, God doeth new call us in a speciall way by a singular peice of dispensatione, and knowing that all quho are acquainted with God in the land will make conscience of it, wee conceave it expedient that the quhole land be humbled for the causses following.

1. The continued ignorance and profanitie of the bodie of the land, and the obstinacey and incorrigiblenes of maney, notwithstanding of all the caires that God hath takin upon us by his word, and by his workes of mercy and judgement, to teache us in the knowledge of his name, and to refraine us from the eivell of our wayes.

2. The manifest provocations of the kinges housse wiche we feare are not throughlie repented off, nor forsaken by him to this day; togidder with the crooked and precipitant wayes that wer takin by sundrie of our statesmen for caring on the trettey with the king.

3. The bringing home with the king a grate maney malignants, and indevoring to keepe some of them about him, and maney of them in the kingdome, notwithstanding of publicke resolutions to the contrarey.

4. The not purging of the kinges familie from malignant and profane men, and the constituting of the samen of weill affected and godlie persons; albeit it hathe beine oftin pressed upone the parliament and comittee of Estaits, undertaking and promessed to be performed by them.

5. The leveing of a most malignant and profaine guard of horsse to be aboute the king, quho having beine sent for to be purgit aboute 2 dayes before the defaite, were suffred to be and feight in our armey.

6. The exceiding grate slaknes of maney and aversnes and untowardnes of some in the cheiffe judicatories of the kingdome and in the armey, in guid motione and publick deuties, especially in thesse thinges that concerne the purging of judicatories and the armey from malignant and scandalous persons, and filling all places of powre and trust with men of knowen integritie and trust, and of a blamles and Christiane conversatione; togider with grate inclinations to keepe and bring in malignants to the judicatories and to the armey, as if the land could not be gydit and defendit without thesse; and grate repyning and craying out against all that is done to the contrarie, and studding to make the same ineffectual.

7. The exceiding grate diffidence of some of the cheiffe leaders of our armey, and others amongest us quho thought wee could not be saved bot by ane numerous armey; who quhen wee have gottin many thousands togider, wold not hazard to acte aney thing, notwithstanding that God offred faire opportunities and advantages, and fitted the spiritts of the souldiers for ther deutie; for carnall confidence that was in maney of the armey, to the dispysing of the enimey and promising victorie to themselves without eying of God.

II. Take Christ's rule, 'By their fruits ye shall know them.' There is a great party in the land that adhere to malignant principles, bring forth malignant fruits, and tread malignant paths, as may appear in these instances. 1. A great many of these who have been formerly engaged in such courses, and under church censures, did lately conjoin together and rise in arms, and drew away the king* from

8. The lousnes, insolencie and oppressione, of maney in the armey, and the litle or no caire that was taken by maney to preserve the corne, by wich it hath come to passe that verey much of the food of the poore people of the land have beine neidlesly destroyed; and quhile wee even remember this, we wishe that the prophanitie and oppressione of sundrie of oure officers and souldiers in Ingland, quhen we were fighting for the assistance of the parliament of that kingdome, may not be forgottin, because it was matter of stumbling in that land, so it is lyke it is ane of the causses of the sore indignatione now manifested against us by the hands of thesse men.

9. Our grate unthankfullnes for former mercies and deliverances, and even for maney tokins of the Lords favor and goodness towards our present armey quhile they wer togider, and the grate impatience of spirit that was to be seine in maney thesse weekes past, quhilk made them limitt the Lord, and to compleine and weerie of his delaying of ane deliverance.

10. The enving and eyeing of the kings intrest and quarrell by maney, without subordinatione to religione and the liberties and saveties of this kingdomes.

11. The carnall selve seiking and crooked way of sundrie in our judicatories and armies, quho make ther employments and places rather ane matter of intrest and gain and preferment to themselves then of advancing religione and righteousness in the land.

12. The not putting difference betwix thesse that fear God, and thesse that fear him not, for our services, our companie, our employments, bot acompting all men alyke, maney times preferring thesse quho have nothing of God in them.

13. The exceiding grate negligence that is in grate ones, and maney others, in performing the deuties in ther families notwithstanding of our former soleme acknowledgment of the samen; as also, our neglecte of the deuties of mutuall edificatione, and grate unfruitfullness and barrennes that is to be seine amongest all sorts of persons; togider with the following of deutie with a grate deall of mixture of carnall affections and fleschly wisdome wich grives the Spirit of God, and takes away muche of the beutie of the Lords image from our judicatories.

As we wold be humbled for thesse thinges, so wold wee also intreat the Lord that he wold sanctifie this affliction to his people that they nather dispysse his chestisings, nor faint quhen they are rebukit of him; bot that they may beare his indignatione patiently, and cleive steadfestly to the treuthe, and the covenants, and the causse of God without yeilding to the power of the enimey, or receaving ther errors, or complaying ather with them on the one hand, ore malignants on the other, and that the Lord wold poure out of his Spirit upon the people, that ther spirits may be raissed unto ther deutie, and that they may be filled and furnished of God with wisdome and resolutione to acte against their enimies for the honor of God, ther awen preservatione; and that the Lord wold not suffer them to be tempted above that whiche they are able to beare, bot that he wold break the yoke of ther oppressors from off ther neckes, and give them salvatione and deliverance; earnestly to intreat the Lord in private and in publicke that he wold preserve with us the ordinances of Jesus Christe, the kingdom, the kings maties persone, the ministrie, from the power of ther enimies, quho seekes the destruction of all."—Id. pp. 102—107.—Ed.]

‖ [See the Acts of the Parliaments of Scotland, Anno 1650, xxx Novembris, vol. vi. p. 544.—Ed.]

* ["About this time the king's head was filled by some unhappy men about him, especially Dr. Fraser [who was the king's physician] and Henry Seymour, with many extreme fears. After the affront at Leith, they had raised suspicions in his mind, which, upon the defeat at Dunbar, were increased, but by the separate rising in the west brought near to the head of a design to break the treaty with him, and agree upon his expences with Cromwell. Upon these motions the malignants in the north stept in, and by the forenamed persons began a correspondence for the raising of the north for his present service, under the conduct of Middleton. So many noblemen were on this unhappy enterprise. Crawford was given out for its head and contriver, albeit he professed to me his opposition to it. Lauderdale knew of it; but he has said so far to me, that I believe him he opposed it to his power. However, the thing was so foolishly laid, and the king, by the counsels of these about him, was so various in giving order for that rising, sometimes commanding and then countermanding to rise, that all the party was put in a confusion; yet, by the information of these foresaid fools, the king being put in fear, that Lorn, going timely to bury a soldier, was drawing together his regiment to lay hands on him, contrary to his former resolutions; he took horse with some two or three, as if it had been to go a hawking, but crossed Tay, and stayed not till he came to Clowe in Angus. By the way he repented of the journey, and meeting with Lauderdale at Diddup, and Balcarras coming from Dundee by accident, was almost persuaded by them to return; yet by Diddup and Buchan he was kept in Clowe. But when he came to that miserably-accommodated house, and in place of the great promised forces, he saw nothing but a small company of Highlanders, he presently sent for Robert Montgomery, who was near with his regiment, and without more ado, did willingly return, exceedingly confounded and dejected for that ill-advised start. When it was first blazed abroad, it filled all good men with great grief, and to my own heart it brought one of the most sensible sorrows that in all my life I had felt. Yet his quick return of his own accord, and his readiness to give all satisfaction for that failure, and his kind receiving by the committee of states, among whom he ever sat after his return (though never before) turned our grief

the public councils of the kingdom, and refused to lay down arms till they got conditions agreeable to their mind; which course of theirs was justly declared by the commission to carry upon it the stamp of malignancy in an eminent way. 2. The seeking to promote and establish an arbitrary power in the person of the king, as it hath been still the endeavour of the malignant party, so it hath been always taken by the kirk of Scotland as one of their characters; and that there is a party now in Scotland who still hold that principle, and drive this design of arbitrary power, is evident. First, because these same men, who were lately in arms, did not only take up arms upon the king's simple warrant, and without the knowledge, and contrary to the mind of the committee of estates; but also received the act of indemnity,* and laid down arms, in obedience to the king's majesty, without so much as mentioning or acknowledging the committee of estates, as is to be seen in a paper subscribed by them,† and in the remonstrance of the commission of the General Assembly, dated at Perth, Nov. 29, 1650, the words whereof are these: "Your lordships should likewise consider, whether it doth not encroach upon the present constitution of government of this kingdom, and will not involve your lordships in the guilt of these men's sin, if you shall accept of their laying down of arms, merely upon the profession of obedience to the king's command, without any expression of their respect and obedience to the committee of estates, or any acknowledgment of their sin and offence, which we hope you will look upon as a most unnatural and unseasonable rending of the kingdom, in the time of this heavy oppression by a common enemy, and exposing the kingdom to all misery and ruin."‡ Second, It may be remembered that in the first model of the agreement which was made at Breda,§ that clause which doth concern the determining of civil matters in the interval of parliament, by such as are authorized by parliament for that effect, and the king's majesty hearkening to their advice, was wholly left out; and any who are acquainted with expressions and inclinations of sundry great ones in the land, are not ignorant of their dislike of a committee of estates, and their desire to have the administration of matters, in the interval of parliament, wholly devolved upon the king's council. And the same spirit that would draw

suddenly into joy, his absence not lasting above two full days. Yet all men were not so soon satisfied.

"Sundry of them who had been on the plot, fearing a discovery and punishment, flew to arms; Lewis Gordon, Ogilvie, Athol, and others, under Middleton's command, putting out a number of fair pretexts for their rising. This might have destroyed all; yet, by God's mercy, all was quickly quieted. D. Leslie, with all his horse, marched towards them; the king wrote earnestly to them to lay down. The committee of estates sent a fair act of indemnity, and so without more ado they went home."—Baillie's Letters, vol. ii. p. 356.

Middleton, like the Marquis of Montrose, had been at one time a covenanter. After the Restoration, he was appointed to open the Scottish parliament, as his Majesty's commissioner. But this did not prevent him from taking part in the debate, when the Act Rescissory, by which the presbyterian form of church polity was completely destroyed, was under consideration. Mr. David Dickson, along with some others, was delegated by the presbytery of Edinburgh to present to the Earl of Middleton a petition upon this subject. Middleton told Mr. Dickson "he was mistaken if he thought to terrify him with papers,—he was no coward." Mr. Dickson dryly replied, "They knew well he was no coward ever since the bridge of Dee." This was a skirmish which took place on the 19th of June, 1638, in which Middleton had displayed great zeal for the covenant, in opposition to Charles I. He took no notice of Mr. Dickson's sarcastic remark.—Kirkton's 'History of the Church of Scotland,' p. 118.—Ed.]

* [This was the "Acte of Pardon and Indemnitie, granted by the King and Comittee of Estaites to the Northerne Rebells, 26 October, 1650, and proclaimed at the mercat crosse of Perth, the 29th ditto, by Rosse Heraulde, A. L." See Balfour's Annales, vol. iv. p. 132.—Ed.]

† [He refers to "The Northerne Band and Othe of Engagement sent by Mideltone to L. Generall David Lesley, 26th of October, 1650." Middleton and the other subscribers of the Bond promise and swear that they "shall manteine the trew religione, as it is established in Scotland; the covenant, league and covenant, the Kings Majesties persone, prerogative, gratnes and authoritie; the previllidges of parliament and freedome of the subjects."—Id. p. 129.—Ed.]

‡ [See the Acts of the Parliaments of Scotland, ut supra.—Ed.]

§ [The reader will find a very interesting account of the negociations at Breda, in "A Brief Historical Relation of the Life of Mr. John Livingston, Minister at Ancrum in Scotland, and last at Rotterdam in Holland," who was one of the commissioners sent from Scotland to Breda (pp. 39—52. Glasgow, 1754). Dr. Cook, who quotes from the MS., does not seem to have been aware that the Life of Livingston was ever printed. See his 'History of the Church of Scotland,' vol. iii. p. 177, *note*.—Ed.]

business from the committee to a cabinet council, would at last draw them from the parliament itself; because that is also, if not more, crossing to private interests and designs than a committee of estates. Third instance. There is a party in the land who as in their hearts they do envy, and in their tongues do traduce men that have been steadfast and faithful in the covenant and cause of God; so do they endeavour to the utmost of their power, to bring them into disgrace and contempt, and to get them removed from power and trust, and, upon the other side, study with no less diligence to get places of power and trust, in the army and elsewhere, filled with such as either have been open enemies or secret underminers. Fourth instance. Are there not many who oppose the kingdom of Jesus Christ and work of reformation, not only by holding up that old calumny of malignants, concerning the seditious and factious humour of ministers, and their stretching of themselves beyond their line, and by mocking all faithful and free preaching of the word, and by bearing down the power of godliness, deriding and hating all the lovers and followers thereof, by being impatient of the discipline and censures of the church; but also looking upon the government of the church with an evil eye, and strongly inclining, some of them, that church government be put in the hands of a few prelates, most of them that it may be wholly devolved upon the civil government? Fifth instance. There is still a party in the land that endeavour to have the state of the question altered, and to have religion left out of the same; that it being stated upon civil interest, they may take to themselves a greater latitude in their way of carrying on business. This was holden forth to be the design of the malignant party in the year 1648, as appears in the Declaration of the Commission that year in March: and there was a necessary and seasonable warning given against it by the Commission in their Declaration, of the date July 1650.

III. Besides those who are excommunicated, there are yet in the land a considerable number of persons of chief note, who do still lie under censures of the church; some because of their accession to the late unlawful engagement; others because of their accession to the late course of rebellion, about the time of the king's escape from Perth; besides many others of less note.

IV. We suppose that it is most certain and unquestionable, that there was lately a malignant party and faction in the land, very numerous and powerful. How many men of blood, murderers of their brethren, as unnatural and barbarous as the Irish* they once joined with, against their country,—how many have watched all opportunities for troubling the peace of the kingdom, and rejoiced in the day of its calamity? How many were the oppressors of those who called on the Lord's name in the time of the Engagement?† What multitudes of profane and ungodly

* [" Immediately after the Scots army had marched into England to the parliament's assistance, did the King commissionate Montrose to raise a war in Scotland, by which he made account either to oblige the covenanters to recall their army out of England, or at least to make that nation smart for their boldness. And this, indeed, he did effectually; for landing in the West Highlands, with a party of bloody Irish papists, who had been but a little before fleshed in the cruel massacre of the innocent protestants, he overran the whole country, and beat the covenanters' forces in six bloody conflicts. His war, I believe, was the most cruel in the world." (Kirkton's History, p. 43.) " Montrose's History is written in good Latin (supposed to be by Bishop Wishart), but with as little truth as most in the world." Id. p. 122.—Ed.]

† [Sir James Turner and Colonel Urrey were sent to the west of Scotland, with their respective regiments, in 1648, to overawe, and reduce to obedience, those who were averse to Hamilton's Engagement. (Guthry's Memoirs, p. 272, second edition.) This service seems to have been perfectly congenial to the habits and taste of Sir James Turner, " who appears," says Sir Walter Scott, (' Tales of a Grandfather,' vol. ii. p. 211. Edin. 1829), " by the account he gives of himself in his Memoirs, to have been an unscrupulous plunderer, and other authorities describe him as a fierce and dissolute character." On coming to Glasgow, the way he took, as he himself tells us with considerable *gusto*, " to make the hardest headed Covenanter in the toune to forsake the kirk and side with the Parliament," was to quarter on suspected persons " two or three troopers and halfe a dozen musketeers." In the same heartless strain he proceeds to say:—" Finding my Glasgow men groune prettie tame, I tenderd them a short paper, which whoever signed, I promisd, sould be presentlie easd of all quartering. It was nothing bot a submission to all orders of Parliament, agreeable to the Covenant. This paper was afterward, by some merrie men, christend Turner's Covenant." (' Memoirs of his own Life and Times,' by Sir James Turner, pp. 53, 54, printed at Edinburgh, by the Bannatyne Club, in 1829.) As he was deprived of his rank by the Act of Classes in 1649, Sir James Turner was one of those " pretended penitents," of whom, according

mockers of all godliness, and haters and persecutors of the godly, swarming everywhere? If this be truth, as it is indeed, we may say, who hath heard such a thing? Who hath seen such a thing? Shall a nation be born at once? And have they so soon learned to do well, who have been so long accustomed to do evil? When did this catholic conversion fall out, and by what means? Hath the act of indemnity and pardon such influence, to justify these men from all their butcheries and barbarous cruelties? The adding of three thousand to the church in one day, was miraculous in the days of miracles. But behold, a greater miracle than that in the days when miracles are ceased, many thousands added to the church of the friends of the cause of God in one day, and that not by preaching, which is the power of God unto salvation; not by spiritual weapons, which are mighty through God; but by the carnal weapon of an act of indemnity, and the example of one man, the king's conjunction in the cause, which at the best hath not such evidence of reality as to convince any, and change their mind. Sad experience, and the constant testimony of the church of Scotland proves, that malignancy is a weed that hath deeper and stronger roots than to be plucked up so easily; and that, though there be some, yet there be but few in the land who have been once engaged in that way, that have really and indeed abandoned and come off the same.

The point shall more appear by taking off objections that are made to the contrary. It is objected, 1. That these who were formerly esteemed malignants, did oppose the work of God because they could not be persuaded in conscience, that the covenant and cause were contrived and carried on in a warrantable way, those who were most instrumental in it, seeming to them not only to act without authority, but against authority. But so it is, that the king hath now joined in the covenant and added his authority to it, and therefore it needs not be feared that these men will any more oppose it; nay it may be expected, they will no less zealously promove the ends thereof than they did formerly oppose the same.

Answer. This argument supposeth some things that are false, some things at best doubtful, and some things dangerous.

I. It supposeth two falsities. 1. That it was a ground and principle of conscience and respect to the king's authority that made these men to oppose the covenant and work of reformation. If it was the conscience and conviction of the unwarrantableness of it for the want of authority, that stirred them up to oppose the covenant and cause; then why did they subscribe it and join in the defence of the same against the king? 2. It supposeth that the only ground, why they did oppose and undermine the same, was, because the king was of a contrary mind, and refused to join in the covenant, and ratify the same by his authority, which also is false:

to Bishop Burnet, "all churches were full" after the passing of the Public Resolutions. ('Memoires of the Duke of Hamilton,' p. 425.) "Martii 12. 1651. The qlk day was given in ane lettre from the comission of the kirk, the tenour whereof follows,—Reverende and loving brethrene, having received a petition how general adjutant James Turner, acknowledgeing verie humblie his sin, in ye great accession he had to that unlawful engadgement against England, and particularlie his impious carriage in your citie by perturbing divine service, he seems to be verie sensible of his former miscarriage. We however still continue him under conference wt presbyteries hear. Bot if we shall find him in a condition to mak publik satisfaction, we desyre to know of you, if he can com and staye there wt safetie, and without danger from the enemie, that he may satisfie in ye kirk of Glasgow, which we thinke the most convenient place for removing the scandal, that if he can be secur, he may be appoynted to com to you, and if not, we may tak such other course as shall be thought most convenient. We have no more to say, bot commending you in all thingis to ye Lordis direction, we remain your loving brethrene the comissioners of ye generall assemblie. Perth, 13 Feb. 1651. Sic subscribitur, Mr. Robert Douglas, Moderator." (Records of the Presbytery of Glasgow.)

What Principal Baillie says of the oppressive conduct of Sir James Turner at Glasgow, during the time of the Engagement, is this:—"Some regiments of horse and foot were sent to our town, with orders to quarter on no other but the magistrates, council, session, and their lovers. These orders were executed with rigour. On the most religious people of our town, huge burdens did fall. On some 10, on some 20, on others 30 soldiers and more, did quarter, who, beside meat and drink, wine, and good cheer, and whatever they called for, did exact cruelly their daily pay, and much more. In ten days, they cost a few honest but mean people, 40,000 lb., besides plundering of those whom necessity forced to flee from their houses." Letters and Journals, vol. ii. p. 294.—Ed.]

for there were several other grounds and causes of so doing besides this. We shall name a few, leaving the rest to a further scrutiny. (1.) The natural enmity that is in the hearts of all men against the Lord and his anointed, his work and his people, and the power of godliness, which doth effectually work in the children of disobedience. (2.) An enmity against the power of parliament and laws. (3.) An enmity against the union of the kingdoms. (4.) An enmity against the power of presbyteries, and the discipline of the church, to which are opposed, a sinful desire of breaking the bonds, and casting away the cords of the Lord and his anointed; a desire to establish an arbitrary power and unlimited monarchy; a desire to establish a lordly prelatical power in the persons of a few, or to have the government of the church wholly dependent on the civil power; a desire to dissolve the union of the kingdoms, that they may be thereby weakened and less able to resist malignant designs against religion and liberties; a desire to live loosely without bands in regard of personal reformation.

II. It supposeth something that is at best doubtful; to wit, that the king hath really joined unto the cause of God, there being small evidences of it, and many presumptions to the contrary; especially, 1. His bringing home with him into the kingdom, a number of eminent, wicked, and known malignants; his countenancing of, and familiar conversing with such in this nation since his coming,* and correspondence with others of them abroad; his deserting of the public councils of the kingdom, to join to a party of bloody and wicked men, raised in arms with his knowledge and by his warrant. 2. His not being convinced of any guilt in his father, because of his opposition to the cause and covenant, notwithstanding of all the blood of the Lord's people shed by him in that opposition. For verifying whereof, we appeal to the knowledge of some noblemen and ministers, who have occasion to know his mind, and to be serious with him in this thing.

III. It supposeth something that is of very dangerous consequence. 1. That these men's zeal to the cause or against it, doth ebb and flow according to the king's being against it or for it. Since they follow the cause not for itself but for the king, will they not desert it when the king forsakes it? Can they be accounted real friends of the cause who are known to favour it only, *ad nutum principis*,†—as

* [" Stirling, 27 Sept. 1650. The comittee of Estaits, considering the necessarey deutie lying upone them in prosecutione of the acte of parliament, and according to the frequent and serious remonstrances of the commissione of the churche for purging of the kings familey of al profaine, scandalous, malignant, and disaffected persons; and that it be constituted of such as are pious, and weill affected to the cause and covenant, quho have not opposed the same by ther counsells and actions. And lykewayes considering the grate offence hes beine taken that the persons after nominated have not removed from courte nor depairted out of the kingdome respectively; and having taken also into consideratione the report of the sub-comittee, appoynted to think on the purging of the kings familey, doth heirby therfor ordaine and command, The French Marques of Villaneuffe, The Earle of Cleveland, Lord Wentworthe his son, Viscount Grandeson, Lord Volmett, Lord Withringtone, Robert Long, Secretarey, Sr Edward Walker, Garter, Mr. Progers, Groome of His Maties Bed chamber, Master Lane, Master Marche, Colonell Darcey, Mr. Antoney Jacksone, Major Jacksone, Colonell Loes, Master Oder Under Secretary, Lord St. Paule, Sr Philipe Musgrave, Sr Faithful Fortskew, Sr Timothey Featherstons, L.-Coll. Meutis, Collonell Carbraithe, to depairt the courte within 24 houres, and to remove out of the kingdome within 20 dayes after intimatione; and Doctor Fraser and Sr George Melveill to withdraw from the court within 24 houres." (Sir James Balfour's Annales of Scotland, vol. iv. pp. 109, 110.) Sir Edward Walker, whose name is included in the above list, says, " Money being ordered for my transportation, which I never got I was connived at for about three months, and therein had the opportunity to collect and write my observations of the Affairs as they then stood. Yet upon Friday the 4th of October, I was, by Sir James Balfour, lyon king of arms, commanded from court, which I presently obeyed, and about a month after imbarqued for Holland, where I resided several years after." (Historical Discourses. See " Contents" folio. Lond. 1705.) The circumstances in which this zealous royalist was placed, together with his national prejudices, may account for his extreme credulity, in believing that the clergy of Scotland, after the battle of Dunbar, offered up such impious prayers as he has ascribed to them. (Id. p. 182.) It was not to be expected that Mr. Hume would neglect the opportunity which was thus afforded him of covering with ridicule the Scottish covenanters. (See Hume's Account of the Battle of Dunbar.) Rapin vindicates the conduct of the Estates, in requiring the removal, from about the person of the king, of some of his friends and attendants, " men," he says, " whose principles and maxims were directly opposite to the interests of Scotland, and who were the kingdoms reputed enemies." Hist. of Eng. vol. ii. p. 581. Lond. 1833.—Ed.]

† [" At the nod of a prince."—Ed.]

the comedian, *ait, aio ; negat, nego ?** Is it not all one to follow the cause for the king, and for a man's own interest and advantage ? Both are alike extrinsic and adventitious to the cause, both are alike changeable. Eccebulus under Constantius was a precise Christian ; under Julian a persecuting apostate ; and then again under the next Christian emperor became a Christian. And it is like if he had outlived that emperor till a heathen succeeded, he should have paganized the second time. 2. That very principle that is pretended to unite them to the cause is in itself most dangerous, both to the privileges of parliament and liberties of the people, and to our religion beside. Their principle of opposition was, "They conceived the way followed could not be warrantable without the king's consent and warrant ; that people might not vindicate their own just rights and liberties, and their religion, without the king's concurrence, or against him." Now then, the principle of their conjunction to the cause must be this, because it is now clothed with authority which it had not before, and which now makes it warrantable. This principle therefore includes in the bosom of it, the establishing of unlimited and absolute power in kings ; the unlawfulness of defensive wars against tyranny and oppression ; the king's negative voice ; and the dependent power of parliaments upon his pleasure : all which are principles destructive of the cause and our liberties, and the very characters † of our enemies from the beginning. Thus they have changed their way, but not their principles, and are now the more dangerous that they may not be looked upon as enemies, but as friends. Seeing it is manifest, that it is not the love of the cause that constrains them, and they know it was not that principle that persuaded the king, but mere necessity, contrary to his own inclination, may we not certainly expect, that according to their principles they will labour to set at freedom the king, whom they conceive imprisoned and captivated by the power of necessity within the limits and bounds of a regulated monarchy, and to loose him from all these chains of involuntary treaties and agreements, and rigid laws and parliaments, that he may then act in freedom and honour according to his own inclination and theirs both ? And then farewell religion and liberties.

Objection 2: The most part of these who were formerly malignant, have now repented of that sin, and make profession of their resolution to adhere to the covenant and cause of God, and to bestow their lives and estates in defence thereof. Therefore they are not now to be esteemed malignants.

Answer. We would wish from our hearts that we had no answer to this argument; then should we yield the point in hand, and yield it cheerfully, that there is no malignant party now in Scotland. But, alas! that we have so much evidence convincing our consciences and persuading them to deny what is objected. We acknowledge some have indeed repented, and such we desire to embrace and receive with all tenderness and love, as godly Christians, worthy to be intrusted. But yet the most part of them do still bring forth the same malignant fruits. Their ungodly and wicked practices testify to their face that they have nothing to do to take his covenant in their mouth, seeing they hate to be reformed. The late rising in arms, contrary to their solemn and particular engagements, their bearing down and reproaching the godly, and such as are of known integrity, their studying to fill places of trust with men formerly enemies or underminers, their continuing in their profane and loose walking,—all these are more convincing evidences of their retaining their old principles than any extorted confessions or professions ; for sinister respects and ends can be no probable signs of their repentance and change.

We desire these things to be remembered, 1. That the Engagement ‡ was car-

* [That is, "He says, I say ; he denies, I deny." It is the parasite Gnatho that is referred to. Terence makes the shameless sycophant proclaim his own infamy :—

Quicquid dicunt, laudo ; id rursum si negant, laudo id quoque.
Negat quis? Nego. Ait? Aio.—Eunuchi Act. ii. Sc. ii.

"Whatever they say, I applaud : if again they deny that, I applaud that too. Does any one deny a thing? I deny it. Does he affirm it? I affirm it."—Ed.]

† [That is, the characteristics.—Ed.]

‡ [For an account of the origin, progress, and unsuccessful issue of Hamilton's Engagement, or the Unlawful Engagement, as it was also called, the reader may consult Stevenson's History of the Church and State of Scotland, book iv. chapter x. ; Cook's History of the Church of Scotland, vol. iii. p. 149.—Ed.]

ried on, not by open and professed enemies, but such as had made public profession of their repentance, and were thereupon admitted to trust. 2. That upon consideration of the hypocrisy and instability of these men appearing in that and other particulars, the kirk and kingdom of Scotland did take upon themselves strait bonds and engagements to exclude such from trust, until such time as they had given real evidences of the reality of their repentance, and of abandoning their former principles and ways, of which this kirk was to judge impartially as in God's sight. 3. That it hath been confessed and preached by many godly ministers, and was given in by sundry in the time of the search of the Lord's controversy against the land, in November last at Perth, and hath been bemoaned and regretted by many of the people who feared God; that there is a great deal of sin and guilt lying on the kirk of Scotland, for the sudden receiving of scandalous persons, especially malignants, to the public profession of repentance before there was in them any real evidence of their forsaking their former principles and ways.

Objection 3. None are now to be esteemed malignants, in reference to employment and trust, but such as stand judicially declared by kirk and state to be so: for certainly, men are not to lie under the burden of so great a reproach, upon the private whisperings and common reports of others; otherwise, honest men may be wronged, and there shall be no end of confusion, or terminating this controversy, there being no certain rule to walk by in it.

Answer. We acknowledge that surmisings, whisperings, and reports of others are not sufficient, but that a rule is needful. All the question will be, What is that rule? And though the judicial debarring of judicatories be not all, but it must be ruled by another rule, yet are we willing to take it for so much: for even that will prove there is yet a malignant party in Scotland, because many are standing under church censures, [albeit we are sorry there is so much precipitancy and haste in taking off the censures.*] These involved in the late rebellion are standing under a sentence of the commission, † declaring them to be following their old malignant designs; few of them are yet admitted to profession of repentance. We desire it may be considered, that the rule holden forth by the kirk of Scotland 1648, for admitting of persons to trust, is of larger extent than judicial sentence or censure; to wit, that they be such against whom there is no just cause of exception or jealousy. 2. Albeit a judicial trial or censure be indeed necessary, for inflicting punishment or censure upon men, yet it is not necessary for avoiding association with them, or debarring them from trust. 3. If none were to be accounted malignants, but they who are judicially declared to be such, what needed the kirk of Scotland have frequently taken so much pains, to give characters to know them by, there being so clear and compendious a way beside? Hath there not been always in the land secret underminers as well as open enemies? And hath not faithful men avoided the one as well as the other? 4. The General Assembly, 1648, declared the taking in of these who followed James Graham ‡ to be an association with malignants, though most part of them were then released from church censures.

* [Old MS.—Ed.]

† [" Pearth, Novemb. 29, 1650.—The Comis. of the Gen. Assemb. considering the great sin and offence these men are guilty of, who have had accessione to the late Rebellione in ye north; therefore they doe appoint that all these persons that were actually in arms at the late rebellione, and all such as subscribed the Bond and Declaratione emited by them, to be suspended from the communione till the nixt Gen. Assemb. to which they are hereby refered for further censure; and for all others that had any accessione, by counsel or otherwise, to that rebellione, or to the King's withdrawing from his Counsell, refers to Presbytries to try diligently in their severall bounds, these persons and the degree of their guiltines, and to report the same, with the evidences and proofs thereof, to the nixt meeting of this Commissione. A. Ker."—'The Waters of Sihor.' Wodrow MSS. vol. xvii. pp. 44, 45.—Ed.]

‡ [James, Marquis of Montrose. After his forfeiture by the Scottish parliament, he was usually styled in their Acts and proclamations *James Graham*, and sometimes *James Graham, late Earl of Montrose.* Bishop Guthry says (Memoirs, p. 175,) that it was considered a proof of malignancy to distinguish him and the Earl of Airly by their titles. In a letter to Principal Baillie, 19th March, 1649, Mr. Spang mentions that he was admitted to an audience by the Prince of Orange at the Hague. Something was said by the Prince, which led Mr. Spang to suspect he alluded to Montrose. "I hoped," says Mr. Spang, "his Highness did not mean of that man, whose apostacy, perjuries, and unheard of cruelty, had made him so odious, in all our country, that they could not hear of his name. He presently gave me to understand he meant not him or any such; for by the

SECTION II.

THAT THE PRESENT PUBLIC RESOLUTIONS, EXPRESSED IN THE COMMISSION'S ANSWER TO THE PARLIAMENT'S QUERY, * AND THE ACT OF THE LEVY, † DO NOT EXCLUDE THAT PARTY.

In the next place, upon supposal and proof, that there is a malignant party and faction still in the land, it is needful to examine, whether the exceptions contained in the answer of the Commission to the Parliament's Query, and inserted into the Act of Levy, be so comprehensive as to include all that party. The exceptions be four. 1. Such as are excommunicated. 2. Such as are forfaulted. 3. Such as are notoriously profane or flagitious. And, 4. Such as have been from the beginning, and continue still, or at this time are, obstinate enemies and opposers of the covenant and cause of God. That these are not comprehensive of the whole malignant party in the land, appears.

First, The rules of the General Assembly framed for the exclusion of all such as ought not to be employed in our armies, are far more comprehensive. The rule is for employing of such only as are of a Christian and blameless conversation, which is turned over by their commissioners into a negative, all that are not notoriously profane or flagitious. Another is, for intrusting only these who have been of known integrity and constant friends to the cause of God from the beginning, which is also turned over into a negative, all that have not been constant enemies.

comportment of our Scottish noblemen at court now, he perceives how odious *James Graham* must be at home; for they will not salute or speak to him; nay, not look where they think he is: and this I have observed with my own eyes." Baillie's Letters and Journals, vol. ii. p. 323.—Ed.]

* [On the 14th of December 1650, an answer was returned to parliament, "be the commissioners of the general assemblie to the quære, givin in to thame be the estattis of parliament, anent the persones to be admitted to ryse in armes, and joyne with the forces of the kingdome, and in what capacitie, for defence thereoff, aganes the armie of sectaries, &c." (Acts of the Parliaments of Scotland, vol. vi. p. 554.) The Answer of the Commission, after a declaration that it is the duty of parliament to use all necessary and lawful means for the defence of the land, and a description of the enfeebled state of the kingdom, contains the following exposition of their views: "In this case of so great and evident necessity, we cannot be against the raising of all fencible persons in the land, and permitting them to fight against this enemy for defence of the kingdom; excepting such as are excommunicate, forfaulted, notoriously profane or flagitious, and such as have been from the beginning, and continue still, or are at this time, obstinate and professed enemies, and opposers of the Covenant and cause of God: and for the capacity of acting, that the Estates of Parliament ought to have, as we hope they will have special care, that in this so general concurrence of all the people of the kingdom, none be put in such trust or power as may be prejudicial to the cause of God; and that such Officers as are of known integrity and affection to the cause, and particularly such as have suffered in our former armies, may be taken special notice of."—'A True Representation of the Rise, &c. of the Present Division in the Church of Scotland,' pp. 10, 11. London, 1657. 'The Answer of the Commission of the General Assemblie to the Quæree Propounded to them from the Parliament,' pp. 2, 3. Aberdeen, Printed by James Brown, 1651.—Ed.]

† ["*Act of Leavie.* At Perth, the twentie third day of December, one thousand six hundred and fiftie yeiris, the Kingis Majestie and Estaits of parliament, being verie sensibill of the dangerous and distressed conditione of this kingdome, and most desyreous, according to the law of God and nature, in discharge of there public trust, to use all lawful and necessarie means for the saiftie and defence of religione, his Majesties persone and royal authoritie, laws and liberties of the kingdome, aganis an armie of sectaries, who most unjustlie and perfidiouslie, contrarie to the solemne league and covenant and treaties, have invaded, and are by all actis of hostilitie destroying the same, Thairfore hes statute and ordained that all fensible men, within the sherrefdomes of Fyiff, and Kinross, Clakmanan, Stirling, Dumbartane, Argyll, Boott, Perth, Forfar, Kincardine, Aberdeine, Bamff, Murray, Nairne, Inverness, Ross, Sutherland, Cromartie, Caitnes, and Orknay, cum to an randevouze in the severall divisions of ilk schyre respective, to be set doun and appoyntit be the comitties of war in ilk schyre, according to the number of the regimentis efter specifit. The haill hertofore noblemen, gentlemen, and utheris to burt and landwart lyfrenteris, woodsetteris, and all other fensible men, betwixt thriescore and sixteine, with all there horses fitt for service, and their haill armes for horsemen and footmen (except such as are excommunicate, forfeited, notoriouslie profane or flagitious, and such as have beene from the beginning, and continew still, or are at this tyme, obstinat and professed enemies and opposeris of the covenant and caus of God). Out of the quhilk haill number of fensible persones, in ilk division, all such as are vigorous and able men for war are heirby appoynted to be drawin out, and put in Regimentis, as is efter specifit, with there best horses and arms, so many as are serviceable horses, and the rest on foot, with their best armes, twa part musquettis and third part pickis, and all with swords. The horsemen to be armed with pistollis, hulsteris or syidpistollis, and launces," &c. &c.—'Acts of the Parliaments of Scotland,' vol. vi. pp. 560—562.—Ed.]

All such, by the Answer, are capable of some trust and employment. The rules agreed upon by the assembly, and ratified by act of parliament, anno 1649, and renewed upon occasion of this invasion, were that no officer nor soldier that followed James Graham should be permitted in the army, nor any officer that was in the Engagement, except such as, upon real evidence of repentance, were particularly recommended by the church, nor any common soldier, but upon sufficient testimony of his repentance. Now, since it is proved that the most part of all such continue still malignants, and retain their old principles, and that the bulk and body of the people are called forth by the public resolution, without such exceptions as were conceived before necessary, for the exclusion of that party, it follows clearly, that the malignant party is not excepted in the present resolutions.

Second. Few of these who were in the late rebellion, and declared, not many days since, to be following a most malignant design and course, are contained under these exceptions; because very few of them are excommunicated or forfaulted: and though more of them be indeed flagitious and profane; yet very few of them will fall under the compass of the exception, notoriously flagitious. Many wicked things will be said to concur to make up a profane man. Some acts will not serve; a habit must be demonstrated: and though that were showed, yet there must be also a notoriety of it, which imports a man to be famous for looseness and profanity; and there are none almost, if any in the land, who have been professed enemies from the beginning, and continue so to this day. James Graham was not such. It is the matter of our sad complaint, that whilst many are enemies, they make profession and semblance of friendship.

Third. These exceptions do not comprehend any who are under censure for malignancy or profanity, except such as are under the sentence of excommunication; and that even such may not be excluded, lest the rule be transgressed, by admitting and employing excommunicated persons, 'tis withal resolved, that these persons shall be relaxed from that sentence, that so they may be immediately in the same capacity of employment with others, whatever formerly hath been their opposition or defection. Some exceptions must be made, for honesty and credit's sake. But the nearest and readiest way is taken to make them ineffectual.

Fourth. These exceptions do not only not reach these who were upon the unlawful engagement, and have not as yet given sufficient proof of their abandoning their malignant principles and courses; but come not the length of comprehending these men of blood who followed James Graham, and in the most barbarous and cruel way, shed the blood of their own brethren and God's people. Because the most part of these are not excommunicated nor forfaulted, nor notoriously flagitious and profane, nor such as have from the beginning been, and still are enemies. If any will say, that such are comprehended under these exceptions, why did the commission express the exceptions in such terms, as to men's common apprehension do not include many, especially seeing there are known rules, particular and distinct, without ambiguity, and seeing there is such a propension in rulers to employ all without difference, which would undoubtedly take advantage of any thing that seemed to look that way.

It is likewise manifest, that the second part of the answer, relating to the capacity of acting, is loaded with the same inconvenience. 1. There is no positive determination of the qualifications of persons to be intrusted, as in former times it was agreed on by the Assembly and their Commissioners, but that is now referred to the discretion of the parliament; together with such diminutive terms, as give them great latitude to go upon. Before, no trust was given to such persons. Now, it is allowed they shall have some trust: and how much is not determined, nor what degree of it is prejudicial to the cause; which it appears, the parliament's proceedings in nomination of officers unquestioned by the Commission, is a good commentary to expound that they may have any trust, except to be general officers. 2. Our former established rule was, that no persons should be intrusted, but such as are of known integrity, and have been constant friends of the cause. But how far is this diminished? They who are such, only recommended to be especially taken notice of. Less could not be said by any. More ought to have been said by the Commission. And though no such notice be taken of such by the parliament; but on the contrary, those who have been most faithful, and suffered in the late defeat at Hamilton,* are used as enemies, worse than malignants in former times; yet there is no testimony given against such things. *Quantum mutatus ab illo cœtu qui quondam fuit !*†

Before we enter upon the chief question, we offer these manifest and known truths to consideration.

(1.) The occasion of contriving and subscribing first the national covenant, and then the solemn league and covenant, was, the designs and practices of the popish, prelatical and malignant party, against religion and the work of reformation in these kingdoms. (2.) Since the contriving and subscribing of the same, it hath

* [This disastrous attack was made by the forces in the west, from whom had proceeded, what was called, the Western Remonstrance, which had been condemned both by the Committee of Estates, and the Commission of the church. ('Causes of the Lord's Wrath in Scotland,' p. 60, printed in the year 1650.) "Befoir this feight at Hammilton, Collonell Ker inquyred the judgement of his inferiour officeris the nicht befoir, quhat thai thocht of the caice of effaires, as they then stood; and schewed thame that he wold joyne with nane quho wes not for the Remonstrance, nor yit with those quho wold not declyne the Stait,—I meane the committee of Estait as it then stood." (Nicol's 'Diary of Transactions in Scotland,' p. 37.) The following letter from Cromwell describing the defeat at Hamilton, is interesting in itself as well as on account of the writer. "Sir, I have now sent you the results of some treaties amongst the enemy, which came to my hand this day. The Major-General, and Commissary-Generall Whaley marched a few days ago towards Glasgow, and the enemy attempted his quarters in Hamilton, and entred the town; but by the blessing of God, by a very gracious hand of Providence, without the losse of 6 men, as I hear of, he beat them out, kild about 100, took also about the same number, amongst which are some prisoners of quality, and near 100 horse (as I am informed), the Major-Gen. being in the chase of them, to whom also I have since sent the addition of a fresh party. Col. Kerre (as my messenger this night tells me) is taken, his Lieutenant-Col. and one that was sometimes Major to Collonel Straughan, and Kerres Captain-Lieutenant. The whole party is shattered; and give me leave to say it, if God had not brought them upon us, we might have marched 3000 horse to death, and not have lighted on them: and truly it was a strange Providence brought them upon him. For I marched from Edenburgh on the north side of Cloid, appointed the Major-General to march from Peebles to Hamilton, on the south side of Cloid. I came thither by the time expected, tarryed the remainder of the day, and untill neer 7 o'clock the next morning, apprehending the Major-Gen. would not come by reason of the waters. I being retreated, the enemy took encouragement, marched all that night, and came upon the Major-General's quarters about two houres before day, where it pleased the Lord to order as you have heard.

"The Major-Gen. and Commissary-Gen. (as he sent me word) were still gone on in the prosecution of them, and saith, that except 150 horse in one body, he heares they are fled by 16 or 18 in a company, all the country over. Robin Montgomery was come out of Sterling, with 4 or 5 regiments of horse and dragoons, but was put to a stand when he heard of the issue of this businesse. Straughan and some other officers had quitted some 3 weeks or a month before this businesse, so that Ker commanded this whole party in chief.

"It is given out that the malignants will be all (almost) received and rise unanimously and expeditiously. I can assure you, that those that serve you here, find more satisfaction in having to deale with men of this stamp, then others, and it is our comfort that the Lord hath hitherto made it the matter of our prayers, and of our endeavours (if it might have been the will of God), to have had a Christian understanding between those that feare God in this land, and ourselves; and yet we hope it hath not been carryed on with a willing failing of our duty to those that trust us; and I am persuaded the Lord hath looked favourably upon our sincerity herein, and will still doe so, and upon you also, whilst you make the interest of God's people yours. Those religious people of Scotland, that fall in this cause, we cannot but pitty and mourne for them, and we pray that all good men may do so too. Indeed there is at this time a very great distraction, and mighty workings of God upon the hearts of divers, both ministers and people, much of it tending to the justification of your cause. And although some are as bitter and as bad as ever, making it their businesse to shuffle hypocritically with their consciences and the covenant, to make it lawfull to joyne with malignants, which now they do (as well as they might long before) having taken in the head of them; yet truly others are startled at it; and some have been constrained by the work of God upon their consciences, to make sad and solemn accusations of themselves, and lamentations in the face of their supream authority, charging themselves as guilty of the blood shed in this warre, by having a hand in the treaty at Breda, and by bringing the king in amongst them. This lately did a Lord of the Session, and withdrew; and lately Mr. James Leviston, a man as highly esteemed as any for piety and learning, who was a Commissioner for the Kirk at the said treaty, charged himselfe with the guilt of the blood of this war, before their assembly, and withdrew from them, and is retired to his own house. It will be very necessary to encourage victuallers to come to us, that you take off customes and excise from all things brought hither for the use of the army. I beg your prayers, and rest your humble servant, O. Cromwell. Edinburgh, 4 Dec. 1650."—Sev. Proc. in Parl. Dec. 12 to 19, apud Cromwelliana, pp. 94, 95.—Ed.]

† [That is, "How much changed from that assembly which was formerly!" (Quantum mutatus ab illo Hectore, qui, &c. *Virg. Æneid,* lib. ii. ver. 274.)—Ed.]

been the continual endeavour of that party, sometimes by undermining, and sometimes by open opposition, to undo the same, and to bear down all those that clave honestly thereto, and faithfully prosecute all the ends thereof. (3.) That there hath been these many years past, and still is, such a party, in all the three kingdoms, considerable for number, power, and policy. (4.) That that party hath always prosecuted their design, under a colour of zeal and respect to the king's authority and interest. (5.) That that party hath always been the authors and abettors of much bloodshed, many miseries, and sad calamities to these nations. (6.) That the people of God in these kingdoms have taken upon themselves a most solemn and sacred bond of an oath and covenant to discover them, and bring them to condign punishment. (7.) That it hath been one of the predominant sins of Scotland under the bond of the covenant, to comply with them. (8.) That indignation and wrath from the Lord hath been following that party and their designs these years past. (9.) That compliances with them hath always been cursed to us of God. (10.) That few of that party do really abandon and forsake their corrupt principles and way, and join cordially in the cause and covenant. (11.) That many of them do, after the profession of their repentance for their opposition to the cause and covenant of God, relapse frequently into the same sin. (12.) That sudden receiving of many of them to fellowship and trust, and too great credulity in believing their professions, hath often cost this land very dear. (13.) That upon consideration of the deep treachery and hypocrisy of these men, and the sad consequences following upon sudden receiving of them, without evidence of a change, after long and renewed experience, this land renewed their obligations more strictly in the solemn engagement. (14.) That there hath been a design driven these two years past, to get that party again in power and trust. (15.) That this design hath been testified against by the public resolutions of the judicatories unto this time. (16.) That as it hath been driven at very cunningly and actively, by many instruments and arguments of several sorts, so hath it gained ground piece and piece, until at length many of them are brought into the court, and to the army and judicatories in the country. And now, by the public resolutions, they are generally to be employed and intrusted. Thus the design is accomplished. But, (17.) These men do not satisfy themselves with some degree of power, but endeavour to engross the whole power of the kingdom into their own hands, and study to bring into contempt, and cull out these who have been and do continue constant in the cause of God. (18.) That having power into their hands, they must act according to their own principles, and for establishing their own ends. And lastly, That these principles and ends are destructive to the covenant and work of reformation.

SECTION III.

THAT THE EMPLOYING OF, AND ASSOCIATING WITH THE MALIGNANT PARTY, ACCORDING AS IS CONTAINED IN THE PUBLIC RESOLUTIONS, IS SINFUL AND UNLAWFUL.

If there be in the land a malignant party of power and policy, and the exceptions contained in the Act of Levy do comprehend but few of that party, then there need be no more difficulty to prove, that the present public resolutions and proceedings do import an association and conjunction with a malignant party, than to gather a conclusion from clear premises. But that such a conjunction is in itself sinful and unlawful, and besides, a violation of our solemn oaths and engagements, a backsliding from our principles and professions, and a walking contrary to the whole tenor and current of our former resolutions and practices, is now to be made manifest.

First. We reason from that constant, standing and perpetual rule, which the Lord gives concerning the modelling and carriage of the armies of his people in all their wars: Deut. xxiii. 9, 'When the host goeth forth against their enemies, then keep thee from every wicked thing.' And after, 'If there be among you any man that is unclean, by reason of uncleanness that chanceth him by night, then shall he go abroad out of the camp; he shall not come within the camp.' (If for ceremonial uncleanness he was to be excluded, much more for moral, as our divines reason from the Old Testament in the point of excommunication; and if for uncleanness not voluntary, much more for voluntary wickedness.) The reason of all is given ver. 14. 'For the Lord thy God walketh in the midst of the camp, to deliver thee, and to give up thine enemies before thee. Therefore shall thy camp be holy, that he see no unclean thing in thee, and turn away from thee.' Even as they would expect a blessing of the Lord, so ought they to keep their camp holy, as he is holy. He gives not such a strict rule for the competency of number, as for the qualifications of the persons, as being the principal thing. Therefore the present conjunction with so many ungodly and wicked men, that have formerly declared themselves enemies to God and his people, and to this day give no evidence to the contrary, is sinful and unlawful.

Second. The Lord hath frequently in scripture declared his dislike and hatred of such associations and conjunctions. The scriptures cited in the General Assembly's declaration in the year 1648, against the Engagement, * are sufficient proof of this. We shall take the argument as it is formed by the commissioners of that assembly, in their answer to the observations of the committee of estates upon the assembly's declaration, p. 7. "Every engagement in war, that is pretended to be for religion, and hath in it a confederacy and association with wicked men, enemies of true religion, is sinful and unlawful. But the present engagement in war, as it is held forth in the public resolutions, is pretended to be for religion, and yet hath in it a confederacy and conjunction with wicked men, and enemies of true religion." Ergo, The second proposition is evident from the two first sections.

The first proposition is proved from those scriptures forementioned. God forbade conjunctions and confederacies with the enemies of his cause and people: not only the Canaanites, (Exod. xxxiv. 12, 15. Deut. vii. 2.) and other heathens, such was Asa his covenant with Benhadad, (2 Chron. xvi. to ver. 10.) Ahaz his confederacy with the king of Assyria, (2 Kings xvi. 7, 10. 2 Chron. xxviii. 16.) but also with wicked men of the seed of Abraham, as Jehoshaphat's with Ahab, (2 Chron. xviii. 3. 'And Ahab king of Israel said unto Jehoshaphat king of Judah, Wilt thou go with me to Ramoth-Gilead? And he answered him, I am as thou art, and my people as thy people, and we will be with thee in the war,' compared with chap. xix. 2. 'And Jehu the son of Hanani the seer, went out to meet him, and said to king Jehoshaphat, Shouldst thou help the ungodly, and love them that hate the Lord? therefore is wrath upon thee from before the Lord,') and with Ahaziah, (2 Chron. xx. 35. 'And after this did Jehoshaphat king of Judah join himself with Ahaziah king of Israel, who did very wickedly,') which being reproved for, he would not again join with Ahaziah, 1 Kings xxii. 49. 'Then said Ahaziah the son of Ahab unto Jehoshaphat, Let my servants go with thy servants in the ships: But Jehoshaphat would not.' And then Amaziah's association with 100,000 of Israel, 2 Chron. xxv. 7, 8, 9, 10. 'But there came a man of God to him, saying, O king, let not the army of Israel go with thee: for the Lord is not with Israel, to wit, with all the children of Ephraim. But if thou wilt go, do it, be strong for the battle: God shall make thee fall before the enemy: for God hath power to help and to cast down. And Amaziah said to the man of God, But what shall we do for the hundred talents which I have given to the army of Israel? And the man of God answered, The Lord is able to give thee much more than this. Then Amaziah separated them, to wit, the army that was to come to him out of Ephraim, to go home again: wherefore their anger was greatly kindled against Judah, and they returned home in great anger.' The sin and danger of such associations may further appear from Isa. viii. 12, 13. 'Say ye not, A confederacy, to all them to whom this people shall say, A confederacy; neither fear ye their fear, nor be afraid. Sanctify the Lord of hosts himself, and let him be your fear, and let him be your dread;' Jer. ii. 18. 'And now,—what hast thou to do in the way of Assyria, to drink the waters of the river?' Psal. cvi. 35. 'But were mingled

* ["Ult. July, 1648. Post Meridian. Sep. xxi. *A Declaration of the General Assembly concerning the present dangers of Religion, and especially the unlawful engagement in War, against the kingdom of England.* Together with many necessary exhortations and directions to all the Members of the Kirk of Scotland." Records of the Kirk of Scotland, pp. 498—505. Edited by A. Peterkin.—Ed.]

among the heathen, and learned their works;' Hosea v. 13. 'When Ephraim saw his sickness, and Judah saw his wound, then went Ephraim to the Assyrian, and sent to king Jareb: yet could he not heal you, nor cure you of your wound;' and chap. vii. 8, 11. 'Ephraim, he hath mixed himself among the people: Ephraim is a cake not turned. Ephraim also is like a silly dove without heart: they call to Egypt; they go to Assyria,' 2 Cor. vi. 14, 15. 'Be ye not unequally yoked together with unbelievers; for what fellowship hath righteousness with unrighteousness? and what communion hath light with darkness? And what concord hath Christ with Belial? or what part hath he that believeth with an infidel?' And if we should esteem God's enemies our enemies, and hate them with perfect hatred, how can we then join with them as friends? Psal. cxxxix. 21.

The committee of estates at that time endeavoured to elude the strength of these scriptures, and vindicate their engagement from the falling within the compass of them. But the commission of the Assembly that year took the mask off their evasions. Would to God we had no other party to deal with now! It was the evil and complaint of that time, that church and state were divided. But what an evil time are we now fallen into, that the union of those in this point, is the complaint of many of the godly? The commission, in their letter to Stirling presbytery,* sets up the committee's answer in a new dress, and holds it out for satisfaction to our consciences. All that is answered may be reduced to three or four heads.

I. There is made a great difference between an invasive and defensive war as if in the one, choice of instruments ought to be sought; but in the case of just and necessary defence, all subjects may be employed.†

To which we answer, 1. That the scriptures cited conclude most expressly against conjunctions of that kind in defensive wars. Such was Asa's covenant, such was Ahaz his confederacy. Were not the reproofs of the prophets directed particularly against the people's seeking of help from Egypt and Assyria, in the case of heir own just and necessary defence? Jer. ii. 18; Hosea v. 13; and vii. 8, 11; Isa. viii. 12, 13; 2 Chron. xvi. to ver. 10. 2. The law and rule given, Deut. xxiii. is general, regulating all their wars whether defensive or offensive; and it is strange that any should imagine such a difference where the law makes none; nay, when the ground of the law is moral and general, equally respecting all wars. Is there any ground of conscience, why wicked persons may not be kept in the camp when we invade others, and yet these may be employed and intrusted when we defend ourselves? If there be any reason to prefer the one to the other in this point, we conceive defensive war should have the preference, because when the Lord brings upon us an unjust invasion, he is ordinarily pursuing a controversy against us. And therefore we ought to be most tender and circumspect, that there be no un-

* [At a meeting of the Committee of Estates, on the 6th of January, 1651,—"Rege Presente. The letter from the Presbytery of Stirling to the Commission of the Generall Assembly, still disclaiming the kings intereste, and the unity of all the subjects of the land to assist their countrey against the comon enimey, redd; with the Commission of the Generall Assemblies ansuer therto, redd lykwayes, approvin and ordained to be published and printed." (Balfour's Annales, vol. iv. p. 235.) The Commission of the Assembly complained, that the letter of the Ministers of the Presbytery of Stirling, which was printed at Edinburgh, 1651, had prefixed to it "the false and odious title of *A Remonstrance of the Presbytery of Stirling against the present conjunction with the malignant partie.*" ('Answer of the Commission,' &c. dated Perth, 6 Jan. 1651. p. 19. Printed at Aberdeen, 1651.) What Binning now advances is in vindication of the Letter of the Presbytery of Stirling, and in reply to the Answer of the Commission. Mr. James Guthrie, and Mr. David Bennet, Ministers at Stirling, were charged by the committee of Estates with framing this Letter, and summoned to appear before them, at Perth, on the 19th of February, 1651, to answer for their conduct.—'Acts of Parl,' vol. vi. p. 578.—Ed.]

† ["And first, we shall desyre every one seriously to consider the case and condition wherein the kingdome is engaged, and standeth at this tyme; that now we are not upon an engagement of invasive warre, but upon necessary defence against a forraign enemy, who hath not only injustly invaded us, but also (through the holy permissive providence of God) slaine many of our brethren with the sword, subdued a great part of the land, is oppressing the people of God therein, and following his injust designes and intentions against the rest of the kingdome; that in this case, in the ordinary way of providence, according to which men must act, unlesse they would be guilty of tempting God, there is need of, and ought to be employed against the enemy, such a competency of power as is requisit in right and warrantable prudencie, and may be had, not being of itself sinful. This certainly is mans duety, whatever God, out of his soveraignity, hath done, or may doe, in the case of want, or disproportion of meanes."—'Answer of the Commission,' ut supra, p. 6.—Ed.]

clean thing in the camp, and put away every wicked thing from us, even the appearance of evil, lest we add oil to the flame of his indignation, and he seeing such an unclean thing in us, turn yet further from us, except we say, that we need not take care to have God in the camp with us, when we are upon just and necessary defence, seeing our cause is so good. 3. There is more hazard and danger to our religion and liberties in having a wicked malignant army at home among us, than abroad in another nation. While they are here, they have the power of the sword, and can command all; but there might be some hope and endeavour for vindicating our own liberties and religion while they are abroad, as it fell out in the time of the Engagement.

II. It is answered, that there is a difference between this case and the Engagement, because there was then no necessity of choosing such instruments, a competency of power might be had; but now it is not so, and therefore the scriptures mentioned do not militate against the present case. *Answer* 1. The scriptures cited will obviate this. What made Israel and Judah run to Egypt and Assyria for help, but their weakness and necessity? Their wound was incurable, and their bruise grievous, as Jeremiah often laments, and particularly chap. viii. 20—22; and x. 19, &c.; and yet this did not excuse them for going to Egypt or Assyria to heal their wound, Hosea v. 13, and vii. 8, 11. The scripture holds out infidelity and distrust in God as the ground of such association, (2 Chron. xvi. 7—9; Isa. viii. 12, 13,) which proceeds from the incompetency of means as the occasion of it. 2. Suppose there was a necessity for the calling forth the body of the common people, yet certainly there is no necessity of employing any such persons of whom the question is, and putting them in places of trust. There is none can deny but there are, besides all secluded persons, many that might fill the places of trust and power. Therefore the plea of necessity is but a pretence to cover some design, that under its specious and plausible covering, the power of the land may be engrossed into the hands of malignants; and so by this means all power and trust may return, as the rivers to the sea or fountain, as they judge the king; that so in his person there may be established an unlimited and arbitrary power. 3. Necessity is a very plausible argument and strong plea to carnal reason for any thing; but it cannot be a good ground, in point of conscience, for that which is sinful in itself. Now that this is sinful in itself appears, from the word of God simply condemning such associations, upon moral, and so general and perpetual grounds. Now, in such a case of necessity, we are called either to trust in God, in the use of competent means, seeing in such cases we have so many promises; or, if all help be gone which God allows us to make use of, we must wait on him till he brings salvation with his own arm.

But because the plea of necessity is the strongest that is made use of for the present public resolutions, we must consider it a little more. It is alleged, that the best part of the land is under the feet of the enemy, and so no help can be had from it; and for other parts of the land which are yet free, there is not much choice of persons; and the testimony of faithful men in the state declares, that when all that are called forth of these places are gathered, it cannot amount to a power competent enough; and therefore in such a question of the existence of second means, the knowledge whereof immediately depends on sense and experience, these who are not acquainted should give credit to the testimony of faithful witnesses; and that a competency of power must be had, according to the ordinary way of Providence, in relation to which we must act, except we would tempt God by requiring of him wonders.*

* ["In such parts of the kingdome, as are yet free from the oppression of the enemy, and so out of which any men can be raised, there is not a possibility to get such a competencie of power, unlesse there be a more generall calling foorth of the body of the people than hath been before: this as it is most certain in itselfe, so it is most apparent, and evident unto all, that doe understand these parts of the kingdome. And whereas faithfull and honest men in the State, well acquainted with the severall shyres of that part of the kingdome, have publickly declared, that when all shall be brought together, that can be called foorth of these parts, according to publick resolution, there will scarce be a competent power against the power of the enemy, we cannot but much wonder, if any, not so acquainted therewith, shall hold the contrary, and not give credit to the declaration of honest and faithfull men, especially in authority; the matter being such, as in the immediate know-

Answer. Suppose the enemy's army to consist of 20,000 or above, are there not more fencible persons in the shires on the north side of Forth? Believe it who please, we cannot stop our own consciences, and put out our own eyes. Let the rolls of several shires be looked to, and it shall confute that testimony. Nay, are there not more persons, not formerly secluded, in all those shires? What meant the levy appointed immediately after Dunbar? Was not 10,000 foot, and 1,400 horse put upon these shires which are not under the power of the enemy, and yet the rules of exclusion were not abandoned? Now all these, or most part of them, are yet in the country not levied. Money was taken instead of men; the levies obstructed, so that there was little addition to the strength of the forces that remained; the forces diverted by the insurrection of the malignants in the north,* at the king's command or warrant,—all which hath such pregnant presumption of a design carried on to necessitate the kingdom to employ that party, by the cunning politicians of the time, by obstructing the levies; raising the malignants, and then pacifying them by an act of indemnity, and at last openly and avowedly associating with them. Thus the design is accomplished which was long since on foot.

2. If satisfying courses had been studied by the public judicatories to carry on all the godly in the land with their resolutions, there had accrued strength from the parts of the land be-south Forth, which would have compensated all that competency of power that the conjunction of the malignants makes up: and, it may be, would have been more blessed of God. 3. If there be no help required nor expected from those parts of the kingdom be-south Forth, wherefore did the commission write to the presbyteries in those bounds that they might concur actively in their stations for the furtherance of the levies, and choose ministers to go out with them?

III. It is answered, That the confederacies reproved were unlawful, because they were either with heathens, or with idolaters, strangers, and foreigners. This is answered to the case of Amaziah, &c., and so it seems not to make against the present case, the employing all subjects in the just and necessary defence of the kingdom.†

Answer 1. This answer at one blow cuts off all the strength of the General Assembly's reason against the association with malignants in that year. There might be some few persons idolaters, but there was no party and faction such, and yet they can deny association with the English malignants from those scriptures; yea, not only with them, but with our own countrymen that were in rebellion with James Graham, who were neither idolaters nor foreigners. We need no

ledge thereof dependeth on sense, and, as to those that have not that knowledge, pertaineth to humane faith, which giveth credit to the testimony *testium idoneorum*, of competent witnesses, such as these are whom we have designed."—Id. pp. 6, 7.—Ed.]

* [" 1650, Oct. This moneth the malignant pairtie of this kingd. did ryse in armes in the north: they emited a declaratione. The Comission of the Gener. Ass. emitted a warning, deated att Stirling, 24 Oct. 1650, against them, to be read in the severall churches. L. G. Da. Lesley was sent north with some horsemen against them."—Lamont's Diary, p. 23. Printed at Edinburgh, 1830.—Ed.]

† [" We need say no more, unlesse there were some show of proofe to the contrary. Yet we shall say somewhat particularly to one place, that which is said in the case of Amaziah's associating with, and taking to him the Israelits for help in his just defence, (2 Chron. xxv. 7. 'O king, let not the army of Israel goe with thee, for the Lord is not with Israel, even with all the house of Ephraim,') as being mainly urged, and as it seems most to stick with some in the present businesse, to which sundry things may be answered, which clear the present businesse from the force thereof. 1. The Israelits were idolaters, and forrainers; not so in our case, in either respect. But it is alledged, that the reason why Amaziah is disswaded from taking their assistance is, because God was not with them, and therefore, the same reason having place in manie of these, whom the present resolution comprehendeth, the disswasion hath the same force against them. Therefore 2. God's not being with them may be either conceived and understood, in regard of the estate of grace and reconciliation with God, but how-so-ever that with many of them God was not in this regard, yet the reason cannot be alledged in this sense, because then it would follow by the argument, that we might not take the help of any man out of the estate of grace, for our just and necessary defence, which none will admit; or it may be understood of God's assistance, and prospering providence simply. But neither can it be taken thus, because it is certain and clear, that God was often with them in this sense, in their own cause and quarrells. Therefore it must needs be conceived, in regard of their profession, and religion, which was corrupt and idolatrous. Now the reason thus understood hath not place in our businesse. 3. Yet doe we not find that Amaziah is commanded to exclude any of the subjects of his own kingdom, from acting in that defence, or reproved for not doing of it, notwithstanding many of them no doubt were naughty and corrupt in their way, 2 Kings xiv. 4."—'Answer of the Commission,' p. 12.—Ed.]

other answer than the Commission at that time gave to the committee of estates using that same evasion, *pag.* 10, 11. 2. The ground and reason whereupon such associations are condemned, is more general and comprehensive. Jehoshaphat was reproved for joining with Ahab, because he was 'ungodly, and hated the Lord,' which is properly, in our terms, because he was a malignant and profane man. It was a strange mocking of scripture to restrict ungodliness, in that place, to the sin of idolatry. Confederacy with the Canaanites and other nations was forbidden on this ground, 'that the people be not insnared, and learn not their works.' Now, is not the company of, and communion with ungodly men, of the same general profession, but mockers and haters of the power thereof, as infectious and insnaring? Nay, it is more apt to insnare because of the profession. Paul would have as much distance kept with a brother walking unorderly as a pagan. For such a one as walks contrary to his profession of the true religion, does evidence more ungodliness and wickedness, than an ignorant and superstitious papist that walks precisely according to his profession. There is some principle of conscience stirring in the one; but it is seared in the other with a hot iron. God ranks such, who are uncircumcised in heart, with the uncircumcised in flesh. Ought not his people to do so too? 3. The rule of modelling armies and purging the camp is most comprehensive, Deut. xxiii. Not only idolaters and foreigners, but every wicked thing, and unclean thing, was to be removed out of the camp. Now, seeing those examples are transgressions of this law, what reason is there to make the only ground of reproving and condemning of them to be, because idolaters were associated with, as if any other might be joined with, that is not an idolater? 4. That reason against Amaziah's conjunction with Israel is wrested, by some expounding it thus. God is not with them, is not understood, in regard of a state of grace, as appears, nor in regard of God's prospering providence; because he was often with them in that regard: but it must be understood in regard of an idolatrous profession. But we reply, that it is true it is not understood in regard of a state of grace, nor simply in regard of his prospering providence; but *ut plurimum*,* the Lord for the most part crossing them till they were cut off from being a nation. But especially it is to be meant in regard of a course opposite to God, according as the Lord speaks, 2 Chron. xv. 2. 'The Lord is with you while ye be with him, but if ye forsake him he will forsake you.' If any will restrict this to idolatry, he hath no ground from scripture for such a limitation; but being engaged in the business, he wrests the scriptures to his own destruction. Sure we are, there are many palpable forsakings of God, and God's forsaking of men, beside idolatry and false worship. 5. That which is said, 'That God did not command Amaziah to dismiss any of his own subjects.' Either it makes not much to the present business, or else it strikes against the law of God itself, that commanded such strict purging of the camp. From whom I pray you? Certainly from wicked Israelites, from wicked countrymen. Therefore, if there was any such among the men of Judah, he ought to have put them out of the army as well as the Israelites. Nay, the command of dismissing the Israelites, was, really and upon the matter, a command to purge his camp of all that was of the stamp of the Israelites. It is strange that the civil difference of strangers and citizens should make such difference in the point of conscience. Ought we not to hate the Lord's enemies with a perfect hatred, not as Englishmen, not as strangers, but as enemies? Levi knew not his brother. This was his honour. But many now for respect to their brethren, know not God. It is the moral quality that the law of God respects, without respect of persons and countries. To be a citizen, if not qualified, doth no more plead for employment, *in foro conscientiæ** and before God, than to be a stranger and qualified doth impede trust and employment *in foro conscientiæ* and before God.

IV. It may be answered (and it is by some), That those scriptures plead, that there should be no conjunction with wicked men in a quarrel of religion; but seeing our present business is the defence of the kingdom, all subjects, as subjects, stand

* [That is, "chiefly." The strict signification of *ut plurimum* is, *as much as possible*.—Ed.]
† ["At the bar of conscience."—Ed.]

in capacity of employment for that end, though in reference to the defence of religion there must be a choice.

Answer 1. The Commission have vindicated themselves in a letter to Stirling presbytery from that imputation, that it is said, they state the quarrel and cause merely upon civil things in the answer to the parliament's query.* But certainly there is just ground given to these that are watching for any such thing, to state the cause so; because they do, contrary to all former custom and practice, mention the defence of the kingdom only, as it had been of purpose to make the employing of all members of the body or subjects of the kingdom for its defence more plausible. But we answer to the point. The associations and conjunctions that are condemned in the cited scriptures, are some of them for civil quarrels so far as we know; some of them in the point of just and necessary defence of the kingdom, and yet that doth not justify them. 2. The rule given them, Deut. xxiii., was regulating all their wars, and clearly holds forth, that all subjects, as subjects, and members of the politic body, though as such there is an obligation lying on them to defend the whole, yet are not in actual and nearest capacity to the performance of that duty, if they be wicked and unclean. And the reason is, because the Lord would have the wars of his people his own wars, and all that they do, to his glory, Num. xxi. 14; 2 Chron. xx. 15; Col. iii. 17. More especially in such solemn undertakings, there ought to be a difference between his people, acting for self-defence, and other nations. 3. Although the defence of the kingdom and defence of the cause, be different in themselves, yet are they inseparable. Whoever is intrusted with the defence of the kingdom really and *de facto*,† he is *eo ipso* ‡ intrusted with the defence of the cause. Therefore the people of God, who ought always to have religion first in their eye, ought, especially in raising forces for self-preservation, to level at religion, and direct the choice of instruments in relation to that mark, that they destroy not Christians, while they save subjects, and preserve our bodies to destroy our souls.

Third Reason. That which is dissonant from and contrary unto all our former resolutions and proceedings, oaths and engagements, confessions and humiliations, must needs be most unlawful, or they themselves, as to that point, were unlawful. But the present resolutions and proceedings are dissonant from, and contrary to all these. Ergo, either our present or our former resolutions and practices were unlawful: either we were wrong before, or we are not right now. The second proposition may be made manifest from, 1. The present resolutions are contrary to the solemn league and covenant in the fourth article and the sixth,—to the fourth, because we put power in the hands of a malignant party, power of the sword, which is inconsistent in the own nature of it with either actual punishing of them, or endeavouring to bring them to punishment; unless it be intended to bring them all forth, and expose them to the slaughter for a sacrifice for the land, which may be the Lord's mind indeed, howbeit they know not his thoughts,—and to the sixth article, because it is a declining to the contrary party, even that party against whom the covenant was at the making expressly contrived. And as the declaration of the General Assembly 1648, hath it, it is a joining with one enemy to beat another, with a black devil to beat a white.§

* [" Doeth our mentioning onlie the kingdome, in that resolution, import a separation of the kingdome, and the cause, in the quarrell agaynst our enemie? Or what logick can draw out such a consequence out of it? Wee do think that the kingdome being in danger by this enemie, the cause also is in danger, and the defending of the kingdome will be the defending of the cause also. And we trust no instruments shall bee employed for the defence of the kingdom to the prejudice of the cause."—' Answer of the Commission,' ut supra, p. 19.—Ed.]

† [" In point of fact."—Ed.]

‡ [" On that very account."—Ed.]

§ [Bishop Hall quaintly remarks, that " No devil is so dangerous as the religious devil." "Suppose the ends of this Engagement to be good, (which they are not,) yet the meanes and ways of prosecution are unlawful, because there is not an equall avoiding of rocks on both hands, but a joyning with malignants to suppresse sectaries, a joyning hands with a black devill to beat a white devill. They are bad physicians who would so cure one disease as to breed another as evil or worse." (' A Declaration of the Gen. Assembly concerning the present dangers of Religion.' Rec. of the Kirk of Scotland, p. 501.) In the year 1649, the Scottish parliament passed an " Act against Consulters with Devils and Familiar Spirits," &c. (' Acts of the Parl. of Scot.' vol. vi. p. 359.) It was supposed that the power of some of these was employed in particular instances for the ben

It is most ingeniously answered, that the present resolutions are not contrary to the covenant, because such as are described in the covenant are not allowed to be employed, meaning that these men are not now malignants. What needs men make such a compass to justify the public resolutions, seeing there is so easy and ready a way straight at hand? This one answer might take off all the arguments made against them, that there is no malignant party now, which is the foundation that being removed all the building must fall to the ground. But we have in the first article evinced that, which had been scandalous to have proved, if it had not been questioned. If it were indeed true, that no malignants are allowed to be employed, what need the Commission in their letter to Stirling presbytery take so much pains from scripture and reason to justify the present resolutions, when the clearing of that one point had cleared all? As for the declaration of the Assembly, anno 1648, it is answered, *that none are to be employed, that continue notourly* in the courses of malignancy*, which was done that year. Whereas the malignant party that was then associated with, would have engaged to be faithful to all the ends of the covenant; many of them were such as had been in covenant, and made show of their repentance for their defection from it: and so there is no difference in this particular.

2. The Solemn Acknowledgment of public sins is so clear and peremptory in this that it makes us tremble to think on it. *Page* 6, "Should we again break his commandments and covenant, by joining any more in affinity with the people of these abominations, and take in our bosom these serpents, which have formerly stung us almost to death? This, as it would argue much folly and madness, so, no doubt, it would provoke the Lord to consume us till there be no remnant, nor escaping." Let the 6th article also be considered.† Join to this the Declaration of the commission, upon report of this enemy's invading, *p.* 6. where it is declared, that malignants shall not be associated with, nay, not countenanced and permitted to be in our armies. The General Assembly after this, upon the enemy's entry into Scotland, gives serious warning to the rulers, to take heed of snares from that party: and that the rather, because men ordinarily are so taken with the sense of danger, as not to look back to that which is behind them, &c. How often have we sentenced ourselves unto wrath and consumption if we shall fall into this sin again? All these and the like, are endeavoured to be taken off, by saying that our engagements in this point were conceived in a way of prosecution of the cause; but to be no impediment of the just and necessary defence, which we are bound to by nature's law, which no human law can infringe.

But we reply, (1.) It is strange, our prosecution of the cause these years past should be contradistinguished from the defence of it and the kingdom. It was conceived that our war in England was defensive, not invasive, that it was necessitated for the defence even of our kingdom, but it seems it is now questioned. But passing what was acted abroad, certainly all our wars at home were merely defensive, both against unjust invasion and seditious insurrections. Now our so-

efit of mankind. They were therefore distinguished from the others, in the same way that white witches, or persons who used charms and incantations for curing diseases, &c. were distinguished, but not in the eye of the law, from black witches, or those who practised their art for the purposes of mischief. (Whitelock's 'Memorials,' p. 550. See also Sir Walter Scott's 'Tales of a Grandfather,' vol. ii. p. 117.) If we look to the strange confessions of many of the unfortunate creatures who were condemned to suffer death for witchcraft in those days, without adverting to the cruel means that were often resorted to with a view to extort from them such confessions, the credulity of the age will not appear to have been so extraordinary as it has been represented. It is impossible not to admire the singular discretion of Dr. Grey, Rector of Houghton-Conquest, when speaking on this subject. "Nothing," says he, "more plainly discovers the iniquity of those times, than the great numbers of people executed in England and Scotland for witches, *if they were guilty;* or the barbarous superstition of the times, *if they were innocent,* which is the more probable."—'Impartial Examination of the Fourth Volume of Mr. Daniel Neal's History of the Puritans,' p. 96. Lond. 1739.—Ed.]

* [That is, openly persisting. See 'The Answer of the Commission to the Presbytery of Stirling,' p. 11.—Ed.]

† [See 'The Nullity of the Pretended Assembly at Saint Andrews and Dundee,' &c. p. 312. Printed in the year 1652. As many had been under age when the Solemn League and Covenant was first sworn, the Commission of the General Assembly ordained it to be renewed by their Act October 6, 1648, joining to it the "Solemn Acknowledgment of Public sins and Breaches of the Covenant, and a Solemn Engagement to all the Duties contained therein."—Ed.]

lemn engagements were conceived, in relation to our actings at home especially, and modelling our armies for the defence of our liberties and religion. We know well enough that a just invasive war is a rare accident in the world, and that the flock of Jesus Christ is, for the most part, obnoxious to the violence of others, as sheep among wolves, but are not often called to prey upon others. (2.) To call our solemn engagements and declarations grounded upon our oaths and the word of God, human laws and constitutions that must cede to nature's law, is indeed ingenious dealing: because to justify the present proceedings, there can be no more expedite way, than to condemn bypast resolutions for the peremptoriness of them, and to make them grounded on politic considerations, which are alterable: but it imports a great change of principles. We conceive that all human laws that are not for the matter grounded on the word of God, that oblige not conscience, but in the case of scandal, and in regard of the general end, are alterable and changeable, whenever they come in opposition to the law of nature, self-defence, and the law of God written in his word. And therefore that act of parliament, mentioned by the Commission, discharging all subjects from rising without the king's command, which was made use of against our first taking arms, was no ways binding on the subjects not to rise in defence of their religion and liberties when in hazard.* And we wonder that that law should be compared to our solemn engagements, which are grounded upon oaths and God's word, as touching the very matter and substance of them, as if our engagements did no more bind us now, in case of defence, than that law did bind us then. Royalists might be excused for preferring the king's will to God's; but we cannot be pardoned for equalizing them: and especially while we consider that that fore-mentioned act undoubtedly hath been intended for the establishing of an arbitrary and absolute power in the king's hand, that the subjects may not have liberty to save themselves, except the king will. Where God hath given us liberty by the law of nature, or his word, no king can justly tie us; and when God binds and obliges us by any of these, no king or parliament can loose or untie us. (3.) The Declaration of the Commission and Assembly upon this invasion, renews the same bond of our former engagements; yea, and speaks expressly, in the case of fewness and scarceness of instruments, against the unbelief of people that are ready in danger to choose any help.† Therefore that which is said in answer, that at that time there was a choice of instruments which now is not, may indeed condemn and falsify the declarations at that time, in the supposition of the paucity of instruments, and in the application of that doctrine and divine truth to that time, but it doth not speak any thing against the application of that truth therein contained to our time; it being more manifest, that we have greater necessity and less choice of instruments, and so in greater hazard of unbelief, and overlooking what is behind us.

3. It is of all considerations the most confounding, to reflect upon our former humiliations and fasts. How often hath it been confessed to God, as the predominant public sin of Scotland, countenancing and employing the malignant party? But when we call particularly to mind the first solemn fast after the defeat at Dunbar, astonishment takes hold on us, to think, that is now defended as a duty, which, but some months ago, was solemnly confessed as a sin. The not purging of the army, the obstructing of that work, and great inclinations to keep in and fetch in such persons, and the repining at, and crying out against all that was done in the contrary, were then reckoned as the great causes of God's wrath, and his sad stroke upon us. What distraction may this breed in the hearts of the people of the land to hear that same thing complained of as a great sin to-day, and commended as a

* [" We desire it may be remembered that in the beginning of these troubles, anno 1638, when as there were then standing laws in this kingdom, which are not yet repealed to this day, discharging all subjects from rysing in armes, without the kings expresse warrant and command; yet the subjects of this kingdome, perceiving themselves in danger to be destroyed by forraign invasion, did fynd these lawes no wayes to bynd up their hands, from taking armes, for their just defence and selfe preservation,—these lawes, in the intention of the lawgiver, being made for the preservation of the kingdom, and not for the destruction of it."—'Answer of the Commission,' pp. 13, 14.—Ed.]

† [See 'The Waters of Sihor, or the Lands Defectione.' Wodrow MSS. vol. xvii. pp. 39—41, in Bib. Ad. Peterkin's 'Rec. of the Kirk of Scotland,' pp. 619, 620.—Ed.

necessary duty to-morrow? Is not all the land presently called to mourn for the king's sins, of which this is one, the designing a conjunction with the malignant party, and giving them warrant to rise in arms for the defence of the kingdom? Now, how shall they be able to reconcile these in their own minds,—at the same time to mourn for that as a sin in the king, which they hear commended as the duty of the parliament,—to fast to-day for that as the king's sin, which they must go about to-morrow as their own duty? 'Tell it not in Gath, publish it not in Askelon, lest the daughters of the Philistines rejoice.' Heathens may rise in judgment against this generation. *Semper idem velle atque idem nolle hæc demum sapientia est.** If any wise man be *ubique et semper sibi par et idem,*† what ought a godly man to be?

Fourth Reason. That which is an uncertain mean of preservation of the kingdom, and a more certain mean of destruction of religion, is utterly unlawful. But the employing and intrusting of all men promiscuously, according as is holden out in the public resolutions, is at best an uncertain mean of the preservation of the kingdom, and is a more certain mean of the destruction of religion. *Ergo,* It is utterly unlawful. The first proposition cannot be denied. When any less good comes in opposition with a greater good, the lesser good in that respect becomes evil. We may not endanger certainly a greater good for the probable and uncertain attainment of the lesser. The second proposition I know will be denied, as it was denied in the time of the engagement by the committee of estates. They said, the danger of religion was not infallible, that it might eventually fall out so, but not by any casualty. And thus it is pleaded now, that the danger of religion is not inevitable; but that the danger of the kingdom is certain: and so these being laid in the balance together, we ought, to eschew a certain danger of the kingdom's destruction, rather hazard a probable danger of religion.

But we shall clear this and confirm the reason. 1. The danger of the kingdom is indeed great; but it is not so certain and inevitable in case of not employing the malignant party, because there may be some competency of power beside. Now the delivery and preservation of the kingdom from this danger, by conjunction with that party, is rather improbable, because we have sentenced ourselves to destruction if ever we should do such a thing again. We are standing under a curse, whereto we have bound over ourselves; and beside, God is in a special manner pursuing that generation, and hath raised up this enemy for their destruction: so that we may with greater probability expect to partake of their plagues, and to fall under our own curse, than to be delivered, or be instruments of deliverance to the kingdom. Or, at the best, it is uncertain. For what is more uncertain than the event of war? The battle in this sense may be said peculiarly to belong to the Lord. Now, on the other hand, the danger of religion is certain and inevitable, though not simply in itself and absolutely, (because the Lord doth in heaven and earth what he pleases,) yet with a moral certainty and infallibility, which is often as great as physical certainty. Suppose these men having the power of the sword, prevail, will they not employ it according to their principles, and for attaining their own ends, which both are destructive to religion? What is more certain than that men act and speak from the abundance of the heart, when there is no outward restraint? It should be a great wonder if they who are so accustomed to do evil, should cease to do evil, when they have power and convenience to do it. Power and greatness hath corrupted many good men. Shall it convert them? Can men expect other fruits from a tree than the nature of it yields? Will one seek figs on thorns, or grapes on thistles? 2. We do not see what defence it can be, for the present, to the kingdom, at least the godly and well-affected in the kingdom, who will be as much troubled in their persons and estates by that party, as by the common enemy. It is known what threatenings the country is filled with, which vent that inveterate malice and hatred to all the well-affected in the kingdom, which they have kept within their breast of a long time: and now they find opportunity of outing it. It is as clear as daylight, that the most part of all the secluded persons look upon these that opposed them in the Engagement, and shut

* [See Note, page 96.—Ed.]

† [That is, "every where and at all times like himself and the same."—Ed.]

them out of places of trust, and capacity of employment, as enemies, and as great enemies as the sectaries. And that we may know what to expect when they have full power in their hands, they have already so lifted up their head, that no godly man can promise himself security in many places; and especially the faithful gentlemen and people of the West, * who have given more proof of their faithfulness to the cause and kingdom against the common enemy, than any others in the land; yet are they daily suffering violence from these preservators of the kingdom, while they are sufferers under the feet of the enemy. When they have no common enemy, whom, I beseech you, will they prey upon, seeing they do it already while they have an enemy?

But it is replied, That none of the least suspicion are allowed to be in such trust and power, as may be prejudicial to religion; and that an oath is to be taken of all, which is to be conceived as particular, binding, and strict as possible.

Answer 1. What a manifest receding is it from former principles, that it is now conceived, that all places of trust, excepting some few of eminent note, may be filled with secluded and debarred persons, without the prejudice of religion! It is certain that most part of the officers, nominated by the parliament and shires, are not only such, of whom there is just ground of suspicion, but such as have been enemies by actual opposition to the cause of God, or known underminers thereof. Can it be said in good earnest, that none, of whom is any suspicion, shall have such trust as may be prejudicial? Sure we are, there are many just grounds of suspicion and jealousy of general persons,† who have chief trust in our armies: and this the public judicatories are not ignorant of. 2. Oaths and covenants are but like green cords about Samson to bind these men. Would we have them yet once again perjured? Then may we tender an oath to them. Put power in their hand, and then make them swear to employ it well. 'Tis as ridiculous as to give a madman a sword, and then persuade him to hurt none with it. There is no more capitulation with such persons, retaining their old principles, than with the floods or winds. These whom that sacred bond of covenant hath not tied, what oath can bind? Except you can change their nature, do not swear them to good behaviour. Can a leopard change his spots?

Fifth Reason. That which gives great offence and scandal, and lays a stumbling-block in the way, both of the people of the land and our enemies, especially in the way of the godly, that is unlawful. But the present association and conjunction with all persons in the kingdom (excepting a few, if any) is scandalous and offensive to the whole land, to the godly especially, and also to the enemy. Therefore it is unlawful. The *major* ‡ is beyond all exception, if we consider how peremptory Christ and his apostles are in the point of offence, which yet few Christians do consider. We ought not only to beware of the offence of the godly, but even of wicked men, even of our blaspheming enemies. 'Give no offence neither to the Jew nor Gentile, nor to the church of God.' Christ would not offend and scandalize his malicious enemies. The *minor* § is proved. 1. There is great offence given to the godly in the kingdom by the public resolutions, concerning that conjunction with the malignant party, under the name and notion of subjects. (1.) Because it is known that the most part of them are tender in that point, what fellowship they act with; and this hath been remonstrate unto the commission and committee of estates, from several synods. Now the present resolution layeth that stumbling-

* [We learn from Principal Baillie, ('Letters and Journals,' vol. ii. p. 363,) that Binning had identified himself with the Association of the West, which was required to dissolve itself, by an Act of the Scottish parliament, passed 28th Decem., 1650.—Ed.]

† [Or, general officers.—Ed.]

‡ [The *first* or *principal proposition* in the preceding syllogism.—Ed.]

§ [(Minor probatur,) that is, *the second proposition* in the preceding syllogism. It will be perceived that the arguments of the author are constructed according to the rules of the Aristotelian logic. A familiar acquaintance with this mode of reasoning continued to be cultivated, at this time, by all who wished to excel in public disputations. (Professor Jardine's 'Outlines of Philosophical Education in the University of Glasgow,' p. 12. Glas. 1825.) In the Westminster Assembly, the different speakers often presented their opinions under the form of syllogisms, which were impugned and defended by employing the usual terms and technical formalities of the dialectic art.—See Lightfoot's 'Journal of the Proceedings of the Assembly of Divines.' Works, vol. xiii. pp. 123, 157, 203—205, &c.—Ed.]

block in their way, that they cannot act in the defence of the kingdom, because there is no way left them for the performing of that duty, but that which they in their consciences are not satisfied with. It is a sad necessity and snare that is put upon them, that they cannot perform their bound duty, which they are most desirous of, without sin, because of the way that is taken. (2.) Is it not matter of offence and stumbling to them, to be necessitated by law to that which was their affliction? The mixture that was in our armies was their grief; and their comfort was that the judicatories were minting at* their duty to purge them. But now there is no hope of attaining that; all doors are shut up by the public resolutions. (3.) It undoubtedly will weaken their hands, and make their hearts faint, so that they cannot pray with affection and in faith, for a blessing upon such an army, † the predominant and leading part whereof have been esteemed, and are really enemies to God and his people. (4.) Is it not a great offence that any thing should proceed from the public judicatories that shall lay a necessity upon many godly in the land, to suffer, because they cannot in conscience go along with it? *Next,* It scandalizeth the whole land. What may they think within themselves, to see such dissonancy and disagreement between present and former resolutions and practices? What may they judge of this inconstancy and levity of the commission, and thus be induced to give no respect and reverence to them in their resolutions? Is it not, at least, a very great appearance of evil to join with that party, that we did declare and repute, but some few weeks since, to be wicked enemies of religion and the kingdom, and look henceforth on them as friends without so much as any acknowledgment of their sin had from them? Shall not they be induced to put no difference between the precious and the vile, not to discern between him that fears God and him that fears him not, when the public resolutions put no difference? Then, how will it confirm all the malignant party in their wickedness? May they not think our solemn vows and engagements, our rigid resolutions and proceedings, were but all contrived and acted out of policy; and that interest and advantage, and not conscience, principled them? Have they not an occasion given them to persecute all the godly, and vent their long harboured malice against these who have been most zealous for reformation and purging of the land? Nay, they are put in the capacity that they have desired, for acting all their resolutions, and accomplishing their designs. And last of all, the present proceedings will not only encourage and animate the common enemy, but confirm them in all the imputations and calumnies they have loaded our church with. May they not have ground to think, that we are but driving on a politic design, and do not singly aim at God's glory,—that it is not grounds of conscience that act us, but some worldly interest, when they look upon the inconstancy and changeableness of our way and course, which is so accommodated to occasions and times? Can they think us men of conscience, that will join with all these men of blood, before we will so much as speak with them? It is replied, that the scandal is taken, and not given, which must not be stood upon in the case of a necessary duty. But, 1. We cleared, that there is no necessity of that conjunction; therefore the scandal is given, seeing it is known beforehand that it will be taken. 2. There are many grounds of offence given by the present resolutions, as appears by what is said. If it were no more, it is a great appearance of evil; it is very inductive of many evils; a most fit occasion of all that is spoken; and besides, it is in itself sinful; contrary to God's word, and our oaths.

Sixth Reason. That which makes glad all the wicked and enemies of God in the land, and sad many, if not most part, of the godly, hath much appearance and evidence, if not certainty, of evil. But the public resolutions and proceedings are such. *Ergo,*—Or thus:—That which makes glad all the wicked, and heightens

* [Aiming at.—Ed.]

† [Mr. Robert Ramsay, Principal of the University, reminded the Presbytery of Glasgow at their first meeting in June, 1651, "that Mr. Hew Binnen had expresslie protested that it wes not lawfull for us to pray for ye successe of the armie, as it was constitute, and becaus of those who now have power in the same. And farther, the said Mr. Hew Binnen, when notice wes taken of these words, repeated them over and over agane, and avowed, he wold pray for a blessing to them, yt is, that yei might be converted, but, that he could not pray for success to them as yei are now constitute."—'Records of the Presbytery of Glasgow.'—Ed.]

the hopes and expectations of the malignant party, and makes sad none almost but the godly, and discourages their spirits; that, proceeding from the public judicatories, cannot be right and lawful. But so it is, that that which proceeds from the public judicatories makes glad all the hearts of the wicked, and makes sad none almost but the godly; heightens the hopes of the malignants, and makes them say, their day is coming, 'lo we have seen it;' and discourages the godly, and makes them almost say, 'Our hope is cut off, our glory is departed.' *Ergo,* It cannot be right, at least it hath a great and convincing appearance of evil.

This argument may be thought more popular than either philosophical or scriptural. But such an argument the General Assembly, 1648, made use of against the Engagement. It is no ways imaginable, how the wicked and ungodly in the land would so insult and rejoice in this day, if they saw not some legible characters upon it, which were agreeable to their own principles and ends. The children of God are, for the most part, led by the Spirit of God, and taught the way they should choose, John xvi. 13; Psal. xxv. 12. So that readily they do not skunner* at courses approven of God. But the children of the world being, at best, led by their own carnal minds and senses, and, for the most part, acted by a spirit of disobedience and enmity against God, they use not to rejoice at things that do not suit with their carnal hearts, and are not engraven with the character of that which is imprinted in their spirits. We see now that the wicked walk on every side, when the vilest men are exalted. And when the wicked rise, the righteous is hidden; and when they bear rule, the people mourneth: but when righteous men are in authority, the people do rejoice; and when the righteous rejoiceth, there is great glory, Ps. xii. 8; Prov. xxviii. 12; and xxix. 2.

Seventh Reason. That which is the accomplishment and perfecting of the malignant design that hath been driven on these years past, especially since the Unlawful Engagement, cannot be a course approven of God. But the present course is the accomplishment of that design. *Ergo,* That there hath been a design, for a long time, driven and endeavoured, both at home and abroad, with much policy and industry, by many turnings and windings, and by arguments of several kinds, as the exigence of the times did furnish,—and that the design was, to have all such persons in trust and power again, who had been secluded, that so they might compass their own ends,—hath not been denied hitherto: and we are persuaded no man that fears God, and observes the times, is ignorant of it. Let the public papers of the treaty at Breda,† and the public papers of this kingdom and church at home, be consulted. They bear witness for us. Was not the foundation of it laid in Holland, and many of them in both nations, brought home with the king contrary to public resolutions, and by the prevailing influence of some in the state, kept in the kingdom, contrary to public resolutions? Was not the work of purging judicatories and armies obstructed; the godly discountenanced and discouraged; great endeavours used to raise the malignants in the South and in England; and, since the defeat, to raise all without exception in the North; but when that could not be obtained, by the withstanding of honest men in the state? The levies appointed, which would have been a considerable force for the defence of the kingdom, were rendered wholly ineffectual; partly by taking money for men; partly by raising the malignant party; and then pretending to go against them, they were pacified by an act of indemnity: the fruit and result of all which is, this present conjunction with them, and putting the power of judicatories and armies in their hand. Thus the design is completed.

Eighth Reason. That which will increase the Lord's indignation and controversy against the land yet seven times more, that is very unlawful and unseasonable. But so it is, that confederacy and association with the people of these abominations, will increase the Lord's indignation and controversy seven times more. *Ergo,* The assumption was as manifest and uncontroverted as the proposi-

* [Or shudder.—Ed.]

† [For the Instructions given by the Scottish parliament to the Commissioners who went to Breda, see 'Acts of the Parliament of Scotland,' vol. vi. pp. 513, 514. A copy of the Treaty itself agreed upon by his Majesty Charles II. and the Scottish Commissioners, and afterwards ratified by parliament, will be found in Thurloe's State Papers, vol. i. pp. 147, 148.—Ed.]

tion, a few months ago, but it is begun now to be questioned by some, *qui quod sciunt nesciunt, quia sapiunt.** But we shall evince it. 1. We are standing under such a sentence, which we deliberately and sincerely passed upon ourselves, in the days of our vows to God, that if we did ever any more join with the people of these abominations, the Lord would consume us till there was no remnant. And this was not done in rashness but in sobriety, and with a scripture precedent, Ezra ix. 12, 13. 2. Our experience hath made this clear to us, we never did mingle ourselves among them, but the Lord did pursue us with indignation, and stamped that sin, as in vive † characters, upon our judgment. God hath set upon that rock, that we have so oft split upon, a remarkable beacon. Therefore we do not only in our solemn engagements, bind ourselves over to a curse, in case of relapsing, but pass the sentence of great madness and folly on ourselves. *Piscator ictu sapit.*‡ Experience makes fools wise, but it cannot cure madness. Did not that mixture provoke God at Dunbar?§ And is this the way to appease him, to revolt more and more? 3. Conjunction and confederacy with that party, doth necessarily infer a communion in blessings and plagues; we must cast in our lot with them, and have all one purse. Now it hath been confessed and declared by this church, that God hath a notable controversy with that party; that this enemy is in an eminent way to bear them down and crush them. Therefore if we join with them, we must resolve to partake of their plagues, and have that controversy pleaded against us also.

It is answered, That indignation need not be feared simply on this account, because the means are lawful and necessary; else, if this have any force, it will conclude, that we should lie down and do nothing, because God's indignation is upon the whole land.

But we reply, 1. Though it be true, that this enemy is the rod of God's indignation against the whole land; yet it is certain to us, and hath been formerly unquestioned, that they are raised up in a special way, to execute God's wrath on malignants, and God doth arm them with power in a signal manner for that end. Besides, the Lord's anger and indignation against his enemies is such, as will burn and none can quench it. It is of another nature than his wrath against his own people, which is a hiding of his face for a moment. He corrects us in measure and judgment, but leaves us not altogether unpunished. But he makes an end of other nations, especially these that rise up to actual enmity and hatred of his people, and shedding of their blood. And therefore, if any man would not meet with wrath and sore displeasure, he would stand at a distance with such as God hath appointed for destruction; we mean, as long as they carry in their foreheads the mark of the beast. When God hath such a remarkable controversy against a people, then 'he that helpeth and he that is helped shall both fall together,' Isa. xxxi. 3. All that is in league with them, shall fall with them by the sword, Ezek. xxx. 5. and xxxii. 21. 2. Since it is known that the malignant party have not changed their principles, and so they cannot but in prosecuting this war establish their old quarrel and follow it, viz. the king's arbitrary power, the interest of man above God's, or the kingdom's interest; we leave it to be judged impartially, whether or not these that associate with them, do espouse that quarrel and interest, at least expose themselves to all that wrath and indignation, which hath hitherto followed that quarrel, seeing they must have common blessings and curses. Will not that quarrel holden up by most part of the army, be a wicked thing, an Achan in the camp, that will make God turn away from it, and put Israel to shame?

* [That is, "who, because they are wise, are ignorant of that which they know." (Tu pol, si sapis, quod scis, nescis. Terent. Eun. iv. 4. 54.)—Ed.]

† [That is, *lively* or *distinct* characters.—Ed.]

‡ ["A fisherman is made wise by a bite." A Greek proverb, the original of this (Ὁ ἁλιευς πληγεις νουν φυσει), has been preserved in a fragment of Sophocles. Erasmi Adagiorum Chil. Quat. p. 41. Coloniæ, 1612. Scholiastes Græci In Sophoc. Tom. iii. p. 602. Argentorati. 1788.—Ed.]

§ ["Another consequence of this defeat [at Dunbar] was, that every one blamed the other; the one side for purging out too many who might have been of service against the enemy; and these again blamed their opposites for being too remiss, and not well enough purged."—Memoirs of the Life of the Rev. Robert Blair, p. 113. Edin. 1755.—Ed.]

Having thus established the truth; in the next place, we come to take off what objections are made to the contrary.

First. It is argued from human authority. The uncontroverted and universal practice of all nations in all generations, is, to employ all subjects in the case of necessary just defence. It was the practice of our reformers, who took into the congregation, and received all that, upon acknowledgment of their error, were willing to join, though they had been on the contrary faction. Such an universal practice of Christian nations, though it be not the ground of our faith, yet it is apparent that it cannot want reason for it.*

Answer 1. This will plead as much against the exceptions added in the answer to the query and act of levy; for seeing other nations except none, in the case of necessary defence, why should we except any? And if once we except any upon good and convincing grounds, upon the same ground we ought to except far more. 2. Mr. Gillespie, in his Treatise of Miscellany Questions,† makes mention that the city of Strasburg, 1529, made a defensive league with Zurich, Berne, and Basil; because they were not only neighbours, but men of the same religion. And the Elector of Saxony refused to take into confederacy those who differed from him in the point of the Lord's supper; lest such sad things should befall him, as befell these in Scripture, who used any means of their own defence. This rule was good *in thesi*, ‡ though in that case misapplied. Now then, if they made conscience of choosing as the means of their own defence, a confederacy with foreigners; may not the same ground lead us to a distance from our own countrymen, as unqualified, who have nothing to commend them but that they are of the same nation, which is nothing in point of conscience? 3. The practice of other nations, that are not tender in many greater points, cannot be very convincing: especially, when we consider that the Lord hath made light to arise, in this particular, more bright than in former times. God hath taken occasion of illustrating and commending many truths unto us in this generation, from the darkness of error, and of making straight many rules, from the crookedness of men's practice and walking. Is not the Lord now performing the promise of purging out the rebels from among us and them that transgress? God hath winked at former times of ignorance. But now, the Lord having cleared his mind so to us, how great madness were it to forsake our own mercy, and despise the counsel of God against our own souls? (1.) As for that instance of our reformers, there could not have been any thing brought more prejudicial to that cause, and more advantageous for us. After they were twice beaten by the French in Leith, and their forces scattered, and the leaders and chief men of the congregation forced to retire to Stirling; John Knox, preaching upon the eightieth Psalm, and searching the causes of God's wrath against them, condescends upon this as the chief cause, that they had received into their councils and forces, such men as had formerly opposed the congregation, and says, God never blest them since the Duke had come among them. See Knox's Chron.§ (2.) It cannot be showed that ever they took in a party and faction of such men, but only some few persons; which, though it was not altogether justifiable, was yet more excusable. But now the public resolutions hold forth a conjunction with all the bloody murderers in the kingdom (excepting very few), and these without profession of repentance in many, and without evidence of the reality of it almost in any. (3.) These persons were not such as had once joined with the congregation,

* [Answer of the Commission, *ut supra*, p. 8.—Ed.]

† [P. 178. Edin. 1649.—Ed.]

‡ [Or as a general principle.—Ed.]

§ [In opposition to what is here affirmed, it is stated in the pamphlet entitled, 'A True Representation of the Present Division in the Church of Scotland,' (p. 15.) that the Scottish Reformers did not look upon their conjunction with the Duke of Chatelherault and his followers, "as a cause of that sad stroak, as some would make the world believe, from Mr. Knoxes Sermon at Sterlin. For in the heads of that Sermon, printed in the History of the Church of Scotland, p. 217. *Edit. Edinburgh*, 1644, in 4to., there is no mention of any such thing, but only of their carnal confidence; that possibly they had not sincerely repented of their former opposition; and that they who were late come in were made to feel in their own hearts, how bitter a cup they had made others to drink before them. Nor doth he (as our Brethren's tenets now lead them) presse them to purge out such as were lately admitted, but doth only presse repentance upon all of them."—Dr. M'Crie presents his readers with an analysis of this sermon of the "great Apostle of the Scots," as he was called by Beza.—See 'Life of Knox,' pp. 192, 193 sixth edit.—Ed.]

and relapsed and became enemies to it; but they turned to the protestant religion from popery. But ours is a different case.

Second. It is argued from scripture. Three scripture instances are brought to justify the present proceedings. The first instance is from the practice of God's people in the book of Judges, who, when for defection from religion they were brought under oppression, yet when any governor was raised by God for their defence, they gathered and came all out promiscuously, notwithstanding a great part of them had been in the defection. Yet it is not found that their governors are reproved for this, but rather sad curses on them that came not out to the work, Judges v. 15, 16, 17, 23. The second instance is from the story of the kings, very like the first. When, after defection, gracious reforming kings arose, and had to do against foreign invasion, we find them not debarring any subjects, but calling them out promiscuously. Neither is this laid to their charge, that they called out such and such subjects, though we may perceive by the story of the prophets, that the greater part of the body of the people were wicked, &c.

We answer to these two instances jointly. 1. We may by the like reason prove, that which is as yet uncontroverted (we know not how long), that we ought at no time to make choice of instruments, neither in case of prosecution of the cause and the invasion of others, nor yet in the time when choice is to be had; and so, that all our former engagements, resolutions, and proceedings, in the point of purging judicatories and armies, was superfluous and supererogatory, because we read not that the reforming kings and judges, whenever they had an invasive war, and in the times that they had greatest plenty and multitudes of people, did ever debar any of their subjects from that service, but called them out promiscuously. Neither is this laid to their charge; though we may perceive that the greater part of the people were wicked under the best kings. Therefore we may lawfully employ any subjects of the kingdom in any of our wars. And we may look upon all indifferently, without any discerning of persons that fear God and them that fear him not, as in good capacity to be intrusted, even when otherwise we have choice of good instruments. Certainly it follows, by parity of reason. For if you conclude that, from the calling forth all promiscuously, and no reproof given for it, in the case of necessary defence; then we may conclude, from the calling forth of all promiscuously, and in the case of an invasive war, and no reproof recorded, that neither, in such a case, is it sinful to make no difference; and that with strong reason, because it being more easy in such a case to choose instruments, and no necessity pleading for it; if it had been sinful, the prophets would have rather reproved it, then rebuked them for using such means in a case of necessity. 2. We may argue after that manner, that in the case of necessary just defence, there should be no exceptions made at all of any persons, because we read not that the judges or kings debarred any subjects, neither that they were rebuked for so doing. Therefore the instances militate as much against the exceptions added in the answer to the query, as against us; unless it be said that there were no such persons among that people, which were as groundless rashness as to say that they gave all evidence of repentance. 3. Seeing the judges and the reforming kings of Judah were so accurate and exact in cleaving to the law of God, and walking according to it in all other things; it were more charitable and Christian judgment to say, that since they are not reproved for any fault in this particular, that they were also exact to walk according to the rule, (Deut. xxiii.) in so great a point as this. 4. Men's practice is often lame and crooked, and therefore must be examined according to the rule; but it were not fair dealing to accommodate the rule to men's practice. Seeing then we have so clear and perfect a rule (Deut. xxiii.), which must judge both their practice and ours; we see not how their practice can be obtruded as a rule upon us, which itself must be examined according to a common and general rule. If it be not according to that law, we hold it to be sinful in itself, and so no precedent for us; albeit the prophets did not reprove it in express and particular terms (as they did not reprove man-stealing, &c.), yet they rebuked it by consequence, in as far as they rebuked the kings for association with wicked Israelites, which is condemned upon grounds common to this very case in hand. 5. We see not any ground for such promiscuous calling forth of the people by the judges. Barak's business, as that of Jephthah and Gideon, was done by no great multitudes of people, but a few choice men. 6. As the oppression was heavy and continued long; so the repentance of the people was solemn, and their deliverance a fruit of this. 7. Their case and ours is very different. None of Israel or Judah did fight against the profession of the true religion, and shed the blood of their fellow-subjects who were for the defence of the same. Israel in the days of the judges, and Judah in the time of the reforming kings, was not divided the one half against the other, upon opposition and defence of the true religion, and the better part, after many experiences of the treachery and enmity of the most of the worst part, solemnly engaged to God, not to admit them to employment and trust, but upon real evidence of repentance, of which they should judge as in the sight of God. And last of all, did ever Israel or Judah, in the days of their judges and reforming kings, admit into their armies a party and faction of such as had given no real evidence of their abandoning their former course; and such a party, as had been long studying to get the power of armies and judicatories in their own hands for attaining their own ends? But all those are in our case.

The third instance from scripture, is from 1 Sam. xi., which is alleged to be a clear practice, and stamped with divine approbation. In the case of Jabesh-Gilead besieged by a foreign enemy, Saul commands all to come forth for defence of their brethren, under pain of a severe civil censure. Now, what Saul did in this business, the Spirit of God is said to act him to it; and what the people did, was from the fear of God, making them obey the king. And then Samuel in this acting concurs jointly, and makes no opposition. And last of all, the people came forth as one man, and yet (chap. x. 27.) many men of Belial were among them, who malignantly opposed Saul's government, contrary to God's revealed will.

To which we answer, 1. The stamp of divine approbation is not apparent to us; success doth not prove it. Neither the Spirit coming on Saul, nor the fear of God falling on the people, will import a divine approbation of all that was done in the managing that war. That motion of the Spirit is no sanctifying motion, but a common, though extraordinary, impulse of Saul's spirit to the present work, which, doubtless, was in the king of Babylon, whom God raised up, fitted and sent for the destruction of many nations: albeit that work in his hand was iniquity. That fear of God that fell upon the people, was but a fear of the king imprinted by God, and it is more peculiarly attributed to God, because the people did despise and contemn him, which makes their reverence and fear to be a more extraordinary thing upon a sudden. Then Samuel, not opposing the course in hand, doth no more import his approbation of all that was done in it, than his not reproving the men of Belial doth prove that he approved of their opposition. 2. It doth not appear that the men of Belial were a great faction and party; there is something in ver. 12. speaks against it. It is not like the people would put a faction and party to death. 3. Neither doth it appear that they were in the army. For that which is said, that all the people came out as one man, doth only import, that the body and generality of them came forth; and that it was a wonder so many came forth so suddenly at the command of the king, who was but mean and abject in their eyes. It is certain that all fencible persons were not present, because the whole army being numbered, ver. 8, was but 330,000. And who will say there was no more men in Israel, when they had 600,000 such, and above, before their coming into the land? Seeing then, many have staid at home, it is most probable that these men of Belial would not come, seeing they despised Saul's mean and low condition in their heart, and thought him unfit to lead their armies, till he should prove what was in him. That which is said, ver. 12, doth not prove they were in the camp. It might be conveniently spoken of absent persons. 4. It is not certain that these men were wicked and scandalous in their conversation, haters of godliness and of their brethren; but that they stood at distance only with Saul, in the point of his election, which indeed was blame-worthy, seeing God had revealed his mind in it. And therefore they are called men of Belial, as Peter was called Satan, for opposing Christ's suffering.

Some other scriptures are alleged by some, as David's employing of such men, &c., all which are cleared in Mr. Gillespie's Treatise of Miscellany Questions, quest. 14.

Third. It is argued from reason. And, 1. That which any is obliged to do for another's preservation by the law of God and nature, and which he cannot omit without the guilt of the other's destruction, that may the other lawfully require of him to do when he needs it, and when it may be done without the undoing of a greater good. But so it is, that every subject is obliged by the law of nature, oath and covenants, and the law of God, to endeavour to their power, the preservation of the kingdom against unjust violence. And the safety of the kingdom stands in need of many subjects' assistance who were secluded. And it may be done without undoing a greater good than is the preservation of religion. *Ergo*,

This argument hath an answer to it in the bosom of it. (1.) We shortly deny the assumption, in relation to the two last branches, both that the kingdom's preservation stands in necessity of these men's help; and that their help tends not to the undoing of a greater good, seeing there is no reason given to confirm these two points, wherein the nerve of the business lies. We refer to a reason of our denial of them given p. 22.* (2.) It is true that the obligation to such a duty lies upon all; but that obligation is to be brought into act and exercise in an orderly and qualified way, else what need any exceptions be in the act of levy? Excommunicated persons are under the same obligation, yet the magistrate is not actually obliged to call such, but rather to seclude them. Are not all bound to come to the sacrament who are church members? Yet many are not in a capacity to come, and so ought neither to presume to come nor be admitted. Are not all subjects obliged to defend the cause of God, and to prosecute it? And yet many, because of their enmity to the cause of God, are actually incapable of employment in the defence or prosecution thereof. (3.) The law of nature is above all human laws and constitutions, they must cede whenever they come in opposition to it. *Salus populi* is *suprema lex* † in relation to these. But, in relation to the law of God, it is not so. Sometimes the law of nature must yield to positive commands of God. Abraham must sacrifice his son at God's command. The law of nature obliges us to the preservation of ourselves; but it does not oblige to every mean that may be found expedient to that end, unless it be supposed lawful and approven of God. Therefore the Lord in his written word doth determine what means we may use for that end, and what not. But, (4.) We conceive that the law forbidding association and confederacy with known wicked and ungodly persons, is included in the law of nature, as well as the law that obliges us to self-preservation. That is grounded on perpetual reason, as well as this. Nature bids me preserve myself, and nature binds me to have one friend and foe with God. The heathens had a notion of it. They observed, that Amphiaraus, a wise and virtuous man, was therefore swallowed up in the earth with seven men and seven horses, because he had joined himself and associated with Tydeus, Capaneus, and other wicked commanders marching to the siege of Thebe. Mr. Gill. Miscell. Quest. chap. 14. p. 171.‡

* [See page 495 of this edition.—Ed.]

† ["The safety of the people" is "the highest law."—Ed.]

‡ ["The very heathens had a notion of the unlawfulnesse of confederacies with wicked men. For, as Victorinus Strigelius on 2 Chron. 25, noteth out of Æschylus his tragedy, intituled *Seven to Thebe*, Amphiaraus a wise vertuous man was therefore swallowed up in the earth, with seven men, and seven horses, because he had associat himself with Tydeus, Capaneus, and other impious commanders marching to the siege of Thebe." ('Gillespie's Miscel. Quest.,' p. 178.) Æschylus makes Eteocles give the following description of the character of Amphiaraus, and foretell his destiny:—('Septem cont. Thebas,' ver. 597.)

"Nothing worse
In whate'er cause than impious fellowship;
Nothing of good is reap'd: for when the field
Is sown with wrong, the ripened fruit is death.
So this seer
Of temper'd wisdom, of unsullied honour,
Just, good, and pious, and a mighty prophet,
In despite to his better judgment join'd
With men of impious daring, bent to tread
The long, irremeable way, with them
Shall, if high Jove assist us, be dragg'd down
To joint perdition"—Potter.

Regarded simply as a poetical fiction, the account which Statius has given of the fate of Amphiaraus is particularly striking and beautiful.—(Thebaid. lib. vii. ver. 815—823.)—Ed.]

2. The second reason is framed thus *in hypothesi.** Such as are excluded are a great part, if not the greater part, of the remnant of the land, if rules of exclusion be extended impartially. Now, they having their lives and liberties allowed them, must either in these things be insured by the interposing of a competent power for their defence, or else they must have liberty to act for themselves. But so it is, that we cannot interpose a competent power for their protection. *Ergo,* They must have liberty to act for themselves. *Nam qui dat vitam, dat necessaria ad vitam.*†

We answer, (1.) It is not certain that such as are excluded are the greater part of the land. However, it is certain, that though the rule had been kept, and endeavours had been used to walk according to it, yet many whom it excludes would have been taken in. There is a great difference between endeavour of duty, and attaining its perfection. If the rule had not been quite destroyed, so great offence could not have been taken, though it had not been strictly urged in all particulars. (2.) We still affirm, upon evident grounds to us, that there is a power competent in the land, beside the malignant party, which may protect the land and insure their lives and liberties. (3.)‡ We are persuaded many of that party, who have been so deeply involved in blood-guiltiness and barbarous cruelties, should neither have lives nor liberties secured to them, because they ought not to be permitted to live. But the not taking away so much guilty blood from the land by acts of justice, is the cause that so much innocent and precious blood is now shed. Our rulers have pardoned that blood which God would not pardon: and therefore would not pardon it to the land because they pardoned it to the murderers.

SECTION IV.

THAT IT IS NOT LAWFUL FOR THE WELL-AFFECTED SUBJECTS TO CONCUR IN SUCH AN ENGAGEMENT IN WAR, AND ASSOCIATE WITH THE MALIGNANT PARTY.

Some convinced of the unlawfulness of the public resolutions and proceedings, in reference to the employing of the malignant party, yet do not find such clearness and satisfaction in their own consciences as to forbid the subjects to concur in this war, and associate with the army so constituted. Therefore it is needful to speak something to this point, That it is as unlawful for the subjects to associate and join in arms with that party as it is for the parliament to employ them. For these reasons.

1. The scriptures before cited against associations and confederacies with wicked and ungodly men do prove this. The command prohibiting conjunction with them and conversing, &c. is common both to magistrates and people ; for the ground of it is common to both:—The people's insnaring, helping of the ungodly, &c. It were strange doctrine to say, that it is not lawful for the parliament to associate in war with the malignants, lest the people be insnared: and yet it is lawful for the people to associate with them upon the command of the parliament, seeing the insnaring of the people hath a more immediate connexion with the people's conjunction with them, nor§ with the parliament's resolution about it. Had it not been a transgression in all the people to have joined with these men before the parliament's resolution about it? How then can their resolution intervening loose the people from their obligation to God's command? Shall it be no sin to me, because they sin before me? Can their going before me in the transgression, exempt me from the transgression of that same law which obliges both them and me? 2. The people were reproved for such associations as well as rulers, though they originated from the rulers. The prophets speak to the whole body. 'What hast thou to do in the way of Egypt?' &c. Jer. ii. 18. And Isa. xxxi. 'Wo to them that go

* ["A Hypothetical Proposition is one which asserts not absolutely, but under an hypothesis, indicated by a conjunction. An hypothetical syllogism is one on which the reasoning depends on such a proposition."—Whately's 'Elements of Logic,' p. 388.—Ed.]

† ["For he who gives life, gives the things which are necessary to life."—Cic. De. Offic. lib. i. cap. 4.—Ed.]

‡ [The MS. in my possession, which will be afterwards described, has no part of this third answer. In place of it, I find the following passage: "And though there had been disproportion of numbers betwixt us and the enemy; yet we cannot but still say, it had been a way much better beseeming the people of God, and in which there would have been much more peace and consort, to have hazarded on our duty, with such a disproportion, than to have taken in the malignant party for making it up."—Ed.]

§ [Than with.—Ed.]

down to Egypt.' Psal. cvi. 'They mingled themselves,' &c. The Lord instructed Isaiah, and in him all his own people, all the children whom God had given him, saying, 'Say ye not, A confederacy, to all them to whom this people shall say, A confederacy,' Isa. viii. 12. When all the people were going on in such a mean of self-defence, the Lord instructed him and the disciples among whom the testimony was sealed, that they should not walk in the way of this people. When Jehoshaphat was reproved for helping the ungodly, were not all his people reproved that went with him? They were the helpers of the ungodly as well as he. If Amaziah had refused to dismiss the army of Israel whom God was not with, doubtless it had been the subject's duty to testify against it, and refuse to concur and act in such a fellowship.

3. If the association and conjunction with malignants be only the sin of the parliament, and not the sin of the people, who do upon their command associate with them; then we cannot see how people can be guilty of association with malignants at any time, and in any case. To join with them in an ill cause is not lawful indeed. But neither may we join with good men in an evil cause. Suppose then the cause be good and necessary (as no war is just if it be not necessary), in what case or circumstances shall association with them be unlawful for the people? If it be said, in case the magistrate command it not; we think that strange divinity, that the sole command of the magistrate should make that our duty, which in absence of his command is our sin, and that not because of the absence of his command but from other perpetual grounds. Certainly, whenever association with them is a sin, it is not that which makes it a sin, because the magistrate commands it not, but because God forbids it. And it is as strange, that the unlawful and sinful resolution of parliament should make that lawful to me which otherwise had been unlawful. It is known that human laws oblige not, but as they have connexion with God's word. Now if that law, enjoining a confluence of all subjects for the defence of the kingdom, be contrary to the word, in as far as it holds out a conjunction with malignant and bloody men, how can it be lawful to me, in obedience to that ordinance, to associate with these men? If it be said to be lawful in the case of necessity, that same necessity is as strong a plea for the magistrate's employing them, as for the people's joining with them: and if it do not justify that, it cannot excuse this. If the lawfulness of the mean must be measured by the justice and necessity of the end; then certainly any mean shall be lawful in the case of just and necessary defence; then we may employ Irish cut-throats; then we may go to the devil for help, if expediency to compass such a necessary and just end be the rule of the lawfulness of the mean.

4. The whole land is bound by the covenant and solemn engagement not to associate with the malignant party. *Ergo,* It is as sinful for the people to join with them as for the magistrate to employ them. Are we not all bound by covenant, to endeavour to bring malignants to condign punishment, and to look on them as enemies? And is not conjunction and confederacy with them, on the people's part, as inconsistent in its own nature with that duty, as the magistrate's employing them is inconsistent with his covenanted duty? When all the people did solemnly engage themselves not to join any more with the people of these abominations, was the meaning of it, we shall not join until our rulers join first; or, we shall not join with them in an ill cause? No indeed; but, we shall not employ them in a good cause, or join with any party of them in it. If that engagement be upon every one in their station, let us consider what every man's station in the work is. The ruler's station and calling is to choose instruments, and levy forces for the defence thereof. The subject's station and calling is, to concur in that work, by rising in defence of the cause and kingdom. Now, what did the subject then engage unto? Certainly, unless we mock God, we must say, that as the magistrate engaged not to employ that ungodly generation in a good cause, so the subject engaged not to join with any such party even in a good cause. If this be not the meaning of our engagements and vows, we see not how the subjects are in capacity to break them, as to that precise point of association.

In sum, All the reasons that are brought to prove the unlawfulness of the public resolutions, may with a little variation be proportionably applied to this present question. Therefore we add no more but a word to an objection or two.

Objection 1. A necessary duty, such as self-preservation is, cannot be my sin. But it is the subject's necessary duty to rise in defence of the kingdom. *Ergo*,

Answer. A necessary duty cannot be a sin in itself, but it may be a sin in regard of some circumstances, in which it ceases to be a necessary duty. It is a necessary duty to defend the kingdom. But it is neither a duty nor necessary to do it in such a conjunction and fellowship, but rather a sin. If I cannot preserve myself, but by an unlawful mean, then self-preservation in such circumstances is not my duty.

Objection 2. Jonathan did assist Saul in a war against the Philistines invading the land, and no doubt many godly joined and died in battle. Now this is commended in scripture, as may be seen in David's funeral* upon them; although it was known that Saul was an hater of God's people and a persecutor, and that God had a controversy with him, and that these 3,000 that assisted him against David were also ungodly and wicked men.

Answer 1. These scriptures speak nothing to commend that particular act of Jonathan's conjunction in war with his father. David in his epitaph speaks much to the commendation of both Saul and Jonathan, as of excellent warriors, and of Jonathan as a kind and constant friend to him; but there is nothing touched of that point. If that place be pressed, it will follow with much more evidence, that Saul was as good a man as Jonathan, and that the people of God had great loss in his death. But none of these must be pressed rigorously from a speech wherein he vents his affection and grief. 2. Suppose the natural bond of Jonathan to Saul his father, and the civil bonds of the people to Saul their king, did oblige them to join with him against the common enemy; yet we think they ought not to have associated with these persecuting servants, and the 3,000 that pursued David, but they ought to have pleaded for a purging of the army. 3. It is not probable that there were many godly persons employed in that army. David complains of that time, (Psal. xii.) that the godly man ceased, and the faithful from among the children of men: and that the wicked walked round about when the vilest men were exalted. 4. Many of the laws of God have not been much taken notice of, even by godly men, until the Lord hath taken occasion to reprove them particularly, and so to mind† them of their duty. It is likely the rule, (Deut. xxiii.) had not been considered till the time of Jehoshaphat and Amaziah. ‡[However it be, they had not so many solemn and particular ties of oaths, and covenants, and vows, and confessions, as we have lying on us. 5. Let no man wonder that such particular escapes are not always reproved in scripture, who considers that the fathers' polygamy, though so frequent among them, was not laid to their charge.

Objection 3. Separation from the army, because of the sin of magistrates, in employing such unqualified persons, is paralleled to separation from church worship, because of the sin of the false worshippers, and because the guides of the church do not exclude them. *Answer* 1. We have particular commands about this, and many examples of it, which we have not about separation from a true church, and lawful worship. Union and conjunction with an enemy renders conjunction, and their fellowship, more dangerous and infectious than conjunction in a church state. Judah might not separate from these Israelites in lawful ordinances, or from the ordinance [because] of their presence. And yet they might not help them nor take help from them. Paul did not exhort any to separate from the worship at Corinth, because of the presence of scandalous persons at it: and yet he charges them not to converse with such brethren as walk disorderly. Notwithstanding of union in church and state, we may look on many as such as should not be joined with in some other bonds. It is not lawful for a godly man to marry a profane woman: though a visible professor, he may not join in such a tie, although he ought not to separate from church worship for her presence. *Besides*, there is a conjunction in arms for one cause, as necessarily makes men partakers of the same

* [Dirge, or some such word, is wanting here.—Ed.]

† [That is, put them in mind.—Ed.]

‡ [The remaining part of the Section is not contained in either of the two preceding editions of the 'Case of Conscience,' but is taken from a MS. in the handwriting of the period, with the use of which I have been favoured by my friend, David Laing, Esq., Secretary to the Bannatyne Club. This MS. terminates with Section IV.—Ed.]

blessings and cursings; and therefore we should give the more diligent heed, when we partake with them in lawful things. 3. Are we all tied, by such particular oaths and solemn vows, not to join with the scandalous persons of a congregation in lawful worship, as we are, not to associate with the malignant party in the defence of the cause of God, and kingdom? It cannot be said. Therefore the cases are not paralleled.

We shall close all with a testimony of one of the Lord's most faithful witnesses, Mr. Gillespie, whose light in this case was once very seasonably held forth, and effectual to the preventing of the declining of this land: and we hope it will not be wholly forgotten by them, with whom it had weight then. In his letter to the General Assembly, 1648, he sayeth, "I am not able to express all the evils of compliance, they are so many. Sure I am, it were a hardening of the malignant party, a wounding of the hearts of the godly, a great scandal to our brethren of England, an infinite wronging of those who, from their affection to the covenant and cause of God, have taken their life in their hand; who, as they have been strengthened and encouraged, by the hearing of the zeal and integrity of the well-affected in this kingdom, and how they oppose the late Engagement, so they would be as much scandalized to hear of a compliance with malignants now. Yea, all that hear of it may justly stand amazed at us, and look on us as a people infatuated, that can take in our bosom the fiery serpents, that have stung us so sore. But above all, that which would heighten these sins to the heavens is this, that it were not only a horrible backsliding, but a backsliding into that very sin, which was especially pointed at, and punished by the prevalency of the malignant party; God justly making them thorns and scourges, who were taken in as friends, without any real evidence, or fruits of repentance. Alas! shall we split twice upon this same rock, yea, run upon it, when God has set a beacon on it? Shall we be so demented as to fall back to the same sin, which was engraven in great letters in our late judgment? Yea, I may say, shall we thus out-face and out-dare the Almighty, by protecting his and our enemies, when he is persecuting them; by making peace and friendship with them, when the anger of the Lord is burning against them; by setting them on their feet, when God hath cast them down? O! shall neither judgments nor deliverances make us wise? I must here apply to our condition the words of Ezra; 'And after all this is come upon us for our evil deeds, and for our great trespasses, seeing that thou our God hast punished us less than our iniquities deserve, and hath given such deliverance us this; should we again break thy commandments, and join in affinity with the people of these abominations, wouldest thou not be angry with us till thou hast consumed us, so that there should be no remnant nor escaping?' O happy Scotland! if thou canst now improve aright, and not abuse this golden opportunity, but if thou wilt help the ungodly, or love them that hate the Lord, wrath upon wrath, and woe upon woe, shall be upon thee from the Lord.

"This testimony of a dying man (who expects to stand shortly before the tribunal of Christ) I leave with you my reverend brethren," &c. And again in his Testimony against association and compliance with malignants, written two days before his death, he says, "Seeing now, in all appearance, the time of my dissolution is very near, although I have, in my latter will, declared my mind of public affairs; yet I have thought good to add this further testimony, that I esteem the malignant party in these kingdoms the seed of the serpent, enemies to piety, and Presbyterian government, (pretend what they will to the contrary,) a generation that have not set God before them. With the malignants are to be joined the profane and scandalous, from all which, as also from heresies, and errors, the Lord I trust is about to purge his churches. I have often comforted myself, and still do, with the hopes of the Lord's purging of this polluted land; surely the Lord has begun, and will carry on that great work of mercy, and will purge out the rebels. I know there will be always a mixture of hypocrites, but that cannot excuse the conniving at gross and scandalous sinners. This purging work, which the Lord is about, very many have directly opposed, and said, by their deeds, we will not be purged nor refined, but we will be joining, and mixing ourselves with those whom the ministers preach against, as malignant enemies to God and his cause. But let him that is filthy, be filthy still; and let wisdom be justified of her children. I recommend to them that fear God, sadly and seriously to consider, that the Holy Scripture doth plainly hold forth, 1. That the helping of the enemies of God, or joining and mingling with wicked men, is a sin highly displeasing. 2. That this sin hath ordinarily insnared God's people into divers other sins. 3. That it hath been punished of God with grievous judgments. 4. That utter destruction is to be feared, when a people, after great mercies and judgments, relapse into this sin, Ezra ix. 13, 14. Upon the said and the like grounds, for my own exoneration, that so necessary a truth want not the testimony of a dying witness of Christ, also the unworthiest of many thousands, and that light may be held forth, and warning given, I cannot be silent at this time, but speak by my pen, when I cannot by my tongue; yea, now also by the pen of another, when I cannot by my own; seriously and in the name of Jesus Christ, exhorting all that fear God, and make conscience of their ways, to be very tender and circumspect, to watch and pray that they be not insnared in that great dangerous sin of conjunction, or compliance with malignant or profane enemies of the truth, under whatsomever prudential considerations it may be varnished over, which if men will do, and trust God in his own way, they shall not only not repent it, but to their greater joy and peace of God's people, they shall see his work go on, and prosper gloriously. In witness to the premises, I have subscribed the same with my hand at Kirkaldy,* December 15th, 1648. Mr. Frederick Carmichael,† at Markinch, and Mr. Alex. Moncreiff,‡ minister at Scoonie,

Sic Sub[r].

GEORGE GILLESPIE.
F. C. *Witness.*
A. M. *Witness.*"]

* [Mr. George Gillespie, who was the son of Mr. John Gillespie, Minister of Kirkaldy, was at this time one of the Ministers of Edinburgh; but he had gone to Kirkaldy for the benefit of his health. He was one of the Commissioners from the Church of Scotland, to the Westminster Assembly. In his letters from London, Principal Baillie, who was also one of the Scottish Commissioners, speaks of his youthful colleague in terms of high admiration. "Of a truth," he says, respecting him, in a letter dated March 26, 1644, "there is no man whose parts in a public dispute I do so admire. He has studied so accurately all the points ever yet came to our assembly, he has gotten so ready, so assured, so solid a way of public debating, that, however there be in the assembly divers very excellent men, yet in my poor judgment, there is not one who speaks more rationally and to the point, than that brave youth has done ever." ('Letters and Journals,' vol. i. p. 451. See also, pp. 407, 419, 431.) Gillespie's 'Treatise of Miscellany Questions,' which was published after his death, in 1649, contains a chapter entitled, "Another most useful Case of Conscience discussed and resolved, concerning associations and confederacies with idolaters, infidels, heretics, or any other known enemies of truth and godliness." (pp. 169—193.) This, it will be observed is, with very little variation, the title of the Tractate of Binning. It is probable, that they who first undertook the publication of Binning's MS. were led to adopt this title from the similarity of the views, as well as the identity of the subjects of the two authors. When the Commission of the church met at Perth, in December, 1650, for the purpose of considering the *query* of the parliament as to the persons who ought, or ought not, in present circumstances to be employed, in the defence of the country,—it was not likely that the published opinions of Gillespie upon such a subject would be overlooked. But says Baillie, when giving an account of this meeting, "The question was alleged to be altered from that which Mr. Gillespie writes of."—'Letters and Journals,' vol. ii. p. 365.—ED.]

† [The name of "M. F. Carmichael" is attached to a warrant, which is dated Sept. 1, 1651, and bears to be subscribed by certain commissioners of the church, authorizing George Ogilvy of Barras, to deliver up to Lord Balcarres, the Registers of the Kirk that were in his house. (Reg. of Deeds, 6 March, 1701. Dr. M'Crie's Mem. of Veitch and Brysson, Append. p. 525.) There can be little doubt that these were the original records of the church, which were produced and identified at the meeting of the General Assembly at Glasgow, in the year 1638. (Id. p. 497. 'Rec. of the Kirk,' vol. i. pp. 22—24, Edited by A. Peterkin.) It is boldly asserted by Gordon, parson of Rothiemay, that the old authentic records of the Assemblies were at that time in the hands of Archbishop Spottiswood, who had carried them with him, he says, to London, though he more cautiously adds, in a *nota*, "It is *very uncertaine* if the registers presented wer the principalls, or if only copyes." ('History of Scots Affairs,' vol. i. pp. 146, 147. Aberdeen, Printed for the Spalding Club, 1841.) Keith tells us in what way these records afterwards came into the possession of Mr. Archibald Campbell, a Scottish non-juring clergyman residing in London, by whom they were most unjustifiably detained from the Church after the Revolution, and subsequently gifted to Sion College, the governors of which being expressly restricted from permitting them to pass out of their custody. ('Hist. of the Aff. of Church and State in Scot.,' p. 497.) After some delay on the part of the governors, the long-concealed records, bound up in three volumes, and embracing the whole period between 1560 and 1616, were given up by them for inspection, in the year 1834,

SECTION V.

SCRIPTURES SHOWING THE SIN AND DANGER OF JOINING WITH WICKED AND UNGODLY MEN.

WHEN the Lord is punishing such a people against whom he hath a controversy, and a notable controversy, every one that is found shall be thrust through: and every one joined with them shall fall, Isa. xiii. 15. They partake in their judgment, not only because in a common calamity all shares, (as in Ezek. xxi. 3.) but chiefly because joined with and partakers with these whom God is pursuing; even as the strangers that join to the house of Jacob partake of her blessings, chap. xiv. 1. To this purpose is Isa. xxxi. 2, 3. and Ezek. xxx. 5, 6, 8. The mingled people and those that are in league with Egypt partake in her plagues, and those that uphold that throne that God so visibly controverts with, their power shall come down, and all its helpers shall be destroyed, as it is Jer. xxi. 12, 20, 24. And this is the great reason of these many warnings to go out of Babylon, Jer. l. 8. and li. 6. Remember that passage, 2 Kings i. 9, 10, 11, 12. The captain and messenger of the king speaks but a word in obedience to his wicked master's command, and the fifty are but with him, and speak not: but their master's judgment comes on them all.

Consider how many testimonies the wise king, in his Proverbs, gives against it. Chap. i. from ver. 10, to 19. 'My son, if sinners entice thee, consent thou not. If they say, Come with us, let us lay wait for blood, let us lurk privily for the innocent without cause. Let us swallow them up alive as the grave, and whole as those that go down into the pit. We shall find all precious substance, we shall fill our houses with spoil. Cast in thy lot among us, let us all have one purse. My son, walk not thou in the way with them; refrain thy foot from their path. For their feet run to evil, and make haste to shed blood,' &c. Here are the practices and designs of wicked men expressed in their own nature. But certainly they would colour them over with fair pretences. Their purpose is to undo men, especially godly men that classed and purged them. Yea, it is the profession of many, and they scarce lie privily, or have so much wisdom as to conceal their designs till their fit opportunity: but before the power be confirmed in their hand, they breathe out cruelty against all the innocent in the land, and promise themselves great gain by it, and are already dividing their estates among them, saying we 'shall find all precious substance,' ver. 13. But, my son, if thou fear God, though they entice thee with specious arguments of nature, and necessity, and country privileges, yet consent not. Venture not thy stock in one vessel with them. Cast not in thy lot among them. 'Walk not in the way with them: refrain thy foot from their path:' for they are not come to the height of iniquity, they are running on to it. And if thou join, thou wilt cast thyself in a miserable snare; for either thou must go on with them to their designed and professed evils, or be exposed to their cruelty.

Chap. ii. from ver. 10. to the end. 'When wisdom entereth into thine heart, and knowledge is pleasant to thy soul; discretion shall preserve thee, understanding

to the Select Committee of the House of Commons on Church Patronage. ('Minutes of Evidence,' pp. 126, 355, 374.) Dr. Lee, one of the witnesses before the Committee, declared, after examining them, he was quite certain that they were "authentic records." (Id. p. 450). The loss of such invaluable archives, soon after this, which now appears to be placed beyond all doubt, in consequence of the destruction of the House of Commons by fire, is much to be deplored.—ED.]

‡ [At the Restoration, Mr. Moncrieff was ejected from his parish, for the part he had acted in framing or sanctioning the "Remonstrance," and the "Causes of the Lord's wrath," which was ingenuously confessed by him. ('Acts of the Parliaments of Scotland,' vol. vii. p. 367.) Wodrow has collected various particulars regarding the life, character, and subsequent sufferings, for conscience' sake, of this pious and useful minister. ('Hist. of the Suff. of the Ch. of Scot.,' vol. i. pp. 197—200.) As he was persecuted, during the Usurpation, for persisting in praying publicly for the king, he had thus the singular misfortune of being punished both for his loyalty and his supposed disloyalty. Mr. Moncrieff has had a niche assigned to him by Howie among the *Scots Worthies.* (pp. 411—415. Dumfries, 1835.) Mr. James Guthrie, Minister at Stirling, who was imprisoned at the same time with his friend, Mr. Moncrieff, and afterwards executed, was accused at his trial of compiling "the Remonstrance." This he denied, affirming he could prove, by hundreds of witnesses, that he was at Stirling at the time, many miles distant.—See his Defences, 'Acts of the Parl. of Scot.,' vol. vii. Append. p. 37.—ED.]

shall keep thee: to deliver thee from the way of the evil man, from the man that speaketh froward things; who leave the paths of uprightness, to walk in the ways of darkness,' &c. If thou take the word of God for a lamp to thy feet, and it enter into thy soul, and be received in love and affection, it will certainly keep thee from the evil men's way, who have already left the righteous paths to walk in the ways of darkness, who rejoice in nothing so much as in the sorrows and miseries of the godly, and delight in one another's wickedness. And it will keep thee chaste to thy husband Christ Jesus, and preserve thee from committing fornications with Egypt as Aholah and Aholibah, and joining so nearly with the degenerated seed of Abraham, who are but as strangers. For come near their house and paths, and they will lead thee to destruction with them, or make thee a more miserable life. But these that go to them return not again quickly. They are like fallen stars. Shall they ever be set in the firmament again? It is safest to walk with good and righteous men: for God's blessing and promise is on them. His curse and threatening is on the wicked. Therefore thou may fear wrath on that account, if thou join with them.

Chap. iv. ver. 14—20. 'Enter not into the path of the wicked, and go not in the way of evil men. Avoid it, pass not by it, turn from it, and pass away. For they sleep not except they have done mischief: and their sleep is taken away except they cause some to fall. For they eat the bread of wickedness, and drink the wine of violence. But the path of the just is as the shining light, that shineth more and more unto the perfect day. The way of the wicked is as darkness: and they know not at what they stumble.' It was said, chap. iii. 23. that the man who keeps wisdom and the fear of God in his heart, should walk in the way and not stumble. That safety hath ease in it here. Their steps are not straitened, as when a man walks in steep and hazardous places, who cannot choose but it will be. If a man enter into the path of wicked men, he must either go along in their way with them, and then it is broad indeed; or, if he think to keep a good conscience in it, he will be pinched and straitened. Therefore it is most free for the mind and conscience to avoid and pass by that way: 'for they sleep not,' &c. They will never be satisfied till they have done a mischief, they will live upon the ruins of the poor country. And how wilt thou join in that? Or how can thou eschew it, if thou walk with them? If it were no more, it is a suspected by-path, that thou never travelled into. O pass by it: or, if thou be entered, turn out of it. If thou wilt enter upon the apprehension of some light and duty in it, know that it is but evening, the sun is setting, and thou wilt be benighted ere it be long: and thou shalt stumble then, and not know whereupon, even on that, thou seest not now and thinkest to eschew and pass by. Then from ver. 23, to the end. 'Keep thy heart with all diligence: for out of it are the issues of life,' &c. Except thou keep thy heart and whole man, thou cannot escape falling into some temptation. O keep thy heart diligently on the knowledge and love of the truth. Take heed to thy words. Look not a-squint but directly to that which is good. Give not a squint look to any unlawful course, for the necessity or utility, it may be, that seems to attend it. But look straight on, and ponder well the way thou walkest in, that thou run to no extremity either to one parte or other; that thou walk in the middle way between profanity and error. Thou heldest these ways hitherto for extremes. Ponder, I beseech thee, then, before thou walkest in any of them. See whether they be really come to thee, or thou to them. Mark who is changed.

Chap. v. 8, to the 15. 'Remove thy way far from her; and come not near the door of her house; lest thou give thine honour unto others, and thy years unto the cruel. Lest strangers be filled with thy wealth, and thy labours be in the house of a stranger. And thou mourn at last when thy flesh and thy body are consumed; and say, How have I hated instruction, and my heart despised reproof; and have not obeyed the voice of my teachers, nor inclined mine ear to them that instructed me!' &c. If thou would be safe from snares, remove from the way and house of the strange woman. Thou must fall in Aholah and Aholibah's whoredoms, (Ezek. xxiii.) except thou come not near them. If thou keep not from that assembly and congregation, thou shall be 'almost in all evil.' If thou join with them, thou cannot but partake of their sins and plagues; and so thou shalt say after, when thou cannot well mend it, ' I was near gone, my steps almost gone,' and all the assembly of his people shall witness to it.

Chap. vi. 16, 17, 18, 24, 25. ' These six things doth the Lord hate, yea seven are an abomination unto him. A proud look, a lying tongue, and hands that shed innocent blood, an heart that deviseth wicked imaginations, feet that be swift in running to mischief. To keep thee from the strange woman, from the flattery of the tongue of a strange woman. Lust not after her beauty in thine heart; neither let her take thee with her eye-lids.' This describes both our enemies, the malignant party and the sectarian. Pride, violence, cruelty, lying, is the very character of the one. Flattery, beauty of pretended religion, false witnessing and charging of the Lord's people, and seeking to sow discord among these that were one in heart and work, is the character of the other. Now, keep thee from both these abominations: and do not think it is in thy power not to be infected with the contagion of their fellowship. ' Can a man take fire in his bosom and his clothes not be burnt? Can one go on hot coals and not burn his feet?' So whoever associates and goes in friendly to either of them ' shall not be innocent,' ver. 27, 28, 29.

Chap. vii. 14, &c. ' I have peace-offerings with me, this day have I paid my vows.' They pretend religion on both sides. And our church says, the malignants have satisfied them, and repented, even like the peace-offerings and vows of the whore. She began with her devotion, that she might with more liberty sin more, and have that pretence to cover it; and by means of her offerings, she got a feast of the flesh; even as they by profession of repentance are admitted to trust; and by offering for the like sin, a new sin is covered, and vows undertaken never to be kept. Therefore take heed of these snares. 'For she hath cast down many strong,' ver. 26. Many a tall cedar hath fallen by that fellowship. It is the way to hell, ver. 27. See chap. viii. 13.

Chap. x. shows us the very different estate of the godly and wicked, both in regard of light and knowledge concerning duty, and of blessings promised. Ver. 6, 9, 11, 20, 23. ' Blessings are upon the head of the just: but violence covereth the mouth of the wicked. He that walketh uprightly, walketh surely: but he that perverteth his ways, shall be known. The mouth of a righteous man is a well of life: but violence covereth the mouth of the wicked. The tongue of the just is as choice silver: the heart of the wicked is little worth. It is as a sport to a fool to do mischief: but a man of understanding hath wisdom,' &c. Ver. 24, 25, 28, 31, 32, which show us, that if the Lord's mind be revealed to any concerning the present courses, it must be to his poor people that wait on him, and not to all the wicked and ungodly in the land, who almost only are satisfied and clear in the course, who yet before were never satisfied. And beside, though the Lord be chastising his people, yet one may join with them without fear of wrath and indignation on that account, and with hope of partaking of their blessings, when he cannot and dare not join with a wicked party pursued with wrath and indignation in the same dispensation, which may be more clear from chap. xi. 3, 5, 8. ' The integrity of the upright shall guide them: but the perverseness of transgressors shall destroy them. The righteousness of the perfect shall direct his way: but the wicked shall fall by his own wickedness. The righteous is delivered out of trouble, and the wicked cometh in his stead.' And verses 10, 11, show the different condition of people under wicked rulers and godly. All the wicked now rejoice. None shouts but they. They think their day is come. The godly generally hang their head and are discountenanced, even as Psal. xii. The 21 and 31 verses show, that when godly men are chastised and punished in the earth for their sins, ' much more the wicked,' especially when the godly were chastised for partaking with them, according to 1 Pet. iv. 17, 18; Isa. x. 12, and xlix. 26.

Chap. xii. 13. ' They are snared by the transgression of their lips.' Their ordinary common speeches they drop out with, declare them, and make their cause, more hateful than other pretences, it is covered with, would permit. Yea, they speak like the piercings of a sword, against the godly, ver. 18. If our state and church had a lip of truth, they would speak always the same thing. They would not carry in their talk and writings, as now every common understanding perceives. We may find their writings made up of contradictions. For ' a lying tongue is but for a moment,' ver. 19. It is but for a moment indeed before the judicatory; and then out of doors it contradicts itself, as in the mock repentances. But sorrow and anguish will come to these, who before they would speak of terms of peace with one enemy, would associate in war with another. 'But to the counsellors of peace is joy,' ver. 20. The present course contradicts this. Ver. 26. 'The righteous is more excellent than his neighbour: but the way of the wicked seduceth them.' They think these malignants better than the west country forces. They would condescend to any terms to get their help, though it were to reverse the Act of Classes,* to give them indemnity, yea, not so much as to condemn their way: but they will not so much as clear the state of the quarrel, or choose a better general † for all their help. Their way seems good in their own eyes, ver. 15. But it were wisdom to hearken to the counsel of the godly.

Chap. xiii. 10. 'Only by pride cometh contention: but with the well-advised is wisdom.' There is nothing keepeth up our contention and wars but pride: no party will condescend to another. We will not say we have done wrong in bringing in the king. They will not say they have done wrong in invading. But it were wisdom to fall lower and quit those interests. Ver. 16. 'Every prudent man dealeth with knowledge: but a fool layeth open his folly.' A wise man would count before the war, if he can accomplish it: and if he cannot, then he would send messengers of peace, and cede in all things he may without sin. If it be but more honour and wealth to our king,‡ should we destroy the kingdom to purchase that? Our rash and abrupt proceedings show our folly. Ver. 20. 'He that walketh with wise men shall be wise: but a companion of fools shall be destroyed.' A man will be, must be, assimilated to his company, and then partake of their judgment or blessings.

* [The parliament of Scotland passed the *Act of Classes* on the 23d of January, 1649. It was entitled an Act "for purging the Judicatories, and other places of Public trust." Those whom it declared to be incapable of sitting in parliament, or of holding any civil or military appointment, were divided into four classes. The disqualification of such as, on account of their supposed greater criminality, were placed in the first class, was to continue for life; that of the second class for ten years; that of the third class for five years; and that of the fourth class for one year only, provided they gave previously sufficient evidence of their penitence.—'Acts of the Parl. of Scots,' vol. vi. p. 352.—Ed.]

† ["After the woful rout at Dunbar, in the first meeting at Stirling, it was openly and vehemently pressed to have David Lesly laid aside, as long before was designed, but covertly by the chief purgers of the times. The man himself did as much press as any to have liberty to demit his charge, being covered with shame and discouragement for his late unhappiness, and irritated with Mr. James Guthrie's publick invectives against him from the pulpit. The most of the committee of estates, and commission of the kirk, would have been content to let him go; but finding no man tolerably able to supply his place, and the greatest part of the remaining officers of horse and foot peremptory to lay down, if he continued not; and after all trials finding no maladministration on him to count of, but the removal of the army from the hill the night before the rout, which yet was a consequence of the committee's order, contrary to his mind, to stop the enemy's retreat, and for that end to storm Broxmouth house as soon as possible. On these considerations the state, unanimously did with all earnestness entreat him to keep still his charge: against this order, my Lord Wariston, and, as I suppose Sir John Cheesly, did enter their dissent. I am sure Mr. James Guthrie did his, at which, as a great impertinency, many were offended. Col. Strachan offered to lay down his charge, being unwilling more to be commanded by D. Lesly. Some more inclined to do so; but all were quieted by this expedient."—Baillie's Letters, vol. ii. p. 350.—Ed.]

‡ [The religious zeal of Binning, his patriotism, and his dread of arbitrary power were, it is clear, stronger than his loyalty. Sir Edward Walker, however, vouches for the loyalty, at this period, of the Scottish nation in general. "For the disposition of the people," he says, (Hist. Disc. p. 194.) "they are generally for the king and his government, being most under the notion of Malignants and Engagers, about 100 of 120 noblemen being in that condition. Most of the Gentry are very loyal, and in a manner all the common people." Binning's language respecting Charles II. at the time of passing the Public Resolutions, appears to have startled his co-presbyter, Principal Baillie, who writes thus in a letter which was first designed for his friend Mr. Dickson, but afterwards sent to Mr. Spang at Campvere.—"Mr. Patrick [Gillespie] and Mr. James Guthrie, wherever they came, uttered their passion. I heard one who had married Mr. Patrick's sister's daughter report to Mr. Douglas, that Mr. Hugh Binning, with Mr. Patrick, in Kirkaldy, had spoke like a distracted man, saying to Mr. Douglas's own wife, and the young man himself, and his mother-in-law, Mr. Patrick's sister, 'that the commission of the kirk would approve nothing that was right; that a hypocrite ought not to reign over us; that we ought to treat with Cromwell and give him security not to trouble England with a king; and whoever marred this treaty, the blood of the slain in this quarrel should be on their heads.' Strange words if true."—Letters, vol. ii. p. 363. The ungrateful, impolitic, and barbarous treatment which his Scottish subjects received from Charles II.

Chap. xiv. He that is accustomed to speak truth in private, will in his common speech be a faithful witness in public : but a man accustomed to lying, dissembling, swearing in private, will not stick to forswear himself, to make professions and vows contrary to his mind in public, ver. 5. (and also chap. xii. 17. and vi. 19.) Such men seek wisdom and make a show of religion, but find it not; whereas it is easy to godly men to find it, to find repentance and salvation, ver. 6. Go away from foolish men, and break off society with ungodly men. Be not privy to their counsels. Use them not as special friends, when thou perceivest that all means are used in vain to reclaim them from their damnable way and principles, ver. 7. The knowledge a godly man hath serves to direct his way, and is given of God for it. But all the wit and skill of such wicked men is deceit. They themselves are beguiled by it in opinion, and practice, and hope. And they also beguile others, ver. 8. Sin makes fools agree : but among the righteous, that which is good makes agreement (in the old translation*), ver. 9. It is only evil will unite all the wicked in the land as one man. For it is a sport to them to do mischief, chap. x. 23. Albeit our way seem right in our eyes, yet because it is a backsliding way, and departing from unquestionably right rules, the end will be death, and we will be filled with our own devices. O! it shall be bitter in the belly of all godly men when they have eaten it! ver. 12, 14. and chap. i. 31. 'The simple believeth every word;' giveth credit to every vain word that is spoken. But a prudent man looketh well to men's goings, ponders and examines whether their professions and practices agree, what weight is in their words, by the inspection of their deeds, and of their ordinary speaking, and does not account a coined word before a judicatory sufficient to testify repentance. And as he gives not present credit to their professions, who have so often proven treacherous, so he himself scares at every appearance of evil, and keeps himself from it; whereas foolish souls rage and are confident, think any thing lawful if they can have any pretence for it, or use of it, ver. 15, 16. Then, what a great difference is between wicked men and godly men, both in their lot, when God is correcting both, and in their disposition! Wisdom that rests in the one's heart, is manifested; wickedness in the other's heart appears also. In the midst of such men there is no other thing, ver. 32, 33.

Chap. xv. 8, ('The sacrifice of the wicked is an abomination to the Lord; but the prayer of the upright is his delight,') expresses how provoking a thing the outward professions and sacrifices of wicked men, continuing in their wickedness; what an abomination that commonly called public repentance, or ecclesiastical holiness is, when men are visibly unholy and ungodly in their conversation. And therefore he pleaded always with that people, that his soul abhorred their external ceremonies, because of the uncleanness of their hands. He pleaded that he never commanded them, though indeed he did command them. Yet those were aberrations and departings from the express rule and command,—to accept or be pleased with these sacrifices and ceremonies,—when there was no evidence of real repentance. To this purpose are chap. xxi. 4, 27; Isa. i. 11; and lxvi. 3; Jer. vi. 20; and vii. 22; Amos v. 22,—all which show that it is but a mocking of the Lord, and perverting of his law, and profaning of his ordinances, to accept the profession of repentance in those who walk contrary thereto, and to count them ecclesiastically holy enough, who say, they repent, though a thousand actions witness the contrary. Of such the Lord says, 'What hast thou to do to take my covenant in thy

after the Restoration, must be held to be a proof of the sagacity at least of Binning, and a justification of the suspicion with which he and some of the other Protesters regarded him. It is not unlikely that, in their case, the strong appeal to the fears of the English and Scottish presbyterians, as the supposed friends of monarchy, contained in Milton's 'Tenure of Kings and Magistrates,' which was published but two years before this, had not failed altogether of its effect.—Ed.]

* [I have not been able to discover to what "old translation" the author alludes. But Wilcox puts the same interpretation, that he does, upon the ninth verse of this chapter. "*Sinne,* (viz. which the wicked and ungodly men commit, and they know one of them by another,) *maketh fools to agree,* (viz. one of them with another: q. d. their partaking in wickednesse joineth the wicked's minds, one of them towards another;) *but among the righteous,* (i. e. good and holy people,) *that which is acceptable* (viz. before God and good men) *maketh agreement* (viz. among themselves: q. d. good things onlie tie good men's minds together)". *A Short yet Sound Commentarie Written on that Worthie Work called the Prouerbs of Salomon.* London, 1624.—Ed.]

mouth, seeing thou hatest to be reformed?' Psal. l. 16, 17. They have no right to it. They should not be admitted to it: for it is a taking the Lord's name in vain. The 16th verse tells us, that it had been better to possess our own land in quietness, than to venture what we have for the uncertain conquest of England, and restitution of the king, parallel with Eccl. iv. 8.

Chap. xvi. 7. 'When a man's ways please the Lord, he maketh even his enemies to be at peace with him.' Can our States'* way then please the Lord, seeing they cannot find the way of peace,—they will not walk in it; and seeing they make the godly in the land to fall out with them, and none to be at peace but the wicked, who may thereby get opportunity to crush the godly? Ver. 17. 'The highway of the upright is to depart from evil.' This is the highway only, to depart from evil, not carnal policies, nor advantages. He thinks the stepping aside to any of these is not the highway. Can then men change their way, and go cross to it, and keep the right way in both? No, the godly have this high way and keep it. Chap. xvii. 11. 'An evil man seeketh only rebellion; therefore a cruel messenger shall be sent against him.' Evil men seek only rebellion, and delight in no other thing. But the King of kings shall send a cruel messenger; he arms men with wrath and power against them. Ver. 13, speaketh sadly to the English, and to our State, that rewarded the west country evil for good. Ver. 14, 19, tell us how we should advise before we begin a war, and leave no mean of composing difference and strife unessayed. We did more in it than the English, but not all we might have done. Ver. 15, with chap. xviii. 5, is a dreadful sentence against the public judicatories, that all their resolutions, papers, and practices, justify the wicked and ungodly as honest faithful men, and condemn all approven faithful men, that cannot go along in such courses, or were earnest to have them repent, as both malignants and sectaries. Do they not pronounce all malignants friends, and absolve them from the sentences and classes they stand under? And do they not put the godly in their place? They relax the punishment of the one, and impute transgression to the other, and so bring them under a law. See Exod. xxiii. 7; Prov. xxiv. 24; Isa. v. 23, and the 29th verse of this chapter. It is not good to punish godly men, who have given constant proof of their integrity, for abstaining from such a course, at least having so much appearance of evil, that many distinctions will never make the multitude to believe that we are walking according to former principles, because their sense observes the quite contrary practices, &c.

Chap. xviii. 2, ('A fool hath no delight in understanding, but that his heart may discover itself,') shows, that if the present cause and course were of God, and tended so much to his glory, fools or wicked men would have no such delight in it. For they delight in nothing but what is agreeable to their humour, to discover themselves, &c. Ver. 3. gives the true reason, why our public judicatories and armies are so base and contemptible, why contempt and shame is poured on them; because, 'when the wicked comes, then also comes contempt, and with the vile man reproach.' Ver. 13. 'He that answereth a cause before he hears it, it is folly and shame unto him.' Many pass peremptory sentence upon the honest party in the west, before they hear all parties, and be thoroughly informed, and this is a folly and shame to them. They hear the state and church, and what they can say for their way; and indeed they seem just, because they are first in with their cause, and they will not hear another. But he that comes after will make inquiry, and discover those fallacies. Ver. 24. 'There is a friend that sticketh closer than a brother.' A godly neighbour, not so near in natural bonds to us, that is a surer friend than many brethren in the flesh. These bonds of country and kindred, should all cede to God's interest. See chap. xvii. 17.

Chap. xix. 22. 'A man's desire is his kindness: and a poor man is better than a liar.' The godly, that cannot concur in the public cause, being disabled, through an invincible impediment of sin lying in the way and means made use of, are better friends, and have more real good-will to the establishment and peace of the land, than any ungodly man, let him be never so forward in the present course. Ver. 10. Pleasure and its attendants are not comely for a wicked man, (i. e. a foolish

* [The Estates, or parliament.—Ed.]

man) much less for a servant, (i. e. men enthralled in their lusts,) to rule over princes (i. e. godly men, highly privileged by God). All things that are good do ill become them ; but worst of all to have power and superiority over good men, ver. 25, joined with chap. xxi. 11. Ringleaders of wickedness, refractory and incorrigible persons, should have been made examples to others ; and this would have prevented much mischief. The scripture gives ground for putting difference between the scorner and simple, seducers and seduced.

Chap. xx. 6 ; xxi. 2, and xvi. 2. 'Most men will proclaim every one his own goodness ; but a faithful man who can find ?' It is no great wonder that malignants say they repent ; and the state and church say they keep the same principles. For who will say any evil of himself ? Ver. 8. Magistrates should scatter away evil men with their countenance, by denying it to them, and looking down on them. How, then, do our rulers gather them ? Ver. 3, shows that war and strife should not be kept up but in extreme necessity. Fools 'will be meddling.' Ver. 11, shows that the best way of judging of men is by their doings and fruits, not strained words and confessions. But those who, upon a bare profession, pronounce a notour* malignant a friend, having no proof of his integrity, and will not have any judged such, but such as judicially are debarred, yet contrary to all the testimony of works and fruits, judge and condemn honest men as traitors, though not judicially convicted. Certainly divers measures are an abomination to the Lord, as in ver. 10. Then in ver. 25. sacrilege is described, and covered perjury, which is a snare to the soul that commits it. He 'devoureth that which is holy,' i. e. applieth to a common use these things God hath set apart, and commanded to be kept holy, as our profaning of repentance and absolution, by casting such pearls to swine ; and for our own advantage, making a cloak of them to bring in wicked men, contrary to the very nature and institution of the ordinance ; also our prostituting of our covenant and cause, most holy things, to maintain unholy or common interests,—our committing his holy things to them that will devour them. 'And after vows to make inquiry,' to dispute now, that we did not bind ourselves in the case of necessity, not to employ wicked men, whereas the ground is perpetual and holds in all cases, shows either temerity, in swearing,—or impiety, in inquiring afterward and changing. See Deut. xxiii. 21. Then ver. 26. 'A wise king scattereth the wicked, and bringeth the wheel over them.' O that our magistrates were so wise ! Is the act of levy a scattering of the wicked ? Is the act of indemnity a bringing the wheel over them ? Psal. ci. 8. 'I will early destroy,' &c.

In Chap. xxi. 10. 'The soul of the wicked desireth evil, his neighbour findeth no favour in his eyes.' The wicked's principles can carry nowhere but to evil, and to do evil to good men. Ver. 8. His way and life is full of horrible and tragical chances. But a good man's work is easy and pleasant, directs to a good and peaceable end, Isa. xxvi. 7. Ver. 12. A righteous man should have his wit about him, to consider ungodly houses and families, and persons that God hath visible controversies with, that he may not communicate with them in their judgments. Ver. 16. It is a sad wandering out of the way, when a man leaves the congregation of the living to abide among the dead,—dead in sins and appointed to death. It is a great judgment as well as sin. Ver. 27, with the 4, and places before cited, show how abominable the external professions and pretences of wicked men are, when contradicted by their practice ; especially if they do it but out of a wicked mind, when they intend to effect some mischief, under the colour of repentance and being reconciled to the church, as Absalom's vow at Hebron : as Balaam and Balak and the Pharisees, who under pretence of long prayers devoured widows' houses ; as Jezebel's fast ; and as the people, (Isa. lviii. 4.) who fasted for strife and debate, and to strike with the fist of wickedness. All men know that the church is the ladder to step up upon to go to preferment, and repentance the door to enter to places of trust.

Chap. xxii. 3. 'A prudent man foreseeth the evil and hideth himself, but the simple pass on and are punished.' He is a wise man that knows the judgment of the Lord, as the stork and swallow the time of their coming ; that in the consideration of sins and threatenings, and comparing things spiritual with spiritual, appre-

* [That is, notorious or manifest.—Ed.]

hendeth judgment coming on such a course and such a party, and hides himself, goes aside, retires to a covert, by avoiding these evils, and the least fellowship with them that bring it on, and eschewing such a society as hath the cloud hanging directly above their head. But simple idiots and blind worldlings go on headlong, and dread nothing, and are punished, ver. 5. Most grievous plagues and punishments, and all manner of unhappiness, encumbereth their wicked life. Therefore he that would keep himself pure and clean (1 John v. 18.), and save his own soul, shall be far from them, shall keep himself far from such people. He prays with Job, 'Let their counsel be far from me.' Job xxi. 16, 17. Because their good is not in their hand, their candle is oft put out, &c. And he resolves with Jacob, My soul shall not enter into their secret, to have such intimacy with them as join counsels with them, Gen. xlix. 6. And ver. 10, 11, Cast out of thy company, family, jurisdiction, the scorner that contemns the godly men, and mocks instruction: for such men are infectious, and able to corrupt all they converse with. But cast him out, and contention shall go out with him. It is such only that mars the union of the godly, that stirs up strife, and foments divisions. Thou shalt have more peace, and be more free from sin and shame. But sound-hearted upright men, who deal faithfully, not to please but to profit,—you should choose these to intrust and rely upon; these should be friends of kings. Ver. 14. As a harlot's allurements are like pits to catch men, so the allurements of wicked ungodly men, their power, policy, &c., and their fair speeches and flatteries, are a deep ditch to catch men into this spiritual whoredom and fornication spoken of Ezek. xxiii. And he whom God is provoked with, by former wickedness, falls into it, Eccl. vii. 26. Ver. 24, 25. 'Make not friendship with an angry man: and with a furious man thou shalt not go,' &c. And is not association in arms with such, as friends against an enemy, a making friendship with them we are sworn to hold as enemies? If we may not converse with a furious passionate man, how then with men of blood, enraged, whose inveterate malice hath now occasion to vent against all the godly? For thou wilt learn his ways, as we have always seen it by experience, and thou wilt get a snare to thy soul. If thou go not in his ways you cannot agree, you will fall out and quarrel, and that is a snare to thee. Ver. 28. 'Remove not the ancient landmark which thy fathers have set.' If it be so dreadful and accursed to remove our neighbour's marks and bounds, O! how much more to change and alter God's landmark, his privileges, oaths and covenants, &c. And chap. xxiii. 10, 11. Deut. xix. 14. and xxvii. 17.

Chap. xxiii. 1, 7. 'When thou sittest to eat with a ruler, consider diligently what is before thee. For as he thinketh in his heart so is he,' &c. Consider diligently what men are, not what they pretend and seem to be. For as they think, so are they, not as they pretend with their tongue and countenance, but as they think in their heart, which is better evidenced by their common and habitual speaking and walking, than any deliberate and resolved profession contrived of purpose. But if thou consider not this, the morsel thou hast eaten thou shalt vomit up. Thou shalt dearly pay for thy credulity, and lose all thy sweet words. Ver. 23. 'Buy the truth and sell it not,' &c. Do not we sell the truth, and cause, and all, into the hands of the enemies of all? whereas we ought to ransom the kingdom's liberty and religious interest, with the loss of all extrinsic interest that does but concern the accession of one's honour. Yet we sell, endanger, and venture all for that.

Chap. xxiv. 1. 'Be not thou envious against evil men, neither desire thou to be with them.' Godly men's hearts are often tickled to be acquainted with, in league and friendship with wicked men, when they have power, that they may not be hurt by them. But seeing there is no society between light and darkness, let not the godly desire to be with them, (as in chap. xxiii. 17,) but rather to be in God's fear always. That is good company. The reason is (verse 2.) their heart studies the destruction of the godly, (why then should thou walk with thine enemy?) and you shall hear nothing but mischief in their lips. Ver. 12. It is not according to men's words but works they should be judged. And why do not we follow that rule in our judging? Do we mock God as one mocks another? Job xxxiv. 11. Psal. lxii. 12. Jer. xxxii. 19. Rom. ii. 6. Ver. 21, &c. Men given to change, false deceitful men, meddle not with such, if thou either fear God or respect man.

For such will be sure to no interest but their own. Their calamity shall come suddenly. Therefore have nothing to do with them. For 'who knoweth the ruin of them both,' of them and all other wicked men, or of both them and the king, if wicked? Also to the wise and godly this belongs, 'It is not good to have respect of persons in judgment,' whether he be king or nobleman. A righteous state respects not the person of the prince and mighty, saith Job. But he that says to the righteous, you are wicked sectaries, and also malignants, because ye will not approve all their resolutions; and to the wicked, 'thou art righteous;' to the malignants, you are the honest men, the blessed of the Lord,—who did ever to this day fall under Meroz' curse, should the people approve him? No certainly,' Him shall the people curse, and the nations shall abhor him,' or them. But a blessing on them that would reprove our sins and search them out, ver. 25. The malignant party are even speaking so: as the classers and purgers did to us, even so will we do to them. But God will render to them according to their work, ver. 29.

Chap. xxv. 2. 'It is the honour of kings to search out a matter.' It is a king and judge's glory to search out a matter, to try dissemblers before they trust them. God's glory is to pardon. Man's glory is to administer justice impartially. Ver. 4, 5, show what need there is of purging places of trust, especially about the king. Dross cannot be melted. Take what pains you will, it will not convert into a vessel and become useful. This mixed in, obstructs all equity, justice, and piety, where it is. The ruler should be the refiner to purge away this dross, and the army, or judicatory, or kingdom, is a vessel. You shall never get a fined vessel for use and service till you purge away the dross, Psal. ci. 4. Then, (ver. 8.) we should follow peace with all men as much as is possible, never to begin strife or draw the sluice of contention. But if we be wronged, we should not for all that go out hastily to strife, till, 1. The justice and equity of the cause appear. 2. That the matter whereabout we contend be of great moment, a ground to found a war upon. 3. That we first use all means of peace and agreement possible. 4. That we overmatch not ourselves with those who are too strong for us, (see chap. xvii. 14.) 'lest' thou be brought to that extremity that 'thou know not what to do.' Thus Christ adviseth, Luke xiv. 31. I am persuaded this would plead much in reason to yield security to England, so be it our wrong were repaired, and no more done. Ver. 19. shows what the employment of unfaithful men, who mean nothing less than they pretend, is. They fail when most is expected, and hurt beside, as Job's friends, chap. vi. 15. And ver. 26. A righteous and upright man, consenting with a wicked man in sin, or, through fear of him, not daring to do his duty, turning to him and his way, or dallying and flattering him in his iniquity, is like 'a troubled fountain,' is not good and profitable for edification nor correction, having troubled the purity of his soul through the mud of carnal respects and interests. Corruption within is the mire; the wicked's seducements are like the beast's trampling it with his foot. And he is like a corrupt, infected, and poisoned fountain, more ready to infect and draw others by his example. Ver. 27. A man should not seek honour and preferment that is base and shameful. None of the trees longed for sovereignty but the bramble.

Chap. xxvi. 1. 'As snow in summer and as rain in harvest; so honour is not seemly for a fool.' It is as unseemly, prodigious, and destructive a thing, to give honours, promotions, and trust to a wicked man, as snow and much rain in harvest; a reproach and punishment more becomes him than honour, the reward of goodness (as ver. 3.); a whip, rod, and bridle are more for him, to restrain him from wrong and provoke him to goodness. Ver. 6. He that commits an errand or business to a wicked man, and intrusts him with it, is as unwise in so doing, as if he did cut off the messenger's feet he sent. He deprives himself of the means to compass it. He sends a lame man to run an errand. He is punished by himself as if he had cut off his own feet, and procureth sorrow and discontent to himself, as if he were compelled to drink nothing but what is contrary to his stomach. Ver. 7. All good speeches halt and limp in evil men's mouths; for there is no constancy in their mouths. Within they are very rottenness. 'Out of the same mouth come blessing and cursing,' James iii. 10. Their very words agree not; the public and extraordinary crosses the private and ordinary. And their actions have less harmony with their words. Professing they know God, in works they deny him, &c. Ver. 8. To give a madman a weapon, what else is it but to murder? To bring shot to an ordinance which may do much mischief to himself and others, is to be accessory to that mischief. So to give 'honour to a fool.' He hath given power to them, and put them in a capacity to do evil, and set them on work again to perfect their designs against good men. Ver. 9. As a drunken man, with a thorn in his hand, can make no use of it, but to hurt himself and others; so wicked men's good speeches and fair professions commonly tend to some mischief. These but cover their evil designs: and yet the covering is shorter than that it can hide them. Ver. 10. Wicked rulers (look the margin*) grieve and molest the subjects; and the means to effect this is, to employ the fool and transgressor, to give offices and countenance to evil men, which may be instruments of their lust; so Abimelech, Judges ix. 4; so Jezebel, 1 Kings xxi. 10; so in Neh. vi. 12. Ver. 11. The dog, feeling his stomach surcharged, goes to the grass,—as our malignants to profess repentance,—and casts up that which troubles him, by a feigned confession. But because there is no change in his nature, he is inwardly stirred by his old principles to lick up that vomit, to commit and practise what he professed repentance for; yea, and to profess the same he pretended sorrow for. When power is confirmed in their hand they will return to their folly. Ver. 17. What else is our interposing ourselves in the king's quarrel concerning England, though we have interest in it to endeavour it in a peaceable way, if he were fit for it; yet in comparison of our kingdom and religion's safety, which may be ruined by war, it is no such matter as belongeth to us. And so it falls out, we are like a man taking a dog by the ears to hold him: we have raised up many enemies, and provoked them to bite us. We cannot hold them long from destroying him; and we provoke them more by holding them, in espousing his quarrel, as Jehoshaphat joining with Ahab. We had done well to interpose ourselves between the king and them to make peace, but to side with one party was not well done. Verses 18, 19. Furious and bloody men take all opportunities to hurt others, especially good men; and so deceive those employed. But they do it under a pretence. As a scorner reproacheth under a pretence of sport; so they, under other pretences, of wrongs done, of the country's defence, &c. Verses 20, 24, show the way to prevent trouble and keep peace. As a contentious turbulent person would inflame a whole country and put them by the ears; so a person, though not contentious in his own nature, yet having many contentious interests following him, which he will not quit, or commit to God's providence, as our king was. O it is the destruction of a nation to have such a person among them. He hath broken the peace of two kingdoms. Verses 23, 24, 25, 26. Burning lips, hot and great words of love and friendship, and a wicked heart revenging its enmity, and minding nothing less than what is spoken, is like a potsherd, a drossy piece covered over with the fairding† of hypocrisy; or, like a sepulchre garnished and painted, he dissembles and speaks vanity, and flatters. Psal. xii. 3. But he lays up his wicked purposes close within him till a time of venting them. Therefore when he speaks so fair and courteously, be not confident of him, trust him not too far till thou have proof of his reality. Put not thyself and thy dearest interests into his mercy. This is wisdom, and not want of charity, Jer. xii. 6; Micah vii. 5; Cain, Joab, and Judas, are proofs of this. It may be covered a time, but not long. *Naturam expellas furca licet; usque recurret.*‡ All the world shall be witness of it, Psal. cxxv. So then, (ver. 21.) the calumniator and false accuser, who openly professes his hatred and malice, and the flatterer that seems to be moved with love, both of them produce one effect, viz., ruin and calamity.

Chap. xxvii. 3, 4. 'A stone is heavy, and the sand weighty: but a fool's wrath is heavier than them both,' &c. We see what we may expect of the enraged, exasperated malignant party. Their wrath against all the godly, for their faithful secluding and purging them out of places of trust, is weighty and insupportable like the sand of the sea. It will crush them under it if God support not. It is

* [In the margin of the authorized version the verse is translated thus: 'A great man grieveth all, and he hireth the fool, he hireth also transgressors.'—Ed.]

† [That is, violent blowing. *Cairding*, however, is not unlikely the proper word, *a caird* being in Scotland the name of a tinker.—Ed.]

‡ ["Although you expel nature by violence, she will still return."—*Hor. Epist.* lib. i. ep. 10. ver. 24.—Ed.]

like a swelling river, or a high spring-tide, it goes over all banks, since the state and church have drawn the sluice and let it out. But when it is joined with envy and malice, against godliness and piety itself, who can stand before that? No means can quench that heat. Ver. 6. Faithful men's reproofs, remonstrances, and warnings, applied in love and compassion, are better than an enemy's kisses and flatteries, than his oils and ointments are. Therefore we would pray against the one, and for the other; that God would smite us with the mouth of the righteous, but keep us from the dainties of the wicked Joabs, Judases, and Ahithophels. Verse 8. speaks sadly against ministers that withdraw from their charges so unnecessarily, as a bird that wandereth too long from her nest: the young starve for cold or famine, or are made a prey. So these who, having no necessary call to be elsewhere, especially not being members of the Commission, yet stay not with their flocks, are guilty of their soul's ruin. Ver. 10. O how doth this speak against the present course of judicatories! They have forsaken their old faithful friends, when they proved ever constant, and have gone in to their wicked countrymen's house in the day of their calamity. But a neighbour in affection and piety, is nearer than a brother in flesh and near in habitation.

Chap. xxviii. 1. 'The wicked fleeth when no man pursueth: but the righteous is bold as a lion.' Wicked men are now chosen for stoutness and courage, but they have no sure foundation for it. It is but like the rage and temerity of a madman or drunkard. But godly men, once satisfied in grounds of conscience about their duty, would have been bold as lions. A good conscience would have made them bold, Psal. cxii. 7, 8; Lev. xxvi. 36. Now, ver. 2, behold the punishment of our sins, our governors are changed; there is almost a total alteration, and we are faces about, which cannot but bring ruin to the land, especially when men of understanding and piety are shut out. Ver. 4, with chap. xxix. 27. It is a great point and argument of declining and forsaking the law of God, when men praise the wicked, change their names though they themselves be not changed, and leave off contending with, or declaring against them, and do rather plead for them. But godly men, that keep the law, contend with, discountenance, and oppose them; as David, 'I hate them that hate thee,' and earnestly contend with them. Thus they are kept from partaking with other men's sins. Ver. 5. It is not very likely that all the ungodly should now understand the duty of the times and discern the right way, and that so many that fear God understand it not, seeing the Lord's secret is revealed to them, Psal. xxv. 14. Verses 6, 7. A poor man, and weak means, if they be of upright men, are better and stronger than many rich and strong perverters. A companion of evil men and a keeper of the law agree not in one person; the one is an honour, the other a shame to all that have interest in them. Ver. 9. Their prayers and professions are abomination; no acceptation of those that turn away their ears from obedience to the law, who walk contrary to it. Ver. 10. These cunning and crafty men that have enticed some godly men, and led them on in the present course, shall themselves smart for it, when the godly seduced shall see good things after all this. Ver. 12. When wicked men have power and trust, good men hide and retire themselves from such a congregation or assembly of the wicked. See chap. x. 10, 11. Should we thus choose our own plague, tyranny, oppression, calamity, and misery, and cast away our own glory? Then, (ver. 13.) repentance requires true and ingenuous confession, and real forsaking. If both these join not, it is but a covering and hiding of sin. If a man confess, and yet walk and continue in them, he is but using his confession as a covering to retain his sins; and such shall not find mercy of God, or prosper before men. Ver. 14. It is not so despisable a thing to fear alway, and to be very jealous of sin as it is now made. It is counted a reproach to have any scruples at the present course. But happy is he that abstaineth from all appearance of evil; but he that emboldeneth himself, and will not question any thing that makes for advantage, falls into mischief. Ver. 15, 17. show the lamentable condition of a people under wicked rulers. They are beasts and not men towards the people, especially towards the best, Dan. vii. 4, 5; Zeph. iii. 3. Ver. 17. How doth that agree with our sparing of bloody men, of our soliciting for their impunity, of our pardoning them? Are they not, by the appointment of God's law, ordained for destruction, and haste to it? Should any then stay them? Should they not then far less employ them? And, (ver. 24.) if it be so heinous to take our father's goods upon this pretence, because they are our own, how much more sacrilege is it to rob God of his interests, and give over his money to bankrupts, and say it is no transgression to rob the land of its defence, and make them naked, as Ahaz his confederacy did? Certainly it is murder. Ver. 28. and chap. xxix. 2. and xi. 12. and xxviii. 28. are to one purpose. We have forsaken our own mercy and wronged our own souls; and destroyed ourselves in choosing our own judgment, and making our own rod to beat us withal. Chap. xxix. 1. We being so often reproved by his word and providence for the sin of association with the wicked, and being so lately punished for it; and having so lately reproved ourselves for it in our declarations and fasts, yet to harden our necks, what can we expect but utter destruction, and that without remedy, as we sentenced ourselves? Ezra ix. 13. and xiv. 13; Isa. xxx. 13, 14. Shall not this iniquity be to us a breach ready to fall, even this iniquity of going down to Egypt for help, &c. Then, (ver. 6.) there is a snare to entrap thy feet in the sins of the wicked; if thou be joined with them, thou cannot well escape. Ver. 8. Wicked profane contemners of God and his people bring ruin on a city or commonalty, they set it on fire and blow it up. But godly men pacify wrath, turn away judgments, and purge all from provocations, which is the only means to turn it away. Ver. 16. shows, when wicked men gather together, and grow in state and power, they grow worse, and sin with greater boldness; and transgression then overflows the land, *tanquam ruptis repagulis.** There is no obstacle. See Psal. xii. And ver. 24. shows, he that is partner and fellow-receiver with a thief, or conceals such offenders, endangers his own destruction: and he that stays with, and associates with wicked men, must hear cursing and cannot bewray it. He will see many abominations, that though he would he cannot remedy. Ver. 25. Fear of man and of the land's danger, hath brought many into a snare, to run from the Lord to an arm of flesh: but he that trusts in the Lord shall be safe. Ver. 27. Here is the deadly enmity between the two seeds, they cannot reconcile well. See ver. 10. and chap. xxi. 3. It is no wonder the godly abominate such men who are God's enemies and the land's plague.

Chap. xxx. 11, 14. describes the malignant party, who make nothing of the godly magistrates or their mother church and land, but curse, malign, oppose as much as they could, and are oppressors, monstrous tyrants, mankind beasts, or beastly men. The subject of their cruelty is the godly afflicted man. They eat up all and will not leave the bones, as the prophet complains, 'I lie among men whose teeth are as spears and arrows, and their tongue a sharp sword.' And then, ver. 12, 13, 20. describe our enemies, the invaders. They think themselves godly and righteous, yet are not purged from their filthiness. They are given up to strong delusions to believe lies; and there is no lie greater than this, that they are a godly party in a godly cause and way. They wipe their mouth after all their bloodshed, and say, I have done no evil. They wash their hands, as Pilate, as if they were free of the blood of these just men, whose souls cry under the altar. Ver. 21—23. It is a burden to the world and a plague to mankind, when servants, unworthy men, and persons unfit for high places are set in authority, and when wicked men have their desire of plenty and honour; (chap. xix. 10.) and when an odious woman, or men of hateful vicious dispositions, come to preferment and are espoused by a state;—nought they were while alone, but worse now when they have crept into the bed and bosom of the state: her roots were nought before; but now she is planted in rank mould, and will shoot forth her unsavoury branches and blossoms,—and when handmaids, kept in a servile estate because of their disposition and quality, get their masters ushered out, and they become heirs, at least possessors of the inheritance or trust. Ver. 33. shows how necessarily war and contention follow upon unnecessary provocations by word or deed, such as we have given many to England, though indeed they have given moe.† And lastly, chap. xxxi. 20, 26, 31. shows how word and work should go together, and men should be esteemed and praised according to their works and fruit of their hands.

* ["Having burst, as it were, its floodgates."—Ed.]

† [That is, more.—Ed.]

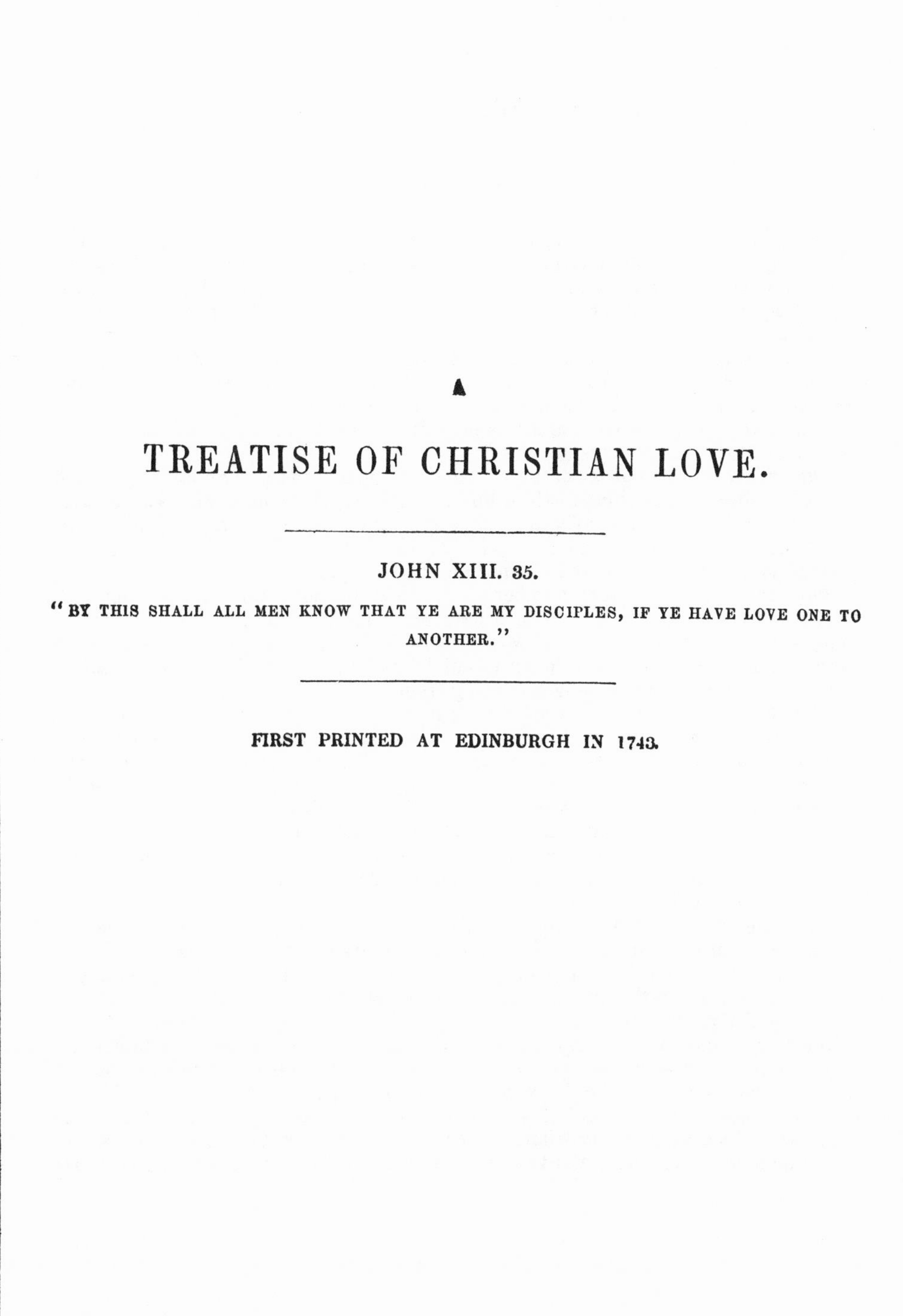

A

TREATISE OF CHRISTIAN LOVE.

JOHN XIII. 35.

"BY THIS SHALL ALL MEN KNOW THAT YE ARE MY DISCIPLES, IF YE HAVE LOVE ONE TO ANOTHER."

FIRST PRINTED AT EDINBURGH IN 1743.

TO THE READER.

This treatise concerning Christian Love, was composed by the pious and learned Mr. Hugh Binning, who was minister of the gospel at Govan, near to Glasgow. He was much celebrated and esteemed in this church, for several practical treatises, frequently printed for the benefit of the public ; but this is not inferior to any of them.

Though there have been many excellent discourses in late years on this divine subject, yet, considering that there never was a time wherein a treatise of this kind was more seasonable and necessary than the present, when the love of many, of too, too many, is waxed cold, and this holy fire is almost extinguished, this cannot be thought to be superfluous.

The author was a minister of a most pacific temper ; and this amiable grace and virtue did illustriously shine forth in him : and in this discourse, he breathes with a spirit of love in the most affecting and gaining manner ; so that, I dare say, that, though it be above ninety years since he composed it, it does not fall short of any performance of this kind that has since appeared in public.

This treatise, with a great number of excellent sermons, preached by this able minister of the gospel, many of which have never been printed, in a manuscript in folio, was found in the late Rev. Mr. Robert Wodrow, minister at Eastwood his library ; and all care has been taken to publish it faithfully, without any alteration, either by adding or diminishing any thing from it.

This divine subject of Christian love he lays a great stress upon ; he shows, that there is a greater moment and weight in Christian charity, than in the most part of those things for which some Christians bite and devour one another. It is the fundamental law of the gospel, to which all positive precepts and ordinances should stoop. Unity in judgment is very necessary for the well-being of Christians ; and Christ's last words persuade this, that unity in affection is most essential and fundamental. This is the badge that he left to his disciples : if we cast away this upon every different apprehension of mind, we disown our Master, and disclaim his token and badge.

Mr. Binning treats of this subject in a most sublime and pathetic strain ; he explains the nature of this grace, discourses of the excellent properties and blessed effects and fruits of it, in a ravishing and captivating manner. There is such a variety of beauties in this treatise, that they deserve to be noticed in this preface ; and particularly, his admirable commentary on the 13th chapter of the First Epistle to the Corinthians, wherein he outstrips all that went before him: and, in fine, he enforces the exercise of this grace with the most convincing arguments, and the most powerful motives. And now, not to detain the reader from the perusal, it is earnestly wished, that the end of the publication may, by the blessing of God, be obtained ; which is, that Christians in our days may be as the primitive ones,—of one mind and of one heart, and that they may love one another with a pure heart fervently.

A TREATISE

CONCERNING

CHRISTIAN LOVE.

CHAPTER I.

The beauty and excellency of this world consists, not only in the perfection and comeliness of each part in it, but especially in the wise and wonderful proportion and union of these several parts. It is not the lineaments and colours that make the image, or complete beauty; but the proportion and harmony of these, though different severally. And truly that is the wonder, that such repugnant natures, such different parts, and dissentient qualities, do conspire together in such an exact perfect unity and agreement, in which the wisdom of God doth most appear, by making all things in number, weight, and measure. His power appears in the making all the materials of nothing; but his wisdom is manifested in the ordering and disposing so dissonant natures into one well-agreeing and comely frame: so that this orderly disposition of all things into one fabric, is that harmonious melody of the creation, made up as it were of dissonant sounds, and that comely beauty of the world, resulting from such a proportion and wise combination of divers lines and colours. To go no further than the body of a man, what various elements are combined into a well-ordered being, the extreme qualities being so refracted and abated as they may join in friendship and society, and make up one sweet temperament!

Now, it is most reasonable to suppose, that, by the law of creation, there was no less order and unity to be among men, the chiefest of the works of God. And so it was indeed. As God had moulded the rest of the world into a beautiful frame, by the first stamp of his finger, so he did engrave upon the hearts of men such a principle, as might be a perpetual bond and tie to unite the sons of men together. This was nothing else but the law of love, the principal fundamental law of our creation, love to God, founded on that essential dependence and subordination to God; and love to man, grounded upon that communion and interest in one image of God. All the commandments of the first and second table are but so many branches of these trees, or streams of these fountains. Therefore our Saviour gives a complete abridgment of the law of nature and the moral law, 'Thou shalt love the Lord thy God with all thy heart, and with all thy soul, and with all thy mind; this is the first and great commandment. The second is like unto it, Thou shalt love thy neighbour as thyself,' Matth. xxii. 37, 38, 39. And therefore, as Paul says, 'Love is the fulfilling of the law,' Rom. xiii. 10. The universal debt we owe to God is love in the superlative degree, and the universal debt we owe one another is love in an inferior degree; yet of no lower kind than that of ourselves. 'Owe no man any thing, but to love one another' (Rom. xiii. 8.), and that collateral with himself, as Christ speaks. Unto these laws all other are subordinate, and one of them is subordinate to the other, but to nothing else. And so, as long as the love of God may go before, the love of man should follow; and whatever doth not untie the bond of divine affection, ought not to loose the knot of that love which is linked with it. When the uniting of souls together divides both from God, then indeed, and only then, must this knot be untied that the other may be kept fast.

But this beautiful and comely frame of man is marred. Sin hath cut in pieces that divine love that knit man to God; and the dissolving of this hath loosed that link of human society, love to our neighbour. And now all is rents, rags, and distractions, because self-love hath usurped the throne. The unity of the world of mankind is dissolved; one is distracted from another, following his own private inclinations and inordinate affection, which is the poison of enmity, and seed of all discord. If the love of God and of one another had kept the throne, there had been a co-ordination and co-working of all men in all their actions, for God's glory and the common good of man. But now self-love having enthroned itself, every man is for himself, and strives, by all means, to make a concurrence of all things to his own interest and designs. The first principles of love would have made all men's actions and courses flow into one ocean of divine glory and mutual edification; so that there could not have been any disturbance or jarring amongst them, all flowing into one common end. But self-love hath turned all the channels backward towards itself; and this is its wretched aim and endeavour, in which it wearies itself, and discomposes the world, to wind and turn in every thing, and to make, in the end, a general affluence of the streams into its own bosom. This is the seed of all division and confusion which is among men, while every man makes himself the centre, it cannot choose but all the lines and draughts of men's courses must thwart and cross each other.

Now, the Lord Jesus having redeemed lost man, and repaired his ruins, he makes up this breach, especially restores this fundamental ordinance of our creation, and unites men again to God and to one another. Therefore he is our peace, he hath removed the seeds of discord between God and man, and between man and man. And this is the subject of that divine epistle which the beloved apostle, full of that divine love, did pen, 'God is love, and in this was the love of God manifested, that God sent his only begotten Son into the world. And he that loveth is born of God, and knoweth God; but we love God, because he loved us first, and if God so loved us, we ought also to love one another,' 1 John iv. This is the very substance of the gospel, a doctrine of God's love to man, and of man's love due to God, and to them who are begotten of God; the one declared, the other commanded. So that much of the gospel is but a new edition or publication of that old ancient fundamental law of creation. This is that paradox which John delivers, 'I write no new commandment unto you, but an old commandment, which you had from the beginning: again, a new commandment I write unto you, which thing is true in him and you; because the darkness is past, and the true light now shineth,' 1 John ii. 7, 8. It is no new commandment, but that primitive command of love to God and men, which is the fulfilling of the law; and yet new it is, because there is a new obligation superadded. The bond of creation was great, but the tie of redemption is greater. God gave a being to man, that is enough. But God to become a miserable man for man, that is infinitely more. Fellow-creatures, that is sufficient for a bond of amity. But to be once fellow-captives, companions in misery, and then companions in mercy and blessedness, that is a new and stronger bond. Mutual love was the badge of reasonable creatures in innocency. But now Jesus Christ hath put a new stamp and signification on it; and made it the very differential character and token of his disciples, 'By this shall all men know that ye are my disciples, if ye love one another.' And therefore, when he is making his latter will, he gives this testamentary commandment to his children and heirs, 'A new commandment give I unto you, that ye love one another, as I have loved you, that ye also love one another.' New indeed! For though it be the same command, yet there was never such a motive, inducement, and persuasive to it as this. God so loved that he gave me, and I so loved that I gave myself, that is an addition more than all that was before, John xiii. 34, 35.

There is a special stamp of excellency put on this affection of love, that God delights to exhibit himself to us in such a notion. 'God is love,' and so holds out himself as the pattern of this. 'Be ye followers of God as dear children, and walk in love,' Eph. v. 1, 2. This is the great virtue and property which we should imitate our Father in. As God hath a general love to all the creatures, from whence the river of his goodness flows out through the earth, and in that, is like the sun conveying his light and benign influence, without partiality or restraint, to the whole world, but his special favour runs in a more narrow channel towards these whom he hath chosen in Christ; so in this a Christian should be like his Father, and there is nothing in which he resembles him more than in this, to walk in love towards all men, even our enemies. For in this he gives us a pattern, Matt. v. 44, 45. 'But I say unto you, Love your enemies, bless them that curse you, do good to them that hate you, and pray for them which despitefully use you, and persecute you; that ye may be the children of your Father which is in heaven: for he maketh his sun to rise on the evil and on the good, and sendeth rain on the just and on the unjust.' To do good to all, and to be ready to forgive all, is the glory of God; and certainly it is the glory of a child of God to be merciful as his Father is merciful, and good to all, and kind to the unthankful. And this is to be perfect as he is perfect. This perfection is charity and love to all. But the particular and special current of affection will run toward the household of faith, those who are of the same descent, and family, and love. This drawn into such a compass, is the badge and livery of his disciples. These two in a Christian are nothing but the reflex of the love of God, and streams issuing out from it. A Christian walking in love to all, blessing his enemies, praying for them, not reviling or cursing again, but blessing for cursing, and praying for reviling, forgiving all, and ready to give to the necessities of all, and more especially, uniting the force of his love and delight, to bestow it upon these who are the excellent ones, and delight of God, such a one is his Father's picture, so to speak. He is partaker of that divine nature, and royal spirit of love. Gal. vi. 10. 'As we have therefore opportunity, let us do good unto all men, especially unto them who are of the household of faith.' 1 Thess. iii. 12, 13. 'And the Lord make you to increase and abound in love one towards another, and towards all men, even as we do towards you: to the end he may establish your hearts unblameable in holiness before God, even our Father, at the coming of our Lord Jesus Christ, with all his saints.'

It is foretold by our Lord Jesus Christ, that in the last days the 'love of many shall wax cold,' Matt. xxiv. 12. And truly this is the symptom of a decaying and fading Christian and church. Love is the vital spirits of a Christian, which are the principles of all motion and lively operation. When there is a deliquium* in these, the soul is in a decay; it is so comprehensive an evil, as alone is sufficient to make an evil time. And besides, it is the argument and evidence, as well as the root and fountain, of abounding iniquity, because this is the epidemical disease of the present time, love cooled, and passion heated, whence proceed all the feverish distempers, contentions, wars and divisions, which have brought the church of God near to expiring. Therefore being mindful of that of the apostle, Heb. x. 24, I would think it pertinent to consider one another, and provoke again unto love and to good works. It was the great charge that Christ had against Ephesus, 'Thou hast left thy first love.' I shall therefore show the excellency and necessity of this grace, that so we may remember from whence we have fallen and repent, that we may do the first works, lest he come quickly and remove our candlestick, Rev. ii. 4, 5.

CHAPTER II.

1. Then, it might endear this Christian virtue unto us, that God propones himself as the pattern of it, that Christ holds out himself as the rare example of it for our imitation. It is what doth most endear God to creatures, and certainly it must likewise appreciate them one to another. 1 John iv. 7, 8 'Beloved, let us love one another: for love is of God; and every one that loveth, is born of God, and knoweth God. He that loveth not knoweth not God; for God is love.' Matt. v. 44, 45, 'But I say unto you, Love your enemies, bless them that curse you, do good to them that hate you, and pray for them which despitefully use you, and persecute you; that you may be the children of your Father which is in heaven: for he maketh his sun to rise on the evil and on the good, and sendeth rain on the just and on the unjust.' Eph. v. 1, 2, 'Be ye therefore followers of God, as dear children; and walk in love, as Christ also hath loved us, and hath given himself

* [That is, a deficiency.—Ed.]

for us, an offering and a sacrifice to God, for a sweet smelling savour.' John xiii. 35. 'By this shall all men know that ye are my disciples, if ye love one another.' Now the following of so rare an example, and imitating of so noble and high a pattern, doth exalt the soul into a royalty and dignity, that it dwells in God and God in it, 1 John iv. 16. This is the highest point of conformity with God, and the nearest resemblance of our Father. To be like him in wisdom, that wretched aim, did cast men as low as hell; but to aspire unto a likeness in love, lifts up the soul as high as heaven, even to a mutual inhabitation.

II. It should add an exceeding weight unto it, that we have not only so high a pattern, but so excellent a motive, 'God so loved;' and 'herein is love, not that we loved God, but that he loved us, and sent his Son to be the propitiation for our sins;' therefore, 'If God so loved us, we ought also to love one another,' 1 John iv. 9, 10, 11. 'Walk in love, as Christ also hath loved us, and hath given himself for us," Eph. v. 2. Here are the topics of the most vehement persuasion. There is no invention can afford so constraining a motive, God so loving us, sinful and miserable us, that he gave his only begotten Son, that we might live through him; and Christ so loving us, that he gave himself a sacrifice for sin. O then! who should live to himself, when Christ died for others? And who should not love, when 'God spared not his own Son, but delivered him up for us all?' 'God commendeth his love to us, in that while we were yet sinners, Christ died for us,' Rom. viii. 32. and v. 8. and xiv. 7, 8.

III. Join to this so earnest and pressing a command, even the latter will of him to whom we owe that we are, and are redeemed. That is the burden he lays on us. This is all the recompence he seeks for his unparalleled love, 'This is my command, that as I have loved you, ye love one another,' John xiii. 34. Your goodness cannot extend to me, therefore I assign all the beneficence and bounty ye owe to me, I give it over to these whom I have loved, and have not loved my life for them. Now, says he, whatsoever ye would count yourself obliged to do to me, if I were on the earth among you, do it to these poor ones whom I have left behind me, and this is all the testimony of gratitude I crave. Matth. xxv. 34 to 40. 'Then shall the King say unto them on his right hand, Come ye blessed of my Father, inherit the kingdom prepared for you from the foundation of the world. For I was an hungered, and ye gave me meat. I was thirsty and ye gave me drink. I was a stranger, and ye took me in: naked, and ye clothed me. I was sick, and ye visited me. I was in prison, and ye came unto me. Then shall the righteous answer him, saying, Lord, when saw we thee an hungered, and fed thee? or thirsty, and gave thee drink? When saw we thee a stranger, and took thee in? or naked, and clothed thee? Or when saw we thee sick, or in prison, and came unto thee? And the King shall answer, and say unto them, Verily I say unto you, Inasmuch as ye have done it unto one of the least of these my brethren, ye have done it unto me.' 'These ye have always with you, but me ye have not always.' It is strange how earnestly, how solicitously, how pungently he presses this exhortation, John xiii. 34, 35, 'A new commandment I give unto you, that ye love one another as I have loved you, that ye love one another. By this shall all men know that ye are my disciples, if ye have love one to another;' and xv. 12 and 17, 'This is my commandment, that ye love one another as I have loved you. These things I command you, that ye love one another;' and his apostles after him, 1 Thess. iv. 9, 'But as touching brotherly love, ye need not that I write unto you; for ye yourselves are taught of God to love one another.' Coloss. iii. 14, 'And above all these things, put on charity, which is the bond of perfectness.' 1 Pet. iv. 8, 'And above all things have fervent charity among yourselves: for charity shall cover the multitude of sins.' But above all, that beloved disciple, who being so intimate with Jesus Christ,—we may lawfully conceive he was inured to that affectionate frame by his converse with Christ,—has been most mindful of Christ's testamentary injunctions. He cannot speak three sentences but this is one of them. All which may convince us of this one thing, that there is a greater moment and weight of Christianity in charity than in the most part of these things for which Christians bite and devour one another. It is the fundamental law of the gospel, to which all positive precepts and ordinances should stoop. Unity in judgment is very needful for the well-being of Christians. But Christ's last words persuade this, that unity in affection is more essential and fundamental. This is the badge he left to his disciples. If we cast away this upon every different apprehension of mind, we disown our Master, and disclaim his token and badge.

IV. The apostle Paul puts a high note of commendation upon charity, when he styles it the bond of perfection. 'Above all things,' says he, 'put on charity, which is the bond of perfectness,' Col. iii. 14. I am sure it hath not such a high place in the minds and practice of Christians now, as it hath in the roll of the parts and members of the new man here set down. Here it is above all. With us it is below all, even below every apprehension of doubtful truths. An agreement in the conception of any poor petty controversial matter of the times, is made the badge of Christianity, and set in an eminent place above all which the apostle mentions, in tho 12th verse, 'bowels of mercies, kindness, gentleness, humbleness of mind, meekness, long-suffering :' Nay, charity itself is but a waiting handmaid to this mistress.

But let us consider the apostle's significant character he puts on it. It is a bond of perfection, as it were, a bundle of graces, and chain of virtues, even the very cream and flower of many graces combined. It is the sweet result of the united force of all graces. It is the very head and heart of the new man, which we are invited to put on, 'Above all put on charity.' All these fore-mentioned perfections are bound and tied together, by the girdle of charity and love, to the new man. When charity is born and brought forth, it may be styled *Gad*,* for a *troop* cometh, *chorus virtutum*,† "a troop or company of virtues" which it leads and commands. Charity hath a tender heart, for it hath 'bowels of mercies,'—such a compassionate and melting temper of spirit, that the misery or calamity, whether bodily or spiritual, of other men, makes an impression upon it. And therefore it is the Christian sympathy which affects itself with others' afflictions. If others be moved, it moves itself through comsort and sympathy. This is not only extended to bodily and outward infirmities, but, most of all, to infirmities of mind and heart, error, ignorance, darkness, falling and failing in tentation. We are made priests to God our Father, to have compassion on them who are ignorant and out of the way ; for that we ourselves are also compassed with infirmity, Rev. i. 6. and Heb. v. 2. Then, love hath a humble mind, 'humbleness of mind,' else it could not stoop and condescend to others of low degree ; and therefore Christ exhorts above all to lowliness. 'Learn of me, for I am meek and lowly in heart.' If a man be not lowly, to sit down below offences and infirmities, his love cannot rise above them. Self-love is the greatest enemy to true Christian love, and pride is the fountain of self-love, because it is impossible that, in this life, there should be an exact correspondence between the thoughts and ways of Christians. Therefore it is not possible to keep this bond of perfection unbroken, except there be a mutual condescendence. Self-love would have all conformed to it; and if that be not, there is the rent presently. But humbleness of mind can conform itself to all things, and this keeps the bond fast. Then charity, by the link of humility, hath meekness chained unto it, and kindness. Love is of a sweet complexion, meek and kind. Pride is the mother of passion, humbleness the mother of meekness. The inward affection is composed by meekness, and the outward actions adorned by gentleness and kindness. O that sweet composure of spirit! The heart of the wicked is as the troubled sea, no rest, no quiet in it, continual tempests raising continual waves of disquiet. An unmeek spirit is like a boiling pot, it troubles itself and annoys others. Then, at length, charity, by lowliness and meekness, is the most durable, enduring, long-suffering thing in the world ; 'with long-suffering, forbearing one another in love.' These are the only principles of patience and longanimity. Anger and passion is expressed in scripture under the name of haste ; and it is a sudden, furious, hasty thing, a rash, inconsiderate, impatient thing, more hasty than speedy. Now the special exercises and operations of these graces are in the 13th verse, 'forbearing one another, and forgiving one another,' according to Christ's example. And indeed these are so high and sublime works, as charity must yoke all the fore-mentioned graces, unite them all in one troop, for the accomplishing of them. And the great and sweet fruit of all this is comprehended in the 15th verse, 'The peace of

* [Gen. xxx. 11.—ED.] † [Vide Cic. de Offic. lib. iii. cap. 33.—ED.]

God rule in your hearts, to the which ye are called in one body.' Peace with God is not here meant, but the peace which God hath made up between men. All were shattered and rent asunder. The Lord hath by his Son Jesus Christ gathered so many into one body, the church; and by one Spirit quickens all. Now where love is predominant, there is a sweet peace and harmony between all the members of this one body. And this peace and tranquillity of affections rules and predominates over all these lusts, which are the mineries * of contentions, and strifes, and wars.

V. Add unto this another special mark of excellency that this apostle puts on charity, or Christian love: 'The end of the commandment is charity, out of a pure heart, of a good conscience, and of faith unfeigned,' 1 Tim. i. 5. If this were duly pondered, I do believe it would fill all hearts with astonishment, and faces with confusion, that they neglected the weightier matters of the law, and overstretched some other particular duties, to fill up the place of this, which is the end, the fulfilling of the law. It appears by this that charity is a cream of graces. It is the spirit and quintessence extracted out of these cardinal graces, unfeigned faith, a good conscience, a pure heart. It is true, the immediate end of the law, as it is now expounded unto us, is to drive us to believe in Jesus Christ, as it is expressed, Rom. x. 4. 'Christ is the end of the law for righteousness to every one that believeth.' But this believing in Christ is not the last end of it. Faith unfeigned in a Mediator is intentionally for this, to give the answer of a good conscience in the blood of Christ, and to purify the heart by the water of the Spirit, and so to bring about at length, by such a sweet compass, the righteousness of the law to be fulfilled by love in us, which by divine imputation is fulfilled to us. Now consider the context, and it shall yield much edification. Some teachers (1 Tim. i. 4.) exercised themselves and others in endless genealogies, which, though they contained some truth in them, yet they were perplexing, and brought no edification to souls. Curiosity might go round in such debates, and bewilder itself as in a labyrinth: but they did rather multiply disputes than bring true edification in the faith and love of God and men. Now, says he, they do wholly mistake the end of the law, of the doctrine of the scripture. The end and great purpose of it is love, which proceeds from faith in Christ, purifying the heart. This is the sum of all, to worship God in faith and purity, and to love one another. And whatsoever debates and questions do tend to the breach of this bond, and have no eminent and remarkable advantage in them, suppose they be conceived to be about matters of conscience, yet the entertaining and prosecuting them to the prejudice of this, is a manifest violence offered to the law of God, which is the rule of conscience. It is a perverting of scripture and conscience to a wrong end. I say then, that charity and Christian love should be the moderatrix of all our actions towards men. From thence they should proceed, and according to this rule be formed. I am persuaded if this rule were followed, the present differences in judgment of godly men, about such matters as minister mere questions, would soon be buried in the gulf of Christian affection.

VI. Now to complete the account of the eminence of this grace, take that remarkable chapter of Paul's, 1 Cor. xiii., where he institutes the comparison between it and other graces, and in the end pronounces on its behalf, 'the greatest of these is charity.' I wonder how we do please ourselves, as that we had attained already, when we do not so much as labour to be acquainted with this, in which the life of Christianity consists, without which faith is dead, our profession vain, our other duties and endeavours for the truth unacceptable to God and men. 'Yet I show you a more excellent way,' says he in the end of the former chapter. And this is the more excellent way, charity and love, more excellent than gifts, speaking with tongues, prophesying, &c. And is it not more excellent than the knowledge and acknowledgment of some present questionable matters, about governments, treaties, and such like, and far more than every punctilio of them? But he goes higher. Suppose a man could spend all his substance upon the maintenance of such an opinion, and give his life for the defence of it, though in itself it be commendable, yet if he want charity and love to his brethren, if he overstretch that point of con-

* [Or mines.—Ed.]

science to the breach of Christian affection, and duties flowing from it, it profits him nothing. Then certainly charity must rule our external actions, and have the predominant hand in the use of all gifts, in the venting of all opinions. Whatsoever knowledge and ability a man hath, charity must employ it, and use it. Without this, duties and graces make a noise, but they are shallow and empty within. Now he shows the sweet properties of it, and good effects of it, how universal an influence it hath on all things, but especially how necessary it is to keep the unity of the church.

Charity 'is kind' and 'suffereth long,' (μακροθυμεῖ,) it is longanimous or magnanimous and there is indeed no great, truly great, mind but is patient and long-suffering. It is a great weakness and pusillanimity to be soon angry. Such a spirit hath not the rule of itself, but is in bondage to its own lust; but 'he that ruleth his spirit is greater than he that taketh a city.' Now, it is much of this affection of love that overrules passion. There is a greatness and height in it, to love them that deserve not well of us, to be kind to the unfaithful, not to be easily provoked, and not soon disobliged. A fool's wrath is presently known. It is a folly and weakness of spirit, which love, much love cures and amends. It suffers much unkindness, and long suffers it, and yet can be kind.

'Charity envieth not.' Envy is the seed of all contention, and self-love brings it forth. When every man desires to be esteemed chief, and would have pre-eminence among others, their ways and courses must interfere one with another. It is this that makes discord. Every man would abate from another's estimation, that he may add to his own. None lives content with his own lot or station, and it is the aspiring beyond that, which puts all the wheels out of course. I believe this is the root of many contentions among Christians,—the apprehension of slighting, the conceit of disrespect, and such like, kindles the flame of difference, and heightens the least offence to an unpardonable injury. But charity envieth not where it may lie quietly low. Though it be under the feet of others, and beneath its own due place, yet it envieth not, it can lie contentedly so. Suppose it be slighted and despised, yet it takes it not highly, because it is lowly in mind.

'Charity is not puffed up, and vaunteth not itself.' If charity have gifts and graces beyond others, it restrains itself, with the bridle of modesty and humility, from vaunting or boasting, or any thing in its carriage that may savour of conceit. Pride is a self-admirer, and despises others, and to please itself it cares not to displease others. There is nothing so incomportable * in human or Christian society, so apt to alienate others' affections: for the more we take of our own affection to ourselves, we shall have the less from others. O these golden rules of Christian walking! Rom. xii. 10, 16, 'Be kindly affectioned one to another with brotherly love; in honour preferring one another. Mind not high things, but condescend to men of low estate. Be not wise in your own conceits.' O but that were a comely strife among Christians, each to prefer another in unfeigned love, and in lowliness of mind, each to esteem another better than himself! Philip. ii. 3. 'Knowledge puffeth up,' says this apostle (1 Cor. viii. 1.) 'but charity edifieth.' It is but a swelling and tumour of the mind, but love is solid piety and real religion.

Then charity doth nothing unseemly, 'behaveth not itself unseemly,' 1 Cor. xiii. 5. Vanity and swelling of mind will certainly break forth into some unseemly carriage, as vain estimation, and such like; but charity keeps a sweet decorum in all its carriage, so as not to provoke and irritate others, nor yet to expose itself to contempt or mockery. Or the word may be taken thus, it is not fastidious. It accounts not itself disgraced and abused, to condescend to men of low estate. It can with its Master bow down to wash a disciple's feet, and not think it unseemly. Whatsoever it submit to in doing or suffering, it is not ashamed of it, as that it were not suitable and comely.

'Charity seeketh not her own things.' Self-denial and true love are inseparable. Self-love makes a monopoly of all things to its own interest; and this is most opposite to Christian affection and communion, which puts all in one bank. If every one of the members should seek its own things, and not the good of the whole body,

* [Or, unsuitable.—Ed.]

what a miserable distemper would it cause in the body? We are called into one body in Christ, and therefore we should look not on our own things only, but every man also on the things of others, Philip. ii. 4. There is a public interest of saints' mutual edification in faith and love, which charity will prefer to its own private interest. Addictedness to our own apprehension, and too much self-overweening and self-pleasing, is the grand enemy of that place to which we are called into one body. Since one Spirit informs and enlivens all the members, what a monstrosity is it for one member to seek its own things, and attend to its own private interest only, as if it were a distinct body!

Charity 'is not easily provoked.' This is the straight and solid firmness of it, that it is not soon moved with external impressions. It is long-suffering, it suffers long and much. It will not be shaken by violent and weighty pressures of injuries; where there is much provocation given, yet it is not provoked. Now to complete it, it is not easily provoked at light offences. It is strange how little a spark of injuries puts all in a flame, because our spirits are as gunpowder,—so capable of combustion through corruption. How ridiculous, for the most part, are the causes of our wrath! For light things we are heavily moved, and for ridiculous things sadly, even as children who fall out among themselves for toys and trifles, or as beasts that are provoked upon the very show of a colour, as red or such like. We would save ourselves much labour, if we could judge before we suffer ourselves to be provoked. But now we follow the first appearance of wrong; and being once moved from without, we continue our commotion within, lest we should seem to be angry without a cause. But charity hath a more solid foundation. It dwells in God, for God is love; and so is truly great, truly high, and looks down with a steadfast countenance upon these lower things. The upper world is continually calm and serene. No clouds, no tempests there, no winds, nothing to disturb the harmonious and uniform motion: but it is this lower world that is troubled and tossed with tempests, and obscured with clouds. So a soul dwelling in God by love, is exalted above the cloudy region. He is calm, quiet, serene, and is not disturbed or interrupted in his motion of love to God or men.

Charity 'thinketh no evil.' Charity is apt to take all things in the best sense. If a thing may be subject to diverse acceptations, it can put the best construction on it. It is so benign and good in its own nature, that it is not inclinable to suspect others. It desires to condemn no man, but would gladly, as far as reason and conscience will permit, absolve every man. It is so far from desire of revenge, that it is not provoked or troubled with an injury. For that were nothing else but to wrong itself because others have wronged it already; and it is so far from wronging others, that it will not willingly so much as think evil of them. Yet if need require, charity can execute justice, and inflict chastisement, not out of desire of another's misery, but out of love and compassion to mankind. *Charitas non punit quia peccatum est, sed ne peccaretur,** it looks more to prevention of future sin, than to revenge of a bypast fault; and can do all without any discomposure of spirit, as a physician cuts a vein without anger. *Quis enim cui medetur irascitur?* "Who is angry at his own patient?"

Charity 'rejoiceth not in iniquity.' Charity is not defiled in itself, though it condescend to all. Though it can love and wish well to evil men, yet it rejoiceth not in iniquity. It is like the sun's light that shines on a dunghill, and is not defiled, receives no tincture from it. Some base and wicked spirits make a sport to do mischief themselves, and take pleasure in others that do it. But charity rejoices in no iniquity or injustice, though it were done to its own enemy. It cannot take pleasure in the unjust sufferings of any who hate it, because it hath no enemy but sin and iniquity, and hates nothing else with a perfect hatred. Therefore whatever advantage should redound to itself by other men's iniquities, it cannot rejoice, that iniquity, its capital enemy, should reign and prevail. But it 'rejoiceth in the truth.' The advancement and progress of others in the way of truth and holiness is its pleasure. Though that should eclipse its own glory, yet it looks not on it with

* ["Charity does not inflict punishment because an offence has been committed, but lest an offence should be committed."—Ed.]

an evil eye. If it can find out any good in them that are enemies to it, it is not grieved to find it and know it, but can rejoice at any thing which may give ground of good construction of them. There is nothing more beautiful in its eyes than to see every one get their own due, though it alone should come behind.

Charity 'beareth all things.' By nature we are undaunted heifers, cannot bear any thing patiently. But charity is accustomed to the yoke,—to the yoke of reproaches and injuries from others, to a burden of other men's infirmities and failings. We would all be borne upon others' shoulders, but we cannot put our own shoulders under other men's burden, according to that royal law of Christ, Rom. xv. 1. 'We that are strong ought to bear the infirmities of the weak, and not to please ourselves:' and Gal. vi. 2. 'Bear ye one another's burdens, and so fulfil the law of Christ;' that is the law of love, no question.

Charity 'believeth all things.' Our nature is malignant and wicked, and therefore most suspicious and jealous, and apt to take all in the worst part. But charity hath much candour and humanity in it, and can believe well of every man, and believe all things as far as truth will permit. It knows that grace can be beside a man's sins. It knows that itself is subject to such like infirmities. Therefore it is not a rigid and censorious judger; it allows as much latitude to others as it would desire of others. It is true it is not blind and ignorant. It is judicious, and hath eyes that can discern between colours. *Credit omnia credenda, sperat omnia speranda.* "It believes all things that are believable, and hopes all things that are hopeful." If love have not sufficient evidences, yet she believes if there be some probabilities to the contrary, as well as for it. The weight of charity inclines to the better part, and so casts the balance of hope and persuasion; yet being sometimes deceived, she hath reason to be watchful and wise, for 'the simple believeth every word.' If charity cannot have ground of believing any good, yet it hopes still. *Qui non est hodie, cras magis aptus erit,** says charity, and therefore it is patient and gentle, waiting on all, if peradventure God may 'give them repentance to the acknowledging of the truth,' 2 Tim. ii. 25. Charity would account it both atheism and blasphemy, to say such a man cannot, will not find mercy. But to pronounce of such as have been often approven in the conscience of all, and sealed into many hearts, that they will never find mercy, that they have no grace, because of some failings in practice and differences from us, it were not in sobriety but madness. It is certainly love and indulgence to ourselves, that make us aggravate other men's faults to such a height. Self-love looks on other men's failings through a multiplying or magnifying glass; but she puts her own faults behind her back. *Non videt quod in mantica quæ a tergo est.*† Therefore she can suffer much in herself but nothing in others; and certainly much self-forbearance and indulgence can spare little for others. But charity is just contrary. She is most rigid on her own behalf, will not pardon herself easily, knows no revenge but what is spoken of 2 Cor. vii. 11, self-revenge, and hath no indignation but against herself. Thus she can spare much candour and forbearance for others, and hath little or nothing of indignation left behind to consume on others.

'Charity never faileth.' This is the last note of commendation. Things have their excellency from their use and from their continuance; both are here. Nothing so useful, no such friend of human or Christian society as charity, the advantage of it reacheth all things. And then, it is most permanent and durable. When all shall go, it shall remain. When ordinances, and knowledge attained by means and ordinances, shall evanish, charity shall abide, and then receive its con-

* ["He that is not inclined to-day will be more inclined to-morrow." This is reversing the saying of the poet:—

Qui non est hodie, cras *minus* aptus erit.
Ovid. Remed. Amor. ver. 94.—Ed.]

† ["She does not see what is in the bag behind her."

Sed non videmus manticæ quod in tergo est.
Catul. Carm. xxii. ver. 21.

There is an allusion here to one of the fables of Æsop. Jupiter, says Æsop, placed two bags upon men. The one, which contained their own faults, he put upon their back; and the other, which was filled with the faults of others, he suspended from their neck, upon their breast. In this way, we cannot see our own misdeeds, but, perceiving those of others, we censure them freely. Phæd. Fab. Æsop, lib. iv. fab. 10.—Ed.]

summation. Faith of things inevident and obscure shall be drowned in the vision of seeing God's face clearly. Hope of things to come shall be exhausted in the possession and fruition of them. But love only remains in its own nature and notion, only it is perfected by the addition of so many degrees as may suit that blessed estate. Therefore, methinks it should be the study of all saints who believe immortality, and hope for eternal life, to put on that garment of charity, which is the livery of all the inhabitants above. We might have heaven upon earth as far as is possible, if we dwelt in love, and love dwelt in and possessed our hearts. What an unsuitable thing might a believer think it, to hate him in this world whom he must love eternally; and to contend and strive with these, even for matters of small moment, with bitterness and rigidity, with whom he shall have an eternal, uninterrupted unity and fellowship? Should we not be assaying here how that glorious garment suits us? And truly there is nothing makes a man so heaven-like or God-like as this, much love and charity.

Now there is one consideration might persuade us the more unto it, that here we know but darkly and in part, and therefore our knowledge, at best, is but obscure and inevident, ofttimes subject to many mistakes and misapprehensions of truth, according as *mediums* represent them. And therefore there must be some latitude of love allowed one to another in this state of imperfection, else it is impossible to keep unity, and we must conflict often with our own shadows, and bite and devour one another for some deceiving appearances. The imperfection and obscurity of knowledge should make all men jealous of themselves, especially in matters of a doubtful nature, and not so clearly determined by scripture. Because our knowledge is weak, shall our love be so? Nay, rather let charity grow stronger, and aspire unto perfection, because knowledge is imperfect. What is wanting in knowledge, let us make up in affection, and let the gap of difference in judgment be swallowed up with the bowels of mercies, and love, and humbleness of mind. And then we shall have hid our infirmity of understanding as much as may be. Thus we may go hand in hand together to our Father's house, where, at length, we must be together.

CHAPTER III.

I MAY briefly reduce the chief persuading motive to this so needful and so much desiderated grace into some three or four heads. All things within and without persuade to it, but especially the right consideration of the love of God in Christ, the wise and the impartial reflection on ourselves, the consideration of our brethren whom we are commanded to love, and the thorough inspection into the nature and use of the grace itself.

In consideration of the FIRST, a soul might argue itself into a complacency with it, and thus persuade itself, 'He that loveth not, knoweth not God; for God is love,' 1 John iv. 8. And since he that hath known and believed the love that God hath to us, must certainly dwell in love, since these two have such a strait indissoluble connexion, then, as I would not declare to all my atheism and my ignorance of God, I will study to love my brethren. And that I may love them, I will give myself to the search of God's love, which is the place, *locus inventionis,** whence I may find out the strongest and most effectual *medium** to persuade my mind, and to constrain my heart to Christian affection.

First, then, when I consider that so glorious and great a Majesty, so high and holy an One, self-sufficient and all-sufficient, who needs not go abroad to seek de-

* [These are terms (locus inventionis, *the place or topic of invention;* and medium, *the argument or middle term of a syllogism*) which, belonging to the dialectic art, were employed by the schoolmen. All the arts and sciences have certain general subjects connected with them which presuppose particular facts, axioms, and rules. These general subjects, being used in the *invention* of arguments, were called topics or common places. "They were so called by Aristotle, as if they were the seats from which arguments were to be brought forth." (Sic appellatæ ab Aristotele sunt hæ quasi sedes, e quibus argumenta promuntur.) Cic. Top. cap. ii.—ED.]

light, because all happiness and delight is enclosed within his own bosom, can yet love a creature, yea and be reconciled to so sinful a creature, which he might crush as easily as speak a word; that he can place his delight on so unworthy and base an object, O! how much more should I, a poor wretched creature, love my fellow-creature, ofttimes better than myself, and, for the most part, not much worse? There is an infinite distance and disproportion betwixt God and man; yet he came over all that to love man. What difficulty should I have then to place my affection on my equal at worst, and often better? There cannot be any proportionable distance betwixt the highest and lowest, between the richest and poorest, between the most wise and the most ignorant, between the most gracious and the most ungodly, as there is between the infinite God and a finite angel. Should then the mutual infirmities and failings of Christians, be an insuperable and impassable gulf, as between heaven and hell, that none can pass over by a bridge of love to either? 'If God so loved us,' should not we love one another? 1 John iv. 11. And besides, when I consider that God hath not only loved me, but my brethren who were worthy of hatred, with an everlasting love, and passed over all that was in them, and hath spread his skirt over their nakedness, and made it a time of love, which was a time of loathing, how can I withhold my affection where God hath bestowed his? Are they not infinitely more unworthy of his than mine? Since infinite wrongs hath not changed his, shall poor, petty, and light offences hinder mine? That my love concenter with God's on the same persons, is it not enough?

Next, That Jesus Christ, the only begotten of the Father, full of grace and truth, who was the Father's delight from eternity, and in whom he delighted, yet, notwithstanding, could rejoice in the habitable places of the earth, and so love poor wretched men, yet enemies, that he gave himself for them; that God so loved that he gave his Son, and Christ so loved that he gave himself a sacrifice for sin, both for me and others, O! who should not, or will not be constrained, in beholding this mirror of incomparable and spotless love, to love others? (1 John iv. 9, 10, 11. 'In this was manifested the love of God towards us, because that God sent his only begotten Son into the world, that we might live through him. Herein is love, not that we loved God, but that he loved us, and sent his Son to be the propitiation for our sins. Beloved, if God so loved us, we ought also to love one another.' Eph. v. 2. 'And walk in love, as Christ also hath loved us, and hath given himself for us, an offering and a sacrifice to God for a sweet smelling savour,') especially when he seems to require no other thing, and imposes no more grievous command upon us for recompence of all his labour of love. John xiii. 34, 35. 'A new commandment I give unto you, That ye love one another; as I have loved you, that ye also love one another. By this shall all men know that ye are my disciples, if ye have love one to another.' If all that was in me did not alienate his love from me, how should any thing in others estrange our love to them? If God be so kind to his enemies, and Christ so loving that he gives his life for his enemies to make them friends, what should we do to our enemies, what to our friends? This one example may make all created love to blush and be ashamed. How narrow, how limited, how selfish is it!

Thirdly, If God hath forgiven me so many grievous offences, if he hath pardoned so heinous and innumerable injuries, that amount to a kind of infiniteness in number and quality, O how much more am I bound to forgive my brethren a few light and trivial offences? Col. iii. 13. 'Forbearing one another, and forgiving one another, if any man have a quarrel against any; even as Christ forgave you, so also do ye.' Eph. iv. 32. 'And be ye kind one to another, tender-hearted, forgiving one another, even as God for Christ's sake hath forgiven you.' With what face can I pray, 'Lord, forgive me my sins,' when I may meet with such a retortion, thou canst not forgive thy brethren's sins, infinitely less both in number and degree? Matth. vi. 15. 'But if ye forgive not men their trespasses, neither will your heavenly Father forgive your trespasses.' What unparalleled ingratitude were it, what monstrous wickedness, that after he hath forgiven all our debt, because we desired him, yet we should not have compassion on our fellow-servants even as he had pity on us! O! what a dreadful sound will that be in the ears of many Christians, 'O thou wicked servant, I forgave thee all thy debt, because thou desiredst me! Shouldest not thou also have had compassion on thy fellow-servants, even as I had pity on thee? And his lord was wroth, and delivered him to the tormentors, till he should pay all that was due unto him. So likewise shall my heavenly Father do also unto you, if ye from your hearts forgive not every one his brother their trespasses,' Matth. xviii. 32, 33, 34, 35. When we cannot dispense with one penny, how should he dispense with his talents? And when we cannot pardon ten, how should he forgive ten thousand? When he hath forgiven my brother all his iniquity, may not I pardon one? Shall I impute that which God will not impute, or discover that which God hath covered? How should I expect he should be merciful to me, when I cannot shew mercy to my brother? Psal. xviii. 25. 'With the merciful thou wilt show thyself merciful.' Shall I, for one or few offences, hate, bite, and devour him for whom Christ died, and loved not his life to save him? Rom. xiv. 15. and 1 Cor. viii. 11.

In the next place. If a Christian do but take an impartial view of himself, he cannot but thus reason himself to a meek, composed, and affectionate temper towards other brethren. What is it in another that offends me, when if I do search within, I will not either find the same, or worse, or as evil in myself? Is there a mote in my brother's eye? Perhaps there may be a beam in my own; and why then should I look to the mote that is in my brother's eye? Matth. vii. 3. When I look inwardly, I find a desperately wicked heart, which lodges all that iniquity I beheld in others. And if I be not so sensible of it, it is because it is also deceitful above all things, and would flatter me in mine own eyes, Jer. xvii. 9. If my brother offend me in some things, how do these evanish out of sight in the view of my own guiltiness before God, and of the abominations of my own heart, known to his holiness and to my conscience? Sure I cannot see so much evil in my brother as I find in myself. I see but his outside. But I know my own heart; and whenever I retire within this, I find the sea of corruption so great, that I wonder not at the streams which break forth in others. But all my wonder is that God hath set bounds to it in me or in any. Whenever I find my spirit rising against the infirmities of others, and my mind swelling over them, I repress myself with this thought, 'I myself also am a man,' as Peter said to Cornelius when he would have worshipped him. As he restrained another's idolizing of him, I may cure my own self-idolizing heart. Is it any thing strange that weak men fail, and sinful men fall? Is not all flesh grass, and all the perfection and goodliness of it as the flower of the field? Isa. xl. 6. Is not every man at his best estate altogether vanity? Psal. xxxix. 5. Is not man's breath in his nostrils? Isa. ii. 22. And am not I myself a man? Therefore I will not be high-minded but fear, Rom. xi. 20. I will not be moved to indignation, but provoked to compassion, knowing that I myself am compassed with infirmities, Heb. v. 2.

Secondly, As a man may persuade himself to charity by the examination of his own heart and ways; so he may enforce upon his spirit a meek and compassionate stamp, by the consideration of his own frailty, what he may fall into. This is the Apostle's rule, Gal. vi. 1. 'Brethren, if a man be overtaken in a fault, ye that are spiritual,' and pretend to it, 'restore such an one in the spirit of meekness.' Do not please yourselves with a false notion of zeal, thinking to cover your impertinent rigidity by it. Do as you would do if your own arm were disjointed. Set it in, restore it tenderly and meekly, considering yourselves that ye also may be tempted. Some are more given to reproaching and insulting than mindful of restoring. Therefore their reproofs are not tempered with oil that they may not break the head, but mixed with gall and vinegar to set on edge the teeth. But whenever thou lookest upon the infirmities of others, then consider thyself first, before you pronounce sentence on them, and thou shalt be constrained to bestow that charity to others which thou hast need of thyself. *Veniam petimusque damusque vicissim.** If a man have need of charity from his brother, let him not be hard in giving it. If he know his own weakness and frailty, sure he may suppose such a thing may likely fall out that he may be tempted and succumb in it. For there needs nothing for the bringing forth of sin in any but occasion and temptation, as the bringing of

* [" We grant and solicit in our turn this indulgence." Hor. De Art. poet, ver. 11.—Ed.]

fire near gunpowder. And truly he who had no allowance of love to give to an infirm and weak brother, he will be in *mala fide*, in an evil capacity, to seek what he would not give. Now the fountain of uncharitable and harsh dealing is imported in the 3d verse, 'If any man thinks himself to be something when he is nothing, he deceives himself.' Since all mortal men are nothing, vanity, altogether vanity, and less than vanity, he that would seem something, and seems so to himself, deludes himself. Hence is our insulting fierceness, hence our supercilious rigour. Every man apprehends some excellency in himself beyond another. Take away pride, and charity shall enter, and modesty shall be its companion. But now we mock ourselves, and deceive ourselves, by building the weight of our pretended zeal upon such a vain and rotten foundation, as a gross practical fundamental lie of self-conceit of nothing. Now the Apostle furnishes us with an excellent remedy against this in the 4th verse, 'Let a man prove himself and his own work, and then he shall have rejoicing in himself alone, and not in another:'—a word worthy to be fastened by the Master of assemblies in the heart of all Christians! And indeed this nail driven in would drive out all conceit. Hence is our ruin, that we compare ourselves among ourselves, and in so doing we are not wise, 2 Cor. x. 12. For we know not our own true value. Only we raise the price according to the market, so to speak. We measure ourselves by another man's measure, and build up our estimation upon the disesteem of others; and how much others displease, so much we please ourselves. But, says the Apostle, let every man prove his own work, search his own conscience, compare himself to the perfect rule; and then, if he find all well, he may indeed glory of himself. But that which thou hast by comparison with others is not thine own. Thou must come down from all such advantages of ground, if thou would have thy just measure. And indeed, if thou prove thyself and thy work after this manner, thou wilt be the first to reprove thyself, thou shalt have that glory due unto thee, that is none at all. For every man shall bear his own burden, when he appears before the judgment-seat of God. There is no place for such imaginations and comparisons in the Lord's judgment.

Thirdly, When a Christian looks within his own heart, he finds an inclination and desire to have the love of others, even though his conscience witness that he deserves it not. He finds an approbation of that good and righteous command of God, that others should love him. Now hence he may persuade himself:—Is it so sweet and pleasant to me to be loved of others, even though I am conscious that I have wronged them? Hath it such a beauty in my eye, while I am the object of it? Why then should it be a hard and grievous burden to me to love others, though they have wronged me, and deserve it no more than I did? Why hath it not the same amiable aspect, when my brother is the object of it? Certainly no reason for it, but because I am yet carnal, and have not that fundamental law of nature yet distinctly written again upon my heart, 'What ye would that others should do to you, do it to them,' Matth. vii. 12. If I be convinced that there is any equity and beauty in that command, which charges others to love me, forgive me, and forbear me, and restore me in meekness, why should it be a grievous command that I should pay that debt of love and tenderness to others? 1 John v. 3. 'For this is the love of God, that we keep his commandments: and his commandments are not grievous.'

In the third place. Consider to whom this affection should be extended. More generally to all men, as fellow-creatures; but particularly and especially to all who are begotten of God, as fellow-Christians. 'And this commandment have we from him, that he who loveth God love his brother also. Whosoever believeth that Jesus is the Christ is born of God: and every one that loveth him that begat, loveth him also that is begotten of him,' 1 John iv. 21, and chap. v. 1. 'As we have therefore opportunity, let us do good unto all men, especially unto them who are of the household of faith,' Gal. vi. 10. 'O my soul, thou hast said unto the Lord, Thou art my Lord; my goodness extendeth not to thee: but unto the saints that are in the earth, and to the excellent in whom is all my delight,' Psal. xvi. 2, 3. And this consideration the Holy Ghost suggests to make us maintain love and unity. Love towards these runs in a purer channel:—'Ye have purified your souls in obeying the truth through the Spirit unto the unfeigned love of the brethren, see that ye love one another with a pure heart fervently: being born again, not of corruptible seed, but of incorruptible, by the word of God, which liveth and abideth for ever,' 1 Pet. i. 22, 23. We are begotten of one Father, and that by a divine birth; we have such a high descent and royal generation! There are so many other bonds of unity between us, it is absurd that this one more should not join all. 'One Lord, one faith, one baptism, one body, one spirit, called to one hope, one God and Father of all,' Eph. iv. 2—6. All these being one, it is strange if we be not one in love. If so many relations beget not a strong and warm affection, we are worse than infidels, as the apostle speaks, 1 Tim. v. 8. If a man care not for his own house, his worldly interests, 'he is worse than an infidel;' for he has a natural affection. Sure then this more excellent nature, a divine nature we are partakers of, cannot want affection suitable to its nature. Christianity is a fraternity, a brotherhood, that should overpower all relations, bring down him of high degree, and exalt him of low degree: it should level all ranks, in this one respect, unto the rule of charity and love. In Christ there is neither Jew nor Gentile. There all differences of tongues and nations are drowned in this interest of Christ, Col. iii. 11. 'Thou hast hid these things from the wise and prudent, and revealed them unto babes,' Luke x. 21. And 'God hath chosen the weak and foolish to confound the mighty and wise,' 1 Cor. i. 27. Behold all these outward privileges buried in the depths and riches of God's grace and mercy. Are we not all called to one high calling? Our common station is to war under Christ's banner against sin and Satan. Why then do we leave our station, forget our callings, and neglect that employment which concerns us all; and fall at odds with our fellow-soldiers, and bite and devour one another? Doth not this give advantage to our common enemies? While we consume the edge of our zeal and strength of our spirits one upon another, they must needs be blunted and weakened towards our deadly enemies. If our brother be represented unto us under the covering of many faults, failings, and obstinacy in his errors, or such like; if we can behold nothing but spots on his outside, while we judge after some outward appearance, then, I say, we ought to consider him again under another notion and relation, as he stands in Christ's account, as he is radically and virtually of that seed, which hath more real worth in it than all worldly privileges and dignities. Consider him as he once shall be, when mortality shall be put off. Learn to strip him naked of all infirmities in thy consideration, and imagine him to be clothed with immortality, and glory; and think how thou wouldest then love him. If either thou unclothe him of his infirmities, and consider him as vested now with the robe of Christ's righteousness, and all glorious within, or adorned with immortality and incorruption a little hence; or else, if thou clothe thyself with such infirmities as thou seest in him, and consider that thou art not less subject to failing, and compassed with infirmities; then thou shalt put on, and keep on, that bond of perfection, charity.

Lastly. Let us consider the excellent nature of charity, and how it is interested in, and interwoven with all the royal and divine gifts and privileges of a Christian. All of them are not ashamed of kindred and cognation with charity. Is not the calling and profession of a Christian honourable? Sure to any believing soul it is above a monarchy; for it includes an anointing both to a royal and priestly office, and carries a title to a kingdom incorruptible and undefiled. Well then, charity is the symbol and badge of this profession, John xiii. 35. 'By this shall all men know that ye are my disciples, if ye have love one to another.' Then, what is comparable to communion with God, and dwelling in him? Shall God indeed dwell with men, said Solomon? That exalts the soul to a royalty, and elevates it above mortality. *Quam contempta res est homo si supra humana se non exerat!* "How base and contemptible a thing is man, except he lift up his head above human things to heavenly and divine!" And then is the soul truly magnified while it is ascending to its own element, a divine nature. What more gracious than this, for a soul to dwell in God? And what more glorious than this, God to dwell in the soul? *Charitas te domum Domini facit, et Dominum domum tibi. Felix artifex charitas quæ conditori suo domum fabricare potest!* "Love makes the soul a house for the Lord, and makes the Lord a house to the soul. Happy artificer that can build a house for its master!" Love bringeth him, who is the chief among ten thousand, into the chambers of the heart. It lays him all night between its breasts; and is still emptying itself of all superfluity of naughtiness, and purging out all vanity and filthiness, that there may be more room for his Majesty. And then love dwells in God, in his love and grace, in his goodness and greatness. The secret of his presence it delights in. Now this mutual inhabitation, in which it is hard to say whether the Majesty of God does most descend, or the soul most ascend, whether he be more humbled or it exalted; this brotherly love, I say, is the evidence and assurance of it: 'If we love one another, God dwells in us, and his love is perfected in us. God is love, and he that dwelleth in love dwelleth in God, and God in him,' 1 John iv. 12, 16. For the love of the image of God in his children, is indeed the love of God whose image it is, and then is the love of God perfected, when it reacheth and extends from God to all that is God's, to all that hath interest in God: his commandments, (1 John v. 3. 'This is the love of God, that we keep his commandments, and his commandments are not grievous.' 1 John iv. 21. 'And this commandment have we from him, that he who loveth God love his brother also,') his children, (1 John v. 1. 'Whosoever believeth that Jesus is the Christ is born of God, and every one that loveth him that begat, loveth him that is begotten of him,') his creatures, (Mal. ii. 10. 'Hath not one God created us, why do we deal treacherously every man against his brother?') The love of God being the formal, the special motive of love to our brethren, it elevates the nature of it, and makes it divine love. He that hath true Christian love, doth not only love and compassionate his brother, either because of its own inclination towards him, or his misery and necessity, or his goodness and excellency. These motives and grounds do not transcend mere morality, and so cannot beget a love which is the symptom of Christianity. If there be no other motives than these, we do not love so much for God as for ourselves; for compassion interesting itself with another man's misery, finds a kind of relief in relieving it. Therefore the will and good pleasure of God must be the rule of this motion, and the love of God must begin in it and continue it. And truly charity is nothing else but divine love in a state of condescent,* so to speak, or the love of a soul to God manifested in the flesh. It is that love moving in a circle from God towards his creatures, and unto God again, as his love to the creatures begins in himself and ends in himself, 1 John iii. 17. Is it not a high thing to know God aright? 'This is life eternal to know thee, the only true God, and Jesus Christ whom thou hast sent,' John xvii. 3. That is a high note of excellency put on it, this makes the face of the soul to shine; now brotherly love evinceth this, that we know God, 'Beloved, let us love one another; for love is of God; and every one that loveth is born of God, and knoweth God. He that loveth not, knoweth not God; for God is love,' 1 John iv. 7, 8. Love is real light, light and life, light and heat both. 'When your fathers did execute judgment, and relieve the oppressed, &c. was not this to know me? saith the Lord,' Jer. xxii. 15, 16. The practice of the most common things, out of the love of God, and respect to his commands, is more real and true religion than the most profound and abstracted speculations of knowledge. Then only is God known, when knowledge stamps the heart with fear and reverence of his Majesty and love to his name, because then he is only known as he is a true and living God.

Love is real light and life. Is it not 'a pleasant thing for the eye to behold the sun?' Light is sweet, and life is precious. These are two of the rarest jewels given to men. 'He that saith he is in the light, and hateth his brother, is in darkness even until now, and knoweth not whither he goeth; because darkness hath blinded his eyes: but he that loveth his brother abideth in the light, and there is none occasion of stumbling in him,' 1 John ii. 9—11. 'We know that we have passed from death unto life, because we love the brethren: he that loveth not his brother, abideth in death,' 1 John iii. 14. The light of Jesus Christ cannot shine into the heart, but it begets† love, even as intense light begets heat: and where this impression is not made on the heart, it is an evidence that the beams of that Sun of righteousness have not pierced it. O how suitable is it for a child of light to walk

* [Or condescendence.—Ed.]

† [Or, without its begetting love.—Ed.]

in love! And wherefore is it made day-light to the soul, but that it may rise up and go forth to labour, and exercise itself in the works of the day, duties of love to God and men? Now in such a soul there is no cause of stumbling, no scandal, no offence in its way to fall over. When the light and knowledge of Christ possesses the heart in love, there is no stumbling-block of transgression in its way. It doth not fall and stumble at the commandments of righteousness and mercy as grievous, 'therefore love is the fulfilling of the law,' Rom. xiii. 10. And so the way of charity is the most easy, plain, expedient, and safe way. In this way there is light shining all alongst it, and there is no stumbling-block in it. For the love of God and of our brethren hath polished and made it all plain, hath "taken away the asperities and tumours of our affections and lusts." *Complanavit affectus.* 'Great peace have all they that love thy law, and nothing shall offend them.' Love makes an equable and constant motion, it moves swiftly and sweetly. It can loose many knots without difficulty, which other more violent principles cannot cut; it can melt away mountains before it, which cannot be hurled away. Albeit there be many stumbling-blocks without in the world, yet there is none in charity, or in a charitable soul. None can enter into that soul to hinder it to possess itself in meekness and patience. Nothing can discompose it within, or hinder it to live peaceably with others. Though all men's hands be against it, yet charity is against none. It defends itself with innocence and patience. On the other hand, 'He that hateth his brother is in darkness even till now.' For if Christ's light had entered, then the love of Christ had come with it, and that is the law of love and charity. If Jesus Christ had come into the soul, he had restored the ancient commandment of love, and made it new again. As much of the want of love and charity, so much of the old ignorance and darkness remains. Whatsoever a man may fancy of himself that he is in the light, that he is so much advanced in the light, yet certainly this is a stronger evidence of remaining darkness; for it is a work of the darkest darkness, and murdering affection, suitable only for the night of darkness. And such a man knows not whither he goes, and must needs incur and fall upon many stumbling-blocks within and without. It is want of love and charity that blinds the mind and darkens the heart, that it cannot see how to eschew and pass by scandals in others, but it must needs dash and break its neck upon them. Love is a light which may lead us by offences inoffensively, and without stumbling. In darkness men mistake the way, know not the end of it, take pits for plain ways, and stumble in them. Uncharitableness casts a mist over the actions and courses of others, and our own too, that we cannot carry on either without transgression. And this is the misery of it, that it cannot discern any fault in itself. It knows not whither it goeth, calls light darkness and darkness light. It is partial in judgment, pronounces always on its own behalf, cares not whom it condemn, that it may absolve itself.

Is there any privilege so precious as this, to be 'the sons of God?' 1 John iii. 2. What are all relations, or states, or conditions, to this one, to be the children of the Highest? It was David's question, 'Should I be the king's son-in-law?' Alas! what a petty and poor dignity in regard of this, to be 'the sons of God,' partakers of a divine nature? All the difference of birth, all the distinction of degrees and qualities amongst persons, besides this one, are but such as have no being, no worth but in the fancy and construction of them. They really are nothing, and can do nothing. This only is a substantial and fundamental difference. A divine birth carries along with it a divine nature, a change of principles, from the worst to the best, from darkness to light, from death to life. Now, imagine then, what excellency is in this grace, which is made the character of a son of God, of one begotten of the Father, and passed from death to life? 1 John iii. 10, 14. 'In this the children of God are manifest, and the children of the devil: Whosoever doth not righteousness is not of God, neither he that loveth not his brother. We know that we have passed from death unto life, because we love the brethren: he that loveth not his brother, abideth in death.' 1 John iv. 7. 'Beloved, let us love one another: for love is of God; and every one that loveth is born of God, and knoweth God.' And truly it is most natural, if it be so, that the children of our Father love each other dearly. It is monstrous and unnatural to see it otherwise. But besides, there is in this a great deal of resemblance of their Father, whose eminent and signal property it is, to be good to all and kind even to the unthankful; and whose incomparable glory it is to pardon iniquity, and suffer long patiently. A Christian cannot resemble his Father more nearly than in this. Why do we account that baseness in us which is glory to God? Are we ashamed of our birth, or dare we not own our Father? Shall we be ashamed to love them as brethren whom he hath not been ashamed to adopt as sons, and whom Christ is not ashamed to call brethren?

CHAPTER IV.

We shall not be curious in the ranking of the duties in which Christian love should exercise itself. All the commandments of the second table are but branches of it: they might be reduced all to the works of righteousness and of mercy. But truly these are interwoven through other. Though mercy uses to be restricted to the showing of compassion upon men in misery, yet there is a righteousness in that mercy; and there is mercy in the most part of the acts of righteousness, as in not judging rashly, in forgiving, &c. Therefore we shall consider the most eminent and difficult duties of love, which the word of God solemnly and frequently charges upon us in relation to others, especially these of the household of faith.

I conceive we would labour to enforce upon our hearts, and persuade our souls to a love of all men, by often ruminating upon the words of the Apostle, which enjoin us to 'abound in love towards all men,' 1 Thess. iii. 12. And this is so concerning, that he prays earnestly that the Lord would make them increase in it, and this we should pray for too. An affectionate disposition towards our common nature is not a common thing. Christianity enjoins it, and it is only true humanity, Luke vi. 36, 37. 'Be ye therefore merciful, as your Father also is merciful. Judge not, and ye shall not be judged: condemn not, and ye shall not be condemned: forgive, and ye shall be forgiven.' Now in relation to all men, charity hath an engagement upon it to pray for all sorts of men, from that Apostolic command, 1 Tim. ii. 1. 'I exhort therefore, that first of all, supplications, prayers, intercessions, and giving of thanks be made for all men.' Prayers and supplications, earnest prayers out of affection, should be poured out even for them that cannot, or do not pray for themselves. Wherefore are we taught to pray, but that we may be the mouth of others? And since an intercessor is given to us above, how are we bound to be intercessors for others below, and so to be affected with the common mercies of the multitude, as to give thanks too! If man, by the law of creation, is the mouth of the stones, trees, birds, beasts, of heaven and earth, sun and moon and stars, how much more ought a Christian, a redeemed man, be the mouth of mankind to praise God for the abounding of his goodness, even towards these who are left yet in that misery and bondage that he is delivered from?

Next, Charity by all means will avoid scandal, and live honestly in the sight of all men. The apostle says, 'Give none offence, neither to the Jews nor to the Gentiles, nor to the church of God,' 1 Cor. x. 32. And he adds his own example, 'Even as I please all men in all things, not seeking my own profit, but the profit of many, that they may be saved,' ver. 33. Charity is not self-addicted. It hath no humour to please. It can displease itself to profit others. I do verily think there is no point of Christianity less regarded. Others we acknowledge, but we fail in practice. This scarce hath the approbation of the mind. Few do conceive an obligation lying on them to it. But O how is Christianity, the most of it, humanity? Christ makes us men as well as Christians. He makes us reasonable men when believers. Sin transformed our nature into a wild, beastly, viperous, selfish thing. Grace restores reason and natural affection in the purest and highest strain. And this is reason and humanity, elevated and purified,—to condescend to all men in all things for their profit and edification, to deny itself to save others. Whatsoever is not necessary in itself, we ought not to impose a necessity upon it by our imagination and fancy, to the prejudice of a greater necessity, another's edification. Indeed charity will not, dare not sin to please men. That were to hate God, to hate ourselves, and to hate our brethren, under a base pretended notion of love. But I believe, addictedness to our own humours in things not necessary, which have no worth but from our disposition, doth oftener transport us beyond the bounds of charity than the apprehension of duty and conscience of sin. Some will grant they should be tender of offending the saints. But they do not conceive it is much matter what they do in relation to others; as if it were lawful to murder a Gentile more than a Christian. That is a bloody imagination, opposite to that innocent Christian, Paul, who says (Philip. ii. 15.), we should be 'blameless and harmless, the sons of God, without rebuke, in the midst of a crooked and perverse generation,' among whom we should shine 'as lights.' And truly it is humanity elevated by Christianity, or reason purified by religion, that is the light that shines most brightly in this dark world. And he says (in Col. iv. 5.), 'Walk in wisdom toward them that are without,' and (1 Thess. iv. 12.) 'walk honestly toward them that are without,'—avoiding all things, in our profession and carriage, which may alienate them from the love of the truth and godliness, walking so, as we may insinuate into their hearts some apprehension of the beauty of religion. Many conceive, if they do good, all is well—if it be a duty, it matters nothing. But remember that caution, 'Let not then your good be evil spoken of,' Rom. xiv. 16. We would have our eyes upon that too, so to circumstantiate all our duties, as they may have least offence in them, and be exposed to least obloquy of men, 1 Pet. ii. 12. 'Having your conversation honest among the Gentiles: that whereas they speak against you as evil-doers, they may by your good works which they shall behold, glorify God in the day of visitation.'

Then, *Thirdly*, Charity follows peace with all men, as much as is possible, Heb. xii. 14. 'If it be possible, as much as lieth in you, live peaceably with all men,' Rom. xii. 18. Many spirits are framed for contention. If peace follow them, they will flee from it. But a Christian having made peace with God, the sweet fruit of that upon his spirit, is to dispose him to a peaceable and quiet condescendency to others; and if peace flee from him, to follow after it, not only to entertain it when it is offered, but to seek it when it is away, and to pursue it when it runs away. (Psal. xxxiv. 14. which Peter urges upon Christians, 1 Pet. iii. 8, 9, 10, 11.) 'Finally, be ye all of one mind, having compassion one of another: love as brethren, be pitiful, be courteous: Not rendering evil for evil, or railing for railing: but contrariwise, blessing; knowing that ye are thereunto called that ye should inherit a blessing. For he that will love life, and see good days, let him refrain his tongue from evil, and his lips that they speak no guile: Let him eschew evil, and do good: let him seek peace, and ensue it.' I think, since we obtained the mercy to get a Peace-maker between us and God, we should henceforth count ourselves bound to be peace-makers among men. And truly such have a blessing pronounced upon them, Matt. v. 9. 'Blessed are the peace-makers.' The Prince of peace pronounced it, and this is the blessedness, 'they shall be called the children of God,' because he is 'the God of peace;' and to resemble him in these, first in purity, then in peace, is a character of his image. It is true, peace will sometimes flee so fast, and so far away, as a Christian cannot follow it without sin, and that is breach of a higher peace. But charity, when it cannot live in peace without, doth then live in peace within, because it hath that sweet testimony of conscience, that, as far as did lie in it, peace was followed without. Divine wisdom (James iii. 17.), 'is first pure, then peaceable, gentle, and easy to be entreated, full of mercy and good fruits, without wrangling, and without hypocrisy.' If wisdom be peaceable and not pure, it is but a carnal conspiracy in iniquity, earthly and sensual. But if it be pure, it must be peaceable. For the wisdom descending from above hath a purity of truth, and a purity of love, and a purity of the mind and of the affection too. Where there is a purity of truth, but accompanied with envying, bitter strife, rigid judging, wrangling, and such like, then it is defiled and corrupted by the intermixture of vile and base affections, ascending out of the dunghill of the flesh. The vapours of our lusts arising up to the mind, do incrassate pure truth. They put an earthly, sensual, and devilish visage on it.

Charity, its conversation and discourse, is without judging, without censuring,

Matth. vii. 1. Of which chapter, because it contains much edification, I shall speak more hereafter. James iii. 17. 'Without partiality, without hypocrisy.' The words in the original are, αδιακριτος και ανυποκριτος, (without judging and wrangling, and without hypocrisy), importing, that great censurers are often the greatest hypocrites, and sincerity has always much charity. Truly, there is much idle time spent this way in discourses of one another, and venting our judgments of others; as if it were enough of commendation for us to condemn others, and much piety to charge another with impiety. We should even be sparing in judging them that are without, 1 Cor. v. 12, 13. Reflecting upon them or their ways, hath more provocation than edification in it. A censorious humour is certainly most partial to itself, and self-indulgent. It can sooner endure a great beam in its own eye, than a little mote in its neighbour's; and this shows evidently that it is not the hatred of sin, or the love of virtue, which is the single and simple principle of it, but self-love, shrouded under the vail of displeasure at sin, and delight in virtue. I would think one great help to amend this, were to abate much from the superfluity and multitude of discourses upon others. 'In the multitude of words there wants not sin,' and in the multitude of discourses upon other men, there cannot miss the sin of rash judging. I find the saints and fearers of God commended for speaking often one to another, but not at all for speaking one of another. The subject of their discourse (Mal. iii. 16.) certainly was of another strain,—how good it was to serve the Lord, &c.—opposite to the evil communication of others there registered.

Charity is no tale-bearer. It goeth not about as a slander to reveal a secret, though true, Prov. xx. 19. It is of a faithful spirit to conceal the matter, Prov. xi. 13. Another man's good name is as a pledge laid down in our hand, which every man should faithfully restore, and take heed how he lose it, or alienate it by backbiting. Some would have nothing to say, if they had not other's faults and frailties to declaim upon; but it were better that such kept always silent, that either they had no ears to hear of them or know them, or had no tongues to vent them. If they do not lie grossly in it, they think they do no wrong. But let them judge it in reference to themselves: 'A good name is better than precious ointment,' (Eccles. vii. 1.) 'and rather to be chosen than great riches,' Prov. xxii. 1. And is that no wrong, to defile that precious ointment, and to rob or steal away that jewel more precious than great riches? There is a strange connection between these: 'Thou shalt not go up and down as a tale-bearer, nor stand against the blood of thy neighbour,' Lev. xix. 16. It is a kind of murder, because it kills that which is as precious as life to an ingenuous heart: 'The words of a tale-bearer are as wounds, and they go down to the innermost parts of the belly,' Prov. xviii. 8. and xxvi. 22. They strike a wound to any man's heart, that can hardly be cured; and there is nothing that is such a seminary of contention and strife among brethren as this. It is the oil to feed the flame of alienation. Take away a tale-bearer, and strife ceaseth, Prov. xxvi. 20. Let there be but any (as there want not such who have no other trade or occupation), to whisper into the ears of brethren, and suggest evil apprehensions of them, they will separate chief friends, as we see it in daily experience, Prov. xvi. 28. 'Revilers' are amongst these who are excluded out of the kingdom of God, 1 Cor. vi. 10. And therefore, as the Holy Ghost gives general precepts for the profitable and edifying improvement of the tongue, that so it may indeed be the glory of a man; (which truly is no small point of religion, as James expresses, Chap. iii. 2. 'If any man offend not in word, the same is a perfect man;') so that same spirit gives us particular directions about this, 'Speak not evil one of another, brethren. He that speaketh evil of his brother, and judgeth his brother, speaketh evil of the law, and judgeth the law,' (James iv. 11.) because he puts himself in the place of the Lawgiver, and his own judgment and fancy in the room of the law, and so judges the law. And therefore the Apostle Peter makes a wise and significant connection, 1 Pet. ii. 1. 'Laying aside all malice, and all guile, and hypocrisies, and envies, and all evil-speakings.' Truly, evil-speaking of our brethren, though it may be true, yet it proceeds out of the abundance of these, in the heart, of guile, hypocrisy, and envy. While we catch at a name of piety from censuring others, and build our own estimation upon the ruins of another's good name, hypocrisy and envy are too predominant. If we would indeed grow in grace by the word, and taste more how gracious the Lord is, we must lay these aside, and become as little children, without guile, and without gall. Many account it excuse enough, that they did not invent evil tales, or were not the first broachers of them; but the Scripture joins both together. The man that 'shall abide in his tabernacle' must neither vent nor invent them, neither cast them down nor take them up, 'He backbiteth not with his tongue, nor taketh up a reproach against his neighbour;' (Psal. xv. 3.) or *receiveth not* or *endureth not*, as in the margin. He neither gives it nor receives he it, hath not a tongue to speak of others faults, nor ear to hear them. Indeed he hath a tongue to confess his own, and an ear open to hear another confess his faults, according to that precept, 'Confess your faults one to another.' We are forbidden to have much society or fellowship with tale-bearers; and it is added, Prov. xx. 19. 'And meddle not with such as flatter with their mouth,' as indeed commonly they who reproach the absent, flatter the present; a backbiter is a face-flatterer. And therefore we should not only not meddle with them, but drive them away as enemies to human society. Charity would in such a case protect itself, if I may so say, by 'an angry countenance,' an appearance of anger and real dislike. 'As the north wind drives away rain,' so that entertainment would drive away a 'backbiting tongue,' Prov. xxv. 23. If we do discountenance it, backbiters will be discouraged to open their pack of news and reports: and indeed the receiving readily of evil reports of brethren, is a partaking with the unfruitful works of darkness, which we should rather reprove, Eph. v. 11. To join with the teller is to complete the evil report; for if there were no receiver there would be no teller, no tale-bearer, 'Charity covers a multitude of sins,' 1 Pet. iv. 8; and therefore 'above all things have fervent charity among yourselves,' says he. What is above prayer and watching unto the end, above sobriety? Indeed, in reference to fellowship with God, these are above all; but in relation to comfortable fellowship one with another in this world, this is above all, and the crown or cream of other graces. He whose sins are covered by God's free love, cannot think it hard to spread the garment of his love over his brother's sins. Hatred stirreth up strife, all uncharitable affections, as envy, wrath. It stirreth up contentions, and blazeth abroad men's infirmities. But 'love covereth all sins,' concealeth them from all to whom the knowledge of them doth not belong, Prov. x. 12. Love in a manner suffers not itself to know what it knoweth, or at least to remember it much. It will sometimes hoodwink itself to a favourable construction. It will pass by an infirmity and misken* it, but many stand still and commune with it. But he that covereth a transgression seeks love to bury offences in. Silence is a notable mean to preserve concord, and beget true amity and friendship. The keeping of faults long above ground unburied, doth make them cast forth an evil savour that will ever part friends. Therefore, says the wise man, 'He that covereth a transgression seeketh love: but he that repeateth a matter separateth very friends,' Prov. xvii. 9. Covering faults christianly, will make a stranger a friend; but repeating and blazing of them will make a friend not only a stranger, but an enemy. Yet this is nothing to the prejudice of that Christian duty of reproving and admonishing one another, Eph. v. 11. 'Have no fellowship with the unfruitful works of darkness, but rather reprove them.' Love commands to reprove in the 'spirit of meekness,' (Gal. vi. 1.) as a man would restore an arm out of joint. And therefore thou 'shall not hate him in thy heart, but shall in any ways reprove him, and not suffer sin upon him,' Lev. xix. 17. And he that reproves his brother after this manner from love, and in meekness and wisdom, 'shall afterward find more favour of him than he that flatters with his tongue,' Prov. xxviii. 23. To cover grudges and jealousies in our hearts, were to nourish a flame in our bosom, which doth but wait for a vent, and will at one occasion or other burst out. But to look too narrowly to every step, and to write up a register of men's mere frailties, especially so as to publish them to the world; that is inconsistent with the rule of love. And truly, it is a token of one 'destitute of wisdom to despise his neighbour; but a man of understanding will hold his peace.' He that has most defects himself, will find maniest † in others, and strive to vilify them one way or other; but a wise man can pass by frailties, yea, offences done to him, and be silent, Prov. xi. 12.

* [Overlook it.—ED.]

† [Most.—ED.]

CHAPTER V.

Humility is the root of charity, and meekness the fruit of both. There is no solid and pure ground of love to others, except the rubbish of self-love be first cast out of the soul; and when that superfluity of naughtiness is cast out, then charity hath a solid and deep foundation: 'The end of the command is charity out of a pure heart,' 1 Tim. i. 5. It is only such a purified heart, cleansed from that poison and contagion of pride and self-estimation, that can send out such a sweet and wholesome stream, to the refreshing of the spirits and bowels of the church of God. If self-glory and pride have deep roots fastened into the soul, they draw all the sap and virtue downward, and send little or nothing up to the tree of charity, which makes it barren and unfruitful in the works of righteousness, and fruits of mercy and meekness. There are obstructions in the way of that communication, which only can be removed by the plucking up of these roots of pride and self-estimation, which prey upon all, and incorporate all in themselves, and yet, like the lean kine that had devoured the fat, are never the fatter or more well-favoured.

It is no wonder, then, that these are the first principles that we must learn in Christ's school, the very A B C of Christianity: 'Learn of me, for I am meek and lowly in heart, and ye shall find rest unto your souls,' Matth. xi. 29. This is the great Prophet sent of the Father into the world to teach us, whom he hath, with a voice from heaven, commanded us to hear: 'This is my well-beloved Son, hear him.' Should not the fame and report of such a Teacher move us? He was testified of very honourably, long before he came, that he had the Spirit above measure, that he had 'the tongue of the learned;' (Isa. l. 4.) that he was a greater prophet than Moses, (Deut. xviii. 15, 18.) that is, the wonderful Counsellor of heaven and earth, (Isa. ix. 6.) the 'Witness to the people,' a Teacher and 'Leader to the people.' And then, when he came, he had the most glorious testimony from the most glorious persons,—the Father and the Holy Ghost,—in the most solemn manner that ever the world heard of, Matth. xvii. 5. 'Behold, a voice out of the cloud, which said, This is my beloved Son, in whom I am well pleased; hear ye him.' Now, this is our Master, our Rabbi, Matth. xxiii. 8. This is the 'Apostle and High Priest of our profession (Heb. iii. 1.); 'the light of the world and life of men,' John viii. 12. and vi. 33, 51. Having, then, such a Teacher and Master, sent us from heaven, may we not glory in our Master? But some may suppose, that he who came down from heaven, filled with all the riches and treasures of heavenly wisdom, should reveal in his school unto his disciples, all the mysteries and profound secrets of nature and art, about which the world hath ploded since the first taste of the tree of knowledge, and beaten out their brains to the vexation of all their spirits, without any fruit, but the discovery of the impossibility of knowing, and the increase of sorrow by searching. Who would not expect, when the Wisdom of God descends among men, but that he should show unto the world that wisdom, in the understanding of all the works of God, which all men have been pursuing in vain; that he by whom all things were created, and so could unbowel and manifest all their hidden causes and virtues, all their admirable and wonderful qualities and operations, as easily by a word, as he made them by a word; who would not expect, I say, but that he should have made this world, and the mysteries of it, the subject of all his lessons, the more to illustrate his own glorious power and wisdom? And yet behold, they who had come into his school and heard this Master and Doctor teach his scholars, they who had been invited to come, through the fame and report of his name, would have stood astonished and surprised to hear the subject of his doctrine; one come from on high to teach so low things as these, 'Learn of me, I am meek and lowly.' Other men that are masters of professions, and authors of sects or orders, do aspire unto some singularity in doctrine to make them famous. But behold our Lord and Master, this is the doctrine he vents! It hath nothing in it that sounds high, and looks big in the estimation of the world. In regard of the wisdom of the world, it is foolishness, a doctrine of humility from the most High! A lesson of lowliness and meekness from the Lord and Maker of all! There seems, at first, nothing in it to allure any to follow it. Who would travel so far as the college of Christianity to learn no more but this, when every man pretends to be a teacher of it?

But truly there is a majesty in this lowliness, and there is a singularity in this commonness. If ye would stay and hear a little longer, and enter into a deep search of this doctrine, we would be surcharged and overcome with wonders. It seems shallow till ye enter, but it has no bottom. Christianity makes no great noise, but it runs the deeper. It is a light and overly knowledge of it, a small smattering of the doctrine of it, that makes men despise it, and prefer other things; but the deep and solid apprehension of it will make us adore and admire, and drive us to an *O altitudo!* 'O the depth both of the wisdom and knowledge of God!' Rom. xi. 33. As the superficial knowledge of nature makes men atheists, but the profound understanding of it makes men pious, so all other things, *vilescunt scientia,* "grow more contemptible by the knowledge of them." It is ignorance of them which is the mother of that devout admiration we bear to them. But Christianity only, *vilescit ignorantia, clarescit scientia,* "is common and base, because not known." And that is no disparagement at all unto it, that there is none despises it, but he that knoweth it not; and none can do any thing, but despise all besides it that once knows it. That is the proper excellency and glory of it.

All arts and sciences have their principles, and common axioms, of unquestionable authority. All kind of professions have some fundamental doctrines and points which are the character of them. Christianity hath its principles too. And principles must be plain and uncontroverted; they must be evident by their own light, and apt to give light to other things. All the rest of the conclusions of the art are but derivations and deductions from them. Our Master and Doctor follows the same method. He lays down some common principles, some fundamental points of this profession, upon which all the building of Christianity hangs: 'Learn of me, for I am meek and lowly.' This was the high lesson that his life preached so exemplarily, and his doctrine pressed so earnestly; and in this he is very unlike other teachers, who impose burdens on others, and themselves do not so much as touch them. But he first practises his doctrine, and then preaches it. He first casts a pattern in himself, and then presses to follow it. Examples teach better than rules, but both together are most effectual and sure. The rarest example and noblest rule that ever was given to men, are here met together.

The rule is about a thing that has a low name, but a high nature. Lowliness and meekness in reputation and outward form, are like servants; yet they account it no robbery to be equal with the highest and most princely graces. The vein of gold and silver lies very low in the bowels of the earth; but it is not therefore base, but the more precious. Other virtues may come with more observation; but these, like the Master that teaches them, come with more reality. If they have less pomp, they have more power and virtue. Humility, how suitable is it to humanity! They are as near of kin one to another, as *homo* and *humus*;* and therefore, except a man cast off humanity, and forget his original, the ground, the dust from whence he was taken, I do not see how he can shake off humility. Self-knowledge is the mother of it, the knowledge of that *humus* would make us *humiles.*† Look to the hole of the pit from whence thou art hewn. A man could not look high that looked so low as the pit from whence we were taken by nature, even the dust; and the pit from whence we are hewn by grace, even man's lost and ruined state. Such a low look would make a lowly mind. Therefore pride must be nothing else but an empty and vain tumour, a puffing up. 'Knowledge puffeth up,' not self-knowledge. That casts down, and brings down all superstructures, razes out all vain confidence to the very foundation, and then begins to build on a solid ground. But knowledge of other things without, joined with ignorance of ourselves

* [The word *homo* (man) has been supposed to be derived from *humus* (the ground), because man sprang from the earth. Quintillian's objection to this derivation of the word is, that all other animals have the same origin, (quasi vero non omnibus animalibus eadem origo. Instit. Orator. lib. i. cap. 6.) Such an objection however has but little force. For though, according to the account which Moses gives of the creation, the earth at the command of God, not only brought forth man, but other creatures, (Gen. i. 24.) man alone was called *Adam*, (אדם) because he was formed of the dust of the *ground*, (אדמה adamah,) Gen. ii. 7.—Joseph. Antiq. lib. i. cap. i.—Ed.]

† [That is, "humble beings."—Ed.]

within, is but a swelling, not a growing; it is a bladder or skin full of wind; a blast or breath of an airy applause or commendation, will extend it and fill it full. And what is this else but a monster in humanity; the skin of a man stuffed or blown up with wind and vanity, to the shadow and resemblance of a man; but no bones or sinews, nor real substance within? Pride is an excrescence. It is nature swelled beyond the intrinsic terms or limits of magnitude, the spirit of a mouse in a mountain. And now, if any thing be gone without the just bounds of the magnitude set to it, it is imperfect, disabled in its operations, vain and unprofitable, yea, prodigious-like. If there be not so much real excellency as may fill up the circle of our self-estimation, then surely it must be full of emptiness and vanity fancy and imagination must supply the vacant room, where solid worth cannot extend so far. Now, I believe, if any man could but impartially and seriously reflect upon himself, he would see nothing of that kind, no true solid and real dignity to provoke love; but real baseness and misery to procure loathing. There is a lie in every sin; but the greatest and grossest lie is committed in pride, and attribution of that excellency to ourselves which is not. And upon what erroneous fancy, which is a sandy and vain foundation, is built the tower of self-estimation, vain gloriation, and such like? Pride, which is the mother of these, says most presumptuously, 'By the strength of my hand I have done it, and by my wisdom; for I am prudent,' (Isa. x. 13.) 'I am, and none else besides me,' Isa. xlvii. 10. It is such a false imagination, as 'I am of perfect beauty,' I am and none else, 'I am a god,' (Ezek. xxvii. 3. and xxviii. 2.) which swells and lifts up the heart. Now what a vain thing is it, an inordinate elevation of the heart upon a false misapprehension of the mind? The 'soul which is lifted up, is not upright in him,' Hab. ii. 4. It must be a tottering building that is founded on such a gross mistake.

Some cover their pride with the pretence of high spiritedness, and please themselves in apprehensions of some magnanimity and generosity. But the truth is, it is not true magnitude, but a swelling out of the superabundance of pestilent humours. True greatness of spirit is inwardly and throughout solid, firm from the bottom, and the foundation of it is truth. Which of the two do ye think hath the better spirit, he that calls dust, dust, and accounts of dung as dung; or he that, upon a false imagination, thinks dust and dung is gold and silver, esteems himself a rich man, and raises up himself above others? Humility is only true magnanimity; for it digs down low, that it may set and establish the foundation of true worth. It is true, it is lowly, and bows down low. But as the water that comes from a height, the lower it comes down the higher it ascends up again; so the humble spirit, the lower it fall in its own estimation, the higher it is raised in real worth and in God's estimation. He that humbles himself shall be exalted, and he that exalts himself shall be abased,' Matt. xxiii. 12. He is like a growing tree, the deeper the roots go down in the earth, the higher the tree grows above ground; as Jacob's ladder, the foot of it is fastened in the earth, but the top of it reaches the heaven. And this is the sure way to ascend to heaven. Pride would fly up upon its own wings. But the humble man will enter at the lowest step, and so goes up by degrees, and in the end is made manifest. Pride catches a fall,* and humility is raised on high: it descended that it might ascend. 'A man's pride shall bring him low, but honour shall uphold the humble in spirit,' Prov. xxix. 23. 'Pride goeth before destruction, and an haughty spirit before a fall.' But 'before honour is humility,' Prov. xvi. 18. and xviii. 12. The first week of creation, as it were, afforded two signal examples of this wise permutation of divine justice; angels cast out of heaven, and man out of paradise; a high and wreched aim at wisdom brought both as low as hell. The pride of angels and men was but the rising up to a height, or climbing up a steep to the pinnacle of glory, that they might catch the lower fall: But the last week of the creation, to speak so, shall afford us rare and eminent demonstrations of the other; poor, wretched, and miserable sinners lifted up to heaven by humility, when angels were thrown down from heaven for pride. What a strange sight, an angel, once so glorious, so low; and a sinner, once so wretched and miserable, so high! Truly may any man

* [See note page 168.—Ed.]

conclude within himself, 'Better it is to be of an humble spirit with the lowly, than to divide the spoil with the proud,' Prov. xvi. 19. Happy lowliness that is the foundation of true highness! But miserable highness that is the beginning of eternal baseness! 'Blessed are the poor in spirit: for theirs is the kingdom of heaven,' Matt. v. 3. Blessedness begins low, in poverty of spirit. And Christ's sermon upon blessedness begins at it, but it arises in the end to the riches of a kingdom, a heavenly kingdom. Grace is the seed of glory; and poverty of spirit is the seed, first dead, before it be quickened to grow up in fruits. And indeed the grain 'is not quickened except it die,' (1 Cor. xv. 36.) and then it gets a body, and 'bringeth forth much fruit,' John xii. 24. Even so grace is sown into the heart, but it is not quickened except it die in humility, and then God gives it a body, when it springs up in other beautiful graces, of meekness, patience, love, &c. But these are never ripe till the day that the soul get the warm beams of heaven, being separated from the body, and then is the harvest a rich crop of blessedness. Holiness is the ladder to go up to happiness by, or rather our Lord Jesus Christ as adorned with all these graces. Now these are the steps of it mentioned Matt. v., and the lowest step that a soul first ascends to him by, is poverty of spirit, or humility. And truly the spirit cannot meet with Jesus Christ till he first bring it down low, because he hath come so low himself, as that no soul can ascend up to heaven by him, except they bow down to his lowliness, and rise upon that step.

Now a man being thus humbled in spirit before God, and under his mighty hand, he is only fit to obey the apostolic precept, 'Be ye all of you subject one to another,' 1 Pet. v. 5. Humility towards men depends upon that poverty and self-emptying under God's mighty hand, ver. 6. It is only a lowly heart that can make the back to bow, and submit to others of whatsoever quality, and condescend to them of low degree, Rom. xii. 16; Eph. v. 21. But the fear of the Lord humbling the spirit, will easily set it as low as any other can put it. This is the only basis and foundation of Christian submission and moderation. It is not a complemental condescendence. It consists not in an external show of gesture and voice. That is but an apish imitation. And indeed pride often will palliate itself under voluntary shows of humility, and can demean itself to undecent and unseemly submissions to persons far inferior; but it is the more deformed and hateful, that it lurks under some shadows of humility. As an ape is the more ugly and ill-favoured, that it is liker a man, because it is not a man; so vices have more deformity in them, when they put on the garb and vizard of virtue. Only it may appear how beautiful a garment true humility is, when pride desires often to be covered with the appearance of it, to hide its nakedness. O how rich a clothing is the mean-like garment of humility and poverty of spirit! 'Be ye clothed with humility,' 1 Pet. v. 5. It is the ornament of all graces. It covers a man's nakedness by uncovering of it. If a man had all other endowments, this one dead fly, would make all the ointment unsavoury, pride. But humility is *condimentum virtutum*, as well as *vestimentum*.* It seasons all graces, and covers all infirmities. Garments are for ornament and necessity both. Truly this clothing is alike fit for both, to adorn and beautify whatsoever is excellent, and to hide or supply whatsoever is deficient, *ornamentum et operimentum*.†

The apostle Paul gives a solemn charge to the Romans (Rom. xii. 3.), that no man should think high of himself; but soberly, according to the measure of faith given. That extreme undervaluing and denial of all worth in ourselves, though it be suitable before God (Luke xvii. 6, 7, 10; Prov. xxx. 2, 3; Job xlii. 6; 1 Cor. iii. 7.), yet is uncomely and incongruous before men. Humility doth not exclude all knowledge of any excellency in itself, or defect in another, it can discern; but this is the worth of it, that it thinks soberly of the one, and despises not the other. The humble man knows any advantage he has beyond another, but he is not 'wise in his own conceit.' He looks not so much upon that side of things, his

* [Humility is "the seasoning of the virtues," as well as "the garb." Cicero represents suavity of speech and manners to be the seasoning of friendship (condimentum amicitiæ). De Amicitia, cap. 18.—Ed.]

† [That is, "an ornament and covering."—Ed.]

own perfections and others' imperfections. That is very dangerous. But he casts his eye most on the other side, his own infirmities and others' virtues, his worst part and their best part, and this makes up an equality or proportion. Where there is inequality, there is a different measure of gifts and graces, there are diverse failings and infirmity, and degrees of them. Now, how shall so unequal members make up one body, and join unto one harmonious being, except this proportion be kept, that the defects of one be made up by the humility of another? The difference and inequality is taken away this way, by fixing my eye most upon my own disadvantages and my brother's advantages. If I be higher in any respect, yet certainly I am lower in some, and therefore the unity of the body may be preserved by humility. I will consider in what I come short, and in what another excels, and so I can condescend to them of low degree. This is the substance of that which is subjoined: (Rom. xii. 16.) 'Mind not high things, but condescend to men of low estate. Be not wise in your own conceits.' And this makes us meet in honour to prefer one another; taking ourselves up in the notion of what evil is in us, and another up in the notion of what good is in him. Rom. xii. 10, 'Be kindly affectioned one to another, with brotherly love, in honour preferring one another.' Thus there may be an equality of mutual respect and love, where there is an inequality of gifts and graces; there may be one measure of charity, where there are different measures of faith, because both neglect that difference, and pitch upon their own evils and another's good.

It is our custom to compare ourselves among ourselves, and the result of that secret comparison is estimation of ourselves, and despising others. We take our measure, not by our own real and intrinsic qualifications, but by the stature of other men's; and if we find any disadvantage in others, or any pre-eminence in ourselves, in such a partial application and collation of ourselves with others (as readily self-love, if it find it not, will fancy it), then we have a tacit gloriation within ourselves, and a secret complacency in ourselves. But the humble Christian dares not make himself of that number, nor boast of things without his measure. He dare not think himself good, because, *deterioribus melior*, "better than others who are worse." But he judges himself by that intrinsic measure which God hath distributed unto him, and so finds reason of sobriety and humility; and therefore he dare not stretch himself beyond his measure, or go without his station and degree, 2 Cor. x. 12—14. Humility makes a man compare himself with the best, that he may find how bad he himself is. But pride measures by the worst, that it may hide from a man his own imperfections. The one takes a perfect rule, and finds itself nothing. The other takes a crooked rule, and imagines itself something. But this is the way that unity may be kept in the body, if all the members keep this method and order, the lowest to measure by him that is higher, and the higher to judge himself by him that is yet above him; and he that is above all the rest, to compare with the rule of perfection, and find himself further short of the rule than the lowest is below him. If our comparisons did thus ascend, we would descend in humility, and all the different degrees of persons would meet in one centre of lowliness of mind. But while our rule descends, our pride ascends. The scripture holds out pride and self-estimation as the root of many evils, and humility as the root of many good fruits among men. 'Only through pride comes contention,' Prov. xiii. 10. There is pride at least in one of the parties, and often in both. It makes one man careless of another, and out of contempt not to study equity and righteousness towards him; and it makes another man impatient of receiving and bearing an injury or disrespect. While every man seeks to please himself, the contention arises. Pride in both parties makes both stiff and inflexible to peace and equity; and in this there is a great deal of folly. For, by this means, both procure more real displeasure and dissatisfaction to their own spirits. 'But with the well-advised is wisdom.' They who have discretion and judgment will not be so wedded to their own conceits, but that in humility they can forbear and forgive for peace' sake. And though this seem harsh and bitter at first, to a passionate and distempered mind, yet, O how sweet is it after! There is a greater sweetness and refreshment in the peaceable condescendence of a man's spirit, and in the quiet passing by any injury, than the highest satisfaction that ever revenge or contention gave to any man. 'When pride comes, then comes shame: but with the lowly is wisdom,' Prov. xi. 2. Pride groweth to maturity and ripeness. Shame is near hand it, almost as near as the harvest. If pride come up, shame is in the next rank behind it. But there is a great wisdom in lowliness. That is, the honourable society that it walks in. There may be a secret connection between this and the former verse, 'divers and false balances are abomination to the Lord: but a just balance is his delight.' Now, if it be so in such low things as merchandise, how much more abominable is a false spiritual balance in the weighing of ourselves! Pride hath a false balance in its hand, the weight of self-love carries down the one scale by far.

Lowliness of mind is the strongest bond of peace and charity. It banishes away strife and vain-glory, and makes each man to esteem another better than himself, (Philip. ii. 3.) because the humble man knows his own inside, and only another's outside. Now certainly the outside is always better and more specious than the inside; and therefore a humble man seeing nothing but his neighbour's outside, and being acquainted throughly with his own inside, he esteems another better than himself. Humility, as it makes a man to think well of another, so it hinders him to speak evil of his brother. James iv. He lays down the ground-work in the 10th verse, 'Humble yourselves in the sight of the Lord, and he shall lift you up.' He raises his superstructure, verses 11, 12. 'Speak not evil one of another, brethren. He that speaketh evil of his brother, and judgeth his brother, speaketh evil of the law, and judgeth the law: but if thou judge the law, thou art not a doer of the law, but a judge. There is one lawgiver, who is able to save, and to destroy: who art thou that judgest another?' For truly the very ground of evil-speaking of that nature, is some advantage, we conceive, that may redound to our own reputation, by the diminution of another's fame. Or, because we are so short-sighted in ourselves, therefore we are sharp-sighted towards others; and because we think little of our own faults, we are ready to aggravate other men's to an extremity. But in so doing we take the place of the judge and law upon us, which judges others, and is judged by none. So we judge others, and not ourselves. Neither will we suffer ourselves to be judged by others. This is to make ourselves the infallible rule, to judge the law.

Humility levels men to a holy subjection and submission to another, without the confusion of their different degrees and stations. It teaches men to give that respect and regard to every one that is due to his place or worth; and to signify it in such a way as may testify the simplicity of their estimation, and sincerity of their respect. Eph. v. 21, 'Submit yourselves one to another in the fear of God.' 1 Pet. v. 5, 'All of you be subject one to another, and be clothed with humility.' Now, if humility can put a man below others, certainly it will make him endure patiently and willingly to be placed in that same rank by others. When others give him that place to sit into, that he had chosen for himself, will he conceive himself wronged and affronted, though others about him think so? Nay, it is hard to persuade him of an injury of that kind, because the apprehension of such an affront hath for its foundation the imagination of some excellency beyond others, which lowliness hath razed out. He hath placed himself so low for every man's edification and instruction, that others can put him no lower; and there he sits quietly and peaceably. *Bene qui latuit bene vixit.** Affronts and injuries fly over him, and light upon the taller cedars, while the shrubs are safe.

Qui cadit in plano, (vix hoc tamen evenit ipsum,)
Sic cadit, ut tacta surgere possit humo.†

He sits so low, that he cannot fall lower: so a humble man's fall upon the ground is no fall indeed, but in the apprehension of others; but it is a heavy and bruising fall from off the tower of self-conceit.

Now the example that is given us, 'Learn of me,' is certainly of greater force to

* [Crede mihi; bene qui latuit, bene vixit: et intra
Fortunam debet quisque manere suam.
"Believe me, he who has not attracted the notice of the world has lived well; and every one ought to keep within his own proper sphere." Ovid Trist. lib. iii. eleg. iv. ver. 25.—Ed.]

† [" He who falls on a smooth surface, (yet this rarely happens,) falls in such a way that he can rise again from the ground he has touched." Ovid. ut supra, ver. 17.—Ed.]

persuade a man to this humble, composed, and quiet temper of spirit, than all the rules in the world. That the Son of God should come down and act it before our eyes, and cast us a pattern of humility and meekness; if this do not prevail to humble the heart, I know not what can. Indeed this root of bitterness, which is in all men's hearts by nature, is very hard to pluck up; yea, when other weeds of corruption are extirpated, this poisonable one, pride, groweth the faster, and roots the deeper. Suppose a man should be stript naked of all the garments of the old man, this would be certainly nearest his skin, and last to put off. It is so pestilent an evil, that it grows in the glass window as well as on the dunghill; and, which is strange, it can spring out of the heart, and take moisture and aliment from humility, as well as from other graces. A man is in hazard to wax proud that he is not proud, and to be high-minded because he is lowly. Therefore, it is not good to reflect much upon our own graces, no more than for a man to eat much honey.

I know not any antidote so sovereign as the example of Jesus Christ, to cure this evil; and he himself often proposes this receipt to his disciples, (John xiii. 13—17.) 'Ye call me Master and Lord: and ye say well; for so I am. If I then, your Lord and Master, have washed your feet, ye also ought to wash one another's feet. For I have given you an example, that ye should do as I have done to you. Verily, verily, I say unto you, the servant is not greater than his lord; neither he that is sent greater than he that sent him. If ye know these things, happy are ye if ye do them.' Matt. xi. 29, 30, 'Take my yoke upon you, and learn of me; for I am meek and lowly in heart: and ye shall find rest unto your souls. For my yoke is easy, and my burden is light.' Matt. xx. 27, 28, 'And whosoever will be chief among you, let him be your servant: Even as the Son of man came not to be ministered unto, but to minister, and to give his life a ransom for many.' Might not that sound always in our ears, the servant is not above his lord, the 'Son of man came not to be ministered unto, but to minister?' O! whose spirit would not that compose? What apprehension of wrong would it not compensate? What flame of contention about worth and respect would it not quench? What noise of tumultuous passions would it not silence?' Therefore, the apostle of the Gentiles prescribes this medicine, (Phil. ii. 5—8,) 'Let this mind be in you, which was also in Christ Jesus: who, being in the form of God, thought it not robbery to be equal with God; but made himself of no reputation, and took upon him the form of a servant, and was made in the likeness of men; and being found in fashion as a man, he humbled himself, and became obedient unto death, even the death of the cross.' If he did humble himself out of charity, who was so high, how should we humble ourselves, both out of charity and necessity, who are so low! If we knew ourselves, it were no strange thing that we were humble; the evidence of truth would extort it from us. But here is the wonder, that he who knew himself to be equal to God, should notwithstanding become lower than men; that the Lord of all should become the servant of all, and the King of glory make himself of no reputation! That he pleased to come down lowest, who knew himself to be the highest of all, no necessity could persuade it, but charity and love hath done it. Now, then, how monstrous and ugly a thing must pride be after this! That the dust should raise itself, and a worm swell; that wretched miserable man should be proud, when it pleased the glorious God to be humble; that absolute necessity shall not constrain to this, that simple love persuaded him to! How doth this heighten and elevate humility, that such an one gives out himself, not only as the teacher, but as the pattern of it: 'Learn of me, for I am meek and lowly in heart, and ye shall find rest unto your souls.'

SEVERAL SERMONS

UPON

THE MOST IMPORTANT SUBJECTS

OF

PRACTICAL RELIGION.

FIRST PRINTED AT GLASGOW 176[illegible].

THE PUBLISHER TO THE READER.

THERE are no sermons I know of any divine or pastor in this kingdom, that have been more frequently printed, or more universally read and esteemed, than the elegant and judicious discourses of Mr. Binning, which were published after his death, at different times, in four small volumes. As there was a great demand for these valuable writings, about twenty six years ago ; so these printed copies of them were compared with his own manuscript copy now in my hand, carefully revised, and then printed, in a large 4to of 641 pages, by Robert Fleming, Printer at Edinburgh, in the year 1735, to which was prefixed a short account of his Life, chiefly taken from the large memoirs of his Life, that the Reverend Mr. Robert M'Ward, some time minister of the gospel at Glasgow, wrote, in a long letter to the Reverend Mr. James Coleman, Minister of the gospel at Sluys in Flanders, who translated Mr. Binning's Sermons into High Dutch, and printed them for the benefit of the Christian congregations in Holland and Flanders. Some of the most memorable particulars of this great man's life have been also published, anno 1753, by the reverend, learned, and industrious Mr. John Wesley, late Fellow of Lincoln college, Oxford, in his Christian Library, which contains about fifty volumes in 8vo of Extracts from, and Abridgments of, the choicest pieces of practical Divinity, we have printed in our language. It is prefixed to Mr. Binning's Sermons upon the first and part of the second chapters of the first Epistle of John, in the 29th volume of that useful work.† * * *

Mr. Binning's elegant and judicious Treatise of Christian Love was first printed from a manuscript in my hand, at Edinburgh, 1743, in an octavo pamphlet of forty-seven pages, in short print, by Robert Fleming, to which he hath prefixed a short preface. And the publisher tells us, " That he had revised about twenty-four sermons, upon very edifying and profitable subjects, to print in a separate volume, from which they [his readers] should receive as great improvement and satisfaction, as from any of his printed treatises, which every person may easily discover from the style and language to be Mr. Binning's genuine compositions, as his manner of writing can scarcely be imitated by any other person." These sermons were carefully transcribed some little time ago, and revised by the assistance of a friend, and are now printed in this small volume.* * * And not to detain the reader further from the serious and candid perusal of this book, I shall only add, that I have faithfully transcribed these sermons from the manuscript copy without the smallest alteration of his sentiments. I have endeavoured to rectify a few grammatical errors of the transcribers and the old form of spelling, and altered a few words not now used in our modern sermons, for words of the same meaning. As I have added several sermons of this author upon the kingdom of God, which I transcribed since the proposals of this book were printed ; so I could not insert the sermons upon Acts xxvi. 18 ; Acts xiv. 11, 12, without almost doubling the price, which I feared would not be agreeable to some of the encouragers of this work. I intend to put the other sermons I have transcribed, or may yet copy, into the hands of some friends to revise before they be printed ; as also Mr. M'Ward's Life of this worthy gentleman, taken from his own papers.* * *

It is my sincere wish, that all the readers of this book may be builded up in spiritual wisdom and goodness unto eternal life.

BROUSTERLAND,
September 12th, 1760.

† [A relation of the principal circumstances in Binning's life follows.—ED.]

PRACTICAL SERMONS.

Sermon I.

1 John iii. 23.—"*And this is his commandment, That we should believe on the name of his Son Jesus Christ, and love one another.*"

It is a common doctrine often declared unto you, that the most part of those who hear the gospel do run, in their pretended course to heaven, either upon a rock of dashing discouragement, or the sands of sinking presumption. These are in all men's mouths; and no question they are very dangerous, so hazardous, as many fools make shipwreck either of the faith, or a good conscience,—of the faith, by running upon and dashing upon the rock,—of a good conscience, by sitting down upon the quicksand. But I fear that which is commonly confessed by all is cordially believed by few, and so, little regarded in our course and conversation. All Christians pretend to be making a voyage heaven-ward, and that is only home-ward. Now the gospel is given us to direct our course, and teach us how to steer between these two hazards, both safely and surely. This is the shore that shall guide us, and conduct to our intended haven, that is heaven, if we set our compass by it, and steer our course accordingly. Yet strange it is to behold the infinite wanderings and errors of men, on the one hand or the other:—some presuming upon the news of mercy, and the sound of God's grace, to walk after the imagination of their own hearts, and to live and continue in sin, for which Christ died, that he might redeem us from it, fancying a possibility of living in sin, and escaping wrath, and so abusing the tender of grace to promote licentiousness;—others, again, apprehending the wrath of God, and their just deservings, abusing the notion of God's justice, and the perfection of his holiness, to the prejudice of the glory of his grace and mercy, and their own salvation. This is certainly the cunning sleight of Satan, with the deceitfulness and ignorance of our own hearts, that leads men, and sometimes one and the same man, at diverse times, to contrary misapprehensions of divine truths. The wind of temptation gets fires to one corner of the house and then to another, and sometimes over-persuades the notion of mercy, and another time overstretches the apprehension of his justice; and yet in effect there is no true persuasion of any of them, but a cloud or shadow is apprehended instead of them.

Now I say, there is one cure for both these,—the right apprehension of the gospel in its entire and whole sum, the right uptaking of the light which shines in a dark place, and is given to lead us to our place of rest—to have a complete model, and a short summary of the gospel, always in our heart and eye. For truly it is the apprehending of parcels of divine truth, which leads men into such opposite mistakes and courses. To remedy this, we have some brief comprehensive models of the gospel set down by the Holy Ghost, and none in better terms than this here: 'This is his commandment, that ye believe,' &c. You have it in two words, faith and love. This is the form of sound words which we should hold fast, 2 Tim. i. 13. This is the mould of doctrine delivered by Christ and his Apostles. It is the separation of these two in some men's fancy, that leads too many in such paths of destruction. Truly they can as little be divided as the sun's light and heat, but the motions and shadows of them may, and it is the following the shadows of some of them which shipwrecks souls. Now not only the common multitude of the hearers of the gospel are in hazard of this, but even God's own children, who have believed in him.

The taking up of these things apart, creates the heart much trouble and perplexity, and occasioneth much sin and stumbling. I do think it is the ignorance and advertency of this conjunction, that makes our case both more sad and sinful than otherwise it would be. And these two indeed have a mutual influence upon one another, loosing reins to sin more freely, for it unquestionably disturbs the soul's peace, and procures it much bitterness. And again, the quitting hold of the promise of grace in Christ Jesus, and the indulging our own sad and sullen apprehensions, cannot but in the issue disable the soul from the duties of love, and expose it unto the violence of every temptation. As these two do mutually strengthen one another, the faith of Jesus Christ, and the lively apprehension of his grace and goodness, so they are the most noble and effectual persuasives to live unto him, and to walk in love. Besides, faith is the mean and way which God hath appointed to convey his influence unto the soul; and then again, love carrying itself actively in duties to God and men, bestirring itself for God and those who are beloved of God, it brings in a supply to faith, and returns by a straight compass to the spring from whence it first issued, and increases it still more. Believing on the name of the Son sends forth the stream of holy affection to him, and all begotten of the Father, and this returns again by the circuit of obedience to his commands and submission to his easy yoke, to unbosom itself in the fountain from whence it first issued; and whereas faith was at first one simple soul adherence to a Saviour, and a hearty embracing of him, this accession of the fruits of it exalts it unto that height of assurance, and gives that evidence which it wanted; and faith being thus strengthened, and rooted, and built up to the top of assurance of God's grace, love, and salvation, it becomes more able to bear the yoke of his commands, which are not grievous. The spring of believing, thus swelled by the concurrence of so many streams, it breaks forth the more, and sends out more love and delight in God, and more charity, compassion, and meekness towards men. And this is the circle and round Christianity runs, until that day come that the head-spring of faith shall be obscured and shrivelled up in the great sea of the love of God, which shall overflow all the saints' graces in due time, when we shall see God face to face.

This is a true Christian, which this apostle so beloved of God describes. Here is one under a commandment, and not above it, as some fondly conceive. He is a keeper of his commands, and a doer of these things which are pleasant in God's sight. This is no legal notion, if it be right taken.

It is not the bondage of the creature to be under the command of God, truly it is the beauty and liberty of a reasonable soul. Some speak of all subjection unto a law as slavery, but is it not an infinitely greater slavery to be at liberty to sin, and serve our own lusts? O wretched and base liberty! the Son indeed makes us truly free, and that from sin; and he is truly a Redeemer who redeems us from all iniquity, John viii. 32; Psal. cxxx. ult.; Tit. ii. 14.

But this commandment here spoken of, would not indeed be gospel, unless there was a prior command, a brighter precept, given by the Father to the Son. I find two commands given by the Father, and received by the Son, which two you may conjoin and make one of, as here faith and love are made one commandment. The first is, John x. 18, 'I lay down my life of myself, no man taketh it from me. This commandment have I received from my Father,' and no other. John xii. 49, 50, 'The Father gave me a commandment, what I should say and speak, and I know that his commandment is life everlasting.' This is more expressly and clearly set down, John vi. 39, 40, 'This is the Father's will that sent me, that of all that he gave me I should lose none, but raise them up at the last day. This is the will of him that sent me, that every one which seeth the Son, and believeth on him, should have everlasting life.' Here, then, beloved in the Lord, is the foundation of our hope, and that which makes all commandments given by God to us to come under a gospel notion, that which makes Christ's yoke easy, and his burden light, and his commands not grievous. The great commandment was imposed upon our Saviour. The great weight of that wrath due to our sins was put upon his shoulders. This was the Father's will, that he should lay down his life for his sheep; this command he received willingly, and obeyed faithfully and fully. And by his obedience to this, that great obligation to satisfy God's justice, and pay a ransom for our souls is taken off us ; inasmuch as he died, justice cannot come and demand it at our hand. Now, therefore, there is another commandment given to Christ, which directly concerns us, and it is this in substance : " I will and command that thou who hast come in the place of sinners, and resolvest to die for them, that thou give eternal life to whom thou wilt, even to as many as believe in thy name ; I give to thee the absolute disposal of life and death ; I command thee to preach life everlasting to all pious souls, that shall flee unto thee upon the apprehension of the danger of death, and that thou bestow that life upon them, and raise them up at the last day to be partakers of it.' This is the commission the Father gave to the Son, a sweet commission for poor sinners, and the charter of our salvation. And for this errand he was anointed with the Holy Spirit, and sent into the world; nay, the commission extends further than grace, even to eternal glory also. Christ has received commandment of the Father, to give repentance and remission of sin, both to give faith, and love, and all other graces, else it were defective. Thus Christ comes instructed to the world. He lays open his commission in preaching the gospel. He obeys the first commandment in his own person, by offering up himself upon the cross a sacrifice for sins, and he is about the fulfilling the next commandment, that is, the giving life to them that believe : and that he may accomplish it, having ascended himself unto heaven to intercede for us, he also sent his ambassadors into the world, to whom he hath committed the word of reconciliation, and he gives them commission to publish and proclaim this commandment in his own name. This is his command, that ye ' believe on the name of his Son Jesus Christ.' And this we do proclaim in his name, since he has gotten a commandment to give life everlasting to believers. This, then, is his charge to you, to come and receive it from him. Come and embrace him, and ye shall have life and all in him. This is the hardest and heaviest burden he imposes upon you, the weight of your life and salvation he hath taken upon himself. But O! now come and lay hold on him, who is thus offered unto you. Know that you are lost and undone in yourselves, consider the impossibilities you lie under to escape his wrath. Behold the anger of God hanging over your head, ready to be revealed in flaming fire, and a tempestuous cloud of eternal misery. Will ye consider that ye are born heirs of wrath ? Your natural inheritance is in the lake of fire ; and whatsoever your endowments by nature, or your privileges by birth be, nothing shall exeem you from this. Shall not then this Saviour be welcome to you ? For truly faith is but a cordial salutation and embracement of our blessed Redeemer. The soul brings him into the house, and makes him welcome, and he is standing ready to come in to your heart, and to bring in salvation with him.

Now whatever soul hath obeyed this commandment by belief of the truth, and receiving of Christ into the heart, there is but one commandment behind, and it is not grievous, viz., love me, and love one another ; love me, and live unto me. This is an easy yoke ; and there is good reason for it, though it had never been required to love him, and live to him, who loved not his life unto the death for us. There is mention made only of brotherly love here, but certainly the other love to God flowing from the sense of his love, is the right wing of the soul, and brotherly love the left; and by these the pious soul mounts up to heaven with the wings of an eagle. The love of our brother is but the fruit and consequent of this love, but it is set down as a probation, and clear evidence of the love of God in our souls.

Love is commanded as the very sum and substance of the whole law, as the fountain of all other duties. Things are compacted in their causes, and lie hid within the virtue of them. Truly this is the way to persuade and constrain you to all the duties of godliness and righteousness, of piety towards God, and charity towards men,—if once we could fasten this chain of affection upon your hearts, and engage your souls by love to God and man. We cannot but beat the air, while we seek to persuade you to the serious practice of religious duties, of prayer in secret and in your families, of reading and meditation upon the word, of sanctifying the Sabbath, of dealing justly and moderately with all men, of sobriety and temperance in your conversation, of denying ungodliness and worldly lusts, of walking humbly with God and towards men, of restraining and subduing your inordinate lusts and passions; I say, it is almost in vain to press these things upon you, or expect them from you, till once the Spirit of power and love enter into your hearts; and indeed the spirit of love is a powerful spirit, the love of God possessing the heart within, cannot but conform all within and without to his love and good pleasure. Love only can do these things which are pleasant in his sight, for it doth them pleasantly, heartily, and cheerfully; and God loves a cheerful giver, a cheerful worshipper. Brotherly love is rather expressed, because little or not at all studied by the most part. Other duties to God, if men come not up in practice to them, yet they approve them in their soul and mind. But there is scarce a notion of the obligation of charity and love towards our brethren, yea, not so much as in the minds of Christians let be in their practice. It is the special command which Christ left to his disciples when he was going away, John xiii. 35. But, alas! we have forgotten it, it is so long since.

Sermon II.

1 John iii. 23.—"*This is his commandment, that,*" &c.

We commonly make many rules in religion, and turn it into a laborious art, full of intricate questions, precepts, and contentions. As there hath been a great deal of vanity in the conception of speculative divinity, by a multitude of vain and unedifying questions which have no profit in them, or are beneficial to them that are occupied therein, but only have stirred up strife and envy, and raised the flame of contention in the Christian world; so I fear that practical divinity is no less vitiated and spoiled in this age amongst true Christians (by many perplexed cases relating to every condition), than the other among the schoolmen. Hereby it seems to me, that Christ and his apostles did not suppose it to be so perplexed a business as we now do make it; neither did the hearers weary themselves or others with so many various objections against the practice of the fundamental commandment of the gospel, believing in Jesus Christ. The plain nature of the gospel being holden forth and received, I am persuaded, was and is able (like the sun arising in brightness) to dispel and scatter all these mists and clouds which do arise both in the one and other, from ignorance at first, and which are elevated to a greater height by the custom of the times. The matter, my brethren, is not so dark as you make it. Here it is plainly and simply expressed: 'This is his commandment, that ye believe in the name of his Son;' and then, 'love one another.' Ye all know that we had commandments given us by God, which were by nature impressed on the heart of man; but by his fall into sin, the tables of the law (which I may say were in Adam's mind and heart, understanding and affection), those two tables were broken in the fall, and since there could be no obedience, because of ignorance and perversion, the tables breaking in pieces, their ruptures have produced these two opposite principles. The fall of man hath broken his mind, and so darkened his understanding, and broken his will, and put it in a wrong set. This appointed it, set it in a posture of enmity against God. However, we are by this fall utterly disabled to stand up before God in acceptable obedience. There is no man breathing, how blameless soever he be before the world, but must fall down as guilty before God in many things, yea, in all things. But the law being thus obliterated out of men's consciences, as he lost ability to obey, so he lost almost all conscience of sin and disobedience. He not knowing his charge and obligation, could not accuse himself for falling in rebellion. Therefore it pleased the Lord to cause the law to be written in tables of stone in mount Sinai. He transcribes the commandments over again, that all the world may see their obligation, and how infinitely short they have come in their subjection, and how just their condemnation may be. For this purpose, the Lord causes proclaim the old bond in the ears of men with great majesty and authority, as it became the Lawgiver, that all may become guilty, and stop their mouth before God, Rom. iii. 19. He would once have all men knowing that they are under infinite breaches of his commandments, that they may see themselves also subject to his judgment. Now, what do you think of a soul that stands at the foot of this mountain, and hears a dreadful accusation read against it, to all which the conscience within must subscribe unto, and both together pronounce the person guilty and liable to eternal punishment? I say, what can such a soul do, who has with trembling heard his voice? Satisfaction there cannot be given for an infinite offence against an infinite nature. The curse and sentence which was the sanction and confirmation of this commandment is just, and there appears no way how, without violation of God's justice, it can be repealed. Obedience to these commandments is now both impossible and unprofitable;—impossible, I say, because of the weakness and wickedness of the flesh, that has no ability nor willingness but to offend and disobey; and unprofitable, because it cannot at all relax the former sentence of condemnation. Now obedience, being a present duty, cannot pay old debts, or satisfy for our former rebellions, and so it must leave a man to seen condemnation. I fear this is a puzzle that all consciences must come unto here, or elsewhere. Here is a strait indeed.

But yet there is an enlargement, there is a way found out of bringing the soul out of the miry clay, and deep pit of misery; and it is this, God hath found out a ransom for himself, without our procurement, or consent, or knowledge. He hath provided a satisfaction to his justice in his Son Jesus Christ. Having laid upon him our iniquities, he exacts of him our deserved punishment, and makes him a curse who knew no sin. Now this being done, the Lord sends forth to all poor sinners who are trembling at mount Sinai this proclamation,—this is my last and most peremptory command, that ye believe in the name of my Son Jesus Christ. This is my well-beloved Son, in whom I am well-pleased, hear ye him. Have ye heard me the lawgiver condemning you? Now go and hear him, the Mediator and Saviour, absolving you, for I have committed all judgment unto him. Though I pronounce the sentence in this world against you, yet I have committed all the execution of it to him, and if you come to him, you may prevent it. You have broken all my former commandments, and I have pronounced a sentence against you for that. But now I give a new commandment instead of all the former, which if you obey, then the sentence of death is relaxed. You who cannot obey the law and give satisfaction in your own persons, I charge you to flee unto my Son Christ, who hath given me full satisfaction both to the curse, by suffering, and to the command, by obedience, and lay hold on his righteousness as your own, and in him ye are justified, and delivered from all these sentences and hard writings against you. I give a new commandment as the cure and remedy of all broken commandments. Believe on this name, in which is salvation. Take his obedience and suffering for your cure, and present me with that, I shall be as well satisfied as with your own personal satisfaction.

This now is very plain business. All commands are broken. There is yet one published in the gospel to help all, and it is in substance to embrace and welcome Jesus Christ for all, to seek our life and salvation in him, to take him as a priest to offer sacrifice for us, and expiate our sins, and to come to him as a prophet to seek wisdom and illumination, and all grace from him; to choose him as our King, henceforth to submit to his easy yoke of government. Now I say there will be no more debates about this. Will ye yet dispute whether ye may believe or not? Will ye inquire after this whether you have a warrant or not? Truly such a question would occasion much jealousy and provocation among men. If a man had signified as much willingness by command, by invitation, by request, by frequent repetition of these, yet to call in question or dispute whether or not I may go to such a person, will he make me welcome, were it not the greatest affront I could put upon him? Would it not alienate his affection more than any thing, to be jealous of his real kindness to me.

I would desire to hold out unto you the sin, the danger, and the vanity of such a way. I say the sin is great, it is no less than the highest and most heinous disobedience to the gospel, which of all others is of the deepest dye. You have disobeyed the law, and broken all the ten commandments. And will ye therefore disobey the gospel, too, and break this fundamental commandment? Is it not enough that ye have broken the rest, and will ye break this also, which was given for the cure of all?

Consider, I say, this is his commandment. Now commands should be obeyed, and not disputed, coming from an infallible and uncontrollable authority. Would ye not silence all the rebellions of your hearts against the commands of praying, hearing, reading, dealing justly, and walking soberly, with this one word, it is his command, it is his sovereign will? And why do ye not see the stamp of that same authority upon this? Now if you consider it aright, it hath more authority upon it than upon others, because it is his last command, and so would be taken as most pungent and weighty. When your hearts rise up to question and dispute this matter, I pray you cut all these knotty objections with the sword of his commandment. You use to go about to loose them by particular answers and untie them at leisure with art and skill, but truly it would be a readier and wiser course to cut them in pieces at one stroke, by this piercing and pungent precept. If your reasons and scruples be weighty, and you cannot get answers to overbalance them, I pray you put this weighty seal of divine authority into the balance, and sure I am it will weigh down all. Consider then the danger of it. It is the last and most peremptory command, after which you may expect no other, but the execution of justice. How sad and severe is the certification, 'He that believeth not is condemned already,' and 'the wrath of God abideth on him.' There needs no new sentence to be pronounced against you. Why? Because, if you believe not, that prior sentence of the law is yet standing above your heads to condemn you, that wrath abides on you. This is the only way to remove it, to come to him, who hath taken it on himself, after the breach of all commands. Ye have this retreat, this refuge to flee unto, a new command to come unto the Son, and have life ; but after this disobedience of the Son, you have none. There is nothing after unbelief, but ye are turned over, or rather left over, in the hand of the law and divine justice. Therefore it is the most dangerous and damnable thing to disobey this. It is to refuse the very remedy of sin. Consider also what vanity and uselessness is in these debates. What an unreasonable and senseless thing is it to dispute against our own soul, and against our own happiness! All is wrapt up here, and we do no less than the highest act of self-murder that can be. He that hateth me, wrongs his own soul. What an unreasonable thing then is it, because ye are miserable, to refuse mercy ; because ye are unclean, therefore to maintain that ye are not to come to the blessed fountain of cleansing ; because ye have broken the rest of the commands, therefore ye may not obey this? Is there any sense or reason in such things ; because I am a sinner, therefore I will not come to a Saviour? Alas! to what purpose was the Son sent and given, and for what end came he? Was it not to seek and to save such as are lost and undone, and to deliver them from misery? What do you gain by such questions? For at length you must turn and enter in at the door of a naked command and promise, when you have wearied yourselves to find that in your hearts which is not in them, to seek waters in the wilderness, and springs in the desert, qualifications and graces in your own hearts to warrant your boldness in coming to the promise. I say, when you have sought and all in vain, you must at length come to this fountain in which is all grace and happiness. If you had what you seek, yet if ye would indeed believe in Christ, you must deny them and look upon yourselves as ungodly, to be justified by faith. Why then do you grasp after that which can do you no good, (though you had it,) I mean, in point of your acceptation? Consider it, my beloved, that the honour of God and your own happiness lies most in this, nay not only that, but your holiness too, which you pretend to seek after, lies in it. Till you come to Christ, it is in vain to seek it elsewhere.

Sermon XXI.

1 John iii. 23.—"*And this is his commandment,*" &c.

There are different tempers of mind among men, some more smooth and pliable, others more refractory and froward. Some may be persuaded by love, who cannot be constrained by fear. With some a request will more prevail than a command. Others again are of a harsher disposition. Love and condescension doth rather embolden them, and therefore they must be restrained with the bridle of authority. It would seem that the Lord hath some regard to this in the administration of the gospel. He accommodates himself to the diverse dispositions of men, and (if we may say with respect to him which yet can be no disrespect, seeing he hath humbled himself lower) he doth become all things to all men, that he may gain some. You see the gospel sometimes running in the channel of love and kindness, sometimes in the channel of authority and majesty. God sometimes stoopeth down to invite, and affectionately to beseech sinners to come unto his Son for life. He hath prepared a marriage and banquet for us in Christ. He hath made all things ready for the receiving, for the eating, and he sends forth his servants to entreat and invite all such, who have no bread and clothing, who are poor and lame, to this wedding. He gives an hearty invitation to all that stand at an infinite distance from God, and so are feeding upon empty vanities without him, to come and enjoy the riches of his grace, which runs as a river in Christ between these two golden banks, the pardon of sin, and the purification of our soul from its pollution. You have a hearty invitation, Isa. lv. 1, 2, 3, 'Ho, every one that thirsteth, come to the waters.' But he comes yet lower to request and obtest poor sinners, as if he could have advantage by it; he will not stand* to be a supplicant at any man's door, to beseech him to be reconciled to God, 2 Cor. v. 14, 19, 20. As if we could do him a favour and benefit, he requests us most earnestly. Truly it is strange that this doth not melt the heart, and make it fall down into the belief and obedience of the truth. Affection is the most insinuating and prevailing thing with an ingenuous spirit, most of all when it is accompanied with majesty in the person that hath it, and humility in the carriage and disposition. For a great personage to descend out of love, to affectionate and humble requests and solicitations, this cannot but have a mighty influence on any spirit that is not wild and savage. But because the heart of man is desperately wicked, and hath lost that true ingenuity and nobleness of spirit, and is now become stubborn and froward, as a wild ass, or as a swift dromedary traversing her ways, therefore the Lord takes another way of dealing with men suitable to their froward natures; he gives out his royal statute backed with majesty and authority; "This is his command," &c.—that when fair means could not prevail, other means more terrible might reduce lost rebellious men. He hedges in our way with threatenings and promises annexed to the commandment, 'He that believeth has everlasting life, but he that believeth not is condemned already, and shall not see life, but the wrath of God abideth on him.' He declares all men traitors if they come not in to his Son, to be reconciled to God, before the decree of wrath pass forth.

Truly it is a wonder that there should be any need either of an invitation, or a request, or a command, or a threatening; that we should need to be invited, or requested, or commanded, or threatened to our own happiness. Might not a bare and simple offer, or proposal of Jesus Christ, his nature, and offices, of the redemption and salvation purchased by him, suffice? What needed more, but to declare unto us that we are lost and utterly undone by nature, and that there is a refuge and remedy provided in Christ? Surely in any other thing of little importance, we needed no entreaty. Were it not a good enough invitation to a man that is like to starve for hunger, to cast meat freely before him; or to a man that is in hazard of drowning, to cast a cord to him? We would seek no other persuasion to go and dig for a treasure of gold, than to show us where it is hid. But strange is the rebellious and perverse disposition of man's heart. What an enmity is in it to the ways of God! What strange inclination to self-murder, ever since man destroyed himself! We cannot express it unto you; but you may perceive it well enough, both by the Lord's frequent obtesting, and protesting to us in his word, and the experience of the great barrenness of all such means. Whence is it, I pray you, that there should need so many means to persuade you to that which is your own advantage, and to call you to shun the ways of destruction? And whence is it that notwithstanding of all those invitations, entreaties, commandments, promises, and threatenings often sounding in your ears, yet the most part are not reduced to

* [That is, he will not refuse.—Ed.]

obedience, nor reclaimed from the ways of death, and do not take hold of the path of life. Truly it may plainly point out to you the desperate wickedness of the heart, the stubbornness and rebelliousness of our disposition, and if once we could persuade you of this, we had gained a great point which few do seriously consider, and so do not abhor themselves.

The commandments mentioned in the text are these two, to believe in Christ, and to love our brother. It is no wonder they are recommended with so much seriousness and earnestness; for they are both the most comprehensive, and the most pleasing commandments. They are most comprehensive; for it appears that all the commands spoken of in the preceding verse, are summed up in this one precept, 'And this is his commandment,' &c. And that they are most pleasant in God's sight is evident, for the true Christian being described from this, that he does these things that are pleasing in God's sight,—that he is one that studies to conform himself to his good pleasure, this is subjoined, as the two most pleasing exercises of Christianity, 'This is his commandment,' that is, his pleasing commandment, that ye should believe in Christ, and love one another.

This command of believing in Jesus is comprehensive, because it takes in all precepts, and that under a threefold consideration. It takes them all in as broken and transgressed by men, as fulfilled by Christ, and also takes them all in as a rule of righteousness, according to which the believer ought henceforth to walk.

The command of believing in Christ doth first of all import this,—that a sinner should examine himself according to the law of God,—that he should lay his whole life and course, his heart and ways, down before the perfect and holy commandments,—that he may stop his own mouth with shame and silence, and find himself guilty before God. Many use to speak of humiliation preparatory to believing, and the work of the law preparatory to the gospel. But truly I conceive it would be more fitly expressed, if it were holden out thus, that it is one of the essential ingredients in the bosom of believing, and one of the first articles of the gospel-law, to charge all sinners to acknowledge their sin and misery, to discern their own abounding iniquity, and danger of perishing by it, how guilty they are before God, and how subject to his judgment, that so finding themselves undone, they may have recourse to a Saviour.

Truly the Spirit's work is to convince of sin, and then of righteousness, and when we are commanded to believe, the first part of our believing is crediting and subscribing to the law, to the justice and righteousness of God against us; and then the believing and acknowledging the gospel is the end and purpose to that. 'Ye believe in God, believe also in me.' This takes in completely the two books of saving faith towards God as a Lawgiver and Judge, and faith towards our Lord Jesus Christ as a Saviour and Redeemer; and it doth but beget misapprehensions in many, when the one is looked upon as a condition without which we shall not be welcome to the other. Truly, I think, both are proposed as essentials of saving faith; none of them in such a way as to procure right and warrant to the other, but only in such an order as is suitable to any reasonable nature to be wrought upon, and that is all. It is only required of you, upon that account, because fleeing unto a Saviour for refuge is a rational and deliberate action, which necessarily includes the sense of misery without him. But the sense of sin and misery is not urged as one thing which ye should go about to prepare, and fit yourselves for more welcome at Christ's hand as commonly it is taken. Here it is easy to understand how the command of believing belongs unto all who hear it, even to the vilest and grossest sinners, who are yet stout, hard-hearted, and far from righteousness, (Isa. xlvi. 12.) those who are spending their money for that which is not bread, and their labour for that which satisfies not, and those whose hearts are uncircumcised, and their lives profane. And yet the commandment of coming to the Son and believing on him for life, is extended unto them all. All are invited, requested, commanded, and threatened to this duty. There is no bar of exclusion set down in the gospel to hold out one, and let in another; as many suppose these promises, that sound condition-wise, to be limitations, and restrictions of the right and warrant to persons to believing. Indeed it is true, all are not exhorted at the first hand to assurance of God's love, and an interest in Christ. There is no question that none have right to this seal, but them who have believed and set to their own seal to the character or truth of the word. But all are charged to believe in Christ, that is, out of a sense of their own lost estate, to embrace a Saviour for righteousness and strength. Neither is there any fear that men can come too soon to Christ. We need not set down exclusions or extractions, for if they be not sensible of sin and misery, they will certainly not come to him at all. And therefore the command that enjoins them to believe on the Son, charges them also to believe that they are lost without him. And if the most presumptuous sinners would once give obedience to this commandment, really there would be no fear of presumption in coming too soon unto Jesus. A sense of sin is not set as a porter, to keep out any who are willing to come in; but rather to open the door, and constrain them that were unwilling to enter in: so that if the least measure of that can do this, we are not to stand till we have more, but to come to the Prince exalted to get remission of sins, and more true gospel-sorrow which worketh repentance unto salvation from dead works. You should not therefore understand any promises in the scriptures so, as if there were any conditions set down to seclude any from coming, who are willing to come. For they do but declare the nature and manner of what they are invited to, that no man may mistake believing, and take his own empty presumptions or fancies, which embolden him to sin more, for that true faith which is full of good fruits.

Now, in the text, the pious soul, having once subscribed to the guilt and curse of all the commandments, by believing the law, he looks also upon the Son, Jesus Christ, and finds the law fulfilled, the curse removed, all satisfied in him. He finds all the commandments obeyed in his person, all the wrath due for the breach of them pacified and quenched by his sufferings. And he gives a cheerful and cordial approbation of all this. He receives Christ as the end of the law for righteousness, which Christ made up by obedience and suffering to supply our disobedience. We should stay or rest upon this, as that which pacifies the Father's wrath to the full. This is what gives the answer of a good conscience, and pacifies every penitent soul, and secures his title to heaven. Now this presents God with a full atonement and obedience to all the law, which he accepts from a believer as if it were his own. This is the large comprehension of believing; it takes in its arms, as it were, in one bundle,* all the precepts and curses, and devolves them over on Christ, puts them in an able hand, and then takes them all, as satisfied and fulfilled by him, and holds them up in one bundle to the Father. And hence it proceeds, in the third place, that believing on the Son takes in all again, to be the rule of walking, and the mark to aim at. Finding such a perfect exoneration of bygones † in Christ, and standing in such favour with God, the soul is sweetly constrained to love and delight in the divine laws. And truly this is the natural result of faith. I wish you may rightly observe this conjunction, that this is inseparably knit with it, love to God and men, delight to do his will, to love him, and live unto him. Do not deceive yourselves with vain words. If you find not the smartness of the gospel, and the doctrine of grace laying this restraint upon the heart, ye are yet in your sins. This is the reasoning of a believing soul: Shall I, who am dead unto sin, live any longer therein? Shall I not delight in those commandments, when Christ hath delivered me from the curse of the law? Though such a one fall, and come short, yet the pressure of the heart is that way. But then attend unto the order, ye must first believe on the Son, and then love him, and live unto him. Ye must first flee unto his righteousness, and then the righteousness of the law shall be wrought in you. Therefore do not weary yourselves to no purpose. Do not wrong your own souls by seeking to prevent this order, which was established for your joy and salvation. Know that you must first meet with satisfaction in all the commands of Christ, before obedience to any of them be accepted, and having met with that, know that the sincere endeavour of thy soul, and the affectionate bensal ‡ of thy heart to thy duty, is accepted. And if ye find yourselves thereafter surcharged with guilt and unanswerable walking, yet ye know the way is to begin at this again, to believe in the Son. This is the round you must walk, as long as ye are in the body. When you are defiled, run into the fountain; and when you are washed,

* [Parcel.—Ed.] † [Such a disburdening of former offences.—Ed.] ‡ [Inclination.—Ed.]

study to keep your garments clean; but if defiled again, get your hearts washed from wickedness. 'These things,' says John, 'I write to you that ye sin not,' who believe. but if any sin, who desire not to transgress, you have a propitiation for the sins of the whole world.

Now love is a very comprehensive command. It is the fulfilling of the whole law, Rom. xiii. 10; Matth. xxii. 37, 38. It is indeed the true principle and pure fountain of our obedience unto God and men. All fruits of the Spirit are moral virtues that grow out of the believer. Whether pleasant unto God, or refreshing unto men, they are all virtually in this root of love, all the streams are compacted in this fountain. Therefore he names one for all, viz. brotherly-love, which is the bond of perfection, Col. iii. 14. It is a bundle of many divine graces, a company or society of many Christian virtues combined together. They are named bowels of mercies, long-suffering, kindness, humbleness of mind, meekness, forbearance, and forgiveness, all which are tied to the believer's girdle by charity; so that where love is, every good comes. After it a troop of so many sweet endowments and ornaments also come, and where this is wanting, (as truly it is the epidemical disease of the time,) there are many sins abounding; for when iniquity abounds 'the love of many shall wax cold,' Matt. xxiv. 12. Oh that is our temper or rather our distempered nature,—love cold, and passion hot! When charity goes away, these wild and savage beasts of darkness come forth, viz. bitter envying and strife, rigid censuring and judging, unmercifulness and implacableness of spirit upon others' failings and offences. Self-love, that keeps the throne, and all the rest are her attendants. For where self-love and pride is, there is contention, strife, envy, and every evil work, and all manner of confusion. Thus they lead one another as in a chain of darkness, Prov. xiii. 10; James iii. 16. Think not that love is a complimental word, and an idle motion of loving; it is a more real thing, a more vital thing. It hath bowels of mercy, they move themselves when others are moved, and they bring their neighbour's misery into the inmost seat of the heart, and make the spirit a solemn companion in misery. And it is also exercised in forbearing and forgiving. Charity is not easily provoked, therefore it can forbear; is easily appeased, therefore it can forgive: it is not soon displeased, or hard to be pleased, 'forbearing' and forgiving 'one another in love.' Study then this grace more. See it to be the fulfilling of the law; for 'the end of the commandment is charity, out of a pure heart, a good conscience, and faith unfeigned.' The end of the law is not strife and debate, nor such intricate and perplexed matters as minister endless questions and no edification. Though men pretend conscience and scripture, yet the great end of both is violated, that is charity, which mainly studies edification in truth and love. And therefore it is a violent perversion of the commandment, or word, to overstretch every point of conscience, or difference, so far as to the renting of Christian peace and unity. What hath kindled all these flames of bloody war, what hath increased all these fiery contentions among us, but the want of this? As James says of the tongue, so I may speak of uncharitableness and self-love, they set on fire the course of nature, and they are set on fire of hell. The true zeal and love of God, is like that elementary fire of which they speak, that in its own place hath a temperate heat, and doth not burn or consume what is about it. But our zeal is like the fire that is mixed with some gross matter, a preying, devouring, and consuming thing, zeal down in the lower region of man's heart; it is mixed with many gross corruptions, which are as oil and fuel to it, and gives it an extreme intemperate destroying nature.

But then consider, that this commandment of love is our Lord and Saviour's last testamentary injunction to his disciples, John xiii. 34, 35. 'A new commandment I give unto you, that ye love one another; as I have loved you, that ye also love one another. By this shall all men know that ye are my disciples, if ye have love one to another.' It is Christ's latter-will, and given us as a token and badge of discipleship. Every profession hath its own signs and rules, every order their own symbol, every rank their own character. Here is the differential or peculiar character and livery of a Christian, brotherly-love,—'By this shall all men know that ye are my disciples, if ye have love one to another,' &c. I remember a story of a dying father who called his sons to him on his death-bed, and having sent for a bundle of arrows, he tried them one by one if they could break them; and when they had all tried this in vain, he caused loose the bundle, and take the arrows one by one, and so they were easily broken: by which he gave them to understand, that their stability and strength would consist in unity and concord, but, if love and charity were broken, they were exposed to great hazard.* I think our Lord and Saviour gives such a precept unto his disciples at his departure out of this world,—'A new command I give unto you,' &c. (John xiii. 34.)—to show them that the perfection of the body, into which they were all called as members, consisted in that bond of charity. And indeed love is not only a bond or bundle of perfection in respect of graces, but in regard of the church too. It is that bond or tie which knits all the members into one perfect body, Col. iii. 14, 15, 16. Without this bond, all must needs be rents, rags, and distractions.

Now I shall add but one word of the other, that these commands are pleasing in God's sight. And truly believing in the Son must be grateful to him, not only from the general nature of obedience to his will, but also because this doth most honour both to the Father and to the Son. The Father counts himself much honoured, when we honour the Son; and there is no honour the creature can be in a capacity to give unto him like this, to cast all our hope, and hang all our happiness upon him, (John v. 23, 24.) to set to our seal that he is true and faithful, (John iii. 33.) which is done by believing. But most of all, this is pleasing in his sight because the Father's good pleasure concentres in the same point with the soul's good pleasure, that is, on the well-beloved Son, Christ. Therefore faith must needs be well-pleasing to the Father; for what is faith else but the soul's complacency and satisfaction in the Son. As the Father is already well-pleased with his death and sufferings, so he propones and holds him out in the gospel, that you may be as well-pleased with him as he is. This is believing indeed, to be pleased with him as the Father is pleased, and this pleases the Father too. Oh that you could understand this! The gospel is not brought unto you, that you may reconcile God, and procure a change in his affection; but for this end, to beseech you to be reconciled unto God, to take away all hostile affections out of your heart. And this is the business we have to do, to persuade you that the Father holds him abundantly contented with his Son. 'This is my beloved Son, in whom I am well-pleased.' And to move you to be as well contented with him as he is, he says, 'Hear him. I hear him for you, hear ye him for me. I hear him interceding for you, hear ye him beseeching you.' Now this may take down all ground of jealousy concerning our welcome and acceptance; it cannot but be an acceptable and pleasing thing to God, that the affection and desire of the soul fall in and embosom itself with his good pleasure upon Christ his Son.

And then, in the next place, it is well-pleasing to God that ye love one another, not only because he shall see his own image and likeness in your love; (for there is nothing in which a Christian more eminently resembles his Father, or more evidently appears to be a child of the Highest, than in free loving all, especially the household of faith, and forbearing and forgiving one another, and so he cannot choose but like it well;) but especially, because your love concentres too, and meets upon the same objects with his love, these whom the Father so loved, that he gave his only begotten Son for them; and the Son so loved them, that he gave himself for them. If these be thy delight, and thou forbear them as the Father and the Son hath done, that conspiracy of affections into one point cannot but be pleasing unto him. Now, if these please him so well, whom should they not please?

Sermon XV.

JAMES iii. 14.—"*But if ye have bitter envying and strife in your hearts, glory not,*" &c.

It is a common evil of those who hear the gospel, that they are not delivered up to the mould and frame of religion that is holden out in it, but rather bring religion

* [De Agricola filios suos docente. ÆSOP. Fab. p. 98. Oxon. 1653.—ED.]

into a mould of their own invention. It was the special commendation of the Romans, that they obeyed from the heart that form of doctrine into which they were delivered, (Rom. vi. 17.) that they who were once servants, or slaves of sin, had now become voluntary captives of truth, and had given themselves up to the gospel, to be modelled and fashioned by it; and if so, then certainly the most substantial points of religion would be most deeply engraven upon them. Every thing would have its own due place with us, if we were cast in the primitive mould of godliness; but when we cast godliness in a mould of our own apprehension, they cannot choose but a miserable confusion and disorder will follow in the duties of religion. For according as our fancy and inclination impose a necessity upon things, so we do pursue them, and not according to the real weight that is in them. I find the scripture laying most weight upon the most common things, placing most religion in the most obvious and known things; and for other things more remote from common capacity, I find them set far below, in the point of worth and moment, even these things that seem least. But I find that order quite perverted in the course of Christians. Some particular points that are not so obvious to every understanding, are put in the first place, and made the distinguished character of a Christian; and others again, in which true and undefiled religion doth more consist, are despised and set in a low place, because of their ceremonies. I think this apostle hath observed this confusion, and hath applied himself to remove it, by correcting the misapprehensions of Christians, and reducing their thoughts and ways to the frame of true Christianity. Even as Christ dealt with the Pharisees, who brought in such a confusion in religion, by imposing a necessity upon ceremonies, and an indifferency upon the very substance itself, truly, I think, it may be said unto us, you tithe mint, anise, and cummin, and pass over judgment and the love of God: these things ye ought to have done, and not to leave the other undone. Ye neglect the weightier matters of the law, judgment, mercy, faith and truth, and in the room of these ye have misplaced things, that are higher in God's esteem from an apprehension of their necessity. Thus by your traditions and opinions of things so remote from the kingdom of God, ye have made the unquestionable commandments of God of none effect, Matth. xv. 6. You think possibly, if this apostle was coming out to preach unto you this day, that he would certainly resolve you in many controverted points, and would bring some further light to the debates of the time. But truly I think if he knew the temper of our spirits, he would preach over this sermon to us again: 'My brethren, be not many masters,' &c. I suppose he would bring that old primitive light of pure and undefiled religion, the splendour of which our present ways and courses could not endure, but would be constrained to hide themselves in darkness. What would you think of such a sermon as this, 'If any man among you seem to be religious, and bridleth not his tongue, this man's religion is vain?' Jam. i. 26. 'If any man offend not in word, the same is a perfect man,' Jam. iii. 2. This is accounted a common and trivial purpose. But believe it, sirs, the Christian practice of the most common things, hath more religion in it than the knowledge of the profoundest things; and till you learn to do what you know, it is a mockery to study to know further what to do. There is a strange stirring of mind after more light and knowledge in some particulars of the time. But I would fain know, if there be as much ardour and endeavour to practise that which we have already. To him that hath shall be given; to him that makes use of his knowledge for the honour of God, and the good of mankind, and their edification, more shall be given; but from him that hath not, shall be taken away even that which he hath, and yet really and cordially hath not, because he hath no use of it. Therefore he may by inquiry find more darkness, because his old light shall rather be put out. Do you not all know that ye should bridle your tongues, that it is a great point of that Christian victory over the world to tame and danton * that undantoned wild beast, to quench that fire-brand of hell? Do ye not all know that we should be swift to hear, slow to speak, and slow to wrath? And as the apostle Paul speaks on another subject, 'Doth not even nature itself teach you' when you have but one tongue, and two ears, that ye should hear much, and speak little?

* [Subdue.—Ed.]

Are not our ears open, and our tongue enclosed and shut up, to teach us to be more ready to hear than to speak? Now I say, till Christians learn to practise these things that are without all controversy, you may make it your account never to want controversy, and never to get clearness. For to what purpose should more light be revealed, when that which is revealed is to no purpose?

But it is in vain to think to reform the tongue, till you have the heart first reformed. They say the belly hath no ears. Truly the tongue is all tongue, and has no ears to take an admonition or instruction. We must, then, with the apostle, retire into the heart, and abate from the abundance of the superfluity and naughtiness that is within; and therefore our apostle descends to the cure of pride, envy and strife in the heart, that are fountains of all that pestiferous flood which flows out of every man's mouth. 'Is there any wise man among you?' &c. And indeed this is the orderly proceeding both of nature and grace. Nature begins within to probe among the superfluous and noisome humours which abound in the body, and desolate the members, and doth not think it sufficient to apply external plasters. Grace must begin within too, to purge the heart, for out of the abundance of the heart the mouth speaks, the eye looks, and the feet walk. If there be no destroyer in the members or outward man, it is not the prescriving of rules and cautions that will suffice to restrain, to abate, or to cure, but the disease must be ripped up to the bottom, the cause found within, as our apostle doth here. Hence, says he, proceed all these feverish distempers among you, your hot and passionate words, your evil speakings and reproachings, your contentions and wars about matters either civil or religious. Whence are all these? From a vain persuasion of wisdom, from a foolish imagination of some excellency in yourselves, and some inward affection to be accounted something of among men. 'Who is a wise man,' &c. You would be accounted wise, and so you do account yourselves, and this begets strife and envy in the heart, and predisposeth the mind to strife and contention with others. Aud therefore he takes the mask off, by deciphering the very nature of such a wisdom; he embowels that pretended wisdom in religion and gives it its own name, and because things are best known, and most livelily comprehended in their opposition and comparison with one another, he shows wherein true wisdom and religion consist, and sets the one against the other, that the deformity of the one and the beauty of the other may appear. We shall then speak a word of this that is supposed, and then of that which is expressed, the descriptions of true wisdom, and pretended wisdom. I conceive this interrogation, 'Is there a wise man among you?' imports chiefly these two: one is,—that it is the natural disease of all men to esteem themselves something, and desire to be esteemed such by others; another is, —that the misapprehension of that wherein true wisdom and excellency doth especially consist, is the ground of many miscarriages in the seeking or venting of that.

It was an ancient remark, that 'vain man would be wise, though he be born like a wild ass's colt.' Empty man is wise in his own eyes, and would be so in other men's too. He hath no reality nor solidity, but is like these light things which the wind carries away, or the waters bear above, and tosses hither and thither; yet he apprehends some solid and real worth in himself, and would impose that apprehension upon others. And truly this is a drunkenness of mind, which makes a man light and vain, to stagger to and fro. It is a giddiness of spirit, that makes him inconstant and reeling, but insensible of it. Though he be born as stupid and void of any real wisdom and excellency, as a wild ass's colt, yet he hath this madness and folly superadded to all that natural stupidity, that he seems to be wise and understanding; and truly it was a more ancient disease than Job's days. We may trace the steps of its antiquity to be from the very beginning, and there we shall find the true original of it. What was it, I pray you, did cast the angels out of heaven, down to the lowest hell, to be reserved in chains for everlasting darkness? I do not conceive what their natures so abstracted from all sensual lusts could be capable of, but this spiritual darkness and madness of self-conceit, and an ambitious aspiring after more wisdom, whence did flow that mal-content and envious humour, in maligning the happiness of man. And this was the poison that Satan, the chief of these angels, did drop into man's nature, by temptations and suggestions of an imaginary wisdom and happiness; 'You shall be as gods knowing good and evil.'

And truly this poison is so strong and pestilent, that having once entered into the body, it spreads through all the members; it infects all the posterity that were in Adam's loins. Being once distilled into the lump, it diffuses itself through the whole, such a strange contagion is it. That wretched aim at a higher wisdom, hath thrown us all down into this brutish and stupid condition, to be like wild asses' colts. Yet this false and fond imagination of wisdom and excellence remains within us, which is so much the nearer madness, that now there is no apparent ground left for such a fairly.* And if one of a cubit's height, should imagine himself as tall as a mountain, and accordingly labour to stretch out himself, we would seek no other sign of madness. Truly this malignant and poisonable humour is so subtile that it hath insinuated itself into all the parts and powers of the soul, and steals in without observation into all our thoughts, purposes, affections, ways, and courses. It is of so infectious and pestiferous a nature, that it defiles all that is in the man, and all that comes out of the man.

The apostle speaks of covetousness, that it 'is the root of all evil.' Truly I think that comprehends many inordinate affections in it. Now, both self-love and earth-love arise from some false imagination of that which is not. Whether it be an imagination of some excellency in ourselves, or some worth in these worldly and earthly things, man first makes a god of it, and then worships it. Therefore covetousness is called idolatry, self-idolatry, and earth-idolatry. We first attribute some divinity to ourselves, like these people (Isa. xliv. 17.) to their idols. We then fall down and worship ourselves; but we do not consider in our heart, that we are but dust. And then we ascribe some divinity to the perishing things of the world, and then worship them; but do not consider that they are earthly and perishing vanities. Thus we feed upon ashes, a deceived heart hath turned us aside, and we cannot deliver our own souls, by discovering the lie that is in our right hand. We feed partly on the element of the air, by seeking that of others that we have of ourselves; and partly upon the element of the earth, by the love of this world. And these two degenerated evils, are the root of all evils, self-estimation, and creature-affection.

I think this apostle in this one word, 'Is there any wise man among you,' or any endowed with knowledge? and that word, 'glory not,' strikes at the root of all the forementioned and aftermentioned evils. From whence I say doth that promptitude and bensal† to speak, that slowness and difficulty to hear, that readiness and inclination to pride, (reproved, James i. 19, 20.) proceed? Is it not from an overweening conceit of our own wisdom, that we are so swift to speak, and so slow to hear, and that we would teach others, and yet be taught of none? We are so much in love with our own apprehensions, that we imagine they shall find as much esteem and affection among men; and so being like barrels full of liquor, in our own conceit, we are like to burst, if we vent not, and are as incapable of taking from others as of retaining what is within. The word of God was a fire in Jeremiah's heart that would have consumed him, if he had not given it vent. Truly self-love is a fire that must vent one way or other, or it would burn up all within by displeasure, and then it is the over-apprehension of some excellency in ourselves, which so disposes us to anger, that makes us combustible matter, like the spirit of gunpowder; for the least spark of injury or offence, will set all in a flame. It is certainly the fond imagination of some great worth in ourselves, that is the very immediate predisposition to the apprehension of an injury. Humility cannot be affronted, it is hard to persuade of an injury. Why? Because there is no excellency to be hurt or wronged. Therefore Christ conjoins these, 'meek and lowly in heart,' (Matth. xi. 29,) lays poverty of spirit down as the foundation of meekness, Matth. v. 3—5. Whence is it that we accept of men's persons by judging according to the outward appearance, and are so ready to displease our brethren, especially these who are inferior to us in body, or mind, or estate? Is it not from this root, self-admiration? This makes us elevate ourselves above others, and to intrude ourselves among these who are chiefest in account. Whence doth our unmercifulness and rigidity towards other men proceed, but from this fountain, that we allow so

* [Such a wonder.—Ed.]

† [Violent inclination.—Ed.]

much licence and indulgence to ourselves, that we can have none to spare for others, and that we do not consider that we ourselves stand in need of more mercy from God, and cannot endure a mixture of judgment in it? Therefore we have judgment to others without mercy, James ii. 13. And is not this self-pleasing humour the fountain of that contentious plea after the pre-eminence, and censorious liberty of judging others, and usurping authority over them? James iii. 1, 'My brethren, be not ye many masters.' Truly this is the root of all contentions and strifes. It is this which rents all human and Christian society. This looses all the pins of concord and unity. This sets all by the ears, and makes all the wheels reel through other. The conceit of some worth beyond others, and the imagination of some pre-eminence over them, even in the best creatures—he best, and he best, that is the plea; he greatest, and he greatest, that is the controversy. As bladders puffed up with wind, they cannot be kept in little room, but every one presses another; but if the wind were out, they would compact in less room, and comply better together. The apostle implies this, when he puts every man in mind of his own failing, 'in many things we offend all;' and if this were considered, it would abate our security, and cool our heat and fervour, and moderate our rigour towards others. There would not be such strife about places of power and trust, if we were not swelled in our own apprehensions to some eminency. And is not this the very fountain which sends out all these bitter streams of the tongue, these evil-speakings one of another, these sharp and immoderate censures of our neighbours? Truly this is it, every man accounts himself to be wiser and more religious than his brother, to have more knowledge, and so he cannot endure any difference in opinion; to have more holiness, and so he cannot bear any infirmity in practice. But the way to help this, would be to humble ourselves before God, James iv. 10. Lowliness and meekness are the ground stones of these Christian virtues which preserve Christian-society, Eph. iv. 2, 3. And is not this, I pray you, the foundation of wars, strifes, contentions, and jealousies? 'From whence come wars and fightings among you?' Is it not from these imperious lusts which war in our members? Only from pride cometh contention, Prov. xiii. 10. The head-spring of all envy, also issues out from pride, and this divides, in many streams and waters, all our courses and ways, with putrified and pestilent corruptions. While every man hath this opinion of himself, all is done in strife, no condescendence, no submission one to another, Phil. ii. 3. While all make themselves the centre, it cannot otherwise happen, but designs, courses, thoughts, and ways, must interfere and jar among themselves. Self-seeking puts all by the ears, as you see children among themselves, if an apple be cast to them. Any bait or advantage of the times yokes them in that childish contention, who shall have it? All come, strive, and fight about it, and it is but a few can have it, and these that get it cannot keep it long. Others will catch it from them. Now what vain things are these, which can neither be gotten, nor kept, but by strife? Oh that we could seek better things, which may be both sought and kept, without emulation or strife!

Now the other thing is, that the misapprehension of that wherein true excellence consists is the ground of many evils: 'Who is a wise man?' &c. You all affect the title, and ye seek the thing, as ye suppose. But alas! ye mistake that wherein it consists. Truly there is in all men (ever since we tasted of the tree of knowledge of good and evil) a strange innate desire of knowledge, and affectation of wisdom, and desire of excellence. But since the first endeavour in paradise succeeded ill, there hath nothing gone well since. We weary ourselves to catch vanities, shadows, and lies. 'How long, O ye sons of men, will ye love vanity, and follow after lies?' That divinely taught prophet could not but pity the children of men. And as Paul speaks to the Athenians of another purpose, 'Him whom ye ignorantly worship, we show unto you,' so he declares unto men that which they ignorantly and vainly seek elsewhere. This I assure you consists in this, that ye show out of a good conversation your works with meekness and wisdom.

All our mischief proceeds from this, that we misapprehend and mistake that which we would gladly have. And so once being in the wrong way, that cannot lead to our purposed end; the faster we run, the farther we go from it. The more we move in affection and diligence, the less we indeed promove in reality to the attaining what we seek. How greatly have we fallen! I might instance this in many things, but I shall be content with these two. There is a desire in all men after happiness, but there is a fundamental error in the imagination supposing it to consist in the enjoyment of temporal pleasure, honour, advantage, or the satisfaction of our own natural inclinations. Now this leads all mankind to a pursuit after these things. But how base a scent is it? And how vain a pursuit is it? For the faster they move in that way, the further they are from all solid and true contentment. Again, in all godly men, there is something of this rectified, and they suppose religion to be the only true wisdom, and this wisdom the only true happiness. But oftentimes there are even mistakes in that too. As many of the world call sweet bitter, and bitter sweet, because of the vitiated and corrupted palate; so the godly, being in some measure distempered, call that which is not so sweet sweetest, and that which is not so bitter, bitterest. They change the value of things, and misplace them out of that order in which God hath set them. One great mistake is this. We impose a great deal of weight and moment upon these things in religion, which are but the hay and stubble, or pins in the building, and we esteem less that wherein the foundation and substance of true religion consists. We have an over-apprehension of a profession, and an undervaluing thought of practice. We overstretch some points of knowledge, and truth of the least value;* and have less value for the fundamental statutes of the gospel, faith and love, mercy and judgment. This our Saviour reproved in the Pharisees. 'I will have mercy (says God) and not sacrifice.' A ceremony of opinion in some particulars of the time hath more necessity with us than the practice of true godliness: and this is the root of the most part of these vain janglings, strifes of words, and perverse disputings of men, whereof cometh envy, strife, malice, evil surmisings, and no edification in faith and love, which were so frequent in the primitive times, and so often hammered down by Paul. This is it, a misapprehension of the value of them. Fancy imposes a worth and necessity upon them. But Paul doth always oppose unto them true godliness (1 Tim. vi. 3. chap. iv. 7.), and prescribes that as the cure, that true godliness in practice of what we know, and charity towards our brethren, may be bigger in our apprehension, and higher in our affection. Would ye then know, my brethren, wherein true religion consists, and wherein genuine Christianity stands? It is in showing out of a good conversation, our works with meekness and wisdom.' I reduce it to these two words, in joining practice to knowledge, and meekness to both; and this makes our religion to shine before men, and glorify our heavenly Father.

Wherein then do ye think this mystery of wisdom which the gospel reveals consists? Not in the profound and abstracted speculations of God, or the secrets of nature,—a work about which learned men have racked their inventions, and beaten their brains to no other purpose, than the discovery of the greatness of man's ignorance. It doth not consist in the sounding of the depths of divinity, and loosing all these perplexing knots of questions, and doubts, which are moved upon the scripture, in all which men really bewray their own ignorance and misery. 'The world by wisdom knew not God.' Living right is the first point of true wisdom. It costs many men great expenses to learn to know their own folly, to become fools, that they may become wise, 1 Cor. iii. 18. Man became a fool by seeking to become wiser than God made him; and that is all the result of our endeavours after wisdom since, Rom. i. 22. But here is the great instruction of Christianity, to bring man down low from the height of presumption and self-estimation, and make him see himself just as he is by nature, a fool, and a wild ass's colt. Nebuchadnezzar had much ado to learn this lesson. It cost him some years brutality to learn to know his brutishness, and when that was known his understanding returned to him.

Now this is the first and hardest point of wisdom. When it is once learned and imprinted on the heart, O what a docility is in the mind to more! What readiness to receive what follows! It makes a man a weaned child, a little simple child, tractable and flexible as Christ would have all his disciples. A man thus emptied and vacuated of self-conceit, these lines of natural pride being blotted out, the soul is as a *tabula rasa*, 'an unwritten table,' to receive any impression of the law of God that

* [That is, truths of little value.—Ed.]

he pleases to put on it; and then his words are all 'plain to him that understandeth, and right to them that find knowledge,' Prov. viii. 9. Then I say it is not difficult to understand and to prove what is the good and acceptable will of God, Rom. xii. 2; Eph. v. 10—17. It is not up unto heaven, that thou shouldest say, who shall ascend to bring it down? Neither is it far down in the depth, that thou shouldest say, who shall descend and bring it up from hence? But it is near thee, 'in thy mouth, and in thy heart,' &c. Rom. x. 6, 7, 8. 'He hath showed thee, O man, what is good, and what is required of thee, but to do justly, to love mercy, and to walk humbly with thy God,' Micah vi. 8. There is the plain sign of Christian wisdom, the abridgment of all that is taught in the school of Christ. Here is the course of moral philosophy, 'The grace of God hath appeared, to teach us to deny ungodliness, and worldly lusts, and to live soberly, righteously, and godly in this world.' And when the scholar is brought along by these degrees, he is at length laureated* in that great day of our Saviour's appearance. Then he hath the degree of glory and immortality conferred upon him. He is a candidate of immortality and felicity, Tit. ii. 12, 13.

We are in the Christian school like many scholars who labour to know so many things, that indeed they know nothing well; as the stomach that devours much meat, but digests little, and turns it not into food and aliment, incorporates it not into the body. We catch at many great points of truth, and we really drink in none of them; we let none sink into the heart, and turn into affection and practice. This is the grand disease of the time, a study to know many things, and no study to love what we know, or practise any thing. The Christian world is all in a flame, and the church is rent asunder by the eager pursuit and prosecution of some points of truth, and this is the clamour of all men, who will show us our light? Who will discover some new thing unto us? But in the mean time we do not prove the unquestionable acceptable will of our God; like a fastidious squeamish stomach, that loathes what it receives, and always longs for something else. Thus the evil is vented here. Who is a wise man, do ye think? Not he who knows many things, who hath still a will to controversy, who hath attained some further light than others of them; not he, brethren, but he that shows out of a good conversation, his works with meekness of wisdom, he that proves and practiseth as well as knows, the good will of God. 'For hereby do we know that we know him, if we keep his commandments. He that saith, I know him, and keeps not his commands, is a liar, and the truth is not in him,' 1 John ii. 3, 4. This proves that knowledge is not in the head, but in the heart, and that it is not captivated and shut up in the mind, but that a man is delivered up as a captive to the truth, Rom. vi. 16.

All men complain of the want of light and knowledge, though perhaps none think they have much. But is the will of God so dark and intricate? Is it so hard to understand? Truly it is plain, 'He hath showed thee what is good,' he hath showed thee what to do; but that thou neglectest to do, and therefore men know not what to do further. Do ye not all know that ye should walk soberly, righteously, and piously, and humble yourselves to walk with God, and in lowliness of mind each should esteem another better than himself? Ye should forbear and forgive one another, as God for Christ's sake hath forgiven you. Ye should not seek great things for yourselves, especially when God is plucking up what he hath planted, and casting down what was built. Ye should mind your country above more, and live as sojourners here. Are not these words of wisdom all plain and obvious to the meanest capacity? Now, my beloved, with what face can ye seek more knowledge of God, or inquire for more light into his mind, when you do not prove that known and perfect will of his? When you do not occupy your present talent, why do ye seek more? 'To him that hath shall be given.' Truly it is the man that fears and obeys as far as is revealed, to whom God shows his secret, and teaches the way he should choose, Psal. xxv. 12. I know not a readier way to be resolved in doubtful things, than to study obedience in these things that are beyond all doubt. To walk in the light received, is the highway to more light. But what hope is there of any more light from the Lord, when our ways and courses, and dispositions and

* [In the Scottish universities, they were said to have *laureated,* who had a degree conferred upon them, as they were "crowned with laurel leaves." Ev. Un. Com. vol. i. p. 153. Lond. 1837.—Ed.]

practices, even in our endeavours after more knowledge, cannot endure the light of that shining will of God, that is already revealed? In ordering our conversation, we catch at the shadow of our points of truth, and lose the substance that was in our hands, lowliness, meekness, charity, long-suffering, sobriety of mind and actions, and heavenly-mindedness. All these substantials we let go, that we may get hold of some empty unedifying notions. We put out our candle that is already enlightened, that is, the knowledge of good conversation, that we may seek more light; and that is the way to find darkness and delusion. Because they received not the truth in love, that they might be saved, God gave them up to strong delusions, and the belief of lies, 2 Thess. ii. 10, 11. There is the ground of delusions, truth received, but not loved or obeyed, many things known, but the stamp and seal not impressed on the heart we express in the conversation. Therefore God is provoked to put out that useless light of truth, and deliver that man captive to delusions, who would not deliver his soul a captive to truth. And is not this righteousness, that he who detained the known truth in unrighteousness of affection and conversation, be himself detained and incarcerated by strong delusions of mind and imagination?

As a good conversation and good works should be joined to knowledge, and meekness must be the ornament of both, this meekness of wisdom is the great lesson that the wisdom of the Father came down to teach man: 'Learn of me, for I am meek.' And truly the meekness of that substantial wisdom of God Jesus Christ, is the exact pattern and copy, and the most powerful motive and constraint to this kindness of Christian wisdom. Our Saviour did not cry nor lift up his voice in the streets. He made little noise, nor cried with pomp, he was not rigorous, nor rigid upon sinners. Though he was oppressed and afflicted yet he opened not his mouth; being reviled, he reviled not again; being cursed, he blessed. Though he could have legions of angels at his command, yet he would show rather an example of patience and meekness to his followers, than overcome his enemies. If many of us, who pretend to be his disciples, had the winds, rains, heavens, and elements at our commandment, I fear we would have burned up the world. We would presently have called for fire from heaven, to devour all whom we conceived enemies to him, or ourselves, and that under the notion of zeal. Zeal it is indeed, but such as is spoken of in the next verse: 'If ye have bitter envying (the word is bitter zeal) in your hearts, glory not, nor lie against the truth.' Christ's zeal was sweet zeal. It might well consume or eat him up within, but it did not devour others without. 'The zeal of thy house (says he) hath eaten me up.' But our zeal is like the Babylonian furnace, that burnt and consumed these that went to throw the pious children into it. At the first approaching it gets without the chimney, and devours all around it. If the meekness or gentleness of a person who received the greatest injuries that ever any received, and to whom the greatest indignities were done, and who endured the greatest contradiction of sinners, if his calm composed temper do not soften our spirits, mitigate our sharpness, and allay onr bitterness, I know not what can do it. I do not think but if any man considered how much long-suffering God exercises towards him, how gentle and patient he is, after so many provocations; how Jesus Christ doth still forgive infinite numbers of infinite wrongs done to his grace, how slow he is to wrath, and easy to be entreated, surely such a man would abate much of his severity towards others; he would pursue peace with all men, and esteem little of wrongs done unto him, and not think them worthy of remembrance, he would not be easily provoked, but he would be easily pacified. In a word, he could not but exercise something of that gentleness and meekness in forbearing and forgiving, as Christ also forgave him: and truly there is no ornament of a man like that of a meek and quiet spirit, 1 Pet. iii. 4. It is both comely and precious, it is of great price in God's sight. It is a spirit all composed and settled, all peace and harmony within. It is like the heavens in a clear day, all serene and beautiful; whereas an unmeek spirit is for the most part like the troubled sea, tossed with tempests, winds, and dashed with rains; even at the best, it is but troubled with itself. When there is no external provocation, it hath an inward unrest in its bosom, and casts out mire and dirt. Meekness is so beseeming every man, that it is even humanity itself. It is the very nature of a man restored, and these brutish, wild and savage dispositions put off. Meekness is a man in the true likeness of God.

But passion, and the evils which accompany it, is a man metamorphosed and transformed into the nature of a beast, and that of a wild beast too. It hath been always reckoned that anger is nothing different from madness, but in the continuance of it. It is a short madness. But what is wanting in the continuance is made up in the frequency. When spirits are inclined to it, there is a habitual fury and madness in such spirits. It is no wonder then, these are conjoined, meekness and wisdom, for truly they are inseparable. Meekness dwells in the bosom of wisdom. It is nothing else but wisdom, reason, and religion ruling all within, and composing all the distempered lusts and affections ; but anger rests in the bosoms of fools, it cannot get rest but in a fool's bosom, for where it enters, wisdom and reason must go out, Eccles. vii. 9. 'A fool's wrath is presently known,' Prov. xii. 16. For if there were so much true and solid wisdom as to examine the matter first, and to consider before we suffer ourselves to be provoked, we would certainly quench anger in the very first smoking of an apprehension of a wrong. We would immediately cast it out, for there is nothing so much blinds and dimmeth the eye of our understanding ; and when this gross vapour rises out of the dunghill of our lusts, nothing so much uncovers our shame and nakedness. 'A prudent man covereth shame,' but hastiness and bitterness takes the garment off our infirmity, and exposes us to mockery and contempt, Prov. xii. 16. There is not a greater evidence of a strong solid spirit, than this, to be able to govern this unruly passion, whereas it is taken far otherwise. Meekness is construed by some to be simplicity and weakness ; and many imagine some greatness and height of spirit in the hotter natures, but truly it is far otherwise. 'For he that is slow to anger, is better than the mighty ; and he that ruleth his own spirit, than he that takes a city.' Wrath is an impotency and weakness. It hath no strength in it, but such as ye would find in madmen. But this is true magnanimity, to overcome thyself, and 'overcome evil with good.'

As there is nothing which is a greater evidence of wisdom, so there is nothing a better help to true wisdom than this. For a meek spirit is like a clear running fountain, that ye see the bottom of; but a passionate spirit is like a troubled fountain, the shadow of truth cannot be seen in it. A glass that is pure and cleanly, renders the image lively ; but if it be besmeared with dust, you can see nothing: so is a composed mild spirit apt to discern the truth without prejudice. And indeed it is the meek whom God engages to teach his ways, Psal. xxv. 8, 9. He that receives with meekness the ingrafted word, is in the readiest capacity to receive more. When the superfluity of naughtiness is cast out, and all the faculties of the soul composed to quietness and calmness, then his voice will best be heard, and himself readiest to receive it. Our affection keeps a continual hurry within the tumultuous noise of our disordered lusts, that are always raging and controlling the voice of God, so that we cannot hear his teaching. A passionate temper of spirit is very indocile. There are so many loud sounds of prejudices within, that the truth cannot be heard. But a meek spirit hath all quietness and silence, as Cornelius and his house had waiting for the mind of the Lord. And such he delights to converse with most, and reveal most unto ; for it gets readiest entertainment. Let me tell you, beloved in the Lord, you disoblige the Lord (if I may speak so) and hinder him to reveal any more of his mind to you ; ye disengage him to teach you his way in those dark and untrodden paths, because ye do not study this meekness in the wisdom and knowledge ye have already, nor his meekness and moderation in seeking further knowledge. And it is no wonder he be provoked by it, to choose your delusions, because it is certainly these graces of meekness, charity, patience, gentleness, long-suffering, humbleness of mind, and such like, which go always in a chain together. These are an ornament of grace upon the head, and a crown of glory, and that chain about the neck, Solomon mentions, Prov. iv. 9. Now when you cast off your crown of glory, your noblest ornament, your chain of dignity, should he give such precious pearls to swine ? When you trample under foot the greater commandments of mercy, judgment, sobriety, humility, meekness, and charity, should he reveal lesser commandments, or discover his will in lesser matters ? Consider the manner of expression here, 'Let him show forth out of a good conversation,' &c. Truly it is good works with meekness of wisdom, it is a good conversation, with a true profession, that shows forth a Christian, and shows him most before men. 'Let your light (says Christ) so shine before men.' What is the shining beauty of Christian light? It is the works of piety, charity, equity, and sobriety. These glorify the Father, and beautify all his children. You may easily conceive what that is, that chiefly commends religion to the ignorant world. Is it not the meekness of Christian wisdom? Is it not this harmless simplicity, that divine-like candour, that shines in every true Christian? Will rigidity, severity, passion, blood, violence, persecution, and such like, ever conciliate the hearts of men? Have such persons any beauty, any light in them, except a scorching consuming light? The light of a good Christian is like the light of the sun, of a sweet, gentle, and refreshing nature, conveying influence to all, doing good to the household of faith. Peter will tell you what that is, that will most engage the hearts of the world, to a reverend esteem of true religion, 1 Pet. ii. 12. It is a conversation honest, and void of offence, giving to every one their own due, honouring all men, loving the brotherhood, not using our liberty for a cloak of maliciousness, and not overstretching it, to the loosing of other natural or civil bands. When men see Christianity making us do that really and cheerfully, which even nature itself teacheth all to do, that makes the light of it shining and beautiful. Are not these higher mysteries of faith, than some conceive? It is not other points of truth and profession, that are either above natural reason, or seem something opposite to it, that can engage natural beholders; and far less the prosecution of a temporal worldly interest of the people of God, to the destruction of all opposite to it, at least to the diminishing of all other men's gain and advantage, the engrossing of all earthly privileges into the hands of saints. That is such a thing, that never entered into the heart of the shining lights of the primitive times. O how doth the stream of their exhortations run cross to this notion! I am sure there is nothing, in its own nature, such a stumbling-block to the world, or represents religion so odious and abominable to other men, as when it stands in the way, and intercepts all these natural immunities or privileges of life, or estate. This makes natural men to hate it, even at a distance, and become irreconcilable enemies unto it. Since it will not let them live by it, they are engaged not to let it live by them. I wish indeed all the places of power and trust in every nation, were in the hands of godly men, not so much for the interest of the godly, as for the public interest; because 'men fearing God, and hating covetousness,' can only rule justly and comfortably. But to monopolize all power and trust to such a particular judgment and way (as it is now given out), is truly, I think, inhuman and unchristian. These deserve not power and trust who would seek it, and engross it wholly to themselves.* But there is another thing which savours greatly of the flesh, at least of that spirit which Christ reproved in his disciples, to take away men's lives, liberty, and livelihood given by their Creator, upon every foot of opposition and enmity to our way and interest. Is this to love our enemies, blessing them that curse us, or praying for them that despitefully use us, or persecute us? Let us remember we are Christians, and this is the rule of Christianity, that stops even the mouth of adversaries. But some still find an evasion for this. They will say they are God's enemies, and not my particular enemies only. But I pray you, were not the enemies of Christians in these days more properly enemies to Christ than now? For they had nothing then to persecute them for, but the very profession of that name. And truly I confess in our days we make more particular enemies, by particular injuries and disobligements, than either our profession or practice of religion make. But to put it out of all doubt, we learn that they are persecutors, and do all manner of evil against us, for Christ's name sake. I have said this, because I know nothing that more darkeneth and obscures religion, nor† such worldly and temporal interests, so eagerly pursued; and nothing makes it more to shine among men, than a good conversation with meekness of wisdom.

* [These are the generous sentiments of an enlightened Christian. They would lead us to infer that the author's views, as a Protester, had been modified somewhat before he died, or that he had never taken such high ground, as some others, on this score.—ED.]

† [Than.—ED.]

Sermon V.

JAMES iii. 14.—" *But if ye have bitter envying,*" &c.

THE cunning of Satan, and the deceitfulness of our own hearts, are such that when a grosser temptation will not prevail with conscience in some measure enlightened, then they transform themselves into angels of light, and deal more subtilely with us. And there is no greater subtilty of Satan, nor no stronger self-deceit, than this, to palliate and cover vices with the shadow of virtue, and to present corruptions under the similitude of graces. It is common unto all temptations to sin, to have a hook under their bait, to be masked over with some pleasure or advantage or credit. But when such earthly and carnal pretences do not insinuate strongly unto a believing heart that has discovered the vanity of all that which is in the world, so dare not venture upon sin for all the pleasures which attend it, then he winds about and tames and changes his likeness unto light, conscience, and duty, presents many works of darkness and corruption under the notion of duty and honesty, according as he finds the temper of a man's spirit to be. I can give no instance more pregnant, and even common, than this which is given here, viz. contentions and strivings among brethren, bitter envying, maligning and censuring one another, which are very manifest works of the flesh, and works of darkness, fitter for the night than the day, and for the time of ignorance, nor the time after the clear light hath shined. Now if Satan were about to persuade a church or a Christian of this, how do ye think he would go about it? Would he present some carnal advantage to be gained by it, some more profit or preferment from it? May be that might be very taking with some more unconscientious self-seeking spirits, and I fear it be too much taken with many. But sure it will not relish with every man. It will not entice him that hath the fear of God, and the love of Jesus stirring within him. Therefore he must seek about, and find some false prophet, that may come out in the name of the Lord, and disguise himself, and by such means he will do it. Let a point of truth or conscience come in debate, let a notion of religion, and one far off from an interest in Christ be in the business, and then he can take advantage to make a man overreach himself in it. He will present the truth as a thing of so great weight and consequence, that he must contend for it, and empty all his wit and power and parts for it. This good intention being established, he raises up men's passions under a notion of zeal, and these be promoved under that pretence for such an end. Whatsoever mean may be sought, profitable for that end, all is chosen and followed without discretion or knowledge of what is good or evil. It is apprehended that the good principle of conscience, of duty, and the good intention, may justify all. And by that means he hath persuaded the churches of Christ, and the Christian world, unto more rigidity, severity, cruelty, strife, contention, blood, violence, and such works of darkness, than readily have been found in the times of ignorance. Is Christendom a field of blood, rather than any other part of the world? Truly this is the reproach of Christianity. By this, God's name is daily blasphemed. Here our apostle sets himself to unmask this angel of light, and to decipher him in his own proper nature and notion. He takes off the vizard of religion and wisdom, and lets you see the very image of hell under it; 'But if ye have bitter envying and strife, glory not.' Ye glory as if ye had the truth, you glory in your zeal for it, you boast that ye are the wise men, the religious men; and so you take liberty upon the account of envy, to malign, despise, and contend with others. Glory not, if you cherish such strifes and contentions, to the breach of Christian peace and concord You are liars against the truth, which you profess. Do not think these proceed from true zeal; nay, nay, it is but bitter envy, and bitter zeal. Do not flatter yourselves with an apprehension of wisdom, or knowledge, or religion. That is wisdom indeed; but mark of what nature. It is earthy, sensual, and devilish. And indeed, that is a foolish wisdom, to say no worse of it.

You see, then, what need we have of the exhortation of the apostle (Eph. vi. 11.),

'Put on the whole armour of God, that ye may be able to stand against the wiles of the devil.' Truly we may stand against his darts, and violent open thrusts at our conscience; when we,* being ignorant of his devices, and not acquainted with his depths (2 Cor. ii. 11. Rev. ii. 24.), will not be able to stand against his ways. For we have a great and subtile party to wrestle with, principalities and powers, and spiritual wickedness in high places, or heavenly things (as some render the word). He exercises much wickedness, spiritual invisible wickedness in heavenly and religious things, in which it is hard to wrestle, unless we be endowed with faith, knowledge, and righteousness, and shod with the gospel of peace; the peaceable gospel reducing our spirits to a peaceable temper. I conceive there is nothing the world hath been more abused with, than the notion of zeal, justice, and such like: and there is nothing wherein a Christian is more ready to deceive himself than this. Therefore I conceive the Holy Ghost has undeceived us in this, and hath of purpose used the word zeal as often in a bad sense as in a good one, and usually chooses to express envy and malice by it, though another word might suit as well, and be more proper. So here bitter zeal, ζηλος φθονος, is reckoned among the works of the flesh, Gal. v. 20. And we are exhorted to walk honestly as in the day, not in strife and envy, or zeal. And therefore the apostle rebukes sharply the Corinthians. 'Are ye not carnal, and walk as men, whereas there is among you envying, or zeal, and strife,' 1 Cor. iii. 3. Zeal is a vehemency of affection in any earnest pursuit, or opposition of a thing; and to make it good, it must not only be fixed upon a commendable and good object, but must run in the right channel, between the banks of moderation, charity, and sobriety. If it overflows these, certainly that excess proceeds not simply and purely from the love of God, or the truth, but from some latent corruption or lust in our members, which takes occasion to swell up with it. I find in scripture the true zeal of God hath much self-denial in it. It is not exercised so much concerning a man's own matters, as concerning the matters that are purely and merely concerning God's glory. It is the most flexible, condescending, and forbearing thing in those things that relate to ourselves and our own interests. Thus Moses is commended as the meekest man, when Aaron and Miriam raise sedition against him, Num. xii. 3. He had not affections to be commoved upon that account. But how much is he stirred and provoked upon the apprehension of the manifest dishonour of God, by the people's idolatry? How many are lions in their own cause, and in God's as simple and blunt as lambs? And how much will our spirits be commoved when our own interest lies in the business, and hath some conjunction with God's interest; but if these are parted, our fervour abates, and our heat cools. I lay down this, then, as the fundamental principle of true zeal, it is like charity that seeketh not its own things.

But to make the nature of it clear, I give you three characters of it, verity, charity, and impartiality. I say it hath truth in it, a good thing for the object, and knowledge of that good thing in the subject, for the principle of it. 'It is good to be zealously affected always in a good thing,' Gal. iv. 18. Zeal is an evil thing, hath something of the impatient and restless nature of the devil in it. There is nothing we should be more deliberate and circumspect in, than what to employ or bestow our affections upon. We should have a certain persuasion of the unquestionable goodness of that which we are ardent and vehement to obtain, else the more ardour and vehemency, the more wickedness is in it. The Jews had a zeal for God but not according to knowledge, and that is a blind impetuous self-will. For if a man take a race at his full speed in the dark, he cannot but catch a fall.† The eager and hot pursuits of men are founded upon some gross misapprehensions.

Secondly, There must not only be a goodness supposed in the object, but some correspondence between the worth and weight of that goodness, and the measure of our desires and affections; else there wants that conformity between the soul and truth, which makes a true zeal of God. I mean this, the soul's most vehement desires should be employed about the chiefest good, and our zeal move in relation to things unquestionably good, and not about things of small moment, or of little edification. This is the apostolic rule, that not only we consider that there be

* [Or, *while we, on the other hand*.—Ed.]

† [See note, page 168.—Ed.]

some truth in the thing, but that we especially take notice, if there be so much truth and goodness as requires such a measure of vehemency and affection. Therefore in lesser things we should have lesser commotion, and in greater things greater, suitable to them. Otherwise the Pharisees who exercised their zeal about trifles, and neglected the weightier matters of the law, (Matt. xxiii. 23.) would not have been reproved by Christ. And indeed this is the zeal to which we are redeemed by Christ, Tit. ii. 14. Be ye zealous of good works, of works that are unquestionably good, such as piety, equity, and sobriety. There is nothing more incongruous than to strain at a gnat and swallow a camel, to spend the vital spirits upon things of small concernment to our own or others' edification, and to have nothing to spare for the weightier matters of true godliness. It is as if a man should strike a feather or the air with all his might. He must needs wrest his arms. Even so, to strike with the spiritual sword of our affections, with such vehemency, at the lighter and emptier matters of religion, cannot choose but to disjoint the spirit, and put it out of course, as there is a falsehood in that zeal that is so vehement about a light matter, though it have some good in it. For there is no suitable proportion between the worth of the thing and the vehemency of the spirit. Imagination acts in both. In the one it supposes a goodness, and it follows it; and in the other, it imposes a necessity and a worth far beyond that which really is, and so raises up the spirit to that height of necessity and worth that hath no being but in a man's imagination. I think there is no particular that the apostle doth so much caveat. For I find in 1 Tim. i. 4. he takes off such endless matters that minister questioning rather than godly edifying, and gives us a better subject to employ our zeal upon, ver. 5, the great end and sum of all religion, love to God and man, proceeding from a pure heart, a good conscience, and faith unfeigned, from which we must needs swerve, when we turn aside to such empty and vain janglings, ver. 6. For truly we have but narrow and limited spirits, and it must needs follow, when we give them very much to one thing, that they cannot attend another thing seriously, as Christ declares, (Matt. vi. 24.) 'no man can serve two masters,' &c. And therefore there is much need of Christian wisdom to single out and choose the most proper and necessary object. For as much as we give other things that have not so much connexion with that, we take from it as much: and the apostle counsels us, (1 Tim. iv. 7.) rather to exercise ourselves unto true godliness, and to the most substantial things in it, rather than vain things, and opposition of science, chap. vi. 3—5, 20. There he opposes the wholesome words of Christ, and the doctrine that is according to godliness, unto questions, and strifes of words, whereof comes envy, railings, evil-surmisings, and perverse disputings of men of corrupt minds. And it is very observable that he is pressing the duties of believing servants towards their masters, whether believers or infidels, that the name of God be not blasphemed, nor the gospel evil spoken of. For there is nothing so much exposes it to misconstruction, as when it is stretched and abused unto the prejudice of natural and civil duties, and doubtless there would be many doubts and questions about it in these days, some contending for worldly pre-eminence over the Pagans, and some for the levelling of all Christians. But, says he, 'If any man teach otherwise,' or contend about this, 'he is proud, knowing nothing,' &c. He hath forsaken the substance of true godliness, which consists in good works shining before men, and disabuses the notion of Christian liberty to the dishonour of Christ, and hath supposed gain, a worldly carnal interest of the godly, to be piety, and so pursues that fancy of his own. He renews this in the Second Epistle, (chap. ii. 14—16.) showing that these strifes about words, albeit they seem to be upon grounds of conscience at the beginning, yet they increase unto more ungodliness, ver. 23. And unto Titus he gives the same charge very solemnly, (Tit. iii. 8, 9.) 'I will that thou affirm constantly, that they who believe in God should be careful to maintain good works. But avoid foolish and unlearned questions,' &c. For 'this is a faithful saying.' But again,

Thirdly, Zeal must have charity with it, and this all the scriptures cited prove. It must be so tempered with love, that it vents not to the breach of Christian peace and concord. Charity envieth not, or is not zealous. When zeal wants charity, it is not zeal but envy. And hence it is that there are so frequent and fervent exhortations to avoid such questions as may gender strifes, and contentions, and malice. Now certainly there was some truth in them, and something of conscience also in them. Yet he dissuades entirely the prosecution of them to the rigour, as men are apt to do, but wills us rather to have faith in ourselves. And truly I think the questions that did then engender strifes, and rent the church, were as much if not more momentous nor the most part of these about which we bite and devour one another,—the questions of the law, the circumcision, and eating of things sacrificed to idols, of things indifferent, lawful, or not lawful. Yet all these he would have subordinated unto the higher end of the commandment, charity, 1 Tim. i. 4, 5 And when he exhorts the Corinthians to be zealous for spiritual gifts, he would yet have them excel in these things which edify the church, 1 Cor. xiv. 1—12. 'Covet earnestly the best gifts,' says he, and yet he shows them a more excellent way, and that is charity, (1 Cor. xiii. 1.) to do all these things for the good and edification of the church, rather than of our own opinion, 1 Cor. xii. 3; chap. xiv. 12. I find where the word zeal is taken in a bad sense it hath these works of darkness attending it, wrath, strife, malice, &c. Gal. v. 20; 1 Cor. iii. 3; Rom. xiii. 13. It is accompanied with such a hellish crowd of noisome lusts. Let me add a differential character of it. It is uncharitable, contentious, and malicious. It can do nothing, condescend to nothing, and is conversant about nothing, but what pleases our own humour, for the peace and unity of the church. It is a self-willed impetuous thing, like a torrent that carries all down before it. But truly right zeal runs calmly and constantly within the banks; it will rather consume its own bowels within with grief, than devour others without.

Sermon VI.

Matth. xi. 28.—" *Come unto me, all ye that labour, and are wearied,*" &c.

It is the great misery of Christians in this life, that they have such poor, narrow, and limited spirits, that are not fit to receive the truth of the gospel in its full comprehension; from whence manifold misapprehensions in judgment, and stumbling in practice proceed. The beauty and life of things consist in their entire union with one another, and in the conjunction of all their parts. Therefore it would not be a fit way to judge of a picture by a lineament, or of an harmony by a discrepant, nor of the world by some small parcel of it; but take all the parts together, all the notes and draughts, as conjoined by art in such an order, and there appears nothing but beauty and consent. Even so it falls out in our conceptions of the gospel. The straitness and narrowness of our spirits takes in truth by parcels, disjointed from the whole, looks upon one side of it, and sees not the other. As for example, sometimes there appears unto us our duty and strait obligation to holy walking, and this being seen and considered alone, ordinarily fills the soul with some fears, jealousies, and confusions. Another time, there rises out from under the cloud, the mercy and peace of Christ in inviting, accepting, and pardoning sinners, by his blood, that cleanses from all sin; and in that view (such is our weakness and shortness of sight) there is nothing else presented but pardoning grace; and hence there is occasion given to the corruption of our hearts, to insinuate secretly and subtilely unto us some inclinations to more liberty, and indulgence to the flesh. Thus you see what stumbling in practice, and disorder in walking, this partial way of receiving the truth occasioneth. But it hath no less influence upon the many controversies and differences in doctrine and opinion, about grace and works. For from whence arise these mistakes on both hands, but from the straitness of our apprehensions, that we do not take the truth of God in its full latitude, but being eager upon one part and zealous of it, we almost lose the remembrance, and sometimes fall, in wrangling with the other? Many that proclaim the free grace of the gospel, their fault is, not that they make it freer than it is, for truly it is as free as any Antinomian can apprehend it, but rather because they take it not in its entire and full complexion, which best declares the freedom of it, as comprehending both the pardon of sin and purity from sin, grace towards us and grace within us; and so, while they only plead for the one, they seem at least to oppugn the other. And, in like manner, others apprehending the necessity, beauty, and comeliness of holiness and new obedience, are much in pressing and declaring this in opposition to the other way; in which there may be some mistake, not in making it more meritorious than it is, but at leastwise * in such a manner it may be holden out, as may somewhat obscure the freedom of God's grace. The occasion of both these misapprehensions may be from the scattering of these diverse parcels of truth, as so many pearls in the field of the scripture; one is found here, and one takes it up, as if there were no more; here is repentance, and away he goes with that, without conjoining these scattered pieces into one body. But yet our Saviour sometimes gives us complete sums and models of the gospel, in which he presents all at one view at once, and especially in these words now read. The sum of all the gospel is contained in two words, 'Come unto me,' and 'take my yoke upon you.' All the duty of a Christian, and all his encouragement is here. His duty is to believe in Christ, and to give himself up to his obedience, and become his disciple, and to follow his example; and his encouragement is the rest promised, rest to his soul,—which is the only proper seat of rest or disquiet. It is most capable and sensible of both,—and this rest includes in its bosom, not only peace and tranquillity of mind here, which all the creatures combined cannot give, but all felicity besides; that eternal rest from all the labours of this life, and complacency in the fruition of God for ever. You see, then, what is the full invitation of the gospel. It is nothing else but come, and have rest. "Take on an easy yoke, and ye shall find rest. Come and be happy. Come and receive life. That which you seek elsewhere, both ignorantly and vainly, here it is only to be found. Come (says Christ), and I promise to give it unto you. Wait upon me by obedience, and you shall at length find by experience, that rest which I am willing to give you."

I desire you may consider both the order and the connexion of these integral parts of the gospel. The order of the gospel is a great part of the gospel. In some things method is arbitrary, and it matters not which go before, or which follow after, but here they become essential, and so a great part of the matter itself. There must be first coming to Christ, and then taking on his yoke; first believing, then obeying his commandments. This is as essential an order, as is between the fruit and the root, the stream and the fountain, the sun-beam and the sun. Will any man expect fruit till he plant? There must then first be the implanting of the soul into Christ by faith, and then in due season follow the fruits of obedience by abiding in him. The perverting of this order makes much disorder in the spirits and lives of Christians. But how can it choose but all must wither and decay, if the soul be not planted by this river, whose streams gladden the city of our God, if the roots of it be not watered with the frequent apprehension and consideration of the grace of Christ, or the riches of God's mercy? The way and method of many Christians is just opposite to this. For you labour and weary yourselves, how to attain some measure and satisfaction in the latter, before you adventure the first, to have the heart humbled by godly sorrow, and the soul inflamed by love to God, and the yoke of his obedience submitted unto; while in the mean time you deliberately suspend the exercise of faith, and apprehension of the pardoning grace of Christ. Now, how this can consist either with sound reason or religion, I do not see. For were it not a point of madness to seek fruits from a tree that is lying above ground, and to refuse to plant it till it give some experience of its fruitfulness in the air? And what can be more absurd, than to imagine to have the Spirit of Christ working in the heart godly sorrow, or Christian love, and so renewing it again to his image, and yet withal Christ not received into the heart by faith? Do you not know that this is his first entrance into the soul? He enters there by the door of faith, and a soul enters into him at the door of the promise by faith. How then do ye imagine he shall work in you, before you will admit him to come in to you? Besides, either you ap-

* [Perhaps it should be, *at least, less.*—Ed.]

prehend that you may attain to such gracious qualifications by your own industry without Christ, which is blasphemous to his name and office; for if you may, what need have you of him? Or, if you believe that he is the only treasure of all grace and wisdom, and that all things are delivered to him of the Father, then how do you seek these things without him? It must be wretched folly to seek them elsewhere, and not come to him. And indeed it is observable, that this exhortation to come unto Christ is subjoined unto ver. 27, 'All things are delivered unto me by the Father.' And therefore, seeing all grace, and life, and happiness is enclosed in me, seeing without me there is nothing but a barren wilderness, in which you may toil and labour, and weary yourselves in fruitless pursuits, come hither where it is originally and plentifully seated, and you cannot miss your end, nor lose your labour. And for the farther illustration of this subject, I shall only add that,

Secondly, There is another woful mistake possesses your minds who take up this way; for certainly you must think that there is some worth or dignity in it, whereby you intend to recommend yourselves unto Christ. For to what purpose is that anxious and scrupulous exaction of such previous qualifications, if it be not to give some more boldness and confidence to thy mind, to adventure to believe the promises and come to Christ, because thou thinkest thou canst not come when thou art so unclean and so unworthy? And therefore thou apprehendest that thou canst so purge thyself from sin, and adorn thyself with graces, as may procure some liking, and procure some favour at Christ's hand, which is indeed very opposite to the tenor of the proposal of free grace in the gospel in which there is nothing upon the creature's part required as a condition or qualification to make them the more welcome in coming to Christ.

Let this word then abide with you, 'Come unto me, and take my yoke upon you, and learn of me,' which in substance is this, Come and cast your burdens on me first, and then take my burden upon you. O it is a blessed exchange! Cast your heavy burden upon my back, and take my light burden on yours. For what is it to invite them that labour and are ladened to come, but to come and repose themselves for rest upon him? And that is directly to lay over that which burdens and ladeneth them upon him. There is an unsupportable burden of sin, the guilt of sin, and there is an intolerable weight of wrath; 'Mine iniquities are gone over mine head, (Ps. xxxviii. 4.) and as an heavy burden they are too heavy for me.' And when the wrath of God is joined to this burden, the name of the Lord burning with anger, how may you conceive a soul will be pressed under that burden, which is so heavy, that it will press the mountains into valleys, make the sea flee out of its place, and the earth tremble? Now here is the invitation. Is there any penitent soul that feels the burden of the weight of sin and wrath? Let them come and disburden their souls of care, fear, and anxiety in this blessed port of rest and refuge for poor sinners. Is there a yoke of transgressions wreathed about thy neck, and bound by the hand of God, (Lam. i. 14.) a yoke that neither men nor angels are able to bear? Then, I beseech you, come hither, and put over your yoke upon Jesus Christ. Tie it about him, for God hath laid upon him the iniquities of us all, and he bore our sins. He did bear the yoke of divine displeasure, and it was bound about his neck with God's own hand, with his own consent. Now, here is the actual liberty and the releasement of a soul from under the yoke, here is its actual rest and quiet from under the pain of this burden, when a soul is made to consent unto, and willingly to put over that burden upon Christ. And this freedom and vacancy from the unsupportable yoke of guilt, will certainly dispose the soul, and make it more capable of receiving the easy and portable yoke of his commandments. For you may easily perceive how easy love maketh all things, even difficulties themselves. Let once a soul be engaged that way to Christ, (and there is no possibility of engaging it in affection without some taste and feeling, or believing apprehension of his love and sufficiency for us,) and you will see that the rough way will be made plain, and the crooked way straight, heavy things light, and hard things easy. For what command can be grievous to that soul who apprehends that Christ hath taken the great weight of wrath off it, and carried away the intolerable pain of its guiltiness, which would have pressed and depressed it eternally, without any hope of relaxation or ease? Hath he borne a yoke bound on by the majesty of God, and fastened with the cords of his displeasure? And can it be so heavy to a believing soul to take up that obedience which is fastened with the cords of love? And besides, how much will faith facilitate this, and make this yoke to be cheerfully and willingly submitted to, because it delivers the soul from those unsufferable cares and fears, which did quite enervate its strength, and take away its courage? For, I pray you, what is there in a soul under the fear of wrath, that is not totally disabled by that heavy pressure for any willing or cheerful obedience? The mystery* of the spirit is spent that way, the courage of the soul is defeated, the heart is weakened, and nothing is suitable to the yoke of Christian love and obedience. But when once a soul apprehends Christ, this is a reposition of all his cares and burdens, and comes to exoner† his soul in him, and cast his burthen upon him. Then the soul is lightened as it were for this journey, then he may walk in the ways of obedience, without the pressing fear and pushing anguish of the dread of condemnation of the law. To conclude this head, nothing will make you take up this yoke willingly, or bear it constantly, except you be delivered from the other yoke that was so heavy even to Christ, and that made him cry, 'My soul is exceeding heavy and troubled, and what shall I say? Father, save me from this hour.'

Now, these who are here in the text invited to come unto Christ,—you see them described to be labouring and heavy laden persons. 'Come unto me, all ye that labour,' &c. At least it seems to hold forth a previous qualification and condition of believing, without which we may not venture to come unto Christ. Indeed it is commonly so taken, and mistaken. Many conceive that the clause is restrictive and exclusive, that is to say, that this description of burdened and wearied sinners is a limitation of the command of believing, and that it circumscribes the warrant of coming to Christ, as if none might lawfully come unto him but these that are thus burdened: and thus it is supposed to be a bar, set upon the door of believing at which sinners must enter in to Christ, to hold out, and shut out all those who are not thus qualified for access, which I truly conceive is contrary to the whole strain and current of the dispensation of the gospel. Therefore I take it to be rather declarative, or ampliative, or both. I say, it is partly for declaration, not of the warrant to come, but of the persons who ordinarily do come to Christ. It declares not simply and universally who should come, but those who actually do come unto Christ. Take it thus then. All persons who hear the gospel are invited to come unto our Saviour without exception, the blind, the lame, those on the highways, not only the thirsty and the hungry, (Isa. lv. 1.) but those who have no thirst or hunger for righteousness, but only for things that do not profit (ver. 2.); not only the broken-hearted, that desire to come near to righteousness, but even the stout-hearted that are far from righteousness. Such are commanded to hearken, and incline their ear, Isa. xlvi. 12; lv. 2, 3. Now, this command that reaches all, gives an immediate actual warrant and right to all to come, if they will. For what is required previous to give warrant to obedience, but the command of obedience? And therefore the Jews were challenged, because they would not come to Christ that they might have life. Now then there is no bar of seclusion set upon the door of the gospel, to keep out any soul from entering in. There is no qualification or condition prescribed by the gospel; and without which if he come, he is actually welcomed and received by Christ, whatsoever you suppose he wants. It is true, men's own security and unbelief will exclude them from Christ, but that is no retraction on the gospel's part. It is a bar set on a man's own heart, that shuts him up from coming to the patent entry of the gospel.

Therefore I take it thus, that though all ought to come to Christ, and none that are indeed willing are debarred for the want of any supposed condition, yet none will actually and really come, till they be in some measure sensible of the weight of their sins, and the wrath of God, till they are labouring under the feeling of

* [The word *mystery* seems to be used here in the sense of *energy*. It is sometimes spelt by Scottish writers *mister* and *myster*, and signifies an art or calling, being derived from the old French word *mestier*, a trade. When employed to denote something above human intelligence, it has a different origin (being formed from *μυστηριον*, a secret).—Ed.]

† [Exonerate, or unburthen.—Ed.]

their own misery and desperate condition. And whatsoever be the measure of this, if it give so much uneasiness to a man that he can be content with rest and ease in Christ, he may, and certainly ought, to come unto Jesus, and cast all his burdens upon him. I think then, that way that is in so frequent use among Christians, to sit down, and essay to bring our hearts to some deep humiliation, and so to prescribe and order it, as we will deliberately delay, and suspend the thoughts of believing, till we have attained something of this,—I say, this way crosses the very intention of Christ in uttering these words, and such like. For certainly he meant to take away impediments, and not to cast delays in our way. And therefore I said the word was rather for ampliation, that is, rather to encourage these who accounted themselves excluded, than to exclude any who desire to come. "Come unto me, every one, but especially you that labour, ye should make the greatest haste. Come unto me even though ye apprehend the wrath of God to be intolerable, and have foolishly wearied yourselves in seeking rest by other ways. Ye that are most apprehensive of your sins, and so are apt to doubt of any acceptation,—you that think yourselves worse than any, and so to have least warrant to come to me,—yet come, and I will by no means cast you out, but give rest to your souls." So that it is not intended to exclude those who are most ready to think themselves excluded, because they see so much sin in themselves.

Therefore, my beloved, without further disputing about it, let me exhort you in the name of Jesus Christ, who here invites and commands you, that you would at once put a period to this, and bring it to some conclusion. Since you are diseased and disquieted in yourselves, and cannot find rest in your own bosoms, I beseech you come here, where it is most likely to be found, and it is most certain, if you come you shall find it. Do not continue wrangling and contesting about the matter; for what is that but to increase your labour, and vexation, and add to your heavy burden? It will be so far from giving you any ease in the result of it, that it will rather make your wounds more incurable, and your burdens more intolerable, which is both opposite to the intention of the gospel and the nature of believing. Here then is your rest, here is your refreshing rest. Here it is in quiet yielding to his gracious offers, and silent submitting to the gospel, not in bawling or contending with it, which is truly a contending against ourselves Isa. xxviii. 12, 'This is the rest, wherewith you may cause the weary to rest. It is nowhere else, not in heaven or earth; for there is no back that will take on this burden or can carry it away from us. There is no disburdening of a sinner of guilt and wrath, in any other port or haven, but in Christ, who is the city of refuge. Wheresoever you think to exoner yourselves besides this, you will find no refreshing, but a multiplication of burdens and cares. Your burden shall be rolled over upon you again with double weight. Therefore, my beloved, if you will not hear this, consider what follows, viz. you shall refuse this rest and refreshing and restlessly seek another rest. You may go and be doing, but you shall fall backward, and be broken and snared. Your burden shall fall back upon you, and you shall fall and be broken under it. That which the Lord said to Israel when they would flee to Egypt, is most true in this case: 'In returning, and in rest ye shall be saved; in quietness and confidence shall be your strength:' but alas! they would not, that is a sad close.

Sermon VIII.

MATT. xi. 29.—"*Take my yoke upon you, and learn of me,*" &c.

SELF-LOVE is generally esteemed infamous and contemptible among men. It is of a bad report every where; and indeed as it is taken commonly, there is good reason for it, that it should be hissed out of all societies, if reproaching and speaking evil of it would do it. But to speak the truth, the name is not so fit to express the thing; for that which men call self-love, may rather be called self-hatred. Nothing is more pernicious to a man's self, or pestilent to the societies of men than this; for if it may be called love, certainly it is not self-love, but the love of some baser and lower thing than self, to our eternal prejudice. For what is ourselves, but our souls? Matt. xvi. 26; Luke ix. 25. For our Lord there shows that to lose our souls, and to lose ourselves, is one and the same thing. But what is it to love our souls? Certainly it is not to be enamoured with their deformed shape, as if it were perfect beauty? Neither can it be interpreted, any true love to our souls, to seek satisfaction and rest unto them, where it is not at all to be found; for this is to put them in perpetual pain and disquiet. But here it is that true self-love, and soul-love centereth, in that which our Saviour propounds, namely, to desire and seek the everlasting welfare of our souls, and that perpetual rest unto them, after which there is no labour nor motion any more. Therefore, to draw unto himself the souls of men the more sweetly, and the more strongly too, he fasteneth about them a cord of their own interest, and that the greatest, real rest; and by this he is likely to prevail with men in a way suited to their reasonable natures. 'Come unto me, all ye that labour and are wearied, and I will give you rest.' Self-interest is ordinarily exploded, at least disowned and disclaimed in men's discourses, as a base, wretched, sordid thing, which, though all men act by it, yet they are all ashamed to profess. But yet, if the interest be so high as indeed to concern self, and that which is truly our self, then both nations and persons count it the most justifiable ground of many of their actions, self-preservation. But yet there is a higher interest than that, that relates to the eternal interest of our souls. And truly to own and profess, and prosecute that interest of soul-preservation, of eternal rest to our souls, is neither ignoble, nor unbeseeming a Christian; neither is it any way inconsistent with the pursuance of that more public and catholic interest of God's glory, in respect of which all interests, even the most general and public, are particular and private. For this is the goodness of our God, that he hath bound up his own honour and our happiness in one bundle together; that he hath knit the rest of our precious souls, and the glory of his own name inseparably together: not only to condescend to our weakness, but to deal with us suitably to our natures. He proposes our own interests chiefly, to draw us to himself, and allows this happy self-seeking in which a man loses himself, that he may be found again in Christ. Seeing then it is thus, that elsewhere, wheresoever you turn yourselves, within or without, there is no rest, but endless labour, and fruitless toil, (you find this already by experience, you who apprehend the weight of your sins, and the greatness of divine wrath,) that there is an intolerable pressure upon your souls already, and that this is nothing diminished, but rather augmented, by your vain labours and inquiries after some ease and peace,—your endeavours to satisfy your own consciences, and pacify God's wrath some other way, having filled you with more restless anxiety; and seeing there is a certain assurance of true rest and tranquillity here, upon the easiest terms imaginable, that is, 'come to Jesus Christ, all ye who are disquieted and restless, and he will give you rest,'—O should not this be an invincible and irresistible attractive to your hearts, to draw them to our Redeemer over all impediments? The rest is perfect happiness; and yet the terms are easy. Only come and embrace it, and seek it nowhere else. There is a kind of quietness and tranquillity in the seeking and attaining this rest. All other rests are come to by much labour and business. Here Christ would have you,—who have laboured in vain for rest, and lost your toil and your pains,—to come at it, by ceasing from labour, as it were; that which you could not attain by labour, to come by it, *cunctando* (by keeping quiet), which you could not gain *pugnando* (by fighting). There is a quiet and silent way of believing promises, and rolling yourselves upon Christ offered in them, which is the nearest and most compendious way to this blessed rest and quietness; which, if you think to attain by much clamour and contention of debate or dispute, or by the painful labour and vexation of your spirits, which you call exercise of mind,—you take the way about, and put yourselves further off from it. Faith has a kind of present vacancy and quietness in it, in the very acting of it. It is not a tumultuous thing, but composes the soul to quietness and silence, to a cessation from all other things but the looking upon Christ holden out in the gospel; and this in due time will give greater rest and tranquillity. Consider what the Lord speaks to the people that would take a journey upon them to Egypt, (Isa. xxx. 15.) 'In returning and rest shall ye be saved, in quietness and confidence shall be your strength.' Their peace was near hand, but they would travel abroad to seek it, and they find trouble. Their strength was to sit still and be quiet, and trust in the Lord. Nay, but they would not sit still, but flee and wander abroad to their old house of bondage; and therefore, says the Lord, you shall flee. Now, may not this represent the folly and madness of souls that are under the fear of wrath and sense of sin, and be as it were a type of it? Our rest is in resting on a Saviour, our peace is in quiet confidence in him; it is not far off, it is in our mouth: 'The word is near' (says Paul), it is neither in heaven above, nor in the depth below. We need not go abroad and search for that happiness we want. It is nigh at hand in the gospel; but while we refuse this, and give ourselves to restless agitation and perplexity about it, sometimes we apprehend that we are eased in our travels and endeavours; but it shall prove to us no better than Egypt, a house of bondage. Wheresoever we seek shelter out of Christ, we will find it a broken reed, that not only will fail under us, but in the rent will split our hand, and pierce us through with many sorrows. To conclude then this head, coming to Christ with our burdens is a motion towards rest. For he adds, 'I will give you rest.' But moreover, there is a kind of rest in this motion. It is an easier, plainer, and pleasanter motion, than these troubled and laborious windings and wanderings of our hearts after vanity. He persuades you to walk in this path of pleasantness and peace; and you shall find a great rest at the end of it; 'receiving (says Peter) the end of your faith, the eternal salvation of your souls.'

Now the next thing in the text is, having come to Jesus, and found rest and happiness in him, we must take his yoke upon us. And this is the other integral part of the gospel, of which I desire you to consider these few particulars, that occur in the words,—The order in which it is to be taken on,—The nature of this yoke,—And the most ready and expeditious way of bearing it.

The method and order in which Christ's yoke is to be taken upon us, is first, To come unto our Saviour, and give over the yoke of our transgressions to him, and then to take up the yoke of his commandments from him; to believe in his promises, and rest our souls on them; and to take up the yoke of his precepts, and proceed to motion, and walking in that rest. Now this method hath a double advantage in it, for the real receiving and carrying of Christ's yoke. It gives vacancy and room for it, and it gives strength and furniture* for it. It expels that which would totally disable you to bear it, and brings in that comfortable supply, which will strengthen and enable you to bear it. Consider what posture a soul is put into, that lives under the terror of God, and is filled with the apprehension of the guilt of sin and the greatness of God's wrath. I say, such a soul, till he have some rest from that grievous labour, is fit for no other more pleasant labour, until he be something disburthened of that which is like to press him down to hell. He is not very capable of any new burden, until the yoke of his transgressions that is wreathed about his neck be taken off. Do ye think he can find any vacant room for the yoke of Christ's obedience? When a soul is under the dominion of fear and terror, under the power of grief and anguish, do ye think he is fit for any thing, or can do any thing, but groan in that prison of darkness, under these chains? Such a soul is in bondage, under servitude, and can neither take up this yoke of liberty nor walk in it. The strength and moisture of the spirit is drunk up by the poison of these arrows: and there remains neither attention, affection, nor spirit for any thing else. Therefore here is the incomparable advantage that redounds from this way of coming first to Christ, and exonering our cares and fears in his bosom, and in disburthening our sins upon him, who hath taken them on, and carried them away, as that scape-goat sent unto the wilderness on which they laid the sins of the people. By this means, I say, you shall have a vacancy for the yoke of Christ and liberty to all your faculties, your understanding, will, and affections, (which are no better than slaves and captives, *non sui juris*, while they are under these tyrannous passions of fear and horror,) to attend the obedience of Christ, and the drawing of his yoke. This will relieve your souls out of prison, and then you will be fit for employment.

* [Or harness.—Ed.]

Besides this, there is furniture and help brought into the soul, which enables it to this; and without which, though it were not pressed under a burden of sin and wrath, yet it would neither be able nor willing. There is that supply and strength that faith brings from Christ, which arises from our mystical implantation in him; from hence flows that communication of his grace to a believer. The law came by Moses, but grace and truth by Jesus Christ, John i. 16, 17. Now this efficacy and virtue that is in Christ the head, is transmitted unto the members of his body by believing in him. Indeed the very apprehension of such a Saviour may have some quickening virtue in it; but certainly the great influence of life is annexed to it by his gracious promises, 'Because I live, ye shall live also,' John xiv. 19. 'As the living Father who sent me, lives in himself, and I have life by the Father; so he that believes on me, shall live by me,' John vi. 57. 'Abide in me, and I in you, and ye shall bring forth much fruit.' He hath graciously appointed the derivation of that life to us, to be conjoined with our right apprehensions, and believing meditations of him, making, as it were, faith the opening of his house, to let in his fulness to us. Now, besides this more mysterious and supernatural furniture and supply, there is even something that is naturally consequent to it; some enabling of the soul for holy obedience, flows naturally from the love of Christ. And whenever a believer apprehends what he has done for him, finds some rest and relaxation in him, it cannot but beget some inward warmth of love to him who so loved us. 'Faith worketh by love,' says Paul. The way it goes to action is by affection. It at once inflames that, and then there is nothing more active and irresistible. It hath a kind of indefatigable firmness in it; it hath an unwearied strength to move in the yoke all the day long. In a word, nothing almost is impossible or too hard for it; for it is of the nature of fire to break through all, and over all impediments. Nothing is so easy but it becomes uneasy to a soul under fear; and nothing so difficult but it becomes easy to a soul wherein perfect love has cast out fear. For love makes a soul to move supernaturally in divine things, as a natural or co-natural agent, freely, willingly, and constantly. If they be not suitable to our natures as corrupted, and so, grievous to love, then, as much as it possesses the heart, it makes the heart co-natural to them, and supplies the place of that natural instinct that carries other creatures to their own works and ends, strongly and sweetly, 1 John v. 3; Psal. cxix. 165; Neh. viii. 10; Col. iii. 15. Now you may judge whether or not you can possibly expect so much advantage in any other method or way you take. This I leave to your own consideration and experience.

And so I come to the next thing proposed, *secondly*, To consider what this yoke is, and what is the nature of it. And may I not upon this head justly enough distinguish a twofold yoke, of doctrine and discipline, that is, the yoke of Christ's commandments and laws, which both, in his love and wisdom, he hath imposed upon us, for the regulation of our lives? And this we are to take on by an obedience cheerful, willing, and constant. But there is another yoke mentioned in scripture, namely, the yoke of his chastisements and correcting; such a one as Ephraim (Jer. xxxi. 18.) was tried with, and was long or he could learn to bear it. It is good for a man to bear this yoke in his youth, Lam. iii. 27. Now whether or not this be meant here, I do not contend. The first is the chief intent, and it is not needful to exclude this altogether, since it is not the smallest point of Christianity to take up the one yoke by submission, as well as to take up the other by obedience. However it be, obedience must be taken so largely, as it cannot but comprehend the sweet compliance, and submission of the will to God's will in all cross dispensations, which is no little probation of the loyal and obedient temper of the heart. Both yokes must be taken up, for so Christ speaks of his cross, 'If any man will be my disciple, he must take up his cross and follow me,' Matt. xvi. 24, 25. It must be lifted up upon our shoulders, as it were, willingly, and cheerfully, we actually concurring, as it were, to the bearing of it, and the receiving it. But there is this difference between the one yoke and the other, the one cannot be imposed upon us, neither can we bear it, except we actively and with our own consent and delight take it up. Though God may impose laws upon us, and give us righteous and faithful commandments, which indeed lay a strait obligation and tie upon us, under pain of disloyalty and rebellion, to walk in them; yet it never becomes our yoke, and is never carried by us, until there be a subsequent consent of the soul, and a full condescension of the heart, to embrace that yoke with delight. Till we yoke ourselves unto his commandments, by loving and willing obedience, we have not his yoke upon us. 'Thy people shall be made willing in the day of thy power.' It is not terrors and constraints, but the bands of love will bind us to this yoke. It must be bound upon us by the cords of love, not of fear. He is a true king, not a tyrant; he loves *imperare volentibus*, "to rule every man with his own consent;" but a tyrant "rules every man against his will," *nolentibus imperat.* But as to the other yoke of his discipline, his cross, whether it be for his sake, or whether it be the general cross of our pilgrimage here, and the vicissitudes and changes of this life, it is not in our arbitrament to bear a cross, or have a cross or not. Have it we must, bear it we must, whether we choose or refuse it. There is no man can be exempted from some yoke of this kind. No man can promise himself immunity from some cross or other; if not in poverty, yet in abundance; if not in contempt and reproach, yet in honour and greatness. There is nothing of that kind that will not become weighty with itself alone, though nothing be superadded to it. So then, since every man must have a yoke, he hath only the advantage who takes it up, and bears it patiently. For if he thus sweetly comply and yield to God's will, he will not so much bear his cross, as his cross will bear him. If thou take it up, it will take thee up, and carry thee. If thou submit and stoop willingly to God's good pleasure, thou wilt make it a more easy yoke, and light burden. *Ducunt volentem fata, nolentem trahunt.** If thou be patient, his dispensation will gently and sweetly lead thee to rest; but an impatient soul is dragged and drawn after it against the hair, and yet he must follow it. There is this mighty disadvantage in our impatient unsubjection to God's will, that it makes that a yoke which is no yoke, no cross a cross, an easy yoke hard, and a light burden heavy, and yet notwithstanding we must bear it. A yoke, a cross, we cannot escape, whithersoever we go, whithersoever we turn ourselves, because we carry ourselves about with us, and our own crooked perverse apprehensions of things, which trouble us more than the things themselves. Now consider the reasonableness of taking on the yoke of Christ's obedience. Should we not with David, offer ourselves willingly, and present ourselves even before we are called: 'Lo I come, to do thy will, O God: I delight in thy law, it is in my inward part,' Psal. xl. 8. There is no yoke so reasonable, if you consider it as imposed by Christ our King and Lawgiver. Hath he not redeemed us from the house of bondage, from the vilest and basest slavery, under the most cruel tyrants, Satan, and death, and hell? Heb. ii. 15. Hath he not asserted and restored us into the true liberty of men, and of the sons of God? The Son hath made us free, (John viii. 32.) when we were under the most grievous yoke of sin, and wrath, and the eternal curse of God. He hath put his own neck under it, and become a curse for us, that he might redeem us from the curse of the law; and so he hath carried away these iron-chariots, these yokes of brass and iron, whereby Satan kept us in subjection; and now been established our careful King, not only by the title of the justest and most beneficial conquest that ever was made, but by God's solemn appointment upon the hill of Zion, Psal. ii. 6. And being exalted a Prince to give us salvation, were it not most strange if his kingdom should want laws, which are the life and soul of republics and monarchies? Ought not we to submit to them gladly, and obey them cheerfully? Should not we absolutely resign ourselves to his will, and esteem his commandments concerning all things to be right? What command should be grievous to that soul, which is delivered from the curse of all the commandments, and is assured never to enter into condemnation? If there were no more to say, were it not monstrous ingratitude to withdraw ourselves from subjection to him, or yield obedience to any other strange lords, as our lusts are? Would it not be an unexemplified unthankfulness to requite rebellion to him, for so much unparalleled affection? Since we are not our own, but bought with a price, we are not *sui juris*,† to dispose of ourselves. All reason should say, that he who payed so dear for us should have the use of us. And that is nothing but glory he seeks from us, that

* [Senec. Ep. 107. See note, page 76.—ED.] † [We are not, "of our own authority."—ED.]

we offer and consecrate soul and body to him, to come under his yoke. As for the gain, it redounds all to ourselves, and that as the greater gain too.

Now a word to the last thing proposed, for I can only hint at it. The most excellent and ready way of bearing this yoke, is to learn of him, to present him as our pattern, and to yield ourselves to him, as his disciples and scholars; not only to learn his doctrine, but to imitate his example and practice; 'to walk even as he walked.' And herein is great moment* of persuasion, Christ puts nothing upon you, but what he did take upon himself. There is so much more reason for you to take it up, that it is his own personal yoke, which he himself carried; for he delighted to do the Father's will. It was his meat and drink to work in that yoke. Now there are two things especially wherein he propones himself the exemplar or pattern of our imitation, viz., his humility and meekness of spirit. He was 'meek and lowly in heart.' And these graces have the greatest suitableness to capacitate and dispose every man for taking, and keeping the yoke of Christ. Humility and lowliness bows his back to take on the least of his commands. This makes him stoop low, and makes his shoulders fit for it: and then meekness arms him against all difficulties and impediments that may occur in it.

Sermon VIII.

MATT. xi. 29.—"*Take my yoke upon you,*" &c.

CHRISTIANITY consists in a blessed exchange of yokes between Christ and a pious soul. He takes our uneasy yoke, and gives his easy yoke. The soul puts upon him that unsupportable yoke of transgressions, and takes from him the portable yoke of his commandments. Our burden was heavy, too heavy for angels, and much more for men. It would crush under it all the strength of the creatures; for who could endure the wrath of the Almighty? Or, 'what could a man give in exchange for his soul?' Nay, that debt would drown the whole creation, if they were surety for it. Notwithstanding, Christ hath taken that burden upon him, being able to bear it, having almighty shoulders, and everlasting arms for it. And yet you find how heavy it was for him, when it pressed out that groan from him, 'Now is my soul sore amazed, very heavy, and exceeding sorrowful even unto death, and what shall I say?' That which carried it away from us, hath buried it in his grave, whither it pressed him down. It gets him very low under it, but he hath got above it and is risen again; and whereas in vain there was a stone put above him, and sealed, he hath rolled a stone above that yoke and burden, that it cannot be able to weigh down any believing soul to hell: for that weight which depressed his spotless soul, would have depressed the sons of men to eternal darkness. Now for his burden, we observe that it is of another nature, to speak properly, than other burdens. It is not a heavy yoke or burden, but a state of liberty, an ornament, a privilege. It is a chain of gold about a saint's neck, to bind Christ's laws about them; every link of that chain is more precious than rubies or diamonds. If there be any burden in it, it is the burden of honour, the burden of privilege, and incomparable dignity; *honos* not *onus* or *onus honoris*.† This is that which he puts upon us, or rather that which a believer receives from him. Now I will not have you so to take it, as if Christ did not propose the terms thus, "If you will be willing to take on the yoke of my laws, I will take on the yoke of your sins and curses." Nay, it is not such an exchange as is thus mutually dependent; for it hath pleased the Father without consulting us, and the Son without our knowledge or consent, to conclude what to do with the heavy and unsupportable burden of sinners. The Father 'laid upon him the iniquities of us all; and he' of his own accord 'hath borne our griefs, and carried our sorrows,' (Isa. liii. 4—6.) and that

* [That is, weight or force.—ED.]

† [That is, "*the honour,* not *a load,* or *a load of honour.*"—ED.]

burden did bruise him; yea, 'it pleased the Lord to bruise him,' and it pleased himself to be bruised. O strange and unparalleled love, that could digest so hard things, and make so grievous things pleasant! Now I say, he having thus taken on our burden already, calls upon us afterward, and sends forth proclamations, and affectionate invitations, "Come unto me, all ye poor sinners, that are burdened with sin, and wearied with that burden; you who have tired yourselves in these by-ways, and laboured elsewhere in vain, to seek rest and peace: you have toiled all night and caught nothing, come hither, cast your net upon this side of the ship, and you shall find what you seek. I have undertaken your yoke and burden, why then do you laden yourselves any more with the apprehension of it? The real and true burden of wrath I have already carried away, why then do ye weary yourselves with the imagination of it? Only come to me, and see what I have done, and you shall find rest and peace."

Now this being proponed absolutely unto sinners, and they being invited to consent to that which Christ has done in their name, in the next place he comes to impose his easy yoke upon us, not at all for any recompence of what he hath done, but rather for some testimony of gratitude and thankfulness on our part, and for the manifestation of grace and love on his part. I do indeed conceive, that the imposition of the yoke of Christ's laws upon believers, is as much for the declaration of his own love and goodness, as the testification of our thankfulness. If you consider the liberty, the beauty, and the equity of this yoke, it will rather be construed to proceed from the greatest love and favour, than to tend any way to recompence his love. Herein is perfect liberty, Psal. cxix. 32, 45. It is an enlargement of heart, from the base restraint and abominable servitude of the vilest lusts, that tyrannize over us, and keep our affections in bondage. O how narrow bounds is the liberty of the spirits of men confined unto, that they serve their own lusts! Sin itself and the lusts of the flesh, are a grievous yoke, which the putting on of this yoke looses thee from: and when the heart is thus enlarged with love and delight in Christ, then the feet unfettered, may walk at liberty, and run in the way of God's commandments. 'I will walk at liberty,' when I have a respect to thy ways, Psal. cxix. 45. O how spacious and broad is that way in reality, which to our first apprehension and the common construction is strait and narrow! The truth is, there is no straitness, no bondage, no scantiness, but in sin. That is the most abominable vassalage, and the greatest thraldom of the immortal spirit; to be so basely dragged by the flesh downward, to the vilest drudgery, and to be so pinched and hampered* within the narrowness of created and perishing things. To speak properly, there is no slavery but this of the spirit; for it is not so contrary to the nature and state of the body, (which by its first institution was made a servant,) to be under the dominion of men, and further we cannot reach. Yea, it is possible for a man, while his body is imprisoned, to be yet at greater freedom than those who imprisoned him. As his mind is, so he is. But to be a servant of sin and unrighteousness, must totally degrade the soul of man. It quite defaces that primitive glory, and destroys that native liberty, in which he was created. Therefore to have this sin taken off us, and the yoke of Christ's obedience put on us, to be made free from sin, and become the servants of righteousness, that is the soul's true liberty, which sets it forth at large to expatiate in the exceeding broad commandments, and in the infinite goodness of God, where there is infinite room for the soul.

When, then, I consider how beautiful this is for a reasonable spirit, to be under the law of him that hath made it and redeemed it, I cannot but think that Christ doth rather beautify and bless, than burden. The beauty of the world consists in that sweet order, and harmonious subordination of all things, to that law God hath imposed upon them, or engraves upon their natures. If we should suppose but one of the parts of the world to swerve from the primitive institution, what a miserable distraction would ensue? How deformed would this beautiful and adorned fabric become? How much more is it the beauty, grace, and comeliness of an intelligent being, to be under the law of him that gave him a being, and to have that written in his

* [Confined.—Ed.]

heart,—to be in a manner transformed by the shining glory of these laws, to be a living law? What is it, I pray you, deforms these fallen angels, and makes them devils? Why do we paint a good angel in a beautiful and comely image, while the devils are commonly represented in the most horrid, ugly, and monstrous shape and visage? Is it not this that makes the difference, that the one is fallen from a blessed subordination to the will of God, and the other keeps that station? But both are equal in nature, and were alike in the beginning.

Add unto this, the equity of Christ's yoke. There is nothing either so reasonable in itself, or yet so suitable to ourselves. For what is it that he puts upon us? Truly no new commandment; it is but the old command renewed. It is no new law, though he hath conquered us, and hath the right of absolute dominion over us; yet he hath not changed our fundamental laws. He changes only the present tyrannical yoke of sin: but he restores us, as it were, to our fundamental liberty we formerly enjoyed, and that sin forced us from, when it conquered us. Christ's yoke is not a new imposition. It is but the ancient yoke that was bound upon man's nature by God the Creator. The Redeemer doth not invent or contrive one of his own; he only looses off the yoke of iniquity, and binds on that sweet yoke of obedience and love to God. He publishes the same laws, many of which are already written in some obscure characters upon our own minds; and he again writes them down all over in our hearts. There is nothing superadded by Jesus Christ, but a chain of love to bind this yoke about our necks, and a chain of grace and truth to keep his laws. And truly these make the yoke easy, and take away the nature of a burden from it. O what mighty and strong persuasions! O what constraining motives of love and grace doth the gospel furnish, and the rarest cords to bind on Christ's yoke upon a reasonable soul,—cords of the most unparalleled love!

I shall only add unto all this, that as herein Christ hath expressed or completes the expression of his love upon his part; so upon our part it becomes us to take on his yoke, in testimony of our thankfulness. We owe our very selves unto him. What can be more said? We owe ourselves once and again; for we are twice his workmanship, first created by him, and then renewed or created again unto good works. We are bought with a price, we are not our own. Can there be any obligation imagined beyond this? Let us therefore consecrate ourselves to his glory. Let all who believe the gospel dedicate themselves to its obedience, not so much for salvation to themselves, as their obligation to their Saviour. We are not called so much to holiness and virtue that we may be saved, as, because we are saved, to be blameless before God in love. O how gracious and honourable a disposition of this kind would it be, to serve him more out of gratitude for what he hath done, than merely for the reward that he will give!

Sermon IX.

Rom. xv. 13.—"*Now the God of hope fill you with all joy and peace in believing,*" &c.

It is usual for the Lord in his word to turn his precepts unto promises, which shows us, that the commandments of God do not so much import an ability in us, or suppose strength to fulfil them, as declare that obligation which lies upon us, and his purpose and intention to accomplish in some, what he requires of all: and therefore we should accordingly convert all his precepts unto prayers, seeing he hath made them promises. This gives us ground, as it were, to retort his commands by way of requests and supplications. The scripture here gives us a precedent, and often elsewhere hath made his command a promise. It is then in the next disposition, and nearest capacity, to be turned into the form of a supplication. The joy promised in the preceding verse is elsewhere commanded; and this immediately disposes the sinner to receive a new form of prayer, from a believing heart, and that not only for himself, but for others. You see how frequently such holy and hearty wishes are interjected in his writings. And indeed such ejaculations of the soul's desires, whether kept within, or vented, will often interrupt the thoughts and discourses of believers; but yet they break no sentence, they mar no sense, no more than the interposition of a parenthesis. Such desires will follow by a kind of natural resultance upon the lively apprehension of any divine excellent thing, and secret complacency in it; and a stirring of the heart to be possessed with it, will almost prevent deliberation. Such an attractive power the excellency of any object hath in the heart, that it draws it and engages it almost before any consultation be called about it. Now there is something of this in these objects which we are naturally delighted with. All at least that they want the apprehension supplies, and this draws the heart forcibly after them, as it were, without previous advisement. Yet because of the limitation, emptiness, and scarcity of these things, commonly the desires of men are contracted much within themselves, and run towards a monopoly of these things. They are so poor and narrow, that they cannot be enjoyed of more, without division, and the dividing them cannot be without diminution of each man's contentment; and therefore men's wishes ordinarily are stinted within their own satisfaction and possession, and cannot without some restraint of reason extend further to other men. But this is the vast difference between spiritual things and bodily, eternal things and temporal, that there is no man possessed of spiritual good, but he desires a community. It is as natural upon the apprehension of them to enlarge the soul's wishes to other men, because there is such excellency, abundance, and solidity discovered in them, as that all may be full, and none envy or prejudge another. They are like the light that can communicate itself to all, and that without diminution of its splendour. All may see it without prejudice one to another. They are such an ocean that every one may fill their vessel, and yet nothing less for them that come after. And therefore the soul that wishes largely for itself, will not find that inward discontent at the great abundance of another, which is the inseparable shadow of earthly and temporal advantages. It is cross to men's interest, that love gain or preferment, or any such thing, that others grow rich, or are advanced high in the world, for it intercepts what they desire. But it is not at all the interest of a godly soul that others be worse than himself; but rather the salvation and happiness of all men is that interest which alone he espouses.

Now for this, my beloved, before we proceed further, you may find how the pulse of your souls beats, and what your temper is, by considering what is the ordinary unrestrained and habitual wishes of your hearts. Certainly as men are inclined so they affect, and so they desire; and these unpremeditated desires that are commonly stirred up in the hearts of men, argue much the inward temper and inclination of the heart, and give the best account of it. I think if men would reflect upon themselves, they will find that earthly things are vain, while they put on another beauty, and have a more magnificent representation in their minds; and so draw after them the choicest of their affections, that they cannot spare much real affection for spiritual things, which are apprehended more slightly and darkly, and make the lighter and more superficial impression. But certainly this will be the most natural beating of a holy heart, and the ordinary breathing of it, to desire much of this spiritual treasure for themselves and others. You know what the thoughts and discourses of merchants turn most upon. It is to have good winds, fair weather, good markets, and all things that may facilitate gain: and husbandmen wish for good seasons, timely showers, and dry harvests, that there may be plenty. And generally what men's hearts are set upon, that they go abroad fervently and incessantly in longing desires after. Now truly this is the Christian's inward motion, and this is his salutation, wherewith he congratulateth others: 'The God of hope fill you with all peace and joy in believing.' His gain lies in another airth.* His plenty is expected from another field, and that is from above, from the God of hope, the sweetest name (if all the rest be answerable) to be dealt withal, either for gain or plenty; for it is hope that makes labour sweet, and if it answer expectation then all is well. Therefore, in the sowing the seed of prayers and supplications,

* [See note, page 115.—Ed.]

with tears, for this harvest of joy, and in trafficking for this treasure of peace, it is good that we have to do with the God of hope, who cannot make us ashamed ; for he that soweth must sow in hope, 1 Cor. ix. 10. And therefore, though we sow in tears, yet let us mingle hope therewith, and the harvest shall be joy, and the plenty, affluence of peace in the Holy Ghost. Now if we believed this, would not our sorrows be deep, and our labours sweet ?

In the words you have read, there is the highest wish of a holy heart for himself and them he loves best ; that one desire, if he had no occasion ever to present himself to God, but once, that he would certainly fall upon, or some such like, to be filled after this manner with all peace and joy in believing. These are the fruits of the Spirit he desires to be filled with, and feed upon,—peace as an ordinary meal, and joy as an extraordinary desert, or as a powerful cordial ; and to supply what here is wanting at present, the hope of what is to come, and that in abundance. This is even an entertainment that a believer would desire for himself, and these who have his best wishes, while he is in this world. He would despise the delicacies of kings, and refuse their dainties, if he might sit at this table that is spread on the mountain of God's church, a full feast which fills the soul with peace, joy, and hope, as much as now it is capable of. Now these precious fruits you see in the words show the root that brings them forth, and the branch that immediately bears them. The root is the God of hope, and the power of the Holy Ghost. And a soul being ingrafted as a living branch by faith into Christ, receives virtue to bring forth such pleasant fruits, so that they grow immediately upon the branch of believing ; but the sap and virtue of both come from the Holy Ghost, and the God of hope. Or to take it up in another like notion. This is the river which gladdeneth the city of God with its streams, that waters the garden of the Lord with its threefold stream. For you see it is parted in three heads, and every one of them is derived from another. The first in the order of nature is peace,—a sweet, calm, and refreshing river, which sometimes overflows like the river Nilus ; and then it runs in a stream of joy, which is the high spring-tide : but ordinarily it sends forth the comfortable stream of hope, and that in abundance. Now this threefold river hath its orginal high, as high as the God of hope, and the power of the Holy Ghost, but the channel of it is situated low, and it is believing in Christ.

To begin then with the first of these. Truly there is nothing can be spoken that sounds more sweetly in the ears of men than peace and joy. They need nothing to commend them, for they have a sufficient testimonal, and letters of recommendation written upon the affections of all men. For what is it that all men labour and seek after but this ? It is not any outward earthly thing that is desired for itself, but rather for the peace and contentment the mind expects in it. And therefore, this must be of itself the proper object or good of the soul, which, if it can be had immediately, without that long and endless compass about the creatures, certainly a man cannot but think himself happy, and will have no missing of other things ; as if a man could live healthfully and joyfully without meat, and without all appetite for it, no doubt but he would think himself the happiest man in the world, and would think it no pain to him to want the dainties of princes, but rather that he were delivered from the wearisome necessity others laboured under. Just so is it here, there is nothing would persuade a man to travel, and toil all his lifetime, about the creatures, and not to suffer his soul to take rest, if he did believe to find that immediately without travel, which he endures so much travel for. And therefore the believing Christian is only a wise man, who is instructed where the things themselves, true peace and joy, do lie, and so seeks to be filled with the things themselves, for which only men seek other things ; and not as other men who catch at the shadows, that they may at length find the substance itself, for this were far about, and labour in vain.

Peace is so sweet and comprehensive a word, that the Jews made their usual compellation, 'Peace be unto you ;'* importing all felicity, and the affluence of

* [The friendly salutation which the steward of Joseph addressed to his master's brethren, when they went a second time toEgypt to purchase corn, was (שלום לכם Shalum leikoum) "Peace be to you." After the lapse of so many ages, it is interesting to know that this still continues to

all good. And indeed our Saviour found no fitter word to express his matchless good-will to the well-being of his disciples nor this (Luke xxiv. 36.), when he saluted them after his resurrection, 'Peace be unto you,' which is as much as if he had wished absolute satisfaction, all contentment and happiness that themselves would desire. Now this peace hath a relation to God, to ourselves, and our brethren. I will exclude none of them from the present wish; for even brotherly concord and peace suits well with the main subject of this chapter, which is the bearing of our neighbours' infirmities, and not pleasing ourselves, and such like mutual duties of charity. But certainly the other two relations are most intrinsic to happiness, because there is nothing nearer to us than the blessed God; and next to him, there is nothing comes so near us as ourselves. The foundation of all our misery, is that enmity between man and God, which is as if heaven and earth should fall out into an irreconcilable discord, and upon that should follow the suspension of the light of the stars, and the withdrawing of the influences of heaven, and the withholding the refreshment of the early and latter rain. If such dissension fell between them, that the heavens should be as brass to the earth, and would refuse the clouds when they cry for rain, or the herbs and minerals when they crave the influences from above, what a desolate and irksome dwelling-place would the earth be? What a dreary habitation would we find it? Even so it is between God and men. All our being, all our well-being, hangs upon the good aspect of his countenance. In his favour is all our life and happiness; yet since the first rebellion, every man is set contrary to God, and in his affections and actions denounces war against heaven, whence hath flowed the sad and woful suspension of all these blessings, and comfortable influences, which only beautify and bless the soul of man. And now there is nothing to be seen but the terrible countenance of an angry God, the revengeful sword of justice shaken in the word; all above us as if the sun were turned into blackness, and the moon into blood, and behold trouble and darkness, and dimness of anguish.

Now whenever a soul begins to apprehend his enmity and division in sad earnest, there follows an intestine war in the conscience. The terrors of God raise up a terrible party within a man's self, and that is the bitter remembrance of his sins. These are mustered and set in order in battle-array against a man, and every one of these, as they are thought upon, strike a dart into his heart. They shoot an arrow dipped in the wrath of God, the poison whereof drinketh up his spirit, Job vi. 4. Though the most part of souls have now a dead calm, and are asleep like Saul in the field in the midst of his enemies, or as Jonas in the ship in the midst of the tempest, yet when they awake out of that deep stupidity, God will write bitter things against them, and make them to possess their iniquities; and they shall find that he hath numbered their steps, and watched over their sin, and sealed it as in a bag, to be kept in record. Then he will renew his witnesses against them, and put their feet in the stocks, and they shall then apprehend that changes and war are against them, and that they are set as a mark against God, and so they will be a burden to themselves, Job vii. 20. O what a storm will it raise in the soul! Now to lay this tempest, and calm this wind, is the business of the gospel, because it reveals these glad tidings of peace and reconciliation with God, which can only be the ground of a perfect calm in the conscience. Herein is the atonement and propitiation set forth, that which by its fragrant and sweet smell hath pacified heaven, and appeased justice; and this only is able to pacify the troubled soul, and lay the tumultuous waves of the conscience, Eph. ii. 13—20; Col. i. 19—22. This gives the answer of a good conscience, which is like the sweet and gentle breathing of a calm day after a tempest, 1 Pet. iii. 21. Now it is not so much God reconcileable to sinners, as God in Christ reconciling sinners to himself, 2 Cor. v. 19. Though some men be always suspicious of God, yet they have more reason to suspect their own willingness. For what is all the gospel but a declaration of his love, and laying down the enmity, or rather, that he had never

be, with little variation, the common salutation of friends in the East. Salam aleikoum, "Peace be with you," is immediately acknowledged by a similar greeting, Aleikoum salam, "To you be peace."—Ed.

hostile affections to his elect, and so was all this while providing a ransom for himself, and bringing about the way to kill the enmity? And having done that by the blood of Christ, he will follow us with entreaties of reconcilement, and requests to lay down our hostile affections, and the weapons of our warfare; and for him we have no more ado but to believe his love, while we were yet enemies. This, I say, carried into the heart with power, gives that sweet calm and pleasant rest to the soul, after all its tossings. This commands the winds and waves of the conscience, and they obey it. It is true that many find no trouble within, and some, upon terrible apprehensions of sin and wrath, find ease for the time in some other thing, as a diversion to some other object, and turning aside with Cain to build cities, to worldly pleasures, or employments, or company, that the noise of them may put the clamours of their conscience to silence. Some parleys and cessations men have, some treaties of this kind for peace with God; but alas! the most part make no entire and full peace. They are always upon making the bargain, and cannot close it, because of their engagements to sin, and their own corrupt lusts. And therefore many do nothing else than what men do in war, to seek some advantage, or to gain time by their delays: but O the latter end will be sad, when he shall arm you against yourselves! Were it not better, now while it is to-day, not to harden your hearts? Now, joy is the effect of peace, and it is the very overflowing of it in the soul, upon the lively apprehension of the love of God, and the inestimable benefit of the forgiveness of sins. It is peace in a large measure, pressed down, and running over, breaking without the ordinary channel, and dilating itself to the affecting and refreshing of all that is in man: 'My heart and my flesh shall rejoice.' This is the very exuberance and high sailing-tide of the sea of peace that is in a believer's heart. It swells sometimes upon the full aspect of God's countenance beyond the ordinary bounds, and cannot be kept within in gloriation and boasting in God. When a soul is so illustrated with the Holy Ghost, as to make a kind of presence and possession of what is hoped for, that makes the soul to enlarge itself in joy. This makes the inward jubilation, the heart as it were to leap for joy. Now, truly this is not the ordinary entertainment of a Christian. It is neither so universal nor constant as peace. These fruits so matured and ripe, like the grapes of Canaan, are not set down always upon the table of every Christian, nor yet at all to some. It is enough that he keep the soul in that healthful temper, that it is neither quite cast down or discouraged through difficulties and infirmities. It is sufficient if God speak peace to the soul, though it be not acquainted with these raptures of Christianity. This hath so much sense in it, that it is not meet to be made ordinary food, lest we should mistake our pilgrimage for heaven, and fall upon the building of tabernacles in this mount. For certainly the soul would conclude it good to be here, and could not so earnestly long for the city and country of heaven, if they had any more but some tastes of that joy to sharpen their desires after the full measure of it. It is a fixed and unchangeable statute of heaven, that we should here live by faith, and not by sense. And indeed, the following of God fully, in the ways of obedience, upon the dim apprehensions of faith, is more praiseworthy, and hath more of the true nature of obedience in it, than when present sweetness hath such a predominant influence. Besides, our vessel here is weak and crazy, and most unfit for such strong liquor as the joys of the Holy Ghost. Some liquors have such a strong spirit in them that they will burst an ordinary bottle; and as our Saviour says, 'No man puts new wine in old bottles, for they will burst,' Matt. ix. 17. Truly the joy of heaven is too strong for our old ruinous and earthly vessels to bear, till the body 'put on incorruption,' and be fashioned like unto Christ's own glorious body; for it cannot be capable of all the fulness of this joy. And yet there is a kind of all fulness of peace and joy in this life, 'fill you with all joy and peace.' Indeed the fulness of this life is emptiness to the next. But yet there is a fulness in regard of the abundance of the world. Their joys and pleasures, their peace and contentation in the things of this life, are but like 'the crackling of thorns under a pot,' that makes a great noise, but vanishes quickly in a filthy security, Eccles. vii. 6. It is such, that like the loudest laughter of fools, there is sorrow at the heart, and in the end of it is heaviness, Prov. xiv. 13. It is but at the best a superfice, an external garb drawn over the countenance, no cordial, nor solid thing. It is not heart-joy, but a picture and shadow of the gladness of the heart in the outward countenance; and whatever it be, sorrow, grief, and heaviness follow at its heels, by a fatal inevitable necessity. So that there is this difference between the joys and pleasures of the world, and dreams in the night; for the present there is more solidity, but the end is hugely different. When men awake out of a dream, they are not troubled with it, that their imaginary pleasure was not true. But the undivided companion of all earthly joys and contentment, is grief and vexation. I wonder if any man would love that pleasure or contentment, if he were assured to have an equal measure of torment after it, suppose the pain of the stone, or such like. But when this misery is eternal, O what madness and folly is it to plunge into it! 'I said of laughter, It is madness; and of mirth, What doth it?' But the Christian's peace and joy is of another nature. Yet as no man knoweth the 'hidden manna,' the 'new name,' and the 'white stone,' but he that hath it, (Rev. ii. 17.) so no man can apprehend what these are, till he taste them and find them. What apprehension, think ye, can a beast form of his own nature? Or what can a man conceive of the angelical nature? Truly this is without our sphere, and that without theirs. Now certainly the wisest and most learned men cannot form any lively notion of the life of a Christian, till he find it. It is without his sphere and comprehension, therefore it is called 'the peace of God which passes all understanding,' (Phil. iv. 7.) a 'joy unspeakable and full of glory,' 1 Pet. i. 8. Suppose men had never seen any other light but the stars of the firmament, or the light of a candle, they could not conceive any thing more glorious than the firmament in a clear night. Yet we that have seen the sun and moon, know that these lights are but darkness unto them. Or, to use that comparison that the Lord made once effectual to convert a nobleman, if a man did see some men and women dancing afar off, and heard not their music, he would judge them mad, or at least foolish; but coming near hand, and hearing their instruments, and perceiving their order, he changes his mind. Even so, whatever is spoken of the joy of the Spirit, or the peace of conscience, and whatsoever is seen by the world of abstaining from the pleasures of the world, the natural mind cannot but judge it foolishness, or melancholy, because they do not hear that pleasant and sweet harmony, and concert of the word and Spirit, in the souls of God's children. Else if they heard the sweet Psalmist of Israel piping, they could not but find an inward stirring and impulse in themselves to dance too.

Now the third stream is hope; 'that ye may abound in hope,' because this is not the time nor place of possession. Our peace and joy here is often interrupted, and very frequently weakened. It is not so full a table as the Christian's desire requires. Our present enjoyments are not able to mitigate the very pain of a Christian's appetite, or to supply his emptiness. Therefore there must be an accession of hope to complete the feast and to pacify the eagerness of the soul's desire, till the fulness of joy and peace come: and if he have spare diet otherwise, yet he hath allowance of abundance of hope, to take as much of that as he can hold, and that is both refreshing and strengthening. Truly there is nothing men have, or enjoy, that can please, without the addition of hope unto it. All men's eyes are forward to futurity, and often men prejudice themselves of their present enjoyments, by the gaping expectation of, and looking after things to come. But the Christian's hope being a very sure anchor cast within the vail, upon the sure ground of heaven, it keeps the soul firm and steadfast; though he be not unmoved, yet from tossing or floating; though it may fluctuate a little, yet his hope regulates and restrains it. And it being an helmet, it is a strong preservative against the power and force of temptations. It is that which guards the main part of a Christian, and keeps resolutions after God untouched and unmaimed.

Now, my beloved, would you know the fountain and original of these sweet and pleasant streams? It is the God of hope, and the power of the Holy Ghost. There is no doubt of power in God, to make us happy and give us peace. But power seems most opposite to peace, especially with enemies, and it seems whatsoever he can do, yet that his justice will restrain his power from helping us. But there is no doubt but the God of power, as well as hope, both can and will do it. He hath this style from his promises and gracious workings, because he hath given us ground of hope in himself. He is the chief object of hope, and the chief cause of hope in us too. Therefore we would look up to this fountain, for here all is to be found.

But I haste to speak a word of the third thing proposed, viz. The channel that these streams run into; It is believing, not doing. Indeed this stream once ran in this channel. But since paradise was defaced, and the rivers that watered it turned another way, this hath done so too. It is true, that righteousness and holy walking is a notable mean to preserve this pure, and unmixed, and constant. For indeed the peace of our God will never lodge well with sin, the enemy of God, nor can that joy, which is so pure a fountain, run in abundance in an impure heart. It will not mix with carnal pleasures and toys. But yet the only ground of true peace and joy is found out by believing in another. Whatsoever ye do else to find them, dispute and debate never so long about them, toil all night and all day in your examinations of yourselves, yet you shall not catch this peace,—this solid peace, and this surpassing joy, but by quite overlooking yourselves, and fixing your hearts upon another object, that is, Jesus Christ. 'Peace and joy in believing,' and what is that believing? Mistake it not. It is not particular application at first. I delight rather to take it in another notion, for the cordial assent and consent of the soul to the promises of the gospel. I say but one word more, viz. meditation and deep consideration of these truths is certainly believing, and believing brings peace, and peace brings joy.

Sermon X.

MATTH. xi. 16.—"*But whereunto shall I liken this generation?*"

WHEN our Lord Jesus, who had the tongue of the learned, and spoke as never man spake, did now and then find a difficulty to express the matter herein contained, 'What shall we do?' The matter indeed is of great importance; a soul-matter, and therefore of great moment; a mystery, and therefore not easily expressed. No doubt he knows how to paint out this to the life, that we might rather behold it with our eyes, than hear it with our ears; yet he uses this manner of expression, to stamp our hearts with a deep apprehension of the weight of the matter, and the depth of it. It concerns us all, as much as we can, to consider and attend unto it.

Two things are contained here: The entertainment Christ gets in the world, of the most part; and, The entertainment he gets from a few children, of whom he is justified. I say, it concerns you greatly to observe this,—for Christ observed it very narrowly,—what success both his forerunner and himself had. Christ begins here to expostulate with the multitudes, and with the scribes and Pharisees about it. But ere all be done he will complain to the Father. He now complains unto you, that he gets not ready acceptance amongst you, if it be possible that you may repent of the great injury done to the Son of God, no not so much to Christ, as your own souls; for 'all who hate me love death, and he that sinneth against me wrongeth his own soul,' Prov. viii. 36. Wo unto your souls, for you have not hurt Christ, by so much despising him. Ye have not prejudiced the gospel, but ye have rewarded evil to yourselves, Isa. iii. 9. I say, Christ now complains of you to yourselves, if so be you will bethink yourselves in earnest, and return to yourselves; but if ye will not, he will at length complain to the Father. When he renders up the kingdom, and gives an account of his administration unto God, he will report what entertainment ye gave his word. For he will say, "I have laboured in vain, and spent my strength for nought with such a man. All threatenings, all entreaties would not prevail with him to forsake his drunkenness, his swearing, his covetousness, his oppressions," &c. You know Christ's last long prayer, John xvii. He gives an account in it what acceptance he had among men, when he is finishing his ministry. These are the men he now speaks unto in the text, 'Whereunto shall I liken this generation?' Thus he speaks of them to his Father, 'O righteous Father, the world hath not known thee, but I have known thee.' Well then, this is not so light a matter as ye apprehend. Ye come to hear daily, but know ye not that ye shall give an account of your hearing? Know ye not that there is one who observes and marks all the impressions which the word makes on your consciences? He knows all the blows of the sword of the word, that returns making no impression on your consciences. Christ says to the multitudes here, 'And what went ye out for to see?' I pray you what went ye out to see, seeing ye have not believed his report? Why went ye out unto the wilderness? Know ye who spake, or in whose authority? May we not speak in these terms unto you, when we consider the little fruit of the gospel? What do you come to see, and what do ye come to hear every Sabbath, and other solemn days? I pray you ask at your own hearts, what your purpose is. Wherefore do ye come together so often? Men are rational in their business. They do nothing but for some purpose. They labour, and plough, and sow, in order to reap. They buy and sell to get gain. They have many projects and designs they still seek to accomplish. And shall we be only in matters of salvation and damnation so irrational? Shall we in the greatest thing of the greatest moment, because of eternal concernment, be as perishing brutish beasts, that know not what we aim at? Christ will in the end ask you, what went ye out of your own houses so often to hear? What went you out to see? I pray you what will ye answer? If ye say, we went to hear the word of the Lord, then he shall answer you, and why did not ye obey it? Then why did ye not hear it as my word, and regard it more? If ye shall say, we went to hear a man speak some good words unto us, for an hour or two, then is Christ also engaged against you, because he sent him, and ye despise him; for he says, 'He that despises me, despises him that sent me:' so ye shall be catched both the ways. If ye think this to be God's word, I wonder why ye do not receive it, with the stamp of his authority in your hearts. Why do ye not bow your hearts to it, for it shall endure for ever, and judge you? Why do you sit* so many fair offers, so many sad warnings? Are not the drunkards warned every day by this word, that the curse of the Lord shall come upon them? Is not every one of you, according to your several stations and circumstances, warned to forsake your wicked ways, and your evil thoughts, to flee from the wrath to come, before the decree of the Lord pass forth, and before his fury burn as an oven? And if ye think these to be the true words of the eternal God, and the sayings of the Amen, the faithful and true witness, and the truth itself; if ye believe it as ye profess to do, why do ye not get out of the way of that wrath, which continues upon these sinners daily? Shall ye escape the judgment of God? Shall not his word overtake you, though ministers that speak unto you will not live for ever? But these words they speak will surely take hold of you, as they did your fathers, so that ye shall say, 'Like as the Lord of hosts hath said he will do unto us, so hath he done,' Zech. i. 6. If ye do not think this is God's word, I beseech you, why do you come hither so oft? What do ye come to hear? Why take ye so much needless pains? Your coming here seems to speak that ye think it to be God's word, and yet your conversation declares more plainly that ye believe it not. Yet Christ takes notice of you: and O that ye, beloved, would search yourselves that so ye might hear the word as in the sight of the all-seeing God, and in his sight, who will judge you according to it: a sermon thus heard, would be more profitable than all that ever ye heard. Now to what purpose speak we of these things unto you, and why do we choose this discourse, when ye expect to hear public things? I will tell you the reason of it. Because I conceive this is the great sin of the times, and the most reprehensive and fountain sin, the root of all our profanity and malignity, even this which Christ points out in this similitude. The great blessing and privilege of Scotland is the gospel. Ye all must grant this. Now, then, the great misery and sin of this nation is, the abuse and contempt of the glorious gospel; and if once we could make you sensible of this, ye would mourn for all other particular sins.

The words are very comprehensive. Ye shall find in them the different manifestations of God in his word, reduced to two heads. The Lord either mourns to

* [To sit an offer is, not to accept it.—Ed.]

us to make us mourn, or joys to us to make us dance. A similitude and likeness is the end of all the manifestations of himself, that we be one with him. Therefore when he would move our affections in us, he puts on the like, and clothes himself, in his word and dispensation, with such a habit as is suitable. So ye have both law and gospel. He laments in the one, he pipes in the other. Both sad and glad dispensations of his providence may be subordinate to these ; the one, I mean his judgments, representing that to our eyes which his law did to our ears, making that visible of his justice, which we heard ; the other, I mean mercies, represents that to our eyes, which the gospel did to our ears, making his good-will, his forbearance, and long-suffering, and compassion visible, that men might say, ' As we have heard, so have we seen in the city of our God.' Now these should stir up suitable affections in men. This is their intendment and purpose, to stir up joy and grief, sorrow for sin, on the one hand, and joy in the Lord's salvation on the other hand ; hatred of sin by the one, and the love of Christ by the other.

But what is the entertainment * these get in the world ? Ye shall see it different. In some it meets with different affections, or it makes them, and moves them, and these do justify wisdom. The accomplishment and performance of God's purposes, in the salvation of souls, justifies his word. They justify Christ by believing in him ; Christ justifies us, by making us to believe in him, and applying his own righteousness to us. He that believes justifies the word, and Christ in the word, because he sets to his seal that God is true ; and Christ likewise justifies the believer, by applying his righteousness unto him. The believer justifies wisdom, by acknowledging it as the Father's wisdom ; Christ justifies the believer by making him and pronouncing him righteous, and a son of God. But in others, and in these a great many, it generally meets with hard hearts, stupid and insensible, incapable of these impressions. You know music is very apt to work upon men's spirits, and doth stir up several passions in them, as joy or grief. Now Christ and his ministers are the musicians that do apply their songs to catch men's ears and hearts, if so be they may stop their course and not perish. These are blessed Sirens † that do so, and pipe, day and night, in season and out of season, some sad and woful ditties of men's sin and God's wrath, of the day of judgment, of eternal punishment, that if it be possible, men may fore-apprehend these ills, before they fall into them without recovery. These are the boys in the market-places that strive to sadden your hearts, and make you lament in time, before the day of howling, and weeping, and gnashing of teeth. These also have as many joyful and glad ditties, sweetening the sad. It may be, diverse men have diverse parts of this harmony. John had the woful and sad part, Christ took the joyful and glad part ; so the one answered the other, and both made a complete harmony. It may be, one man in one spring mixes these two, and makes good music alone. The one part is intended to move men to grief, and mourn once, that they may not mourn for ever ; the other to comfort in the meantime these that mourn, to mix their mourning with their hope of that blessed delivery in Jesus Christ. Now what is the entertainment these get from the most part? They can neither move men to one affection nor another ; they will neither mourn nor dance. As the children complain of some rude and rustic spirits, that are uncapable of music, and cannot discern one spring ‡ from another, so does Christ com-

* [Reception.—Ed.]

† [The heathen mythologists represented the Sirens to be three in number, and described them as effecting the destruction of mariners, by luring them from their course with their singing.

—" They the hearts
Enchant of all, who on their coast arrive.
The wretch, who unforewarn'd approaching, hears
The Sirens' voice, his wife and little ones
Ne'er fly to gratulate his glad return ;
But him the Sirens sitting in the meads
Charm with mellifluous song, although he see
Bones heap'd around them, and the mouldering skins
Of hapless men, whose bodies have decay'd."
Hom. Od. lib. xii. v. 39. Cowper's Translation.

‡ [That is, one tune from another.—Ed.]

plain of a generation of men ; they can neither repent nor believe, they care for none of these things. His threatenings and denunciations of wrath are a small thing to them, and his consolations appear also to be inconsiderable. Their souls are otherwise taken up, that they have no sense to discern the transcendent excellency of eternal things. We would then press upon your consciences these three things. First, That the word of God, comprehending the law and gospel, contains both the saddest ditties, and the most joyful and sweet songs in the world. Next, We would discover unto you the great sin, and extreme stupidity of this generation, of which ye are a part, that ye may know the controversy God hath with the land. And then at length, we would labour to persuade you to the right use of this gospel, and justifying of wisdom, if ye would be his children.

The law is indeed a sad song and lamentation, it surpasses all the complaints and lamentations among men. Ye know the voice in which it was given at Sinai. It was delivered with great thunders, great terrors accompanied it. The law is a voice of words and thunder, which made these that heard it entreat that it should not be spoken to them any more ; for they could not endure the word that was commanded, Heb. xii. 18, 19. Ye would think if they were holy men, they would not be afraid of it, but so terrible was that sight, and that voice, that it even made holy Moses himself exceedingly fear and quake. It made a great host, more numerous than all the inhabitants of Scotland, to tremble exceedingly. And why was it so sad and terrible ? Even because it was a law that publishes transgression ; for 'by the law is the knowledge of sin.' If there were no fear of judgment and wrath, yet I am sure there is none that can reasonably consider that excellent estate in which he was once, that throne of eminency above the creatures, that height of dignity in conformity and likeness to God, that incomparable happiness of communion with the supreme Fountain of life ; none I say, none can duly ponder these things, but they will think sin to be the greatest misery of mankind. They must be affected with the sense of that inestimable treasure they lost. And how sad a consideration is it to view that cloud of beastly lusts, of flesh and earth, that was interposed between the Sun of righteousness, and our souls, which hath made this perpetual eclipse, this eternal night and darkness ! How sad is it to look upon our ruin, and compare it with that stately edifice of innocent Adam ! How are we fallen from the height of our excellency, and made lower than the beasts, when we were once but a little lower than the angels ! But then if ye shall consider all that followed upon this, the innumerable abominations of men, so contrary to that holy law and God's holiness, that hath flowed from this corrupt fountain, and hath defiled so many generations of men, that they are all bruises and putrified sores, and in nothing sound from the head to the foot,—the soul within becomes the sink of all pollution, the members without the conduits it runs through, and weapons of unrighteousness against our Maker. And what a consideration is this alone, how vile and ugly doth that holy and spiritual law make the most refined and polished civilian ? He that hath poorest naturals,* most extracted from the dregs of the multitude, oh how abominable will he appear in this glass, in this perfect law of liberty ! So that men would despise themselves, and repent in dust and ashes, if once they did see their own likeness. Ye would run from yourselves as children that have been taken up with their own beauty, but are spoiled with the small pox. Let them look unto a glass, and it will almost make them mad. But if we shall stay, and hear out the trumpet which sounds louder and louder, there will be yet more reason of trembling. For it becomes a voice publishing judgment and wrath, for therein is the wrath of God 'revealed from heaven, against all ungodliness and unrighteousness of men,' Rom. i. 18. It speaks much of all men's sins, 'that every mouth may be stopped ;' but the voice waxed louder and louder, the spring grows still sadder, that 'all the world may become guilty before God,' Rom. iii. 19. It publishes first the command; and then follows the sad and weighty curse of God, 'Cursed is every one that abides not in all things which are written in the law,' (Gal. iii. 10.) as many curses as breaches of the law. And what a dreadful song is this ! Ye 'shall be punished with everlasting destruction, from the

* [Or gifts of nature.—Ed.]

presence of the Lord, and the glory of his power?' If he had said, ye shall be eternally banished from God, what an incomparable loss had this been? Men would lead an unpleasant life, who had fallen from the expectation of an earthly kingdom; but what shall it be to fall from the expectation of a heavenly kingdom? But when withal there is an eternal pain with that eternal loss, and an incomparable pain with incomparable loss, everlasting destruction from God's presence, joined with this; always to be destroyed, and never to be made an end of! It is the comfort of bodily torments, and even of death itself, that it shall be quickly gone, and the destruction ends in the destruction of the body, and so there is no more pain. But here is an eternal destruction,—not a dying, and then a death, but an eternal dying without tasting death. Now consider (if ye can indeed think) what it is to have a law of enmity, and a hand-writing of ordinances against us, as many curses written up in God's register against us, as there were transgressions of the law multiplied, and God himself engaged to be against us, to have no mercy on us, and not to spare us! Could any heart endure, or any hands be strong, if they would duly apprehend this? Would the denunciation of war, the publishing of affliction, the sentence of earthly judges, would they once be remembered beside this? If ye would imagine all the torments and rackings that have been found out by the most cruel tyrants against men, all to be centred in one, and all the grief and pain of these who have died terrible deaths, to be joined in one, what would it be to this! It would be but as a drop of that wrath and vexation that wicked souls find in hell, and are drowned into, and that everlastingly without end.

But we must not dwell always at mount Sinai. We are called to mount Zion, the city of the living God, to hear a sweet and calm voice of peace, to hear the sweet and pleasant songs of the sweet Psalmist of Israel, and of our glorious Peacemaker, Christ Jesus, the desire of all nations, and the blessing of all the families of the earth. His song is a joyful sound, and blessed are they that hear it. I am come, says Christ, 'to seek and to save that which was lost.' I am come to save sinners, and the chief of sinners. Let all these who find their spirits saddened by the terrible law, or who find themselves accursed from the Lord, and cannot be justified by the law of Moses, come unto me. Cast your souls upon me, and ye shall find ease to them. Are ye pressed under the heavy burden of sin and wrath? Come unto me, and I will give you ease. Put it over upon me. Do ye think yourselves not wearied nor burdened enough, and yet ye would be quit of sin and misery? Do your souls desire to embrace this salvation? Come unto me, and I will not cast you out. Whoever comes, on whatsoever terms, in whatsoever condition, I will in no case cast you out. Do not suppose cases to exclude yourselves. I know no case. Ye who cannot be justified by the law of Moses, come unto me, and ye shall be justified 'from all things from which ye could not be justified by the law of Moses.' Ye who have no righteousness of your own, and see the righteousness of God revealed with wrath against you, now come to me, I have a righteousness of God, beside the law, and will reveal it to you. Ye have a band of enmity, and handwriting of ordinances against you; but come unto me, for I have cancelled it in the cross, and slain the enmity, so it shall never do you any harm. In a word, this is the messenger whose feet are beautiful, that publishes glad tidings of peace. This is the Mediator, who reconciles us unto God. The whole gospel and covenant of grace is a bundle of precious promises. It is a set of pleasant melodious songs, that may accompany us through our wearisome pilgrimage, and refresh us till we come unto the city, where we shall all sing the song of the Lamb. What a song is liberty to captives and prisoners, light to them that sit in darkness, opening of the eyes to the blind, gladness of spirit to those who are heavy in spirit! Ye would all think salvation and remission of sins a sweet song. But if ye would discern it, ye would find nothing sweeter in the gospel than this redemption from all iniquity, from sin itself, and from all kind of misery. How lovely and pleasant a thing is that! When Christ hath piped unto you, the remission of all sins in his own blood, then he plays the most sweet spring, the renunciation of sin, and dying to this world, by his death and resurrection. Many listen to the song of justification, but they will not abide to hear out all the song. He is our sanctification and redemption, as well as our righteousness. Always to whomsoever he is pleasant, when he puts his yoke upon them, he will be more pleasant in bearing it. Whosoever gladly hears Jesus singing of righteousness and holiness, they shall also hear him sing of glory and happiness. Those who dance at the springs of righteousness and sanctification, what an eternal triumph and exultation waits on them, when he is singing the song of complete redemption!

Are these things so? Is this the law, and this the gospel? Do they daily sound in our ears, and what entertainment, I pray you, do they get from this generation? Indeed, Christ's complaint hath place here, whereunto shall our generation be likened? For he hath lamented to us, and we have not mourned; he hath piped to us, and we have not danced. We will neither be made glad nor sad by these things. How long hath the word of the Lord been preached unto you, and whose heart trembled at it? Shall the lion roar, and the beasts of the field not be afraid? The lion hath roared often to us. God hath spoken often, who will not fear? And yet who doth fear? Shall a trumpet be blown in the city, in congregations every day, that terrible trumpet of Mount Sinai that proclaims war between God and men, and yet will not the people be afraid? Amos iii. 6, 8. Have not every one of you heard your transgressions told you? Are ye not guilty of all the breaches of God's holy law? Hath not the curse been pronounced against you for these, and yet who believes the report? Ye will not do so much as to sit down and examine your own guiltiness, till your mouth be stopped, and till ye put it in the dust before God's justice. And when we speak of hell unto you, and of the curses of God passed upon all men, you bless yourselves in your own eyes, saying, peace, peace, even though ye walk in the imagination of your own hearts, add sin to sin, and 'drunkenness to thirst,' Deut. xxix. 20. Now, when all this is told you, that many shall be condemned and few saved, and that God is righteous to execute judgment, and render vengeance on you, ye say within yourselves, For God's sake, is all this true? But where is the mourning at his lamentations, when there is no feeling or believing them to be true? Your minds are not convinced of the law of God, and how shall your hearts be moved? Christ Jesus laments unto you, as he wept over Jerusalem, 'How often would I have gathered thee, and thou wouldst not!' What means he? Certainly, he would have you to sympathize with your own condition. When he that is in himself blessed, and needs not us, is so affected with our misery, how should we sympathize with our own misery! God seems to be affected with it, though there be no shadow of turning in him. Yet he clothes his words with such affections, 'Why will ye die?' 'O that my people had hearkened unto me!' He sounds the proclamation before the stroke, if it be possible to move you to some sense of your condition, that concerns you most nearly. Yet who judges himself that he may not be judged? The ministers of the Lord, or Christians, may put to their ear, and hearken to men in their retiring places, but who repents in dust and ashes, and says, 'What have I done?' Jer. viii. 6. But every man goes on in his course without stop. The word ye hear on the Sabbath-day against your drunkenness, your oppressions, your covetousness, your formality, &c., it doth not lay any bands on you to keep you from these things. Long may we hearken to you in secret, ere we hear many of you mourn for these things, or turn from them. Where is he that is afraid of the wrath of God, though it be often denounced against him? Do not men sleep over their time, and dream of escaping from it? Every man hath a refuge of lies he trusts in, and will not forsake his sins.

Again, on the other hand, whose heart rejoices within them to hear the joyful sound? Because men do not receive the law, and mourn when he laments, they cannot receive the gospel. It cannot be glad news to any but the soul that receives sad tidings, the sentence of death in its bosom. Therefore Christ Jesus is daily offered, and as often despised, as a thing of nought, and of no value. Ye hear every day of deliverance from eternal wrath, and a kingdom purchased unto you, and ye are no more affected, than if we came and told you stories of some Spanish conquest, that belonged not unto you. Would not the ears and hearts of some men be more tickled with idle and unprofitable tales, that are for no purpose but driving away the present time, than they are with this everlasting salvation? Some men have more pleasure to read an idle book, than to search the holy scriptures, though in them this inestimable jewel of eternal life be hid. The vain things of this present world have a voice unto you of pleasure, and profit, and credit. They will pipe unto you, and ye will listen unto their sound; but ye know not that the dead are there, and that it is the way to the chambers of hell. These indeed are Sirens* that entice passengers by the way with their sweet songs, and having allured them to follow, lead them to perishing. Here is the voice that is come down from heaven, the 'Word that was with God;' and he is 'the way, the truth, and the life.' He is gone before you, and undertakes to guide you. He comes and calls upon simple men. The Father's Wisdom calls the simple ones to understand wisdom, to find life and peace. Will ye then so far wrong your own souls as to refuse it? And yet the most part are so busied with this world and their own lusts, that the sweetest and pleasantest offers in the gospel sound not so sweet unto them as the clink of their money, or the sound of oil and wine in a cup. Any musician would affect them more than the sweet singer of Israel, the anointed of the God of Jacob. Always † these souls that have mourned and danced according to Christ's motions, and whose hearts have exulted within them at the message and word of reconciliation,—blessed are ye. Ye are of another generation, children of wisdom, ye who desire to hear his voice. 'Let me hear thy voice,' O thou that dwellest in the gardens; the companions hear thy voice, 'for thy voice is sweet, and thy countenance is comely.' If this be the voice of thy heart, blessed art thou. Thou mayest indeed dance, who hath rejoiced in his salvation, or who hath mourned at his lamentation; thy dancing is but yet coming, for his piping is but yet coming. When all the companies of wisdom's children shall be gathered together in that general assembly of the first-born, Christ Jesus, the head of all principalities, and in special the head of the body the church, shall lead the ring; and there shall be eternal praises and songs of those that follow the Lamb. They shall echo into him, who shall begin that song of the hallelujah, Salvation, blessing, honour, glory, and power to the Lamb, &c.

Now, whereunto shall this generation be likened, that are not affected with these things? What strange stupidity and senselessness is it, that men are not affected with things of so great and so near concernment? It would require the art of men to express the obstinacy of some Christian professors, or rather a pen steeped in hell. He would be thought unnatural that would not grieve at his friend's death or loss. And what shall they be called that will not sympathize with themselves, that is, their souls? If we speak to you of corporal calamities, and ye could not be moved, it were great stupidity. But what stupidity is it, that men will not consider their own souls? What shall ye profit, if ye lose your precious souls, and be cast away? It is the greatest loss that is told you, and the greatest gain. Your affections are moved with perishing things, every thing puts them up or down, and casts the balance with you. What deep ignorance and inconsideration is it, that ye who can mourn for loss of goods, of children, of health, of friends, that ye cannot be moved to sorrow for the sin of your soul, for the eternal loss of your soul! Other sorrows cannot profit you, but this is the only profitable mourning. If ye were told your sin and misery, to make you despair and mourn eternally, ye had some excuse to delay, and forget it as long as ye can. But when all this is told you, that you may escape from it, will ye not consider it? When ye are desired to mourn, that ye may be comforted for ever, will ye not mourn? We would have you to anticipate the day of judgment, that ye may judge yourselves, and then ye shall not be judged. What folly and madness is this to delay it till endless, irremediless mourning come, a day that hath no light mixed with darkness! Those that now mourn at that law, and for their sin, and dance at the promises of the gospel, may well be called children of wisdom; and O how may this generation be said to be begotten of foolishness, as their father, and wildness as their mother! For is there any such folly as this, to lose a man's self absolutely and irrecoverably, for that which they cannot have always? Is there any such folly as to refuse this healing medicine, for the little bitterness which is in it, and then to incur eternal death?

* [See note, page 595.—Ed.]

† [In the ancient Scottish dialect, as in this instance, *always* is frequently synonymous with *although, however, notwithstanding*.—Ed.]

Now what should we do then? What doth the word of God call you to do? This is it, to mourn and rejoice, and this is to justify wisdom. These two are the pulse of a Christian. According as he finds his grief and joy, so is he. All of you have these affections, but they are not right placed. They are not pitched upon suitable objects. The worldling hath no other joy but carnal mirth, no other grief but that which is carnal; these are limited within the bounds of time. Some loss, or some gain, some pleasure or pain, some honour or dishonour, these are the poles all his affections turn about on. Now then we exhort and beseech you, as ye would flee from the wrath to come, consider it now and fear it. As ye would not partake with this untoward generation in their plagues, so be not like them in their stupidity.

Ye are called to consider your sins and God's wrath, that ye may turn unto the Lord, and then you will hear the voice of peace crying unto thee, 'Be of good comfort, thy sins are forgiven thee.' If ye submit unto the justice of God, or unto the holiness and righteousness of his law in condemning you, you justify wisdom in part: but ye who have justified wisdom thus far, do not condemn wisdom after it. Justify the gospel, in believing upon Jesus Christ. Receive it as a true and faithful saying with your hearts, and this shall justify you. And if ye justify the wisdom of God in prescribing the righteousness of Christ unto you, ye will also justify wisdom in prescriving a rule of holiness and obedience unto you, and count all his paths pleasantness and peace. Ye must dance at the commandments, as well as the promises, because all God's precepts are really promises. Ye have nothing to do but to believe them, as the way, and then to dance until ye all sing the song of the Lamb with the saints above.

Now if ye believe his law and gospel, and be suitably affected with these, ye are led also to sympathize with all the dispensations of his providence. Doth God lament to you in his works as well as his word? O then, Christians, we exhort you to mourn. Yet mourning because of his lamentable providence, should be joined with rejoicing in his word; 'God hath spoken in his holiness, I will rejoice.' We are a stupid generation, that can neither see, nor hear, neither can we be affected with what we see, nor hear. Do not his judgments go forth as a lamp that burneth, yet who considers? Doth not the lion roar, but who is afraid? Is there not a voice publishing affliction? Hath not God's rod a loud voice, and yet who hears it? Who fears? We do not receive agreeable impressions of the Lord's dealing with us, but every man puts the day of evil far from him. He will not apprehend public rods, till they become personal, and therefore they must become personal. If ye were mourning in a penitent manner, as a repenting soul laments, would not our fast-days have more soul affliction attending them? If ye did dance as God pipes in his providence, would not our solemn feasts have more soul rejoicing, and heavenly mirth? Alas for that deep sleep that has fallen upon so many Christians! How few stir up themselves to take hold upon God, though he hides his face, and threateneth to depart from us? For the Lord is with you while ye are with him; if ye seek him, and feareth for him with all your heart, you will find him, but if ye forsake him he will forsake you.

Sermon IX.*

1 Tim. i. 5.—"*Now the end of the commandment is charity out of a pure heart, and a good conscience, and faith unfeigned.*"

In this chapter the apostle, after the inscription of this epistle, repeats a former commandment that he had given to Timothy, how he should both teach himself, and by his authority, committed unto him by an extraordinary commission, see

* [It is extremely probable that this was one of the probationary discourses which the author delivered before the Presbytery of Glasgow, previous to his ordination. The following is an extract from the Record of that Presbytery. "Dec. 5, 1649. The qlk daye Mr. Hew Binnen made his popular sermon, 1 Tim. i. ver. 5. 'The end of ye commandment is charity,'—Ordaines Mr. Hew Binnen to handle his controversie, this day fifteen dayes, De satisfactione Christi."—Ed.]

that other ministers teach so also. Paul almost in all his epistles, sets himself against legal preachers, and false teachers. It was a common error in the primitive times, to confound the law and grace, in the point of righteousness, or to make free justification inconsistent with the moral law. Therefore our apostle makes it his chief study to vindicate the doctrine of the gospel. He preaches the gospel, and yet is no Antinomian. He preaches the law, and yet is no legal preacher. He exalts Christ more than the Antinomian can do, and yet he presses holiness more than the mere legalist can do. He excludes the law in the point of justification and pardon, and then brings it in again to the justified man's hand. If these words were rightly understood, and made use of, it would put an end to the many useless controversies of the present time, and reform many of our practices.

There are as many practical abuses among Christians concerning the law and the gospel, as there are speculative errors among other sects. In the former verse, he more particularly directs him what to take a care of, that men may neither spend their own, or their neighbour's time, in foolish, unnecessary, or impertinent questions, that tend nothing to the edification of the body of Christ, or in building them up in our most holy faith, the doctrine of Christ Jesus, and faith in it. And in this verse, he shows the true meaning and purpose of the law, and commandment, when he meets these doctors, and draws an argument against them from their own doctrine. They boasted of the law, and were counted very zealous of it; but as it is said of the Jews, they had a zeal of God, but not according to knowledge, because they did not submit unto the righteousness of God. They were also zealous for the commandment, but neither God nor the commandment would give them thanks. Why? Because they wholly mistake and pervert the meaning and purpose of the law. As long as they make the law inconsistent with the gospel, or would mix it with it, in the point of justification, they do it not unto edification in faith (as it is read), and as they ought to do, verses 4, 5, 6. We think this evangelic sentence, but rawly,* yea, legally exponed by many, when they look upon the words as they lie here, 'the end of the commandment is love,' for love worketh no evil, and is the fulfilling of the whole law; and this love is described to be pure and sincere, by the following properties. But we conceive the main business is not to describe love, or to oppose this unto their contentions about trifling questions. We choose rather to understand the text another way, according to the order of nature, which also the words themselves give ground for. 'The end of the commandment is love out of a pure heart,' out 'of faith unfeigned.' So then, according to the phraseology and meaning of the words, love is not first, but faith must be first, and primarily intended; so that the sense of the words is this, The end of the commandment is unfeigned faith, from whence flows a good conscience, a pure heart, and love; or the end of the commandment is faith, which is proved unfeigned by these effects, that it gives the answer of a good conscience, it purifies the heart, worketh by love; the effect of faith which is love, being to our knowledge more sensible than faith itself. We think it then more native † to make a pure heart, and love, marks of unfeigned faith, than faith and a good conscience the marks of love. This exposition is yet more confirmed by parallel places, Rom. x. 4, 'The end of the law is Christ for righteousness, unto them that believe.' This is most principally intended, and even before love. Now it is all one to speak of faith as to speak of Christ. For faith and Christ are inseparably joined, and faith comes not as a consideration in the gospel, abstracted from Christ the object of it, as some enemies of Christ affirm. It justifies us not as an act or work, but as an instrument, whereby we apprehend Christ and his righteousness. For faith abstracted from Christ is but an empty notion, and among the dung and loss that Paul would quit to be found in Christ, Phil. iii. 7—9. Now this sense only fits the scope and purpose, and leads on strongly against the false teachers. When Paul brings his argument from the law, which they defended against the gospel, they made the commandment to contradict the gospel. Paul makes the commandment to contradict them, and agree with the gospel, and to be so far from disagreeing with it, that it hath a great affinity with it as the mean to the end, as that which is unperfect, without its own complement and perfection.

* [That is, coldly.—Ed.]

† [Natural.—Ed.]

Faith in Jesus Christ alone for salvation, quieting a man's conscience, is the very intent of the law; and the command was never given since Adam, to justify men by obedience to it, but to pursue men after Christ. And to satisfy you more fully, and clear it up, he says, though the end of the command be not to justify, but to pursue a man from it to Christ, yet the command suffers no prejudice by this means, but rather is established by faith, the end of it: because this faith persuades the heart, and makes a man obey out of love to God, whereas before it should never have gotten any obedience, while men sought salvation by it.

You see then, there is an admirable harmony and consent between these things that are set at variance, both in the opinion and practice of the times. For what seems more contrary than the cursing commanding law, and the absolving promising gospel? Yet here they are agreed. Doth not justice go cross to mercy in the ordinary notion? Yet here there is a friendly subordination of justice to mercy, of the law to the gospel. Behold how faith is environed with the law, commanding and cursing on the one hand, and obedience to the command on the other hand, how faith is the middle party. A good conscience could never meet with the command since Adam's fall. A pure heart, and the obedience of love, had casten out* with the command; but here is the union, the meeting of old friends. Faith is the mediator, as it were, and the gospel comes between them, and so they dare meet again. Christ Jesus, who is our peace to make two one, comes in the middle, and takes away the difference. The law never meets with an obedient servant, or friend, till it meet first with Christ. It can find none righteous in all the world, none upright. Here you have the law's command and curse reconciled with the gospel's promise, and absolution reconciled with new obedience unto the command; the command leading to Christ, and Christ leading the man just back again to the command; the command serving Christ's design, and Christ serving the command. And this is the round that the believer shall go about in, until sin shall be no more. He shall be put over from one hand to another, till Christ shall be all in all. The command shall put him to Jesus, and Christ shall lead him back again, under a new notion, to his old master.

We may consider in the text a twofold relation that faith stands in; the relation of an end, and of a cause. Faith hath the relation of an end unto the commandment, of a cause unto a good conscience, and a pure heart, and love; for these are said to be out of faith, which notes this dependence of a cause and fountain. The command is for faith, and a pure heart and love are from faith. We shall use no other division, but consider the method of these effects that flow from faith. There is an order of emanation and dependence. There is a chain here. The first link nearest faith is a good conscience. The second link is a pure heart. The third is love; the hand follows the heart, and the heart follows the conscience.

We need not be subtile in seeking our purpose on these words; we think there is more in the plain words than we can speak of. We shall only resolve the verse in these propositions, without more observations. *First*, Faith in Jesus Christ is the end of the commandment, or law. *Secondly*, There is a faith feigned, and a faith unfeigned, a true and a false faith. *Thirdly*, Unfeigned faith gives the answer of a good conscience. *Fourthly*, Faith purging the conscience, purifies the heart. *Fifthly*, Faith purifying the heart, works by love. Here then is the substance of all the gospel, and all this makes up an entire complete end. Faith purifying the heart, purging the conscience, and working by love, is the end of the commandment.

First, The end of the commandment or law (for a part is put for the whole) is faith in Christ, or Jesus Christ apprehended by faith, which is all one. For ye cannot abstract faith from Christ, for the whole gospel is a shadow without him. Grace and glory is but a beam of the Sun of righteousness, that if ye come between it and Christ, it evanishes presently, Rom. x. 4, 'Christ is the end of the law for righteousness to every one that believes.' And if Christ be the end of the law, then faith is the end of it, because faith is the profession of Christ, and union with him. But consider, I. That the end is not taken here for the consumption or destruction of a thing. Christ is not the end of the law in that sense; though indeed, if the

* [Fallen out, or quarrelled.—Ed.]

Antinomian speak ingenuously, his sense would be this, Christ makes an end of the law, contrary to Christ's own express meaning, 'I came not to destroy the law but to fulfil it,' Matt. v. 17. II. The end is either the intention or scope of a thing; the original word imports both. III. There is an end principally and directly intended in the thing, or work itself; and an end adventitious, and of the work. We may speak either of the end the law, of its own nature, is ordained unto, or the end of the Lawgiver in promulgating the law. These may be different. Next, concerning the law, consider, I. That the law may be taken strictly in a limited sense, as it comprehends only the command, and the promise of life, and the curse on the breach of it: and in this sense, it is frequently taken in Paul's epistles to the Romans, and Galatians, and opposed to faith and the gospel, as the gospel contains promises of salvation to penitent sinners. Or, II. It may, or useth to be so extended, as to comprehend all the administrations made under Moses, or all God's mind revealed under the Old Testament: now, in this sense, it comprehends the gospel, and covenant of grace in it, as we shall hear. I. Faith in Christ is the intention and scope of the law. Indeed faith in Jesus is not the intention of the law itself, as it is only made up of commandments, promises, and curses. For the law as it commands, hath nothing to do, but to be a rule and obligation to men, and as it curses, it condemns men, and speaks nothing of Jesus Christ, or a way to make up the breach of the law. The gospel is not contained in the law, but rather accidental to it. For Jesus Christ comes with the gospel, as if some unexpected cautioner would come in, when the Judge is, as the angel that held Abraham's hand,—when he was to slay his son, and offer him up a burnt-offering,—giving sentence to deliver him. It is an exception from the curse.

But Christ is directly intended and pointed out by the law. If ye consider the whole administration of Moses, that is, the law and covenant of works, though it was preached after the fall, yet it was never preached alone without the gospel, and so if ye consider the whole administration of God's mind and ordinances, Christ is principally aimed at. For, 1. The doctrine Moses delivered in mount Sinai contained a covenant of grace. If you look to the preface of the ten commandments, it is even the chief gospel-promise, and article of the covenant, For how could God come to terms with men after sin, but in terms of grace? and on no other terms can man stand before God, nor God be his God. And likewise, seeing the gospel was preached in paradise, and afterwards to Abraham, God could not be false in his promise made to Abraham, neither could the promulgation of the law that followed make that null which went before, Gal. iii. 17. What meant all the ceremonial law? It shadowed out Jesus Christ, the only sacrifice and propitiation. And this is the sum of the gospel salvation to penitents believing in Christ, and looking through the sacrifices unto him; and thus David's righteousness was the imputation of righteousness, and not inherent holiness, Psal. xxxii. 1, 2; Rom. iv. 5. But 2. It uses to be a question, whether the law delivered upon mount Sinai was a covenant of works or not. Some say, that the law which was delivered upon mount Sinai was indeed a covenant of works, though they confess it was preached with the covenant of grace, and not delivered to them to stand by it, or of intention to get righteousness by it, but to be subservient to the covenant of grace. Others speak absolutely that the law upon mount Sinai was a covenant of grace. We conceive this is but a contention about words. The matter is clear in itself, (1.) That neither is now the gospel preached without the law, as ye may see in Christ's sermon upon the mount, and his sermon to the young man, (Matt. chapters v, vi, vii. Mark x. 17,) nor yet was then the law preached without the gospel, as ye may see in Exod. chap. xx. The preface to the commandments, and the second command contains much of the gospel in them. Deut. xxx. 6, 7, &c. compared with Rom. x. 6, &c, where Paul notes both the righteousness of faith and of the works of the law. (2.) Those who say the law on mount Sinai was a covenant of works, do not assert that God gave it to be a covenant of works, out of intention that men should seek salvation thereby, but they make it only a schoolmaster to lead us unto Christ, and to discover our sinful condition: and those who say it was a covenant of grace, consider it in relation to God's end of sending it, and as it takes in all the administration and doctrine of Moses. So there needs be no difficulty here. The matter seems clear, that the covenant of works was preached by Moses, and so it was by Paul, (Rom. x. Gal. iii.) and that neither Paul nor Moses preached the covenant of works, but as a broken covenant; not as such that men could stand unto, or be saved by. No man can preach the gospel, unless he preach the covenant of works; not because both concur to the justification of a sinner, but because the knowledge of a man's own lost condition under the one, presses him to flee to the other.

Now I say, Christ Jesus, or faith in him, is the scope and intention of the law. It is the scope and intention of the lawgiver, in giving out the law. God hath never given a command or curse since Adam's fall, but for this end, to bring sinners unto Christ. This is the end revealed, and appointed by him in his word. This we shall clear from some texts of scripture, because it is very material, Rom. v. 20, 21. It might be questioned from the former words, since death hath reigned before Moses, for sins against nature's light, what means the new entry of the written law? What was the end of the promulgation of it on mount Sinai? He answers, 'the law entered that sin might abound;' that is, the world knew not sin, the letters of nature's light were worn out and rusty; men thought not of their miserable condition by nature, and did not charge themselves before God: therefore a new edition and publication of the law must be given, that all men may know how much they owe, and how they were guilty in a thousand things they never dreamed of. But wherefore serves this? That grace might superabound where sin had abounded. The Lord would have sin abounding in men's knowledge, and their charge to be great and weighty, that God's pardoning grace might be more conspicuous, and the discharge more sweet. We also learn, (Gal. iii. 19.) that the same question was moved, 'Wherefore then serves the law?' Seeing the covenant of grace was preached to Abraham, what meant the publishing of a covenant of works upon mount Sinai? He answers, 'It was added because of transgression, till the seed should come, to whom the promise was made;' and as it is said, Rom. v. 13, 'For until the law sin was in the world.' It abounded in all places of the world before the law came; but men did not impute it unto themselves, nor condemn themselves as guilty. Therefore the law was added to discover many hidden transgressions, and to show them the curse they deserved. Now this law is not against the promise or covenant of grace, (ver. 21.) which it behoved to be if it were not given of intention to drive men to Christ. But the 22d verse speaks out clearly the end of it, 'the scripture hath concluded all men under sin,' and under the curse both. To what end? That the promise by faith in Christ might come, or be given to believers. And ver. 24, 'The law' was a 'schoolmaster' and teacher, to lead us unto Christ. The very doctrine of a command impossible for man to keep, was, as it were, a proclamation of Christ Jesus to him, a complete teaching of the necessity of some other way of salvation. The law exacted obedience rigorously, even such as we could not perform, and cursed every degree of disobedience. This, if there were no more, speaks that a man cannot stand to such terms, and therefore he must flee to Jesus Christ, who mends the broken covenant.

Again, the apostle, 2 Cor. iii. 13, 14, while he speaks of the excellency of the ministry of the gospel beyond the ministry of Moses, notwithstanding all the material glory that accompanied that ministration, as the shining of Moses' face, &c. now opens up a great mystery here,—Moses' face shining while he was with God upon the mount. This holds forth the glory of the law as in respect of God. By counsels and inventions they saw no more but temporal mercies in it, and were not able to fix their eyes on that glory; the carnal Israelites did not break through the ministry of the law and death, to see Jesus there, because a vail was upon their hearts. They thought God had been dealing with them in the terms of a covenant of works, and they would stand to all God had said, and undertook indeed very fairly, 'All which God hath commanded, we will do, and be obedient.' But though* they perverted God's meaning of the law, and did not see Jesus intended; for they did not look steadfastly to the end of that mystery. Now what was it the

* [Some words are omitted here, which may be supplied thus:—though *they said this*, they perverted God's meaning of the law, &c.—Ed.]

vail hid them from? For the same vail is yet on them to this day, while they read Moses and the prophets, and when they shall be converted it shall be done away in Christ, they shall then see him in Moses' law. So then, the end of this ministry of the law was Jesus Christ, and this they could not behold.

Now from all this it is very clear, that Jesus Christ, or faith in him, was the great purpose and end of the law, and covenant of works. The world was lying in sin, and none sought God, no not one; neither knew they well what sin was. Therefore God sends his gospel from mount Sinai, and publishes his law in a terrible manner, that they might know the way and manner of the God they served, and see that their obligation was infinitely beyond their ability or performance. But, poor souls! they clearly mistake the matter, and stand to the terms of the covenant of works, as if they were able to perform them. But God did not leave them so. For he adds a ceremonial law, and sacrifices, to shadow out Christ Jesus. Now, says God, though ye have undertaken so well, yet I know you better than ye do yourselves. Ye will never keep one word of what you say. Therefore, when ye sin bring a sacrifice, and look to my Son, the Lamb that is to be slain and offered up, and ye shall have pardon in him.

II. Christ Jesus apprehended by faith, is the accomplishment and perfection of the law. 1. Because Christ Jesus, or faith laying hold upon him, accomplishes the same end that the law was ordained for of itself. The law was appointed to justify men, that it might be a rule of righteousness according to which men might stand before God and live. Now when the law was weak through the flesh, and could not give life, (Rom. viii. 3; Gal. iv. 21.) and the law ordained to life, wrought more death, and made sin exceeding sinful, (Rom. vii. 10—13.) therefore Jesus Christ came in the flesh, to do what the law was unable to do, and to bring many sons unto glory, that the just might live by faith, Gal. iii. 11. The law should never have gotten its end, no man should have stood before God, but the curse only would have taken place, and the promise would have been of no effect. Therefore, Jesus comes, and gives obedience to the law, and delivers men from the curse of it, and by faith puts men in as good, and even in a better condition, than they would have been by the promise; so that the justified sinner may come before God, as well as innocent Adam, and have as great confidence and assurance, and peace by faith, as he could have had by inherent holiness. Imputed righteousness comes in as a covering over the man's nakedness, and doth the turn* of perfect inherent holiness.

2. Christ, or faith laying hold on him, is the end or accomplishment of the law, because faith in Christ fulfils the righteousness of the law, in respect of a believer's personal obedience. Although the believer gave not perfect obedience, and so cannot stand in terms of justice, yet he gives sincere and upright obedience, which the law should never have got. The command wrought sin and death, by occasion of corruption, and never would any point of it be fulfilled by men. For as long as the curse was standing, no obedience could be acceptable till justice was satisfied, and though that might have been dispensed with, yet there is none that are righteous, none seek after God. No good principles of obedience were in us, but all are corrupt, and have done abominable works, and all our righteousness is as a menstruous cloth; and though upright obedience could have been yielded, yet the law exacted perfect obedience. But now faith in our Redeemer absolves a man from the curse of the law, so that now he is not looked upon as an enemy, but a friend; and then it puts a man upon obedience to the command from new motives and principles: and thus the righteousness of the law is fulfilled in us, who walk after the Spirit, Rom. viii. 4. And that imperfect obedience is accepted of God, and received off his hand, by virtue of the sacrifice and atonement of Christ. The law would accept of no less, no not of nine commandments, if the tenth was broken. But now God in Christ accepts of endeavours and minting,† and so is the law in some way or other accomplished. And faith leads a man on till he be perfected. He walks by faith from strength to strength, till he appear before God, and be made holy as he is holy. Faith in Christ is the end of the law.

* [Serves the purpose.—Ed.]

† [Imperfect attempts.—Ed.]

3. Because whatever faith wants of perfect and personal obedience, it makes up in Christ's obedience; and thus is the law thoroughly accomplished, for what it wants in the believer it gets in Christ. Paul would have the Romans take this way, Rom. vi. 11. 'Likewise reckon ye yourselves dead indeed unto sin, but alive unto God through Jesus Christ.' Ye may gather by good consequence, that since Christ hath died to sin as a public person, so ye should die with him unto sin, and mortify sin with him. And thus may ye have consolation against your imperfect personal mortification. Ye were thoroughly mortified in Christ. So the believer may look unto Jesus, as one who hath given obedience even unto the death, and that, not in his own name but for us; that the imperfect holiness and obedience of every sound believer, may have his complete righteousness to cover it, and come next the Father's eye. And thus is the law fulfilled ; and this way doth faith not make void, but establish the law, Rom. iii. 31. And as the law got better satisfaction in the sufferings of Christ, who became a curse for us, than in all the punishment we could endure, so it gets more satisfaction to the command by his obedience than if our personal had been perfect. Christ was 'made under the law, that we might receive the adoption of sons,' (Gal. iv. 4.) and the Son's being made under the law is of more worth than all our being under it. Now faith puts that obedience of God-Man in the law's hand. When we do God's will, he brings out Christ Jesus, 'Lo, (says he) I come, I delight to do thy will,' Psal. xl. 7—9. In a word, faith in Jesus accomplishes the law, in the commands, in the promise, in the curse, as might be easily shown, if your time would allow.

(1.) In the curse, because it lays hold upon Christ, who was 'made a curse for us,' (Gal. iii. 13.) and so gives complete satisfaction to the Lord's justice in that point. It holds up the sacrifice and propitiation of our Saviour ; and justice says, I am satisfied. It holds up the ransom, (Job xxxiii. 24.) and therefore Christ says, 'Deliver them from going down to the pit, for I have found a ransom.' Again we also observe, (2.) That faith in Christ also fulfils the commandments of the law, because it is the fountain of new obedience unto the law. It hath a respect unto all God's righteous judgments. It purifies the heart into the obedience of them, and it works by love, and so it is the end of the law for righteousness. It not only gives the answer of a good conscience unto all challenges and curses from Christ's blood, but daily derives virtue out of Jesus Christ, to bring forth fruit unto God. What it cannot reach by doing, it supplies by believing, and laying hold upon Christ's obedience. And this is the righteousness of the law fulfilled in us. Let us also,

(3.) Look upon the promise of life, and it is accomplished also by faith in Christ. For the law could not have given life, and so the promise would now be in vain ; but Christ by faith justifies the sinner, and he lives, yea, hath eternal life in him, and so all the three are strengthened and established. Faith is the most comprehensive commandment, 1 John iii. 22, 23. It is put for all the commandments, (1.) By acknowledgment of the breach of all ; and so it magnifies the law, and makes it honourable, and subscribes to the sentence of justice and the authority of the command. (2.) By satisfaction, because it gives a price for the breach of it, and puts the Cautioner* in the craver's hand. (3.) By obedience, because after this, it hath a respect to all God's laws, and endeavours after new obedience to every one of them.

The improvement of all this is extremely plain. Use I. It may serve to discover unto us how we disappoint God of his end in giving unto us the command. And the law was given for the best purposes. But, 1. The most part of men have no end, no use of the law. God hath given it for some end, but they know it not. They live without God, and without rule in the world. Men walk as if there was no law, nor command, nor curse. There are but two ends the command was ordained for ; the first instituted end which it naturally tends unto is life, (Rom. vii. 10.) and the second end for which God hath appointed it since the first is missed, is to pursue men to Jesus Christ, and convince them of sin, to make them once die that they may live, Rom. vii. 9. But the most part know neither of these ends.

* [A Scottish forensic word corresponding to *Surety*.—Ed.]

A carnal profane generation will not seek life by the righteousness of the law; their iniquities testify against them even to their face, and their sin is found hateful. There is not so much as an endeavour among too many Christian professors, either to approve themselves unto men, or their own consciences in their outward walking. They walk without any regard of a command, or rule, as it were by guess. Their own rule is what pleases them best. What suits their humours, and crosses God's word, that they will do, as if they knew not the curse, or were afraid of the sentence of condemnation. They walk in peace, and have no changes, they walk in the imagination of their vain hearts. They cannot say, and none will say for them, they seek life by the law, their contempt of it is so palpable ; and yet no other end of it they know: so it is to them as if God had never appointed it. Again,

2. There are many wrong and false ends, or uses of the law, when we make it the immediate mean to life and righteousness, and seek justification by it. And this was the end that these false teachers would have made of it. This is the end that the Israelites looked to: 'All that the Lord hath commanded, will we do.' O that was a great undertaking! Poor men, they knew not what they said. They thought upon no other thing but obedience to the command, and so made it a covenant of works. Thus did the people that followed Christ, John vi. 28. And the young man that came to Christ said, 'What good thing shall I do, to inherit eternal life?' Here doing was preferred to living by faith, Rom. x. 1—23. The Jews did so, and missed the right way. And few of you will take* with this, that ye seek to be justified by your own works ; and yet, it is natural to men, they will not submit to God's righteousness. There is need of submission to take Christ. O would not any think all the world would be glad of him, and come out and meet him bringing salvation? Would not dyvours† and prisoners be content of a deliverance? Were it any point of self-denial for a lost man, to grip a cord cast unto him? Yet here must there be submission to quit your own righteousness. It were of great moment to convince you of this, that ye are all naturally standing to the terms of a covenant of works, ye who are yet alive, and the commandment hath not slain you, with Paul, Rom. vii. 9, 11. Ye are yet seeking life by the law, if ye have not applied the curse unto yourselves. After application of yourselves to the command, ye are yet seeking life by it. Ye adorn yourselves with some external privileges, in some external duties of religion, some branches of the second table duties, and come to God with these. Some think to satisfy God for their faults, with an amendment in time to come. Some think God cannot punish some faults in them, because they have some good things in them. Ask many men the ground of their confidence, and in all the world they know not how to be saved, unless their prayers do it, or their keeping the kirk.‡ But this is not the end that God hath sent out the law for. Ye cannot now stand to such a bargain. The law is now weak through the flesh, and it is now impossible for it to give life. Though you would pray never so much, all is but abomination. And would not many of you think ye were in a fair venture for heaven, if no man living could lay any thing to your charge, but were you unblameable in all the duties of the first and second table? [Could you say,] though you know nothing as by yourselves, that you were frequent and fervent in prayer, reading, and meditation ; and as far advanced as Paul, or David, or Moses, or Job, sure ye would think yourselves out of doubt of heaven? Nay, but in this, ye may see ye are seeking righteousness by the law. Though ye were so far advanced, yet God, who is of purer eyes than to behold iniquity, would look to your sins, and pass by your righteousness, and all that would be as menstruous rags before him ; and therefore Paul was much wiser, who said, 'though I know nothing by himself, yet am I not hereby justified.' 3. Many make the law an end, when God hath only made it a mean. God hath appointed the law for some other use, namely, to be subservient to Christ and the gospel. But oftentimes we make the law the end of all God's speaking to us, and so conclude desperate resolutions from it, (Rom. vii. 9.) 'When the law came, sin revived,

* [Acknowledge this.—Ed.]
† [A name formerly given to bankrupts in Scotland.—See Act James VI. par. 23, cap. 18.—Ed.]
‡ [Attending the church.—Ed.]

and I died.' Here the man is slain by the commandment, and not yet come to the healing Physician at Gilead. We use to gather desperation of the command, when it presses so perfect and exact obedience, such as we cannot yield. When it craves the whole sum, without the abatement of a farthing, we sit down under the sense of an impossibility to obey, and will not so much as mint* at obedience. Because we cannot do as we ought, we will not do as we can. Because we cannot do in ourselves, we conclude nothing can be done at all. This is to make the command the last word, and the end of God's speaking. Doth not the child of God frequently sit down and droop over his duty, while he looks upon the Egyptian taskmaster, the command, charging the whole work and portion of brick, and giving no straw to work upon? So are many in duties. While the aim and eye is upon some measure according to the perfect rule, the hands fall down feeble, and none is wrought at all, and they do not look if there be another word from God posterior to the command, a word of promise. We use also to gather desperate conclusions of the curse, and make the law according to which we examine ourselves, the end of God's manifesting his mind unto us, and do not look upon it as a way leading to some other thing. When ye have tried yourselves, and applied your own ways and state unto the perfect rule, God's verdict of all men's condition is true in you, 'all have sinned, and come short of the glory of God;' 'there is none righteous, no, not one;' and so if necessitated to apply the dreadful sentence of the judgment to yourselves, ye stay there, and sit down to lodge with the sentence of condemnation, as if that were God's last word to sinners. Is not this to make the law the end, which is but appointed for another end? The curse is not irrepealable. Why then do ye pass peremptory conclusions, as if there was no more hope, but it were perished from the Lord?

Use II. To discover unto us the right end and use of the law, the great design and purpose of God in making such a glorious promulgation of the law on mount Sinai, and delivering it by the ministry of angels, in the hands of a mediator. The end which God hath been driving at these six thousand years, is this only, that men may come to Jesus Christ and believe in him. The end wherefore the covenant of works hath been preached since Adam's fall, is only this, to make way for a better covenant of grace, that men may hearken to the offer of it. Now faith in Jesus Christ hath two special actings, either upon Christ for justification of the person, and eternal life and salvation; or for sanctification of the person and actions, in the fruits of new obedience. And in the text, unfeigned faith is described from both these, and gives the answer of a good conscience, that is, of absolution from the curse, by the blood of Jesus, and makes him as quiet as he had never sinned. And then it purifies the heart, and worketh by love.

Now the law is a mean appointed of God, and instituted to lead to both these, and Christ in these. The law is appointed to lead a man to faith in Christ, for salvation and righteousness; and the suitableness of it to that end, we comprehend thus. 1. It convinces of sin. 'The law entered that the offence might abound,' and 'was added because of transgressions,' Rom. v. 20; Gal. iii. 19. This is the end of God's sounding the trumpet, and declaring our duty, 'that every mouth may be stopped' before God, and that none may plead innocence before his tribunal. While men are without the law, they are alive, and think well of themselves; but the entering of the commandment in a man's conscience, in the length, breadth, and spirituality of it, makes sin to appear exceeding sinful. Sin was in the house before, but was not seen before, and now when the bright beam of a clear, spiritual, holy law, carrying God's authority upon it, is darted into the dark soul, O what ugly sights appear! The house is full of motes. Ye cannot turn the command where it will not discover innumerable iniquities, an universal leprosy. For all the actions that were called honest, civil, and religious before, get a new name, and and they being seen in God's light, are called rottenness, and living without the law, Rom. vii. 9. &c. Think ye, but the woman of Samaria knew her adultery, before Christ spake to her? Nay, but Christ speaks according to the law, and makes it a mean of faith. He tells her all that ever she did. He tells her indeed

* [Aim at.—Ed.]

what she knew before, but in another manner. Men know their actions, but the Lord discovers the sinfulness of them, as offensive to God's holy majesty, and pure eyes. It will force a man to give his sin the right name; it will take away all excuses and shifts, and aggravate sin, that it may become exceeding sinful. But further, 2. This is not the last end of it. Not only is it ordained to stop all mouths, but to make all flesh guilty before God, 'For by the deeds of the law shall no flesh be justified,' Rom. iii. 18, 19. It convinces of an impossibility to stand before God, and so it kills a man. And now the man asks, 'What shall I do to be saved?' He cannot stand before God in terms of justice, where none can stand, and so either must some other delivery come, or he is gone. Now here he is put from making satisfaction, 'Who can abide with everlasting burnings?' He sees himself standing under the stroke of justice; and where can he go from God's presence? If he go to heaven, he is there; if to hell, he will find him out; the light and darkness are alike to him, Psal. cxxxix. 7—11. Not only the cries of sinful man, but of wretched and miserable man, are heard from him! Now these are the steps the law proceeds by. But it must not stay there, or else it is not come to the end of it. It must put a man within the doors of the covenant of grace. The law is a messenger sent to pursue a man out of his own house of self-confidence and security, he was like to perish in, and not to know it. Now by discovering his sinful and cursed condition, it brings him out of himself, and out of all created things. But the end is not yet attained, till it put him in Christ's hand, and enter him in the border of the city of refuge: and this is the end of the abounding of sin by the law, that grace may superabound, Rom. v. 20. And this is the end of the concluding him under sin, and making him guilty before God, that the promise of faith may be given him, and another righteousness revealed by faith, Rom. iii. 20, 21; Gal. iii. 23. And now he is at peace, being justified by faith, and rests as a stone in its own place (Rom. v. 1, 2.); and the law hath nothing to do with him; he is out of its jurisdiction. 3. Now when it hath pursued him unto Christ for salvation, yet the command is still useful, and appointed yet for faith in Jesus, in performing new obedience. The Christian's daily walking is but the turning of the old round, as the sun doth this day go about the compass it did the first day; so his life is but a new conversion still. When he is now settled on Jesus for salvation, he must yet be put by* the command. It discovers his daily sins, and so he is put to Jesus, the open Fountain for all sin and uncleanness. And the command comes out in perfection, and discovers his shortcoming and inability, and therefore he is put to Jesus for strength. And this is the end of the perfect rule upon believers, that they, comparing duty with their ability, may be forced to make up their inability for duty by faith in Christ.

Use III. We may know from this what great encouragement we have to believe, and how great warrant, since not only God commands faith itself (1 John iii. 23.), but he hath appointed faith to be the end of all other commands, and hath given the whole law for this end. For 'without faith it is impossible to see God.' Faith is that which God loves best in all obedience. What is it that makes faith so precious? Certainly not the act itself, but the precious object of it, Jesus Christ, in whom the Father is well-pleased. Faith glorifies God in his justice and mercy most, and abases the creature. Now what an obligation lies on us to believe? It is usual to question a right and warrant of faith, when we have no doubt of other commands. But, in all reason, any command might be questioned before faith. There is no duty admits of less disputing. Hath not God put it out of all controversy? What warrant have ye to pray, or to sanctify the Sabbath? Is it not because God commands these duties? And do ye not go about them in obedience to God, notwithstanding of the sense of your own inability? How comes it then that ye make any more scruple of this? Hath not the same authority that gave the ten commands, given also this new command? And shall not disobedience be rebellion, and worse than witchcraft?† But when, besides all this, it is the

* [Near the command.—Ed.]

† [A belief in the prevalence of witchcraft at this time seems to have pervaded all ranks and classes. An Act of Parliament was passed against it on the 1st of February, 1649.—Ed.]

appointed end of all the commands, so that ye may say, it is commanded in all the commands and the whole law,—command and curse is a virtual kind of commanding faith,—then what shall disobedience be? When ye break one command, ye are guilty of all. Much more here, not only because of God's authority stamped upon all, but because it is the common end of all. If ye could once come to believe that ye had as good warrant to believe in Christ as to abstain from cursing God's name, and as great obligation, what could ye answer for disobedience?

Use IV. This is a point of great consolation also. What more terrible than the law? Nothing in all the world. Nothing in all the word so dreadful as the trumpet on Sinai, sounding louder and louder. The judge and law gives voice. Yet if ye could look to the end of it, and if the vail that was on the Jews' heart be not upon yours, O how comfortable shall it be! Doth not a command and curse form a dead sound in an awakened man's ears, and strike unto his heart like a knife? But if he knew this, it would be a healing medicine. Would not many sinners wish there would be no such thing in the Bible as a condemning law, when they cannot get it escaped? But look to the end of it, and see gospel saving doctrine in the very promulgation of it. When it was published, it made the Jews all to tremble and cry out, and even holy Moses himself was afraid. But there is more consolation than terror here. This condemning law is delivered in a Mediator's hand, even Jesus Christ, Gal. iii. 19, 20. Who was he that spake out of the cloud, and fire, and came and set down his throne on Sinai, accompanied with innumerable angels? Deut. xxxiii. 2; Acts vii. 53. It was Jesus Christ that spoke to Moses in the mount, and in the bush also, Acts vii. 35, 38. Is it then the Mediator's law, whose office it is to preach glad tidings, and the day of salvation? Sure then it needs be dreadful to no man. For if he wound, he shall heal, and he comes to bind up the broken-hearted. Ye may look on the command and curse as messengers sent by mercy, to prepare you, and make his way straight before his face. The end of the law is not to condemn you, to stop your mouth, and make you guilty. That is not the last work it is appointed for; but the Mediator hath another end, to bring you to the righteousness of faith, to save you without yourselves. Therefore ye may more willingly accept the challenge, since it comes in so peaceable terms. What should be terrible to you in all God's word and dispensation, since the ministry of condemnation and death is become the port* of heaven and life? What must all his other dealings be? Surely there is nothing in the world, but it must lead to this end also. Prosperity and adversity, the end of them is faith, conviction and challenges. Be not then as men without hope, when you are challenged, for the challenge comes from a Mediator who would have you saved.

Use V. You may see hence how injurious they are to grace who cry down the law. The Antinomian cannot be a right defender and pleader for faith (the end of the command), when he opposes the command that leads to that end. He cannot exalt Christ aright, or lead men to him, when he will not come under the pedagogue's hand to be led to Christ. The law, even as a covenant of works, is of perpetual use to a believer, because it lays a blessed necessity upon him to abide with Christ. It is a guard put before the door, to keep him, as it was a schoolmaster to bring him to Christ; and makes a man subordinate to the gospel as a mean to the end, and so it ought to be used. So then it is against the truth [to say] that the Israelites were under the law; and not Christians. The law came not to be a mean of life and righteousness unto them, but that the offence might abound, that so grace might superabound. The law was not intended, but Christ was intended; and this end they could not fix their eyes upon, by reason of the hardness of their hearts. It is also false, that Christian believers are wholly exeemed † from the command and law. No, he hath use of all that leads to Jesus Christ; and the law itself becomes gospel under that notion. The command stands in its integrity, that he may be convinced of shortcoming and inability, and so may believe in Christ. The curse also stands, and condemns him for new sins, that he may believe in Christ, who justifies the ungodly. Again, it is not truth, that the law is no mean

* [Portal, or gate.—Ed.]

† [Excempted.—Ed.]

of conversion, though not in its own virtue and power, but as it is delivered in a Mediator's hand, and applied by the Spirit of grace and the gospel.

Use VI. We exhort you not to disappoint God of his end; and if he hath given the law for this end, never rest till ye be at the end. Let the law enter into you once, or enter ye into it. Ye cannot come to Jesus unless it lead you. Let it enter into your consciences, with God's power and authority as his law, and examine yourselves by it, else ye shall never believe in Christ. 2. Accept all the challenges of the law, let it enter till your mouth be stopped. Read your obligation well, that ye may see how much ye owe. 3. Let faith be the issue and result of all the applications of the law to yourselves. Ye go in the law's hand to Christ, but sit not down with it, or else you will not go free till ye have paid the last farthing. Make faith in Christ the end of the curse condemning you, that he may absolve you; the end of the command, commanding, that he may give strength and fulfil in you the righteousness of the law. God never sent a condition to you, but that you may believe, and be established. 4. Let it be your exercise to travel between an impossible command, and Christ Jesus by faith, through whom all things are possible. Write always down how much ye owe, that ye may see grace superabounding, Sit not down to examine the duty, or go not about it in your own strength. Be not discouraged though ye find no strength. Ye are called in such a case to believe. Nay, in a word, what is all the Christian's employment? Faith exhausts it all. Look on the command, and it calls for believing. Look upon the curse and it calls also for believing.

Sermon XII.

1 Tim. i. 5.—"*Now the end of the commandment,*" &c.

We come now, as was proposed, to observe, *Thirdly,** That faith unfeigned is the only thing which gives the answer of a good conscience towards God. Conscience, in general, is nothing else but a practical knowledge of the rule a man should walk by, and of himself in reference to that rule. It is the laying down a man's state, and condition, and actions beside the rule of God's word, or the principles of nature's light. It is the chief piece of a man. The man is as his conscience is. It is a man's lord. As a wing to a bird, or as a rudder to a ship, so is conscience to a man in all his ways. The office of conscience is ordinarily comprehended in three styles it gets. It is a law or rule, a witness, and a judge; or a light, a register, and a recorder, and an executioner. For the conscience its first act is some principle of nature's light, obliging it as a rule to walk by, or some revealed truth of God, whereof the conscience is informed. Now the conscience, in the second place, comes to examine itself according to the rule, and there it bears witness of a man's actions or state, and faithfully records and depones.† And at length the conscience pronounces the sentence upon the man, according as it has found him, either accusing or excusing, condemning or absolving. Now a good conscience is diversely taken in scripture, I. A good conscience is an honest clean conscience, bearing testimony of integrity and uprightness in walking, such as Paul had, 2 Cor. i. 12, 'Our rejoicing is this, the testimony of our conscience, that in simplicity, and godly sincerity, we have had our conversation in the world.' Heb. xiii. 18, 'We trust we have a good conscience, in all things willing to live honestly.' Acts xxiv. 16, 'Herein do I exercise myself in having a conscience void of offence, towards God and man.' 1 Pet. iii. 16, 'Having a good conscience, that whereas they speak evil of you, as of evil-doers, they may be ashamed that falsely accuse your good conversation in Christ.' II. A good conscience is a conscience calmed and quieted, that hath gotten an answer to all challenges

* [The illustration of the second proposition found in the text, "There is a faith feigned, and a faith unfeigned, a true and a false faith," (p. 602,) is omitted. We may conclude that this was the subject of a separate sermon, which has been lost.—Ed.]

† [Deposes or testifies.—Ed.]

the blood and resurrection of Jesus, 1 Pet. iii. 21. And this we take to be meant here. The good conscience is the conscience that is sprinkled with Christ's blood, from dead works, to serve the living God, Heb. ix. 14. For the guilty man that comes to Christ, and washes in the fountain opened for sin, hath no more conscience of sins, Heb. x. 2. And therefore it is called a pure and clean conscience, 2 Tim. i. 3, 'I thank God, whom I serve from my forefathers, with a pure conscience,' &c.; the stain of guilt is taken away. Now I say, faith only gives the answer of a good conscience. The man that comes to Christ hath an ill conscience, when he hath examined himself according to the law, and given out faithful witness of his own state and condition, and accordingly pronounced sentence,—a sentence condemnatory. He finds himself lying under God's curse, and so the conscience from a judge turns a tormentor, and begins to anticipate hell, and prevent* the execution of wrath. All the world cannot answer this challenge, or absolve from this sentence, until faith come and give a solid answer, that may be a ground of peace. And its answer is good and sure, because it dips the conscience in the blood of the Son of God. For the blood of bulls and of goats could not do it, the redemption of the soul was precious. Faith puts the soul over head and ears in the fountain opened, and it comes out like snow, or wool, though it were like scarlet or crimson. The law condemned, and the conscience subscribed itself sinful, and concluded itself lost in sin; but faith in Christ pleads before mercy's throne, where judgment and justice also sit. It pleads its cause over again, and gets the former sentence repealed. The conscience gave in the charge against the man, but faith sits down and writes the discharge; and so he is as free as if all his debt was paid, or never contracted. Faith puts the Cautioner in the creditor's hand, and goes free. As the law writes down a charge of sin and curses, faith sets against it as many sufferings in Christ, as many blessings in the Blessing of all nations. And when the conscience that condemned itself by faith again absolves itself, O what a calm, what a perfect peace is it then kept in! What a continual feast doth it enjoy! Prov. xv. 15. Make him never such a great man in the world, he would utterly despise it, and count himself more blessed in the pardon of sin, and the friendship of God, than all the enjoyments of this world. He is better in some respect than if he had never sinned, for his sin is, as it were, not before God. And withal he hath got not only acquittance from guilt, but acquaintance with Jesus Christ, the Blessing of the nations, and the Desire of all the families of the earth. Now may he triumph and boast in Christ Jesus, Who shall condemn? It is God that justifies, it is Christ that died, and is risen again. He may say with David, 'I will not fear, though my iniquities compass me about;' and with Job, 'If he cause quietness, who can give trouble?' We observe then that,

I. Before a man come to Christ, he has an ill conscience; for either he is at peace with himself, and absolves himself, saying, I shall have peace, though I walk in the abominations of my heart, Deut. xxix. 19; or he also says, 'Because I am innocent,' therefore God will turn away his wrath, Jer. ii. 35. He cries peace, peace, when there is no peace, (Ezek. xiii. 10.) and that is but a desperate condition, and a bad conscience, if any can be so called. This is the secure and seared conscience, that either doth not judge itself, because a man hath beaten it flint hard, or is constantly absolving itself upon false grounds. That is the conscience that in all the creation is nearest the desperate conscience, that shall never have a good answer. His sin is but lying at the door like Cain's, and shall enter in when judgment comes. He is but flattering himself in his own eyes, till his iniquity be found hateful, and till sudden destruction comes as an armed man. Look upon Deut. xxix. 20. and see such a man's case. There is no peace for him, the Lord will not pity nor spare him, but pour upon him all the curses of the law, even when he blesses himself in his own eyes. In short, he is such as is awakened to see where he is, and condemns himself according to the word; and that is a better and a more hopeful conscience than the former, yet it is but an ill conscience. Conscience doth act its part aright, and in so far it is good, but the man is but in a miserable condition. Withal it gives such a wound to the soul, as none can bear it. All the

* [That is, foresee or anticipate.—Ed.]

sad affections which take up men's spirits come in, and this is the worm which never dies in hell, and the fire which shall never be quenched. Anger, grief, hatred, despair, always dwell with an ill conscience. This is both the resemblance of hell, and the sparks which come from that devouring fire. But II. When the troubled conscience, tossed up and down, and looking upon all hands for help, and all refuge failing them, and no person caring for their soul, when it gets once a look of Jesus, and roweth unto his shore, O what a change! He commands the winds to calm, and the waves to cease, and says unto him, Son, be of good comfort, thy sins are forgiven. Faith finds in Jesus ample grounds of answering all challenges, of silencing all temptations, of overcoming all enemies, and commands the soul to go into its place of refuge. 'Return unto thy rest, O my soul, for the Lord hath dealt bountifully with thee,' &c. Psal. cxvi. 7—9.

We shall now shut up all with the application in some uses. Use I. We may learn hence how few have a good conscience. Faith is a rare thing, but a good conscience is much rarer. And here we may notice, 1. That the conscience which is dead and sleeping, is not a good conscience: every quiet and calm conscience is not a good one. Ye may dream over your days with the foolish virgins, and take rest in a pleasing delusion, and cry peace, peace, and yet the end of it will be worse than the beginning. A conscience that acts not at all, nor judges itself, is, as it were, no conscience; either ignorance hath blinded it, and keeps it in the dark, or wickedness hath stopped its mouth. You think your conscience good because it tells you few of your faults, it troubles you not; but that conscience must once speak, and do its office, it may be in a worse time for you. 2. It is not a good conscience that always speaks good, and absolves the man. God may condemn when it absolves. When ye walk according to false principles and grounds, and either take a wrong rule, or know not how to apply the rule to yourselves, shall God approve of false judgment? Your conscience is erring and deludes you. But, 1. The good conscience is not only a quiet conscience, but a quieted conscience. It not only hath peace, but peace after trouble. Ye then that have no peace, but what ye had all your days, it is but a mere fancy. The answer of a good conscience quiets the distempered mind, it comes by the sprinkling and washing of Christ's blood. He that hath peace on solid grounds with God, hath once taken up his enmity against him. 2. The good conscience hath been once an evil conscience, when it met with the command. The man has once been under the law, before he came to faith, and examined himself, and his conscience condemned him as not righteous, and out of Christ. Ye then that never examined your state, according to the perfect and holy law, and never judged yourselves, ye cannot believe in Jesus, and so can have no good conscience. 3. The good conscience flows nearest from faith answering the challenges of the law. Some have had sore distempers of conscience, and puddling exercises of terror. But how they were eased or quieted they cannot tell, but their spring-tide ebbed, and they bubbled no more. It went away at will, and did wear out with time. This is not a good conscience, that knows not distinctly the grounds of faith to oppose to the law's condemnation. Some turn to build cities with Cain, and pass the time pleasantly, or in some business, that they may beguile their challenges. But this is not the conscience that faith makes good. Now, set apart all these who do not examine themselves at all, nor judge themselves, but live in a golden dream, who have never been arraigned before God's tribunal, or summoned by his deputy to appear before his judgment-seat; and join unto these all persons who, judging themselves, take other rules of absolution than the word gives, who after trial absolve themselves, and withal those, who, condemning themselves, yet flee not unto this city of refuge, this blood of sprinkling, to get a solid answer in the word to all their challenges, and O how few are behind! It is but as the gleaning after the vintage. Nay, many believers have not a good conscience, though they have a right to it, because they settle not themselves on the grounds of faith, and go not on from faith to faith. There must be some sense of faith, before faith answer rightly, and give peace to the mind.

Use II. Ye see the way to get a good conscience. Believe much, and maintain your faith. It is as simple and poor a mistake as can befall a soul. Ye think because ye have not peace after your believing, therefore it was not unfeigned and true faith: and therefore ye will not believe, because ye cannot get peace. But believe that ye may have a good conscience. Would ye know your sins are pardoned before ye believe? How precious should faith be unto you, when by faith ye may not only overcome the world, but, as it were, overcome God in judging, that the soul may be justified when it is judged? Ye will not get challenges* answered by your own integrity and uprightness, or by your performing of duties. No, no, these cannot be sufficient grounds of your peace. Lay down the solid and satisfying grounds of faith, of imputed righteousness, and of salvation by Jesus Christ, and this shall be a foundation of lasting peace. Sense makes not a good conscience; there is much lightness and vanity in it, and the rule it proceeds by is changeable, but faith establishes the soul, and makes it not ashamed.

Sermon XIII.

1 Tim. i. 5.—"*Now the end of the commandment,*" &c.

Fourthly, Faith purging the conscience purifies the heart (Acts xv. 9.), and hope also purifies the heart (1 John iii. 3.), which is nothing else but faith in the perfection and vigour of it. This includes, I. That the heart was unclean before faith. II. That faith cleanses it, and makes it pure. But 'who can say, I have made my heart pure (Prov. xx. 9.), I am clean from my sin?' Is there any man's heart on this side of time, which lodges not many strange guests? In answer to this we may observe, that there is a legal purity, and a gospel purity. A legal purity is a sincere and full conformity to God's holy will and command, in thought, affections, inclinations, and actions; and, in this sense, who can say, I have made my hands clean? The old corruption sticks to the heart, and cannot be thoroughly scraped out; there are many lurking holes for uncleanness to lie hid in. Corruption is engrained in him, and it will not be the work of one day to change it. The whole head is sick, and the whole body full of sores. All the corners of the heart are full of filthiness and idols; and though the house be now sweeped and garnished, and all things look better in it, yet there are many hidden places of rottenness undiscovered, and it is the soul's continual exercise to purify itself as he is pure. But evangelical purity and cleanness is that which God reconciled in Christ takes to be so, and that which in Christ is accepted, and is a fount of his clean Spirit dwelling in the heart. The heart formerly was a troubled fountain, that sent out filthy streams, as a puddle. Corruption was the mud among the affections and thoughts; but now a pure heart is like a clear running water, clean and bright like crystal. Now this purity consists in the washing of regeneration, and sanctification by the Spirit of holiness. Jesus Christ came both by water and blood, 1 John v. 6. He came by blood, to sprinkle and purge the conscience, that it might have no more conscience of sins, Heb. x. 2; ix. 14. And he also came by water, that is, the washing and cleansing virtue of the Spirit of grace, to purge and cleanse us from all filthiness of the flesh and spirit. There are two things in sin that Jesus came to destroy, the guilt and offence of sin, whereby the sinner is bound over to condemnation, and lies under the Judge's curse; and the spot of sin, which also Christ came to destroy. He did both in his own person, and he is to perfect this in us personally, who were judicially reckoned one with him, Rom. vi. 3—12; 1 John iii. 5. Now Jesus Christ hath come with blood to sprinkle the conscience from dead works, and give it a good answer to the challenges of the law, and an ill conscience. And he hath come likewise with water, to wash and cleanse us from the spots, and filth, and power of sin. The first removes the guilt, the latter removes the filth of sin, and both are done by faith, which is our victory over the world; and this is the way how faith overcomes the world by the water and blood, 1 John v. 4—6. The blood of Jesus Christ is holden by faith with a twofold virtue of

* [Charges, or accusations.—Ed.]

cleansing, from the guilt, and from the filth of sin, and thus cleanses us from all unrighteousness, 1 John i. 7. According to the promise of the covenant (Ezek. xxxvi. 25, 26.), the application of the blood of sprinkling hath two effects. One is for justification, 'ye shall be clean;' another is, 'from all your filthiness and idols will I cleanse you,' that is sanctification. I. Now this purity consists in this, that the pure heart regards not iniquity in the inward man, nor delights in sin, Psal. lxvi. 18. He sets not up his idols in God's place, Ezek. xxxvi. 25. The cleansing of the heart is from idols. Although he cannot get himself purified as Christ is pure, and though iniquity be in his heart, yet he regards it not. He looks not upon it as a guest approven and accepted. Sin may be an intruding guest, but sin is not welcomed with all his heart. He dare not take that pleasure in sin that another man would do. He hath a worm that eats up his pleasure when he departs from God, or his thoughts go a-whoring from him. The unbelieving man's heart is a house full of idols, but the entry of faith by God's Spirit makes their Dagon to fall. But, II. The pure heart hath much of the filthiness taken away that filled it before, and so it is denominated from the best part. It is washed and cleansed from a sea of corruption, and the body of sin that did reign within the heart was formerly like an impure fountain, that sent out nothing but rotten stinking waters. Unto him were all things unclean, for his heart and conscience was defiled, Tit. i. 15. Nothing was pure to him, it ran continually in a stream of unclean thoughts and affections. But now he is purified, and to the believer 'all things are pure:' the ordinary strain and current of his thoughts and affections run more clearly free of the earthly quality they had, more sublimated, more spiritualized, and he is named by that. Though, it may be, temptation may trouble the fountain, and make it run unclean and earthly, yet it will settle again, and come into its own posture, and the dreg fall to the bottom, and the clean water of the Spirit be the predominant. But a standing puddle will run foul as long as it runs, corruption goes through all. It is not a corner of the heart, but the whole heart.

III. A pure heart is like a running fountain; if it be defiled, it is always casting out the filth, and is about returning to a right state. But an impure heart is like a standing puddle that keeps all it gets. If by temptation the pure heart and affections be stirred, and the filth that is in the bottom come up to the brim, it hath no rest nor peace in that condition, but works it out again; and it hath this advantage, that it is purer and clearer after troubling nor* it was before. For much of the filth would run out that had been lying quiet before. But an impure heart keeps all, and vents none. If ye trouble it, ye will raise an ill smell, and when it settles, it falls but to the bottom again, and there is as much to work upon the next time. In a word, the believer when he sins, and his heart goes wrong, he weeps over his heart, and has no peace till it be cleansed. He washes in the fountain of Christ's blood. When a natural transgression gets up, he sets himself against it and the root of it both, and bears down the original corruption, which is the fountain of all sin (Psal. li. 5.), and at every descent he brings away something of that puddle. He is upon the growing hand by the exercise of faith and repentance. Look upon him after he has seen and been sensible of his sins, and ye would say it is not the man ye saw: he hates sin more than he did formerly. We also notice,

IV. That purity is sincerity and uprightness (James iv. 8.), 'Purify your hearts, ye double-minded.' Hypocrisy is filthiness and abominable to God. He then is a sincere man, that hath any honesty of heart toward God. When his actions are not right, his heart doth not approve them, Rom. vii. When he cannot come up to his duty, his desire comes before performance. A sincere man hath a respect to all God's commandments.

V. The pure man is still purifying himself 'even as God is pure.' As he who hath called him is holy, so he is holy in all manner of conversation. He never thinks he is clean enough, and so he aspires after greater purity, and is named a saint, rather from his aim and endeavour, than from his attainment. He cries, unclean, unclean, am I, and holy, holy, Lord God, art thou. He hath taken up his lodging near the opened fountain, and dwells there, never to remove thence, till he

* [Than.—Ed.]

have his robes clean and white in the blood of the Lamb. No unclean thing can enter into heaven, and he is trimming himself against that day, and setting apart all superfluity of naughtiness, and filthiness, and still all his righteousness is as menstruous rags. He is cleansing his house, every day casting out something, searching out all the corners of it, lest the unclean thing, and the Babylonish garment be hid. His pattern is to walk even as Christ walked, 1 John ii. 6.

Now faith and a good conscience have influence on this purifying the heart. I. Because faith lays hold upon the cleansing virtue of Christ's blood. It applies Jesus Christ who came by water and blood, and his blood purges the conscience from dead works, to serve the living God. The blood that was offered up by the eternal Spirit, of how great virtue must it be when applied to the heart and conscience, Heb. ix. 14. No wonder it makes that like wool which was formerly like scarlet. Now faith in Jesus Christ applies that blood. It is the very hand that sprinkles it. Faith takes up house beside the opened fountain, and dwells there. Faith takes Jesus for sanctification as well as justification, 1 Cor. i. 30. Faith looks upon a judicial union with Christ crucified, and sees his perfect offering once offered to sanctify all, and therefore makes continual applications with David, 'Purge me with hyssop, and I shall be clean; wash me, and I shall be whiter than the snow.' II. Faith purifies the heart, because it lays hold on the promises, and makes use of the word, 2 Cor. vii. 1. Faith having such promises, cleanses the man from all filthiness of the flesh and spirit. The proper order of faith is the word, and the word is the truth by which we are sanctified and made clean, John xvii. 17. There are many precious promises of sanctification and holiness, and faith draws the virtue of purifying the heart out of the promises, and applies the promise to his impure heart, and it is purged. III. Faith purifies the heart also by provocation and upstirring, in as far as it gives the answer of a good conscience. For the man who hath gotten a solid answer to all his objections in Christ's blood, and hath the continual feast of joy and peace in believing, O how will he abhor himself, and repent in dust and in ashes! Faith takes up God's holiness and purity, and loathes itself with Job, and cries, unclean. The believer will thus reason and conclude,—shall I any more delight and live in sin, since I am dead unto it by Jesus Christ? Rom. vi 1, 2. He falls in with the beauties of holiness, and so cannot abide his own. Faith begets hope, and hope purifies the heart. Shall then the man who expects to see God, and be a citizen of the new Jerusalem, where no unclean thing can enter, shall he walk in his former lusts, like the wicked world, and not make himself ready for the continuing city he goes to, and adorn himself for the company of the blessed God and angels?

Let us now conclude, by applying all which hath been said in some uses. Use I. We may see from what hath been hinted, how little faith is among you. Faith purifies the heart, but if ye examine yourselves, your hearts will be found unclean, and such as the Holy Ghost cannot dwell in. The temple in which God's Holy Spirit resides must touch no unclean thing, 2 Cor. vi. 16, 17. Are not many men's corruptions rank and lively? Unclean hands are an infallible demonstration of an unclean heart, James iv. 8. These things which proceed out of the heart may teach you what is within the heart. The streams may let you know what is in the fountain, Mark vii. 15—22; James iii. 11, 12. What need ye any more proof of yourselves? Sinners, look to your hands, and your outward man, and learn from them to know your hearts. These things proceed out of the heart and defile the whole man. The profanity of the most part of men's practices, cursing and swearing, &c., is a bitter stream that cannot proceed from a good fountain. It is a wonder how the world satisfy themselves with a dream of faith. What influence hath your faith had upon your heart and conversation? Are ye not as earthly and worldly as ever, as unclean as ever? Ye think your hearts good; but if your conversation be not good, your hearts are not good. Will any person think his sins are pardoned, when he wallows in them? Do they believe they shall obtain the remission of these sins they are not purging themselves from? No, no, the blood and water must go together, and the Spirit's sanctifying with Christ's justifying.

Use II. The children of God may hence gather the ground and reason of their little progress in sanctification. Why are your hearts so unclean, and why is there so much corruption yet living in your thoughts and affections, that it cannot keep within the heart, but, as a full fountain, must run out in streams of external actions? It is even this, ye do not believe much, and though this be told you, yet ye will not believe it; ye take ways of your own to purge out your corruptions, and it will not do. All your resolutions, prayers, sad experiences, &c., are of no more virtue than the blood of bulls and goats. Ye must then apply the blood of the Son of God, which was offered up by the eternal Spirit. It is but a poor fancy to suspend believing till ye see a pure heart. How shall ye get a pure heart? Is it not folly to forbear planting till ye see fruits, or to pluck up your tree because it bears not the first day? Abide in Christ, and ye shall bring forth much fruit. Believe, and believe, and believe again, till faith be answered by a good conscience, till that sweet echo be given unto the Lord's comforting voice, 'Thy sins, which are many, are forgiven thee.' Be much in laying hold upon the precious promises, and then your heart shall fall out of love with this present evil world, and shall relish spiritual things. But who will believe this report? Ye go away convinced that this is the only way to purify yourselves, and yet ye continue puddling in your old way. May God persuade your hearts to do better.

Sermon XIV.

1 Tim. i. 5.—" *Now the end of the commandment,*" &c.

Fifthly. Faith purging the conscience, and purifying the heart, works by love. Love is the fruit of faith. Love is the stream that flows out of a pure heart and a good conscience. By love, we mean principally love to God, or Jesus Christ, and then love to the saints next to our Saviour. This is often mentioned in scripture, 'Hope maketh not ashamed, (Rom. v. 5.) because the love of God is shed abroad in your hearts by the Holy Ghost.' This love is the consequence of the peace which a justified man obtains by faith, Rom. v. 1, 2; 2 Cor. v. 14. The constraining love of Christ flows from this ground, that a man judges Christ to have died for him, from faith's taking up of Christ in that noble expression of his love, (John v. 40, 42.) 'And ye will not come unto me that ye may have life. I know you, that ye have not the love of God in you.' Faith works by love. Love is faith's hand put out in action for Christ; and as the mind commands the outward man, whether it will or not, so doth faith command love, Eph. iii. 17. The rooting and building up in love is a fruit of Christ's dwelling in the heart by faith. Love is the branch that grows in faith's root. These are often joined together, and comprehend the substance of the law and gospel, 1 Tim. i. 14; 2 Tim. i. 13. Faith fulfils the obedience to the gospel, and love is the fulfilling of the whole law, (Rom. xiii. 10.) so that faith leads a man back again to the command, that he fled to faith from. Faith hath reconciled them and taken up the difference. We shall then show how faith and a good conscience and a pure heart contribute to love.

First. Faith is the eye and sense of the soul to take up Jesus Christ. Nothing is loved but as it is known and apprehended to be good. The affections of themselves are blind, and cannot go forth but as led by the direction of faith. Faith is the mind to present love's object. The world sees no beauty nor form in the commands, that they should desire them. Even Jesus Christ himself is but foolishness to a natural mind, he neither knows his need of him, nor Christ's suitableness to his need. But faith is the first opening of the eyes, when we are turned from darkness to light, and from the power of sin and Satan unto God, Acts xxvi. 18. Christ becomes the believer's wisdom, righteousness, sanctification, and redemption, 1 Cor. i. 30. The day-spring from on high visits them who sit in darkness, to guide their feet in the way of peace, Luke i. 78, 79. The light of the knowledge of the glory of God shining in the face of the Sun of righteousness, doth arise and shine into their hearts. The man sees himself in a dangerous condition, and says, Oh! where am I? And faith discovers, on the other hand, all things in Christ

Jesus suitable to such a case. He sees nothing but vanity, emptiness, and misery, sin, and condemnation in the creature; he sees grace, mercy, holiness ,righteousness and free salvation in Christ. Set these beside one another, and judge ye if the soul cannot choose to run out in affection and longing desire. Oh! says he, to be one with him. Faith presents all the motives and attractives of the heart, and then there needs no more to make it love. Faith discovers a man's self unto himself, and lets him see all misery within, complete wo within doors, and it holds forth bread without the ports * for the saint, and salvation for the lost. It brings in an amiable person, who is fairer than the children of men, who is all love, and hath no spot in him. Is it not a sweet word, a Redeemer to captives, a Saviour to sinners? And will not the soul rise up, and go forth out of itself? And will it not choose to flit † unto him who is the desire of all nations? Will it not go unto him for food and clothing? Love then is the soul's journey and motion towards Jesus, whom faith hath brought in such a good report of. But,

Secondly. When faith hath given the answer of a good conscience, and brought Jesus nearer hand to the soul, or the soul nearer unto him, then love is stronger, and grows like a fire that many waters cannot quench. It is like jealousy, that is cruel as the grave, many floods cannot drown it. Union is the ground of love; union in nature, or sympathy, or likeness, is the ground of affection. According as faith brings Christ nearer to the heart, the flame increases. All things are desired and loved as good, but more desired, as not only good in themselves, but good unto us. Gold in the Indies will not much move the heart; but bring it hither, and ye shall see who loves it. The first act of faith puts a man in great need of a Saviour, and discovers a possibility of redemption through Jesus, and in so far he is loved. But when once faith has gone that length as to make a good conscience, and to calm and silence the woes of a troubled mind, by the actual application of that desired possible redemption, and when it can particularly apply the common salvation, O then what burning affection! 'Who is a God like unto thee, who pardoneth iniquity, and passest by the transgression of his heritage, because he delights in mercy?' 'Whom have I in heaven but thee? and there is none upon earth that I desire besides thee.' 'I will love the Lord, because he hath heard my voice, I will call upon him so long as I live,' as if it had never loved before. They will love much to whom much is forgiven. Love, without such a faith, is full of jealousies and suspicions; but when faith hath brought in Christ to dwell in the heart, then it is rooted and built up in love, (Eph. iii. 17.) and then perfect love casts out fear, 1 John iv. 18. Love before such an assurance, is but a tormenting love, and hath much fear in it, saying, Oh I may want him, and then I will be more miserable than if I had not known him! But faith, giving the answer of a good conscience, casts out horror and fear, and then perfects love, and the soul then closes with Christ as a Mediator and friend, and closes with God as a merciful Father, now reconciled unto him through Christ, and not any more as a stern or severe Judge. But,

Thirdly. When faith hath purified the heart, and cleansed the affections, then the soul burns with a purer flame of affection and zeal to God, and is, as it were, delivered from the earthly weight put upon it. When the heart is purified, love is like the flame; whereas, if he be not so purged, there may be some heat and fire latent in the ashes, covered with corruption. But a pure heart is a spiritual heart, and minds spiritual things, (Col. iii. 1.) and it is a heart going back unto its own place; Christ hath touched it with his own heart, and with his salvation, and it looks aye ‡ sure to him in the heavens. The love of the world is inconsistent with the love of the Father, 1 John ii. 15. The love of the world plucks the heart downward; and the lusts of the flesh are so many weights upon the believer, that he cannot mount up in a spiritual cloud of divine affection to Jesus Christ. But the pure and spiritual heart is now more refined, and delivered from these impediments, and it is like a pure lamp of oil burning upward. When a man's heart is engaged to any thing of this world, love cannot be perfect. For love is a man's master, and no man can serve two masters.

* [Gates.—Ed.] † [Remove.—Ed.] ‡ [Always.—Ed.]

Sermon XV.

MATT. vi. 33.—"*But seek ye first the kingdom of God and his righteousness,*" &c.

THIS is a part of Christ's long sermon. He is dissuading his disciples and the people from carnal carefulness and worldly-mindedness. The sermon holds out the Christian's diverse aspects towards spiritual and external things. What is the Christian's disposition in regard to the world, how should he look upon food, raiment, and all things necessary in this life? 'Be careful for nothing.' 'Take no thought for your life, what ye shall eat, or drink,' &c. Seek them not as your chief good. But what is his disposition towards spiritual and eternal things, and how ought ye to look upon them? Seek them, set your heart upon them, look upon them as your treasure, and where your treasure is, let your heart be there also. So then you see here two callings and employments of a man in the world,—two universal callings that comprehend all men, one natural to us, and unlawful, the other divine, and lawful, the one paganish, the other Christian. What is the employment of all men out of Christ? There are many different callings and employments among men. One spends his time and thoughts one way, and another another way, but all of them agree in one general, whatever they are. Their heart is here. The thoughts they have are bounded and circumscribed in this present world. They are careful for nothing else but what concerns their back and belly,* or their name and credit. Take the best of them, whose employment seems most abstracted from the common affairs and distractions among men, yet their affections run no higher than this present world. On the other hand, what should be the exercise and employment of a Christian? It is even this, whatever he be, or whatever his occupation be among men, he drives a higher trade with heaven, that should take him up. The world gets but his spare hours. He is upon a more noble and high project. He aspires after a kingdom. His heart is above where Christ is, and where his treasure is. And these things exhaust his affections and pains. Christ Jesus once takes the man's heart off these baser things, that are not worthy of an immortal spirit, let be† a spirit who is a partaker of a divine nature. But because the creature cannot be satisfied within itself, its happiness depends upon something without itself, (and this speaks out the vanity of the creature, and something of God, that is peculiar to him, to be self-sufficient,) therefore Christ changes the object of the heart, and fixes the spirit upon a nobler and divine exercise. Since the spirit of a man cannot abide within doors without starving, it must run out upon something; therefore Jesus Christ hath described its bounds and way, its end and period. Before, a man sought many things, because not one was satisfying, that the want of one might be supplied by another; and therefore he was never near the borders of contentment and happiness, because still a thousand things are wanting. But now, Christ puts the soul upon a satisfying and self-sufficient object. And here the streams of affection may run in one current, and need not divide or go contrary ways.

First. We have here then the Christian's calling and employment in this world, opposed to the carefulness and worldly-mindedness of the men of this world, 'Seek ye the kingdom of God.' *Secondly.* His encouragement and success in two things; one is expressed, the other implied. That which is expressed, is seeking the kingdom of God, of grace and glory. If ye seek this kingdom, all temporal things shall be laid to your hand, all these things that ye need 'shall be added unto you.' The other imported is, ye shall get the kingdom who seek it. For the words, 'added unto you,' suppose the first and principal intent to be gotten. Then the Christian's success and encouragement is this, ye shall have the thing ye seek and more also. It was said to Solomon, 'Because thou hast sought wisdom, therefore thou shalt get all other things.' Because, O Christian, thou sought the kingdom of God, and not this present world which Satan is prince of, therefore thou shalt get according to

* [A proverbial expression, signifying food and raiment.—ED.]

† [Much less.—ED.]

thy word, and thou shalt also get what thou asked not, 1 Kings iii. 11—13. He hath success in the main business, and there is a superplus besides, some accession to his portion, that comes of will, so to speak. The kingdom of God in the New Testament is sometimes restricted to the elect, the word of the gospel, and the administration of it, by the Spirit of grace in the hearts of his people. This is frequently called 'the kingdom of heaven,' and 'of God,' Matth. xiii. 33. Sometimes the kingdom of God is taken for the state of grace, a new principle of spiritual life, that grows up to the perfect day, and this kingdom is within us, Luke xvii. 21. It is taken also for heaven, the kingdom of glory, Luke xxii. 16. Both these must be sought after, (Luke xii. 31.) and received, (Luke xviii. 17.) and must suffer violence, Matth. xi. 12. The righteousness thereof may be taken for the righteousness of God by faith, Rom. x. 3; chap. iii. 21, 22; 2 Cor. v. 21; Rom. iv. 11, 13; Rom. ix. 30; chap. x. 6; Heb. xi. 7; Phil. iii. 9.

We would observe here. I. That the Christian his name and occupation is to be a wanter and a seeker. II. The great exercise and employment he should have in this world, that which should swallow up his affections, thoughts, and endeavours, should be the kingdom of God and his righteousness, which is clearly expressed in three things. 1. His first and chief care should be to be at peace with God, and to be adorned with Christ's righteousness. 2. To have the kingdom of God within him, a throne of judgment erected for Christ to rule the whole man, by his Spirit according to the word. 3. To be made an heir here, and a possessor hereafter, of the everlasting kingdom of glory. 4. No man can either be a subject of God's gracious kingdom here, or his glorious kingdom hereafter, without the imputed righteousness of the Son of God; and whoever seeks righteousness must also seek the kingdom of God. These are joined together, and there is a great opposition between seeking of the world, and seeking grace and glory. Whoever is careful in these things cannot be diligent here. But rather seek the kingdom of God (Luke xii. 31.) also implies, 5. That whatever a man be, or his profession be, except he seek this way of righteousness, and yield himself unto God's kingdom of grace, and unless Christ rule in him, he is but a pagan, or infidel Gentile, in God's account. We return to the first of these, namely.

1st. That the Christian is a seeker. This is the ordinary description of a child of God, Psal. xxiv. 6; Psal. xxvii. 8. Many, at this time, call themselves Seekers.* They profess they seek a true church, and seek ordinances purely dispensed, but find none. But the child of God, the good Christian that seeks according to Christ's appointment, seeks not these things as if they were not, but he seeks God in ordinances, he seeks Christ in the church, he seeks grace and glory, honour and immortality, and eternal life. He is in the church, he hath the ordinances rightly administered, yet he wants the most part, till he find Jesus Christ in all these. Many seek corn, wine, or any worldly good thing, saying, 'Who will show us any good?' Fie upon such a lax and indifferent spirit, that hath no discretion or sense of things that are good, that sees not one thing needful, and no more good than is necessary. But the child of God is a seeker different from these also, he seeks the favour and countenance of God, Psal. iv. 6, 7. He seeks wisdom above all things, Prov. ii. 4. He seeks but one good thing, because there is but one good thing necessary. The seeking Christian is a wanter, one that hath nothing, and finds it so. He wants, and knows he wants, else he would never seek. What wants he? Nay, rather ask, what hath he? It may soon be told what he hath, but it is hard to tell what he wants. Look what he hath, and ye find little or nothing, and therefore ye may conclude he wants all things. The text tells what he wants. (1.) He wants righteousness. (2.) He wants grace. (3.) He wants glory, and hath no

* ["The sect of *Seekers* hold that there are not at this time, neither have been for many ages past, any true ministers or ambassadors of Christ." (Gillespie's Miscellany Questions, p. 1. Edinburgh, 1649.) A few years before this, Laurence Clarkson, a *Seeker*, published a pamphlet entitled "The Pilgrimage of Saints." Edwards, in his Gangræna (Part I. p. 24; Part II. p. 6. London, 1646), refers to it for an account of the opinion of the Seekers. Clarkson declared that in these days there ought to be no churches built, no sacraments administered; that the saints, as pilgrims, wander here as in a temple filled with smoke, not being able to find religion; and that, on this account, 'waiting for a church,' and for the coming of the Spirit, as the apostles did, they ought to seek "knowledge of any passenger, of any opinion or tenet whatsoever."—ED.]

right to it. Men seek not what they carry from the womb. Therefore all men have come into the world with three great wants. (1.) Ye want righteousness. Ye cannot stand before God in the terms of strict justice. There is nothing ye have, or can do, but it is a menstruous cloth, Isa. lxiv. 6. All your religion and prayers will never commend you to God's holy justice. The scripture hath passed this sentence upon you all, 'There is none righteous, no not one,' Rom. iii. 10. The righteousness that the law of God requires is perfect, and complete, and exact. Either lay down the whole sum, or if it want a farthing it is no payment. Keep all the nine commands, but if ye break the tenth the nine will not suffice. Now all of you have sinned and corrupted your ways, and it is impossible to make up the want. As the redemption of the soul is precious and ceases for ever, so the broken and dyvour* man having become a bankrupt, shall never make up or pay his debt to all eternity. He hath once broken the command, and all your keeping afterwards will not stand for the obedience ye should always have given to it. Therefore sinners of the posterity of Adam, and wretched men by nature, see this great want and impossibility to recover it in yourselves. (2.) Ye likewise want all grace by nature. There is no delusion more ordinary than this, that the world thinks grace is very common. But believe it, Sirs, that all men came from the womb without grace, get it as ye will. Look what the scripture speaks of the whole race of Adam, 'There is no fear of God before their eyes,' Rom. iii. 18. They are without Christ, without hope, and without God in the world, aliens from the covenants of promise, Eph. ii. 1—3, 12. Let grace be as common as can be, yet all of you once wanted it. Ye have it not by birth, nor by education, nor by baptism. Ye think perhaps a baptized soul cannot be graceless, but know it for a truth that ye have neither legal righteousness nor evangelical holiness. All of you have wofully fallen from righteousness, and therefore ye lie, with Adam's posterity, without hope in the world. Grace and truth must come from above by Jesus Christ. Grace and glory are the gifts of God. (3.) The sinner also comes short of the glory of God, Rom. iii. 23. All sinners are born heirs of hell and wrath, without the hope of happiness. There is none born with a title to the kingdom of heaven, or any right to it. Man in his fall lost his right to eternal life and immortality, and hath purchased a doleful right to the Lord's wrath and to hell-fire. Ye think it strange that any christened or baptized person should be damned, but the scripture knows no difference. 'Neither circumcision nor uncircumcision availeth any thing, but a new creature, and faith which worketh by love.' Neither to be a member of the visible church nor a pagan avails any thing, 'for all have sinned and come short of the glory of God.' Now what have ye since ye want righteousness? Ye want grace and ye want glory, and in the place of these ye have unrighteousness, all sin, all God's curses and wrath, and this makes up complete misery. In a word, ye want God and Christ, and this is all, and enough for all, Eph. ii. 12. Ye have, by nature, more sibness† with Satan, and nearer relation to him, than to God; and if ye want God, what can ye have beside? Your abundance is want. As all things are theirs who are Christ's, so nothing is theirs who are not God's. In short, there is not in all the creation such a miserable creature as man, whom God hath magnified and exalted above the angels, and the rest of the works of his hands. Now all men want these, but no man knows this but the Christian, whose eyes Christ hath opened, and to whom he hath given eye-salve. Laodicea was blind and saw not, but she thought she was rich enough, when she had nothing, Rev. iii. 17, 18. The man, who will discourse well on all the miseries of this life, and human infirmities, may be ignorant of these things. There is no man but knows some want. But what is it he misses? Nothing but what concerns his present being and well-being in this world, and so the world may supply it. But the Christian wants something this vain world will not make up. 'Whom have I in heaven but thee? And there is none upon the earth I desire beside thee,' says the soul that hath found God. And whom want I in heaven but thee? (Psal. lxxiii. 25, 26.) says the soul that seeks God. He wants God's favour, and the light of his reconciled countenance, Psal. iv. 6. If ye ask him, what seek ye, what want ye in all the world? He an-

* [See note, page 607.—Ed.]

† [Kindred alliance.—Ed.]

swers, 'And now, Lord, what wait I for?' My heart and 'my hope is in thee,' Psal. xxxix. 7. None needed ask at Mary, 'Whom seekest thou?' Any body that knows her, knows her want. It is he, the Christ Jesus, and she thinks all the world should want him, and seek him with her, and thinks no body should be ignorant of him; for she speaks to the gardener, as if there had been no other in the world, John xx. 15. But,

2dly. His wants put him to seeking, to diligence. He misses something, and O it is a great something, infinitely more than he is worth in the world! He wants being and well-being. He thinks himself as good as lost, and he comes at length to some point of resolution, with the lepers of Samaria, (2 Kings vii. 3, 4.) 'Why sit we here till we die? If we enter into the city there is famine, if we sit still we perish, if we go out we may find bread.' And so the poor soul, with Mordecai and Esther, comes to this conclusion, 'If I perish, I perish;' nothing but perishing as I am, I will go and seek salvation in Jesus Christ, and it may be I will find it. Who knows but he may turn again? Resolution is born a man at first, a giant. It goes out to the utmost border of want the first day. Wanting makes desire, and desire, attended with some hope, makes up resolution and purpose; and when the soul is thus principled, then in the third room,* it comes forth to action. Desire and hope give legs to the soul for the journey; and now the wanting Christian ye shall find with his hand in every good turn, his feet in every ordinance. Ye shall find him praying, reading, and hearing. It is true, resolution is born a man; and practice is born but a child, and scarcely will come up in many years to the stature of resolution. Always† diligence and violence is the qualification of his practice; (Heb. xi. 6; Matth. xi. 12.) and this is written upon his using of means, 'How love I the Lord! I am sick of love.' The Christian's diligence in the use of means proclaims his earnest desire to obtain, whereas many a man's practice speaks but a coldrife and indifferent spirit. That is a neutral who cares not whether he obtain or miss. Some Christians have some missings of God, and spiritual things, but alas! their want, and sight of want, makes them twice miserable, because it puts not their hand to action. The slothful and sluggard's desire slays him, because his hands refuse to labour, Prov. xxi. 25. O! but he finds many difficulties in the way. Though he have half a wish, or a raw‡ desire after Christ, yet it never comes farther than a conditional wish. A beggar may wish to be a king. He comes to no purpose in it, and therefore his way is called a hedge of thorns. Whereas a seeking Christian finds a plain path where he goes, Prov. xv. 19. The sluggard says, 'There is a lion in the way, and a lion in the streets.' He concludes upon the means and duties of religion before ever he try them, Prov. xxii. 13. Prov. xix. 24. How lazy is he! He will not bring his hand out of his bosom, when he hath put it in. Thus the lazy and secure Christian is a brother to a great waster, his desire consumes him. He hath no more religion than a spunk § of desire; and he sits down with this spark of his own kindling, and the life of religion thrives not upon his hand, Prov. xviii. 9, 12. His seeking must have violence with it, Matth. xi. 12. But we may also observe concerning the Christian, that he is,

3dly. Defined on this side of time as a seeker. In heaven he is an enjoyer, and he seeks no more; for how can the ox low over his fodder? He sits down to eat the fruit and sweat of his labour, and well may he triumphantly say, as the ancient philosopher said, "I have found, I have found."‖ But here he is a seeker still. Whatever he miss, he is still a seeker, and whatever he find, he is yet a

* [Or, in the third place.—Ed.] † [Notwithstanding.—Ed.] ‡ [A cold desire.—Ed.]

§ [That is, a glimmering, or slight degree of desire.—Ed.]

‖ [This was the exclamation of Archimedes, the celebrated geometrician of Syracuse, (Ευρηκα, Ευρηκα,) after discovering, when in the bath, a method of detecting the quantity of alloy, which a fraudulent artisan had mixed with the gold of Hiero's crown. (Plut. Mor. et Phil. Op. p. 1094.) An exclamation somewhat similar was uttered by Cicero, when, searching for the tomb of Archimedes in the neighbourhood of Syracuse, he at length perceived it covered with thorns and brambles. (Cic. Tusc. Quest. lib. v. cap. 23.) But if they had cause to be delighted, much more surely had Philip the apostle reason to be so, when addressing Nathanael, he cried out in ecstacy,—"We have found him of whom Moses in the law and the prophets did write, Jesus of Nazareth, the son of Joseph!" John i. 45.—Ed.]

seeker. He is named not from his finding, but his seeking, not from his enjoyment or attainment, but from his endeavour and aim. Though he find righteousness in Jesus, and remission of sins, yet he is a seeker of grace; though he be justified, yet he seeks holiness. There are many who would seek no more of God than pardon of sin. Let him deliver them from hell, and they will trouble God with no more requests. Doth not some of your own consciences speak, that ye would seek no more from Christ than to be saved from an ill hour, and to be found in him; whereas Paul was not content with this, but made an holy gradation, as we read, Philip. iii. 8, &c. He desired to know the power of Christ's resurrection, and to be made conformable to him by any means; and now, when he is found in Christ, and justified, he counts not himself well, or perfect and complete, or to have attained that which he struggled earnestly for. Would not many be content with a Saviour, but they love not to hear of a king to rule over them, nor of his laws to regulate their lives by? They love an imputed holiness, as well as righteousness. But the true seeker seeks grace within him. Though he be justified, or freed from guilt and condemnation, and have the righteousness of Christ to cover him, and though he should never come into condemnation for sin, yet he seeks the death and destruction of it in his soul, and the life of holiness implanted and perfected in his inward man. Though he is sure of heaven, yet he would have God's image upon his spirit, and whole man.

4thly. Whatever degree of grace he have or attain, yet he is still a wanter, and still a seeker. He counts not himself to have attained, or to be already perfect, but presses forward to gain the mark and prize of God's high calling, Phil. iii. 13, 14. He stands at no pitch, but forgets what is behind, and overlooks it; he thinks it not worthy to come in reckoning. There is still so much before his hand, that he apprehends it to be lost time to reckon what is passed. His aim is to perfect holiness in the fear of God. He endeavours to be holy as God is holy, who is the completest pattern of unspotted purity and uprightness, and to be holy in all manner of conversation. He goes from strength to strength, till he appear blameless before God; he seeks grace for grace, Psal. lxxxiv. 5—8. And truly the man who seeks the exact copy or pattern, Jesus Christ, who is gone before his people into heaven, and he who knows the spiritual command in all its dimensions, he will not say 'I have found,' but will still want more than he hath, and seek what he wants. There are some professors who have attained some pitch and degree, as it were, the first day, and never advance further. They have gotten a gift of prayer, some way of discharging duties, some degree in profession, and they want no more. Look on them some years after, and ye would say, they have sought no more. And truly he who seeks no more shall never be able to keep what he hath already, as a fire must soon die away if ye add not new fuel to it. Christians are not green in old age, because they have come to a pitch in their religion, and stand there. No, religion should not come to its stature hereaway.* This is but the time of its minority. Grace should be still on the growing hand. The grace of God is but a child here. Heaven and eternity make up the man. Glory is the man, who was once the child grace.

5thly. The good Christian is still a seeker till Christ be all in all, till he apprehend that for which he is apprehended. As long as he is in this world he is a seeker. Whereof, ye will say? Not only of more grace here, but of glory hereafter. Here he hath no continuing city, but he seeks one to come, Heb. xiii. 14. He is a pilgrim on earth, embracing the promises afar off, and seeking his country, even heaven itself, Heb. xi. 13, &c. All your present enjoyments in this world, your own houses and lands, would not make you think yourselves at home, if ye were Christians at the heart. Ye would miss consolation, ye would want happiness in the affluence of all created things. And therefore, Christians, do ye want nothing when all things go according to your mind? Is there no hole in your heart that a world cannot fill up? This is not well. Ye ought to seek a city, while ye are in your own country, and ye should never think yourselves at home till ye be in heaven. The Christian gets some taste of the fruits of the land, some clusters in

* [In the present world.—Ed.]

the wilderness and house of his pilgrimage, and this makes him long to be there. This inflames the soul's desire, and turns it all in motion to seek that which was so sweet. If hope be so sweet, what shall the thing possessed be? If a grape brought a savour and taste so refreshful, what must the grapes plucked from the tree of life be, and the rivers of pleasures, which are at God's right hand, for evermore be? Sit not down then, Christians, upon your enjoyments, whether they be worldly or spiritual, but aspire to high things.

Sermon XVI.

MATTH. vi. 33.—"*But seek ye first the kingdom of God,*" &c.

II. THE Christian's chief employment should be to seek the kingdom of God, and the righteousness thereof. 'Seek first,' &c. Upon this he should first and chiefly spend his thoughts, and affections, and pains. We comprehend it in three things. *First,* He should seek to be clothed upon with Christ's righteousness, and this ought to take up all his spirit. This is the first care and the chief concern. Did not this righteousness weigh much with Paul, when he counted all things but loss and dung, that he might be found in Christ, not having his own righteousness, but the righteousness which is by faith in Jesus Christ? Phil. iii. 8, 9. Now this righteousness is of more concernment than all the world beside. For it is God's righteousness, (Rom. x. 3, 4; 2 Cor. 5. 21.) and this holds out a threefold excellence in it. (1.) It is God's righteousness, because he alone devised it, and found it out. All the world could not have imagined a way possible to save lost mankind, or ever one sinner of that wretched number. Satisfaction to justice was needful, and there was none righteous among Adam's posterity. But here God himself in his everlasting counsel hath found it out, and all hath flowed from his love. The mission of Jesus Christ to be the propitiation for our sins, comes from this blessed fountain, 1 John iv. 9, 10; Rom. iii. 24, 25. God hath been framing this righteousness from all eternity, and even this world seems to be made for this end. All God's dispensation with Adam, his making a covenant of works with him, his mutability and liableness to fall, and so governing all things in his holy providence that he should fall from his own righteousness, and involve all his posterity in the same condemnation with himself,—all this seems to be in respect of God's intention and purpose, even ordained for this end, that the righteousness of Jesus Christ might be commended to you, far more than all the dispensation of the law upon Sinai, more than the curse and the command, the thunder and the lightning. The very condemnation of the scripture was all in God's own mind and revealed will also, as the means appointed to lead sinners to this righteousness, Rom. x. 4. Therefore, how precious should that be to us, that God keeps and preserves the world for?

(2.) By this righteousness alone, we can stand before God, and therefore it is termed God's righteousness; and is not this enough to make it lovely in the eyes of all men? This is the righteousness without the law, though it was witnessed both by the law and the prophets. This is the only righteousness that justifies, when all men are found guilty before God, Rom. iii. 19, &c. Now, what is it in this world can profit you, if ye want this? Condescend * upon all your pleasures and heart-wishes, let you have them all, and now, poor soul, pray what hast thou? Though thou hast gained the world, thou losest thy soul, that thou should use the world with? Let you then get what you so eagerly pursue in the world, what will ye do when your soul is required by the hand of justice? 'Then whose shall these things be?' Luke xii. 20, 21. By all these things, a man neither knows love nor hatred, as Solomon speaks of external enjoyments, Eccles. ix. 1. But hear the way, O men! how ye may stand before God; here it is only. Will it profit you to enjoy the world, and bless God? And when all these things leave you, and ye

* [Specify or enumerate.—ED.]

leave them, what will ye do,—for riches will not go to the grave with you? All that is here cannot help you in that day, when ye must stand before the Judge of all flesh. If a man be not found in Christ he is gone, and if he be found in him, then the destroying angel passes by, death hath a commission to do him good, God is become his friend in Jesus. If ye could walk never so blamelessly in this world, all this will not come as righteousness in God's sight, nor stand before him. It is only the righteousness of Christ that can be a covering to sinners. But,

(3.) This is God's righteousness, because it is the righteousness of Christ who is truly God, and so it is divine. This is the most excellent piece in all the creation, that comes from Jesus Christ his life, death, and resurrection. And let all men's inherent holiness blush here and be ashamed. Let all your prayers, good wishes, your religious obedience be ashamed, let them evanish as the stars before the sun. The righteousness of Christ is the bright sun that makes all the dim sparkles of nature, civil honesty, and even religious education, disappear. Let even angels blush before him, for they are not clean in his sight, but may be charged with folly. Innocent Adam was also a glorious creature, but the second Adam, the life-giving Spirit and the Lord from heaven, hath an infinitely transcendent and supereminent excellency and prerogative beyond him, and all the creation of God. Look then upon this Jesus how he is described, as the 'brightness of the Father's glory and the express image of his person,' (Heb. i. 1—3; Col. i. 15, &c.) and wonder that such a glorious one should become our righteousness, that he should take our sins upon him, (2 Cor. v. 21; 1 Pet. ii. 24.) and make over his righteousness to us. This is the righteousness of the saints in heaven, Rev. xix. 8. This is the glory of the spirits of just men made perfect. Think ye, my friends, that the glorious saints shall wear their own holiness upon their outside in heaven? No, no, the righteousness of Christ shall cover them, and that shall be the upper-garment that all the host of heaven must glory in. Now this is the thing that the child new-born, if he had the use of reason, should first cry for, before he ever get the breast, to be reconciled to God in Christ. Would ye then spend your time and thoughts upon other things, if ye knew what need ye have of his righteousness, and how suitable it were to your need? Should not the beggar seek food and clothing? Should not the sick man seek health, and the poor man riches? Here they are all in Christ's righteousness. Ye are under the curse of God. This righteousness redeems from the curse. Ye are sinners, and none of you righteous, no not one. But Christ was made sin for us, that we might be made the righteousness of God in him. O sinners, wonder at the change! Hath Christ taken on your sins, that his righteousness might become yours, and will ye not do so much as seek it? But many a man beguiles his own soul, and thinks he seeks this righteousness in the gospel. Therefore ye would know what it is to seek his righteousness. If ye seek it, ye want your own righteousness. And who of you have come this length, to judge yourselves that ye be not judged? It is a great difficulty to convince the multitude of sin. That general notion, that we are all sinners, is but the delusion that many souls perish in. Never any will deny themselves to seek another righteousness, till they be beaten and driven out of their own. There is need of submission to take and receive this righteousness, let be to seek it. And now tell me, can ye say that ye have seen all in yourselves as dung and dross, that ye count all things but loss for the excellency of the knowledge of Christ Jesus, (Phil. iii. 8, 9.) that ye have seen all your own privileges and duties loss, and are ye even sensible that prayer will no more help you than the cutting off a dog's neck? Ye that lay so much weight upon your being baptized, and upon outward privileges, are ye void of righteousness? No, ye seek to establish your own, and do not submit to the righteousness of God. In a word, all who are ignorant of this righteousness of God in Christ, ye all seek to establish your own. There needs more. But not one of twenty of you can tell what this is, it is a mystery. Ask at any of you, how ye shall be saved, ye will say, by prayer to God, and the mercy of God. Ye cannot tell the necessity of Christ's coming into the world.

Secondly, Ye must see an impossibility to attain a righteousness, or to stand before God another way. When ye miss this righteousness and are convinced of sin, it is not the running to prayer will help or mend it. When ye see the broken covenant, ye fall upon doing something, to mend your faults, with some good turns; and some will make a few good works answer all the challenges of sin. Alas! this is a seeking of your own righteousness. Many a poor broken man seeks to make up his fortune. Poor wretched sinners are building up the breach of the old covenant, putting up props under an old ruinous house, seeking to establish it, and rear it up again. But ye will never seek Christ till ye cannot do better, till ye be desperate of helping yourselves without him. Now I appeal to your consciences. Who among you was ever serious in this matter, to examine your own condition, whether you were enemies or friends? Ye took it for granted all your days. But never a man will betake himself to an imputed righteousness, but only he that flies, taking with* his enmity, and is pursued by the avenger of blood, and flies in to this righteousness as a city of refuge.

Thirdly, Ye must seek this righteousness, and what is it to seek it? It is even to take it and to receive it. It is brought to your door. It is offered. And the convinced sinner hath no more to do but hearken, and this righteousness is brought near unto him. Prayer to God, and much dealing with him, is one of the ways of obtaining this righteousness. But coming to Jesus Christ is the comprehensive short gate;† and therefore it is called 'the righteousness of faith,' and 'the righteousness of God by faith.' Now shall ye be called seekers of Christ's righteousness, who will not receive it when it is offered? Ye who have so many objections and scruples against the gospel, and the application of it, ye in so far are not seekers, but refusers of the gospel, and disobedient. Christ's righteousness should meet with a seeker not a disputer. Any thing God allows you to seek, certainly he allows you to take and receive it, when it is brought unto you. And therefore, whoever have need of Jesus Christ, not only refuse him not, but stay not till they find him come to them. This is a noble resolution, I will give myself no rest till I be at a point in this. Seek him as a hid treasure, as that which your happiness depends upon.

(1.) The kingdom of grace is worthy of all your affections and pains. That despised thing in the world called grace is the rarest piece of the creation, and if we could look on it aright, we would seek grace, and follow after it. Grace extracts a man out of the multitude of men that are all of one mass. Grace separates him from the rest of the world, and to this purpose are these usual phrases in scripture, 'Such were some of you;' 'Once ye were darkness, but now are ye light in the Lord;' 'Among whom ye had your conversation in times past, fulfilling the desires of the flesh.' All men are alike by nature and birth, there is no difference. Grace brought to light by the gospel makes the difference, and separates the few chosen vessels of glory and mercy from the world; and now 'they are not of the world, as I am not of the world.' All the rest of men's aims and endeavours cannot do this. Learning makes not a man a Christian. Honour makes not a man differ from a Gentile or Pagan. Riches make you no better than infidels. Speak of what ye will, you shall never draw a man entirely out of the cursed race of Adam, never distinguish him from Gentiles before God, till the Spirit of regeneration blow where he listeth. And this is grace's prerogative, beyond all other things. All other excellent gifts, even the gift of preaching, praying, all these are common, so to speak, and in a manner befall to all alike. Your external calling is but common, but he gives grace to all his chosen ones. But (2.) Grace puts a man in a new kingdom. It draws a man out of Satan's kingdom, and makes him a king, who before was a subject. The man was led captive by sin and Satan at their pleasure. He served his own corrupt lusts and the prince of this world. Sin reigneth in his mortal body, whatever his passion and corruption did put him to, he could have no bridle, but as a horse went on to the battle. And ye may see daily that there is scarce one of an hundred that is master of himself. He is a servant of sin; but grace makes him a priest and a king, Rev. i. 6; chap. v. 8, 10. He can now command himself. Sin reigned before unto death, but now grace reigns through righteousness unto eternal life, Rom. v. 20, 21. And O! but this victory over a man's self is more than a man's conquering a strong city. This victory is more than all the triumphs and

* [Acknowledging.—Ed.]

† [Path or way.—Ed.]

trophies of the world's conquerors. For they could not conquer themselves, the little world, but were slaves to their own lusts. Some men talk of great spirits that can bear no injury. Nay, but such a spirit is the basest spirit. The noble spirit is that spirit which can despise these things, and be above them. Grace puts men upon a throne of eminence above the world. The Spirit of God makes a man of a noble spirit. (3.) Grace translates a man from Satan's kingdom to God, and makes him a subject, a free-born subject, of God or Christ's kingdom, and therefore Christ is the 'King of saints,' Rev. xv. 3. Our Lord and Saviour hath an 'everlasting kingdom,' 2 Pet. i. 11. We were subjects of the powers of darkness, but grace makes the translation into the kingdom of God's own dear Son, Col. i. 13. Now what an unspeakable privilege is this, to be one of Christ's subjects, who is our dear Saviour and King! Surely we must all be great courtiers. David, the great king of Israel, had this for his chief dignity, his style of honour, 'the servant of the Lord,' as kings use to write down themselves; and this was his title, 'servant of God.' Paul gloried much in this, 'Paul, an apostle and servant of Jesus Christ.' And surely all the families of heaven and earth may think it their highest honour to get liberty to bow their knees to Jesus, the 'King of kings, and Lord of lords,' the first-born of God's creation. The converted man is turned from the power of Satan to God. Mark but the emphasis of these two terms. Mark the whence or from,—that it is from Satan, the great destroyer of mankind, the first transgressor and deceiver. And how great is his power, tyranny, and dominion! He had us all in chains reserved for the day of judgment. But to what a happy change grace turns us, *from* him! But the term *to*, which is more admirable; it is to God, to Christ, to true religion, to God himself most High. And O! but this must be a more wonderful and excellent change than our conversion from darkness to light, from hell to heaven. These are but shadows of this glorious conversion. (4.) Grace makes a man likewise a 'partaker of the divine nature,' 2 Pet. i. 4. This is the image and glory of God. This is the imitation and resemblance of God's spotless holiness and purity, 'Be ye holy, as I am holy,' 1 Pet. i. 15, 16. Every creature hath some dark characters of God. Some things speak his power, some things his wisdsm, but this he hath called his own image. And so the Christian is more like unto God than all the world beside. This is the magnifying of a man, and making him but 'a little lower than the angels,' Psal. viii. 3, 4. Therefore God loves grace better than all the creation. Holiness is a great beauty, and God requires to be worshipped in the beauties of it. Albeit grace be often clouded with infirmities, and sometimes is reckoned despicable, because of the vessel it is in, yet it is precious as the finest gold, and more precious than any rubies. It is like gold in ashes, not the less excellent in itself, though it appear not so. But sin is the devil's image and likeness, and therefore Satan is called the father of sinners. 'Ye are of your father the devil, and the lusts of your father ye will do.' O but sin hath an ugly shape! It is the only spot in the face of the creation which God's soul abhors. For he loves righteousness, and hates iniquity, Psal. xlv. 6, 7. But there is one thing more, (5.) That may commend grace to all your hearts. Grace is the way to glory. It gives title and right to, or at least declares it. It is inseparably joined with it. Grace is glory in the bud, and glory is the flower of grace: grace is young glory, and glory is old grace. Without holiness it is impossible to see God's face in peace. No man can come unto heaven without grace. Glorification is the first link of the chain, Rom. viii. 30. But sanctification must intervene first. No unclean thing can enter into heaven; but he that gives grace, gives glory, Psal. lxxxiv. 11. Heaven cannot receive many of you, because ye have not holiness. But it may commend holiness unto you, that it ministers an abundant entrance 'into the everlasting kingdom of our Lord and Saviour Jesus Christ.' As much as eternity is beyond the poor span of your time, so much is grace and holiness, whereon depends your everlasting condition, preferable to all things of this present vain world. O! but the children of men have many vain pursuits of the creature, that when it is had is nothing and vanity. Ye labour to secure an inch of your being, and to have contentment here in this half day, and never look beyond it to many millions of ages, when ye are to continue. Your honour, your pleasure, your gain, your credit, many such things like these can have no influence on tne next world. These cannot go through death with you. Only grace and holiness, begun here, are consummated in glory, and make the poor man, that was miserable for a moment, eternally happy.

Sermon XVIII.

MATTH. vi. 33.—"*But seek ye first the kingdom of God, and his righteousness, and all these things shall be added unto you.*"

THE perfection even of the most upright creature, speaks always some imperfection in comparison of God, who is most perfect. The heavens, the sun and moon, in respect of lower things here, how glorious do they appear, and without spot! But behold, they are not clean in God's sight! How far are the angels above us who dwell in clay! They appear to be a pure mass of light and holiness; yet even these glorious beings cannot behold this light without covering their faces. These God may charge with folly, 'God is light,' saith the apostle, 1 John i. 5. This is his peculiar glory, for 'in him there is no darkness at all.' Is there any thing more excellent and divine than to seek God, and find him, and enjoy him? Yet even that holds forth the emptiness of the creature in its own bosom, that cannot be satiated within, but must come forth to seek happiness. Nay, even the greatest perfection of the creature speaks out the creature's own self-indigence most, because its happiness is the removal from itself unto another, even unto God the fountain of life.

Now the enjoyment of this 'kingdom of God' mentioned in the text, holds forth man's own insufficiency for well-being within himself. But seeking this kingdom declares a double want, a want of it altogether. Not only hath he it not in himself, but not at all, and so must go out and seek it. God is blessed in himself, and self-sufficient, and all-sufficient to others. Without is nothing but what has flowed from his inexhausted fulness within; so that, though he should stop the conduit, by withdrawing his influence, and make all the creatures to evanish as a brook, or a shadow, he should be equally in himself blessed. 'Darkness and light are both alike to thee,' says David in another sense, Psal. cxxxix. 11, 12. And indeed they are all one in this sense, that he is no more perfected and bettered, when all the innumerable company of angels, and the spirits of just men made perfect, follow him with an eternal song, nor * before the mountains and hills were, when nothing was brought forth. Many thousand more worlds would add nothing to him, nor diminish anything from him. It is not so with man, he is bounded and limited, he cannot have well-being in his own breast. He was indeed created with it in the enjoyment of God, which was his happiness; so that he had it not to seek, but to keep; he had it not to follow after, but to hold it still fast. But now, alas! he hath lost that, and become miserable. Once all Adam's posterity were void of happiness. By catching at a present shadow of pleasure, and satisfaction to his senses, he lost this excellent substance of blessedness in communion with God. Now, how shall this be recovered again? How shall this pearl of great price be found?

Certainly we must agree upon two principles, and according to them walk, ere we come within reach of this. It is a great question that is of more moment than all the debates among men,—how shall man's ruin be made up, and the treasure be found? If ye think it concerns you, I pray you hearken to this, and condescend † upon these two grounds, that the question may be right stated. One is, we have all lost happiness, fallen from the top of our excellency into the lowest dungeon of misery. We are cast down from heaven to hell. There needs not much to persuade you of the truth of this in general. But alas! who ponders it in their

* [Than.—ED.]

† [Fix upon.—ED.]

hearts? And until ye think more seriously upon it, ye will never be serious in the search for reparation of it. All of you by your daily experience find that ye are miserable creatures. Ye have no satisfaction nor contentment. Ye are compassed about with many infirmities and griefs. But this is but an appendix of your misery. All the calamities of this life are but a consequent, a little stream of that boundless ocean of misery that is yet insensible to you. Therefore enter into your own hearts, and consider what Adam once was, and what ye now are, nay, what ye will all quickly be, if God prevent it not. We are born heirs of wrath and hell. It is not only the infinite loss of that blessed sight of his face for evermore, which an eternal enjoyment of creature pleasures could not compensate the want of, one hour ; but it is the kingdom of darkness, and the devil that we are all born to inherit. Let this then once take root in your heart, that ye are in extreme misery, and that a remedy must be provided, else ye must perish. Now when this principle is established, ye must agree upon this also. "But out of myself I must go. Blessedness I must have. It is not in me. While I look in, there is nothing but all kind of emptiness, and, which is worse, all kind of misery. Not only the common lot of creatures (that none is sufficient to its own well-being) is incident to me, but I have lost that being which I had in another, which was my well-being, and do now possess, or shall shortly possess, all misery." Now, are ye settled upon these two? I am not happy, I must go out of myself to find it. It is not in me, in my flesh dwells no good thing, in my spirit and flesh both, is nothing good. Ask then this great question, Whither shall I go? What shall I do to find it? All men know they must seek it. But Christ tells where they shall seek it, and whither they shall go. The word of the gospel is for this very purpose to answer this question. If we were sensible that we had lost happiness, certainly we would be earnest in this question, where shall it be recovered? What shall I seek after? And no answer would satisfy but the gospel itself, that directs unto the very fountain of life, and holds 'forth the kingdom of God' as the true happiness of men to be sought. 'Seek ye first,' says Christ, 'the kingdom of God,' and the righteousness thereof. Here only is a solid answer. Seek me, for I am eternal life, I am the life and the light of men. Oh! that your souls answered, with David, 'Thy face, Lord, I will seek.' Peter had sought and found, and thought himself well, so that he answers Christ with great vehemency, when he said unto his disciples, 'Will ye also leave me?' Peter saith, Leave thee, Lord, 'to whom should we go but unto thee, for thou hast the words of eternal life? And we believe and are sure, that thou art the Christ, the Son of the living God,' John vi. 66, &c. It were all the absurdity in the world to leave thee, or to go to any other thing for life itself. Shall not death be found, if I leave life? It were madness not to seek thee, but what shall it be called to leave thee, when I have found and tasted thee to be so good? Every man misses happiness and justification within himself, and so is upon the search after it. But is it not strange, that all the experiences of nations and generations conjoined in one, cannot hold forth even a probable way of attaining it? Gather them all in one, the sum and result is, 'We have heard the fame thereof with our ears,' but 'it is hid from the eyes of all living,' as we read more fully, and should apply, what Job said of wisdom, to the true happiness of man, Job xxviii. 12, to the end of that chapter. Certainly there is some fundamental and common mistake among men. They know not what was once man's happiness, and so it is impossible they can seek the right remedy. Look upon us all, what do we seek after? It is some present thing, some bodily and temporal thing, that men apprehend their happiness lies in ; and so whether they attain it or not, or being attained, it doth not answer our expectation ; and thus still are we disappointed, and our base scent becomes a vain pursuit, whether we overtake it or not. Every man proposes this within himself as the principle of his life and conversation, what shall I seek after? What shall I spend most of my time and affections upon, to drive at? And alas! all men, save those whose eyes the Spirit openeth, err in the very foundation. One man propones honour to himself, another pleasure, and a third riches; and the most part seek all of them, some accommodation and satisfaction in a present world. And almost every man conceives he would be blessed, if he had that which he wants, and sees another have.

Now while men's designs are thus established, all must be wrong. The ship is gone forth, but it will never land on the coast of happiness. And thus we see men seek many things. They are divided among many thoughts and cares, because no one thing is found that can satisfy, and so we have put ourselves upon an endless journey to go through all the creatures. Neither one nor all together have what we want, and neither one nor all can be had or possessed with assurance, though we had it. But the gospel comes to lay a right foundation, and frame a right principle within us. 'Seek ye first the kingdom of God.' Here is the principal design that should be driven at; and if men would make it, and follow it, O how should they be satisfied with the fulness of that kingdom, the vast dimensions of it, the incorruptibleness of it!

Now there is one of two you must fall upon, either many things, or one thing. All that a man can seek after is here ranked. On the one side is many things, 'all these things,' that is, food, raiment, honour, pleasure, and such like, that concern the body, or men's condition here in this world, and these things a man hath need of, verses 31 and 32, 'Therefore take no thought, saying, What shall we eat? or, what shall we drink? or, wherewithal shall we be clothed? (for after all these things do the Gentiles seek;) for your heavenly Father knoweth that ye have need of these things.' Nay, there is but one thing that is set up against all these many things, namely, 'the kingdom of God and his righteousness.' Now without all controversy the more unity be, there will be the more satisfaction. If all other things be equal, it is a kind of torment to have so many doors to go to for help. If a man could have all in one, he would think many things a great vexation and burden. If any one thing had in it as much as to answer all our necessities, that one thing would be of great price, beyond many things, having but so much virtue among them all. I shall suppose then, that there were real satisfaction and happiness to be found in the affluence and conjunction of all created things here, that there was some creature that could answer every necessity of men; yet, I say, would ye not exchange all that variety and multitude, if ye could find one thing that did all that to the full, that so many did, but no more? Then certainly ye would choose a variety in one thing, beyond the scattered satisfaction in many things. But when it is not to be found in all these things, and though it were, yet all these are not consistent together, then of necessity we must make another search. I say then, in the name of Jesus Christ, that if ye seek satisfaction in this present world, ye shall be disappointed. Ye may be all your days sowing and ploughing, but ye shall not see the harvest. Ye shall never reap the fruit of your labour, but in the end of your days shall be fools, and see yourselves to have been so, when ye thought yourselves wise. I shall also suppose that ye have attained what ye have with so much vexation toiled for, that ye had your barns and coffers full, that all the varieties of human delights were still attending you, that ye were set upon a throne of eminency above others, and in a word, that ye had all that your soul desired, so that no room was left empty for more desire, and no more grief entered into your hearts. Are ye blessed for all that? No certainly, if ye do but consider that with all ye may lose your own souls, and that quickly, and that your spirits must remove out of that palace of pleasure and delight into eternal torment, and then count, are ye blessed or not? What gained ye? It is madness to reckon upon this life, it is so inconsiderable when compared with eternity. A kingdom, what is it, when a man shall be deprived for evermore of the kingdom of God, and inhabit the kingdom of darkness under the king of terrors? Do ye think a stageplayer a happy man that for an hour hath so much mirth and attendance, and for all his lifetime is kept in prison without the least drop of these comforts? Will not such a man's momentary satisfaction make hell more unsatisfying, and add grounds of bitterness to his cup? For it is misery to have been happy.

Nay, but this is a fancied supposal. All this, how small soever it be, was never, and never shall be, within the reach of any living. Ye may reckon beforehand, and lay down two things as demonstrated by scripture and all men's experience. One is,—'all is vanity and vexation of spirit' under the sun. All that ye can attain by your endeavours for an age, and by sweating and toiling, will not give you one hour's satisfaction, without some want, some vexation, either in wanting or possessing. Nay, though you had all, it could not give you satisfaction. The soul could not feed upon these things. They would be like silver and gold, which could not save a starving man, or nourish him as meat and drink doth. A man cannot be happy in a marble palace, for the soul is created with an infinite capacity to receive God, and all the world will not fill his room. Another is,—that it is impossible for you to attain all these things. One thing is inconsistent with another, and your necessity requires both. Now then, how shall ye be satisfied when they cannot meet? I think, then, the spirits of the most part of us do not rise very high to seek great things in this world, we are in such a lot among men. I mean that we have not great expectation of wealth, pleasures, honours, or such like. Oh then so much the more take heed to this, and see what ye resolve to seek after! Ye do not expect much satisfaction here. Then I pray you hearken to this one thing, seek the kingdom of God.

This kingdom of heaven and righteousness are equivalent unto, nay they exceedingly surpass, all the scattered perfections and goodness among these many things, or all things that God hath promised to add to them in the text. Why should I say equivalent? Alas, there is no comparison; 'For I reckon (says Paul, Rom. viii. 18, 19.) that the sufferings of this present time are not worthy to be compared with the glory that shall be revealed in us. For the earnest expectation of the creature waiteth for the manifestation of the sons of God.' What this kingdom is in itself, is beyond our conception; but all these things which God will add thereunto, are to be considered only as an appendix to it. Is not heaven an excellent kingdom? All that ye are now toiling about, and taking thought for, these, 'all these things' (as a consequent to itself), food and raiment, and such like, 'shall be given you' as your heavenly Father judges fit. 'For godliness (says the apostle, 1 Tim. iv. 8.), is profitable unto all things, having the promise of this life,' as well as of 'the life to come.' I think then, if all men would but rationally examine this business, they would be forced to cry out against the folly and madness of too many men, who have their portion only in this life, Psal. xvii. 14. What is it ye seek? Ye flee from godliness as your great enemy. Ye think religion an adversary to this life, and the pleasures of it. Nay, but it is a huge mistake; for it hath the promise of this life, and that which is to come. Ye cannot abide to have Christ's kingdom within you. Ye will not have him to rule over you. Ye will not renounce self, and your own righteousness. But consider, O men, that here is that which ye should seek after. Here is wealth, and honour, and long life, and pleasures at God's right hand for evermore. Ye seek many things first, and ye will not seek this one thing needful, Luke x. 41, 42. But here is the way to get what ye seek more certainly and solidly, 'Seek first the kingdom of God and his righteousness,' and all these other things will come of will. Ye need not seek them, for your heavenly Father knows best what ye need. Behold what a satisfying portion this kingdom is! When the pitch and height of men's attainments in this world is but a consectary, an appendicle of it, what must this kingdom be in itself, when all these things follow as attendants? Here then is one thing, worth all, and more than all, even Jesus Christ, who is all in all, Col. iii. 10, 11. Ye speak of many kingdoms, nay, but here is one kingdom, the kingdom of grace and glory, that hath in it eminently all that is scattered among all things. It unites us to Jesus Christ, 'in whom all the fulness of the Godhead dwells; and ye are complete in him, who is the head of all principality and power,' Col. ii. 9, 10. In his house is fatness, and ye shall be satisfied with this, and drink of these rivers of everlasting pleasures that are at his right hand, Psal. xxxvi. 8, 9; xvi. 11. When the pious Psalmist was overcharged with the very forethought and apprehension of this, he says: 'How excellent is thy loving-kindness, O God! therefore the children of men put their trust under the shadow of thy wings,' Psal. xxxvi. 7. 'O how great is thy goodness, which thou hast laid up for them that fear thee, which thou hast wrought for them that trust in thee!' Psal. xxxi. 19, 20. When the sight of it afar off, and the taste of it in this wilderness, is of so much virtue, what shall the drinking of that well-head be, when the soul shall be drowned in it?

As these things are divided,—on the one side, many things, and on the other, one kingdom more worth than all, so are men divided accordingly. On the one hand are the nations and Gentiles, on the other a poor handful. Ye my disciples, 'Seek ye,' says Christ, 'first the kingdom of God, and his righteousness, and all these things,' what ye shall eat, and what ye shall drink, or wherewithal ye shall be clothed, 'shall be added.' For after all these things the Gentiles seek, and your Father knoweth that ye have need of them. 'Fear not, little flock, for it is your Father's good pleasure to give you the kingdom,' Luke xii. 29, 31. Now this division hath been always in the world, 'For many say, (Psal. iv. 6, 7.) Who will show us any good?' But they who have their affections gathered in one channel toward one thing, are as it were but one man. But, Lord, 'lift thou up the light thy countenance upon us; thou hast put gladness in my heart more than in the time that their corn and wine increased.' Here then is even the course of the world, the way of the multitude. They have their way scattered, their gain lies in many arts. Many things they must seek, because they forsake the one thing necessary. When they forsake the one fountain of living water, they must dig up, and hew out to themselves many broken cisterns, that can hold no water, no one to help another. This is even proclaimed by the conversation of a great part of the world. Do ye not declare this, by your eager pursuit of this world, and the things of it, and your careful thoughts of it, that ye have no mind* of eternity, or the kingdom to come? Ye seek nothing but things here, and these do not descend after you. Be persuaded, I beseech you, be persuaded of this, that when ye have your hearts below, that ye are no better, the most part of you, than pagans. Ye have this pretence, that it is necessary to live and follow some calling. It is true indeed. But is it not more necessary to live for ever after death, than for a moment? Godliness will not prejudge this life or thy calling; but ye seek after these things, as if ye were to live eternally in this vain world. Ye could toil no more, take no more thought for a million of ages, than ye do now for the morrow. This prejudges and shuts out all thoughts of heaven or hell. Ye are called to a kingdom. This is offered unto you. Will ye be so mad as to refuse it, and embrace the dunghill, and scrape it still together? We declare unto you in his name, who is truth itself, that if ye will be persuaded to be Christians indeed, ye shall have these outward things ye have need of, without care and anxiety, which now ye are tormented for. And for superfluities, what need ye care for them? A reasonable man should despise them, and much more a Christian. If ye would not be as pagans without the church, ye must be sober in these things, mortified and dead unto them. There shall be no real difference between thee and a heathen, in the day of appearing before Christ's tribunal, O Christian, except thou hast denied and despised this world, and sought principally the things that are above. Is Christianity no more, I pray you, but a name? Ye would all be called Christians. Why will ye not be so indeed? For the name will never advantage you, but in the day of judgment it shall be the greatest accession and weight unto your guiltiness, and also to your judgment. Ye would all now be accounted Christians; but if ye be not so in truth, and in deed, the day will come that ye shall wish from your soul ye had wanted the name also, and had lived among these Gentiles and pagans whose conversation ye did follow. For it shall be more tolerable for the covetous worldly pagan in that day, than the covetous Christian.

Oh that ye were once persuaded that there is an inconsistency in them, who seek these many things, and this one kingdom. 'But seek ye first the kingdom of God, and his righteousness,' in opposition to the Gentiles seeking of many things. Ye may seek the world, but if ye seek it, seek it as if ye sought it not; if ye use it, use it as if ye used it not, or use the world as these who do not abuse it, knowing that the fashion thereof passes away. Certainly ye cannot with all seek grace and glory, 1 Cor. ii. 29, 32. Therefore Christ says to enforce his exhortation, (Matth. vi. 24.) 'No man can serve two masters, for either he will hate the one, and love the other, or else he will hold to the one, and despise the other: ye cannot serve God and mammon.' I fear many of you conceive that this belongs not to you. Those who are not naturally covetous and greedy, who are not still in anxiety and perplexity about the things of the world, will possibly conceive themselves

* [That is, no thought of eternity.—Ed.]

free. Nay, but look upon the division that Christ makes. Was there not many a heathen man among the nations, as free of that covetousness noted among men? Were there not as gallant spirits among them, that cared as little for riches as any of us,—nay, men every way of a more smooth and blameless carriage than the most part of us are? Yet behold the construction that Christ puts on them, 'after all these things do the nations seek.' I think many of them have declaimed more against the baseness of covetous spirits, * than many Christian preachers, and in the very practice of it have outstripped the most part of the Christian world. Yet in the scripture sense, even all these who have cried down the world, are but lovers of it, and of themselves too. How can this be? It is certain every man is composed of desires and breathings after some thing without himself. Some men's desires are more shallow and low than others. One man hath honour in admiration, and may despise riches. Another follows his pleasure, and may neglect both these. Nay, possibly a man may be moderate in all these things, so that none can challenge him, and yet he is but a lover of the world. It is the master he serves, and the idol he worshippeth; because no man wants one, or many idols, something to take up his affection and desires. Now though such a man seems moderate in these, in comparison of others whose hearts run more after them, yet, because there is no other thing, that does take up his heart so much as these, he is but in Christ's account among the heathen nations. Some of you are not in great expectations; ye have but mean projects, ye seem content with few things, ye are not vexing yourselves as others do, but let the world come and go as it pleases, without much disquiet. This, I say, may be the temper of some natural spirits, yet I ask such of you, is there any thing else ye seek more after, or spend more time and thought upon, and what is that? Is there any other thing ye are more taken up with, than your present ease and accommodation in this life? No certainly, ye cannot say so, however your projects be mean and low, yet they are confined within time and things present, and the kingdom of grace and glory comes not much in your mind. Then, I say, thou art but a lover of the world. Mammon is thy god. Thou seekest not the kingdom of heaven, and shalt not obtain it. For that which the nations seek after is thy predominant.

Will ye then, I beseech you, gather in your hearts to consider this. Is it a light matter we speak of, life or death? Doth it not concern you as much as you are worth? Therefore consider it as seriously as if you were going hence to be no more. Many of you will not grant worldly-mindedness a sin. When ye make it a god, and sacrifice unto it, ye fancy that ye are seeking heaven. I pray you do not deceive your souls. Give them as good measure as ye would do your bodies in any thing. Would ye say ye were seeking after any thing, I suppose to find such a friend to speak to, would ye, I say, think that ye earnestly desired to see that friend, and sought him, if ye did all the day take up your time with other petty business that might be done at any time? How can ye imagine ye seek not the world but heaven, when, if ye would look back upon the current and stream, both of your affections and endeavours, ye would find they have run this way toward your present ease and satisfaction? Ye do not give one entire hour to the thought of Jesus Christ and his kingdom, it may be, in a whole week.

Are ye then seekers of the kingdom? If ye did but examine one day how it is spent, ye might pass a judgment upon your whole life. Do ye seek that first which is fewest times in your thoughts, and least in your affections, and hath least of your time bestowed on it? Alas, do not flatter yourselves. That ye seek first which is

* [Quid non mortalia pectora cogis
Auri sacra fames?
Virg. Æneid, lib. iii. ver. 56.

"O sacred hunger of pernicious gold!
What bands of faith can impious lucre hold?"
Dryden's Translation.

Nihil enim est tam angusti animi, tamque parvi, quam amare divitias: nihil honestius, magnificentiusque, quam pecuniam contemnere, si non habeas: si habeas, ad beneficentiam liberalitemque conferre. "There is no surer characteristic of a narrow and little mind than to love riches; nothing more amiable and noble than to despise money, if you possess it not,—if you possess it, to be beneficent and liberal in the use of it." Cic. De. Offic. lib. i. cap. 20.—Ed.]

often in your mind, which uses to stir up your joy or grief, or desire most. It is this present world only, and this present world is your portion. Ye shall lose the kingdom of heaven by seeking to make the world sure. As for the children of God, ye who will be his disciples, (to such he speaks here,) it becomes not you to be like the heathens. Ye ought, most of all, to adorn your holy profession, your high calling to a kingdom above. If then ye seek these things below, as if ye sought them not, ye ought to make religion your main business, else ye are not indeed religious. If Christianity take not up a man, he hath not the thing, but the name. 'Seek first,' that is, chiefly, principally, and above all, 'the kingdom of od and his righteousness.' Nay, this is more strange, it is a first that hath no second. Seek this first, so as if ye sought nothing else, and all things necessary here shall be superadded to the seeking and finding of this kingdom.

This is that which I would have engraven on all our hearts, that there is a necessity of making Christianity our calling and trade, our business and employment, else we must renounce it. It will take our whole man, our whole time, not spare hours, and by-thoughts. Ye have a great task to accomplish, a great journey to make. If ye give not all diligence to add to your faith virtue, knowledge, temperance, patience, godliness, brotherly-kindness, and charity, ye are certainly blind, and see not afar off, and have not been purged from your old sins, 2 Pet. i. 5—11. This imports that those who make not religion their great comprehensive study, do neither know eternity, nor see into it. Oh, how may this word strike into the hearts of many Christians, and pierce as a sword! Is our lazy, indifferent, and cold service at some appointed hours, 'all diligence?' Or, is it diligence at all? Is there not more diligence and fervour in other things than this, to add grace to grace? Who is covetous of such a game? Are not many more desirous of adding lands and houses to their lands and houses, and money to their stock, than to add to their faith virtue? &c. Who among you is enlarging his desires, as the grave, after conformity to Jesus Christ, and the righteousness of his kingdom, that this treasure of grace may abound? Alas, we are poor mean Christians, because we are negligent! For 'the hand of the diligent maketh rich,' Prov. x. 4. But we become poor in grace, because we deal with a slack hand. Is there any great thing that is attainable without much pains and sweating? *Difficilia quæ pulchra.**

Think ye to come to a kingdom by sleeping through some custom of godliness? 'Seest thou a man diligent in his business? that man shall stand before kings, he shall not stand before mean men,' Prov. xxii. 29. This advances him to be a courtier. And is not this business of Christianity more considerable to be diligent about when it advances a man into the court of heaven, into his presence in whose favour is life, and whose loving-kindness is better than life? And not only so, but if ye be diligent here ye shall obtain a kingdom. 'Seek first the kingdom of God.' 'The hand of the diligent shall bear, rule: but the slothful shall be under tribute,' Prov. xii. 24. If ye make this your business, and spend your spirits in it, ye shall be kings and priests with God in the kingdom above, that may suffer many partakers without division or emulation. It is he that overcomes, that shall have the new name, the white raiment, the crown of life, and all the glorious things which are promised to them that overcome in the second and third chapters of the Revelation. O what glad tidings are these! This is the gospel of peace. This is the joyful sound that proclaims unto us so great, so excellent things as a kingdom, the kingdom of God, an everlasting kingdom like God, a kingdom glorious as he is, a kingdom suitable to his royal Majesty, and the magnificence of his palace above. Are we called into this by the gospel, and would ye know what is the sum thereof? It is this: Ho! every one that will have great things, ho! every one that will be a king to God, and to bear rule over kings in the great day, come, here it is, overcome yourselves here in the Lamb that hath overcome, follow Jesus the captain of your salvation, who for the joy and glory which was set before him, despised all the glory of this world, and the pains and shame of the cross, Heb. xii. 1, 2. 'Why do ye spend your money for that which is not bread, and your labour for that which satisfieth not?' Isa. lv. 1, 2, 3. All ye toil about, what is it? Children's

* [That is, "It is difficult things that are admired."—Ed

fancies. Such houses and kingdoms as they build in the sand. Why spend ye your time and labour upon earthly things that are at an end? Here is a kingdom worthy of all men's thoughts, and affections, and time. The diligent shall have it. Gird up the loins of your mind, and seek it as the one thing needful. Many of you desire this kingdom, but alas! these are sluggard's wishes, ye have fainting desires after it. Your desires consume and waste you. But ye put not forth your hand, and so ye have nothing. 'The soul of the sluggard desireth and hath nothing; but the soul of the diligent shall be made fat,' Prov. xiii. 4. Do ye see any growing Christian, but he that is much in the exercise of godliness, and very honest in it? See ye any fat souls, but diligent souls? Our barrenness and leanness hath negligence written upon it. Do ye not wonder that we are not fat and flourishing, as palms and cedars in the courts of our God? Certainly it is no wonder. Is it not a wonder that our sleeping away secure, keeps so much as the leaves of a profession upon us? Therefore Christians, let this be your name, Seekers; but seekers of what? Not of any new religion, but of the good old kingdom of God, proponed to us in the gospel. And remember that the seeker must seek diligently, if he think that which he seeks worthy of finding. 'He that comes to God must believe that he is, and that he is the rewarder of them that diligently seek him,' Heb. xi. 6. Your seeking will proclaim your estimation of what ye seek. It will be written on it, what your desires are. Many men's unfrequent and lazy prayers have this written upon them in legible characters, I care not whether God grant or not. Diligence speaks affection, and affection principles* diligence. And if ye be seekers, ye must be so still, till ye find, and have no more want. When ye have done all, ye must stand, Eph. vi. 10, 16. When ye have found all, ye must seek. Ye do but find in part, because the kingdom of God is but coming in the glory and perfection of it. Nay, I believe the more ye find, the more ye will seek, because tasting what this kingdom is, can best engage the affection and resolution after it. Seeking is an exercise suitable to a Christian in this state of pilgrimage. Enjoyment is for his own country, heaven. And shall not the bitterness and pains of seeking, sweeten the enjoyment of this kingdom when it is found? This will endear it and make it precious. Yet it needs no supereminent and accessory sweetness, it is so satisfactory in itself. Christians, remember your name. When you have attained all, still seek more. For there is more to be found here than ye have yet found. It is sitting down on our attainments that makes us barren and lean Christians. Desires and diligence are the vital sap of a Christian. Enlarge once your desires as the grave, that never says I have enough. And ye have good warrant so to do, because that which ye are allowed to desire is without bounds and measure. It is inexhaustible, and when once desires have emptied the soul, and made it capable of such a great kingdom, then let your study be henceforth to fill up that void with this kingdom. Let your diligence come up to desires, and at length ye shall be what ye would be, ye shall find what ye sought.

Sermon XVIII.

MATT. vi. 33.—"*But seek ye first the kingdom of God,*" &c.

O 'seekest thou great things for thyself,' says God to Baruch, (Jer. xlv. 5.) 'seek them not.' How then doth he command us in the text to seek a kingdom? Is not this a great thing? Certainly it is greater than those great things he would not have Baruch to seek after, and yet he charges us to seek after it. In every kind of creatures there is some difference, some greater, some lesser, some higher, some lower; so there are some men far above others in knowledge, understanding, strength, and such like. Yet such is the order God hath made, that the lowest angel is above

* [Excites.—ED.]

the highest man, so that in comparison of these, the greatest man is but a mean worm, a despisable nothing. Among things created, some are greater, some lesser. 'When I consider the heavens, the work of thy fingers,' says David, 'the moon and stars which thou hast ordained: What is man, that thou art mindful of him? and the son of man that thou visitest him?' Psal. viii. 3, 4. But when all these are compared with God, then the difference of greater and lesser disappears. In the night there are different lights, the moon and stars, 'and one star,' says Paul, 'differeth from another in glory.' Some are of the first, some of the second, and most of them the third magnitude. Nay, but let the sun arise—and all these are alike, they are all darkness when compared with the sun's brightness. What then are angels and men to God, who is a light inaccessible and full of glory, whom no eye hath seen or can see? 'All nations before him are as nothing, yea, they are counted to him less than nothing, and vanity,' Isa. xl. 12—19; 1 Tim. vi. 15, 16. The sun himself shines not before him, and the moon gives not her light. Now is it not so proportionably here? If we stay within the sphere of temporal and worldly things, some are great, some small, some things of greater, some things of less consequence, greater or smaller in their appearance to us, and in men's fancies. But if we go further and look into eternity, then certainly all these will appear small and inconsiderable. This earth seems very spacious, and huge in quantity unto us who dwell upon it. We discern mountains and valleys, sea and land, and do make many divisions of it. But if one man were above where the sun is, and looked down upon the earth, he would consider it but as one point almost invisible, that had no proportion to the vast dimensions of heaven. Even so it is here, while men abide within their own orb, their natural understanding, and do compare time only with time, and temporal things with temporal, riches with poverty, honour with disgrace, pleasure with pain, learning with ignorance, strength with weakness, pleasant lands and goodly houses with wildernesses and wild deserts where none do well. It is no wonder, I think, that those who compare themselves with some that commend themselves, are not wise, 2 Cor. x. 12, 13. There is but one perfect pattern they should look to, if they would not be deceived. While ye stay your thoughts within these bounds, ye apprehend in yourselves great odds between one thing and another. But if once the Spirit of God enlightened your eyes, and made you to see far off, if ye were elevated above your own station, to the watch-tower of the holy scriptures, to behold off* these, by the prospect of saving faith, things that are afar off, such as heaven and hell, eternity, salvation and condemnation, O how would all these differences in a present world evanish out of sight, in the presence of these vast and infinite things! Food and raiment are great things to the most part of men, therefore do they toil so much about them, and take so much thought for them, how to feed, and how to be clothed, how to have a full and delicate table, and fine clothes! Again, many others apprehend some greatness and eminency in honour and respect among men; others in pleasure and satisfaction to their senses, even as a beast would judge. Others apprehend some worth and excellence in great possessions, in silver and gold beside them, and have a kind of complacency in these. But if once this kingdom of God entered into your heart, if ye saw the worth of it, the vast dimensions of it, the pleasure, honour, and profit of it, then certainly all other things would appear to be mean and low, not worth a thought beforehand. Advantage and disadvantage would be all one to you. Honour and dishonour, evil report and good report, pleasure and pain, would have no distance from one another; this gain, this honour, this pleasure of the kingdom of God, would so overmaster them, so outshine them.

Nay, I may say, if ye but knew your immortal souls, or your own worth beyond the rest of the creatures, such as silver, gold, lands, houses, &c., I am confident ye would fall in your esteem of them. They would appear but low, base things in regard of the soul. Suppose even this world came in competition, (the gain of it now seems great gain,) but I pray you, if ye laid all that world in the balance with your soul, what would weigh most? Christ holds it forth to a rational man, to judge of it; 'What shall it profit a man, if he shall gain the whole world, and lose

* [From these, as from mount Pisgah.—Ed.]

his own soul, or be cast away?' Would ye account yourselves gainers, when ye have lost yourselves? Matt. xvi. 26; Luke ix. 25. Is not a man better than meat? Are not your souls more precious than the finest gold? When you lose your souls, whose shall these be? 'What shall a man give in exchange for his soul?' And if there be no one more to possess or use, what profit is it? This then that we have in hand is one thing of greatest moment and concernment in the world. Let me then beseech you to weigh these things in the balance of the sanctuary,—your souls, and this world, the kingdom of God, and many temporal things, such as food and raiment. Ye never enter into the comparison of these things in your mind. If ye did, would ye not see to which side the balance would turn? Therefore we would have you look upon these words of our Saviour, which are the just balance of the sanctuary. Behold how the question is stated, how the comparison goeth. It is not whether I shall want food and raiment, and other necessary things here, or the kingdom of God hereafter? It is not thus cast—in the one balance, the present life and its accommodations, in the other, the life to come and God's kingdom. Indeed if it were so, without all controversy this kingdom would carry it. I say, if there were an inconsistency supposed between a life here, and a life hereafter, suppose no man can be godly, except he be miserable, poor, naked, afflicted, extremely indigent, yet I say the balance thus casten, would be clear to all men that judged aright. Would not eternity weigh down time? Would not an immortal soul weigh down a mortal body? What proportion would the raiment of wool, or gold, or silk have to the white and clean linen, the robes of righteousness, the robes of saints, and to the crown of glory that fadeth not away? What proportion would our perishing pleasures have to the rivers of pleasures, pure, unmixed, undefiled pleasures at God's right hand for evermore? Would ye thus rate this present span, inch, and shadow of time, if ye considered the endless endurance of eternity? I am sure reason itself might be appealed unto, though faith were not to judge.

Though it would hold well enough so, yet our Lord Jesus Christ states the controversy otherwise, and holds out another balance, that it may be the more convincing and clear, if it were possible even, to overcome natural consciences with the light of it. And it is this, in the one hand you may see food and raiment, things that belong to this life; and, on the other hand, you may behold the kingdom of God, and his righteousness, grace, and glory; and, besides that, even all these other things that ye did see in the other hand, food, raiment, &c., 'all these things shall be added.'

Wisdom, in the Proverbs, uses such a device to catch poor, foolish, and simple men: 'Happy,' says Solomon, 'is the man that findeth wisdom, and the man that getteth understanding. For the merchandise thereof is better than the merchandise of silver, and the gain thereof than fine gold. She is more precious than rubies: and all the things thou canst desire are not to be compared unto her.' Here is the weight of wisdom in itself. See how ponderous it is of itself; so heavy that it may weigh down all that come within the compass of desire, and certainly its compass is infinite. But, he adds, 'Length of days are in her right hand, and in her left hand riches and honour. Her ways are ways of pleasantness, and all her paths are peace. She is a tree of life to them that lay hold upon her.' She is a tree of life in herself, though she had no accession of other things, 'and happy is every one who retaineth her,' Prov. iii. 13—19.

Now, O men, if ye will not be allured with the beauty and excellency of the princess, wisdom herself, then, I pray you, look what follows her. That which now ye are pursuing after with much labour and pains, and all in vain too, is here in her train. Look how the comparison is stated. Christ Jesus would catch us with a holy guile, and, if it had success, O! it would be a blessed guile to us. Ye have large and airy apprehensions of temporal things, which ye call needful, and ye cannot behold eternal things. Ye know not the worth of this kingdom. Ye conceive that godliness is prejudicial unto you in this life, that the kingdom of grace will make you miserable here; and that ye cannot endure. Ah, be not mistaken, come and look again. If godliness itself will not allure you, if the kingdom itself will not weigh with you, then, I pray you, consider what an appendix, what a consectary these have. Consider that the sum is added to the principal, which ye so much seek after. But ye refuse the principal, the kingdom. Ye have not right thoughts of godliness; 'for godliness is profitable unto all things, having the promise of the life that now is, and that which is to come,' 1 Tim. iv. 8. Now, is not this 'a faithful saying?' If ye believe it so to be, is it not 'worthy of all acceptation?'

Ye may have things necessary here, food and raiment. And if ye seek more, if ye will be rich, and will have superfluities, then ye shall fall into many temptations, snares, and hurtful lusts, which shall drown you in perdition, 1 Tim. vi. 8—11. Nature and reason might check such exorbitances, for nature is content with few things. Therefore believe that 'godliness with contentment is great gain.' Ye are now only seeking temporal gain, but that is neither great gain, nor gain at all, when ye lose your soul. For that is an irrecoverable and incomparable loss. Ye may have these outward things, God's blessing, and peace with them, and heaven too, if ye choose this kingdom before all things, and above all things. But if ye give these other things the pre-eminence, it is uncertain if ye will get what ye seek, and ye shall certainly be eternal losers beside. If there were no more but this kingdom alone, it might weigh all down. If heaven and earth were laid in a balance, would not heaven, if it were ponderous according to its magnitude, weigh down the earth exceedingly out of sight? Would it not evanish as a point? Even so, though this kingdom of grace and glory were alone, in opposition to all these things that ye take thought for, it would weigh them down eternally. Look what the weight of glory was to Paul, when he says, 2 Cor. iv. 17, 'For our light affliction, which is but for a moment, worketh for us a far more exceeding and eternal weight of glory, while we look not at the things which are seen, but at the things which are not seen; for the things which are seen are temporal, but the things which are not seen are eternal.' The weight of glory is eternal, and far exceeds any thing temporal. The one scale of the balance goes up, as it were, eternally out of sight, out of thought; the one goes up for lightness and vanity, and the other goeth down, for weight and solidity, out of sight, and out of the thought and imagination. If ye looked upon these things which are invisible and eternal, as Paul did, it would be so with you also.

But when withal the earth and its fulness is in the scale with God's kingdom and righteousness, will not these, with that accession, weigh down the earth alone? Is it food and raiment that ye seek? Then I say, food and raiment is on this kingdom's side also. And ye shall be more sure of these things, because ye have God's promise for them. The wicked have not his word and promise for prosperity, even not so much as to answer their necessities, but only they may sometimes prosper in the world, in his providence. But God's people shall have him engaged in their need for their temporal being here in this world: 'O fear the Lord, ye his saints, for there is no want to them that fear him. The young lions do lack and suffer hunger, but they that seek the Lord shall not want any good thing,' Psal. xxxiv. 9, 10. Godliness hath the promise of this life. Now, then, ye are more assured of temporal things by these means than any monarch can be. The world's stability depends only upon a command. But your food and raiment here is grounded upon a promise; and though heaven and earth should fail and pass away, yet not one jot of truth shall fail. God indeed may change his command if he pleases, but not his promises. Now, then, let all the world judge, come and see this balance, how on the one hand are food, raiment, and all things needful for this present life; on the other hand, these same thing necessary for our bodies, and well-being here, and that more solidly and sweetly flowing from God's love, grounded on a promise,—I think this weighs down already, if we should say no more. But then behold what more is on his right hand. There is a kingdom of God beside, an eternal kingdom, and this weighs down eternally. All this world is but an accession and addition to it. The promises of this life are not your portion and inheritance, they are but superadded to your portion, so then we have as much beside, an inheritance incorruptible and undefiled, as the world have for their inheritance, yea, and more sure and more sweet beside. We might with reverence change that verse which Paul has on this consideration: 'If we had hope only in this life, we were of all men most miserable,' 1 Cor. xv. 19. He speaks thus be cause of afflictions and persecutions. But on this consideration we might say, If we have hope in Christ only in this life, we were *not* of all men most miserable, but most blessed, because we have all these things added to us, without toil and vexation, without care and anxiety, by divine promise and providence; with God's blessing and favour, what the world takes thought for, rendeth their hearts for, toils their bodies for, and yet are not sure of success, or if they get them, they get a curse with them.

Now when the balance is thus presented, what is your choice? What will ye seek after? Will ye seek this present world, and lose the kingdom of heaven? Or will ye choose to 'seek first the kingdom of God and his righteousness,' and then ye shall have in this world what is good for you? The choice is soon made in men's judgments. Ye dare not any of you deny, but it ought thus to be. But who seriously ponders these things till their minds affect their hearts? Who will sit down to meditate upon them, and pass a resolute and well-grounded choice upon deliberation? Remember what Christ says, 'No man can serve two masters.' Ye may indeed have both these things, and the kingdom. But ye cannot seek them both, they are not so consistent. 'But seek first the kingdom of God,' and then all these things shall be given you.

Now there is no more need of any second seeking. For 'all these things shall be added' as an accessory to the first. O see then, ye whose projects and thoughts are towards present things,—ye spend the prime and flower of your affections, and time upon them,—ye cannot also seek the kingdom of heaven. Unless ye seek them as if ye sought them not, ye cannot seek this blessed kingdom. If ye seek not this kingdom as the one thing necessary, and your seeking proclaim that ye account it so, ye do not seek it aright. If ye be careful and troubled about many things, ye proclaim that ye do not think there is but one thing needful; ye do not, like Mary, choose the good part which shall not be taken from you, Luke x. 41, 42. If ye would abandon the distracting care of the world, and let all your anxiety and care vent itself here upon the kingdom of God, all these things would be added besides the kingdom itself. 'Seek the kingdom of God *and his righteousness.*' I conceive this is added to make us understand the better what it is, and what is the way to it. The kingdom of God is the kingdom of grace, in which he rules in us by his Spirit. For Jesus Christ is come for this end, and made grace to superabound over the abounding of sin, that as sin reigned unto death, so grace might reign through righteousness unto eternal life by Jesus Christ our Lord (Rom. v. 21.); that as sin had a throne in us, so grace might have a throne, and subject the whole man, rendered obedient to that rule of righteousness that he here holds forth in his word. But this kingdom of God also includes the kingdom of glory, wherein these who overcome this world by faith in the Son of God, reign as kings set upon thrones with God the Father of all. Now because the most part, when they heard of the kingdom of God, dreamed of nothing but a state of happiness in heaven, and passed over the way to it, which is holiness, and they thought not upon the kingdom of grace, which is preparatory unto, and disposes us for the kingdom of glory, therefore Christ exhorts us also to seek his righteousness, opposite to the righteousness of the scribes and Pharisees, who satisfied themselves with a mere walk before men. This was man's righteousness but not God's. This righteousness may be also opposed to the rags of our own righteousness, that we seek to cover ourselves with, Isa. lxiv. 6. The apostle says of the Jews, Rom. x. 3, 4, 'For they being ignorant of God's righteousness, and going about to establish their own righteousness, have not submitted themselves to the righteousness of God. For Christ is the end of the law for righteousness to every one that believeth.'

Now here is the business, and I would have you to conceive it right. The gospel calls you to a kingdom. This is certainly more than all earthly kingdoms. But how shall ye come to it? Not at the nearest hand, not *per saltum.** No, believe it, ye must come and enter this way, before ye compass the end, and the way to this kingdom is by another kingdom, namely righteousness. It is the kingdom of grace within us, and the

* [That is, not "by a leap."—Ed.]

fruit of it is this: Deny thyself, and follow me, Matt. xvi. 24—26. Overcome yourselves, and your corrupt lusts, and ye shall be more than conquerors. Kingdoms are gotten by conquest. But here is the greatest conquest and triumph in the world, for a man to overcome himself. He that rules himself and his own spirit, is greater than he that taketh a city, Prov. xvi. 32. Other conquerors but overcome men like themselves, and yet are overcome by themselves, and their own passions, and so are but slaves indeed. But if ye deny yourselves, and resign yourselves to Jesus Christ, ye shall be more than conquerors, Rom. viii. 37. This then is the kingdom ye must seek first, and it is the first step to the throne of glory. If ye would have a throne after this life, you must have a throne of grace in your hearts. 'If the Son shall make you free, then shall ye be free indeed.' They truly are kings who are most subject to God above themselves, and free from the bonds of creatures. This is the glorious liberty of the children of God, to have liberty from him to make sin a captive. It is a righteous kingdom, a kingdom of righteousness. Therefore ye must here study righteousness and holiness, 'for the grace of God that hath appeared to all men, and bringeth salvation, teacheth us, that denying all ungodliness, and worldly lusts, we should live soberly, righteously, and godly in this present world: looking for the blessed hope, and the glorious appearing of the great God, and our Saviour Jesus Christ,' &c. Tit. ii. 11, &c. All men love the salvation it brings. But do ye love the lessons it teaches you? Ye would all be glad to have that blessed hope, and obtain the salvation which the saints look for, when Christ shall appear again in glory. But how few learn and practise what the gospel teacheth, to mortify and deny your corrupt lusts, and live daily in the practice of sobriety, equity, and piety! O if this were engraven upon your hearts, that ye might study to do that in this present world, which this precious grace and gospel teaches us to do in it! Know ye not, brethren, that all your pains in seeking heaven, are not about heaven itself immediately, but the way to it, which is holiness? Without this, no man shall see the Lord, ye need not seek the kingdom of glory, hope for it, and look for it. But seek grace and righteousness in this world, and if ye obtain them, ye have not much to do, but to look for the blessed hope and Christ's glorious appearance to judgment. For if ye have sought and got grace here, Christ will come with grace and glory at the day of his revelation. Will ye consider that ye are redeemed by Christ? But from what is it? From hell only, and eternal death only? No, no, for we are redeemed from all iniquity, as well as the curse of the law and the wrath to come, Matt. i. 21; Tit. ii. 14. This deliverance from sin is the greater and best half of our redemption. Consider also to what ye are redeemed. Is it to happiness and glory only? No certainly, but unto grace also. For Christ 'gave himself for us, that he might purify us unto himself a peculiar people, zealous of good works.' These things should ministers teach and exhort, and above all things press them upon men's consciences. We are redeemed from all our enemies to serve God without fear, in holiness and righteousness all the days of our life, Luke i. 74, 75. Yea, glory is not glory, except it be complete grace; so we must call the kingdom of glory. If ye believed that it was nigh you, ye would look then for the perfection of grace. And will ye not love the beginning of it here?

But this is not all. There is yet more here to comfort us. Seek the righteousness of God. There is a righteousness of God by faith, manifested in the gospel for lost sinners, who have nothing to cover them. Now I say ye must so seek inherent grace, as ye may not make it your covering, and the only foundation of your confidence. Sinners, the thing which ye first seek and find, is to be clothed with God's righteousness, that he may see no iniquity within you; and then let it be your daily study henceforth to be adorned and made all glorious within, with grace and holiness. Ye must first renounce all your own righteousness, and then be clothed with the robes of God's righteousness; ye must still renounce it, that grace may appear as the gift of God, and not yours; as his beauty, not your ornament. If ye be imperfect in your own righteousness, comfort yourselves in the righteousness of God made yours by faith, that worketh by love and purifies your hearts; for, says the apostle, Gal. ii. 16, 17, Though we are not justified by the works of the law, but by the faith of Christ, yet we must keep ourselves from every wicked thing, and perfect holiness in the fear of God; for if while we seek to be justified by Christ, and we ourselves be found sinners, impenitent and impure, is therefore Christ the minister of sin? God forbid.

Sermon XXX.

Matt. vi. 33.—"*Seek first the kingdom of God*," &c.

It may seem strange, that when so great things are allowed, and so small things are denied, that we do not seek them. The kingdom of God and his righteousness are great things indeed, great not only in themselves, but greater in comparison of us. The things of this world, even great events, are but poor, petty, and inconsiderable matters, when compared with these. Yet he graciously allows a larger measure of these great things relating to his kingdom and righteousness, than of those lesser things he hath promised to give his people, and he commands us to seek after these greatest things: 'Seek first the kingdom of God, and his righteousness, and all these things shall be added unto you.'

This indeed is most suitable to his Majesty, and to us also. It is most becoming his royal Majesty when he is to declare his magnificence, and to vent his love, to give such high and eminent expressions of it. A kingdom is a fit expression of a king's love and good-will. Kings cannot give empires, unless they unking themselves. But Christ is the 'King of kings,' and hath prepared a kingdom for them that love him. It is a glorious declaration of God's excellent name, that he is good to all, kind even to the evil and unthankful. His tender mercies are over all his works. The whole earth is full of his riches, and the wretched posterity of Adam have the largest share of his goodness, even since the first defection from him. Nay, but there are other things prepared and laid up for them that seek him; O how great is that goodness! How excellent is that loving-kindness! Psal. xxxi. 19, 20; Psal. xxxvi. 5, 10. These things have not yet entered into the heart of men to consider. If ye could speak the mind of it, then the tongue could express it. If ye could apprehend the wonders of it, then the heart could conceive it; but this the scripture denies, Isa. lxiv. 4. 'For since the beginning of the world, men have not heard nor perceived by the ear, neither hath the eye seen, O God, besides thee, what he hath prepared for him that waiteth for him:' or as Paul writes, 'Eye hath not seen, nor ear heard, neither have entered into the heart of man, the things which God hath prepared for them that love him. But God hath revealed them unto us by his Spirit, who searcheth all things, even the deep things of God,' &c. 1 Cor. ii. 7—14. Is not a kingdom a gift suitable to such a Giver? And is not this kingdom of God every way like himself? These things are prepared by Christ, and there is no more to do, but to give to him that asks, and he that seeks shall find. This righteousness, divine and human, is it not wholly of God's finding out? Is it so glorious, so excellent, as to hide the greatest spots of the creation from his spotless eyes? For even hell itself is naked before him, and destruction hath no covering; even the heavens are not pure in his sight, he chargeth his angels with folly, Job xxvi. 6; chap. iv. 17, 18, 19; chap. xv. 14—17. When all the creatures could not procure the salvation of sinful men, when the depth said, it is not in me, and the sea said, it is not with me, and the heavens and heights said so too, —even angels could not redeem us,—the redemption of the soul was so precious, it would have ceased for ever, if divine wisdom had not found it out, and almighty power brought it to pass. 'Sacrifice and offering thou wouldest not; but a body hast thou prepared for me. Lo, I come, in the volume of the book it is written of me, I delight to do thy will, O my God, yea thy law is within my heart,' Psal. xl. 6, 7, 8; Heb. x. 5—11. All this was with God, and he knew the way thereof. Christ framed this royal robe of his righteousness, by suffering and death, which may cover all our nakedness. He came and sought the human nature with all its infirmities. He became in all things like unto us, sin only excepted. On him God laid our iniquities. For he himself 'bare our sins in his own body,' when he was slain upon the cross or tree, 'that we, being dead unto sin, might live unto righteousness,' 1 Pet. ii. 24 ; 2 Cor. v. 21. Behold what a wonder! Iniquities, and our iniquities, laid upon the immaculate Lamb, Jesus Christ. Our Redeemer hid his divinity, his holiness, and his innocence, as with a vail and covering from the eyes of God's awful justice. He smites the Shepherd, his beloved Son, as he did the rebel creature. It pleased the Father to bruise him and put him to grief, when his soul was made an offering for sin, Isa. liii. 4—11 ; Zech. xiii. 7. Justice did not look through the covering to his innocence, but reckoned and numbered him among transgressors, when he bore the punishment of our sins, and made an atonement for them, Isa. liii. 11, 12 ; Gal. iii. 13, 14.

Now hence it is that the righteousness of Jesus Christ, which he learned in the days of his flesh, and purchased by his death, is prepared for us, to put on: 'Whosoever will, let him come and take it.' Empty yourselves, stripped naked of all kind of coverings, but sin and unworthiness, that which God's holy eye cannot behold, and seek Christ's righteousness to adorn and cover you. Behold it shall hide all your sins and abominations, of whatsoever nature and degree, from the pure and unspotted eyes of God's justice, which are as a flaming fire, to consume what it cannot look upon without abhorrence. Put on this righteousness of God, and justice shall not draw by the covering, to look under it. It shall look upon the sinner as a righteous man, on the slave of Satan as a child of God, on the heir of hell as the heir of heaven, if he sincerely repent of, and forsake his sins, believe in Christ and obey his gospel. 'Behold all things are new ; and all things are of God, who hath reconciled the world unto himself by Jesus Christ,' &c., 2 Cor. v. 17—19 ; Col. i. 19—24. Christ was no worse dealt with for our sins, than we shall be well dealt with for his righteousness. This is the gift of God. And is it not worthy to be sought? Is it not a gift worthy of him to give? Is it not also suitable for us to ask? 'If thou knewest the gift of God, and who it is that saith to thee, Give me to drink ; thou wouldst have asked of him, and he would have given thee living water,' &c., John iv. 10—15. So say I to you, if ye knew the gift of God, what this kingdom is, what this righteousness is, and who is appointed by God to be the treasure-house of all fulness, to be communicated to us, ye would certainly ask of him the water of life. Ye would surely seek this kingdom of God and his righteousness. He doth not value other things. God only hath these things offered in the gospel, in choice of many, therefore are they laid up for some few, whom he makes his peculiar treasure and jewels, Mal. iii. 17 ; Exod. xix. 5, 6. If ye knew a monarch that was a possessor of all this habitable world, and was about to express his singular affection towards some persons, if his kingdom or the half or whole of it was not sufficient, to be a token of it, but he had found out some other thing, and laid it up for them, and distributed the kingdom, the lands and cities among others, certainly ye would think that behoved to be some strange thing of great price. If the Lord was pleased to give you abundance of all things here, make you all great, rich, and honourable persons, then many would seek no other expression of his love. They would think he did well enough to them. But alas! what is it all? He esteems it so little that he often casts it to swine, the profane and wicked world. He fills their belly with his hid treasure, Psal. xvii. 14. He makes his sun to shine, and his rain to fall on the evil and the good, Matt. v. 45. It is a demonstration that it is but a base thing, when it is so common, I mean, in comparison of the portion of his saints. For though these worldly things are good in themselves, yet they are not precious, they are not pearls. Would he cast pearls before dogs and swine? The honourable man's brutishness and ignorance of God may demonstrate to you he cares not for it. 'The Most High ruleth in the kingdom of men, and giveth it to whomsoever he will,' and sometimes 'setteth up over it the basest of men,' Dan. iv. 13—18. If God loved riches well, do ye think he would give them so liberally, and heap them up upon some base covetous wretches? Surely no. But here is the precious thing that is laid up and treasured. The world and its gain seems great, and big in your eyes, ye cannot imagine more, nor wish for more. But alas! how low and base spirits have ye! It is but as the dunghill that the swine feed on, or the husks which the prodigal desired to feed his belly with, when he began to be in want, Luke xv. 13—17. So are all men's worldly pleasures, preferments, and profits. But here are some particular things, that only deserve to be called good, namely, 'the kingdom of God and his righteousness.' And when God had searched the whole world, (to speak with reverence of his glorious Majesty, who needs not inquire into secret things,) when he had looked through all the works of his hand, he sets these apart from all the rest, to be given to the men whom the King shall honour. This kingdom is the substance and accomplishment of heaven's eternal counsel and purpose of grace, which was given in Christ before the world; and it is the end of the Son's redemption of a sinful world, and his intercession for them at God's right hand. 'Father,' says he, (John xvii. 24.) 'I will that those whom thou hast given me, be with me where I am, that they may behold the glory which thou hast given me;' and for other things he makes them as the stones of the field.

Now I say, as this kingdom of God and his righteousness are suitable expressions of his love, according to his magnificence, so they are also suited to our condition and necessities. No question but he would permit us to seek great things in this world, if these things were really great and good, and if they did become such great immortal spirits as we have. Your souls are above all these things. But this kingdom, and this only, is above the soul. Now then, if ye go out to seek these earthly things, ye must go down from the throne of eminency that God hath set your souls upon by creation, and abuse your spirits by stooping to the very dust of your feet, to embrace these things; and, which is worse, ye put yourselves out of that high throne of dignity that ye are exalted to by Christ's redemption, which we may call a second creation. Jesus declared by the infinite ransom he gave, when he offered himself a sacrifice without spot to God, (Heb. ix. 14.) and laid down his life for us, what the worth of your souls was. 'None of them,' saith the Psalmist, 'can by any means redeem his brother, nor give to God a ransom for him; for the redemption of their soul is precious, and it ceaseth for ever,' Psal. xlix. 6—10. Call and assemble all the creatures in heaven and earth, summon gold, silver, precious stones, houses, cities, kingdoms, places of trust and dignity, great learning and parts, and every other thing ye can imagine, let them all convene in a parliament, and consult how men shall be ransomed. All of them combined together, though they make one purse, cannot do it. They cannot pay the least farthing. The Lord Jesus Christ then stepped in here, 'Lo, I come,'—I give the body thou gave me, my life for theirs, 'I delight to do thy will, thy law is in my heart.'

Are your souls then exalted to such great dignity? Is such a price set upon them, and will ye spend them, for that which could not pay the price for them, 'for that which profiteth not?' Ye must go out of yourselves to seek happiness. Then I pray you, go not downward. It is not there, but misery is there. And by going down to the creatures, ye have found it, and cannot lose it to this day. But the kingdom of God is the only thing above. Go up to it. 'Seek these things that are above,' Col. iii. 1—4. 'If then ye be risen with Christ,' through the faith of God's operation, 'set your affection on things above, where Christ sitteth at God's right hand, and not on things on the earth.' These things are but great in your apprehension. If they are at all great indeed, it is only in evil. If then ye seek great things for yourselves, ye may find evil things; ye shall certainly find such evil things as shall drown you in everlasting destruction. 'They that will be rich' (in worldly things), who lay up treasures for themselves, and are not rich towards God, 'fall into temptation, and a snare, and into many foolish and hurtful lusts which drown men in perdition. For the love of money is the root of all evil, which while some coveted after, they have erred from the faith, and pierced themselves through with many sorrows,' 1 Tim. vi. 9, 10. Great things in this world are not always good. To seek them, makes them certainly evil and hurtful. It is not so hurtful to have them, though very dangerous; but it is hurtful, yea, present ruin to seek them. But here is a kingdom that is great, and great in goodness, every way answerable to our necessities. This is the kingdom we should seek above all things.

We would therefore beseech you to be wanters in yourselves, and seekers in Christ; and seekers ye cannot be till ye be wanters, and finders ye cannot be except ye seek in Jesus all satisfaction and remedy of your necessity. This is even the very nature of a Christian, his chief exercise and employment. What then is a Christian's principal study, his great business, his important calling, and what is his success in it? He is a seeker by his employment, or calling here, and he shall certainly find what he asks. But what puts him to seeking? The discovery of his own emptiness, and God's fulness. Therefore study these things most, if ye would be Christians in truth and in deed. It is these two that ye must still pass between; if ye keep them not both in your view at once, ye cannot well perceive any of them, either comfortably, humbly, or profitably.

This is even the sum of Christianity. Look what ye want in yourselves, and make up that in God. Discover your own emptiness and fill it up with God's fulness. 'The liberal soul shall be made fat, and he that watereth, shall be watered also himself,' Prov. xi. 25. Be not niggards here. Be liberally minded, both in seeking and receiving, so shall ye please him best who counts it his glory to give. 'The instruments of the churl are evil, but the liberal deviseth liberal things, and by liberal things he shall stand,' Isa. xxxii. 7, 8. Seek answerable to your own necessity, and God's all-sufficiency, and know no other rule or measure.

Now, Christians, this is your calling and employment here, to be seekers of God's kingdom and righteousness. But shall we come speed? Yes certainly. It is so far put out of question here, that it needs not be expressed. 'Seek first the kingdom of God, and all these things shall be' superadded to you. He thinks it needless to say, *and ye shall find the kingdom of God, and his righteousness*; for it is supposed as a thing unquestionable, and he adds these words, 'and all these things shall be added to you,' to answer the faithlessness of these who could not credit him in temporal things, though they had concredited * to him their immortal souls. Ye do not doubt, then, but ye shall have the kingdom of heaven. Ye do indeed seek it. Many by seeking kingdoms lose here—by seeking to make them more sure, they lose—the hold they have. Many by aspiring to greater things, lose these things they have, and themselves too. But here is the man that is only sure of success,—the man that may reckon upon his advantage before he take pains, if indeed he resolves to take pains for it. This one thing is made sure, eternal life, if ye lay hold on it here by faith, and quit your hold of present things that end in death, Rom. vi. 21. We may well submit to the uncertainty of all other things, as David, who held himself well satisfied with the everlasting covenant God had made with him, which was well ordered in all things and sure, 2 Sam. xxiii. 5. Though the kingdom and house go, it matters not, if he keep this fast. If he take not away his loving-kindness, this is all my comfort, my joy, and my desire. Comfort yourselves with this, amidst the manifold calamities and revolutions of times. Ye see no man can promise himself immunity, or freedom from common judgments. Here ye have no continuing city. Why then do ye not seek one to come, and comfort yourselves in the hope of it? Your rights and heritable securities will not secure your lands and riches for any considerable time. Therefore seek an eternal and sure inheritance, sure mercies. Seek that which ye cannot miss, and having found, cannot lose. Nothing here can you expect either to find, or keep, until ye have found it.

But besides all this, there is an accession to the inheritance. All needful things shall be added, ye shall want 'no good thing,' Psal. lxxxiv. 11. Will not all this double gain and advantage recompense, yea, overcome all the labours of seeking? Shall it not drive away the remembrance of them? Here then is the most compendious and comprehensive way to have your desires in this life granted, to get your necessities supplied. 'Seek first the kingdom of God' and ye shall have them. But if ye seek these things and not heaven, ye shall want this kingdom. I think then it is all the folly and madness in the world, not to take this way, for it is the way to be blessed here and hereafter. And if we choose any other way, it brings no satisfaction here, and it brings eternal misery hereafter. If ye would

* [Intrusted.—Ed.]

be well in this world, seek heaven. Do not think that ye should have heaven, or seek God's kingdom from this sordid principle, that ye shall have all worldly things given you, which God pleaseth to bestow. For no man can seek the kingdom of heaven aright, but he that seeks it for itself. Yet if there were no more to proclaim the madness of men, this would sufficiently suffice, all they can desire or expect is promised with the kingdom ; and yet they will not seek it.

Sermon XX.

1 PET. iv. 7.—"*But the end of all things is at hand: be ye therefore sober and watch unto prayer.*"

IF ye would ask what ye should do till Christ come again, or what should be your exercise and employment in this old age of the world, here ye have it in a word, 'be sober, and watch unto prayer.' When Christ was to go away to his Father, and leave his disciples in this world, as he left them not orphans, or comfortless, without the Comforter, so neither left he them without counsel and direction. The word he left to them was, 'Take heed, watch and pray,' Mark xiii. 33. In this chapter, Peter is mindful of his Lord's direction, as Paul also was, 1 Thess. v. 6. The substance of this chapter is to exhort Christians to a holy conversation, suitable to their high calling. He presses mortification in general, from that which should be of greatest force with a believer's heart,—the strongest and most convincing reason in the world,—union with Christ crucified, even as Paul does, Rom. vi. And then, in the 3d and 4th verses, he argues from their former conversation, ye have sinned enough already, all the rest of your time is over little * to consecrate to God ; according then as ye have advanced Satan's kingdom while under it, so advance Christ's kingdom when it comes to you, and take that noble revenge upon yourselves and sins, so as to bring them both captive to the obedience of Christ. And although the world may think it strange ye walk not with them, yet so much the rather ought ye to aspire after a disconformity to the world. Be then ambitious of being singular in the world. Ye would lay down such a conclusion as this, I am a stranger, and will walk as a stranger. And ye need not think yourselves miserable to be out of so much company, and to be alone. No, if ye knew what was to come upon them, ye would get you out from among them, lest ye be partakers of their plagues. The day of the Lord is coming, and the world must give an account to the Judge of all flesh. Ye may endure their mockings, and all the hard measure which ye get here, for it shall be recompensed unto them. And your lot is the same that other saints had, who now sleep in the Lord. The gospel was preached unto them, and they had the same fruit of it before God, and got everlasting life by it ; yet they were judged in the world as well as you, and were counted base and contemptible. Now, in this verse, he comes to particular exhortations from the former reasons. This text hath two parts: I. An exhortation to some special duties, which are so conjoined in this form of speech that they seem all but one duty. 'Prayer' is the duty, and sobriety and watchfulness are means to it. II. There is a reason given, because 'the end of all things is at hand.' So, then, ye have here the posture the world is in, and the posture a Christian should be in. This is the world's old age. It is declining, albeit it seem a fair and beautiful thing in the eyes of them who know no better, and unto them who are of yesterday, and know nothing. It looks as if it had been created yesterday ; yet the truth is, and a believer knows, it is near the grave. Gray hairs are here and there upon it, though many know it not; and Jesus the Lord is at hand to put an end to it. Now, what should be your condition in the meantime ? What should immortal souls do, that are to remain for ever, and outlive this habitable world ? How should they be employed ? The spirit and soul is to endure longer than the man's possessions,

* [Too little.—ED.]

goods, honour, and place. How, then, should ye look upon these things? Here it is. Be sober in the use of all things. Use the world as if ye used it not, watch unto prayer. Ye are encompassed about with manifold temptations. Therefore watch, and be as men on their way waiting for the Bridegroom. The bride's exercise, since Christ hath ascended unto heaven, should be to say, 'Lord Jesus, come quickly.'

In discoursing upon this subject, I. We shall speak of these three parts of a Christian's duty severally. II. Consider how they help one another, and so jointly speak of them. And then, III. Of the reason and motive to them all, and how it enforces such an exercise. As to the first of these, we observe, that sobriety is a duty becoming every Christian, that is united unto Jesus Christ, and is separated by God's holy calling from the rest of the world. I add these two considerations, because of the preceding verse. For in the first and second verses, he lays down an excellent ground of all kind of mortification, viz. the believer's union with Christ crucified. Jesus Christ suffered and died for us, as a Common Person, to sustain the guilt of our sins. He died as a Cautioner and Undertaker for us, and as our Head and King; and we, by virtue of that, are obliged to crucify sin also. In verses 3d and 4th, the other consideration is set down. There ought to be a vast difference between a believer now, and before his conversion. He should not be the same man, but, as Paul, say, 'I am crucified with Christ, nevertheless I live, yet not I, but Christ liveth in me,' Gal. ii. 20. He should be separated from the world, that all the world may wonder at him, and think it strange to see his conversation. Now I conceive this exhortation is gathered from both these; and the word of reference *therefore* relates to the preceding verse, as well as his reason in the words now read. Now therefore be sober. This sobriety is not limited to meat, drink, or apparel: the object of it is more comprehensive in scripture. It uses sometimes to be expressed singly, without making mention of any particular matter, evidently importing, that sobriety ought to be in all things. That which we ought to be sober in, is certainly the 'all things' spoken of in the reason of sobriety, whose end 'is at hand.' They are most distinctly expressed 1 John ii. 15—17, 'All that is in the world, the lust of the flesh, the lust of the eye, and the pride of life;' all that perishes is not of the Father, but of the world, that is, the world which wicked men frame to themselves. Here then is a large commentary on 'all things.' Therefore whatever is in the world is the matter of sobriety. Whatever comes under the senses calls for sobriety. Whatever comes under the object of the mind is the matter of sobriety. Nay, whatever is corruptible and perishing, or whatever the last day of the Lord's coming shall put an end to, in all these, there must be sobriety exercised. There is a threefold sobriety, 1. Sobriety in the mind, or sober-mindedness, Rom. xii. 3, We ought not to think more highly of ourselves than we ought to think, 'but to think soberly,' 1 Cor. iv. 6, 7; Tit. ii. 6; Rom. xi. 20; 1 Cor. viii. 2. Sobriety of mind is that excellent lesson that Christ Jesus both taught and practised in his humble state: 'Learn of me, for I am meek and lowly in heart,' Matt. xi. 29. Humility is not like Peter, who said, 'Depart from me, for I am a sinful man, O Lord.' 'Lord, thou shalt never wash my feet.' But humility is rather like Mary, that sat down at Christ's feet, and washed them with tears. Sobriety of mind does not undervalue God's gifts and graces, neither doth it overvalue them It thinks of itself according to the measure of grace freely given, (Rom. xii. 3.) and sobriety looks on all its own gifts; and ornaments, as not its own but another's, as free gifts; and therefore it puffs not up a man against his neighbour, though he should see a gift given beyond his neighbour. High-mindedness is like the high bending of a string of an instrument, which easily breaks in two pieces. Sobriety walks with a low sail, and creeps through under the wind; but the high mind is like the cedar, that moves with the wind, and falls when the bowing twig stands still. Some will think the aspiring of the spirit a sign of a better spirit than the humble mind, and so look down upon others. But oh, if they walk safely, they will walk humbly with God.

2. There is also sobriety in the affections, when they are moderate. The objects of this world which come under the affections, are either sinful and unlawful, or in themselves lawful and allowable. Now sobriety towards the first

kind is simple abstinence, towards the second moderation. The rule of the first is, 'Abstain from fleshly lusts which war against the mind' (1 Pet. ii. 11.); and, as it was said in another sense, 'Touch not, taste not, handle not.' 'Have no fellowship with the unfruitful works of darkness,' Eph. v. 11. As a man who would be clean should not touch pitch, and he who would not be burnt should not carry coals in his bosom, so ought the child of God, who walked formerly in the lusts of ignorance, after the custom of this world, to abstain from all appearance of evil (1 Thess. v. 22.); not only from sin itself, but from all the occasions of it, and inducements unto it, all that which hath any appearance of evil. There is no measure of moderation here; a man must not think to give his lusts part, and Christ part. No, he must have all or none. Ye should have no quarters with sin, ye should be out of speaking terms with it. The least motion of the affections and heart that way, is insobriety, and inordinate affections. 3. But sobriety in things lawful is moderation, when the spirit is kept within bounds, Col. iii. 1, 2. And the rule of this is that which Paul prescribes 1 Cor. vii. 29, 'Use the world as not abusing it,' knowing that the fashion of the world doth pass away. Love this world as if ye loved it not. Every thing hath too much of the heart, and Jesus Christ would have his royal palace, his peculiar place here. He may have suitable affections to God's dispensations in this world, (for the Christian wants none of his senses,) yet he ought not to be 'greatly moved,' as David speaks, Psal. lxii. 2. Now we consider this in three things, (1.) In seeking of any thing. (2.) In enjoying of any thing. (3.) In losing or wanting any thing. That rule of Paul's may be applied to all the three, he should seek the world as if he sought it not. He should enjoy the world as if he enjoyed it not. He should want or lose the world as if he lost it not. This sobriety makes him want, in abundance; and abound, in want,—to have nothing, and yet possess all things. All our time and pains and affections are spent out upon these, and turn about on these three points. Desire, attended with care and anxiety, goes out to fetch in any thing that the mind fancies. When the soul hath gotten its desire, it delights and rejoices in it; and when it is frustrated, disappointed, or crossed, it grieves and torments itself. If ye find a Christian sober in these, you find his pulse beat well. (1.) Ye should then seek the world or any thing, as if ye sought it not. We are given to idolize the creatures, and dig broken cisterns, and forsake the fountain of living waters, to seek the creature as if it were God; and the strength of affections uses to be spent on it. Men have big and large apprehensions of the things of this world, and are like foolish children amazed with pictures and dreams. Fancy busks * up and adorns the object with all things suitable, and thus the poor soul is put in expectation of something, and stretcheth out itself, to the utmost of its ability, to purchase that, which being had will not satisfy. The world promises fair to deluded minds that know no better. But the child of God must be sober here. He ought to have a low estimation of all created things, and conclude all under vanity and vexation of spirit, Luke x. 41, 42. Sobriety so seeks, that it can want, because it seeks a better thing that it cannot miss. But the poor worldling seeks this world as his only thing, and if he want it, what hath he more? He must have it, or else he hath nothing. The child of God should seek as a rich man that is satisfied, and needs no more, so that he cares not whether he obtain or not. The worldlings seek it as their portion, their heart and affections are on it; but he seeks it not as his portion, but as an accessory to his inheritance, Matt. vi. 33. Again we observe, (2.) That the good man uses the world, and enjoys it, as if he enjoyed it not. When riches increase, he sets not his heart on them. He is dead to the world, and crucified to it. It is but an unpleasant thing to him, and he to it. He can be refreshed with his meat more than another, because he sees God and his love in it; yet he hath it not as his portion. He is not excessive in gladness for any dispensation cast in the balance, one kind of dispensation or another. That which would make another man think he was half in heaven, or half in hell, it will not add much moment and weight to such a spirit. It is but like the casting in of a feather in a great balance, that will scarcely incline it to either side. (3.) He loses

* [That is, bedecks.—Ed.]

or wants * the world, as if he lost it not. That which would break another man's heart, sobriety will make him go light under, and not be much disquieted for any thing. Why, what is the matter of it? Can it trouble his peace or access to God? Can his portion be removed? What, then, should ail him, for the light of God's countenance is more recompense than all the world? Proceed we now to apply this in some uses.

Use I. It discovers unto the most part of men how little they are advanced in Christianity. Many are insober in the use of the world, and what must their affections be? The works of darkness, that become not the children of God nor the children of the day, are yet common in the visible church. Insobriety in many is palpable, and written on their forehead. That beastly sin of drunkenness abounds in many congregations. But, II. We would even convince the Lord's own children of great short-coming in this duty. Although your carriage before men might pass free of censure of insobriety, yet O! how many things will God put such a construction on! There are many saints that cannot walk soberly in the use of this world. They spend their time upon it, and this is insobriety. Scarce can prayer and communion with God get an hour in the day from their calling; and when ye have to spend, insobriety is written upon many passages of your behaviour. Your meat, and drink, and clothing, should declare that ye are waiting for a better inheritance. But O! how are your affections wedded unto this present world! The current and stream of many of your thoughts go this way, what shall I eat or drink, or what shall I put on for clothing? And ye spend your spirits in projecting, and in following out your projects. There are some evident demonstrations of insobriety in the affections. For, (1.) Most of your thoughts run upon temporal things; and certainly if your hearts were not in this world, your minds would follow your hearts. Christians, too many amongst you spend whole days, and never any object enters into your minds but one thing of the world after another. Your minds are highways for the travellers of this world to come through. It may be ye will steal an hour, or half an hour for prayer, but the rest of your conversation is not in heaven, but void of God. According as every hour furnishes new opportunities, so are your minds here, Phil. iii. 20. And meditation upon spiritual things, that is the nerves and sinews of religion, that is a rare thing. If your affections were not more upon this world than upon Christ Jesus, would not our Saviour be uppermost in your thoughts? Would not Christ interrupt your thoughts of the world? Would not heaven come in the midst of your business, and get a spare look and ejaculation? The world uses to interrupt your thoughts of God, and the mind is given to wander in prayer. But put you upon something temporal, ye can fix your heart as long as you please, and never wander. David was not so. He awaked, and was still with God. He meditates upon him in the night-watches. He remembers him day and night, (Psal. lxiii. 8.) and this made him a lively Christian. But, (2.) If ye be seeking any thing, ye seek it so, as insobriety is stamped upon it. Your seeking of the world is prejudicial to your seeking of God, and takes away much time for prayer. Ye will be so eager in the pursuit of a momentary passing vanity, as ever ye were in the seeking of God, Col. iii. 1, 2. Care and anxiety comes in to be your provision, and ye put not prayer in the place of it, to make your requests known unto God. Ye seek it as if it were your portion and inheritance: surely this is insobriety. (3.) Look upon your affections toward present enjoyments, and are ye sober? Ye can delight in these things, and take the sweetness of them, but the consolations of God are a small thing to you. Any thing adds to your joy and lifts you up. Albeit ye be not in good terms with God, yet ye can take your pleasure in the world. Ye see not a worm and moth in your pleasures, ye are not afraid to fill your belly with honey. Some think themselves made up when they get such a lot. But saints, are ye sober when such a thing changes your condition? O but the children of God look upon this world as David did in his fretting condition, (Psal. xxxviii.) and in his prosperous condition, Psal. xxx. Ye sit down and say, 'My mountain stands strong, and I shall never be moved.' Ye have more delight in your outward lot

* [That is, has no interest in the world.—Ed.]

than ever ye had in Jesus Christ. But, (4.) When any outward thing goes cross to your mind, then your insobriety appears. The taking * of a sad and cross dispensation will evidence how ye sought the world. The taking away of a friend or idol, will declare ye idolized it. As the saints have too longing desires for the things of this world, and look upon them as the paradise of God, not as Paul did, who thought the world a dead thing ; so remove any thing that ye enjoy, and your joy is taken from you. Give you something for which you pray, your sorrow is away, and ye can no more mourn for sin ; and take something away, and your joy is gone, ye cannot delight in God. Ye vex and disquiet yourselves in vain, and are weighed down with it. Are ye not then under the feet of this present world, when it tramples upon you ? Are ye not servants unto it, when your condition altereth and changeth according to the nod of outward things ? Ye may know what puts you up and down: that commands you, and this is not sobriety. Ye are drunk with the creature. The child of God should be like mount Zion, that can never be moved. Therefore,

III. We would exhort all the saints to study more sobriety in this world. We need no more exhortation than what Paul gives, 1 Cor. vii. 29. It is a strange language, saints, ' Set not your affections upon the things of this earth, but on the things which are above,' Col. iii. 1, 2. ' Love not the world, nor the things of the world,' &c., 1 John ii. 15—17. Ye ought to study such a walk abstracted from this world, that ye might be as strangers at home, as sojourners in your own country. The child of God should sit down in his own family among his children, as if he were abroad ; and he ought to be abroad, as if he were at home. Wherefore your life is called a pilgrimage, and ye strangers. Engage not much your heart to any thing of this world. Take but a standing drink and be gone, ye may not lay down your staff and burden, that his may bear you right. (1.) Consider that insobriety is idolatry. Insobriety puts the creature in God's place, and sobriety puts all things in their own place. When a man's heart or affections are set on any thing, that is his idol and his master ; and Christ says, ' Ye cannot serve God and mammon, (Matt. vi. 24.) these two masters. Sure the worldling thinks not that he serves his riches, yet Christ puts that construction upon his loving them well ; Christ calls any thing that is a man's master his god. Now, any thing that the heart goes after is a man's master. That which commands a man's affections commands the whole man, for the affections are the man's master, and they command the man. If ye knew this, ye would be afraid of spending your hearts upon vanity ; ye put that vanity in the place of Jesus Christ, and so your heart is a temple of idols, and the great gospel-promise (Ezek. xxxvi. 25, 26.) hath not gotten place in you. The due place of the creature is to be subservient to the Lord its Maker, to be only the footstool, that he may have the throne. True insobriety puts the creature upon the throne, and worships it. (2.) Insobriety or love to the world hinders the love of God; as much as is added to the one, is taken from the other, 1 John ii. 15. If the love of the world have one grain weight of allowance more than Christ speaks of, that is incompatible with the love of the Father. The creature will suffer a parting of affection, and will be content with a share, like the harlot and false mother that would be content with the divided child ; but God must have all or none, and will not share with the creature. Ye may find it by experience when your hearts have been much set upon any thing in this world, Christ Jesus has not been so pleasant to you, ye have not so much delight in him. Affection must run in the channel ; or it is but weak, if once ye divide the streams. The love of the world makes the heart carnal, it is the defilement of the whole soul, and a weight that easily besets us, that it cannot mount up in a cloud of divine affection to Jesus. Can the needle go to two contrary points both at once ? Can it move to the north and the south at the same time ? Such an opposition is there between the Father, and the things of the world. If then ye turn your face on the creature, ye must turn your back upon God. Think not, Christians, to keep love entire to God, and to set your affections on the world. Solomon's backsliding had this false principle, he thought to retain his integrity,

* [That is, *the way in which you will take or receive.*—Ed.]

and his wisdom should abide with him, though he would try folly and madness, Eccles. vii. 23. But did he not grow more foolish? Did he retain his wisdom? Many have come down from their excellence by this presumption. (3.) Insobriety is the world's sin. It is the sin of the days of your ignorance, when ye walked after the lusts of the Gentiles, and it is a shame for a child of God to be so. This duty* is opposed to their former walking, verses 3d and 4th. There should be a great distance between you and the world, that ye may seem men of diverse countries. Though ye dwell in one city or in one house, ye ought so to walk as men may think it strange, as, it may be, a wonder in the world. O but few Christians give the worldly men occasion to speak of them for holiness, few give them any ground for wondering at and mocking their conversation! Your conversation is so like theirs, that they need not think any thing in it strange. Is it not a shame, saints, to be like pagans? Christ uses such an argument with his disciples to dissuade them from carnal carefulness, Matt. vi. 32. Sobriety is a work of the day, becoming a child of light, as Paul observes, 1 Thess. v. 4—9. importing as much as if it were a shame for the Christian to be found much in love with the world, as it is for a man to be drunk at nine in the morning and staggering in the streets. There ought to be as great a difference between you and the world, as there is between day and night, light and darkness. Since the true light hath shined, to discover a more excellent happiness than the world can give, and since it hath concluded all under vanity, ye are not answerable to your holy calling to have it in any higher estimation. Consider also, (4.) That the world is not your portion. Your life consists not in what you enjoy, your inheritance is above, reserved in the heavens for you. Therefore be sober. If ye believed this, that one day ye shall put on white robes, and be clothed with immortality, would ye so pursue after the world? It is the world's portion, and let them who know no better seek it as their god, and love it as their inheritance; but fie upon believers, that have a hope laid up in heaven, and fixed as an anchor within the vail. Should ye cause your portion to be evil spoken of, by your groping so much after this present world? If ye walked right ye should torment the world, and oblige them to be convinced that ye seek a city to come, and that ye despise all their enjoyments. But, (5.) Insobriety becomes not a reasonable soul and is very unbeseeming a Christian; even so is it to every man. Are ye not better, says Christ, than many sparrows? Is not the life more than meat? Matt. vi. 25; Luke xii. 23, 24. So we may say, Is not the soul better than the perishing creature? O it is the disgrace and debasement of an immortal spirit to be put under the feet of a piece of clay, to be subjected to vanity, and to the poor perishing things of the world. If a man but knew himself, and his natural prerogative above the creatures, let be† his Christian privileges, he would despise the world, and think all that is in it not a satisfying portion for his spirit. He would count it a great disparagement to lodge upon this side of infiniteness and divine fulness. Would ye not think it a base thing to see a king's son sitting down among beggars, and puddling in the filth of the city? God made man to have lordship and pre-eminence over the creatures, and his spirit shall outlive all these things he sees, and looks to; and what a dishonour must it be to spend an immortal spirit on vanity, to have no eye beyond the span of time? As Christ said, 'What hath a man gained, if he lose his own soul?' What gain ye in this world, though all things should befall you according to your contentment; what gain ye, since ye prostitute an immortal soul unto the service of the world, and have made it, to the prince of the world and all things, a servant and slave?

Sermon XXX.

1 Pet. iv. 7.—"*And watch unto prayer.*"

'Watch.' A Christian should watch. A Christian is a watchman by office. This duty of watchfulness is frequently commanded and commended in scripture, Matt.

* [That is, the duty of sobriety.—Ed.]

† [Much more.—Ed.]

xxiv. 42; Mark xiii. 33; 1 Cor. xvi. 13; Eph. vi. 18; 1 Pet. v. 8; Col. iv. 2; Luke xii. 37. David did wait as they that did watch for the morning light. The ministers of the gospel are styled watchmen in scripture: and every Christian should be to himself as a minister is to his flock, he should watch over himself. This imports the Christian's condition in this world, and expresses his exercise in it. Watching is a military posture, and insinuates the Christian's case in this world. He is compassed about with enemies, and therefore he must be a soldier, 2 Tim. ii. 3. 'Thou therefore endure hardness, as a good soldier of Jesus Christ.' The Christian hath a warfare to accomplish in this world, and therefore the church here is militant, and in heaven triumphant, 1 Tim. i. 18. Every Christian should war a good warfare, holding faith and a good conscience. What is the reason that when Christ triumphed upon the cross, and conquered all his enemies, and is ascended on high, that he hath not made all believers conquerors? Is the man that sits with Christ in heavenly places, (Eph. ii. 6.) and he who was dead with Christ, and also risen with him, is he yet a soldier, when Christ hath overcome, and gotten the crown? And the believer, hath he not the victory that Christ obtained? Why then is he put to fight any more? Hath not Christ completely done it? Yes indeed, Christ hath overcome by his own strength, (Col. ii. 15.) and is now on high, yet he will have the poor pieces of contemptible clay to overcome the Archangel,* the immortal spirits. It was not so much for the prince Gabriel, † the messenger of the covenant, the King of saints, to overcome his own creature; but he hath drawn out a battle and warfare to all his followers, that, in the strength of their victory in him already past, they may be made more than conquerors, and that there may be a perpetual song of triumph and victory in heaven, he hath made the saints strong, and hath made the strong weak. He hath set the poor with princes, and the kings on the dunghill. The Christian's heart and grace are like a besieged city, that is blocked up upon every hand, there are enemies without, and false friends within. Its party is great principalities and powers, &c. (Eph. vi. 12.) and these go about continually to spy a breach. In the city, what strength can do, what policy can do, will not be wanting. All things of the world besiege the heart, and every sense is a port to let the enemy in. All a man's negotiation and trading in the world, is as dangerous as the proclaiming a public market in a town, for the country, while the enemy is about it. There is a desperate wicked heart within, that hath deceived many thousands, and would surrender the city upon any occasion. Here are fleshly lusts which war against the soul, (1 Pet. ii. 11.) temptation to sin, and to unbelief. There is a heart within that can conceive and bring forth sin, and needs no temptation, a heart within that can seduce temptation itself, but it follows the tempter: and when to all that a foreign power is added, Oh then, who can stand? Christ himself was tempted, but Satan found nothing in him, and had nothing in him; but when Satan comes he finds all in us, and we are like powder to conceive flame. We can even tempt ourselves, as well as be tempted by another. The Christian keeps a house that the enemy surrounds, and if he sleep he will enter; he is here a pilgrim, and is not yet come home, yet he hath a foul and dangerous way to go through. He is like a servant that his lord hath left, and given provision to, and is to come home when he pleases, Mark xiii. 33; Matt. xxiv. 32. If his master find him sleeping, woe to him. This is his case. What then should his exercise and posture be? He should be a watchman. (1.) Watching is opposed to security and sleeping, Matt. xxiv. 42; Mark xiii. 33. He must keep his eyes open, or else he is gone; (1 Pet. v. 8) be vigilant, lest the devil attack him. The sluggard's destruction comes as an armed man, because of his 'little sleep' and slumber, Prov. vi. 10; and Prov. xx. 13. Security is the Christian's night, when he ceases from his labour, and the adversary does with him according to his pleasure. But the Christian is in a better condition when he is wrestling with temptation, and getting sore blows. When he is at peace and dwells securely, as the people of Laish, he troubles himself with

* [It must be perceived that the reading ought to be, "overcome *like* the Archangel."—Ed.]

† [It is no less obvious that for "the prince Gabriel" we ought to read, *the prince Michael.* See Dan. x. 13, 21. Jude 9. Rev. xii. 7.—Ed.]

nothing, but dreams over his days; but that is a decaying condition. (2.) To watch, is to observe all things, 1 Sam. iv. 13; Luke vi. 7. This is a special point of the watchman's duty, to let nothing pass by without observation, whatever object would come in, to ask at it from whence, and whither. The heart is a highway-side that all things travel through. If the Christian then be not exact in this, to know what comes in, and what is its errand, he may be surprised or he know. He should observe all the motions of the enemy, and be well acquainted with all the subtleties of temptations. He must know his own spirit, or his thoughts; he should also observe all the Lord's motions and dealings with his spirit. It concerns him also to know what is his enemy or friend. Therefore the Christian should get upon the watch-tower of the word, and look through the prospect * of faith round about him, that he may know what his spiritual condition is. But, (3.) The watchman gives warning while it is seasonable, and the enemy far off. He raises the alarm, and all must be in readiness. So ought ye to be. Come to Jesus Christ with all ye observe, inform the Captain of your salvation whose soldiers you are. It is best dealing with temptation far off, and resisting the first motions of sin, for when it comes near hand, it gets many friends within; and it is the watchman's part not to give his judgment of what he sees, but to report only. Do not ye sit down to pass the sentence on any thing, whether it be good or evil, sin or not, but come unto Jesus, and let him speak; for oftentimes we reason according to flesh and blood. (4.) There must be no interruption in this watching. He must give diligent heed to it, Mark xiii. 33; 1 Thess. v. 6. It is a very laborious exercise for a Christian to watch, all his senses will be exercised by it. He must look up, and that steadfastly; he must stand, and when he hath done all, to stand. When he hath overcome he must yet watch, lest he enter into temptation. He is in greater hazard after victory than before, Ezra vi. 13. He must watch when he is come out of one temptation, lest he enter into another. The greatest disadvantage that armies have gotten, hath been after some victory, when they were secure. Therefore we ought to give all diligence, and love not sleep, lest we come into poverty.

From what hath been said, (1.) We see how few are in a warlike posture against Satan. Many serve under Satan's colours, and the strong man keeps the house. They watch not against him, but for him; they fight for him, and not against him. Do not many Christians, in profession, even watch for their sin, how to encompass what they would be at? Many wait on all advantages to get their own heart's desires; they watch against God's word, to hold out conviction. These are the children of darkness, in whom the devil reigns. We also observe from this, (2.) That even the children of God are seldom found watching. There is much woful security among them, and this is the universal complaint, who of you walks as if ye were among enemies? Ye walk as if ye were in a peaceable city without gates, as the people of Laish, who dwelt securely. Ye have no friend in all the world, and yet what unspeakable negligence and sleeping is there among you? The flesh is so weak, that ye cannot watch but one hour for Christ. And O! but the intermission of one hour's watching hath brought down many strong ones. This made a breach upon David that could hardly be made up for ever again. From the words, (3.) We observe, that prayer is a part of a good Christian's exercise. We may be ashamed to speak or hear of this duty. It is true, indeed, our religion is all compendized in this duty. Yet this duty is so little in practice, that our religion must be but little. We would, then, speak somewhat of prayer, and observe,

1. That it is the distinguishing character of a Christian in scripture. The child of God, and the man that calls upon God's name, is all one and the same thing. The wicked man's name is one that calls not upon God, nor seeks him; but the godly call upon their Maker, Acts ix. 11; 1 Cor. i. 2. All the saints in scripture have been praying men. The wicked, or natural man, is not an indigent man, he wants nothing, and therefore seeks nothing from God; but the Christian is one who hath nothing in himself, a beggar by birth, one that is cast out into the open field, and he is still seeking to make up his losses. Praying and wanting goes hand in hand together. Prayer then is the first breathing of the new man. What sign of life would ye know him by? Motion is an infallible sign of life, and this is the

* [That is, the prospective glass.—Ed.]

motion of the new creature. Prayer is the stirring of the soul, and going out of itself for bread, it is the sucking of the breasts of consolation. Grace turns a man's face God-ward and Christ-ward. 2. Prayer is the pouring out of an indigent man's heart in God's bosom. It is the emptying of the soul, and the landing of it on God's lee-shore, Psal. cii. 2; 1 Sam. i. 10; Psal. cxlii. 2, &c. When a pious heart is overwhelmed and sore disquieted, it prays. Prayer emptieth the vessel, and brings the soul above the water again. It is a present ease in the time of trouble. Care and anxiety of spirit plunge the soul over the ears, but prayer brings it again unto dry land, Phil. iv. 6. Care burns and drowns a man's requests, but prayer makes them known to God in every circumstance of life. Therefore prayer is called a 'making known our requests unto God,' and 'the lifting up of our souls unto God,' Psal. xxv. 1, 2. But, 3. Prayer is the provision of a soul; for it is sufficient to do that which carefulness and thoughtfulness undertake to do, and effectuate not, Phil. iv. 6. Prayer does all a man's business. He lives by prayer, as Paul lived by Christ living in him, &c., Gal. ii. 20. He lived the natural life of a Christian by faith. So David says, 'I gave myself unto prayer;' he opposes this unto all that his enemies do against him. Not only doth it ease the spirit of the present burden; but prayer does all his business, because it puts it over into a better hand, viz., the hand of him who cares for us, 1 Pet. v. 6. It is like a child who is under his father's tutory,* and he does nothing himself, but all is done for him, and he needs to do no more but ask, and have; to seek, and find; to knock, and it shall be opened unto him. Prayer hath the promise of all spiritual and valuable blessings, and the promise is true. 4. Prayer speaks a life of indigence and dependence in the creature, and also speaks out the attributes of God, for the supply of all our need, sovereignty, bounty, and good-will in God. It is the travelling of the poor creature between his own emptiness and God's all-sufficient fulness. It acknowledges that he hath nothing, and that God hath all things he can desire to make him happy. Prayer is an act of homage and subjection to our Creator, and it is also an act of love and reverence; for prayer looks upon God, as a Lord, a Father, and a Master. 5. Prayer is the pulse of a Christian, and here ye may find him. If he be vigorous and frequent here, he is well; a decay in this is a woful symptom of a dangerous and dwining† condition. This is the fountain of the spirit of life, and the Spirit's breath. For the Spirit helps our infirmities with groans which cannot be uttered, (Rom. viii. 26, 27.) and according as the Spirit of God dwells in a man, in so far is he a good Christian. If, then, ye would ask how ye should walk here, and thrive in true Christianity, we would only say this, pray fervently and without ceasing. Pray and prosper, and daily be strong, and the Lord shall be with you. He will never fail nor forsake you. Again, consider, 6. That prayer is not so much a duty as a privilege; and if saints knew this, prayer would not so often be a burden unto them. Is there any privilege like this? For prayer is an admission into the secrets of God, it is an emptying of the heart into his bosom. It is a great part of our correspondence with heaven. It is a swift messenger sent thither, that never comes back with ill news. It never returns empty, but accomplishes its intent. Prayer is as it were speaking with God face to face, as a man speaks to his friend; and is it not an honourable privilege, that believers are admitted to him, and may boldly come to him under all their necessities, and have such a sympathizing friend as Jesus? What is wonderful in scripture is, that God hath put that honour upon prayer to be instrumental in obtaining the greatest blessings. Did not the Lord, at the prayer of Moses, dry up the Red sea? Did he not, at the prayer of Elias, withhold and give rain? Did not the prayer of Joshua make the sun to stand still, till he had vanquished his enemies? Wherefore was all this? Could he not have done it unasked? Certainly, but the Lord would put that honour and respect upon prayer in all ages, that it might be a demonstration to all ages and generations, how ready and propense‡ God was to hear prayer. Nay, to speak with reverence, God will submit his own omnipotence to prayer. Command, ask of me, and command me, says the high and holy One, Isa. xlv. 11. O but

* [Or tutelage.—Ed.] † [Declining.—Ed.]
‡ [That is, disposed. The word, though now obsolete, is found in Hooker.—Ed.]

'the effectual fervent prayer' of the righteous avails much! James v. 16. It does a man's business, and upon less expenses; it gives a reward in the hand, and the hope of the things sought. Withal, prayer is like Jacob's getting that within doors, without much toil, which careful Esau goes about all the fields for, and toils all day to obtain. Prayer is the most compendious way of remedy of all things else. It always makes up losses either of the same kind, or better; for if the loss be temporal, if the want be bodily, prayer makes it up with access unto God. It pays in gold. If it give not the same coin, yet it is better.

We have spoken something of prayer for this end, that your hearts may fall in love with it. It is the property of a sincere upright man, that he calls always upon God, whereas the hypocrite will not always do it. Count, then, yourselves as much Christians as ye find of the spirit of prayer and supplication in you; for those that call not on God, their portion is very terrible. God will pour out his wrath upon them. God's face is set against such as do not pray. And I believe the multitude of this visible kirk have this brand upon their face, they call not upon God. God hath taken this character to himself, 'the hearer of prayer,' and those who mock at it, their judgment hasteneth, their damnation slumbereth not.

Sermon XXIX.

1 Pet. iv. 7.—"*Be ye therefore sober, and watch unto prayer.*"

We now come to consider the coherence and connexion these duties have one to another. *First,* Prayer is the principal part of the Christian's employment, and sobriety and watchfulness are subordinate to it. 'Be sober, and watch unto prayer.' (1.) Prayer is such a tender thing that there is necessity of dieting the spirit unto it. That prayer may be in good health, a man must keep a diet and be sober, sobriety conduces so much to its well-being, and insobriety makes prayer fail. Prayer respects a wholesome Christian at his best estate. (2.) Because prayer that is well in itself must have much divine affection in it, that may be the wings of it to rise upon, the oil that may keep the flame, James v. 16. Now insobriety is the moth of divine affection. The love of this world eats out the love of God and spiritual things; as much as the one goes up the other goes down, like the contrary points, 1 John ii. 15. Vehement desires would be a cloud of incense to carry the petition up unto heaven; but the love of this world scatters it, pours water upon the heart, and makes it neither to conceive heat nor flame. To be carnally minded is death, both here and hereafter, Rom. viii. 5—7. It is death to duties, it kills the spiritual life of the soul. Insobriety is carnal-mindedness, and minding of the flesh, so that a man hath no more taste of Jesus Christ than the white of an egg. It quite distempers his taste, and makes that only savoury which is like itself, and all other things bitter. But, (3.) Prayer must have hope in it. For how shall a man pray if he hope not to come speed? If he maintain not a lively hope, he will cool in his petitions. Insobriety is not consistent with hope to the end, 1 Pet. i. 17. He that would hope to the end must lift up his garments that hang side, and take a lick* of every thing by the way; he must not let them hang down, but gird up his affections with the girdle of truth and sobriety. We observe, (4.) That prayer must come out of a pure heart, and God must be worshipped in spirit and in truth, John iv. 23, 24; 2 Tim. ii. 22. Insobriety makes an unclean heart; the lusts of the flesh, and the love of the world defile the spirit, and makes it to send forth impure streams. (5.) There cannot be lodging for the Spirit where there is much love to the world. This grieves the Spirit, and makes him depart from us, and so a man is best to express his own groans, or to have none at all, which is worse. Where the Spirit of the Lord is there is liberty, and the Spirit must have a clean house; ye must touch no unclean thing, if you would have God

* [That is, that hang *low*, and take a *sweep* of every thing by the way.—Ed.]

to receive you into the holy adoption of his children. (6.) Prayer cannot thrive where faith is not in a good condition. For faith purifies the heart which sends out prayer, 1 Tim. i. 5; Acts xv. 9; 2 Tim. ii. 22; and O! but insobriety makes an ill conscience; and faith and a good conscience scarce sail in one bottom.* Both fall and stand together. How then can the soul look that Holy One in the face whose eyes are pure, and cannot look upon iniquity but with abhorrence? how can it look upon his holiness, when it hath been going a-whoring after the world, and forsaking the fountain of living waters? In a word, the heart that is not dead to this present world, will neither pray much nor well; for the heart is otherwise taken up, hath not many wants to spread before God, nor room for spiritual things. The creature gives him no leave to come to God. O but communion with God is a tender thing, and subject to many alterations and changes of weather! A little more mirth than is needful will indispose us for prayer. A little more sadness than is within bounds will also indispose us for this duty. Carefulness and anxiety cannot pray. Therefore it concerns all the saints to keep their hearts with all diligence, to keep themselves unspotted from the world. If ye would keep yourselves in speaking terms with God, ye must not entertain the creature too much. Any excess in your affections will divert the current of them, that they shall not run towards God. And next, ye see a solid reason why ye are so little in prayer, and keep not a praying temper, because ye are too liberal and lavish of your affections upon the world. Christians, how can ye pray, when your affections are upon the things of the earth? Will ye seek heavenly things, or care much for communion with God, when a present world is so much in your eye? Prayer must be wersh† and unsavoury when the world is sweet; and religion turns a compliment, when your hearts are here. Prayer is a special point of your conversation in heaven, and the love of this world keeps your hearts beneath heaven. Your treasure is here, and your hearts can be nowhere else willingly. Ye must then be mortified to the world before ye can pray aright. But we would likewise consider,

Secondly, That sobriety is a great furtherance to watching, and therefore they are usually joined together, 1 Pet. v. 8; 1. Thess. v. 6—9. This is clear. For if a man be not sober, but drink too much of the creature's sweetness, or bitterness, till he lose his feet, he cannot watch, and the enemy will make invasion when he sleeps. Sobriety is the mother of security. A surfeit of any thing indisposes the body for any action. When the mind goes without the bounds of moderation, and stretches its Christian liberty beyond the bounds of edification, it cannot hold waking, a little sleep and slumber overtakes, till poverty and destruction come like an armed man. (2.) When a man hath drunk to excess of the creature and hath his heart engaged to it, he is in an incapacity to discern a friend from an enemy; whatever comes in with his predominant or idol will get fair quarters; though it may be, it will betray him. The love of the world when it stands centry at a man's heart, will keep out true friends. It will hold out Jesus Christ and spiritual things, all that seems to come in contrary terms with itself, and will let in the enemy that will destroy the soul. (3.) Insobriety entangles a man with the snares of the world, and so he cannot be a good soldier of Jesus. I think the conjunction here is expressed more fully, 2 Tim. ii. 2—4. The good soldier of Jesus Christ that wars a good warfare, must not entangle himself with the affairs of this life. He must be sober in the use of all things, or else he cannot be faithful to his master; he will be about his own business when he should be watching. He will not only labour to please the Captain of his salvation, Jesus, but he has many other things to please besides: and if any of his too kind friends come to speak with him, he will leave his duty and go apart with them, the watchman's office will take him up nothing beside. But the insober man cannot give himself wholly to it. Because his idols cry upon him, he will prefer his pleasures before his credit and honesty. Therefore, as ye would not expose your souls and all ye have, to the will of temp-

* [A single word appears to have dropped out here, the absence of which materially changes the meaning of the author, and makes him contradict himself. The sentence, it is conceived, ought to run thus:—faith and a good conscience scarce sail *but* in one bottom, that is, *in one ship*.—Ed.]

† [That is, insipid.—Ed.]

tation, be sober. The devil hath gotten his will of a man that he can force to lie down with the creature, and sleep in its bosom. If once Satan can gild up the world in your eyes, and represent it amiable, and cause high and big apprehensions of it, O, ye are in the greatest hazard from the world of being overcome wholly by it! That was the temptation Satan sought to prevail with Christ by, but he found nothing in him. If the devil hath taken thee up to a mountain to see the glory of the world, and make you fancy a pleasant life here-away,* take heed of it, for ye will drink drunk,† and forget yourselves, and will not discern between good and evil.

Thirdly. Prayer must be watched unto. We must not only pray, but continue 'instant in prayer,' Rom. xii. 12. We must 'continue in prayer, and watch in the same with thanksgiving,' Col. iv. 2. It is a strange expression, and familiar in scripture, Eph. vi. 18. O what a strange word is it! It is either very needless, or else imports the unspeakable necessity of prayer. 'Praying always,' what needed more? But we must pray with all manner of 'prayer and supplication in the Spirit;' and more yet, 'watching thereunto;' and to express the superlative degree of the necessity of prayer, he adds 'with all perseverance.' Since the words at the first view do speak infinitely more than we practise, let many a Christian express their own practice and set it down beside this verse, and blush and be ashamed. The most part of you behoved to speak thus, I pray sometimes morning and evening, when I have nothing to do. And is this praying always, and watching thereunto with all perseverance? To watch unto prayer we conceive speaks these things.

I. To observe all opportunities, occasions, and advantages of prayer,—to be glad of getting any occasion to sit down and pray. It is to seek out occasions and to be waiting for them. Too many use to excuse themselves easily that their other employments take them up, and they think on this account they may omit prayer with a good conscience, as ministers, busied about their calling, and at their book, think it no omission that they pray not often. But alas, is this watching unto prayer? Ye should be as men lying in wait upon some good opportunity to take hold of it. Prayer would hinder no business of that kind, but much further it. Prayer would be the compendious way of it. Ye used not to be challenged when ye get not a commodity ‡ to pray; but do ye seek opportunity when it is not offered? Do ye look after a retiring place, and withdraw from company, when ye cannot pray with company? This were indeed watching unto prayer. But watching unto prayer will make men sometimes uncivil (so to speak, that which it may be would be called uncivility). It will be a very pressing necessity that will draw away the time of prayer, no compliment should hinder you to go to it. If ye got a corner alone, that would invite a man that watches unto prayer. He even seeks it when he finds it not offering itself. The watcher unto prayer will steal much of his time from others, and other employments, and he will not spend time unnecessarily.

II. To watch unto prayer is to accept willingly of all occasions and opportunities offered. O! if such a man find a corner, but it will be seasonable and sweet unto him. If he have nothing to do, and knows not how to pass his time, then he conceives he is called to prayer, and to keep communion with God. But how many opportunities have ye, and what advantage make ye of them? Ye have time and place convenient, all the day or much of it, and yet ye content yourselves with an ordinary set diet. Sure this is not watching. Watching unto prayer would make all emergent occasions welcome, ye would not have any impulse of the Spirit and motion to pray, but ye would follow it, and be led by the Spirit to your duty. Ye would not hear of any rare passage of providence, or any of God's dispensations towards yourselves, and other saints, but you would think it a good call to pray and make the right use and improvement of it.

III. To watch unto prayer is to observe all the impediments of prayer, all the enemies of that precious thing prayer, that ye ought to keep as the apple of your eye. Whatever ye find by experience prejudicial unto prayer, mark that. What

* [Upon the earth.—Ed.]

† ["It is hard to find many who are not tipplers or common drunkards, or will *drink drunk* on occasions and with company." Causes of the Lord's Wrath, p. 17. printed in the year 1653.—Ed.]

‡ [That is, a convenient time or place.—Ed.]

indisposes the spirit and makes it carnal, mark that. What fills you with confusion and astonishment, and what hinders the liberty of your delighting in God, and rejoicing in his promises, mark that; and set yourselves against these. O but many Christians find liberal discoursing, and much mirth, prejudicial to the Spirit's temper, and yet who watches against it?

IV. Watch over your hearts that ye may keep a praying temper, and be still in speaking terms with God. And if ye would still keep a praying temper, 1. Be frequent and often in the meditation of God. Keep yourselves in his presence, as before him, that ye may walk under the sight of his eye, Psal. cxix. 168; Psal. cxxxix. 1—7. Stealing out of God's sight makes the heart bold to sin. The temper of the heart is but like the heat of iron, that keeps not when it is out of the fire, or like the melting of wax. If ye be out of God's sight your hearts will close. But 2. Let no object come through your mind without examination of it. Let not your heart be a highway for all. If a good motion enter, entertain it, and let it not die out. Give it up to God, that he may cherish it. 3. Repel not any motion of the Spirit, but entertain it. There are three things ye would watch over, as, (1.) Yourselves, your own hearts, Prov. iv. 23, &c. ye must keep your heart, and it keeps all. (2.) Watch over your duty, Luke viii. 18. (3.) The time of Christ's coming, his second coming to judgment, Matt. xxiv. 42; Mark xiii. 33. So did David wait and watch till the Lord should return, Psal. cxxx. 5, 6. So did Job wait all the days of his appointed time, till his change came. Now, Christians, where are ye? Is not your practice your shame? It is one among a thousand professors that can be noted for much praying. Who among you can get this commendation that the Holy Ghost gives to Anna, she served God with fasting and prayer night and day? Your morning and evening are the limits of your duty, and it is almost an heresy to go beyond that. Is there any tender well-doing Christian in scripture, but he prayed much? This made David so exemplary, and hath not Jesus Christ gone before you, (Heb. v. 7.) to lead the way? O! but Christ's praying so often in the days of his flesh, and making supplication with strong cries, is a crying witness against the sloth of Christians in this generation. Both people and pastor, how should ye be ashamed? Hath Jesus prayed so long and often, and should not the poor followers, indigent beggars, be all in supplication? The Christian should name himself as David did, 'I gave myself to prayer.' Many a man sits down to his employment and prays not much, because he hath gifts and abilities. But so did not Christ, who was able to save, yet he prayed and went about the Father's work with dependence upon him. And O that ministers would seek all from heaven immediately, and people seek it from heaven also! Think ye that the Spirit will take twice a-day for praying always, and set times for watching thereunto? No, no, we think there is little of this practised in this generation.

Now we come to the reason that is added in the text, 'the end of all things is at hand;' that is, the day of the Lord is at hand. Christ Jesus, who was once here offered for sins, shall again appear without sin, unto salvation, unto them who look and wait for his appearance; and he shall put an end to all these things, either to themselves, by consuming them, or to the use of them. All that ye now dote upon is perishing, and it is not far hence that ye shall see the world in a flame, and all that ye spend your spirits on; and Jesus Christ shall bring salvation to his own saints, therefore be sober and watch. But how is it that the end is said to be at hand? Are not many generations passed since this word was spoken? It is almost two thousand years since, and yet Peter spake of it, and Christ spake of this day, as at hand. Sure it must be nearer us now than it was then. The day of the Lord is at hand: I. Because if we would count years as God doth, we would call the world but of one week's standing, for God counts a thousand years as but one day, 2 Pet. iii. 8, 9. The world thinks he is slack concerning his promise, and asks, 'Where is the promise of his coming?' But believers, think not ye so, reckon years according to the duration of the Ancient of days, and by faith see the Lord's day at your hand, as it were to-morrow still. But, II. It is not without special reason that the New Testament speaks of all the time from Christ's coming to the end, as the last time, as it were but one age or generation immediately preceding the great day, as if the day of judgment were to be, or this generation of the earth would pass. It is of great use to us, because the Lord would have believers in the last age of the world come to some great pitch of mortification and deadness to the world, and hope of immortality, than has been come to before. He would have them be as men waiting for the Bridegroom, and this their exercise,—every one in his generation standing with his loins girded, and his shoes put on ready for the journey, and his lamp in his hand, Luke xii. 37; Mark xiii.; Matt. xxv. He would have all walking as if the day of judgment were to-morrow, as if the King of saints were now entering into the city, and all believers should go out to meet him as their King bringing salvation.

This then is the posture of the world, all things are near run, the fashion of this world passes away, 1 Cor. vii. 29: and the same exhortation is here pressed. This then, I say, is the state all things ye see are in, it is their old age. The creation now is an old rotten house, that is all dropping through, and leaning to the one side. The creature is now subject to vanity and groaning, Rom. viii. 21, 22. The day is not far hence, that this habitable world must be consumed, and O! but many a man's god and idol will then be burnt to ashes. 2 Pet. iii. 10—12, 'The heavens shall pass away with a great noise,' &c. God hath suffered men to live long in this world, that they might come to repentance, and he hath kept it so long for the elect's sake. If it had not been for them, the world should not be unburied till six hours at night;* but when he hath gathered in all the election, then shall an end be put to all the administrations of kingdoms, all governments, all nations. Think ye that God had so much respect to the world, or to the kings of it? No, he would put an end to all the kingdoms of the world, and never let them make their testament, if the elect were completed. If Christ were completed, there would be no marrying or giving in marriage, no more food and raiment, no more laws and government, all your fair lands and buildings must go to the fire. Now ask the question that Peter asks, 'Seeing all things shall be dissolved, what manner of conversation ought ye to have?' And here it is answered, 'Be sober, and watch unto prayer.' Ask at Paul, and he will tell you, (1 Cor. vii. 29, 30, 31.) 'The time is short,' what remains then, but that he that marries be as they who marry not, they that weep as they that wept not, &c. So then here is the duty of those who look for Christ's second coming; Christ hath left it with you till he come again, and put an end to all things: 'be ye sober and vigilant.' But consider what strength this reason hath to enforce this exercise, and how suitable this duty is to them who look for Christ's second coming. 1. In relation to sobriety it hath a twofold force; for, (1.) It is all the absurdity of the world, that ye should so eagerly pursue perishing vanities; that ye should fall in love with the old decrepit world that is groaning under vanity, and very near consumption. The day is coming that the soul shall see all these things destroyed to ashes, and what will it then think of this idol? This is the thing I lost my soul for, and it is gone. And O how tormenting a thing will it be to the conscience! How have I been put by heaven for a thing of nought, for a vanity! Be sober, for the world cannot be a portion to an immortal spirit. Your spirit is immortal, and will continue after these things are gone, and it will outlive this world. Your goods and good name, your pleasures and profits, your lands and rents, all will have an end, and your spirit shall continue after them. Why then will ye choose that for your portion that will take wings and flee from you, or you will leave it? When ye see all burnt up, where then will your god and your portion be? (2.) Christian believers, ye have another portion; for Christ, who comes to put an end to these things, shall appear in glory, and ye shall appear with him in glory. He shall come with salvation to you, Heb. ix. 28; Col. iii. 4. Your life shall appear with him. Your inheritance is above. That sweet Saviour that came unto this world for saving lost sinners, shall come again, and will not think himself complete without you, and till he have all his members at his right hand. And therefore, saints, be sober. While ye are in this world, ye need not any other thing in the interim but the hope of eternal life, to keep your hearts, and hold them up. O but ye will think yourselves well come to it ere it be long. Ye may laugh at the poor, blind, demented†

* [Or, till the evening.—Ed.]

† [That is, *insane* worldlings.—Ed.]

worldlings, who are standing in slippery places, and like children catching a shadow, or labouring to comprehend the wind in their fists. They are but dreaming that they eat and drink, and behold when the great day of awakening comes at the resurrection, they find their souls empty, though while they lived they blessed their own souls, and men blessed them also. Your inheritance is above, and what need ye more that have such a hope? May ye not purify yourselves as he is pure, and purge your hearts from all corruptions, and use this world as strangers, in your passage through it, that owns nothing as their own? Ye have no propriety * here, and therefore ye may the better live as strangers. But, 2. In relation to watching; Christ Jesus is coming, and is near, therefore watch. This Christ himself presses earnestly: Be as men that wait for the coming of their Lord, since he is not far off. Therefore, Christians, ye ought to be upon your feet, and not sit down with the creature. Ye should entertain this hope of his coming, and comfort yourselves by it, and be kept at your duty by it. I may say, there is nothing that is less known among Christians. Christ and his apostles often pressed it, as it seems he would have it the one ever running duty, through all generations. Ye ought then to be ready for Christ's coming, and not be found sleeping. 3. In relation to prayer; for if the end of all things is at hand, and Christ will soon come again, then the Spirit's exercise, and the bride's should be, 'Come, Lord Jesus, come quickly.' Pray Christ back again, and say, Why tarry his chariot wheels? Pray him back with salvation, and hasten his return by prayer. He hath left such a dependent condition, left such an employment for us, as speaks dependence and necessity. This is the time of promises, and we ought to pray for their accomplishment. In heaven there will be no prayer, for prayer shall be swallowed up in praise, faith in vision, and hope in possession. But prayer is a duty suitable to the time, and to the Christian's minority, to his banishment and sojourning. Dream not of an eternity here-away. Learn wisdom to number your days, and apply your hearts to religious wisdom; and if ye die thus, ye may rejoice that so many of the number are passed, and cannot return again.

* [Property.—Ed.]

THE END.

EDINBURGH:
FULLARTON AND MACNAB, PRINTERS, LEITH WALK.